Walt Whitman

GARLAND REFERENCE LIBRARY OF THE HUMANITIES (VOL. 1877)

Advisory Board

Walt Whitman

An Encyclopedia

Editors
J.R. LeMaster
Donald D. Kummings

GARLAND PUBLISHING, INC.
A MEMBER OF THE TAYLOR & FRANCIS GROUP
New York & London
1998

Library of Congress Cataloging-in-Publication Data

Walt Whitman : an encyclopedia / editors, J.R. LeMaster, Donald D. Kummings.
        p.   cm. — (Garland reference library of the humanities ; vol. 1877)
    Includes bibliographical references and index.
    ISBN 0-8153-1876-6 (alk. paper)
    1. Whitman, Walt, 1819–1892—Encyclopedias.   2. Poets, American—
19th century—Biography—Encyclopedias.   I. LeMaster, J.R., 1934– .
II. Kummings, Donald D.   III. Series.
PS3230.W35   1998
811'.3—dc21
[B]   98-14072
                                                    CIP

Cover photograph: Walt Whitman, ca. 1865, probably taken by Mathew Brady.
   By permission Beeghly Library, Ohio Wesleyan University.

Cover Design: Karin Badger

Printed on acid-free, 250-year-life paper
Manufactured in the United States of America

*Dedicated to the more than 200 contributors to this volume
and to the memory of
Gay Wilson Allen (1903–1995)*

Contents

Introduction

Published in 1855, Whitman's *Leaves of Grass* was met, for the most part, by indifference, contempt, and abuse. Ralph Waldo Emerson sent the poet a salutatory letter, declaring that "I find [the book] the most extraordinary piece of wit and wisdom that America has yet contributed," but other responses were far less charitable. For instance, a writer in the London *Critic* claimed that "Walt Whitman is as unacquainted with art, as a hog is with mathematics," and a reviewer in the Boston *Intelligencer* described Whitman's book as a "heterogeneous mass of bombast, egotism, vulgarity, and nonsense," adding that "there is neither wit nor method in his disjointed babbling, and it seems to us he must be some escaped lunatic raving in pitiable delirium." Yet another reviewer characterized the poet as a "scurvy fellow" and his poems as a "gathering of muck." Nearly 150 years later, Whitman is considered by many to be the greatest of all American poets. Moreover, he has emerged as a major figure in world literature, as demonstrated by the recently published *Walt Whitman and the World* (edited by Allen and Folsom, 1995), an anthology surveying the poet's reception and influence in the British Isles, Spain and Latin America, Brazil, Portugal, the German-speaking countries, the Netherlands, France and Belgium, Italy, the former Yugoslavia, Poland, Russia, Sweden, Denmark and Norway, Finland, Israel, India, China, and Japan.

Right from the start, there has been about Whitman and his work an imposing quality. As the poet himself proclaimed in the 1855 *Leaves,* he is large and contains multitudes. His self-assessment was clearly accurate if measured by the subsequent response to him. Since the middle of the nineteenth century, scholars and critics have published on Whitman's life and work a phenomenal, even daunting, volume of commentary, something now in excess of 12,000 books, monographs, dissertations, theses, chapters in books, articles, essays, notes, and reviews. Poets and fiction writers have made countless overt and covert uses of Whitman's writings. Composers have been inspired by *Leaves of Grass,* finding in various poetic texts the basis for hundreds of songs, choral works, cantatas, oratorios, and symphonies. Even sculptors, architects, painters, and photographers have found Whitman a valuable instructor and guide. Here at the close of the twentieth century, if one turns to the Internet and its various search engines—Lycos, Yahoo, Alta Vista, etc.—he or she will find that entry of the poet's name generates thousands of Web sites. One can only conclude that Whitman is among those writers whose life and writings merit discussion in an encyclopedic format.

In Whitman studies, there has never existed a reference book truly comparable to this encyclopedia. There have been good general introductions and critical overviews, such as Gay Wilson Allen's *Reader's Guide to Walt Whitman* or James E. Miller's *Critical Guide to "Leaves of Grass."* There have been massive, critically astute, and profusely detailed biographies, such as David S. Reynolds's *Walt Whitman's America* or Allen's *The Solitary Singer.* Finally, there have been various guidebooks and handbooks, easily the most impressive of which has been Allen's *New Walt Whitman Handbook.* However, each of these books, if considered as a reference tool, falls short of the range and depth of coverage provided by this volume.

Except for this encyclopedia, there is no single source to which one can turn for answers to a set of questions such as the following: What was Whitman's opinion of each of the presidents of the United States from George Washington to Benjamin Harrison? What New York libraries did Whitman have at his disposal? What were the nature and extent of Whitman's borrowings from foreign languages? In what ways was Whitman influenced by his visits to Dr. Henry Abbott's Egyptian Museum, John Plumbe's daguerreotype gallery, and the Phrenological Cabinet of Fowler and Wells? To what extent did Whitman draw on the sentimental tradition? Who were the Hutchinson family singers? Who were the "Mad Poet of Broadway," Frederick B. Vaughan, and Abby H. Price? What was a Bowery B'Hoy? What were Whitman's favorite operas? Who were his favorite authors? What was Whitman's opinion of Shakespeare? Besides Whitman, what "bohemians" frequented Pfaff's Cellar? To what places did Whitman travel? How did Whitman respond to Reconstruction? What were his racial attitudes? What themes run through Whitman's short fiction? How have critics interpreted "Crossing Brooklyn Ferry," "Out of the Cradle Endlessly Rocking," or "The Sleepers"? How do the various editions of *Leaves of Grass* differ from one another? The encyclopedia answers these and countless other questions and, through an alphabetical arrangement of entries and ample cross references, provides its answers in the most accessible manner possible.

Walt Whitman : An Encyclopedia is a reference guide designed for anyone interested in Whitman, from the general reader to the specialist. Its nearly 760 entries are in fact a collection of articles, ranging in length from 3,100 words on the first (1855) edition of *Leaves of Grass* to 140 words on Elizabeth Leavitt Keller. Although constrained by limitations of space, the volume nevertheless makes available at least some commentary on virtually every topic relevant to this major American author's life, intellectual milieu, literary career, and achievements. All articles include brief, selective bibliographies that are intended to guide readers to sources that contain additional information and, in many cases, bibliographies that cite still other sources.

Walt Whitman : An Encyclopedia offers the general reader convenient access to basic and reliable biographical information: the poet's childhood on Long Island; his family life; his education and reading; his early work as printer, reporter, and editor; his relationships with such people as Ralph Waldo Emerson, William Douglas O'Connor, Peter Doyle, Anne Gilchrist, Harry Stafford, Richard Maurice Bucke, and Horace Traubel; his career as author of *Leaves of Grass;* his activities as a Civil War volunteer nurse; his long bout with ill health; his years in Camden, New Jersey, as the Good Gray Poet—in short, the names, dates, places, and events germane to an understanding of Whitman's life and career.

Biography, however, is but one aspect of this encyclopedia. All of Whitman's editions of *Leaves of Grass,* as well as all of his poem clusters, major poems, principal essays, and other notable writings, receive individual attention in articles that provide a general introduction to the primary work, discuss prominent themes, forms, and techniques, identify significant critical approaches and points of scholarly controversy, and furnish a list of suggested supplementary readings. A special feature of this guide is its inclusion of entries on Whitman's novel *(Franklin Evans)* and on each of his more than two dozen short stories—all minor writings, to be sure, but of increasing importance to scholars interested in tracing the sources of *Leaves.* Whitman's connections to newspapers and magazines such as the Brooklyn *Daily Eagle,* New Orleans *Crescent, Democratic Review,* and the *Atlantic Monthly* are explored in brief but trenchant entries. Events, places, and landmarks of significance to Whitman—for example, the Buffalo Free Soil Convention, New York City, Washington, D.C., and the Mickle Street House (Camden, New Jersey)—are vividly described in articles of moderate length. Finally, longer, more general articles treat recurring themes or concepts that have assumed major importance in Whitman studies: his use of language; his attitudes toward democracy, slavery, the Civil War, religion, sexuality, politics, education, art, music, the women's rights movement, science, and pseudoscience; his prosody; his style and techniques; his sources and influences. Still other special features of this guide include sixteen articles on Whitman's impact abroad, a survey of trends in Whitman scholarship, and an assessment of Whitman's legacy.

Most of the articles in this volume synthesize information and thus provide convenient access to material ordinarily treated in a variety of disparate sources; some articles break new ground and suggest areas where additional research is needed. Hence the book serves the average reader or student as a handy, accessible source of basic information and a launching point for more sustained investigation. At the same time, it serves the researcher or teacher as a succinct, reliable guide to the latest thinking on an array of subjects and an overview of the current status of Whitman scholarship. In one way or another, all of the recent preoccupations of Whitman studies are reflected here—the concerns with textual and bibliographic matters, with political opinions, with new historicist and cultural approaches, with psychological explorations, and with the contested issues of sexual identity.

Of the many challenges encountered in undertaking a project of this magnitude, none was more laborious and time-consuming than establishing a list of entries, a set of topics on which articles would be written. Incredibly, we began with a computer-generated list of more than 20,000 names, works, themes, periodicals, places, and miscellaneous subjects. This list was rather quickly reduced to about 5,000 potential topics. However, more than six months would go by before we settled on a final list. Along the way we discovered that not every noteworthy person or poem or essay or theme could be treated in a separate entry. Readers should note, however, that a subject not discussed in its own entry may nevertheless receive attention in an entry devoted to a broad or general topic. For example, there is no entry on Marietta Alboni, and yet comments on this individual can be found in the entries "Principal Influences on Whitman," "Whitman and Music," and "Opera and Opera Singers." Not finding what one is looking for among the alphabetically arranged entries, one should turn to the index, where, chances are, help will be available.

Another challenge to this project was posed by Whitman's habit of incessant revision. He was forever expanding, revising, and reordering the poems of *Leaves of Grass*. He sometimes took lines out of one work and used them in another. He altered the titles of poems, two or three times in some cases. He frequently tinkered with punctuation. In this encyclopedia, unless otherwise explicitly indicated, we have identified poems and poem clusters by their final versions and final titles. Moreover, in checking the accuracy of quotations, titles, punctuation, capitalization, and so forth, we have taken as our authoritative guide the twenty-two-volume edition of *The Collected Writings of Walt Whitman*, relying especially in this edition on *Leaves of Grass: A Textual Variorum of the Printed Poems*, three volumes, edited by Sculley Bradley, Harold W. Blodgett, Arthur Golden, and William White; and *Prose Works 1892*, two volumes, edited by Floyd Stovall.

We have made no effort here to promote a particular view of Whitman's life or to insist on a particular approach to his writings. A reader who delves into this book on certain issues will find that Whitman's contradictoriness is matched by the contradictoriness of his critics. Consider, for instance, the puzzle of Whitman's sexuality. Was he asexual, omnisexual, bisexual, homoerotic, or actively homosexual? A number of critics address this issue, and one finds that they proceed from radically different, even conflicting, assumptions. The diversity of opinion on this issue, and on others as well, is as it should be—an accurate reflection of the present state of Whitman scholarship. In editing, therefore, we have avoided interfering with the judgments of individual contributors, concentrating instead on achieving consistency of format, improving cogency, verifying accuracy of quotations, page references, and factual details, eliminating duplication of information presented in related entries, and ensuring that bibliographies contain sources truly useful to further research.

As far as was possible, the editors equally divided the work required by this book. Donald Kummings invested much of his time in setting up an advisory board, hammering out the list of entries, generating a roster of potential participants, and assigning topics to the volume's more than 200 contributors. J.R. LeMaster expended much of his energy on preparing a prospectus and a set of guidelines for contributors, applying for financial aid, coordinating the computerization of the seemingly endless stream of submissions, and closely editing the entire manuscript. Our work as editors, however, was greatly assisted by the scrupulous efforts and generous help of literally hundreds of individuals.

We are grateful to our advisory board members for their wise counsel in planning this project. Each reviewed our list of proposed topics, suggesting numerous additions, exclusions, combinations, and rewordings, and many of them recommended appropriate scholars to write on particular subjects. We are profoundly indebted to our contributors. Without their expertise, their diligence, their willingness to write articles in the midst of countless other commitments, there would be, quite frankly, no *Walt Whitman : An Encyclopedia*. We gladly express our thanks to a number of people who provided research assistance and clerical support. At Baylor University these include Gay Barton, Brent Gibson, Di Gan, Virginia Ewbank, Heidi Robinson, and Denise Bain; at the University of Wisconsin–Parkside they include Mary Frances Chachula, Louise Jones, Joseph Kane, Donald Lintner, Rita Steckling, and Abigail Streblow. We are pleased to acknowledge Baylor University for released time and financial backing; the University of Wisconsin–Parkside for support from the Committee on Research and Creative Activity, the University of Wisconsin Professional Opportunities Fund, and the Department of English; and Garland Publishing for assistance in ways too numerous to mention here. For help with photographs and illustrations, special thanks go to Ed Folsom, Martin Murray, Joel Myerson, and Geoffrey Sill. Finally, for their forbearance, encouragement, and tangible support, we express our deepest appreciation to our wives, Wanda LeMaster and Patricia Kummings.

J.R. LeMaster
Donald D. Kummings

Chronology

1819	31 May, Walter Whitman born at West Hills, Huntington Township, New York, the second child of Walter Whitman, house builder, and Louisa Van Velsor, both descendants of early settlers on Long Island. Seven other Whitman children survive infancy: Jesse (1818–1870), Mary Elizabeth (1821–1899), Hannah Louisa (1823–1908), Andrew Jackson (1827–1863), George Washington (1829–1901), Thomas Jefferson (1833–1890), and Edward (1835–1892).
1823	27 May, Whitman family moves to Brooklyn expecting housing boom.
1825	4 July, Marquis de Lafayette visits Brooklyn and, according to Whitman's recollection, embraces him.
1825–1830	Attends public school in Brooklyn. Family frequently relocates within city.
1830–1831	Quits school; works as an office boy for lawyer, doctor.
1831–1832	Learns printing trade as apprentice for *Long Island Patriot*.
1832–1835	Summer 1832, works at Worthington's printing house. Fall 1832 to 12 May 1835, works as compositor on *Long Island Star*. 1833, Whitman family moves back to Long Island.
1835–1836	Works as a printer in New York but is unemployed after a great fire in printing district, 12 August 1836.
1836–1838	Teaches school on Long Island at East Norwich, Hempstead, Babylon, Long Swamp, and Smithtown.
1838–1839	Edits weekly newspaper, *Long Islander*, Huntington; works on *Long Island Democrat*, Jamaica.
1840–1841	Fall 1840, campaigns for Martin Van Buren; teaches school on Long Island at Trimming Square, Woodbury, Dix Hills, and Whitestone.
1841	May, moves to New York City; works as a compositor for *The New World*. July, addresses Democratic Party rally in City Hall Park. August, publishes "Death in the School-Room (a Fact)" in *Democratic Review*.
1842	November, *Franklin Evans; or The Inebriate* published as an extra to *The New World*.
1842–1845	Works briefly for the *Aurora, Evening Tattler, Statesman, Democrat,* and *Mirror* and contributes to other papers in New York City.
1845–1846	August 1845, returns to Brooklyn; works for Brooklyn *Evening Star* until March 1846.

1846–1848	March 1846 to January 1848, edits Brooklyn *Daily Eagle*. Attends opera regularly.
1848	January, quits (or is fired) from *Daily Eagle*. February, goes to New Orleans with brother Jeff to edit *Daily Crescent*. May, resigns position and returns to Brooklyn via Mississippi and Great Lakes.
1848–1849	9 September 1848, first issue of Brooklyn *Weekly Freeman*, a "free-soil" newspaper founded and edited by Whitman; office burns after first issue. Spring, *Freeman* becomes a daily; Whitman edits until 11 September 1849. July, examined by phrenologist Lorenzo Fowler.
1849–1854	Operates job-printing office, bookstore, and house building business; does freelance journalism. 31 March 1851, addresses Brooklyn Art Union; writes "Pictures" in 1853.
1855	15 May, takes out copyright on the first edition of *Leaves of Grass,* containing twelve poems and a preface. *Leaves* is printed by the Rome brothers in Brooklyn during first week of July. Father dies on 11 July. Ralph Waldo Emerson writes to poet on 21 July: "I greet you at the beginning of a great career."
1855–1856	November 1855 to August 1856, writes for *Life Illustrated;* writes a political tract, "The Eighteenth Presidency!" Between August and September 1856, phrenologists Fowler and Wells publish second edition of *Leaves of Grass,* containing thirty-two poems, Emerson's letter, and an open letter by Whitman in reply to Emerson. November, visited by Henry David Thoreau and Bronson Alcott in Brooklyn.
1857–1860	Spring 1857 to summer 1859, edits Brooklyn *Daily Times;* unemployed during the winter of 1859–1860; frequents Pfaff's restaurant, a center of New York's literary bohemia.
1860	March, goes to Boston to oversee third edition of *Leaves of Grass,* published by Thayer and Eldridge. Urged by Emerson to "expurgate" the "Children of Adam" poems.
1861–1862	12 April 1861, Civil War begins; Whitman's brother George enlists. Writes freelance journalism; visits the sick and injured at New York Hospital. December 1862, goes to Virginia when he learns that George has been wounded at Fredericksburg; remains in camp two weeks.
1863–1864	Moves to Washington, D.C.; visits military hospitals and supports himself as part-time clerk in Army Paymaster's Office. Becomes friends with William D. O'Connor and John Burroughs. December 1863, brother Andrew dies of tuberculosis aggravated by alcoholism. June 1864, returns to Brooklyn for six months on sick leave. 5 December 1864, has brother Jesse committed to King's County Lunatic Asylum.
1865	Returns to Washington after 24 January appointment to clerkship in Indian Bureau of Department of the Interior. 4 March, attends Lincoln's second inauguration. 14 April, Lincoln assassinated. May, begins printing *Drum-Taps* (New York), but suspends printing to add a sequel commemorating Lincoln. 30 June, discharged from position by Secretary James Harlan, supposedly because of authorship of obscene poetry. Is transferred to a clerkship in Attorney General's Office. Summer, writes "When Lilacs Last in the Dooryard Bloom'd" and "O Captain! My Captain!" October, publishes *Drum-Taps* and *Sequel* (Washington). Begins relationship with Peter Doyle, an eighteen-year-old Confederate horse-car conductor, in Washington.
1866	O'Connor publishes *The Good Gray Poet* (New York: Bunce and Huntington), a defense co-written by Whitman, in response to the poet's firing by Harlan.

1867	John Burroughs supports Whitman in *Notes on Walt Whitman as Poet and Person* (New York: American News Company). 6 July, William Michael Rossetti publishes an appreciation of "Walt Whitman's Poems" in the London *Chronicle*. Fourth edition of *Leaves of Grass* printed in New York; publishes "Democracy," first part of *Democratic Vistas*, in December in the *Galaxy*.
1868	*Poems of Walt Whitman*, selected and edited by Rossetti, published in London (John Camden Hotten, publisher). "Personalism," second part of *Democratic Vistas*, published in the May *Galaxy*.
1869	Develops substantial following in England; Anne Gilchrist and, about this time, Edward Carpenter read Rossetti edition and are attracted to Whitman.
1870	Suffers depression; prints fifth edition of *Leaves of Grass*, and *Democratic Vistas* and *Passage to India*, all in Washington, D.C., and dated 1871. May, Anne Gilchrist publishes "An Englishwoman's Estimate of Walt Whitman" in *The Radical*, Boston.
1871	Algernon Charles Swinburne greets Whitman in *Songs Before Sunrise*; Alfred, Lord Tennyson and John Addington Symonds send affectionate letters. Anne Gilchrist writes a marriage proposal; Whitman politely declines (3 November). Rudolf Schmidt translates *Democratic Vistas* into Danish. 7 September, Whitman reads *After All, Not to Create Only* at American Institute Exhibition in New York City (published in Boston by Roberts Brothers).
1872	1 June, Thérèse Bentzon (Mme. Blanc) publishes critical article on Whitman in *Revue des Deux Mondes*. 26 June, reads "As a Strong Bird on Pinions Free" at Dartmouth College commencement (published in Washington, D.C.). Succumbs to heat prostration; quarrels with O'Connor; writes will.
1873	23 January, suffers paralytic stroke. Mother dies on 23 May. "Song of the Universal" read at Tufts College commencement by proxy. June, Whitman leaves Washington and moves in with his brother George in Camden, New Jersey.
1874	12 July, receives adulatory letter from Carpenter. Midsummer, discharged from his position in Washington. Publishes "Song of the Redwood-Tree" and "Prayer of Columbus" in *Harper's Magazine*.
1876	Publishes "Author's" or "Centennial" edition of *Leaves of Grass* and *Two Rivulets*, a matched set of volumes, and *Memoranda During the War* (all in Camden, New Jersey); and "Walt Whitman's Actual American Position" in *West Jersey Press* (26 January), an unsigned article that leads to an international controversy about America's neglect of Whitman. Befriends Harry Stafford, a printers' employee; frequently visits the Stafford family farm at Timber Creek. September, Anne Gilchrist visits the United States with her children, rents a house, and hopes to marry Whitman.
1877	28 January, lectures on Thomas Paine in Philadelphia. Painted by George W. Waters in New York. May, Edward Carpenter visits Whitman in Camden; Dr. Richard Maurice Bucke visits Whitman and becomes a close friend. Whitman visits Burroughs in Esopus, New York, with Harry Stafford.
1878	Too sick to give planned lecture on "The Death of Abraham Lincoln" in spring. June, visits J.H. Johnston and John Burroughs in New York.
1879	14 April, gives first Lincoln lecture in New York. Anne Gilchrist returns to England. September, travels west as far as Colorado; falls ill, and stays with brother Jeff in St. Louis.
1880	April, gives Lincoln lecture in Philadelphia. January, returns to Camden. June to October, travels in Canada and visits Bucke in London, Ontario.

1881	15 April, gives Lincoln lecture in Boston. August to October, visits Boston to supervise a new edition of *Leaves of Grass* published by James R. Osgood containing the final arrangement of 293 poems. Visits Emerson in Concord.
1882	January, Oscar Wilde visits Whitman in Camden. April, Osgood withdraws edition of *Leaves of Grass* on complaint of Boston District Attorney. Rees Welsh (later David McKay) reprints Osgood edition in Philadelphia and issues *Specimen Days and Collect*. Publicity of Boston "suppression" of Whitman causes unprecedented boom in sales of *Leaves of Grass*. Becomes friends with Pearsall Smith, wealthy Philadelphia glass merchant and prominent Quaker.
1883	McKay publishes Bucke's *Walt Whitman*, a biography written with contributions from Whitman.
1884	March, buys house at 328 Mickle Street, Camden, New Jersey, with royalties from McKay edition of *Leaves of Grass*. June, Carpenter visits a second time. Becomes friends with Horace Traubel, Thomas Harned, Talcott Williams, Thomas Donaldson, and Robert Ingersoll.
1885	July, has heat stroke. Friends, headed by Donaldson, present him with horse and buggy.
1886	Gives Lincoln lecture in Elkton, Maryland; Camden; Philadelphia; and Haddonfield, New Jersey. *Pall Mall Gazette* promotes fund which presents Whitman with eighty pounds. Boston supporters send $800 for purchase of summer cottage on Timber Creek (never built).
1887	14 April, Lincoln lecture in New York City at Madison Square Theater attracts many notables and nets $600, followed by reception at Westminster Hotel. Sculptured by Sidney Morse; painted by Herbert Gilchrist, J.W. Alexander, and Thomas Eakins.
1888	June, suffers another paralytic stroke followed by severe illness. Makes a new will naming Richard Maurice Bucke, Thomas B. Harned, and Horace Traubel as literary executors. Publishes *November Boughs* (Philadelphia: David McKay).
1889	Seventieth birthday party commemorated in *Camden's Compliment to Walt Whitman* (ed. Horace Traubel. Philadelphia: David McKay).
1890	April, delivers Lincoln lecture for the last time, Philadelphia. 19 August, writes to John Addington Symonds; declares Symonds's homosexual interpretation of "Calamus" poems "damnable" and claims to have fathered six illegitimate children. October, Whitman contracts to have $4,000 tomb built for himself in Harleigh Cemetery, Camden, New Jersey.
1891	Publishes *Good-Bye My Fancy* and Deathbed edition of *Leaves of Grass* (both published by McKay, dated 1892). Prepares *Complete Prose Works* (McKay, 1892). Last birthday dinner at Mickle Street. December, catches pneumonia.
1892	26 March, dies at Mickle Street; 30 March, buried in Harleigh Cemetery, Camden, New Jersey.

Posthumous Publications

1893	In *Re Walt Whitman*. Ed. Horace L. Traubel, Richard Maurice Bucke, and Thomas B. Harned. Philadelphia: David McKay.
1896	*Reminiscences of Walt Whitman with Extracts from His Letters and Remarks on His Writings by William Sloane Kennedy*. London: Alexander Gardner.

1897	*Calamus: A Series of Letters Written During the Years 1868–1880 by Walt Whitman to a Young Friend (Peter Doyle).* Ed. Richard Maurice Bucke, M.D. Boston: Laurens Maynard.
1898	*The Wound Dresser: A Series of Letters Written from the Hospitals in Washington During the War of the Rebellion by Walt Whitman.* Ed. Richard Maurice Bucke, M.D. Boston: Small, Maynard and Company.
1899	*Notes and Fragments: Left by Walt Whitman and Now Edited by Dr. Richard Maurice Bucke.* Privately printed.
1900	*Leaves of Grass by Walt Whitman Including a Facsimile Autobiography, Variorum Readings of the Poems, and a Department of Gathered Leaves.* Philadelphia: David McKay.
1902	*The Complete Writings of Walt Whitman Issued Under the Editorial Supervision of His Literary Executors, Richard Maurice Bucke, Thomas B. Harned, and Horace Traubel with Additional Bibliographical and Critical Material Prepared by Oscar Lovell Triggs, Ph.D.* 10 vols. New York and London: G.P. Putnam's Sons, The Knickerbocker Press.
	Letters Written by Walt Whitman to His Mother from 1866 to 1872 Together with Certain Papers Prepared from Material Now First Utilized. Ed. Thomas B. Harned. New York and London: G.P. Putnam's Sons.
1904	*An American Primer by Walt Whitman with Facsimiles of the Original Manuscript.* Ed. Horace Traubel. Boston: Small, Maynard and Company.
	Walt Whitman's Diary in Canada with Extracts from Other of His Diaries and Literary Note-books. Ed. William Sloane Kennedy. Boston: Small, Maynard and Company.
1905	*Lafayette in Brooklyn.* Intro. John Burroughs. New York: George D. Smith.
1913	*Criticism: An Essay.* Newark, New Jersey: Carteret Book Club.
1918	*The Letters of Anne Gilchrist and Walt Whitman.* Ed. Thomas B. Harned. Garden City, New York: Doubleday, Page and Company.
	Visits to Walt Whitman in 1890–91 by Two Lancashire Friends. J. Johnston, M.D., and J.W. Wallace. Includes letters and postcards from Whitman from 29 May 1887 to 6 February 1892. New York: Egmont Arens at the Washington Square Bookshop.
1920	*The Gathering of the Forces by Walt Whitman: Editorials, Essays, Literary and Dramatic Reviews and Other Material Written by Walt Whitman as Editor of the Brooklyn Daily Eagle in 1846 and 1847.* Ed. Cleveland Rodgers and John Black. 2 vols. New York and London: G.P. Putnam's Sons.
1921	*The Uncollected Poetry and Prose of Walt Whitman Much of Which Has Been But Recently Discovered with Various Early Manuscripts Now First Published.* Ed. Emory Holloway. 2 vols. Garden City, New York, and Toronto: Doubleday, Page and Company.
1923	*Poem Describing a Perfect School.* [New York: Simon de Vaulchier].
1927	*The Half-Breed and Other Stories by Walt Whitman Now First Collected.* Ed. Thomas Ollive Mabbott. New York: Columbia University Press.
	Pictures: An Unpublished Poem . . . With an Introduction and Notes by Emory Holloway. New York: The June House; London: Faber and Gwyer, Ltd.

1928	*The Eighteenth Presidency! Voice of Walt Whitman to Each Young Man in the Nation, North, South, East, and West.* Montpellier, France, 1928.
	Rivulets of Prose: Critical Essays. Ed. Carolyn Wells and Alfred F. Goldsmith. New York: Greenberg Publisher.
	Walt Whitman's Workshop: A Collection of Unpublished Manuscripts. Ed. Clifton Joseph Furness. Cambridge, Massachusetts: Harvard University Press.
1930	*A Child's Reminiscence.* Ed. Thomas O. Mabbott and Rollo G. Silver. Seattle: University of Washington Book Store.
1932	*I Sit and Look Out: Editorials from the Brooklyn Daily Times by Walt Whitman.* Ed. Emory Holloway and Vernolian Schwarz. New York: Columbia University Press.
1933	*Walt Whitman and the Civil War: A Collection of Original Articles and Manuscripts.* Ed. Charles I. Glicksberg. Philadelphia: University of Pennsylvania Press.
1936	*New York Dissected . . . A Sheaf of Recently Discovered Newspaper Articles by the Author of "Leaves of Grass."* Ed. Emory Holloway and Ralph Adimari. New York: Rufus Rockwell Wilson, Inc.
1938	*Complete Poetry & Selected Prose and Letters.* Ed. Emory Holloway. London: The Nonesuch Press.
1947	*Walt Whitman's Backward Glance . . . and Two Contributory Essays Hitherto Uncollected.* Ed. Sculley Bradley and John A. Stevenson. Philadelphia: University of Pennsylvania Press.
1949	*Faint Clews & Indirections: Manuscripts of Walt Whitman and His Family.* Ed. Clarence Gohdes and Rollo G. Silver. Durham, North Carolina: Duke University Press.
1950	*Walt Whitman of the New York Aurora, Editor at Twenty-Two: A Collection of Recently Discovered Writings.* Ed. Joseph Jay Rubin and Charles H. Brown. State College, Pennsylvania: Bald Eagle Press.
	Walt Whitman Looks at the Schools. Ed. Florence Bernstein Freedman. New York: King's Crown Press, Columbia University.
1951	*Whitman and Rolleston: A Correspondence.* Ed. Horst Frenz. Bloomington: Indiana University Press.
1955	*Whitman's Manuscripts: "Leaves of Grass" (1860), A Parallel Text.* Ed. Fredson Bowers. Chicago: University of Chicago Press.
1959	*Walt Whitman: An 1855–56 Notebook Toward the Second Edition of "Leaves of Grass."* Ed. Harold W. Blodgett. Additional Notes by William White. Carbondale: Southern Illinois University Press.
1960	*Walt Whitman's Civil War: Compiled & Edited from Published and Unpublished Sources.* Ed. Walter Lowenfels. New York: Alfred A. Knopf, 1960.
1961–1984	*The Collected Writings of Walt Whitman.* General eds. Gay Wilson Allen and Sculley Bradley. New York: New York University Press. *The Correspondence.* Ed. Edwin Haviland Miller. 6 vols. 1961, 1961, 1964, 1969, 1969, 1977; *The Early Poems and the Fiction.* Ed. Thomas L. Brasher. 1963; *Prose Works 1892.* Ed. Floyd Stovall. 2 vols. 1963, 1964; *Leaves of Grass: Comprehensive Reader's Edition.* Ed. Harold W. Blodgett and Sculley Bradley. 1965; *Daybooks and Notebooks.* Ed. William White. 3 vols. 1978; *Leaves of Grass: A Textual Variorum of the Printed Poems.* Ed. Sculley Bradley, Harold Blodgett, Arthur Golden, and

William White. 3 vols. 1980; *Notebooks and Unpublished Prose Manuscripts.* Ed. Edward F. Grier. 6 vols. 1984.

1968   *Walt Whitman's Blue Book: The 1860–61 "Leaves of Grass" Containing His Manuscript Additions and Revisions.* Ed. Arthur Golden. 2 vols. New York: The New York Public Library.

1974   *Walt Whitman's Autograph Revision of the Analysis of "Leaves of Grass" (For Dr. R. M. Bucke's "Walt Whitman").* Introduction by Quentin Anderson, Ed. Stephen Railton. New York: New York University Press.

1993   *The Walt Whitman Archive: A Facsimile of the Poet's Manuscripts.* Ed. Joel Myerson. 3 vols. Vol. 1. *Whitman Manuscripts at the Library of Congress;* Vol. 2. *Whitman Manuscripts at Duke University and the University of Texas;* Vol. 3. *Whitman Manuscripts at the University of Virginia.* New York: Garland.

William A. Pannapacker

Contributors

James E. Barcus, Jr.
Baylor University
Huneker, James Gibbons
November Boughs
Westminster Review, The

Robert W. Barnett
University of Michigan, Flint
Literature
"Poetry To-day in America—Shakspere—
   The Future"

Gay Barton
Abilene Christian University
Chopin, Kate
"Quicksand Years"
"Song of Prudence"

Mark Bauerlein
Emory University
City, Whitman and the
Hegel, Georg Wilhelm Friedrich
"Out of the Cradle Endlessly Rocking"

Amy M. Bawcom
Baylor University
Arnold, George B.
Ashton, J. Hubley
Evening Tattler (New York)
Saturday Press
Van Velsor, Cornelius
Van Velsor, Naomi ("Amy") Williams

Thomas Becknell
Bethel College
Bible, The

Keiko Beppu
Kobe College, Japan
Japan, Whitman in

Lawrence I. Berkove
University of Michigan, Dearborn
Howells, William Dean
Lanier, Sidney
Miller, Joaquin

Martin Bidney
State University of New York, Binghamton
Anderson, Sherwood
Blake, William
Russia and Other Slavic Countries, Whitman in

Alice L. Birney
The Library of Congress
Collectors and Collections, Whitman

Stephen A. Black
Simon Fraser University, Canada
Leaves of Grass
Psychological Approaches

David Haven Blake
United States Air Force Academy
American Revolution, The
"Eighteenth Presidency!, The"
Jackson, Andrew
Paine, Thomas

Ruth L. Bohan
University of Missouri, St. Louis
Painters and Painting
Sculptors and Sculpture

Wesley A. Britton
Grayson County Community College
Clemens, Samuel Langhorne (Mark Twain)
Everson, William (Brother Antoninus)
Hughes, Langston
Jarrell, Randall
Kerouac, Jack
Masters, Edgar Lee
Media Interpretations of Whitman's Life and
   Works

Willis J. Buckingham
Arizona State University
Griswold, Rufus W.
Hale, Edward Everett
Norton, Charles Eliot

Frederick J. Butler
Gulfport, Florida
"Are You the New Person Drawn toward Me?"
"Mystic Trumpeter, The"
"Song at Sunset"

Lorelei Cederstrom
Brandon University, Canada
Canada, Whitman's Reception in
London, Ontario, Canada
Symbolism

Sherry Ceniza
Texas Tech University
Born, Helena
Farnham, Eliza W.
Price, Abby Hills
Price, Helen E.
Whitman, Louisa Van Velsor
Woman's Rights Movement and Whitman, The
Women as a Theme in Whitman's Writing

K. Narayana Chandran
University of Hyderabad, India
"As Consequent, Etc."
"As I Ponder'd in Silence"
"Centenarian's Story, The"
"Darest Thou Now O Soul"
"Earth, My Likeness"
"Sometimes with One I Love"
"Who Learns My Lesson Complete?"

V.K. Chari
Carleton University, Canada
Hindu Literature
India, Whitman in
Mysticism
Reincarnation

Matt Cohen
College of William and Mary
Short Fiction, Whitman's

Robert G. Collmer
Baylor University
"Shakspere-Bacon's Cipher"

Stephen A. Cooper
Baylor University
Smith, Alexander
Warren, Samuel
Williams, Captain John

Angelo Costanzo
Shippensburg University
Correspondence of Walt Whitman, The
Organicism

Philip Dacey
Southwest State University, Marshall, Minnesota
"I Heard You Solemn-Sweet Pipes of the Organ"
"Me Imperturbe"
"To the States"

Christina Davey
Pierce College
Costelloe, Mary Whitall Smith
Hicks, Elias
Smith, Logan Pearsall
Smith, Robert Pearsall

Robert Leigh Davis
Wittenberg University
Civil War Nursing
Memoranda During the War

Susan Day Dean
Bryn Mawr College
Quakers and Quakerism

Thomas K. Dean
Moorhead State University
Garland, Hamlin
Realism

Deborah Dietrich
California State University, Fullerton
American Adam
Journeying
"Myself and Mine"
"Song of Joys, A"

David Breckenridge Donlon
College of William and Mary
Broadway Hospital (New York)
Thayer and Eldridge

Martin K. Doudna
University of Hawaii, Hilo
"Broadway Pageant, A"
"Facing West from California's Shores"
Nature

James Dougherty
University of Notre Dame
Art and Daguerreotype Galleries
Ferries and Omnibuses
"Give Me the Splendid Silent Sun"

Michael R. Dressman
University of Houston, Downtown
American Primer, An
Language
"Slang in America"

David Drews
University of Tennessee, Knoxville
Racial Attitudes

Margaret H. Duggar
Chicago State University
Individualism
"One Hour to Madness and Joy"
"Out of the Rolling Ocean the Crowd"
"To Thee Old Cause"

Renée Dye
Emory University
James, Henry
Jefferson, Thomas
Matthiessen, F.O.

Amy E. Earhart
Texas A&M University
"Ethiopia Saluting the Colors"
Poe, Edgar Allan

Gregory Eiselein
Kansas State University
"Chanting the Square Deific"
Drum-Taps
Leaves of Grass, 1860 Edition
Lincoln's Death
"O Captain! My Captain!"

Betsy Erkkila
Northwestern University
Michelet, Jules
Molinoff, Katherine
New World, The (New York)

Nathan C. Faries
Baylor University
Hudson River
"To Soar in Freedom and in Fullness of
      Power"

Jack Field
New Port Richey, Florida
"Autumn Rivulets"
Mississippi River
"Not Heaving from my Ribb'd Breast Only"
Travels, Whitman's

Ed Folsom
University of Iowa
Bon Echo
Borges, Jorge Luis
Democracy
Dictionaries
Duncan, Robert
Jordan, June
Kinnell, Galway
Native Americans (Indians)
Periodicals Devoted to Whitman
Photographs and Photographers
Rukeyser, Muriel
Traubel, Horace L.
"When I Heard the Learn'd Astronomer"
Wright, James
"Yonnondio"

R.W. French
University of Massachusetts, Amherst
British Romantic Poets
Leaves of Grass, 1891–1892, Deathbed Edition
Personae

Preface to *Leaves of Grass,* 1855 Edition
Reading, Whitman's
"When Lilacs Last in the Dooryard Bloom'd"

Julian B. Freund
Park Forest, Illinois
"Artilleryman's Vision, The"
"Return of the Heroes, The"
"To a Certain Civilian"
"To One Shortly to Die"

Joe Boyd Fulton
Dalton College
"By That Long Scan of Waves"
Metaphysics
"On the Beach at Night Alone"
"Year that Trembled and Reel'd Beneath Me"

Paula K. Garrett
Millsaps College
Pennell, Joseph, and Elizabeth Robins
Whitman (Heyde), Hannah Louisa
Whitman (Van Nostrand), Mary Elizabeth

T. Gregory Garvey
Michigan State University
Douglas, Stephen Arnold
Holloway, Emory
Parton, James
Willis, Nathaniel Parker

Brent L. Gibson
Baylor University
Hartshorne, William
Pre-*Leaves* Poems
Tupper, Martin Farquhar

Sheree L. Gilbert
Arizona State University
"As I Lay with My Head in Your Lap
      Camerado"
"First O Songs for a Prelude"
"Spirit whose Work is Done"

Jonathan Gill
Columbia University
Brooklyn, New York
Treasurer's Office, Solicitor of the

Arthur Golden
City College, City University of New York
      (Emeritus)
Leaves of Grass, Variorum Edition
Leech, Abraham Paul
Walt Whitman's Blue Book

Chanita Goodblatt
Ben-Gurion University of the Negev, Israel
Israel, Whitman in

Mitch Gould
Atlanta, Georgia
Boker, George Henry
Love
Taylor, Bayard

Walter Graffin
University of Wisconsin, Parkside
Chase, Richard Volney
De Selincourt, Basil
Harris, Frank
New York *Times*

Rosemary Graham
St. Mary's College of California
Attorney General's Office, United States
"City Dead-House, The"
Collected Writings of Walt Whitman, The
Complete Writings of Walt Whitman, The
"Over the Carnage Rose Prophetic a Voice"

Charles B. Green
College of William and Mary
Hunkers
Libraries (New York)
Tammany Hall

Christopher O. Griffin
Baylor University
Baxter, Sylvester
Pride

Larry D. Griffin
Dyersburg State Community College
"America [Centre of equal daughters . . .]"
"Death of Abraham Lincoln"
Human Voice
Johnston, Dr. John
Wallace, James William

Kirsten Silva Gruesz
College of William and Mary
American Character
"By Blue Ontario's Shore"

Walter Grünzweig
Universität Dortmund, Germany
Bertz, Eduard
Freiligrath, Ferdinand
German-speaking Countries, Whitman in the
Heine, Heinrich
Herder, Johann Gottfried von
Imperialism

Interculturality
Knortz, Karl
Rolleston, Thomas William Hazen

Huck Gutman
University of Vermont
"As I Ebb'd with the Ocean of Life"
"Drum-Taps"
Ginsberg, Allen
"I Sing the Body Electric"
Williams, William Carlos

Joseph P. Hammond
Arizona State University
Comstock, Anthony
Harlan, James W.
Heywood, Ezra H.
Stevens, Oliver

Maverick Marvin Harris
East Texas Baptist University
"Broadway"
Democratic Party
Immigrants
Lafayette, Marquis de
New Orleans *Crescent*
New Orleans, Louisiana
New Orleans *Picayune*
"To a Historian"

W. Edward Harris
Indianapolis, Indiana
Epictetus
Higginson, Thomas Wentworth
Ingersoll, Robert Green
Lucretius (Titus Lucretius Carus)

Frederick Hatch
San Antonio, Texas
Chase, Salmon P.
Gurowski, Count Adam de
Presidents, United States
Republican Party
Speed, Attorney General James
Whigs

Burton Hatlen
University of Maine, Orono
"Our Old Feuillage"
"Sleepers, The"
"So Long!"
"Song for Occupations, A"
"Song of the Answerer"
"Song of the Banner at Daybreak"
"Song of the Broad-Axe"
"Song of the Rolling Earth, A"

Alan Helms
University of Massachusetts, Boston
"Fast Anchor'd Eternal O Love!"
"Live Oak with Moss"

Andrew C. Higgins
University of Massachusetts, Amherst
Bryant, William Cullen
Douglass, Frederick
Rhetorical Theory and Practice
Symonds, John Addington

Milton Hindus
Brandeis University (Emeritus)
Critics, Whitman's

Bernard Hirschhorn
New York, New York
Education, Views on
"Memories of President Lincoln"
Political Views
"To a President"

Harbour Fraser Hodder
North Brookfield, Massachusetts
Romanticism

Guiyou Huang
Kutztown University of Pennsylvania
"Beginning My Studies"
China, Whitman in
"Sketch, A"
"Unseen Buds"
"When I Read the Book"

Edward W. Huffstetler
Bridgewater College
Indian Affairs, Bureau of
"O Magnet-South"
South, The American
Spontaneity

George Hutchinson
University of Tennessee, Knoxville
Civil War, The
Racial Attitudes
Specimen Days
Stoicism

Jennifer A. Hynes
University of South Carolina, Columbia
Mitchell, Silas Weir
Stoddard, Richard Henry
Temperance Movement
Wright, Frances (Fanny)

Matthew Ignoffo
Eatontown, New Jersey
Cosmic Consciousness
"Dirge for Two Veterans"
"Lo, Victress on the Peaks"

Donald C. Irving
Grinnell College
Carnegie, Andrew
Roughs

John Lee Jellicorse
University of North Carolina, Greensboro
Literariness
Taylor, Father (Edward Thompson)

Robert Johnstone
University of North Carolina, Chapel Hill
"Inscriptions"
Poetic Theory

Sholom J. Kahn
Hebrew University of Jerusalem, Israel
Evil
"To Think of Time"

Martha A. Kalnin
Baylor University
"As I Sit Writing Here"
Denison, Flora MacDonald
Eyre, Ellen
Grey, Ellen

Arnie Kantrowitz
College of Staten Island, City University of New York
Brown, Lewis Kirk
Carpenter, Edward
Sawyer, Thomas P.
Stafford, Harry L.

Karen Karbiener
Columbia University
Long Island Democrat
Long Island Patriot
Long Island Star
Long Islander

Mary Louise Kete
University of Vermont
Sentimentality

Frances E. Keuling-Stout
New York University
Leaves of Grass, 1876, Author's Edition
Preface to *Two Rivulets*
Two Rivulets, Author's Edition

M. Jimmie Killingsworth
Texas A&M University
Human Body
Journalism, Whitman's
Scholarship, Trends in Whitman
Self-Reviews of the 1855 *Leaves*, Whitman's
　　Anonymous

Jerry F. King
Vancouver, Washington
Gosse, Sir Edmund
"Long, Too Long America"
"That Music Always Round Me"

Martin Klammer
Luther College
"Boston Ballad (1854), A"
Compromise of 1850
Free Soil Party
Slavery and Abolitionism
Wilmot Proviso

George Klawitter
St. Edward's University
"Ages and Ages Returning at Intervals"
"As Adam Early in the Morning"
France, Whitman in
"Native Moments"
"We Two, How Long We were Fool'd"

Ronald W. Knapp
Omaha, Nebraska
"Hast Never Come to Thee An Hour"
"I Dream'd in a Dream"
Pantheism
"Song of the Universal"

Denise Kohn
University of Houston
Tyndale, Hector
Tyndale, Sarah Thorn
Whitman, Hannah Brush

Alan E. Kozlowski
Loyola University, Chicago
Arnold, Matthew
["Long I Thought That Knowledge Alone
　　Would Suffice"]
Swinburne, Algernon Charles

Joann P. Krieg
Hofstra University
Birthplace, Whitman's
Bolton (England) "Eagle Street College"

Fritzinger, Frederick Warren
"Italian Music in Dakota"
Long Island, New York

David Kuebrich
George Mason University
Comradeship
Immortality
Religion
Sea, The
Soul, The

Donald D. Kummings
University of Wisconsin, Parkside
Allen, Gay Wilson
"America's Mightiest Inheritance"
Asselineau, Roger
Barrus, Clara
Bibliographies
Internet, Whitman on the
Miller, Edwin Haviland
Miller, James Edwin, Jr.
Teaching of Whitman's Works
White, William

Andrew Ladd
Emory University
Homer
Macpherson, James ("Ossian")
Swedenborg, Emanuel

Lyman L. Leathers
Ohio Wesleyan University (Emeritus)
Music, Whitman's Influence on

J.R. LeMaster
Baylor University
Collect
Prophecy
Redpath, James

Philip W. Leon
The Citadel
Buchanan, Robert
Conway, Moncure Daniel
Dowden, Edward
Drinkard, Dr. William B.
Eakins, Thomas
Osler, Dr. William
Perry, Bliss
Williams, Talcott

Carl Martin Lindner
University of Wisconsin, Parkside
Freedom

Jay Losey
Baylor University
"Hand-Mirror, A"
"Of Him I Love Day and Night"
"Thou Mother with Thy Equal Brood"

Deshae E. Lott
Texas A&M University
O'Connor (Calder), Ellen ("Nelly") M. Tarr
O'Connor, William Douglas

Jerome Loving
Texas A&M University
Biographies
Emerson, Ralph Waldo

Elmar S. Lueth
University of Iowa
Buffalo Free Soil Convention
Centennial Exposition (Philadelphia)
Crystal Palace Exhibition (New York)

William G. Lulloff
Eau Claire, Wisconsin
"Army Corps on the March, An"
"By the Bivouac's Fitful Flame"
"Come Up from the Fields Father"
Franklin Evans
"Mannahatta [I was asking . . .]"
"Vigil Strange I Kept on the Field One
    Night"

Phyllis McBride
Texas A&M University
Feudalism
Shakespeare, William

Patrick McGuire
University of Wisconsin, Parkside
"Angel of Tears, The"
"Bervance: or, Father and Son"
"Boy Lover, The"
"Child and the Profligate, The"
"Death in the School-Room (a Fact)"
"Death of Wind-Foot, The"
"Dumb Kate"
"Fireman's Dream, The"
"Half-Breed, The"
"Last Loyalist, The"
"Last of the Sacred Army, The"
"Legend of Life and Love, A"
"Lingave's Temptation"
"Little Jane"
"Little Sleighers, The"
"Love of Eris: A Spirit Record, The"

"Madman, The"
"My Boys and Girls"
"One Wicked Impulse!"
"Reuben's Last Wish"
"Richard Parker's Widow"
"Shadow and the Light of a Young Man's
    Soul, The"
"Shirval: A Tale of Jerusalem"
"Some Fact-Romances"
"Tomb Blossoms, The"
"Wild Frank's Return"

Alan L. McLeod
Rider College
Australia and New Zealand, Whitman in

Jim McWilliams
Troy, Alabama
Forster, E.M.
"I was Looking a Long While"
St. Louis, Missouri
"To a Western Boy"

Luke Mancuso
St. John's University
Leaves of Grass, 1867 Edition
Leaves of Grass, 1871–1872 Edition
Preface to *As a Strong Bird on Pinions Free*
Reconstruction
Sequel to Drum-Taps

Mordecai Marcus
University of Nebraska, Lincoln
"Proud Music of the Storm"

Ivan Marki
Hamilton College
Leaves of Grass, 1855 Edition
"Starting from Paumanok"

Robert K. Martin
Université de Montréal, Canada
Arvin, Newton
"City of Orgies"
Crane, Hart
"Dalliance of the Eagles, The"
"In Paths Untrodden"
Santayana, George
"Scented Herbage of My Breast"
"To a Stranger"
"What Think You I Take My Pen in Hand?"
"Whoever You are Holding Me Now in
    Hand"

John B. Mason
California State University, Northridge
Catalogues
Oratory
"Passage to India"

Julian Mason
University of North Carolina, Charlotte (Emeritus)
Alcott, Amos Bronson
Fuller, Margaret

N.J. Mason-Browne
Coe College
Canada, Whitman's Visit to
García Lorca, Federico
Pessoa, Fernando
"Reconciliation"

Dena Mattausch
Rockford College
Harned, Thomas Biggs
"Of the Terrible Doubt of Appearances"
Printing Business

John T. Matteson
Columbia University
Clarke, McDonald
Galaxy, The
Harris, Thomas Lake
Humboldt, Alexander von
Liebig, Justus
Neruda, Pablo
Time
West Jersey Press

Susan M. Meyer
Ohio State University
Actors and Actresses
Theaters and Opera Houses

Charles W. Mignon
University of Nebraska, Lincoln
"I Hear America Singing"
"Pioneers! O Pioneers!"

David G. Miller
Mississippi College
Schyberg, Frederik
Stafford, George and Susan M.
Whitman, Jesse W. (grandfather)
Worthington, Richard

James E. Miller, Jr.
University of Chicago (Emeritus)
"Calamus"
"Children of Adam"

Sex and Sexuality
"Song of Myself"

Andy J. Moore
Baylor University
Dana, Charles A.
Hugo, Victor
Joyce, James
Sand, George
Stevens, Wallace

Hadley J. Mozer
Baylor University
"Birds of Passage"
"O Living Always, Always Dying"

Terry Mulcaire
Northwestern University
"As Toilsome I Wander'd Virginia's Woods"
Dialectic
"One's-Self I Sing"
Technology
"To You [Whoever you are . . .]"

Maire Mullins
Saint Xavier University
Beach, Juliette H.
"From Pent-up Aching Rivers"
"Once I Pass'd through a Populous City"
"Spontaneous Me"
"To Rich Givers"
"Woman Waits for Me, A"

Willa Murphy
University of Notre Dame
Ireland, Whitman in

Martin G. Murray
The Washington Friends of Walt Whitman,
    Washington, D.C.
Doyle, Peter
Washington, D.C.
Whitman, Andrew Jackson
Whitman, George Washington

Joel Myerson
University of South Carolina, Columbia
Hotten, John Camden
McKay, David
Rhys, Ernest Percival

Howard Nelson
Cayuga Community College
Bucke, Richard Maurice
"Crossing Brooklyn Ferry"
"Miracles"
"Sparkles from the Wheel"
Timber Creek

Scott L. Newstrom
Grinnell College
Adams, Henry Brooks
Dartmouth College
Harper's Monthly

David Oates
Clark College
"Base of All Metaphysics, The"
"I Hear It was Charged against Me"
"Spirit That Form'd This Scene"
"To a Foil'd European Revolutionaire"
"Year of Meteors (1859–60)"

Steven Olson
Central Washington University
"From Far Dakota's Cañons"
"From Noon to Starry Night"
"Song of the Redwood-Tree"
Space
"To the Leaven'd Soil They Trod"
"Whispers of Heavenly Death"
"Whispers of Heavenly Death" (cluster)

Jon Panish
University of California, Irvine
Brooklyn *Freeman*
Miller, Henry
Radicalism

William A. Pannapacker
Harvard University
American Phrenological Journal
Associations, Clubs, Fellowships,
    Foundations, and Societies
Chronology
"Death's Valley"
Furness, Clifton Joseph
Genealogy
Life Illustrated
Lincoln, Abraham
Lowell, James Russell
North American Review, The
Osgood, James R.
Philadelphia, Pennsylvania
Putnam's Monthly
Washington, George

Maria Clara B. Paro
Universidade Estadual Paulista, Brazil
Portugal and Brazil, Whitman in

Vivian R. Pollak
Washington University
Dickinson, Emily
Motherhood

Kenneth M. Price
College of William and Mary
Dos Passos, John

Stephen Rachman
Michigan State University
American Whig Review
Broadway Journal
"By the Roadside"
Niagara Falls
Shephard, Esther
"Tramp and Strike Questions, The"
Trowbridge, John Townsend

Richard Raleigh
St. Thomas University, Miami, Florida
Hopkins, Gerard Manley
["Hours Continuing Long"]
"Letter to Ralph Waldo Emerson"
"Not Heat Flames Up and Consumes"
"When I Heard at the Close of the Day"
Wilde, Oscar

Katherine Reagan
Pierpont Morgan Library
Binns, Henry Bryan
Canby, Henry Seidel
Kennedy, William Sloane

Julie A. Rechel-White
Grand Valley State University
"Excelsior"
Holmes, Oliver Wendell
Longfellow, Henry Wadsworth
Whittier, John Greenleaf

Dennis K. Renner
Adrian College
Brooklyn *Daily Eagle*
Brooklyn *Daily Times*
Daybooks and Notebooks
Leaves of Grass, 1881–1882 Edition
Legacy, Whitman's
New York *Aurora*
Optimism

David S. Reynolds
Baruch College, City University of New York
Popular Culture, Whitman and

D. Neil Richardson
Georgetown University
"Eidólons"
Smuts, Jan Christian

Susan Rieke
Saint Mary College, Leavenworth, Kansas
"As at Thy Portals Also Death"
"Ashes of Soldiers"
"Songs of Parting"

John Rietz
Henry Ford Community College
Falmouth, Virginia
"Leaves-Droppings"
"My Picture-Gallery"
Whitman, Jesse (brother)
Whitman, Walter, Sr.

Susan L. Roberson
Auburn University
Gilder, Jeannette L.
Gilder, Richard Watson
Johnston, John H. and Alma Calder
Thoreau, Henry David

John F. Roche
Michigan State University
Architects and Architecture
Arts and Crafts Movement
Hartmann, C. Sadakichi

Phillip H. Round
University of Iowa
Boston, Massachusetts
Goethe, Johann Wolfgang von
"O Hymen! O Hymenee!"
"Supplement Hours"

Thomas Sanfilip
Wright College
Health
Italy, Whitman in
Tennyson, Alfred, Lord

Carmine Sarracino
Elizabethtown College
Burroughs, John and Ursula
Riverby
Sarrazin, Gabriel
"To a Common Prostitute"

Steven P. Schneider
University of Nebraska at Kearney
Great Plains and Prairies, The
"Poets to Come"
"Prairie-Grass Dividing, The"
Simpson, Louis

Robert J. Scholnick
College of William and Mary
Science

Steven Schroeder
Roosevelt University
Donaldson, Thomas
Heyde, Charles Louis
Lawrence, Kansas
Leland, Charles Godfrey

John E. Schwiebert
Weber State University
"Beat! Beat! Drums!"
"Bivouac on a Mountain Side"
"Cavalry Crossing a Ford"
"Clear Midnight, A"
"March in the Ranks Hard-Prest, and the
    Road Unknown, A"
"Sight in Camp in the Daybreak Gray and
    Dim, A"
"To the Garden the World"

Charley Shively
University of Massachusetts, Boston
Mexican War, The
Vaughan, Frederick B.

Alan Shucard
University of Wisconsin, Parkside
"Backward Glance O'er Travel'd Roads, A"
Eliot, T.S.
Lawrence, D.H.
Pound, Ezra
Sandburg, Carl

Conrad M. Sienkiewicz
Central Connecticut State University
"Here the Frailest Leaves of Me"
"Recorders Ages Hence"
"These I Singing in Spring"

Jesus Sierra-Oliva
San Diego, California
"Osceola"

Geoffrey M. Sill
Rutgers University, Camden
Camden, New Jersey
Harleigh Cemetery
Mickle Street House (Camden, New Jersey)

Sharron Sims
East Carolina University
Swinton, William

James Perrin Warren
Washington and Lee University
Style and Technique(s)

Jan Whitt
University of Colorado, Boulder
Leaves of Grass Imprints
Rome Brothers, The
Whitman, Nancy

Ted Widmer
Harvard University
Barnburners and Locofocos
Leggett, William L.
New York *Evening Post*
Providence, Rhode Island

Rosemary Gates Winslow
Catholic University of America
Abbott, Dr. Henry
Egyptian Museum (New York)
Prosody

A. James Wohlpart
University of South Florida
"On the Beach at Night"
"Patroling Barnegat"
"Sea-Drift"
"World Below the Brine, The"

Karen Wolfe
Temple University
"Good-Bye my Fancy!"
"Song of the Exposition"
Whitman, Louisa Orr Haslam (Mrs. George)

Sam Worley
Pennsylvania State University
Influences on Whitman, Principal

Arthur Wrobel
University of Kentucky
Democratic Vistas
Phrenology
Pseudoscience

Donald Yannella
Barat College
Duyckinck, Evert Augustus
Gray, Fred
Mathews, Cornelius
Pfaff's Restaurant
Stedman, Edmund Clarence
Swinton, John
Young America Movement

Carol M. Zapata-Whelan
California State University, Fresno
Contradiction
"For You O Democracy"
"Salut au Monde!"
Spain and Spanish America, Whitman in

Walt Whitman

Abbott, Dr. Henry (1812–1859)

During the years *Leaves of Grass* was first being composed, Walt Whitman passed many afternoons in conversation with Dr. Henry Abbott at Abbott's Egyptian Museum on Broadway. In a catalogue published to promote the exhibit, Abbott describes himself as "merely an amateur of antiquity as appeared to me illustrative of the religious and other customs of the ancient Egyptians, in whose country I have passed the last twenty years of my life" (Abbott 3).

An Englishman, Dr. Abbott departed on an expedition to Egypt when his family moved to America upon completion of the education of the children. He stayed in Egypt, practicing medicine, marrying an Armenian, and settling in Cairo. He amassed a collection of over one thousand ancient artifacts, often going into tombs himself for objects and spending by his account $100,000. He brought them to New York to find a buyer, but failing that, he opened the museum in 1853. He returned to Cairo in 1855, and the New-York Historical Society purchased the collection for $34,000 in 1859, a few months before his death.

In an essay written for *Life Illustrated* in 1855, Whitman praises the Egyptians' habit of living in daily awareness of a spirituality made keen by constant reminders of death. Reaching back past Greece and Rome to praise the life and religion of their forerunner, Whitman saw Egypt as alive, energetic, freedom-loving, and great—an older kindred of the American people. This sense of a culture teeming with life was captured by Dr. Abbott's talks of his life in Egypt and the vivid relics Whitman saw. Whitman also read books recommended in Abbott's *Catalogue,* chiefly the first on the list, by Sir John Gardner Wilkinson.

Rosemary Gates Winslow

Bibliography

Abbott, Henry. *Catalogue of a Collection of Egyptian Antiquities, the Property of Henry Abbott, M.D., Now Exhibiting at the Stuyvesant Institute.* New York: J.W. Watson, 1853.

New-York Historical Society. *Catalogue of the Museum and Gallery of Art of the New-York Historical Society.* New York: New York Historical Society, 1893.

Whitman, Walt. "One of the Lessons Bordering Broadway: The Egyptian Museum." *New York Dissected.* 1936. Ed. Emory Holloway and Ralph Adimari. Folcroft, Pa.: Folcroft Library Editions, 1972. 30–40.

See also EGYPTIAN MUSEUM (NEW YORK)

Actors and Actresses

The American theater and its actors were an important cultural influence on Walt Whitman. He attended the theater most regularly as a teenager from 1832–1836 and as a journalist from 1841–1849, and he wrote often about the early American theater in his waning years (1885–1890). During his theater-going years, Whitman attended productions featuring such favorites as Junius Brutus Booth, Charlotte Cushman, Edwin Forrest, Thomas Hamblin, Fanny Kemble, and William Charles Macready as well as lesser-known actors and actresses such as James H. Hackett, Henry Placide, T.D. Rice, Ada Webb, Adah Isaacs Menken, and Clara Fisher. *Specimen Days* (1882), *November Boughs* (1888), and *Good-Bye My Fancy* (1891) are important Whitman sources for the names of plays, theaters, and actors. They may also be found in his early newspaper articles.

Whitman was most impressed by Junius Brutus Booth (1796–1852), the leading tragedian of antebellum America, who was best known for his Shakespearean villain and madman roles: Richard III, Iago, Lear, and Othello. Whitman often commented upon the genius of Booth and called him "one of the grandest revelations of my life, a lesson of artistic expression" (*Prose Works* 2:597). Booth was born in England and in his teen years became the recognized rival of Edmund Kean as a tragedian. He was married twice and came to America in 1821, where he lived a traumatic life. He was most likely a manic-depressive with a serious alcohol problem that finally contributed to the eclipse of his artistic reputation. Booth was the father of the acclaimed tragedian Edwin Booth and the infamous John Wilkes Booth. The elder Booth is a key figure in the development of an American style of acting and was a precursor to Edwin Forrest. Booth was a fiery performer who could scare both audiences and other actors by the vehemence of his acting, and Whitman was impressed by the power of Booth's acting and his ability to totally immerse himself in a role. When acting Iago or Richard, he became those figures in much the same way that Whitman would "become" any number of personae in "Song of Myself."

Another important artistic influence on Whitman was Charlotte Cushman (1816–1876), the first American actress of note. Cushman began her career in Boston and New Orleans before moving to the New York stage. Her most famous roles were as Charles Dickens's Nancy Sykes ("the most intense acting ever *felt* on the Park boards" [*Gathering* 2:326]), Meg Merrilies in Scott's *Guy Mannering,* and Lady Macbeth. Cushman was equally famous for her portrayal of men: Hamlet, Romeo, and Oberon of *A Midsummer Night's Dream.* Whitman called Cushman the greatest performer he had seen and admired her for playing any role that would further her career.

America's first native-born star was Edwin Forrest (1806–1872), a committed Jacksonian Democrat and patriot who was best known for his muscular, booming style in such roles as Othello, Lear, Shylock, and Spartacus. Forrest was at the forefront of an international dispute over British vs. American styles of acting. The British style was best exemplified by William Charles Macready, subdued and rather tame, as opposed to the American style of Forrest, which was much more aggressive and sought to dominate audiences by the sheer force of voice and physique. This dispute came to a head in the infamous Astor Place Riot in 1849. Whitman initially favored the acting style of Forrest and claimed that the actor's performances strongly affected him and "permanently filter'd into [his] whole nature" (*Prose Works* 2:593). He ultimately cooled toward Forrest, however, and barely mentions Macready in his articles.

Thomas Hamblin (1800–1853) played Hamlet in 1825 but was best known for his management of the Bowery Theater. Whitman considered Hamblin great in his role as Arbaces, the Egyptian in *The Last Days of Pompeii,* and called his portrayal of Faulconbridge in *King John* the best performed on the stage. Whitman found Hamblin's comparatively small role superior to that of Charles Kean's King John, but it seems probable that Whitman confused Hamblin's role with that of Booth as King John in 1834. Because Whitman occasionally confused performances, biographical work concerning his interactions with the theater is difficult.

The English actress Fanny Kemble (1809–1893) impressed Whitman in his early days; he claims to have seen her every night she played the Park Theater. Kemble is best remembered by Whitman for her portrayal of Bianca in H.H. Milman's *Fazio,* Lady Townly in Colley Cibber's *The Provoked Husband,* and Marianna in Sheridan Knowles's *The Wife.* Whitman wrote that Kemble's performances "entranced us, and knock'd us about" (*Prose Works* 2:695).

Although Whitman commented upon performances, actors, and the theater in his essays, it is difficult to find instances of their direct influence on his poetry. On the other hand, critics have noted the multiple roles, or personae, assumed by the speaker in "Song of Myself" and throughout *Leaves of Grass.* In his notebooks, Whitman makes the connection, likening his poetic self to an actor and his literary audience to the audience of the theater. The immediate concern of the nineteenth-century American theater and its actors was to develop a style of drama and acting that was specifically American, a concern which Whitman shared, not only for the theater, but also for American literature in general.

Susan M. Meyer

Bibliography

Bogard, Travis, Richard Moody, and Walter J. Meserve. *American Drama.* Vol. 8 of *The Revels History of Drama in English.* London: Methuen, 1977.

Odell, George C.D. *Annals of the New York Stage.* 15 vols. New York: Columbia UP, 1927–1938.

Reynolds, David S. *Walt Whitman's America: A Cultural Biography.* New York: Knopf, 1995.

Stovall, Floyd. *The Foreground of "Leaves of Grass."* Charlottesville: UP of Virginia, 1974.

Whitman, Walt. *The Gathering of the Forces.* Ed. Cleveland Rodgers and John Black. 2 vols. New York: Putnam, 1920.

———. *Prose Works 1892.* Ed. Floyd Stovall. 2 vols. New York: New York UP, 1963–1964.

See also MENKEN, ADAH ISAACS; OPERA AND OPERA SINGERS; THEATERS AND OPERA HOUSES

Adams, Henry Brooks (1838–1918)

Great-grandson of President John Adams and grandson of President John Quincy Adams, Henry Adams was a historian known for his dynamic theory of history and his idea of historical force. He is remembered for his autobiographical *The Education of Henry Adams,* which maintains that his conventional education was incomplete and had to be supplemented by his own experience and study.

Though Adams infrequently mentioned Whitman in his published writing and correspondence, he clearly admired Whitman's poetry and compared other poets to Whitman. More importantly, in *The Education* he praised the "power of sex" evident in Whitman's poetry, which he thought other American authors lacked. The force of procreation found throughout Whitman mirrors Adams's own admiration for the force abundant in the thirteenth-century Virgin figure, which he opposed to the destructive power of the twentieth-century dynamo. In this way, Adams shared with Whitman an anxiety about modern technological culture. While both Whitman and Adams attempted to understand America in terms of historical and cosmic forces, Adams was more elegiac, while Whitman was more progressive and optimistic. Both authors wrote autobiographically, but Whitman's first-person voice contrasts with Adams's writing his *Education* in a third-person omniscient voice.

Scott L. Newstrom

Bibliography
Adams, Henry. *The Education of Henry Adams.* 1906. New York: Modern Library, 1931.

Aspiz, Harold. *Walt Whitman and the Body Beautiful.* Urbana: U of Illinois P, 1980.

Jordy, William H. "Henry Adams and Walt Whitman." *South Atlantic Quarterly* 40 (1941): 132–145.

Miller, Edwin Haviland. *Walt Whitman's Poetry: A Psychological Journey.* Boston: Houghton Mifflin, 1968.

See also SEX AND SEXUALITY; TECHNOLOGY

Africa, Whitman in

It is extremely difficult to assess and describe the impact of Walt Whitman in Africa. In the countries where Arabic is spoken, there is not even any translation of *Leaves of Grass.* There exists one only in the Middle East, which seems to be unknown in Africa. In Black Africa, where the original animism is still so strongly alive under the veneer of Islam or Christianity, there should be a public for a poet who believed in "[l]iving beings, identities now doubtless near us in the air that we know not of" ("Starting from Paumanok," section 10), for a poet who exclaimed, "Surely there is something more in each of the trees, some loving soul . . . O spirituality of things!" ("Song at Sunset"). There seems, however, to have been no echo to Whitman's poetry in any of the innumerable vernacular tongues and dialects. The oral poetry of the "griots" is still very much alive, but it remains profoundly traditional and impervious to outside influences. It is only in the literatures written in the former colonizers' tongues (English or French) that it is possible to encounter the influence of Whitman in the works of writers who have had access to French translations of *Leaves of Grass* or to the text itself. Walt Whitman thus appealed above all to highly literate readers.

Such was the case of Léopold Sédar Senghor (b. 1906), the first African to obtain the *agrégation* in French, Latin, and Greek and teach French and Latin in French *lycées;* he was later to become the first president of the Republic of Senegal. Despite his sound classical education, Senghor heard Whitman's yawp over the roofs of the world. *Leaves of Grass* gave him a greater shock and consequently influenced him more deeply than any other poem he had ever read. Romantic poetry, he said, "was always channelled between the mighty banks of Christianity . . . [w]hereas with Whitman it is truly primeval man and *natura naturans* which get expressed to the rhythm of days and nights, of ebb and flow, a rhythm which, for all its freedom, is strongly stressed" (Senghor 33). Although he treated almost exclusively African themes in his own poetry—*Chants d'Ombre* (Songs of Darkness), *Hosties noires* (Black Hosts), *Éthiopiques, Nocturnes,* etc.—Senghor was encouraged by Whitman's example to reject the constraints of French prosody and express himself in free verse—a medium which also enabled him to preserve the cadences of the oral poetry chanted by the griots in the native tongues he spoke himself, Sérère and Peul. Senghor, however, was an exception. It is symptomatic that *Leaves of Grass* is not taught in the University of Dakar because, as the professor in charge of American Literature there points out, "the very elusive unity of design of *Leaves of Grass* . . . would evade the students' reflections"; it is preferable to teach "full-length novels of quality" (qtd. in Pollet 27).

In South Africa the same phenomenon occurred as in Senegal. A distinguished intellectual, a philosopher this time rather than a poet—Jan Christian Smuts (1870–1950)—came under the spell of *Leaves of Grass* and wrote an important bio-critical essay on Whitman. Smuts was of Boer descent and even fought on the side of the Boers during the Boer War, but he wrote in English and eventually championed the reconciliation of the Boer and British settlers and became prime minister of the Union of South Africa. In his youth, he was firmly rooted in Christianity (Lutheran), classical studies, and German philosophy. During the Boer War, he carried two books in his saddlebags: a Greek New Testament and Kant's *Critique of Pure Reason,* but during his law studies in London he underwent a kind of conversion; he read "everything there was on Whitman in the British Museum." "Whitman did a great service to me," Smuts said, "in making me appreciate the Natural Man and freeing me from much [*sic*] theological or conventional preconceptions due to my very early pious upbringing. It was a sort of liberation. . . . Sin ceased to dominate my view of life . . ." (qtd. in Hancock 48). He felt there was a pre-established harmony between him and Whitman, since they both had Dutch blood and shared the same convictions regarding the world and democracy. Carried away by his enthusiasm, he wrote in the early 1890s *Walt Whitman: A Study in the Evolution of Personality,* which

helped him to crystallize the ideas he developed later in two philosophical treatises: *Inquiry into the Whole* (1911) and *Holism and Evolution* (1926). ("Holism" comes from the Greek word which means "whole.") Like Whitman, he believed that the world is a whole made up of dynamic wholes which are more than the sums of their component parts and tend to absorb more parts, for they obey a creative or emergent evolution inconsistent with bare mechanism. Thus, in his eyes, matter is alive, and the highest whole is Personality, which is characterized by the greatest freedom and creative power, as Whitman's personality showed, passing from a "period of Naturalism" to one of "Emotionalism" and one of "Applied Spiritualism," finally to reach a "Period of Pure or Religious Spiritualism," a harmonious self-realization tending toward the eventual realization of Truth, Beauty, and Goodness in the world. This dynamic optimism plunged its roots into *Leaves of Grass:* "The Lord advances and ever advances, / Always the shadows in front, / Always the outstretched Hand / Helping up the laggards" (Smuts's paraphrase of section 4 of "Faces," Smuts 18). Unfortunately, Smuts found no English publisher for his essay on Whitman, and it remained unpublished in his lifetime. It appeared only in 1973 in Detroit and thus had no impact in Africa.

Though Whitman saluted the "divine-soul'd African . . . superbly destin'd, on equal terms with me" ("Salut au Monde!," section 11), the climate has not been favorable to the growth of *Leaves of Grass* on African soil. However, *Leaves of Grass* has contributed to the growth of a great poet, Léopold Sédar Senghor, and to the foundation of the Union of South Africa and the League of Nations, which were both energetically championed by Jan Christian Smuts.

Roger Asselineau

Bibliography

Allen, Gay Wilson. *The New Walt Whitman Handbook.* 1975. New York: New York UP, 1986.

Asselineau, Roger, and William White, eds. *Walt Whitman in Europe Today.* Detroit: Wayne State UP, 1972.

Hancock, W.K. *Smuts: The Sanguine Years, 1870–1919.* Cambridge: Cambridge UP, 1962.

Pollet, Maurice. "Whitman in Dakar." *The Bicentennial Walt Whitman: Essays from "The Long-Islander."* Ed. William White. Detroit: Wayne State UP, 1976. 27.

Senghor, Léopold Sédar. "The Shock of *Leaves*

of Grass." *Walt Whitman in Europe To-day.* Ed. Roger Asselineau and William White. Detroit: Wayne State UP, 1972. 33.

Smuts, Jan Christian. *Walt Whitman: A Study in the Evolution of Personality.* Ed. Alan L. McLeod. Detroit: Wayne State UP, 1973.

Whitman, Walt. *Chants de la Terre qui Tourne.* Ed. and trans. Roger Asselineau. Paris: Nouveaux Horizons (Éditions Seghers), 1966.

Zell, Hans M., Carol Bundy, and Virginia Coulon, eds. *New Reader's Guide to African Literature.* 2nd ed. New York: Africana Publishing, 1983.

See also INTERCULTURALITY; SMUTS, JAN CHRISTIAN

A

Manuscript page of "After the Supper and Talk." Courtesy of the Library of Congress.

"After the Supper and Talk" (1887)

This poem was first published in *Lippincott's Magazine,* November 1887, and included as the last poem in the First Annex, "Sands at Seventy," 1891–1892 edition. Its earlier title, "So Loth to Depart," was more appropriate, if less euphonious.

In a dozen lines, this lyric describes the pain of a final parting from friends. The first lines suggest little more than a warm departure after a pleasant dinner, but lines 4–6, in parentheses, widen the implications. The leave-taker, never identified, is going on a journey, never to return, and will be present "[n]o more for communion of sorrow and joy." While he is leaving his friends, the darkness deepens and the figure of the departing one grows dimmer. Since Whitman regularly used the journey motif symbolically, the journey may be a journey into death. It may also be associated with Whitman himself, for he often addressed the themes of death and dying in poems written during his final years.

The structure of "After the Supper and Talk" is periodic, a favorite rhetorical device of the poet. Since the poem's strength derives from the reluctance of the departing one to leave his friends, a common human experience, the holding off of the main clause till the end is especially effective. The final line, "Garrulous to the very last," may best be read as abruptly shifting the mood from the somber and melancholy to the playful and teasing. The fact that Whitman knew himself to be loquacious increases the likelihood of his being the central figure. The hesitant, interrupting rhythm well suits the circumstance of the reluctant farewell.

"After the Supper and Talk" can be compared to two other farewell poems, "Good-Bye my Fancy!," the last poem in the Second Annex to the 1891–1892 edition of *Leaves of Grass,* and the longer and more personal "So Long!," which Whitman used as the closing poem of *Leaves* from the 1860 edition on.

David B. Baldwin

Bibliography

Whitman, Walt. *Leaves of Grass: Comprehensive Reader's Edition.* Ed. Harold W. Blodgett and Sculley Bradley. New York: New York UP, 1965.

See also DEATH; "GOOD-BYE MY FANCY!"; "GOOD-BYE MY FANCY" (SECOND ANNEX); "SANDS AT SEVENTY" (FIRST ANNEX); "SO LONG!"

Age and Aging

In January 1888 Whitman published in the New York *Herald* a highly romanticized and sentimentalized poem about the experience of aging which he called "Halcyon Days." In light of the strokes and other illnesses he had suffered during the fifteen years prior to the composition of this poem, it would seem that his depiction of a serene and untroubled old age facing the sunset years with equanimity is not based upon his own experience but is merely a literary or artistic conception, written in the affirmative tone of his early poems. Possibly it is not so much deception, or self-deception, as it is a way of continuing and sustaining the themes and attitudes of his life's work. As he often said in his later years, he was determined to keep as much as possible his own sickness and pain out of his poems; at the same time, however, he wanted to be honest and to put as much of his own personal experiences into them as he could. These contradictory aims account for the conflicting attitudes toward his own aging that appear in his later poems. In the context of *Leaves of Grass* the poems about old age are part of Whitman's philosophy of contraries; he could claim that his loss of energy, weakening mental powers, and even his fears of senility were not to be resisted but were to be thought of as part of the life cycle and part of a greater spiritual totality.

Only two days after the three strokes that came close to killing him in June 1888, Whitman had a remarkable conversation with Horace Traubel in which he examined his current condition in the context of his life, his beliefs, and what he had recently described in "A Backward Glance O'er Travel'd Roads" as his program to "exploit [my own] Personality, identified with place and date, in a far more candid and comprehensive sense than any hitherto poem or book" (Whitman 714).

"As long as I live the Leaves must go on," he said. "The Sands have to be taken as the utterances of an old man—a very old man. I desire that they may be interpreted as confirmations, not denials, of the work that has preceded. . . . I am not to be known as a piece of something but as a totality" (*With Walt Whitman* 1:271–272). "The Sands" he refers to is the "Sands at Seventy" collection, first published in 1888 in the *November Boughs* volume. The poems of his later years are clearly not the work of a poet in fullest command of his powers, but we find occasional flashes that recall his younger self. The dominant themes in the two annexes, "Sands at Seventy" and "Good-Bye my Fancy," as well as in "Old Age Echoes," are old age and death. Speaking to Horace Traubel about their subject matter, Whitman said, "Of my personal ailments, of sickness as an element, I never spoke a word until the first of the poems I call Sands at Seventy were written, and then some expression of invalidism seemed to be called for" (*With Walt Whitman* 2:234). He realized that, if he were to be true to his own stated goal of reflecting the life of an old man in his poems, he had to include references to his sickness and invalidism, since they had become so much a part of his life.

Some of the same painful self-awareness that formerly centered on sexual questions in the "Calamus" poems and elsewhere was in later life directed toward another personal experience: growing old. This questioning mood may be found in "Queries to My Seventieth Year," published about a month before Whitman's sixty-ninth birthday in 1888. It had become clear to him by that time that he would never achieve the national fame and recognition he had hoped for, and after his first stroke he necessarily became more aware of his vulnerability, his oncoming old age, and his mortality. The passages in which he describes the aging Columbus, the "batter'd, wreck'd old man" who ended his life despised and defeated, quite clearly refer to himself as well.

Three poems in the "Sands at Seventy" collection are similarly indirect in their treatment of old age. In one of these, "The Dismantled Ship," he describes an "old dismasted, gray and batter'd ship, disabled, done." "After free voyages to all the seas of the earth," Whitman writes, the ship is "haul'd up at last and hawser'd tight, / Lies rusting, mouldering." Another is "Twilight" (1887), which shows that Whitman was thinking more and more about death—not death in an abstract philosophical way, but his own death, including the death of consciousness.

The contradiction between his own feelings and the posture he wanted to maintain as a poet often gave Whitman trouble. In the fall of 1888, when his immobility forced him to sell his horse and carriage, he remarked to Traubel, "It marks a new epoch in my life: another stage on the down-hill road." Traubel replied, "I shouldn't think with your idea of death that you would speak of it as a *down* road." And Whitman answered, "Sure enough—the word was false: *up* road: up—up: another stage on the up-hill road:

that certainly seems more like me and I want to be like myself" (*With Walt Whitman* 2:273).

Less direct than some others in its use of imagery suggestive of old age is "You Lingering Sparse Leaves of Me." In this poem Whitman compares himself to a tree in autumn, whose "Leaves" are "tokens diminute and lorn—(not now the flush of May, or July clover-bloom—no grain of August now)." Still the lingering sparse leaves are, he says, "my soul-dearest leaves confirming all the rest, / The faithfulest—hardiest—last." Once again we hear a note of insistence—he protests too much in his claims that these last leaves are his best.

"Old Age's Lambent Peaks," Whitman told Traubel, was "an essential poem—it needed to be made" (*With Walt Whitman* 2:289). It characterizes old age as a time to look at the world and at life "in falling twilight." This poem also seems an effort to justify this stage of life, stated in Whitman's characteristic affirmative tone. While the poem stands in opposition to much of what he said as a young man celebrating manly vigor, it is consistent with the attitude in "Song of Myself" and repeated throughout his life that whatever he is experiencing at the moment is for the best.

Donald Barlow Stauffer

Bibliography

Fillard, Claudette. "Le Vannier de Camden: Vieillesse, Poésie, et les Annexes de *Leaves of Grass*." *Études Anglaises* 45 (1992): 311–323.

Stauffer, Donald Barlow. "Walt Whitman and Old Age." *Walt Whitman Review* 24 (1978): 142–148.

Traubel, Horace. *With Walt Whitman in Camden*. Vol. 1. Boston: Small, Maynard, 1906; Vol. 2. New York: Appleton, 1908.

Trent, Josiah C. "Walt Whitman: A Case History." *Surgery, Gynecology and Obstetrics* 87 (1948): 113–121.

Whitman, Walt. *Prose Works 1892*. Ed. Floyd Stovall. Vol. 2. New York: New York UP, 1964.

See also "Backward Glance O'er Travel'd Roads, A"; Death; "Good-Bye my Fancy" (Second Annex); "Halcyon Days"; Health; *November Boughs*; "Old Age Echoes"; "Old Age's Lambent Peaks"; "Prayer of Columbus"; "Sands at Seventy" (First Annex); Traubel, Horace L.; "You Lingering Sparse Leaves of Me"

"Ages and Ages Returning at Intervals" (1860)

"Ages and Ages Returning at Intervals" first appears in the 1860 edition of *Leaves of Grass*, where it is twelfth among the cluster of "Enfans d'Adam." Its position, however, in the final edition (1881) is eighth. Minor variants for the various editions, mostly of punctuation marks, are noted in the *Variorum* (2:362–363). In his emendations of the 1860 edition, Whitman added a new opening line, "With the old, the potent original loins," words he lifted and canceled from line 3 of the poem. In a second review, he restored line 3 to its earlier reading, except for the word "original." However, the poem appeared in subsequent editions with the word restored to line 3 and the new first line of the poem canceled.

Aspiz feels that the poem blends lust and transcendence in the Adamic narrator, furthering the Whitmanesque notion that sexuality is basically spiritual, a notion that Allen also finds in the poem, in the form of Whitman's belief that the soul identifies itself through sex. Miller sees in the poem an attempt to show that Adam's innocence did not die in Eden but rather returns from time to time, significantly here in the "Children of Adam" cluster.

George Klawitter

Bibliography

Allen, Gay Wilson. *Walt Whitman Handbook*. 1946. New York: Hendricks House, 1962.

Aspiz, Harold. "Sexuality and the Language of Transcendence." *Walt Whitman Quarterly Review* 5.2 (1987): 1–7.

Killingsworth, M. Jimmie. *Whitman's Poetry of the Body: Sexuality, Politics, and the Text*. Chapel Hill: U of North Carolina P, 1989.

Miller, James E., Jr. *A Critical Guide to "Leaves of Grass."* Chicago: U of Chicago P, 1957.

Whitman, Walt. *Leaves of Grass: A Textual Variorum of the Printed Poems*. Ed. Sculley Bradley, Harold W. Blodgett, Arthur Golden, and William White. 3 vols. New York: New York UP, 1980.

———. *Walt Whitman's Blue Book*. Ed. Arthur Golden. 2 vols. New York: New York Public Library, 1968.

See also AMERICAN ADAM; "CHILDREN OF ADAM"; SEX AND SEXUALITY

Alcott, Amos Bronson (1799–1888)

Bronson Alcott, educator and philosopher, was born at Spindle Hill, Connecticut, on 29 November 1799. His formal schooling ended when he was thirteen, and he became a peddler. After being impressed by Quaker beliefs in 1822, he adapted many of them to his use as a teacher and thinker, particularly the belief that there is something of God in each person. This informed the teaching he did (beginning in 1824) in a series of schools, primarily in New England, over much of the rest of his life. In 1830 he married Abigail May, and they eventually had four daughters, including Louisa May (1832), the writer. His liberal ideas about education were often controversial and misunderstood, and his difficult-to-read writings were not very helpful. He was a participant in the transcendental movement and moved to Concord, Massachusetts, in 1840, where he lived most of the rest of his life. His family was often in financial uncertainty until the authorial success of Louisa. He was paralyzed by a stroke in 1882 and died in Boston on 4 March 1888.

Walt Whitman and Alcott shared various general beliefs, including those related to transcendentalism and those growing out of the interest of each in Quaker ideas and practice. In the fall of 1856 Alcott went to New York for several months. During the preceding winter he had been introduced to Whitman's 1855 *Leaves of Grass* and found himself enthusiastic about it, so on 4 October 1856 he went to Brooklyn to visit Whitman. Alcott visited with Whitman a number of times over the ensuing weeks and was given a copy of the 1856 *Leaves of Grass*. Although they were different in temperament and demeanor, they came to admire each other and to consider themselves friends, a friendship which lasted the rest of their lives. They not only explored each other's ideas, but Whitman was also glad to be able to discuss Ralph Waldo Emerson with someone who knew Emerson. Over the years, they occasionally corresponded and exchanged things they had published. Their last meeting came on 17 September 1881 when Whitman visited New England. As time passed, Alcott's admiration for Whitman as both man and writer had steadily grown, and he had come to think of Whitman as a wise representative of America and its potential. Whitman thought Alcott's best trait to be his upholding of the supremacy of the spiritual aspects of humanity and life. Alcott wrote to Whitman on 28 April 1868, "I am interested in all you choose to communicate" (*Letters* 435), and on 10 October 1856 he wrote to Abigail Alcott, "I am well rewarded for finding this extraordinary man" (*Letters* 200). In 1888, after Alcott's death, Whitman said, "Alcott was always my friend" (*With Walt Whitman* 1:333) and called him one of "the wise wondering seers . . . quite exceptional" (*With Walt Whitman* 3:267).

Julian Mason

Bibliography

Alcott, A. Bronson. *The Journals of Bronson Alcott.* Ed. Odell Shepard. Boston: Little, Brown, 1938.

———. *The Letters of A. Bronson Alcott.* Ed. Richard L. Herrnstadt. Ames: Iowa State UP, 1969.

Dahlstrand, Frederick C. *Amos Bronson Alcott: An Intellectual Biography.* Rutherford, N.J.: Fairleigh Dickinson UP, 1982.

Shepard, Odell. *Pedlar's Progress: The Life of Bronson Alcott.* Boston: Little, Brown, 1937.

Traubel, Horace. *With Walt Whitman in Camden.* Vol. 1. New York: Small, Maynard, 1906; Vol. 3. New York: Mitchell Kennerley, 1914.

See also EMERSON, RALPH WALDO; QUAKERS AND QUAKERISM; THOREAU, HENRY DAVID; TRANSCENDENTALISM

Allen, Gay Wilson (1903–1995)

For his monumental *The Solitary Singer: A Critical Biography of Walt Whitman* (1955; rev. ed. 1967), for his highly acclaimed and widely consulted guides, the *Walt Whitman Handbook* (1946) and *The New Walt Whitman Handbook* (1975; rpt., with a new introduction and selected bibliography, 1986), for his work (with Sculley Bradley) as General Editor of the 22-volume *Collected Writings of Walt Whitman* (1961–1984), and for his many other monographs, editions, and articles on America's foremost poet, Gay Wilson Allen became internationally known as the dean of Whitman scholars. His first publication on the poet was an article entitled "Biblical Analogies for Walt Whitman's Prosody," which appeared in *Revue Anglo-Américaine* in 1933; his last was *Walt Whitman and the World* (coedited with Ed Folsom), a collection of foreign criticism published in 1995, a few months after his death on August 6.

Born in Lake Junaluska, North Carolina, and educated at Duke University (A.B., 1926;

A.M., 1929) and the University of Wisconsin (Ph.D., 1934), Allen was a dedicated teacher at both Bowling Green State University (1935–1946) and New York University (1946–1969). He stated in 1991 that he "had not planned an academic career as a Whitman scholar, or even as a teacher of American literature" (Allen 92). Had opportunities presented themselves, he likely would have pursued a career in Middle English. However, certain serendipitous occurrences led him into Whitman studies—a fascination with prosody, an interest in connections between Whitman and French historian Jules Michelet, and, most important, his discovery of a Danish biography, Frederik Schyberg's *Walt Whitman* (1933; translated into English by Allen's wife, Evie Allison Allen, 1951). Allen was profoundly influenced by Schyberg's analysis of the successive editions of *Leaves of Grass* and by his discussion of "Whitman in World Literature." In the end, Schyberg inspired Allen to write his own biography of Whitman.

Hailed by critics as perceptive, thorough, and objective, *The Solitary Singer* has been touted for many years as the definitive biography of Whitman. Allen's genius seems to have resided in the artful rendering of lives, for he also wrote major biographies of William James and Ralph Waldo Emerson, as well as biographical studies of Herman Melville, Carl Sandburg, and (with Roger Asselineau) Hector St. John de Crèvecoeur. His life of Whitman prompted the U.S. State Department to send Allen, along with William Faulkner, on a 1955 tour of Japan. It also had much to do with his receipt, in 1977, of the Jay B. Hubbell Medallion for contributions to American literature.

Donald D. Kummings

Bibliography

Allen, Gay Wilson. "History of My Whitman Studies." *Walt Whitman Quarterly Review* 9 (1991): 91–100.

Blair, Stanley S. "The Gay Wilson Allen Papers." *Walt Whitman Quarterly Review* 12 (1994): 106–108.

Christie, N. Bradley. "Gay Wilson Allen." *American Literary Biographers: First Series.* Ed. Steven Serafin. Vol. 103 of *Dictionary of Literary Biography.* Detroit: Gale Research, 1991. 3–12.

See also BIOGRAPHIES; COLLECTED WRITINGS OF WALT WHITMAN, THE; CRITICS, WHITMAN'S; MICHELET, JULES; SCHYBERG, FREDERIK

"America [Centre of equal daughters . . .]" (1888)

"America" first appeared in the New York *Herald* (11 February 1888) and then in the "Sands at Seventy" annex to *Leaves of Grass* in 1891–1892. Whitman, as he had done in 1872 in "As a Strong Bird on Pinions Free" ("Thou Mother with Thy Equal Brood" [1881]), addresses "America" as "Mother." The poem, like many from the "Sands at Seventy" annex, is one sentence. In that single sentence, Whitman displays several oral tendencies, including the catalogue of the country's components, clear parallel structure, and the homeostasis suggested by "the adamant of Time."

Whitman's "America" equalizes both the sons and daughters for whom the "seated Mother" is the "[c]entre." Whitman thus provides another early statement of the equality of the sexes, extending such equality despite age— "all alike endear'd, grown, ungrown, young or old." The sons and daughters make up an admirable family whose members are characteristically "[s]trong, ample, fair, endurable," and "rich." As with the "Earth," "Freedom," "Law," and "Love"—anything that is constant, that is persistent, and that continues uninterrupted—"America" is "[p]erennial." "Chair'd in the adamant of Time" further emphasizes the constancy of Whitman's "Mother."

Whitman's feminine, matriarchal America provides an opposite alternative to the masculine, patriarchal, capitalist America of the late nineteenth century. Like Liberty, the Statue in New York Harbor, and the figures on the obverses of numerous nineteenth- and twentieth-century American coins, Whitman's "Mother" provides readers with powerful associations, including the unlimited potential for revolutionary change in a feminine country where one enjoys the rights of "life, liberty, and the pursuit of happiness."

"America" may be the only poem Whitman ever recorded. Originally recorded in 1890, the cylinder, which contains Whitman reading the first four lines of "America," purportedly was once in the collection of Roscoe Haley (1889–1982). On 5 August 1951, Leon Pearson broadcast Whitman reading "America" on his NBC radio program *Yesterday, Today, and Tomorrow.* Audio-Text Cassettes in the 1970s included the recording in a cassette tape series for classroom use. The Belfer Audio Lab and Archives at Syracuse University holds a similar recording on an acetate disk. How appropriate that Whitman, in the only recording of his voice, should speak out about such an America.

Larry D. Griffin

Bibliography

Folsom, Ed. "The Whitman Recording." *Walt Whitman Quarterly Review* 9 (1992): 214–216.

Whitman, Walt. "America." 1890. *Voices of the Poets: Readings by Great American Poets from Walt Whitman to Robert Frost.* American Literary Voices Audiotape. 14026. Center for Cassette Studies, 1974.

———. *Leaves of Grass: Comprehensive Reader's Edition.* Ed. Harold W. Blodgett and Sculley Bradley. New York: New York UP, 1965.

———. *Leaves of Grass: A Textual Variorum of the Printed Poems.* Ed. Sculley Bradley, Harold W. Blodgett, Arthur Golden, and William White. Vol. 3. New York: New York UP, 1980.

See also AMERICAN CHARACTER; EQUALITY; "SANDS AT SEVENTY" (FIRST ANNEX)

American Adam

Leaves of Grass dramatizes Whitman's attempt to reestablish the Adamic man of the Western world. The *Leaves of Grass* persona projects a world of order and meaning into a sheer vacuum. Companionless, he finds himself in an Adamic condition, in a "vacant, vast surrounding" ("A Noiseless Patient Spider"), and his only recourse is to create a world of splendor and variety for himself.

In the opening lines of "Starting from Paumanok," Whitman provides a description of the genesis of the poetic self. Whitman has his poetic self start from Paumanok; the Native American place name emphasizes America's beginnings and symbolically associates America's and the poet's origins with the creation of the world itself. He concludes section 1 with a metaphor of the solitary singer: "Solitary, singing in the West, I strike up for a New World." In the first two sections of the poem, Whitman places the poetic self in the central procession, developing both his mythic and personal portrait. In section 17 Whitman's Adamic man of the Western world announces a "new race, dominating previous ones and grander far."

In *The American Adam*, R.W.B. Lewis discusses Whitman's persona as an extreme example of the Adamic type: an individual undefiled by inheritance, an innocent. Opening lines like "Out of the cradle endlessly rocking" and "Unfolded out of the folds of the woman, the man comes unfolded" emphasize his newness. Whitman's natural unfallen man is truly awake, like "Adam early in the morning, / Walking forth from the bower refresh'd with sleep" ("As Adam Early in the Morning"). "[H]ankering, gross, mystical, nude," this new Adam makes holy whatever he touches ("Song of Myself," section 20).

Whitman's Adamic hero is a creator and a namer. He gives birth to the human race out of his love affair with himself. "If I worship one thing more than another," he proclaims, "it shall be the spread of my own body" ("Song of Myself," section 24). Whitman realizes that love originates in self-love, that narcissism is an important stage of the growth process. This love is for the whole being: the inseparable body and soul. Like the "noiseless, patient spider [who] launch'd forth filament, filament, filament, out of itself," the New Adam spins his own conditions. He projects his own reality onto the emptiness. In so doing, he creates an image of America in all its diversity, promise, and confusion. Lewis has suggested that Adam integrates the idea of Eve into the concept of himself and the result of his self-love is the conception of the human race. Moreover, playing both Adam and Eve, Whitman's persona gives birth to himself as a poet as well.

The things that Whitman's Adam names come into being because the name is the soul of the concrete reality it represents. In section 16 of "Starting from Paumanok," Whitman focuses on the organic connection between the names of places and their spirits: "Okonee, Koosa, Ottawa, Monongahela, Sauk, Natchez, Chattahoochee, Kaqueta, Oronoco, / Wabash, Miami, Saginaw, Chippewa, Oshkosh, Walla-Walla / Leaving such to the States they melt, they depart, charging the water and the land with names." The words enable the Adamic hero to become one with all the things he names, and through them he is able to connect mystically to the universe. With words, he creates an imagined world and, with his words, he connects to it. The Adamic hero incorporates everything, and this expansive self Whitman called "cosmos."

Whitman's connection of the self to the universe is paradoxical: man is unitary, integral to himself, and, at the same time, he is equal to everything else. "I celebrate myself and sing myself, / And what I assume you shall assume, / For every atom belonging to me as good belongs to you" ("Song of Myself," section 1). He celebrates himself as an enlightened Everyman—the representative man who will attempt to call forth the heroism in his readers.

The powers of genesis are his because he is the poet. In "Song of the Broad-Axe," Whitman's persona first comes before us as a blacksmith, manufacturer of the symbolic ax which creates an American panorama, artifacts shaped from the American forests. This is similar to the poet who with his pen shapes his poems out of the fiber of the United States. The ax and the pen are tools for harmoniously unifying America's schisms. In "Song of the Redwood-Tree," the sequoia becomes a symbol of the material wealth, willing to be felled for the "superber race" of Americans. In contrast to the emphasis on man's creativity and control over nature in "Song of the Broad-Axe," "Song of the Redwood-Tree" focuses on the moral influence of the environment on man.

Consisting of sixteen poems, "Children of Adam" is set in the Garden of Eden. Although beautiful and peaceful, Whitman's Eden is not the Garden of Genesis. Instead, it is an earthly Eden of Delight, the site of bodily joy and sexual fulfillment. When Whitman declares in "Starting from Paumanok" "a world primal again" (section 17), he connects it with newness, expansion, and turbulence. Similarly, Whitman's Adam is strong, vigorous, and sexual, with limbs quivering with the fire "that ever plays through them" ("To the Garden of the World"). Celebrating the physical act of procreation, Whitman proclaims sex to be as fundamental in the physical world as love in the spiritual world. Adam is not debased, he does not carry the burden of original sin, and his body is as sacred as his soul. In Whitman's Eden, all gender differences disappear, and Eve's body and soul are equally perfect.

Critics Thomas Crawley and Harold Bloom assert that Whitman's persona is more like the second Adam than the first. Whitman's New Adam is "well-begotten and raised by a perfect mother" ("Starting from Paumanok," section 1). He reaches out Christlike and offers aid and encouragement to his fellow man. Dispensing biscuits and milk, he offers the bread of life. He identifies with all experience: "All sorrow, labor, suffering, I, tallying it, absorb in myself" ("Chanting the Square Deific," section 2). He walks the hills of Judea with God by his side. He knows that he is deathless and that nothing is final. Crawley argues that the Christ symbol is the most important symbol in *Leaves of Grass* and that the "climactic" passage in "Song of Myself" occurs when Whitman's persona identifies himself and all humans with the crucified Christ. The "friendly and flowing savage" is absorbed into the Christ figure, the symbol of the divinity that lies dormant in civilized man.

In "Passage to India," Whitman proclaims the poet to be the true son of God. Unlike Christ, the poet does not advocate sacrifice. Embracing atheists and skeptics, he accepts all. For Whitman, the material is as important and as divine as the spiritual. "And nothing, not God, is greater to one than one's self is" ("Song of Myself," section 48).

Deborah Dietrich

Bibliography

Bloom, Harold. "Whitman's Image of Voice: To the Tally of My Soul." *Walt Whitman.* Modern Critical Views. Ed. Harold Bloom. New York: Chelsea House, 1985. 127–147.

Crawley, Thomas Edward. *The Structure of "Leaves of Grass."* Austin: U of Texas P, 1970.

Hoffman, Daniel. "'Hankering, Gross, Mystical, Nude': Whitman's 'Self' and the American Tradition." *Walt Whitman of Mickle Street.* Ed. Geoffrey M. Sill. Knoxville: U of Tennessee P, 1994. 1–17.

Lewis, R.W.B. *The American Adam.* Chicago: U of Chicago P, 1955.

Miller, James E., Jr. "America's Epic." *Whitman: A Collection of Critical Essays.* Twentieth Century Views. Ed. Roy Harvey Pearce. Englewood Cliffs, N.J.: Prentice-Hall, 1962. 60–65.

Pearce, Roy Harvey. *The Continuity of American Poetry.* Princeton: Princeton UP, 1961.

See also "AGES AND AGES RETURNING AT INTERVALS"; "AS ADAM EARLY IN THE MORNING"; "CHILDREN OF ADAM"; "SONG OF MYSELF"; "STARTING FROM PAUMANOK"; "TO THE GARDEN THE WORLD"

American Character

As the self-proclaimed "bard of Democracy," Whitman set out both to portray the national character and to reshape it according to his own convictions. The 1855 Preface proclaims that the "genius of the United States" is expressed "most in the common people" (Whitman 5–6): the working men, artisans, farmers, housewives, and "roughs" who populate the panoramic canvases of the poems. In choosing such figures to represent the "splendid average" of the American, Whitman forged a new poetic practice from the principles of self-determination and equality set forth in the Declaration of Independence; *Leaves of Grass* was to be its literary equivalent, a radical statement of separation from European models. Moreover, by depicting women, blacks, and native peoples in the poems, Whitman revised the original revolutionary compact to include those whom it had left out. Although disease, death, and injustice lurk in the poet's field of vision, his catalogue of American attributes—the wholehearted embrace of modernity and progress, a rejection of social hierarchies, frankness of manners, Emersonian self-reliance—is essentially optimistic.

While Whitman was not the first to call for an indigenous American literature, he went beyond native subject matter to democratize poetic language itself: borrowing words from everyday speech, addressing the reader boldly and familiarly. More radically, the very structure of *Leaves* was designed to reflect the national principle of equality. "The United States themselves are essentially the greatest Poem," he writes in the Preface (5), and the book, similarly, is an aggregate of diverse parts, of interconnected responses to the same central theme. The poems together suggest the pluralistic nature of life in the United States, which is "not merely a nation but a teeming nation of nations" (5). As it accumulated more and more "leaves" over the years, the work approached a massive, epic scale appropriate to the rapidly expanding country.

The exuberance of Whitman's early vision reflects a general antebellum faith in America's destined greatness. Whitman was fascinated by advances in natural science and medicine, and particularly by phrenology, the "science of character," with its tantalizing claim to reveal the hidden origins of human behavior. Improving the individual could potentially create a perfect society: "Produce great Persons, the rest follows" ("By Blue Ontario's Shore," section 3). "Song of Myself" relies on the idea that the poet's own character is representative of the nation's: "Walt Whitman, an American, one of the roughs, a kosmos" (section 24, 1855 *Leaves*) embodies all aspects of American reality. Whitman often fictionalizes details of his life as he creates this idealized poetic persona. In *Specimen Days* (1882), for example, he describes his hereditary background as a healthy amalgam of different nationalities, much like the "[g]rand, common stock" of the well-bred, robust race of Americans he praises in *Democratic Vistas* (946). In doing so, he glosses over the actual history of mental and physical illnesses in the family. This discrepancy underscores the strength of Whitman's belief in a fundamental correspondence between the body and the inner character and in well-directed procreative energy as a means to perfect both.

The healthy surge of this new breed could not, however, overcome the most pressing social and political problem of the day, the racial division between black and white. Whitman was aware that the existence of slavery exposed an underlying paradox in his identification of individual freedom as the most basic component of American character. Although hesitant to endorse abolitionism, he opposed the extension of slavery into the Western territories and, in his journalistic writings, excoriated the weakness of compromise-seeking politicians whom he saw as alienated from the will of the people. The increasingly fractious national debates that culminated in the Civil War threatened to undermine the foundations of a poetic and personal philosophy built around the concept of union, contributing to Whitman's artistic crisis of the late 1850s.

Like most of his contemporaries, Whitman saw the war as a struggle to maintain the Union rather than to abolish slavery. Paradoxically, his firsthand experience with wartime devastation provided him with a renewed sense of mission. The task of national healing, as he proposes in *Democratic Vistas* (1871), must begin with a spiritual regeneration. He diagnoses the national body as "canker'd, crude, superstitious, and rotten" (937). Having survived the sectional crisis, postwar America is endangered by soulless mercantilism; the gap between rich and poor is growing, along with the social distinctions that *Leaves* had hoped to erase. His faith in political leaders at an ebb, Whitman insinuates that American poets alone can redeem the nation from the moral corruption and degradation into which it has fallen. Under their guidance, he predicts, humankind will evolve spiritually so as to spread the idea of democracy over the globe. Through this prophetic turn, the later Whitman thus recovers some of his initial optimism.

Readers abroad received *Leaves of Grass* as a major statement on the American character long before most of Whitman's countrymen were willing to do so. Foreign audiences have tended to be both more lavish in their praise and more vocal in their skepticism. D.H. Lawrence, for instance, vividly describes Whitman's all-embracing Self as a careening automobile heedless of what it crushes, and Cuban revolutionary poet José Martí notes uncomfortably that Whitman's image of an America extending from Canada to the Caribbean casts an imperial net over the hemisphere. Many commentators in the United States prefer to separate Whitman's nationalistic claims from his stylistic innovations and his pioneering treatment of sexuality; however, critics such as Betsy Erkkila and Kerry Larson insist that the same principle motivates both his politics and his poetics. Although *Leaves* may not provide a final answer to the challenge of pluralism that is built into the American constitution, its textual design, unifying the many into one, offers an implicit response.

Kirsten Silva Gruesz

Bibliography

Erkkila, Betsy. *Whitman the Political Poet.* New York: Oxford UP, 1989.

Kaplan, Justin. *Walt Whitman: A Life.* New York: Bantam, 1982.

Larson, Kerry C. *Whitman's Drama of Consensus.* Chicago: U of Chicago P, 1988.

Reynolds, David S. *Walt Whitman's America: A Cultural Biography.* New York: Knopf, 1995.

Whitman, Walt. *Complete Poetry and Collected Prose.* Ed. Justin Kaplan. New York: Library of America, 1982.

See also DEMOCRACY; *DEMOCRATIC VISTAS*; EQUALITY; FREEDOM; IMMIGRANTS; INDIVIDUALISM; INTERCULTURALITY; LABOR AND LABORING CLASSES; *LEAVES OF GRASS*; NATIVE AMERICANS (INDIANS); PREFACE TO *LEAVES OF GRASS*, 1855 EDITION; RACIAL ATTITUDES

American Phrenological Journal

Published in New York by Fowler and Wells from January 1851 to April 1861, the *American Phrenological Journal and Repository of Science, Literature and General Intelligence* continued the *American Phrenological Journal and Miscellany,* which was published in Philadelphia by Adam Waldie from October 1838 to December 1850. In May 1861 it merged with *Life Illustrated,* another Fowler and Wells periodical, to form the *American Phrenological Journal and Life Illustrated,* which ran from May of 1861 to December of 1869.

In the late 1840s Whitman developed a professional relationship with phrenologists Lorenzo and Orson Fowler and their partner, Samuel R. Wells. Fowler and Wells sold the first edition of *Leaves of Grass* (1855) in their shop at 308 Broadway, and they permitted Whitman to use the *American Phrenological Journal* to advertise his book and to write his own review, "An English and an American Poet" (October 1855). The review contrasts Alfred, Lord Tennyson's *Maud, and Other Poems* (1855) with *Leaves of Grass* (1855). A statement of literary nationalism, Whitman's review describes Tennyson's poetry as a product of aristocratic decadence, while Whitman's poems are an outgrowth of democratic vitality. Whitman concludes that he will prove "either the most lamentable of failures or the most glorious of triumphs, in the known history of literature" (45).

The similarity in style between Whitman's review in the *American Phrenological Journal* and his 1855 Preface resulted in a controversy. It was not uncommon for writers in this period to review their own books; nevertheless, in an unsigned review in the New York *Daily Times* (13 November 1855) William Swinton accuses Whitman of dishonesty and egotism inconsistent with his poetic ideals.

William A. Pannapacker

Bibliography

Allen, Gay Wilson. *The Solitary Singer: A Critical Biography of Walt Whitman.* 1955. Rev. ed. 1967. Chicago: U of Chicago P, 1985.

Mott, Frank Luther. *A History of American Magazines.* 4 vols. Cambridge, Mass.: Harvard UP, 1938.

[Swinton, William]. "It is a lie to . . . review . . . one's own book." *Walt Whitman: The Critical Heritage.* Ed. Milton Hindus. London: Routledge and Kegan Paul, 1971. 69–77.

Whitman, Walt. "An English and an American Poet." *Walt Whitman: The Critical Heritage.* Ed. Milton Hindus. London: Routledge and Kegan Paul, 1971. 34–48.

See also FOWLER, LORENZO NILES AND ORSON SQUIRE; LIFE ILLUSTRATED; PHRENOLOGY; SELF-REVIEWS OF THE 1855 *LEAVES,* WHITMAN'S ANONYMOUS; SWINTON, WILLIAM; TENNYSON, ALFRED, LORD; WELLS, SAMUEL ROBERTS

American Primer, An (1904)

This is a small book of Walt Whitman's general thoughts and speculations on language, especially American English. Horace Traubel compiled and edited a sheaf of Whitman's handwritten notes to form the book, which he published in 1904 under the title *An American Primer.* The volume contains a short foreword by Traubel that includes the famous quotation of Whitman calling *Leaves of Grass* "only a language experiment." An alternative title for the notes, found on one slip of paper, is "The Primer of Words: For American Young Men and Women, For Literati, Orators, Teachers, Musicians, Judges, Presidents, &c."

The text of the *Primer* is based on 110 manuscript pages that are part of the Feinberg Collection in the Library of Congress. Most of the small sheets of paper on which Whitman wrote these language notes are of various pastel colors, and Traubel identifies them as scraps coming from the paper covers of the unbound copies of the first edition of *Leaves.* The notes date from the mid- to late-1850s, around the time that Whitman published his article on language, "America's Mightiest Inheritance," in *Life Illustrated* (1856). However, Traubel says that some of the notes show "later paper and later handwriting." In addition to the thirty-five pages of Whitman's text in the *Primer* and the five pages of Traubel's foreword, there are three pages of facsimiles of the original manuscript. The *Primer* has been reprinted by City Lights Books, San Francisco (1970), and by others.

Traubel says that Whitman had considered delivering a lecture based on the notes, but nothing ever came of those plans. Although the notes are in no way a finished product, their having been assembled as a unit has increased their prominence among the many collections of Whitman's manuscript jottings. Biographers, critics, and students of Whitman's poetry have used the contents of the *Primer* to gain insights into his theory of language and his notions on such topics as pronunciation, spelling, dialects, naming, and the difference between oral and written English.

The *Primer* contains a series of philosophic pronouncements on the English language in America, along with observations on the history of human language and the relation of that history to American English. Whitman refers to Noah Webster and makes indirect references to other research that he had done as part of his collecting of facts and information about language and its growth.

Whitman says, "*Names* are magic," and spends several pages offering examples of names, especially American place names that he judges most appropriate. He establishes two basic principles for geographic naming. The first is that all aboriginal names "sound good." Thus, if there is an Indian name for a place, such as "Ohio, Connecticut, Ottawa, Monongahela," let it stand. The second principle is that a name fits if it grows out of some feature, person, or historical occurrence associated with a place. He especially approves of slang terms and analogies that the common people so often make. He disapproves of borrowed, European names for American cities, states, rivers, or mountains, and he rejects Spanish saints' names in the West and Southwest. But he allows for the power of certain historical names, including Socrates, Christ, Alfred the Great, and George Washington.

Whitman speaks favorably of the English of African Americans, which he calls the "nigger dialect," and credits it with enriching the American vocabulary and pointing to the future development of American pronunciation for musical purposes, perhaps giving rise to an American grand opera. He expresses distaste for "Yankee" pronunciation, calling it nasal and flat.

The *Primer* has several lists of examples, reinforcing Whitman's various points. The longest list is of twenty-seven different types of vocabularies, arranged much like one of the catalogues in "Song of Myself" or other poems in *Leaves.* A series of commodities listed in the *Primer* (coal, iron, gold, hemp, wool) appear to be the rough material for section 14 of "Starting from Paumanok." There are, also, such characteristic Whitman predilections as his special spelling for "kosmos" and transcendental proverbs such as "*All lies folded in names.*" The *Primer* repeats some of the same observations on the aptness of certain newspaper names and

nicknames that Whitman made in his article "Slang in America" (1885). He registers his objection to naming months and days of the week for European mythological deities. Acting on such feelings in *Leaves,* he resorts to the Quaker usage of "First-Day" for Sunday and "Fourth-Month" for April.

As one who had experienced the disapproval of others, Whitman associates censorship with the deficient and unnatural elements of society and asserts that "the use of strong, cutting, beautiful, rude words" would be forever welcome to the common people. He asserts that the "Real Dictionary" of American English, when it is written, will include all words—the bad as well as the good. And the "Real Grammar" will be liberating rather than restrictive.

Whitman saw a firm connection between his stance as the poet who spoke for all and his encompassing interest in expression through language. Words grow from life. New developments, occupations, and scientific breakthroughs call for new words. The new continent and the new society forming on that continent

Title page of An American Primer. *From* Walt Whitman: A Descriptive Bibliography, *by Joel Myerson,* © 1993 *by University of Pittsburgh Press.*

call for fresh and accurate expression. Although it appeared after the poet's death, *An American Primer* is evidence of his habits of mind early in his poetic career and gives us a glimpse of a portion of that "long foreground" that went into the intellectual and motivational formation of Walt Whitman.

Michael R. Dressman

Bibliography

Bauerlein, Mark. *Whitman and the American Idiom.* Baton Rouge: Louisiana State UP, 1991.

Dressman, Michael R. "'Names are Magic': Walt Whitman's Laws of Geographic Nomenclature." *Names* 26 (1978): 68–79.

Kramer, Michael P. "'A Tongue According': Whitman and the Literature of Language Study." *Imagining Language in America: From the Revolution to the Civil War.* By Kramer. Princeton: Princeton UP, 1992. 90–115.

Warren, James Perrin. "Dating Whitman's Language Studies." *Walt Whitman Quarterly Review* 1 (1983): 1–7.

———. *Walt Whitman's Language Experiment.* University Park: Pennsylvania State UP, 1990.

Whitman, Walt. *An American Primer.* Ed. Horace Traubel. Boston: Small, Maynard, 1904.

———. "The Primer of Words." *Diary in Canada, Notebooks, Index.* Vol. 3 of *Daybooks and Notebooks.* Ed. William White. New York: New York UP, 1978. 728–757.

See also "AMERICA'S MIGHTIEST INHERITANCE"; DICTIONARIES; LANGUAGE; PLACE NAMES; SLANG; "SLANG IN AMERICA"; SWINTON, WILLIAM; TRAUBEL, HORACE L.

American Revolution, The

Whitman hinged his claim to the title of national bard on his being the natural aesthetic outgrowth of the American Revolution's political ideals. Like many of his contemporaries, the poet regarded the revolution as not simply the heroic birth of his country, but as a perpetual mandate for democratic change. Whitman saw in the "haughty defiance of '76" the triumph and promise of New World democracy, and in both his poetry and prose he measured the reality of antebellum America against the founders' generative vision (1855 Preface 7). As the prospect of civil war intensified debates over the nation's civic ideals, Whitman deployed the revolution as a means of expressing his genuine political concerns and demonstrating the value of his literary translations of them.

The event's most significant influence on Whitman may have been in his remarkably civic ambitions for *Leaves of Grass.* Framed by the adoption of two national "compacts," the Declaration of Independence and the Federal Constitution, the American Revolution offered a compelling precedent for how literary performance could announce and effect cultural change. Both texts came under increasing scrutiny when conflicts over states' rights and slavery erupted in the 1850s, and as Kerry Larson has argued, it was during this historical crisis that Whitman's admiration for the Constitution evolved into a literary rivalry. If the Constitution strained under the burden of keeping the nation together, if it struggled to balance individual rights with civic unity, then the "great psalm of the republic" would emerge to create a more stable, comprehensive Union (1855 Preface 8). As Whitman suggests in section 9 of "By Blue Ontario's Shores" (1856), the poet alone could fuse the states into "the compact Organism of a nation." To the government's effort to "hold men together by paper and seal or by compulsion," Whitman promoted a more cohesive "living principle," a force akin to "the hold of the limbs of the body or the fibres of plants." *Leaves of Grass* promised to create the necessary adhesiveness.

Along with these effusive gestures toward the country's most sacred texts, Whitman's interest in the revolution centered on episodes of heroism and camaraderie. The poet, in this respect, appealed to the reverence many Americans felt toward the founding fathers. Sections 35 and 36 of "Song of Myself" (1855), for instance, incorporate the story of John Paul Jones's capture of the British warship *Serapis.* While the poem dramatically recounts Jones's resilience in winning the battle from his sinking ship, it also highlights the suffering neglected by most myths of national heroism. The reader learns that "stacks of bodies and bodies" line the decks; the masts and spars are spotted with "dabs of flesh"; beside the captain's feet lies the cabin boy's corpse (section 36). Whitman not only declines to identify the celebrated battle by name, but he concludes the scene with a chilling description of a surgeon amputating a sailor's limb. The images of "gnawing teeth" and the "swash of falling blood" suggest the body politic's basic vulnerability to its own heroic stands.

Whitman's ambivalence toward the war surfaces again in section 5 of "The Sleepers," another poem included in the 1855 *Leaves*. The section couples accounts of Washington's loss at the battle of Brooklyn (1776) with his emotional farewell to his officers at the war's end (1783). Both scenes emphasize the general's attachment to his men, and the tears he sheds for his "southern braves" as they lie slaughtered on the ground become tears of affection wetting the soldiers' faces as they receive his embraces and kisses. Whitman's juxtaposition of these historical events has aroused divergent critical responses. James Miller suggests that both stories depict the spiritual affection binding democratic men, and in Washington's departing embrace he sees an early version of the "Calamus" poet professing comradeship and love. Larson argues that Washington's anguish in Brooklyn overshadows his triumphant farewell. The general emerges from the poem as a representative mourner, a patriarch stricken with grief as he watches his children die. In Larson's analysis, Whitman's use of Washington foreshadows the mood of "Drum-Taps" more than that of "Calamus." The great father warns his descendants against the horrors of internal conflict.

Before writing "The Sleepers," Whitman had used the revolution for a similar admonitory effect in the satire "A Boston Ballad (1854)." One of the earliest works included in *Leaves of Grass*, the poem responds to the 1854 capture and trial of a fugitive slave in Boston and his subsequent return to the South. Whitman mockingly contrasts the revolution's moral and political idealism with the orderly compliance of antebellum Boston. While "the president's marshal" clears the streets for an invading government cannon, the dead rise from their graves and weep at the city's submissiveness. The satire's political force, as Betsy Erkkila has commented, depends on the ironic equation of the federal government with the British crown. The poem's speaker ridicules the heroic phantoms, and as he commands them to return to their graves, he summons from across the ocean the corpse of King George. The ironic voice of "A Boston Ballad (1854)" sharply contrasts with the sensual dreamer of "The Sleepers," but both poems use the revolution to chide the American people for abandoning their republican heritage.

Like Abraham Lincoln, Whitman was keenly aware of the American Revolution's rhetorical power, and he returned to the figure of Washington in the Civil War poem "The Centenarian's Story" (1865). The poem describes the interchange between a revolutionary war veteran and a "Volunteer of 1861–2." Watching a group of Union recruits drilling in front of a cheering crowd, the feeble veteran recalls the battle of Long Island (1776) and the terrible defeat Washington suffered only weeks after reading the Declaration of Independence to his troops. The veteran recalls the general's confidence even in retreat, and the volunteer pledges to spread the story across the land, calling himself a "chansonnier of a great future." As M. Wynn Thomas observes, it is the poet who ultimately assumes responsibility for the volunteer's oath. In connecting the past with the present, however, the poet also aims to preserve Washington's resolute vision that the veteran witnessed at sunrise.

The poem's effort to turn the revolution into a source of national strength remains inextricable from its description of Washington weeping at the massacre of his Maryland and Virginia brigade. "The Centenarian's Story" is typical of Whitman's treatment of the American Revolution in emphasizing the interplay between democratic heroism and an awareness of human sacrifice. Whitman's portraits of an affective, highly sensitive Washington distinguish the martial patriarch as a man of feeling as well as the leader of a revolutionary cause. Whitman admired the spirit of rebellion, and like Thomas Jefferson, he considered it to be a necessary, universal force. However, while that respect surfaces throughout the poet's rhetoric about American independence, it is significant that even before he adopted the role himself, Whitman was as attracted to the wound-dresser as he was to the defiant founder.

David Haven Blake

Bibliography
Erkkila, Betsy. *Whitman the Political Poet.* New York: Oxford UP, 1989.

Larson, Kerry C. *Whitman's Drama of Consensus.* Chicago: U of Chicago P, 1988.

Miller, James E., Jr. *A Critical Guide to "Leaves of Grass."* Chicago: U of Chicago P, 1957.

Reynolds, David S. *Walt Whitman's America: A Cultural Biography.* New York: Knopf, 1995.

Rule, Henry B. "Walt Whitman's 'Sad and Noble Scene.'" *Walt Whitman Review* 27 (1981): 165–170.

Thomas, M. Wynn. *The Lunar Light of Whitman's Poetry.* Cambridge, Mass.: Harvard UP, 1987.

Whitman, Walt. 1855 Preface. *Walt Whitman's "Leaves of Grass": The First (1855) Edition.* Ed. Malcolm Cowley. New York: Viking, 1959.

———. *Leaves of Grass: Comprehensive Reader's Edition.* Ed. Harold W. Blodgett and Sculley Bradley. New York: New York UP, 1965.

See also HARTSHORNE, WILLIAM; JEFFERSON, THOMAS; PAINE, THOMAS; PRESIDENTS, UNITED STATES; WASHINGTON, GEORGE

American Whig Review

When Whitman contributed his early story "The Boy Lover" in May 1845, this New York monthly was called *The American Review: A Whig Journal of Politics, Literature, Art and Science (1845–1847).* The *Review* was the organ of the embattled Whig party until both party and magazine collapsed after the presidential election of 1852. George H. Colton edited the *Review* in the hopes of selling a profitable mixture of politics and literature which would rival the *Democratic Review.* The magazine gained immediate notice by publishing Edgar Allan Poe's "The Raven" in its February 1845 number. In light of Whitman's previous associations with the *Democratic Review* and his anti-Whig campaigning, the publication of his slight tale and a few other pieces, as Perry Miller observed, gives some indication of Colton's willingness to print the writings of those Democrats who conformed to his conservative style. It also indicates the wide political and literary range of Walt Whitman's search for a literary identity in the 1840s. Whitman continued to read the *Review* through the 1850s, clipping articles on literature which interested him.

Stephen Rachman

Bibliography

Allen, Gay Wilson. *The Solitary Singer: A Critical Biography of Walt Whitman.* 1955. Rev. ed. 1967. Chicago: U of Chicago P, 1985.

Miller, Perry. *The Raven and the Whale: The War of Words and Wits in the Era of Poe and Melville.* New York: Harcourt, Brace, 1956.

Mott, Frank Luther. *A History of American Magazines, 1741–1850.* Cambridge, Mass.: Harvard UP, 1939.

Reynolds, David S. *Walt Whitman's America: A Cultural Biography.* New York: Knopf, 1995.

Whitman, Walt. *The Early Poems and the Fiction.* Ed. Thomas L. Brasher. New York: New York UP, 1963.

See also "BOY LOVER, THE"; DEMOCRATIC REVIEW; WHIGS

"America's Mightiest Inheritance" (1856)

Written near the beginning of Whitman's career, this article on the English language first appeared in the 12 April 1856 issue of *Life Illustrated,* a weekly magazine published by Fowler and Wells. For reasons unknown, Whitman chose not to include "America's Mightiest Inheritance" in the collections of prose he later assembled. His decision not to preserve it in book form perhaps explains why it did not end up in the New York University Press edition of *The Collected Writings of Walt Whitman* (1961–1984). Nevertheless, the article remains accessible, having been reprinted in 1936 in *New York Dissected,* a selection of Whitman's periodical publications.

"Inheritance" is a pastiche. It consists of a set of notes that appear to have been hastily arranged in what is, at best, a rough order. Even if disjointed, however, the essay is provocative. Its thesis is that the English language is the greatest of all the things that have been bequeathed to America by the past. Exhibiting something approaching linguistic chauvinism, Whitman claims that "the English language is by far the noblest now spoken—probably ever spoken—upon this earth. It is the speech for orators and poets, the speech for the household, for business, for liberty, and for common sense. It is a language for great individuals as well as great nations" (55).

In addition to such grandiose claims, Whitman devotes several pages to a history of English, emphasizing the many "tongues" that have contributed to that history. He argues that language is the most enduring of human creations and warns against elegant, artificial, and showy uses of language. He praises lexicographers such as Samuel Johnson, Noah Webster, and Joseph Worcester but maintains that a "perfect" English dictionary has yet to be compiled. He offers advice on pronunciation, and finally, he appends a list of foreign words, mostly French, that are "much needed in English" (61).

Though uneven in quality, "Inheritance" remains one of Whitman's key statements on the subject of language. It represents early evidence of his lifelong preoccupation with the subject. Whitman's other important writings on language include a notebook entitled *Words,* passages scattered throughout the poetry of *Leaves of Grass* and the prose of the prefaces and of *Democratic Vistas,* contributions to William Swinton's *Rambles Among Words* (1859; rev. ed. 1872), an essay called "Slang in America" (1885), and *An American Primer* (1904), a series of notes edited and published by Horace Traubel.

Donald D. Kummings

Bibliography

Folsom, Ed. *Walt Whitman's Native Representations.* Cambridge: Cambridge UP, 1994.

Hollis, C. Carroll. *Language and Style in "Leaves of Grass."* Baton Rouge: Louisiana State UP, 1983.

Warren, James Perrin. *Walt Whitman's Language Experiment.* University Park: Pennsylvania State UP, 1990.

Whitman, Walt. "America's Mightiest Inheritance." *New York Dissected.* Ed. Emory Holloway and Ralph Adimari. New York: Rufus Rockwell Wilson, 1936. 55–65.

See also AMERICAN PRIMER, AN; DICTIONARIES; LANGUAGE; "SLANG IN AMERICA"; SWINTON, WILLIAM

Anderson, Sherwood (1876–1941)

Of Sherwood Anderson's twenty-three books the finest contain his shorter works of fiction: *Winesburg, Ohio* (1919), *The Triumph of the Egg* (1921), *Horses and Men* (1923), and *Death in the Woods* (1933). Anderson's style influenced the minimalism of Hemingway, while his psychoanalytical sophistication impressed Faulkner.

A New Testament (1927) shows Anderson trying to imitate Whitman's quasi-scriptural ambitions, his long-lined free verse, and his concept of an androgynous universal "self." But Anderson only succeeds as a Whitmanesque visionary in "Out of Nowhere into Nothing," the longest tale in *The Triumph of the Egg.* The protagonist Rosalind Wescott is attracted equally to contrasting older men: Walter Sayers and Melville Stoner. Eventually Rosalind transcends both of her male friends, but she learns the most from Walt(er). Her dung-beetle reverie recalls section 24 of "Song of Myself"; Walter's advice to give herself to the night, his praise of Native Americans, and his love of humble weeds and grasses recall sections 21, 39, and 5. Walter teaches Rosalind to be a seer of grasses, and she in effect rewrites "Crossing Brooklyn Ferry" in her epiphany of seagulls. But finally she leaves Walter and Melville both, afoot with her own vision like Whitman in section 33 of "Song of Myself."

In *Tar* (1926) Anderson notes that Dr. Reefy, "[l]ike Walt Whitman," was a nurse in the Civil War (330). Anderson was akin to Hamlin Garland in that both of these regional writers found in Whitman a sense of the depth of ordinary people.

Martin Bidney

Bibliography

Anderson, Sherwood. *A New Testament.* New York: Boni and Liveright, 1927.

———. *Tar: A Midwest Childhood.* New York: Boni and Liveright, 1926.

———. *The Triumph of the Egg.* New York: B.W. Huebsch, 1921.

Bidney, Martin. "Thinking about Walt and Melville in a Sherwood Anderson Tale: An Independent Woman's Transcendental Quest." *Studies in Short Fiction* 29 (1992): 517–530.

Bunge, Nancy L. "The Midwestern Novel: Walt Whitman Transplanted." *The Old Northwest* 3 (1977): 275–287.

See also CATHER, WILLA; GARLAND, HAMLIN; LEGACY, WHITMAN'S

"Angel of Tears, The" (1842)

This short story appeared first in *United States Magazine and Democratic Review* in September 1842. Concerning publication and revisions, see Thomas L. Brasher's edition of *The Early Poems and the Fiction.*

As a story, "The Angel of Tears" is negligible. A fratricide remembers happier times with his brother and is overcome with repentance. God sends Alza, the angel of tears, to the criminal's bedside in prison to soothe the murderer's sleep. The theme of brothers at odds with each other connects "Angel of Tears" to "Wild Frank's Return" (1841) and "Bervance: or, Father and Son" (1841). But the theme is made little of here. When the fratricide remembers pleasant childhood moments with his brother, repentance follows, but no explanation for enmity is given. Only in "Angel of Tears," moreover, has the enmity between brothers led to murder. Asselineau detects in this story the influence of Poe.

Also of interest in this story is Whitman's propensity for capitalized epithets. God, for example, is the Unfathomable, the Master of the Great Laws. Heaven is the Pure Country. God's plan for reckoning good and evil is in the Shrouded Volume (120–122).

Whitman's sympathy for the outcast is prominent. He seems to argue that personal judgment of criminals is inappropriate since their evil acts are as likely the outcome of forces in childhood as are the good acts of people who are not criminals. There is also an implicit criticism, in a veiled reference, to capital punishment, but not as direct or emphatic as Whitman's criticism in other tales, most notably in "Death in the School-Room (a Fact)" (1841).

Patrick McGuire

Bibliography

Asselineau, Roger. *The Evolution of Walt Whitman: The Creation of a Personality.* Trans. Richard P. Adams and Roger Asselineau. Cambridge, Mass.: Harvard UP, 1960.

Whitman, Walt. *The Early Poems and the Fiction.* Ed. Thomas L. Brasher. New York: New York UP, 1963.

See also "BERVANCE: OR, FATHER AND SON"; "DEATH IN THE SCHOOL-ROOM (A FACT)"; POPULAR CULTURE, WHITMAN AND; SHORT FICTION, WHITMAN'S; "WILD FRANK'S RETURN"

Apollinaire, Guillaume (1880–1918)

Guillaume Apollinaire's real name was Wilhelm Apollinaris de Kostrowitsky. He belonged to a cosmopolitan family and received a cosmopolitan education. He was a protean writer— in turn a futurist, a cubist, and a surrealist—a modernist in short. He was a friend of Picasso and like him an admirer of African art. Apollinaire became famous above all as an avant-garde poet with *Alcools* (1913), made up of both traditional and experimental poems deprived of punctuation, and *Calligrammes* (1918), also called "idéogrammes lyriques," which belonged to his cubist period. He thought poetry should enjoy the same liberty as journalism, but considered free verse only one of many possible innovations. He could turn any object, any topic, into something rich and strange.

The poems of Apollinaire are both serious and whimsical, and he was fond of hoaxes, one of which he perpetrated in the *Mercure de France* (to which he was a regular contributor) in the 1 April 1913 (April Fools' Day) issue. Although Apollinaire was neither a disciple of Whitman nor a homosexual, he pretended to quote an anonymous witness of Whitman's funeral in Camden, according to whom "pederasts came in crowds" and indulged in all kinds of rowdy activities to celebrate the death of their fellow homosexual. This pseudo-report was taken seriously by readers, and a controversy followed, which lasted for ten months in the pages of the *Mercure de France* as well as in other journals, until 1 February 1914. Stuart Merrill and Léon Bazalgette, the author of a romanticized biography of Whitman, denied the American poet's homosexuality, whereas Harrison Reeves and the German Eduard Bertz confirmed it. The whole controversy has been described by Henry Saunders and Betsy Erkkila. Federico García Lorca may have had Apollinaire's description of Whitman's funeral in mind when he composed his "Oda a Walt Whitman" in 1929–1930 during his stay in New York. (This poem is part of his *Poeta en Nueva York*.)

Despite his indebtedness to Whitman for some of his own innovations, Apollinaire joined the futurists in their *Manifestes Futuristes* (Milan, 1913) in saying "merde" ("shit") to him as well as to Poe and Baudelaire.

Roger Asselineau

Bibliography

Billy, André, and Henri Parisot. *Guillaume Apollinaire.* Paris: Éditions Seghers, 1947.

Erkkila, Betsy. *Walt Whitman Among the French: Poet and Myth.* Princeton: Princeton UP, 1980.

Lorca, Federico García. *The Poet in New York and Other Poems.* New York: Norton, 1940.

Saunders, Henry S. *A Whitman Controversy—Being Letters Published in the Mercure de France 1913–1914.* Toronto: Henry S. Saunders, 1921.

See also BAZALGETTE, LÉON; BERTZ, EDUARD; FRANCE, WHITMAN IN; SEX AND SEXUALITY

Architects and Architecture

Whitman appears to have acquired only limited experience with the building arts while doing house carpentry in the early 1850s. But architecture was to become a favorite trope in his poetry. Moreover, some of America's most innovative architects took particular inspiration from Whitman.

Whitman was undoubtedly familiar with the sculptor Horatio Greenough, a friend of Ralph Waldo Emerson who wrote books and magazine articles on architectural theory. His essay "Form and Function" is a key text in the development of modern architecture. In addition, Henry David Thoreau's discussion of shelter in the "Economy" section of *Walden* could not have escaped Whitman's notice. Also consonant with Whitman's love of simplicity were the "democratic" cottages widely promoted by Andrew Jackson Downing in the 1840s and 1850s.

In his career as a journalist, Whitman wrote an occasional architectural critique, particularly of churches and public buildings, though buildings appear most often in word sketches of city environs. Similarly, in the prose pieces of *Specimen Days,* architecture serves to evoke a theme or mood, as in "The White House by Moonlight" or, perhaps the most haunting example, the "Patent Office Hospital." An exception is the essay "Wicked Architecture," published in *Life Illustrated* in 1856, where Whitman indicts tenement builders.

Although Whitman often remarked that America's true monuments would be its people, his poetic catalogues contain numerous references to buildings and city sights. In his poetry, architecture usually serves as a symbol for the building of the American commonwealth and for the fulfillment of its destiny, as in "Song of the Broad-Axe," "A Song for Occupations," "By Blue Ontario's Shore," or "Song of the Exposition." Sometimes, as in "A Song of the Rolling Earth," he draws an implicit correlation between the architect and the long-awaited "American bard": "Delve! mould! pile the words of the earth! / Work on, age after age,

nothing is to be lost, / It may have to wait long, but it will certainly come in use, / When the materials are all prepared and ready, the architects shall appear. / I swear to you the architects shall appear without fail" (section 4).

Architectural or engineering images may also serve to represent spiritual perfection or the unfolding of a cosmic drama, as in the Pythagorean symbolism of "Chanting the Square Deific" or in "Passage to India," where the narrator exclaims, "Lo, soul, seest thou not God's purpose from the first? / The earth to be spann'd, connected by network" (section 2).

Many of Whitman's friends and followers wrote on architecture, often for arts and crafts movement magazines. These include Edward Carpenter, William Sloane Kennedy, John Burroughs, and Elbert Hubbard. Near Philadelphia, architect William L. (Will) Price founded the Rose Valley Association in 1901, a crafts community. Whitman confidant Horace Traubel edited Rose Valley's magazine, *The Artsman,* subtitled *The Art That Is Life,* promoting an arts and crafts philosophy with Whitman as a leading prophet. The magazine contained articles on various arts, including architecture.

The turn-of-the-century Chicago School architects were enthusiastic readers of Whitman, whom they found sympathetic to their own attempts to create an indigenous American architecture based on organic functionalist principles. Louis Sullivan wrote Whitman in 1887 to acknowledge his debt to the poet. Traubel reports that Whitman cherished the letter and told him to "keep it near you" (3:26). Sullivan himself wrote Whitman-inspired verse, in addition to prose works like *The Autobiography of an Idea, Kindergarten Chats,* and *Democracy: A Man-Search.*

Before coming to Chicago, Sullivan worked for the important Philadelphia architect Frank Furness, who was the son of the Reverend William Henry Furness, a close friend of Emerson and a Unitarian minister who contributed to Traubel's *The Conservator.* Another son, Professor Horace Howard Furness, Sr., the noted Shakespearean scholar, befriended Whitman, and served as a pallbearer at the poet's funeral.

Sullivan and his one-time employee Frank Lloyd Wright both appear to have been influenced by Whitman scholar Oscar Lovell Triggs, whose Chicago arts and crafts organizations they supported. Wright left Sullivan's employ, coincidentally, the year after Whitman died.

Wright would continue throughout a career that spanned six decades to claim Whitman and Sullivan as his two primary models. In a special issue of *The Architectural Forum* (January 1938), Wright combined drawings and photos of his works with quotes from a number of Whitman poems. Near the end of his life he wrote the following: "Walt Whitman, seer of our Democracy! He uttered primitive truths lying at the base of our new life, the inspirations we needed to go on spiritually with the brave 'sovereignty of the individual'"(59).

Lewis Mumford, perhaps the twentieth century's most influential city historian and urban planning critic, wrote about Whitman, Sullivan, and Wright with equal fervor while promoting his own version of an "organic architecture."

If the "proof of a poet is that his country absorbs him as affectionately as he has absorbed it" (Whitman 26), then Whitman has at very least been absorbed into America's architectural tradition. He continues to be invoked by architects, as in a quotation from "City of Ships" inscribed on the ornamental fence of Cesar Pelli's World Financial Center complex, built in the 1980s in lower Manhattan: "City of tall facades of marble and iron! / Proud and passionate city—mettlesome, mad, extravagant city!"

John F. Roche

Bibliography

Adams, Richard P. "Architecture and the Romantic Tradition: Coleridge to Wright." *American Quarterly* 9 (1957): 46–62.

Egbert, Donald Drew. "The Idea of Organic Expression and American Architecture." *Evolutionary Thought in America*. Ed. Stow Persons. New Haven: Yale UP, 1950. 336–396.

Greenough, Horatio. "Form and Function." *The Roots of Contemporary American Architecture*. Ed. Lewis Mumford. New York: Reinhold, 1952. 32–56.

Matthiessen, F.O. *American Renaissance*. London: Oxford UP, 1941.

Metzger, Charles R. *Emerson and Greenough: Transcendental Pioneers of an American Esthetic*. Berkeley: U of California P, 1954.

Murphy, Kevin. "Walt Whitman and Louis Sullivan: The Aesthetics of Egalitarianism." *Walt Whitman Quarterly Review* 6 (1988): 1–15.

Paul, Sherman. *Louis Sullivan: An Architect in American Thought*. Englewood Cliffs, N.J.: Prentice-Hall, 1962.

Roche, John F. "Democratic Space: The Ecstatic Geography of Walt Whitman and Frank Lloyd Wright." *Walt Whitman Quarterly Review* 6 (1988): 16–32.

Sullivan, Louis. *Democracy: A Man-Search*. 1850. Detroit: Wayne State UP, 1961.

Twombly, Robert. *Frank Lloyd Wright: His Life and Architecture*. New York: Wiley, 1979.

Weingarden, Lauren S. "Naturalized Technology: Louis H. Sullivan's Whitmanesque Skyscrapers." *Centennial Review* 30 (1986): 480–495.

Whitman, Walt. 1855 Preface. *Complete Poetry and Collected Prose*. Ed. Justin Kaplan. New York: Library of America, 1982. 5–26.

Wortman, Marc. "Battery Park City: Utopian Poetics in the Urban Greenhouse." *Yale Review* 79 (1990): 501–508.

Wright, Frank Lloyd. *A Testament*. New York: Horizon, 1957.

See also ARTS AND CRAFTS MOVEMENT; CITY, WHITMAN AND THE; CRYSTAL PALACE EXHIBITION (NEW YORK); ORGANICISM; *SPECIMEN DAYS*

"Are You the New Person Drawn toward Me?" (1860)

Entitled "To a new personal admirer" in an early manuscript, this poem first appeared in the 1860 edition of *Leaves of Grass* as number 12 of the "Calamus" cluster. It appeared under its present title in the 1867 edition.

In this as in other poems, most notably "Whoever You are Holding Me Now in Hand," Whitman employs the technique of addressing the poem to another person, presumably the reader. In both poems, Whitman immediately warns that he is "far different" from what might be supposed. In a number of the "Calamus" poems, including this one, James E. Miller, Jr., suggests the poet is proclaiming his difference—that his outer appearance is by no means an indication of the depth of his "spiritual attachment to others" (65). Such a difference is at the heart of this poem, which asserts an essential duality. Whitman asks if the potential new friend will find in him an ideal, a lover. Will the poet's friendship provide "unalloy'd satisfaction?" Is Whitman "trusty and faithful . . . a real heroic man?" These are lofty qualities many admirers hope to find in great artists. But Whitman then suggests an opposing reality by asking if it "may be all maya, illusion?" He proposes that there is a distinction between the reality of himself and his image in the mind of the potential admirer.

The *Upanishads,* part of Vedic literature, also discriminate between the real world, Brahman, and the world of illusion, maya. In his commentary on the Brahma-Sutras, Sri Sankaracarya discusses the difference between the one who experiences and the thing experienced. Furthermore, he elaborates by pointing out that in reality such a difference does not exist.

In this poem and throughout much of his poetry, Whitman advances the person addressed toward a higher level of understanding of the difference between the illusion of what is experienced and the reality of it.

Frederick J. Butler

Bibliography
Miller, James E., Jr. *A Critical Guide to "Leaves of Grass."* Chicago: U of Chicago P, 1957.
Radhakrishnan, S., ed. *The Principal Upanishads.* Delhi: Oxford UP, 1989.
Sankaracarya, Sri. *Brahma-Sutra-Bhasya of Sri Sankaracarya.* Trans. Swami Gambhirananda. Calcutta: Advaita Ashrama, 1983.
Whitman, Walt. *Leaves of Grass: Comprehensive Reader's Edition.* Ed. Harold W. Blodgett and Sculley Bradley. New York: New York UP, 1965.

See also "Calamus"; Leaves of Grass, 1860 Edition; "Whoever You are Holding Me Now in Hand"

"Army Corps on the March, An" (1865–1866)

The poem "An Army Corps on the March" originally appeared in Walt Whitman's *Sequel to Drum-Taps* (1865–1866). Its original title was "An Army on the March." In 1865 Whitman engaged Peter Eckler to print the first issue of *Drum-Taps* but after Abraham Lincoln's death withdrew the book. In the autumn of 1865 he added the *Sequel,* which included this poem along with seventeen other new poems. Still later, in 1867, the poem became a part of the *Drum-Taps* annex to *Leaves of Grass,* in which both *Drum-Taps* and the *Sequel* appeared with separate title pages and pagination. In 1871 Whitman selected the present title, "An Army Corps on the March," and he also changed the last line of the poem from the original "As the army resistless advances" to "As the army corps advances." The edited poem became a permanent part of the "Drum-Taps" cluster of *Leaves of Grass* and appeared in all future editions.

Determining the exact date of composition is not possible; however, since it was not included in the initial issue of *Drum-Taps,* May 1865, Whitman may have composed it between May and October of that year, when *Drum-Taps* was republished with the *Sequel.*

Like several short poems in "Drum-Taps," "An Army Corps on the March" sketches a realistic free-verse portrait of a Civil War scene including images of "dust cover'd men," horses sweating, wheels rumbling, and first the sound of a single shot "snapping like a whip" and later an "irregular volley" of shots. Whitman probably had witnessed scenes like the one described in the poem when he went south in 1863 in the company of Major Lyman Hapgood. James E. Miller, Jr., cites this poem along with other short poems in this part of the cluster as being "among the best in 'Drum-Taps'" (221).

William G. Lulloff

Bibliography
Allen, Gay Wilson. *The New Walt Whitman Handbook.* 1975. New York: New York UP, 1986.
Miller, James E., Jr. *A Critical Guide to "Leaves of Grass."* Chicago: U of Chicago P, 1957.
Whitman, Walt. *Leaves of Grass.* Ed. Sculley Bradley and Harold W. Blodgett. Norton Critical Edition. New York: Norton, 1973.
———. *Walt Whitman's "Drum-Taps" (1865) and "Sequel to Drum-Taps" (1865–6): A Facsimile Reproduction.* Ed. F. DeWolfe Miller. Gainesville, Fla.: Scholars' Facsimiles and Reprints, 1959.

See also Civil War, The; "Drum-Taps"; Realism; Sequel to Drum-Taps

Arnold, George B. (1803–1889)

As Sherry Ceniza has revealed, Whitman's biographers (Allen, Kaplan, Reynolds, and others) have often mistakenly referred to George B. Arnold as John Arnold; the latter was actually a son of the former. In any event, George B. Arnold was a retired Unitarian minister and a lodger for a number of years in the Brooklyn home of Mrs. Abby Price, one of Whitman's best friends. Helen Price, Abby's daughter, described Arnold as "a Swedenborgian, not formally belonging to the church of that name, but accepting in the main the doctrines of the Swedish seer as revealed in his works" (qtd. in Bucke 27). When Whitman visited the Price household, he often engaged Arnold in intense but friendly arguments, discussing such matters as politics, democracy, spiritualism, Harmonialism, and, most often, Swedenborgianism. According to Justin Kaplan, Arnold inspired Whitman to attend Swedenborgian meetings and to study the Swedish mystic's life and writings. Arnold may also have influenced Whitman to write "Who Was Swedenborg?"—an article published on 15 May 1858 in the Brooklyn *Daily Times*.

Amy M. Bawcom

Bibliography
Bucke, Richard Maurice. *Walt Whitman*. Philadelphia: McKay, 1883.
Ceniza, Sherry. "Walt Whitman and Abby Price." *Walt Whitman Quarterly Review* 7 (1989): 49–67.
Kaplan, Justin. *Walt Whitman: A Life*. New York: Simon and Schuster, 1980.

See also PRICE, ABBY HILLS; PRICE, HELEN E.; SWEDENBORG, EMANUEL

Arnold, Matthew (1822–1888)
Despite certain thematic affinities between the work of Whitman and the British Victorian poet and critic Matthew Arnold, including a belief in literature as a criticism of life, each had little to say about the other. What remains of their mutual comments, preserved in letters and conversations, is rather critical, stemming from the clash of Whitman's inclusiveness and originality against Arnold's advocacy of high culture and tradition.

Most characteristic of Arnold's attitude toward Whitman is his letter to W.D. O'Connor (1866) acknowledging receipt of O'Connor's *The Good Gray Poet,* written to defend Whitman after his dismissal as a clerk in the Indian Affairs Office. In the letter, Arnold states his doubt that the intervention of "foreign expostulators" will be able to effect Whitman's reinstatement. Arnold also states his belief that any public servant in a similar predicament in western Europe would meet a similar fate. Continuing as an advocate of high culture, he comments on the merits and demerits of Whitman's poetry as representative of American literature in general. While many in England found Whitman's poetical worth in his originality, Arnold finds Whitman in particular and American literature in general "displaying an eccentric and violent originality." Whitman and American literature must come "into the European movement," which will not impede America from being "an independent intellectual power" rather than "an intellectual colony of Europe" (qtd. in Perry 177–179). Mentioning Whitman in his article "Theodore Parker" (1867), Arnold believes each has "a genuine American voice, not an echo of English poetry," but that too much is made of this native strain (Arnold 12).

Whitman is similarly cool toward Arnold, comparing their antipathy to oil and water, saying "Arnold is inveterately one thing as I am another" (*With Walt Whitman* 4:37).

Alan E. Kozlowski

Bibliography
[Arnold, Matthew]. "Theodore Parker." *Pall Mall Gazette* 24 Aug. 1867: 12.
Blodgett, Harold W. *Walt Whitman in England*. Ithaca, N.Y.: Cornell UP, 1934.
Perry, Bliss. *Walt Whitman: His Life and Work*. Boston: Houghton Mifflin, 1906.
Traubel, Horace. "Whitman on His Contemporaries." *American Mercury* 2 (1924): 328–332.
———. *With Walt Whitman in Camden*. Vol. 1. Boston: Small, Maynard, 1906; Vol. 2. New York: Appleton, 1908; Vol. 3. New York: Mitchell Kennerley, 1914; Vol. 4. Ed. Sculley Bradley. Philadelphia: U of Pennsylvania P, 1953.

See also BRITISH ISLES, WHITMAN IN THE

Art and Daguerreotype Galleries
In antebellum America the public display of art was mostly confined to galleries connected with the production and the commerce of art. Early in the century, associations of artists began providing casts of European sculpture for classes and exhibiting their own work; art suppliers

offered a few canvases attributed to the masters; and traveler-artists like George Catlin showed, for a fee, their views of the exotic. By the 1840s, Whitman could see European paintings at such dealers as Goupil, Vibert, and the Düsseldorf gallery, or contemporary American work at the annual exhibitions of three New York art associations—the National Academy of Design, the American Art-Union, and the Brooklyn Art Union. The Art-Union showed such artists as Thomas Cole, John F. Kensett, William Sidney Mount, and George Caleb Bingham prior to its yearly lottery of paintings. Landscapes and still lifes were the galleries' favored genres. In the display style of the time, hundreds of paintings crowded the gallery walls, closely spaced from floor to high ceiling. (See Samuel F.B. Morse's painting *The Louvre.*)

As the daguerreotype became fashionable, it proved to be an art more profitable than painting. By 1843 daguerreotypists were expanding their studios into galleries displaying duplicates of their portraits, not just as samples of their art but as advertisements that prominent citizens were among their clientele. People often came not to be photographed, but to see the pictures, mounted in salons as sumptuous as the photographer could afford. In the Brooklyn *Daily Eagle* (2 July 1846) Whitman described a visit to John Plumbe's Manhattan gallery. Besides noting the decor, the crowd, and the hundreds of portraits arrayed from floor to ceiling, he wrote of feeling an "electric chain" passing between himself and the depicted faces: "Time, space, both are annihilated, and we identify the semblance with the reality" (*Gathering* 2:117).

Always the connoisseur of his city's shows, Whitman often reviewed art exhibitions for the *Eagle* in the late 1840s. In 1849–1851 he wrote about art and artists in several New York newspapers and addressed the Brooklyn Art Union. Identifying the hero with the artist, he spoke of the "sublime moral beauty" of rebels and innovators, whether in deeds or in works of art (*Uncollected* 1:246). In section 15 of "Song of Myself" we glimpse the connoisseur in the exhibition gallery and the lady sitting for her daguerreotype; in section 41 Whitman represents himself as a collector bidding for portraits of God. (Like most Americans he gained much of his art experience from the printed engraving and the lithograph.) Whitman's early poem "Pictures" exhibits a gallery of pictures within the poet's skull; Ed Folsom, Miles Orvell, and Richard Rudisill think them daguerreotypes, but Ruth Bohan explains that they must be engravings and lithographs. All find the picture gallery, with its crowded, intense, and various displays, a prototype of the pictorial catalogues in "Song of Myself" and many later poems.

James Dougherty

Bibliography

Bode, Carl. *Antebellum Culture.* Carbondale: Southern Illinois UP, 1970.

Bohan, Ruth L. "'The Gathering of the Forces': Walt Whitman and the Visual Arts in Brooklyn in the 1850s." *Walt Whitman and the Visual Arts.* Ed. Geoffrey M. Sill and Roberta K. Tarbell. New Brunswick, N.J.: Rutgers UP, 1992. 1–27.

Folsom, Ed. *Walt Whitman's Native Representations.* Cambridge: Cambridge UP, 1994.

Orvell, Miles. *The Real Thing: Imitation and Authenticity in American Culture, 1880–1940.* Chapel Hill: U of North Carolina P, 1989.

Rubin, Joseph Jay. *The Historic Whitman.* University Park: Pennsylvania State UP, 1973.

Rudisill, Richard. *Mirror Image: The Influence of the Daguerreotype on American Society.* Albuquerque: U of New Mexico P, 1971

Whitman, Walt. *The Gathering of the Forces.* Ed. Cleveland Rodgers and John Black. 2 vols. New York: Putnam, 1920.

———. *The Uncollected Poetry and Prose of Walt Whitman.* 1921. Ed. Emory Holloway. 2 vols. New York: Peter Smith, 1932.

See also "MY PICTURE-GALLERY"; NEW YORK CITY; PAINTERS AND PAINTING; PHOTOGRAPHS AND PHOTOGRAPHERS; POPULAR CULTURE, WHITMAN AND

"Artilleryman's Vision, The" (1865)

An entry in the Civil War collection entitled *Drum-Taps*, this poem was written in 1865, underwent its final revision in 1881, and is included in the "Drum-Taps" cluster of *Leaves of Grass.* As with other "Drum-Taps" poems, Whitman is portraying scenes from the Civil War. Presented as a dream or a vision, this particular poem represents the horrors of war (like those depicted by World War I poets Wilfred Owen, Rupert Brooke, and Siegfried Sassoon) which the twentieth-century reader associates with the flashbacks of men suffering shell-shock after Vietnam or World Wars I and II.

Whitman's artilleryman describes himself as lying alongside his slumbering wife in a midnight stillness at home, punctuated only by the breath of the couple's infant. As the speaker wakes from sleep, a vision "presses upon me." Then, as he has done in earlier writings on the Civil War, Whitman graphically describes recollected horrors of past battles in a "fantasy unreal," complete with sound effects of rifles discharging, shells exploding, and pistols crackling. The nightmare quality of the poem is replete with images of troops crawling, shells shrieking and exploding, and grape shot humming and whirring like wind as it twists its way toward human flesh. Unique to the artilleryman is the somewhat impersonal nature of his contribution to the event. He fires his cannon and then leans to the side in order to evaluate the carnage he has caused. But this impersonality is soon replaced by a "devilish exultation" and "old man joy," which rises from the depths of his soul as he then averts his eyes from the bloodshed he has just caused.

This poem reveals Whitman's fascination with photography. The Civil War was the first photographed war, and Whitman includes many comparable word pictures, not only of battle scenes, but also of soldiers at rest in camp. His lament at the conclusion of the war that "the real war" will never get into books (Whitman 778) is readily countered by his Civil War portraits such as this poem and others in the "Drum-Taps" cluster.

Julian B. Freund

Bibliography

Folsom, Ed. Introduction. *"This Heart's Geography's Map": The Photographs of Walt Whitman.* Special issue of *Walt Whitman Quarterly Review* 4.2–3 (1986–1987): 1–5.

Fussell, Paul. *The Great War and Modern Memory.* New York: Oxford UP, 1975.

Whitman, Walt. *Complete Poetry and Collected Prose.* Ed. Justin Kaplan. New York: Library of America, 1982.

See also CIVIL WAR, THE; "DRUM-TAPS"; *MEMORANDA DURING THE WAR*; PHOTOGRAPHS AND PHOTOGRAPHERS

Arts and Crafts Movement

Although Whitman was not part of any arts and crafts organization and had little to say on the subject proper, a number of his friends and supporters in England and America were leaders of that movement and saw their poet as embodying its vision of a society based on pride in workmanship rather than on greed. In the years between his death and World War I, Whitman came to be seen as the American Morris by many, especially by leaders of influential arts and crafts societies in Philadelphia and Chicago.

In England, where the movement started under the aegis of John Ruskin and William Morris, a few significant activists had links to Whitman. Chief among these was Edward Carpenter, frequent correspondent and visitor to Camden, as well as an ally of Morris in crafts and socialist organizations. Morris himself was publicly cordial, but remained cool to Whitman's verse.

In 1901 Whitman confidant Horace Traubel, along with the architect Will Price, helped to found the Rose Valley Association of craftsmen near Philadelphia. Traubel edited the crafts periodical *The Artsman;* a regular feature, "Rose Valley Scriptures," presented quotations by Whitman, Morris, Carpenter, and others. Whitmanites also took leading roles in the Morris Society branch in Philadelphia, in Charles Godfrey Leland's Industrial Art School, and in Pennsylvania Academy art circles around Whitman's friend Thomas Eakins.

The Chicago Society of Arts and Crafts was founded in 1897 at Hull House. Key to the Chicago crafts movement was University of Chicago instructor Oscar Lovell Triggs. A Whitman scholar and editor, he also authored *A History of the Arts and Crafts Movement* (1902). Triggs founded the Industrial Art League in 1899, the Morris Society of Chicago in 1903, and the Whitman Fellowship, Western Branch, in 1904. He also started the free-thought magazine *To-Morrow,* with the aid of Parker Sercombe, who replaced Triggs as editor shortly after the magazine's appearance in 1905. Sercombe was also the founder of the curiously titled Walt Whitman–Herbert Spencer Center. Young Carl Sandburg lived at the center while an assistant editor at the magazine in 1906, in between lecture tours on Whitman or socialism. Architects Louis Sullivan and Frank Lloyd Wright, both avid Whitman admirers, were also active in Chicago crafts societies.

Whitman was less admired in Boston, home of the conservative Boston Society of Arts and Crafts, founded in 1897, and its journal *Handicraft*. BSAC founder Charles Eliot Norton had written an early and reasonably favorable review of the 1855 *Leaves of Grass*, the same year Norton met John Ruskin, yet Norton steered the society in an Anglophilic direction contrary to Whitman's. Only one Whitman confederate was active in the BSAC, Boston art critic Sylvester Baxter, who helped organize and publicize the 1897 exhibition that initiated that society and wrote occasional pieces for its journal. Whitman publisher Thomas B. Mosher was based in Maine but was active in Boston arts circles.

Elbert Hubbard, leader of the Roycroft colony at East Aurora, New York, frequently invoked Whitman. Whitman proselytizer Sadakichi Hartmann ghost-wrote for Hubbard in the latter's magazine, *The Philistine*. Ralph Radcliffe-Whitehead, founder of the Byrdcliffe crafts colony near Woodstock, New York, called Whitman's poetry "the one supreme expression of American life in art" (59). Radical crafts advocates like Leonard Abbott and J. William Lloyd also spoke highly of Whitman.

The arts and crafts movement subsided after 1917, though its effects on crafts education and design have persisted. The movement's synthesis of romantic nature aesthetics with utopian politics continued to inform countercultural poets like Kenneth Rexroth, Gary Snyder, Robert Duncan, and Allen Ginsberg.

John F. Roche

Bibliography

Boris, Eileen. *Art and Labor: Ruskin, Morris, and the Craftsman Ideal in America.* Philadelphia: Temple UP, 1986.

Clark, Robert Judson, ed. *The Arts and Crafts Movement in America 1876–1916.* 1972. Princeton: Princeton UP, 1992.

Kahler, Bruce Robert. "Art and Life: The Arts and Crafts Movement in Chicago, 1897–1910." Diss. Purdue U, 1986.

Kaplan, Wendy. *"The Art That Is Life": The Arts & Crafts Movement in America 1875–1920.* Boston: Little, Brown, 1987.

Lears, T.J. Jackson. *No Place of Grace: Antimodernism and the Transformation of American Culture 1880–1920.* New York: Pantheon, 1981.

Radcliffe-Whitehead, Ralph. "A Plea For Manual Work." *Handicraft* April 1903: 58–73.

Roche, John F. "The Culture of Pre-Modernism: Whitman, Morris, & the American Arts and Crafts Movement." *ATQ* 9.2 (1995): 103–118.

See also ARCHITECTS AND ARCHITECTURE; BAXTER, SYLVESTER; CARPENTER, EDWARD; EAKINS, THOMAS; LELAND, CHARLES GODFREY; NORTON, CHARLES ELIOT; TRAUBEL, HORACE L.; TRIGGS, OSCAR LOVELL

Arvin, Newton (1900–1963)

One of the most important American literary critics on the left, an exponent of biographical criticism, Newton Arvin spent virtually all of his career as a professor of English at Smith College. A homosexual, Arvin was forced to retire from Smith in 1960 after a scandal in which he was convicted of the possession of gay male pornography. His death came just after the publication of his last book, a biography of Longfellow.

Widely published as a critic and reviewer, Arvin wrote two major essays on Whitman prior to the publication of his book *Whitman* in 1938. "Whitman's Individualism" (1932) is a critique of "pastel" portraits of the poet that make him appear to be a liberal democrat. Against such views, Arvin insists on Whitman's interest in the masses, the working people of America. Although Arvin grants that Whitman was an individualist in the American tradition, he sees this individualism profoundly modified by Whitman's concept of comradeship.

Whitman carries the argument further; it begins dramatically by evoking a conversation between Whitman and Horace Traubel in which Whitman asserts his fundamental socialism. Arvin addresses the question of Whitman's politics by insisting on his own critical method, that of reading the author in the context of his or her time and place. Arvin stresses the republican enthusiasms of Whitman's youth, with its idealization of Thomas Paine and Frances Wright, as well as his attraction to Quakerism, embodied in the Quaker reformer Elias Hicks. He traces the decline of Whitman's faith in a strong executive and shows Whitman's disgust at post–Civil War politics of greed and corruption.

Arvin's mode of intellectual biography passed out of favor in the years of the New Critics, who saw little merit in Whitman's work other than in some of his lyrics. Because Arvin rarely practiced *explication de texte,* few if any of his readings have passed into the body of accepted Whitman criticism. His significance lies in his identification of a radical Whitman whose work emerged directly from the reform movements of the second quarter of the nineteenth century.

Robert K. Martin

Bibliography

Arvin, Newton. *Whitman.* New York: Macmillan, 1938.

———. "Whitman as He Was Not." *The New Republic* 14 April 1937: 301–302.

———. "Whitman's Individualism." *The New Republic* 6 July 1932: 212–213. Rpt. in *American Pantheon.* Ed. Daniel Aaron and Sylvan Schendler. New York: Delacorte, 1966. 43–50.

See also HICKS, ELIAS; INDIVIDUALISM; LABOR AND LABORING CLASSES; PAINE, THOMAS; RADICALISM; TRAUBEL, HORACE L.; WRIGHT, FRANCES (FANNY)

"As Adam Early in the Morning" (1860)

"As Adam Early in the Morning" appeared as number 15 in the cluster "Enfans d'Adam" of the 1860 edition of *Leaves of Grass.* Whitman made minor variations in punctuation from edition to edition, and in his Blue Book revisions of the 1860 edition, he tried out several titles but settled for the first line title "As Adam Early in the Morning," the first two words of which had not appeared in the 1860 edition (*Blue Book* 2:314).

Allen sees the poem as a kind of epilogue for the "Children of Adam" cluster, celebrating tactile sensation, and Miller notes that the poem opens up the world for modern man to search out his own Eden. Nathanson sees the poem as a perfect example of Whitman's ability to fuse person with voice; a reader is encouraged to touch a body which, in reality, does not exist beyond the confines of the words on the page. Thus the poem evokes a kind of magical or mystical presence of the narrator. Reiss reads the poem as a single sentence moving from a subordinate clause vague in direction to an independent clause that does not satisfy with any

kind of closure. There is in the poem, however, a fusion of Adam with the I-narrator, making the poem in actuality a process for the reader, a creative act.

George Klawitter

Bibliography

Allen, Gay Wilson. *Walt Whitman Handbook.* 1946. New York: Hendricks House, 1962.

Miller, James E., Jr. *A Critical Guide to "Leaves of Grass."* Chicago: U of Chicago P, 1957.

Nathanson, Tenney. *Whitman's Presence: Body, Voice, and Writing in "Leaves of Grass."* New York: New York UP, 1992.

Reiss, Edmund. "Whitman's Poetic Grammar: Style and Meaning in 'Children of Adam.'" *American Transcendental Quarterly* 12 (1971): 32–41.

Whitman, Walt. *Leaves of Grass: A Textual Variorum of the Printed Poems.* Ed. Sculley Bradley, Harold W. Blodgett, Arthur Golden, and William White. Vol. 3. New York: New York UP, 1980.

———. *Walt Whitman's Blue Book.* Ed. Arthur Golden. 2 vols. New York: New York Public Library, 1968.

See also AMERICAN ADAM; "CHILDREN OF ADAM"; *LEAVES OF GRASS,* 1860 EDITION

"As at Thy Portals Also Death" (1881)

"As at Thy Portals Also Death" was written in 1881, specifically for the "Songs of Parting" cluster. An elegy to Walt Whitman's mother, Louisa Van Velsor Whitman, it also reveals Whitman's own sense of the imminence of death, a dominant theme in the cluster. In the beginning of the poem, the speaker admits that he also stands before death and is explicit in saying that he wants to write about his mother before he himself dies. The poem, he asserts, stands as a monument to her, a tombstone set in "these songs," by which he may mean this cluster or the whole of *Leaves of Grass.*

As in the "Songs of Parting" cluster as a whole, the poem exhibits an ambivalent attitude toward death. The speaker declares his mother "buried and gone" and in the same line says, "yet buried not, gone not from me." This contradiction is important to Whitman, who tries in the cluster to subvert death's power. Certainly it supports his idea that he will remain on earth as long as readers continue to read his poetry and that his mother will be remembered as long as the poem is read.

The short ten-line, one-sentence poem manifests a sweeping scope from "divine blending" to "maternity" (by the proximity of these concepts, does Whitman suggest a feminine principle in the deity?), from death's "illimitable grounds" to "sweet old lips" and cheeks and eyes. These paired opposite, or nearly opposite, images suggest questions that underlie the poem, questions also posed by the "Songs of Parting" cluster: What is death? What goes and what remains after death? How does it happen? Is death final? These were perhaps Whitman's personal concerns as he wrote the poem in 1881, but they might also be concerns he had about the American experiment and the present state and future of democracy in America.

Susan Rieke

Bibliography
Allen, Gay Wilson. *The Solitary Singer: A Critical Biography of Walt Whitman.* 1955. Rev. ed. 1967. Chicago: U of Chicago P, 1985.
Carlisle, E. Fred. *The Uncertain Self: Whitman's Drama of Identity.* East Lansing: Michigan State UP, 1973.
Crawley, Thomas Edward. *The Structure of "Leaves of Grass."* Austin: U of Texas P, 1970.

See also DEATH; MOTHERHOOD; "SONGS OF PARTING"; WHITMAN, LOUISA VAN VELSOR

"As Consequent, Etc." (1881)

Published as one of the four new poems in "Autumn Rivulets," a cluster Whitman prepared for his 1881 *Leaves of Grass*, "As Consequent, Etc." is appropriately the very first poem of the cluster. It introduces the poet's metaphor of rivulets, the rivulets being his poems as well as the American currents of progress and reform.

The opening stanza introduces some common themes of "Autumn Rivulets": nature's bountiful store and supply; America's coming of age through years of struggle; the continued vigor and creative will of her people; time and death. The poet's songs are compared to "wayward rivulets" caused by summer rains, underground rills making for the sea, or the reticulated progress of a brook lined with herbs. The disorderly rush of the poet's ideas and images

meets an answering figurative description in these lines.

The rivulets are also "Life's ever-modern rapids," the signs of the nation's progress now manifested in Ohio's fields and woods, Colorado's canyons, Atlantica's bays, and the seas. In fact the poet sees the rivulets as currents that energize, inspire, and transform both himself and his readers—tiny currents, all flowing toward the mystic ocean of one supreme being. This union is further celebrated as "Fusion of ocean and land," as bridging abysses and canyons, the here and the hereafter. The poet is ecstatic at the thought that this mystic power infuses the whole world and runs through forms of life everywhere. The songs are also weeds and shells cast ashore by the sea of time. The singer gathers them all—souvenirs and tokens from a vast mystic sea. He values them for their music, their reverberations, no matter how far or faint. These soundings are important to him, for their "tidings [are] old, yet ever new and untranslatable."

K. Narayana Chandran

Bibliography
Allen, Gay Wilson. *The New Walt Whitman Handbook.* 1975. New York: New York UP, 1986.
Miller, James E., Jr. *A Critical Guide to "Leaves of Grass."* Chicago: U of Chicago P, 1957.
Whitman, Walt. *Leaves of Grass: Comprehensive Reader's Edition.* Ed. Harold W. Blodgett and Sculley Bradley. New York: New York UP, 1965.

See also "AUTUMN RIVULETS"

"As I Ebb'd with the Ocean of Life" (1860)

Whitman's "As I Ebb'd" was first published in the prestigious *Atlantic Monthly* in 1860 and later that year appeared as the opening poem of the "Leaves of Grass" section in the third edition of *Leaves of Grass*. Originally entitled "Bardic Symbols," it was later moved, under its present title, to the "Sea-Drift" section, where it appears as a pendant to the poem "Out of the Cradle Endlessly Rocking." In fact, so marked is its contrast with that poem of a year earlier that it seems its natural partner. Whereas "Out of the Cradle" is about mothers, oceans, poetry, love, and commitment, "As I Ebb'd" is about fathers, the shore, the failure of poetry, personal inadequacy, and profound uncertainty.

Unrelievedly revealing a darkness which contradicts Whitman's heroic self-creation of himself as the poet of democracy, as the celebrator of self, as the good gray poet, "As I Ebb'd" is one of Whitman's most important poems. Nowhere else does Whitman testify so powerfully to what the poem itself is at pains to recognize, that his life was "buoy'd hither from many moods, one contradicting another" (section 4).

The poem is divided into four sections. In the first, "held by this electric self out of the pride of which I utter poems," the poet wanders the shoreline of Long Island at the ebbing of the tide. As his eyes look downward, he notices that the retreating tide has revealed rows of trash, remnants washed ashore by the waves, "Chaff, straw, splinters of wood, weeds, and the seagluten." Thinking like a poet—"seeking types"—Whitman decides to read what he sees as a symbol, hoping to understand as "tokens of myself" ("Song of Myself," section 32) what lies before him.

In the second section, as he meditates on the natural symbol washed up by the waves as a representation of himself in the world, Whitman articulates what is, for him, a stunning discovery: "I too but signify at the utmost a little wash'd-up drift." Seeing an additional parallel between the "lines" of worthless sea-drift and the lines of poetry he has sent out into the world, he acknowledges that the poems he has been writing are arrogant. He admits, with much pain, that his poetic productions do not represent the "real Me [which] stands yet untouch'd, untold, altogether unreach'd."

In the third section, he identifies the "fish-shaped island" on which he stands, an island both solid and phallic in profile, with his father. (In contrast, both section 4 and "Out of the Cradle" identify the ocean with his mother.) His sense of personal worthlessness and inadequacy is related, perhaps autobiographically, to the son's powerlessness in the presence of his father. "I too have bubbled up, floated the measureless float, and been wash'd on your shores, / I too am but a trail of drift and debris." As Paul Zweig notes, "in an odd way, father and failure went together for Whitman" (307). Uncertain and deeply dependent, he throws himself on the breast of his father, seeking to be held close so that he can be comforted and hear "the secret of the murmuring I envy." Whether the murmuring is the fulfillment of adult heterosexual love—father and mother together in the mar-

riage bed—or whether it is homoerotic—the sound of manly passion—is ambiguous, an ambiguity which lends the poem great resonance.

The final section has formal affinities with the final section of "Crossing Brooklyn Ferry," since in both what has been formerly described is now addressed in the imperative, the poet insisting that what exists will hereafter be sufficient for him. Astute readers will note, however, the remarkable dissonance between the celebratory self-confidence of the earlier poem and the saddened acceptance of the whole of "As I Ebb'd." Nowhere is the difference in mood more obvious than between the ecstatic "float" in section 5 of "Brooklyn Ferry" and the passive "floated the measureless float" in section 3 of "As I Ebb'd," where emergence from the primal flux of existence and the uterine fluids signifies no more than the casting up of "drift and debris." The poet's depressive melancholy reaches a nadir in section four, where he envisions himself as a corpse washed up by the waves, lines so shocking that James Russell Lowell, the *Atlantic Monthly*'s editor, cut them from the first published edition. At the close of the poem Whitman's persona embraces the depressive role; contrary to almost all his other poetry, the poet submits without objection to passivity, powerlessness, and subservience.

As Whitman reads symbolically the detritus at his feet left by the retreating tide, so readers of the poem read Whitman's self-presentation symbolically. Readers see it as a break with Whitman's previous poetry, especially the ecstatic self-celebration of "Song of Myself." They read it as documenting a crisis of confidence in Whitman, a profound uncertainty about the worth of his poems and his existence, although some see Whitman's passive acceptance in the fourth part as a subdued resolution to that crisis. Additionally, there are critics who see the poem in historical and psychological contexts. Betsy Erkkila looks to its composition at the historical moment when the nation was coming undone, about to fall into fratricidal war: "No longer sustained by the ensemble of a national democratic order . . . Whitman's drowned poet projects the shipwreck of an entire culture" (169). Edwin Miller sees the collapse of the social order as revealing, through this poem, the substrate of all Whitman's poetry: "despite the . . . expressed desire to be the poetic spokesman of democracy . . . the real subject matter is the restoration of infantile relationships" (46). The renewal of a bond with his father is what the poem signifies to Paul Zweig: "His hurt has enabled him to see his father as if for the first time, and draw from him a kind of negative strength: the ability to endure and thrive in failure" (309).

Huck Gutman

Bibliography

Bromwich, David. "Suburbs and Extremities." *Prose* 8 (1974): 25–38.

Erkkila, Betsy. *Whitman the Political Poet.* New York: Oxford UP, 1989.

Miller, Edwin Haviland. *Walt Whitman's Poetry: A Psychological Journey.* New York: New York UP, 1968.

Nathanson, Tenney. *Whitman's Presence: Body, Voice, and Writing in "Leaves of Grass."* New York: New York UP, 1992.

Waskow, Howard J. *Whitman: Explorations in Form.* Chicago: U of Chicago P, 1966.

Zweig, Paul. *Walt Whitman: The Making of the Poet.* New York: Basic Books, 1984.

See also ATLANTIC MONTHLY, THE; "CROSSING BROOKLYN FERRY"; LEAVES OF GRASS, 1860 EDITION; LONG ISLAND, NEW YORK; "OUT OF THE CRADLE ENDLESSLY ROCKING"; SEA, THE; "SEA-DRIFT"; "SONG OF MYSELF"; WHITMAN, WALTER, SR.

"As I Lay with My Head in Your Lap Camerado" (1865–1866)

"As I Lay with My Head in Your Lap Camerado" first appeared in Whitman's separately published *Sequel to Drum-Taps* (1865–1866). *Sequel* was printed in Washington and was first bound with *Leaves of Grass* in 1867. "As I Lay" was moved elsewhere in the 1871 and 1876 editions and returned to "Drum-Taps" in 1881. The 1881 version excludes a parenthetical passage which followed line 4.

Placed in the concluding pages of "Drum-Taps," "As I Lay" urges the camerado onward, down an unknown road. The war is over, but the fight continues. The resolution is only temporary as "words are [now] weapons" and restlessness a contagion. The struggle for union and a true democracy will continue.

While critics agree that "As I Lay" belongs in "Drum-Taps" as a Civil War poem, some also read it as a restatement of Whitman's "Calamus" themes. The speaker's marginal status, "all have denied me," and his rebellion against

---

"all the settled laws" are characteristic of this earlier cluster. The hope that "we shall be victorious" in the last three lines suggests the possibility of survival and acceptance both for the union of the lovers and the union of the nation. One becomes a metonymy for the other.

Sheree L. Gilbert

Bibliography

Allen, Gay Wilson. *The New Walt Whitman Handbook.* 1975. New York: New York UP, 1986.

Askin, Denise T. "Retrievements Out of the Night: Prophetic and Private Voices in Whitman's *Drum-Taps.*" *American Transcendental Quarterly* 51 (1981): 211–223.

Cady, Joseph. "*Drum-Taps* and Nineteenth-Century Male Homosexual Literature." *Walt Whitman: Here and Now.* Ed. Joann P. Krieg. Westport, Conn.: Greenwood, 1985. 49–60.

Davis, Robert Leigh. "Whitman's Tympanum: A Reading of *Drum-Taps.*" *American Transcendental Quarterly* 6.3 (1992): 163–175.

Whitman, Walt. *Walt Whitman's "Drum-Taps" (1865) and "Sequel to Drum-Taps" (1865–6): A Facsimile Reproduction.* Ed. F. DeWolfe Miller. Gainesville, Fla.: Scholars' Facsimiles and Reprints, 1959.

See also "CALAMUS"; CIVIL WAR, THE; COMRADESHIP; "DRUM-TAPS"; "OVER THE CARNAGE ROSE PROPHETIC A VOICE"; SEQUEL TO DRUM-TAPS; "VIGIL STRANGE I KEPT ON THE FIELD ONE NIGHT"

"As I Ponder'd in Silence" (1871)

The second in a group of nine (later twenty-four) opening poems called "Inscriptions" (1871 *Leaves of Grass*), "As I Ponder'd in Silence" strikes the keynote of war, the epic theme of the volume.

As Whitman reflects on his poems, he has a vision of a "Phantom" rising before him. The poet is awestruck and identifies the Phantom as the "genius of poets of old lands." The Phantom asks the poet rather menacingly whether he understands that there is only one supreme and perennial *"theme for ever-enduring bards,"* namely, war. Whitman's reply, rather defensive in tone and claim, follows. He too sings of war.

In his books, claims the poet, he wages an ongoing war, now advancing, now retreating, but nonetheless risky or challenging for that. He sees the world itself as a theater of war where man fights for life and death in a bid to save his body and soul. It is these battles he celebrates, the bravery of these fighters he admires.

"As I Ponder'd" is one of those very early poems that introduces the by-now-familiar topos of Whitman's dialogue with a visionary figure, usually the shade of a heroic ancestor. The passages in italics here mark the dialogue discreetly from the silent pondering, a technique Whitman uses with great effect in such poems as "Song of the Redwood-Tree," "Out of the Cradle Endlessly Rocking," and "Out of the Rolling Ocean the Crowd."

K. Narayana Chandran

Bibliography

Allen, Gay Wilson. *The New Walt Whitman Handbook.* 1975. New York: New York UP, 1986.

Crawley, Thomas Edward. *The Structure of "Leaves of Grass."* Austin: U of Texas P, 1970.

Whitman, Walt. *Leaves of Grass: Comprehensive Reader's Edition.* Ed. Harold W. Blodgett and Sculley Bradley. New York: New York UP, 1965.

See also "INSCRIPTIONS"

"As I Sit Writing Here" (1888)

"As I Sit Writing Here" first appeared in the New York *Herald,* 14 May 1888. Later that year, Whitman collected "Writing" into *November Boughs* under the section "Sands at Seventy." Also later that year, "Sands at Seventy" was reprinted as an annex to *Leaves of Grass* in *Complete Poems and Prose.*

Whitman's attempt to record universal experiences and his self-proclaimed role as poet of body and soul force him to write even about the unpleasantness of aging. In "Writing" Whitman voices his concerns that advancing age is filtering into his poetry, making him a weaker poet. His body becomes a metaphor for poetic activity: both succumb to the burdens of age. Instead of a free flow of ideas expressed through a natural process, Whitman's poetry is stopped up—constipated. Time has made him "dull" and "querulous." "Lethargy" slows his writing so that he produces shorter poems. "Whimpering

ennui" causes him to question his ability to write. By acknowledging his advanced age in his writing, however, Whitman attempts to put himself in control of his querulousness. He hopes that by his forcing the reader to participate in his aches and "glooms," the reader will experience aging with him and thus overlook the weaknesses seeping into his poetry.

Martha A. Kalnin

Bibliography

Fillard, Claudette. "Le Vannier de Camden: Vieillesse, Poésie, et les Annexes de *Leaves of Grass.*" *Études Anglaises* 45 (1992): 311–323.

Stauffer, Donald Barlow. "Walt Whitman and Old Age." *Walt Whitman Review* 24 (1978): 142–148.

Thomas, M. Wynn. "A Study of Whitman's Late Poetry." *Walt Whitman Review* 27 (1981): 3–14.

Whitman, Walt. *Leaves of Grass: Comprehensive Reader's Edition.* Ed. Harold W. Blodgett and Sculley Bradley. New York: New York UP, 1965.

See also AGE AND AGING; HEALTH; *NOVEMBER BOUGHS*; "SANDS AT SEVENTY" (FIRST ANNEX)

"As Toilsome I Wander'd Virginia's Woods" (1865)

In the fall of 1862, on a trip to the Union army camps in Falmouth, Virginia, in search of news about his wounded brother, George, Walt Whitman came as close as he ever would to the Civil War's front lines. A short but thematically dense lyric describing the poet's encounter with the grave and epitaph of a soldier buried on the march, "As Toilsome I Wander'd Virginia's Woods" seems likely to be one of a handful among the poems in "Drum-Taps" that derive from Whitman's own experiences during this visit to the front.

The soldier's epitaph—"Bold, cautious, true, and my loving comrade"—is perfectly Whitmanesque, both in its free verse form and its masterfully dense and emotionally turbulent evocation of paradox. The first half of the line sets up a logic of antithesis—boldness matched by caution—that becomes a submerged echo, battling with the manifest meaning of the rest of the line. The latent meaning submerged within "my loving comrade" as the antithesis of "true," in other words, is falseness, inconstancy.

Loving intimacy, the line suggests subtly, is founded in its opposite, in heartbreak and loss.

This paradoxical emotional logic, according to which death becomes the perfection of intimacy, is at the heart of Whitman's great elegiac masterpieces "Out of the Cradle Endlessly Rocking" (1860) and "When Lilacs Last in the Dooryard Bloom'd" (1865). Along with those poems, "Toilsome" suggests that the experience of profound loss, evoked in poetic form, can provide an enduring basis for a democratic community of feeling. "My book and the war are one," Whitman would assert in "To Thee Old Cause" (1871); in "Toilsome" that claim means that a certain poetic distance from the war—the distance of epitaph or elegy—can actually serve to produce an emotionally genuine experience of the war, where the effect of poetry is to make loss feel intimately present.

Terry Mulcaire

Bibliography

Kaplan, Justin. *Walt Whitman: A Life*. New York: Simon and Schuster, 1980.

Maslan, Mark. "Whitman's 'Strange Hand': Body as Text in *Drum-Taps*." *ELH* 58 (1991): 935–955.

Reynolds, David S. *Walt Whitman's America: A Cultural Biography*. New York: Knopf, 1995.

Snyder, John. *The Dear Love of Man: Tragic and Lyric Communion in Walt Whitman*. The Hague: Mouton, 1975.

See also CIVIL WAR, THE; "DRUM-TAPS"; FALMOUTH, VIRGINIA

"Ashes of Soldiers" (1865)

"Ashes of Soldiers" was written in 1865 and first appeared in *Drum-Taps* as "Hymn of Dead Soldiers." In 1871 Walt Whitman added the first two stanzas and placed it in the "Passage to India" annex, where it remained until its 1881 position in "Songs of Parting." The addition of this and other Civil War poems to "Songs of Parting" intensifies this cluster's emphasis on death.

In the poem, the speaker's retrospective musings call forth the metonymic ashes of the war's dead soldiers, and in his silent vision of them he moves among a vast army of the "Phantoms of countless lost." He commands no trumpets and drums as he merges in loving companionship with the ashes of the soldiers, whose dearness to him is signified by the repetition of the possessive "my." They are with him always, he says, and he mourns their loss in line 30: "Dearest comrades, all is over and long gone."

However, in line 31 the speaker turns sharply from his sorrow to consider the paradoxical notion that his companions still live. They live, he says, in his "immortal love" for them. He then constructs a metaphoric process which amounts to an idea of resurrection; the soldiers perdure in the "fœtor" he calls "Perfume" rising from the earth which holds their bodies. As he breathes this sweet perfume, the soldiers live in him; in fact, they "nourish and blossom" as he fills himself with them and almost becomes them. The speaker's voice rises to an ecstatic pitch as he prays to love, asking love to make him a fountain in order that he might exhale them from him, thus causing them to live "like a moist perennial dew," present forever on the earth, in the speaker's present time. Thus, the breathing process becomes a metaphor for resurrection and immortality.

In this interpretation, Whitman mourns naturally the loss of those he knew and nursed in the Civil War and laments the loss of their love for one another. But a political Whitman also grieves for the loss of his early democratic ideals and for the vision of the Union shattered by the Civil War. Perhaps the poet's carefully constructed idea of resurrection is a way to retain some hope in the American democratic experiment. The last line of the poem reveals both the poet's concern for the Union and his grief over dead comrades as it includes "the ashes of all dead soldiers South and North" in the poem's moving, elegiac vision.

Susan Rieke

Bibliography

Crawley, Thomas Edward. *The Structure of "Leaves of Grass."* Austin: U of Texas P, 1970.

Hutchinson, George B. *The Ecstatic Whitman: Literary Shamanism & the Crisis of the Union*. Columbus: Ohio State UP, 1986.

Thomas, M. Wynn. *The Lunar Light of Whitman's Poetry*. Cambridge, Mass.: Harvard UP, 1987.

See also CIVIL WAR, THE; COMRADESHIP; *DRUM-TAPS*; "SONGS OF PARTING"

Ashton, J. Hubley (1836–1907)

Lawyer, government official, and professor at Georgetown University, J[oseph] Hubley Ashton was one of the founders of the American Bar Association and a long-time friend of William Douglas O'Connor, who was among Whitman's closest associates and most fervent admirers.

In January 1865, in his capacity as Assistant Attorney General of the United States, Ashton played a key role in finding Whitman a full-time government clerkship in the Bureau of Indian Affairs within the Department of the Interior. Something of a sinecure, this job enabled Whitman to write his poetry and, at the same time, perform his ministrations as a nurse in the Civil War hospitals in and around Washington, D.C. In June, however, Whitman was dismissed from this position by Secretary of the Interior James W. Harlan because Harlan had discovered, on or in Whitman's desk, Whitman's personal, marked copy of the 1860 *Leaves of Grass* (the so-called Blue Book) and had found in it passages of poetry he deemed offensive and immoral. Ashton attempted to intervene with Harlan on Whitman's behalf, but to no avail. However, Ashton again made a signal contribution, this time by finding a clerkship for Whitman in the office of the Attorney General, a position he would occupy for the next eight years.

Although he would eventually claim that his interventions on Whitman's behalf were all due to the promptings of the poet's devoted friend William O'Connor, Ashton nevertheless demonstrated his own active interest in Whitman's affairs in Washington.

Amy M. Bawcom

Bibliography

Allen, Gay Wilson. *The Solitary Singer: A Critical Biography of Walt Whitman.* 1955. Rev. ed. 1967. Chicago: U of Chicago P, 1985.

Loving, Jerome. *Walt Whitman's Champion: William Douglas O'Connor.* College Station: Texas A&M UP, 1978.

Traubel, Horace. *With Walt Whitman in Camden.* Vol. 3. 1914. New York: Rowman and Littlefield, 1961.

See also Attorney General's Office, United States; Civil War Nursing; Harlan, James W.; Indian Affairs, Bureau of; O'Connor, William Douglas

Asselineau, Roger (1915–)

Born in Orléans, France, Roger Maurice Asselineau was educated at the Université de Paris–Sorbonne, where he received degrees in 1935, *Licence ès Lettres;* 1938, *Agrégation d'anglais;* and 1953, *Doctorat ès Lettres.* After teaching briefly at the Université de Lyon, he returned to the Sorbonne, there to serve as Professor of American Literature from 1960 to 1983. In 1954, Asselineau published his massive doctoral dissertation, calling it *L'Évolution de Walt Whitman.* A few years later, aided by Richard P. Adams and Burton L. Cooper, he translated his 569-page book into English. Harvard University Press published the translation in two volumes: *The Evolution of Walt Whitman: The Creation of a Personality* (1960) and *The Evolution of Walt Whitman: The Creation of a Book* (1962). This two-part study was promptly recognized as a major contribution to the effort to demythologize the poet, and Asselineau was well on his way to becoming one of the foremost Whitman scholars of our time.

Asselineau's *Evolution* advances the thesis, venturesome in its day, that homosexuality is the key to Whitman's personality and poetry. Because of a struggle with homosexual desires, Asselineau argues, Whitman was unstable, tormented; he used his poetry as a means to discharge his turbulent passions. His art was, in effect, not only compensatory, a substitute for physical gratification, but therapeutic. Whitman's poetry saved him.

In addition to *The Evolution of Walt Whitman,* Asselineau published a French translation of *Leaves of Grass* (*Feuilles d'herbe,* 1956), as well as a bilingual edition (1972). He wrote the long chapter on Whitman in *Eight American Authors: A Review of Research and Criticism,* edited by James Woodress (rev. ed., 1971). In 1980, he published *The Transcendentalist Constant in American Literature,* a collection of essays in which Whitman is a central figure. Finally, in 1992, the centennial of the poet's death, he edited a special Whitman issue of *Études Anglaises.* Although Asselineau wrote books on other authors, such as Mark Twain, Sherwood Anderson, Ernest Hemingway, Edgar Allan Poe, and St. Jean de Crèvecoeur (with Gay Wilson Allen), his primary focus, for more than fifty years, has been on Whitman.

Donald D. Kummings

Bibliography

Asselineau, Roger. "My Discovery and Exploration of the Whitman Continent (1941–1991)." *Walt Whitman Quarterly Review* 9 (1991): 15–23.

See also BIOGRAPHIES; CRITICS, WHITMAN'S; FRANCE, WHITMAN IN; SEX AND SEXUALITY

Associations, Clubs, Fellowships, Foundations, and Societies

Although Whitman did not organize groups in any formal way, from the 1860s to the 1890s he attracted disciples, primarily in the United States, Canada, and England. Whitman's American admirers—William D. O'Connor, Richard Maurice Bucke, John Burroughs, Thomas Harned, William Sloane Kennedy, and Horace Traubel—sometimes presented the poet as a new messiah, and English admirers Edward Carpenter, James Wallace, and Dr. John Johnston made pilgrimages to Camden and wrote books about the experience. In the last few years of Whitman's life his disciples began to organize themselves into cultlike associations with shrines, scriptures, icons, and rituals. While Whitman was sometimes embarrassed by the excesses of his admirers, he encouraged groups like the antecedents of the Walt Whitman Fellowship and the "Eagle Street College," whose construction of "Walt Whitman" was generally consistent with the image he wished to present. On the other hand, Whitman resisted Sadakichi Hartmann's unauthorized attempt to make himself the head of a Whitman fund-raising society in Boston in 1887. In the decades after Whitman's death, however, new associations became less religious, and the poet became a central figure in a variety of cultural movements. The versions of Whitman that emerged were often created in the image of his admirers: Whitman the socialist, Whitman the communist, Whitman the feminist, Whitman the democrat.

The group that became the Walt Whitman Fellowship began informally as early as 1887, when Whitman's friends began to celebrate his birthday with a dinner held on 31 May. In a few years these dinners developed into publicity and fund-raising affairs, the largest of which was in 1889, when a committee including Harned, H.L. Bonsall, and Geoffrey Buckwalter rented a hall in Camden and sent notices to admirers, friendly critics, and authors the world over. The celebration was covered by the local press, and enough money was raised to buy Whitman a wheelchair. The numerous testimonial speeches and telegrams were collected by Traubel in *Camden's Compliment to Walt Whitman* (1889). After Whitman's death in 1892, his friends gathered again in Philadelphia on 31 May and named themselves the "Walt Whitman Reunion Association," dedicated to keeping "fresh in our hearts the memories of our departed friend, the poet," and to extending "the influence of his writings where they are not understood and loved" (White 69). In June, John H. Johnston, a jeweler and patron of Whitman from New York, was named chairman of the association. The members had a "Whitman Night" at New York's Twilight Club in the fall, and they celebrated Whitman's birthday in New York in 1893.

In 1894 the association met again in Philadelphia, and after voting down titles such as "Society" and "Comradeship," the thirty-six members renamed themselves the "Walt Whitman Fellowship: International." Its purposes were threefold: to bring together people interested in Whitman, to establish Whitman fellowships all over the world, and to publish works relating to Whitman. The founding members included Daniel Garrison Brinton, Bucke, Burroughs, Harned, Robert Ingersoll, Johnston, David McKay, Traubel, and his wife, Anne Montgomerie Traubel. A professor at the University of Pennsylvania, Brinton was named president, and Horace Traubel soon became secretary-treasurer, a position he held until his death in 1919. From 1895 to 1900 the fellowship alternated its annual gatherings between Philadelphia and Boston, and from 1901 to 1919 they met in New York. During these years membership climbed as high as 240, and branches of the fellowship were formed in Boston, New York, Philadelphia, and Knoxville, Tennessee. Other branches were proposed for Chicago, Atlanta, Los Angeles, and San Francisco in the United States, and London, Bolton, and Liverpool in England. The fellowship continued its celebrations for twenty-five years, and it attracted a diverse membership of writers, artists, and politicians, including Max Eastman, John Erskine, Walter Lippman, F.B. Sanborn, E.C. Stedman, Clement Wood, Marsden Hartley, John Sloan, Alfred Stieglitz, Max Weber, and Samuel L. Jones, the mayor of Toledo. According to one member, the meetings were a gathering of "Socialists, anarchists, communists, painters, poets, mechanics, laborers, business men," each of whom shared a love of Whitman (White 67). Before the fellowship ended in 1919 with the death of its chief organizer, Horace Traubel, it had published 123 "Walt Whitman Fellowship Papers," containing many important essays on Whitman. The fellowship eventually became a parent group for several other Whitman organizations that continued through the twentieth century.

While the Walt Whitman Fellowship: International was active in the United States, another group of Whitman's admirers continued its activities in England. Around 1885 some friends in Bolton, Lancashire, became interested in Whitman and began to meet regularly at the house of James William Wallace on Eagle Street. The group called itself the "Eagle Street College," but it became known as the Bolton Whitman Fellowship. Its members were mostly middle-class men; among them were two bank clerks, an accountant, two assistant architects, two law clerks, a couple of tradesmen, a clergyman, and a doctor. Wallace and Dr. John Johnston, the leaders of the group, began to correspond with Whitman in 1887. They regularly sent the poet letters of homage and cash gifts, and Whitman responded with affectionate letters, photographs, and copies of his books. In 1890 Johnston visited Whitman in Camden and made a pilgrimage to the poet's birthplace on Long Island. Later that year Johnston published a pamphlet, "Notes of a Visit to Walt Whitman and His Friends in 1890," and received Whitman's approval to send copies of it to numerous friends in England and America. At this time the leaders of the Bolton Fellowship came into contact with several important English Whitman enthusiasts (Edward Carpenter, William Michael Rossetti, and John Addington Symonds) and with leaders of the Whitman Fellowship in America (Bucke, Burroughs, Harned, and Traubel). In 1891 Wallace, accompanied by Bucke, visited Whitman in Camden and the birthplace on Long Island, and later published his own account, "Visits to Walt Whitman and His Friends, Etc., in 1891" (1917). The Bolton group remained active until the death of Wallace in 1926. Members continued to meet on Whitman's birthday at the house of James Ormrod for a time, and Wallace's adopted daughter, Minnie Whiteside Bull, maintained a correspondence with Whitman's American enthusiasts, particularly Anne Montgomerie Traubel, until the 1950s. Largely

through her efforts an important collection of Whitmaniana and the proceedings of the "Eagle Street College" remain in Bolton's Central Library. Harold Hamer published a catalogue of the collection in 1955.

Several other groups of Whitman enthusiasts emerged in the United States and Canada in the first decades after Whitman's death. Not personally associated with Whitman, these groups tended to be less religious in their devotion and more interested in Whitman as literary figure or as a spokesman for social and political reform. The long-surviving Iowa Schoolmasters' Walt Whitman Club was founded in Cedar Falls, Iowa, in 1895 by J.T. Merrill and O.J. Laylander, both Iowa school officials who wanted students to become more familiar with Whitman's writings. The club began with a dozen members, and in 1896 Merrill was elected "Chief Walt" for life, and Laylander became "Scribe Walt." (Ordinary members were called "Waltlets.") They held regular initiation rituals followed by a banquet with speeches and toasts from "Brother Walts." Some Iowans suspected the club of radical intentions, but it seems to have been simply a fraternal society for the promotion of Whitmanesque attitudes, and it may be that Whitman eventually became incidental to the networking activities it facilitated among the leading educators of the state. Among its membership were at least twenty Iowa college presidents, fifty superintendents of schools, and numerous principals, deans, and professors. From 1895 to 1970 the Whitman Club had 290 members, a large percentage of whom have been associated with the University of Iowa, sponsor of *The Walt Whitman Quarterly Review* (1983–).

The Walt Whitman Fellowship of Chicago also maintained a long unbroken history. Founded in 1906 by Dr. Morris Lychenheim, it continued to hold annual meetings on 31 May until at least the late 1950s. Noted criminal lawyer Clarence Darrow was a supporter of the fellowship in 1919, and he spoke at their 1925 meeting. A fiftieth-anniversary celebration was held in 1956 and attended by Senator Paul Douglas, Louis Untermeyer, Francis Winwar, and Walter Blair.

Although not founded as a Whitman association, New York's Sunrise Club championed Walt Whitman at dinners attended by several hundred members in the late 1890s. Around 1918 one of its members started an annual gathering dedicated to Whitman. Led by James

F. Morton, over the next decade the group swelled to several hundred people who met to discuss Whitman, read poems, and visit Whitman's birthplace on Long Island. Meanwhile, the "Writers' Club" of New York, organized in 1917, protested Whitman's exclusion from New York University's Hall of Fame. Their leader, J. George Frederick, organized annual trips to Whitman's birthplace which included ceremonial addresses and readings. The two leaders, Morton and Frederick, formed the "Whitman Society" in New York in 1924, which continued its expeditions to Long Island. Around 1928 they planned a *Walt Whitman Magazine,* which was halted by the beginning of the depression in 1929. The Whitman Society disbanded shortly after Whitman was accepted into the Hall of Fame in 1931.

The Walt Whitman Fellowship of Canada was founded in 1915 in Toronto and held annual meetings with speeches and music on Whitman's birthday for at least fifteen years. Its members included Henry S. Saunders, a noted collector of Whitmaniana, who served at times as president. Another Canadian association, the Whitman Club of Bon Echo, Ontario, existed for only a few years, headed by Flora Mac-Donald Denison, former president of the Canadian Woman Suffrage Association. She published six issues of *The Sunset of Bon Echo* from 1916 to 1920 and organized the erecting of a monument to "Old Walt" on scenic Bon Echo Rock in 1919.

The spirit of reform and political radicalism never entirely left the Whitman associations that continued in various forms through the twentieth century, but the interests of the two principal organizations that remain today, the Walt Whitman Association and the Walt Whitman Birthplace Association, are primarily the preservation of the houses in which Whitman was born and died, the maintenance of archives of Whitman materials, and the education of the public about Whitman. Nevertheless, in both cases the need to acquire government funding has necessitated a political construction of Whitman quite different from those of other associations.

What is now the Walt Whitman Association originated in 1919 when J. David Stern, publisher of the Camden *Daily Courier,* and his wife, Juliet Lit Stern, urged the city to purchase Whitman's former house at 330 Mickle Boulevard. As a result of their efforts the house was purchased by the city of Camden and dedicated as a memorial museum in 1923. A committee of remaining members of the Walt Whitman Fellowship: International, including Anne M. Traubel and her daughter, was created to advise the city and to appoint a curator for the house. The committee became the Walt Whitman Foundation, chaired by Whitman's former physician, Alexander McAlister, and it resumed the annual celebrations of Whitman's birthday. In 1940 a board of trustees, chaired by Ralph W. Wescott, formed a corporation in order to raise funds to preserve the house and to build a library next door. In 1945 ownership of the house was transferred from Camden to the State of New Jersey. From 1948 to 1955 the *Walt Whitman Foundation Bulletin* was published and expanded to *The Walt Whitman Newsletter,* which continued until 1958. According to a leaflet inserted in the first issue of the *Bulletin,* the promotion of Whitman was a "vital step towards world democracy, tolerance and peace," and in March 1950 the *Bulletin* included an essay by Cleveland Rodgers contrasting Whitman with Marx.

In 1965, the foundation was reincorporated as the Walt Whitman Association and elected Dr. Harold W. Barnshaw president. In 1984 the association prevailed on the state to restore the building next to the house as a library, and the following year it aided the initiation of a Whitman Studies program at Rutgers University directed by David Reynolds. From 1979 to 1991 the association sponsored *The Mickle Street Review,* and since 1987 it has published a newsletter, *Conversations.* The house remains open for tours, the library is open by appointment to visiting scholars, and the association continues to hold meetings, readings, and Whitman-related events for the general public.

Closely related to the Walt Whitman Foundation, the Walt Whitman Birthplace Association was organized in 1949 by Cleveland Rodgers to purchase Whitman's birthplace in West Hills, Huntington, Long Island, from its former owner and to preserve it. Rodgers succeeded, in part, by presenting Whitman as an anticommunist poet, and in 1951 the Birthplace Association took over the house, holding a dedication on 31 May 1952. In 1957, to ensure its long-term security, title to the house was given to New York State under an agreement that would make it a State Historic Site operated by the Birthplace Association. The house remains open to the public, and the Birthplace Association continues to hold celebrations of Whitman's birthday and maintains a library and a visitor center with exhibits, presentations, and educational programs. The Birthplace Association published the *Walt Whitman Birthplace Bulletin* (1957–1961) and *The Long Islander* (1969–1974); since 1979 it has published a literary journal, *The West Hills Review,* and it has published a newsletter, *Starting From Paumanok,* since 1985. Its Poet-in-Residence Program has attracted Robert Bly, Allen Ginsberg, Galway Kinnell, and Adrienne Rich.

It is impossible to calculate how many other Whitman groups have sprung up and disappeared, leaving perhaps a memorial room at school or library, a collection of books, a few issues of a hand-printed newsletter, or nothing at all. There was a Walt Whitman Society of National Librarians in Hempstead, Long Island; a Walt Whitman Foundation of Los Angeles; a Whitman Society of London; a Whitman Society of Australia; a group in Vienna headed by Roswitha Ballabene; a Société de Walt Whitman in Paris; and a Walt Whitman Society of America formed briefly by Cleveland Rodgers in the early 1950s. Many other groups, no doubt, still exist and continue to be formed unnoticed by the larger community of Whitman admirers.

William A. Pannapacker

Bibliography

Dyson, Verne. "The Whitman Societies." *Walt Whitman Birthplace Bulletin.* "I. The Walt Whitman Reunion Association (1887)." 1.2 (1958): 14–17; "II. The Walt Whitman Fellowship: International (1894)." 1.3 (1958): 3–7; "III. The Walt Whitman Fellowship, Bolton, England: 'Eagle Street College' (1885)." 1.4 (1958): 18–21; "IV. The Walt Whitman Fellowship of Chicago (1906)." 2.1 (1958): 11–12; "V. The Walt Whitman Fellowship of Toronto (1915)." 2.1 (1958): 12–13.

Frederick, J. George. "The Attempts to Form Whitman Societies." *Walt Whitman Birthplace Bulletin* 2.1 (1958): 16–17.

Hamer, Harold. *A Catalogue of Works by and Relating to Walt Whitman in the Reference Library, Bolton.* Bolton, England: Libraries Committee, 1955.

Hendrick, George. "Flora MacDonald Denison's *The Sunset of Bon Echo.*" *Walt Whitman Birthplace Bulletin* 3.2 (1960): 3–5.

———. "Walt Whitman and Sadakichi Hartmann." *Emerson Society Quarterly* 11 (1958): 50–52. Rpt. in *Walt Whitman Birthplace Bulletin* 3.1 (1959): 15–19.

Johnston, John, and James William Wallace. *Visits to Walt Whitman in 1890–1891 by Two Lancashire Friends.* London: George Allen and Unwin, 1917.

Krieg, Joann P. "Walt Whitman in the Public Domain: A Tale of Two Houses." *Long Island Historical Journal* 6.1 (1993): 83–95.

Petersen, William J. "The Walt Whitman Club." *The Palimpsest* 51 (1970): 323–348.

Traubel, Horace. *With Walt Whitman in Camden.* 9 Vols. Vol. 1. Boston: Small, Maynard, 1906; Vol. 2. New York: Appleton, 1908; Vol. 3. New York: Mitchell Kennerley, 1914; Vol. 4. Ed. Sculley Bradley. Philadelphia: U of Pennsylvania P, 1953; Vol. 5. Ed. Gertrude Traubel. Carbondale: Southern Illinois UP, 1964; Vol. 6. Ed. Gertrude Traubel and William White. Carbondale: Southern Illinois UP, 1982; Vol. 7. Ed. Jeanne Chapman and Robert MacIsaac. Carbondale: Southern Illinois UP, 1992; Vols. 8–9. Ed. Jeanne Chapman and Robert MacIsaac. Oregon House, Calif.: W.L. Bentley, 1996.

White, William. "The Walt Whitman Fellowship: An Account of Its Organization and a Checklist of Its Papers." *Papers of the American Bibliographical Society* 51 (1957): 67–84, 167–169.

See also AUSTRALIA AND NEW ZEALAND, WHITMAN IN; BIRTHPLACE, WHITMAN'S; BOLTON (ENGLAND) "EAGLE STREET COLLEGE"; BON ECHO; BRITISH ISLES, WHITMAN IN THE; BUCKE, RICHARD MAURICE; BURROUGHS, JOHN AND URSULA; CAMDEN, NEW JERSEY; CANADA, WHITMAN'S RECEPTION IN; CARPENTER, EDWARD; DENISON, FLORA MACDONALD; HARNED, THOMAS BIGGS; HARTMANN, C. SADAKICHI; INGERSOLL, ROBERT GREEN; JOHNSTON, DR. JOHN; JOHNSTON, JOHN H. AND ALMA CALDER; KENNEDY, WILLIAM SLOANE; MCKAY, DAVID; MICKLE STREET HOUSE; O'CONNOR, WILLIAM DOUGLAS; PHILADELPHIA, PENNSYLVANIA; ROSSETTI, WILLIAM MICHAEL; SYMONDS, JOHN ADDINGTON; TRAUBEL, HORACE L.; WALLACE, JAMES WILLIAM

Atlantic Monthly, The

The *Atlantic Monthly: A Magazine of Literature, Art and Politics* was the inspiration of Free-Soiler Francis Underwood and writers such as Ralph Waldo Emerson, Oliver Wendell Holmes, and James Russell Lowell. Founded as a monthly whose cultural mission would be to guide the age in literature and the arts, the magazine was also firmly antislavery in political orientation. Lowell, editor of the *Atlantic* from November 1857 until June 1861, was interested in promoting the work of American writers and published works by Harriet Beecher Stowe, John Greenleaf Whittier, Henry David Thoreau, Thomas Wentworth Higginson, and Henry Wadsworth Longfellow, as well as younger unknowns, such as Louisa May Alcott and Thomas Bailey Aldrich. Although Lowell promoted the works of a variety of American writers, the contributors were generally New Englanders, especially during the early years of the magazine.

Ambivalent about his public reception in the late 1850s, Whitman sought an opportunity for publication in the *Atlantic*. "Bardic Symbols" (later entitled "As I Ebb'd with the Ocean of Life") appeared in the *Atlantic* in April 1860. Evidently finding the suggestion of suicide too graphic for the pages of the *Atlantic*, Lowell deleted two lines from the fourth stanza which Whitman later restored in the 1860 edition of *Leaves of Grass*. Whitman nonetheless offered Lowell three additional poems written during the first months of the Civil War (later included in *Drum-Taps*), but the editor refused them, apparently finding them too topical for lasting interest. James T. Fields, the next editor of the *Atlantic*, published "Proud Music of the Sea-Storm" in February of 1869, later reprinted in *Passage to India* (1871).

Susan Belasco Smith

Bibliography

Allen, Gay Wilson. *The New Walt Whitman Handbook*. 1975. New York: New York UP, 1986.

Greenspan, Ezra. *Walt Whitman and the American Reader*. Cambridge: Cambridge UP, 1990.

Mott, Frank Luther. *A History of American Magazines*. 5 vols. Cambridge, Mass.: Harvard UP, 1938–1968.

Myerson, Joel. *Walt Whitman: A Descriptive Bibliography*. Pittsburgh: U of Pittsburgh P, 1993.

Sedgwick, Ellery. "The Atlantic Monthly." *American Literary Magazines: The Eighteenth and Nineteenth Centuries*. Ed. Edward E. Chielens. New York: Greenwood, 1986. 50–57.

See also "As I Ebb'd with the Ocean of Life"; "Proud Music of the Storm"

Attorney General's Office, United States

Whitman worked in the Attorney General's Office from July 1865 until he left Washington in January of 1873. His friends William O'Connor and J. Hubley Ashton arranged this position within twenty-four hours of his dismissal from the Office of Indian Affairs.

The job in the Attorney General's Office was not, by Whitman's own account, very difficult. He kept up a wide correspondence during this time and in his letters often described the work as "light and modest," leaving him "plenty of leisure" (Whitman 265). Whitman used this leisure to continue his visits to the injured in the war hospitals. Though the war had been over for a year, a good number of injured men, whom he referred to as "the old dregs & leavings of the war . . . who have no place to go" (276), were slowly dying or recovering while the federal government went about the business of putting the nation back together.

As a "third class clerk" earning sixteen hundred dollars a year, Whitman's primary duty was to copy out letters and legal documents from drafts written by the Attorney General and his assistant. He boasted to one of his younger correspondents, a soldier he had nursed during the war years, that he was personally responsible for copying out the Attorney General's communications with "the big men," the president, Secretary of State, and other such department heads (Whitman 283). Much of the work done in the Attorney General's office involved the legal status of Southern property owners. As Whitman explained, "all the rich men & big officers of the reb army have to get special pardons, before they can buy or sell, or do anything that will stand law" (265). In letters to his mother, he alluded to scandal and intrigue surrounding the buying and selling of such pardons.

During his tenure at the Attorney General's Office, Whitman from time to time insinuated himself into legal affairs, as when at the prompting of his friend Abby Price he made a personal plea to Attorney General Henry Stanbery for the pardon of a Massachusetts postal clerk jailed for theft. During that year, Abby Price also asked Whitman to do some lobbying on behalf of her dressmaking business, offering him a thousand dollars if he could convince members of Congress to exempt dress ruffles from new taxes they were levying.

For the most part, however, Whitman spent these postwar years in Washington as an observer. Continuing to work among wounded veterans, witnessing the rancorous Congressional battles over Reconstruction and the attempt to impeach Andrew Johnson, he remained keenly aware of how deeply the nation was wounded by the Civil War. It was during this time that he first conceived of the idea for the series of essays—"Democracy," "Literature," and "Personalism"—that would eventually become *Democratic Vistas*. Perhaps the most explicitly political prose work Whitman was to write, this effusive essay offers the divided nation a vision of a utopian future where, as Whitman first projected in the Preface to the 1855 *Leaves of Grass,* poets would wield more power than politicians.

Rosemary Graham

Bibliography

Kaplan, Justin. *Walt Whitman: A Life.* New York: Simon and Schuster, 1980.

Reynolds, David S. *Walt Whitman's America: A Cultural Biography.* New York: Knopf, 1995.

Stampp, Kenneth M. *The Era of Reconstruction: 1865–1877.* New York: Knopf, 1966.

Whitman, Walt. *The Correspondence.* Ed. Edwin Haviland Miller. Vol. 1. New York: New York UP, 1961.

See also ASHTON, J. HUBLEY; CIVIL WAR, THE; CIVIL WAR NURSING; *DEMOCRATIC VISTAS;* INDIAN AFFAIRS, BUREAU OF; O'CONNOR, WILLIAM DOUGLAS; PRICE, ABBY HILLS; RECONSTRUCTION; WASHINGTON, D.C.

Australia and New Zealand, Whitman in

Within twenty years of the publication of *Leaves of Grass* there seems to have been an interest in the author in New Zealand, and by 1885 there was a small but dedicated following in Australia. But Whitman's influence was principally in outlook and philosophy; his poetic technique was apparently too modern and iconoclastic for even his most devoted admirer, Bernard O'Dowd.

Professor Macmillan Brown, head of the department of English at the then small Canterbury College in Christchurch, New Zealand, claimed, in a letter now in the Dunedin Public Library, to have visited Whitman in February 1875. There is, however, no corroborative evidence for this visit or for his assertion that he had contributed an article on Whitman to the *Press* in Christchurch. Nonetheless, Whitman studies in New Zealand continued and were advanced by W.H. Trimble, librarian of the Hocken library in Dunedin, and his wife, Annie E. Trimble. The couple first read Whitman in 1896, became avid collectors of Whitmaniana, and during the winter of 1903 gave a series of lectures that were published as *Walt Whitman and Leaves of Grass: An Introduction* (1905). Annie Trimble privately published two hundred copies of *Walt Whitman and Mental Science: An Interview* (1911), an exercise of her imagination which, through its style, suggested a verbatim report of an actual conversation. About this time the Trimbles and their friend Isaac Hull Platt produced a concordance to *Leaves of Grass* that was purchased by Henry S. Saunders and presented to the Brown University library in 1931. In the September 1909 *Atlantic Monthly* Mrs. Trimble contributed an article on the trio's concordance-making, saying that it required "about four years of steady work" with little encouragement (Trimble 365). They were told, "Nobody reads Whitman except a few cranks like yourselves" (364).

An undated and privately printed *Catalogue of a Collection of Walt Whitman, Compiled by the Owner, W.H. Trimble* indicated the ardor of the enthusiast to amass a unique antipodean archive. In more recent times Professor Sydney Musgrove of the University of Auckland published *T.S. Eliot and Walt Whitman* (1952), which demonstrates with some persuasion that Eliot owed more to Whitman in matters of poetic technique than is generally allowed.

In Australia, Whitman was warmly received by a small group of men and women interested in matters of literary and religious (or philosophical) importance; they were, in general, not academic folk and not in the urban centers or attached to intellectual cliques. The cynosure of this group was Bernard O'Dowd, a recusant Catholic who was for a time assistant librarian in the Supreme Court Library in Melbourne, and later Chief Parliamentary Draughtsman for the State of Victoria. While only nineteen, living in the country town of Ballarat, O'Dowd was introduced to Whitman's poetry by a local journalist, Tom Bury, who wrote as Tom Touchstone for the Ballarat *Courier.* O'Dowd's reading of *Drum-Taps,* we are told by Nettie Palmer and Victor Kennedy, came "as a clean, hot wind, blowing the cobwebs and dust of ages before it" (Kennedy and Palmer 53). The democratic content of Whitman's verse appealed to O'Dowd more than its innovations in style, but the appeal was insistent, and this intellectual encounter of 1885 became the turning point of O'Dowd's life. He said that the "wonderful stimulus of [his] communion with Walt Whitman" led to a reconsideration of his nationalism, religious beliefs, and general philosophy (qtd. in Anderson, *Bibliography* ix). Whatever Tom Bury's motivation in bringing Whitman to O'Dowd's notice, the experience changed O'Dowd's life; he carried his copy of *Leaves of Grass* with him always and wore a boutonniere of grass as a symbol of his commitment to all that Whitman represented.

O'Dowd, one of the most admirable and modest of Australia's poet-democrats, responded so completely to Whitman's message that he became (in the words of one of Australia's great literary critics, A.G. Stephens) "like a priest without a frock; a priest devoted . . . to the service of humanity" (qtd. in Kennedy and Palmer 126). On 6 August 1889 O'Dowd commenced a letter to Whitman, addressed as "My Revered Master," which he never finished and, thus, never sent. In it he says that he and four friends were studying a newly acquired complete edition of *Leaves of Grass* and that he was "passionately fond of Walt Whitman"—to the point of "defending your very faults" (qtd. in Anderson, *Bernard O'Dowd* Twayne 26). By 1890 O'Dowd had become one of the mainstays of the Australeum, a study and discussion group established after the pattern of the American lyceums and Chautauquas. He addressed this and most of the other cultural and literary associations in the Melbourne metropolis on Whitman.

On 12 March 1890 O'Dowd sent his first complete letter to Whitman, thus inaugurating a correspondence that lasted until 1 November 1891 and that assumed the character of a religious experience for the small group of admirers gathered around O'Dowd in Melbourne.

O'Dowd's wife's uncle, a cabinetmaker, built a special box (a sort of Ark of the Covenant) to house the letters, offprints, galleys, photographs, and reviews that arrived from Camden, New Jersey. These eventually became the property of the State Library of Victoria, and O'Dowd's letters to Whitman became part of the magnificent collection of Charles E. Feinberg of Detroit, Michigan.

The intensity of the O'Dowd commitment to Whitman can be judged from the salutations of the letters; they address the poet as master, bard, prophet, apostle, and other similarly reverential appellations. Whitman never failed to mention all the members of the Australeum whose names had been provided to him. The brief correspondence was intense and quasi-religious in its Melbourne part, appreciative and avuncular in its Camden part.

Shortly after Whitman's death O'Dowd contributed a number of obituary notices and literary appreciations (some anonymously) to Australian papers and periodicals. These were followed by public lectures on various topics related to Whitman, all marked by an evangelistic enthusiasm. In "Poetry Militant," the presidential address for the Literature Society of Melbourne in 1909, O'Dowd observed that "The world does not yet fully know, as it shall know, its deep debt of gratitude to the courage of poets like Walt Whitman" (O'Dowd 23), adding that Whitman, like Nietzsche, was both Destroyer and Creator (28). He concluded his address by asserting that the case for militant poetry is best made in Whitman's "The Answerer." Until his death in 1953, O'Dowd was unswerving in his belief in the significance of Whitman's contribution to the development of the democratic spirit and of modern poetic technique, though he himself was unable to renounce traditional forms—especially the quatrain and the rhymed couplet.

A Scottish visitor to Australia, William Gay, had a high opinion of Whitman and in 1895 wrote a pamphlet, *Walt Whitman: His Relation to Science and Philosophy,* in which he demonstrated for the members of the Australian Association for the Advancement of Science—with commendable lucidity—that Whitman embraced all the fundamental questions of knowledge and that he was "a great man" (Gay, rpt. in McLeod, *Australia and New Zealand* 82). The editor of Gay's *Poetical Works* (1911) noted that Gay admired Whitman's matter rather than his idiosyncratic style.

A

J. Le Gay Brereton, later to become professor of English in the University of Sydney, in 1894 contributed two articles on *Leaves of Grass* to the university's literary magazine, *Hermes*. "He expresses the modern man," Brereton writes. "He stands naked and is not ashamed . . . he voices the claims of each and all" (Brereton, "Hints on Walt Whitman's 'Leaves of Grass,'" rpt. in McLeod, *Australia and New Zealand* 67). This evaluation is representative of all subsequent Australian criticism of Whitman. Even in music he was honored; the noted Australian pianist and composer Percy Grainger dedicated his "Marching Song of Democracy" (1916) to the Good Gray Poet.

While Whitman's poetic technique only slowly gained a following in Australia and New Zealand, his ideas were readily accepted. These essentially egalitarian countries could have found no American poet more congenial than Walt Whitman.

Alan L. McLeod

Bibliography

Anderson, Hugh. *Bernard O'Dowd*. New York: Twayne, 1968.

———. *Bernard O'Dowd (1866–1953): An Annotated Bibliography*. Sydney: Wentworth, 1963.

Kennedy, Victor, and Nettie Palmer. *Bernard O'Dowd*. Melbourne: Melbourne UP, 1954.

McLeod, A.L. "Walt Whitman in Australia." *Walt Whitman Review* 7 (1961): 23–35.

———, ed. *Walt Whitman in Australia and New Zealand: A Record of His Reception*. Sydney: Wentworth, 1964.

O'Dowd, Bernard. *Poetry Militant: An Australian Plea for the Poetry of Purpose*. Melbourne: Lothian, 1909.

Trimble, A.E. "Concordance-Making in New Zealand." *The Atlantic Monthly* September 1909: 364–367.

See also INTERCULTURALITY; LEGACY, WHITMAN'S

"Autumn Rivulets" (1881)

The first appearance of "Autumn Rivulets" as a named cluster occurred in the 1881 edition of *Leaves of Grass*. Situated between sections titled "Memories of President Lincoln" and "Whispers of Heavenly Death," "Autumn Rivulets" signaled a change in focus for Whitman from the physical nature of the preceding poems (in the 1881 edition) to a more spiritual outlook. The use of the word "Autumn" in the title suggests the age, maturity, and reflective spirit of the poet and nation, while "Rivulets" warns the reader of the eclectic nature of the poems within.

The thirty-eight poems in "Autumn Rivulets" first appeared in nine separate editions. Such a mixture is ample evidence of Whitman's continual and purposeful reshaping of *Leaves*. The "clusters" (a number of poems grouped under a single title), which first began appearing in the 1860 edition, were perhaps an attempt to shape a thematic framework to his opus, although the individual poems in each cluster do not always conform to the implied theme (as is the case in "Autumn Rivulets").

The 1881 edition was originally published by James R. Osgood of Boston, but on 1 March 1882 it was classified as obscene literature by the Boston district attorney. Because Whitman refused to remove two poems, "To a Common Prostitute" (number 18 in "Autumn Rivulets") and "A Woman Waits for Me" (in the "Children of Adam" cluster), Osgood abandoned the edition. Later that year Rees Welsh and Co. in Philadelphia agreed to publish the book.

The opening poem of "Autumn Rivulets" is titled "As Consequent, Etc." It is a combination of the first two poems in the second volume of the 1876 ("Centennial") edition of *Leaves*, "Two Rivulets" and "Or from that Sea of Time." That volume, called *Two Rivulets*, combined poetry and prose in an unorthodox attempt to expand *Leaves*. By 1881 the second volume had disappeared; the prose would appear again in 1891–1892, when a volume completely devoted to prose was issued along with the Deathbed edition of *Leaves of Grass*.

"As Consequent, Etc." embodies the symbolism of the cluster's title, more so than any other poem in the group: the "songs of continued years," like "wayward rivulets," are "all toward the mystic ocean tending." The poet brings "A windrow drift of weeds and shells" which share "eternity's music" and "[w]hisper'd reverberations" from his life and the lives of many Americans, "joyously sounding." The second selection in the cluster, "The Return of the Heroes," continues a healing motif and looks toward a hopeful present and future (after the horrors of the Civil War). The nation trades guns for "better weapons" (section 7), the "labor-saving implements" (section 8) with which to grow food and rebuild the continent. For America, autumn implies harvest, bounty, and growth; for Whitman, a time when "my soul is rapt and at peace" (section 5).

After these two opening poems, the remaining thirty-six follow no common pattern or theme, justifying the promise (in "As Consequent") of "wayward rivulets in autumn flowing." Yet there is a common sense of compassion and inclusiveness, especially for the broken and fallen, in several poems of the cluster. Some notable examples are "The City Dead-House," "The Singer in the Prison," "You Felons on Trial in Courts," and "To a Common Prostitute." There is also a celebration of the healing quality of nature, taking what is unknown or unwanted and raising it to new purpose, as in "This Compost," "Unnamed Lands," and "Wandering at Morn."

Two of the most famous poems in the cluster are selections that originally appeared in the first edition of *Leaves* (1855): "There Was a Child Went Forth" and "Who Learns My Lesson Complete?" Other notable poems in "Autumn Rivulets" include "Vocalism," "Laws for Creations," and "Unfolded Out of the Folds."

Scholars disagree as to the importance of the clusters which, like "Autumn Rivulets," follow "Drum-Taps" in the 1881 *Leaves*. Many critics, such as Gay Wilson Allen, believe that the final edition, and this cluster specifically, suffers from Whitman's revisions and shuffling of poems, preferring a more chronological arrangement. Others, including Thomas Crawley and James Perrin Warren, argue that in the 1881 edition the poet achieves his goal of an organically unified *Leaves*, with thematic progression reflecting youth to maturity, physicality to spirituality, and private passions to a public persona. In this sense, "Autumn Rivulets" is a pivotal cluster, a harbinger of Whitman's shift in priorities which also provides transition: acknowledgment of the past, celebration of the present, and hope for the future.

Jack Field

Bibliography

Allen, Gay Wilson. *The New Walt Whitman Handbook.* 1975. New York: New York UP, 1986.

——. *The Solitary Singer: A Critical Biography of Walt Whitman.* 1955. Rev. ed. 1967. Chicago: U of Chicago P, 1985.

Crawley, Thomas E. *The Structure of "Leaves of Grass."* Austin: U of Texas P, 1970.

Lizotte, Paul A. "'Time's Accumulations to Justify the Past': Whitman's Evolving Structure in 'Autumn Rivulets.'" *Emerson Society Quarterly* 26 (1980): 137–148.

Miller, James E., Jr. *A Critical Guide to "Leaves of Grass."* Chicago: U of Chicago P, 1957.

Warren, James Perrin. "The 'Paths to the House': Cluster Arrangements in *Leaves of Grass*, 1860–1881." *ESQ* 30 (1984): 51–70.

Whitman, Walt. *Leaves of Grass: Comprehensive Reader's Edition.* Ed. Harold W. Blodgett and Sculley Bradley. New York: New York UP, 1965.

See also "As Consequent, Etc."; "City Dead-House, The"; *Leaves of Grass,* 1881–1882 Edition; "Return of the Heroes, The"; "There was a Child Went Forth"; "This Compost"; "To a Common Prostitute"; "Unfolded Out of the Folds"; "Who Learns My Lesson Complete?"

B

"Backward Glance O'er Travel'd Roads, A" (1888)

Walt Whitman published "A Backward Glance O'er Travel'd Roads" in *November Boughs* (1888), not long before his seventieth birthday. Although he put the entire essay together from segments of four previously published essays—"A Backward Glance on My Own Road," "How 'Leaves of Grass' Was Made," "How I Made a Book," and "My Book and I"—"A Backward Glance" is a unified statement of the influences on Whitman and of his purposes in the composition of *Leaves of Grass*. The essay is also, to a lesser extent, a document of poetic theory.

Among the influences, Whitman names Sir Walter Scott's poetry; the Bible; Shakespeare; Ossian; and, in the best available translations, Homer, Aeschylus, Sophocles, the Nibelungen cycle, ancient Hindu poetry, and Dante. But where he read them was also of great importance; "those mighty masters" did not overwhelm him, he says, because he had read them in "the full presence of Nature" (723). He names Edgar Allan Poe, too, as influential—not Poe's poems, which he did not admire, but Poe's idea that "there can be no such thing as a long poem" (723) (an extraordinary notion for the expansive Whitman to praise!). Of all the external influences that Whitman mentions, however, the "Secession War," as he calls the American Civil War, is clearly the most salient. He calls the period from 1863 through 1865 "the real parturition years" (more than 1776–1783) of "this henceforth homogeneous Union" and claims that without the experience of those years, "'Leaves of Grass' would not now be existing" (724), an extravagant claim reflecting the effect that the war had on him. It is noteworthy that in this late self-examination Whitman omits from his list of influences Ralph Waldo Emerson, whom Whitman had extolled decades before for bringing him from simmering "to a boil."

Nevertheless, Emerson's expression "autobiography in cipher" reverberates through Whitman's statement of his main purpose in writing *Leaves of Grass* (Miller 37). The center, "to which all should return from straying however far a distance, must be an identical body and soul, a personality—which personality," Whitman recalls, "after many considerations and ponderings I deliberately settled should be myself—indeed could not be any other" (723). Toward the end of this retrospective essay Whitman reemphasizes the biographical imperative that drove his composition, speaking of "an attempt, from first to last, to put *a Person,* a human being (myself, in the latter half of the Nineteenth Century, in America,) freely, fully and truly on record" (731).

Establishing himself as the universal paradigm, Whitman carried out his other intentions for *Leaves*. He wanted to make process, which he calls "Suggestiveness" in the essay, his approach: "I round and finish little, if anything; and could not, consistently with my scheme. . . . I seek less to state or display any theme or thought" than to cause "you, reader . . . to pursue your own flight" (725). Other qualities which he aimed to suffuse through his *Leaves* were "Comradeship . . . Good Cheer, Content, and Hope." He wished to instill in his reader habits of "vigorous and clean manliness, religiousness, and . . . *good heart*" (725). He wanted to explain that although science and technology may seem to be destroying the majesty of the human soul, they are enhancing it. He intended to make his poems agents of light, and to make them gender neutral and geographically impartial. He set out to sing a song of "Sex and Amativeness, and even Animality," whereby he might change his readers' perception of sexuality (727–728). He wanted to impart a sense of religion and morality—a "record of that entire faith . . . which is the foundation of moral America"—along with his transcendental belief in nature as an expression of a spiritual entity (729).

Of course, some of Whitman's stated intentions for *Leaves* were chauvinistic: to chant "the great pride of man in himself," which is essential for an American as "counterpoise to the leveling tendencies of Democracy" (726); to "help the forming of a great aggregate Nation . . . through the forming of myriads of fully develop'd and enclosing individuals" (726); "to show that [Americans], here and today, are eligible to be the grandest and the best" (727); and to proclaim and help fulfill the prediction "that the crowning growth of the United States is to be spiritual and heroic" (729).

As with any poet's contribution to poetic theory, Whitman's in "A Backward Glance" mirrors his own purposes and practice. Thus, when he asks for "a readjustment of the whole theory and nature of Poetry" (719)—despite all the "divine works" of the poetic tradition, to which he pays greater homage in this essay than he cared to pay earlier in his life—he insists that "the first element" of excellence in poetry must be "a sufficient Nationality" (718). He well knows, he says, that his *Leaves* could have grown only in "the latter half of the Nineteenth Century" and only in "democratic America, and from the absolute triumph of the National Union arms" (718). Finally, he postulates, quoting Taine, that all original art is "self-regulated" and "lives on its own blood" (730).

Far from being the maudlin retrospective of a failing old man, "A Backward Glance" concludes with a strong reiteration of the core of Whitman's poetic theory and a reflection of his undying optimism. He avers first, "what Herder taught to the young Goethe, that really great poetry is always . . . the result of a national spirit," and second—here Whitman's spirit can still be seen soaring—"that the strongest and sweetest songs yet remain to be sung" (731–732).

Alan Shucard

Bibliography

Bradley, Sculley, and John A. Stevenson. Introduction. *Walt Whitman's Backward Glances*. By Walt Whitman. Ed. Bradley and Stevenson. Philadelphia: U of Pennsylvania P, 1947. 1–13.

Miller, James E., Jr. *The American Quest for a Supreme Fiction: Whitman's Legacy in the Personal Epic*. Chicago: U of Chicago P, 1979.

Whitman, Walt. "A Backward Glance O'er Travel'd Roads." *Prose Works 1892*. Vol. 2. New York: New York UP, 1964. 711–732.

See also BIBLE, THE; CIVIL WAR, THE; EMERSON, RALPH WALDO; INFLUENCES ON WHITMAN, PRINCIPAL; LEAVES OF GRASS; NOVEMBER BOUGHS; POETIC THEORY; PREFACE TO LEAVES OF GRASS, 1855 EDITION

Barnburners and Locofocos

These colorful political terms described subsets of the New York Democratic party in the 1830s and 1840s. The "Locofocos" originated in October 1835 at a rowdy Tammany Hall meeting. Tammany bosses tried to end the meeting by shutting off the lights, but a group of radicals responded by lighting "locofocos" (a type of match) and continuing on their own. They were fiercely opposed to monopolies (particularly in the banking world) and fought Tammany Hall on many local issues, despite their allegiance to the Democratic party.

The Locofocos (known more prosaically as the Equal Rights party) peaked between 1835 and 1837. They enjoyed little success at the ballot box, but their vituperative defense of democracy inspired many, particularly the incipient Northern laboring class, and Martin Van Buren incorporated some of their ideas into his monetary policy. Thereafter, Democrats were collectively nicknamed Locofocos. (Nathaniel Hawthorne called himself "the Locofoco Surveyor" in his preface to *The Scarlet Letter*.)

The term "Barnburners" applied to several groups. It stemmed from an adage about a Dutch farmer who burned down his barn to rid it of rats, connoting a militant group obsessed with one issue. In the early 1840s, it designated New York Democrats opposed to state fiscal policy, but by the mid-1840s it described a more serious schism—Democrats against the expansion of slavery. These "Barnburners" would break off from the party to join the Free Soil campaign in 1848. Whitman was active in the campaign and supported Barnburner causes at the Brooklyn *Daily Eagle,* though the paper was owned by a "Hunker" (a traditional Democrat), which probably led to his dismissal in January 1848.

Ted Widmer

Bibliography

Byrdsall, Fitzwilliam. *The History of the Loco-Foco or Equal Rights Party.* New York: Clement and Packard, 1842.

Donovan, Herbert D.A. *The Barnburners: A Study of the Internal Movements in the Political History of New York State and of the Resulting Changes in Political Affiliation, 1830–1852.* New York: New York UP, 1925.

Trimble, William. "Diverging Tendencies in New York Democracy in the Period of the Locofocos." *American Historical Review* 24 (1919): 396–421.

See also BROOKLYN *DAILY EAGLE;* DEMOCRATIC PARTY; FREE SOIL PARTY; HUNKERS; POLITICAL VIEWS; TAMMANY HALL

Barrus, Clara (1864–1931)

After earning an M.D. degree from Boston University in 1888, Barrus was a general practitioner of medicine in Utica, New York (1889–1893), and a psychiatrist at the State Hospital in Middletown, New York (1893–1910). However, she is best known today as the companion, assistant, literary executor, and authorized biographer of John Burroughs, naturalist, writer, and devoted friend of Walt Whitman. Of the various books on Burroughs authored or edited by Barrus, the most important are *Our Friend John Burroughs* (1914), *John Burroughs, Boy and Man* (1920), *The Life and Letters of John Burroughs* (2 vols., 1925), *The Heart of Burroughs's Journals* (1928), and *Whitman and Burroughs, Comrades* (1931). While all of these books contain references to Whitman, the most complete account of the relationship between poet and naturalist is to be found in *Whitman and Burroughs, Comrades.* Gay Wilson Allen has described this book as a "record of one of the most important friendships in the poet's life [and] a distinguished contribution to scholarship, containing much new material on Whit-

man's reputation at home and abroad, and sound, intelligent critical judgments" (16–17). Burroughs used the term "Whitmanesque" to describe Barrus herself (qtd. in Renehan 220).

Donald D. Kummings

Bibliography

Allen, Gay Wilson. *The New Walt Whitman Handbook.* 1975. New York: New York UP, 1986.

Renehan, Edward J., Jr. *John Burroughs: An American Naturalist.* Post Mills, Vt.: Chelsea Green, 1992.

See also BURROUGHS, JOHN AND URSULA

"Base of All Metaphysics, The" (1871)

The poem addresses an audience of "gentlemen" with a last word of wisdom, claiming to reveal not only the foundation but also the "finalè" of "all metaphysics." The poem's speaker is apparently the "old professor" parenthetically described in lines four and five (a manuscript gives the title "The Professor's Answer"). The speaker reviews his studies of philosophers, "Greek and Germanic systems," and even Christ and Christianity. He declares that beneath all is the grounding fact of love and community, exemplified as comradeship, friendship, married and filial love, and political concord.

This is the only complete poem added in any edition to the original 1860 "Calamus" cluster. It replaced two poems not included after the 1860 edition: ["Long I Thought That Knowledge Alone Would Suffice"] and ["Hours Continuing Long"]. Positioning "Base" immediately after "Of the Terrible Doubt of Appearances" allows Whitman to emphasize philosophical concerns that recur often in "Calamus" and *Leaves,* and which were of particular interest to him at the time: appearance versus underlying reality and the connection or disconnection of the one and the many.

In typical Whitman fashion, such intellectual questioning is not so much answered as it is gotten through—by penetrating to the level of felt experience instead of relying on mere ratiocination and book learning. In this case, Whitman intuits the mystery of love at the center, holding all together—a perception he shares with mystics and sages of both West and East.

Whitman's language moves in two directions: love is both "base and finalè," both foundation and pinnacle. In hourglass fashion, after

B

establishing the base through an enumeration of the many philosophical systems he has studied, the speaker draws all into one climactic focus—comradely love and friendship—and again expands that focus into the finalè of ever-enlarging circles of social cohesion, bonding family members, cities, and countries.

This conclusion may be seen as an example of an often-noted tendency in successive editions of *Leaves* (especially after 1860) toward muting, sublimating, or generalizing the sexual materials. While Miller sees the concluding list as a hierarchy, Martin criticizes it as a descent from the emotionally honest to the diffusely vague. Whitman similarly universalizes and expands the meaning of affection in two other notable works of 1871, "Passage to India" and the long essay *Democratic Vistas*.

David Oates

Bibliography

Allen, Gay Wilson. *The New Walt Whitman Handbook*. 1975. New York: New York UP, 1986.

Chari, V.K. *Whitman in the Light of Vedantic Mysticism*. Lincoln: U of Nebraska P, 1964.

Hanson, R. Galen. "A Critical Reflection on Whitman's 'The Base of All Metaphysics.'" *Walt Whitman Review* 18 (1972): 67–70.

Killingsworth, M. Jimmie. "Whitman's Sexual Themes during a Decade of Revision: 1866–1876." *Walt Whitman Quarterly Review* 4.1(1986): 7–15.

Martin, Robert K. *The Homosexual Tradition in American Poetry*. Austin: U of Texas P, 1979.

Miller, James E., Jr. *A Critical Guide to "Leaves of Grass."* Chicago: U of Chicago P, 1957.

Stovall, Floyd. *The Foreground of "Leaves of Grass."* Charlottesville: UP of Virginia, 1974.

See also "Calamus"; Comradeship; Love; Metaphysics; Mysticism

Baxter, Sylvester (1850–1927)

Sylvester Baxter was a Boston journalist and publicist largely associated with the Boston *Herald* and involved in the improvement and historical preservation of Boston and New England. Most of his writings concern the publicizing or evaluation of Boston's industrial, cottage, and leisure complexes, but Baxter also wrote about Mexico and New Mexican Indians and produced two collections of poetry.

Baxter first met Whitman in April 1881 at one of the poet's Lincoln lectures. That the two were amiable associates is evidenced by Whitman's writing to Baxter later in that year, asking for help in finding a room in Boston while the poet was seeing his forthcoming edition of *Leaves of Grass* through press. Baxter repeatedly wrote favorable reviews of Whitman's work, which certainly increased the poet's esteem for, and, thereby, association with the Boston journalist.

On 6 December 1886 Baxter promoted a government pension to support the poet, and in early 1887 Congressman Henry B. Lovering of Massachusetts introduced the twenty-five-dollar-per-month pension bill into the House. Apparently it passed committee but was then dropped, probably due to Whitman's objection to the idea. A substantial monetary gift from admirers in England most likely influenced Whitman in his decision.

Despite the abandonment of the pension bill, Baxter continued to work on the poet's behalf. In 1887, he and William Sloane Kennedy raised $800 to build a cottage for Whitman on Timber Creek, where he had spent several summers beginning in 1876 at the farm of George and Susan Stafford. Unfortunately, after assuming full control of both the money and the executive decisions regarding location and construction of the cottage, Whitman had to use the money for more urgent financial demands.

Christopher O. Griffin

Bibliography

Gohdes, Clarence, and Rollo G. Silver, eds. *Faint Clews & Indirections: Manuscripts of Walt Whitman and His Family*. Durham: Duke UP, 1949.

Whitman, Walt. *The Correspondence*. Ed. Edwin Haviland Miller. Vol. 4. New York: New York UP, 1969.

See also Boston, Massachusetts; Kennedy, William Sloane; Leaves of Grass, 1881–1882 Edition; Timber Creek

Bazalgette, Léon (1873–1929)

Léon Bazalgette belonged to a French-English family and divided his life between Paris and an old water mill in Normandy. The millpond was his Walden. A lover of nature and a sentimental socialist with anarchist leanings, Bazalgette admired both Henry David Thoreau and Whitman and wrote biographies of both. He was also in touch with Horace Traubel and contributed to the *Conservator*. In 1908 he published *Walt Whitman: L'Homme et son oeuvre* (several times reprinted), which gave an idealized image of the poet *ad usum delphini,* so to speak. In particular, he took up H.B. Binns's story of a romantic love affair in New Orleans. This biography was followed in 1909 by a complete translation of *Leaves of Grass* (several times reprinted), which is still the only complete French translation, but is faulty and rather awkward in places, more literal than literary. André Gide objected to the suppression of all signs of Whitman's homosexuality and undertook a translation of his own. Bazalgette was more interested in the content than in the form of *Leaves of Grass,* in Whitman's politics than in his artistry. He also wrote a book on Whitman's philosophy: *Le Poème-Evangile de Walt Whitman* (1921, but written in 1914) and later translated *Specimen Days* under the title of *Pages de Journal* (1926). His biography of Whitman was translated in 1920: *Walt Whitman: The Man and His Work* (reprinted in 1970) by Ellen Fitzgerald, who abridged it, especially as regards the New Orleans episode, and censored the more sensual passages.

Roger Asselineau

Bibliography

Allen, Gay Wilson. *The New Walt Whitman Handbook*. 1975. New York: New York UP, 1986.

Erkkila, Betsy. *Walt Whitman Among the French: Poet and Myth*. Princeton: Princeton UP, 1980.

Masson, Elsie. "Walt Whitman, ouvrier et poète." *Mercure de France* 68 (Aug. 1907): 385–390.

Pucciani, Oreste F. *The Literary Reputation of Walt Whitman in France*. 1943. New York: Garland, 1987.

Special issue of *Europe* on Léon Bazalgette (78, June 1929) with contributions by Stefan Zweig, Panaït Istrati, Waldo Frank, John Dos Passos, Sherwood Anderson, and others).

See also BINNS, HENRY BRYAN; BIOGRAPHIES; FRANCE, WHITMAN IN; GIDE, ANDRÉ

Beach, Juliette H. (1829–1900)

Journalist, editor (1869–1871), and owner (1868–1900) of the *Orleans Republican,* a newspaper published in Albion, New York, Beach also wrote and published prose and poetry in magazines and newspapers. Her patriotic verse was widely circulated during the Civil War. She married Calvin Beach (1830–1868) in 1850; at his death Juliette became owner, manager, and editor of the newspaper, unusual for a woman in the nineteenth century.

Beach and her husband occasionally visited New York City, and they knew Henry Clapp, editor of the *Saturday Press*. Clapp advised Whitman to send a copy of the 1860 *Leaves of Grass* to Juliette Beach for review. On 2 June 1860 a review was published in the *Saturday Press*. It was unfavorable, calling the "Children of Adam" poems "disgusting," describing Whitman as a poet who possessed "strength and beauty—but . . . no soul" (qtd. in Giantvalley 13), and advising Whitman to "drown himself" (qtd. in Furness 425). Calvin Beach, who had intercepted *Leaves of Grass* and read it, apparently wrote this first review himself and submitted it to the *Saturday Press* unsigned. Clapp mistakenly appended Juliette's initials to it, and a week later had to print a retraction.

On 23 June a second review of *Leaves of Grass* appeared in the *Saturday Press*. This time the review, written by Juliette Beach and signed "A Woman," described *Leaves of Grass* as "the standard book of poems in the future of America" and Whitman as "an embodiment of the new 'National Genius'" (qtd. in Giantvalley 14).

According to Ellen O'Connor, this incident sparked a correspondence between Whitman and Beach which went on for many years (although no letters have been found), and it was for Beach that Whitman wrote "Out of the Rolling Ocean the Crowd" (1865).

Maire Mullins

Bibliography

Allen, Gay Wilson. *The Solitary Singer: A Critical Biography of Walt Whitman*. 1955. Rev. ed. 1967. Chicago: U of Chicago P, 1985.

Callow, Phillip. *From Noon to Starry Night: A Life of Walt Whitman*. Chicago: Ivan R. Dee, 1992.

B

"Death of Mrs. C.G. Beach." Obituary. *Orleans Republican* 20 June 1900.

Furness, Clifton Joseph. Rev. of *American Giant: Walt Whitman and His Times,* by Frances Winwar. *American Literature* 13 (1942): 423–432.

Giantvalley, Scott. *Walt Whitman, 1838– 1939: A Reference Guide.* Boston: Hall, 1981.

"History of 'Republican' Written by Fred G. Beach." *Orleans Republican* 24 July 1928.

Holloway, Emory. "Washington (1863– 1873)." *The Uncollected Poetry and Prose of Walt Whitman.* 1921. Ed. Holloway. Vol. 1. Gloucester, Mass.: Peter Smith, 1972. lviii–lix n15.

Kaplan, Justin. *Walt Whitman: A Life.* New York: Simon and Schuster, 1980.

See also CLAPP, HENRY; "OUT OF THE ROLLING OCEAN THE CROWD"; SATURDAY PRESS

"Beat! Beat! Drums!" (1861)

Written shortly after the first battle of Bull Run (July 1861), "Beat! Beat! Drums!" was published in the Boston *Daily Evening Transcript* on 24 September 1861. It was reprinted in the New York *Leader* and *Harper's Weekly Magazine* on 28 September and was included in *Drum-Taps* in 1865. In 1871 the poem was incorporated into the body of *Leaves of Grass* as part of the "Drum-Taps" cluster, where it remained through subsequent editions.

Among the so-called mobilization poems Whitman wrote during the opening months of the Civil War, "Beat!" is one of relatively few that employ a quasi-traditional verse structure and form. The work is organized into three stanzas of seven lines each, with a refrainlike repetition occurring across stanzas in the opening and closing lines of each. Like other of Whitman's more successful traditional poems, however, "Beat!" combines traditional and free verse elements. For instance, meter is variable, ranging from dactylic to iambic to iambic-anapestic; line lengths within stanzas are also variable; and Whitman's customary structuring devices of anaphora and parallelism are also pervasive.

The poem depicts peacetime scenes being dashed aside by the frenzy of war. Despite its overt bellicosity, many scholars have detected signs of thematic ambivalence: in the speaker's persistent questions; in the protests of the peace-loving (e.g., the old man, the child, and the mother in stanza three); and in Whitman himself, for whom the war and its totalizing structures were an unwelcome but necessary means of redeeming a divided and increasingly materialistic democracy.

John E. Schwiebert

Bibliography

Erkkila, Betsy. *Whitman the Political Poet.* New York: Oxford UP, 1989.

Schwiebert, John E. *The Frailest Leaves: Whitman's Poetic Technique and Style in the Short Poem.* New York: Lang, 1992.

Thomas, M. Wynn. *The Lunar Light of Whitman's Poetry.* Cambridge, Mass.: Harvard UP, 1987.

White, William. "'Beat! Beat! Drums!' The First Version." *Walt Whitman Review* 21 (1975): 43–44.

Whitman, Walt. *Walt Whitman's "Drum-Taps" (1865) and "Sequel to Drum-Taps" (1865–6): A Facsimile Reproduction.* Ed. F. DeWolfe Miller. Gainesville, Fla.: Scholars' Facsimiles and Reprints, 1959.

See also CIVIL WAR, THE; "DRUM-TAPS"

"Beginning My Studies" (1865)

This poem first appeared in the 1865 *Drum-Taps* where, according to Roger Asselineau, it did not belong because its theme is irrelevant to that collection; in 1871 Whitman transferred it to the "Inscriptions" cluster.

E. Fred Carlisle views the poem as Whitman's identification of the first stage of the self's meeting with the world. The poet's attachment to the actual, physical world serves as a bridge to "partial fulfillment and self-transcendence" (Carlisle 97). Thus the poet is articulating his concern with the thing-in-itself and his wish to experience the real world. James Dougherty presents a similar reading; Whitman finds a self-conscious delight in consciousness and confesses the pleasure of being the connoisseur of one's own experience. V.K. Chari reinforces this reading and establishes the theme of the self as essential to the comprehensive intent of Whitman's poems because the subject matter of his poetry is the nature of experience itself, "the fact of human consciousness" (Chari 19). According to these readings, the poem explores the nature of subject-object relationship and offers the key to a large portion of Whitman's poetry; its "mere fact consciousness" explains the fundamental meanings of Whitman's poems and largely determines their forms and techniques. Gay Wilson Allen, on the other hand, reads the poem as Whitman's declaration not to become a systematic or aggressive student of philosophy.

In theme and tone "Beginning My Studies" resembles "When I Heard the Learn'd Astronomer." Both display a disdain for bookish knowledge and for authorities as represented by learned astronomers. The poet evinces greater interest in and curiosity about the actual facts than in figures and charts from books and classrooms. He seems to be content with what he is and with the actual physical forms whose presence his senses can feel; he is equally pleased to enjoy the consciousness of those matters and sing them "in ecstatic songs."

Guiyou Huang

Bibliography

Allen, Gay Wilson. *Walt Whitman Handbook*. 1946. New York: Hendricks House, 1962.

Asselineau, Roger. *The Evolution of Walt Whitman: The Creation of a Personality*. Trans. Richard P. Adams and Roger Asselineau. Cambridge, Mass.: Harvard UP, 1960.

Carlisle, E. Fred. *The Uncertain Self: Whitman's Drama of Identity*. East Lansing: Michigan State UP, 1973.

Chari, V.K. *Whitman in the Light of Vedantic Mysticism*. Lincoln: U of Nebraska P, 1964.

Dougherty, James. *Walt Whitman and the Citizen's Eye*. Baton Rouge: Louisiana State UP, 1993.

See also "INSCRIPTIONS"; "WHEN I HEARD THE LEARN'D ASTRONOMER"

Berryman, John (1914–1972)

Whitman's influence on John Berryman, one of America's most significant post-World War II poets, was most keenly felt in Berryman's prize-winning *The Dream Songs* (1969).

James E. Miller, Jr., contends that *The Dream Songs* inherits Whitman's legacy as regards the "personal epic"—the attempt as Berryman put it, echoing Whitman, "to record a

personality . . . and through him, the country" (qtd. in Miller 238). Like Whitman, Berryman sought to be a "spiritual historian" for his time, and his long poem is a "wisdom work" on the conduct of life (Miller 237, 240). Though more formally regular than Whitman's verse, *The Dream Songs* mimics the loosely organized, open-ended structure of "Song of Myself" (1855). Berryman creates an alter ego called "Henry" or "Mr. Bones," who converses throughout *The Dream Songs* with an unnamed interlocutor. These conversations mirror the interplay in *Leaves of Grass* among the poet's speaking "I," his self, his soul, and the character "Walt Whitman."

Like many other significant poets of the 1950s and 1960s, Berryman used the example of Whitman to help him break free of the then dominant influence of T.S. Eliot, upon whose dense, highly allusive, tightly controlled verse Berryman had modeled his early poetry. This change of poetic allegiance is signaled in Berryman's posthumously published essay on Whitman (1976).

Carl Smeller

Bibliography

Berryman, John. *The Dream Songs*. New York: Farrar, Straus and Giroux, 1969.

———. "'Song of Myself': Intention and Substance." *The Freedom of the Poet*. New York: Farrar, Straus and Giroux, 1976. 227–241.

Miller, James E., Jr. *The American Quest for a Supreme Fiction: Whitman's Legacy in the Personal Epic*. Chicago: U of Chicago P, 1979.

See also LEGACY, WHITMAN'S; PERSONAE

Bertz, Eduard (1853–1931)

The main claim to fame of Eduard Bertz, novelist, philologist, and self-declared sexual researcher, is his friendship and long-term correspondence with British novelist George Gissing, whom he came to know after he was forced to emigrate from Germany to England for political reasons. In 1881 he moved to Rugby, Tennessee, where he lived in Thomas Hughes's utopian community until 1883.

After he returned to Germany, his new project became Walt Whitman, whose writings he had come to know in the United States. In a letter congratulating Whitman on his seventieth birthday, he vowed that "[i]f life and strength lasts, this pen of mine shall help to reveal you to the German people" (qtd. in Grünzweig, "Adulation" 7). However, this project had already been entrusted to Johannes Schlaf, a naturalist German author. Since Schlaf had the support of Horace Traubel and other Whitmanites on both sides of the Atlantic, Bertz, feeling rejected, shifted the nature of his interest in Whitman.

In 1897 Bertz signed a petition to liberalize German laws regulating homosexuality, and in 1905 he published a book-length article on Whitman in the yearbook of the *Wissenschaftlich-Humanitäre Komitee* (Scientific-Humanitarian Committee), which supported homosexuals scientifically, medically, and legally. Bertz's thesis that Whitman was a (sexually inactive) homosexual was in line with the committee's attempts to create a more favorable public attitude by demonstrating the "social usefulness" of homosexuals.

Schlaf, although himself a signer of the petition, felt that this revelation would hurt his own Whitman project and the rapidly growing popularity of Whitman in Germany. Supported by Traubel and other Whitmanites, he wrote a pamphlet contesting Bertz's claim. Bertz, in turn, now considering himself a victim of a homosexual conspiracy and coverup, wrote two vicious monographs attacking Schlaf and Whitman. Although he claimed that by exposing or revealing Whitman he had sought only to break the hostile public silence regarding homosexuality, the paranoiac discourse of parts of these books reveals clearly homophobic attitudes.

The debate resurfaced eight years later in France. When French Whitmanite Léon Bazalgette disputed the truth of Guillaume Apollinaire's hoax regarding orgiastic events at Whitman's funeral, Bertz intervened by taking Apollinaire's side and again attempted to prove Whitman's homosexuality.

The narrowness of the views expressed in this debate should not obscure its significance. The German battle surrounding Whitman's homosexuality was, internationally, one of the earliest public discussions of an author's gayness and also forms a chapter in the legal and human emancipation of homosexuals in Germany.

Walter Grünzweig

Bibliography

Bertz, Eduard. *Der Yankee-Heiland: Ein Beitrag zur modernen Religionsgeschichte*. Dresden: Reissner, 1906.
———. "Walt Whitman: Ein Charakterbild." *Jahrbuch fur sexuelle Zwischenstufen* 7 (1905): 153–287.
———. *Whitman-Mysterien: Eine Abrechnung mit Johannes Schlaf*. Berlin: Gose and Tetzlaff, 1907.
Grünzweig, Walter. "Adulation and Paranoia: Eduard Bertz's Whitman Correspondence (1889–1914)." *Gissing Journal* 27.3 (1991): 1–20 and 27.4 (1991): 16–35.
———. *Constructing the German Walt Whitman*. Iowa City: U of Iowa P, 1995.
Lang, Hans-Joachim. "Eduard Bertz vs. Johannes Schlaf: The Debate on Whitman's Homosexuality in Germany." *A Conversation in the Life of Leland R. Phelps. America and Germany: Literature, Art and Music*. Ed. Frank L. Borchardt and Marion C. Salinger. Durham, N.C.: Duke UP, 1987. 49–86.
Schlaf, Johannes. *Walt Whitman Homosexueller?* Minden: Bruns, 1907.

See also APOLLINAIRE, GUILLAUME; GERMAN-SPEAKING COUNTRIES, WHITMAN IN THE; SEX AND SEXUALITY; TRAUBEL, HORACE L.

"Bervance: or, Father and Son" (1841)

"Bervance: or, Father and Son" was published in *United States Magazine and Democratic Review* in December 1841.

The technique of this story is unusual in Whitman's work in that a first narrator introduces another narrator, Bervance *père*, who then tells his own tale. The first narrator is presumably Whitman since the introductory paragraph is signed "W.W."

Bervance's tale is in the form of a confession. As in "Wild Frank's Return," the father prefers his older son, and he and the second son have a dispute. Young Luke Bervance is sent to an asylum, where when the father neglects him he becomes wildly deranged. Upon escape, Luke visits Bervance, who is horrified at his son's insanity. After blaming and cursing his father, the madman flees and is never heard from again. But the father, in his soul, sees his maniac son and hears the curse over and over.

Reynolds reads the story as Whitman's attempt to purge his psychological demons, perhaps oedipal in nature. Kaplan sees this story as comparable to the work of Edgar Allan Poe, and Allen sees it as part of Whitman's compulsive interest in cruel fathers. The story also relates to another frequent theme of Whitman's fiction: the separating of two brothers.

Patrick McGuire

Bibliography

Allen, Gay Wilson. *The Solitary Singer: A Critical Biography of Walt Whitman.* 1955. Rev. ed. 1967. Chicago: U of Chicago P, 1985.

Kaplan, Justin. *Walt Whitman: A Life.* New York: Simon and Schuster, 1980.

Reynolds, David S. *Walt Whitman's America: A Cultural Biography.* New York: Knopf, 1995.

Whitman, Walt. *The Early Poems and the Fiction.* Ed. Thomas L. Brasher. New York: New York UP, 1963.

See also SHORT FICTION, WHITMAN'S; "WILD FRANK'S RETURN"

Bible, The

As was the work of many of his contemporaries, Walt Whitman's poetry was deeply influenced by the Bible, both thematically and stylistically. Nearly two hundred direct biblical quotations, allusions, and paraphrases have been documented by critic Gay Wilson Allen. However, Whitman's use of the Bible went far beyond the borrowing of language, themes, and patterns. As Herbert J. Levine has shown, Whitman anticipated that *Leaves of Grass* would itself be a new, American "bible" of democracy.

One of Whitman's earliest works, "Shirval: A Tale of Jerusalem" (1845), is a fictionalized retelling of the story of Jesus's raising the widow's dead son at Nain, taken from the gospel of Luke (7:11–16). Late in life, reflecting upon his work, Whitman identified the Old and New Testaments first among the literary inspirations for his poetry ("A Backward Glance O'er Travel'd Roads"). Evidence of Whitman's admiration for the Bible can be found most conspicuously in his prose, where he quotes widely from both the Old and New Testaments. In his essay "The Bible as Poetry" (*November Boughs*), Whitman expresses effusive praise for the Bible's emotional vigor, its unifying ideas, and its spiritual purpose. Whitman offers a particularly moving recollection in *Specimen Days* of being asked by a dying soldier to read from the Bible; the poet selects the chapters describing the crucifixion of Christ, and the wasted soldier then asks him to read the chapter on the resurrection.

In his poetry, however, Whitman rarely quotes the Bible directly and uses the word "bible" only a few times. But allusions to the Bible abound—especially allusions to Christ, the most prominent symbol in *Leaves of Grass,* according to Thomas Crawley. Identifying more than one hundred passages referring to the Christ idea, Crawley explains Whitman's frequent parallels to Christ as the structural key to his vision—the creation of a unifying personality like the Christ of the Bible. In such poems as "To Him That was Crucified," and throughout "Song of Myself," Whitman identifies himself with the New Testament Christ; he sees himself "[w]alking the old hills of Judæa with the beautiful gentle God by my side" ("Song of Myself," section 33). Whitman adheres to biblical tradition, Crawley explains, in believing that God is revealed in the human, but Whitman sought to free this idea of incarnation from its historical orientation in the Bible and to give it a universal and mythic significance. "I am the man," he says; "I suffer'd, I was there" ("Song of Myself," section 33). In short, it was the humanism of Christ that Whitman most admired, the fact that he was the "brother of rejected persons" ("Think of the Soul," 1871 *Leaves*). Horace Traubel recalled Whitman as saying that in its humanism, *Leaves of Grass* was completely compatible with the Bible.

Considerable evidence indicates that Whitman intended *Leaves of Grass* to be a sacred text. In an 1857 notebook entry, Whitman wrote: "The Great Construction of the New Bible / Not to be diverted from the principal object—the main life work" (*Notebooks* 1:353). In his sweeping analysis of American society, *Democratic Vistas,* Whitman laments the absence of "genuine belief" in American life and concludes that the nation can only regain its spiritual vitality through a reconciliation of the individual and the mass. *Leaves of Grass* deliberately addresses that objective. Levine claims that Whitman's democratic vision, the reconciliation of the solitary self and the mass, is informed by Whitman's blending of two biblical patterns—the Old Testament narrative (a national motif) and the New Testament narrative (a personal motif). Whitman, then, presents himself as the democratic ideal, projecting himself as an Americanized Jesus, a divine self who identifies and empathizes with all people.

In his vision of a nation of divine persons, Whitman assumes a prophetic voice reminiscent of Old Testament prophets. Indeed, he alludes to biblical prophets almost as frequently as to Christ. Like the role of the biblical prophets, Herbert Schneidau argues, Whitman's prophetic role was that of a gadfly, in his condemning of social privilege and arrogance and his accepting in turn the resulting abuse and rejection. Whitman also draws upon various other rhetorical strategies learned from biblical genres: the epistles, the gospels, and the wisdom and apocalyptic books.

As a "scriptural" poem, "Song of Myself" bears witness to the experience of God in the world and in doing so makes the world itself into a sacred text where one finds "letters from God dropt in the street" (section 48). Throughout the poem, as Levine has shown, Whitman's language echoes that of biblical writing: creeds and petitions ("I believe in you my soul" and "Loafe with me on the grass" [section 5]), revelations and wisdom. But from the outset "Song of Myself" also subverts biblical themes. Section 3, for example ("I do not talk of the beginning or the end"), seems to stand in resistance to the overall historical momentum of the Bible from Genesis to Revelation. Or again, in "A Song for Occupations," while Whitman admits that bibles are divine, he hastens to add, "It is not they who give the life, it is you who give the life" (section 3). Whitman's use of the Bible is complex and becomes, in his later work, deeper and more difficult to discern, Gay Wilson Allen observes. Perhaps Whitman's relationship to the Bible can best be summed up in his own expectation of the disciple he seeks: "He most honors my style who learns under it to destroy the teacher" ("Song of Myself," section 47).

Thomas Becknell

Bibliography

Allen, Gay Wilson. "Biblical Echoes in Whitman's Works." *American Literature* 6 (1934): 302–315.

Bercovitch, Sacvan. "The Biblical Basis of the American Myth." *The Bible and American Arts and Letters*. Ed. Giles Gunn. Philadelphia: Fortress, 1983. 219–229.

Berkove, Lawrence I. "Biblical Influences on Whitman's Concept of Creatorhood." *Emerson Society Quarterly* 47.2 (1967): 34–37.

Crawley, Thomas. "The Christ-Symbol in *Leaves of Grass.*" *The Structure of "Leaves of Grass."* Austin: U of Texas P, 1970. 50–79.

Frye, Northrop. *The Great Code: The Bible and Literature*. New York: Harcourt Brace Jovanovich, 1982.

Levine, Herbert J. "'Song of Myself' as Whitman's American Bible." *Modern Language Quarterly* 48 (1987): 145–161.

Munk, Linda. "Giving Umbrage: The Song of Songs Which Is Whitman's." *Journal of Literature and Theology* 7.1 (1993): 50–65.

Schneidau, Herbert. "The Antinomian Strain: The Bible and American Poetry." *The Bible and American Arts and Letters*. Ed. Giles Gunn. Philadelphia: Fortress, 1983. 11–32.

Whitman, Walt. *Notebooks and Unpublished Prose Manuscripts*. Ed. Edward F. Grier. 6 vols. New York: New York UP, 1984.

See also Reading, Whitman's; Religion; "Shirval: A Tale of Jerusalem"; "Song of Myself"; Style and Technique(s)

Bibliographies

Although bibliographical resources on Walt Whitman have been sizable since early in this century, only in recent years have they exhibited anything approaching cohesion, comprehensiveness, and accessibility. Such resources tend to fall into two general categories: primary or descriptive bibliographies, those compilations that identify and describe, often in technical detail, the writings by Whitman—books, pamphlets, collected editions, separately published poems, articles and essays, stories, letters, notebooks, unpublished manuscripts, etc.; and secondary bibliographies, those compilations that enumerate, annotate, or evaluate the scholarly and critical writings about Whitman and his work.

In the first category the indispensable resource is Joel Myerson's *Walt Whitman: A Descriptive Bibliography* (1993). This volume surpasses in both scope and detail all previous attempts to describe what Whitman wrote. Nearly 1,100 pages long, its various sections document (1) all books and pamphlets wholly by Whitman, not only the editions and reprintings that appeared in English and other languages during his lifetime but also those published in English through 1991; (2) all collected editions of Whitman's writings through 1991; (3) all miscellaneous collections through 1991; (4) all titles in which Whitman poems, prose works, or letters appear for the first time in a book or pamphlet; (5) all first-appearance contributions by Whitman to American and English magazines and newspapers through 1991; (6) all proof copies, circulars, and broadsides of poetry and prose through 1892; (7) poetry and prose reprinted in books and pamphlets through 1892; (8) separate publications of individual poems and prose works through 1991; and, finally, (9) publications containing material possibly by Whitman. Because this bibliography is clearly organized and meticulously indexed, its user has easy access to a wealth of information.

Much less spacious and detailed than the Myerson book but valuable nevertheless is the long chapter on Whitman in volume 9 of Jacob Blanck's *Bibliography of American Literature* (1991), which was edited and completed by Michael Winship. For more than seventy years, people in Whitman studies who needed bibliographic particulars on primary sources had to rely, for the most part, on *A Concise Bibliography of the Works of Walt Whitman* (1922) by Carolyn Wells and Alfred F. Goldsmith or on *The Bibliography of Walt Whitman* (1920) by Frank Shay. The work of Winship and Myerson, the latter in particular, now radically diminishes the importance of these earlier volumes.

Two other resources provide illuminating information on primary materials: *The Walt Whitman Archive* (1993), edited by Joel Myerson, and *Whitman at Auction, 1899–1972* (1978), compiled by Gloria A. Francis and Artem Lozynsky. A multivolume work of more than 2,000 pages, the *Archive* photographically reproduces many of the most important Whitman manuscripts now located in the collections at the Library of Congress, Duke University, the University of Virginia, and the University of Texas. *Whitman at Auction* reproduces in facsimile over forty catalogues that were printed for various auction sales involving Whitman material. Cited at the end of this essay are still other items, such as exhibition catalogues, that describe writings by Whitman.

The essential books in the category of secondary bibliographies are *Walt Whitman, 1838–1939: A Reference Guide* (1981) by Scott Giantvalley and *Walt Whitman, 1940–1975: A Reference Guide* (1982) by Donald D.

Kummings. These two comprehensive volumes provide fully annotated year-by-year lists of nearly 8,200 items—book-length studies, monographs, dissertations, articles, chapters or passages in books, notes, reviews, and significant incidental references. Access to entries is facilitated by author, title, and subject indexes. For a supplement to Giantvalley's book, one should see his "*Walt Whitman, 1838–1939: A Reference Guide:* Additional Annotations" (1986). For bibliographies of secondary writings published after 1975, one should consult the *MLA International Bibliography* (annually issued in print form or on CD-ROM) and the *Walt Whitman Quarterly Review* (formerly the *Walt Whitman Review*). With each issue concluding with "A Current Bibliography," the *WWQR* contains the most complete listings.

Anyone interested in critical or evaluative bibliographies should peruse initially the annual surveys in *American Literary Scholarship* (1963–). While not inclusive, these overviews nevertheless try to assess the best of a given year's publications. Other resources illuminating in their judgments of Whitman scholarship include Roger Asselineau's chapter on the poet in *Eight American Authors* (1971); Ed Folsom's "The Whitman Project: A Review Essay" (1982); Jerome Loving's chapter in *The Transcendentalists* (1984); William White's "Whitman in the Eighties: A Bibliographical Essay" (1985); Donald D. Kummings's discussion of "Materials" in *Approaches to Teaching Whitman's "Leaves of Grass"* (1990); and David S. Reynolds's "Bibliographic Essay on Walt Whitman" (1992). Not to be overlooked are Gay Wilson Allen's *The New Walt Whitman Handbook* (1986) and M. Jimmie Killingsworth's *The Growth of "Leaves of Grass"* (1993), both of which contain excellent critiques of many of the major biographical and critical books on Whitman.

Listed below are other informative items, including three bibliographies of bibliographies.

Donald D. Kummings

Bibliography

Primary

Anon. *Walt Whitman: Catalogue of an Exhibition held at the American Library, London, March–April, 1954.* London: United States Information Service, 1954.

Blanck, Jacob. "Walt Whitman: 1819–1892." *Bibliography of American Literature,*

Volume Nine: Edward Noyes Westcott to Elinor Wylie. Ed. Jacob Blanck and Michael Winship. New Haven: Yale UP, 1991. 28–103.

Brewer, Frances J., comp. *Walt Whitman: A Selection of the Manuscripts, Books and Association Items Gathered by Charles E. Feinberg: Catalogue of an Exhibition Held at the Detroit Public Library.* Detroit: Detroit Public Library, 1955.

[Dubester, Henry J., et al., comps.]. *Walt Whitman: A Catalog Based Upon the Collections of the Library of Congress.* With Notes on Whitman Collections and Collectors, by Charles E. Feinberg. Washington: Library of Congress, 1955.

Francis, Gloria A., and Artem Lozynsky, comps. *Whitman at Auction, 1899–1972.* Detroit: Bruccoli Clark/Gale, 1978.

Frey, Ellen Frances. *Catalogue of the Whitman Collection in the Duke University Library.* 1945. Port Washington, N.Y.: Kennikat, 1965.

Hamer, Harold. *A Catalogue of Works by and Relating to Walt Whitman.* Bolton, England: Libraries Committee, 1955.

Holloway, Emory, and Henry S. Saunders. "Whitman." *The Cambridge History of American Literature.* Ed. William Peterfield Trent et al. Vol. 3. New York: Putnam, 1918. 551–581.

[Kebabian, Paul, et al.]. *Walt Whitman: The Oscar Lion Collection.* New York: New York Public Library, 1953.

Kennedy, William Sloane. "A Bibliography of Walt Whitman's Writings." *The Fight of a Book for the World: A Companion Volume to "Leaves of Grass."* By Kennedy. West Yarmouth, Mass.: Stonecroft, 1926. 237–272.

Miller, Edwin Haviland, and Rosalind S. Miller. *Walt Whitman's Correspondence: A Checklist.* New York: New York Public Library, 1957.

Myerson, Joel. *Walt Whitman: A Descriptive Bibliography.* Pittsburgh: U of Pittsburgh P, 1993.

———, ed. *The Walt Whitman Archive: A Facsimile of the Poet's Manuscripts.* 3 vols. 6 parts. New York: Garland, 1993.

Randle, Betty, ed. *Catalogue of the Collection of Walt Whitman Literature Presented to the Dunedin Public Library by W.H. Trimble.* Dunedin, New Zealand: Dunedin Public Library, 1975.

Shay, Frank. *The Bibliography of Walt Whitman.* New York: Friedmans, 1920.

Stark, Lewis M., and John D. Gordon, comps. *Walt Whitman's "Leaves of Grass": A Centenary Exhibition from the Lion Whitman Collection and the Berg Collection of the New York Public Library.* New York: New York Public Library, 1955.

Triggs, Oscar Lovell. "Bibliography of Walt Whitman." *The Complete Writings of Walt Whitman.* Ed. Richard Maurice Bucke, Thomas B. Harned, and Horace L. Traubel. Vol. 10. New York: Putnam, 1902. 139–233.

Wells, Carolyn, and Alfred F. Goldsmith. *A Concise Bibliography of the Works of Walt Whitman.* Boston: Houghton Mifflin, 1922.

White, William. "Walt Whitman: A Bibliographical Checklist." *Walt Whitman Quarterly Review* 3.1 (1985): 28–43.

———. "Walt Whitman's Journalism: A Bibliography." *Walt Whitman Review* 14 (1968): 67–141.

———. "Walt Whitman's Poetry in Periodicals: A Bibliography." *Serif* 11 (1974): 31–38.

———. "Walt Whitman's Short Stories: Some Comments and a Bibliography." *Papers of the Bibliographical Society of America* 52 (1958): 300–306.

Secondary

Allen, Gay Wilson. *The New Walt Whitman Handbook.* 1975. New York: New York UP, 1986.

Asselineau, Roger. "Walt Whitman." *Eight American Authors: A Review of Research and Criticism.* Ed. James Woodress. Rev. ed. New York: Norton, 1971. 225–272.

Boswell, Jeanetta. "Walt Whitman." *The American Renaissance and the Critics.* By Boswell. Wakefield, N.H.: Longwood Academic, 1990. 411–502.

———. *Walt Whitman and the Critics: A Checklist of Criticism, 1900–1978.* The Scarecrow Author Bibliographies, No. 51. Metuchen, N.J.: Scarecrow, 1980.

Chanover, E. Pierre. "Walt Whitman: A Psychological and Psychoanalytic Bibliography." *Psychoanalytic Review* 59 (1972): 467–474.

Folsom, Ed. "Prospects for the Study of Walt Whitman." *Resources for American Literary Study* 20 (1994): 1–15.

———. "The Whitman Project: A Review Essay." *Philological Quarterly* 61 (1982): 369–394.

Giantvalley, Scott. "Walt Whitman, 1819–1892." *Research Guide to Biography and Criticism.* Ed. Walton Beacham. Washington: Research Publishing, 1985. 1265–1270.

———. *Walt Whitman, 1838–1939: A Reference Guide.* Boston: Hall, 1981.

———. "*Walt Whitman, 1838–1939: A Reference Guide:* Additional Annotations." *Walt Whitman Quarterly Review* 4.1 (1986): 24–40.

Howard, Patsy C., comp. "Walt Whitman." *Theses in American Literature 1896–1971.* Ann Arbor, Mich.: Pierian, 1973. 238–244.

Jason, Philip K. *Nineteenth-Century American Poetry: An Annotated Bibliography.* Pasadena, Calif.: Salem, 1989. 146–188.

Johnson, Thomas H., and Richard M. Ludwig. "Walt(er) Whitman." *Literary History of the United States: Bibliography.* 4th ed. Ed. Robert E. Spiller et al. Vol. 2. New York: Macmillan, 1974. 759–768, 997–1001, 1310–1313.

Killingsworth, M. Jimmie. *The Growth of "Leaves of Grass": The Organic Tradition in Whitman Studies.* Columbia, S.C.: Camden House, 1993.

Kummings, Donald D. "Materials." *Approaches to Teaching Whitman's "Leaves of Grass."* Ed. Kummings. New York: MLA, 1990. 3–22.

———. "Walt Whitman Bibliographies: A Chronological Listing, 1897–1982." *Walt Whitman Quarterly Review* 1.4 (1984): 38–45.

———. *Walt Whitman, 1940–1975: A Reference Guide.* Boston: Hall, 1982.

Loving, Jerome. "Walt Whitman." *The Transcendentalists: A Review of Research and Criticism.* Ed. Joel Myerson. New York: MLA, 1984. 375–383.

Nilon, Charles H. "Whitman, Walt." *Bibliography of Bibliographies in American Literature.* By Nilon. New York: Bowker, 1970. 159–165.

Reynolds, David S. "Bibliographic Essay on Walt Whitman." *Walt Whitman and the Visual Arts.* Ed. Geoffrey M. Sill and Roberta K. Tarbell. New Brunswick: Rutgers UP, 1992. 175–182.

Ruppert, James. "Whitman, Walt." *Guide to American Poetry Explication.* Vol. 1. Boston: Hall, 1989. 199–234.

Tanner, James T.F. "Walt Whitman Bibliographies: A Chronological Listing, 1902–1964." *Bulletin of Bibliography* 25 (1968): 131–132.

Thorp, Willard. "Walt Whitman." *Eight American Authors: A Review of Research and Criticism.* Ed. Floyd Stovall. New York: Norton, 1963. 271–318. Bibliographical Supplement by J. Chesley Mathews, 445–451.

White, William. "Whitman in the Eighties: A Bibliographical Essay." *Walt Whitman: Here and Now.* Ed. Joann P. Krieg. Westport, Conn.: Greenwood, 1985. 217–224.

Woodress, James. "Whitman, Walt." *Dissertations in American Literature, 1891–1966.* Rev. ed. Durham, N.C.: Duke UP, 1968. [90–92].

See also COLLECTED WRITINGS OF WALT WHITMAN, THE; COLLECTORS AND COLLECTIONS, WHITMAN; MEDIA INTERPRETATIONS OF WHITMAN'S LIFE AND WORKS

Binns, Henry Bryan (1873–1923)

A minor English poet and biographer, Henry Bryan Binns was the author of *A Life of Walt Whitman* (1905) and *Walt Whitman and His Poetry* (1915). Binns's life of Whitman, the first major biographical work to appear after the poet's death, is of particular interest for having been the first to print one of the great Whitman myths: that Whitman fathered an illegitimate child during a visit to New Orleans in 1848. In his biography, Binns claims that Whitman met and fell in love with a highborn Southern woman whose family, probably due to class prejudice, prevented the marriage and refused to recognize Whitman's paternity. Despite careful research by many subsequent biographers, however, no absolute proof of the affair, or its issue, has ever been found. Binns appears to have based his conjectures on hearsay and a too literal interpretation of certain passages of Whitman's correspondence and poetry. Lack of evidence, however, did not stop scores of writers from repeating the fantastic story, which has persisted in the literature until recent times.

Published biographical information on Binns is scant. Born in Ulverston, Lancashire, in 1873, he produced works on a variety of topics between 1902 and 1922. Notable among these is a Lincoln biography, *Abraham Lincoln* (1907), and (sometimes publishing under the pseudonym Richard Askham) several books of poetry.

Katherine Reagan

Bibliography

Binns, Henry Bryan. *A Life of Walt Whitman.* London: Methuen, 1905.
———. *Walt Whitman and His Poetry.* London: Harrap, 1915.
Loving, Jerome. "The Binns Biography." *Walt Whitman: The Centennial Essays.* Ed. Ed Folsom. Iowa City: U of Iowa P, 1994. 10–18.

See also NEW ORLEANS, LOUISIANA

Biographies

Fifteen biographies of Whitman have been published since 1883, not counting biographical studies such as John Addington Symonds's *Walt Whitman: A Study* (1893), Edward Carpenter's *Days with Walt Whitman* (1906), Basil De Selincourt's *Walt Whitman: A Critical Study* (1914), Newton Arvin's *Whitman* (1938), or Frederik Schyberg's *Walt Whitman* (1951). Of these, at least two are adolescent or purely romantic biographies, Cameron Rogers's *The Magnificent Idler: The Story of Walt Whitman* (1926) and Frances Winwar's *American Giant: Walt Whitman and His Times* (1941). There are also "pre-biographies" or hagiographies written by close associates of the poet. The naturalist John Burroughs's *Walt Whitman as Poet and Person* (1867) was co-written by Whitman to promote the fourth edition of *Leaves of Grass;* William Douglas O'Connor's *The Good Gray Poet,* a forty-six-page pamphlet published in 1866, was done by an inspired enthusiast and (along with Burroughs) one of the poet's closest friends.

In fact, the "first" biography was also partly written, or revised, by Whitman, Richard Maurice Bucke's *Walt Whitman* (1883). It differs from those by Burroughs and O'Connor mainly in that Whitman deleted as much myth as he added as a silent coauthor. Mainly, he discarded Bucke's attempt to make him more of a prophet than a poet. But he allowed to stand the notion that the poet had traveled America (including one year instead of three months in New Orleans) before emerging with his poetic vision. Today the biography, a collector's item, is valued mainly as a sourcebook because more than half of its 236 pages are devoted to testimonies by contemporaries.

The next full-fledged biography, and the first book written largely away from the influence of Whitman's disciples (sometimes referred to as "Whitmaniacs"), was Henry Bryan Binns's *Life of Walt Whitman* (1905). It brought together on the fiftieth anniversary of the publication of the 1855 *Leaves of Grass* most of the known facts about the poet's life and attempted to link Whitman with the emerging international stature of the United States. While Binns benefited from biographical material supplied by literary executor Horace Traubel, the British biographer resisted Traubel's attempts to control his thesis. Binns was the first biographer to embellish Whitman's 1890 letter to John Addington Symonds about having had six illegitimate children by suggesting that the poet while in New Orleans in 1848 had experienced a literary awakening as the result of "an intimate relationship with some woman of higher social rank" (51). Binns may also be the first biographer to attempt to ward off the rumors of the poet's homosexuality, suggested by Edward Carpenter (who published Symonds's letter in his 1906 *Days with Walt Whitman*) and exploited as Whitman's "sex pathology" in Eduard Bertz's *Der Yankee-Heiland* in 1905.

Perhaps unfairly, the importance of Binns's scholarship was quickly overshadowed by Bliss Perry's *Walt Whitman: His Life and Work* (1906), the first "unauthorized" American life of the poet. That is to describe, however, its outcome, not its process, which depended heavily upon information from Whitman associates such as Traubel and Ellen O'Connor Calder, the widow of William Douglas O'Connor. Traubel attacked the book in *The Conservator,* his journal devoted to the worship of Whitman, for its selective appreciation of *Leaves of Grass* and Perry's effort to make a "gentleman" out of the "man." Perry, who soon afterward became a professor of literature at Harvard and the editor of the *Atlantic Monthly,* acknowledged that, except for his "immodest" but not indecent poems, Whitman would be read universally, but Perry's tone was often condescending (e.g., when discussing the rumor about illegitimate children, he chided Whitman for parental irresponsibility). Yet it was probably because of Perry's affiliation and literary Brahmin status that his biography was influential in the eventual acceptance of Whitman as a national poet. No objective criticism had done so much for Whitman's reputation since Edmund Clarence Stedman's assessment of Whitman's poetry in *Poets of America* (1885), based upon his essay on *Leaves of Grass* in the November 1880 issue of *Scribner's Magazine.*

The first of three French biographies, Léon Bazalgette's *Walt Whitman: L'Homme et son oeuvre,* appeared in French in 1908 (with a bowdlerized English edition by Ellen Fitzgerald appearing in 1920). It was a romanticized version of Whitman's life, but Bazalgette also speculated on Whitman's sexual activities, even hinting that the poet's huge sense of diversity might have led him to indulge in same-sex activities. This material, especially Bazalgette's speculation on the New Orleans period, was omitted from Fitzgerald's "translation."

Binns and Perry held the field for scholarly biography until the publication of Emory Holloway's *Whitman: An Interpretation in Narrative* in 1926. Even though it has no notes, its information is fully reliable, if not its speculation about the poet's sexuality, which Holloway was determined to see as primarily heterosexual, or bisexual at most. In arguing against the poet's homosexuality, Holloway elaborated on Binns's theory about the New Orleans romance and speculated that Whitman fell in love with a Creole woman. Holloway's book, which won the Pulitzer Prize in 1927, was the most visible product of many years of groundbreaking research that appears more systematically in his edition of *Uncollected Poetry and Prose* (1921). There he printed the manuscript version of "Once I Pass'd Through a Populous City" in which the "woman" is a "man," but he ignored this fact in his subsequent biography. Generally, he believed that the confusion about Whitman's sexual preferences stemmed from the poet's failure to distinguish between "the sort of affection which most men have for particular women and that which they experience toward members of their own sex" (Holloway 168–169). For all its faults, *Whitman: An Interpretation in Narrative* held the field as the most original and reliable biography until the publication of Gay Wilson Allen's *The Solitary Singer* in 1955.

The second French biography appeared in 1929, Jean Catel's *Walt Whitman: La naissance du poète.* It was the first full-length psychobiography of the poet, in which Catel discounted Whitman's public life and external activities and interpreted the first edition of *Leaves of Grass* as the writer's retreat into a fantasy world which compensated for all Whitman's failures both professional and personal. Whereas his French predecessor Bazalgette had hinted reluctantly that Whitman may have been bisexual, Catel had no reservations in pronouncing the poet homoerotic. Catel examines the "foreground" exhaustively to argue for its negative influence upon *Leaves of Grass.* He also believed that after the first edition Whitman retreated from his original candor and attempted to cover up its embarrassing truths.

The next two important biographies before Asselineau and Allen were written by a renowned man of American letters and the author of *Spoon River Anthology* (1915), Edgar Lee Masters, and a renowned literary editor and critic, Henry Seidel Canby. While both studies are dependable, neither *Whitman* (1937) nor *Walt Whitman: An American* (1943) is definitive or useful to more than the reader of popular nonfiction. Using the then current sexual pathologist's term for homosexual, Masters described Whitman as a "Uranian," whose personal warmth led to the intimacy found in *Leaves of Grass* and especially the "Calamus" poems. Making no apologies about Whitman's homosexual tendencies, he thought the poet cleverly translated his sexual energy and inaugurated the movement, better realized in the twentieth century, toward acceptance of sex and psychology in American literature. Canby, on the other hand, avoided the psychological in his effort to explore Whitman's social and intellectual background. Canby found a merely symbolical America within *Leaves of Grass,* but he felt the poetry was the product of a real America, its strength, tenacity, and probity, which—it seemed to be implied in the first years of World War II—would always endure. While not denying the possibility that Whitman was homosexual, this literary historian (who would write the Whitman chapter in *The Literary History of the United States,* 1948) refused to theorize where there was no empirical evidence. Canby's biography was the most up to date for its time in terms of scholarship, even though he did not intend a scholarly biography.

The current era of Whitman biography began with studies by Roger Asselineau and Gay Wilson Allen. In the French tradition of treating the life and the work in tandem,

B

Asselineau wrote *L'Évolution de Walt Whitman* in 1954 (translated into English in two volumes in 1960 and 1962 by Asselineau and Richard P. Adams as *The Evolution of Walt Whitman*). Picking up where Catel left off in his book, the biography begins after the first edition of *Leaves of Grass,* but the narrative contains numerous flashbacks that utilize the most up-to-date scholarly information for the 1950s. For Asselineau there is no doubt that Whitman was a homosexual, but it was literature (more than, if not in lieu of, actual homosexual liaisons) that allowed the expression of his homoerotic passion. In his focus on *Leaves of Grass,* Asselineau sees the successive editions in relation to important episodes and crises in the poet's life. The biography is most successful in its imaginative apprehension of Whitman's psychological situations as he turns life into literature.

More documentary and perhaps less speculative is Allen's life of Whitman, which sifts through all the information available at the time and treats the life from start to finish. It has stood for forty years as the principal compendium of facts about the poet's life and work. Allen gathered this vast and scattered information before most modern editions of the poet's papers; hence, today the citations are often to superseded sources. Writing near the end of the New Critical period, in which an author's work was considered without reference to the times and culture, Allen nevertheless saw his "Solitary Singer" as much involved and influenced by his milieu. It is the most complete biographical picture available today.

Joseph Jay Rubin's *The Historic Whitman* is a biography of Whitman in the "foreground" of *Leaves of Grass* as revealed by an analysis of newspaper articles and historical documents. It presents information about Whitman not found in Allen, but its organization is not the most effective way of highlighting such information. Often, it makes claims that are historically incorrect with regard to Whitman, yet overall it reimmerses Whitman in the political age that fostered his revolutionary poetry. Justin Kaplan's *Walt Whitman: A Life* (1980) takes advantage of Rubin's discoveries in one of the most readable biographical narratives of Whitman yet written. Otherwise, Kaplan relies for the most part on information found in Allen and elsewhere between 1955 and 1980, but this information is recast to place the poet within the myths and expectations of late twentieth-century culture and popular culture.

Paul Zweig's *Walt Whitman: The Making of the Poet* (1984) is a poet's view of the life of Whitman from the late 1840s, when he lived in New Orleans, to the beginning of the Civil War. It is a stimulating if not altogether reliable portrait of the poet during his most important years. In Zweig's lively and enthusiastic prose there is an element of hero worship that ties this biography to hagiographies written by O'Connor, Burroughs, and Bucke. It adds no original information about the poet's life, but the colorful portrait of Whitman the poet is freshly conceived. It has been said that a biography is a novel that dare not speak its name, but British novelist Philip Callow might well have added "A Novel" after the main title of his *From Noon to Starry Night: A Life of Walt Whitman* (1992). Poorly documented and rife with minor biographical errors, Callow's biography, like Zweig's but without his stronger command of the material, celebrates Whitman instead of analyzing him or chronicling his life with any hint of originality. As a foreign biography, it resembles Bazalgette's in its portrait of the poet as vigorously in love with life freed from convention and pregnant with possibility. The most recent biography is David S. Reynolds's *Walt Whitman's America: A Cultural Biography* (1995). True to its subtitle, this life is written in the fashion of the New Historicism, where it is thought that the culture is frequently more important than the author in producing original works. Reynolds is a master at this kind of scholarship, and his book brings out all the background to Whitman's "long foreground." The biography covers the entire life but is concerned mainly with the author's life up to the Civil War.

Jerome Loving

Bibliography

Allen, Gay Wilson. *The Solitary Singer: A Critical Biography of Walt Whitman.* 1955. Rev. ed. 1967. Chicago: U of Chicago P, 1985.

Asselineau, Roger. *The Evolution of Walt Whitman.* 1954. 2 vols. Cambridge, Mass.: Harvard UP, 1960–1962.

Bazalgette, Léon. *Walt Whitman: L'Homme et son oeuvre.* Paris: Societe du Mercure de France, 1908.

Binns, Henry Bryan. *A Life of Walt Whitman.* London: Methuen, 1905.

Bucke, Richard Maurice. *Walt Whitman.* Philadelphia: McKay, 1883.

Callow, Philip. *From Noon to Starry Night: A Life of Walt Whitman.* Chicago: Ivan R. Dee, 1992.

Canby, Henry Seidel. *Walt Whitman: An American.* Boston: Houghton Mifflin, 1943.

Catel, Jean. *Walt Whitman: La naissance du poète.* Paris: Rieder, 1929.

Holloway, Emory. *Whitman: An Interpretation in Narrative.* New York: Knopf, 1926.

Kaplan, Justin. *Walt Whitman: A Life.* New York: Simon and Schuster, 1980.

Masters, Edgar Lee. *Whitman.* New York: Scribner's, 1937.

Perry, Bliss. *Walt Whitman: His Life and Work.* Boston: Houghton Mifflin, 1906.

Reynolds, David S. *Walt Whitman's America: A Cultural Biography.* New York: Knopf, 1995.

Rubin, Joseph Jay. *The Historic Whitman.* University Park: Pennsylvania State UP, 1973.

Zweig, Paul. *Walt Whitman: The Making of the Poet.* New York: Basic Books, 1984.

See also ALLEN, GAY WILSON; ARVIN, NEWTON; ASSELINEAU, ROGER; BAZALGETTE, LÉON; BERTZ, EDUARD; BINNS, HENRY BRYAN; BUCKE, RICHARD MAURICE; BURROUGHS, JOHN AND URSULA; CANBY, HENRY SEIDEL; CARPENTER, EDWARD; CATEL, JEAN; DE SELINCOURT, BASIL; HOLLOWAY, EMORY; MASTERS, EDGAR LEE; O'CONNOR (CALDER), ELLEN ("NELLY") M. TARR; O'CONNOR, WILLIAM DOUGLAS; PERRY, BLISS; PSYCHOLOGICAL APPROACHES; SCHYBERG, FREDERIK; SEX AND SEXUALITY; STEDMAN, EDMUND CLARENCE; SYMONDS, JOHN ADDINGTON; TRAUBEL, HORACE L.

"Birds of Passage" (1881)

First appearing in the 1881 *Leaves of Grass*, the "Birds of Passage" cluster grouped seven previously published poems: "Song of the Universal" (1876), "Pioneers! O Pioneers!" (1865), "To You [Whoever you are . . .]" (1856), "France, The 18th Year of these States" (1860), "Myself and Mine" (1860), "Year of Meteors (1859–60)" (1865), and "With Antecedents" (1860). The poems, initially published under various titles between 1856 and 1876, appeared in different clusters, annexes, supplements, and companion volumes until their final nesting place in "Birds."

Whether all of the clusters in *Leaves* constitute unified groupings is debatable, certain clusters seeming purposeful to some critics and nearly haphazard to others. The title "Birds of Passage" suggests as an organizing principle the cyclical migrations of birds and the associated ideas of flight, movement, and change. As suggested by the title, the poems explore several types of progression: cosmic (from imperfection to perfection), cultural (the shift of civilization from East to West), and personal (from self-deprecation to self-affirmation). These migrations cross physical expanses, such as the North American continent and the Atlantic ocean, as well as nonmaterial ones like time and history. The title, then, does establish a principle of organization for the cluster—certainly broad and, perhaps, loose, yet not arbitrary.

Despite the cluster title, only one poem, "Song of the Universal," incorporates explicit bird imagery. An "uncaught bird," illustrating the flight of the universal, the good, or the soul, is pictured "hovering, hovering, / High in the purer, happier air" above the "mountain-growths disease and sorrow" (section 3). In lieu of any recurring bird imagery, the dominant motif illustrating progression is America's role as the culmination (at least momentarily) of cosmic and cultural evolution, an idea appearing most prominently in "Pioneers! O Pioneers!" and "Song of the Universal" and to a lesser extent in "France the 18th Year of These States" and "With Antecedents." "To You," "Myself and Mine," "Year of Meteors," and "With Antecedents" primarily illustrate more personal types of progression, whether it be the reader's self-actualization, the poet's poetic agenda, the poet's brief physical existence, or the reader and poet's tallying of the past.

Besides those of Thomas Edward Crawley and James E. Miller, Jr., few studies systematically examine the unity of the clusters and the significance of their placement in *Leaves*. For Crawley, "Birds" functions as a transitional cluster between the first part of *Leaves*, which is more concerned with the physical (the journey motif and the land being unifying principles), and the second part, which is more concerned with the spiritual (the voyage motif and the sea now becoming dominant). Miller treats the cluster as the confrontation of the self—the paradigmatic American self Whitman offers for usage—with time and history (that self having been introduced earlier, particularly in "Song of Myself").

While none of the poems in "Birds" occupies a central place in the Whitman canon, they are important expressions of Whitman's belief in an orderly progression of all things toward perfection—an idea of central importance in the poet's philosophy.

Hadley J. Mozer

Bibliography

Crawley, Thomas Edward. *The Structure of "Leaves of Grass."* Austin: U of Texas P, 1970.

Miller, James E., Jr. *A Critical Guide to "Leaves of Grass."* Chicago: U of Chicago P, 1957.

Warren, James Perrin. "The 'Paths to the House': Cluster Arrangement in *Leaves of Grass, 1860–1881.*" *ESQ* 30 (1984): 51–70.

Whitman, Walt. *Leaves of Grass: Comprehensive Reader's Edition.* Ed. Harold W. Blodgett and Sculley Bradley. New York: New York UP, 1965.

See also LEAVES OF GRASS, 1881–1882 EDITION; "MYSELF AND MINE"; "PIONEERS! O PIONEERS!"; "SONG OF THE UNIVERSAL"; "TO YOU [WHOEVER YOU ARE . . .]"; "YEAR OF METEORS (1859–60)"

Birthplace, Whitman's

Whitman was born in West Hills, Long Island, New York, in a two-story frame house built by his father. It is believed that Walter Whitman, Sr., intended the house as an example of various styles of construction he was able to provide, since it contains some features innovative for the time. Among these are the corbeled chimney and the storage closets set in the fireplace walls. The staircase, too, is unusual in that it is topped with a short riser, a feature also found in another house in the area believed to have been built by Whitman, Sr. Large twelve-over-eight-pane windows bring ample light and air into the farmhouse. The dining wing appears to be older than the main part of the house and may have been on the property before the larger main section was built.

The Whitman family moved from West Hills to Brooklyn in 1823, but Whitman is known to have returned to the house on at least two occasions. One visit was with his father in 1855, shortly before the latter's death, and the other was in 1881, when Whitman was accompanied by Dr. Richard Maurice Bucke.

Whitman's birthplace, West Hills, Long Island, taken by Ben Conklin, 1902. By permission, Walt Whitman Birthplace Association.

Only three owners held title to the property between 1823 and 1949, at which time the Walt Whitman Birthplace Association, formed for the express purpose of purchasing the house, acquired it. Within those years the house was a private residence, a boardinghouse for farm laborers, and a tea room. In 1957 the association turned the property over to New York State and it became a State Historic Site open to the public.

Difficulties surrounded the purchase by the association, some of which arose from the claim that Whitman's poetry was being used effectively as propaganda by communist nations and their sympathizers. A concerted effort by many Long Island communities, and especially by school children who made coin contributions, enabled the purchase to go forward. Similar objections raised during the McCarthy era almost prevented state acquisition, but Governor Averell Harriman signed a bill making the Whitman Birthplace Long Island's first State Historic Site. The bill marked a shift downward from the manor and mansion sites selected in previous years to a recognition of sites connected to the middle and lower classes.

The Birthplace Association maintains a small library available to scholars and the general public. An annual celebration of Whitman's birth is held at the birthplace, continuing a tradition of celebration begun by Whitman's friends in his lifetime.

Joann P. Krieg

Bibliography

Allen, Gay Wilson. *The Solitary Singer: A Critical Biography of Walt Whitman*. 1955. Rev. ed. 1967. Chicago: U of Chicago P, 1985.

Dyson, Verne. "This House of Memories." *Walt Whitman Birthplace Bulletin* 2 (1959): 17–19.

Krieg, Joann P. "Walt Whitman in the Public Domain: A Tale of Two Houses." *The Long Island Historical Journal* 6.1 (1993): 83–95.

See also LONG ISLAND, NEW YORK

"Bivouac on a Mountain Side" (1865)

Composed during the Civil War, "Bivouac on a Mountain Side" was first published in *Drum-Taps* (1865) and incorporated into the body of *Leaves of Grass* in 1871 as part of the "Drum-Taps" cluster, where it remained through subsequent editions. "Bivouac" is one of several "Drum-Taps" poems remarkable for their concise and photographic precision of imagery.

The poem depicts an army halting at close of day. The speaker's eye takes in a valley, "barns and . . . orchards," a mountain spread with "clinging cedars," and—punctuating the scene—the "numerous camp-fires" and "large-sized" shadows of men and horses. The poem offers a view that is both arrestingly literal and symbolic. The literal image, which seems to be almost instantaneously observed by the speaker's eye, invites comparison with the then nascent art of photography, which fascinated Whitman. At the same time, items like the "large sized" shadows and "eternal stars," with their intimation of the larger-than-life struggle in which these troops are involved, seem to suggest the profounder significances Whitman continually observed in the war.

John E. Schwiebert

Bibliography

Dougherty, James. *Walt Whitman and the Citizen's Eye*. Baton Rouge: Louisiana State UP, 1993.

Erkkila, Betsy. *Whitman the Political Poet*. New York: Oxford UP, 1989.

Matthiessen, F.O. *American Renaissance*. 1941. London: Oxford UP, 1974.

Waskow, Howard. *Whitman: Explorations in Form*. Chicago: U of Chicago P, 1966.

Whitman, Walt. *Walt Whitman's "Drum-Taps" (1865) and "Sequel to Drum-Taps" (1865–6): A Facsimile Reproduction*. Ed. F. DeWolfe Miller. Gainesville, Fla.: Scholars' Facsimiles and Reprints, 1959.

See also CIVIL WAR, THE; "DRUM-TAPS"

Blake, William (1757–1827)

Introspective psychological mythmaker and political as well as cosmic visionary, poet-artist William Blake wrote and illustrated verse of astonishing originality. To the Victorian writer A.C. Swinburne, Blake seemed so deeply akin to Whitman as almost to encourage belief in the transmigration of souls. Whitman saw himself and Blake as fellow mystics but thought the English poet somewhat too dizzy and wild. Yet Whitman knew little of Blake's work before

Swinburne's book came out in 1868; the only ascertainable influence is the design for Whitman's tomb, which the American poet adapted from a Blake engraving.

Apparent contradictories in Whitman's writing—especially about good and evil—are often actually productive contraries in a Blakeian sense. In his manifesto *The Marriage of Heaven and Hell* (1790) Blake presents a law of contraries: energy and order, desire and reason must be "married" or paired in a creative tension; similarly, body and soul are inseparable in a human being. Whitman, too, is poet of both body and soul, poet of progress through the tension of contraries, the "advance" of "opposite equals" ("Song of Myself," sections 3, 21, 48). In *The Four Zoas* (1797–ca. 1810) Blake sees imagination extending its range from the infinitely small to the infinitely great; imagination can encompass the universe, which becomes its metaphorical cosmic body. The cosmic body vision is at the heart of Whitman's work as well ("Song of Myself," section 31). Such imaginative expansiveness helps Blake and Whitman unite the intensity of lyric with the scope of epic.

Finally, Blake and Whitman are kindred mythmakers. In Whitman's "Chanting the Square Deific" the myth-map of four mental forces parallels Blake's scheme of "four Zoas," two pairs of mutually contrasting forces within Universal Man. On each poet's mental map, a Rebel (Luvah, Satan, or passion) faces a Reconciler (Tharmas, Hermes-Christ-Hercules, or intuitive compassion), and a Lawgiver (Urizen, Jehovah-Brahma-Kronos, or reason) confronts a Law-transcender (Urthona, Santa Spirita, or imagination). Blake's and Whitman's mental mappings are richly suggestive and psychologically acute.

Martin Bidney

Bibliography

Askin, Denise T. "Whitman's Theory of Evil: A Clue to His Use of Paradox." *ESQ* 28 (1982): 121–132.

Bidney, Martin. "Structures of Perception in Blake and Whitman: Creative Contraries, Cosmic Body, Fourfold Vision." *ESQ* 28 (1982): 36–47.

Blake, William. *The Complete Poetry and Prose of William Blake*. Rev. ed. Ed. David V. Erdman. New York: Doubleday, 1988.

Kaplan, Justin. *Walt Whitman: A Life*. New York: Simon and Schuster, 1980.

Pease, Donald. "Blake, Whitman, Crane: The Hand of Fire." *William Blake and the Moderns*. Ed. Robert J. Bertholf and Annette S. Levitt. Albany: State U of New York P, 1982. 15–38.

Swinburne, Algernon Charles. *William Blake: A Critical Essay*. 1868. Ed. Hugh J. Luke. Lincoln: U of Nebraska P, 1970.

See also BRITISH ROMANTIC POETS; MYSTICISM; ROMANTICISM

Boker, George Henry (1823–1890)

George Henry Boker, a wealthy Philadelphian, served as ambassador to Turkey (1871–1875) and Russia (1875) and is best known for *Francesca da Rimini* (staged 1855), a popular play about adultery among the Italian nobility. Boker was dissatisfied with his theatrical career and desperately wanted a following for his *Plays and Poems* (1856). Boker's suppressed *Sonnets: A Sequence on Profane Love* (1929) are thought to be inspired by his wife, Julia, and a mistress, Angie King Hicks.

Whitman had the "kindliest" thoughts of Boker (*With Walt Whitman* 6:266) and spontaneously referred to him during a discussion with Horace Traubel: "He is pretty genuine, after all: the fellows say he holds off . . . but I don't know. Boker is genuine, has quality" (*With Walt Whitman* 2:476–477). In contrast to Whitman's concept of manly love, Boker's conception of comradeship was feminine rather than masculine, as indicated by his letter to his friend Bayard Taylor: "We have both . . . an almost feminine tenderness for those we love . . . are you laughing at me for making love to you, as if you were a green girl?" (qtd. in Evans 115).

Mitch Gould

Bibliography

Evans, Oliver H. *George Henry Boker*. Boston: Twayne, 1984.

Traubel, Horace. *With Walt Whitman in Camden*. Vol. 2. New York: Appleton, 1908; Vol. 6. Ed. Gertrude Traubel and William White. Carbondale: Southern Illinois UP, 1982.

See also PHILADELPHIA, PENNSYLVANIA; TAYLOR, BAYARD

Bolton (England) "Eagle Street College"

Among the birthday greetings Whitman received in 1887 were an unexpected gift of money and an expression of admiration from two Englishmen who were completely unknown to him. They were J.W. Wallace and Dr. John Johnston, both of Bolton, a cotton manufacturing town not far from Manchester in the Lancashire district of northern England. Wallace and Johnston were the leaders of a small band of Whitmanites who met weekly at Wallace's home on Eagle Street. So earnest were their discussions at these gatherings that Johnston dubbed the group the "Eagle Street College." Whitman acknowledged the gift warmly, which was repeated in succeeding years, and in 1890 met Johnston for the first time when the doctor arrived at Mickle Street in Camden. The following year Wallace made the same journey. While in America, both men also visited various friends and associates of Whitman, meetings which they recounted in a jointly written volume published in 1917.

The story of the "College" itself, however, ranges beyond these brief contacts, for in the closing years of his life Whitman wrote a steady stream of messages, sometimes on a daily basis, to this unlikely group of admirers. These were not literary critics or scholars, in the usual sense, but bank clerks, clergymen, manufacturers, assistant architects (including Wallace), and, of course, the physician, Dr. Johnston. Originally their meetings ranged freely over many subjects, but three or four were already students of Whitman, so gradually the poet became the principal subject of their papers, readings, and discussions.

Once the direct contact had been made with Whitman through Johnston's visit, it never lessened, having been intensified by Wallace's stay in Camden. The ties between the poet and the Bolton group were made deeper by the gifts of books, magazines, and photographs that flowed between England and America, including Whitman's gift of the stuffed canary which in life had brought him much pleasure and which he made the subject of a poem, "My Canary Bird" (1888). Others were also brought into the relationship—John Burroughs; R.M. Bucke, who visited Bolton; and Horace Traubel, who became one of Wallace's most constant correspondents and remained so until Traubel's death. In England the "College" contacts included Edward Carpenter and John Addington Symonds.

Despite the literary luster of Carpenter and Symonds, it was the working-class status of the collegians themselves that appealed to Whitman, and in them he believed he had found the audience for which he aimed. Later the circle of friends became part of the English socialist movement, but while Whitman was alive their ideal was democracy, by which they meant the elimination of the class system in England and the improvement of the conditions of workers. Therein lay Whitman's great appeal for them, for they understood him to be the divinely inspired prophet of world democracy.

The "Eagle Street College" did not disband or lose its direction after Whitman's death, but continued to work toward the high objectives its members believed Whitman had set. Virginia Woolf once paid respect to their long devotion to Whitman, and the "College" so inspired their townsmen that the Bolton Library maintains the collegians' books, correspondence, and manuscripts in its local history collection. Included among the artifacts is the stuffed canary still in its original case.

Joann P. Krieg

Bibliography

Blodgett, Harold. *Walt Whitman in England.* Ithaca, N.Y.: Cornell UP, 1934.

Johnston, J., and J.W. Wallace. *Visits to Walt Whitman in 1890–1891.* 1917. New York: Haskell House, 1970.

Salveson, Paul. *Loving Comrades: Lancashire's Links to Walt Whitman.* Bolton, England: Worker's Educational Association, 1984.

Woolf, Virginia. "Bolton and Walt Whitman." *Times Literary Supplement* 3 Jan. 1918.

See also Associations, Clubs, Fellowships, Foundations, and Societies; British Isles, Whitman in the; Johnston, Dr. John; Wallace, James William

Bon Echo

Bon Echo is a sixty-four-hundred-acre tract of wilderness land on Upper and Lower Mazenaw Lakes in Ontario, 175 miles northeast of Toronto. It is now an Ontario Provincial Park, but from 1916 through the early 1920s, it was the center of Whitman activities in Canada. At the time, Bon Echo had a large inn and cottages, and the estate was operated by the Canadian suffragist and spiritualist Flora MacDonald Denison as a summer resort. Instrumental in founding the Canadian Whitman Fellowship in 1916, MacDonald Denison decided to dedicate Bon Echo to the poet. She held meetings of The Whitman Club of Bon Echo; edited and published *The Sunset of Bon Echo*, a little magazine devoted to Whitman; and arranged to turn the face of the four-hundred-foot-high granite cliff overlooking the lakes into a monument to Whitman. The cliff was named "Old Walt" and was dedicated during the summer of 1919 (the centennial of the poet's birth) by MacDonald Denison and Horace Traubel (who died at Bon Echo just days after the dedication ceremony).

During the fall of 1919, stonemasons carved an inscription on the face of the cliff in two-foot-high letters:

OLD WALT

1819–1919

DEDICATED TO THE DEMOCRATIC IDEALS OF

WALT WHITMAN

BY

HORACE TRAUBEL AND FLORA MACDONALD

"MY FOOTHOLD IS TENON'D AND MORTISED IN GRANITE

I LAUGH AT WHAT YOU CALL DISSOLUTION

AND I KNOW THE AMPLITUDE OF TIME"

(Greenland and Colombo 202)

When Flora MacDonald Denison died in 1921, her ashes were scattered in the lake at the base of Old Walt. Her son Merrill unsuccessfully took over the operation of Bon Echo; it became a boys' camp in the early 1930s, then fell into disuse. Merrill rededicated Old Walt in 1955, the centennial of the first edition of *Leaves of Grass,* then donated the land to Canada in 1959. Bon Echo opened as a public park in 1965.

Ed Folsom

Bibliography

Greenland, Cyril, and John Robert Colombo, eds. *Walt Whitman's Canada.* Willowdale, Ontario: Hounslow, 1992.

See also ASSOCIATIONS, CLUBS, FELLOWSHIPS, FOUNDATIONS, AND SOCIETIES; CANADA, WHITMAN'S RECEPTION IN; CANADA, WHITMAN'S VISIT TO; DENISON, FLORA MACDONALD; PERIODICALS DEVOTED TO WHITMAN; TRAUBEL, HORACE L.

Borges, Jorge Luis (1899–1986)

Jorge Luis Borges, the Argentinian essayist, poet, and master of the short story, was a great admirer of Whitman. He wrote several important essays on Whitman, who also figures as the subject of several of his poems, and he translated a large selection of *Leaves of Grass* into Spanish (*Hojas de hierba,* 1969). Much of the work from Borges's sixty-year writing career has been translated into English, most notably *Labyrinths* (1964), *Other Inquisitions* (1964), and *Selected Poems* (1968).

Borges was most intrigued by the phenomenon he named the "two Whitmans: the 'friendly and eloquent savage' of *Leaves of Grass* and the poor writer who invented him" ("Note" 68). In this double figure of the fictional expansive Whitman and the actual limited Whitman, Borges found a cracked mirror image of his own divided self, and he came to identify with both the "lonely, unfortunate man whose life was short of happiness" and the "semi-divine hero espousing democracy" ("Poet of Democracy" 305). Borges also insisted that one of Whitman's great accomplishments was to make of his reader a fictional character. Borges's fascination with metafictional worlds led him to see Whitman as the original metafictionist, "making a character out of the writer and the reader" (Foreword xvii), and he believed this accomplishment was never equaled.

In his poem "Camden, 1892" Borges imagines an aged Whitman living out his tedious final years, feeling quite remote from the robust fictional Whitman he had created. The final line of the poem is "Yo fui Walt Whitman" ["I was Walt Whitman"], a line spoken at once by the elderly Whitman and by Borges himself. Blind and frail in his final decades, Borges continued to claim a kinship with the Camden sage.

Ed Folsom

Bibliography

Borges, Jorge Luis. "The Achievements of Walt Whitman." *Texas Quarterly* 5.1 (1962): 43–48.

———. Foreword and "Camden, 1892." *Homage to Walt Whitman.* Ed. Didier Tisdel Jaén. Tuscaloosa: U of Alabama P, 1969. xiii–xvii, 2–3.

———. "Note on Walt Whitman." *Other Inquisitions, 1937–1952.* Trans. Ruth L.C. Simms. Austin: U of Texas P, 1964. 66–72.

———. "Walt Whitman, Man and Myth." *Critical Inquiry* 1 (1975): 707–718.

———. "Walt Whitman, Poet of Democracy." *Commonweal* 22 May 1981: 303–305.

See also SPAIN AND SPANISH AMERICA, WHITMAN IN

Born, Helena (1860–1901)

Helena Born moved with her friend Miriam Daniell from England to the Boston area in 1890. Born in Devonshire, England, Born moved with her parents to Bristol and in time became active in the socialist movement, working especially hard for better pay and working conditions for women. A well-educated woman, she read voraciously, coming to admire Whitman while still living in England.

Born was one of the early members of the Boston Branch of the Walt Whitman Fellowship, where she and Helen Tufts Bailie, her close friend and loyal admirer, actively joined with others to support Whitman's poetry and prose. After Born's death in 1901, Tufts (Bailie) saw to it that Born's writings were collected and published in a book titled *Whitman's Ideal Democracy*. This book, whose title essay was originally published in *Poet-Lore* in 1899, contains articles on writers other than Whitman, though the majority of them focus on him.

Born found Whitman's concept of democracy to be at one with her own. Though her communal side responded to Whitman's call for national unity through a strong public structural grounding, Whitman's call for the strong individual—for self-knowledge and pride—touched her own experience deeply. She felt such a message had special appeal to women. Born is one of a long list of women in the nineteenth and early twentieth centuries who felt Whitman to be a valid spokesperson for women's rights.

Sherry Ceniza

Bibliography

Born, Helena. *Whitman's Ideal Democracy and Other Writings*. Ed. Helen Tufts. Boston: Everett, 1902.

See also DEMOCRACY; WOMAN'S RIGHTS MOVEMENT AND WHITMAN, THE

"Boston Ballad (1854), A" (1855)

This poem, written in 1854 but first published in the 1855 *Leaves of Grass*, satirizes the indifference of Boston's citizens during the return by federal marshals of the fugitive slave Anthony Burns. The poem demonstrates that Walt Whitman opposed the Fugitive Slave Law because of his objection to federal interference in areas of state and local sovereignty, not because of sympathy for the fugitive slave.

In perhaps the most celebrated fugitive slave case in the antebellum period, Anthony Burns, an escaped slave from Virginia, was arrested in Boston on 24 May 1854 and placed in the federal courthouse. The Fugitive Slave Law, enacted as part of the 1850 Compromise, empowered federal marshals to compel citizens and communities to cooperate in the return of fugitive slaves. The law had been enforced generally without incident since its enactment, but passage of the Kansas-Nebraska Act, just two days prior to the arrest, had outraged many Northerners. (The Act essentially repealed the terms of the 1820 Missouri Compromise and allowed Kansas to be organized as a slave state.) While Burns was in custody, a biracial group attempted to rescue him in an attack on the courthouse. The attempt failed, one of the guards was killed, and federal troops were called in to secure order. A week-long trial found that Burns should be returned to his master in Virginia.

The delivery of Burns from the courthouse to the wharf was a spectacle unparalleled in the brief history of the Fugitive Slave Law. According to the New York *Times,* more than 10,000 troops, including the entire Boston police force and various companies of United States Marines, escorted Burns under arms. More than 20,000 persons lined the streets, jeering the police and cheering Burns. Nationally, crowds numbering into the thousands stood vigil to protect escaped slaves from arrest by federal marshals in Milwaukee, Chicago, and elsewhere. The Burns case, coupled with the Kansas-Nebraska Act, wholly altered Northern antislavery sentiment.

Whitman was so outraged by the Burns affair that he wrote "A Boston Ballad (1854)," his first poem in four years. The speaker of the poem is apparently one of the many Bostonians who have come to see "the show," with little interest in its causes. His excitement about the federal troops is suddenly interrupted when he sees at the back of the march "bandaged and bloodless" phantoms, Revolutionary War heroes who have returned from the dead to protest the violation of republican ideals for which they had died. When these phantoms level their crutches as they would muskets to show the course of action required, the speaker understands this merely as a senile gesture, and urges instead a proper respect for the federal show of power. Horrified at the indifference of the citizens, the revolutionaries retreat. The speaker then realizes the "one thing that belongs here," and he convinces the mayor to send a committee to England to exhume the corpse of King George III and bring it to be crowned in Boston.

Whitman's ironic depiction of complacent Bostonians contradicts what he probably knew about the public ferment in Boston, given exhaustive press coverage in the New York newspapers. But even more striking in the poem is the absence of Anthony Burns. By eliding the fugitive slave from the narrative, Whitman suggests that the Fugitive Slave Law should be resisted not to protect the freedom and rights of blacks, but to protect the freedom of Northern white communities from an invasive federal power whose tyranny is as heinous as the return of British monarchs.

Martin Klammer

Bibliography

Campbell, Stanley W. *The Slave Catchers: Enforcement of the Fugitive Slave Law, 1850–1860*. Chapel Hill: U of North Carolina P, 1970.

Malin, Stephen. "'A Boston Ballad' and the Boston Riot." *Walt Whitman Review* 9 (1963): 51–57.

Rubin, Joseph Jay. *The Historic Whitman*. University Park: Pennsylvania State UP, 1973.

See also BURNS, ANTHONY; COMPROMISE OF 1850; *LEAVES OF GRASS*, 1855 EDITION; SLAVERY AND ABOLITIONISM

Boston, Massachusetts

Boston, the capital of Massachusetts, was founded in 1630 by English Puritans under the leadership of John Winthrop, a Suffolk lawyer. Boston was early on a center for the literary culture of English-speaking America, establishing within its jurisdiction a printing press at Cambridge, Massachusetts, in 1638 and another in Boston proper in 1675. The city's im-

portance to American literary culture was sustained in the nineteenth century by the establishment of the prestigious publishing houses of Ticknor and Fields and James Osgood, and the founding of two important journals—the *North American Review* in 1815 and the *Atlantic Monthly* in 1857.

Whitman's ongoing relationship with Boston was both symbolic and actual, at times bringing him face to face with an actual city of well-wishers and publishers, and at other times, with a symbolic metropolis of abolitionist strength and, just as often, Victorian hypocrisy. But it was the old city's crooked streets and "multitudinous angles" that most delighted the poet, and in *Specimen Days* he describes its haphazard beauty in language that reflects his own improvisational poetics: "crush up a sheet of letter paper . . . throw it down, stamp it flat, and that is a map of old Boston" (*Prose Works* 1:265).

Whitman's first public recognition of Boston refers to the symbolic city, recording its struggles with the slave question in "A Boston Ballad (1854)," a near doggerel satire written in 1854 on the transport of fugitive slave Anthony Burns. The poet actually visited Boston for the first time on 15 March 1860, in order to oversee the publication of the third edition of *Leaves of Grass* by the firm of Thayer and Eldridge. Almost as soon as he arrived, Ralph Waldo Emerson called on him, and, as Whitman recalled later, spent much of his time trying to convince the poet not to include the "Children of Adam" poems in the forthcoming edition. Within days, Emerson had acquired borrowing privileges for him at the Boston Athenaeum, the venerable private library frequented in Whitman's day by the likes of Henry Wadsworth Longfellow (with whom he shared a "short but pleasant" visit), James Russell Lowell, and Oliver Wendell Holmes. For the next few months, Whitman divided his time in the Massachusetts capital between reading proof sheets and sauntering along Boston Common, discovering on these walks that "Everybody here is so like everybody else—and I am Walt Whitman!" (*Correspondence* 1:50). On Sunday mornings, he liked to visit the Seaman's Chapel to hear the Methodist minister Edward Thompson Taylor deliver his sermons in the powerful nautical language that Herman Melville had reproduced in *Moby-Dick* in the oratory of "Father Mapple"; Whitman eventually produced an essay on the subject, "Father Taylor (and Oratory)" (1887). During his visit Whitman also took time out from his work to attend the trial of Frank B. Sanborn, who was being tried for aiding some of John Brown's followers. It was on this trip, as well, that Whitman met William Douglas O'Connor, who would become one of his most vehement and vigilant supporters.

Whitman would not return to Boston until April 1881, when he traveled to the city to deliver his Lincoln lecture in the Hawthorne Room of the St. Botolph Club on the anniversary of the president's death. In August of that year, Whitman found himself back in the city, this time to supervise a new edition of *Leaves of Grass* to be brought out by James R. Osgood, one of America's leading publishers. He quickly settled into the routine he had developed twenty-one years before, reading page proofs in a small office in the forenoon and strolling on Boston Common or meeting with friends in his time off. It was during this trip that Frank Sanborn took Whitman to Concord to visit the rapidly aging Emerson, with whom the poet sat quietly during their several evenings together, soaking up his early mentor's aura and chatting with Mrs. Emerson about the personal life of Henry David Thoreau, who had died in 1862. While in Concord, Whitman also visited "Sleepy Hollow" cemetery and the graves of Nathaniel Hawthorne and Thoreau; took in the Old Manse, where Hawthorne had written several of his best tales; and toured the Concord battlefield, where the Revolutionary War had begun.

While in Boston completing the page proofs to the 1881 edition, Whitman received news that President Garfield had died of the wounds inflicted by an assassin's bullet more than a year before, and he responded with "The Sobbing of the Bells," inserting the freshly composed poem into the "Songs of Parting" cluster just before the pages were set.

In March 1882, after Osgood had printed three issues of the book amounting to two thousand copies, the Boston district attorney ordered the publisher to cease publication, having officially declared *Leaves* to be obscene literature. After agreeing to revise "a half a dozen . . . words or phrases" (*Correspondence* 3:267), Whitman found the district attorney unwilling to budge and finally reached a settlement with Osgood in May in which he received the plates, dies, and remaining copies of the edition (along with one hundred dollars) and the freedom to seek another publisher.

Phillip H. Round

Bibliography

Allen, Gay Wilson. *The Solitary Singer: A Critical Biography of Walt Whitman.* 1955. Rev. ed. 1967. Chicago: U of Chicago P, 1985.

Baxter, Sylvester. "Walt Whitman in Boston." *New England Magazine* 6 (1892): 714–721.

Furness, Clifton J. "Walt Whitman Looks at Boston." *New England Quarterly* 1 (1928): 353–370.

Kaplan, Justin. *Walt Whitman: A Life.* New York: Simon and Schuster, 1980.

Whitman, Walt. *The Correspondence.* Ed. Edwin Haviland Miller. 6 vols. New York: New York UP, 1961–1977.

———. *Prose Works 1892.* Ed. Floyd Stovall. 2 vols. New York: New York UP, 1963–1964.

See also ATLANTIC MONTHLY, THE; "BOSTON BALLAD (1854), A"; "DEATH OF ABRAHAM LINCOLN"; EMERSON, RALPH WALDO; LEAVES OF GRASS, 1860 EDITION; LEAVES OF GRASS, 1881–1882 EDITION; LONGFELLOW, HENRY WADSWORTH; NORTH AMERICAN REVIEW, THE; O'CONNOR, WILLIAM DOUGLAS; OSGOOD, JAMES R.; SANBORN, FRANKLIN BENJAMIN (FRANK); STEVENS, OLIVER; TAYLOR, FATHER (EDWARD THOMPSON); THAYER AND ELDRIDGE

"Boy Lover, The" (1845)

This short story was first published in *American Review,* May 1845. For publication particulars and revisions, see Brasher's edition of *The Early Poems and the Fiction.*

"The Boy Lover" is a first-person account of a love story. It is unusual in that four young men fall in love with the same girl, the beautiful Ninon. When she dies unexpectedly, the four men grieve, but one of them less violently, less openly than the others. This one, Matthew, maintains an even temper and dies of grief unexpressed: "The shaft, rankling far down and within, wrought a poison too great for show, and the youth died" (308). Matthew's brother is the narrator, now an old man reminiscing. He reminds his readers that they will grow old and have to measure their happiness, and he extols love as "the child-monarch that Death itself cannot conquer" (302–303).

Through his choice of narrator, Whitman is able to characterize the passion of the four boys with the immediacy of a first-person viewpoint, while still allowing for the sentimentality of the ending: death through grief. Grief as a cause of death is a pervasive theme in Whitman's fiction; it is implicit in "Death in the School-Room (a Fact)" (1841) and explicit in "Dumb Kate" (1844) and in number 1 of "Some Fact-Romances" (1845).

Little critical attention has been given to "The Boy Lover."

Patrick McGuire

Bibliography

Whitman, Walt. *The Early Poems and the Fiction*. Ed. Thomas L. Brasher. New York: New York UP, 1963.

See also "DEATH IN THE SCHOOL-ROOM (A FACT)"; "DUMB KATE"; SENTIMENTALITY; SHORT FICTION, WHITMAN'S; "SOME FACT-ROMANCES"

British Isles, Whitman in the

Despite Walt Whitman's efforts to put wildly favorable words into the mouths of his British reviewers, the first (1855) edition of *Leaves of Grass* was met in London for the most part either with frosty silence or with scathing condescension: "Walt Whitman is as unacquainted with art, as a hog is with mathematics," snorted the *Critic* (Allen and Folsom 22). In a private letter of 1866, Matthew Arnold deplored the "eccentric and violent originality" of the poetry (Allen and Folsom 25). Yet by 1876 Whitman's friends in England were sufficient in number to muster a hefty subscription to help the by then ailing and impoverished poet. This action lent at least some credence to Whitman's claims that England had been much readier than his native country to recognize his genius. And yet no complete, unexpurgated edition of *Leaves of Grass* was published in Britain during the author's lifetime.

Although Whitman's late-nineteenth-century admirers in Britain were a fairly motley crowd, they were by and large middle class, bookish, socially and politically radical, and more attracted to the gospel he preached than convinced by his means of preaching it. Inclined as many of them were to view him as prophet, pioneer, and liberator, they valued his writings for their egalitarian spirit, healthy optimism, spiritual uplift, cosmic vision, nature philosophy, frank physicality and sexual openness.

Their attraction to him was often a function of their reaction against established Victorian practices and values, a reaction that in some cases could be accommodated within the mainstream sociopolitical reform movements of the period, but in other cases contributed to a developing counter-culture, including utopian socialism, an inchoate feminism, and attempts to liberalize, or even revolutionize, sexual issues.

Whitman was disappointed in his hopes that W.M. Rossetti's 1868 publication of a bowdlerized selection from *Leaves of Grass* would take Britain by storm, but it was nevertheless a landmark edition that more or less coincided with the switch of readers' interests from European to American literature, following the ending of the Franco-Prussian war (1870). By then, the anti-democratic prejudice that had helped prolong Britain's colonialist attitude toward the United States had been eroded by the steady democratization of British politics, and the great Education Acts of the seventies also helped produce a new breed of reader, avid for transatlantic reading matter. But, unlike the work of Nathaniel Hawthorne and Ralph Waldo Emerson, Whitman's poetry still appealed only to a minority. Even discriminating writers like George Eliot and Gerard Manley Hopkins expressed only a nervous interest in his work; Alfred, Lord Tennyson responded to Whitman's personal overtures in carefully measured tones of baffled respect; and Algernon Charles Swinburne ended as fierce enemy to the poetry, although he had begun as brilliant advocate of its Blakeian power of visionary utterance. It was, in fact, by relating Whitman to William Blake, or to Percy Bysshe Shelley, that many radicals were able to claim him as heir to a British tradition of revolutionary poetics. It was in these terms that Henry Salt recommended Whitman's poetry to proletarian readers in his radical anthology *Songs of Freedom* (1884), intended to challenge Francis Turner Palgrave's enormously influential *Golden Treasury* (1851). The popular journalistic pieces about Whitman by James Thomson ("B.V."), author of *The City of Dreadful Night* (1880), were, however, much more effective attempts at crossing the class barrier and drawing the poetry to the attention of the lower classes with whom Whitman so yearned to connect.

That Whitman's work could indeed appeal to politicized sections of the lower middle classes was proved when a group of working men in industrial Bolton (Lancashire) began discussing his work and entered into prolonged correspondence with Whitman himself. The poet was so touched by their interest that he later bequeathed to them the stuffed body of the little canary bird whose singing had consoled him in old age. As the labor movement began to turn to the new secular religion of socialism, the new "labor churches" in several industrial towns, including Birmingham, adopted Whitman as their prophet. His poetry, or at least the diluted Whitmanesque poetry of his British epigone, Edward Carpenter, affected the climate of thinking of the Independent Labor party and was an acknowledged influence on the great Keir Hardie, elected the first Labor party M.P. in 1900. By the turn of the century Whitman was a significant presence in the thinking of many working class progressivist groups, and it was probably in this context that the young D.H. Lawrence first encountered him. But as the labor movement was increasingly forced by economic and political circumstances into militant unionism and the politics of class struggle, Whitman's writing lost its appeal.

In the earlier period, when Whitman's poetry excited the attentions of crusading middle-class socialists, one of his most devoted acolytes was Ernest Rhys, who believed strongly in producing cheap books to educate the masses and was later instrumental in establishing the enormously influential Everyman Library. Rhys was one of many British visitors to Whitman's little house in Camden, others including the young Oscar Wilde and the famous actor Sir Henry Irving. Rhys's Welshness is a reminder that Whitman's appeal extended to all the nationalities of the British Isles. Other Welsh writers who came under his influence were the colorful communist dentist and populist versifier T.E. Nicholas (Niclas y Glais), the great Welsh-language poet Waldo Williams, and of course Dylan Thomas, who kept a photograph of Whitman pinned to the wall of the Laugharne boathouse that served as his "study." Whitman's poetry was translated into Welsh by M. Wynn Thomas in 1995.

Since Ossian, Robert Burns, and Thomas Carlyle had meant so much to Whitman, it was appropriate that Scottish writers and academics should take a particular interest in his work. Three important studies of his work appeared in Scotland even before his death. The young Robert Louis Stevenson was besotted with his poetry; the Edinburgh town planner and poly-math Patrick Geddes was enthusiastic about his social utopianism; and the omnivorousness of Whitman's imagination appealed enormously to that giant, maverick figure of the modern Scottish Renaissance, Hugh MacDiarmid. Such contemporary poets as Robert Crawford, W.T. Herbert, and the veteran experimentalist Edwin Morgan are therefore only the latest in a long line of distinguished Scottish Whitmanians.

Similarly, the contemporary Ulster poets Tom Paulin and Paul Muldoon, drawn respectively to Whitman's antiauthoritarianism and his tangy use of the vernacular, have behind them a century of Irish interest in his writing. Even the great modernists W.B. Yeats and James Joyce were passingly taken with him, unlike the poet Patrick Kavanagh, who memorably dismissed him as "a writer who tried to bully his way to prophecy" (qtd. in Allen and Folsom 18). Among his many Irish admirers were Sean O'Casey, Frank O'Connor, Padraic Colum, Oscar Wilde, and AE (George Russell), but his appeal extended well beyond Irish literary circles to include labor leader James Larkin and freedom fighter James Connolly. Indeed, Whitman's nationalistic poetry contributed significantly to the cultural fashioning of an independent Ireland, as is evident both from the letters of the young Yeats and from the early writings of Standish O'Grady, one of the key figures in the Irish literary awakening during the closing years of the last century.

O'Grady studied at Trinity College, Dublin, with Edward Dowden, a representative figure of the Anglo-Irish Ascendancy whose early study of Whitman in *The Poetry of Democracy* (1878) provided a judicious assessment of his unorthodox talent, much appreciated by the poet himself. Others who wrote in measured, academic terms were the distinguished bookmen George Saintsbury and Edmund Gosse (who memorably described Whitman's poetry as "literature in the condition of protoplasm" [Allen and Folsom 48]). But in the latter part of the nineteenth century the most strikingly original British response to Whitman was expressed in a much more excited, and exciting, form. "An Englishwoman's Estimate of Walt Whitman" (1870) consisted of remarkable letters about Whitman's poetry written to W.M. Rossetti by Anne Gilchrist, the widow of a great Blake scholar. Hearing in the poetry a call to resensualize the female body and to shatter the Victorian constraints on female sexuality, Gilchrist responded with an emotional nakedness conveyed through surges of ecstatic prose. Her writing departed from the "masculine," rational norm in ways that approximate to what feminists would now call *écriture féminine* (womanly writing). Gilchrist also wrote love letters to Whitman himself and eventually took her family to Boston to visit him, probably with a view to taking him as her spouse or partner. In the face of Whitman's kind but distant response, however, her ardor cooled to a warm respect and steadfast friendship.

Whitman's real sexual orientation, guardedly expressed in "Calamus" and guardedly recognized by the English Jesuit poet Gerard Manley Hopkins in a remarkable private letter to Robert Bridges (1882), was intuited by three important British disciples. The freethinking Edward Carpenter, whose *Towards Democracy* (1883) consisted of over five hundred closely printed pages of Whitmanesque poetry, claimed (unconvincingly) in old age to recall in detail how he had granted the aged Whitman his sexual favors. Havelock Ellis included Whitman in his pantheon of sexually liberated cosmic philosophers, precursors of a new age. Most interesting of all, the frail scholar-aesthete John Addington Symonds credited Whitman not only with breathing into him a new robust spirit of physical health but also with a celebration of comradeship conceived of as passionate male bonding. However, when Whitman was privately pressed by Symonds in 1890 to admit his homoeroticism, he reacted with alarm, angrily repudiating the imputation and claiming to have fathered six children. Some recent scholars have read this incident not as an outright denial by Whitman of his homosexuality but as a rejection of that kind of homosexual character (aesthetic, upper-class, "effeminate") which to him Symonds seemed to represent.

Another figure preoccupied with the turbid sexuality of Whitman's writing was D.H. Lawrence, whose obsession with his work was reflected in the many essays he drafted on the subject before the appearance of the epoch-making chapter in *Studies in Classic American Literature* (1923). At once infatuated with Whitman and exasperated by him, Lawrence wrote in wonderfully comic terms of the American's grossly egotistical voraciousness. But he also recognized his "classic" greatness and his massive importance as the originator of free verse. Probably the only great British writer to have benefited creatively from Whitman's example, Lawrence drew upon the rhythms of *Leaves of Grass* in writing his

own fluid "poetry of the moment." Other writers who honored Whitman, but whose style was not marked by his, included the ascetic nineties poet Lionel Johnson; the war poets Isaac Rosenberg and Ivor Gurney; the liberal humanist and homosexual author of *A Passage to India*, E.M. Forster; the major modernist novelist Virginia Woolf; and the eccentric genius John Cowper Powys.

While naturalized Americans such as Thom Gunn and David Hockney have recently demonstrated how much Whitman's work can still matter to British poets and artists, for most of this century the study of Whitman in Britain has been largely confined to academic scholars, men and women of letters, and freelance critics. Regardless of whether they have belonged to the nativist, conservative, anti-American tradition or to the progressivist, modernist, Poundian tradition, British poets have tended to overlook Whitman. But, as the novelist Anthony Burgess pointed out, distinguished British composers have remedied this deficiency: Ralph Vaughan Williams's *A Sea Symphony* and *Toward the Unknown Region*, Frederic Delius's *Sea-Drift*, Gustav Holst's *Dirge for Two Veterans,* and Sir Arthur Bliss's *Morning Heroes* are all important works based on Whitman's poetry.

M. Wynn Thomas

Bibliography

Allen, Gay Wilson. *The New Walt Whitman Handbook*. 1975. New York: New York UP, 1986.

Allen, Gay Wilson, and Ed Folsom, eds. *Walt Whitman & the World*. Iowa City: U of Iowa P, 1995.

Blodgett, Harold. *Walt Whitman in England*. 1934. New York: Russell and Russell, 1973.

Clarke, Graham, ed. *Walt Whitman: Critical Assessments*. 4 vols. Robertsbridge: Helm Information, 1994.

Crawford, Robert. *Devolving English Literature*. Oxford: Clarendon, 1992.

Gohdes, Benjamin. *American Literature in Nineteenth-Century England*. Carbondale: Southern Illinois UP, 1944.

Grant, Douglas. *Purpose and Place: Essays on American Writers*. London: Macmillan, 1965.

Hindus, Milton, ed. *Walt Whitman: The Critical Heritage*. London: Routledge and Kegan Paul, 1971.

Lease, Benjamin. *Anglo-American Encounters: England and the Rise of American Literature.* Cambridge: Cambridge UP, 1981.

Murphy, Francis, ed. *Walt Whitman: A Critical Anthology.* Harmondsworth: Penguin, 1969.

Perlman, Jim, Ed Folsom, and Dan Campion, eds. *Walt Whitman: The Measure of His Song.* Minneapolis: Holy Cow!, 1981.

See also ARNOLD, MATTHEW; BOLTON (ENGLAND) "EAGLE STREET COLLEGE"; BUCHANAN, ROBERT; CARPENTER, EDWARD; DOWDEN, EDWARD; FORSTER, E.M.; GILCHRIST, ANNE BURROWS; GOSSE, SIR EDMUND; HOPKINS, GERARD MANLEY; INTERCULTURALITY; IRELAND, WHITMAN IN; JOYCE, JAMES; LABOR AND LABORING CLASSES; LAWRENCE, D.H.; MUSIC, WHITMAN'S INFLUENCE ON; RHYS, ERNEST PERCIVAL; ROSSETTI, WILLIAM MICHAEL; STEVENSON, ROBERT LOUIS; SWINBURNE, ALGERNON CHARLES; SYMONDS, JOHN ADDINGTON; TENNYSON, ALFRED, LORD; WILDE, OSCAR

British Romantic Poets

While Whitman was reasonably well acquainted with the works of the British Romantic poets, none of them mattered to him as did William Shakespeare, Sir Walter Scott, Thomas Carlyle, and Alfred, Lord Tennyson, his favorite British writers. His readings in Romantic poetry were fleeting, tangential, and largely insignificant, except insofar as they influenced him by negative example and made him ever more confident of the directions, both artistic and thematic, in which he wanted to go.

Politically, the British Romantics were suspect, since Whitman believed they shared in the attachment to Old World feudalism that made British writers irrelevant, if not inimical, to the needs and concerns of nineteenth-century democratic America. A notebook entry probably dating from 1855 or 1856 specifically rebuked Robert Southey, Samuel Taylor Coleridge, and William Wordsworth for turning away from human rights in order to embrace "kingcraft, priestcraft, obedience, and so forth" (*Notebooks* 5:1778).

Even where Whitman found much to admire, he generally qualified his views. Robert Burns, for example, appealed to Whitman because of his democratic sympathies as well as his attractive personality, yet Burns was finally found wanting. In an 1882 essay, "Robert Burns As Poet and Person," Whitman condemned the Scottish poet for one telling defect, a lack of spirituality that prevented him from rising to the heights of the truly great, like Homer or Shakespeare, or even to the levels of such lesser eminences as Tennyson and Ralph Waldo Emerson. The criticism may reflect the importance that Whitman attached in his later years to his own growing sense of spirituality.

Blake, too, was found deficient, despite the force of his prophetic energies. In 1868 Whitman read A.C. Swinburne's *William Blake*, which concluded with a laudatory comparison of Whitman and Blake. While Whitman responded courteously to this comparison, in his own mind he was intent on putting some distance between himself and the British poet. In a manuscript fragment of the time, Whitman noted that he and Blake were both "mystics, extatics," but went on to record a major difference: while Blake's visions were "wilful & uncontrolled," he, Whitman, "never once loses control, or even equilibrium" (*Notebooks* 4 1502–1503). Ten years later, Whitman had apparently not changed his opinion, as he referred in an 1878 newspaper article to Blake's "half-mad vision" (*Prose Works* 2:670).

Whitman also found Wordsworth to be significantly flawed. In a marginal annotation of 1849, Whitman scribbled, "Wordsworth lacks sympathy with men and women" (qtd. in Stovall 128). For a poet of Whitman's extensive sympathies, such a charge would be conclusive. All indications are that Whitman found in Wordsworth's poetry too much attention to nature, too little to humanity. Furthermore, as noted above, Whitman considered Wordsworth a political reactionary, far removed from Whitman's democratic values.

In 1847 Whitman briefly reviewed in the Brooklyn *Eagle* two prose works by Coleridge, whom Whitman praised for being "like Adam in Paradise, and almost as free from artificiality" (*Uncollected* 1:131). The characterization is such as Whitman would have gladly claimed for himself. As for the poetry, however, Coleridge's use of the mythical and supernatural was too remote from Whitman's own practices to be appealing. In an 1880 entry in *Specimen Days*, Whitman complained of the "lush and the weird" then in favor among readers of poetry (*Prose Works* 1:232). The second adjective would seem to apply to Coleridge, as the first would apply to Percy Bysshe Shelley and John Keats.

In 1888 Whitman claimed to have read all of Keats's poetry, but the response was conventional and superficial: "he is sweet—oh! very sweet—all sweetness: almost lush: lush, polish, ornateness, elegancy" (*With Walt Whitman* 3:83). Whitman had little use for Keats, considering him too remote from the times, thematically as well as stylistically, to compel attention. In a note probably dating from the 1850s, Whitman complained that Keats's poetry reflected the sentiments of the classical deities of twenty-five hundred years earlier rather than the concerns of its own age. "Of life in the nineteenth century," Whitman wrote, "it has none any more than the statues have. It does not come home at all to the direct wants of the bodies and souls of the century" (*Notebooks* 5:1770).

Shelley, too, represented the "lush" in poetry that Whitman rejected. Particularly objectionable was Shelley's prolific use of figurative language, so far removed from the strong, simple language that Whitman valued. Shelley's extensive use of classical mythology, like Keats's, also provided cause for rejection, and while Whitman could admire Shelley's ethereal qualities, he knew they were not for him. Shelley, Whitman remarked to Horace Traubel in 1888, "was not sensual—he was not even sensuous" (*With Walt Whitman* 1:41). The same year, again speaking to Traubel, Whitman remarked that he was not a reader of Shelley, then added, "Shelley is interesting to me as Burns is, chiefly as a person: I read with most avidity not their poems but their lives . . ." (2:345). Whitman was often more interested in poets' biographies than in their poetry.

Such is the case with George Gordon, Lord Byron, although Whitman apparently knew the poetry well enough by the mid-1840s to quote from it. In an 1848 review he referred to Byron's "fiery breath" (*Uncollected* 1:121), and forty years later the metaphor still held. As Whitman remarked to Traubel in 1888, "Byron has fire enough to burn forever" (*With Walt Whitman* 1:41). He further commented that his attitude toward Byron had remained unchanged during all those years. Whatever the concern with the poetry, however, the biography was of particular interest.

In an 1880 entry in *Specimen Days,* Whitman grouped Byron with Burns, Friedrich von Schiller, and George Sand as representatives of the admirable type of person in whom "the

perfect character, the good, the heroic, although never attain'd, is never lost sight of, but through failures, sorrows, temporary downfalls, is return'd to again and again" (*Prose Works* 1:231). In 1889, Whitman remarked to Traubel that Byron (in contrast to Keats) "prospered" under "scurrility, abuse, contempt" (*With Walt Whitman* 6:154). Whitman apparently saw in Byron an example of courage and fortitude in the face of adversity that served his own needs in difficult times. Early in 1889, Whitman listed Byron and his poetry among those poets and works referred to as "my daily food" (*With Walt Whitman* 4:67). That Byron is cited along with such longtime favorites as Homer, Epictetus, and Scott would seem to indicate high regard.

Even so, on various grounds the British Romantic poets as a group had little appeal for Whitman. Particularly objectionable, in his view, were the ornate and decorated qualities of their language, the apparent lack of concern for ordinary humanity, and the remoteness from the life of the century. In sum, they represented, as Whitman fully recognized, directions opposed to his own.

R.W. French

Bibliography

Price, Kenneth M. *Whitman and Tradition: The Poet in His Century.* New Haven: Yale UP, 1990.

Stovall, Floyd. *The Foreground of "Leaves of Grass."* Charlottesville: UP of Virginia, 1974.

Traubel, Horace. *With Walt Whitman in Camden.* 9 vols. Vols. 1–3. 1906–1914. New York: Rowman and Littlefield, 1961; Vol. 4. Ed. Sculley Bradley. Philadelphia: U of Pennsylvania P, 1953; Vol. 5. Ed. Gertrude Traubel. Carbondale: Southern Illinois UP, 1964; Vol. 6. Ed. Gertrude Traubel and William White. Carbondale: Southern Illinois UP, 1982; Vol. 7. Ed. Jeanne Chapman and Robert MacIsaac. Carbondale: Southern Illinois UP, 1992; Vols. 8–9. Ed. Jeanne Chapman and Robert MacIsaac. Oregon House, Calif.: W.L. Bentley, 1996.

Whitman, Walt. *Notebooks and Unpublished Prose Manuscripts.* Ed. Edward F. Grier. 6 vols. New York: New York UP, 1984.

———. *Prose Works 1892.* Ed. Floyd Stovall. 2 vols. New York: New York UP, 1963–1964.

———. *The Uncollected Poetry and Prose of Walt Whitman.* 1921. Ed. Emory Holloway. 2 vols. Gloucester, Mass.: Peter Smith, 1972.

See also BLAKE, WILLIAM; CARLYLE, THOMAS; FEUDALISM; INFLUENCES ON WHITMAN, PRINCIPAL; READING, WHITMAN'S; SCOTT, SIR WALTER; SHAKESPEARE, WILLIAM; TENNYSON, ALFRED, LORD

"Broadway" (1888)

This rather short poem by Whitman first appeared in the 10 April 1888 issue of the New York *Herald* and ended up in the "Sands at Seventy" cluster in the final (1891–1892) edition of *Leaves of Grass.* Since Whitman died shortly thereafter (26 March 1892), it has remained unaltered. The original manuscript is in the Clifton Waller Barrett Collection at the University of Virginia.

Given Whitman's love for New York City, a poem celebrating its grandeur is not surprising. As a young man he loved to stroll down Broadway in his frock coat with a boutonniere in the lapel, reveling in the sights, sounds, and smells of the famous street. Sometimes he rode on top of an omnibus all day long, seated by the driver; often he "took refuge" at Pfaff's, a famous Swiss restaurant that was a favorite haunt of New York's literary Bohemia.

By using emotional bursts instead of complete sentences, Whitman expresses in the poem's eleven lines the excitement of the street that unceasingly teems with "hurrying human tides" and "endless sliding, mincing, shuffling feet!" People of all types and with various intents scurry about: the passionate, gamblers, lovers true or false, evil people, blissful people, sad people. The street is the portal and arena for long lines, rich windows, huge hotels, wide sidewalks, and wondrous tales, if flagstones could but talk.

Though small itself, this poem shows Whitman's appreciation for the variety of American life, with its "vast, unspeakable show and lesson."

Maverick Marvin Harris

Bibliography

Asselineau, Roger. *The Evolution of Walt Whitman: The Creation of a Personality.* Trans. Richard P. Adams and Roger Asselineau. Cambridge, Mass.: Harvard UP, 1960.

See also CITY, WHITMAN AND THE; NEW YORK CITY; "SANDS AT SEVENTY" (FIRST ANNEX)

Broadway Hospital (New York)

While his visits to the Civil War hospital in Washington are more famous, Whitman actually began visiting the sick at New York Hospital in the 1850s. The institution, known as the Broadway Hospital, though it was just off Broadway on Pearl Street, engaged Whitman's attention especially during the early years of the Civil War. He was interested both in the hospital itself as a scientific institution and in the human suffering he witnessed there.

Although he was interested in helping all those confined, before the war broke out Whitman particularly concerned himself with the circumstances of the stage drivers he met there. Dr. D.B. St. John Roosa, in an article for the 20 June 1898 edition of the *Mail and Express* (New York), recalled, "No one could see him [Whitman] sitting by the bedside of a suffering stage driver without soon learning that he had a sincere and profound sympathy for this order of men" (30). Whitman also cultivated a relationship with the physicians, who allowed him great freedom in the hospital, even occasionally permitting him to witness surgical operations.

After the war began, Whitman wrote several articles based on his experiences at New York Hospital. The first was published in March of 1862 in the New York *Leader,* under the pseudonym of Velsor Brush, a combination of his mother's maiden name (Van Velsor) and his paternal grandmother's maiden name (Hannah Brush). The articles were part of a series entitled "City Photographs," which included four articles on the Broadway Hospital. In one of these Whitman wrote, "What a volume of meaning, what a tragic poem there is in every one of those sick wards!" (qtd. in Masur 47). In these articles, he repaid the doctors' kindness to him by calling for greater support, public and private, of the city hospitals, which he regarded as important democratic institutions.

During the early years of the war, Whitman continued to make regular visits to the hospital, but he focused his attention mostly on the war-wounded housed there, wishing to cheer them and relieve the monotony of their days. It was during this time that Whitman developed the skills that he used so effectively at the Civil War hospitals in Washington. In one of his articles for the *Leader,* he observed that the wounded responded especially well to small gifts of food or reading matter left for them by a compassionate lady (who preferred not to allow Whitman to use her name in the paper). When in December 1863 Whitman began his ministrations to the wounded in Washington, he was already a practiced caretaker. He recalled his experiences at the New York Hospital, in particular remembering the effects of the anonymous lady's gifts, and always tried to have something on hand to give the soldiers he met, which he bestowed upon them affectionately.

David Breckenridge Donlon

Bibliography

Allen, Gay Wilson. *The Solitary Singer: A Critical Biography of Walt Whitman.* 1955. Rev. ed. 1967. Chicago: U of Chicago P, 1985.

Masur, Louis. "'The Experience Sweet and Sad': Whitman's Visits to New York Hospitals." *Seaport* 26 (Spring 1992): 46–49.

Roosa, Dr. D.B. St. John. Untitled article in Henry Stoddard's "World of Letters." *Mail and Express* 20 June 1898: 30.

See also CIVIL WAR NURSING

Broadway Journal

As editor of the *Broadway Journal,* Edgar Allan Poe printed Whitman's brief article "Art-Singing and Heart-Singing" in late 1845. The short-lived weekly was the pet project of Charles F. Briggs, author of *The Adventures of Harry Franco* (1839); Henry C. Watson; and a former schoolteacher, John Bisco, who very much wanted New York to have a review devoted exclusively to literature. When Poe joined the staff, however, the *Journal* soon became a forum for his critical obsessions, most notably his charges of plagiarism against Henry Wadsworth Longfellow. By the fall of 1845, Poe was wholly in charge of its editorial content and used Whitman as a correspondent, thanking him for his contributions in the Editorial Miscellany for 22 November 1845. The *Journal* ceased publication in January 1846.

"Art-Singing and Heart-Singing," which appeared in the 29 November 1845 issue, was a revision of an article for the Brooklyn *Star* entitled "Heart-Music and Art-Music." In both articles (and subsequent reprints), Whitman celebrated the authentically American singing of the Cheneys, a family quartet from New Hampshire then appearing in New York. Whitman declared that "the subtlest spirit of a nation is expressed through its music" ("Art-Singing" 318). In the Cheneys he found what he called "heart-singing" or a natural, democratic music, and he claimed for it a power similar to what he would claim for his poetic vision in *Leaves of Grass.*

In *Specimen Days,* Whitman recalled meeting Poe at the *Journal*'s offices, describing him as "very kindly and human, but subdued, perhaps a little jaded" (702). Whitman's brief connection with the *Journal* offers a glimpse into his early forays into music criticism and musical nationalism and suggests that Poe presided in a small way over Whitman's nascent ideas of American "singing."

Stephen Rachman

Bibliography

Allen, Gay Wilson. *The Solitary Singer: A Critical Biography of Walt Whitman.* 1955. Rev. ed. 1967. Chicago: U of Chicago P, 1985.

Miller, Perry. *The Raven and the Whale: The War of Words and Wits in the Era of Poe and Melville.* New York: Harcourt, Brace, 1956.

Mott, Frank Luther. *A History of American Magazines, 1741–1850.* Cambridge, Mass.: Harvard UP, 1939.

Whitman, Walt. "Art-Singing and Heart-Singing." *Broadway Journal* 29 November 1845: 318–319. Rpt. in *The Uncollected Poetry and Prose of Walt Whitman.* Ed. Emory Holloway. Vol. 1. Garden City, N.Y.: Doubleday, Page, 1921. 104–106.

———. *Specimen Days. Complete Poetry and Collected Prose.* Ed. Justin Kaplan. New York: Library of America, 1982. 675–926.

See also MUSIC, WHITMAN AND; POE, EDGAR ALLAN

"Broadway Pageant, A" (1860)

This occasional poem first appeared as "The Errand-Bearers" in the New York *Times* on 27 June 1860 and was reprinted in *Drum-Taps* (1865) as "A Broadway Pageant (Reception Japanese Embassy, 16 June 1860)." Significant as an early precursor of "Passage to India," it was prompted by the celebration welcoming the Japanese envoys who had just arrived in New York City from Washington, D.C., after ratifying the first diplomatic and commercial treaty between the United States and Japan.

The first section of the poem vividly describes the scene as an estimated half million New Yorkers, including Whitman, turned out to watch the visitors from Japan make their stately way in carriages down Broadway. The remaining two sections are concerned not with the Japanese delegation itself but with the larger meaning of this first diplomatic visit from an Asian country. Like "Facing West from California's Shores," written a few years earlier, "A Broadway Pageant" reflects both the popular nineteenth-century American interest in Asia and the progress in Whitman's thought toward the idea that receives its fullest expression in "Passage to India."

"Facing West" speaks of a "circle almost circled"; "A Pageant" asserts, "The ring is circled" (section 3); and "Passage" refers to the "rondure of the world at last accomplish'd" (section 4). The speaker in "Facing West" looks toward Asia, "the house of maternity"; the speaker in "A Pageant" sees Asia as "the Originatress," the "all-mother," the "long-off mother" (sections 2 and 3); and the speaker in "Passage" sees Asia as "the cradle of man" (section 6). And just as "A Pageant" depicts Asia as the source of human origins, with a reference to "the race of eld" (section 2), so "Passage" honors "the myths and fables of eld" (section 2)—the only two uses of the word "eld" in *Leaves of Grass.*

"A Pageant," nevertheless, is inconsistent in its presentation of the relationship between the United States and Asia. The references toward the end of section 2 to "America the mistress," a "new empire," and "a greater supremacy" seem to suggest a Manifest Destiny extending across the Pacific. Yet section 3 counsels the young American nation—addressed as "Libertad"—to be humble and considerate of the "venerable Asia." Although this inconsistency is not resolved, the use of the verbs "justified" and "accomplish'd" in the penultimate line of the poem points the way to their key use in section 5 of "Passage," where the full reconciliation of East and West is depicted.

Martin K. Doudna

Bibliography

Doudna, Martin K. "'The Essential Ultimate Me': Whitman's Achievement in 'Passage to India.'" *Walt Whitman Quarterly Review* 2.3 (1984): 1–9.

Dulles, Foster Rhea. *Yankees and Samurai: America's Role in the Emergence of Modern Japan: 1791–1900.* New York: Harper and Row, 1965.

Miner, Earl Roy. "The Background, Date, and Composition of Whitman's 'A Broadway Pageant.'" *American Literature* 27 (1955): 403–405.

Smith, Henry Nash. *Virgin Land: The American West as Symbol and Myth.* 1950. New York: Random House, 1970.

Sugg, Richard P. "Whitman's Symbolic Circle and 'A Broadway Pageant.'" *Walt Whitman Review* 16 (1970): 35–40.

See also "Facing West from California's Shores"; Japan, Whitman in; "Passage to India"

Brooklyn *Daily Eagle*

For the two years of his Brooklyn *Daily Eagle* editorship beginning in March of 1846, Walt Whitman's most difficult challenge was reconciling his evolving political convictions with regional and presidential politics. The *Eagle* was the Democratic party organ in Kings County, which gave Whitman responsibility for leadership in political communication only a river ferry crossing away from New York's diverse journalistic interpretations of important developments in Washington. It was the time of territorial expansion to the Pacific and Gulf coasts, which destabilized sectional coalitions sustaining the Union. Whitman lost the position in January of 1848, when he could not reconcile his editorial devotion to free-soil principles with a Democratic party platform moderate on the slave issue. The last straw was his decision to publish a point-by-point rebuttal of a statement by Lewis Cass, the Democratic candidate, instead of the statement itself.

Thomas Brasher's definitive study of Whitman's *Eagle* editorials establishes the scope and competence of Whitman's commentary on the political and social developments of the day. Although Whitman was not a distinguished journalist, he was a serious, innovative political communicator who, like Horace Greeley, began to explore the potential of the penny press as an agent of reform. Whitman framed his interpretations of political events from the perspective of working-class interests, as he understood them, in opposition to commercial greed and the political corruption he blamed on the remaining influence of Old World aristocracies. His *Eagle* editorials display an impressive richness of specific policy analysis and knowledge about everything from local lighting, safety, and health issues to banking, tariffs, and Constitutional theory.

Whereas only a few literary items appeared during Whitman's 1842 *Aurora* editorship, in the *Eagle* Whitman displaced advertisements on the front page with two columns of literary coverage. He published more than one hundred small items on fiction alone. These items are not critical of European influence, but other articles in the *Eagle* display early signs that Whitman was developing a theory of postcolonial literature much like that of the Young America movement advanced by the *Democratic Review*, which had published Whitman's early fiction.

Brasher finds evidence that despite Whitman's occasional reflection of the negrophobia of his time and his fear that abolitionists were undermining the agreement to leave slavery alone in original Southern states, Whitman was beginning to accept the argument that slavery was incompatible with Christianity and the equalitarian ideals of the revolutionary fathers. Brasher also discerns a surprisingly militaristic expansionism in the early months of Whitman's *Eagle* editorship. In a detailed allegorical fable, Whitman likens critics of President Polk's military ventures in Texas to children betraying their own mother, even when some of her property has been "stolen by a neighbor" (qtd. in Brasher 90). The allegory is so elaborate that it seems to preview Whitman's analogical imagination in *Leaves of Grass*.

Although earlier critics expressed puzzlement over the difference between the literary quality of Whitman's journalism and his best poems, some critics now discern important continuities in Whitman's transition from editorialist to poet. In fact, they believe that political embroilments during Whitman's *Eagle* editorship led directly to the literary intentions of *Leaves of Grass*.

At first, Whitman's *Eagle* editorials celebrated party disputes as the lifeblood of self-government and supported the expansionist Democratic presidency of James Polk. By the end of his editorship, however, Whitman was afraid that political parties only heightened prospects for disunion, and he had become so disillusioned by Polk's support for the expansion of slavery that in the first issue of the free-soil newspaper he later started, he asked God to forgive New Yorkers who had helped make Polk president.

By the time he was fired, Whitman's free-soil rhetoric had become strident, and sentences from editorials were being structured in the participial rhythms of free verse. In notebooks from this period, Whitman mentions writing a great book and begins to write lines of experimental poetry on the same subjects that provoked his most impassioned *Eagle* editorials—poetry about slavery and about the survival of the Union and Republicanism as bastions of free labor.

Eagle editorials display Whitman's thinking about subjects to which he returns in his mature poetry. He celebrates the "communion" between writer and reader (qtd. in Brasher 24), covers the fine arts from sculpture to theater and ballet, denounces nativism, argues that capital punishment is "as clearly contrary to the laws of Christ as was wanton murder" (qtd. in Brasher 151), and decries the low wages for women that seem to contribute to prostitution. *Eagle* articles about ferries display Whitman's ambivalence toward this profitable form of mechanized transportation, which, like the growing market economy, was transforming American life.

Of more than eight hundred Whitman items that have been identified from the *Eagle*, some five hundred have been reprinted in modern periodicals or collections of his journalism.

Dennis K. Renner

Bibliography

Allen, Gay Wilson. *The Solitary Singer: A Critical Biography of Walt Whitman.* 1955. Rev. ed. 1967. Chicago: U of Chicago P, 1985.

Bergman, Herbert. "Walt Whitman as a Journalist, 1831–January, 1848." *Journalism Quarterly* 48 (1971): 195–204.

Brasher, Thomas L. *Whitman as Editor of the Brooklyn Daily Eagle.* Detroit: Wayne State UP, 1970.

Erkkila, Betsy. *Whitman the Political Poet.* New York: Oxford UP, 1989.

Reynolds, David S. *Walt Whitman's America: A Cultural Biography.* New York: Knopf, 1995.

Rubin, Joseph Jay. *The Historic Whitman.* University Park: Pennsylvania State UP, 1973.

Thomas, M. Wynn. *The Lunar Light of Whitman's Poetry.* Cambridge, Mass.: Harvard UP, 1987.

See also BROOKLYN *FREEMAN;* DEMOCRATIC PARTY; JOURNALISM, WHITMAN'S; POLITICAL VIEWS; SLAVERY AND ABOLITIONISM

Brooklyn *Daily Times*

Walt Whitman had published two editions of his poems when he returned to full-time editing in 1857 for the Brooklyn *Daily Times,* after an interim of nine years. His return may have been motivated by the need for income, since he had just been sued for defaulting on a loan, but he may also have been attracted by the political match. The *Times* had supported John C. Frémont, the Free Soil party's presidential candidate for whom Whitman had drafted an impassioned campaign pamphlet, "The Eighteenth Presidency!" Whitman edited the *Times* from early spring of 1857 until midsummer 1859, when the evidence suggests that discontent over his viewpoints on church issues led to his resignation or dismissal.

The *Times* editorship, like his other newspaper appointments, placed Whitman in a position to frame significant political developments in the United States as episodes in an ongoing narrative of imperiled self-government. Ten years earlier, as editor for the Brooklyn *Eagle,* Whitman wrote about the defeat of the Wilmot Proviso, which would have prohibited slavery in the territories. Now, writing for the *Times,* he interpreted the dispute over whether Kansas should be a slave or free state as the decisive event in the long struggle between the two contenders for the future of the country—a proslavery Southern "aristocracy" afraid that political power would shift irrevocably away from slave states if the West became free soil, and free-labor advocates who feared the reverse.

In May 1857, within months after he began editing the *Times,* Whitman wrote the editorials "Kansas and the Political Future" and "White Labor, versus Black Labor." He published fifteen major items on developments in Kansas and Washington from the fall of 1857 through November 1858. For the 1858 Congressional election the *Times* editor abandoned the traditional format of a newspaper editorial to publish an election-eve public address he wrote urging voters to reject a Brooklyn congressman who had voted with the Buchanan administration for a proslavery constitution in Kansas. Lines of the address, "To the Voters of the Vth Congressional District" (1 November 1858), were double-spaced, which called attention to the oratorical form. This deliberate rhetorical strategy, like Whitman's notes about becoming a free-soil orator, suggests that he grew increasingly anxious about the political power of slave states during his work for the *Times.*

Scholars disagree about the correlation between the political events Whitman wrote about for the *Times* and the 1860 edition of his poems. Some believe that personal relationships, not politics, inspired the most significant new poems in the third edition of *Leaves,* but biographers have begun to explore connections between dominant themes in Whitman's new poems and the gloomy climate of economic depression and sectional conflict portending disunion while Whitman wrote for the *Times.* Many new poems—some written early in his *Times* editorship, others during or soon after—display themes of despair and manly love or "adhesiveness," the phrenological borrowing Whitman associated with solidarity and political resistance.

Whitman's *Times* articles display the humanitarian concerns of his earlier journalism, but most editorials in the *Times* were factual and less passionate, perhaps because Whitman had lost confidence in the press as an agent of reform. Nonetheless, the responsibility of filling columns for a daily newspaper gave Whitman a chance to comment on most of the political issues of his day—comments that are sometimes paradoxical or contradictory. Whitman published without comment derogatory references to black Americans in Kansas ("Good for Governor Walker!," 6 June 1857), yet he counters the argument of a Southern newspaper that hiring slaves out for pay makes them too independent. If this is so, Whitman observes, then slaves are as capable as white Americans and deserve the rights of citizenship ("A Southerner on Slavery," 27 November 1858). He calls for privatizing canals to avoid political corruption from government ownership ("The State Canals," 27 January 1859), but he favors government regulation to curb profiteering by ferry companies ("Free Ferries," 31 June 1857) and argues that government should pass laws to protect workers from accidents caused by corporate greed in the construction industry ("The Moral of the Remsen Street Accident," 19 October 1857). Whitman expresses sympathy for the poor and unemployed, yet he warns that leaders of "mobs" in the streets are "the real enemies of the poor" ("Aggravations by the Unemployed," 21 November 1857). He approves of universal suffrage in the United States, yet he concedes that in Europe—because paupers are so poorly educated—suffrage would lead to "universal confiscation" ("Universal Suffrage," 7 January 1859).

Although Gay Wilson Allen provides a thorough biographical discussion of Whitman's work for the *Times,* the scholarly examination of Whitman's political thought in *Times* editorials is incomplete. Perhaps because Whitman's stint with the *Times* has often been considered less pertinent to his poetry than his journalism before *Leaves* was first published in 1855, only 125 of more than 900 *Times* items by Whitman have been reprinted.

Dennis K. Renner

Bibliography

Allen, Gay Wilson. *The Solitary Singer: A Critical Biography of Walt Whitman.* 1955. Rev. ed. 1967. Chicago: U of Chicago P, 1985.

Bergman, Herbert. "Walt Whitman as a Journalist, March, 1848–1892." *Journalism Quarterly* 48 (1971): 431–437.

Erkkila, Betsy. *Whitman the Political Poet.* New York: Oxford UP, 1989.

Reynolds, David S. *Walt Whitman's America: A Cultural Biography.* New York: Knopf, 1995.

See also FREE SOIL PARTY; JOURNALISM, WHITMAN'S; *LEAVES OF GRASS,* 1860 EDITION; POLITICAL VIEWS; SLAVERY AND ABOLITIONISM

Brooklyn *Freeman*

In 1848, a few months after Whitman returned to Brooklyn, New York, from his brief sojourn working for the New Orleans *Crescent* in Louisiana, he became the editor of a political newspaper called the Brooklyn *Freeman.* Although Whitman's association with the paper, a free-soil vehicle, lasted only a year, his editorship of the *Freeman* is notable because it includes some of his most passionate antislavery journalism

and marks a transitional period in his life during which his cynicism about American politics began to direct his attention to other areas.

Whitman returned to Brooklyn in June of 1848 in the midst of a particularly turbulent political season. The recent selection of Senator Lewis Cass, a foe of the Wilmot Proviso, as the candidate of the Democratic party had angered those who, like Whitman, staunchly opposed the spread of slavery into the newly acquired territories. As a result, radical Democrats were forming a third party—the Free Soil party—as an alternative. Elected to represent Kings County, Whitman attended the Free Soil convention in Buffalo in early August.

After the convention, Whitman continued his political activities as a member of the Free Soil General Committee for Brooklyn and as the editor of the Brooklyn *Freeman,* the new Free Soil newspaper. Published initially with the financial backing of Whitman's friend, Judge Samuel V. Johnson, the *Freeman* commenced publication as a weekly newspaper on 9 September 1848. The first issue of the paper is the only one that has survived. Asking for the reader's tolerance of its superficial unattractiveness, this issue contains some of Whitman's most fiery and pointed rhetoric regarding slavery. Unlike the more moderate stand on the extension of slavery that he espoused when he was the editor of the Brooklyn *Daily Eagle,* Whitman used the *Freeman* to exclaim: "[W]e shall oppose, under all circumstances, the addition to the Union, in the future, of a single inch of *slave land,* whether in the form of state or territory" (qtd. in Rubin 211).

However, Whitman and the Brooklyn Free-Soilers were dealt a blow the day after the first issue was published when a massive fire swept through the area of town housing the newspaper's office. After losing all of its equipment and supplies in the fire, the *Freeman* was not published again until almost two months later. On 1 November Whitman rushed the newspaper back into print to get in a final word on the upcoming election. Acknowledging the superior power of the more conservative faction of the Democratic party, Whitman positioned the Free-Soilers as the conscience of the party and the nation.

Despite the Free-Soilers' defeat in the 1848 presidential election and again in the spring elections of 1849, Whitman continued to publish the *Freeman,* even converting it to daily publication in May (again with the financial help of Judge Johnson). In June, looking ahead to the next presidential election, Whitman sought to boost the candidacy of a politician whose principles and integrity he admired: Senator Thomas Hart Benton of Missouri. Whitman put Benton's name on the masthead of the newspaper and in his editorials lauded Benton's achievements and potential.

Whitman's optimism was short-lived, however. By early September, it had become clear that most members of the radical wing of the Democratic party were not as determined as he to hold fast to their principles. Unwilling to compromise his integrity, Whitman published his resignation from the editorship on 11 September 1849. Predictably, Whitman's departure from the *Freeman* was interpreted by his friends as confirmation of his strong character and by his enemies as further evidence of his weakness.

Jon Panish

Bibliography
Allen, Gay Wilson. *The Solitary Singer: A Critical Biography of Walt Whitman.* 1955. Rev. ed. 1967. Chicago: U of Chicago P, 1985.
Brasher, Thomas L. *Whitman as Editor of the Brooklyn Daily Eagle.* Detroit: Wayne State UP, 1970.
Reynolds, David S. *Walt Whitman's America: A Cultural Biography.* New York: Knopf, 1995.
Rubin, Joseph Jay. *The Historic Whitman.* University Park: Pennsylvania State UP, 1973.

See also BROOKLYN, NEW YORK; BUFFALO FREE SOIL CONVENTION; DEMOCRATIC PARTY; FREE SOIL PARTY; JOURNALISM, WHITMAN'S; POLITICAL VIEWS; SLAVERY AND ABOLITIONISM; WILMOT PROVISO

Brooklyn, New York

Walt Whitman lived for almost three decades in Brooklyn, New York, longer than his association with any other city, and although the word itself appears relatively few times in *Leaves of Grass*—only nine times, compared to forty-six mentions of Manhattan—Brooklyn held a crucial place in the poet's memory and imagination. If Manhattan signified culture to Whitman, and Long Island meant the beauties of nature, Brooklyn was his home.

Whitman spent his earliest years on Long Island and moved to Brooklyn only in 1823, but throughout his life he remained proud of an older family connection to Brooklyn. In letters and essays, as well as in "The Sleepers" and "The Centenarian's Story," Whitman recalled George Washington's battle of Brooklyn, during which a great-uncle supposedly died. *Specimen Days* nostalgically records the day in 1823 when the Whitmans moved from Long Island to a house on Front Street, a waterfront area where, as the poet put it in *Good-Bye My Fancy,* the young Whitman "tramp'd freely about the neighborhood and town" (*Complete* 1282). In the years after their arrival the family lived in various homes.

The Brooklyn that Whitman knew as a child was largely rural. Incorporated in 1816, it changed its status from village to city only in 1834, and did not become one of the boroughs of New York City until 1898. In the 1820s Brooklyn's population numbered only seven thousand, and there were no streetlights or sidewalks, no fire or police department, no water, garbage, or sewage services. Although Whitman later remembered the Brooklyn of his childhood as "one huge farm and garden" (*Whitman's New York* 147), the area where the Whitmans lived, near the port and ferry terminals, was chaotic and dirty, densely populated with white and African-American sailors, carpenters, butchers, clerks, street vendors, artisans, waiters, and bartenders.

Starting in 1825 Whitman attended Brooklyn's first public school, District School 1, at the corner of Adams and Concord streets, and it was in that year that during dedication ceremonies for the Apprentices' Library at the corner of Henry and Cranberry streets he was embraced by General Lafayette. It was also in Brooklyn that the youthful Whitman saw two more figures who would later play an important role in his writings: the preacher Elias Hicks and President Andrew Jackson. In the 1820s Whitman also attended Sunday school, though not regular services, at St. Ann's, a new Episcopalian church at the corner of Sands and Washington streets. Whitman left school around 1830 to work as an office boy for local businesses, including two lawyers and a doctor. The next year Whitman became an apprentice at the Fulton Street print shop of the *Long Island Patriot.* During this time Whitman lived with his family or as a boarder at various residences on Henry, Liberty, and Fulton streets.

In the early 1830s Whitman began spending more of his free time across the East River, in Manhattan. Even though Brooklyn's population had by this time doubled, Manhattan was indisputably the center of the region's culture and nightlife. In Manhattan, accessible by a quick, inexpensive, exciting ferry ride, Whitman introduced himself to the worlds of music, theater, and art. In 1836 Whitman followed his family back to Long Island, and it was not until August 1845 that they returned to Brooklyn, to a house on Prince Street. The next month he began working at the *Long Island Star.* This job initiated what would be Whitman's second of a long series of involvements with Brooklyn newspapers, including the Brooklyn *Daily Eagle,* on Fulton Street, and the Brooklyn *Freeman,* on Orange Street and later at the corner of Middagh and Fulton streets. During this time Whitman lived alone or with his family in a variety of houses—including one on Myrtle Street, where Whitman in addition to his newspaper activities ran a bookstore and print shop.

The Brooklyn in which Whitman lived and about which he wrote in the years before the Civil War was in the midst of an enormous growth spurt—one that he and his family tried to capitalize on in an endless series of real estate deals, which accounts for their nomadic existence. The city's population grew from 40,000 in 1845 to 100,000 in 1850 and to 250,000 in 1855. Then the third-largest city in the United States, Brooklyn had absorbed the villages of Bushwick, Greenpoint, and Williamsburg and supported 27 public schools, 13 ferries to Manhattan, and 130 churches. In his newspaper articles and editorials from the 1840s and 1850s Whitman celebrated Brooklyn's growth, especially as opposed to what he called the "Gomorra" across the river; he detailed minute changes in street life, parks, schools, shops, churches, and politics, all of which he noticed and discussed during his daily strolls. In these writings Whitman also lamented the relentless urbanization that meant the loss of trees and increased urban squalor.

It was while Whitman was working as an editor and later during the early 1850s as a house builder in Brooklyn that he assembled the notebook fragments that became the 1855 edition of *Leaves of Grass.* The building in which he helped the Rome brothers set type for this first edition was still standing on the corner of Cranberry and Fulton streets as of the early 1960s. During the mid-1850s Whitman was living with his family

on Ryerson Street, in a house that still exists, but because the Whitmans bought and sold properties so often in an effort to capitalize on the city's surging real estate market, it is not clear where Emerson's famed December 1855 visit to Whitman took place. Although history records visits by Bronson Alcott and Henry David Thoreau later in the decade as adventurous trips into the working class hinterlands of New York, in the 1850s Whitman counted among his Brooklyn friends such renowned artists as Henry Kirke Brown, Frederick A. Chapman, Gabriel Harrison, Charles L. Heyde, Walter Libbey, Jesse Talbot, and John Quincy Adams Ward.

From 1857 until 1862 Whitman worked as the editor of the Brooklyn *Daily Times,* on Grand Street and later on South Seventh Street, and then at the Brooklyn *Daily Standard,* where he published his most extended writing on Brooklyn. "Brooklyniana" appeared in twenty-five installments from 8 June 1861 through 1 November 1862 and consisted of what he called "authentic reminiscences," or "gossiping chronicles" (*Whitman's New York* 3, 87). The series, which was reprinted as a volume called *Walt Whitman's New York* in 1963, informally tells the social history of Brooklyn, with sections including Manhattan and Long Island, and consistently presents Brooklyn as a place central to the story of the United States.

In 1862 Whitman left Brooklyn for Washington, D.C., never to settle in his beloved hometown again. He made annual visits—he was at his mother's home in Brooklyn when he heard the news of President Lincoln's assassination—until the early 1870s, when his poor health made travel difficult. Nonetheless, he returned to the area in 1878, 1879, and 1881, and lectured in New York in 1887.

The place of Brooklyn in Whitman's poetic imagination remains largely implicit. More than half of Brooklyn's appearances in *Leaves of Grass* pertain to its liminal status, either as one terminal of the ferry to Manhattan in "Crossing Brooklyn Ferry" or as the namesake of the Brooklyn Bridge in "Song of the Exposition." "The Sleepers" briefly remembers the battle of Brooklyn, as does "The Centenarian's Story," in which an elderly veteran watching Civil War recruits training below a hill in Washington Park recalls the earlier Revolutionary War battle. Here Whitman presents Brooklyn as a living part of American history, a part perhaps not appreciated enough in the 1860s ("Centenarian's Story").

Jonathan Gill

Bibliography

Allen, Gay Wilson. *The Solitary Singer: A Critical Biography of Walt Whitman.* 1955. Rev. ed. 1967. Chicago: U of Chicago P, 1985.

Berman, Paul. "Walt Whitman's Ghost." *The New Yorker* 12 June 1995: 98–104.

Brasher, Thomas L. *Whitman as Editor of the Brooklyn Daily Eagle.* Detroit: Wayne State UP, 1970.

Brouwer, Norman. "'Cross from Shore to Shore': Whitman's Brooklyn Ferry." *Seaport* 26 (1992): 64–67.

Keller, James. "Brooklyniana." *Seaport* 26 (1992): 70–71.

Reynolds, David S. *Walt Whitman's America: A Cultural Biography.* New York: Knopf, 1995.

Rubin, Joseph Jay. *The Historic Whitman.* University Park: Pennsylvania State UP, 1973.

Whitman, Walt. *Complete Poetry and Collected Prose.* Ed. Justin Kaplan. New York: Library of America, 1982.

———. *Walt Whitman's New York: From Manhattan to Montauk.* Ed. Henry M. Christman. New York: Macmillan, 1963.

See also BROOKLYN *DAILY EAGLE;* BROOKLYN *DAILY TIMES;* BROOKLYN *FREEMAN;* "CENTENARIAN'S STORY, THE"; "CROSSING BROOKLYN FERRY"; FERRIES AND OMNIBUSES; HICKS, ELIAS; JACKSON, ANDREW; LAFAYETTE, MARQUIS DE; *LEAVES OF GRASS;* PRINTING BUSINESS; ROME BROTHERS, THE; "SLEEPERS, THE"; *SPECIMEN DAYS*

Brown, Lewis Kirk (1843–1926)

Lewis (aka Lew or Lewy) K. Brown left his family's farm near Elkton, Maryland, to join the Union army. Walt Whitman met him in February 1863 in the Armory Square Hospital in Washington, D.C., where Brown was recovering from a wound in the left leg, which he had received in a battle near Rappahannock Station in August 1862.

His affectionate nature made him receptive to Whitman's nurturing ministrations, and it was through Brown that Whitman formed close attachments to several other wounded soldiers. Whitman reported in letters to Brown's friend Sergeant Thomas P. Sawyer that Brown gave him a kiss "half a minute long" (Whitman 91)

and that he hoped to live with both Sawyer and Brown after the war was over, suggesting that his interest in the two young soldiers (among others) may have been more than paternal. Although his feelings for Sawyer may have been even stronger than those he felt for Brown, Whitman's letters to Brown say the sight of Brown's face was "welcomer than all," and he refers to Brown as "my darling" (Whitman 119).

On 5 January 1864 Brown's leg was amputated five inches below the knee, and Whitman spent two nights on a cot near his bed to see him through the painful experience. Brown left the army in August 1864, and a year later he was employed as a clerk in the Treasury Department. As late as 1867, Whitman wrote to Hiram Sholes that Brown was well and that he saw him often. In 1880 Brown became Chief of the Paymaster's Division and remained in that position until his retirement in 1915.

Arnie Kantrowitz

Bibliography

Allen, Gay Wilson. *The Solitary Singer: A Critical Biography of Walt Whitman.* 1955. Rev. ed. 1967. Chicago: U of Chicago P, 1985.

Shively, Charley, ed. *Calamus Lovers: Walt Whitman's Working Class Camerados.* San Francisco: Gay Sunshine, 1987.

Whitman, Walt. *The Correspondence.* Ed. Edwin Haviland Miller. Vol. 1. New York: New York UP, 1961.

See also CIVIL WAR NURSING; SAWYER, THOMAS P.

Bryant, William Cullen (1794–1878)

William Cullen Bryant was perhaps the most famous American poet in the first half of the nineteenth century, and, as editor of the New York *Evening Post* for almost fifty years, one of America's leading newspaper editors. Bryant was an accomplished poet at an early age, publishing his first poems at age thirteen and writing his important poems "To a Waterfowl" and "Thanatopsis" by age twenty-one. But poetry would always be an avocation for Bryant. He spent the first part of his professional life as a lawyer, until he became the editor of the *New York Review* in 1825. Two years later he began working for the *Evening Post* and in 1829 became its editor-in-chief.

During this time, Bryant had been steadily establishing himself as America's premier poet, publishing his first book, *Poems,* in 1821, and writing a series of influential essays on American poetry. Though Bryant's overall output is not large, he continued to write poems for the rest of his life, publishing his last book of poems at age seventy and a translation of the *Iliad* and *Odyssey* in his late seventies.

As editor of the *Evening Post,* Bryant's consistent editorial policies and his refusal to take sensational positions helped to forge a long-lived and widely respected newspaper in a time when the average newspaper specialized in the sensational and lasted less than a year. Under Bryant, the *Post* became a strong supporter of the abolitionist movement and of the fledgling Republican party.

Bryant was important to the young Whitman because of his dual position as leading poet and leading newspaper editor of New York. While writing for the Brooklyn *Eagle* in 1847, Whitman called Bryant "one of the best poets in the world!" (qtd. in Brown 325). Many of Whitman's early poems echo Bryant's best work, and while Whitman and Bryant would part stylistically, some of the older poet's themes, particularly his notion of the democracy of the dead articulated in "Thanatopsis," would become important focal points for the younger poet.

But as important as Bryant was as a role model for Whitman, he was more important as a figure with whom Whitman could contrast himself. Bryant's editorial voice was reasoned and restrained, while the young newspaper editor Walter Whitman often wrote fiery diatribes, designed to stir up his readers. Years later, the image-conscious Whitman would point to two pictures, one of the solid, well-dressed Bryant and the other of the casual loafer Whitman, and offer them as a study in contrast.

Andrew C. Higgins

Bibliography

Brown, Charles H. *William Cullen Bryant.* New York: Scribner's, 1971.

Bryant, William Cullen. *The Letters of William Cullen Bryant.* Ed. William Cullen Bryant II and Thomas G. Voss. 2 vols. New York: Fordham UP, 1975.

———. *The Poetical Works of William Cullen Bryant.* Ed. Parke Godwin. 2 vols. New York: Appleton, 1883.

———. *The Prose Writings of William Cullen Bryant.* Ed. Parke Godwin. 2 vols. New York: Appleton, 1884.

McLean, Albert F. *William Cullen Bryant.* Updated ed. Boston: Twayne, 1989.

Price, Kenneth M. *Whitman and Tradition: The Poet in His Century.* New Haven: Yale UP, 1990.

Ringe, Donald A. "Bryant and Whitman: A Study in Artistic Affinities." *Boston University Studies in English* 2 (1956): 85–94.

See also JOURNALISM, WHITMAN'S; NEW YORK *EVENING POST;* READING, WHITMAN'S

Buchanan, Robert (1841–1901)

Born in Aversall, Lancashire, poet and critic Robert Buchanan grew up in Scotland and attended the University of Glasgow. He became acquainted with Dickens, George Eliot, and Browning, but ran afoul of the Pre-Raphaelites with his article "The Fleshly School of Poetry," appearing in the *Contemporary Review* of October 1871, in which he attacked the eroticism in their work. Dante G. Rossetti and Algernon Charles Swinburne were his particular targets, both of whom ironically also admired Whitman at that time. Swinburne, who later wrote some strongly deprecating remarks about Whitman, also unleashed his vitriol on Buchanan, calling him a "hack rhymester" (qtd. in Stephens 795). Though Buchanan later apologized to Rossetti, whom he never met, this article irreparably damaged his career.

Lamenting the lack of his critical and popular reception in America, Whitman wrote to Rudolf Schmidt of Copenhagen in January 1872 that "Robert Buchanan, Swinburne, the great English and Dublin colleges [Edward Dowden], affectionately receive me and doughtily champion me" (Whitman 1001). In stark contrast to his condemnation of the "fleshly" Pre-Raphaelites, Buchanan regarded Whitman as a moral poet and admired his pioneering spirit. He solicited from friends funds to send to Whitman in 1876 and 1877, and in 1884 he traveled to Camden and met Whitman, forming a lasting friendship with him and calling him in 1898 "Socrates in Camden" (qtd. in Cassidy 32).

Philip W. Leon

Bibliography

Browning, D.C., comp. *Everyman's Dictionary of Literary Biography*. New York: Dutton, 1969.

Cassidy, John A. *Robert W. Buchanan*. New York: Twayne, 1973.

Stephens, James, Edwin L. Beck, and Royall H. Snow, eds. *Victorian and Later English Poets*. 1934. New York: American, 1949.

Whitman, Walt. *Complete Poetry and Selected Prose and Letters*. 1938. Ed. Emory Holloway. London: Nonesuch, 1967.

See also British Isles, Whitman in the; Dowden, Edward; Swinburne, Algernon Charles

Bucke, Richard Maurice (1837–1901)

Bucke was a Canadian physician and student of the human mind who became one of Whitman's most devoted friends and supporters in the poet's later years. He was Whitman's first biographer, and his book *Cosmic Consciousness* (1901), which features Whitman and Bucke's messianic view of him, has won its author a minor but enduring fame.

After several years of wandering, work, and adventure—including a battle with Shoshone Indians and a trek through the Rocky Mountains in winter that cost him one of his feet and part of the other due to frostbite—Bucke received an inheritance which allowed him to attend McGill University Medical School. Further study in Europe followed. Bucke then returned to Canada, married, and for several years lived the life of a small town doctor. In 1876 he was appointed superintendent of a hospital for the insane, his profession from then on. He gained a reputation as one of the leading "alienists" of his day, and his approach to treatment of the mentally ill was progressive, deemphasizing alcohol, drugs, and physical restraints in favor of useful work and a more healthful living environment.

Always a wide-ranging reader, Bucke first encountered Whitman's work in 1867. He read Whitman's poetry with intensity and fascination for several years, committing much of it to memory. (It has been alleged that eventually Bucke knew all of *Leaves of Grass* by heart.) One evening in 1872 Whitman's poetry led to one of the key experiences of Bucke's life. After an evening of reading poetry (William Wordsworth, John Keats, Percy Bysshe Shelley, and especially Walt Whitman) aloud with friends, he experienced an overwhelming state of illumination and joy; he felt himself literally surrounded with light from an inner fire. The man of science with strong introspective and metaphysical leanings was from this time on a mystic as well.

Something similar occurred when he finally met Whitman in person. In Philadelphia on professional business, Bucke crossed the river to Camden and looked the poet up. Though their visit was outwardly unremarkable, after parting Bucke found himself in a state of "mental exaltation." This feeling continued for the next six weeks, and Bucke's devotion to Whitman continued for the rest of his life.

Many people have judged Whitman extraordinary in a variety of ways, but none has made a larger claim for him than Bucke. He believed that Whitman was not only a great writer but a breakthrough in humanity's psychic and moral evolution comparable to Buddha or Jesus; in fact, Bucke felt that Whitman surpassed even these. Bucke dedicated *Man's Moral Nature* (1879), his first book on his theory of evolving consciousness, "to the man of all men past and present that I have known who has the most exalted moral nature—Walt Whitman."

Bucke's biography of Whitman (1883) was an unconventional book, as much an anthology of documents about the poet as a biography. It was also a collaboration; Whitman advised throughout, revised Bucke's text, and wrote significant portions of the book himself. Always uncomfortable with Bucke's inclination to view him as a demigod, Whitman's reworking of Bucke's text removed such claims, emphasizing instead the robustness of his personality. Bucke continued to devote much time and energy to writing, editing, and overseeing the publication of Whitman materials, including poetry, prose, correspondence, and criticism. Along with Horace Traubel and Thomas Harned, he served as Whitman's literary executor. *Cosmic Consciousness* was in a sense the book that Whitman would not let him write in the biography, because it does not merely present Bucke's theory of moral and spiritual evolution but also uses Whitman as central example.

Besides his literary efforts on Whitman's behalf, Bucke was also a medical consultant throughout the last years of the poet's life. Their correspondence includes a steady stream of advice from Bucke, who also treated Whitman directly when he visited. He was on hand during a crisis in 1888, and Whitman credited Bucke with having brought him through. Bucke's role was not just that of a self-appointed disciple and intellectual/mystical apostle; he was also an extremely dependable, knowledgeable, and practical man, and a loyal friend.

In 1880 Whitman spent the summer with Bucke at his home in Canada. His observations of religious services at the asylum are recorded in a haunting entry in *Specimen Days* (1882). They traveled together down the St. Lawrence River, and the following year, in preparation for the biography, they visited places important in Whitman's earlier years in Long Island and Manhattan. The 1880 visit was the basis for an engaging but factually unreliable Canadian feature film, *Beautiful Dreamers* (1992), with Rip Torn as Whitman and Colm Feore as Bucke.

Howard Nelson

Bibliography

Bucke, Richard Maurice. *Calamus: A Series of Letters Written During the Years 1868–1880 by Walt Whitman to a Young Friend (Peter Doyle).* Boston: Laurens Maynard, 1897.
———. *Cosmic Consciousness: A Study in the Evolution of the Human Mind.* 1901. New York: Dutton, 1969.
———. *Man's Moral Nature: An Essay.* New York: Putnam, 1879.
———. *Richard Maurice Bucke, Medical Mystic: Letters of Dr. Bucke to Walt Whitman and His Friends.* Ed. Artem Lozynsky. Detroit: Wayne State UP, 1977.
———. *Walt Whitman.* 1883. New York: Gordon, 1972.
———. *The Wound Dresser: A Series of Letters Written from the Hospitals in Washington.* Boston: Small, Maynard, 1898.
Coyne, James H. *Richard Maurice Bucke: A Sketch.* Rev. ed. Toronto: Saunders, 1923.
Jaffe, Harold. "Bucke's *Walt Whitman:* A Collaboration." *Walt Whitman Review* 15 (1969): 190–194.
Shortt, S.E.D. "The Myth of a Canadian Boswell: Dr. R.M. Bucke and Walt Whitman." *Canadian Bulletin of Medical History* 1 (1984): 55–70.
Traubel, Horace L., Richard Maurice Bucke, and Thomas B. Harned, eds. *In Re Walt Whitman.* Philadelphia: McKay, 1893.
Whitman, Walt. *Specimen Days.* Vol. 1 of *Prose Works 1892.* Ed. Floyd Stovall. New York: New York UP, 1963.

See also BIOGRAPHIES; CANADA, WHITMAN'S RECEPTION IN; CANADA, WHITMAN'S VISIT TO; COSMIC CONSCIOUSNESS; LONDON, ONTARIO, CANADA

Buffalo Free Soil Convention (1848)

Held on 9–10 August 1848, the national Free Soil convention in Buffalo, New York, brought together delegates from nineteen states and molded the diffuse elements of the free soil movement into a short-lived political party, whose main goal was to prevent the extension of slavery into the Western territories. Democrats, Whigs, Liberty Men, and abolitionists rallied around the slogan "Free Soil, Free Speech, Free Labor, and Free Men" (Blue 74), nominating Martin Van Buren for president and Charles Francis Adams for vice-president. While the adopted party platform renounced the extension of slavery, it did not question the existence of slavery in the South or demand full civil rights for blacks.

Walt Whitman attended the Buffalo convention as one of fourteen delegates from Brooklyn. As editor of the Brooklyn *Daily Eagle* between March 1846 and January 1848, Whitman had repeatedly spoken out in favor of the 1846 Wilmot Proviso, the legislative attempt to keep slavery out of any new territories acquired from Mexico. Whitman viewed the extension of slavery as detrimental to American democracy and as unfair competition for white workers eager to settle in the West. Like many other Free-Soilers, he was not immediately concerned about slavery as a moral dilemma. Upon return from Buffalo, Whitman was appointed a member of the Free Soil General Committee for Brooklyn and began editing the Brooklyn *Weekly Freeman,* a Free Soil paper established with the help of Judge Samuel V. Johnson. Whitman stayed with the *Freeman* from September 1848 until September 1849, when he resigned in reaction to a political compromise between New York Free-Soilers and Democrats. Although Whitman ceased being active on behalf of the Free Soil party after his resignation, his interest in free-soil principles continued. On 14 August 1852 Whitman wrote a letter to

Senator John Parker Hale of New Hampshire, urging him to accept the presidential nomination of the Free-Soilers, who now campaigned under the name of Free Democrats.

Elmar S. Lueth

Bibliography

Blue, Frederick J. *The Free Soilers: Third Party Politics, 1848–54.* Urbana: U of Illinois P, 1973.

Dyer, Oliver. *Phonographic Report of the Proceedings of the National Free Soil Convention at Buffalo, N.Y.* Buffalo: Derby, 1848.

Erkkila, Betsy. *Whitman the Political Poet.* New York: Oxford UP, 1989.

Klammer, Martin. *Whitman, Slavery, and the Emergence of "Leaves of Grass."* University Park: Pennsylvania State UP, 1995.

Rubin, Joseph Jay. *The Historic Whitman.* University Park: Pennsylvania State UP, 1973.

See also BROOKLYN *FREEMAN*; FREE SOIL PARTY; POLITICAL VIEWS; SLAVERY AND ABOLITIONISM; WILMOT PROVISO

Burns, Anthony (1834–1862)

Anthony Burns was a runaway slave who escaped from his owner in Virginia, fled to Boston, and found employment. His previous owner, upon learning of Burns's new life, had Burns arrested and jailed in Boston on 24 May 1854 under the auspices of the Fugitive Slave Law. Massachusetts abolitionists were enraged, and Thomas Wentworth Higginson even tried to break Burns out of the Boston jail. The rescue attempt failed, and a thousand federal troops conducted Burns in chains through the streets of Boston to the ship which took him back to slavery in Virginia. Two years later Northern sympathizers purchased and freed him; they then sent him to Oberlin College to study for the ministry, after which he became a Baptist minister in Canada. His health had been bad for years, and he died at the age of only twenty-eight.

The government's handling of the Burns incident motivated Whitman to write "A Boston Ballad (1854)" and to include it the next year in the first edition of *Leaves of Grass.* Although he does not mention Burns by name in the poem, Whitman focuses on the government's violation of individual liberty.

Linda K. Walker

Bibliography

Campbell, Stanley W. *The Slave Catchers: Enforcement of the Fugitive Slave Law, 1850–1860.* Chapel Hill: U of North Carolina P, 1970.

Reynolds, David S. *Walt Whitman's America: A Cultural Biography.* New York: Knopf, 1995.

Rossbach, Jeffrey. *Ambivalent Conspirators: John Brown, The Secret Six, and a Theory of Slave Violence.* Philadelphia: U of Pennsylvania P, 1982.

See also "BOSTON BALLAD (1854), A"; HIGGINSON, THOMAS WENTWORTH; SLAVERY AND ABOLITIONISM

Burroughs, John (1837–1921) and Ursula (1836–1917)

John Burroughs first met Whitman in 1864, while Burroughs was in Washington, D.C., looking for work. After his marriage to Ursula North in 1857, Burroughs foundered financially. Against the wishes of his conventional wife, who had grown up in affluence as the daughter of a prosperous New York farmer, Burroughs hoped to become a writer, thus his interest in Walt Whitman. In 1862 he had frequently visited Pfaff's beer cellar, a bohemian watering hole and the center of literary life in Manhattan. There Burroughs championed Whitman in literary arguments, anticipating at every moment a meeting with the poet himself.

That meeting did not take place at Pfaff's, but rather by chance on the streets of Washington, D.C., as Whitman made his way to an army hospital to tend wounded soldiers. Always trying to recruit fresh help, Whitman invited Burroughs to come along. In an earlier desperate attempt at employment, Burroughs had briefly worked on a crew that buried Union soldiers whose bodies were transported to Washington. Nursing the horribly wounded was as repugnant to Burroughs as handling mangled corpses, and he soon left his job in the hospitals. But Burroughs and Whitman, who quickly began calling him "Jack," had struck up an enduring friendship.

Whitman encouraged Burroughs to develop a literature of nature that was scientifically precise in its observations and factuality and at the same time poetic in its praise of nature. Under Whitman's guidance, Burroughs developed as a writer and began to sell pieces to magazines while working as a clerk for the Department of Treasury and, later, as a bank examiner. Burroughs in turn influenced Whitman by sharpening Whitman's eye for precise detail in observing nature.

Whitman became a regular guest at the Burroughs's house for Sunday breakfast. He befriended Ursula, nicknaming her "Ursa." The Burroughs's marriage had been strained from the outset by sexual incompatibility; Whitman attempted to reconcile the two.

Even though their courtship had been completely chaste, John's attraction to the slender, attractive Ursula North had been powerfully erotic, perhaps even solely erotic. On their wedding night, however, the devoutly religious Ursula portentously fell to her knees at the side of the bed they would share for the first time and urged John to join her in prayer. After five troubled years of marriage, Ursula consulted ministers in Olive, her hometown in the Catskills, and concluded that her husband's sexual demands were immoral and intolerable. She prescribed a separation of two months, July and August 1862, so that John could learn the value of chastity. The separation, however, lasted until February 1864, by which time John had learned not the value of chastity but rather the ease of finding accommodating female company. Even after their reunion, John remained unfaithful.

Whitman sided with Ursula. He told John that his "wantonness" was the one flaw in an otherwise beautiful and admirable character. As for Ursula's sexual unresponsiveness, Whitman blamed it on John's failure sufficiently to inspire Ursula to love him. Whitman frequently visited the lonely Ursula when John's job as bank examiner required him to travel, as it often did. In 1873 Whitman's visits suddenly ceased because of the stroke he suffered; Ursula, in turn, then became a frequent visitor to the ailing poet, bringing him food and taking him out for carriage rides. She even offered him a room in the Burroughs's Washington home at 1332 V Street, which offer Whitman appreciated but declined.

Burroughs's first work on Whitman was *Notes on Walt Whitman* (1867). The work was so extensively revised and rewritten by Whitman himself that it should properly be considered a collaborative effort. In it we see Whitman

shaping his public personality, even at the expense of accurate biography; for example, Whitman is alleged to have traveled to the western United States, although in fact his first such trip took place decades later.

In *Whitman, A Study* (1896), his second major work on the poet, Burroughs is, as always, the Whitman disciple, but he turns his naturalist's eye on Whitman as an original specimen: a poet whose work transcends the usual categories of art, who is as much the prophet as the poet. Whitman was commonly attacked for his lack of artistic polish and literary refinement; Burroughs and others defended him against these charges by in turn attacking the limitations of "the literary."

In 1901, nine years after Whitman's death, John Burroughs met the great love of his life, Clara Barrus, who was a physician affiliated with the state psychiatric hospital at Middletown, New York. She wrote Burroughs an admiring letter, and he invited her to visit him at Slabsides, his "hermit's retreat" about a mile from Riverby, the home he had built on the banks of the Hudson. Barrus was thirty-three, Burroughs sixty-four; he referred to her as "Whitmanesque," a "new woman" who was his intellectual equal as well as his lover. She became his live-in companion after Ursula's death in 1917, and then his literary executor and biographer.

Carmine Sarracino

Bibliography

Barrus, Clara. *Whitman and Burroughs, Comrades*. Boston: Houghton Mifflin, 1931.

Burroughs, John. *Birds and Poets*. Boston: Houghton Mifflin, 1877.

———. *Notes on Walt Whitman as Poet and Person*. New York: American News, 1867.

———. "The Poet of the Cosmos." *Accepting the Universe*. By Burroughs. New York: Wise, 1924. 316–328.

———. *Whitman, A Study*. 1896. St. Clair Shores, Mich.: Scholarly, 1970.

Renehan, Edward J., Jr. *John Burroughs, An American Naturalist*. Post Mills, Vt.: Chelsea Green, 1992.

Wyman, Mary A. "Burroughs and Whitman—Naturalist and Mystic." *The Lure for Feeling in the Creative Process*. By Wyman. New York: Philosophical Library, 1960. 104–128.

See also BARRUS, CLARA; HUDSON RIVER; NATURE; RIVERBY; SCHOLARSHIP, TRENDS IN WHITMAN; WASHINGTON, D.C.

"By Blue Ontario's Shore" (1856)

One of the most heavily revised compositions in all of *Leaves of Grass,* this long poem lays out the central features of Whitman's democratic idealism and describes the poet's role in fostering it. The poem first appears in 1856, liberally borrowing key passages from the prose Preface to the first edition (1855) and serving a similar purpose as a manifesto for the book as a whole. Following the mutations of "By Blue Ontario's Shore" over the years offers revealing glimpses into the refinement of Whitman's Americanist thought—particularly as it responds to the trauma of the Civil War—as well as the evolution of his style.

The original 1856 title, "Poem of Many In One," alludes to the national motto that Whitman incorporated into his philosophy of composition. ("E Pluribus Unum" was another designation he considered for it.) Just as the Union forms one political entity out of the separate states, *Leaves of Grass* fuses many poems into one interrelated whole. As the poem explains, the bard of democracy is entrusted with the task of linking together the diverse individuals who make up this young "Nation announcing itself" (section 2) by celebrating the greatness of their daily lives. The poet is the glue that holds this American mosaic together; he is the "equalizer," the "arbiter of the diverse" (section 10). As he imagines himself literally "incarnating this land" (section 6), stretching to accommodate its rapid growth across the continent, Whitman characteristically uses the human body as a metaphor for the body politic. This organic relationship between the poet and the country he has "affectionately . . . absorbed" (section 13) is expressed through sexual imagery as well; both creative and procreative energies represent the larger force that unifies part and whole.

The poem's reappearance as the first of the "Chants Democratic" in the third edition (1860) suggests its continuing importance as a prefatory statement of purpose. By 1867, however, it undergoes a dramatic change of tone, reflecting the intervening events of the Civil War, which shattered Whitman's ideal of a unified nation. Now titled "As I sat Alone by Blue Ontario's Shore," it begins not with a celebration of America's greatness, but with the somber image of a solitary poet musing upon "the dead that return no more." Turning for comfort to the "Mother" of democracy, he confronts the devastating legacy of the war by railing against the "enemies" that sought to destroy the Union. However, he goes on to peer prophetically into the future, envisioning democracy "with spreading mantle covering the world" (section 17). The geographical growth of the nation will be accompanied by a more mature spiritual understanding of "the great Idea" (sections 10, 11, 14, 20)—democratic individualism. As its ultimate position following the "Memories of President Lincoln" section indicates, the poem in its final version responds to the wounds of the war by placing recent events within a larger, prophetic perspective of the nation's destiny.

Perhaps because of its indebtedness to the Preface (especially evident in sections 5–6 and 9–12), critics have divided sharply on the merit of "Blue Ontario" as a work of poetry. Some New Critics, notably Howard Waskow, complain that there is too much message and not enough music in it. But as Thomas Crawley points out, Whitman here perfects many of the techniques, such as the catalogue and the incantatory phrase, that are hallmarks of *Leaves.* Moreover, the genesis of the poem suggests a radical fluidity between prose and poetry that reinforces Whitman's importance as an innovative user of language. (On the other hand, some of the revisions to "Blue Ontario" also indicate an increasing linguistic conservatism, as he tones down both its strident nationalism and its boldly sexual images.)

The most useful readings of this poem, such as those of M. Wynn Thomas, Betsy Erkkila, and James E. Miller, Jr., grow out of the idea that Whitman's poetics are inseparable from his understanding of political, spiritual, and bodily union. Along with "Starting from Paumanok," "Song of the Broad-Axe," and "Song of Myself," "By Blue Ontario's Shore" stands as a major statement of Whitman's philosophy of democratic individualism.

Kirsten Silva Gruesz

Bibliography

Crawley, Thomas Edward. *The Structure of "Leaves of Grass."* Austin: U of Texas P, 1970.

Culbert, Gary A. "Whitman's Revisions of 'By Blue Ontario's Shore.'" *Walt Whitman Review* 23 (1977): 35–45.

Erkkila, Betsy. *Whitman the Political Poet.* New York: Oxford UP, 1989.

Miller, James E., Jr. *"Leaves of Grass":
America's Lyric-Epic of Self and Democracy.* New York: Twayne, 1992.
Thomas, M. Wynn. *The Lunar Light of
Whitman's Poetry.* Cambridge, Mass.:
Harvard UP, 1987.
Waskow, Howard J. *Whitman: Explorations
in Form.* Chicago: U of Chicago P, 1966.

See also DEMOCRACY; POETIC THEORY; PREFACE TO *LEAVES OF GRASS*, 1855 EDITION

"By That Long Scan of Waves" (1885)

First published in August of 1885 with seven other poems in the group *Fancies at Navesink,* "By That Long Scan of Waves" was later incorporated into "Sands at Seventy" in the 1889 printing of *Leaves of Grass.* The poem serves as a summation of Whitman's career and poses a tableau wherein the light and dark playing on the "long scan of waves" recalls for the poet all the positive and negative experiences of his life.

As in other poems, Whitman uses the image of the sea with its continuous roll and flow to suggest both the passage of time and timelessness. Whitman's use of sea imagery also suggests, as Mark Bauerlein observes, a primordial mother figure that unites birth and death in an endless cycle. Thus, in "Waves" each wave recalls a "by-gone phase" of the poet's life: youth, joy, travels, studies, the Civil War. Reflecting on his life with "old age at hand," Whitman fears that despite his "grand ideal," the totality remains "a nothing." The "grand ideal" may refer to *Leaves of Grass,* with the "scan" of the waves suggesting poetic meter. Even in 1889, the dominant literary establishment still rejected Whitman's poetry, and in "A Backward Glance O'er Travel'd Roads" (1888) he laments the public's "anger and contempt" (Whitman 562).

Whitman consoles himself in "Waves" with the certainty that, while his efforts may be unappreciated, they are still "some drop within God's scheme's ensemble." Compared to major works like "Crossing Brooklyn Ferry" (1860), "Waves" receives little critical attention, but it chronicles a moment in the poet's life and plays a significant, albeit small, part in Whitman's own ensemble.

Joe Boyd Fulton

Bibliography
Bauerlein, Mark. *Whitman and the American
Idiom.* Baton Rouge: Louisiana State UP,
1991.

Whitman, Walt. *Leaves of Grass: Comprehensive Reader's Edition.* Ed. Harold W. Blodgett and Sculley Bradley. New York: New York UP, 1965.

See also "SANDS AT SEVENTY" (FIRST ANNEX); SEA, THE

"By the Bivouac's Fitful Flame" (1865)

This poem was originally published in *Drum-Taps* (1865) and appeared again when Whitman reissued *Drum-Taps* along with *Sequel to Drum-Taps (Since the Preceding Came from the Press): When Lilacs Last in the Door-Yard Bloom'd and Other Pieces* (1865–1866). The poems in both volumes were added to *Leaves of Grass* in 1867 as annexes and many were included in the "Drum-Taps" cluster in the 1871–1872 and subsequent editions of *Leaves of Grass.* The date of composition of the poem is not possible to determine; however, many of the poems in the "Drum-Taps" collection probably were written when Whitman was at home in Brooklyn in 1861–1862.

The speaker in the poem is an invented persona who relates his thoughts as he sits by the "bivouac's fitful flame." With the reminders of the war all around, the speaker focuses on his thoughts "Of life and death, of home and the past and loved." Like many others in the "Drum-Taps" cluster, this poem paints a word picture of a Civil War scene. Here the battlefield scene serves as a contrast with the thoughts of the narrator. His thoughts are not of war but of "those that are far away." The thoughts come winding around the speaker in a procession, and he absorbs the experiences—the memories invoked by this procession of thoughts. The narrator's consciousness alternates between the "tender and wondrous" procession of thoughts and the stark reality of the camp: tents, woods, and fire. Whitman's free verse is given form by the same alliterative opening and closing words. Personification invests the scene around the speaker with life: the "fitful flame" and "shrubs and trees . . . watching me."

William G. Lulloff

Bibliography
Dougherty, James. *Walt Whitman and the
Citizen's Eye.* Baton Rouge: Louisiana
State UP, 1993.
Schwiebert, John E. *Whitman's Poetic Technique and Style in the Short Poem.* New
York: Lang, 1992.

Whitman, Walt. *Walt Whitman's "Drum-Taps" (1865) and "Sequel to Drum-Taps" (1865–6): A Facsimile Reproduction.* Ed. F. DeWolfe Miller. Gainesville, Fla.: Scholars' Facsimiles and Reprints, 1959.

See also CIVIL WAR, THE; "DRUM-TAPS"

"By the Roadside" (1881)

Sandwiched between the astonishing poems of ebbing in "Sea-Drift" and the bloody battle poetry of "Drum-Taps," the twenty-nine poems grouped in "By the Roadside" have an interstitial and miscellaneous quality. They first appeared as a cluster in the sixth edition of *Leaves of Grass* (1881–1882), bringing together three new poems with two from the 1855 edition, sixteen from the 1860 edition, five from *Drum-Taps* (1865), one from the 1867 edition, and two from *Passage to India* (1871). The grouping is not often discussed as a whole; Gay Wilson Allen, Sculley Bradley, and Harold W. Blodgett see little more connecting the poems than the poet's experience as a roadside observer.

In part this response is prompted by the varied subject matter and the way many of the poems gathered here matter-of-factly take place by roads, such as "The Dalliance of the Eagles" (1880), "The Runner" (1867), or the parade in "A Boston Ballad (1854)" (1855). Perhaps more important, if "Roadside" has appeared minor and fugitive to scholars it is because Whitman quite deliberately offers contrapuntal relief to the epochal groupings it lies between. In his periodic rearrangements and orchestrations of the poetic movements of *Leaves of Grass,* Whitman settled on hiatal moments of frustrated rebellion and social complaint to give "Roadside" its most abiding theme. The first two poems in the sequence, "A Boston Ballad (1854)" and "Europe, The 72d and 73d Years of These States" (1850) (originally titled "Resurgemus"), respond with overtly political comment to, in the case of the former, the 1854 Fugitive Slave Law controversy and, in the case of the latter, the revolutionary turmoil which swept Europe in 1848. "Liberty," he writes in "Europe," "let others despair of you—I never despair of you." The rest of the cluster is largely comprised of brief lyric "Thoughts" and imagistic snapshots such as "A Farm Picture" (a poem which anticipates William Carlos Williams's "The Red Wheelbarrow" in its photographic minimalism), which emphasize the

observing, spectatorial quality of Whitman's perspective. But the sequence is punctuated by two political poems, "To a President" (1860) and "To the States, To Identify the 16th, 17th, or 18th Presidentiad" (1860), which refer scornfully to the administrations of Fillmore, Pierce, and Buchanan. Returning to the motif of failed rebellion, "Roadside," as a retrospective organization of Whitman's poetic history, subtly invokes the aura of ineffectual struggles and mediocre, one-term administrations.

In this context, the briefer, more personal poems in the cluster, such as "O Me! O Life!" (1865) and "I Sit and Look Out" (1860), emphasize the frustrations of the poet in his struggle to realize what might be termed a socially efficacious poetic rebellion ("all the meanness and agony without end I sitting look out upon, / See, hear, and am silent") and the abiding quality of his commitment to that struggle in spite of setback ("the powerful play goes on, and you may contribute a verse"). The road in this cluster helps Whitman to claim for his *Leaves* continuity between his political and poetic struggles while traveling between the great movements of his poetic career. The roadside is a figure for the site where, as Kenneth Burke and Alan Trachtenberg have suggested, Whitman translates the political into the experiential, and "Roadside" records the tribulations of that translation. The late poems that Whitman added to the group, such as "Roaming in Thought (After reading Hegel)" (1881), stress the continuity of that translation and indicate how Whitman's growing Hegelian idealism throughout the latter stages of his career served to help him fashion unities from the disparate movements of his verse.

Stephen Rachman

Bibliography

Allen, Gay Wilson. *The New Walt Whitman Handbook.* New York: New York UP, 1975.

———. *The Solitary Singer: A Critical Biography of Walt Whitman.* 1955. Rev. ed. 1967. Chicago: U of Chicago P, 1985.

Burke, Kenneth. "Policy Made Personal: Whitman's Verse and Prose—Salient Traits." *"Leaves of Grass" One Hundred Years After.* Ed. Milton Hindus. Stanford: Stanford UP, 1955. 74–108.

Crawley, Thomas Edward. *The Structure of "Leaves of Grass."* Austin: U of Texas P, 1970.

Trachtenberg, Alan. "Whitman's Visionary Politics." *Walt Whitman of Mickle Street: A Centennial Collection.* Ed. Geoffery M. Sill. Knoxville: U of Tennessee P, 1994. 94–108.

Whitman, Walt. *Leaves of Grass.* Ed. Sculley Bradley and Harold W. Blodgett. Norton Critical Edition. New York: Norton, 1973.

See also "Boston Ballad (1854), A"; "Dalliance of the Eagles, The"; "Europe, The 72d and 73d Years of These States"; "Hand-Mirror, A"; "Hast Never Come to Thee an Hour"; "I Sit and Look Out"; "To a President"; "To Rich Givers"; "To the States, To Identify the 16th, 17th, or 18th Presidentiad"; "When I Heard the Learn'd Astronomer"

C

"Calamus" (1860)

The "Calamus" poems had their origin in a sequence entitled "Live Oak with Moss," which survived in manuscript (published, 1955, in Fredson Bowers's *Whitman's Manuscripts*). This sequence of twelve poems contained a sketchy account of "manly attachment" that ended in separation. Other poems were added to this core to comprise the forty-five poems of the "Calamus" cluster in 1860. In subsequent editions of *Leaves of Grass,* Whitman dropped or shifted a few "Calamus" poems, ending with a total of thirty-nine in 1881.

The poems of the "Calamus" cluster, companion to the "Children of Adam" cluster, celebrate friendship and "manly attachment" (or "adhesiveness," a term that Whitman adopted from phrenology, as he did "amativeness" for heterosexual love). In setting these clusters together in his book, he appears to be following a tradition of the personal essay, from Montaigne to Emerson: writing on love and friendship by drawing on personal experience as a basis for philosophical generalizations. Whitman explained his title "Calamus" in the following way: "[I]t is the very large and aromatic grass, or root, spears three feet high—often called 'sweet flag'—grows all over the Northern and Middle States. . . . The récherché or ethereal sense, as used in my book, arises probably from it, Calamus presenting the biggest and hardiest kind of spears of grass, and from its fresh, aromatic, pungent bouquet" (*Poetry and Prose* 941). In his nude portrait of himself in section 24 of "Song of Myself," the phallic suggestiveness of Calamus (or sweet flag) is made explicit: "Root of wash'd sweet flag! timorous pond-snipe! nest of guarded duplicate eggs!"

"In Paths Untrodden" opens the "Calamus" cluster with a straightforward resolution "to sing no songs to-day but those of manly attachment," concluding "I proceed for all who are or have been young men, / To tell the secret of my nights and days, / To celebrate the need of comrades." The next poem, "Scented Herbage of My Breast," initially introduces an extraordinarily copious imagery entwining "[t]omb-leaves," "body-leaves," "tall leaves," "sweet leaves," until, finally, in the middle of the poem the poet exclaims: "Emblematic and capricious blades I leave you, now you serve me not, / I will say what I have to say by itself." The poet spins an opaque web of images and, feeling himself getting entangled in his weaving, tosses it all aside and begins to speak directly: "I will sound myself and comrades only, / I will never again utter a call only their call." The drama of the poem is essentially about writing the poem, or about the giving up on the writing of the poem and turning to direct speech in its place.

This playfulness with the reader continues in the next poem, "Whoever You are Holding Me Now in Hand." The very title leads the reader to expect a love scene, with the poet's hand held by one of his comrades. But this is not the case. The reader quickly discovers that it is the reader's hand caught in the title. The poet turns the reader into the seducer, saying "before you attempt me further, . . . [t]he whole past theory of your life and all conformity to the lives around you would have to be abandon'd." The poet (becoming his book) gives the reader a chance to escape, but then entices him or her by suggesting a trial in some hidden spot—"in some wood," "back of a rock," or "on the beach." There he will permit the reader to kiss him with the "comrade's long-dwelling kiss or the new husband's kiss" and will allow himself to be thrust beneath the reader's clothing to rest against heart or hip. Readers discover, perhaps to their dismay, that they have been propositioned by a book! The poet himself is ready to escape, requesting his release with a riddle: "For all is useless without that which you may guess at many times and not hit, that which I hinted at; / Therefore release me and depart on your way."

"These I Singing in Spring," the fifth poem in the "Calamus" cluster, portrays the poet going to the pond-side alone but soon surrounded in imagination by a gang of comrades—"the spirits of dear friends dead or alive." The poet, accompanied by this ghostly "great crowd" and wandering in search of "tokens," soon comes upon a place sacred to his memory: "O here I last saw him that tenderly loves me, and returns again never to separate from me, / And this, O this shall henceforth be the token of comrades, this calamus-root shall, / Interchange it youths with each other! let none render it back!" At the end of the poem, the poet begins to discriminate among his "cloud of spirits": not all of them are worthy of receiving the phallic-like Calamus-root. Indeed, it is reserved for a few: "I will give of it, but only to them that love as I myself am capable of loving."

The "Calamus" poems celebrate adhesiveness and manly love but rarely portray such a relationship at any length. At times, the intensities of feeling the poet celebrates seem more real in memory and imagination than in fact. For example, in "Of the Terrible Doubt of Appearances," after describing the big philosophical questions that defy human answer, the poet reveals that for him the questions are "curiously answer'd" by his friends, his "lovers." Such a relationship charges him with "untold and untellable wisdom": "He ahold of my hand has completely satisfied me." A similar portrait is painted in "When I Heard at the Close of the Day"; even though the poet's name has been received "with plaudits in the capitol," even though he has accomplished his plans, still he is not happy. Only when his friend and lover returns is he happy. The poem concludes with a bedroom scene, the poet lying awake content listening to the waters roll in on the shore: "For the one I love most lay sleeping by me under the same cover in the cool night, / In the stillness in the autumn moonbeams his face was inclined toward me, / And his arm lay lightly around my breast—and that night I was happy." Again, the poem appears to be a treasured recollection, the more valued for its rarity in the poet's life; that night must provide comfort for the many others spent alone. The passion of adhesiveness seems to be manifested in the simplest of gestures—the holding of a hand, the encircling of an arm.

Though the poet celebrates adhesiveness and associates the love of comrades with some of the tenderest, most memorable moments of his life, he also sometimes reveals the pain he has felt. "Trickle Drops," the bloodiest of all Whitman's poems, might well be read as an anguished confessional poem—indeed the opposite of celebratory. The blood-drops come from his face, from his forehead and lips, and from his breast—"from within where I was conceal'd." The drops are "confession drops" that "stain every page, stain every song I sing, every word I say." The poet exhorts the drops to saturate his pages "with yourself all ashamed and wet." The shortest of the "Calamus" poems, "Here the Frailest Leaves of Me," is similarly confessional, but less self-lacerating: "Here the frailest leaves of me and yet my strongest lasting, / Here I shade and hide my thoughts, I myself do not expose them, / And yet they expose me more than all my other poems."

"Sometimes with One I Love" portrays the poet as feeling jealous rage for fear that he "effuse[s] unreturn'd love." He discovers, however, there is recompense, even for "unreturn'd love": "I loved a certain person ardently and my love was not return'd, / Yet out of that I have written these songs." Perhaps this poem reveals the secret as to why there is so much celebration of adhesiveness in "Calamus" but so little portrayal of it in any extended sense. "Sometimes with One I Love" may be paired with "Not Heaving from my Ribb'd Breast Only," one of the most visually negative of Whitman's poems: fourteen lines begin with "Not" and two others with "Nor" in this seventeen-line poem! Along with "Trickle Drops," this is one of Whitman's most tortured poems, a long periodic sentence filled from beginning to end with heaving, sighing, panting, and chattering, a portrait of an unhappy, almost despairing man ("in sighs at night in rage dissatisfied with myself"). The source of the rage is finally disclosed in the last two lines: "Not in any or all of them O adhesiveness! O pulse of my life! / Need I that you exist and show yourself any more than in these songs." These two poems reveal that the poet has lived a largely lonely life suppressing his adhesiveness, his only compensation the creation of his poems.

These poems may reveal the reason Whitman emphasized the social dimension of the "Calamus" poems when he referred to them in later years, as, for example, in his 1876 Preface to *Two Rivulets:* "Important as they are in my purpose as emotional expressions for humanity, the special meaning of the *Calamus* cluster of *Leaves of Grass,* (and more or less running through that book, and cropping out in *Drum-Taps,*) mainly resides in its Political significance" (*Comprehensive* 751). That "political" dimension is explicit in "For You, O Democracy" and "The Base of All Metaphysics." In the first of these, the poet announces his aim to make "the continent indissoluble," "the most splendid race," "inseparable cities"—all "By the love of comrades, / By the manly love of comrades." Many readers have found this poem naive or unconvincing.

"The Base of All Metaphysics," however, has not received its due. The poet become professor explains the base for all past metaphysical speculation—Plato, Socrates, Christ, Fichte, Schelling, Hegel, etc.—as contained in "The dear love of man for his comrade, the attraction of friend to friend, / Of the well-married husband and wife, of children and parents, / Of city for city and land for land." In *Civilization and Its Discontents* (1930), Sigmund Freud presents in his nonpoetic prose a vision of social bonding quite compatible with Whitman's: "Man's discovery that sexual (genital) love . . . provided him with the prototype of all happiness [inspired him to] . . . make genital eroticism the central point of his life. . . . The love which founded the family continues to operate in civilization both in its original [sexual] form . . . and in its modified form as aim-inhibited affection." Freud believed that "aim-inhibited love" was originally "fully sensual love, and it is so still in man's unconscious. Both—fully sensual love and aim-inhibited love—extend outside the family and create new bonds with people who before were strangers" (qtd. in Miller, *Leaves* 54). Freud would have seen that in such poems as "To a Stranger" the poet provides an example of the kind of bonding derived from such "aim-inhibited love." The poem is addressed to a "[p]assing stranger": "You give me the pleasure of your eyes, face, flesh, as we pass, you take of my beard, breast, hands, in return."

As a poet Whitman probably had more conscious access to his unconscious than do most people. In the last "Calamus" poem he describes himself as "[f]ull of life now, compact, visible," but he speaks to those readers who have come after him, who themselves are "compact, visible," seeking him in his poems—"Fancying how happy you were if I could be with you and become your comrade; / Be it as if I were with you. (Be not too certain but I am now with you.)" ("Full of Life now"). The poet is confident that his readers, whatever their sexuality, overt or suppressed, will respond imaginatively to such an appeal cast primarily in physical terms.

During the nineteenth century, Whitman's sex poems in "Children of Adam" and elsewhere in *Leaves* became subjects of controversy and created many problems for the Good Gray Poet, but the "Calamus" pieces were largely accepted as innocent poems of comradeship and brotherly love. In the twentieth century, the two clusters have exchanged positions in the reputation of *Leaves;* the sex poems have found acceptance, but the "Calamus" poems are charged with depicting "unnatural" sexuality. Most recently, however, with the advent of the rights movement for gays and lesbians (allied with the rights movement for blacks and women), the "Calamus" cluster has come to be celebrated as a homosexual manifesto. Too often in the debate about "Calamus," proponents for one or another interpretation forget that it is a cluster of *poems* which, like all genuine poetry, yields itself most fully only after one attends to the subtlety and complexity of its techniques and themes.

James E. Miller, Jr.

Bibliography

Black, Stephen A. *Whitman's Journeys into Chaos.* Princeton: Princeton UP, 1975.

Erkkila, Betsy. *Whitman the Political Poet.* New York: Oxford UP, 1989.

Fone, Byrne R.S. *Masculine Landscapes: Walt Whitman and the Homoerotic Text.* Carbondale: Southern Illinois UP, 1992.

Killingsworth, M. Jimmie. *Whitman's Poetry of the Body: Sexuality, Politics, and the Text.* Chapel Hill: U of North Carolina P, 1989.

McKinley, John. "Shooting the Moon: Over-Reading Homoeroticism in Whitman's 'Calamus.'" *Walt Whitman Centennial International Symposium.* Ed. Manuel

Villar Raso, Miguel Martinez Lopez, and Rosa Morillas. Granada, Spain: U of Granada P, 1992. 146–150.

Martin, Robert K. *The Homosexual Tradition in American Poetry*. Austin: U of Texas P, 1979.

Miller, Edwin Haviland. *Walt Whitman's Poetry: A Psychological Journey*. New York: New York UP, 1969.

Miller, James E., Jr. *A Critical Guide to "Leaves of Grass."* Chicago: U of Chicago P, 1957.

———. *"Leaves of Grass": America's Lyric-Epic of Self and Democracy*. New York: Twayne, 1992.

Moon, Michael. *Disseminating Whitman: Revision and Corporeality in "Leaves of Grass."* Cambridge, Mass.: Harvard UP, 1991.

Pollak, Vivian R. "Death as Repression, Repression as Death: A Reading of Whitman's 'Calamus' Poems." *Walt Whitman of Mickle Street: A Centennial Collection*. Ed. Geoffrey M. Sill. Knoxville: U of Tennessee P, 1994. 179–193.

Thomas, M. Wynn. "Whitman's Achievements in the Personal Style in *Calamus*." *Walt Whitman Quarterly Review* 1.3 (1983): 36–47.

Whitman, Walt. *Leaves of Grass: Comprehensive Reader's Edition*. Ed. Harold W. Blodgett and Sculley Bradley. New York: New York UP, 1965.

———. *The Poetry and Prose of Walt Whitman*. Ed. Louis Untermeyer. New York: Simon and Schuster, 1949.

———. *Whitman's Manuscripts: "Leaves of Grass" (1860)*. Ed. Fredson Bowers. Chicago: U of Chicago P, 1955.

See also "Base of All Metaphysics, The"; "Children of Adam"; Comradeship; "For You O Democracy"; "Here the Frailest Leaves of Me"; "In Paths Untrodden"; *Leaves of Grass*, 1860 Edition; "Live Oak with Moss"; Love; "Not Heaving from my Ribb'd Breast Only"; "Of the Terrible Doubt of Appearances"; "Scented Herbage of My Breast"; Sex and Sexuality; "Sometimes with One I Love"; "These I Singing in Spring"; "To a Stranger"; "Trickle Drops"; "When I Heard at the Close of the Day"; "Whoever You are Holding Me Now in Hand"

Camden, New Jersey

Camden is described by one Whitman biographer as "unlovely," an appropriate term for the late-twentieth-century city that has survived eighty years of decline since it reached its greatest glory in the 1920s. But during Whitman's residence in Camden from 1873 to 1892, the city was still young and growing, vigorous and raw-boned much as Brooklyn, New York, had been in the 1830s during Whitman's youth. This is one reason why Whitman gradually formed a strong attachment to his adopted city.

Camden began as a refuge for a group of Irish Quakers seeking relief from religious persecution. Between 1681 and 1700, they settled on the eastern shore of the Delaware River across from Philadelphia on a tract of land bordered by Pennsauken Creek to the north and Timber Creek to the south. These waterways, along with Newton Creek and Cooper's Creek, which also joined the Delaware at this point, made the tract a natural center for transportation between Philadelphia and the West Jersey towns of Salem, Woodbury, Haddonfield, and Burlington, all of which had large Quaker populations. Several ferry companies provided transit across the river, William Cooper's giving the town its early name of Cooper's Ferry. His descendant Jacob Cooper laid out the streets of the town and sold building lots in 1764, naming it in honor of Charles Pratt, Earl of Camden and friend of the American colonies. The town was incorporated by the New Jersey legislature in 1828, although it was little more than a collection of separate villages lying at some distance from each other. The town's three public gardens were sufficiently wooded that John James Audubon was able to conduct his ornithological studies there in the late 1820s and early 1830s.

Camden tripled in population between 1828 and 1840, from eleven hundred to about thirty-three hundred, in part because it continued to provide transportation for the emerging industrial economy of the region. A sixty-mile railroad between Camden and Amboy, New Jersey, completed in 1834, provided a direct link between Philadelphia and New York; another in 1852 connected Camden with Atlantic City. Ferry services improved as a result of the railroads, with modern slips at the ends of five city streets. Gas street lamps were first lit in 1852, tracks were laid down for horse-drawn streetcars, and a waterworks was built in 1854. A cholera epidemic in 1866 forced the construction of a sewer system, which in turn created a demand for iron pipes. Among the employees taken on by local foundries in November 1868 was a pipe inspector from Brooklyn named George Washington Whitman.

George Whitman, Walt's younger brother, worked part-time in Camden for several years while also running a construction business and inspecting pipes in Brooklyn. By 1871, however, he was employed full-time in Camden, which enabled him to marry Louisa Orr Haslam and take a house at 322 Stevens Street. He brought his mother, Louisa Van Velsor Whitman, and his brother Edward to live with them in August 1872 and soon began construction of a three-story house on a corner lot at 431 Stevens Street. Before he could finish it, his mother became ill and died in May 1873. Still partially paralyzed by a stroke he had suffered four months earlier in Washington, Walt Whitman hastened to Camden to see his mother, arriving on 20 May, three days before her death. He intended to stay only until his strength returned, but his convalescence was very slow. In September he moved with George's family into the new house at 431 Stevens, and in 1874 he was dismissed from his clerkship in Washington, leaving him a permanent resident of Camden.

Whitman never regained the strength of mind or body that he had enjoyed prior to his stroke, but the last eighteen years of his life were by no means barren of literary activity. In February and March 1874 he published two poems in *Harper's Monthly,* "Song of the Redwood-Tree" and "Prayer of Columbus," and in June the *Daily Graphic* published "Song of the Universal," the three poems together comprising a reaffirmation of his belief in the self and the new world of America. In 1876 he published those and other new poems in the Centennial edition of *Leaves of Grass,* the only edition to cite Camden as its place of publication. That two-volume edition also included *Two Rivulets,* a collection of prose and poetry that Whitman hoped would "set the key-stone to my democracy's enduring arch" (Whitman 467). The inclusion of prose signified his determination to become known as a prose writer as well as a poet, and a major portion of his labor in the late 1870s and 1880s went into writing the essays finally published in 1891 as the *Complete Prose Works,* a longer volume than *Leaves of Grass.* Many of these essays, such as "Scenes on Ferry and River—Last Winter's Nights," eloquently express the depth of Whitman's attachment to Camden and Philadelphia.

Walt Whitman with friend and phaeton driver Bill Duckett. By permission, Rare Books Division, New York Public Library.

In 1884 George Whitman moved his family to a farm twelve miles from Camden, but Walt refused to go with them. He had a circle of friends and admirers, including the lawyer Thomas B. Harned and his brother-in-law, Horace Traubel, and George and Susan Stafford, with whom Whitman summered in Laurel Springs on a branch of Timber Creek. He had a stream of visitors who knew to look for him in Camden, and he enjoyed the ferryboat rides to Philadelphia immensely. So when an opportunity arose to buy a two-story frame house on Mickle Street for $1,750, he took it, paying the price with his royalties and a loan. He acquired a housekeeper, Mrs. Mary Davis, and spent his days by the front window, looking out and talking with neighbors; or riding in the buggy bought for him through a subscription arranged by Thomas Donaldson; or editing his manuscripts and recalling details of his biography to Horace Traubel. His birthday each year was celebrated with a dinner, the grandest being a banquet in Camden on 31 May 1889, with orations by twelve notable locals and greetings from many more, published as *Camden's Compliment to Walt Whitman.*

When Whitman died in 1892, his funeral was attended by over three thousand viewers who filed past the casket in the Mickle Street house and thousands more who lined the avenue as Whitman was carried to his tomb in Harleigh Cemetery. The Camden *Post* editorialized that Camden would someday be "America's Stratford," Whitman's name giving the city "a glamour second only to that of Avon" (Dorwart and Mackey 94). The city acquired Whitman's house on Mickle Street in 1921, located the original furniture which had been dispersed through the neighborhood, and restored the home as a memorial to the poet. An eight-story hotel in downtown Camden, finished in 1925, was named for Whitman, and a new bridge across the Delaware River was named for him in 1957. Although much of Walt's neighborhood has been lost to urban renewal and George's house at 431 Stevens Street burned down in 1994, Walt's house at 328 Mickle Street and two adjoining properties are now a New Jersey State historic site, offering the original dwelling, a library and visitor's center, and a park with a lifesize statue of Walt with a butterfly on his outstretched fingertip. In these ways, Camden has continued to pay its compliments to its most famous and best-loved resident.

Geoffrey M. Sill

Bibliography

Allen, Gay Wilson. *The Solitary Singer: A Critical Biography of Walt Whitman.* 1955. Rev. ed. 1967. Chicago: U of Chicago P, 1985.

Canby, Henry Seidel. *Walt Whitman: An American.* Boston: Houghton Mifflin, 1943.

Dorwart, Jeffrey M., and Philip English Mackey. *Camden County, New Jersey, 1616–1976: A Narrative History.* Camden County, N.J.: Camden County Cultural and Heritage Commission, 1976.

Kaplan, Justin. *Walt Whitman: A Life.* New York: Simon and Schuster, 1980.

Loving, Jerome M. Introduction. *Civil War Letters of George Washington Whitman.* Ed. Loving. Durham: Duke UP, 1975. 3–35.

Traubel, Horace. *With Walt Whitman in Camden.* 9 vols. Vols. 1–3. 1906–1914. New York: Rowman and Littlefield, 1961; Vol. 4. Ed. Sculley Bradley. Philadelphia: U of Pennsylvania P, 1953; Vol. 5. Ed. Gertrude Traubel. Carbondale: Southern Illinois UP, 1964; Vol. 6. Ed. Gertrude Traubel and William White. Carbondale: Southern Illinois UP, 1982; Vol. 7. Ed. Jeanne Chapman and Robert MacIsaac. Carbondale: Southern Illinois UP, 1992; Vols. 8–9. Ed. Jeanne Chapman and Robert MacIsaac. Oregon House, Calif.: W.L. Bentley, 1996.

———, ed. *Camden's Compliment to Walt Whitman.* Philadelphia: McKay, 1889.

Whitman, Walt. *Prose Works 1892.* Ed. Floyd Stovall. Vol. 2. New York: New York UP, 1964.

See also DAVIS, MARY OAKES; HARLEIGH CEMETERY; HARNED, THOMAS BIGGS; MICKLE STREET HOUSE; PHILADELPHIA, PENNSYLVANIA; STAFFORD, GEORGE AND SUSAN M.; STAFFORD, HARRY L.; TIMBER CREEK; TRAUBEL, HORACE L.; WHITMAN, GEORGE WASHINGTON; WHITMAN, LOUISA ORR HASLAM; WHITMAN, LOUISA VAN VELSOR

Canada, Whitman's Reception in

Walt Whitman left America only once, and that was to visit Canada from 3 June to 29 September 1880. Dr. Richard Maurice Bucke, devotee of Whitman's poetry and philosophical perspectives, accompanied Whitman from his home in Camden, New Jersey, to Bucke's home near London, Ontario, where Bucke was the director of the London Asylum for the Insane. They spent most of the summer quietly on the "ample and charming garden and lawns of the asylum" (*Prose Works* 1:237) while Bucke gathered information for the biography of Whitman he was writing.

Later that summer, Bucke and Whitman took an extensive trip through southern Ontario and Quebec, traveling by railroad to Toronto, where they boarded a steamship on

Lake Ontario. The two toured the Thousand Islands on the St. Lawrence, with overnight stops at Kingston, Montreal, and Quebec (City). They eventually left the St. Lawrence, heading north on the Saguenay River to Chicoutimi, Quebec.

Although Whitman kept a diary of his visit, wrote several brief letters to friends during his stay, and composed a piece about his travels that was sent to several newspapers in hope of publication, Canada did not seem to inspire his creative imagination to any great degree. His writings about Canada are for the most part details of the landscape and weather, with a few generalizations about the cities he visited and people he met. He notes, for example, the "amplitude and primal naturalness" of the Thousand Islands, which present a "sane, calm, eternal picture, to eyes, senses, and the soul" (*Diary* 23–24). The French signs on the streets and stores of Montreal captured Whitman's attention, but he found the principal character of the city in the display of steamships along the wharves. He was as impressed with the trees and "grand rocky escarpments" of Mount Royal Park as with the "handsome shops" of St. James street or the church of Notre Dame de Lourdes. He found the city of Quebec, its rocky banks littered with "rafts, rafts of logs everywhere," to be "as picturesque an appearing city as there is on earth" (*Diary* 30). Whitman described the Saguenay as less appealing, referring to the "dark-water'd river" and its environs as "a dash of the grimmest, wildest, savagest scenery on the planet" (*Diary* 30).

In notes at the end of the Canadian diary headed "? For lecture—for conclusion?" Whitman attempted to bring his impressions of Canada together more coherently and formulate his ideas about the Canadian national character. He praises Canada as "a grand, sane, temperate land . . . the home of an improved grand race of men and women; not of some select class only, but of larger, saner, better masses" (*Diary* 40–41). This concurs with his comments in *Specimen Days,* where he describes Canadians as "hardy, democratic, intelligent, radically sound, and just as American, good-natured and *individualistic* [a] race, as the average range of the best specimens among us." Whitman tempers these superlatives a bit by adding that the "element" he just described, "though it may not be the majority, promises to be the leaven which must eventually leaven the whole lump" (*Prose*

Works 1:240). He emphasizes that the elements of the Canadian environment, "the best air and drink and sky and scenery of the globe," are the "sure foundation-nutriment of heroic men and women" (*Diary* 42).

Whitman also assesses the quality of Canadian social values. He was greatly impressed with the humane treatment of the inmates at the London Asylum under Dr. Bucke's care, and further study of Canadian institutions led him to praise Canadian benevolence as a mark of an exceptional civilization (*Diary* 43). He admired the Canadian school system, as well as the "advanced and ample provision" for the "maimed, insane, idiotic, blind, deaf and dumb, needy, sick and old, minor criminals, fallen women" and "foundlings" (*Diary* 43).

The most controversial of Whitman's comments about Canada are his suggestions for open trade between the United States and Canada and his prediction of a political union between the two countries. In an article published in 1880 in the London [Ontario] *Advertiser,* Whitman urges a "zollverein" between the two nations "for commercial purposes." He reminds Canadians of the practical considerations of such an agreement, noting that they might "abolish the frontier tariff line, with its double sets of custom house officials now existing between the two countries," and "agree upon one tariff for both, the proceeds of this tariff to be divided between the two governments on the basis of population" (*Prose Works* 1:240). Whitman sees Canada's reluctance to enter such a partnership to be based upon the fear of "loosen[ing] the bonds between Canada and England" and dismisses this as a sentiment which rather foolishly "overrides the desire for commercial prosperity" (1:241). In a parenthetical comment Whitman adds: "It seems to me a certainty of time, sooner or later, that Canada shall form two or three grand States, equal and independent, with the rest of the American Union" (1:241). This united statehood would make the Great Lakes and the St. Lawrence, whose length he had just traveled, not a "frontier line, but a grand interior or mid-channel" (1:241). There is no indication of the response of the London readers to these suggestions, but heated arguments over the free-trade agreement a century later and the line of customs houses still guarding the border attest to the optimism of Whitman's suggestions.

Canada inspired only a few lines in *Leaves of Grass,* and in these Whitman relies upon rather stereotyped views of "Kanada" (which he always spells thus) as a place of ice and snow. In "Starting from Paumanok" he writes of the "Kanadian cheerily braving the winter, the snow and ice welcome to me" (section 14). Similarly in "Song of Myself" he finds himself "At home on Kanadian snow-shoes or up in the bush, or with fishermen off Newfoundland" (section 16). Even when he stands "By Blue Ontario's Shore," his perspective is cosmic rather than particular, envisioning a phantom demanding bards rather than noting details of the Ontario landscape. A particular reference to the "black stream" of the Saguenay, which echoes the color emphasis in the diary (32), appears in "Thou Mother with Thy Equal Brood" (section 2). The inclusion of a detail from Canada here suggests, once more, his vision of a United States of North America.

If Canada failed to inspire Whitman's poetry, the reverse is also true. In spite of the vital role the landscape plays in Canadian literature and the need for a cosmic vision capable of uniting a continental culture, very few poets have been influenced by Whitman in their depiction of the physical or spiritual dimensions of Canada. This is not to say that Canadians lacked an interest in Whitman, for he has inspired a coterie of devoted followers, beginning with Dr. Bucke. Perhaps the most memorable achievement of one of the numerous Whitman fellowships and clubs is the dedication to the poet in 1919 of a mile-long granite rock face in what is now Bon Echo Provincial Park in Ontario, where Whitman's name remains inscribed today.

An overview of Canadian poetry, however, reveals only peripheral attention to Whitman, consisting of an occasional passing reference to Whitman's "barbaric yawp," the striking of a fleeting cosmic perspective when addressing the vast Canadian landscape, a salute to Whitman in depictions of the vagabond rebel on the road, or an outright denunciation of Whitman's gauche American expansiveness among university poets.

Perhaps most puzzling is the fact that the daunting Canadian landscape, which seems to cry out for the bravado and all-encompassing sweep of a voice like Whitman's, has instead inspired very ordinary versifying. In an early study of Canadian literature, Desmond Pacey posed the question that may be fundamental to the problem of Whitman's influence. Referring to the landscape poet Bliss Carman, Pacey asks:

"When there was a . . . Whitman to be listened to, how should . . . a Carman make his voice heard?" (5). Another of the best-known Canadian nature poets, Wilson MacDonald, whose works at times aspire to Whitman's cosmic vision, has also suffered from the comparison. The "too obvious echoes of Whitman" (Pacey 117) which color his philosophic perspectives are uneasily caught within the regular rhyme and metrical patterns he prefers. Even poets like Tom MacInness and Robert Service, who are devoted to depictions of Whitman-like individualists confronting the frontier, confine the slangy speech of their bohemian characters to strict rhythms, thereby inhibiting their verse.

There has also been a deliberate resistance to Whitman on the part of poets trained in the university, who tend to align themselves with the cool condescension of the British literary tradition rather than with Whitman's expansive cosmic consciousness. Phyllis Webb, for example, in a prose-verse declaration of her poetics, decries Whitman's bold posture as "assertive . . . open mouth, big-mouthed Whitman, yawp, yawp . . . howling. Male" (668). Toronto poet Raymond Souster, however, forges a conciliation with Whitman which typifies the reaction of many twentieth-century poets. His free-verse lines echo Whitman's voice as he tells the reader to "Get the poem outdoors" and urges the Canadian poet to yawp "loud and then louder so it / brings the whole neighbourhood out" (122–123). But Souster's Whitmanesque vision is often darkened by contemporary cynicism. In "The Lilac Poem," with its many obvious references to Whitman, Souster notes that he wants to write about the flower's "beauty" and "star-shining" but is hampered by knowing that "tomorrow [it] lies forgotten" (113). Canadian poetry is just beginning to come into its own as a cultural expression and, in many of the younger poets, seems to be developing a voice which blends rural and urban perspectives and incorporates both British and American traditions. On the whole, however, Canadian poets still have much to learn from Whitman's assured voice and his all-embracing sense of selfhood in their quest to express the Canadian identity.

It may be that Whitman's most significant influence upon Canadian culture is to be found not in poetry but in art. In particular, the mystical landscapes of Canada's "Group of Seven" artists provide Whitman's cosmic perspectives with another medium of expression. Whitman's influence is especially apparent in the paintings of Lawren Harris, prime mover of the group, whose work reveals the spiritual qualities of the northern landscape. Harris was an early convert to the Bucke/Whitman version of cosmic consciousness and holds the "distinction of being the sole Canadian ever" to review Bucke's book on Whitman (Greenland and Colombo 227). In the final phase of his career, Harris gave up representational art, as he tried to re-create a cosmic perspective in flowing natural shapes that suggest rock, wave, snow, and earth. In these paintings and in the lines from "Song of Myself" carved on the granite rock face at Bon Echo, Whitman has achieved a visible presence uniting him for all time with the Canadian landscape he admired.

Lorelei Cederstrom

Bibliography

Greenland, Cyril, and John Robert Colombo, eds. *Walt Whitman's Canada*. Willowdale, Ontario: Hounslow, 1992.

Pacey, Desmond. *Creative Writing in Canada*. Toronto: Ryerson, 1952.

Souster, Raymond. "The Lilac Poem" and "Get the Poem Outdoors." *15 Canadian Poets Plus 5*. Ed. Gary Geddes and Phyllis Bruce. Toronto: Oxford UP, 1978. 113, 122.

Webb, Phyllis. "On the Line." *20th Century Poetry & Poetics*. Ed Gary Geddes. 3rd ed. Toronto: Oxford UP, 1985. 666–672.

Whitman, Walt. *Prose Works 1892*. Ed. Floyd Stovall. 2 vols. New York: New York UP, 1963–1964.

———. *Walt Whitman's Diary in Canada*. Ed. William Sloane Kennedy. Boston: Small, Maynard, 1904.

See also BON ECHO; BUCKE, RICHARD MAURICE; CANADA, WHITMAN'S VISIT TO; DENISON, FLORA MACDONALD; INTERCULTURALITY; LEGACY, WHITMAN'S; LONDON, ONTARIO, CANADA

Canada, Whitman's Visit to

In the summer of 1880, shortly after a journey to the western United States, Whitman spent four months in Canada. He did so at the invitation of Dr. Richard Maurice Bucke, a fervent admirer who was much taken with the poet's mystical attributes. For the most part, Whitman stayed with the Buckes in London, Ontario, but he went on a number of excursions. In a photograph of him taken at the time, he has the look of a latter-day biblical patriarch, bundled up in a greatcoat, walking stick in hand, leaning casually against a parapet.

In his biography of Whitman (published in 1883), Bucke relies heavily on the observations he made during the poet's visit. Extensive and detailed, those observations include a quasi-medical inventory of Whitman's physical measurements and traits. Among other things, Bucke is struck by the inordinate size of his visitor's ears, which are "remarkably handsome" (Bucke 49). And he is persuaded that Whitman's acuity of hearing is such that he is able to hear the growth of vegetation.

Bucke reports that during his stay Whitman was happiest when strolling out of doors. He had a special fondness for flowers and children. He was often singing a little tune to himself and liked to recite poetry (including Tennyson's "Ulysses"). He read the newspapers every day, but the rest of his reading was for the most part erratic. From time to time, he wrote letters to the Canadian papers, reporting and reflecting on his situation, and sent out copies of these in lieu of personal correspondence. Apparently Whitman was not very talkative that summer and had scarcely anything at all to say about *Leaves of Grass*. Asked why he had never married, he replied that he could not have tolerated the constraints of marriage. In the context of a conversation about religion, he remarked that he "never had any particular religious experiences . . . never had any . . . distrust of the scheme of the universe" (qtd. in Bucke 61).

Whitman himself was keeping a diary during those summer months. Some elements of it would be subsequently dressed up for inclusion in *Specimen Days* (1882). Considerably edited, the rest would appear as *Walt Whitman's Diary in Canada* in 1904. His own account of events was that of a good-natured and observant tourist rather than a holy man. In fact, the first observations of the diary set the tone for everything which follows: "Calm and glorious roll the hours here—the whole twenty four. A perfect day, (the third in succession)" (*Daybooks* 3:611). Whitman was evidently much impressed by what he saw of Canadians and Canadian life. He made an impromptu visit to a school in Sarnia, Ontario, and came away with a strongly favorable impression of its students. He rode around in a bus in Toronto and found it a dynamic and engaging city. In Montreal he was the guest of a Dr. Hunt and wrote: "Genial host, delightful quarters, good sleep" (*Daybooks* 3:632).

From a technical standpoint, Whitman's original and unedited diary is a fascinating document. As was the case with a number of the poet's notebooks and journals, it was used as a repository for every kind of scribble and discursive exercise imaginable. Lists of Canadian crops, mailing addresses, and columns of figures rub elbows with fragmentary reminiscences, half-formed prose poems, and curious, small-scale anticipations of the poetic movement imagism. Above all, the diary contains elliptical and evocative characterizations of Canadian scenery and wildlife. The language of such passages is at times impressively vivid and affecting, and their rough edges afford them an unsettled, contemporary quality all their own.

N.J. Mason-Browne

Bibliography

Bucke, Richard Maurice. *Walt Whitman.* 1883. New York: Johnson Reprint Corporation, 1970.

Doyle, James. "Whitman's Canadian Diary." *University of Toronto Quarterly* 52.3 (1983): 277–287.

Greenland, Cyril, and John Robert Colombo, eds. *Walt Whitman's Canada.* Willowdale, Ontario: Hounslow, 1992.

Lynch, Michael. "Walt Whitman in Ontario." *The Continuing Presence of Walt Whitman.* Ed. Robert K. Martin. Iowa City: U of Iowa P, 1992. 141–151.

Whitman, Walt. *Daybooks and Notebooks.* Ed. William White. 3 vols. New York: New York UP, 1978.

———. *Specimen Days. Complete Poetry and Collected Prose.* Ed. Justin Kaplan. New York: Library of America, 1982. 869–926.

Zweig, Paul. *Walt Whitman: The Making of the Poet.* New York: Basic Books, 1984.

See also BUCKE, RICHARD MAURICE; CANADA, WHITMAN'S RECEPTION IN; LONDON, ONTARIO, CANADA

Canby, Henry Seidel (1878–1961)

One of Whitman's many biographers, Henry Seidel Canby is most often remembered as a literary journalist and educator. Born in Wilmington, Delaware, on 5 April 1878 to Edward Tatnall Canby, a banker, and Ella Augusta Seidel, he earned his Ph.D. from Yale in 1905. During the course of his more than fifty-year career as an editor and writer, Canby looked for ways to make scholarly writings on literary topics accessible to a nonscholarly audience. In 1920, after several years on the Yale faculty, he became editor of the *Literary Review,* later moving on to found the *Saturday Review of Literature* in 1924. In 1926 he advanced his campaign to make good books available to the general public when he became the first chairman of the board of judges of the Book-of-the-Month Club, a position he held until 1958. Canby began writing on a variety of literary topics while still at Yale. By the time he published *Walt Whitman: An American* (1943), he had already edited selections of poems by Henry Wadsworth Longfellow and Robert Louis Stevenson and written *Thoreau: A Biography* (1939) and numerous other books and articles on American literature and the writing of English. According to his memoirs, he developed an interest in Whitman after he read Whitman's poems "intensively" in the 1920s (*American Memoir* 406). Canby's biography of Whitman relies heavily on its predecessors and does not break new scholarly ground. It did, however, accomplish the author's goal of bringing Walt Whitman to the attention of a wider audience.

Katherine Reagan

Bibliography

Canby, Henry Seidel. *American Memoir.* Boston: Houghton Mifflin, 1947.

———. *Walt Whitman: An American.* Boston: Houghton Mifflin, 1943.

See also BIOGRAPHIES

Carlyle, Thomas (1795–1881)

Thomas Carlyle was a controversial but highly influential Victorian social critic, philosopher, historian, biographer, and translator. He fused elements of his Calvinist upbringing—an insistence on duty and the primacy of an elite caste—with German romanticism, gleaned especially from the writings of Schiller and Goethe.

Born in Ecclefechan, Scotland, in 1795, Carlyle attended Edinburgh University, which he left before receiving a degree. After his marriage to Jane Baillie Welsh in 1826, Carlyle moved to Craigenputtock, where he wrote numerous essays that were collected in *Critical and Miscellaneous Essays* (1838). He also wrote *Sartor Resartus* (1833–1834), in which a fictional philosopher, Diogenes Teufelsdröckh, resolves a crisis of belief. Although the book was initially criticized by a number of confused readers, *Sartor* eventually drew praise from figures such as Ralph Waldo Emerson.

In 1834, Carlyle and his wife moved to Chelsea, where he completed *The French Revolution* (1837). Carlyle also began to lecture; his May 1840 lectures were published in *On Heroes, Hero Worship & the Heroic in History* (1841), a characteristic insistence that great individuals must exert their powerful influence to provide coherence in desperate times. Carlyle's tenets were further outlined in works such as *Chartism* (1839) and *Past and Present* (1843). While in Chelsea, the Carlyles entertained a circle of admirers that included such figures as John Stuart Mill; Charles Dickens; John Forster; Robert Browning; Alfred, Lord Tennyson; Harriet Martineau; and Carlyle's biographer, James Anthony Froude. Carlyle became known as the "Sage of Chelsea."

Carlyle's later writings were increasingly conservative and antidemocratic, as evidenced in *Latter-Day Pamphlets* (1850), *Occasional Discourse on the Nigger Question* (1853), *History of Friedrich II of Prussia, Called Frederick the Great* (1858–1865), and *Shooting Niagara: and After?* (1867). Carlyle condemned overly liberal views on such issues as human rights and prison reform, and opposed emancipating American and West Indian slaves. His more stringent conservatism alienated many of his followers, most notably Mill. The death of his wife in 1866 devastated Carlyle, who spent most of his final years completing the autobiographical *Reminiscences* (1887). When he died in 1881, Carlyle was buried, as he wished, at Ecclefechan rather than Westminster Abbey.

Walt Whitman was very familiar with Carlyle's writings, as evidenced by the Carlylean images that appear in his poetry and his notes on German philosophy, which seem to come directly from Carlyle. Whitman reviewed several of Carlyle's books while he was a journalist with the Brooklyn *Daily Eagle,* and he claimed that *Democratic Vistas* (1871) was written in response to *Shooting Niagara.* Horace Traubel notes that during his time at

Camden Whitman read many books by and about Carlyle.

Despite Whitman's interest in Carlyle, Carlyle was much less attentive to Whitman. In 1856 Emerson sent a copy of *Leaves of Grass* (1855) to Carlyle, which prompted him to say: "'It is as though the town-bull had learned to hold a pen'" (qtd. in Wilson 6:926). Whitman wrote to Carlyle and even sent him a copy of *Vistas,* but apparently Carlyle never responded.

Whitman disagreed with a number of Carlyle's beliefs. Carlyle insists in his *Occasional Discourse* that blacks are naturally inferior to whites, and although Whitman was no abolitionist, he treated the black race more sympathetically. In addition, the strict political and social aristocracy that Carlyle endorsed clashed with Whitman's ideal democracy. As he states in his essays on Carlyle, it was not Carlyle's specific pronouncements that Whitman admired but his outspoken voice of protest. Whitman recognized Carlyle's conservatism and distaste for democracy (especially American democracy) but praised his overpowering individualism, his honesty, and his attempts to reform the age. Whitman considered Carlyle a powerful and necessary literary voice of his time: "[W]ithout Carlyle there would be no literature" (Traubel 478).

Matthew C. Altman

Bibliography

Carlyle, Thomas. *The Works of Thomas Carlyle.* Ed. H.D. Traill. Centenary ed. 30 vols. London: Chapman and Hall, 1896–1899.

Cumming, Mark. "Carlyle, Whitman, and the Disimprisonment of Epic." *Victorian Studies* 29 (1986): 207–226.

Froude, James Anthony. *Thomas Carlyle: A History of His Life in London 1834–1881.* 2 vols. London: Longmans, Green, 1884.

———. *Thomas Carlyle: A History of the First Forty Years of His Life, 1795–1835.* 4 vols. London: Longmans, Green, 1882.

Paine, Gregory. "The Literary Relations of Whitman and Carlyle with Especial Reference to Their Contrasting Views on Democracy." *Studies in Philology* 36 (1939): 550–563.

Smith, Fred Manning. "Whitman's Debt to Carlyle's *Sartor Resartus.*" *Modern Language Quarterly* 3 (1942): 51–65.

———. "Whitman's Poet-Prophet and Carlyle's Hero." *PMLA* 55 (1940): 1146–1164.

Traubel, Horace. *With Walt Whitman in Camden*. Ed. Gertrude Traubel. Vol. 5. Carbondale: Southern Illinois UP, 1964.

Whitman, Walt. "Carlyle from American Points of View." *Prose Works 1892*. Ed. Floyd Stovall. Vol. 1. New York: New York UP, 1963. 254–262.

———. "Death of Thomas Carlyle." *Prose Works 1892*. Ed. Floyd Stovall. Vol. 1. New York: New York UP, 1963. 248–253.

Wilson, David Alec. *Life of Thomas Carlyle*. 6 vols. London: Kegan Paul, 1929–1934.

See also BRITISH ISLES, WHITMAN IN THE; DEMOCRACY; *DEMOCRATIC VISTAS;* READING, WHITMAN'S

Carnegie, Andrew (1835–1919)

An industrialist and philanthropist, Carnegie gave small sums to subscriptions for Whitman in 1887 and in 1888, reportedly because he felt "triumphant democracy disgraced" upon hearing that British, not Americans, were raising money for the destitute poet (Whitman 85, n1). It is unlikely that the two ever met, but a literary exchange occurred when Carnegie sent his books with a "friendly inscription" and Whitman sent a copy of *Leaves of Grass* in return (Whitman 146–147).

Some friends criticized Whitman's association with Carnegie because of his exploitation of the working class, but Whitman defended Carnegie's generosity to him (Traubel 254). Reynolds draws several connections between the two, especially their praise of American technology as in Carnegie's *Triumphant Democracy* (1886) and Whitman's "Song of the Exposition" (1871).

Danielle L. Baker and Donald C. Irving

Bibliography

Carnegie, Andrew. *Triumphant Democracy*. 1886. New York: Doubleday, 1933.

Reynolds, David S. *Walt Whitman's America: A Cultural Biography*. New York: Knopf, 1995.

Traubel, Horace. *With Walt Whitman in Camden*. Ed. Sculley Bradley. Vol. 4. Philadelphia: U of Pennsylvania P, 1953.

Wall, Joseph F. *Andrew Carnegie*. Pittsburgh: U of Pittsburgh P, 1989.

Whitman, Walt. *The Correspondence*. Ed. Edwin Haviland Miller. Vol. 4. New York: New York UP, 1969.

See also "DEATH OF ABRAHAM LINCOLN"

Carpenter, Edward (1844–1929)

Like Walt Whitman, Edward Carpenter was an inspirational writer. Carpenter gave up the advantages of an affluent family and Cambridge education to live openly as a homosexual with his lover, George Merrill, among the workers of Sheffield in the north of England. He was a socialist who spoke out for the labor movement and for women's rights in the late nineteenth and early twentieth centuries, but he was also a student of sexuality, especially of homosexuality. His work in that field and the spiritual side to his writing were both influenced by Walt Whitman.

Carpenter's writings include *Civilisation, Its Cause and Cure* (1889), an appreciation of the virtues of preindustrial cultures; *Love's Coming of Age* (1895), a commentary on feminism and free love; and *Towards Democracy* (1905), a poetic and spiritual summons to human improvement. He examined his own experience in *My Days and Dreams* (1890). In *The Intermediate Sex* (1908) and *Intermediate Types Among Primitive Folk* (1919), he explored homosexuality as an instinctive behavior which premodern societies incorporated openly into their religious and cultural lives. Since there was no vocabulary for homosexuality at the time, Carpenter used the term "Uranian" to discuss the phenomenon, an allusion to the sky god Uranus.

Although Whitman was not a socialist, his writing had a profound effect on Carpenter, who made the long trip to America primarily as a pilgrimage to his literary and spiritual inspiration. He visited the poet for several weeks in 1877 and again in 1884. In 1906 he published an account of his visits to America, *Days with Walt Whitman*, writing a respectful, even somewhat glorified, portrait of his idol.

It was not until the 1966 publication of a memoir by Gavin Arthur entitled *The Circle of Sex* that the intimate details of Carpenter's visits were revealed. Arthur slept in bed with Carpenter, who was an old man at the time, and described a gentle body-stroking with the hands, which led not to a spilling of seed, but to "a far more intense orgasm of the whole nervous system, in which oneself, as a unit, reunites with the Whole" (Arthur 135). When Arthur asked Carpenter if that had been his experience with Whitman, Carpenter assented (Arthur 136), leaving us with our only description of Whitman's sexual behavior, an area otherwise shrouded in mystery and controversy.

In his emulation of Whitman, Carpenter became one of the first of many disciples, spreading Whitman's message into another country and another century.

Arnie Kantrowitz

Bibliography

Allen, Gay Wilson. *The Solitary Singer: A Critical Biography of Walt Whitman.* 1955. Rev. ed. 1967. Chicago: U of Chicago P, 1985.

Arthur, Gavin. *The Circle of Sex.* New Hyde Park, N.Y.: University Books, 1966.

Carpenter, Edward. *Days with Walt Whitman.* New York: Macmillan, 1906.

Grieg, Noel. Introduction. *Edward Carpenter: Selected Writings.* By Edward Carpenter. Vol. 1. London: GMP, 1984. 10–77.

See also BRITISH ISLES, WHITMAN IN THE; SEX AND SEXUALITY

Carpenter, George Rice (1863–1909)

Professor of rhetoric and literature, first at Harvard (1888–1890), then at MIT (1890–1893), and finally at Columbia University (until his death), where he made significant contributions to its character and growth, Carpenter wrote many rhetoric textbooks and literary histories. He was best known for *Episode of the Donna Pietosa* (1888), which won him accolades from the Dante Society; sketches of Henry Wadsworth Longfellow (1901) and John Greenleaf Whittier (1903); and his biography of Walt Whitman (1909), part of the English Men of Letters Series.

Although now superseded by more recent and more thoroughly researched biographies, Carpenter's *Walt Whitman* was well received, especially by reviewers unaware that much of the information came (unacknowledged) from Bliss Perry's earlier biography of Whitman (rev. ed., 1908). Carpenter also relied on Richard Maurice Bucke (1883), whom he quotes several times; he shares Bucke's vision of Whitman as mystic, but tones down Bucke's ecstatic rhetoric.

Carpenter's biography—often reviewed favorably by his contemporaries as an objective and fair treatment of Whitman—certainly contributed to the more widespread acceptance of the poet in the early twentieth century. His view of Whitman primarily as a religious seer (whom he likens in his conclusion to St. Francis of Assisi) and his vision of *Leaves of Grass* as revealing the mystic unity of all things, however, seem now somewhat archaic and quaint.

Joseph Andriano

Bibliography

Carpenter, George Rice. *Walt Whitman.* 1909. New York: Macmillan, 1924.

Wright, Ernest Hunter. "Carpenter, George Rice." *Dictionary of American Biography.* Ed. Allen Johnson. Vol. 3. New York: Scribner's, 1946. 511–512.

See also BIOGRAPHIES

Catalogues

Whitman's catalogues, his long lists, have been the most notorious stylistic feature of his poetry. Especially in the first half of the twentieth century, when poetic compression and precision were highly valued by literary critics, Whitman's catalogues earned him considerable condemnation, having been likened to the telephone directory and the Sears Roebuck catalogue. In addition, they have fueled most of the parodies that have been made of his poems. More recently, many of Whitman's readers have explained the catalogues as an integral part of both his stylistics and his poetic theory.

Whitman's source of inspiration for the catalogues may have been Homer, but more likely the Old Testament of the Bible. They appear in abundance in the first edition of *Leaves of Grass* and frequently thereafter until 1860; then they diminish and eventually disappear. The diminishing of a device through which Whitman expresses his faith in the expansiveness and all-inclusiveness of American democracy is evidence of the psychological devastation he suffered at the onset of the Civil War.

With the catalogue technique, Whitman seeks to encompass the nation and even the universe. It is difficult to think of any category of qualities, objects, persons, or occupations that is not catalogued by Whitman somewhere. As he projects the persona of the bard, whom he sometimes calls the "Sayer," he simultaneously extends himself out into the universe and enfolds all into himself. In "Song of Myself," he refers to this role as "the caresser of life," one who moves "To niches aside and junior bending, not a person or object missing, / Absorbing all to myself and for this song" (section 13).

The use of the catalogues is also a logical extension of Whitman's transcendental understanding of the nature of language. For the transcendentalist, all items within the universe are connected through chains of correspondences. Nothing exists in isolation, and words themselves contain and evoke relationships. Although he would eventually join those who condemned Whitman's catalogues, Emerson recommended the reading of the dictionary because of the evocative power of individual words. A few years before his death, Whitman echoed Emerson when he said to Horace Traubel, "They call the catalogues names, but suppose they do? It *is* names: but what could be more poetic than names?" (Traubel 324). Whitman's notebooks further illustrate the poet's fascination with words.

When Whitman is at his best, the catalogues are stylistically much more controlled and unified than they seem upon first encounter. Despite their appearance as spontaneous outpourings, they are often connected by both logic and grammar. Perhaps reflecting a popular early form of psychology termed "Associationalism," the catalogues relate one thing to another through a chain of associated thought. Sometimes, as Stanley K. Coffman has shown of "Crossing Brooklyn Ferry," the catalogues are organized grammatically so that words, phrases, and clauses of the same type are repeated and then expanded into complete grammatical constructions. Very often, as in the long catalogues of "Song of Myself," Whitman uses the poetic device of anaphora, in which a single word is repeated at the beginning of successive lines or clauses.

Sometimes Whitman's readers are embarrassed to admit that they skim the catalogues, but skimming seems almost unavoidable because of their length, repetition, and parallelism. Critics argue about whether Whitman's poems are essentially oral or visual in quality. Certainly the sweeping, broad lines of the first edition (Whitman had to revert to a smaller format in order to get the second edition published) emphasize the visual aspect of the poetry. One's eyes sweep across the page, just as the poet sweeps across the universe, pulling all unto himself and his vision. Whitman anticipated the motion picture camera, presenting items which, like the frames of celluloid film, are individual but also part of a moving picture. Whitman was not uniformly successful in controlling the catalogue technique, however. Some of his weaker attempts, such as those in "Song of the Broad-Axe," resemble the parodies that they inspired. Yet at his best, Whitman uses the catalogues to give an expansive, exhilarating quality to his poems.

John B. Mason

Bibliography

Coffman, Stanley K., Jr. "'Crossing Brooklyn Ferry': A Note on the Catalogue Technique in Whitman's Poetry." *Modern Philology* 51 (1954): 225–232.

Mason, John B. "Whitman's Catalogues: Rhetorical Means for Two Journeys in 'Song of Myself.'" *American Literature* 45 (1973): 34–49. Rpt. in *On Whitman: The Best from "American Literature."* Ed. Edwin Harrison Cady and Louis J. Budd. Durham, N.C.: Duke UP, 1987. 187–202.

Miller, Edwin Haviland. *Walt Whitman's "Song of Myself": A Mosaic of Interpretations.* Iowa City: U of Iowa P, 1989.

Traubel, Horace. *With Walt Whitman in Camden.* Ed. Sculley Bradley. Vol. 4. Philadelphia: U of Pennsylvania P, 1953.

See also PARODIES; POETIC THEORY; STYLE AND TECHNIQUE(S)

Catel, Jean (1891–1950)

Jean Catel was the first French academic critic who undertook a thorough study of *Leaves of Grass*. He did his research at Harvard and the Library of Congress after World War I and obtained a doctor's degree at the Sorbonne. His two dissertations were published. The major one was entitled *Walt Whitman: La naissance du poète* (1929). The minor one was on *Rythme et langage dans la 1re édition des "Leaves of Grass"* (1930). Catel was a poet and an artist by temperament, and, unlike Léon Bazalgette, was more interested in Whitman's aesthetics than in his politics. In *La naissance du poète* he rejects all previous interpretations of Whitman's personality. He does not, like Richard Maurice Bucke, need a mystical experience to explain the birth of the poet nor, like Henry Binns, a romantic love affair in New Orleans. By means of a searching analysis of the rough drafts and text of the 1855 *Leaves,* Catel reached the conclusion that Whitman originally was a maladjusted and introverted young man who found compensation for his failings and failures in poetry. His poems surged out of his unconscious, liberating his homosexual eroticism and everything American society obliged him to repress. They were the expression of his autoeroticism and enabled him to build up his "identity," his soul, free of external constraints. Catel argues that Whitman identified himself with what his imagination called up and, thanks to Emerson's transcendentalism, succeeded in spiritualizing the physical world. The result was a form of poetry which anticipated symbolism.

In *Rythme et langage* Catel insists on the oral character, the "vocal style," of *Leaves of Grass* and shows how much it owes to the spoken language and to oratory and its rhythms, primacy being given to rhythm over meaning. Catel also did pioneer work by publishing *The Eighteenth Presidency!* (1928) for the first time. He had the luck of finding a set of the proofs in a Boston bookshop. He had it translated by Sylvia Beach and Adrienne Monnier and the translation was published in *Le Navire d'Argent* (1 March 1926).

Roger Asselineau

Bibliography

Allen, Gay Wilson. *The New Walt Whitman Handbook.* 1975. New York: New York UP, 1986.

Pucciani, Oreste F. *The Literary Reputation of Walt Whitman in France.* 1943. New York: Garland, 1987.

See also BIOGRAPHIES; FRANCE, WHITMAN IN

Cather, Willa (1873–1947)

Willa Cather, American novelist, journalist, and critic, is best known for her fiction about immigrant life and pioneer experience in the Midwest and Southwest. Her novel *O Pioneers!* (1913), named for Whitman's poem, incorporates Whitman's lyrical style and sense of cosmic unity in all of nature.

Cather may have first read Whitman between 1891 and 1895, while attending the University of Nebraska. Her early attitude toward him was mixed, reflecting the competing influences of European and American models on her

artistic development. Susan Rosowski argues for British rather than American romantic influences on Cather. Carl Van Doren and Edward Wagenknecht, however, compare her with Whitman and Sarah Orne Jewett, and Judith Fryer, citing a column that Cather wrote for the Lincoln *Courier* (1895), calls Whitman and Henry James her literary masters. In a column in the *Nebraska State Journal* (1896), Cather criticizes Whitman's all-inclusive, prosaic language, but she praises his "primitive elemental force" (*The World* 1:280), passion for nature, and celebration of life. As she matured, her attraction to Whitman deepened.

O Pioneers! evokes Whitman in style and theme. Bernice Slote notes its loose structure, contrasts, and repetitive symbols; James Woodress its epigraphic poem celebrating the land and the pioneering spirit of those who cultivate it *(Willa Cather);* and David Stouck its epic qualities. John Murphy finds parallels with "Song of Myself": a unity of self and nature, achieved through Alexandra Bergson's love of the land; a procreative urge, evident in the rich seasonal harvests and Emil Bergson and Marie Shabata's romance; and an assurance of life after death. Cather also borrows from Whitman in her depiction of comradeship between Alexandra and Carl Linstrum. Whitman's influence is also apparent in other fiction by Cather. She alludes to "Passage to India" and "Crossing Brooklyn Ferry" in her novel *Alexander's Bridge* (1912), to Whitman's doctrine of the "open road" in her novel *My Ántonia* (1918), and to "Out of the Cradle Endlessly Rocking" in her 1932 story "Two Friends."

Cather's use of Whitman places her in a predominantly male American literary tradition; as Hermione Lee notes, however, Cather transforms as well as reflects masculine forms. She also combines romantic celebrations of nature and westward expansion with modernist regret and nostalgia.

Carol J. Singley

Bibliography

Cather, Willa. *The World and the Parish: Willa Cather's Articles and Reviews, 1893–1902.* Ed. William M. Curtin. 2 vols. Lincoln: U of Nebraska P, 1970.

Comeau, Paul. "The Doctrine of the Open Road in *My Ántonia.*" *Approaches to Teaching Cather's "My Ántonia."* Ed. Susan J. Rosowski. New York: MLA, 1989. 150–155.

Fryer, Judith. *Felicitous Space: The Imaginative Structures of Edith Wharton and Willa Cather*. Chapel Hill: U of North Carolina P, 1986.

Lee, Hermione. *Willa Cather: A Life Saved Up*. London: Virago, 1973.

Murphy, John J. "Cather's 'Two Friends' as a Western 'Out of the Cradle.'" *Willa Cather Pioneer Memorial Newsletter* 31.3 (1987): 39–41.

———. "A Comprehensive View of Cather's *O Pioneers!*" *Critical Essays on Willa Cather*. Ed. John J. Murphy. Boston: Hall, 1984. 113–127.

Rosowski, Susan J. *The Voyage Perilous: Willa Cather's Romanticism*. Lincoln: U of Nebraska P, 1986.

Slote, Bernice. "Willa Cather: The Secret Web." *Five Essays on Willa Cather: The Merrimack Symposium*. Ed. John J. Murphy. North Andover, Mass.: Merrimack College, 1974. 1–19.

Stouck, David. *Willa Cather's Imagination*. Lincoln: U of Nebraska P, 1975.

Van Doren, Carl. *Contemporary American Novelists, 1900–1920*. New York: Macmillan, 1922.

Wagenknecht, Edward. "Willa Cather." *Sewanee Review* 37 (1939): 221–239.

Woodress, James. "Whitman and Cather." *Études Anglaises* 45.3 (1992): 324–332.

———. *Willa Cather: A Literary Life*. Lincoln: U of Nebraska P, 1987.

See also LEGACY, WHITMAN'S; "PIONEERS! O PIONEERS!"

"Cavalry Crossing a Ford" (1865)

Written during the Civil War, "Cavalry Crossing a Ford" was first published in *Drum-Taps* (1865) and incorporated into the body of *Leaves of Grass* in 1871 as part of the "Drum-Taps" cluster, where it remained through subsequent editions of *Leaves*. "Cavalry" is one of several "Drum-Taps" poems remarkable for their concise and photographic precision of imagery.

The poem depicts a unified scene of varied images rendered in a single moment. The literal image, which seems to be almost instantaneously observed by the speaker's eye, invites comparison with the then nascent art of photography. Yet the poem's spare imagery deftly shades into the symbolic. Depicting individual figures ("each person a picture") engaged in collective action, the poem exemplifies Whitman's balanced celebration of the individual and the democratic "en-masse"—the individualism tempered by community and camaraderie that he sees as indispensable to the survival of union and democracy.

Some critical interest (e.g., Howard Waskow, John Schwiebert) has focused on the roles readers play in "Cavalry" and other "imagistic" Whitman poems. Lacking the strong and rather discursive speaker-persona of "Song of Myself," these poems focus more exclusively on the image itself, without authorial guidance or explanation, thus emphasizing the reader's creative role in making meaning. Such a view coincides with Whitman's own contention that a poem should not be a finished product but a beginning, that the reader "must himself or herself construct indeed the poem" (Whitman 425).

John E. Schwiebert

Bibliography

Erkkila, Betsy. *Whitman the Political Poet*. New York: Oxford, 1989.

French, Roberts W. "Reading Whitman: 'Cavalry Crossing a Ford.'" *The English Record* 27 (1976): 16–19.

Schwiebert, John E. *The Frailest Leaves: Whitman's Poetic Technique and Style in the Short Poem*. New York: Lang, 1992.

Waskow, Howard J. *Whitman: Explorations in Form*. Chicago: U of Chicago P, 1966.

Whitman, Walt. *Prose Works 1892*. Ed. Floyd Stovall. Vol. 2. New York: New York UP, 1964.

See also CIVIL WAR, THE; "DRUM-TAPS"; PHOTOGRAPHS AND PHOTOGRAPHERS

"Centenarian's Story, The" (1865)

Included as one of the fifty-three poems in *Drum-Taps* (1865) and later incorporated into the "Drum-Taps" cluster, "The Centenarian's Story" conjures up America's revolutionary past, especially the Battle of Long Island (27 August 1776), which took place in Washington Park, Brooklyn, at Fort Greene. Whitman had earlier called this poem "Washington's First Battle," referring to the part played by the General in the Centenarian's tale.

The poem has three discrete parts: the Volunteer's address-cum-invitation to the Veteran to recount his war memories; the Veteran's account of the war of Brooklyn Heights; and a "Terminus" that helps us see the narrator as a "chansonnier of a great future" exhorting his compatriots to hold firm through the mad fury of the Civil War.

The Volunteer's opening section introduces the terrain, "the plain below [where] recruits are drilling and exercising." He asks the Centenarian why the latter trembles and clutches his hand so convulsively. He assures the old man that "the troops are but drilling"; there is no reason for worry or panic.

The Centenarian begins to answer the Volunteer by recalling how he himself had taken part in a war on "this hilltop, this same ground." He sees the ground now "re-peopled from graves," the engines of war remounted, and the men resuming action. He also remembers the Declaration of Independence read aloud there, the army on parade, and the General standing in the midst of it all holding his unsheathed sword. The Centenarian recalls one scene in particular—the steady march of a brigade made up of young men from the South that confronts death headlong. Memory unwinds yet another spool as the Veteran calls up the alarm and dismay on the perspiring General's face, the wringing of his hands in shame and anguish. The battle over, the General beats a retreat at night. When everyone thinks that the situation warrants capitulation, the General thinks otherwise. And so, recalls the Centenarian, at the break of day, the General's face betrays no sign of despair or resignation.

The poet speaks the "Terminus." His voice is now heard as distinct from the solicitous Volunteer's and the elegizing Veteran's. "I must copy the story," he says, "and send it eastward and westward," a message hopeful and heroic enough to be relayed far and wide. The implicit parallel between the battle of Long Island and the first battle of Bull Run is hard to ignore. The defeat of the Union is, in a way, a trial of the new nation's democratic strength. The "hills and slopes of Brooklyn" now symbolize the values of democratic dharma for which the Americans must fight, even among themselves, so that those values can still be upheld.

Whitman's sophistication in framing the Centenarian's tale is of considerable contemporary interest. The visionary sequence of the middle part is framed by two brief narratives, the first initiatory, and the second summary. While the tale itself is rather extravagant (even baroque) in style, the framing narratives are appropriately analytical, factual, and self-reflexive by turns.

K. Narayana Chandran

Bibliography
Burrison, William. "Whitman's *Drum-Taps* Reviewed: The Good, Gray, Tender Mother-Man and the Fierce, Red, Convulsive Rhythm of War." *Walt Whitman: Here and Now*. Ed. Joann P. Krieg. Westport, Conn.: Greenwood, 1985. 157–169.
Cavitch, David. *My Soul and I: The Inner Life of Walt Whitman*. Boston: Beacon, 1985.
Dougherty, James. *Walt Whitman and the Citizen's Eye*. Baton Rouge: Louisiana State UP, 1993.

See also AMERICAN REVOLUTION, THE; BROOKLYN, NEW YORK; CIVIL WAR, THE; "DRUM-TAPS"; WASHINGTON, GEORGE

Centennial Exposition (Philadelphia)

Commemorating the 100th anniversary of American independence, the Centennial Exposition opened in Philadelphia's Fairmount Park on 10 May 1876. Inaugurated by President Ulysses S. Grant and Emperor Dom Pedro II of Brazil, the exposition included 31,000 exhibitors from 56 countries and colonies. Over a six-month period, close to 10,000,000 visitors came to Fairmount Park, which offered such spectacular sights as a 1,400-horsepower steam engine and the future arm and torch of the Statue of Liberty. By closing day in November, the Centennial Exposition had set a new record for attendance at international fairs and had boosted America's reputation as an industrial and economic power.

In the spring of 1875, while Fairmount Park was little more than a construction site, Walt Whitman began collecting material for a new edition of his writings to coincide with the opening of the Centennial Exposition. He probably hoped that the timely appearance of this Centennial edition would convince the exposition committee to let him write the official poem for the opening ceremony. In *Two Rivulets*, the second volume of the Centennial edition, Whitman included a poem entitled "Song of the Exposition" and prefaced it with remarks about the Centennial Exposition. In the preface,

Whitman invites the muse mentioned in the poem to Philadelphia and praises "those superb International Expositions." The poem had originally been published under the title *After All, Not to Create Only* in 1871, when Whitman had delivered it as the inaugural poem at the 40th Annual Exhibition of the American Institute in New York.

Despite Whitman's efforts to get the attention of the Philadelphia exposition committee, he did not receive an invitation to participate in the opening ceremony. Instead, the honor to write for the Centennial Exposition went to three other poets. Bayard Taylor, who ironically had satirized Whitman's inaugural poem in 1871, delivered an ode at the exposition's Fourth of July celebration. Sidney Lanier wrote a cantata for the opening ceremony, and John Greenleaf Whittier contributed a hymn. Although Whitman had tried more consistently than any of these poets to write about America in his poetry, his controversial reputation made him an unlikely choice for the exposition committee. In the end, Whitman came to the Centennial Exposition as an ordinary visitor, paying the same fifty cents admission as everyone else. Living with his brother George in Camden, New Jersey, Whitman did not have to travel far to get to the exposition. He was still weak from a paralytic stroke suffered in 1873, however, and there is little to suggest that the exposition made much of an impression on him after it had started.

Elmar S. Lueth

Bibliography

Allen, Gay Wilson. *The Solitary Singer: A Critical Biography of Walt Whitman.* 1955. Rev. ed. 1967. Chicago: U of Chicago P, 1985.

Ingram, J.S. *The Centennial Exposition, Described and Illustrated.* Philadelphia: Hubbard Brothers, 1876.

Kaplan, Justin. *Walt Whitman: A Life.* New York: Simon and Schuster, 1980.

Post, Robert C., ed. *1876: A Centennial Exhibition.* Washington, D.C.: National Museum of History and Technology, 1976.

See also CAMDEN, NEW JERSEY; LANIER, SIDNEY; *LEAVES OF GRASS*, 1876, AUTHOR'S EDITION; PHILADELPHIA, PENNSYLVANIA; "SONG OF THE EXPOSITION"; TAYLOR, BAYARD; TECHNOLOGY; *TWO RIVULETS*, AUTHOR'S EDITION; WHITTIER, JOHN GREENLEAF

"Chanting the Square Deific" (1865–1866)

One of Walt Whitman's most important religious statements, this poem first appeared in *Sequel to Drum-Taps* (1865–1866). The origins of the poem stretch back to the early 1850s, however. Trial lines appear in "Pictures," an unpublished poem written before 1855; further trial lines took shape in an 1860–1861 notebook; and Whitman scribbled trial titles— "Quadriune" and "Deus Quadriune"—on the contents page of his personal, heavily-marked copy of *Leaves of Grass.* In 1871 Whitman placed "Chanting" in *Passage to India.* He then revised the poem and moved it to the "Whispers of Heavenly Death" cluster in the 1881 *Leaves of Grass.*

"Chanting" evokes the supreme being as a four-person deity. In each of the poem's four stanzas, a separate side of the divine square speaks, announcing and describing himself or herself. The first is the eternal Father God, the uncreated creator, known as Jehovah, Brahma, Saturnius, or Kronos. An unmerciful keeper of the law, He represents justice. Mercy and love characterize the second figure, God's human aspect, God incarnate, who goes by the names Christ, Hermes, and Hercules. The third face of God is Satan. Rejecting the Father's authority and Consolator's love, he is belligerent and outcast—but, in Whitman's theology, a necessary part of the cosmos. Santa Spirita speaks in the final stanza. She is the Holy Spirit whose ethereal presence pervades and unites the four-person deity and all creation. Recasting the masculine *Spirito Santo* into a feminine form, Whitman creates a female deity who symbolizes life and the unity of all things.

Whitman thought of "Chanting" as an expression of spiritual egalitarianism, a representation of the four equal, necessary, eternal sides of the universe. "Chanting" is inclusive. It deems democracy a spiritual condition and conceives a religion suitable to a democratic country. It encompasses all faiths, placing Jehovah next to Kronos and Hermes next to Christ without distinction or preference. The theology of "Chanting" is notable for its similarly egalitarian conception of the deity as female, a feminine divine principle who exists beyond death, beyond good and evil. Perhaps most striking is Whitman's inclusion of Satan as member of the Godhead—the addition that makes the Christian trinity into a distinctively Whitmanesque quaternity. Merging righteousness with rebelliousness, accepting the unacceptable, including the excluded, "Chanting" makes "the denied God" (as Whitman calls Lucifer in "Pictures" [*Comprehensive* 645]) an integral part of the deity and an eternal part of the universe.

In the late nineteenth and early twentieth centuries, "Chanting" drew criticism for its heretical, anti-Trinitarian view of God and its audacious deifying of Satan. But it is not merely this heterodoxy that makes the inclusion of Satan arresting. Satan's incorporation within the Godhead implies that the presence of God depends upon an absence, the defiance of God, God's negative image. Lucifer's antithetic presence is also related to the poem's Hegelianism—its spiritual dialectic, its embrace of negativity and contradiction and synthesis of antagonistic forces.

The appearance of "Chanting" in *Sequel to Drum-Taps* suggests that Whitman offered the poem as a postwar message of reconciliation and religious consolation. From this perspective, it comments allegorically on the war: Satan is the South ("plotting revolt," "brother of slaves," "warlike" [section 3]) and Jehovah the North, seeking righteousness; the Consolator could be Abraham Lincoln or perhaps a wound dresser and the Santa Spirita probably the poet himself through whose songs comes peace and the spiritual preservation of the Union. Whitman later decided to downplay the poem's historical significance and emphasize its theological meaning by deleting a war allusion and moving the poem out of the Civil War clusters and into the explicitly religious "Whispers of Heavenly Death."

The historical relevance of "Chanting" and its outline of a new American religion make it a revealing text for understanding Whitman in his culture, while its allegorical suggestiveness make it a poem rich with interpretive possibilities.

Gregory Eiselein

Bibliography

Allen, Gay Wilson. *The Solitary Singer: A Critical Biography of Walt Whitman.* 1955. Rev. ed. 1967. Chicago: U of Chicago P, 1985.

Hollis, C. Carroll. *Language and Style in "Leaves of Grass."* Baton Rouge: Louisiana State UP, 1983.

Mancuso, Luke. "'Chanting the Square Deific': Whitman Confronts Structural Evil in Post-War America." *Symposium* 8 (1990): 15–33.

Sixbey, George L. "'Chanting the Square Deific'—A Study in Whitman's Religion." *American Literature* 9 (1937): 171–195.

Whitman, Walt. *Leaves of Grass: Comprehensive Reader's Edition.* Ed. Harold W. Blodgett and Sculley Bradley. New York: New York UP, 1965.

———. *Walt Whitman's "Drum-Taps" (1865) and "Sequel to Drum-Taps" (1865–6): A Facsimile Reproduction.* Ed. F. DeWolfe Miller. Gainesville, Fla.: Scholars' Facsimiles and Reprints, 1959.

See also DEMOCRACY; DIALECTIC; EVIL; RELIGION; *SEQUEL TO DRUM-TAPS;* "WHISPERS OF HEAVENLY DEATH" (CLUSTER)

Chase, Richard Volney (1914–1962)

A Columbia University professor, Chase wrote books on prominent American literary figures and issues, including *Herman Melville: A Critical Study* (1949), *Emily Dickinson* (1951), and *The American Novel and Its Tradition* (1957). As a Whitman scholar, his two books *Walt Whitman Reconsidered* (1955) and *Walt Whitman* (1961) undertook to revise previous interpretations by emphasizing Whitman's modern, paradoxical, and comic qualities, none of which, according to Chase, had received adequate attention. "Song of Myself" is the first modern poem in that it incorporates prose elements and expands subject matter to include the entire spectrum of life. Also, at the heart of Whitman's work are paradox and contradiction, modern attributes, which appear in the poet's vacillation between praising the individual self and extolling the democratic mass, between being a cheerleader for and a critic of American society.

Chase took issue with critics who overemphasized Whitman's philosophical and religious qualities. Instead, in the best poems, such as "Song of Myself," "Crossing Brooklyn Ferry," and "Out of the Cradle Endlessly Rocking," Chase saw Whitman's strength and true subject to be his presentation of the development of an often-divided self against the backdrop of energetic but chaotic cultural and social conditions, which he alternately praised and decried. The many contradictions that result from the topic of a self sometimes at odds with its own and its culture's values produced, in Chase's view, a comic tone in much of Whitman's poetry, a tone as characteristic of his work as the more praised lyrical one. While Chase found it ironic that the poet was unappreciated by the general public for which he wrote, he contended that, because of his many masks and contradictions, Whitman is America's spokesman.

Walter Graffin

Bibliography

Chase, Richard. *Walt Whitman*. University of Minnesota Pamphlets on American Writers 9. Minneapolis: U of Minnesota P, 1961.

——. *Walt Whitman Reconsidered.* New York: William Sloane Associates, 1955.

See also HUMOR; SCHOLARSHIP, TRENDS IN WHITMAN

Chase, Salmon P. (1808–1873)

Born in New Hampshire, Chase grew up in Ohio, establishing a legal practice in Cincinnati in 1830. An early and ardent crusader against slavery, in 1840 Chase left the Democrats to join the Liberal party and later the Free Soil party, serving as chairman of the convention in Buffalo (1848) to which Whitman was a delegate. U.S. senator (1849–1855) and governor of Ohio (1856–1860), Chase was a candidate for the Republican presidential nomination (1860). As Secretary of the Treasury (1861–1864) he ably performed the difficult task of financing the Civil War, and as Chief Justice of the U.S. Supreme Court (1864–1873), he presided over the impeachment trial of President Johnson (1868).

Having heard that Whitman's writings "have given him a bad repute" (qtd. in Allen 311), as Secretary of the Treasury Chase would not offer Whitman a position in the Treasury Department and even kept Emerson's letter of recommendation. In *The Solitary Singer,* Gay Wilson Allen suggests that Chase was being cautious because of his political ambitions, though noting that Chase was religious and conservative in social matters and may therefore have acted upon his beliefs. Efforts by Chase to achieve the presidency in 1868 and 1872 were greeted with scorn by Whitman, who called Chase "the meanest and biggest kind of a shyster" (Whitman 35).

Frederick Hatch

Bibliography

Allen, Gay Wilson. *The Solitary Singer: A Critical Biography of Walt Whitman.* 1955. Rev. ed. 1967. Chicago: U of Chicago P, 1985.

Belden, Thomas G. and Marva R. *So Fell the Angels.* Boston: Little, Brown, 1956.

Blue, Frederick J. *Salmon P. Chase: A Life in Politics.* Kent, Ohio: Kent State UP, 1987.

Myerson, Joel, ed. *Whitman in His Own Time.* Detroit: Omnigraphics, 1991.

Vexler, Robert I. *The Vice-Presidents and Cabinet Members.* Dobbs Ferry, N.Y.: Oceana, 1975.

Whitman, Walt. *The Correspondence.* Ed. Edwin Haviland Miller. Vol. 2. New York: New York UP, 1961.

See also TROWBRIDGE, JOHN TOWNSEND

"Child and the Profligate, The" (1841)

This important short story initially appeared under the title "The Child's Champion" in *New World,* 20 November 1841. After much revision, the story appeared with its present title in *Columbian Magazine,* October 1844. See Thomas L. Brasher's edition of *The Early Poems and the Fiction* for publication particulars and revisions.

Thirteen-year-old Charley, the only child of a poor old widow, works for a greedy farmer. One evening, music lures Charley into a tavern, where a one-eyed seaman brutally tries to force the boy to drink brandy. A wealthy young man, Langton, who has been living a dissolute life, rescues Charley. Charley and his mother give purpose to the profligate's life, and as Langton saves them from their once-inescapable poverty, he is reformed.

The story's obvious didactic purpose is the reformation of a wastrel in contrast to the dissolution of the other characters. The vulnerability of the poor and the greed of Charley's employer are also part of its didacticism. Its temperance theme appears in other stories by Whitman, most notably his novel *Franklin Evans; or The Inebriate. A Tale of the Times* (1842).

Moon has noted homoeroticism in the interaction between the seaman and young Charley, which Reynolds parallels to the interaction between Tim and Lugare in "Death in the School-Room" (1841). Moreover, Moon connects "Calamus" number 29 (1857) to elements of the story. A more gentle homoeroticism is evident, perhaps, in Charley's relationship with his rescuer, on whose bosom, in the earliest version of the story, Charley rests his cheek as they sleep through the night. But not all critics agree; Callow and Kaplan see the love between the boy and the man as devoid of any sexual content.

Patrick McGuire

Bibliography

Callow, Philip. *From Noon to Starry Night: A Life of Walt Whitman.* Chicago: Ivan R. Dee, 1992.

Kaplan, Justin. *Walt Whitman: A Life.* New York: Simon and Schuster, 1980.

Moon, Michael. *Disseminating Whitman: Revision and Corporeality in "Leaves of Grass."* Cambridge, Mass.: Harvard UP, 1991.

Reynolds, David S. *Walt Whitman's America: A Cultural Biography.* New York: Knopf, 1995.

Whitman, Walt. *The Early Poems and the Fiction.* Ed. Thomas L. Brasher. New York: New York UP, 1963.

See also "DEATH IN THE SCHOOL-ROOM (A FACT)"; *FRANKLIN EVANS*; SHORT FICTION, WHITMAN'S

"Children of Adam" (1860)

Originally entitled "Enfans d'Adam" in the 1860 edition of *Leaves of Grass,* this cluster of poems celebrating sexuality was called "Children of Adam" in 1867 and thereafter. The poems, openly "singing the phallus" and the "mystic deliria," were too bold for their time and often got Whitman into trouble. His relationship with Ralph Waldo Emerson cooled after he refused Emerson's advice in 1860 to drop the sex poems; in 1865 he lost his job in the Interior Department in Washington for writing "indecent" poems; and he had to withdraw the 1881 edition of *Leaves* from publication in Boston when the Society for the Suppression of Vice found it immoral.

On conceiving the idea for the "Children of Adam" cluster, Whitman jotted in a notebook: "Theory of a Cluster of Poems the same *to the passion of Woman-Love* as the *Calamus-Leaves* are to adhesiveness, manly love" (*Notebooks* 1:412). Whitman appropriated two terms from phrenology to distinguish the two kinds of relationships he describes here: "adhe-siveness," or comradeship, and "amativeness," or heterosexual love. In pairing his poems on friendship with poems on love, Whitman was following masters of the personal essay, from Montaigne to Emerson, who in their prose compared and contrasted the two most fundamental, and generally complex, relationships in life. Whitman's intention is programmatic: he challenges the traditional ecclesiastic view of sexuality as inherently evil. The symbolism basic to the structure of the "Children of Adam" cluster is announced in the title: human beings are all descendants of Adam and Eve, who, after eating the forbidden fruit from the Tree of Knowledge, "knew that they were naked" and covered their nakedness with "fig leaves" (Genesis 3:7). For their act of disobedience, they were cast out of the Garden of Eden. In effect, Whitman exhorts a return to the Garden by recovering the sexual innocence of Adam and Eve before the Fall.

The voice heard in the "Children of Adam" cluster, as revealed in "Ages and Ages Returning at Intervals," is that of a "chanter of Adamic songs" who, "[l]usty, phallic," wanders through "the new garden the West" and the great cities, "bathing" his songs in sex. This chanter identifies himself specifically as Adam in the opening and closing poems of the cluster, "To the Garden the World" and "As Adam Early in the Morning." In the first he is walking with Eve, content, taking delight in the "quivering fire that ever plays" through his limbs; in the latter he emerges from his "bower refresh'd with sleep" and urges, "Touch me, touch the palm of your hand to my body as I pass, / Be not afraid of my body."

Although the poet does not portray himself as Adam in the other "Children of Adam" poems, he assumes the voice of the "chanter of Adamic songs." "From Pent-up Aching Rivers," second in the cluster, has the tone of a defiant proclamation ("what I am determin'd to make illustrious, even if I stand sole among men"). Images seem to tumble out with an increasing speed and intensity, creating finally the impression of a montage of sexuality in all its many and varied manifestations. The rhythmic urgency of the poem, beginning with the "pent-up aching rivers" seemingly at flood-tide, has something of the urgency of the universal sexual drive.

Although Whitman considered using "Song of Procreation" as his title for this poem, he decided against it probably because he came to realize that the poem was more clearly a celebration of all sexuality however expressed— "The mystic deliria, the madness amorous, the utter abandonment." The poem embraces autoeroticism ("From native moments, from bashful pains, singing them"), homoeroticism ("From exultation, victory and relief, from the bedfellow's embrace in the night"), hetero-eroticism ("The female form approaching, I pensive, love-flesh tremulous aching"), and what might be called cosmo-eroticism ("Of the mad pushes of waves upon the land, I them chanting"). In brief, Whitman's poem portrays the sex drive as a "pent-up aching river" or a "hungry gnaw" present day and night that demands release or relief, whatever form that release takes.

The third poem in "Children of Adam," "I Sing the Body Electric," originally appeared in the 1855 *Leaves*. It dominates the "Children of Adam" cluster by its sheer length and, like "From Pent-up Aching Rivers," celebrates sexuality as a mysterious primal energy contained within the human body: "The love of the body of man or woman balks account, the body itself balks account" (section 2). In section 2 the "chanter of Adamic songs" provides a random catalogue of men and women engaging in various activities—the "swimmer naked," "the female soothing a child," the "wrestle of wrestlers," the "march of firemen"—and then concludes: "Such-like I love— I loosen myself, pass freely, am at the mother's breast with the little child, / Swim with the swimmers, wrestle with wrestlers, march in line with the firemen, and pause, listen, count." By such lines the poet reveals the sensual pleasure, rooted unconsciously in sexuality, that all feel in seeing such scenes; great painters and novelists have always been attuned to such primal responses.

Sections 5–9 of "Body Electric" focus alternately on the bodies of women and men and are, in effect, a series of idealized portraits of nudes. To some readers they may seem a bit perfunctory, presenting predictable catalogues of the female and male bodies, interspersed with affirmations that everything named (including "the womb, the teats, nipples," "man-balls, man-root") are not just "of the soul" but "are the soul!" (section 9). The poet's technique, however, is full enough of the unexpected to reward the reader.

Section 5 begins "This is the female form," then suddenly veers away from cataloguing into a metaphoric sketch of love-making that must

be counted among Whitman's greatest lines: "Ebb stung by the flow and flow stung by the ebb, love-flesh swelling and deliciously aching, / Limitless limpid jets of love hot and enormous, quivering jelly of love, white-blow and delirious juice, / Bridegroom night of love working surely and softly into the prostrate dawn, / Undulating into the willing and yielding day, / Lost in the cleave of the clasping and sweet-flesh'd day." The metaphoric "bridegroom" and "prostrate dawn" are evocative of heterosexual love. But the initial focus on the phallus in orgasm is suggestive of homosexual love. There is enough ambiguity or indirection (the bridegroom is "night," the dawn is prelude to "day") to make it impossible to decide definitively. One might ask, what difference does it make? The point is that, contrary to those critics who assume Whitman to be sincere and persuasive only in his poems of adhesiveness, he could write with great power poems of amativeness that would appeal to all readers, whatever their sexuality. In this regard, it is useful to recall the many women among Whitman's readers who pointed to his sexual themes as one of the strongest of his attractions—Anne Gilchrist, who fell in love with the poet upon reading *Leaves of Grass;* Kate Chopin, who adapted some of Whitman's sexual themes for her own fiction; and Muriel Rukeyser, who found Whitman's handling of his sexual themes a model to admire.

After "Body Electric," two poems appear that were included in the 1856 edition: "A Woman Waits for Me" (originally "Poem of Procreation") and "Spontaneous Me" (originally "Bunch Poem"). In "A Woman Waits for Me" the poet assumes the role of Adam as everyman, contributing his vital part to the continuation of humankind. "Sex contains all" not only in the sense that it is the mystic deliria, key to human happiness, but it literally contains "all" the human beings of the future. As the poet drains his "pent-up rivers" into the "woman who waits" for him, "warm-blooded and sufficient," he wraps in her "a thousand onward years." The "crops" he "so lovingly" plants now will produce still other "loving crops from the birth, life, death, immortality."

"Spontaneous Me" is a powerful outpouring of "pent-up" sexual images, but it seems to move toward a climax of some sort. A curious line in the middle of the poem—"The body of my love, the body of the woman I love, the body of the man, the body of the earth"—epitomizes the confusion felt in reading the poem. The spontaneous poet is revealing inchoate sexual feelings that originate from within and that are capable of being directed to any one of a number of bodies: the body of his "love" or of the woman, man, or earth he loves. Masturbatory images dominate the latter half of the poem, as in "the pulse pounding through palms and trembling encircling fingers." In the closing lines, the poet refers to a "wholesome relief, repose, content" and adds: "And this bunch pluck'd at random from myself, / It has done its work—I toss it carelessly to fall where it may." "Bunch" has at least two meanings: it is, in some obscure sense, the semen (a bunch of sperm?) ejaculated by his own hand, and the lines of the poem he has just written, also by his own hand, for which these are the closing lines. Semen or poem—each will "fall where it may": the first perhaps in the woods or in the sea, the poem among the manuscripts destined to become the *Leaves*.

The remaining poems of "Children of Adam" all celebrate sexuality and sexual feeling consonant with the program announced in "From Pent-up Aching Rivers," but they are sparse on images of man-woman, or heterosexual, love. The poems appear to promise a particular sexual experience or partner—"One Hour to Madness and Joy," "Out of the Rolling Ocean the Crowd," "We Two, How Long We were Fool'd," "I am He that Aches with Love," "Once I Pass'd through a Populous City," "I Heard You Solemn-Sweet Pipes of the Organ"—but instead they offer a generalized celebration of sexuality or ambiguity about the sex of the partner. "Once I Pass'd," for example, was originally addressed not to a woman but to a man (Emory Holloway's discovery of this in the 1920s subverted his enthusiasm for Whitman). There remain three additional, as yet unmentioned poems in "Children of Adam." Containing one of the rare references to the female genitalia in *Leaves*, "O Hymen! O Hymenee!" is a short paean to married love. "Native Moments," on the other hand, celebrates the "midnight orgies of young men," more adhesive than amative in its sentiment. In the penultimate poem of the cluster, "Facing West from California's Shores," the voice of the "chanter of Adamic songs" no longer sounds so confident as at the beginning, instead ending on a plaintive note: "But where is what I started for so long ago? / And why is it yet unfound?"

In "A Backward Glance O'er Travel'd Roads" (1888), Whitman wrote his final reply to those readers and critics who condemned him and his work for his frank avowal of sexuality. He said: "'Leaves of Grass' is avowedly the song of Sex and Amativeness, and even Animality. . . . the espousing principle of those lines so gives breath of life to my whole scheme that the bulk of the pieces might as well have been left unwritten were those lines omitted" (*Comprehensive* 572). Readers today are more prone to agree with Whitman than with the squeamish critics of his own time. "Children of Adam" should be read for what it purports to be, not a paean to heterosexual love, but a celebration of sexuality in all its varied forms—auto-, homo-, hetero-, cosmo-eroticism. Whitman was right to deal with all of these as a whole and, in a sense, as one; he realized that they are much more alike than different, that they hold much more in common than not. All these forms of sexuality take their origins from the same source, the "mystic deliria" of the universal sex drive.

James E. Miller, Jr.

Bibliography
Allen, Gay Wilson. *The New Walt Whitman Handbook*. 1975. New York: New York UP, 1986.
Black, Stephen A. *Whitman's Journeys into Chaos: A Psychoanalytic Study of The Poetic Process*. Princeton: Princeton UP, 1975.
Holloway, Emory. *Free and Lonesome Heart: The Secret of Walt Whitman*. New York: Vantage, 1960.
Larson, Kerry S. *Whitman's Drama of Consensus*. Chicago: U of Chicago P, 1988.
Lawrence, D.H. *Studies in Classic American Literature*. 1923. New York: Viking, 1964.
Miller, James E., Jr. *A Critical Guide to "Leaves of Grass."* Chicago: U of Chicago P, 1957.
Reiss, Edmund. "Whitman's Poetic Grammar: Style and Meaning in 'Children of Adam.'" *Whitman in Our Season: A Symposium*. Ed. B. Bernard Cohen. Hartford: Transcendental Books, 1971. 32–41.
Whitman, Walt. *Leaves of Grass: Comprehensive Reader's Edition*. Ed. Harold W. Blodgett and Sculley Bradley. New York: New York UP, 1965.

———. *Notebooks and Unpublished Prose Manuscripts*. Ed. Edward F. Grier. 6 vols. New York: New York, 1984.

See also "Ages and Ages Returning at Intervals"; "As Adam Early in the Morning"; "Calamus"; "Facing West from California's Shores"; "From Pent-up Aching Rivers"; Human Body; "I Heard You Solemn-Sweet Pipes of the Organ"; "I Sing the Body Electric"; *Leaves of Grass*, 1860 Edition; "Native Moments"; "O Hymen! O Hymenee!"; "Once I Pass'd through a Populous City"; "One Hour to Madness and Joy"; "Out of the Rolling Ocean the Crowd"; Sex and Sexuality; "Spontaneous Me"; "To the Garden the World"; "We Two, How Long We were Fool'd"; "Woman Waits for Me, A"

China, Whitman in

Of the vast number of foreign writers China has introduced and translated, none other seems to have enjoyed the kind of respect and popularity that Whitman holds. His free verse helped start China's New Poetry movement in the first decades of the twentieth century, and he is one of the very few foreign writers for whom biographies have been written in China.

Whitman was first introduced into China in 1919, a year marked by great turmoil and patriotic passion that witnessed the famous May Fourth movement. This movement was an essential component of the larger New Culture movement, characterized by a cry for the downfall of Confucianism and the adoption of two Western ideals: science and democracy. In the wake of the May Fourth movement, Tian Han, later known as one of China's foremost playwrights and poets, published the introductory essay, "The Poet for the Common People: Commemorating the Centennial Anniversary of Whitman's Birthday," in the inaugural issue of *Young China,* a radical journal for contemporary intellectuals.

The importance and accomplishment of this long essay cannot be overestimated. It reached a large audience of intelligentsia, and essays on and translations of Whitman soon began to surface in journals and newspapers. Tian's essay was certainly read by Guo Moruo, then studying in Japan, who would come to be known as the apostle of Whitman and recognized as the most important voice in Chinese

new poetry (that is, vernacular poetry as opposed to the traditional, classic poetry that had reigned in Chinese literature for two thousand years). Guo not only read Whitman's poetry in English and Japanese; he also translated some of the poems into Chinese, though only a small portion of his translations have survived. Guo thought that the spirit of the American poet was identical with the Chinese May Fourth spirit.

As a result of Tian's high praise and Guo's imitation of Whitman, a considerable number of "new culture" poets and writers turned to Whitman for inspiration and began to write poetry and prose in vernacular Chinese. Among them was Ai Qing, perhaps second only to Guo as a significant twentieth-century Chinese poet. Ai's poetry reflects the influence of a number of foreign writers, including Whitman and Charles Baudelaire. Ai and Guo both share Whitman's tendency to use long, irregular lines to contain unconstrained thoughts. Whitman's influence is not limited to poets; important Chinese writers in a variety of genres embraced Whitman as a model in the 1930s, 1940s, and 1950s, but Guo and Ai were among the strongest advocates of free verse, and their work best represents Whitmanian qualities.

Whitman has also been used in China for political purposes. In 1955 the 100th anniversary of the first publication of *Leaves of Grass* sparked a renewed interest in the American poet. That in turn led to the publication of new translations of and essays on Whitman, including some East European writings translated into Chinese, such as Maurice Mendelson's influential *Life and Work of Walt Whitman: A Soviet View*. That same year—two years after the Korean War, which involved both the United States and China—the World Peace Council convened in Beijing, where Whitman was lauded as a peace-loving, democratic poet as contrasted to the warlike, imperialistic U.S. government. Thus Whitman was turned into a propaganda tool against his own country. Among the politicians making use of Whitman was Yuan Shuipai, a high official in the Ministry of Propaganda, who claimed that in the Cold War Whitman would be on the side of the peace-loving Chinese, rather than on that of the American government.

Whitman was not seriously studied in the academy until the late 1970s, when China reopened its doors to the West and Whitman made a triumphant return. He has been taught to English majors in Chinese university classrooms ever since. Six complete Chinese translations of *Leaves of Grass* have been published in Mainland China and Taiwan. Of all the Chinese translators of Whitman, Chu Tunan was the earliest and perhaps also the best known. He started rendering Whitman into Chinese in the 1930s during imprisonment for political activities against the then Nationalist rule. Chu was better known as a successful politician who, before his death in the early 1990s, served as a vice chairman of the Standing Committee of the National People's Congress (the highest legislative body of China), but he is remembered by literary scholars as a pioneering and able translator of Whitman. Using Chu's partial translation, Li Yeguang completed a translation of the entire *Leaves of Grass*. Li also wrote *A Critical Biography of Whitman*, perhaps the first Whitman biography of its kind in China. No less notable is the work that Zhao Luorui has done on Whitman. With a doctorate in American literature from the University of Chicago in the 1940s, Zhao taught at and is a retired member of Beijing University; she single-handedly completed another translation of *Leaves of Grass*, in addition to publishing many essays and articles on Whitman.

The efforts of these first-generation Chinese Whitman scholars have paid off handsomely. Whitman is now available to students and scholars who cannot read English. In recent years, many younger scholars have appeared in universities and research institutes who are conducting research and writing master's theses and doctoral dissertations on Whitman. Clearly, there is a bright future for Whitman studies in China.

Guiyou Huang

Bibliography

Cohen, Mark. "Whitman in China: A Revisitation." *Walt Whitman Review* 26 (1980): 32–35.
Fang, Achilles. "From Imagism to Whitmanism in Recent Chinese Poetry: A Search for Poetics That Failed." *Indiana University Conference on Oriental-Western Literary Relations.* Ed. Horst Frenz and G.L. Anderson. Chapel Hill: U of North Carolina P, 1955. 177–189.
Huang, Guiyou. "Whitman in China." *Walt Whitman & the World.* Ed. Gay Wilson Allen and Ed Folsom. Iowa City: U of Iowa P, 1995. 406–428.
———. *Whitmanism, Imagism, and Modernism in China and America.* Selinsgrove: Susquehanna UP, 1997.
Kuebrich, David. "Whitman in China." *Walt Whitman Quarterly Review* 1.2 (1983): 33–35.
Li, Shi Qi. "Whitman's Poetry of Internationalism." *West Hills Review* 7 (1987): 103–110.
Palandri, Angela Chih-Ying Jung. "Whitman in Red China." *Walt Whitman Newsletter* 4.3 (1958): 94–97.
Wang, Yao. "The Relation Between Modern Chinese Literature and Foreign Literature." *Chinese Literature* 38.3 (1988): 149–160.

See also INTERCULTURALITY

Chopin, Kate (1850–1904)

The fiction of Kate O'Flaherty Chopin depicts late nineteenth-century Creole Louisiana. Her collections of short stories were critical and popular successes, but her final novel, *The Awakening* (1899)—for which she is now best known—was greeted with almost universally hostile criticism for its sensuousness and its sympathetic treatment of an adulterous woman.

Chopin admired both Whitman's prose writings and *Leaves*, and his influence is evidenced particularly by her convention-breaking, open treatment of sexuality. Echoes of Whitman are especially pervasive in *The Awakening*, which alludes to "Song of Myself" and "Out of the Cradle" in its reference to the sensuous murmur and touch of the sea, its recurrent bird imagery, and its association of protagonist Edna Pontellier with Whitman's "bold swimmer" ("Song of Myself," section 46) and "twenty-ninth bather" (section 11). Edna is also a prototype of the ideal woman Whitman depicts in "A Woman Waits for Me" and *Democratic Vistas*.

Nonetheless, the novel's treatment of female sexuality differs from Whitman's, especially in its darker view of motherhood. Certain of its passages even suggest a darker, un-Whitmanesque view of passion and sexuality itself. In "The Storm," however, a story written after *The Awakening*, Chopin depicts an unrestrained sexual encounter in a positive manner reminiscent of the "Children of Adam" poems.

Chopin was powerfully influenced by Whitman, although the relationship of her writing to his was more dialogic than derivative. She honored him in the manner he urged upon his followers; she learned under him how to "destroy the teacher" ("Song of Myself," section 47).

Gay Barton

Bibliography

Barton, Gay. "'Amativeness, and Even Animality': A Whitman/Chopin Dialogue on Female Sexuality." *Journal of the American Studies Association of Texas* 27 (1996): 1–18.

Bloom, Harold. Introduction. *Kate Chopin: Modern Critical Views*. Ed. Harold Bloom. New York: Chelsea House, 1987. 1–6.

Chopin, Kate. *The Awakening: An Authoritative Text, Biographical and Historical Contexts, Criticism*. Ed. Margo Culley. 2nd ed. New York: Norton, 1994.

Leary, Lewis. "Kate Chopin and Walt Whitman." *Walt Whitman Review* 16 (1970): 120–121.

Loving, Jerome. *Lost in the Customhouse: Authorship in the American Renaissance*. Iowa City: U of Iowa P, 1993.

Price, Kenneth M. *Whitman and Tradition: The Poet in His Century*. New Haven: Yale UP, 1990.

See also LEGACY, WHITMAN'S; MOTHERHOOD; SEX AND SEXUALITY; WOMEN AS A THEME IN WHITMAN'S WRITING

"City Dead-House, The" (1867)

This poem in "Autumn Rivulets" finds the poet of *Leaves of Grass* grieving over the body of a prostitute lying dead outside the city morgue. Prostitution was a visible social problem in mid-nineteenth-century New York, and prostitutes appeared frequently in Whitman's writing.

As a journalist Whitman's attitude toward prostitutes was fairly conventional. He could be contemptuous or full of pity. Occasionally he would be unequivocally defensive, pointing the finger of blame at his middle-class readers. In an editorial from the 1840s, he decried the "evils and horrors connected with the payment . . . for women's labor—sewing, bookbinding, umbrella work," and warned his readers that such economic injustice "is an evil . . . that . . . sows a public crop of other evils" (*Uncollected* 1:137). In another he challenged the self-image of his complacent, middle-class audience: "'What?' says the reader, 'poor pay? Do you think my getting my shirts made so cheaply, or my buying clothes at a low price,

has anything to do with female crime?'" (*Gathering* 1:150–151).

As a poet, however, Whitman often presented himself as one who has the unique capacity to understand the prostitute. In the first extended catalogue of "Song of Myself," he comforts a "tipsy" prostitute with "pimpled neck," braving the jeers of an urban crowd: "I do not laugh at your oaths nor jeer you" (section 15). In that same poem, he promises to include the prostitutes in the litany of "long dumb voices" he intends to let sound through his poems (section 24). In the 1860 edition he boasts that he will "take for my love some prostitute" ("Enfans d'Adam" number 8).

The dead prostitute in "The City Dead-House" is a mysterious figure. She is a "divine woman" whose body the poet likens to a "house once full of passion and beauty," an edifice "more than all the rows of dwellings ever built . . . or all the old high-spired cathedrals." But, in seeming contradiction, he also calls her body a "fearful wreck—tenement of a soul" and "house of madness and sin, crumbled, crush'd." He imagines her "talking and laughing," but asserts that she was "dead even then." Now, this dead "[u]nclaim'd, avoided" figure is mourned only by the poet, who offers "one breath from . . . tremulous lips" and "one tear dropt" for her.

Thus, in his final poetic engagement with the prostitute, the poet appears torn. In the space of just a few lines, he reiterates the culture's alternating sympathy and condemnation, but at the same time he also signals his own identification with and attraction toward this being whose erotic life intrigues him.

Rosemary Graham

Bibliography

Reynolds, David S. *Walt Whitman's America: A Cultural Biography*. New York: Knopf, 1995.

Stansell, Christine. *City of Women: Sex and Class in New York, 1789–1860*. New York: Knopf, 1986.

Whitman, Walt. *The Gathering of the Forces*. Ed. Cleveland Rodgers and John Black. 2 vols. New York: Putnam, 1920.

———. *The Uncollected Poetry and Prose of Walt Whitman*. Ed. Emory Holloway. 2 vols. Garden City, N.Y.: Doubleday, Page, 1921.

See also "AUTUMN RIVULETS"; "TO A COMMON PROSTITUTE"

"City of Orgies" (1860)

This "Calamus" poem, which acquired its present title in 1867, was originally called by its first line, "City of my walks and joys!," when published as number 18 in the "Calamus" series in 1860. The manuscript is composed of seven lines (against the published version of nine), with line 5 of the published version not yet present, and the later lines 7 and 8 arranged as a single line.

The poem is characteristic of Whitman's structures of negation. After two apostrophes, there are five successive lines beginning with "Not" or "Nor," followed by two positive evocations of the city's offer of love. Much that Whitman rejects in the poem—the city's pageants, tableaux, or spectacles, its processions and bright windows—is indeed attractive, but it is as nothing compared to the satisfaction offered by "the frequent and swift flash of eyes offering me love."

The poem testifies vividly to Whitman's interest in the city as a subject of poetry and to his attempt to capture the reality of the contemporary urban environment. Located in a section of *Leaves* dominated by the pastoral tradition, it speaks to Whitman's project of writing desire in terms of the multiple possibilities of the new city. Parallel to this wish to write urban desire is an attempt to constitute a community of desire. Whitman's scene of cruising begins the process of creating the modern urban homosexual as an identity. While many of the poems follow a tradition of love poetry that seeks the perfect partner, this poem celebrates another tradition of multiple partners and desires.

Because of its challenge to concepts of romantic love, the poem has been much attacked by critics such as Edwin Miller for depicting the pathetic and "desperate delights of an isolate" (162). Robert Martin, on the other hand, sees it as a celebration of a democratic "sensual awareness" (74) that seeks "Lovers, continual lovers." Perhaps because of its challenge to dominant views of love and sexuality, the poem has not often been discussed in detail.

Robert K. Martin

Bibliography

Martin, Robert K. *The Homosexual Tradition in American Poetry*. Austin: U of Texas P, 1979.

Miller, Edwin Haviland. *Walt Whitman's Poetry: A Psychological Journey*. Boston: Houghton Mifflin, 1968.

See also "CALAMUS"; CITY, WHITMAN AND THE; SEX AND SEXUALITY

City, Whitman and the

After growing up in rural Long Island and the busy village of Brooklyn, Whitman spent his adult life living in and writing about the American city. Whether editing city newspapers such as the Brooklyn *Daily Eagle* or the New Orleans *Crescent,* or composing poetic catalogues of downtown spectacles, Whitman devoted much of his work to representing what he saw in the faces of laborers, what he heard exchanged on the sidewalks, what he felt pulsing all around him as he stood on the corner of, say, 15th and F streets in Washington, D.C. He resided in New York during the forties and fifties (except for a brief stay in New Orleans in 1848), writing articles about city politics and the cultural scene before leaving newspaper work in the mid-fifties to begin his experiments in poetry. He stayed in Washington during and after the Civil War, serving first as a volunteer nurse in the hospitals before securing a minor post in the Department of the Interior in 1865. Finally, he settled in Camden, New Jersey, writing and revising poetry and prose and receiving visitors who had come to pay homage to America's bard. Whitman's lifelong immersion in numerous American cities renders him America's first great poetic celebrant of metropolitan life, a sensitive recorder of urban experience. Ever fascinated by street scenes, by the "blab of the pave" ("Song of Myself," section 8), by the pageantry of Broadway at noon and the expectant rush of commuters on Brooklyn ferry, Whitman always sought to transcribe the workaday routines and proletarian intercourse of the city and to give them just as much poetic value as that traditionally ascribed to nature and aristocrats.

Whitman's glorification of the American city assumes many different forms in his writings. In *Leaves of Grass* he includes numerous poems and passages documenting the sights and sounds of urban life in all its splendor and modernity and ferment, as well as revealing its despair and exhaustion and crime. With its exuberant lists of butcher-boys and blacksmiths and machinists and prostitutes and suicides, ballrooms and wharves and hospitals and shop windows, "Song of Myself" is the most copious repository of Whitman's episodic or even single-line descriptions of city scenes. (This is why

Ralph Waldo Emerson, when recommending the book to Thomas Carlyle, said to Carlyle that he might find the volume to be nothing more than "an auctioneer's inventory of a warehouse"—6 May 1856 [Norton 2:283].) Other poems such as "City of Orgies," "A Song for Occupations," "A Broadway Pageant," "Mannahatta," and "Give Me the Splendid Silent Sun" contain the same quotidian urban data, though often Whitman counterbalances his city notes with compendious images of nature. In detailing the city, Whitman tends to adopt an attitude of pure observation, of an innocent vision taking in indiscriminately all that it sees: "Where the city's ceaseless crowd moves on the livelong day, / Withdrawn I join a group of children watching, I pause aside with them" ("Sparkles from the Wheel"). Stepping out of the crowd's endless movement, Whitman pauses simply to watch, to let impressions accrue in his impartial democratic consciousness. He strives to reduce his experience of things to unbiased perception and reach a point of view unaffected by political and social distinctions, one equivalent to the ingenuous eye of children. That way, the city will appear lower class but not low, dirty but not corrupt, commercial but not mercenary, chaotic and violent but not evil. The usual moral conclusions will not apply, and the city will retain its poetic character.

Whitman's unmediated, present-oriented poetic descriptions of the city contrast sharply with the nostalgic reminiscences that make up much of his prose accounts of the city. While some of his prose writings contain diary notes of his stay in Washington during the war and of his "western jaunt" across the Rockies from St. Louis to Kansas City to Denver and his trips to Canada and Boston and Philadelphia, Whitman also composes several remembrances that look back upon a city that was but no longer is. Written in the 1870s and 1880s, first printed in newspapers but later gathered into *Specimen Days & Collect* (1882), *November Boughs* (1888), and *Good-Bye My Fancy* (1891), Whitman's chronicles of "The Old Bowery," "New Orleans in 1848," "Old Brooklyn Days," "Broadway Sights," "Washington Street Scenes," and so on record the American city just as it is moving from town to metropolis (the years 1840–1860). His warm memorializations of a then new urban world and its now bygone customs and vanished technologies are tinged with Whitman's personal reflections on what it all meant to him, how it made him feel. For

example, his note on "Omnibus Jaunts and Drivers" begins with a few facts about the main bus lines in New York and the "Rabelaisian" character of the drivers. Whitman then records how often he would ride the bus from one terminus to the other absorbing the Broadway milieu from the passenger perspective. Finally, he asserts that "the influence of those Broadway omnibus jaunts and drivers and declamations and escapades undoubtedly enter'd into the gestation of 'Leaves of Grass'" (*Prose Works* 1:19).

A less personal account of the nineteenth-century American city appears in another sizable body of Whitman's prose writings: his journalism work in the 1830s and 1840s, plus the series on "Brooklyniana" (city history and culture) published in 1861–1862. Working mainly for New York and Brooklyn newspapers, Whitman wrote stories and editorials on a variety of municipal issues and events: school reform in Queens County, factionalism in the state Democratic party machinery, increases in suburban burglaries, rowdyism among city firemen, deficient mental health care facilities, poor city sanitation, swill milk, and so on. He also reviewed plays and opera and an occasional ballet presented in New York theater houses. These years of daily reportage Whitman always recalled fondly (see, for example, "Starting Newspapers," *Prose Works* 1:286–289), and he correctly attributed much of the material of *Leaves of Grass* to his reporter identity. Covering the city's political, social, and cultural scene put Whitman in the observational attitude of the populist writer, and eventually of America's epic poet. To bring the news of the city to the city's inhabitants, Whitman had to mingle among all classes and in all neighborhoods, to witness trials and parades and elections and other municipal events, to assess the cultural status of New York arts, and then to translate his perceptions into a public discourse. That is, Whitman had to become what he calls in *Leaves of Grass* the "Answerer," the one who faces the confusions and discords of the masses and resolves them into a democratic idiom.

Herein lies what makes Whitman's representations of the American city important: not so much his panoramic descriptions of city workers and settings or his factual accounts of marches on Pennsylvania Avenue as his visionary idea of city life in the New World. The American city to Whitman is much more than a mere concentration of persons, dwellings, and marketplaces. It is an idyllic realization of what

Whitman calls the paradox of "Democracy": the development of free, unique, myriad individuals within an aggregate, equalizing, consolidating society. As Whitman puts it in *Democratic Vistas,* democracy balances two opposing principles—"the leveler, the unyielding principle of the average" and the "principle [of] individuality, the pride and centripetal isolation of a human being in himself" (*Prose Works* 2:391). That is, while the American city brings people together as social and economic functions (boss, employee, merchant, consumer, bus-driver, neighbor, policeman, etc.) contributing to the overall liveliness and prosperity of the city, these city identities only serve to highlight the singularity of every individual involved. In the metropolis, American citizens become lost in the crowd, submerged in a prodigious congregation of carriages and goods and department stores and tenements that accepts all persons but tends to homogenize them. Yet, because American society ideally is organized on egalitarian principles, every laborer and consumer feels equally valuable in the city's bustling operation, and thereby stands out as a unique personality at the same time he or she stands for a portion of humanity. The city is the site of representative democracy, where the crowd (*demos*) has a legitimate political voice, but no more than that of any individual member. Of course, various social and political inequities still prevail, but that can change, for with "eligibility" (one of Whitman's favorite words) characterizing each citizen's status, American society is always open to progress and reform. And that potential is most easily reached in the city, whose concentration of persons demands from them a greater cooperation and understanding than rural society requires.

A theater of passions and incidents, teeming with conflicts and conciliations, mixing classes, races, occupations, nationalities, and sexualities, Whitman's American city is the social analogue of Whitman's inclusive democratic poetry: "I will not have a single person slighted or left away" ("Song of Myself," section 19); "This is the city and I am one of its citizens, / Whatever interests the rest interests me, politics, wars, markets, newspapers, schools" (section 42). Like Whitman's poetics of integration, the city levels those distinctions of persons (wealth, title, privilege) which lead to artificial hierarchies and privileges. However, in massing citizens together indiscriminately in the same streets and stores and parks, the city does not sink individuals into an anonymous, powerless existence. Citizens' close socioeconomic relations properly manifest a natural fellowship that enlivens people's lives, a communal bond that guarantees their vital participation in democracy. While Edgar Allan Poe or Nathaniel Hawthorne might discover in the crowded city a nightmarish dissipation of personal identity, Whitman finds in the bustling thoroughfares and saloons and churches and offices a cosmic energy that enhances the personhood of those partaking of it.

Of course, to understand the city as an expression of "a deep, integral, human and divine principle, or fountain, from which issued laws, ecclesia, manners, institutes" (*Prose Works* 2:390), citizens must see urban living and working conditions as a result, a creation, a poem. They are not an end in themselves nor do they originate in themselves or in simple materialistic human needs. Rather, the city spectacle and the experiences it yields are but one grand materialization of numerous spiritual currents and tendencies. This is why Whitman says in his first Preface, "The United States themselves are essentially the greatest poem" (*Prose Works* 2:434). The United States and all its cities have a spiritual import, a substratum of "spinal meaning" (396) wherein resides the "democratic genius" (394), the "ensemble-Individuality" (396) shaping New World politics.

There is a threat to this municipal spiritualism only if urban relations become disconnected from the natural attachment of souls they should represent, if, say, business relations rest not upon a spirit of cooperation but upon a drive of competition. To Whitman, the best antidote to the decay of urban ideals would be to maintain intimate ties with nature: "American Democracy, in its myriad personalities, in factories, work-shops, stores, offices—through the dense streets and houses of cities, and all their manifold sophisticated life—must either be fibred, vitalized, by regular contact with outdoor light and air and growths, farm scenes, animals, fields, trees, birds, sun-warmth and free skies, or it will certainly dwindle and pale" (*Prose Works* 1:294).

Mark Bauerlein

Bibliography
Andrews, Malcolm. "Walt Whitman and the American City." *The American City: Literary and Cultural Perspectives.* Ed. Graham Clarke. New York: St. Martin's, 1988. 179–197.

Brasher, Thomas. *Whitman as Editor of the Brooklyn Daily Eagle*. Detroit: Wayne State UP, 1970.

Norton, Charles Eliot, ed. *The Correspondence of Thomas Carlyle and Ralph Waldo Emerson*. 1884. 2 vols. Boston: Houghton Mifflin, 1896.

Weimer, David R. "Mast-Hemm'd Mannahatta: Walt Whitman." *The City as Metaphor*. By Weimer. New York: Random House, 1966. 14–33.

Whitman, Walt. *Leaves of Grass: Comprehensive Reader's Edition*. Ed. Harold W. Blodgett and Sculley Bradley. New York: New York UP, 1965.

———. *Prose Works 1892*. Ed. Floyd Stovall. 2 vols. New York: New York UP, 1963–1964.

———. *Walt Whitman's New York: From Manhattan to Montauk*. Ed. Henry M. Christman. New York: Macmillan, 1963.

See also BOSTON, MASSACHUSETTS; "BROADWAY PAGEANT, A"; BROOKLYN, NEW YORK; CAMDEN, NEW JERSEY; "CITY OF ORGIES"; "GIVE ME THE SPLENDID SILENT SUN"; NEW ORLEANS, LOUISIANA; NEW YORK CITY; "SONG OF MYSELF"; "SPARKLES FROM THE WHEEL"; WASHINGTON, D.C.

Civil War, The (1861–1865)

Whitman often spoke of the importance of the Civil War to *Leaves of Grass*. He told his disciple Horace Traubel that it was "the very centre, circumference, umbillicus, of [his] whole career" (*With Walt Whitman* 3:95). In the poem "To Thee Old Cause" he wrote, "My book and the war are one," and elsewhere he wrote that his poems turned on the war as a wheel on its axle. What Whitman liked to call the "Four Years War" indeed represented for the poet a pivotal event in universal history, a sacred conflict between democracy and its internal as well as external antagonists. It proved his poetry's validity and anchored his personal history, with all its private anguish, to the public life of the nation.

Whitman heard of the firing on Fort Sumter while walking down Broadway around midnight, 12 April 1861. Three days later he recorded in his journal a resolution to purify and "spiritualize" his body, to drink only water and to avoid late suppers and fatty meats. This ritual self-purification reflected Whitman's view of the war, from the beginning, as a purgative rite for the country.

Indeed, it is difficult to understand his response to the war without understanding his despair for the country before it broke out—a despair that finds expression in his ecstatic poetry and the crescendo of prose attacks on "cringers, suckers, dough-faces, lice" of humanity (politicians) between 1855 and 1860 (1855 Preface 18). Whitman believed the causes of the war lay not in Southern secessionism alone but rather in lingering "feudal" elements and corruption that infected both the South and the North. Hence, like Lincoln, Whitman viewed it as a war within one identity.

But the war not only preserved and purified the Union; it proved as well that American democracy was breeding a race of heroes in the common people—a new type of human being. This proof Whitman found through personal experience in the hospitals, in the way the boys and men (in Whitman's view at least) faced suffering and death without complaint or fear, in the way they expressed selfless affection for each other and, indeed, for Walt Whitman. Here was America, "brought to Hospital in her fair youth" (*Correspondence* 1:69), and yet, sadly, the closest approximation to true democratic community Whitman would ever know.

Until the very end of 1862, Whitman had no direct experience of the war, for all his interest in it, and he never took up arms. Like most Northerners, he expected the "secessionists" to be quickly defeated and was appalled when early engagements, beginning with the first battle of Bull Run, indicated that this was not to be. Whitman remained in New York during the first year and more, occasionally visiting a hospital for the sick and wounded, and following the conflict in the newspapers. His brother George, on the other hand, enlisted early and would fight in many of the war's major battles yet emerge practically unscathed.

On 16 December 1862, the Whitmans learned that George had been wounded at Fredericksburg, Virginia, and Walt set off to find him. After canvassing the hospitals in Washington, he found George still with his company across the Rappahannock from Fredericksburg, his cheek pierced by shrapnel but on the mend. Walt stayed with his brother slightly over a week, witnessing the dead on the battlefield, visiting the wounded in hospitals, and touring the camps.

He left on 28 December with responsibility for conducting a contingent of wounded soldiers to the hospital authorities in Washington. Here he settled into a rooming house where an acquaintance, William Douglas O'Connor, was staying with his wife, Nellie, and took meals with them. His relationship with these two became among the most important of his career, as they formed the nucleus of his first circle of fervent supporters and, in the end, helped make him famous.

After finding a part-time job as a copyist in the Army Paymaster's Office, Whitman was able to support himself and visit the soldiers in the hospitals. Soon he began to find his real calling in the war—providing aid, comfort, and encouragement to the sick, wounded, and dying. At the same time he wrote journalistic pieces for the New York papers describing the conditions of the hospitals and, more movingly, the emotional condition of the hospitalized. Whitman had found a way of actively employing the qualities celebrated in his poetry. He took on a healing function equivalent to that of his shamanistic persona in early poems such as "The Sleepers," and his homoeroticism could be openly and safely expressed, employed in the cause of his beloved country. He also found a new employment for his poetic powers as he strove to become the bard of the war.

Whitman's routine was to rest after his office work, bathe, dress in fresh clothes, eat a good meal, and put in four to five hours touring the hospitals. He would often pack a knapsack with fruit, tobacco, paper, envelopes, and the like for individual distribution to the soldiers—materials chiefly paid for with money raised from relatives and friends. He entered the hospitals well rested, sweet-scented, and cheerful in appearance. Though he might often break down hours after a visit, he took care to steel himself to the agonies he witnessed for as long as he was in the presence of the soldiers, to keep his spirits high. He was not so much a "wound-dresser," as his poem of that title suggests, as a healer of the spirit, an affectionate comrade or "uncle," whose curative abilities were nonetheless deeply respected at a time when doctors' interventions often did more harm than good. Whitman never read his poetry to the men—in fact, he apparently never told them he was a poet—but he would recite Shakespeare or passages from the Bible. He would also hold the men's hands, kiss them, write letters for them. Some of Whitman's most admirable prose can

Walt Whitman, ca. 1865, probably taken by Mathew Brady. By permission, Beeghly Library, Ohio Wesleyan University.

be found in letters informing parents, with exquisite tact, of the exact circumstances and manner of the death of a son.

While absorbed in this work, Whitman was also making contact with the men who would later be crucial in building his reputation. He met John Burroughs in 1863; along with O'Connor, Burroughs became one of Whitman's most important early publicists, although they differed on abolitionism and racial matters. Whitman's experience in the war also firmed his resolve to dedicate his life to poetry. He wrote his friend Charles W. Eldridge on 17 November 1863 that he had determined to devote himself increasingly to "the work of [his] life, . . . making poems . . . I *must* be continually bringing out poems—now is the hey day" (*Correspondence* 1:185). He came to see his relation to the war as equivalent to that of Homer to the Trojan War. He wished to be identified with it through all later generations.

Throughout this period, however, Whitman was also afflicted with ongoing family difficulties, his brother Andrew dying of a painful throat disease in late 1863 and his older brother, Jesse, gone mad from syphilis, abusive to all around him. On 5 December 1864 Walt would commit Jesse to a lunatic asylum. By that date, the family knew brother George was missing in action—actually a prisoner of war, as they later found out, at which point Walt would begin pulling strings to secure his release through prisoner exchange.

Also in 1864 Whitman proposed a book composed of his diary entries and observations on the war. Above all, he worked on his new collection of poetry, *Drum-Taps,* which he regarded initially as a project independent of *Leaves of Grass,* even artistically superior to it. As he sent the new manuscript to the printer, Richmond fell to the Union Army and Lee surrendered at Appomattox—events that, Whitman believed, would "shape the destinies of the future of the whole of mankind" (*Correspondence* 1:258). Yet in the end these events would be vastly overshadowed by tragedy in the assassination of President Lincoln.

The Saturday after Good Friday, 15 April 1865, Whitman and his family read the news of Lincoln's assassination. Walt and his mother, Louisa, did not eat that day but sat silently as the sky darkened and the rain fell in dreary accompaniment to their sorrow. Later, Whitman would get a firsthand report of the assassination from his friend Peter Doyle, an Irish immigrant and former Confederate soldier whom Whitman had met when Doyle was an out-patient in Washington. Doyle's description would form the basis of Whitman's later speech, "Death of Abraham Lincoln," which in old age he gave religiously on the date of the murder. Essentially, the death of the president encapsulated the entire meaning of the war and proved its sacred quality. That it so well epitomized national tragedy suggested that only God could have written the script: "The whole involved, baffling, multiform whirl of the Secession period," Whitman would argue in his speech, came to a head in that single "fierce deed" ("Death" 11). In a sense, it proved the universal and even religious significance of the war; it was democracy's originary moment, its rite of crucifixion. Whitman ceased thinking of the nation as having been born during the Revolution. He began to see the Civil War and assassination as America's true "parturition and delivery"; the nation had been "born again, consistent with itself" ("Death" 12).

But what if Whitman's reading of the war, and with it Lincoln's death, were wrong? If the poet had deceived himself and democracy had not been truly and permanently saved, then America, he believed, would be a spectacular failure and his life's work wasted—both nation and poet victims of "a destiny . . . equivalent, in its real world, to that of the fabled damned," as he wrote in *Democratic Vistas* (*Prose Works* 2:424). Fear of such self-deceit is one of the keys to Whitman's later years. The war, which seemed to have revealed the very ground of meaning through blood-sacrifice, became the sacred center of the poet's view of both himself and history. He avoided any radical questioning of the motion of history, which helps explain the dramatic shift in his poetry away from personal crisis and ecstasy to stoic detachment, reminiscence, and meditation. Simultaneously, a greater focus upon the problem of temporality as such, of being in time, emerges in all his work as the poet moves not only closer to his own death but also further from the "umbilicus" of his career, those sacred experiences that had revealed the ground of meaning in history.

In incorporating *Drum-Taps* into *Leaves of Grass* and, throughout the last quarter century of his life, expanding as well as reorganizing that work into a cathedral-like form, Whitman gave the Civil War a central position. He devoted the heart of his autobiography, *Specimen Days,* to his memoranda from the war period. Whitman does not provide a comprehensive view of the war; most glaring is an almost total absence of reflection upon slavery and emancipation, except for the awkward "Ethiopia Saluting the Colors" (which, nonetheless, would be much admired by some black writers of later years). The whole epic story of black American experience of the conflict lies outside Whitman's reach—and, for that matter, the reach of every other poet and novelist of the period, as Daniel Aaron has pointed out. Nonetheless, it is right to remember Whitman as our greatest poet of the first modern war.

George Hutchinson

Bibliography

Aaron, Daniel. *The Unwritten War: American Writers and the Civil War.* New York: Knopf, 1973.

Allen, Gay Wilson. *The Solitary Singer: A Critical Biography of Walt Whitman.* 1955. Rev. ed. 1967. Chicago: U of Chicago P, 1985.

Erkkila, Betsy. *Whitman the Political Poet.* New York: Oxford UP, 1989.

Fredrickson, George M. *The Inner Civil War: Northern Intellectuals and the Crisis of the Union.* New York: Harper and Row, 1965.

Glicksberg, Charles I., ed. *Whitman and the Civil War.* Philadelphia: U of Pennsylvania P, 1933.

Hutchinson, George B. *The Ecstatic Whitman: Literary Shamanism & the Crisis of the Union.* Columbus: Ohio State UP, 1986.

Reynolds, David S. *Walt Whitman's America: A Cultural Biography.* New York: Knopf, 1995.

Thomas, M. Wynn. "Fratricide and Brotherly Love: Whitman and the Civil War." *The Cambridge Companion to Walt Whitman.* Ed. Ezra Greenspan. Cambridge: Cambridge UP, 1995. 27–44.

———. *The Lunar Light of Whitman's Poetry.* Cambridge, Mass.: Harvard UP, 1987.

Traubel, Horace. *With Walt Whitman in Camden.* 9 vols. Vol. 1. Boston: Small, Maynard, 1906; Vol. 2. New York: Appleton, 1908; Vol. 3. New York: Mitchell Kennerley, 1914; Vol. 4. Ed. Sculley Bradley. Philadelphia: U of Pennsylvania P, 1953; Vol. 5. Ed. Gertrude Traubel. Carbondale: Southern Illinois UP, 1964; Vol. 6. Ed. Gertrude Traubel and William White. Carbondale: Southern Illinois UP, 1982; Vol. 7. Ed. Jeanne Chapman and Robert MacIsaac. Carbondale: Southern Illinois UP, 1992; Vols. 8–9. Ed. Jeanne Chapman and Robert MacIsaac. Oregon House, Calif.: W.L. Bentley, 1996.

Whitman, Walt. *The Correspondence.* Ed. Edwin Haviland Miller. 6 vols. New York: New York UP, 1961–1977.

———. "Death of Abraham Lincoln." *Memoranda During the War & Death of Abraham Lincoln.* Ed. Roy P. Basler. Bloomington: Indiana UP, 1962. 1–14.

———. 1855 Preface. *Complete Poetry and Collected Prose.* Ed. Justin Kaplan. New York: Library of America, 1982. 5–26.

———. *Prose Works 1892.* Ed. Floyd Stovall. 2 vols. New York: New York UP, 1963–1964.

See also BURROUGHS, JOHN AND URSULA; CIVIL WAR NURSING; "DEATH OF ABRAHAM LINCOLN"; DOYLE, PETER; "DRUM-TAPS"; FALMOUTH, VIRGINIA; LINCOLN, ABRAHAM; *MEMORANDA DURING THE WAR;* O'CONNOR, WILLIAM DOUGLAS; *SPECIMEN DAYS;* WASHINGTON, D.C.; WHITMAN, GEORGE WASHINGTON

Civil War Nursing

Military nursing in 1861 was a brutal and haphazard affair. Performed by convalescent veterans, regimental musicians, or those soldiers "least effective under arms," nursing involved little or no formal training and was stigmatized as a sign of inability or cowardice. Capable soldiers shunned the work and hospital observers emphasized the absence of any meaningful system of nursing care. Afflicted soldiers sometimes concealed their wounds to avoid being taken to hospitals they saw as little better than prisons or morgues.

At the outbreak of the war, reformers from a wide range of social organizations met at the Cooper Institute in New York to establish a training program for military nurses. That meeting, led by Elizabeth Blackwell, resulted in the formation of the Women's Central Association for Relief, the core of the United States Sanitary Commission, later headed by Henry Bellows. In addition, Dorothea Dix was appointed "Superintendent of Female Nurses" and charged with recruiting women for an army nursing corps. "[O]ur Florence Nightingale," as Louisa May Alcott called her, Dix transformed military nursing into an organized profession and her ideas about nursing, medicine, disease, and hospital design were drawn from Nightingale's work in the Crimea.

Although he held an appointment from the Christian Commission, a branch of the YMCA, Whitman took pride in his status as a volunteer nurse and "consolant" of the wounded. Like Mary Ann Bickerdyke and Clara Barton, Whitman worked outside of any agency or institution and saw himself as an advocate for the private soldier. Working in the crowded, chaotic wards of Washington hospitals like the Armory Square, the Judiciary Square, and the Patent Office, Whitman wrote letters for afflicted soldiers, dressed wounds, distributed gifts of money, clothing, and food, and read aloud from William Shakespeare, Sir Walter Scott, Miles O'Reilly, and the Bible. Whitman's hospital visits strengthened his belief in the dignity of common people, the crucial issue of his Civil War. Profoundly moved by the courage and comradeship of wounded soldiers on both sides of the line, Whitman felt that he had glimpsed in the military hospitals the very expression of a democratic America, and he cherished that glimpse as a turning point in his own life, what he later termed "the very centre, circumference, umbillicus, of my whole career" (Whitman 15).

Robert Leigh Davis

C

Walt Whitman, ca. 1864, taken by Alexander Gardner. Courtesy of the Library of Congress.

Bibliography

Adams, George Worthington. *Doctors in Blue: The Medical History of the Union Army in the Civil War.* New York: Henry Schuman, 1952.

Fredrickson, George M. *The Inner Civil War: Northern Intellectuals and the Crisis of the Union.* New York: Harper and Row, 1965.

Greenbie, Marjorie Barstow. *Lincoln's Daughters of Mercy.* New York: Putnam, 1944.

Murray, Martin G. "Traveling with the Wounded: Walt Whitman and Washington's Civil War Hospitals." *Washington History: Magazine of the Historical Society of Washington, D.C.* 8.2 (1996–1997): 58–73, 92–93.

Reverby, Susan M. *Ordered to Care: The Dilemma of American Nursing, 1850–1945.* Cambridge: Cambridge UP, 1987.

Whitman, Walt. *Walt Whitman's Civil War.* Ed. Walter Lowenfels. New York: Knopf, 1960.

Wood, Ann Douglas. "The War Within a War: Women Nurses in the Union Army." *Civil War History* 18 (1972): 197–212.

See also BROADWAY HOSPITAL (NEW YORK); CIVIL WAR, THE

Clapp, Henry (1814–1875)

Journalist, editor, and reformer, Clapp was born in Nantucket, a bastion of Quaker reform sensibility, and entered the abolitionist cause in the 1830s as a lecturer. He continued his reform activities as the editor of a temperance newspaper and subsequently as secretary to the American champion of Fourierist socialism, Albert Brisbane. Although not much is known about Clapp in the 1850s, the decade before he met Whitman, he appears to have developed his reform attachments in relation to free-love doctrine. Free love was a politics associated with Fourierism which upheld the sanctity of sexual love outside marriage and spurned the coerciveness of unions legitimated by church and state. In 1855 Clapp was among those arrested in New York City while attending a meeting of the Free Love League, a discussion group of men and women led by the anarchist and sex radical Stephen Pearl Andrews. In 1858 he appeared at a gathering of prominent reformers in Rutland, Vermont, who met to discuss free love, women's rights, and other reforms. Quite possibly it was Clapp who introduced Whitman to free-love thought.

Whitman probably met Clapp in 1859, when he began to frequent Pfaff's saloon, the bohemian meeting place in Manhattan which Clapp also frequented. The place was a daily rendezvous for journalists of scant means but high literary ambitions. The two were close in age and congenial in their political sympathies. Whitman's career was at a low ebb, and he found in Clapp critical literary support as he prepared the third edition of *Leaves of Grass* for publication. In 1858 Clapp had founded a literary journal, the *Saturday Press,* which was dedicated to publishing new and unknown American writers and to flouting convention and the reigning literary establishment. Clapp's chief contribution to Whitman's eventual success lay in his comprehension of how publicity, even scandal, could obviate the need for the critical and moral approval which Whitman had thus far failed to secure, especially from the Boston literati. Clapp encouraged Whitman's own incipient tendencies toward self-promotion, sensing their value in an increasingly commercial literary market. The *Saturday Press* made it a point to stir up weekly any and all praise or condemnation of the poet. Whitman remembered that "Henry was right: better to have people stirred against you if they can't be stirred for you—better than not to stir them at all" (Traubel 237). Twenty items on Whitman and/or *Leaves of Grass* appeared throughout 1860, including reviews from other journals, both negative and positive, advertisements and parodies of Whitman's style.

Clapp's journal folded in 1860. He worked as a journalist and theater critic in New York until his death.

Christine Stansell

Bibliography

Howells, William Dean. *Literary Friends and Acquaintance.* 1900. Bloomington: Indiana UP, 1968.

Lalor, Eugene. "The Literary Bohemians of New York City in the Mid-Nineteenth Century." Diss. St. John's U, 1977.

Parry, Albert. *Garrets and Pretenders: A History of Bohemianism in America.* New York: Covici, Friede, 1933.

Stansell, Christine. "Whitman at Pfaff's: Commercial Culture, Literary Life and New York Bohemia at Mid-Century."

C

Walt Whitman Quarterly Review 10 (1993): 107–126.

Traubel, Horace. *With Walt Whitman in Camden.* Vol. 1. Boston: Small, Maynard, 1906.

Winter, William. *Old Friends, Being Literary Recollections of Other Days.* New York: Moffat, Yard, 1909.

See also "Out of the Cradle Endlessly Rocking"; Pfaff's Restaurant; *Saturday Press*

Clare, Ada (Jane McElheney) (1836–1874)

Born to a well-to-do family in Charleston, the woman who would become known as Ada Clare left home at nineteen to earn her living as a writer in New York. A prolific essayist, poet, and short-story writer, she won a following in the magazines and newspapers and became a celebrity in the New York demimonde. In the mid-1850s she gave birth to an illegitimate son, probably the child of the pianist Louis Gottschalk, and defiantly presented herself as an unmarried mother, "Miss Ada Clare." A confessional novel, *Only a Woman's Heart* (1866), bears upon these events. Along with her friend Adah Menken, Clare frequented the bohemian Pfaff's saloon, where she befriended Whitman and made a place for herself in the circle of newspapermen who gathered there. She was one of Henry Clapp's featured writers in his *Saturday Press.* Whitman was sufficiently impressed by Clare to make her into one of the "sights" cited in his newspaper articles recounting his New York rambles (later collected in *New York Dissected* [1936]). From the mid-1860s, Clare supplemented her writing with a hard-working, although mostly unsuccessful, stage career. She spent time in San Francisco and Hawaii as a feted literary celebrity. She died in New York in 1874 of rabies, which she contracted from the dog of a theatrical agent.

Christine Stansell

Bibliography

Parry, Albert. *Garrets and Pretenders: A History of Bohemianism in America.* New York: Covici, Friede, 1933.

Stoddard, Charles Warren. "Ada Clare, Queen of Bohemia." *National Magazine* Sept. 1905: 637–645.

See also Clapp, Henry; Menken, Adah Isaacs; Pfaff's Restaurant; *Saturday Press*

Clarke, McDonald (1798–1842)

McDonald Clarke, the so-called Mad Poet of Broadway, was a street drifter and poet who influenced Whitman early in the latter's career. A familiar figure in lower Manhattan from his arrival in 1819 until his death, Clarke suffered intermittent attacks of insanity and spent time in the asylum on Blackwell's Island, now Roosevelt Island. When lucid, he spent much of his time wandering up and down Broadway and scribbling verse. His poems, which filled several published volumes, ranged in mood from social satire to the desolate, brooding romanticism that characterized his best work. On 5 March 1842, while in jail for vagrancy, Clarke was found dead, having drowned in water flowing from an open faucet. The young Whitman was captivated both by Clarke's writings and his eccentric career. In the *Aurora,* Whitman described Clarke as possessing "all the requisites of a great poet" and hailed him as "a true son of song" (*Aurora* 106). Whitman imitated Clarke's unconventional dress, as well as his techniques of varying the lengths of lines and mixing slang with high poetic diction. In the 18 March 1842 *Aurora,* two weeks after Clarke's death, Whitman published his own tribute to Clarke, "The Death and Burial of McDonald Clarke." The poem, which laments the failure of the public to embrace and honor the poet during his lifetime, concludes: "Darkly and sadly his spirit has fled, / But his name will long linger in story; / He needs not a stone to hallow his bed; / He's in Heaven, encircled with glory" (*Early* 26).

John T. Matteson

Bibliography

Jillson, Clark. *Sketch of M'Donald Clarke.* Worcester, Mass.: n.p., 1878.

Reynolds, David S. *Walt Whitman's America: A Cultural Biography.* New York: Knopf, 1995.

Whitman, Walt. *The Early Poems and the Fiction.* Ed. Thomas L. Brasher. New York: New York UP, 1963.

———. *Walt Whitman of the New York Aurora.* Ed. Joseph Jay Rubin and Charles H. Brown. State College, Pa.: Bald Eagle, 1950.

See also Pre-Leaves Poems

"Clear Midnight, A" (1881)

The last manuscript draft of "A Clear Midnight" appears on the back of a letter dated 2 December 1880. The poem was published in *Leaves of Grass* 1881 as the final piece in the cluster "From Noon to Starry Night."

Stylistically and thematically, "Clear Midnight" is characteristic of much of Whitman's later poetry. First, like most of the verse Whitman wrote after the Civil War, the poem is short. Second, it employs traditional poetic diction (e.g., archaisms such as "thy," "Thee," and "thou") and a quasi-traditional rhythm (note especially the second line, which scans iambically). Third, the poem reflects the aging poet's growing preoccupation with themes of death, spirituality, and the soul. As in "Passage to India," the major long poem of Whitman's later years, the soul is seen as symbolically voyaging. The poet invokes his soul to forgo transient preoccupations in favor of a daring and symbolic voyage into night and the unknown—"the wordless."

John E. Schwiebert

Bibliography

Asselineau, Roger. *The Evolution of Walt Whitman: The Creation of a Book.* Trans. Roger Asselineau and Burton L. Cooper. Cambridge, Mass.: Harvard UP, 1962.

Schwiebert, John E. *The Frailest Leaves: Whitman's Poetic Technique and Style in the Short Poem.* New York: Lang, 1992.

Whitman, Walt. *Walt Whitman's Workshop: A Collection of Unpublished Manuscripts.* 1928. Ed. Clifton Joseph Furness. New York: Russell and Russell, 1964.

See also "FROM NOON TO STARRY NIGHT"; SOUL, THE

Clemens, Samuel Langhorne (Mark Twain) (1835–1910)

Clemens, popular for his fiction written under the pseudonym "Mark Twain," and Whitman are often compared as vernacular writers of nineteenth-century American democracy. Clemens's *Adventures of Huckleberry Finn* (1885) is often considered the literary companion piece to *Leaves of Grass*, both works subjects of book bannings that were eventually hailed as turning points in American literature.

Comparisons include the authors' similar backgrounds, time spent as apprentice printers, their personae as self-made, rough-hewn artists, and their sympathy with downtrodden peoples. Both championed American idioms and speech and the individual against conformist society.

Yet the two showed only perfunctory interest in each other. Whitman said Twain "might have been something. He comes near being something: but he never arrives" (qtd. in Kaplan 339). In turn, Twain noted, "If I've become a Whitmanite I'm sorry—I never read 40 lines of him in my life" (qtd. in Gribben 2:764). This claim is probably an exaggeration; Clemens's personal copy of *Leaves of Grass* contains many of his marginal comments, and in 1892 Clemens-owned Charles L. Webster and Company published *Selected Poems, by Walt Whitman* with Whitman's special permission.

Clemens provided financial support for Whitman on several occasions, including one hundred dollars for a horse and buggy and two hundred dollars for a cottage to "make the splendid old soul comfortable" (qtd. in Bergman 3). In 1889 Clemens sent Whitman a complimentary copy of *A Connecticut Yankee in King Arthur's Court*.

In 1884 Clemens grouped Whitman with other writers in an anecdote, and he attended Whitman's 1887 eulogy for Lincoln at Madison Square Theater in New York. His ambivalent feelings about Whitman were reflected on Whitman's seventieth birthday, when Clemens sent an impersonal, ambiguous telegram, and in an unfinished essay, "The Walt Whitman Controversy," in which Clemens worried about the sexual frankness in *Leaves of Grass*, saying the book should not be read by children.

Wesley A. Britton

Bibliography

Bergman, Herbert. "The Whitman-Twain Enigma Again." *Mark Twain Journal* 10.3 (1957): 3–9.

Gribben, Alan. *Mark Twain's Library: A Reconstruction.* 2 vols. Boston: Hall, 1980.

Kaplan, Justin. "Starting from Paumanok . . . and from Hannibal: Whitman and Mark Twain." *Confrontation* 27–28 (1984): 338–347.

See also INDIVIDUALISM; LANGUAGE; PERSONAE

Collect (1882)

Specimen Days & Collect was issued by Rees Welsh and Company in 1882, shortly after James R. Osgood and Company withdrew its November 1881 issue of *Leaves of Grass* from circulation in April of 1882, apparently because of a warning from a Boston district attorney over obscenity charges. As a result of the Boston banning, sales of Whitman's books increased sharply, and Rees Welsh and Company was apparently eager to capitalize on the market. In "One or Two Index Items" Whitman explains that the contents of *Specimen Days & Collect* consist mostly of "memoranda already existing" (*Complete* 927). He also explains that he was hurried by the printer to rush the volume into print. On the surface the result seems to be that Whitman's *Collect* is a strange assortment of pieces with no apparent purpose but to meet the needs of the printer.

One should bear in mind, however, that *Collect* was published with *Specimen Days,* and the latter seems to be purposeful as autobiography, especially the Civil War section. As reminiscence *Collect* also has great value, and that Whitman placed *Democratic Vistas* first was no accident. *Democratic Vistas* embodies most, if not all, of Whitman's major themes—including his emphasis upon the modern and his ideas on personality (Personalism) and the relation of the person to nature, to the state, and to some higher spiritual entity, i.e., the person as both body and soul. That he considered the European personality as a continuation of feudalism is clear, and that he hoped to cultivate a new democratic personality in America is even clearer. But one must ponder the meaning of the title *Collect*. The title can be dismissed as merely referring to a collection of pieces selected at random, or it can be viewed as having religious significance. It could be that Whitman's title also refers to the brief prayer coming just before the epistle in the communion service in many Western churches as well as in morning and evening prayers in Anglican churches. Why else would Whitman place "Origins of Attempted Secession" next, in the very first sentence of which he writes, "I consider the war of attempted secession, 1860–65, not as a struggle of two distinct and separate peoples, but a conflict (often happening, and very fierce) between the passions and paradoxes of one and the same identity—perhaps the only terms on which that identity could really become fused, homogenous and lasting" (*Complete* 994)?

And why would he follow "Origins of Attempted Secession" with the Preface to *As a Strong Bird on Pinions Free* (1872)? In the new union of states Whitman sees anew the possibility of a genuinely democratic nation, but his yearning neither begins nor ends with politics. As in "Starting from Paumanok" (1860) he sees the interconnectedness of love, democracy, and religion, and that he does may explain his misgivings about the future of democracy as well as his own future as America's bard. *Collect,* particularly the second section, "Notes Left Over," is full of doubts and misgivings. The best treatment of this subject is to be found in chapter 12 of Betsy Erkkila's *Whitman the Political Poet*. John Snyder also treats the subject of doubts and misgivings under what he calls "Whitman's new version of a persistent theme, the tragedy of time and space" (164), and in doing so he refers the reader to "Origins of Attempted Secession," "Poetry To-day in America—Shakspere—the Future," and "Death of Abraham Lincoln." *Collect,* writes Snyder, is notable because of its "important statements about the tragic absoluteness of the Civil War and Lincoln's death" (246). As has been generally recognized, Whitman's major work after the Civil War was written in prose, and *Collect,* like *Specimen Days,* stands as a companion piece to *Leaves of Grass*. After the Civil War, Whitman watched as his dream of a Jeffersonian America gave way to the social reality of corrupt government and a capitalistic enterprise which divided people into social and economic classes reminiscent of European feudalism of the Middle Ages, and this bothered him. For clear evidence that such was the case one should read in "Notes Left Over" such essays as "The Tramp and Strike Questions," "Democracy in the New World," "Foundation Stages—Then Others," "Who Gets the Plunder?," and "Our Real Culmination."

In his *Walt Whitman: A Descriptive Bibliography* Joel Myerson did Whitman enthusiasts of all kinds a great service by supplying a transcription of Whitman's *Specimen Days & Collect*. The transcription makes clear that *Collect* includes three sections. The first consists of 10 titles, some of which are speeches and the last of which consists of two letters. The second section consists of 21 notes under the title of "Notes Left Over." And the third is an appendix entitled "Pieces in Early Youth 1834–'42," consisting of 14 selections of early prose and poetry which have generally been ignored.

When Justin Kaplan selected the contents of *Complete Poetry and Collected Prose,* he included all three sections in order but placed only the first under the title *Collect,* and when Floyd Stovall edited the second volume of *Prose Works 1892,* he excluded the appendix.

That little has been made of Whitman's *Collect* is no surprise, especially because of its being rushed into print. The fact remains, however, that Whitman chose these pieces as well as those in *Specimen Days,* and if either work seems disjointed, the reader should not overlook a technique Whitman relied on in writing and organizing his poems, i.e., symphonic treatment of theme. Nor should the reader overlook the oft-repeated adage that Whitman must be read whole—that a part will not suffice, will not stand for the whole. The pieces in *Collect* can best be explained as memories of a paralyzed man looking back while at the same time contemplating death.

J.R. LeMaster

Bibliography

Erkkila, Betsy. *Whitman the Political Poet.* New York: Oxford UP, 1989.

Myerson, Joel. *Walt Whitman: A Descriptive Bibliography.* Pittsburgh: U of Pittsburgh P, 1993.

Snyder, John. *The Dear Love of Man: Tragic and Lyric Communion in Walt Whitman.* The Hague: Mouton, 1975.

Whitman, Walt. *Complete Poetry and Collected Prose.* Ed. Justin Kaplan. New York: Library of America, 1982.

———. *Prose Works 1892.* Ed. Floyd Stovall. Vol. 2. New York: New York UP, 1964.

See also "DEATH OF ABRAHAM LINCOLN"; DEMOCRACY; *DEMOCRATIC VISTAS*; "POETRY TODAY IN AMERICA—SHAKSPERE—THE FUTURE"; PREFACE TO *AS A STRONG BIRD ON PINIONS FREE*; PREFACE TO *TWO RIVULETS*; *SPECIMEN DAYS*; "TRAMP AND STRIKE QUESTIONS, THE"

Collected Writings of Walt Whitman, The (1961–1984)

In 1955, as Whitman scholars around the world were celebrating the hundredth anniversary of *Leaves of Grass,* New York University Press announced plans to publish the most ambitious collection of Whitman's work to date. Under the general editorship of Gay Wilson Allen, who would be joined at a later date by Sculley Bradley, the initial idea was "to print everything, so that the *Collected Writings* could be called absolutely complete" (Allen 11). However, as the project progressed, the editors had to modify their original intent. Nearly thirty years after it was begun, falling short of while in some ways exceeding what had been envisioned, New York University Press deemed the *Collected Writings* project complete.

In a 1963 article Allen described the project as "probably the most difficult, gigantic, and problem-haunted undertaking in the whole field of American letters" (7). Many factors contributed to the complexity of the project. To begin with, all but two of the nine versions of *Leaves of Grass* published in Whitman's lifetime were published by Whitman himself. This meant, Allen explained, that acting as his own publisher, Whitman "kept extra sheets of each printing, and frequently had batches of these bound up for special distribution. It was easy, therefore, for him to vary the contents of these small batches, and how many 'issues,' or variants, exist for some editions is still not definitively known" (Allen 8).

Further complicating matters was the fact that what remained of Whitman's notebooks, correspondence, and other papers at the time of his death had been divided up among his three literary executors, Richard Maurice Bucke, Thomas Harned, and Horace Traubel, who then published parts of their portions in varying formats. Traubel quoted much of Whitman's correspondence in *With Walt Whitman in Camden.* Whole letters were published by Bucke in *Calamus,* which contains Whitman's letters to Peter Doyle, and in *The Wound Dresser,* a collection of letters and newspaper articles Whitman wrote while working in the hospitals around Washington, D.C, and in Harned's *Letters Written by Walt Whitman to his Mother from 1866 to 1872.* Bucke also published a collection of Whitman's notebook jottings in *Notes and Fragments.* All of this "uncollected" material was then gathered by the three executors and included in their ten-volume *Complete Writings of Walt Whitman,* published in 1902 by G.P. Putnam's Sons. Although this ten-volume set offered a great resource to Whitman scholars, it was never "complete," nor had it been prepared by professional scholars.

After publishing from their portions of Whitman's legacy, Bucke, Harned, and Traubel further divided much of it among others who sold or gave it away, resulting in the widespread scattering of Whitman's literary remains among private collections and libraries. In the years that followed the publication of *Complete Writings,* more of Whitman's uncollected writings—notes, letters, and journalism—continued to emerge in editions that varied widely in terms of organization and editorial standards.

When Allen and the advisory editorial board of *Collected Writings* took on this "most difficult, problem-haunted" project in 1955, they hoped to bring together as much of this scattered material as was possible and to present it in a format consistent with the exacting standards of modern scholarship. Collector Charles E. Feinberg, who had devoted his career (and considerable financial resources) to acquiring all he could of Whitman's letters, manuscripts, and notebooks, made his private collection available for the project. Some additional eighteen hundred manuscripts were tracked down by sending out letters to fifteen hundred libraries and private collections. This, and the fact that there was no single agency or institution providing the necessary financial support, meant that the collection emerged much more slowly and much less systematically than the editors had initially imagined.

As it now stands, *The Collected Writings of Walt Whitman* comprises twenty-two volumes grouped under seven titles. Each set begins with an introduction by the editor(s), explaining the arrangement of the material and the methodology used in collecting it and suggesting how Whitman students and scholars might use the material. All of the sets are characterized by thorough, detailed annotations offering biographical information and cross references to the poetry or other published work where relevant. Each set reprints a standardized "Chronology of Whitman's Life and Work" as an appendix.

The *Correspondence,* edited by Edwin Haviland Miller, consists of six volumes, the first five of which are arranged chronologically. The sixth, published eight years after what was thought to be the "final" fifth volume, contains letters that surfaced in the intervening years as well as an index to the whole.

The Early Poems and the Fiction, edited by Thomas L. Brasher, consists of one volume and contains all of Whitman's "pre-*Leaves* verse and . . . tales" (xv) published in newspapers and literary magazines in the 1840s, as well as the complete text of Whitman's temperance novel, *Franklin Evans.*

Prose Works 1892, edited by Floyd Stovall, consists of two volumes, containing "all (except the juvenilia) of the contents of Whitman's final edition of his *Complete Prose Works* in 1892" (1:vii). Included in the two volumes are *Specimen Days & Collect, November Boughs,* and the prose portions of *Good-Bye My Fancy.* Since all of the material in Whitman's 1892 edition had been published previously, Stovall's task was "to record the evolution of the printed text" (1:ix). Notes provide information about the origin of each piece, and each volume concludes with a section containing "Prefaces and Notes Not Included in *Complete Prose Works 1892,*" which provides a fuller context for those excerpts and fragments Whitman cut and pasted together in order to create the original collections. Through the textual notes and appendix Stovall provides "every variant reading of every earlier printed text which Whitman used, in whole or in part, in the 1892 *Complete Prose*" (1:ix).

Leaves of Grass: Comprehensive Reader's Edition, edited by Harold W. Blodgett and Sculley Bradley, consists of one volume. The poems are arranged exactly as Whitman indicated he wanted the final version of *Leaves of Grass* to appear in his note to the 1892 edition. The *Comprehensive Reader's Edition* also includes Whitman's "uncollected" and "excluded" poems—those which were at one time or other part of *Leaves of Grass,* but left out of the 1892 edition—as well as the prefaces and "annexes" ("A Backward Glance O'er Travel'd Roads," "Old Age Echoes"). Some manuscript fragments are also included. The *Norton Critical Edition* of *Leaves of Grass* is based on the *Comprehensive Reader's Edition.*

Daybooks and Notebooks, edited by William White, consists of three volumes. The first two contain the complete text of two "Daybooks" Whitman kept between 1876 and 1889, in which for the most part he recorded the names and addresses of people to whom he sent copies of his books, and made notes of letters written and received, money spent and money earned. White explains that "Whitman never really made up his mind what he wanted [the "Daybook"] to be" (1:xxii). For in between the minutiae of his business dealings, Whitman also recorded literary and social activities, notes about "his friendships, his habits, his health, the weather" (1:xii). These books also contain lists of the names of young men (often followed by brief descriptions of their appearance or occupation), which biographers have noted with interest. The third volume edited by White contains the complete text of a diary Whitman kept during a trip to Canada to visit Dr. Richard Maurice Bucke in the summer of 1880, some miscellaneous journals and "autobiographical notes," the entirety of the clippings and notes he made on the English (and sometimes the French) language, and a transcription of the manuscript notes that were edited and published by Horace Traubel in 1904 as *An American Primer.* This third volume also provides an index to the Daybooks.

Leaves of Grass: A Textual Variorum of the Printed Poems, edited by Sculley Bradley, Harold W. Blodgett, Arthur Golden, and William White, consists of three volumes. In their preface the editors explain that the *Comprehensive Reader's Edition* and the *Textual Variorum* "are complementary volumes." "The *Comprehensive Reader's Edition* honors the poet's preference" for the 1892 edition. The work of the *Textual Variorum* "makes explicit the poet's indefatigable struggle to achieve that preference" by enabling the reader to see "a record of how *Leaves of Grass* developed over the separate editions and impressions spanning thirty-seven years" (1:ix). The editors present each poem in the chronological order in which it first appeared in *Leaves of Grass,* regardless of its placement in or exclusion from the final edition. The text of each poem, however, is "the poem's latest form in an edition—presumably Whitman's final choice." Notes containing textual variants are "given in strict chronological order from the earliest edition to the last" (1:xix–xx). The editors' introduction recounts the publication history of *Leaves* and explains the confusion surrounding the number of editions and the status of the "annexes" and "supplements." The *Variorum* also provides a listing of the chronological order of the poems, a list of all collated editions, supplements, and impressions consulted, and an essay and table tracing the evolution of the cluster arrangements in *Leaves of Grass.* The title pages and tables of contents from all collated editions, supplements, and imprints are included as illustrations.

The final title in the NYU *Collected Writings* is the six-volume *Notebooks and Unpublished Prose Manuscripts,* edited by Edward F. Grier. The manuscripts and notebooks could not be arranged either in "a strict chronological order" or a strictly topical one. Instead, Grier used a combination of these. Part 1, vol-

umes 1–3, "contains material more or less biographical" and is arranged in "loosely chronological" order (1:xix). Part 2, volumes 4–6, "is arranged according to more sharply defined topics, such as Projected Poems, Oratory, Politics, Explanations, and Words, with a considerable chronological range in each category" (1:xix).

Plans for an eighth title bringing together all of Whitman's journalistic writings, edited by Herbert Bergman, were postponed. As Allen explained in 1963, this aspect of the project was perhaps the "most baffling" of all, because of the difficulty of authenticating unsigned editorials and newspaper articles. A good number of these, from the Brooklyn *Eagle* and the Brooklyn *Times,* have been published and attributed to Whitman, since they appeared while he was editor at those papers. Bergman's task was to find "some objective means of identifying Whitman's work" (11). At this time, the first two volumes of a projected five are scheduled for publication by Peter Lang Press. These volumes will be bound and printed in the same manner as the New York University editions and published under the auspices of the advisory board of the *Collected Writings.*

Rosemary Graham

Bibliography

Allen, Gay Wilson. "Editing the Writings of Walt Whitman: A Million Dollar Project Without a Million Dollars." *Arts and Sciences* 1.2 (1963): 7–12.

Folsom, Ed. "The Whitman Project: A Review Essay." *Philological Quarterly* 61 (1982): 369–394.

Myerson, Joel, ed. *Walt Whitman: A Descriptive Bibliography.* Pittsburgh: U of Pittsburgh P, 1993.

Whitman, Walt. *The Collected Writings of Walt Whitman.* Gen. ed. Gay Wilson Allen and Sculley Bradley. 22 vols. New York: New York UP, 1961–1984.

———. *The Correspondence.* Ed. Edwin Haviland Miller. 6 vols. New York: New York UP, 1961–1977.

———. *Daybooks and Notebooks.* Ed. William White. 3 vols. New York: New York UP, 1978.

———. *The Early Poems and the Fiction.* Ed. Thomas L. Brasher. New York: New York UP, 1963.

———. *Leaves of Grass: Comprehensive Reader's Edition.* Ed. Harold W.

Blodgett and Sculley Bradley. New York: New York UP, 1965.

———. *Leaves of Grass: A Textual Variorum of the Printed Poems*. Ed. Sculley Bradley, Harold W. Blodgett, Arthur Golden, and William White. 3 vols. New York: New York UP, 1980.

———. *Notebooks and Unpublished Prose Manuscripts*. Ed. Edward F. Grier. 6 vols. New York: New York UP, 1984.

———. *Prose Works 1892*. Ed. Floyd Stovall. 2 vols. New York: New York UP, 1963–1964.

See also ALLEN, GAY WILSON; COLLECTORS AND COLLECTIONS, WHITMAN; *COMPLETE WRITINGS OF WALT WHITMAN, THE; CORRESPONDENCE OF WALT WHITMAN, THE; DAYBOOKS AND NOTEBOOKS; LEAVES OF GRASS, 1891–1892 EDITION; LEAVES OF GRASS, VARIORUM EDITION; NOTEBOOKS AND UNPUBLISHED PROSE MANUSCRIPTS; PRE-LEAVES POEMS; SHORT FICTION, WHITMAN'S*

Collectors and Collections, Whitman

Whitman's work habits ensured that gathering his personal papers would occupy many future generations of collectors and curators. He habitually scribbled on odd scraps of paper, on backs of poetry drafts or envelopes. He kept perhaps hundreds of handmade notebooks containing random thoughts, jotted ideas, or drafts of poetry. He was so involved in the printing, binding, and sales of his volumes that his proofs often bear important holographic corrections, and unique issues of his books might include bound-in manuscript pages or printing plates left over from other editions. He was an avid letter writer, and his vast network of correspondents across the United States, England, and throughout Europe saved thousands of his personal writings. Though most of the papers have been collected and placed in public repositories, many are privately held, or are still surfacing after more than a century.

Collectors, then, begin with Whitman himself—who was photographed in his last years surrounded by his manuscripts scattered over every surface of his bedroom in Camden, New Jersey. He was, however, generous during his lifetime and often handed a manuscript page to a visiting friend, or enclosed one in a letter. By dividing his legacy of literary and personal papers among three different heirs, Whitman almost assured a complex future for his manuscripts, with the involvement of multiple collectors thereafter. In 1892 the books and papers were shared out among the three literary executors: Richard Maurice Bucke, Thomas B. Harned, and Horace L. Traubel. Of these three only the Harned share remains relatively intact. Dr. Bucke's share changed hands several times and was partially dispersed at auction in 1935, but a large portion of it ended up in the Trent Collection at Duke University. Traubel continued to collect, and his share was partially reassembled by Charles E. Feinberg, who arranged for his Whitman collection and the Traubel papers to join the Harned group in the Library of Congress.

Some other early collectors of note were John Burroughs, William W. Cohen, B. Thomas Donaldson, H. Buxton Forman, William F. Gable, Alfred F. Goldsmith, William Sloane Kennedy, Thomas Bird Mosher, John Quinn, William M. Rossetti, Edmund C. Stedman, Gertrude Traubel, Carolyn Wells, and George M. Williamson. The next generations of collectors featured Charles E. Feinberg, Oscar Lion, Harriet Chapman Sprague, and Leonard Levine, among many others all over the world. Each year, new collectors emerge and unknown or long-lost items come to public notice.

A list of the major public repositories of manuscripts, letters, and related papers follows.

1. **Manuscript Division, Library of Congress, Washington, D.C. 20540–4780.** The largest Whitman repository was begun by Thomas Biggs Harned in 1918 when he deposited his share of the Whitman papers in the capital city where the poet had spent ten important years. The Harned collection numbers approximately three thousand manuscript items alone, including twenty-five notebooks, major sets of correspondence with Anne Gilchrist, James R. Osgood, and T.W.H. Rolleston, and a group of Lincolniana. By the time of a 1955 exhibit at the Library of Congress, the Whitman manuscript holdings had grown to include twenty-seven additional collections, including those of John Burroughs, Charles N. Elliot, George S. Hellman, Hannah Whitman Heyde, Carolyn Wells Houghton, Helen Price, and the Whitman family.

The gift/purchase acquisition of the Charles E. Feinberg collection (approximately twenty-two thousand manuscript items) between 1969 and 1979 gave the Library of Congress the largest Whitman collection in the world. Feinberg donated the famous letter from Emerson to Whitman (1855), the only extant manuscript page from the 1855 *Leaves of Grass*, as well as commonplace books, notebooks, family and general correspondence, drafts and proofs of prose and poetry, memorabilia, and the papers for early major works about Whitman. The Horace and Anne Montgomery Traubel Papers (including Horace's original diary notes for *With Walt Whitman in Camden*) and the Gustave Wiksell Papers (largely on the Whitman Fellowship) expand coverage from primary manuscript materials to Whitman friends and followers.

2. **Duke University Library, Durham, NC 27706.** The Trent Collection features much of Dr. Bucke's share of Whitman's manuscripts which was auctioned in London in 1935. Dr. and Mrs. Josiah C. Trent donated the collection in 1942 and later augmented it to a total of some 650 manuscript items. It includes drafts of and ideas for poems, experiments in prose, notes for essays and lectures, records of literary and cultural studies, autobiographical and travel notes, Whitman letters to friends and associates (including an especially rich William Sloane Kennedy file), letters to the poet from friends and family, manuscripts and drafts of Dr. Bucke's biography of Whitman, and a group of clippings annotated by the poet. The professional papers of Whitman scholar Gay Wilson Allen are in the Jay B. Hubbell Center for American Literary Historiography; dated from 1801 to 1988, they consist of roughly fifty-five hundred items.

3. **Humanities Research Center, University of Texas, Box 7219, Austin, TX 78712.** Among the 575 items of manuscripts, notebooks, correspondence, and other documents are marked proofs for "By the Roadside."

4. **New York Public Library, 5th Ave. and 42nd St., New York, NY 10018.** In the Henry W. and Albert A. Berg Collection of English and American Literature and in the Oscar Lion Collection are approximately 550 manuscripts, letters, and documents, including the poet's famous "Blue Book" copy of the third edition of LG.

5. **Special Collections/Manuscripts, Alderman Library, University of Virginia, Charlottesville, VA 22903.** Some 322 manuscripts of poems, essays, letters, biographical sketches, and notes

are in the Barrett collection. The most notable item is the manuscript for the 1860 edition of LG (microfilmed as M–568).

6. **Beinecke Rare Book and Manuscript Library, Yale University, New Haven, CT 06520.** The Van Sinderen collection includes manuscripts formerly in the Donaldson Collection and lists over two hundred items. These include diaries and notebooks as well as correspondence with John Burroughs, Samuel Langhorne Clemens, and others, as well as poetry and other prose.

7. **Other significant collections** include: John Carter Brown Library, Brown University, Providence, R.I.; Henry E. Huntington Library and Museum, San Marino, Calif.; Pierpont Morgan Library, New York, N.Y.; Charles Patterson Van Pelt Library, University of Pennsylvania, Philadelphia, Pa.; William Sloane Kennedy Memorial Collection, Rollins College, Winter Park, Fla.: Ohio Wesleyan University, Delaware, Ohio.

To quote for publication from unpublished manuscripts, permission of the copyright holder is required if the rights have not been clearly dedicated (i.e., put in the public domain). In addition, it is a courtesy to ask the owner of the document for permission and for proper form of citation; some repositories require this permission. The Whitman copyright on unpublished writings would have been inherited by the heirs of Horace Traubel, but that line apparently ended with the disappearance during World War II of his grandson Malcolm.

No comprehensive facsimile edition of Whitman manuscripts exists, but many sections of the major holdings in public repositories have been published by Joel Myerson in *The Walt Whitman Archive: A Facsimile of the Poet's Manuscripts* (New York: Garland, 1993). This set includes three volumes in six physical books: parts one and two of volume 1 include the poetry portions of the Feinberg/Whitman collection at the Library of Congress (reels 15–19 of L.C. microfilm); part one of volume 2 reproduces much of the collection at Duke University, while part two of this volume shows a portion of the collection at the University of Texas; volume 3 shows the University of Virginia manuscript collection.

Edwin Haviland Miller's edition of Whitman correspondence authoritatively identifies letters to or from the poet and provides location of originals if known. The letters are printed in Miller's *The Correspondence of Walt Whitman* (New York: New York UP, 1961–1977), 6 vols. The sixth volume of this set is a supplement with a composite index, which should be used with Miller's subsequent publication, *The Correspondence of Walt Whitman. A second supplement with a revised calendar of letters written to Whitman* (Iowa City: *Walt Whitman Quarterly Review,* 1991).

Early work in ordering and identifying the fragments of Whitman's prose and poetry manuscripts, including notebooks, was pioneered by Dr. Bucke in his *Notes and Fragments* (London, Canada: 1899) and augmented by Emory Holloway in *The Uncollected Poetry and Prose of Walt Whitman, Much of Which Has Been But Recently Discovered* . . . (Garden City, N.Y.: Doubleday, Page, 1921). This was followed by Clifton Joseph Furness in his *Walt Whitman's Workshop. A Collection of Unpublished Manuscripts* (Cambridge, Mass.: Harvard UP, 1928). Clarence Gohdes and Rollo Silver edited manuscripts of Whitman and his family in *Faint Clews and Indirections* (Durham, N.C.: Duke UP, 1949).

Some of the important specific groups of manuscripts receiving editing attention include those in Fredson Bowers's *Whitman's Manuscripts: "Leaves of Grass" (1860), A Parallel Text* (Chicago: U of Chicago P, 1955). Arthur Golden's *Walt Whitman's Blue Book: The 1860–61 "Leaves of Grass" Containing His Manuscript Additions and Revisions* (New York: New York Public Library, 1968), 2 vols., is a facsimile of the book in the Oscar Lion Collection plus a textual analysis. William White edited the commonplace books and some notebooks in *Walt Whitman: Daybooks and Notebooks* (New York: New York UP, 1978), 3 vols. Edward F. Grier reedited prose texts in *Walt Whitman: Notebooks and Unpublished Prose Manuscripts* (New York: New York UP, 1984), 6 vols.

Two major exhibits in 1955, at the Detroit Public Library and at the Library of Congress, marked the centennial of the first edition of *Leaves of Grass* and produced the catalogues listed below. Some notable exhibits of Whitman manuscripts in recent decades have been presented by the New York Public Library, the John Hay Library of Brown University, and the Van Pelt-Dietrich Library Center of the University of Pennsylvania.

Alice L. Birney

Bibliography

Berg Collection. *Dictionary Catalog of the Henry W. and Albert A. Berg Collection of English and American Literature. 5* vols. Boston: Hall, 1969. 2 supps., 1975, 1983.

Broderick, John C. "The Greatest Whitman Collector and the Greatest Whitman Collection." *Quarterly Journal of the Library of Congress* 27 (1970): 109–128. [Description of the Library's then new Whitman collection and salute to its collector, Charles E. Feinberg]

"Catalog of the Sesquicentennial Exhibit Held in the Library of Congress from May 1969 to January 1970." *Quarterly Journal of the Library of Congress* 27 (1970): 171–176. [Exhibit of 200 items from the first installments of the Feinberg collection]

"Charles E. Feinberg Collection of the Papers of Walt Whitman, The" (unpublished finding aid: Manuscript Division, Library of Congress, 1984). [Detailed register of manuscript items, with list of images transferred to Prints and Photographs Division]

Exhibition of the Works of Walt Whitman, An. Detroit Public Library, Detroit, Mich.: February and March, 1955. [Highlights much of what would become the Feinberg-Whitman Collection of the Library of Congress]

"Feinberg-Whitman Collection, The." *Library of Congress, Acquisitions, Manuscript Division: 1979.* Washington, D.C.: Library of Congress, 1981.

Francis, Gloria A., and Artem Lozynsky, comps. *Whitman at Auction, 1899–1972.* Detroit: Gale Research Company, 1978.

Frey, Ellen Frances. *Catalogue of the Whitman Collection in the Duke University Library, Being a Part of the Trent Collection.* Durham, N.C.: Duke University Library, 1945. [Reprint: Port Washington, N.Y.: Kennikat, 1965]

National Union Catalog of Manuscript Collections, The. Washington, D.C.: Library of Congress, 1959–1993.

Robbins, J. Albert, et al., comps. *American Literary Manuscripts.* 2nd ed. Athens: U of Georgia P, 1977.

Ten Notebooks and a Cardboard Butterfly
    Missing from the Walt Whitman Papers.
    Washington, D.C.: Library of Congress,
    1954. [Four notebooks and the butterfly
    were returned in 1995.]
Walt Whitman: A Catalog Based Upon the
    Collections of the Library of Congress.
    Washington, D.C.: Reference Depart-
    ment, Library of Congress, 1955. [High-
    lights from the Thomas Harned-Walt
    Whitman papers and 27 additional
    Whitman collections in the Library of
    Congress, on the occasion of the centen-
    nial exhibit]

See also BIBLIOGRAPHIES; BUCKE, RICHARD
MAURICE; HARNED, THOMAS BIGGS; INTER-
NET, WHITMAN ON THE; TRAUBEL, HORACE
L.; WHITMAN (HEYDE), HANNAH LOUISA

Columbus, Christopher (ca. 1451–1506)

Christopher Columbus was the Genoese explorer traditionally thought of as the first European to land in the Americas. Walt Whitman
used the figure of Columbus several times in his
poetry, referring to him in "Passage to India"
(1871) as "[h]istory's type of courage, action,
faith" (section 6).

In "Passage to India," Whitman argued
that Columbus's dream of finding a route to the
Indies had finally been realized with the completion of the Suez Canal, the transatlantic telegraph, and the transcontinental railroad.

When he wrote "Prayer of Columbus"
(1874), Whitman was recovering from his first
stroke and mourning the recent deaths of his
mother and sister-in-law. In the poem, he identifies with the sick and elderly Columbus who
has run ashore in Jamaica on his fourth and last
voyage (1502–1504). "Prayer" is a dramatic
monologue in which a Job-like Columbus im-
plores God to accept him on his own terms.

"A Thought of Columbus" (1892), the last
poem Whitman wrote, was published posthumously. In it, Whitman presents Columbus looking west from Europe with the first voyage yet
to come and the New World "only a silent
thought."

Like most nineteenth-century Americans,
Whitman idealized Columbus. Much of this
mythologizing came from his reading of Washington Irving's The Life and Voyages of Christopher Columbus (1828).

                                    Ned C. Stuckey-French

Bibliography

Allen, Gay Wilson. The Solitary Singer: A
    Critical Biography of Walt Whitman.
    1955. Rev. ed. 1967. Chicago: U of Chi-
    cago P, 1985.
Irving, Washington. The Life and Voyages of
    Christopher Columbus. 1828. Ed. John
    Harmon McElroy. Boston: Twayne,
    1981.
Morison, Samuel Eliot. Admiral of the Ocean
    Sea: A Life of Christopher Columbus.
    Boston: Little, Brown, 1942.
Shurr, William H. "The Salvation of America:
    Walt Whitman's Apocalypticism and
    Washington Irving's Columbus." Walt
    Whitman of Mickle Street: A Centennial
    Collection. Ed. Geoffrey M. Sill. Knox-
    ville: U of Tennessee P, 1994. 142–150.
Whitman, Walt. Leaves of Grass: A Textual
    Variorum of the Printed Poems. Ed.
    Sculley Bradley, Harold W. Blodgett,
    Arthur Golden, and William White. 3
    vols. New York: New York UP, 1980.

See also "PASSAGE TO INDIA"; "PRAYER OF
COLUMBUS"; "THOUGHT OF COLUMBUS, A"

"Come Up from the Fields Father" (1865)

The poem "Come Up from the Fields Father"
was first published in Whitman's Drum-Taps
(1865). Subsequently, the poem was included
unchanged, except for minor variations in
punctuation, as a part of the "Drum-Taps" cluster in all future editions of Leaves of Grass.

The poem, a narrative, realistically relates
the reaction of a mother and her family as they
learn of the death of their son and brother in
battle. This poem contains no mention of patriotic duty, no mention of heroism, and no mention of loyalty to a cause. As biographer Gay
Wilson Allen points out, war had become an
"observed reality" to Whitman. As he visited
the hospitals and had seen the results of war,
death no longer was "theoretical or mythical"
(Allen 339).

This poem focuses on the mother's feelings
as she learns of her son's death. Her overt
expression of grief seems honest and heartfelt.
Perhaps Whitman is recalling his mother's reaction when she learned of her son George's wounding near Fredericksburg. Allen reports that
"Mother Whitman was almost frantic" (281).
Perhaps Whitman is recalling the many letters
he wrote home from the hospitals for wounded

soldiers. He has envisioned what receiving his letters must have been like for families of the hospitalized soldiers.

In a sharp contrast with the war, the opening lines of the poem depict nature's harvest on an Ohio farm: "apples ripe in orchards hang," while ripe grapes adorn the trellis. In this tranquil, pastoral scene, the "farm prospers well." The war, however, goes on, and the message about Pete, the grief-stricken mother's only son, causes the omniscient narrator to conclude in the final stanza that she wishes that she might follow, seek, and "be with her dear dead son."

This poem is a favorite of editors and is often anthologized. It seems to validate the theory of a supernatural maternal tie to a child. The mother knows the son is dead, although the letter says he is wounded and will be better. She knows in her heart that "he is dead already." The last stanza relates the mother's anguish over the following days. The son will "never be better," but the mother "needs to be better."

William G. Lulloff

Bibliography

Allen, Gay Wilson. *The Solitary Singer: A Critical Biography of Walt Whitman.* 1955. Rev. ed. 1967. Chicago: U of Chicago P, 1985.

Miller, James E., Jr. *A Critical Guide to "Leaves of Grass."* Chicago: U of Chicago P, 1957.

———. *Walt Whitman.* New York: Twayne, 1962.

Whitman, Walt. *Leaves of Grass.* Ed. Sculley Bradley and Harold W. Blodgett. Norton Critical Edition. New York: Norton, 1973.

———. *Walt Whitman's "Drum-Taps" (1865) and "Sequel to Drum-Taps" (1865–6): A Facsimile Reproduction.* Ed. F. DeWolfe Miller. Gainesville, Fla.: Scholars' Facsimiles and Reprints, 1959.

See also CIVIL WAR, THE; "DRUM-TAPS"

Complete Writings of Walt Whitman, The (1902)

Upon his death, Whitman left his literary legacy in the hands of the three men who had been among his closest companions and fiercest champions during the last twenty or so years of his life: Horace L. Traubel, Richard Maurice Bucke, and Thomas B. Harned. In their zeal to ensure what they saw as Whitman's rightful place in American literature, immediately following Whitman's death they began to publish from among the letters, manuscript notes, prose fragments, and other writings Whitman had left behind. Their efforts culminated ten years after Whitman had died in the first comprehensive collection of Whitman's work: the ten-volume *Complete Writings of Walt Whitman*, published by G.P. Putnam's Sons in 1902, illustrated with manuscript facsimiles and numerous photographs and paintings of the poet.

As a scholarly resource, the *Complete Writings* has been surpassed and replaced by the New York University Press's *Collected Writings*. As the editors of the New York University collection have shown, Traubel, Bucke, and Harned's was never actually "complete." Moreover, it was put together by adoring friends who had no training in the exacting standards of modern scholarship. Yet, for anyone interested in tracing the development of Whitman's reputation after his death, the *Complete Writings* cannot be overlooked.

The first three volumes contain the entirety of the final, authorized version of *Leaves of Grass* arranged by Whitman in 1891–1892, to which he appended the following note opposite the table of contents: "As there are now several editions of L. of G., different texts and dates, I wish to say that I prefer and recommend this present one, complete, for future printing, if there should be any; a copy and a fac-simile, indeed, of the text of these 438 pages."

The first volume includes a biographical and critical essay which rehearses much of the information—and defensive adulation—that had characterized William Douglas O'Connor's *The Good Gray Poet* (1866), Bucke's *Walt Whitman* (1883), and John Burroughs's *Whitman: A Study* (1896). The introductory essay also offers a useful catalogue of the growing body of Whitman criticism that was beginning to emerge at the turn of the century not only in the United States, but in Europe as well.

The third volume of *Leaves of Grass* includes variorum readings, together with first drafts of certain poems, rejected passages, and poems dropped along the way. These were arranged and edited by Oscar Lovell Triggs, of the University of Chicago.

Volumes 4–10 of the *Complete Writings* comprise *Complete Prose Works*, numbered separately as volumes 1–7. The first three of these volumes reprint prose works published by

Whitman during his lifetime. The remaining volumes reprint collections of letters, manuscripts, and notes of Whitman, as well as some essays by the executors drawing on that material.

Volume 1 contains part of *Specimen Days* (originally published as *Specimen Days & Collect* in 1882); volume 2 contains the remainder of *Specimen Days* and part of *Collect*. The third volume contains the rest of *Collect*, all of *November Boughs* (1888), and the first part of *Good-Bye My Fancy* (1891), which is continued in the fourth volume. Also in volume 4 is a reprinting of *The Wound Dresser: A Series of Letters Written from the Hospitals in Washington During the War of Rebellion*, which Bucke had originally edited and published in 1898.

Volume 5 of *Complete Prose Works* reprints all of *Calamus: A Series of Letters Written During the Years 1868–1880 by Walt Whitman to a Young Friend (Peter Doyle)*, another title published by Bucke as a volume unto itself in 1897. *Calamus* also includes an account of an interview with Doyle, conducted after Whitman's death. Also included in this volume is *Letters Written by Walt Whitman to his Mother*, edited by Harned and issued as a single volume simultaneously with the *Complete Writings*. Harned wrote three essays, based on manuscript material he inherited, and included them in this volume: "Walt Whitman and Oratory," "Walt Whitman and Physique," and "Walt Whitman and His Second Boston Publishers."

Volume 6 of *Complete Prose Works* contains most of *Notes And Fragments*, another collection edited and first published by Bucke in 1899 from among his share of Whitman's legacy. Bucke's introduction to the *Complete Writings* version explains that the notes that were published as part one of the original *Notes and Fragments* were used by Triggs in his *Variorum Readings* or *Rejected Lines and Passages* in the *Leaves of Grass* section of *Complete Writings*. From the haphazard and accidental bundles and scrapbooks he inherited, Bucke arranged the material into the following categories: "Notes on the Meaning and Intention of 'Leaves of Grass'"; "Memoranda from Books and from His Own Reflection—Indicating the Poet's Reading and Thought Prefatory to Writing 'Leaves of Grass'"; "Shorter Notes, Isolated Words, Brief Sentences, Memoranda, Suggestive Expressions, Names and Dates"; "Notes on English History"; and "List of Certain Magazine and Newspaper Articles Studied and Preserved by Walt Whitman and Found in his Scrapbooks and Among His Papers." The first three appear in volume 6 of *Complete Prose*, the last two in the final, seventh volume. Two bibliographical essays by Oscar Lovell Triggs, "The Growth of 'Leaves of Grass'" and "Bibliography of Walt Whitman," round out the seventh volume and the collection.

Rosemary Graham

Bibliography

Myerson, Joel, ed. *Walt Whitman: A Descriptive Bibliography*. Pittsburgh: U of Pittsburgh P, 1993.

Whitman, Walt. *The Complete Writings of Walt Whitman*. Ed. Richard Maurice Bucke, Thomas B. Harned, and Horace L. Traubel. 10 vols. New York: Putnam, 1902.

See also BUCKE, RICHARD MAURICE; BURROUGHS, JOHN AND URSULA; COLLECT; COLLECTED WRITINGS OF WALT WHITMAN, THE; DOYLE, PETER; HARNED, THOMAS BIGGS; LEAVES OF GRASS, 1891–1892 EDITION; LEAVES OF GRASS, VARIORUM EDITION; NOVEMBER BOUGHS; O'CONNOR, WILLIAM DOUGLAS; SPECIMEN DAYS; TRAUBEL, HORACE L.; TRIGGS, OSCAR LOVELL; WHITMAN, LOUISA VAN VELSOR

Compromise of 1850

The Compromise of 1850 was the term given to five statutes enacted by Congress in September 1850 that sought to resolve the bitter disputes about slavery between representatives of the North and South. The basic provisions of the compromise established territorial governments in Utah and New Mexico that allowed states formed out of these territories to decide the slavery question for themselves, admitted California under a constitution prohibiting slavery, abolished the slave trade in Washington, D.C., and enacted a stringent Fugitive Slave Law which amended the original 1793 statute. As a Free-Soiler, Walt Whitman was strongly opposed to the compromise and wrote editorializing poems in hopes of discouraging its passage.

Regional divisions over slavery had remained tense since 1846, when the introduction of the Wilmot Proviso incited national debates over whether territory gained from Mexico should be organized as slave or free. By 1850 such tensions threatened to sever the Union. When President Zachary Taylor in his January 1850 address urged Congress to admit California immediately and New Mexico soon thereafter as free states, a faction of Southerners threatened disunion. In an attempt to avert crisis, Henry Clay of Kentucky offered an omnibus bill of compromise resolutions that came to be known as the 1850 Compromise. Clay's resolutions were intended to balance the interests of North and South, but the provisions allowing for the organization of western territories as slave states were anathema to Whitman and Free-Soilers who opposed the extension of slavery on the principle that it would discourage the migration of white labor. Moreover, the Fugitive Slave Law, which included a provision compelling local citizens to assist federal marshals in the return of fugitive slaves, was denounced by Whitman and most Northerners as an intrusion of federal authority.

Whitman saw the entire bill as a capitulation to those who threatened secession. From March to June of 1850 Whitman wrote four poems for New York newspapers in which he urged Northern Congressmen to oppose compromise and excoriated those whom he felt had surrendered their antislavery principles in the face of disunionist threats. While none of the poems bear the marks of his later poetry—one is a satire, two others employ extended biblical analogies—for the first time Whitman has worked the issue of slavery into the form of poetry.

Prevailing Unionist sentiment led to passage of the bill, which provided a measure of national harmony on slavery until the Kansas-Nebraska Act of 1854 once more divided the nation. The 1850 Compromise was a bitter disappointment to Free-Soilers and to Whitman, who had been fighting the extension of slavery since 1846. With his antislavery hopes frustrated, Whitman largely took leave from politics and journalism until the mid-1850s.

Martin Klammer

Bibliography

Klammer, Martin. *Whitman, Slavery, and the Emergence of "Leaves of Grass."* University Park: Pennsylvania State UP, 1995.

McPherson, James M. *Battle Cry of Freedom: The Civil War Era.* New York: Oxford UP, 1988.

Rubin, Joseph Jay. *The Historic Whitman.* University Park: Pennsylvania State UP, 1973.

Whitman, Walt. *The Early Poems and the Fiction.* Ed. Thomas L. Brasher. New York: New York UP, 1963.

See also FREE SOIL PARTY; SLAVERY AND ABOLITIONISM; WILMOT PROVISO

Comradeship

Comradeship was, for Whitman, a complex and multifaceted theme in both his life and his poetry. He conceived of it as a crucial form of religious experience which provided humans with an existential sense of God's presence in this world and living proof of a transcendent spiritual realm and the soul's immortal destiny. On a political level, comradeship was to elevate the male personality and refine its coarser elements, creating an unprecedented male intimacy and bonding that would unify the United States citizenry (for Whitman, politics remained largely a male preserve) and create new forms of international solidarity. Comradeship was also to serve an important artistic function, uniting readers with the poet and each other in bonds of timeless mystical affection.

But the aspect of Whitman's comradeship to receive the most attention in the last twenty years is its alleged homosexual dimensions. Groundbreaking work in the field of gay studies has produced a widely accepted critical understanding which asserts that Whitman was the first self-proclaimed homosexual in modern literature and that his homosexuality formed the imaginative source and thematic center of his politics and his poetry. This approach has brought a needed corrective to Whitman scholarship which had, in keeping with the prejudices of an earlier time, treated homosexuality as a pathology to be primly overlooked or confined to the margins of critical discussion. Yet despite its positive contributions, this construction of a gay Whitman has various problematic features which invite further scrutiny. For while there is abundant evidence that Whitman was strongly attracted to other males, it is less clear whether he engaged in homosexual relations and celebrated gay love in his poetry or instead repressed and sublimated his homosexuality into more culturally acceptable forms of religious, political, and artistic expression.

Fredson Bowers and others have speculated that "Calamus," the sequence of poems which constitutes Whitman's primary poetic treatment of comradeship, was inspired by an actual love relationship Whitman had with another man. This may or may not have been the case, but what is beyond dispute is that Whitman conceived of the love he felt for other men as religious and as a crucial aspect of his spiritual life. Writing in 1870 to Benton Wilson, one of the Union soldiers he met in his hospital work, Whitman emphasized "our love for each other—so curious, so sweet, I say so *religious*" (*With Walt Whitman* 2:370). When Horace Traubel told the elderly poet that his correspondence of 1863 to Union veteran Elijah Fox was "better than the gospel according to John for love," Whitman responded that the sentiments of the letter were "the most important something in the world—something I tried to make clear in another way in Calamus" (*With Walt Whitman* 2:380).

Whitman always conceived of comradeship as an essential feature of his religious vision. In "Starting from Paumanok," written in conjunction with "Calamus," he describes "two greatnesses," love and democracy, which are informed by a "third one rising inclusive and more resplendent," that is, the "greatness of Religion" (section 10). In "Calamus" itself, Whitman gives primary emphasis to the spiritual meaning of "manly love." It is the love of comrades, he announces in the opening poem, rather than "pleasures, profits and conformities," which he needs to "feed" his "soul" ("In Paths Untrodden"). This theme is further established in the second poem as Whitman affirms that the experience of loving comradeship raises his soul to a heightened state ("how calm, how solemn it grows to ascend to the atmosphere of lovers") and instills in him a sense of integration into a more real spiritual order: the "real reality" which transcends the natural world, making it, in comparison, seem but a mere "mask of materials" or "show of appearance" ("Scented Herbage of My Breast"). Elsewhere in the sequence he also calls attention to how friendship culminates in a spiritual love that is part of a higher spiritual reality, referring, for example, to how it liberates his soul so that, becoming "disembodied" and "[e]thereal," it "float[s] in the regions" of spiritual love ("Fast Anchor'd Eternal O Love!").

Whitman believed this elevated state of loving consciousness was an anticipatory experience of the life his soul would know more fully after death. Because this love was a mystical prolepsis of immortality, he spoke of love and death as meaning "precisely the same" and as being "folded inseparably together" ("Scented Herbage of My Breast"). But in closely associating love and death, Whitman's point is not, as routinely (mis)interpreted, that the love of comrades paradoxically leads to death but that it anticipates the greater love the soul will know in the afterlife when united with God, "The great Camerado, the lover true for whom I pine" ("Song of Myself," section 45).

For purposes of analysis, comradeship may be spoken of as having political dimensions, but these are also religious because Whitman envisaged both his ideal citizens and his ideal state as fundamentally religious. The spiritual marrow of Whitman's politics is most clearly and succinctly revealed in *Democratic Vistas,* where he asserts that his envisioned future democracy is to be a "sublime and serious Religious Democracy" (*Prose Works* 2:410) and insists that its citizenry must be thoroughly infused with an "all penetrating Religiousness" (*Prose Works* 2:398). Friendship among religious citizens in a religious polity would necessarily be suffused with spirituality. Whitman imagined a future democratic individualism that would find its needed counterbalance in a comradeship that "fuses, ties and aggregates, making the races comrades, and fraternizing all," and both were "to be vitalized by religion" because "at the core of democracy, finally, is the religious element" (*Prose Works* 2:381).

In its aesthetic function, comradeship is equally religious. Whitman wished to beget a passionate, timeless spiritual relationship between himself and his readers. His poetry was to "arouse and set flowing in men's and women's hearts, young and old, endless streams of living, pulsating love and friendship, directly from them to myself, now and ever" (*Prose Works* 2:471). These bonds of love would not, he proclaimed, be severed by death: "I cannot be discharged from you! not from one any sooner than another! / O death! O for all that, I am yet of you unseen this hour with irrepressible love" ("Starting from Paumanok," section 14). Much as nineteenth-century American Protestants saw themselves as receiving spiritual sustenance from Christ in their efforts to establish the heavenly city in America, Whitman dreamed of future generations of "Americanos, a hundred millions" who would turn to him for inspiration as they worked to build his ideal religious democracy: "With faces turn'd sideways or backwards towards me to listen, / With eyes retrospective towards me" ("Starting from Paumanok," section 2).

When considering the meaning of comradeship, it is still germane to recall Whitman's exchange with John Addington Symonds, the bisexual British scholar who, over a period of nearly two decades, repeatedly inquired about the meaning of "Calamus." Finally responding in 1890, Whitman asserted, in tones of bewildered outrage, that he found Symonds's suggested gay reading "damnable" (*Correspondence* 5:73). Recent scholarship dismisses this reply by interpreting it not as a rejection of a gay reading but as merely an indication of Whitman's distaste for Symonds's use of current European medical terminology for homosexuality (Erkkila 167) or for his "aristocratic or connoisseur or feminized" model of homosexuality (Martin 177).

Such explanations strain belief, and they become even more problematic when the letter to Symonds is paired with another of Whitman's equally forceful repudiations of a homosexual reading from the same period. In this case Whitman speaks not to an upper-class European but a fellow working-class American. In December 1888 Whitman gave Horace Traubel, the painstaking biographer of his final years, another letter he had written from Washington during the Civil War to his friend Hugo Fritsch in New York. Whitman told Traubel the letters would help him to "clear up some things [about "Calamus"] which have been misunderstood: you know what: I don't need to say." Following this, Whitman went on to complain that the world was "so topsy turvy, so afraid to love, so afraid to demonstrate . . . that when it sees two or more people who really, greatly, wholly care for each other . . . they wonder and are incredulous or suspicious or defamatory." Indulging himself in an unusual fit of pique, Whitman asserted that people inevitably come to false conclusions "about any demonstration between men—any," and then they "gossip, generate slander . . . the old women men, the old men women, the guessers, the false-witnesses— the whole caboodle of liars and fools" (*With Walt Whitman* 3:385–386).

These forceful rejections of a possible homosexual theme in "Calamus" should be paired with Whitman's own personal reflections in his notebooks around 1870 in which he anguishes over his affection for Peter Doyle (considered the closest of Whitman's various male friends), referring to it as an "*abnormal* PERTURBATION" and a "diseased, feverish disproportionate adhesiveness" (*Notebooks* 2:887–890). This language indicates that Whitman felt his affection was excessive, and if this attraction contained any conscious sexual dimensions, these appear to be clearly disapproved of as pathological. In short, what limited extra-textual references we have to Whitman's views on homosexuality (if the notebook entry can be so counted) are expressions of strong disapproval.

The grounds for questioning the current homosexual reading of comradeship are further strengthened if one keeps in mind that antebellum culture contained several traditions— among them romanticism, transcendentalism, and phrenology—that encouraged intimate male friendship and often invested it with religious significance (Reynolds 391–398). Also, in nineteenth-century America it was neither uncommon, nor necessarily occasion for comment, for men to share a bed; for example, the young Abraham Lincoln slept openly for four years with his friend Joshua Speed. The existence of these traditions of male friendship and bedsharing explains how in an age when homosexuality was considered immoral, abnormal, and even criminal, Whitman might publish lines like the following: "For the one I love most lay sleeping by me under the same cover in the cool night, / In the stillness in the autumn moonbeams his face was inclined toward me, / And his arm lay around my breast—and that night I was happy" ("When I Heard at the Close of the Day").

That Whitman would compose this vignette and that his contemporaries did not find it offensive indicates that nineteenth-century Americans were considerably less inclined than moderns to equate intimate inter-male affection with homosexuality. The souls not only of Victorian moralists but also of even such sensitive readers as Ralph Waldo Emerson and Henry David Thoreau sometimes shrank from Whitman's poetry, but this was not in response to detected suggestions of homosexuality but because of its candid presentation of the human anatomy and heterosexual love. Attention to our culture's changing perceptions of male friendship cautions against readily interpreting Whitman's poems of "manly love" as homosexual texts.

Much of the textual evidence for a gay reading of comradeship is also far from compelling. The primary argument from Whitman's fiction is based on a highly questionable reading of a short story of 1841, "The Child's Champion," which maintains that the sipping of a drink is to be read as fellatio and that the kicking of a boy's back is suggestive of anal rape. Homosexual interpretations of the poetry also contain problematic elements. The reading of "Song of Myself" as a homosexual dream or fantasy repeatedly strains the textual evidence, e.g., the interpretation of the male bathers (section 11) as a "fantasy of mass fellatio" or of the passage on touch (sections 28–29) as ending with anal intercourse. Equally unconvincing is the frequent reading of section 5 of "Song of Myself," in which Whitman describes the union of his body and soul, as actually being a depiction of homosexual oral sex.

Nor is there persuasive evidence for a gay interpretation of Whitman's life. The extensive body of letters Whitman wrote to Civil War soldiers, and especially Peter Doyle, usually considered his most intimate "camerado," is perhaps the best record we have of his male friendships. This correspondence is noteworthy not for its romantic passion, of which there is little, and certainly not for its eroticism, of which there is none, but rather for its expression of parental love. The persona that emerges is not that of an erotic lover but of an older friend who also serves as a caring, and at times doting, father and mother.

Pointing to these problematic features of the current gay reading does not refute such an interpretation but rather calls for its reexamination. For such a review, several guidelines might be suggested. The first would be to give serious consideration to Whitman's insistence to Symonds that "L of G is only to be rightly construed by and within its own atmosphere and essential character" (*Correspondence* 5:72). At a very minimum, this would mean relating comradeship to Whitman's pervasive religious purposes and the culture of nineteenth-century male friendship (which included intensely affectionate, nonsexual relationships). Also, given Whitman's own strong repudiations, it seems that a proposed gay reading should not present homosexuality as the core of his personality and the central theme of his poetry, but rather emphasize Whitman's tentativeness and confusion about his sexual identity and the indeterminacy inherent in his treatment of male friendship. Finally, a gay reading might be more strongly argued if based not on authorial intent but on a hermeneutic stressing the fusion of the horizons of the text and the modern reader.

Some two years before penning his strong denunciation to Symonds, Whitman allowed to Traubel that he himself sometimes experienced moments of personal puzzlement about "Calamus": "perhaps I don't know what it ["Calamus"] all means—perhaps never did know. My first instinct about all that Symonds writes is violently reactionary—is strong and brutal for no, no, no. Then the thought intervenes that I maybe do not know all my own meanings"

(*With Walt Whitman* 1:76–77). Perhaps this comment is part of a long elaborate ruse Whitman wove throughout his final years to mislead Traubel, skillfully camouflaging his earlier effort to proclaim a gospel of gay love while yet keeping open the possibility of a future gay reading. Or perhaps it is a sincere admission of puzzlement and a clear illustration that Whitman was capable of a profound humility. Either way, the passage points to the intricacies surrounding Whitman's comradeship and the need for modesty in interpretation. Perhaps such factors as the complexity of Whitman's personality, the indeterminacy of his poetic style, the ineffable nature of mystical experience, the fluidity of sexual desire, and the inevitable subjectivity of interpretation combine to defy any clear determination of what Whitman meant by comradeship.

David Kuebrich

Bibliography
Erkkila, Betsy. "Whitman and the Homosexual Republic." *Walt Whitman: The Centennial Essays.* Ed. Ed Folsom. Iowa City: U of Iowa P, 1994. 153–171.
Martin, Robert K. *The Homosexual Tradition in American Poetry.* Austin: U of Texas P, 1979.
———. "Whitman and the Politics of Identity." *Walt Whitman: The Centennial Essays.* Ed. Ed Folsom. Iowa City: U of Iowa P, 1994. 172–181.
———. "Whitman's 'Song of Myself': Homosexual Dream and Vision." *Partisan Review* 42 (1975): 80–96.
Reynolds, David S. *Walt Whitman's America: A Cultural Biography.* New York: Knopf, 1995.
Symonds, John Addington. *Walt Whitman: A Study.* London: Nimmo, 1893.
Traubel, Horace. *With Walt Whitman in Camden.* Vol. 1. Boston: Small, Maynard, 1906; Vol. 2. New York: Appleton, 1908; Vol. 3. New York: Mitchell Kennerley, 1914.
Whitman, Walt. *The Correspondence.* Ed. Edwin Haviland Miller. 6 vols. New York: New York UP, 1961–1977.
———. *Notebooks and Unpublished Prose Manuscripts.* Ed. Edward F. Grier. 6 vols. New York: New York UP, 1984.
———. *Prose Works 1892.* Ed. Floyd Stovall. 2 vols. New York: New York UP, 1963–1964.

C

Comstock, Anthony (1844–1919)

Anthony Comstock, a prominent late nineteenth-century moralist, threatened to suppress the 1881 edition of *Leaves of Grass*. The founder and leading spirit of the New York Society for the Suppression of Vice, and a special agent of the Post Office Department, Comstock considered Whitman's book not merely offensive, but plainly illegal.

Comstock had lobbied heavily for the passage of a federal anti-obscenity bill which, when passed in 1873, became popularly known as the Comstock Law. Supported by this statute, he pressured the Boston district attorney into advising Whitman's publisher, James R. Osgood, that the book could not be legally published without alteration. At first, Whitman agreed to self-censorship; but upon receiving the full list of objections, he refused to make even the slightest revision. When Osgood bowed to the threats of Comstock and the district attorney, Whitman secured continued publication with David McKay of Rees Welsh and Company. Although Comstock never took active measures to thwart further publication, he did arrest Ezra Heywood for distributing two of the objectionable poems through the mail.

Comstock's warnings and Heywood's trial piqued public interest in *Leaves of Grass*, increasing sales and allowing Whitman to enjoy steady royalty payments for the first time in his career.

Joseph P. Hammond

Bibliography

Barrus, Clara. *Whitman and Burroughs, Comrades.* Boston: Houghton Mifflin, 1931.

Bremner, Robert. Introduction. *Traps for the Young.* 1883. By Anthony Comstock. Cambridge, Mass.: Harvard UP, 1967. vii–xxxi.

Loving, Jerome. *Walt Whitman's Champion: William Douglas O'Connor.* College Station: Texas A&M UP, 1978.

Contradiction

"Do I contradict myself? / Very well then I contradict myself. / (I am large, I contain multitudes.)" ("Song of Myself," section 51). Whitman's famous question and answer summarize his philosophy of philosophies. His elastic, eclectic "I" inviting conflicts and embracing inconsistencies "gives up" to the reader "my contradictory moods." Party to a transcendentalism that dismisses "foolish consistency" as the "hobgoblin" of little minds, elbowing an Emerson in whom, as Whitman said, "there is hardly a proposition . . . which you cannot find the opposite of in some other place" (qtd. in Asselineau 377), the poet does justice to Keats's theory of negative capability (an acceptance of conflicting ideas) and incarnates his own version of the Hegelian synthesis of opposites. For Whitman, contradiction is the conjunction of "local" or temporal inconsistencies which cannot touch yet can in fact lead to universal truths. There are several types of contradiction in Whitman: apparent contradiction, which is paradox; about-faces of opinion; ambivalent pronouncements; and a text at odds with Whitman's affirmations. Whitman plots contradiction, but it also sneaks up on him.

As James Miller observes, Whitman cultivates contradiction from the beginning lines of *Leaves of Grass* in "One's-Self I Sing." The tension strung between the "simple separate person" singing for, and standing out from, the "En-Masse" starts the movement of opposites which will push Whitman's verse now strongly, now feebly, through its directions and indirections, bald affirmations and "faint clews." It is in the amorous wrestle between the I and the All, the Me and the Not Me, that Whitman distinguishes and unites opposing elements. His role as poet-prophet is to individuate and reconcile. In *Democratic Vistas* (1871), where Whitman examines the stunted democracy that blooms in *Leaves of Grass*, he speaks of the people as being like "our huge earth itself, which, to ordinary scansion, is full of vulgar contradictions" (*Prose Works* 2:376). It is the artist's mind, "lit with the infinite," transcending the differences of an assumed ensemble, that can transform the "ungrammatical, untidy, . . . ill-bred" average of *Democratic Vistas* (2:376) into the divine oneness of *Leaves of Grass*.

In an effort to transcend the dead-end vision of such "ordinary scansion" or of what he calls in *Specimen Days* (1882) the "malady" of "seems," Whitman's protean "I" would distinguish and penetrate the (sur)faces of his ensemble in poems like "Faces" and "The Sleepers." In such an extension and uncovering of identity, he would illustrate the resolution of what he saw as the contradiction between the necessary yet isolating pride of individualism and the outward-reaching sympathy needed for a cohesive democracy. The synthesis of the two, as Roger Asselineau notes, would result in Whitman's personalism, the self-reliance of the individual as integral member of a healthy democratic "En-Masse."

So zealous was Whitman in his effort to transcend temporal obstacles to a healthy personalism in democratic union that he would appear to dismiss not just apparent contradiction but also the presence of death and evil as surface blips. The breezy "It is just as lucky to die" ("Song of Myself," section 7) seems to deny death as much as the oracular riddle "Great is goodness . . . Great is wickedness" ("Great Are the Myths") dismisses evil. Yet these early pronouncements—contradicted elsewhere in *Leaves of Grass*—crudely illustrate Whitman's acceptance (comparable to that of Vedantic mysticism) of the competing forces of existence. The poet who would commemorate not only goodness, growth, and harmony, but also evil, death, and chaos, sees the latter as a condition on the way to the ideal. This form of Hegelianism occurred in Whitman even before he had a real exposure to German idealism. As Whitman states in his 1855 Preface, "The poets of the kosmos advance through all interpositions and coverings and turmoils to first principles" (*Leaves* 723). In his later "The Base of All Metaphysics," Whitman expresses his admiration for Hegel, seeing himself as poetic representative of the German's philosophy of evolution through negative and positive forces.

There are contradictions in *Leaves of Grass*, however, that are neither markers of truths nor potential Hegelian solutions. Because *Leaves of Grass* as an evolving text spans decades, the poet contradicts himself simply by changing his mind: "If I have said anything to the contrary, I hereby retract it," he announces, or "Now I reverse what I said" ("Says," sections 2 and 7). Whitman even contradicts his defense of contradiction in the famous "Respondez!" (suppressed in 1881), where he loses patience with conflict, declaring with uncharacteristic sarcasm, "Let men and women be mock'd . . . Let contradictions prevail! let one

thing contradict another! and let one line of my poems contradict another!" (*Neglected* 28).

Whitman would appear to ignore the fact that some of the views in his ideological grab bag not only conflicted with but threatened to undermine some of his declarations in *Leaves of Grass*. The poet of brotherhood has been taken to task for his problematic stances on slavery, Native Americans, women, and foreign policy as issued sporadically in his prose. Moreover, Betsy Erkkila finds that there are crises in *Leaves of Grass,* unplotted, in which the text inadvertently contradicts Whitman's affirmations, reflecting the uncontainability of social and historical conflicts that the poet would resolve and absorb in his verse.

If Whitman invited, defended, deplored, and ignored contradiction, he did so containing the opposing elements of the seen and the unseen worlds he assumed. The poet of the body and of the soul, the "solitary singer" of the enmasse, the American Adam of archaisms and neologisms, and the radical conservative and conservative radical, Whitman was a master, as Hart Crane observed, at coordinating opposites.

John Addington Symonds compared Whitman to the universe—at first sight contradictory. Malcolm Cowley saw the poet's ideas as pell-mell driftwood in a flooding river. D.H. Lawrence likened Whitman's synthetic personalism to an "awful pudding" (178). But Whitman's "system" was contradiction; it allowed for what he called the "vast seething mass of materials" (*Leaves* 743) of an America at an historical crossroads. Whitman the artist would offer no fixed system as the path to the ideal, admitting, "when it comes to . . . tying philosophy to the multiplication table—I am lost—lost utterly." He could only offer his capacity for contradictions that the reader would accept, reject, or resolve. As he conceded: "I am not Anarchist, not Methodist, not anything you can name. Yet I see why all the ists and isms . . . exist—can see why they must exist and why I must include them all" (Traubel 71).

Carol M. Zapata-Whelan

Bibliography

Asselineau, Roger. *The Evolution of Walt Whitman: The Creation of a Book.* Trans. Roger Asselineau and Burton L. Cooper. Cambridge, Mass.: Harvard UP, 1962.

Erkkila, Betsy. *Whitman the Political Poet.* New York: Oxford UP, 1989.

Folsom, Ed, ed. *Walt Whitman: The Centennial Essays.* Iowa City: U of Iowa P, 1994.

Klammer, Martin. *Whitman, Slavery, and the Emergence of "Leaves of Grass."* University Park: Pennsylvania State UP, 1995.

Lawrence, D.H. *Studies in Classic American Literature.* 1923. Garden City, N.Y.: Doubleday, 1951.

Miller, James E., Jr. *A Critical Guide to "Leaves of Grass."* Chicago: U of Chicago P, 1957.

Perlman, Jim, Ed Folsom, and Dan Campion, eds. *Walt Whitman: The Measure of His Song.* Minneapolis: Holy Cow!, 1981.

Teller, Walter. *Walt Whitman's Camden Conversations.* New Brunswick, N.J.: Rutgers UP, 1973.

Traubel, Horace. *With Walt Whitman in Camden.* 1908. Vol. 2. New York: Rowman and Littlefield, 1961.

Whitman, Walt. *Leaves of Grass.* Ed. Sculley Bradley and Harold W. Blodgett. Norton Critical Edition. New York: Norton, 1973.

———. *The Neglected Walt Whitman: Vital Texts.* Ed. Sam Abrams. New York: Four Walls Eight Windows, 1993.

———. *Prose Works 1892.* Ed. Floyd Stovall. 2 vols. New York: New York UP, 1963–1964.

Zapata-Whelan, Carol. "'Do I Contradict Myself?': Progression Through Contraries in Walt Whitman's 'The Sleepers.'" *Walt Whitman Quarterly Review* 10 (1992): 25–39.

See also DEMOCRACY; DEMOCRATIC VISTAS; "FACES"; HEGEL, GEORG WILHELM FRIEDRICH; "ONE'S-SELF I SING"; "SLEEPERS, THE"; "SONG OF MYSELF"; TRANSCENDENTALISM

Conway, Moncure Daniel (1832–1907)

Born in slave-holding Virginia, Moncure D. Conway belonged to a distinguished family and was a direct descendant of a signer of the Declaration of Independence. After graduating from Dickinson College (B.A., 1849; M.A., 1852) he practiced law in Virginia, but shortly thereafter abandoned the law and turned to the ministry. He began to read Emerson, with whom he corresponded, and in 1852 entered the Unitarian Divinity School in Cambridge, Massachusetts. From 1854–1857 he was a minister of the Unitarian church in Washington, D.C., where he earned a reputation as an abolitionist. At the urging of Emerson, Conway visited Whitman in New York in 1855 shortly after publication of the first edition of *Leaves of Grass.*

Conway left Washington for Boston in 1863, becoming the editor of *Commonwealth.* That same year he visited England to deliver speeches and sermons on slavery, and he accepted an offer to become the minister at South Place Chapel in London, where he remained until 1884. In 1867 Whitman and Conway corresponded concerning an edition of Whitman's poems which William M. Rossetti wanted to bring out in England. In a letter to Conway, Whitman seemed to allow Rossetti to substitute words for "onanist" and "father-stuff." He also explains that "'Calamus' is a common word here" in America and that its use should not offend an English audience (Whitman 941). But a later letter to Rossetti recanted this position: "I cannot and will not consent, of my own volition, to countenance an expurgated edition of my pieces" (Whitman 942). Rossetti ultimately published a selected edition of Whitman's poems, changing no words, but omitting poems he thought might be offensive.

Upon his return to America in 1885, Conway settled in New York City, where he published treatises and discourses in newspapers and magazines. Conway published several biographies, among them works on Thomas Carlyle (1881), Edmund Randolph (1888), George Washington (1889), Nathaniel Hawthorne (1890), and Thomas Paine (1892).

Philip W. Leon

Bibliography

Conway, Moncure D. *Autobiography.* Vol. 1. Boston: Houghton Mifflin, 1904.

D'Entremont, John. *Southern Emancipator: Moncure Conway, the American Years, 1832–1865.* New York: Oxford UP, 1987.

Ridgely, J.V. "Whitman, Emerson and Friend." *Columbia Library Columns* 10 (1960): 15–19.

Whitman, Walt. *The Poetry and Prose of Walt Whitman.* Ed. Louis Untermeyer. New York: Simon and Schuster, 1949.

See also EMERSON, RALPH WALDO; ROSSETTI, WILLIAM MICHAEL

Cooper, James Fenimore (1789–1851)

Influenced by Long Island, as was Walt Whitman, James Fenimore Cooper was an American prose writer best known for *The Last of the Mohicans* (1826) and *The Deerslayer* (1841). Although Whitman did not consider Cooper an influence, he did read many of Cooper's works, admiring in particular *The Red Rover* (1827), a swashbuckling romance.

Cooper, like Whitman, used the sea as an image throughout his work. However, Cooper differed from Whitman in his treatment of nature. Cooper regarded nature as a fixed object to be observed (see Peck 28), while Whitman viewed it as a mutable entity to be experienced. Cooper's largely conservative social and political views also contrasted sharply with Whitman's. Nevertheless, in the writing of fiction, Whitman at times revealed an indebtedness to Cooper, in both "theme and manner" (Kaplan 117).

Jennifer J. Stein

Bibliography

Berbrich, Joan D. *Three Voices from Paumanok: The Influence of Long Island on James Fenimore Cooper, William Cullen Bryant, and Walt Whitman*. Port Washington, N.Y.: Friedman, 1969.

Kaplan, Justin. *Walt Whitman: A Life*. New York: Simon and Schuster, 1980.

Peck, H. Daniel. *A World by Itself: The Pastoral Moment in Cooper's Fiction*. New Haven: Yale UP, 1977.

See also LONG ISLAND, NEW YORK; READING, WHITMAN'S

Correspondence of Walt Whitman, The (1961–1977)

The thousands of letters written by Walt Whitman during his lifetime to family, friends, and acquaintances have been collected in six volumes of *The Correspondence of Walt Whitman* (New York University Press, 1961–1977), edited by Edwin Haviland Miller, and in a Special Double Issue of the *Walt Whitman Quarterly Review* (University of Iowa, 1991), also edited by Edwin Haviland Miller. In 1990, Professor Miller chose 250 of the most interesting and moving letters and placed them into an edition of *Selected Letters of Walt Whitman*.

Of course, many other books containing Whitman's correspondence have appeared in scattered fashion and of uneven quality in the years following the poet's death in 1892, but Miller's work is the most exhaustive and responsible compilation available. It deals with all of the previously published pieces and adds, in newly collected correspondence, about sixty percent to the total of extant Whitman letters. Miller carefully and thoroughly annotates the individual items in the correspondence, providing information on topical references and identifying both the persons Whitman wrote to and the names of those mentioned in the letters.

Postcards and letters written by Whitman are still being discovered every year, many of which have been published in the *Walt Whitman Quarterly Review*. However, if modern readers of the letters want to acquire a proper perspective and deeper understanding of Whitman's letter writing, they must take into consideration some of the numerous letters the poet received from his correspondents. Although many of these pieces, such as the ones from his mother, are still unpublished, many others can be found in various collections. What emerges from these letters is a fuller picture of the persons Whitman was writing to and a clearer awareness of the topics he was responding to. This approach to an examination of the letters provides insights into the extent of the relationships Whitman had with his correspondents and increases an understanding of what he was expressing to those he wrote to over the years.

In reading Whitman's many letters, scholars looking for literary discussions by the great poet are frequently disappointed. However, those writers seeking autobiographical materials are usually rewarded in their efforts because Whitman's correspondence dealt mostly with personal matters. When Whitman wrote a letter to his mother or to the parents of a dead or wounded soldier, he would express himself in a simple, natural style of language focusing on down-to-earth concerns and on human emotions relating to love and death.

Thus, most of the letters he wrote are not on artistic theories of literature. In fact, many pieces are about mundane business matters of publication and the promotion of his works of poetry. The earliest letters, which are among those that have come to light in recent years and are included in *Selected Letters*, date from 1840 and 1841 and reveal Whitman's concern for his self-image as he assumes various poses and postures in describing his schoolteaching experiences at Woodbury, Long Island. This behavior, plus Whitman's unhappiness and loneliness, comes through in the biting language, pretentious diction, and strained comparisons in the letters he sent to his friend Abraham Paul Leech.

In his poetry Whitman was always cognizant of his audience, and the same awareness of his readers can be seen in the letters. This is why when he writes to his mother and other family members, who he knows have little understanding of his creative work, Whitman uses a plain, practical mode of expression as he concentrates on financial worries, health concerns, and matters of day-to-day living. Addressing publishers and editors, Whitman is strictly business, asking for certain amounts of money for his poems or making sure the printing schedule for his work is on target. The letters to his longtime friends and admirers, such as Ralph Waldo Emerson, William Douglas O'Connor, Richard Maurice Bucke, and John Burroughs, are mostly detailed, factual descriptions of Whitman's current affairs, printing successes or disappointments, and personal condition and needs. Although the style of writing he uses in his correspondence to his friends is sophisticated and congenial, even here the letters rarely touch on literary topics and seldom achieve artistic levels of expression.

The most revealing and touching epistolary pieces of prose by Whitman, however, are in the letters he wrote for the wounded and dying soldiers he visited in the overcrowded, bloody hospitals during the Civil War years. Here Whitman's human qualities of caring, sacrifice, and affection are revealed in the lines written for worried and grieving families. Whether he is explaining a young man's agonizing recovery from battlefront wounds or describing the last hours of a dying soldier, Whitman's words are those of compassion and concern. The letters plainly demonstrate the poet's purpose in these communications. Whitman takes the place of the absent family members. Although they cannot be there with their loved ones, the kind, gray-bearded poet is there dispensing as much love and comfort to the young soldiers as he possibly can. Thus, Whitman enables a mother, father, sister, brother, or wife to feel some assurance in knowing that the wounded loved one is not suffering without a caring person nearby. In the letters he writes to the family members of those young men who died, Whitman gives the comforting message that their loved ones were not alone during their last agonizing moments on earth.

Whitman also corresponded with soldiers he had met in the hospitals who had recovered from their wounds and returned home. These letters show the depth of the poet's affectionate ties with the men he visited in the wards. His letters to two of the soldiers, Thomas P. Sawyer and Elijah Douglass Fox, show the extent of Whitman's attachment and love for these men.

Also of significance are the letters Whitman wrote to two other young men to whom he became fondly connected. His affectionate bond with Peter Doyle, the Washington, D.C., streetcar conductor he met in late 1865, is a testament to Whitman's manly attachment that he celebrated in his "Calamus" poems. Later, when Whitman had settled in Camden in the 1870s and 1880s, he became a close friend to another young man, Harry Stafford. The letters reveal the genuine love of the aging Whitman for these two men. How much Doyle and Stafford reciprocated his affection is somewhat uncertain, but the letters demonstrate the poet's strong commitment to his relationships with both young men.

As previously noted, Whitman's letters are rarely of a literary quality, but they frequently provide glimpses into the mind of the poet. Whether corresponding with his many friends, writing to his admirers in England, or composing practical business letters to send to his publishers and editors, Whitman's overriding purpose was to ensure that his great body of poetry would be preserved and thrive in American literature. His world was his poetry, and most of what he wrote reveals this preoccupation. In Whitman's letters the reader observes if not the making of a poet, the advertisement and preservation of one.

Because much of Whitman's correspondence deals with daily occurrences and matter-of-fact details, some readers have tended to dismiss his letters as tedious and inconsequential. However, as is evidenced in his poetry, Whitman regarded the physical world as vital and essential. In "Crossing Brooklyn Ferry," he expresses the idea that all the material objects and images of life, what Whitman calls the "dumb beautiful ministers," serve to furnish their parts "toward eternity" and "toward the soul" (section 9). This is why Whitman thought it important that he inform his family members and friends of the daily minutiae of living. To him these were the hard objects and everyday scenes that in their accumulative power and symbolic nature offered the clues that would lead to the deeper realities.

Angelo Costanzo

Bibliography

Folsom, Ed. "Prospects for the Study of Walt Whitman." *Resources for American Literary Study* 20 (1994): 1–15.

Whitman, Walt. *The Correspondence*. Ed. Edwin Haviland Miller. 6 vols. New York: New York UP, 1961–1977.

———. "The Correspondence of Walt Whitman: A Second Supplement with an Updated Calendar of Letters Written to Whitman." Ed. Edwin Haviland Miller. *Walt Whitman Quarterly Review* (Special Double Issue) 8.3–4 (1991): 1–106.

———. *Leaves of Grass: Comprehensive Reader's Edition*. Ed. Harold W. Blodgett and Sculley Bradley. New York: New York UP, 1965.

———. *Selected Letters of Walt Whitman*. Ed. Edwin Haviland Miller. Iowa City: U of Iowa P, 1990.

See also BUCKE, RICHARD MAURICE; BURROUGHS, JOHN AND URSULA; *COLLECTED WRITINGS OF WALT WHITMAN, THE*; DOYLE, PETER; EMERSON, RALPH WALDO; LEECH, ABRAHAM PAUL; O'CONNOR, WILLIAM DOUGLAS; SAWYER, THOMAS P.; STAFFORD, HARRY L.; WHITMAN, LOUISA VAN VELSOR

Cosmic Consciousness

Canadian psychiatrist Richard Maurice Bucke, M.D. (1837–1902), met Whitman in Philadelphia (18 October 1877), instantly befriended him, and wrote the poet's first biography (*Walt Whitman*, 1883). At Bucke's invitation, Whitman visited the doctor's insane asylum in London, Ontario, for four months during the summer of 1880, an event dramatized in the film *Beautiful Dreamers* (Hemdale Pictures, 1992). Thomas B. Harned and Horace L. Traubel joined Bucke as Whitman's literary executors.

Bucke's book *Cosmic Consciousness* (1901) defined the state of mystical illumination which Bucke believed was evident in such people as Buddha, Moses, Socrates, Jesus, Mohammed, Dante, Wordsworth, and Whitman. These people possessed a profound awareness "of life and order in the universe," "a state of moral exaltation," and "a sense of immortality" (3).

According to Bucke, Cosmic Consciousness caused all doubts about God and the purpose of life to dissolve in a sudden revelation of universal truth and beauty. This spiritual awakening was mankind's "Saviour" (6). Under its influence, a person's soul would be revolutionized through intuitive discovery that the whole universe is alive and good. All religions would melt into one powerful state of heightened spiritual awareness, a state which Buddha called Nirvana, Jesus called the Kingdom of God, St. Paul called Christ, Mohammed called Gabriel, Dante called Beatrice, and Whitman called My Soul.

Bucke believed that he himself attained Cosmic Consciousness early in the spring of 1873 while reading the works of William Wordsworth, Percy Bysshe Shelley, John Keats, Robert Browning, and especially Walt Whitman. The doctor wrote that Whitman was the "best, most perfect, example the world has so far had of the Cosmic Sense" (225). In Bucke's view, Whitman revealed his own moment of cosmic illumination in section 5 of "Song of Myself" (Bucke used *Leaves of Grass*, 1855 and 1891–1892); "As in a Swoon" (this poem appeared in only three editions: *Leaves of Grass*, 1876, which Bucke used; *Good-Bye My Fancy*, 1891; *Complete Prose Works*, 1892); and "Hast Never Come to Thee an Hour" (Bucke used *Leaves of Grass*, 1891–1892). These passages describe a dramatic revelation during which Whitman ecstatically discovered the mystical interconnection of everything in the universe and the love, both erotic and divine, which is the basis of all existence.

Bucke traced the transformation in Whitman's personality, themes, and writing styles to this moment of cosmic awakening. While describing Whitman's pre-illumination writings as "of absolutely no value," Bucke maintained that the enlightened Whitman wrote poetry so powerful that each page expressed the words "ETERNAL LIFE" written in "ethereal fire" (226). Viewing the poet almost as a god, the enthralled doctor even adopted Whitman's appearance of full beard and broad-rimmed hat.

Bucke summed up Whitman's Cosmic Consciousness as a complete freedom from fear of sin or death resulting in a transcendent awareness of eternal life. Bucke believed that Whitman's illumination was greater than that of Buddha and St. Paul, but not as clear as that of Jesus. While warning that the attainment of the cosmic faculty must not be used to gratify human vanity, Bucke felt that this highest state of consciousness was nevertheless "truly Godlike" (232).

Matthew Ignoffo

Bibliography

Bucke, Richard Maurice. *Cosmic Consciousness: A Study in the Evolution of the Human Mind.* 1901. New York: Dutton, 1969.

——. *Richard Maurice Bucke, Medical Mystic: Letters of Dr. Bucke to Walt Whitman and His Friends.* Ed. Artem Lozynsky. Detroit: Wayne State UP, 1977.

Ignoffo, Matthew. "The Intellectual American Revolution: Whitman as 'New Age' Poet." *Christian New Age Quarterly* July–Sept. 1989: 1, 6, 12.

Lozynsky, Artem. "Dr. Richard Maurice Bucke: A Religious Disciple of Whitman." *Studies in the American Renaissance: 1977.* Ed. Joel Myerson. Boston: Twayne, 1978. 387–403.

Lynch, Michael. "Walt Whitman in Ontario." *The Continuing Presence of Walt Whitman.* Ed. Robert K. Martin. Iowa City: U of Iowa P, 1992. 141–151.

Shortt, S.E.D. "The Myth of a Canadian Boswell: Dr. R.M. Bucke and Walt Whitman." *Canadian Bulletin of Medical History* 1 (1984): 55–70.

See also BUCKE, RICHARD MAURICE

Costelloe, Mary Whitall Smith (1864–1945)

Philadelphia-born Mary Whitall Smith Costelloe, a Quaker, was a political activist and an art historian and critic. She was well known in England for lectures on social reform (1885–1890) and in America for those on art criticism (1903–1904; 1909). As Mary Logan, she wrote most of her works about art, including *Guide to the Italian Pictures at Hampton Court* (1894) and "The New Art Criticism" (1895). She wrote travel books as Mary Berenson (1930; 1935; 1938). Ernest Samuels provides a useful list of many of Costelloe's works; however, Barbara Strachey should be consulted for more reliable biographical information.

Costelloe, daughter of Hannah Whitall and Robert Pearsall Smith, was educated at Smith and Harvard Annex (Radcliffe). She married Benjamin Francis Conn Costelloe in England (1885). Following the death of her first husband, Costelloe married Bernard Berenson in Italy (1900). Her friendship with Whitman began at Christmas time in 1882. He visited the Smith home in Germantown, Pennsylvania, at the invitation of Costelloe's father, who knew about his daughter's admiration for Whitman. Having read *Leaves of Grass* at Smith, Costelloe proclaimed herself a "Whitmanite" and eschewed social conventions and restrictions (Berenson 36). In 1889 Whitman praised Costelloe for pursuing activities outside her home and described her as "a true woman of the new aggressive type" (Traubel 188). In England, Costelloe helped promote interest in Whitman. Her article "Walt Whitman at Camden. By One who has been there" appeared in the 23 December 1886 *Pall Mall Gazette,* one of that periodical's series of works focusing on Whitman between late 1886 and mid-1887.

Costelloe became the poet's "staunchest living woman friend" (*Correspondence* 4:89).

Christina Davey

Bibliography

Berenson, Mary. *Mary Berenson: A Self-Portrait from Her Letters & Diaries.* Ed. Barbara Strachey and Jayne Samuels. New York: Norton, 1983.

Samuels, Ernest. *Bernard Berenson: The Making of a Connoisseur.* Cambridge, Mass.: Harvard UP, 1979.

Strachey, Barbara. *Remarkable Relations: The Story of the Pearsall Smith Family.* London: Gollancz, 1980. Rpt. as *Remarkable Relations: The Story of the Pearsall Smith Women.* New York: Universe Books, 1982.

Traubel, Horace. *With Walt Whitman in Camden.* Ed. Sculley Bradley. Vol. 4. Philadelphia: U of Pennsylvania P, 1953.

Whitman, Walt. *The Correspondence.* Ed. Edwin Haviland Miller. 6 vols. New York: New York UP, 1961–1977.

See also PHILADELPHIA, PENNSYLVANIA; SMITH, LOGAN PEARSALL; SMITH, ROBERT PEARSALL

Cowley, Malcolm (1898–1989)

Born in 1898, Malcolm Cowley received his A.B. from Harvard University and served in World War I. Afterward, Cowley lived in Greenwich Village until, frustrated with America's hostility toward art, he returned to France and became acquainted with the dadaists, several French writers, and a number of Americans, including Ernest Hemingway. In 1923, Cowley returned to New York City, where he published

Exile's Return (1934), a literary history of the "lost generation" of writers that matured during and after World War I. From 1934 until his death in 1989, Cowley wrote a number of memoirs and collections of criticism, including *The Dream of the Golden Mountain: Remembering the 1930's* (1980).

Although he initially disliked Whitman's poetry, Cowley's views began to change while he was in France, where Whitman was greatly admired. In a series of articles that originally appeared in the *New Republic* in 1946 and 1947, Cowley insisted that the early versions of Whitman's poems are his most powerful, for they were written before Whitman had adopted the persona of the gray bard of democracy. Like the members of Cowley's "lost generation," Whitman's early and honest sense of alienation sparked a genuine creative impulse that was obscured by later revisions; the early Whitman, Cowley felt, was the real poet. In 1955, Cowley reviewed Gay Wilson Allen's *The Solitary Singer* (1955) and completed "Whitman: A Little Anthology," which commemorated the centennial anniversary of the first publication of *Leaves of Grass*. Cowley also edited the 1855 edition of *Leaves*, which was published in 1959.

Cowley was a prominent literary critic whose perspectives on literature and culture crystallized the thoughts of a generation. Cowley's opinions on Whitman thus represent a modern and considered evaluation of a poetic forebear to American writers of the twentieth century.

Matthew C. Altman

Bibliography

Bak, Hans. *Malcolm Cowley: The Formative Years*. Athens: U of Georgia P, 1993.

Cowley, Malcolm. "Walt Whitman, Champion of America." Rev. of *The Solitary Singer*, by Gay Wilson Allen. New York *Times Book Review* 6 Feb. 1955: 1, 22.

———. "Walt Whitman: The Miracle." *New Republic* 18 March 1946: 385–388.

———. "Walt Whitman: The Philosopher." *New Republic* 29 September 1947: 29–31.

———. "Walt Whitman: The Poet." *New Republic* 20 October 1947: 27–30.

———. "Walt Whitman: The Secret." *New Republic* 8 April 1946: 481–484.

———. "Whitman: A Little Anthology." *New Republic* 25 July 1955: 16–21.

Whitman, Walt. *The Complete Poetry and Prose of Walt Whitman*. Ed. Malcolm Cowley. 2 vols. New York: Pellegrini and Cudahy, 1948. Rpt. as *The Works of Walt Whitman: The Deathbed Edition in Two Volumes*. 2 vols. New York: Funk and Wagnalls, 1968.

———. *Walt Whitman's "Leaves of Grass": The First (1855) Edition*. Ed. Malcolm Cowley. New York: Viking, 1959.

See also LEAVES OF GRASS, 1855 EDITION

Crane, Hart (1899–1932)

An important American modernist poet, Crane was a native of Ohio who spent most of his creative years in New York City. Influenced in his early work, including the volume *White Buildings* (1926), by the French symbolists, Crane remained an Americanist, drawing upon materials from the American past. His major work, *The Bridge* (1930), can be seen as a response to T.S. Eliot, offering a more affirmative vision grounded in the American experience and centered on the Brooklyn Bridge as architectural accomplishment and figure of transcendence.

There is little visible evidence of Crane's reading of Whitman in the early poems, with the exception of the idyllic male bonding across class lines in "An Episode of Hands" (1920). In *The Bridge* Whitman becomes a major guide to the American experience, Vergil to Crane's Dante. Crane's use of Whitman was a great source of anxiety among his modernist friends and colleagues, particularly Yvor Winters and Allen Tate. Winters thought Whitman a pernicious influence, lacking a moral or ethical system, which would inevitably lead to suicide.

Whitman was an early enthusiasm of Crane's, and his interest was furthered by Isadora Duncan's public evocation of "Calamus." Whitman's male comradeship was important to Crane in supporting his own view of the potential for social change. Whitman's role as a poet of the Civil War and of potential renewal after that carnage offered Crane a model for his own celebration of national renewal after World War I.

Crane's principal use of Whitman occurs in the "Cape Hatteras" section of *The Bridge*, which begins with an epigraph from section 8 of "Passage to India." Whitman is evoked as the figure who can return the poet from the scenes of personal and natural disaster to healing in the native soil. Like Whitman, Crane seeks to reclaim a native Indian heritage, thus fulfilling

Columbus's journey, and to assert the power of "adhesiveness." Taking Whitman as his guide and mourning with him the dead of the war, victims of a lust for power, Crane is able to achieve a vision of love. Whitman's "Crossing Brooklyn Ferry" is revealed as the source of mythic vision and of Crane's particular myths of national joining. Quoting "Recorders Ages Hence," Crane makes it clear that his turn to Whitman owes much to the shared tradition of the "Calamus" poems, of the ability of male friendship to restore a lost pastoral.

Robert K. Martin

Bibliography

Crane, Hart. *The Letters of Hart Crane, 1916–1932.* 1952. Ed. Marc Simon. Berkeley: U of California P, 1965.

———. *The Poems of Hart Crane.* Ed. Marc Simon. New York: Liveright, 1986.

Hammer, Langdon. *Hart Crane & Allen Tate: Janus-Faced Modernism.* Princeton: Princeton UP, 1993.

Martin, Robert K. *The Homosexual Tradition in American Poetry.* Austin: U of Texas P, 1979.

Parkinson, Thomas. *Hart Crane and Yvor Winters: Their Literary Correspondence.* Berkeley: U of California P, 1978.

Yingling, Thomas E. *Hart Crane and the Homosexual Text: New Thresholds, New Anatomies.* Chicago: U of Chicago P, 1990.

See also LEGACY, WHITMAN'S

Creeley, Robert (1926–)

Robert Creeley, one of America's foremost post–World War II poets, is best known for his association with Black Mountain College, the experimental North Carolina college whose faculty and students included some of the most innovative writers, composers, choreographers, and artists of the 1950s and 1960s.

Like other poets in the 1950s, Creeley found in *Leaves of Grass* a model that enabled him to break through the aesthetic dominance of T.S. Eliot's "objectivity" to forge a poetry of personal emotions. Just as important, Creeley gained access through Whitman to the American literary tradition of attention to place and to physical detail. In the introduction to his selection of Whitman's poetry (1973), Creeley also cites Whitman's formal influences on him: the thematic organization of Whitman's poems as "fields of activity" rather than "lines of order," Whitman's variable prosody and structural repetitions, and his flexibility of diction and openness of tone (Introduction 13–18).

One of his few direct references to Whitman, Creeley's poem "Just Friends" (1958) parodies Whitman's famous lyric with the opening line "Out of the table endlessly rocking" (*Collected* 163). Creeley's poetry bears little overt resemblance to Whitman's but takes from Whitman the insistence that only by speaking in an "intensely personal" voice can a poet come to what is common to all (Introduction 7).

Carl Smeller

Bibliography

Creeley, Robert. *The Collected Poems of Robert Creeley: 1945–1975.* Berkeley: U of California P, 1982.

———. Introduction. *Whitman: Selected by Robert Creeley.* By Walt Whitman. Ed. Creeley. Harmondsworth: Penguin, 1973. 7–20.

Foster, Edward Halsey. *Understanding the Black Mountain Poets.* Columbia: U of South Carolina P, 1995.

See also LEGACY, WHITMAN'S

Critics, Whitman's

According to Samuel Johnson, no one has ever been written up or down except by himself. The observation could stand as a summation of the history of Walt Whitman criticism. From the moment he chose to disclose his existence in 1855, he seems to have invited the attention of two kinds of readers who, like himself, were also writers: those bent upon confirming and building up his extravagant estimate of his own importance and those no less stubbornly insisting on rejecting it and tearing down his image. It would be hard to find another writer about whom extremes of opinion have varied and fluctuated more widely. Occasionally, this fluctuation has been present in individual readers, going from strongly negative to positive in Henry James, and in the opposite direction, from enthusiasm to cutting sarcasm, in the case of the poet A.C. Swinburne. Antipathy has reached inspired heights in such writers as Peter Bayne and Knut Hamsun, and this makes their spluttering, abusive reaction almost an even match for the unrestrained hero worship of William Douglas O'Connor and William Sloane Kennedy. But after the wild enthusiasts and the brutal critics have done their best and worst, we are still left with the texts of Whitman himself—with *Leaves of Grass, Specimen Days,* and *Democratic Vistas*—and it is these that must finally determine what we ourselves think. Only one other writer may be helpful in adding to these texts, and that is Horace Traubel, whose patient transcriptions of Whitman's talk with his friends during the last four years of his life dwarf the labors of Boswell.

Johnson's impatience with cant should act as a warning against trendiness in criticism. Both are shields to ward off the labor and pain of thinking for ourselves and bringing to the originality of Whitman our own originality. The academy at best, Whitman once told Traubel, has its eyes set in the back of its head. It is naturally retrospective, not prospective. Whitman himself, at different times, was both—in youth more prospective than retrospective; in age, the opposite. Like many another young prospector, he failed to become rich; and, like others who survive long enough to merit a retrospective look, he benefited from the compassion and charity of his audience. His real career, it might even be said, did not begin until the moment of his death in 1892. It did not occur to anyone to preserve his last domicile until almost thirty years later, in the wake of World War I. From being the most modest of structures on Mickle Street in Camden, New Jersey, in the 1890s, it has survived and expanded to become the most notable landmark on what is known as Mickle Boulevard.

A bridge connecting Camden to Philadelphia, though a controversial suggestion to begin with, has finally been named in honor of him, and the tomb he designed for himself and his family in Harleigh Cemetery has become the focal point of reverent pilgrimages for tourists. Meanwhile, his reputation has undergone changes in deference to the varying political, social, and aesthetic fashions of different times. In the twenties, he was taken as the type of everything that was new, modern, and revolutionary in the arts; in the thirties, he was captured by the left, who gave to his greeting of Comrade their own particular meaning. After World War II, he gave encouragement to dreamers of an American Century and nationalists of various kinds. In the rebellious sixties, he was seen as the venerated ancestor of the beats and those who bravely struck out for the Open Road. In the seventies and eighties, he became the poster figure for gay liberation and those who celebrated their exit from confining closets of conformity. He has never lacked serious biographers and critics who tailored his image to accord with the changing tastes of various decades. Yet all the time there was the warning sign he had set up for the benefit of future biographers, cautioning them against the easy assumption that they were able to encompass him and understand him better than he had ever been able to understand himself.

Fortunately, the prying and prurience that have been in fashion for a long time are showing signs of exhaustion. By giving way to boredom, they are preparing the way for a restoration of a healthier and more balanced approach to the intentions of the writer. This is the case in such a book as David Kuebrich's *Minor Prophecy,* which is inclined to take at face value the aspirations of Whitman to compose the "psalm" of the Republic. Without stressing unduly the religious context in which his work must be seen, such an approach is consonant with the aims of a man who confesses his pleasure in the construction of new houses of worship in his borough of Brooklyn and his curiosity about what was enacted there which took him even into a synagogue where he might hear Hebrew chanting in its traditional form (which he troubled to mention not only in his journalism but in his more serious "Salut au Monde!").

A bracing change for the better is also to be found in such a volume as David Reynolds's *Walt Whitman's America: A Cultural Biography,* which no lover of Whitman's poetry can resist reading thoroughly or learning from, no matter how much of Whitman or about him he or she has read before.

An emerging impulse exists to return to the supposedly outworn image of Whitman in his later years as the Sage of Camden. This is the Whitman who did his best to slow down the eagerness of his young socialist friend Horace Traubel. There are few things in Whitman's published work better than the words Traubel recorded one day: "We must be resigned, but not too much so; we must be calm, but not too calm; we must not give in, yet we must give in some. That is, we must grade our rebellion and conformity both" (qtd. in Hindus, "Centenary" 14). In David Reynolds's biography, we see Whitman as a man who worked continually to live up to his own carefully balanced advice, in politics and in art, as well as in the teaching he transmitted to his friends and disciples. Reynolds does not hesitate to give a fuller account of the consequences of Whitman's sexual orientation than any biographer has given before, but he does not emphasize it unduly or allow it to skew and unbalance the portrait as a whole. What emerges clearly is a Whitman who was no godless atheist (as some of his ill-informed admirers mistakenly surmised), but one who could sincerely sing the praises of his adored father figure, Abraham Lincoln, and who had the liveliest intuitions of the immortality to which both he and his model were destined and which he proposed generously to share with common humanity as a whole.

Milton Hindus

Bibliography

Allen, Gay Wilson. *The New Walt Whitman Handbook.* 1975. New York: New York UP, 1986.

Aspiz, Harold. *Walt Whitman and the Body Beautiful.* Urbana: U of Illinois P, 1980.

Asselineau, Roger. "Walt Whitman." *Eight American Authors: A Review of Research and Criticism.* Ed. James Woodress. Rev. ed. New York: Norton, 1971. 225–272.

Giantvalley, Scott. *Walt Whitman, 1838–1939: A Reference Guide.* Boston: Hall, 1981.

Hindus, Milton. "The Centenary of *Leaves of Grass.*" *"Leaves of Grass" One Hundred Years After.* Ed. Hindus. Stanford: Stanford UP, 1955. 3–21.

———, ed. *Walt Whitman: The Critical Heritage.* London: Routledge and Kegan Paul, 1971.

Killingsworth, M. Jimmie. *The Growth of "Leaves of Grass": The Organic Tradition in Whitman Studies.* Columbia, S.C.: Camden House, 1993.

Kuebrich, David. *Minor Prophecy: Walt Whitman's New American Religion.* Bloomington: Indiana UP, 1989.

Kummings, Donald D. *Walt Whitman, 1940–1975: A Reference Guide.* Boston: Hall, 1982.

Miller, Edwin Haviland, ed. *A Century of Whitman Criticism.* Bloomington: Indiana UP, 1969.

Murphy, Francis, ed. *Walt Whitman: A Critical Anthology.* Harmondsworth: Penguin, 1969.

Reynolds, David S. *Walt Whitman's America: A Cultural Biography.* New York: Knopf, 1995.

Woodress, James, ed. *Critical Essays on Walt Whitman.* Boston: Hall, 1983.

See also Biographies; Legacy, Whitman's; Scholarship, Trends in Whitman

"Crossing Brooklyn Ferry" (1856)

"Crossing Brooklyn Ferry" first appeared in the second edition of *Leaves of Grass* under the title "Sun-Down Poem." It received its present title in 1860, and Whitman revised the poem through the various editions. Thoreau named it and "Song of Myself" as his favorite Whitman poems, and he was only one of the first in a long line of readers who have ranked "Crossing" among Whitman's best. It is one of those mid-length lyrics that offered Whitman what some critics have felt to be his most effective form—not so sprawling as "Song of Myself" but with enough space to allow him some musical and thematic amplitude. "Crossing" is generally regarded, along with "Out of the Cradle Endlessly Rocking" and "When Lilacs Last in the Dooryard Bloom'd," as one of his supreme achievements in this mode.

Late in life Whitman commented, "My own favorite loafing places have always been the rivers, the wharves, the boats—I like sailors, stevedores. I have never lived away from a big river" (Traubel 71). In his younger adult years and again in old age, his river experiences were especially connected with ferries—the latter crossing the Delaware between Camden and Philadelphia, the former crossing the East River between Brooklyn and Manhattan. Both of these periods are acknowledged in entries in *Specimen Days:* "I have always had a passion for ferries; to me they afford inimitable, streaming, never-failing, living poems" (16), and "What communion with the waters, the air, the exquisite *chiaroscuro*—the sky and stars, that speak no word, nothing to the intellect, yet so eloquent, so communicative to the soul" (183). He had written about ferries in his journalism. He editorialized against rate increases, and used the hustle and bustle of the ferries as an image of the frantic pace and impersonality of modern life—no doubt among the earliest protests against the rat-race of the urban commuter. In "Crossing" he looks at ferries and ferry riding from a quite different perspective.

"Crossing" says nothing about the poet's reason for crossing the river; the focus is not on a purpose or destination but on the act of crossing itself and the surrounding spectacle: the water, the people, the sun going down, the boats and docks and city in the distance. The poem describes the daily experience of a mid-nineteenth-century New York ferry rider, mundane enough to most but glorious to Whitman. At the same time it makes the trip the basis for a profound meditation on time and flux and how we exist both within and outside them.

"Crossing" is a very visual poem, conveying a strong sense of particular detail, the play of light, and vista; a number of critics have compared it to painting in its effects, including that of the luminists, Turner, and the popular panorama paintings of the day. It is also richly symbolic, and its symbolic implications arise naturally from the setting and images. The river, the ebb and flow of tides, the boat, the shuttling from one shore to the other—some of the oldest, richest images of the human imagination presented themselves to Whitman in his ferry riding; in his daily experience he was moving among archetypes.

Whitman grasped not just the larger fundamental images that resonate throughout the poem; he used discrete particulars strikingly as well. For example, leaning on the rail of a ferry is a particularly apt image of standing still and moving simultaneously and of the paradox of existing in both particular moments and a ceaseless flow of time. Similarly, "the fine centrifugal spokes of light round the shape of my head in the sunlit water" (section 3) is perfectly accurate in its observation, entirely native to the scene, and at the same time uncannily suggestive and appropriate in a poem in which ordinary human beings going about their daily business have a kind of transcendence, so that the poet asks, "What gods can exceed these that clasp me by the hand . . . ?" (section 8). These examples only begin to suggest the symbolic resonances and possibilities of the poem.

Critics have disagreed about the degree to which the poem is psychological, and psychologically troubled—that is, how much it expresses doubts and struggles in its author, whether feelings of isolation, fear of actual intimacy in life as opposed to intimacy in poems, or gender identity. Psychological critics find a good deal of conflict sublimated into the poem's imagery and tend to emphasize the poem as process, a way of coping or groping toward a resolution Whitman may or may not achieve or fully believe. Of course, many critics are by training and temperament disposed to look for the dark, and some, as if by reflex, view any affirmation, let alone one as far-reaching as Whitman's here, as suspect or regressive. Other critics, while not denying psychological content, see the poem as more philosophical—an Emersonian poem in that it conveys a transcendent apprehension of reality, an achieved vision, and does so with a certain degree of didacticism and composure. Even Edwin Haviland Miller, one of the best-known of Whitman's psychological critics, finds the poem placid, circling rather than journeying or diving and lacking the psychological exploration or turmoil of such poems as "The Sleepers" or "Out of the Cradle."

Whatever directions critics take in their readings of "Crossing," all include the fundamental theme of time and flux, which Whitman introduces in the first section as he addresses first the physical scene itself, then the people riding the ferry with him, and then those who will come after him, far into the future. He makes large claims from the outset: that he sees in all things a "simple, compact, well-join'd scheme" (section 2) and that time and place "avail not" (section 3)—a transcendental claim of unity and cohesion in the universe and throughout time. The conscious purpose of the poem is to communicate this sense of unity; not just to explain it, but to convey it in the most immediate way.

How does one go beyond individual identity, flux, and time? The poem offers at least three ways: through the physical world itself; through shared human nature and experience; and through works of art (and especially this work of art).

In addition to being a poem of cumulative, orchestral, meditative beauty, "Crossing" is also a poem of memorable lines and phrases. One of those lines, in fact, suggests the effect very well: "I too had been struck from the float forever held in solution" (section 5). Just as an individual person is catalyzed out of a flow—both the bodily fluids of parents and the flow of life itself—the poem turns on certain phrasings that seem "struck," precipitated sharply and suddenly, out of the larger meditative and rhetorical movement. Two such phrases, which critics have focused on and any reader would take note of, express the key point of the importance of the things of this world, of physical reality. Near the beginning of the poem Whitman calls the sights and sounds around him "glories strung like beads on my smallest sights and hearings" (section 2); near the end, he refers to objects and physical surroundings as "dumb, beautiful ministers" (section 9). The pun on religion harks back to Whitman's 1855 Preface and his suggestion that priests will soon be supplanted by the physical world itself, poetically perceived. Though Whitman did not foresee the demise of the ferries, he knew that people in the

C

future would, like him, see the gulls turning in late afternoon light, the rise and fall of tides, the river flowing, and the sun, and in that he felt a kind of immortality. (Later, when the Brooklyn Bridge was being built, the threat to ferries became apparent, and Whitman registered far less enthusiasm for that particular modern engineering wonder than would be expected of him.)

Another of the poem's memorable lines, "The dark threw its patches down upon me also" (section 6), expresses the second way that Whitman finds unity across time. The dark patches at first refer to "curious abrupt questionings" (section 5) that stir within him. Then he goes well beyond doubts to a litany of human frailties and failings, all of which, he tells the reader, he was as subject to as anyone. This empathy creates another bond between poet and reader, present and future. Some critics have found this confession unconvincing, too general or easy. (One of the acts to which Whitman did seem to attach some real guilt, masturbation, was removed from the catalogue when he cut the phrase "solitary committer" in later editions.) But even some who feel this way find another aspect of the poem's reaching out to the reader remarkable. Whitman raised the direct address to the reader, a common enough device in pre-twentieth-century literature, to an entirely different level, not artificial, but strangely, convincingly intimate. "Crossing" is one of the outstanding examples of this, both in individual lines, such as "Who knows, for all the distance, but I am as good as looking at you now" (section 7), and in its overall effect. To what degree Whitman meant this ghostly, vivid presence to be taken literally is left to the reader's judgment and imagination.

The idea of art as a means of transcending time is one that "Crossing" shares with other works, such as John Keats's "Ode on a Grecian Urn." What perhaps makes "Crossing" distinctive in its treatment of this theme is its dynamic, kinesthetic quality. A number of critics have commented on the way the poem creates a sense of motion, how, through imagery and linguistic devices, everything within it seems to be flowing, swirling, moving. The experience-caught-in-art seems here more like a motion picture than a carving.

"Crossing" has long been admired for its artistic control. Theme, imagery, rhythm, and symbolism work together to a degree that Whitman rarely achieved, and the poem has a for-mal quality without sacrificing freshness. Whatever the artistry or alchemy he brought to bear, in "Crossing" Whitman wrote a poem that fits startlingly well his description of the experience-poems that ferry riding gave him personally again and again: "inimitable, streaming, never-failing, living poems" (Whitman 16).

Howard Nelson

Bibliography

Black, Stephen A. *Whitman's Journeys into Chaos: A Psychological Study of the Poetic Process.* Princeton: Princeton UP, 1975.

Cavitch, David. *My Soul and I: The Inner Life of Walt Whitman.* Boston: Beacon, 1985.

Coffman, Stanley K., Jr. "'Crossing Brooklyn Ferry': A Note on the Catalogue Technique in Whitman's Poetry." *Walt Whitman: A Collection of Criticism.* Ed. Arthur Golden. New York: McGraw-Hill, 1974. 61–71.

Dougherty, James. *Walt Whitman and the Citizen's Eye.* Baton Rouge: Louisiana State UP, 1993.

Geffen, Arthur. "Silence and Denial: Walt Whitman and the Brooklyn Bridge." *Walt Whitman Quarterly Review* 1.4 (1984): 1–11.

Miller, Edwin Haviland. *Walt Whitman's Poetry: A Psychological Journey.* New York: New York UP, 1968.

Miller, James E., Jr. *A Critical Guide to "Leaves of Grass."* Chicago: U of Chicago P, 1957.

Orlov, Paul A. "On Time and Form in Whitman's 'Crossing Brooklyn Ferry.'" *Walt Whitman Quarterly Review* 2.1 (1984): 12–21.

Thomas, M. Wynn. *The Lunar Light of Whitman's Poetry.* Cambridge, Mass.: Harvard UP, 1987.

Traubel, Horace. *With Walt Whitman in Camden.* Vol. 2. 1908. New York: Rowman and Littlefield, 1961.

Whitman, Walt. *Specimen Days.* Vol. 1 of *Prose Works 1892.* Ed. Floyd Stovall. New York: New York UP, 1963.

See also BROOKLYN, NEW YORK; FERRIES AND OMNIBUSES; *LEAVES OF GRASS,* 1856 EDITION; NEW YORK CITY; PSYCHOLOGICAL APPROACHES; SYMBOLISM; TIME

Crystal Palace Exhibition (New York)

As the main attraction of the Exhibition of the Industry of All Nations, the Crystal Palace opened its doors in New York on 14 July 1853, two years after the original Crystal Palace had been a great success at the World's Fair in London. The palace, an imposing structure of iron and glass with a 148-foot dome at the center, contained 173,000 square feet of exhibition space and allowed some 6,000 exhibitors from 24 nations to display everything from cannons to artificial flowers. The palace also housed a sculpture show and the largest collection of paintings ever assembled in America. Despite its impressive scale, the privately organized exhibition did not draw as many visitors as expected, and the organizers soon found it necessary to hire P.T. Barnum to help with promotion. A fire completely destroyed the palace on 5 October 1858.

In an article for the Brooklyn *Daily Times,* Walt Whitman called the Crystal Palace "an original, esthetic, perfectly proportioned, American edifice" (qtd. in Greenspan 7–8). For almost a year after the opening of the exhibition, he was an enthusiastic and frequent visitor to the palace, browsing through the displays both during the day and at night, both alone and with friends. Whitman especially enjoyed the vast collection of paintings, which he preferred to see at night when the palace was lit by thousands of gas lamps. The exhibition also allowed Whitman to indulge his interest in photography. A large display of daguerreotypes included local exhibitors from New York and Brooklyn, among them Gabriel Harrison, who in 1854 took the picture of Whitman that inspired the frontispiece for the first edition of *Leaves of Grass.*

Much of the public response to the Crystal Palace exhibition celebrated it as an example of America's industrial potential and as a step toward peaceful cooperation between nations. Theodore Sedgwick, the president of the Crystal Palace association, hoped that the exhibition would unite the continents of Europe and America, and Horace Greeley welcomed the palace as a place where America could self-confidently measure its strengths and weaknesses in a cosmopolitan setting. The optimistic atmosphere generated by this exhibition which temporarily fused commerce, science, technology, and art into a harmonious whole likely affected Whitman as he tried to conceive of a national poetry. Both Paul Zweig and Ezra Greenspan detect echoes of Whitman's Crystal Palace experience in the 1855 edition of *Leaves of Grass.*

Elmar S. Lueth

Bibliography

Allen, Gay Wilson. *The Solitary Singer: A Critical Biography of Walt Whitman.* 1955. Rev. ed. 1967. Chicago: U of Chicago P, 1985.

Greeley, Horace. *Art and Industry as Represented in the Exhibition at the Crystal Palace, New York: 1853–54.* New York: Redfield, 1853.

Greenspan, Ezra. *Walt Whitman and the American Reader.* Cambridge: Cambridge UP, 1990.

Rubin, Joseph Jay. *The Historic Whitman.* University Park: Pennsylvania State UP, 1973.

Zweig, Paul. *Walt Whitman: The Making of the Poet.* New York: Basic Books, 1984.

See also Leaves of Grass, 1855 Edition; Painters and Painting; Photographs and Photographers; Sculptors and Sculpture; Technology

C

D

"Dalliance of the Eagles, The" (1880)

This late poem is one of the very few from this period to show Whitman at his very best. Although the poem is surprising in its return to traditional metrical forms, it is as erotically powerful as anything Whitman ever wrote. The poem is in part responsible for Whitman's shift to publisher David McKay after his publisher James R. Osgood indicated his willingness to meet a charge of obscenity by deleting it. The poem has been read as symbolically presenting a democratic female sexuality. It certainly offers a view of sexuality in which both partners are active participants. Whitman has freed the depiction of sexuality from the confines of romantic evasion, allowing for a sexual desire to be seen in violently physical terms.

The poem above all is a kind of tone poem, a composition whose rhythms enact the subject matter. Beginning with the strikingly trochaic "Skirting," emphasized by its alliteration with the first word of the second line, "Skyward," linking himself to the two birds mating in midair, Whitman creates a world of motion and energy through an overwhelming presence of present participles. The ten lines of the poem contain a remarkable series of fifteen present participles, a rushing progression only briefly halted at the moment of mating, in line 7 and the first half of line 8.

In such active movement, the two birds are glimpsed only momentarily and registered only as body parts—claws, wings, beaks. They come together as "a swirling mass" until they reach a moment of stasis, when they join, "twain yet one," to achieve a tenuous "still balance" before returning to themselves and resuming their individual flights. The final line captures them verbally and metrically, having regained their individuality and their linked desires: "She hers, he his, pursuing," with a final amphibrach capturing the movement of the poem in miniature.

Robert K. Martin

Bibliography

Aspiz, Harold. "Whitman's Eagles." *The Mickle Street Review* 7 (1985): 84–90.
Mirsky, D.S. "Poet of American Democracy." 1935. Trans. Samuel Putnam. *Walt Whitman: A Critical Anthology.* Ed. Francis Murphy. Harmondsworth: Penguin, 1969. 238–255.

See also "BY THE ROADSIDE"; STEVENS, OLIVER

Dana, Charles A. (1819–1897)

Charles Dana was a prominent American journalist and editor for fifty years. At age twenty-one he was a member of the Brook Farm cooperative community, where he met Horace Greeley. In 1847 Greeley employed Dana as city editor and, two years later, as managing editor of the New York *Tribune,* where he gained notoriety for his support of the Civil War and the antislavery cause.

As editor of the *Tribune* Charles Dana wrote the first published review of *Leaves of Grass* on 23 July 1855. Although this review praised Whitman's "bold stirring thoughts," and his "genuine intimacy with nature," Dana revealed his mixed feelings about this new poetry; he added that its language, "too frequently reckless and indecent, will justly prevent [Whitman's] volume from free circulation in scrupulous circles" (Dana 23). As an act of friendship to Whitman, and with the poet's permission,

Dana also published in the New York *Tribune* on 10 October the famous 1855 letter from Emerson.

While on the staff of the *Tribune,* Dana came up with the idea for a *New American Cyclopaedia,* the first American reference work, and he edited this from 1858 to 1864. During the early years of the Civil War, Greeley asked for Dana's resignation because of their ideological differences; Lincoln then appointed Dana as a special investigating agent of the War Department and later Assistant Secretary of War. After the war, in 1868, he became editor and part-owner of the New York *Sun,* and remained in control of this newspaper for twenty-nine years, until his death. In 1888 Horace Traubel asked Whitman if Dana had been his friend, and Whitman replied, "Yes. Dana wishes me well. The *Sun* always treats me well" (Traubel 140).

Andy J. Moore

Bibliography
Allen, Gay Wilson. *The New Walt Whitman Handbook.* 1975. New York: New York UP, 1986.
Dana, Charles A. "The First Notice: 1855." *Walt Whitman: The Critical Heritage.* Ed. Milton Hindus. New York: Barnes and Noble, 1971. 22–23.
Traubel, Horace. *With Walt Whitman in Camden.* Vol. 3. 1914. New York: Rowman and Littlefield, 1961.
Wilson, James. *The Life of Charles A. Dana.* New York: Harper, 1907.

See also NEW YORK *TRIBUNE*

"Darest Thou Now O Soul" (1868)

First published in *Broadway Magazine* (London) in October 1868, "Darest Thou Now O Soul" was subsequently placed in the cluster entitled "Whispers of Heavenly Death." In the 1881 edition of *Leaves of Grass,* the cluster opens with this poem. As a challenge, or a taunting invitation to the soul, it proposes a daring plunge into the "unknown"—death, the mysteries and vagaries of which make up the themes of "Whispers of Heavenly Death."

The prospect of this awesome enterprise is, however, made less intimidating in stages. This is done so marvelously by the poet that the exciting journey into the unknown, the thrill of prospective discovery with practically no help— "No map there, nor guide"—becomes a real

adventure with the self. The poem assumes the grandeur of a spiritual quest when it begins to talk about the loosening of material bonds and the imperviousness of the poet and his soul to "darkness, gravitation, sense, [or] any bounds bounding us." As they enter that celestial realm, what awaits them is sheer fulfillment: "O joy! O fruit of all!"

Remarkable for its stanzaic regularity and discrete pauses between the stanzas, the poem dramatizes stages of spiritual ascent iconically. In its five stanzas of three lines each, each line ends with an extra word or two, elongating the lines successively. This ladderlike structure, along with a movement that thematically advances us toward the better known or the more distinct, underscores the poem's theme of soul's progress. Rhythmic uncertainties dissolve in the last stanza, which glories in a potential discovery or self-fulfillment.

K. Narayana Chandran

Bibliography
Allen, Gay Wilson. *The New Walt Whitman Handbook.* 1975. New York: New York UP, 1986.
Miller, James E., Jr. *A Critical Guide to "Leaves of Grass."* Chicago: U of Chicago P, 1957.
Schwiebert, John E. *The Frailest Leaves: Whitman's Poetic Technique and Style in the Short Poem.* New York: Lang, 1992.
Whitman, Walt. *Leaves of Grass: Comprehensive Reader's Edition.* Ed. Harold W. Blodgett and Sculley Bradley. New York: New York UP, 1965.

See also DEATH; SOUL, THE; "WHISPERS OF HEAVENLY DEATH" (CLUSTER)

Dartmouth College

Dartmouth College was founded at Hanover, New Hampshire, in 1769 under a charter issued by George III. Walt Whitman read the poem "As a Strong Bird on Pinions Free" (later retitled "Thou Mother with Thy Equal Brood") for the Dartmouth commencement on Wednesday, 26 June 1872. Whitman found it an honor to be speaking at a college for the first time and wrote the poem for the occasion. But he apparently was unaware that his selection was based on the desire of the students in Dartmouth's United Literary Society to outrage the conservative faculty with a notorious poet. Charles

Ransom Miller, in particular, was the student who convinced his classmates to ask Whitman to address their graduating class. Before leaving for New Hampshire, Whitman prepared a number of laudatory press releases (including copies of his poem) for eastern newspapers, but these releases for the most part were ignored. Whitman's commencement recitation lasted twenty-five minutes, and his delivery was ineffective, being both inaudible and monotonous. Nonetheless, in a letter to Peter Doyle remarking on the commencement, Whitman seemed to feel his poem had been received well. Yet perhaps he was aware of his waning poetical powers, for his Preface to the publication of *As a Strong Bird on Pinions Free* (1872) remarked "it may be that mere habit has got dominion of me, when there is no real need of saying anything further" (*Prose Works* 2:459).

Scott L. Newstrom

Bibliography

Allen, Gay Wilson. *The Solitary Singer: A Critical Biography of Walt Whitman.* 1955. Rev. ed. 1967. Chicago: U of Chicago P, 1985.

Blodgett, Harold W. "Walt Whitman's Dartmouth Visit." *Dartmouth Alumni Magazine* 25 (1933): 13–15.

Bond, Fraser F. *Mr. Miller of "The Times": The Story of an Editor.* New York: Scribner's, 1931.

Perry, Bliss. *Walt Whitman: His Life and Work.* Boston: Houghton Mifflin, 1906.

Whitman, Walt. *The Correspondence.* Ed. Edwin Haviland Miller. Vol. 2. New York: New York UP, 1961.

———. *Prose Works 1892.* Ed. Floyd Stovall. 2 vols. New York: New York UP, 1963–1964.

See also "THOU MOTHER WITH THY EQUAL BROOD"

Darwin, Charles (1809–1882)

Charles Darwin was the author of several books, published during Walt Whitman's lifetime, that were of considerable interest to him. *The Origin of Species* appeared in 1859, though no American edition of the book was available until after the Civil War. Other books that Whitman was at least aware of were *The Movements and Habits of Climbing Plants* (1865), *The Variation of Animals and Plants under Domestication* (1868), *The Descent of Man* (1871), and *Selection in Relation to Sex* (1871).

As the originator of the doctrine of evolutionary development through the process of sexual selection, Darwin was of great interest to Whitman. Nevertheless it is clear that Whitman's evolutionary pronouncements do not always agree with those of the distinguished scientist. While some scholars have observed in Whitman's poetry certain examples of sexual selection, the struggle for existence, and an emphasis upon the variety of life forms, others note that Whitman's essential spirituality and idealism do not fully conform to the rigors of Darwinian natural selection. Essentially, Whitman was a believer in the process of "becoming," a doctrine that was held by many intellectuals during the nineteenth century.

Some scholars find evidence of Darwinian concepts in Whitman's literary works, but others (Harold Aspiz, for example) believe that Whitman drew his evolutionary concepts from Jean Baptiste Lamarck (1744–1829).

James T.F. Tanner

Bibliography

Allen, Gay Wilson. *The Solitary Singer: A Critical Biography of Walt Whitman.* 1955. Rev. ed. 1967. Chicago: U of Chicago P, 1985.

———. *Walt Whitman Handbook.* 1946. New York: Hendricks House, 1962.

Aspiz, Harold. *Walt Whitman and the Body Beautiful.* Urbana: U of Illinois P, 1980.

Beaver, Joseph. *Walt Whitman: Poet of Science.* New York: King's Crown, 1951.

Conner, Frederick William. *Cosmic Optimism: A Study of the Interpretation of Evolution by American Poets from Emerson to Robinson.* Gainesville: U of Florida P, 1949.

Reynolds, David S. *Walt Whitman's America: A Cultural Biography.* New York: Knopf, 1995.

See also EVOLUTION; LAMARCK, JEAN BAPTISTE; SCIENCE

Davis, Mary Oakes (1837 or 1838–1908)

Mary Oakes Davis was Walt Whitman's housekeeper at 328 Mickle Street in Camden, New Jersey, from 1885 until the poet's death in 1892. Davis is known for her steadfast, patient service to Whitman, who grew increasingly infirm, kept irregular habits, and often frustrated Davis's efforts to impose order on the household. She worked for him without pay and after his death successfully sued his estate for lost wages.

Mary Oakes had a long history of nursing the ill and elderly. In Camden, she cared for a dying schoolmate and her husband, and took charge of their two children. She married a sea captain named Davis, but was soon widowed. Whitman became acquainted with her in 1884, when he brought her clothes to mend and ate meals at her house at 412 West Street. After he purchased his Mickle Street house, he proposed that—since he owned a home but no furniture and she owned furniture but paid rent—they combine households. She moved into the house on 24 February 1885, with no formal agreement, bringing with her several pets and an orphan girl she cared for. Whitman left her one thousand dollars in a revised will of 1891; he left his house to his brother Edward.

Critics agree that Whitman—crippled and increasingly dependent—greatly benefited from Davis's services. Horace Traubel leaves no doubt of her attentive care, especially as the poet's health declined. The fairness of Whitman's bargain with the housekeeper is less clear. The arrangement apparently favored Whitman: Davis received no wages for her work and, as Gay Wilson Allen notes, claimed after Whitman's death that she had paid most of the grocery bills. David Reynolds notes that Whitman kept a careful eye on his pocketbook; however, Davis, accustomed to self-sacrifice, may have allowed his financial impositions. The precise nature of Whitman and Davis's relationship is also a matter of speculation. Emory Holloway wonders whether Davis had romantic feelings that Whitman did not return; Henry Seidel Canby suggests that he viewed her as a mother substitute. Davis's strongest defender is Whitman's nurse, Elizabeth Leavitt Keller, who portrays Davis as selflessly devoted to Whitman and subject to his manipulations as well as to neighbors' gossip about an unmarried couple living together. Whitman's arrangement with Davis required mutual accommodation: she rendered loyal service but little understood the poet's idiosyncrasies or genius; he acknowledged her care but may have underestimated its value.

Carol J. Singley

Bibliography

Allen, Gay Wilson. *The Solitary Singer: A Critical Biography of Walt Whitman.* 1955. Rev. ed. 1967. Chicago: U of Chicago P, 1985.

Canby, Henry Seidel. *Walt Whitman: An American.* Boston: Houghton Mifflin, 1943.

Holloway, Emory. *Whitman: An Interpretation in Narrative.* New York: Knopf, 1926.

Keller, Elizabeth Leavitt. *Walt Whitman in Mickle Street.* New York: Kennerley, 1921.

Reynolds, David S. *Walt Whitman's America: A Cultural Biography.* New York: Knopf, 1995.

Traubel, Horace. *With Walt Whitman in Camden.* 9 vols. Vol. 1. Boston: Small, Maynard, 1906; Vol. 2. New York: Appleton, 1908; Vol. 3. New York: Mitchell Kennerley, 1914; Vol. 4. Ed. Sculley Bradley. Philadelphia: U of Pennsylvania P, 1953; Vol. 5. Ed. Gertrude Traubel. Carbondale: Southern Illinois UP, 1964; Vol. 6. Ed. Gertrude Traubel and William White. Carbondale: Southern Illinois UP, 1982; Vol. 7. Ed. Jeanne Chapman and Robert MacIssac. Carbondale: Southern Illinois UP, 1992; Vols. 8–9. Ed. Jeanne Chapman and Robert MacIsaac. Oregon House, Calif.: W.L. Bentley, 1996.

See also CAMDEN, NEW JERSEY; KELLER, ELIZABETH LEAVITT; MICKLE STREET HOUSE

Daybooks and Notebooks (1978)

Literary authorship was a developing profession in the United States during Walt Whitman's lifetime, and its business was sometimes primitive—in Whitman's case, operated from a trunk where he kept records of copies of *Leaves of Grass* sold, correspondence with publishers, and payments received. Whitman called the journals in which he kept track of business details "Daybooks." They have been included, along with assorted notebooks and a diary from his visit to Canada, in the three-volume *Daybooks and Notebooks* (1978), part of the New York University Press series *Collected Writings of Walt Whitman*.

The first two volumes display typed transcriptions of Whitman's hand-written business accounts, begun when orders were brisk for the ten dollars Centennial reprinting of his poems and prose. The fifteen small notebooks in volume three, mostly from the 1850s, reveal the poet's thinking about language, politics, and poetry; they also contain experimental lines of poems for the early editions of *Leaves of Grass*. Such notebooks are planning documents for authorship, recording a poet's strategies and rationale for trying to invent new forms of poetry for New World readers.

The daybooks are business records, not a diary, but when sales of the Centennial reprinting declined, Whitman began adding brief personal notes that kept the account pages going. He recorded payment of utility bills, other household details, and some family notes. Brief descriptions of the weather and his health also appear—"depress'd condition," he writes 29 November 1891, four months before his death; "bad all thro Nov" (2:605).

When newspapers published articles about Whitman, he obtained copies and sent them to a dozen or more friends and supporters, carefully listed in the daybooks, an effort that may reveal the isolation experienced by a nineteenth-century author. The clippings were assurance that Whitman mattered to the rest of the world.

The routine business entries—"sent Old age's voices to H M Alden [*Harper's* editor]," followed by a postscript, "sent back to me rejected," and "David McKay paid me $88.56 for royalty &c," for example (2:535)—are the necessary records for someone who needs income from many separate transactions that have to be monitored carefully, not forgotten. Longfellow, who also managed the promotion of his own poetry during the same period, kept similar records, which William Charvat used in a 1944 article, illustrating the economic underpinnings of nineteenth-century literary history in the United States.

The very informality of this new literary business—cultivating the patronage not of royalty or a coterie but of citizen-consumers who could be reached only through newspapers, magazines, and distribution offices of small regional publishers—has consigned most such accounting records to trash collection or, at best, to manuscript holdings of major libraries. The New York University volumes, supported by the National Endowment for the Humanities and edited by William White, whose notes identify most individuals mentioned in the day-

books, placed primary materials within reach of undergraduate and graduate students.

This is especially important for the details of publishing. Whitman's notebooks and diary entries, which provide grist for perennial Whitman critical debates and reveal the political and literary agenda of a poet-in-the-making, have always been more accessible than his business records. Biographers and editors of collections of Whitman's work have quoted heavily or published extensive passages from his notebooks, but not from the daybooks.

The Canada diary in volume three displays Whitman in the full power of observation at age sixty-one, capable of extensive train and ferry excursions despite his partial paralysis from a stroke, and as excitable about the world as he ever was.

Daybooks and Notebooks—while not as substantive as materials published in the six volumes of *Notebooks and Unpublished Prose Manuscripts* in the *Collected Writings* series— would have been sufficient evidence for Charvat to have drawn more parallels between Whitman and Longfellow as public poets than he was able to draw without having examined Whitman's records. Still, Charvat's 1960s study of literary authorship in the United States is the most illuminating perspective for approaching Whitman's *Daybooks and Notebooks*.

Dennis K. Renner

Bibliography

Asselineau, Roger. "Walt Whitman—*Daybooks and Notebooks*." *Études Anglaises* 32 (1979): 106.

Charvat, William. "Longfellow's Income from His Writings, 1840–1852." *The Profession of Authorship in America, 1800–1879*. Ed. Matthew J. Bruccoli. New York: Columbia UP, 1992. 155–167.

Loving, Jerome. "Walt Whitman: *Daybooks and Notebooks*." *Modern Philology* 76 (1979): 420–424.

Whitman, Walt. *Daybooks and Notebooks*. Ed. William White. 3 vols. New York: New York UP, 1978.

Zweig, Paul. "Walt Whitman: *Daybooks and Notebooks*." *The New York Times Book Review* 16 April 1978: 9, 28, 29.

See also American Primer, An; Canada, Whitman's Visit to; Collected Writings of Walt Whitman, The

De Selincourt, Basil (1876–1966)

English critic and biographer, De Selincourt wrote on Blake and Meredith, as well as Whitman. His 1914 critical biography of Whitman was one of the first to focus mainly on Whitman's style and techniques, perceptively noting that his poetic unit was the line and that the line was determined not by meter but by the thought contained therein. De Selincourt also praised the musical qualities in Whitman's writing, saying that he used words as though they were notes. According to Gay Wilson Allen, he was also the first to assert Whitman's organizational deficiencies, especially in *Leaves of Grass,* which, according to De Selincourt, had so misleading an arrangement that it somewhat compromised the work's greatness. De Selincourt concluded his evaluation of Whitman by labeling him a spokesman not just for America, but for the ever-changing, life-enhancing spirit of mankind.

Walter Graffin

Bibliography

Allen, Gay Wilson. *The New Walt Whitman Handbook.* 1975. New York: New York UP, 1986.

De Selincourt, Basil. *Walt Whitman: A Critical Study.* 1914. New York: Russell and Russell, 1965.

See also BIOGRAPHIES

Death

Whitman's treatment of death had cultural and personal origins. In an era of tragically high mortality rates, the literary drama of death among writers like Charles Dickens, Harriet Beecher Stowe, and Emily Dickinson often assumed a passionate spirit of assurance about the possibility of heaven. Thus Whitman's generation revered George Washington largely because Parson Weems's biography of him illustrated his patient submission to death—an attitude reflected in dozens of Whitman's poems expressing his own calm readiness for death. Even deathbed watching, a practice widely believed to have instructive and moral value, had a counterpart in Whitman's vigils beside the beds of the sick and dying.

This "very great post mortem poet" (Lawrence 17), who proclaimed that "nothing can happen more beautiful than death" ("Starting from Paumanok," section 12), expressed a passion for death that "becomes the inevitable extension for life" (Dutton 3). Whitman also benefited from "a practical familiarity with disease and death which has perhaps never before fallen to a great writer" (Ellis 111). He was attracted to hospitals and to scenes of violent death, apparently visiting cholera victims, whose ravaging disease was almost always fatal, as early as the 1840s. He was drawn to injured and dying firemen and horse-car drivers—one of whom is eulogized in "To Think of Time," a poem which Whitman develops into a meditation on death and into a proclamation of his own immortality. "Song of Myself," "The Sleepers," "Song of the Broad-Axe," and a few "Drum-Taps" poems contain emotionally "irretrievable" images of violent death in sea and land battles and in drownings. However, acknowledging that the horror of so many deaths was the central truth of the Civil War, Whitman reserved his most graphic reportage for two prose works—*Memoranda During the War* and *Specimen Days.* His postwar poems, singularly free from dramatizing the deaths of others, were largely concerned with death as a divine mystery and with the persona's dramatic awaiting of his own death.

Perhaps because the human consciousness "does not believe in its own death," says Sigmund Freud, "it behaves as if it were immortal" (296). Understandably, Whitman was drawn to the drama of his own death and immortality. Despite his contention that death was "some solemn immortal birth," a noble "parturition" ("Whispers of Heavenly Death"), various passages in the poems suggest his fear of what Paul Tillich called "the darkness of the no more" (537) and seem to lack a serene certainty of his own immortality. Because he could not hope to celebrate his own immortality without confronting the (often exhilarating, often frightening) prospect of his own mortal annihilation, the tense interplay between his fears of perishing and his convictions of eternal life endow the poems with dramatic excitement.

Whitman perceived existence as a continuum. "In no man who ever lived was the sense of eternal life so absolute," said Dr. Richard Maurice Bucke (257). Speculating that something drives mankind toward "promotion" through "birth, life, death, burial" ("To You [Whoever you are . . .]"), he speculated that humans were "ferried" into their mortal state from "the float forever held in solution" ("Crossing Brooklyn Ferry," section 5), carrying with them acquired qualities from one state of existence to the next. In accordance with "[t]he law of promotion and transformation" ("To Think of Time," section 7), he said, "the dead advance as much as the living advance" ("Song of the Broad-Axe," section 4). To describe the exit from mortal life, the poems employ a broad range of metaphors—sunsets, ebb tides, dormant seeds, and particularly "homeward bound" and "outward bound" journeys ("The Sleepers," section 7) whose ultimate goal is to meet God "on perfect terms" ("Song of Myself," section 45).

Yet Whitman's stubborn faith in immortality, as he conceded, remains vague, undefined. Although the word "soul" appears some 240 times in the poems—chiefly referring to the essential immortal element in one's being—his concept of the afterlife specifies no heaven, no hell, no mode of existence. An early notebook entry declares that "our immortality is located here upon earth—that we are immortal" (qtd. in Schwartz 28), and the conclusion to the 1856 version of "I Sing the Body Electric" states that the body and its wonders *are* the soul. But generally Whitman maintains that he can "laugh at what you call dissolution" ("Song of Myself," section 20), declaring that the "excrementitious" body is left behind on the soul's eternal journey. In the afterlife, the soul's immaterial body, "transcending my senses and flesh . . . finally loves, walks, laughs, shouts, embraces, procreates" ("A Song of Joys"). "Do you enjoy what life confers?" asks a canceled passage; "you shall enjoy what death confers." The first (1855) edition ends with the affirmation that "death holds all parts together . . . death is great as life."

In his later years, he told a scientist that immortality could be proved intuitively but not demonstrated scientifically. He claimed to say better things about death than did the theologians. "Immortality is revelation," he insisted; "it flashes upon your consciousness out of God knows what." He said that his own insight into death "came long ago" in a vision (Traubel xvii–xxii). Was this the moment of "cosmic consciousness" antedating the appearance of *Leaves of Grass* that Dr. Bucke ascribed to Whitman or—like some of the poems—a bit of mythical autobiography?

The dozen poems of the first edition include "To Think of Time" (originally "Burial Poem"), which, with a not unusual undertone of repressed hysteria, expresses Whitman's be-

lief that "the exquisite scheme" and "all preparation" indicate a progression from mortal life to "nothing but immortality" (section 9). Much of the strength of "Song of Myself" stems from the persona's joyous conviction that all existence in this life and beyond adheres to a divine plan: "It is not chaos or death—it is form, union, plan—it is eternal life—it is Happiness" (section 50). The persona avers that "All goes onward and outward" (section 7), that "There is not stoppage" (section 45), that death is beneficial, and that the persona can wait millions of years to attain perfection. The poem's conclusion (sections 49–52) enacts the persona's death, disintegration, and his transformation into an omnipresent essence that will afford us "good health"—one of several assertions in the poems that Whitman and his book are immortal.

Three of the death-oriented poems in the second edition (1856) illustrate Whitman's practice of demonstrating immortality by analogy. "On the Beach at Night Alone" (originally "Clef Poem") declares that "A vast similitude interlocks" the evidence of spiritual growth through life and death. The persona's terror of dissolution in "This Compost" is allayed by perceiving the similitude between immortality and nature's cyclic renewal. "Crossing Brooklyn Ferry" casts Whitman as a benign Spiritualist incarnation, "disintegrated yet part of the scheme," looking down at the living "many hundred years hence" and invoking "the similitudes of the past and those of the future" (section 2)—the continuity of the spirit through life and death.

The introductory poem of the third (1860) edition, "Starting from Paumanok," announced Whitman's intention to "make poems of my body and of mortality . . . of my soul and of immortality" (section 6). (In fact, he made no more significant poems about his body.) In "Scented Herbage of My Breast" and "Out of the Cradle Endlessly Rocking," the poet searches for words to express the conjoined ecstasy of love and death. And in the thanato-erotic "So Long!"—the poem that closes this and all subsequent editions—the immortal Whitman persona becomes "a melodious echo, passionately bent for, (death making me really undying)." He imagines himself achieving an almost physical intimacy with the reader—"disembodied, triumphant, dead," springing "from the pages into your arms—decease calls me forth." In later poems Whitman rarely voices a terror of annihilation or tries to establish tactile contact with the living, but his more philosophic attitude toward death deprives these poems of a measure of passion and tension.

Whitman apparently expected his wartime poems to describe "passions of demons, slaughter, premature death" ("Song of the Banner at Daybreak"), but viewing the carnage from his Washington vantage, he decided instead to filter his reactions to the omnipresence of death and dying through the sensitive consciousness of a poet-observer who attended the wounded and dying and watched the dead. *Drum-Taps* (1865) characterizes "perennial sweet death" ("Pensive on Her Dead Gazing") as a healing agent and national reconciler. Whitman's great formal elegy "When Lilacs Last in the Dooryard Bloom'd," aside from its renderings of personal and national grieving, contains the incomparable apostrophe to, and celebration of, death, the *"strong deliveress,"* whose mystery the poet links with "the knowledge of death" (mortality and the war's carnage) and "the thought of death" (the promise of immortality) (section 14).

The title page of *Passage to India* announced that the poet would henceforth sing "The voyage of the Soul—not Life alone, / Death—many Deaths, I sing" (*Variorum* 3:xi). The poem "Passage to India," possibly intended to anchor a volume of poems about the soul, is, in effect, an elegy for himself, a prayer for release from life and the launching of his bodiless soul—"thou actual Me"—on its infinite voyage to the godhead. The 1876 volume, which Whitman called "almost Death's book," proposes "a more splendid Theology" and "diviner songs" (*Comprehensive* 744, 753) and illustrates two late tendencies—a celebration of the bodiless soul as the "permanent . . . body lurking there within thy body . . . the real I myself" ("Eidólons") and, in poems large and small, the poet's patient leave-taking and welcoming of death.

The 1881 edition—the definitive arrangement of the poems—ends with a group of five major death-oriented poems dating from 1855 to 1871, followed by clusters of poems (composed at various times) titled "Whispers of Heavenly Death," "From Noon to Starry Night," and "Songs of Parting." The two annexes of old-age poems, chiefly the lyrical good-byes of the "dismasted," "weak-down" poet, conclude, respectively, with minor masterpieces of affecting readiness for death: "After the Supper and Talk" and "Good-Bye my Fancy!"

Whitman's intensely personal, poetic, and philosophic engagement with death, which has fascinated readers and inspired disciples, is basic to the understanding of *Leaves of Grass*.

Harold Aspiz

Bibliography

Bucke, Richard Maurice. *Cosmic Consciousness: A Study in the Evolution of the Human Mind.* 1901. New York: Dutton, 1951.

Douglas, Ann. "Heaven Our Home: Consolation Literature in the Northern United States, 1830–1880." *Death in America.* Ed. David A. Stannard. Philadelphia: U of Pennsylvania P, 1975. 49–68.

Dutton, Geoffrey. *Whitman.* New York: Grove, 1961.

Ellis, Havelock. *The New Spirit.* 1890. New York: Boni and Liveright, 1900.

Freud, Sigmund. "Our Attitude Toward Death." *The Standard Edition of the Psychological Works of Sigmund Freud.* Ed. James Strachey. Vol. 14. London: Hogarth, 1964. 289–300.

Lawrence, D.H. "Whitman." *Whitman: A Collection of Essays.* Ed. Roy Harvey Pearce. Englewood Cliffs, N.J.: Prentice-Hall, 1962. 11–23.

Nathanson, Tenney. *Whitman's Presence: Body, Voice, and Writing in "Leaves of Grass."* New York: New York UP, 1992.

Saum, Lewis O. "Death in the Popular Mind of Pre-Civil War America." *Death in America.* Ed. David A. Stannard. Philadelphia: U of Pennsylvania P, 1975. 30–48.

Schwartz, Jacob. *Manuscripts, Autograph Letters, First Editions and Portraits of Walt Whitman.* Collected by Richard Maurice Bucke. New York: American Art Association, Anderson Galleries, 1936.

Stovall, Floyd. Introduction. *Walt Whitman: Representative Selections.* Rev. ed. New York: American Book, 1939. xi–lii.

Tillich, Paul. "The Eternal Now." *The Meaning of Death.* Ed. Herman Feifel. New York: McGraw-Hill, 1939. 30–38.

Traubel, Horace. Introduction. *The Book of Heavenly Death.* By Walt Whitman. Portland, Maine: Mosher, 1907. xvii–xxii.

Whitman, Walt. *Leaves of Grass: Comprehensive Reader's Edition.* Ed. Harold W. Blodgett and Sculley Bradley. New York: New York UP, 1965.

———. *Leaves of Grass: A Textual Variorum of the Printed Poems.* Ed. Sculley Bradley, Harold W. Blodgett, Arthur Golden, and William White. 3 vols. New York: New York UP, 1980.

See also "After the Supper and Talk"; "Crossing Brooklyn Ferry"; *Drum-Taps;* "From Noon to Starry Night"; "Good-Bye my Fancy!"; Immortality; *Memoranda During the War;* "On the Beach at Night Alone"; "Out of the Cradle Endlessly Rocking"; "Passage to India"; "Prayer of Columbus"; Reincarnation; "Scented Herbage of My Breast"; "Sleepers, The"; "So Long!"; "Song of Myself"; "Songs of Parting"; Soul, The; *Specimen Days;* "This Compost"; "To Think of Time"; "When Lilacs Last in the Dooryard Bloom'd"; "Whispers of Heavenly Death" (cluster)

"Death in the School-Room (a Fact)" (1841)

This short story, Whitman's first published fiction, appeared in the *United States Magazine and Democratic Review,* August 1841. Whitman reprinted it more than any other of his stories. For publication information see William White and G.R. Thompson; see also Thomas L. Brasher's edition of *The Early Poems and the Fiction.*

The story involves Lugare, a sadistic teacher, and sickly Tim Barker, only child of a widow, who is falsely accused of theft. When he begins beating Tim, who is apparently asleep, Lugare learns that he is really beating a corpse. The sentimentality of "Death in the School-Room" underscores Whitman's opposition to corporal punishment. This opposition to violence connects it with his fictional indictments of capital punishment, "One Wicked Impulse!" (1845) and "The Half-Breed: A Tale of the Western Frontier" (1845).

Reynolds observes that the "terrible pain" that "lurks" in some of the poetry first enters Whitman's work in this story (52–53). Along with "Wild Frank's Return" (1841) and "Bervance: or, Father and Son" (1841), the story suggests in Whitman a compulsive interest in cruel authority figures, especially fathers. The beating in this story has been tied to the seaman's forcefulness in "The Child and the Profligate" (1841), both resonating with the homoeroticism in Whitman's personality.

Patrick McGuire

Bibliography

Allen, Gay Wilson. *The Solitary Singer: A Critical Biography of Walt Whitman.* 1955. Rev. ed. 1967. Chicago: U of Chicago P, 1985.

Reynolds, David S. *Walt Whitman's America: A Cultural Biography.* New York: Knopf, 1995.

Thompson, G.R. "An Early Unrecorded Printing of Walt Whitman's 'Death in the School-Room.'" *Papers of the Bibliographic Society of America* 67 (1973): 64–65.

White, William. "Two Citations: An Early Whitman Article and an Early Reprinting of 'Death in the School-Room.'" *Walt Whitman Quarterly Review* 5.1 (1987): 36–37.

Whitman, Walt. *The Early Poems and the Fiction.* Ed. Thomas L. Brasher. New York: New York UP, 1963.

See also "Bervance: or, Father and Son"; "Child and the Profligate, The"; "Half-Breed, The"; "One Wicked Impulse!"; Short Fiction, Whitman's; "Wild Frank's Return"

"Death of Abraham Lincoln" (1879)

Walt Whitman delivered his "Death of Abraham Lincoln" lecture for the first of at least eight, and possibly as many as thirteen, times in New York in 1879.

In this lecture Whitman eulogizes Abraham Lincoln, calling him the "first great Martyr Chief" of the United States of America (*Prose Works* 2:509). Whitman's subject is how the impact of Lincoln's death will ultimately filter into all of America. He himself promises to commemorate Lincoln each year until his own death. Whitman reminisces about seeing Lincoln for the first time in 1861: stepping from a barouche onto the sidewalk in New York, with great courage Lincoln faced a silent and unfriendly crowd. Living in Washington during the next four years, Whitman recalls seeing Lincoln there several times, sometimes on the street and occasionally at Ford Theater. Whitman claims that from the Civil War a "great literature will yet arise" (*Prose Works* 2:502). He then launches into a moving first-person report of the actual events of the assassination on 14 April 1865. He writes as if he were a member of the crowd at the theater who heard the screams and felt the tension of the near rioting that followed. Actually, Whitman was in New York when Lincoln was shot.

Whitman's "Reading Book," deposited by Thomas Harned in the Library of Congress, contains eighteen poems—some by Whitman, some by other poets he admired—from which he often read following the Lincoln lecture. Among these poems are "O Captain! My Captain!" (1865), "Proud Music of the Storm" (1869), and "To the Man-of-War-Bird" (1876) (Whitman, *Workshop* 204–206, n43).

After Whitman gave the Lincoln lecture at Association Hall in Philadelphia on 15 April 1880, a Philadelphia *Press* writer reported a straightforward delivery in "a tone only sufficiently higher than he would make use of in talking to a friend to make sure that the most distant hearer would catch every word" (Whitman, *Memoranda* 33–34). Whitman's delivery moved many members of the audience to tears, and he concluded with a reading of his "O Captain! My Captain!" Whitman also delivered the Lincoln lecture in Boston in 1881. Audience member William Dean Howells called the experience "an address of singular quiet, delivered in a voice of winning and endearing friendliness" (74). One of Whitman's four deliveries of the address in 1886 was at the Chestnut Opera House in Philadelphia. Stuart Merrill (1863–1915) claims that Whitman's "recital was as gripping as the messenger's report in Aeschylus" (55). Among the audience members who heard Whitman give the Lincoln lecture at Madison Square Theater in New York on 14 April 1887 were Andrew Carnegie, Mary Mapes Dodge, Daniel Coit Gilman, John Milton Hay, James Russell Lowell, Charles Eliot Norton, Augustus Saint-Gaudens, and Mark Twain (Whitman, *Memoranda* 40). In "Memoranda" in *Good-Bye My Fancy* (1891), Whitman reports delivering the Lincoln lecture for the last time on 15 April 1890, in the Arts Room in Philadelphia (*Prose Works* 2:684).

Larry D. Griffin

Bibliography

Howells, William Dean. *Literary Friends and Acquaintance: A Personal Retrospect of American Authorship*. New York: Harper, 1900.
Merrill, Stuart. "Walt Whitman." 1912. Trans. John J. Espey. *Walt Whitman Newsletter* 3 (1957): 55–57.
Whitman, Walt. *Memoranda During the War & Death of Abraham Lincoln*. Ed. Roy P. Basler. Bloomington: Indiana UP, 1962.
———. *Prose Works 1892*. Ed. Floyd Stovall. 2 vols. New York: New York UP, 1963–1964.
———. *Walt Whitman's Workshop: A Collection of Unpublished Manuscripts*. Ed. Clifton Joseph Furness. Cambridge, Mass.: Harvard UP, 1928.

See also LINCOLN, ABRAHAM; LINCOLN'S DEATH

"Death of Wind-Foot, The" (1842)

This short story, as well as the story "Little Jane" (1842), initially appeared as part of Whitman's novel *Franklin Evans* (1842). "The Death of Wind-Foot," with slight revisions, appeared in *American Review,* June 1845. The title was changed to "The Death of Wind-Foot. An Indian Story" when the story was reprinted in *Crystal Fount and Rechabite Recorder,* 18 October 1845. For publication history and revisions, see Brasher's edition of *The Early Poems and the Fiction.*

Tribal hatred and revenge are the basic themes of this story about three Native Americans. Unrelenting, chief of a brave tribe, tells his son, Wind-Foot, of the long-standing enmity between them and the Kansi tribe. Unrelenting tells of killing a Kansi while the man's son watched. A guest in Unrelenting's lodge overhears the story and, in a rage, lays plans to kill Wind-Foot. The guest is the now grown son of the dead Kansi. He takes Wind-Foot captive and manages to kill him only after he has been mortally wounded by Unrelenting. Unrelenting is left childless.

Here, as in Whitman's novella "The Half-Breed: A Tale of the Western Frontier" (1845), Native Americans are not mere stock characters. Whitman humanizes the lonesome chief, who, Job-like, has endured the deaths of his wife and all his other children. He is soothing and fatherly and warm to his son. Wind-Foot has the boyish enthusiasm of an adolescent learning to hunt and the disappointment of not hunting well. The unnamed guest, however, is duplicitous and wild and animal-like.

This short story has received little critical attention.

Patrick McGuire

Bibliography

Folsom, Ed. *Walt Whitman's Native Representations*. Cambridge: Cambridge UP, 1994.

Whitman, Walt. *The Early Poems and the Fiction*. Ed. Thomas L. Brasher. New York: New York UP, 1963.

See also FRANKLIN EVANS; "HALF-BREED, THE"; "LITTLE JANE"; NATIVE AMERICANS (INDIANS); SHORT FICTION, WHITMAN'S

"Death's Valley" (1892)

On 28 August 1889, Henry Mills Alden, editor of *Harper's New Monthly Magazine*, wrote Whitman to request a poem to accompany *The Valley of the Shadow of Death* (1867) by the American landscape painter George Inness (1824–1894). Whitman complied with "a little poemet," which he sent on 30 August (*Correspondence* 4:376). The poem, however, did not appear in *Harper's* until the month after Whitman's death in March 1892. This issue was, in part, a memorial to Whitman with J.W. Alexander's portrait of Whitman as the frontispiece and a recent sketch of Whitman by Alexander above the text of "Death's Valley," which appeared on the reverse of the page.

The painting depicts Psalm 23.4: "Yea, though I walk through the valley of the shadow of death, I will fear no evil: for thou art with me." Whitman's title complicates the reference, for it may also refer to Death Valley, California, which was named in 1849. The poem itself is in free verse; it has no regular meter, the lines are irregular in length, and it contains no rhyme. Appropriately, "Death's Valley" echoes the diction and cadence of the Psalms, and it makes frequent use of alliteration and repetition.

In its published form, "Death's Valley" does not describe Inness's painting so much as respond to it. Written in the first person, the poem begins with an apostrophe to the painter, "I . . . enter lists with thee, claiming my right to make a symbol too." The speaker's right to make the symbol is based on having witnessed death in all circumstances and stages of life. Lines 5–11 suggest Whitman's service as a nurse during the Civil War and echo passages from *Drum-Taps* (1865) and *Specimen Days* (1882). The conceit of life as a "hard-tied knot" suggests the tourniquets used in the Civil War to stop the fatal flow of blood. Like the merciful hand of a "Wound-Dresser," "God's beautiful eternal right hand" loosens the knot, and "Sweet, peaceful, welcome Death" results. "Death's Valley" also contains numerous allusions to "Song of Myself." The poem is an appropriate obituary for Whitman, for it summarizes his experiences in the context of a meditation on death.

Manuscripts of "Death's Valley" are in the Feinberg and Barrett collections.

William A. Pannapacker

Bibliography

Whitman, Walt. *The Correspondence*. Ed. Edwin Haviland Miller. 6 vols. New York: New York UP, 1961–1977.

———. "Death's Valley." *Harper's New Monthly Magazine* April 1892: 707–709.

See also DEATH; "OLD AGE ECHOES"

Democracy

"Democracy" is the organizing concept that unites Whitman's poetics, politics, and metaphysics. Democracy always remained for Whitman an ideal goal, never a realized practice. He saw democracy as an inevitable evolutionary force in human history, and he did all he could to urge the evolution along, but he was under no illusions that a functioning democratic society would come easily or quickly. As part of his democratic effort, he tried to invent a poetry as open, as nondiscriminatory, and as absorptive as he imagined an ideal democracy would be. He tried, in other words, to construct a democratic voice that would serve as a model for his society—a difficult task, since he was well aware that his nation and his world were still filled with antidemocratic sentiments, laws, customs, and institutions, and he knew that no writer could rise above all the biases and blindnesses of his particular historical moment. Whitman believed, however, that the United States in the nineteenth century had the opportunity to become the first culture in human history to experience the beginnings of a true democracy.

In Webster's 1847 *American Dictionary of the English Language* (the dictionary Whitman depended on), democracy is defined as "a form of government, in which the supreme power is lodged in the hands of the people collectively, or in which the people exercise the powers of legislation," and the definition ends with a single example: "Such was the government of Athens." This dictionary makes no mention of American democracy. Whitman took issue with this definition; when he talks about the evolution of democracy, he virtually ignores Athenian democracy. For Whitman, human history is not so much a back-and-forth struggle between democratic and antidemocratic forces as it is an unbroken evolution away from feudalism toward the natural and rational democratic future. So, when Whitman defines democracy, his definition contains no past examples or models, but instead looks only toward the future, which of course makes the act of definition impossible: "We have frequently printed the word Democracy," he writes in *Democratic Vistas*. "Yet I cannot too often repeat that it is a word the real gist of which still sleeps, quite unawaken'd." He goes on to say that it is a "great word, whose history, I suppose, remains unwritten, because that history has yet to be enacted" (*Prose Works* 2:393). Democracy, in other words, is the most significant word in the American language and yet remains a word for which there is still no definition, because no society has yet lived the history that would illustrate it. Whitman assumed "Democracy to be at present in its embryo condition" (2:392), and he always professed that "the fruition of democracy. . . . resides altogether in the future" (2:390).

Whitman also disagreed with Webster's emphasis on the "form of government" as the essential aspect of a democracy. For Whitman, a democratic literature was the most essential factor, for as long as the imagination of the country remained shackled by feudalistic models of literature, by romances that reinforced power hierarchies and gender discrimination, and by a conception of literary production that put authorship only in the hands of the educated elite, then democracy would never flourish, regardless of the form of government. Whitman was finally more intrigued with the way a democratic self would act than the way a democratic society would function, and the defining of this revolutionary new self, he knew, was a job for the poet. A democracy, then, would require a new kind of imaginative relationship between reader and author, a more equalizing give and take, and so Whitman constructed a poetry that directly addressed his readers and challenged them to act, speak, and respond. He also constructed a poetry that required of the reader acts of imaginative absorption, a breaking down of the barriers of bias and

convention, and an enlarging of the self. He argued vehemently that "a new Literature," and especially "a new Poetry, are to be, in my opinion, the only sure and worthy supports and expressions of the American democracy" (*Prose Works* 2:416). His belief in the power of literature to shape a democracy was so strong that he occasionally expressed doubts about whether Shakespeare, for example, should be taught in American schools, because he represented "incarnated, uncompromising feudalism, in literature," and "there is much in him ever offensive to democracy" (2:522). The greatest duty of the American poet, Whitman believed, was to write the "epic of democracy" (2:458), to go about the business of "making a new history, a history of democracy, making old history a dwarf" (2:423). The poet of democracy would change a nation's reading habits, and in so doing would create the imaginative energy necessary to break down feudalistic assumptions and to construct a new democratic frame of mind.

Whitman was not a naive apologist for democracy. He regularly cast a skeptical eye on American culture, and he was keenly aware of the many shortcomings of the then current state of American democracy as well as of some of the basic contradictions of democratic theory. "A majority or democracy may rule as outrageously and do as great harm as an oligarchy or despotism," he wrote in *Specimen Days* (*Prose Works* 1:260). And in his "Notes Left Over," he worried about the "dark significance" of the "total want" of any "mutuality of love, belief, and rapport of interest, between the comparatively few successful rich, and the great masses of the unsuccessful, the poor"—such "a problem and puzzle in our democracy" haunted Whitman as much in the late nineteenth century as it does many Americans today (*Prose Works* 2:534). While his faith in democracy as the "destin'd conquerer" of history was strong, his awareness that there were "treacherous lip-smiles everywhere" was just as strong, and his poems articulated "the song of the throes of Democracy" every bit as much as its victories ("By Blue Ontario's Shore," section 1).

Whitman regularly noted the failings and sad ironies of his nation's often faltering attempts to build a democratic culture, and he believed that there could be "no better service in the United States, henceforth, by democrats of thorough and heart-felt faith, than boldly exposing the weakness, liabilities and infinite corruptions of democracy" (*Prose Works* 2:529).

While he could use "the words America and democracy as convertible terms," he at the same time worried that the "United States are destined either to surmount the gorgeous history of feudalism, or else prove the most tremendous failure of time" (2:363). So he became a severe critic of America's shortcomings even while he also looked beyond the failings to future possibilities. During the Civil War, for instance, Whitman castigated the U.S. military for its feudalistic and antidemocratic organization, and yet he also argued that two of the great "proofs" of democracy in America were the voluntary arming of troops in the Civil War and the peaceful disbanding of the armies after the war was over (*Prose Works* 1:25). The military thus at once offered distressing and hopeful signs, as it, like much of American society, struggled to discover the implications of democratic reformation.

Whitman chose to view democracy as a force of nature, an antidiscriminatory law manifested in the fullness of the natural world: "Democracy most of all affiliates with the open air, is sunny and hardy and sane only with Nature" (*Prose Works* 1:294). The word "democracy," he said, is the "younger brother of another great and often-used word, Nature . . ." (*Prose Works* 2:393). So the new democratic poet would take his lessons from nature, as he made clear in his 1855 Preface: "He judges not as the judge judges but as the sun falling around a helpless thing" (2:437). "Not til the sun excludes you do I exclude you," he wrote in "To a Common Prostitute." Whitman thus developed a new edge to the word "discrimination," a word that was undergoing important changes in connotation in the second half of the nineteenth century, shifting from meaning simply "the making of a distinction" to suggesting something significantly more sinister in a democratic society, where the very act of making distinctions in respect to quality, of setting up hierarchies of value, came to be perceived as an antidemocratic process that "discriminated against" those who did not share decision-making authority. Whitman was inventing the definition of the word that we are most familiar with today as he explored ways that the act of discriminating produced victims—those who were discriminated against. "The earth," he wrote in "A Song of the Rolling Earth" (section 1), "makes no discriminations." This nature-based, nondiscriminating democracy, then, becomes the poet's "pass-word primeval" (as he calls it in "Song of Myself," section 24): "I speak the pass-word primeval, I give the sign of democracy, / By God! I will accept nothing which all cannot have their counterpart of on the same terms." Whitman's development of his long-lined free verse and his absorptive catalogues that melded presidents and prostitutes in the same line were all part of his attempt to break out of the discriminating poetry of the past and open literature to a democratic sensibility.

By the time he wrote *Democratic Vistas*, his most extended analysis of democracy, Whitman was less sanguine than he had been about democracy's inevitable success. He begins the essay by alternately agreeing with and disputing Thomas Carlyle's famous attacks on democracy. As Whitman builds a case for the continuing evolution of American democracy and the need for a more spiritual phase of democracy to replace the material phase that the country seemed mired in after the Civil War, he wrestles with the thorny problems of democratic theory, especially the irresolvable tension between the many and the one, between the social cohesion necessary to make a democracy work and the equally important necessity of individual freedom. For Whitman, the issue was always the negotiation of the "democratic individual" with "democratic nationality" (*Prose Works* 2:463). He came to name his provisional solution to this problem "Personalism," a blending of the one and the many, a balancing of individuality with camaraderie, what he had earlier identified (in his 1855 Preface) as the oscillating relationship between sympathy and pride: the love for one's democratic and equal others in all their diversity balanced against the pride in one's own identity. In order to "counterbalance and offset" the "materialistic and vulgar American democracy," Whitman looked to "the development, identification, and general prevalence of that fervid comradeship, (the adhesive love, at least rivaling the amative love . . .)" (2:414n). Democracy, in other words, would require new forms of affection, a fervid friendship that would bind citizens to each other in ways previously unimaginable.

The key for Whitman was always to enlarge the self, to work toward a democratic conception of selfhood as absorptive, nondiscriminating, receptive, and loving. For Whitman, a democratic self was one that came to recognize vast multitudes of possibility within its own identity, one that could imagine how one's own identity, given altered circumstances, might incorporate the identity of anyone in the culture, from the most marginalized and despised to the most exalted and powerful. To experience democratic selfhood, then, meant a radical act of imagining how one could share an identity with every member of the society, a radical act of learning to love difference by recognizing the possibility of that difference within a multitudinous self, a self that had been enlarged by nondiscriminatory practice and by love that crossed conventional boundaries.

While many early commentators viewed Whitman's ideas about democracy as either vague or naive or both, recent critics have found Whitman's thinking about the issue to be complex, serious, and illuminating. In 1990, for example, major political theorists debated Whitman's concepts of democracy in the pages of the journal *Political Theory,* where George Kateb called him "perhaps the greatest philosopher of the culture of democracy" (545).

Ed Folsom

Bibliography
Kateb, George. "Walt Whitman and the Culture of Democracy." *Political Theory* 18 (1990): 545–571. [With commentaries on Kateb's essay by David Bromwich, Nancy L. Rosenblum, Michael Mosher, and Leo Marx; 572–599.]
Whitman, Walt. *Prose Works 1892.* Ed. Floyd Stovall. 2 vols. New York: New York UP, 1963–1964.

See also AMERICAN CHARACTER; CARLYLE, THOMAS; COMRADESHIP; *DEMOCRATIC VISTAS;* FEUDALISM; INDIVIDUALISM; POETIC THEORY

Democratic Party
The Democratic party is the older of the present two major political parties in the United States and is, in fact, the oldest political party in the world. Commonly called the "party of the people," from its beginnings it has drawn members and a power base essentially from such citizens as small farmers, producers, small mercantile traders, and blue collar workers, though both major parties tend to be heterogeneous groups organized to win elections for the purpose of controlling policymaking more than homogeneous groups agreed upon clearly defined programs. Walt Whitman was associated with the Democratic party from the early 1830s

until his defection to the newly formed Republican party twenty years later.

Whitman's workingman heritage, which came from his father, a member of the Workingman's party, led him to the Democratic party early in life. At the age of twelve Whitman worked for the *Long Island Patriot,* a weekly paper that served as the organ of the Democratic party in Kings County. He had a good record in the party at first and felt quite at home in Tammany Hall. Actively involving himself in the affairs of the party, he campaigned vigorously for Martin Van Buren in 1840 and later for James K. Polk, served as the secretary of the General Committee of the Kings County Democratic party in 1846, and wrote and stumped in support of the candidates and doctrines of the Democratic party in New York State—one time addressing a Democratic rally in City Hall Park attended by fifteen thousand people.

Whitman felt that the Democratic party championed that which was noblest and most progressive in a republican form of government. Thus, he held expansionist views based upon the doctrine of Manifest Destiny and felt the Democratic party should promote the ideal of democracy southward even into Central America. In his writings, especially those while editor of the Brooklyn *Daily Eagle,* he espoused the Jeffersonian-Jacksonian ideas that were fundamental to the Democratic party's philosophy at the time: diminished government, free trade, opposition to a national bank, resistance to morality laws, hostility to trade unions, and belief in America as a noble experiment in liberty.

Though not an abolitionist, Whitman firmly believed that slavery should be disallowed in any state entering the Union. Within the Democratic party, liberals who avidly held to the free-soil position ("Barnburners" and "Locofocos") were opposed by conservatives whose sympathies lay with the Southern Democrats favoring slavery ("Hunkers"). The Wilmot Proviso of 1846 (ultimately defeated), which prohibited slavery in any territory acquired from Mexico, split the Democratic party in New York. The failure of the party in New York to take a stand on the issue, Whitman believed, cost it the local election in November 1847 and the presidential election in 1848. The national Democratic party, fearing the alienation of Southern Democrats if it took a stand to support the free-soil position, chose to compromise and support the policy of letting prospective states choose whether to allow slavery or not—which later the Kansas-Nebraska Bill of 1854 provided.

During the bitter controversy, Whitman, as editor of the Brooklyn *Daily Eagle,* unabashedly stated his support for the Wilmot Proviso and other liberal views. The compromise in the Democratic party clearly angered him, for he felt that by compromising, the party had unjustly resorted to chicanery and subterfuge. He blamed the social conditions of the period on control of the Democratic party by slave-owning Southern Democrats. Eventually, his editorials favoring "free soil" and his attacks on the policy of the Democratic party were more than Isaac Van Anden, owner of the *Eagle* and a Hunker, could abide. Whitman was fired.

Shortly thereafter, Whitman accepted the editor's position of the New Orleans *Crescent.* But this position was short-lived, for after only three months (25 February–25 May 1948) he returned to edit a Free Soil Democratic paper, the Brooklyn *Freeman.* Whitman was becoming more and more disenchanted with the Democratic party, however, for after being fired from the *Eagle* for his "radical" position on free soil and then being deserted financially by Free Soil Democrats, he felt the politicians in the Democratic party had betrayed not only him but also the fight for liberty and justice. Indignant, he aligned himself with the newly formed Republican party in the 1856 election, though he never became politically active after this time.

His indignation can be seen in "Blood-Money" (1850), "Dough-Face Song" (originally published as "Song for Certain Congressmen") (1850), and "The House of Friends" (1850).

Maverick Marvin Harris

Bibliography

Allen, Gay Wilson. *The New Walt Whitman Handbook.* 1975. New York: New York UP, 1986.

———. *The Solitary Singer: A Critical Biography of Walt Whitman.* 1955. Rev. ed. 1967. Chicago: U of Chicago P, 1985.

Kaplan, Justin. *Walt Whitman: A Life.* New York: Simon and Schuster, 1980.

Whitman, Walt. *The Early Poems and the Fiction.* Ed. Thomas L. Brasher. New York: New York UP, 1963.

———. *The Gathering of the Forces.* Ed. Cleveland Rodgers and John Black. 2 vols. New York: Putnam, 1920.

Winwar, Frances. *American Giant: Walt Whitman and His Times.* New York:

Tudor, 1941.

Zweig, Paul. *Walt Whitman: The Making of the Poet.* New York: Basic Books, 1984.

See also BARNBURNERS AND LOCOFOCOS; FREE SOIL PARTY; HUNKERS; POLITICAL VIEWS; REPUBLICAN PARTY; TAMMANY HALL; WILMOT PROVISO

Democratic Review

The *United States Magazine and Democratic Review* (October 1837–December 1851), a monthly magazine designed to promote the liberal politics of the Democratic party, as well as to provide a forum for contemporary American literature, was jointly edited by John L. O'Sullivan and Samuel D. Langtree. Often called simply the *Democratic Review,* it was published under that title from January–December 1852, then as the *United States Review* (January 1853–January 1856), and later as the *United States Democratic Review* (February 1856–October 1859). Although there were a variety of owners, publishers, and editors throughout the years of publication, the magazine retained its liberal political orientation and earned, under the sole editorship of John L. O'Sullivan in the 1840s, a reputation for excellence in literature. Nathaniel Hawthorne published twenty-five essays and tales in the magazine, including "Rappaccini's Daughter" and "The Artist of the Beautiful." Other contributors included Ralph Waldo Emerson, Evert Duyckinck, Edgar Allan Poe, James Fenimore Cooper, Horatio Greenough, William Cullen Bryant, James Russell Lowell, William Gilmore Simms, William Ellery Channing, and Henry David Thoreau. Whitman, who was a practicing journalist, largely writing articles and editing newspapers during the decade of the *Democratic Review*'s greatest distinction in literature, was an enthusiastic supporter and saw the magazine under O'Sullivan's leadership as being "of a profounder quality of talent than any since" (*Uncollected* 2:15).

Eager to find new outlets for his own work, especially in a magazine of such quality, Whitman published ten works in the *Review* during 1841–1845. Nine of these were undistinguished and melodramatic tales: "Death in the School-Room (a Fact)" (August 1841); "Wild Frank's Return" (November 1841); "Bervance: or, Father and Son" (December 1841); "The Tomb Blossoms" (January 1842); "The Last of the Sacred Army" (March 1842);

"The Child-Ghost; a Story of the Last Loyalist" (May 1842); "A Legend of Life and Love" (July 1842); "The Angel of Tears" (September 1842); and "Revenge and Requital: A Tale of a Murderer Escaped" (July–August 1845). Whitman also published "A Dialogue [Against Capital Punishment]" (November 1845), his contribution to the progressive campaign to abolish the death penalty. Later, long after O'Sullivan's years as editor of the *Review,* Whitman published one of his several self-reviews of *Leaves of Grass,* "Walt Whitman and His Poems" (September 1855), proclaiming the author of this work as an American bard, "self-reliant, with haughty eyes, assuming to himself all the attributes of his country" (Price 9).

Susan Belasco Smith

Bibliography

Allen, Gay Wilson. *The Solitary Singer: A Critical Biography of Walt Whitman.* 1955. Rev. ed. 1967. Chicago: U of Chicago P, 1985.

Chielens, Edward E., ed. *American Literary Magazines: The Eighteenth and Nineteenth Centuries.* New York: Greenwood, 1986.

Fishkin, Shelley Fisher. *From Fact to Fiction: Journalism and Imaginative Writing in America.* New York: Oxford UP, 1985.

Greenspan, Ezra. *Walt Whitman and the American Reader.* New York: Cambridge UP, 1990.

Mott, Frank Luther. *A History of American Magazines.* 5 vols. Cambridge, Mass.: Harvard UP, 1938–1968.

Myerson, Joel. *Walt Whitman: A Descriptive Bibliography.* Pittsburgh: U of Pittsburgh P, 1993.

Price, Kenneth M., ed. *Walt Whitman: The Contemporary Reviews.* Cambridge: Cambridge UP, 1996.

Whitman, Walt. *The Early Poems and the Fiction.* Ed. Thomas L. Brasher. New York: New York UP, 1963.

———. *The Uncollected Poetry and Prose of Walt Whitman.* Ed. Emory Holloway. 2 vols. Garden City, N.Y.: Doubleday, Page, 1921.

See also SELF-REVIEWS OF THE 1855 *LEAVES,* WHITMAN'S ANONYMOUS; SHORT FICTION, WHITMAN'S

Democratic Vistas (1871)

This lengthy prose work, published in an eighty-four-page pamphlet in 1871, comprises a trilogy of essays Walt Whitman originally intended for publication in the *Galaxy* magazine. Two appeared in the *Galaxy:* "Democracy" in December 1867 and "Personalism" in May 1868; he submitted the third, "Orbic Literature," to the *Galaxy,* but it did not appear.

The text of *Democratic Vistas,* which Whitman variously described as "memoranda" and "speculations," some of which date to the middle 1850s, shows evidence of Whitman's familiar propensity to tinker. Textual variations are evident in its several versions—from the "Rough Draft," *Galaxy,* pamphlet, and *Two Rivulets* (1876) versions to the *Specimen Days & Collect* version. The various additions and deletions, however, are minor and do not alter Whitman's purpose.

The immediate impulse for the writing of *Democratic Vistas* was the publication, in Horace Greeley's *Tribune* on 16 August 1867, of the complete text of Thomas Carlyle's *Shooting Niagara: And After?,* a blistering critique of democratizing trends, specifically enfranchisement legislation, in England and America. Carlyle's and Whitman's essays belong to a larger body of writings that appeared during the third quarter of the nineteenth century and attempted to address the spectacle of a putative moral and spiritual collapse. Unable to discern the providential arm operating through engineering marvels, a frenzied economic development, vulgar consumerism, and widespread social fragmentation, writers in this country and England attempted to recenter the concept of culture, conceiving of it as a beneficent instrument of political reconstruction. For them, the force of culture had the potential to integrate national life through its conceptualization of a common heritage and to elevate the intellectual, aesthetic, and moral faculties of citizens. Unlike his English counterparts, however, Whitman insistently defended the principles associated with the democratic, egalitarian ideal. As he points out in an anonymous review of *Democratic Vistas,* the essay attempts to demonstrate how freedom and individualism could not only "revolutionize & reconstruct politics, but Religion, Sociology, Manners, Literature & Art" as well (qtd. in Warren 79). The culture, he envisioned, would hold up a forgotten ideal that might yet recall people to perfection.

In taking up the challenge of reconstructing his country, Whitman assumes several roles: that of a Jeremiah—harsh and uncompromising in his detailing of America's many spiritual and moral failures; a cultural diagnostician who looks below the surface of America's body politic to "the inmost tissues, blood, vitality, morality, heart & brain" (qtd. in Warren 79) in order to determine a course of treatment; and a visionary seer who anticipates the unfolding of the Great Republic of the future comprised of superbly developed individuals whose freedom lies in their obedience to eternal spiritual laws.

Whitman's prose style in *Democratic Vistas* has been justly described as diffuse, tortured, and murky—one that seemingly dramatizes Whitman in his role as poet-prophet speaking out of a visionary trance. His procedure is no less obscure despite his statement near the beginning that describes it as dialectical: "I feel the parts harmoniously blended in my own realization and convictions, and present them to be read only in such oneness, each page and each claim and assertion modified and temper'd by the others" (363). There is some reason to argue that Whitman counters visionary projections with actualities and explores various sets of antitheses—individual and mass, material and spiritual, present and future—but whether he ever achieves a synthesis, or simply resorts to placing his trust in the familiar nineteenth-century theory of history as an irreversible record of democracy's advance, remains moot.

Democratic Vistas appears to be structured, roughly, according to the three *Galaxy* essays. From this perspective, Whitman initially surveys the "canker'd" present of post-Reconstruction America (369); he then describes his program for developing individualism, which he calls "Personalism," as it is nurtured by the emergence of a "New World literature" (405), the subject of the final part of his essay.

In the first part, Whitman inveighs, with apocalyptic fervor, against the awful discrepancy between "democracy's convictions, aspirations and the people's crudeness, vice, caprices" (363). Fixing his "moral microscope" on post-Reconstruction American society, he surveys a "dry and flat Sahara" (372). His indictment is uncompromising and comprehensive: he accuses American society of hypocrisy, business of a greed that borders on "depravity," and political life, both local and national, of being "saturated in corruption, bribery, falsehood, mal-administration"; he describes churches as "dismal phantasms" and conversation as a mere "mass of badinage"; literature, he asserts, exhibits little more than "scornful superciliousness" (370). He is also distressed by the unmistakable signs of society's fragmentation, its fabric seemingly in imminent danger of being torn apart by a divisiveness he attributes to vestiges of feudalism—competing factions and classes, racial and gender tensions, distinctions between mass and polite culture, party politics, and incipient conflicts between labor and capital—as traditional standards retreat before the advance of accelerating change. He acknowledges that "the fear of conflicting and irreconcilable interiors, and the lack of a common skeleton, knitting all close, continually haunts me" (368). Commenting that "We sail a dangerous sea of seething currents, cross and under-currents, vortices—all so dark, untried," he asks with good reason, "and whither shall we turn?" (422).

The answer for Whitman lies in the transformation of the American nation and the mind of its people by a new class "of native authors, literatuses, . . . sacerdotal, modern, fit to cope with our occasions, lands, permeating the whole mass of American mentality, taste, belief, breathing into it a new breath of life . . . with results inside and underneath the elections of Presidents or Congresses" (365). Such a literature would speak to the "common people, the life-blood of democracy" (388), and "with an eye to practical life" (396) provide them with "a basic model or portrait of personality for general use" (397). The "mental-educational part" of Whitman's model would attend to everything from a program of stirpiculture aimed at producing an ideal birthstock for the new democracy of the future, to the commonplaces of "food, drink, air, exercise, assimilation, digestion," and even manners and dress (397). Such a literature would "raise up and supply through the States a copious race of superb American men and women, cheerful, religious, ahead of any yet known" (395).

On a more sublime note, but no less pragmatic, Whitman values this literature for its moral and political efficacy. Such a literature would be the instrument by which American government would achieve its highest potential, namely "to develop, to open up to cultivation, to encourage the possibilities of all beneficent and manly outcroppage, and of that aspiration for independence, and the pride and self-respect latent in all characters" (379). Acting in concert with a beneficent government, this literature would foster a radical individualism which he names "Personalism." While recognizing that "the virtue of modern Individualism" potentially conflicts with "the ancient virtue of Patriotism, the fervid and absorbing love of general country" (373), Whitman nevertheless hopes that such a reformulation might restore a much needed balance between the desire for personal liberty and communal solidarity. The "Personalism" he proposes projects an "image of completeness in separatism, of individual personal dignity, of a single person, either male or female, characterized in the main, not from extrinsic acquirements or position, but in the pride of himself or herself alone" (374). This construct retains Whitman's two great faiths: "the democratic republican principle," namely "the theory of development and perfection by voluntary standards, and self-reliance" (362) and the common citizenry whose capacity for heroism and patriotism were confirmed for him during the Civil War. Conceding, however, that individualism potentially "isolates," he postulated the existence of a universal force called adhesiveness that could counter the excrescences of individualism while reconnecting the individual to the larger political body. This force fuses and binds "all men, of however various and distant lands, into a brotherhood, a family . . . making the races comrades, and fraternizing all" (381).

The ideal manifestation of "Personalism" was to be found in a spiritualized future democratic state. Whitman's anticipation of this state's unfolding draws on a theory that measured historical change in terms of progress through various stages. For Whitman, civilization advanced from a "feudal, ecclesiastical, dynastic world" (366) to the American present of economic development and material abundance; the next stage entailed the emergence of a "sublime and serious Religious Democracy" (410). The "Vistas" in the title of Whitman's essay are those of the prophet-seer's glimpses into the features of this higher, religious-spiritual democracy. What he envisions is a homogeneous society, animated by a "fervid and tremendous IDEA, melting everything else with resistless heat, and solving all lesser and definite distinctions in vast, indefinite, spiritual, emotional power" (368). Such a society is characterized by "the copious production of perfect characters among the people" (392–393) who are trained "in sanest, highest freedom" so as

to "become a law, a series of laws, unto [themselves]" (375). Here the presence "of a sane and pervading religiousness" (393) undergirds a "rich, luxuriant, varied personalism" (392). In this construct, we are given Whitman's most explicit statement about democracy's agency for spiritualization.

Undoubtedly, *Democratic Vistas* is long on visionary lyricism and a bit short in practical suggestions. Richard Chase faults Whitman for being too sanguine in entertaining a view of history as a force that necessarily nurtures democracy; Arthur Golden for willfully blinding himself to the "canker'd" body politic of Reconstruction America and hoping it would simply disappear; David Marr for contradicting the spirit of democratic plurality in his yearning for a unitary national literature; and Betsy Erkkila for his failure to achieve any convincing reconciliation between vision and reality. However, as Harold Aspiz points out, *Democratic Vistas* needs its visionary content to give it substance, while Alan Trachtenberg notes that the split Whitman observed between literary and mass culture prophetically anticipates the condition we find ourselves in today.

Arthur Wrobel

Bibliography

Aspiz, Harold. "The Body Politic in *Democratic Vistas*." *Walt Whitman: The Centennial Essays*. Ed. Ed Folsom. Iowa City: U of Iowa P, 1994. 105–119.

Chase, Richard. *Walt Whitman Reconsidered*. New York: William Sloane Associates, 1955.

Erkkila, Betsy. *Whitman the Political Poet*. New York: Oxford UP, 1989.

Golden, Arthur. "The Obfuscations of Rhetoric: Whitman and the Visionary Experience." *Walt Whitman: The Centennial Essays*. Ed. Ed Folsom. Iowa City: U of Iowa P, 1994. 88–102.

Grier, Edward F. "Walt Whitman, the *Galaxy*, and *Democratic Vistas*." *American Literature* 23 (1951): 332–350.

Mancuso, Luke. "'Reconstructing is still in Abeyance': Walt Whitman's *Democratic Vistas* and the Federalizing of National Identity." *ATQ* 8 (1994): 229–250.

Marr, David. *American Worlds Since Emerson*. Amherst: U of Massachusetts P, 1988.

Scholnick, Robert J. "The American Context of *Democratic Vistas*." *Walt Whitman: Here and Now*. Ed. Joann P. Krieg. Westport, Conn.: Greenwood, 1985. 147–156.

Trachtenberg, Alan, ed. *Democratic Vistas: 1860–1880*. New York: George Braziller, 1970.

Warren, James Perrin. "Reconstructing Language in *Democratic Vistas*." *Walt Whitman: The Centennial Essays*. Ed. Ed Folsom. Iowa City: U of Iowa P, 1994. 79–87.

Whitman, Walt. *Democratic Vistas. Prose Works 1892*. Ed. Floyd Stovall. Vol. 2. New York: New York UP, 1964. 361–426.

See also CARLYLE, THOMAS; COMRADESHIP; DEMOCRACY; EQUALITY; FEUDALISM; FREEDOM; *GALAXY, THE*; INDIVIDUALISM; RELIGION

Denison, Flora MacDonald (1867–1921)

Flora Merrill grew up in rural Canada, and in 1892 she married Howard Denison. She worked as a businesswoman, a journalist, and a suffragist. Though Denison is best known for her efforts in the women's suffrage movement, she also established a Whitman club and edited *The Sunset of Bon Echo,* the club's journal.

Denison was profoundly influenced by Whitman's poetry. She saw Whitman as a self-expressive, democratic poet who wanted to destroy systems based on the inequality of men (and women). Her position as a regular columnist ("Flora MacDonald") for the Toronto *Sunday World* provided her the opportunity to disseminate Whitman's ideals and to speak for women and labor groups. After her term as president of the Canadian Suffrage Association (1911–1914), Denison founded Bon Echo, a resort for Whitman enthusiasts, on her own land as a Canadian monument to Whitman, believing that "Canada needs Whitman" (Denison, "Whitman" 4). She also edited *Sunset,* occasionally contributing articles about Whitman which reflect Whitman's stylistic influence. By founding a society for Whitman, providing a meeting place for it, and producing a journal, Denison helped to increase the popularity of Whitman's poetry.

Martha A. Kalnin

Bibliography

Denison, Flora MacDonald. "Flora MacDonald." *The Sunset of Bon Echo* 1.1 (1916): 7–9.

———. "Whitman." *The Sunset of Bon Echo* 1.1 (1916): 3–4.

Denison, Merrill. "Flora MacDonald Denison, Bon Echo, and Whitman." *Walt Whitman Birthplace Bulletin* 1 (1957): 17–19.

"Denison, Mrs. Flora MacDonald." *The Macmillan Dictionary of Canadian Biography*. Ed. W.A. McKay. 4th ed. Toronto: Macmillan, 1978. 206–207.

Stafford, Albert Ernest. "Crusts and Crumbs." *The Sunset of Bon Echo* 1.1 (1916): 12–15.

See also BON ECHO; CANADA, WHITMAN'S RECEPTION IN

Denver, Colorado

A city founded just east of the Rocky Mountains, Denver City was named after James W. Denver, governor of the Kansas Territory, in November 1858. The economy of Denver rose and fell with the successes and failures of the gold and silver mines in the nearby mountains. Railroads connected Denver to the national economy in 1870, and the following two decades were periods of tremendous population growth. When Colorado was granted statehood in 1876, Denver became its state capital.

Walt Whitman traveled to Denver in September of 1879 with J.M.W. Geist, E.K. Martin, and William W. Reitzel, at a time when the silver mines were drawing thousands of hopeful prospectors and curious tourists. Impressed by the mountain scenery and the organization of the city, Whitman also noted that the men of Denver had become a type unique to the Rocky Mountain region. He disapproved, on the other hand, of the attempts of Denver women to imitate eastern fashions. Nevertheless, Whitman stayed in Denver's American Hotel, one of the elegant buildings that had begun to replace the original log cabins of the city. Whitman spent a day visiting the Rocky Mountains during his stay in Denver, and he began the trip eastward the next day. This trip to Colorado was too late to influence much of Whitman's poetry, but his memories of Denver became a frequent part of his later correspondence and conversation.

Timothy Stifel

Bibliography

Eitner, Walter H. *Walt Whitman's Western Jaunt*. Lawrence: Regents Press of Kansas, 1981.

Ubbelohde, Carl, Maxine Benson, and Duane A. Smith. *A Colorado History*. 3rd ed. Boulder: Pruett, 1972.

See also ROCKY MOUNTAINS; TRAVELS, WHITMAN'S; WEST, THE AMERICAN

Dialectic

"Do I contradict myself?" Whitman asks at the end of "Song of Myself" (1855). "Very well then . . . I am large, I contain multitudes" (section 51). This impulsive, democratic embrace of contradiction, Whitman would claim years later, expressed at a deep level a rigorous and explicitly Hegelian dialectical logic which would become more explicit, and more important, in Whitman's later, post–Civil War work. "Only Hegel is fit for America—is large enough and free enough," he would write in an unpublished lecture on German philosophy (*Notebooks* 6:2011). In Whitman's adaptation of Hegel, the clash of contradictions—between individualism and democracy, life and death, civil war and union, nature and the machine—would become a source of energy for the emergence of a higher, spiritualized synthesis that was the historical destiny of American democracy. Of course, Hegel so described sounds much more like the expansive and free-wheeling Walt Whitman than the political conservative he actually was. Whitman clearly put Hegel to his own uses, embracing his philosophy in a schematic sense, but applying it idiosyncratically to the United States.

Whitman's most important sources in learning about Hegel were secondary works, especially Frederick Hedge's *Prose Writers of Germany* (1847) and Joseph Gostwick's *German Literature* (1849). By reading in such sources, Whitman had become familiar with Hegelian concepts by the time he began to produce *Leaves of Grass*. In some of his later work the Hegelian fingerprints are clearly visible; "Chanting the Square Deific" (1865), for example, is almost programmatic in its unfolding of a dialectic capped by the emergence of "spirit." "Passage to India" (1871) represents the movement of history itself as the unfolding of a progressive dialectical scheme, an idea which Whitman attributes properly to Hegel in a piece from *Specimen Days* entitled "Carlyle from American Points of View" (1882), in which he rejects Thomas Carlyle's pessimism about modern civilization and praises Hegel's "American" historical optimism.

Hegelian ideas represented for Whitman a way to invigorate Emersonian transcendentalism, removing the lingering phenomenological barrier it left between the individual philosophical subject, conceived by Ralph Waldo Emerson as disembodied mind or spirit, and the external realms of the physical body, of nature, and of society. At the same time, however, in just this opening up of the self to the body, and thus to a sensuous interplay with others and with nature, Whitman moves farthest from the valorization of universal reason over particular sensuous experience that characterizes the tradition of philosophical idealism which produced Hegel. For Hegel, as for Emerson, it was a founding assumption that the world, known truly, was most like a mind. Whitman's variation on this philosophical tradition was that the world, known dialectically not simply by reason, but also by physical, sensuous experience, was most like a human body; and the poems which come out of this sensuous epiphany— "Song of Myself" (1855), for example, or "Out of the Cradle Endlessly Rocking" (1860)—are those which readers over the years have agreed are Whitman's best. For whatever reason, then (perhaps out of a bid for intellectual respectability), it seems that Whitman protests Hegel's greatness, and influence, a little too much.

Indeed, as critics of Whitman ranging from F.O. Matthiessen to M. Wynn Thomas have pointed out, in his turn to sensuousness Whitman's thinking is much closer to the dialectical materialism of Karl Marx, who overturned Hegelian idealism by arguing that the full range of sensuous experience in the world determined rational consciousness and not the other way around. The evidence of Whitman's direct acquaintance with Marxist thought is slender, but the affinities between Whitman and Marx remain numerous and provocative: Whitman was sympathetic to the socialist movements of 1848, harshly critical of the rich and powerful, and an ardent advocate of labor. According to a perhaps apocryphal story recounted by Walter Grünzweig in *Constructing the German Walt Whitman,* Marx favored Whitman's poetry (particularly "Pioneers! O Pioneers!"), and Whitman was widely popular and officially accepted (however odd the latter may seem) in the German Democratic Republic (159–160).

If Whitman's links to Marxist dialectics mark the extent of his political and economic radicalism, however, they also highlight its limits. For Marx, dialectical materialism pointed to the abolition of both wealth and poverty in a socialist utopia, where the sufferings caused by the exploitation and alienation of the working classes would be overcome once and for all. But for Whitman, an exploited industrial proletariat was a European problem, not a problem with capitalism per se. For him, the end of a sensuous dialectic between self and world, as he would insist in poem after poem, is death; only in death does the self overcome alienation once and for all and merge with the world. Although this is a poetic image rather than a philosophical proposition, it implies in philosophical terms Whitman's sense that alienation, and more generally the problems of the human condition, were not finally obstacles to be overcome, but potential sources of beauty to be incorporated into an aesthetic view of the world, in which suffering, sorrow, and pain will always be essential moments in an endless and ultimately positive dialectical progress.

In practical terms, this means that Whitman accepted the basic premises of a liberal political economy, not simply despite their failings and contradictions but in a sense because of them. Thus in *Democratic Vistas* (1871) Whitman suggests that the internal contradictions afflicting American democracy will themselves become, by a process of dialectical transformation, a form of cultural "nutriment," feeding its further growth (*Complete* 470). Whitman's treatment of private property may serve to clarify this claim. On the one hand, he expresses what might be called the negative moment of a dialectical perspective on a property-based society, when he attacks the base materialism of modern industrial society, its widespread greed and selfishness, and its corresponding lack of concern with a shared culture, with the higher matters of literature, art, and spirituality. On the other hand, he insists that democracy requires "owners of houses and acres, and with cash in the bank—and with some cravings for literature, too" (471). The dialectical turn comes here when the acquisitive drive turns seamlessly into "cravings for literature"; selfish materialism is not eliminated but rather transformed into the very thing that redeems it. Democratic literature, in other words,

is the form of private property that transforms the problems of liberal society into advantages, that transforms a hostility to higher culture into the desire to produce and acquire that culture. Proprietary acquisitiveness is not simply what threatens to drive Americans apart, he suggests; it is also what promises to hold them together.

However sound or unsound this logic may be in political terms, it is arguably central to Whitman's poetics, which are more deeply grounded, finally, in the sensuous embrace of dialectical tension and contradiction than in a vision of dialectical synthesis. Such would seem to be the point of his choice in *Democratic Vistas* of the Civil War as a symbol of America's power to balance contradictions. Such, too, may be the point of his call there for "great poems of death" to crown the literary culture of the United States (*Complete* 497) and of his encouragement to true believers in the historically appointed triumph of democracy: "Thus national rage, fury, discussion, etc., better than content," he urges (473), and "*Vive,* the attack—the perennial assault" (472).

Terry Mulcaire

Bibliography

Breitweiser, Mitchell. "Who Speaks in Whitman's Poems?" *Bucknell Review* 28.1 (1983): 121–143.

Grünzweig, Walter. *Constructing the German Walt Whitman.* Iowa City: U of Iowa P, 1995.

Hegel, Georg Wilhelm Friedrich. *Phenomenology of Spirit.* Oxford: Clarendon, 1977.

Kojève, Alexandre. *Introduction to the Reading of Hegel: Lectures on the Phenomenology of Spirit.* Ed. Alan Bloom. Ithaca, N.Y.: Cornell UP, 1969.

Marx, Karl. *Economic and Philosophic Manuscripts of 1844.* Moscow: Foreign Languages Publishing House, 1959.

Marx, Karl, and Friedrich Engels. *The German Ideology.* 1938. New York: International Publishers, 1972.

Maslan, Mark. "Whitman and His Doubles: Division and Union in *Leaves of Grass* and Its Critics." *American Literary History* 6 (1994): 119–139.

Matthiessen, F.O. *American Renaissance.* New York: Oxford UP, 1941.

Stovall, Floyd. *The Foreground of "Leaves of Grass."* Charlottesville: UP of Virginia, 1974.

D

Thomas, M. Wynn. *The Lunar Light of Whitman's Poetry.* Cambridge, Mass.: Harvard UP, 1987.

Whitman, Walt. *Complete Poetry and Selected Prose.* Ed. James E. Miller, Jr. Boston: Houghton Mifflin, 1959.

———. *Notebooks and Unpublished Prose Manuscripts.* Ed. Edward F. Grier. Vol. 6. New York: New York UP, 1984.

See also CONTRADICTION; DEMOCRATIC VISTAS; HEGEL, GEORG WILHELM FRIEDRICH; INFLUENCES ON WHITMAN, PRINCIPAL

Dickens, Charles (1812–1870)

Author of such classic novels as *Oliver Twist* (1838), *Bleak House* (1853), and *Great Expectations* (1861), Charles Dickens, like Whitman, was a journalist as well as a creative writer. Because in both his fiction and nonfiction Dickens advocates social reform, Whitman declared Dickens to be a democratic writer.

Whitman makes this declaration in a February 1842 *Brother Jonathan* article entitled "Boz and Democracy." Whitman responds to critics of Dickens who argued that the novelist's portrayal of wicked, lower-class characters undermined the cause of democracy. Whitman counters: "'A democratic writer,' I take it, is one, the tendency of whose passages is, to destroy those old land-marks which pride and fashion have set up . . . one whose lines are imbued, from preface to finis, with that philosophy which teaches to pull down the high and bring up the low. I consider Mr. Dickens to be a democratic writer" ("Boz" 243).

Whitman continues his defense of Dickens's portrayal of wicked characters in an April 1842 New York *Aurora* article attributed to him entitled "Dickens and Democracy." Here, the author insists that Dickens is a lover of humanity and a believer in human virtue, and only portrays vice in order to thwart it by negative example. Whitman makes his final assertion of Dickens's democratic sentiments in an 1846 Brooklyn *Daily Eagle* article entitled "Boz and His New Paper" in which Whitman claims Dickens is "staunch for the Democratic movement" (*Gathering* 2:257).

Except for these newspaper pieces, Whitman's writings contain few references to Dickens. Whitman does, however, summarize his attitude toward Dickens in an 1888 conversation with Horace Traubel. In response to

Traubel's query about Whitman's "general feeling towards Dickens," Whitman responds that it is one "of great admiration" (Traubel 553).

Vickie L. Taft

Bibliography
Traubel, Horace. *With Walt Whitman in Camden.* Vol. 2. New York: Appleton, 1908.

Whitman, Walt. "Boz and Democracy." *Brother Jonathan* 26 February 1842: 243–244.

———. *The Gathering of the Forces.* Ed. Cleveland Rodgers and John Black. 2 vols. New York: Putnam, 1920.

———. *Walt Whitman of the New York Aurora.* Ed. Joseph Jay Rubin and Charles H. Brown. State College, Pa.: Bald Eagle, 1950.

See also READING, WHITMAN'S

Dickinson, Emily (1830–1886)

An American poet who once mockingly defined herself as a "Nobody," the reclusive, posthumously published, psychologically powerful Dickinson is often competitively compared with the expansive, gregarious Whitman who self-identified as a "kosmos." Feminist critics in particular have been fascinated by the contrasts between them: Dickinson writing richly elliptical, intimate lyrics for herself and for carefully selected private audiences; Whitman writing dazzlingly capacious prose poems for the world at large and for aggressively imagined future generations. Such comparisons between the public and the private poet, though radical oversimplifications of two enormously complex careers, are perhaps inevitable. Dickinson claimed never to have read Whitman's poetry, which her friend the influential editor Josiah Gilbert Holland branded as "disgraceful." And Whitman had never heard of her. Yet during the 1890s, when Dickinson's work was first published, reviewers compared her to Whitman because of her unprecedented transgressions of form. In that sense, Whitman's free-verse style helped to prepare the way for Dickinson's critical reception, which though belated, justified her belief that "Each Life Converges to some Centre." For Dickinson, that center was her poetry.

Highly educated, an avid correspondent and voracious reader, Dickinson had a local reputation as "the Myth of Amherst" before her death at the age of fifty-five of Bright's disease, a kidney disorder. But only eleven of her nearly eighteen hundred short poems were published during her lifetime. She never persuasively explained her choice of a noncareer, instead defining her poetic identity through a series of paradoxical contradictions, in which selecting "her own Society" was mysteriously at odds with her longing for fame. "I smile when you suggest that I delay 'to publish,'" she explained in 1862 to Thomas Wentworth Higginson, a radical reformer and literary critic with whom she had just initiated a crucial correspondence, "that being foreign to my thought, as Firmament to Fin." Yet she added the caveat, "If fame belonged to me, I could not escape her" (*Letters* 2:408). Dickinson's cult of nonpublication—for such it was—seemingly depended on the theory that a woman poet who valued her spiritual autonomy could not risk the commodification of her art through print. Time has justified both her caution and her self-confidence.

Vivian R. Pollak

Bibliography

Dickinson, Emily. *The Letters of Emily Dickinson.* Ed. Thomas H. Johnson. 3 vols. Cambridge, Mass.: Harvard UP, 1958.
———. *The Poems of Emily Dickinson.* Ed. Thomas H. Johnson. 3 vols. Cambridge, Mass.: Harvard UP, 1955.
Diehl, Joanne Feit. *Women Poets and the American Sublime.* Bloomington: Indiana UP, 1990.
Gilbert, Sandra M. "The American Sexual Poetics of Walt Whitman and Emily Dickinson." *Reconstructing American Literary History.* Ed. Sacvan Bercovitch. Cambridge, Mass.: Harvard UP, 1986. 123–154.
Pollak, Vivian R. *Dickinson: The Anxiety of Gender.* Ithaca, N.Y.: Cornell UP, 1984.
Salska, Agnieszka. *Walt Whitman and Emily Dickinson: Poetry of the Central Consciousness.* Philadelphia: U of Pennsylvania P, 1985.
Sewall, Richard B. *The Life of Emily Dickinson.* 2 vols. New York: Farrar, Strauss and Giroux, 1974.

See also HIGGINSON, THOMAS WENTWORTH

Dictionaries

Comprehensive dictionaries of American English were a new phenomenon in Whitman's lifetime, and he quickly fell in love with them. Whitman was still a schoolboy when Noah Webster issued his *American Dictionary of the English Language,* and he was a young man when the great "war of the dictionaries" broke out between Webster's successors and Joseph Emerson Worcester, who issued more conservative, British-oriented dictionaries that sought to counter Webster's brasher and more nationalistic wordbooks. Beginning in the 1840s and lasting until the 1870s, Webster and Worcester dictionaries competed against each other for the right to define the scope, direction, and rules of American English. Each edition of each dictionary increased in size, often dramatically. Whitman owned copies of both Webster and Worcester, and for a while he even considered entering the battle himself; he made substantial notes for his own dictionary, perhaps imagining a battle of the W's—Webster, Worcester, and Whitman. He kept lists of words he felt should be included in an American dictionary, he noted odd pronunciations, and he singled out useful foreign words and phrases that he thought the language would do well to absorb. He took careful notes on the long introductory essay in Webster's dictionary, arguing with Webster as he struggled to arrive at his own theory of language, a theory he expressed most fully in his set of notes now known as *An American Primer.*

In the *Primer,* he propounded a program for expanding the American lexicon by creating needed new words and by recognizing and celebrating words that had been excluded from the standard lexicon for various discriminatory reasons. He said we needed a "Real Dictionary," by which he meant one that would be fully inclusive, as democratic as his own idealized America, accepting and recognizing "all words that exist in use, the bad words as well as any" (*Daybooks* 3:734–735). Such a dictionary would be compiled by the "true lexicographer" (*Notebooks* 5:1704), who would go among all social classes, all races, all occupations, and gather the actual words in use.

Whitman's imagined Real Dictionary would far exceed even Webster's in size and scope, but he was nonetheless exhilarated by the phenomenal growth in each Webster edition, and he kept a careful record of the exponential increase in the number of words in the American language. For him, a dictionary was like the compost heap of language, the place where the culture stored the word-elements out of which all poetry and history would arise; a nation could, in some essential way, only be as large and as open as its dictionaries, which provided the words to express its ideals and laws and stories.

So it is not surprising that dictionaries appear in Whitman's poems, from his inclusion of the "lexicographer" among the experts of "positive science" and "exact demonstration" in "Song of Myself" (section 23), to his expression of frustration about the words that have not yet appeared in our dictionaries, and thus the crucial thoughts that are still literally beyond expression: "There is that in me—I do not know what it is . . / It is not in any dictionary, utterance, symbol" ("Song of Myself," section 50). In "A Song of the Rolling Earth," Whitman calls on poets to write "the dictionaries of words that print cannot touch" (section 3)—that is, to reach their voices out to the things and ideas that language has not yet named, that humans have remained ignorant of because language has not yet evolved to the point where it can express them. As with so much else in Whitman, dictionaries were evolutionary organisms, growing quickly, absorbing new arenas of experience, and piling up words that would eventually make a democracy speakable and thus possible.

Whitman continued to use dictionaries assiduously throughout his life; he once made a note to himself to "get in the habit of tracing words to their root-meaning" (*Daybooks* 3:725), and etymological science—which was just developing during his adult life—was a source of real fascination for him: "Every principal word . . . in our language," he wrote, "is a condensed octavo volume, or many volumes" (*Notebooks* 5:1699). As late as 1891, he was still trading a copy of the latest issue of *Leaves of Grass* for a copy of the newest Merriam *Webster's,* and he was also following the great flowering of lexicography and etymological science evident in the first volumes of the *Oxford English Dictionary,* appearing in the decade before Whitman's death. It is useful to remember Whitman's love of dictionaries when reading his poems, for his words often play on the etymologies and definitions of the particular dictionaries he was consulting at the time he wrote each poem.

Ed Folsom

Bibliography

Cmiel, Kenneth. *Democratic Eloquence: The Fight Over Popular Speech in Nineteenth-Century America.* New York: William Morrow, 1990.

Dressman, Michael Rowan. "Walt Whitman's Plans for the Perfect Dictionary." *Studies in the American Renaissance,* 1979. Ed. Joel Myerson. Boston: Twayne, 1979. 457–474.

Folsom, Ed. *Walt Whitman's Native Representations.* Cambridge: Cambridge UP, 1994.

Whitman, Walt. *Daybooks and Notebooks.* Ed. William White. 3 vols. New York: New York UP, 1978.

———. *Notebooks and Unpublished Prose Manuscripts.* Ed. Edward F. Grier. 6 vols. New York: New York UP, 1984.

See also AMERICAN PRIMER, AN; FOREIGN LANGUAGE BORROWINGS; LANGUAGE; SLANG

"Dirge for Two Veterans" (1865)

This poem, first published in *Sequel to Drum-Taps* (1865–1866), continued essentially unrevised through the remainder of its publication history. The poet's English biographer, John Bailey, called it "incomparably fine" (qtd. in Whitman 314n).

One of Whitman's few poems with a formal structure, each quatrain begins and ends with short lines of as few as four syllables, while the two middle lines are as long as fifteen syllables. This cadence echoes the short-long-long-short drum beats in the dirge that Whitman is listening to as he attends the funeral of a father and son who died in the Civil War.

The poem employs alliteration in its line endings ("sunbeam . . . Sabbath"), as well as iteration ("round moon . . . phantom moon . . . silent moon") and assonance ("moon . . . bugles . . . through . . . soothe . . . you"), yet the lack of true rhyme also creates a kind of dissonance. Whitman addresses the dead as "my soldiers" as if he himself embodies all America, thus expressing national gratitude as well as grief. He dramatizes the poem's theme by personifying the moon as a "sorrowful vast phantom" weeping for the children she has lost. The sound devices and imagery produce a powerful lament over the death of two generations that gave their blood to preserve the Union.

The final stanza hints at the healing which results from the tragedy: the war dead are memorialized by celestial light, martial music, and the poet's love. Preceding the more optimistic and mystical "Over the Carnage Rose Prophetic a Voice," the mournful "Dirge" becomes an expression of America's hope that the extraordinary love epitomized in the sacrifice of the father and son will eventually conquer all hatred and division.

Matthew Ignoffo

Bibliography

Bensko, John. "Narrating Position and Force in Whitman's *Drum-Taps*." *Walt Whitman Centennial International Symposium*. Ed. Manuel Villar Raso, Miguel Martinez Lopez, and Rona Morillas Sanchez. Granada: Universidad de Granada, 1992. 33–43.

Burrison, William. "Whitman's *Drum-Taps* Reviewed: The Good, Gray, Tender Mother-Man and the Fierce, Red, Convulsive Rhythm of War." *Walt Whitman: Here and Now*. Ed. Joann P. Krieg. Westport, Conn.: Greenwood, 1985. 157–169.

Davis, Robert Leigh. "Whitman's Tympanum: A Reading of *Drum-Taps*." *ATQ* 6 (1992): 163–175.

Ignoffo, Matthew. *What the War Did to Whitman*. New York: Vantage, 1975.

Whitman, Walt. *Leaves of Grass: Comprehensive Reader's Edition*. Ed. Harold W. Blodgett and Sculley Bradley. New York: New York UP, 1965.

See also CIVIL WAR, THE; "DRUM-TAPS"; "OVER THE CARNAGE ROSE PROPHETIC A VOICE"; *SEQUEL TO DRUM-TAPS*

Donaldson, Thomas (1843–1898)

Thomas Donaldson was a Philadelphia attorney who authored a number of government documents on American Indians and the law of public domain as it related to the American West. Whitman noted meeting Donaldson, then an agent for the Smithsonian Institute, on 10 October 1882. He characterized him as "my stout, gentlemanly friend, free talker" (356). Whitman met Bram Stoker at Donaldson's house in 1884 and visited with Stoker again in 1885 when Donaldson accompanied Stoker to the poet's residence in Camden. Donaldson secured annual ferry passes for Whitman that made it possible for him to range beyond Camden to Philadelphia in spite of his reduced mobility. After the winter of 1884–1885, when Donaldson realized that Whitman had become almost house-bound, he was instrumental in raising money for a horse and buggy with which he surprised him in 1885. He was a pallbearer at Whitman's funeral in 1892.

Steven Schroeder

Bibliography

Donaldson, Thomas. *Walt Whitman the Man*. New York: Harper, 1896.

Whitman, Walt. *The Correspondence*. Ed. Edwin Haviland Miller. Vol. 3. New York: New York UP, 1964.

See also PHILADELPHIA, PENNSYLVANIA

Dos Passos, John (1896–1970)

In 1938 Jean-Paul Sartre hailed John Dos Passos as the greatest writer of his generation. Although Dos Passos's reputation has slipped in the intervening years, he remains widely admired for his innovations in fictional technique. Whitman was of central importance to his career from his first essay, "Against American Literature" (1916), which asked, "[S]hall we pick up the glove Walt Whitman threw at the feet of posterity?" (38), to his last work, *Century's Ebb* (1975), a posthumously published novel addressed to the poet.

The illegitimate son of a prominent Portuguese-American lawyer who wrote a treatise on Anglo-Saxon supremacy, John Madison (as Dos Passos was known until 1912) grew up as a loner who identified with the powerless. A leftist political orientation marks his early work, culminating in his trilogy, *The 42nd Parallel* (1930), *1919* (1932), and *The Big Money* (1936). These novels, reissued with a prologue and an epilogue, make up the monumental *U.S.A.* trilogy (1938). Using four modes—"newsreel," biography, narrative, and "camera eye"—Dos Passos successfully blends history and fiction. He invokes Whitman periodically in *U.S.A.*, most notably perhaps in his account of the execution of Nicola Sacco and Bartolomeo Vanzetti, a climactic moment in the novel.

In the final decades of his career Dos Passos turned to the political right. Once a fellow traveler with the Communist party, he became an admirer of Joseph McCarthy. Despite his fundamental shift in outlook, Dos Passos maintained his admiration for Whitman, asking, in his final book, "Here, now, today, if you came back to us, Walt Whitman, what would you say?" (*Century's Ebb* 13).

Kenneth M. Price

Bibliography
Baker, John D. "Whitman and Dos Passos: A Sense of Communion." *Walt Whitman Review* 20 (1974): 30–33.
Dos Passos, John. "Against American Literature." *John Dos Passos: The Major Nonfictional Prose.* Ed. Donald Pizer. Detroit: Wayne State UP, 1988. 36–38.
———. *Century's Ebb: The Thirteenth Chronicle.* Boston: Gambit, 1975.
Hughson, Lois. "In Search of the True America: Dos Passos' Debt to Whitman in *U.S.A.*" *Modern Fiction Studies* 19 (1973): 179–192.
Price, Kenneth M. "Whitman, Dos Passos, and 'Our Storybook Democracy.'" *Walt Whitman: The Centennial Essays.* Ed. Ed Folsom. Iowa City: U of Iowa P, 1994. 217–225.
Weeks, Robert P. "The Novel as Poem: Whitman's Legacy to Dos Passos." *Modern Fiction Studies* 26 (1980): 431–446.

See also LEGACY, WHITMAN'S

Douglas, Stephen Arnold (1813–1861)

As United States senator from Illinois and chairman of the Committee on Territories between 1847 and 1859, Stephen Douglas is important for his role in debates concerning the expansion of slavery. During the late 1840s he articulated the doctrine of "popular sovereignty," which asserted that the federal government should leave legislation regarding slavery to the discretion of individual states. Douglas sought to institute this doctrine through the Kansas-Nebraska Act, which he pushed through Congress in 1854. Douglas's bill was perceived as a threat by Northern abolitionists and working class whites because it implied a repeal of the Missouri Compromise (1820).

Debate over the Kansas-Nebraska bill preoccupied the nation as Whitman composed the first edition of *Leaves of Grass,* but he did not explicitly mention Douglas until four years later, during the Lincoln-Douglas debates. Writing for the Brooklyn *Daily Times* in 1858, Whitman

editorialized that "of the two, Mr. Lincoln seems to have had the advantage thus far in the war of words" (Whitman 96). Nonetheless, Douglas won re-election to the Senate and earned a place in Whitman's esteem. Whitman wrote that Douglas's election represented "a victory of the independent representative over the party dictator" (98). This remark is less a jibe at Lincoln's position in the Republican party than an expression of respect for Douglas, who had become a maverick within the Democratic party. Whitman's appreciation of Douglas's victory reflects a transitional phase in his own political loyalties. Like Douglas's, Whitman's lifelong loyalty to the Democratic party was being tested by the Democrats' strong proslavery stance. Though both men opposed slavery, they also yearned for a compromise that might preserve the Union. In this respect, Douglas's advocacy of popular sovereignty is analogous to Whitman's free-soilism. When national unity proved impossible to maintain, Douglas advised a vigorous prosecution of war and supported his rival from Illinois, Abraham Lincoln.

T. Gregory Garvey

Bibliography
Erkkila, Betsy. *Whitman the Political Poet.* New York: Oxford UP, 1989.
Johannsen, Robert W. *Stephen A. Douglas.* New York: Oxford UP, 1973.
Reynolds, David S. *Walt Whitman's America: A Cultural Biography.* New York: Knopf, 1995.
Whitman, Walt. *I Sit and Look Out: Editorials from the Brooklyn Daily Times.* Ed. Emory Holloway and Vernolian Schwarz. New York: Columbia UP, 1932.

See also DEMOCRATIC PARTY; FREE SOIL PARTY; LINCOLN, ABRAHAM; SLAVERY AND ABOLITIONISM

Douglass, Frederick (1818–1895)

Orator, writer, newspaper editor, and activist, Frederick Douglass was born a slave on the eastern shore of Maryland. He learned to read at age nine while working for his owner's brother in Maryland, and then escaped in 1838 to the North, where he became active in the abolitionist movement, working with people like William Lloyd Garrison. Douglass soon became a popular figure on the abolitionist circuit, telling his story of his experiences in and escape from slavery. In 1845 Douglass published *The Narrative of the Life of a Slave,* the first of three autobiographies he would write in his life.

In 1847 Douglass began his own newspaper, *The North Star,* in part because of his belief that blacks should take leadership roles in the abolitionist movement. He was a speaker at the 1848 Free Soil party convention in Buffalo, where Whitman, who was participating as a delegate from Brooklyn, heard him speak. Years later, writing for the Brooklyn *Daily Times,* Whitman would praise Douglass's voice as "loud, clear and sonorous" (qtd. in Reynolds 123).

From the beginning of the Civil War, Douglass campaigned ceaselessly to frame the war as a struggle against slavery. In 1876 he became the first African American appointed to a government post that required Senate approval when Rutherford B. Hayes appointed him United States marshal of the District of Columbia, and he later went on to become minister to Haiti.

Though he never met Whitman, Douglass offers a number of interesting parallels to the poet. Both men spent the main portion of their literary careers rewriting one book, both men were passionately involved in politics, and for both men the Civil War was a watershed event that required them to rethink their approach to life, literature, and politics.

Andrew C. Higgins

Bibliography

Andrews, William L., ed. *Critical Essays on Frederick Douglass.* Boston: Hall, 1991.

Douglass, Frederick. *The Life and Writing of Frederick Douglass.* Ed. Philip S. Foner. 5 vols. New York: International, 1950–1955.

———. *My Bondage and My Freedom.* 1855. Urbana: U of Illinois P, 1987.

———. *Narrative of the Life of Frederick Douglass, an American Slave.* 1845. New York: St. Martin's, 1993.

McFeely, William S. *Frederick Douglass.* New York: Simon and Schuster, 1991.

Sundquist, Eric J., ed. *Frederick Douglass: New Literary and Historical Essays.* New York: Cambridge UP, 1990.

See also Buffalo Free Soil Convention; Civil War, The; Slavery and Abolitionism

Dowden, Edward (1843–1913)

Born in Cork, Ireland, Edward Dowden was educated at Queen's College, Cork, and at Trinity College, Dublin, where he became professor of English literature in 1867. His substantial literary reputation rests upon his prolific writings about William Shakespeare; he also wrote biographies of Robert Southey, Robert Browning, Percy Bysshe Shelley, and Montaigne. Whitman called Dowden "one of the best of the late commentators on Shakspere" (Whitman 884). As did so many other British scholars and writers, Dowden readily accepted Whitman as the new poet, the new voice of America. He included in his *Studies in Literature, 1789–1877* (1887) a long essay on Whitman, ranking him with other luminaries and praising his poetry's originality and its musical qualities despite the absence of an immediately discernible prosody. Dowden viewed Whitman as the representative of a new democracy in art, noting in particular that his subject matter included such figures as "all who toil upon the sea, the city artisan, the woodsman and the trapper" (Dowden 489).

Philip W. Leon

Bibliography

Dowden, Edward. "The Poetry of Democracy: Walt Whitman." *Studies in Literature, 1789–1877.* By Dowden. 4th ed. London: Kegan Paul, Trench, 1887. 468–523.

Whitman, Walt. *The Poetry and Prose of Walt Whitman.* Ed. Louis Untermeyer. New York: Simon and Schuster, 1949.

See also British Isles, Whitman in the; Ireland, Whitman in

Doyle, Peter (1843–1907)

The romantic friendship that Walt Whitman shared with Peter Doyle embodied the "love of comrades" celebrated in Whitman's "Calamus" poems. Their thirty-year friendship (1865–1892) left a legacy of loving letters from the older man to his younger companion which are invaluable reference points for the student seeking to understand Whitman's emotional and sexual nature.

Doyle and Whitman met one winter's evening in Washington, D.C. The twenty-one-year-old Doyle was the conductor on a Pennsylvania Avenue horsecar, and the forty-five-year-old Whitman was the car's sole passenger. Doyle recalled, "We were familiar at once—I put my hand on his knee—we understood . . . From that time on, we were the biggest sort of friends" (qtd. in Bucke 23).

In some respects Doyle seems an unlikely companion for "America's poet." Born in Limerick, Ireland, on 3 June 1843, and reared in America's South, Doyle came into manhood armed as a Confederate soldier against the Union that Whitman held so dear. A marginally literate workingman, Doyle was no intellectual or social match for Whitman, the well-known poet and federal employee whose Washington friends included Lincoln's former secretary, John Hay, Ohio Congressman James Garfield, and Attorney General J. Hubley Ashton.

Yet, in ways that mattered more, Doyle was precisely the kind of man Whitman loved best. The poet always followed his own admonition, laid down in the Preface to the 1855 *Leaves of Grass,* to "go freely with powerful uneducated persons" (Whitman 715). In his youthful grace and good health, Doyle was a welcome tonic for the war-weary Whitman, who had spent the previous two years in Washington's army hospitals nursing the wounded. They spent long afternoons riding the streetcars, or eating fresh fruits at Center Market. Evenings were reserved for moonlit walks along the Potomac River that had Whitman reciting Shakespeare's sonnets to Doyle, and Doyle relating his favorite limericks to Whitman. Whitman also relished the opportunity to be part of the young man's large family circle. It included Doyle's widowed mother, Catherine, and his younger brother Edward and sister Margaret, for whom Pete made a home. Also nearby were the families of married brothers James and Francis, and aunt Ann and uncle Michael Nash, whom Whitman counted among his dear friends.

Doyle is usually associated with Whitman's "Calamus" poems, although he did not serve as

Walt Whitman with Peter Doyle, the poet's close friend and companion. Courtesy of the Library of Congress.

the muse for these tender verses first published in 1860. The satisfaction that Whitman derived from his relationship with Doyle, however, may have influenced him to drop several of the more anxiety-ridden "Calamus" poems in editions of *Leaves of Grass* brought out after 1865. Whitman's expressed affection for the former Confederate artilleryman reinforced the theme of reconciliation in the poet's war writings. The eyewitness narrative of Lincoln's assassination found in *Memoranda During the War* (1875–1876) may have been inspired by Doyle, who was at Ford's Theater on that fateful Good Friday.

A stroke that Whitman suffered on 23 January 1873 caused him to settle later that year in Camden, New Jersey, with his brother George and sister-in-law Louisa. The intensity of Whitman's friendship with Doyle waned with time and distance. In New Jersey, Harry Stafford provided Whitman with a measure of the companionship that Doyle was not there to give.

In the mid-1880s Whitman and Doyle renewed their intimacy when Doyle—now employed by the Pennsylvania Railroad as a baggage master—settled in Philadelphia and made weekly visits to Whitman in Camden. The round-the-clock presence of caretakers during the poet's last years eventually alienated Doyle, whose calls became infrequent. Before Whitman's death on 26 March 1892, Doyle explained to Whitman the reason why he visited so rarely, and the old man understood. Doyle attended Whitman's funeral at Harleigh Cemetery.

Peter Doyle made a lasting contribution to Whitman biography in 1897 when he allowed Richard Maurice Bucke to edit and publish Whitman's letters to Doyle, which Doyle had entrusted to Bucke in 1880. Included with the letters was Bucke's interview of Doyle, which Henry James in his 1898 review of the book called "the most charming passage in the volume" (260).

Doyle was a member of the Walt Whitman Fellowship and enjoyed the friendship of Horace and Ann Traubel, Gustave Percival Wiksell, and publisher Laurens Maynard. Doyle continued to work for the Pennsylvania Railroad until his death on 19 April 1907 at age 63. Peter Doyle is buried in Congressional Cemetery in Washington, D.C.

Martin G. Murray

Bibliography

Bucke, Richard Maurice, ed. *Calamus: A Series of Letters Written During the Years 1868–1880 by Walt Whitman to a Young Friend (Peter Doyle)*. Boston: Small, Maynard, 1897.

James, Henry. "Henry James on Walt Whitman, 1898." *Walt Whitman: The Critical Heritage*. Ed. Milton Hindus. London: Routledge, 1971. 259–260.

Murray, Martin G. "Pete the Great: A Biography of Peter Doyle." *Walt Whitman Quarterly Review* 12 (1994): 1–51.

Whitman, Walt. *Leaves of Grass: Comprehensive Reader's Edition*. Ed. Harold W. Blodgett and Sculley Bradley. New York: New York UP, 1965.

See also "CALAMUS"; COMRADESHIP; WASHINGTON, D.C.; SEX AND SEXUALITY; STAFFORD, HARRY L.

Drinkard, Dr. William B. (1842–1877)

In 1873 Dr. William Beverly Drinkard of Washington, D.C., treated Whitman when he suffered the first of his paralytic strokes. Drinkard attended Georgetown University and the Lycée Imperial, Orléans, France. He studied for a time in Paris and London before returning to Washington, where he received his M.D. from the National Medical College in 1866. Elected professor of anatomy at the National Medical College, he also was a founder of the Washington Children's Hospital.

On 23 January 1873 Whitman suffered a paralysis of his left leg. He wrote his mother, assuring her that he had "a first-rate physician Dr. Drinkard" (Whitman 192). Drinkard treated Whitman with electric shock for several weeks, rubbing his leg and thigh for about twenty minutes with an imperceptible current, giving, perhaps, a new perspective to Whitman's term "body electric." Drinkard's treatment record says Whitman's "habits of life, tastes and mental constitution are, I think, the most natural I have ever encountered" (qtd. in Feinberg 836–837).

Philip W. Leon

Bibliography

Barnshaw, Harold D. "Walt Whitman's Medical Problems While in Camden." *Academy of Medicine of New Jersey Bulletin* 16 (1970): 35–39.

Feinberg, Charles E. "Walt Whitman and His Doctors." *Archives of Internal Medicine* 114 (1964): 834–842.

Whitman, Walt. *The Correspondence*. Ed. Edwin Haviland Miller. Vol. 2. New York: New York UP, 1961.

See also HEALTH

"Drum-Taps" (1865)

"Drum-Taps" is a cluster of forty-three poems about the Civil War, and stands as the finest war poetry written by an American. In these poems Whitman presents, often in innovative ways, his emotional experience of the Civil War. The cluster as a whole traces the sequence of Whitman's varying responses, from initial excitement (and doubt), to direct observation, to a deep compassionate involvement with the casualties of the armed conflict. The mood of the poems varies dramatically, from excitement to woe, from distant observation to engagement, from belief to resignation. Written ten years after "Song of Myself," these poems are more concerned with history than the self, more aware of the precariousness of America's present and future than of its expansive promise. In "Drum-Taps" Whitman projects himself as a mature poet, directly touched by human suffering, in clear distinction to the ecstatic, naive, electric voice which marked the original edition of *Leaves of Grass*.

First published as a separate book of fifty-three poems in 1865, the second edition of *Drum-Taps* included eighteen more poems (*Sequel to Drum-Taps*). Later the book was folded into *Leaves of Grass* as the cluster "Drum-Taps," though many individual poems were rearranged and placed in other sections. By the final version (1881), "Drum-Taps" contained only forty-three poems, all but five from *Drum-Taps* and *Sequel*. Readers looking for a reliable guide to the diverse issues raised in the cluster would be advised to turn to the fine study by Betsy Erkkila. Interested readers will find the more ironic and contemplative poems of Herman Melville's *Battle-Pieces and Aspects of the War* (1866) a remarkable counterpoint to Whitman's poems.

The first eight poems in the sequence express Whitman's exuberance, and his doubts, as America headed into a fratricidal war. Deeply threatened by a divided nation, Whitman insists that the American union should be maintained at all costs. His perspective on the war was very close to that of Abraham Lincoln, who likewise maintained that the central issue in the war was the preservation of the Union. (Most of their contemporaries saw slavery, not the Union, as the war's most pressing issue.) Since Whitman's earlier prose and poetry had explored a parallel between an American political union which was comprised of diverse states, and even more diverse peoples, and the coherence of the poet's own identity, formed of his large and diverse needs and interests, he felt the threat of the nation's dissolution keenly on personal as well as political grounds.

The opening poems of "Drum-Taps" represent a call to arms, a passionate cry to defend the imperiled nation. Most readers find these poems overly rhetorical, though M. Wynn Thomas argues cogently that the long colloquy "Song of the Banner at Daybreak" vividly presents a dialectical opposition between democratic brotherhood and democratic renewal (disturbingly, renewed through violence), an opposition deeply embedded in Whitman's own consciousness. A similar colloquy occurs in "The Centenarian's Story"; a veteran of Washington's campaign recalls for a Civil War volunteer the heroism of war, while simultaneously recollecting, "It sickens me yet, that slaughter!"

Following are four poems unique in Whitman's work, precise word-pictures of men at war which have been variously and oppositely described as imagist, naturalist, subjective, and objective. What is clear and unarguable is the manner in which these four poems exploit a mode of seeing associated with the discovery of photography. They possess the same visual clarity, the same precise focus, found in contemporary photographs of the war, such as those taken by Mathew Brady. Photography was in Whitman's time a novel technology, and the Civil War provided an important opportunity to explore the aesthetic and communicative powers of the new medium of film. Whitman's vision is shaped in these four poems by this new art.

The poems describe an army either at march or at rest: at march in "Cavalry Crossing a Ford," at rest as day ends and night descends in "Bivouac on a Mountain Side"; marching toward combat in "An Army Corps on the March," sleeping at night as seen by a sleepless soldier who sits beside his campfire in "By the Bivouac's Fitful Flame." Each reveals the lyric beauty of a collective body of men moving or resting. Whitman presents to the reader the immediacy of military experience, the sense of being part of an army and observing it from the midst of a military campaign. Informed by the many letters he received from his brother George during his four years of service in the Union army, by conversations he had with wounded soldiers, and by his own trips to the front lines, the four poems are recreations of the perceptions that would have been available to an ordinary soldier.

The following group of five poems confront, in measured but deeply moving fashion, the injury, death, and suffering occasioned by the Civil War. The first, "Come Up from the Fields Father," is a poem of sentiment, since it draws its emotional power from family tragedy. Recounting the experience of a mother inconsolable when she learns of the injury and death of her son in battle, Whitman uses maternal loss to convey the ineradicable pain occasioned by the violence of war. That the poem is held in critical disfavor by some critics today reveals more about changes in literary sensibility, from sentimentality to ironic distance, than it does about the poem itself.

"Vigil Strange I Kept on the Field One Night" is an elegiac meditation on the comradeship felt on the battlefield. Whitman always sought the comradeship he celebrated so powerfully in the "Calamus" sequence. The Civil War, despite or perhaps because of its violence, disruption, and widespread suffering, paradoxically allowed him to experience that comradeship on the most profound level. The narrator in "Vigil Strange" reveals his intimate relation with the soldier who dies by his side in battle, and to whose corpse he returns at night. The imagery of the poem ("one touch of your hand to mine O boy . . . son of responding kisses . . . you dearest comrade . . . I faithfully loved you . . . boy of responding kisses") conveys physical love as well as intimacy. The biographer Paul Zweig sees in Whitman's ability to touch and comfort soldiers—Whitman nursed and nurtured over eighty thousand injured men in Washington hospitals during the war—an acceptance of the human body and of the profound links between all men. He perceptively points out that prior to the cataclysm of the Civil War and Whitman's active involvement in nursing wounded soldiers, the poet had only been able to prophesy and not experience this comradeship. The critic Joseph Cady sees "Vigil Strange" as Whitman's attempt, in a culture that as yet had no word for "homosexual," to present to readers the physical and emotional tenderness that he recognized could exist between men.

An essential companion to reading "Drum-Taps" is Whitman's autobiographical memoir, *Specimen Days*. The large central portion of that work recounts Whitman's daily experiences and meditations during the Civil War. Consonant with the middle section of "Drum-Taps," it reveals that for the poet the dominating metaphor for the war is a hospital filled with injured men who must be nursed or, if dying, comforted. Whitman's early enthusiastic response to the war shifted dramatically when his brother George was injured in December 1862 and Whitman went to the front in Virginia to seek him out. From this time forward, Whitman would spend most of his days visiting military hospitals, primarily in the nation's capital, to comfort and nurture the wounded solders, Union and Confederate, who were convalescing there.

"A March in the Ranks Hard-Prest, and the Road Unknown" describes a battlefield hospital. Its narrator takes on the role of nurse, attendant to the sufferings of injured soldiers. Entering a church converted into a hospital, he sees a young man dying of a stomach wound amid a crowd of wounded companions. This is the poetry of witness: although he at first finds the scene "a sight beyond all the pictures and poems ever made," Whitman proceeds to record this wartime scene and claim it for poetry. "Then before I depart I sweep my eyes o'er the scene fain to absorb it all, / Faces, varieties, postures beyond description, most in obscurity, some of them dead . . . These I resume as I chant, I see again the forms, I smell the odor." As happens in war, the soldiers must move on, and the poet-narrator must leave the hospital. Still, he is aware that, even in extremity, a human bond has been established: "But first I bend to the dying lad, his eyes open, a half-smile he gives me." Such intimacy is all the poet has to sustain him. Beyond it, in a world of pain and suffering and dying, there is only "darkness, / Resuming, marching, ever in darkness marching, on in the ranks, / The unknown road still marching." The imperative of life is to continue, even though moving onward must proceed through a darkness that is metaphorical as well as actual.

There is general agreement that "The Wound-Dresser," which Whitman placed at the center of every version of "Drum-Taps," is the thematic center toward which the sequence moves. Questioned by young people long after the war about what the war was like, the old veteran who narrates the poem summarizes not only Whitman's own experience, but the overall structure of the poems in the "Drum-Taps" sequence: "Arous'd and angry, I'd thought to beat the alarum, and urge relentless war, / But soon my fingers fail'd me, my face droop'd and I resign'd myself, / To sit by the wounded and soothe them, or silently watch the dead." The first section of the poem ends with the entreaties of the young listeners: "[W]hat saw you to tell us? / What stays with you latest and deepest?"

In the second section, the old veteran recalls his experiences as a soldier, only to say that they are not what was most memorable. Adopting the pose of the worshiper—this is both humility before suffering, and reverence for the war which provided Whitman what he claimed was the most profound experience of his life— he returns "with hinged knees" to his deepest memory. "Bearing the bandages, water and sponge, / Straight and swift to my wounded I go." The section concludes with the old veteran once again bending his knees, "onward . . . [w]ith hinged knees and steady hand to dress wounds."

In the third section, the veteran recalls soldiers not in their totality but in their individuality, each defined by the specificity of his wound. "Such was the war," Whitman writes in *Specimen Days*. "It was not a quadrille in a ballroom" (Whitman 779). The veteran understands anew the courage it took to face the devastation: the loss of limbs, the putrefaction of flesh, the suffering, the presence of death. "I am faithful, I do not give out," the veteran asserts. At the same moment he reveals that although he goes about his rounds with a professional manner, he is deeply moved, "a burning flame" flaring deep within his breast.

Returning through memory to the hospitals, in section 4 the veteran achieves an understanding that such comradeship, providing comfort to one's fellow human beings in need, is the deepest experience that life can offer. "The hurt and wounded I pacify with soothing hand, / I sit by the restless all the dark night, some are so young, / Some suffer so much, I recall the experience sweet and sad." The poem concludes with a remarkable parenthesis, one which lends emphasis to those who read the central portion of "Drum-Taps" as testimony to Whitman's discovery in his own life of that love and comradeship—and physical contact with his fellow

men—which his poetry always celebrates: "(Many a soldier's loving arms about this neck have cross'd and rested, / Many a soldier's kiss dwells on these bearded lips.)." The best commentary on these two lines is Whitman's own description, in *Specimen Days*, of his experiences in military hospitals: "Those three years I consider the greatest privilege and satisfaction . . . the most profound lesson of my life. . . . It arous'd and brought out and decided undream'd-of depths of emotion" (Whitman 776).

Little critical attention has been paid to the poems which follow the climactic "The Wound-Dresser," in large part because they eschew the deep conflicts addressed in early poems of "Drum-Taps" and the direct encounter with the war and its victims that the central poems in the sequence take for their subject. "Look Down Fair Moon" recalls the visual glimpses of earlier poems in the sequence, but without their photographic completeness. "The Artilleryman's Vision" is interesting for two opposing reasons. Its recollection of wartime experience as purely experiential, rather than ethical, prefigures modern concerns with the problematic relation between aesthetics and warfare, and its nocturnal setting, in which a sleepless narrator is forced to recollect his wartime experience, reveals a recognition of what today is called post-traumatic stress syndrome.

Huck Gutman

Bibliography

Cady, Joseph. "*Drum-Taps* and Male Homosexual Literature." *Walt Whitman: Here and Now*. Ed. Joann P. Krieg. Westport, Conn.: Greenwood, 1985.

Erkkila, Betsy. *Whitman the Political Poet*. New York: Oxford UP, 1989.

Glicksberg, Charles I., ed. *Walt Whitman and the Civil War*. Philadelphia: U of Pennsylvania P, 1933.

Thomas, M. Wynn. *The Lunar Light of Whitman's Poetry*. Cambridge, Mass.: Harvard UP, 1987.

Whitman, Walt. *Complete Poetry and Collected Prose*. Ed. Justin Kaplan. New York: Library of America, 1982.

Zweig, Paul. *Walt Whitman: The Making of the Poet*. New York: Basic Books, 1984.

See also "Army Corps on the March, An"; "Artilleryman's Vision, The"; "Bivouac on a Mountain Side"; "By the Bivouac's Fitful Flame"; "Cavalry Crossing a

FORD"; "CENTENARIAN'S STORY, THE"; CIVIL
WAR, THE; CIVIL WAR NURSING; "COME UP
FROM THE FIELDS FATHER"; COMRADESHIP;
DRUM-TAPS; "MARCH IN THE RANKS HARD-
PREST, AND THE ROAD UNKNOWN, A";
PHOTOGRAPHS AND PHOTOGRAPHERS; SEQUEL
TO DRUM-TAPS; "SONG OF THE BANNER AT
DAYBREAK"; SPECIMEN DAYS; "VIGIL STRANGE
I KEPT ON THE FIELD ONE NIGHT";
"WOUND-DRESSER, THE"

Drum-Taps (1865)

Drum-Taps (1865) is Walt Whitman's volume
of poems about the Civil War, but the roots of
this book predate the war. In 1860, Thayer and
Eldridge advertised a forthcoming Whitman
volume titled *Banner at Day-Break* (a foreshadowing of "Song of the Banner at Day-Break"
from *Drum-Taps*). Thayer and Eldridge went
bankrupt in 1861, however, and the volume
never materialized. During the war's initial
years, Whitman wrote several war poems.
Later, while working as a hospital volunteer, he
wrote several more. In 1863—after journeying
to Washington, D.C., to find his wounded brother, and witnessing the sick and wounded soldiers convalescing there—Whitman resolved to
publish a book of poems about the war. He
could not find a publisher, however, in part
because of a sluggish wartime book market.
Eager to see his book published, Whitman made
his own arrangements and, on 1 April 1865,
signed a contract with Peter Eckler for five hundred copies of *Drum-Taps*.

Two weeks later, John Wilkes Booth assassinated Abraham Lincoln. Whitman quickly
inserted a poem commemorating Lincoln's burial ("Hush'd be the Camps To-day"), and a few
copies of the first issue, a seventy-two-page
volume with fifty-three poems, were bound and
distributed. Yet Whitman soon realized that
Drum-Taps would be incomplete without significant testimony about Lincoln's death. In the
autumn of 1865 Whitman contracted with Gibson Brothers, well-known Washington printers,
to produce one thousand copies of *Sequel to
Drum-Taps,* an appendix of poems about Lincoln and the war's end. *Drum-Taps* and its
twenty-four-page *Sequel* containing eighteen
additional poems were bound together, and
Whitman arranged for Bunce and Huntington
to market the book. *Drum-Taps* appeared in a
simple brown cloth cover with the words DRUM
TAPS on the front and back.

Whitman eventually integrated *Drum-Taps*
into *Leaves of Grass*. In 1867 *Drum-Taps* and
the *Sequel* appeared as appendices to *Leaves of
Grass*. In 1871 Whitman began to incorporate
the poems into *Leaves of Grass* proper: he
placed many of them in a cluster titled "Drum-
Taps" and distributed others throughout *Leaves
of Grass*.

Drum-Taps begins with a patriotic call to
arms and ends with "psalms of the dead" ("Lo,
Victress on the Peaks"). The contrast between
the early martial poems like "Drum-Taps"
(later titled "First O Songs for a Prelude")
and the later elegiac poems like "Vigil Strange I Kept
on the Field One Night" reflects an evolution
in Whitman's attitude toward the war—a movement from enthusiasm to grief. Alluding (perhaps unintentionally) to both the percussion
sound that calls soldiers into battle (drum taps)
and the bugle call blown at military funerals
(taps), the book's title suggests *Drum-Taps*'s
two very different rhetorics.

Nonetheless, patriotic pieces and elegies
for the dead are not the only kinds of poems in
Drum-Taps. There are several poems devoted to
the vivid, realistic representation of a war scene
such as "Bivouac on a Mountain Side" or "Cavalry Crossing a Ford" and others that portray
humanitarian caretaking as in "The Dresser "
(later "The Wound-Dresser") and "A March in
the Ranks Hard-Prest, and the Road Unknown." *Drum-Taps* also contains poems that
have no explicit connection to the war, poems
like "When I Heard the Learn'd Astronomer."
Drum-Taps has no poems about slavery or African Americans, an omission that emphasizes
Whitman's view that the war was about the
Union, not slavery.

Whitman initially considered *Drum-Taps*
a more controlled and artistic volume of poems, a departure from *Leaves of Grass*. Many
of the *Drum-Taps* poems are sustained, formal
efforts to control expression and emotion, and
they often use military or mourning rituals
and symbols to mask private feelings. Some of
the poems—"O Captain! My Captain!" for
example—are more conventional, more stylistically regular. The presentation of sexuality in
Drum-Taps is less overt than in "Calamus" or
"Children of Adam." Likewise, the handling of
death in *Drum-Taps* tends to be less morbid-
romantic and more immediate and realistic than
in *Leaves of Grass*. Eventually, however, as he
revised and rearranged his poems, Whitman
began to see these war lyrics as central to *Leaves*

D

of *Grass*. And the books do share many similar concerns. The homoerotic aspects of "Vigil Strange" or "The Dresser" are continuations of the "Calamus" project, just as "When Lilacs Last in the Dooryard Bloom'd" extends Whitman's meditation on death in ways similar to those in "Out of the Cradle Endlessly Rocking."

Critics and the reading public mostly ignored *Drum-Taps*. It sold fewer copies than the 1860 *Leaves of Grass* and received fewer reviews. Still, Franklin B. Sanborn gave *Drum-Taps* a mixed-to-favorable notice and championed Whitman as a patriot, and Whitman's friend John Burroughs wrote an important extended essay defending "Walt Whitman and His 'Drum-Taps'" for the *Galaxy*. *Drum-Taps* also garnered the attention of Henry James and William Dean Howells, both of whom disparaged the book as indefinite, prosaic, and artistically unseemly.

Individual poems from this volume became quite popular, however. "O Captain! My Captain!" and "Come Up from the Fields Father" were highly regarded and widely anthologized throughout the nineteenth century, just as "Lilacs" has been widely praised in the twentieth. In recent years, critics have devoted increasing attention to *Drum-Taps,* admiring it as Whitman's attempt to forge poetic meaning out of the war.

Gregory Eiselein

Bibliography

Allen, Gay Wilson. *The Solitary Singer: A Critical Biography of Walt Whitman.* 1955. Rev. ed. 1967. Chicago: U of Chicago P, 1985.

Erkkila, Betsy. *Whitman the Political Poet.* New York: Oxford UP, 1989.

Myerson, Joel. *Walt Whitman: A Descriptive Bibliography.* Pittsburgh: U of Pittsburgh P, 1993.

Thomas, M. Wynn. *The Lunar Light of Whitman's Poetry.* Cambridge, Mass.: Harvard UP, 1987.

Whitman, Walt. *Leaves of Grass: A Textual Variorum of the Printed Poems.* Ed. Sculley Bradley, Harold W. Blodgett, Arthur Golden, and William White. 3 vols. New York: New York UP, 1980.

———. *Walt Whitman's "Drum-Taps" (1865) and "Sequel to Drum-Taps" (1865–6): A Facsimile Reproduction.* Ed. F. DeWolfe Miller. Gainesville: Scholars' Facsimiles and Reprints, 1959.

See also "Bivouac on a Mountain Side"; "Cavalry Crossing a Ford"; Civil War, The; "Come Up from the Fields Father"; Death; "Drum-Taps"; "First O Songs for a Prelude"; Lincoln's Death; "March in the Ranks Hard-Prest, and the Road Unknown, A"; "O Captain! My Captain!"; *Sequel to Drum-Taps*; "Song of the Banner at Daybreak; "Vigil Strange I Kept on the Field One Night"; "When Lilacs Last in the Dooryard Bloom'd"; "Wound-Dresser, The"

"Dumb Kate" (1844)

This short story first appeared in *Columbian Magazine,* May 1844, under the title "Dumb Kate.—An Early Death." Revised, it was given its current title in *Specimen Days & Collect* (1882). For further publication history and revisions, see Brasher's edition of *The Early Poems and the Fiction*.

"Dumb Kate" is a slight tale. Kate, the beautiful, deaf and dumb daughter of a tavern owner, is seduced by a wealthy young man. The villain moves to New York, where his business prospers. Sick at heart, Kate languishes and dies. A little boy throws a weak but lovely flower on her grave, and she becomes the subject for gossipmongers on their Sunday strolls.

In the original version, Whitman emphasizes the "sweet intoxication, as well as the madness" of love (252, n9). Consequently, Kate is less blameworthy. Originally, Whitman also included a paragraph warning moralists not to judge Kate. Without this didacticism, the story may be viewed as an exercise in irony or ironic endings: villainy prospers while innocence loses both her reputation and her life; gossips say uncharitable things after church service; and the weak but lovely flower tossed so easily into the grave becomes a fitting symbol of Kate herself.

The theme of grief as a cause of death connects this story to other Whitman tales, most notably "The Boy Lover" (1845). Also, Whitman's warning against the judgment of Kate is related to a similar injunction in "The Angel of Tears" (1846).

Very little critical attention has been given to "Dumb Kate."

Patrick McGuire

Bibliography
Whitman, Walt. *The Early Poems and the Fiction.* Ed. Thomas L. Brasher. New York: New York UP, 1963.

See also SHORT FICTION, WHITMAN'S

Duncan, Robert (1919–1988)

Robert Duncan taught at the Black Mountain School in North Carolina and was associated with other Black Mountain poets like Robert Creeley and Charles Olson, who generated a movement known as "projective verse." Projective verse was conceived as a kind of "breath poetics," in which the poetic line is determined by the poet's breathing instead of by any imposed conventions. For these poets, Whitman with his long free-verse lines was the obvious precursor. Duncan's various books of poems, including *The Opening of the Field* (1960), *Roots and Branches* (1964), and *Selected Poems* (1993), all owed something to his understanding of Whitman, and he articulated his debt to Whitman in two essays published in *Fictive Certainties* (1985).

In those essays, Duncan speaks of "the adventure of Whitman's line" and sees Whitman's "great insight" as the development of a "new line" that derives from his "ideas of democracy, of faring forth where no lines are to be drawn between classes or occupations, between kinds of intelligence, between private and public" (*Fictive* 203). Duncan continually seeks a connection with Whitman, both formally ("Let me join you again this morning, Walt Whitman, . . . even now my line just now walking with yours" [*Fictive* 207]) and spiritually ("It is across great scars of wrong / I reach toward the song of kindred men / and strike again the naked string / old Whitman sang from" [*Opening* 64]). Like Hart Crane and other twentieth-century American poets who have carried on a dialogue with Whitman, Duncan's concern is both to extend Whitman's inventions and to delineate the unsettling developments in American culture since Whitman's time.

Ed Folsom

Bibliography
Duncan, Robert. *Fictive Certainties: Essays.* New York: New Directions, 1985.
——. *The Opening of the Field.* New York: New Directions, 1960.
——. *Selected Poems.* New York: New Directions, 1993.
——. *A Selected Prose.* New York: New Directions, 1995.
Johnson, Mark, and Robert DeMott. "'An Inheritance of Spirit': Robert Duncan and Walt Whitman." *Robert Duncan: Scales of the Marvelous.* Ed. Robert J. Bertholf and Ian W. Reid. New York: New Directions, 1979. 225–240.

See also CRANE, HART; CREELEY, ROBERT; LEGACY, WHITMAN'S

Duyckinck, Evert Augustus (1816–1878)

Whitman and Evert Augustus Duyckinck, near contemporaries, nationalistic Young Americans, and contributors to the movement's main periodical outlet, John L. O'Sullivan's *United States Magazine and Democratic Review,* labored as journalists in New York during the 1840s and early 1850s. Duyckinck probably served as the *Review*'s literary editor and was coeditor and part owner of other radically nationalistic journals such as *Arcturus* (1840–1842) and the early *Literary World* (1847–1853). Aside from ideological sympathies, however, Duyckinck—son of a New York publisher, Columbia educated, and an attorney—had little in common with the poet, and Whitman received virtually no acknowledgment from the man who promoted Melville and Poe.

The reasons for Duyckinck's virtually ignoring Whitman are perhaps self-evident. Duyckinck was a complex man; an intellectual and littérateur committed to the democratic principles and social change of Jacksonian America, he was also profoundly religious, an active participant in the hierarchical and conservative Protestant Episcopal Church. Though he was not a reactionary, Duyckinck's deep religious faith would probably have been the principal barrier to a full appreciation of and taste for Whitman's subjects and prosody, and possibly even the man himself. It is true that Duyckinck and his brother's most enduring work, the *Cyclopaedia of American Literature* (1855), the place where an entry on Whitman would have been most appropriate, was well along in production in 1855 when the first edition of *Leaves* appeared, and the same plates were used for the 1856 and 1863 printings. However, the latter did not even include Whitman in its Supplement, nor was he acknowledged in the 1875

D

revised and reset printing. Whitman himself was not surprised to have been omitted from the Ducykincks' *Cyclopaedia*. He commented to Traubel in 1888 that he was "not even today accepted in New York by the great bogums—much less then." Whitman recalled having met Evert Duyckinck and his brother, George: "they were both 'gentlemanly men' . . . both very clerical looking—thin—wanting in body: men of true proper style, God help 'em!" (Traubel 139).

Duyckinck, however, is associated with the reprinting of one Whitman poem in an 1857 collaborative anthology with Robert Aris Wilmot, *The Poets of the Nineteenth Century*. In addition, in the early 1850s Duyckinck and his brother-in-law gained control of Justus Redfield's publishing house and thus may have had a financial interest in the firm in 1871 when it published Whitman.

Donald Yannella

Bibliography

Chielens, Edward E., ed. *American Literary Magazines: The Eighteenth and Nineteenth Centuries*. New York: Greenwood, 1986.

Pritchard, John Paul. *Criticism in America*. Norman: U of Oklahoma P, 1956.

Stafford, John. *The Literary Criticism of "Young America": A Study in the Relationship of Politics and Literature*. Berkeley: U of California P, 1952.

Traubel, Horace. *With Walt Whitman in Camden*. Vol. 1. 1906. New York: Rowman and Littlefield, 1961.

Yannella, Donald. "Evert Augustus Duyckinck." *Antebellum Writers in New York and the South*. Vol. 3 of *Dictionary of Literary Biography*. Ed Joel Myerson. Detroit: Gale, 1978. 101–109.

———. "Writing the '*Other* Way': Melville, the Duyckinck Crowd, and Literature for the Masses." *A Companion to Melville Studies*. Ed. John Bryant. New York: Greenwood, 1986. 63–81.

See also DEMOCRATIC REVIEW; MATHEWS, CORNELIUS; YOUNG AMERICA MOVEMENT

E

Eakins, Thomas (1844–1916)

Thomas Eakins is now regarded as the greatest practitioner of realism in nineteenth-century American art. With the exception of his studies in France and Spain (1866–1870), Eakins spent his entire life in Philadelphia.

A controversial figure, Eakins was fired from his teaching position at the Pennsylvania Academy of Fine Arts for removing the loincloth from a male model during an anatomy class with female students present. He shocked the art world with *The Gross Clinic* (1875), showing the surgeon Dr. Samuel D. Gross with his blood-covered scalpel in hand. (Gross's widowed daughter-in-law married Whitman's doctor, William Osler.) His equally sanguinary portrait of Dr. D.H. Agnew, *The Agnew Clinic* (1889), shows among the students in the gallery of the operating theater Dr. Nathan M. Baker, Whitman's nurse for two years and a witness to Whitman's will of 29 June 1888.

Eakins asked Whitman's permission to paint his portrait in 1887 (the date appears in the painting) but did not complete it until 1888. Eakins donated the portrait to Whitman, and upon Whitman's death it passed to Dr. Richard Maurice Bucke, whose heirs later sold it to its present owner, the Pennsylvania Academy of Fine Arts, which had censured Eakins.

Whitman admired Eakins's inclination to unorthodox behavior and a willingness to shock established authority. Both were outside the mainstream of their artistic endeavors, and both saw in the human form an inherent beauty not requiring enhancement with a sympathetic brush, pen, or lens. Evidence exists suggesting that Eakins, a pioneer in photographic art, took multiple photographs of Whitman posing nude.

Philip W. Leon

Bibliography

Folsom, Ed. "Whitman Naked?" *Walt Whitman Quarterly Review* 11 (1994): 200–202 and back cover.

Johns, Elizabeth. *Thomas Eakins: The Heroism of Modern Life*. Princeton: Princeton UP, 1983.

Leon, Philip W. *Walt Whitman and Sir William Osler: A Poet and His Physician*. Toronto: ECW, 1995.

Rule, Henry B. "Walt Whitman and Thomas Eakins: Variations on Some Common Themes." *Texas Quarterly* 17 (1974): 7–57.

Wilmerding, John, ed. *Thomas Eakins (1844–1916) and the Heart of American Life*. London: National Portrait Gallery, 1993.

See also PAINTERS AND PAINTINGS; PHOTOGRAPHS AND PHOTOGRAPHERS

"Earth, My Likeness" (1860)

Published as "Calamus" number 36 in the third (1860) edition of *Leaves of Grass*, "Earth, My Likeness" acquired its present title in 1867.

Critics have often read the poem as a simple love lyric, or perhaps more restrictively as a homosexual song addressed to a young athletic lover. Neither reading tells us why Whitman finds likeness in Earth, whom he addresses here as a person. The likeness is not so much in their looks as in a deeper force or vigor that they share. Both the earth and the poet are full of "fierce" energies that might burst unless ventilated. Whitman talks specifically about "an athlete" and himself who are enamored of each other. How long, he wonders, can this intense longing be suppressed?

Read with no specific awareness of the poet's homoerotic passion, the poem documents the yearnings of a devout soul for comprehending love's mystery, its fierce and terrible spirituality. Alternatively, the poet fancies that only one of the many athletic readers/lovers for whom he feels a similar "fierce and terrible" passion would appreciate the point of his comparison: the poet and earth are pregnant with possibilities of fierce knowledge or passion. "I dare not tell it in words, not even in these songs," says Whitman, who seems to grant himself and the readers of "Calamus" expectations of candor and plain speech.

K. Narayana Chandran

Bibliography

Helms, Alan. "'Hints . . . Faint Clews and Indirections': Whitman's Homosexual Disguises." *Walt Whitman: Here and Now.* Ed. Joann P. Krieg. Westport, Conn.: Greenwood, 1985. 61–67.

Kuebrich, David. *Minor Prophecy: Walt Whitman's New American Religion.* Bloomington: Indiana UP, 1989.

Miller, James E., Jr. "'Calamus': The Leaf and the Root." *A Century of Whitman Criticism.* Ed. Edwin Haviland Miller. Bloomington: Indiana UP, 1969. 303–320.

Whitman, Walt. *Leaves of Grass: Comprehensive Reader's Edition.* Ed. Harold W. Blodgett and Sculley Bradley. New York: New York UP, 1965.

See also "CALAMUS"; SEX AND SEXUALITY

Education, Views on

Convinced that "an ignorant people cannot form a wise government" (*Whitman Looks* 101), Walt Whitman commended tax-supported schools for their protection of republican institutions and for their assurance of the success of the common school movement, a Jacksonian reform. He also supported free public high schools and believed that newspapers should keep citizens informed about public school education issues. To achieve his educational objectives—good citizenship, moral character, and intellect—he wrote a stream of editorials on classroom conditions, educational principles and practices, and school reforms for the Brooklyn *Evening Star* (1845–1846), the Brooklyn *Daily Eagle* (1846–1848), and the Brooklyn *Daily Times* (1857–1859). Further, as a reporter, he visited several schools in Brooklyn and Manhattan, observing classroom instruction and recommending improvements.

His focus was on developing the potential of the average child, seeking good standards to promote effective teaching and learning. As country schools were particularly prone to making poor teacher selections, Whitman advocated the careful screening of applicants to find teachers able to establish a healthy emotional climate in the classroom. He cautioned against rigidity in discipline and inflexibility in classroom management and argued as well for the provision of a pleasant physical environment (including playground space). He believed in the worth of each child as an individual—urging teachers and parents to be alert to the unappealing and unpopular children who seemed more difficult to teach. He also emphasized the importance of teaching children to rely on and think for themselves (ideas which were encouraged by phrenology, a precursor of modern psychology). Whitman was frequently critical of dull teaching methods that relied on mechanical drill and repetition which were commonplace in the teaching of grammar, arithmetic, and geography, for example; instead, he advised teachers and parents to gain an understanding of how children best learn—e.g., through motivation. He also wanted parents to visit schools, confer with teachers frequently, and build up their children's confidence.

Whitman understood the need for the expansion of the free public school system, calling for the acquisition of sites for school building construction. He sought other reforms, including provision for teacher training and supervision (he wanted primary schools to have the most qualified teachers); he also argued for employment of women teachers, improved salaries to raise the quality of teaching, expansion of the curriculum to include American history, vocal music, art, physical recreation, and free, ample, and up-to-date textbooks preferably by the best authors. While corporal punishment was a common practice in his time, Whitman pleaded most energetically for its complete abolition (see his short story entitled "Death in the School-Room (a Fact)" [1841]).

Always personally interested in the schools of New York, he regarded such concern to be a civic obligation of all citizens. Though Whitman's ideas on education were unpopular in his time, they were influenced by his own formal schooling (and probably his Sunday schooling) and his schoolteaching experience. He attended School District No. 1 in Brooklyn (then the only Brooklyn public school) from about 1824 to 1831 when, at age 11, he needed to go to work. Like most large schools of that period, his school used the Lancastrian method of instruction, i.e., a single, authoritarian teacher, assisted by student monitors, for a large class that learned by rote and repetition (typically, girls and boys were on separate floors). In addition, corporal chastisement was used, as Whitman no doubt observed.

At age seventeen Whitman, impelled by severely hard times, became a pedagogue. He taught in some common schools—usually for one three-month term—in Queens County (which then included what is now all of Nassau County) and Suffolk County on Long Island from 1836 to 1841. A teaching profession did not exist then; youths like Whitman, with time to spare and in need of money, were appointed— "chance teachers," as he called them (*Whitman Looks* 26). Still, the inexperienced Whitman did not teach the textbook as teachers then did but instead used the Socratic method of instruction, asking stimulating questions to involve himself and his pupils in discussion and learning. As he realized later, "boarding around" with the parents of his pupils was also a great learning experience for him. His thoughts about school matters may also have been influenced by the lectures on education he had attended in Brooklyn in the 1830s.

Anti-intellectualism in American life still prevails at least to some extent today and during the nineteenth century accounted for the state of public education. Whitman described it thusly: low teacher status, poor pay and lack of job security, and poor and persistent working conditions such as dilapidated school buildings, insufficient ventilation, and overcrowded classrooms. Nevertheless, as his teaching progressed, his respect for his pupils deepened. And it in turn solidified his conviction that the teacher played a pivotal role in their education. Though the job was difficult, he believed the teacher's position was "properly one of the noblest on earth" (*Whitman Looks* 74). (He also thought that proper parenting was crucial to children's success in school.) In *Leaves of Grass* he continued to teach "what I have learnt from America" ("By Blue Ontario's Shore," section 17).

In several educational controversies during the Age of Jackson, Whitman took bold positions. On the issue of secular versus sectarian schooling, he challenged the Catholic officials of New York in 1842 who clamored for government support of their schools. Whitman, who rejected religious creeds, upheld the principle of separation of church and state (many at the time thought that religious and moral training were inseparable). In the debate between nature versus nurture, he agreed with theorists in education and psychology who during the 1830s stressed the environment as a prime determinant of human action, a belief that was rooted in the educational philosophy of Rousseau and Locke—the latter positing the idea of *tabula rasa*. (Interested in debating societies, Whitman helped organize one in Smithtown, Long Island, where he taught from 1837 to 1838. In one of the debates on the issue of heredity versus environment in shaping character, he supported the view that nurture exerted the greater influence.) Whitman also accepted the scientific belief in the inheritability of acquired characteristics (parentage), which overtook the "environmental" school by the late 1840s. He felt, however, that parents could modify their own behavior, which would in turn produce the desired effect on their children. On concrete school issues Whitman greatly respected the views of Horace Mann, a leading contemporary educational reformer who also espoused the theory of democratic education and agitated for change to improve public schools.

Whitman's advanced theories of education and newly tried classroom practices put him in the forefront of the "new education" based on progressive ideas that took hold in the early decades of the twentieth century. Teachers' colleges and schools of education would do well to include Whitman in their curriculum today. Particularly useful in view of perennial social problems is Whitman's notion that investment in public education would, in his words, "preclude ignorance, crime, and pauperism" (*Whitman Looks* 67). Whitman also favored education for young people no longer in school, proposing free evening schools for them. He thought also that education for adult men and women was essential, equating the penny press of his day with the common school. His idea that there was much to learn outside of books was further indication of his extended view of education.

Bernard Hirschhorn

Bibliography

Hitchcock, Bert. "Walt Whitman: The Pedagogue as Poet." *Walt Whitman Review* 20 (1974): 140–146.

E

Hofstadter, Richard. *Anti-Intellectualism in American Life*. New York: Vintage, 1963.
Reynolds, David S. "Walt Whitman and the New York Stage." *Thesis* 9.1 (1995): 4–11.
Whitman, Walt. *The Gathering of Forces*. Ed. Cleveland Rodgers and John Black. Vol. 1. New York: Putnam, 1920.
———. *Walt Whitman Looks at the Schools*. Ed. Florence Bernstein Freedman. New York: King's Crown, 1950.

See also "DEATH IN THE SCHOOL-ROOM (A FACT)"; LONG ISLAND, NEW YORK

Egyptian Museum (New York) (1853–1859)

Owned by Dr. Henry Abbott, a collection of over one thousand artifacts ranging from fragments of cloth, glass, and pottery to human and animal mummies was opened as the Egyptian Museum in 1853 in Brooklyn and exhibited at various locations, including 659 Broadway and the Stuyvesant Institute at 65 Broadway. Dr. Abbott, a native of Britain, spent twenty years in Egypt and, by his account, one hundred thousand dollars acquiring the artifacts. When attempts to sell them in America failed, he put them on exhibit to recover some of the expense. The collection was bought by the New-York Historical Society in 1859 for thirty-four thousand dollars a few months before Abbott's death. Most of the collection is now at the Brooklyn Museum.

Whitman visited the museum frequently and conversed at length with Abbott during the time *Leaves of Grass* was being composed. He wrote an essay in 1855 for *Life Illustrated* recommending the museum. He had also read some of the books Abbott recommended, especially Sir John Gardner Wilkinson's, which Abbott lists first in his catalogue describing the collection.

In the *Life* essay, Whitman presents the artifacts as "tangible representations of the oldest history and civilization now known upon the earth" (Whitman 30). Egyptian ideas provided a pre-European model useful in the rejection of European traditions. He praises the ancient people for the nature and quality of their daily life and religion, comparing the people to Americans as energetic, spiritual, and freedom-loving. A large share of the artifacts were funerary and hence celebrated beliefs and values surrounding life and death. Egyptian tombs were filled with objects used in everyday life; the interiors contained pictures and images of deities and of people going about their daily occupations.

Abbott's collection contained dozens of figures of Osiris, the agricultural god who brought new life on earth and in the afterworld, where he presided as judge and god of life, truth, justice, light, peace, and grace. The Osiris figure (along with Christ in a similar role) may have suggested the expansive encloser of all—the poet/priest/man—in Whitman's poetry. Tapscott suggests that Whitman may have borrowed images, concepts, and the syntactic structure of cataloguing from Egyptian materials. Egyptian references appear throughout the poetry: the leaf of grass is a hieroglyphic; natural objects are indications of reality to the soul; and the poet is the "arbiter of the diverse," the "key" fitting everything in place ("By Blue Ontario's Shore," section 10). Egyptian versions of the belief in the transmigration of souls enter into such poems as "I Sing the Body Electric." Egyptian elements may also have figured in the death elegy for Lincoln.

Rosemary Gates Winslow

Bibliography

Abbott, Henry. *Catalogue of a Collection of Egyptian Antiquities, the Property of Henry Abbott, M.D., Now Exhibiting at the Stuyvesant Institute*. New York: J.W. Watson, 1853.
Gates, Rosemary L. "Egyptian Myth and Whitman's 'Lilacs.'" *Walt Whitman Quarterly Review* 5.1 (1987): 21–31.
Irwin, John T. *American Hieroglyphics: The Symbol of the Egyptian Hieroglyphics in the American Renaissance*. New Haven: Yale UP, 1980.
Richardson, Robert D., Jr. *Myth and Literature in the American Renaissance*. Bloomington: Indiana UP, 1978.
Tapscott, Stephen J. "Leaves of Myself: Whitman's Egypt in 'Song of Myself.'" *American Literature* 50 (1978): 49–73.
Whitman, Walt. "One of the Lessons Bordering Broadway: The Egyptian Museum." *New York Dissected*. 1936. Ed. Emory Holloway and Ralph Adimari. Folcroft, Pa.: Folcroft Library Editions, 1972. 30–40.
Wilkinson, Sir John Gardner. *The Manners and Customs of the Ancient Egyptians*. London: Murray, 1841.
———. *A Popular Account of the Ancient Egyptians*. New York: Harper, 1854.
Williams, Carolyn Ransom. *Catalogue of Egyptian Antiquities*. New York: New York Historical Society, 1924.

See also ABBOTT, DR. HENRY

"Eidólons" (1876)

This poem, included finally in the "Inscriptions" section of the 1881–1882 edition of *Leaves,* was written in 1876. The word "eidōlon" is the Greek word meaning "idol" and in English can be loosely translated as a specter, phantom, or unsubstantial image. Whitman used the word to mean a spiritual image of the immaterial whose essence is unchanging, contrasted to the material world, where change is an appearance, a mere shadow of its true self. The poem is rendered poignant by the fact that Whitman wrote it in his final years, when his physical vitality did not match his inner vigor.

"Eidólons" has been characterized as a poem describing the evolutionary progress of the human soul and, alternatively, a poem of renunciation and detachment in the Eastern spiritual sense. In *Minor Prophecy* David Kuebrich writes that Whitman would maintain himself in "higher stages" than previous inspired bards by wedding a traditional religious world view with the intellectual currents of modernity and in so doing create a new paradigm of spirituality. In the first stanza, Whitman describes an encounter with a "seer" who renounces the "things" of this world in favor of eidólons and demonstrates his belief in the preeminence of the immaterial world. Like "Song of Myself," "Eidólons" is about the detachment from those things that would distract us from the development of our souls. Enlightenment, Whitman seems to be saying, will visit those who realize the dynamic potential of the self-realized person, thereby completing a metaphysical circle in which one becomes truly oneself.

The poem has a cyclical quality, since all stanzas relate to and end with "eidólon(s)," as does life itself. The "eidólon" represents true identity in the poem and is the visionary expression that gives the immaterial its ultimate significance. Whitman, like a true mystic, seeks to demonstrate the incompleteness of our understanding of reality. We see only shadows, forms, or fragments instead of the great whole or, in Whitman's own words, a "round full-orb'd eidólon."

D. Neil Richardson

Bibliography

Holloway, Emory. *Aspects of Immortality in Whitman.* Westwood, N.J.: Kindle, 1969.
Hutchinson, George. *The Ecstatic Whitman: Literary Shamanism & the Crisis of the Union.* Columbus: Ohio State UP, 1986.
Kuebrich, David. *Minor Prophecy: Walt Whitman's New American Religion.* Bloomington: Indiana UP, 1989.
Whitman, Walt. *Notebooks and Unpublished Prose Manuscripts.* Ed. Edward F. Grier. 6 vols. New York: New York UP, 1984.

See also "INSCRIPTIONS"; SOUL, THE

"Eighteenth Presidency!, The" (1928)

"The Eighteenth Presidency! Voice of Walt Whitman to each Young Man in the Nation, North, South, East, and West" occupies a unique position in Walt Whitman's writings, for while the essay stands as the poet's most historically specific critique of American political culture, it remained unpublished until 1928, when it was published separately in both France and the United States and was included in Clifton Furness's edition of unpublished manuscripts, *Walt Whitman's Workshop.* Responding to the 1856 presidential race involving Millard Fillmore, James Buchanan, and John C. Frémont, the manifesto was distributed in proof to several editors, but never actually printed. Whether Whitman grew disenchanted with the essay's biting tone or simply failed to raise the funds necessary for publication remains a significant biographical mystery. For all the ambiguity surrounding its lack of publication, however, "The Eighteenth Presidency!" offers compelling insight into the political anger and anxiety Whitman felt in the 1850s. *Leaves of Grass* at times expresses similar sentiments, but for the most part it labors to transcend them. The essay, in this respect, can be considered the prose counterpart of the poem "Respondez!" (1856). The two works maintain highly ironic, satirical visions of American politics, and Whitman eventually excluded them both from his official canon.

Although Furness suggested that Whitman had written parts of "The Eighteenth Presidency!" before 1856, the essay's intensity and sense of national apocalypse closely match the country's mood that year. The passage of the Kansas-Nebraska Act in 1854 sharply divided the nation along sectional lines, and two years later, Kansas's status as either a free or slave state became the focus of physical conflict on the Kansas-Missouri border and in the Senate chamber itself. "The Eighteenth Presidency!" imputes this violence to the nation's political parties and their inability to overcome the constitutional crises. Addressing America's farmers, laborers, carpenters, and mechanics, the essay points to the gap between the general public and the presidential nominating committees, charging the political establishment with sacrificing the nation's heritage for partisan expediency. Displaying what Betsy Erkkila has described as the self-serving arguments of many Northern abolitionists, Whitman urged his readers to recognize slavery's threat to their own political and economic freedom. "[A]bolish slavery," he cautioned white American workers, "or it will abolish you" (Whitman 1322).

The essay's urgency surfaces most prominently in its caustic and rancorous language. While Whitman's readers are accustomed to his explicit challenges to the presidency, nowhere in *Leaves of Grass* would they be prepared for presidents eating "dirt and excrement" while sitting on cushions of "filth and blood" (1310) or political delegates wracked with syphilis and crawling like serpents across the earth. David Reynolds has traced such statements to the spirit of agitation promoted by reformers during the 1850s. As Kerry Larson has argued, however, Whitman's rhetoric also betrays his own confusion about the political and constitutional dilemmas facing the country. While section 10 of "Song of Myself" depicts the poet as harboring a runaway slave, "The Eighteenth Presidency!" remains ambivalent about the desire to resist slavery's expansion and the need to obey federal law. Whitman, in fact, advises Americans to defy the Fugitive Slave Law with everything from pens to guns, but at the same time he warns that fugitives must be returned in deference to the Constitution. The essay's clearest message may be that while its author is anxious to abolish slavery, he has little sense of how to extract it from the federal Union.

It is fitting, then, that "The Eighteenth Presidency!" tends to depict moral and political controversy as a conflict between generations. In characterizing the 1856 presidential race, Whitman denounces Buchanan and Fillmore not for their partisan platforms, but for their corruption and age. The candidates become "two dead corpses" that "guide by feebleness and ashes" a nation of "live and electric men" (1325). The nominating committees come from "political hearses," the "shrouds inside of the coffins," and the "tumors and abscesses of the land" (1313). In contrast to the 1855 Preface's image of a "wellshaped heir," the youthful poet proudly assuming his station after acknowledging his father's corpse, the bitter young citizens of "The Eighteenth Presidency!" are haunted by bodies that refuse to stay buried and unnaturally rule the earth. As Arthur Golden has suggested, Whitman's vision of a vibrant new race rising to thwart such civic decay serves only to obfuscate his incisive cultural critique. The true crisis of 1856 is that an incompetent, diseased generation threatens to emasculate the nation's youth by keeping them from the republican principles that Whitman considered their birthright.

Whitman's disgust for both Buchanan and Fillmore arises from his conviction that in the country's currently fragile state party platforms were of "no account" and the "right man" was "every thing" (1318). The times demanded a leader who would make "a bold push" (1308), and while the essay refrains from making a specific endorsement, it addresses its discussion of an ideal candidate to John Frémont, the newly formed Republican party's nominee. The "Redeemer President," Whitman advises, must strive to preserve the rights of both individuals and states (1321). As the representative of the people rather than his party, he must be inclusive, not exclusive, and in this respect, he would return the government to the ideals expressed in the Declaration of Independence and the Constitution. These spirited, but vague instructions are indicative of the essay's general preference for discussing the character of potential leaders as opposed to their ideas. Whitman envisions the nation's redeemer as a heroic, bearded Westerner who might cross the Alleghenies and walk into the presidency wearing a working suit and a tan (1308). The image strongly recalls Abraham Lincoln, who in 1856 had yet to establish a national reputation. Scholars have variously praised the passage for being somehow clairvoyant, but perhaps a sounder conclusion would be that it helps explain why Whitman would find such profound meaning in Lincoln's presidency: the poet had called for this representative man long before one had made himself known.

"The Eighteenth Presidency!" is critical to understanding the relations between Whitman's political and poetic sensibilities. The essay's elevation of character over platform and of personality over ideology strongly resembles the trans-partisan vision of *Leaves of Grass*. Whitman's call for a Redeemer President shares much with his projection of a vitally inclusive, national bard. Like the poet of democracy, the Redeemer President promises to represent America's disenfranchised public rather than its political parties.

Indeed, while it makes no mention of poetry or *Leaves of Grass,* "The Eighteenth Presidency!" subtly engages in the similar task of yoking its political commentary with civic self-promotion. The author emerges as a figure who faithfully respects the principles of representation he finds lacking in the culture at large. From his mouth, Whitman announces, Americans can "hear the will of These States" (1323). "The Eighteenth Presidency!" ably demonstrates that this civic persona was useful to the poet across an array of genres and discursive settings.

David Haven Blake

Bibliography

Allen, Gay Wilson. *Walt Whitman Handbook.* 1946. New York: Hendricks House, 1962.

Erkkila, Betsy. *Whitman the Political Poet.* New York: Oxford UP, 1989.

Furness, Clifton Joseph, ed. *Walt Whitman's Workshop: A Collection of Unpublished Manuscripts.* 1928. New York: Russell and Russell, 1964.

Golden, Arthur. "The Obfuscations of Rhetoric: Whitman and the Visionary Experience." *Walt Whitman: The Centennial Essays.* Ed. Ed Folsom. Iowa City: U of Iowa P, 1994. 88–102.

Grier, Edward F. Introduction. *The Eighteenth Presidency!* Ed. Grier. Lawrence: U of Kansas P, 1956. 1–18.

Larson, Kerry C. *Whitman's Drama of Consensus.* Chicago: U of Chicago P, 1988.

Reynolds, David S. *Walt Whitman's America: A Cultural Biography.* New York: Knopf, 1995.

Whitman, Walt. "The Eighteenth Presidency!" *Complete Poetry and Collected Prose.* Ed. Justin Kaplan. New York: Library of America, 1982. 1307–1325.

See also LABOR AND LABORING CLASSES; POLITICAL VIEWS; PRESIDENTS, UNITED STATES; "RESPONDEZ!"; SLAVERY AND ABOLITIONISM

Eliot, T.S. (1888–1965)

Since expatriate T.S. Eliot was an ardent defender of European cultural tradition as the guiding light of American literature, his limited regard for Walt Whitman, redoubtable advocate of American literary independence, is no wonder. In a review article in the London *Athenaeum* in 1919, Eliot complained that Whitman (along with Nathaniel Hawthorne and Edgar Allan Poe) suffered from "the defect of [American] society. . . . Their world was thin; it was not corrupt enough" (qtd. in Howarth 93).

Nevertheless, even though the extent of the influence is debatable, Whitman had an effect on Eliot's work. For example, the hermit thrush's song in the pine trees in the "What the Thunder Said" section of Eliot's *The Waste Land* is an echo of bird songs in Whitman's "Out of the Cradle Endlessly Rocking" and "When Lilacs Last in the Dooryard Bloom'd." In addition, Eliot's question in *The Waste Land* "Who is the third who walks always beside you?" (line 360) resonates with Whitman's "Lilacs," in which the "I" walks "with the knowledge of death as walking one side of me, / And the thought of death close-walking the other side of me, / And I in the middle as with companions" (section 14). Indirectly, it is likely that Whitman influenced Eliot's composition of long lyrical sequences, notably in *The Waste Land.*

In the end, Eliot thought more of Whitman than he cared to admit, acknowledging in his 1926 essay "Whitman and Tennyson" that Whitman was "a great representative . . . of an America which no longer exists" and approving the vision that underlies "all [Whitman's] declamations. . . . When Whitman speaks of the lilacs or of the mocking bird, his theories and beliefs drop away like a needless pretext," Eliot observes, preferring his own pretexts.

Alan Shucard

Bibliography

Canary, Robert H. *T.S. Eliot: The Poet and His Critics.* Chicago: American Library Association, 1982.

Eliot, T.S. "Whitman and Tennyson." *The Nation and Athenaeum* 40 (1926): 426.

Howarth, Herbert. *Notes on Some Figures Behind T.S. Eliot.* Boston: Houghton Mifflin, 1964.

Miller, James E., Jr. "The Waste Land." *The American Quest for a Supreme Fiction: Whitman's Legacy in the Personal Epic.* By Miller. Chicago: U of Chicago P, 1979. 100–125.

Moody, A.D. "T.S. Eliot: The American Strain." *The Placing of T.S. Eliot.* Ed. Jewell Spears Brooker. Columbia: U of Missouri P, 1991. 77–89.

Musgrove, Sydney. *T.S. Eliot and Walt Whitman.* Wellington: U of New Zealand P, 1952.

Strandberg, Victor. "Whitman and Eliot: Two Studies in the Religious Imagination." *Four Quarters* 22 (1973): 3–18.

See also LEGACY, WHITMAN'S

Concord 21 July
Massltts } 1855

Dear Sir,

I am not
blind to the worth of
this wonderful gift of
"Leaves of Grass." I find
it the most extraordinary
piece of wit & wisdom
that America has yet
contributed. I am very
happy in reading it,
as great power makes us
happy. It meets the
demand I am always
making of what seemed
the sterile & stingy Nature,
as if too much handiwork
or too much lymph
in the temperament
were making our
western wits fat & mean.
I give you joy of
your free & brave
thought. I have great
joy in it. I find incom-
parable things said
incomparably well, as
they must be. I find
the courage of treatment,
which so delights us,
& which large perception
only can inspire.
I greet you at the be-
ginning of a great
career, which yet
must have had a
long foreground somewhere,
for such a start. I
rubbed my eyes a little
to see if this sunbeam
were no illusion; but
the solid sense of the book
is a sober certainty.
It has the best merits,
namely, of fortifying
& encouraging.
I did not know
until I, last night, saw

Ralph Waldo Emerson letter (21 July 1855) saluting Leaves of Grass. *Courtesy of the Library of Congress.*

The book advertised in a newspaper, that I could trust the name as real & available for a Post Office. I wish to see

my benefactor, & have felt much like striking my tasks, & visiting New York to pay you my respects.

R.W. Emerson.

Mr Walter Whitman.

Ralph Waldo Emerson letter (21 July 1855) saluting Leaves of Grass. *Courtesy of the Library of Congress.*

Emerson, Ralph Waldo (1803–1882)

Born in Boston on 25 May, Ralph Waldo Emerson was the third of eight children born into a family of Unitarian and Congregational ministers going back to the Puritans. After the age of eight, Emerson grew up without a father. He entered Harvard College in 1817 as the youngest member of his class. It was during his undergraduate days that "Waldo" (as he was called after his junior year) began keeping a journal, or "savings bank," whose life-long entries often served as the first hint of Emerson's sermons, lectures, and essays.

After graduation Emerson assisted his older brother William in the operation of a girls' school in Boston, but Emerson was never comfortable with schoolteaching and soon enrolled in the Harvard Divinity School. This education, which was quite informal at that time, was interrupted several times when Emerson was forced to take to his bed or go to sea or the South to combat recurring bouts of tuberculosis, a frequent malady in the nineteenth century which took early in manhood the lives of Emerson's most promising brothers, Edward and Charles. Following his graduation, Emerson was assigned to the Second Unitarian Church of Boston, where he wrote well over one hundred sermons and otherwise conducted the duties of a clergyman. In arguing for Emerson's lack of warmth to any but the closest relatives, it has been said that Emerson was not comfortable with the hand-holding aspect of a clergyman's duties, but this was generally the least popular aspect of a minister's tasks, which were mainly intellectual. While an active minister, Emerson married Ellen Tucker in 1829, but her health was never strong, and she died of tuberculosis in 1831. Soon afterward, Emerson starting thinking about leaving the ministry; his sermons show him becoming more interested in nature than Scripture as a spiritual guide, and he began to think of Christ as someone who had discovered a divinity that was present in all humankind.

Resigning his position in 1832, he traveled abroad, once again for purposes of health, visiting Italy, Germany, France, and England, and returned with at least part of his first book, *Nature* (1836), drafted either in deed or thought. He joined the Lyceum Movement, which allowed working-class young men the opportunity of educating themselves by giving and hearing lectures on various topics. Emerson gave four in 1835 on the general subject of natural history, but underlying each was the transcendentalist idea that nature was the emblem of the spirit, or God. Successful in his Lyceum lectures, he soon ventured out on his own, announcing a series of lectures each winter, and paying attention to such details as the printing and sale of tickets. For the next fifteen years, this (in addition to what he received from his first wife's estate; he married Lydia ["Lidian"] Jackson in 1835) was Emerson's sole source of income, as he realized no profit from his books until after 1850.

It was during his lecture series "The Times" in New York City in March of 1842 that Emerson first came in contact with Whitman, who heard him deliver "Nature and the Powers of the Poet." As editor of the New York *Aurora,* Whitman wrote that Emerson's lecture was one of the richest and most beautiful compositions he had ever heard anywhere, at any time. By this time Emerson had published his major lectures of the 1830s as well as *Essays* (1841), which Whitman no doubt read, especially the essay entitled "Spiritual Laws" mentioned in one of the poet's editorials in the Brooklyn *Daily Eagle* in 1847. "The Poet" would open *Essays: Second Series* (1844), as the final version of the lecture Whitman had heard in 1842. There Emerson writes that he has looked "in vain" (465) for the poet he had described, one who would in "a meter-making argument" (450) sing of "our log-rolling, our stumps and their politics, our fisheries, our Negroes and Indians, our boasts and our repudiations" (465). He would soon find that poet (though he had thought he had discovered that talent before and was subsequently disappointed) as the author of *Leaves of Grass* in 1855.

Emerson greeted Whitman at the beginning of a "great career" in his letter of 21 July 1855. He promised to visit his "benefactor" and did just that on 11 December, when he sought out the poet in his Brooklyn neighborhood and took him to dinner at the Astor House in Manhattan. Whitman had published without permission Emerson's encomium in the press that fall, but Emerson overlooked the indiscretion to meet the person who had transformed transcendentalist ideas of divinity into democracy. He also apparently overlooked Whitman's second publication of some words from the letter on the spine of the 1856 edition of *Leaves of Grass* (in gold letters) and the full text of the letter in an appendix. When Whitman came to Boston in 1860 in connection with the publication of his third edition, Emerson, who had apparently been given a chance to read the manuscript's new poems, urged him to excise "Enfans d'Adam" ("Children of Adam") because of its perceived obscenity. Whitman listened carefully to Emerson's argument, as the two walked on Boston Common, but he thought that such an excision would be like cutting out a person's virility and kept to his course with the book. The result, in the Boston press at least, was the consensus that Emerson, who had championed an earlier edition of *Leaves of Grass,* and Whitman, who had authored it, had one thing in common: temporary insanity.

This was essentially their last meeting (though Whitman visited Emerson in his senility shortly before his death). Emerson wrote in behalf of Whitman's efforts to secure government employment during the Civil War and in praise of his hospital work, but he began to lose interest in the later editions of *Leaves of Grass* because of their long catalogues and the poet's "religious" tendency to be too consciously transcendental. Yet Whitman may have been inspired by Emerson in part for his crisis poems as he was for those, such as "Song of Myself," that celebrated absolute freedom in nature. Emerson's "Fate" in *The Conduct of Life* (known earlier as a lecture) seems a spiritual blueprint for Whitman's realization in "Out of the Cradle Endlessly Rocking" and "As I Ebb'd with the Ocean of Life" that Transcendentalist Reason (poetical or mystical intuition) could not always calm the Understanding (the senses for empirical reasoning) out of its fear of death. The relationship between these two writers is one of the most important in American literary history, and both kept up their respect for the other until the end. After Emerson's death, Whitman ("At Emerson's Grave") tried to understate his debt to Emerson by aligning him with the traditional literature *Leaves of Grass* had challenged, but he was otherwise always loyal to the man he called "Master" in his open letter in the 1856 edition.

Jerome Loving

Bibliography

Allen, Gay Wilson. *Waldo Emerson.* New York: Viking, 1981.

Emerson, Ralph Waldo. "The Poet." *Essays and Lectures.* Ed. Joel Porte. New York: Library of America, 1983. 445–468.

Loving, Jerome. *Emerson, Whitman, and the American Muse.* Chapel Hill: U of North Carolina P, 1982.

Mott, Wesley T. *"The Strains of Eloquence": Emerson and His Sermons.* University Park: Pennsylvania State UP, 1989.

Richardson, Robert D., Jr. *Emerson: The Mind on Fire.* Berkeley: U of California P, 1995.

Rusk, Ralph D. *Life of Ralph Waldo Emerson.* New York: Scribner's, 1949.

von Frank, Albert J. *An Emerson Chronology.* New York: Hall, 1994.

See also BOSTON, MASSACHUSETTS; INFLUENCES ON WHITMAN, PRINCIPAL; "LETTER TO RALPH WALDO EMERSON"; ORGANICISM; READING, WHITMAN'S; ROMANTICISM; TRANSCENDENTALISM

Epic Structure

For some readers surveying the totality of *Leaves of Grass,* the work displays more unity than variety, and a coherence that resolves many questions into a harmonious, invigorating whole. Among these readers, James E. Miller, Jr., has explained persuasively that the work is no less than an epic, an epic designed to suit the special conditions of a new nation in a given moment of its growth. Miller points out that Whitman himself left many clues, both in his prose and poetry, about his intention to fashion a work of epic proportions (see chapter 18 of Miller's *Critical Guide*). He describes Whitman's epic hero, who is of course none other than Whitman himself, as a man both separate from and part of the crowd, one who is heroic not because superior but because common, whose triumph is that he discovers his own deepest selfhood. Every American is potentially this same kind of hero.

Whitman's democratic epic hero is then engaged in another epic stage, Miller continues, a trial of strength represented by the Civil War. As depicted in the poems of the "Drum-Taps" cluster, the very existence of the nation depends upon the outcome of this war, such a large cause being appropriate to the epic form. In the latter sections of *Leaves of Grass* (from "Proud Music of the Storm" to the end), the hero's mythic nature is built up, providing him with assurances of his immortality. Finally, the New World epic hero is connected as a comrade with no less than God (in "Passage to India"). In his epic, Miller suggests, Whitman has shown the breadth of his faith in science and democracy, especially strong faiths in the nineteenth century. He has also shown a faith in the kind of religious views held in that century, just as the peoples in epics of other centuries lived by certain faiths. Miller concludes by pointing out that no work before or after *Leaves of Grass* can lay claim to being America's epic. Dwelling in the ideal rather than the real, *Leaves* reflects her character, her soul, her achievements, her aspirations. In a later essay, Miller stresses the uniqueness of Whitman's epic by defining briefly its form in these aspects: action, character, setting, and theme, and by examining more closely the interior of *Leaves of Grass* (see chapter 3 of *American Quest*).

Just as other puzzles surrounding Whitman's work may remain after the closest scrutiny, so the reader may have doubts about its form as epic, while at the same time accommo- dating Miller's interpretation. Roy Harvey Pearce's proposal, on the other hand, that "Song of Myself" alone should be considered an epic, or rather "the equivalent of an epic" (83), is unconvincing if only in light of the totality of *Leaves of Grass.*

One doubt arises simply from the way the work is used. Few would sit down and read it cover to cover; the work is ordinarily read in pieces, without damage to the whole. That is the normal way any book of lyric poetry is read. While among the collection are certain great longer poems, there are dozens of highly effective shorter ones that engage the sensitive reader perhaps even more powerfully than some of the more grandiose and public ones because of their very compact and intimate artistry. Can a poet be both lyric and epic? In Whitman's case, it would seem so.

Also, seeing Whitman as the hero of his own work is troublesome, not because he isn't properly at the center for his aims and methods but because to be a hero is always to be special in character and deeds, whereas he is at pains to be thought representative rather than special. Everyone is being invited to join him in a heroic journey to the interior of the self; but the vision of a nation in which everyone becomes heroic simply by accepting his selfhood, his humanity, is stretching the idea of the heroic close to absurdity.

And how is the reader to accommodate the several important places throughout *Leaves of Grass* where Whitman confesses his own blacker side, such evils as sloth, selfishness, greed, concupiscence, envy? Such admirable spots bespeak not heroism but brave recognition of common human frailty. And how are such evils within expiated and controlled? Are all citizens expected to have the same benign, reconciling mechanism with which Whitman's temperament was blessed? As to exterior evils, the only weakness in America's culture he railed against consistently for many years was an issue of social class, namely, narrow respectability and gentility, perhaps a doubtful adversary for an epic hero.

Nor does the internal structure of the work argue for an epic designation, at least not loudly. It is not a book constructed on the dynamic of a journey in search of something desirable yet to be grasped. In the earliest great poem, "Song of Myself," overrated by some as the only indispensable part of *Leaves of Grass,* the search is over before it begins. Here the speaker, at least, has found his faith, the love of comrades, of everyone and everything. He will celebrate them, and every atom of the congenial universe. When he wrote "Song of Myself," Whitman was not an innocent young man. At thirty-seven, as he confidently tells us, he had already experienced what it was to be a carpenter, teacher, printer, writer, and several kinds of editors, as well as an active son and brother. His own battles for identity and direction and faith had largely been won. He would seem to have been better suited to be a guide for others, like Vergil in the *Divine Comedy*, than to set himself up as a hero in search of something, as an epic would call for; and in many sections of "Song of Myself," especially in the last few, he does in fact behave rhetorically like a teacher and guide.

A brief summary of the structural contents of *Leaves of Grass* may or may not cast further doubt on its coherence as an epic. Sections that do show internal consistency, and which proceed in a rough chronology more or less paralleling Whitman's stages of life, are: "Inscriptions," "Children of Adam," "Calamus," "Sea-Drift," "Drum-Taps," "Memories of President Lincoln," "Whispers of Heavenly Death," and "Songs of Parting." Those that are without focus, miscellaneous, are: "By the Roadside," "Autumn Rivulets," "From Noon to Starry Night," "Sands at Seventy," and "Good-Bye my Fancy." Other important miscellaneous long poems, coming after the "Calamus" section, in a grouping not given any title by Whitman, take up over eighty pages of the *Comprehensive Reader's Edition*. Here again the reader is faced with a peculiarity; there is strong evidence for coherence and order of subject matter expected of an epic and only somewhat less strong evidence for little coherence.

In his last years, Whitman discussed with Horace Traubel the possible issuing of *Leaves of Grass* in units of small volumes, as he said, "'Song of Myself' in one, and so on" claiming he "shall never be set at rest" till such separate volumes appeared (*With Walt Whitman* 6:66–67). He also said to Traubel earlier that *Leaves of Grass* is unsatisfactory in pieces, that it "can only find its reflection in ensemble . . . it belongs to bulk, mass, unity: must be seen with reference to its eligibility to express world-meanings rather than literary prettinesses" (*With Walt Whitman* 2:115). Does he contradict himself? Very well. He does.

Whatever arguments may be made against the work's being an epic, *Leaves of Grass* is undeniably of such proportions. It is large. It contains multitudes. While the term *epic* might well be jettisoned in favor of another more flexible one, such as architectonic, with its distinguished tradition it remains suitable for honoring Whitman's truly magnificent accomplishment.

David B. Baldwin

Bibliography

Hansen, Chadwick C. "Walt Whitman's 'Song of Myself'—Democratic Epic." *The American Renaissance: The History and Literature of an Era.* Ed. Marin Abbott and George Hendrick. Die Neueren Sprachen 9. Frankfurt, Germany: Diesterweg, 1961. 77–88.

Köhring, Klaus H. "The American Epic." *Southern Humanities Review* 5 (1971): 265–280.

McWilliams, John P., Jr. *The American Epic: Transforming a Genre, 1770–1860.* Cambridge: Cambridge UP, 1990.

Miller, James E., Jr. *The American Quest for a Supreme Fiction: Whitman's Legacy in the Personal Epic.* Chicago: U of Chicago P, 1979.

———. *A Critical Guide to "Leaves of Grass."* Chicago: U of Chicago P, 1957.

———. *"Leaves of Grass": America's Lyric-Epic of Self and Democracy.* New York: Twayne, 1992.

Nuhn, Ferner. "*Leaves of Grass* Viewed as an Epic." *Arizona Quarterly* 7 (1951): 324–338.

Pearce, Roy Harvey. *The Continuity of American Poetry.* Princeton: Princeton UP, 1961.

Traubel, Horace. *With Walt Whitman in Camden.* Vol. 2. New York: Appleton, 1908; Vol. 6. Ed. Gertrude Traubel and William White. Carbondale: Southern Illinois UP, 1982.

Walker, Jeffrey. *Bardic Ethos and the American Epic Poem.* Baton Rouge: Louisiana State UP, 1989.

Whitman, Walt. *Leaves of Grass: Comprehensive Reader's Edition.* Ed. Harold W. Blodgett and Sculley Bradley. New York: New York UP, 1965.

See also POETIC THEORY; STYLE AND TECHNIQUE(S)

Epictetus (ca.55–ca.125)

Epictetus was one of the Stoic philosophers in the world of the Roman Empire. His name in the Greek means "acquired." He was a slave from his earliest years in Rome, his master a secretary to the emperor, Nero. He attended the lectures of Musonius Rufus and became a follower of the Stoic doctrine.

Epictetus was lame, and, following the death of his master, he was manumitted and became a teacher. No writings are extant although a student, Arrian, published his lectures as *Discourses* and *Encheiridion*. The simplest statement of the Stoic doctrine is that the good life consists of knowing the will of God for our lives and learning to distinguish between those things which are and are not within our power. True education consists in recognizing that the only thing that belongs to a man is his will or purpose. "Men are disturbed not by things," says Epictetus, "but by the views which they take of things" (317).

As a political theorist Epictetus saw humanity as a part of a great system that comprehends both God and humanity. The *polis* we live in is but a pale copy of the true city of God. Human beings can learn to make the city and their own lives more like the will of God. They cannot, however, secure their own welfare unless they contribute to the common welfare. The role of the philosopher for Epictetus was to see the world whole and to grow into the mind of God and make the will of nature his own.

Whitman knew of Epictetus through Frances Wright's *A Few Days in Athens* (1822), which was one of the cherished books of his parents' household. Wright deeply influenced his thinking and approach to life and poetry.

W. Edward Harris

Bibliography

Allen, Gay Wilson. "Walt Whitman and Stoicism." *The Stoic Strain in American Literature: Essays in Honour of Marston LaFrance*. Ed. Duane J. MacMillan. Toronto: U of Toronto P, 1979. 43–60.

Epictetus. "Things Which Are in Our Power." *Source Book in Ancient Philosophy*. Ed. Charles Bakewell. New York: Scribner's, 1907. 317–319.

Goodale, David. "Some of Walt Whitman's Borrowings." *American Literature* 10 (1938): 202–213.

Traubel, Horace. *With Walt Whitman in Camden*. Vol. 2. New York: Appleton, 1908.

Wright, Frances. *A Few Days in Athens*. 1822. New York: Arno, 1972.

See also EPICURUS; STOICISM; WRIGHT, FRANCES (FANNY)

Epicurus (341–270 B.C.)

A native of Samos, Epicurus was a Greek philosopher who founded a school in Athens in 306 B.C. Most of what remains of Epicurus's writings—letters to Herodotus, Pythocles, and Menoeceus; the *Main Principles;* and many of the fragments—appear in the tenth book of the *History of the Philosophers* by Diogenes Laertius.

An atomist, Epicurus professed a materialist ontology akin to that of Democritus. According to Epicurus, all that exists is composed of units of matter that fall eternally through space. Material change occurs because of the natural "swerve" of atoms and the tangential motions caused by their collision.

Known primarily for his ethical philosophy, Epicurus espoused a form of egocentric hedonism that dictated that one ought to maximize one's pleasure and minimize one's pain; pleasure is the standard by which to judge the rightness or wrongness of an action. Epicurus taught that reaching a state of blessedness requires prudence and moderate repose, fulfilling necessary and natural desires and denying unnatural ones.

Whitman was exposed to Epicureanism primarily through the writings of Frances Wright (1795–1852) and Lucretius (94–55 B.C.). Whitman's father attended lectures by Wright, a Scottish neo-Epicurean, and subscribed to her *Free Inquirer*. Whitman read the *Inquirer* and closely studied Wright's *A Few Days in Athens—Being the Translation of a Greek Manuscript Discovered in Herculaneum* (1822). Also, about 1851, Whitman acquired a translation of Lucretius's *De Rerum Natura* (On the Nature of Things), which scholars now contend was probably based on *The Major Epitome* of Epicurus.

Epicurus's notion of prudence may have influenced Whitman's writing, including his definition of the American character—"because prudence is the right arm of independence" (Whitman 63)—and his "Song of Prudence" (1856). Furthermore, Epicurean atheism—its refusal to fear the actions of a fictional god—may be evident in poems such as "Song of

Myself" (1855), where Whitman admires the animals because they "do not make me sick discussing their duty to God" (section 32).

Matthew C. Altman

Bibliography

Allen, Gay Wilson. *The Solitary Singer: A Critical Biography of Walt Whitman.* 1955. Rev. ed. 1967. Chicago: U of Chicago P, 1985.

Epicurus. *Epicurus: The Extant Remains.* Ed. and trans. Cyril W. Bailey. Hildesheim: Georg Olms Verlag, 1975.

Goodale, David. "Some of Walt Whitman's Borrowings." *American Literature* 10 (1938): 202–213.

Jones, W.T. *The Classical Mind: A History of Western Philosophy.* 2nd ed. New York: Harcourt Brace Jovanovich, 1970.

Strodach, George K. *The Philosophy of Epicurus.* Evanston: Northwestern UP, 1963.

Whitman, Walt. *The Uncollected Poetry and Prose of Walt Whitman.* Ed. Emory Holloway. Vol. 2. Garden City, N.Y.: Doubleday, Page, 1921.

Wright, Frances. *A Few Days in Athens— Being the Translation of a Greek Manuscript Discovered in Herculaneum.* 1822. Rev. ed. New York: Bliss and White, 1825.

See also Lucretius; Metaphysics; Wright, Frances (Fanny)

Equality

Whitman's faith in democracy was based on three principles which he inherited from the age of enlightenment: liberty, equality, fraternity— or comradeship, as he preferred to call it. As early as 1855, he proclaimed in *Leaves of Grass:* "Great is liberty! Great is equality! I am their follower . . ." ("Great Are the Myths"). In 1860 he kept repeating: "I announce uncompromising liberty and equality" ("So Long!"); "Of Equality—As if it harmed me, giving others the same chances and rights as myself—As if it were not indispensable to my own rights that others possess the same" ("Thoughts. 4"); and "O equality! O organic compacts! I am come to be your born poet!" ("Apostroph"). He thus insisted with as much vigor on the fundamental equality of all men as on their right to liberty.

Whitman's championship of equality was also based on the teaching of Christ as he had seen it practiced by the Quakers: "I wear my hat as I please indoors or out" ("Song of Myself," section 20). Holding himself up as a point of comparison, he declared: "In all people I see myself, none more and not one a barley-corn less" ("Song of Myself," section 20). He could therefore say "indifferently and alike *How are you friend?* to the President at his levee" and "*Good-day my brother,* to Cudge that hoes in the sugar-field" ("Song of the Answerer," section 1). He refused to make any discriminations, for, according to his philosophy, the mere fact of living conferred a divine character even upon the most despicable being, since every man is the supreme outcome of the evolution of the universe for thousands of years: "Do you think matter has cohered together from its diffuse float . . . For you only, and not for him and her?" ("I Sing the Body Electric," section 6). Besides, he knew from his own experience that education and social origin were of little importance and the most humble being contained infinite potentialities of grandeur: "Always waiting untold in the souls of the armies of common people, is stuff better than anything that can possibly appear in the leadership of the same" (*Comprehensive* 733). So by 1860 Whitman had quite naturally arrived at the notions of "average man" and "divine average," which from that time on were everywhere present in *Leaves of Grass:* "O such themes—equalities! O divine average!" ("Starting from Paumanok," section 10). He went so far as to affirm in 1876, "*You average Spiritual Manhood, purpose of all, pois'd on yourself—giving, not taking law*" ("Song of the Redwood-Tree," section 1).

Nevertheless, although he proclaimed the equality of all men and extolled the average man with genuine fervor, Whitman celebrated great men almost in the same breath: "A great city is that which has the greatest men and women . . ." ("Song of the Broad-Axe," section 4); "Produce great Persons, the rest follows" ("By Blue Ontario's Shore," section 3). The contradiction, however, is more apparent than real, for the great men whom he admired were not like those celebrated by Thomas Carlyle, not statesmen and temporal chiefs "who do not believe in men" ("Thought [Of obedience . . .]"). To Carlyle's heroes Whitman preferred thinkers and prophets—poets like himself, in short, who inspire the masses, or true heroes who sacrifice themselves for the people, or great engineers who work for their well-being. In opposition to Carlyle's hero worship he offered in 1871 a "worship new" of "captains, voyagers, explorers . . . engineers . . . architects, [and] machinists" ("Passage to India," section 2). He thus considered that even in a democratic society of equal men, spiritual and intellectual elites are necessary. He re-affirmed it in *Democratic Vistas:* "[I]t is strictly true, that a few first-class poets, philosophs, and authors, have substantially settled and given status to the entire religion, education, law, sociology, &c., of the hitherto civilized world . . . and more than ever stamp, the interior and real democratic construction of this American continent, to-day, and days to come" (*Prose Works* 2:366–367). For if, as a utopian poet, he unreservedly sang the "divine average," he was quite lucid and illusionless in the prose of *Democratic Vistas* concerning the darker side of human nature. There he admits that "general humanity . . . has always, in every department, been full of perverse maleficence, and is so yet" (2:379). Nonetheless, the Civil War revealed to him the heroism of the average American and confirmed his faith in man "en-masse." When the war was over, he proclaimed the grandeur of the average man: "Never was average man, his soul, more energetic, more like a God . . ." ("Years of the Modern"). He thus wavered between an idealistic and a realistic conception of man, yet firmly concluded that, all men being fundamentally equal, the universal suffrage must guarantee the rights of all and that democracy is the only regime that can ensure the development of a just society: "[G]ood or bad, rights or no rights, the democratic formula is the only safe and preservative one for coming times. We endow the masses with the suffrage for their own sake, . . . perhaps still more . . . for community's sake" (*Prose Works* 2:380–381). Even if democracy is imperfect and only a lesser evil, it respects what Whitman calls "equal brotherhood." Alexis de Tocqueville, though an aristocrat and a conservative, had to acknowledge that the system worked. He admired the social equality he observed in the United States when he visited it in Whitman's time.

Whitman believed in equality because he was an individualist, an upholder of "personalism," who wanted above all to safeguard the rights of the individual, i.e., himself, but he failed to realize that there is an incompatibility between liberty and equality. As Plato pointed out in the *Republic,* in a given society individuals are born intelligent or stupid, good-looking or ugly, dexterous or crippled, strong or weak. Equality is contrary to facts and unnatural. If you want nonetheless to enforce it, you must impose a general leveling down and deny personal liberty, as was done in totalitarian countries. Equality as conceived by the thinkers of the age of enlightenment was equality of opportunity, equality of rights, not complete equality on all planes, as demagogues claim and pretend to believe. Men can be equal only in rights; they can never be totally equal physically and intellectually. If a government wants to impose equality, it will have to impose it by force at the expense of liberty. So the three elements which make up democracy, the three values on which it is based, must be carefully measured. A delicate balance between liberty and equality must be maintained. It is very precarious and rarely obtained. Perfect democracy exists only in *Leaves of Grass*—thanks to Whitman's emphasis on brotherhood.

Roger Asselineau

Bibliography

Allen, Gay Wilson. *The New Walt Whitman Handbook.* 1975. New York: New York UP, 1986.

Asselineau, Roger. *The Evolution of Walt Whitman: The Creation of a Book.* Trans. Roger Asselineau and Burton L. Cooper. Cambridge, Mass.: Harvard UP, 1962.

Erkkila, Betsy. *Whitman the Political Poet.* New York: Oxford UP, 1989.

Whitman, Walt. *Leaves of Grass: Comprehensive Reader's Edition.* Ed. Harold W. Blodgett and Sculley Bradley. New York: New York UP, 1965.

———. *Prose Works 1892.* Ed. Floyd Stovall. 2 vols. New York: New York UP, 1963–1964.

See also COMRADESHIP; DEMOCRACY; FREEDOM; INDIVIDUALISM

"Ethiopia Saluting the Colors" (1871)

Originally written and accepted for publication (but never published) by the *Galaxy* magazine in 1867 as "Ethiopia Commenting," Whitman first placed this poem in *Leaves of Grass* in 1871 and revised it in the 1876 edition with the subtitle "A Reminiscence of 1864." It was placed in the "Drum-Taps" cluster in 1881.

In its final form, the poem recounts an old black woman's watching General Sherman's troops march through her Carolina town on their way to the sea. The woman wears a turban of African colors—yellow, red, and green—as she rises to greet the colors of the army. As Betsy Erkkila notes, the woman's exoticism and exclusion from the dominant American culture is stressed as well as the racial hierarchy accepted by nineteenth-century society.

The speaker contemplates the "hardly human" woman as the colors go by and questions what "strange and marvelous" things she has experienced. The notation of the woman as "hardly human" suggests that the exotic woman remains for Whitman as the Other, the feared. In a brief stanza we are given a glance at what the speaker believes she is thinking; in Whitman's awkward attempt at dialect, she remembers her capture from Africa and the middle passage. The horrors of the middle passage and slavery's abuses are understated as the strangeness of her experiences are emphasized.

By placing the poem in "Drum-Taps" in 1881, Whitman secures the connection between slavery and the Civil War which he first alludes to in the initial poem. The conventional form which Whitman uses—the standard three-line stanzas, internal and terminal rhyme, and alliteration—indicates the difficulty of coming to terms with the black body and suggests a desire for containment.

As one of the few comments on black liberation, the poem offers insight into Whitman's perception of blacks in the United States, suggesting that Whitman had not come to terms with a free black population.

Amy E. Earhart

Bibliography

Erkkila, Betsy. *Whitman the Political Poet.* New York: Oxford UP, 1989.

Klammer, Martin. *Whitman, Slavery, and the Emergence of "Leaves of Grass."* University Park: Pennsylvania State UP, 1995.

Whitman, Walt. *Leaves of Grass.* Ed. Sculley Bradley and Harold W. Blodgett. Norton Critical Edition. New York: Norton, 1973.

See also "DRUM-TAPS"; RACIAL ATTITUDES; SLAVERY AND ABOLITIONISM

"Europe, The 72d and 73d Years of These States" (1850)

This poem was the first published (New York *Daily Tribune*, 21 June 1850) of those later to become a part of *Leaves of Grass* (1855). Called "Resurgemus," in the 1856 edition its title was changed to "Poem of the Dead Young Men of Europe, The 72d and 73d Years of These States."

Both its early date and its two titles reflect Whitman's broad involvement with political matters in his role as editor of and contributor to various newspapers and journals during the 1840s. That he is concerned here with issues in Europe, a region he never visited, suggests that the scope of his vision for humanity was already in place when he was only thirty-one. "Europe" passionately champions the young men who died in the abortive uprisings of 1848 in several European nations, uprisings protesting against arbitrary authority and entrenched royal prerogatives.

Composed of thirty-eight lines, the poem foreshadows dramatic techniques Whitman was to use again and again. It begins with a fresh, immediate image of the rise of the revolutionary impulse, personified with "its hands tight to the throats of kings," opening out to a wail of grief at the failed effort: "O aching close of exiled patriots' lives / O many a sicken'd heart." Using direct address, the poet then speaks to those in power: "And you, paid to defile the People—you liars, mark!" Idealizing the revolutionaries, who scorned to use "the ferocity of kings," the poet records the "bitter destruction" that followed from this mildness, which more likely sprang from a lack of military power.

Out of Whitman's rich visionary imagination appears a phantom, "vague as the night," probably meant to prophesy, in the shape of a fearful death, the ultimate fate of the kings and their retinue. Blunt imagery of the dead young men is followed by a strong message that other young men will carry on the fight. A tone of hope and encouragement dominates the rest of the lyric, most dramatically in line 35: "Liberty, let others despair of you—I never despair of you," the repeating phrase, for emphasis, to become a signature of Whitman's style. Also the loose, trochaic rhythm evident throughout is already a sure sign of Whitman's voice. Still another is the putting of a rhetorical question near the close, followed by a soothing reassurance. In this instance the question is contained in a figure—"Is the house shut? is the master away?"—by which Whitman suggests liberty's temporary absence. He concludes, however, "He will soon return, his messengers come anon."

It is noteworthy that Whitman turned away from specific political topics as he filled out *Leaves of Grass* through the years. Few of his works can be considered partisan, even among his Civil War poems.

David B. Baldwin

Bibliography

Whitman, Walt. *Leaves of Grass: Comprehensive Reader's Edition.* Ed. Harold W. Blodgett and Sculley Bradley. New York: New York UP, 1965.

See also "By the Roadside"; Pre-*Leaves* Poems; Revolutions of 1848; "To a Foil'd European Revolutionaire"

***Evening Tattler* (New York)**

In May or June of 1842, a few weeks after Nelson Herrick and John F. Ropes discharged him (on grounds of "loaferism") as editor of the New York *Aurora,* Whitman began editing yet another paper, the *Evening Tattler,* a small daily that sold for a penny a copy. The *Tattler* had been founded in 1839 by Park Benjamin and Rufus W. Griswold, two individuals who had long since departed by the time Whitman joined the newspaper. During his two or three months at the *Tattler,* Whitman wrote editorials not unlike those he had produced for the *Aurora*—on typical New York characters and scenes. He also continued his feud with Herrick and Ropes, printing accusations and insults whenever possible. At the *Evening Tattler,* which was emblematic of the rough-and-tumble world of nineteenth-century American journalism, where jobs were often tenuous and where invective and vitriol were the order of the day, Whitman, at twenty-three, was nevertheless defining himself as a literary professional.

Amy M. Bawcom

Bibliography

Allen, Gay Wilson. *The Solitary Singer: A Critical Biography of Walt Whitman.* 1955. Rev. ed. 1967. Chicago: U of Chicago P, 1985.

Stovall, Floyd. *The Foreground of "Leaves of Grass."* Charlottesville: UP of Virginia, 1974.

See also Journalism, Whitman's; New York Aurora

Everson, William (Brother Antoninus) (1912–)

Primarily influenced by Robinson Jeffers, poet and printer Everson's career is divided into three parts collected in the ongoing trilogy *The Crooked Lines of God.* The first volume is *The Residual Years* (1944), and the second, *The Veritable Years* (1978), is drawn from his period as Dominican Order Brother Antoninus, his pen name between 1949 and 1966.

Throughout his collection of philosophic essays, *Birth of a Poet* (1982), Everson sees Whitman as an American archetype who first expressed the "New Adam" (102) and lived the role of this archetype in a public life. Whitman "expressed . . . both the populous and the natural wonder" (103) of an American romanticism of "imprecise Homeric" (105) expansiveness. In Whitman, "art is a song of spontaneity and joy, luxuriating in the ambience of the goodness of being" (108).

In 1981, Everson's printing house, Lime Kiln Press, published Everson's setting of the Preface to the 1855 edition of *Leaves of Grass* as a poem, *American Bard,* a publication celebrated in a film of the same name.

Wesley A. Britton

Bibliography

Cherkovski, Neeli. *Whitman's Wild Children.* Venice: Lapis, 1988.

Everson, William. *Birth of a Poet: The Santa Cruz Meditations.* Ed. Lee Bartlett. Santa Barbara: Black Sparrow, 1982.

See also Legacy, Whitman's; Preface to Leaves of Grass, 1855 Edition

---

Evil

W.B. Yeats failed to recognize Whitman's powerful "vision of evil" because he read him superficially. Actually, a fine anthology can be made of Whitman's poetry (and prose) of death, suffering, war, sin, slavery, martyrdom, stoicism, loneliness, "dark" items (in lists), guilt, crime—varieties of evil. Yet a widespread conviction that Whitman somehow shared Emerson's "easy" transcendentalism (which was *not* so easy) filtered out his sense of evil for many critics. Randall Jarrell's 1953 summary is more just: "Whitman specializes in ways of saying that there is in some sense (a very Hegelian one, generally) no evil—he says a hundred times that evil is not Real; but he also specializes in making lists of the evil of the world, lists of an unarguable reality" (227).

One might begin by classifying the various evils noted by Whitman as physical (sickness, pain, decay), psychological (despair, "dark patches," "contrariety"), and social (isolation, prostitution, poverty, civil war)—and after Abraham Lincoln's martyrdom, hypocrisy, bad blood, hollowness of heart (see *Democratic Vistas*). But such categories tend toward generality and abstraction. To dig deeper and soar higher, we may think of religions and philosophies: the theological "problem of Evil" is central for monotheism, of course, but less so for pantheists and "cosmic" mystics, so that Whitman (in "Chanting the Square Deific") made Satan part of his conception of God.

But since Whitman was not a systematic philosopher or theologian, we turn to the textures and bone of his poetry, what Roger Asselineau's biography began to spell out as his personal "evolution": first, as young author, and then as creator of *Leaves of Grass*—the former providing that "long foreground" intuited by Emerson. Every scholar concerned with Whitman's education and milieu links his developing ideas and themes to their historical settings, with their large problems of good and evil: his Calvinistic inheritance; the Unitarian revolt; Methodism and the Great Awakening, as reflected in the "camp meeting" elements in "Song of Myself"; the Long Island Quakerism typified by Elias Hicks; J.L. O'Sullivan's *Democratic Review;* reform politics; free-soil abolitionism; the Civil War and its aftermath; and so forth.

Whitman was an omnivorous reader of the Bible and other classics, including Dante and John Milton, and his "Edgar Poe's Significance" essay (1882) helps explain his appeal in France to the generation of Baudelaire's "Flowers of Evil" and in England to the Pre-Raphaelites and Swinburne. His early writings (from 1841) reflect not only Poe, but also Nathaniel Hawthorne and Herman Melville. Ralph Waldo Emerson, Emanuel Swedenborg, Henry David Thoreau, and John Greenleaf Whittier were also presences in his poetry of good and evil.

Emerging from this mélange, Whitman's "self" confronted not only "all the sorrows of the world, and . . . all oppression and shame" ("I Sit and Look Out"), but death as well, as seen in "To Think of Time," "This Compost," "Out of the Cradle Endlessly Rocking," "The Sleepers," "When Lilacs Last in the Dooryard Bloom'd," and many other poems. Poetry of love and male friendship included strong notes of loneliness and loss; the patriotic "Drum-Taps" included "The Wound-Dresser" and "Vigil Strange." In "Starting from Paumanok" (1860) he declared: "Omnes! omnes! let others ignore what they may, / I make the poem of evil also, I commemorate that part also . . ." (section 7).

Versatile Whitman wrote in prose (fiction, journalism, essays, memoirs) and verse (from early imitations to uniquely original styles and forms), so that we can relate our problematic theme to varieties of genre in both modes. Classic treatments of evil have been in tragedy, comedy, and satire, and some of Whitman's verse experiments were sharply satiric, for example "A Boston Ballad (1854)" and "Respondez!" (1856). But his poetry evades the usual genre classifications. It does seek heroism, but it is finally (despite complications with reference to this point) not "epic." *Leaves of Grass* has many dramatic moments but never achieves full tragedy or comedy. Though such critics as Richard Chase read "Song of Myself" as a "comic drama of the self," both the drama and the comedy are fitful, verging on melodrama, pathos, and sentimentality. (See the discussion of the passage ending "I am the man, I suffered, I was there" in Sholom Kahn, "Whitman's Sense of Evil.") Also, as Thoreau once commented, at many moments Whitman is "Wonderfully like the Orientals," whose sense of evil is quite different from that of Europeans.

Whitman coped with—or transcended—his strong sense of the evil in his life and in the world by writing *Leaves of Grass* and serving as "wound-dresser" in the "hell-scenes" of the Civil War, and he achieved a sanity (termed "higher prudence" in the 1855 Preface) which was stoical, as is evidenced by "Me Imperturbe." In this respect, he was part of a strain pervasive in American literature (as evidenced by Duane MacMillan's collection of essays on stoicism in American literature). Robert E. Lee exemplified those many Americans at war who (so to speak) brought Epictetus to battlefields. Thus, going beyond the usual polarities of evil and good, pessimism and optimism, Whitman was never complacent; his vision of the ultimate triumph of good was the outcome of agonistic struggles powerfully expressed in much of his best poetry.

Sholom J. Kahn

Bibliography

Allen, Gay Wilson. "Walt Whitman and Stoicism." *The Stoic Strain in American Literature: Essays in Honour of Marston LaFrance.* Ed. Duane J. MacMillan. Toronto: U of Toronto P, 1979. 43–60.

Asselineau, Roger. *The Evolution of Walt Whitman.* 2 vols. Cambridge, Mass.: Harvard UP, 1960–1962.

Jarrell, Randall. "Some Lines from Whitman." *A Century of Whitman Criticism.* Ed. Edwin Haviland Miller. Bloomington: Indiana UP, 1969. 216–229.

Kahn, Sholom J. "The American Backgrounds of Whitman's Sense of Evil." *Scripta Hierosolymitana* 2 (1955): 82–118.

———. "The Problem of Evil in Literature." *The Journal of Aesthetics and Art Criticism* 12 (1953): 98–110.

———. "Whitman's Sense of Evil: Criticisms." *Walt Whitman Abroad.* Ed. Gay Wilson Allen. Syracuse: Syracuse UP, 1955. 236–254.

MacMillan, Duane J., ed. *The Stoic Strain in American Literature: Essays in Honour of Marston LaFrance.* Toronto: U of Toronto P, 1979.

Miller, Edwin Haviland, ed. *A Century of Whitman Criticism.* Bloomington: Indiana UP, 1969.

See also "Chanting the Square Deific"; Mysticism; Optimism; Religion; Stoicism

Evolution

Although the theory of evolution—the belief that complex organisms were developed from preexistent simpler forms—is an ancient doctrine, it was only in the nineteenth century that massive scientific data appeared to support the theory systematically.

For students of Walt Whitman's thought, a knowledge of his speculations concerning the theory of evolution helps to clarify the relationship between his mystical idealism and his scientific, materialistic outlook. And scholars interested in Whitman's sources seek to understand the extent to which his evolutionary thought was indebted to Emersonian transcendentalism, German idealism, Oriental religion, and the popular sciences (or pseudosciences) of the period. Scholars continue to debate the question of the poet's most characteristic pronouncements on evolution: were they Lamarckian, Hegelian, Darwinian, mystical, or what?

Whitman was an evolutionist well before the publication of Charles Darwin's *Origin of Species* (1859). As early as 1847, when he was at work on early drafts of what was to become *Leaves of Grass,* he clearly indicated his absorption in evolutionary doctrines, and he was thus not at all upset (as was the case with Thomas Carlyle) when Darwin's work appeared. He was well acquainted with Lamarckian concepts of evolution through his particular interest in phrenology, whose adherents and practitioners clearly preached the doctrine of acquired characteristics as a part of their program of individual self-improvement. And Whitman's reading, as always, was voracious—especially in the popular periodicals, which regularly published articles on evolutionary speculation. The prolific writings of Herbert Spencer (1820–1903) made evolutionary thought accessible to a mass audience in nineteenth-century America.

Like many intellectuals of the nineteenth century, Whitman was interested in the concept of "becoming"—the view that all things are in the process of growth, development, modification, and transformation. In *Leaves of Grass,* this doctrine can easily be seen in the dominant symbol for "perfection," the *seed.* The "seed perfection" is "latent" in the universe, awaiting the appropriate time to reveal itself in the process of becoming. Whitman even viewed his poetic masterpiece, *Leaves of Grass,* as in the process of becoming. Furthermore, the spiritual democracy envisioned by Whitman is clearly an evolutionary concept. Gay Wilson Allen and others have seen evolutionary development as the underlying theme of the "long journey" motif that is pervasive in *Leaves of Grass,* and some also see in Whitman's optimistic view of man's future something akin to Nietzsche's "Superman," an essentially Lamarckian concept.

Whitman believed that the theory of evolution was but one of many ways of looking at the universe, and one not likely to put an end to the mystery of creation. He observed that "In due time the Evolution theory will have to abate its vehemence, cannot be allow'd to dominate every thing else, and will have to take its place as a segment of the circle, the cluster—as but one of many theories, many thoughts, of pro-

E

foundest value—and re-adjusting and differentiating much, yet leaving the divine secrets just as inexplicable and unreachable as before—may-be more so" (Whitman 524).

Although the concept of evolutionary development informs *Leaves of Grass* throughout, scholars and critics have pointed to its presence, especially in "Eidólons," "Song of Myself" (especially sections 31 and 44), "By Blue Ontario's Shore," "Unseen Buds," "The World Below the Brine," "I Sing the Body Electric," and "As I Ebb'd with the Ocean of Life."

James T.F. Tanner

Bibliography

Allen, Gay Wilson. *The Solitary Singer: A Critical Biography of Walt Whitman.* 1955. Rev. ed. 1967. Chicago: U of Chicago P, 1985.
———. *Walt Whitman Handbook.* 1946. New York: Hendricks House, 1962.
Aspiz, Harold. *Walt Whitman and the Body Beautiful.* Urbana: U of Illinois P, 1980.
Beaver, Joseph. *Walt Whitman: Poet of Science.* New York: King's Crown, 1951.
Conner, Frederick William. *Cosmic Optimism: A Study of the Interpretation of Evolution by American Poets.* Gainesville: U of Florida P, 1949.
Reynolds, David S. *Walt Whitman's America: A Cultural Biography.* New York: Knopf, 1995.
Stavrou, C.N. *Whitman and Nietzsche: A Comparative Study of Their Thought.* Chapel Hill: U of North Carolina P, 1964.
Whitman, Walt. *Prose Works 1892.* Ed. Floyd Stovall. Vol. 2. New York: New York UP, 1964.

See also DARWIN, CHARLES; HEGEL, GEORG WILHELM FRIEDRICH; LAMARCK, JEAN BAPTISTE; PSEUDOSCIENCE; SCIENCE

"Excelsior" (1856)

"Excelsior" appeared in the 1856 *Leaves* as "Poem of The Heart of The Son of Manhattan Island"; in 1860 it became number 15 of "Chants Democratic." Then, in 1867, Whitman chose the title "Excelsior" ("more lofty; higher")—the same title Longfellow had chosen for a poem in 1841.

On 12 October 1846, in the Brooklyn *Daily Eagle,* Whitman reviewed *The Poems of Henry Wadsworth Longfellow,* claiming that Longfellow's "beautiful words" were equivalent to those of Bryant and Wordsworth ("The Literary World" 2). In his 1856 "Poem of The Heart," however, Whitman celebrates his own loftiness, his vow to rise, in the future tense: "For I swear I will go farther."

When Whitman changed the title to number 15 of "Chants Democratic," he added two lines in the 1860 Blue Book revisions (never appearing in *Leaves*): "And who has adopted the loftiest motto? / O I will put my motto over it, as it is over the top of this song!" (Whitman, *Blue Book* 1:188). Why, having omitted these "motto lines," did Whitman in 1867 change his title to the New York State motto, "Excelsior"? This title apparently indicates an indictment of Longfellow, who had continued to write sentimental verse while Whitman was nursing wounded soldiers. By using the older poet's title, Whitman makes clear that the "him" in line 10 (in the 1856 through 1867 versions of the poem) refers to Longfellow: "And who has projected beautiful words through the longest time? By God! I will outvie him! I will say such words, they shall stretch through longer time!"

In 1871 Whitman placed "Excelsior" into *Passage to India,* shifting his promissory future statements to rhetorical questions suggesting accomplished fact. Thus the statements in lines 1 and 10 which from 1856 to 1867 read "For I swear I *will go* farther" and "I *will outvie* him" in 1871 became "For lo! *have not* I *gone* farther?" and "*have* I *not outvied* him?" (emphasis added).

Whitman softened toward Longfellow in 1876, when the older poet visited him. He publicly acknowledged Longfellow and recorded their second encounter in "My Tribute to Four Poets." Finally, when they met again in September 1881, Whitman reconciled with the aged poet; while the 1881 *Leaves* was being platecast, he removed the line that indicted Longfellow and his "beautiful words."

Julie A. Rechel-White

Bibliography

Ford, Thomas W. "Whitman's 'Excelsior': The Poem as Microcosm." *Texas Studies in Literature and Language* 17 (1976): 777–785.
Rechel-White, Julie A. "Longfellow's Influence on Whitman's 'Rise' from Manhattan Island." *ATQ* 6 (1992): 121–129.
Whitman, Walt. *The Correspondence.* Ed.

Edwin Haviland Miller. Vol. 3. New York: New York UP, 1964.

———. "The Literary World." Brooklyn *Daily Eagle* 12 Oct. 1846.

———. *Walt Whitman's Blue Book.* Ed. Arthur Golden. 2 vols. New York: New York Public Library, 1968.

See also "FROM NOON TO STARRY NIGHT"; LONGFELLOW, HENRY WADSWORTH

Eyre, Ellen

On 25 March 1862 Ellen Eyre wrote Walt Whitman a love letter referring to pleasures experienced the evening before, but indicating that she wanted to conceal her identity. Though he kept her letter, Whitman writes little else about her. In the summer of 1862, Whitman records telling Frank Sweezey "the whole story . . . about Ellen Eyre" (*Notebooks* 2:488). Also, a photograph Whitman kept at Camden of a young, dark-haired woman, identified as a sweetheart and an actress, might represent her. However, beyond such references, Whitman gives little hint as to the nature or the duration of the relationship.

Because Eyre's letter suggests that Whitman had an affair with a woman, critical efforts focus primarily on identifying Eyre. Most likely, Ellen Grey, an actress, wrote to Whitman as Eyre. In a notebook entry for 1856–1857, Whitman refers to Grey and notes her address, but furnishes no other information. Someone else inscribed "Mrs. Ellen Eyre's" address in Whitman's notebooks; Whitman noted another address underneath it. But no Eyres appear in New York directories between 1859 and 1865. Scholars connect the two mysterious women in light of their similar names. Unfortunately, only

conjecture supports assertions that Grey and Eyre are the same woman.

Critics have suggested other identities for Eyre, but unhappily for contemporary scholars, no new evidence clarifies Eyre's identity, and any attempts to do so depend on meager evidence.

Given the contents of Eyre's letter, critics must recognize the possibility of Whitman's bisexuality. However, because of the lack of information Eyre's impact on Whitman's life is uncertain. Since Whitman respected her pseudonym, one cannot conclusively determine the extent of her influence or ascertain more specific details about their relationship.

Martha A. Kalnin

Bibliography

Allen, Gay Wilson. *The Solitary Singer: A Critical Biography of Walt Whitman.* 1955. Rev. ed. 1967. Chicago: U of Chicago P, 1985.

Hollis, C. Carroll. "Whitman's 'Ellen Eyre.'" *Walt Whitman Newsletter* 2 (1956): 24–26.

Holloway, Emory. "Whitman Pursued." *American Literature* 27 (1955): 1–11.

Kaplan, Justin. *Walt Whitman: A Life.* New York: Simon and Schuster, 1980.

Miller, Edwin Haviland. "Walt Whitman and Ellen Eyre." *American Literature* 32 (1962): 64–68.

Traubel, Horace. *With Walt Whitman in Camden.* Vol. 1. New York: Appleton, 1906.

Whitman, Walt. *Notebooks and Unpublished Prose Manuscripts.* Ed. Edward F. Grier. 6 vols. New York: New York UP, 1984.

See also GREY, ELLEN; SEX AND SEXUALITY

E

"Faces" (1855)

Untitled in the first edition, this exquisite, if sometimes enigmatic, lyric is a testimonial to Whitman's faith in mankind and his belief that "red, white, black, are all deific" (section 4). Titled "Poem of Faces" in 1856 and "A Leaf of Faces" in 1860 and 1867, it acquired its present title in the 1871 edition.

The first two of its five sections, particularly the thirteen-line opening catalogue, contain imagery derived from the popular pseudosciences of physiognomy (the crude analysis of the temperaments by "reading" the features of the face) and phrenology (the analysis of putative mental faculties by interpreting the contours of the head). Physiognomists maintained that the most advanced persons on the evolutionary scale displayed noble Germanic features, the most retarded, crude animalistic features. Underlying both pseudosciences were sexual/evolutionary assumptions. Whitman was aware that "reading" facial and cranial features was largely an intuitive process. Probably expecting that the readers of "Faces" would recognize the poem's physiognomic and phrenological terminology, he identifies the countenance of each passerby by assigning to it a brief (usually pseudoscientific) clue from which the readers could be expected to conjure up an image of the corresponding human type. In poetic terms, this technique is a bold exercise in synecdoche.

Viewing a diverse succession of human beings, the persona declares: "I see them and complain not, and am content with all" (section 1). The persona assures the laggards—those personified by such animalistic features as "the tangling fores of fishes or rats" (section 3), "a

dog's snout" (section 2), a "milk-nosed maggot" (section 2), and other loathsome visages—that they are "my equals" whose "never-erased flow" toward evolutionary perfection he can perceive through "the rims of your haggard and mean disguises" (section 3). In "a score or two of ages," he predicts, they will be "unmuzzled" (their animalistic features cleared away) and be "every inch as good as myself" (section 3), because each person contains "the ovum" of eugenic and spiritual perfectibility (section 4).

In section 4, the vanguard of the evolutionary procession are seen advancing in their "pioneer-caps" to usher in a race of wholesome democratic persons. Their prototype is the "face of a healthy honest boy," "commanding and bearded"—a variant of the Whitman persona, who exemplifies "the programme of all good." In a sensuous passage, the persona is invited to mate with the sexually aggressive, ideal Nordic woman with "the full-grown lily's face" and thus produce a superior progeny. In the closing bucolic vignette (section 5), the "lily" woman has been transformed into a beautiful Quaker grandmother, surrounded by generations of splendid descendants: "The finish beyond which philosophy cannot go." Like some of his feminist contemporaries, Whitman believed that motherhood holds the key to human progress.

"Faces" illustrates Whitman's profound compassion and his faith that an ongoing mystical process will eventually liberate the divinity in each person. Despite its initial linguistic difficulty, the poem is inventive, richly lyrical, and filled with striking images and vital insights into Whitman's thinking in 1855.

Harold Aspiz

Bibliography

Aspiz, Harold. "A Reading of Whitman's 'Faces.'" *Walt Whitman Review* 19 (1973): 37–48.

———. *Walt Whitman and the Body Beautiful*. Urbana: U of Illinois P, 1980.

Fowler, Orson Squire. *Self-Instructor in Phrenology and Physiology*. New York: Fowler and Wells, 1859.

Lavater, Johann Caspar. *Essays on Physiognomy for the Promotion of Knowledge and the Love of Mankind*. 15th ed. London: W. Tegg, 1878.

Sizer, Nelson. *Heads and Faces, and How to Study Them*. 1885. New York: Fowler and Wells, 1891.

Whitman, Walt. *Leaves of Grass: A Textual Variorum of the Printed Poems*. Ed. Sculley Bradley, Harold W. Blodgett, Arthur Golden, and William White. Vol. 1. New York: New York UP, 1980.

See also EVOLUTION; "FROM NOON TO STARRY NIGHT"; PHRENOLOGY

"Facing West from California's Shores" (1860)

The penultimate poem in the "Children of Adam" section of *Leaves of Grass* and an early precursor of "Passage to India," "Facing West" began as a six-line poem probably written in 1856 or 1857. Now in the Barrett Collection at the University of Virginia, the manuscript bears the title "Hindustan, from the Western Sea." The poem was first published in a nine-line version in the third edition of *Leaves of Grass* (1860) as number 10 in the section "Enfans d'Adam." Like the other poems in that section it is untitled. The final version, eleven lines long, incorporates a new first line (which is also used as the title), an eighth line containing the key word "wander'd" twice, and a few minor verbal changes.

Perhaps because "Facing West" is unique among the poems in "Children of Adam" in not referring to love, sexuality, or the human body, Whitman considered transferring it to the "Drum-Taps" section of the fourth edition (1867), as he indicated by a penciled note in his personal copy of the 1860 edition, the Blue Book. But the logic of leaving it with "Children of Adam" lies in its relationship with the first and last poems of that section. The speaker in the first poem, who refers to being accompanied by Eve, is Adam, and the speaker in the last poem compares himself to Adam.

Since the speaker in "Facing West" describes himself paradoxically as "a child, very old," he seems not only to be a descendant of Adam but also to represent all the generations of Adam's descendants. The poem thus adumbrates the theme to be developed later in "Passage to India," particularly section 5, lines 88–92, which speak of the restless wanderings of humanity—children of Adam and Eve—from a common place of origin in Asia.

Martin K. Doudna

Bibliography

Whitman, Walt. *Walt Whitman's Blue Book*. Ed. Arthur Golden. 2 vols. New York: The New York Public Library, 1968.

———. *Whitman's Manuscripts: "Leaves of Grass" (1860)*. Ed. Fredson Bowers. Chicago: U of Chicago P, 1955.

See also "CHILDREN OF ADAM"; "PASSAGE TO INDIA"

Falmouth, Virginia

In December of 1862, Whitman left New York (never to return to live permanently) for Falmouth, Virginia, to search for his brother George, who was listed among the wounded after the battle of Fredericksburg. George's wound was superficial, but Whitman's ten-day visit to the warfront decisively altered his personal life and literary career as the war became the focus of both.

This was the closest he would ever come to witnessing the war firsthand, and although the battle had ended nearly a week before his arrival, his journals, correspondence, and poetry from that period show that its aftermath affected him profoundly. Upon first arriving, he was shocked to see a pile of amputated limbs outside a makeshift hospital. One morning the sight of three fresh corpses on stretchers moved him to make a journal entry that would later be reworked into the poem "A Sight in Camp in the Daybreak Gray and Dim" (1865). He also toured the battlefield, went out on pickets, and under a flag of truce assisted in burying the dead, but what affected him most powerfully were his visits to the sick and wounded. In them he saw not only the rough, large-spirited Americans he celebrated in his poetry but also an image of the Union diseased and dismembered. In his visits, he discovered a mission that would pull him out of his "New York stagnation" (Correspondence 1:61) of the previous few years: he gave the men the personal attention that the overtaxed hospital staff could not, listening empathetically to their stories, bringing them small gifts, and writing letters home for the illiterate or otherwise unable. His experiences and the men's stories also opened a new world of literary materials for Whitman to explore, most notably in Drum-Taps (1865) and Specimen Days (1882). He left Falmouth in charge of a trainload of wounded men bound for the hospitals in Washington, D.C., where he took up residence and continued to nurse the sick throughout the war. Whitman's stay in Falmouth is memorialized in a sketch entitled Fall in for Soup—Company Mess (showing Whitman in a mess line), drawn from life by Edwin Forbes, the popular illustrator.

John Rietz

Bibliography

Allen, Gay Wilson. *The Solitary Singer: A Critical Biography of Walt Whitman*. 1955. Rev. ed. 1967. Chicago: U of Chicago P, 1985.

Forbes, Edwin. *Civil War Etchings*. Ed. William Forrest Dawson. New York: Dover, 1994.

Glicksberg, Charles I., ed. *Walt Whitman and the Civil War*. Philadelphia: U of Pennsylvania P, 1933.

Whitman, Walt. *The Correspondence*. Ed. Edwin Haviland Miller. 6 vols. New York: New York UP, 1961–1977.

———. *Prose Works*. Ed. Floyd Stovall. Vol. 1. New York: New York UP, 1963.

See also CIVIL WAR, THE; CIVIL WAR NURSING; WASHINGTON, D.C.; WHITMAN, GEORGE WASHINGTON

Farnham, Eliza W. (1815–1864)

Helen Price wrote in Richard Maurice Bucke's biography of Whitman that Whitman and Eliza Farnham met at a gathering in the Price home. Farnham, like Helen Price's mother, Abby, was actively engaged in reform movements of the day. She served as matron of Sing Sing prison for four years (1844–1848), worked at the Perkins Institution, nursed the Civil War wounded for a time, lived and worked in California, and perhaps most importantly, wrote and published.

Historically, Farnham belongs to a wide and divergent group of women who agitated for women's rights in the antebellum period, though she was not active in the drive for suffrage. In fact, it was not until 1858 that she addressed a National Woman's Rights Convention. Her two-volume work, *Woman and Her Era* (1864), contains passages from *Leaves of Grass* which support a "new woman" image. Harold Aspiz's 1979 article "An Early Feminist Tribute to Whitman" discusses the Farnham-Whitman connection.

In *Woman and Her Era* Farnham argues for female superiority, believing that biologically speaking, due to their childbearing organs, women were more fully evolved than men and likewise were morally superior. Though Farnham's call for moral superiority was rejected by female activists like Ernestine L. Rose, whose call for reform is grounded in what we now call the social construction argument, Farnham's views offer a window into an aspect of Whitman's thought, historically speaking, specifically his representation of the strong mother.

Sherry Ceniza

Bibliography

Aspiz, Harold. "An Early Feminist Tribute to Whitman." *American Literature* 51 (1979): 404–409.

———. "Walt Whitman, Feminist." *Walt Whitman: Here and Now*. Ed. Joann P. Krieg. Westport, Conn.: Greenwood, 1985. 79–88.

Farnham, Eliza W. *Woman and Her Era*. 2 vols. New York: A.J. Davis, 1864.

See also PRICE, ABBY HILLS; PRICE, HELEN E.; WOMAN'S RIGHTS MOVEMENT AND WHITMAN, THE

"Fast Anchor'd Eternal O Love!" (1860)

Fredson Bowers speculates that this minor, six-line lyric was probably composed sometime between June or July 1857 and the middle of 1858. It first appeared as "Calamus" 38 in the 1860 edition of *Leaves* and was retained in all subsequent editions.

The poem is constructed around a simple distinction between the speaker's love of women and men. The love of women is seen as "Fast-anchor'd" ("Primeval" in 1860) and "resistless," apparently in the sense that it is physical and biological, whereas the love of

F

men is "Ethereal" and "disembodied." Whitman is indebted here to Plato's *Symposium* for this classical distinction between physical and spiritual love, but as elsewhere in his poetry the idea seems more borrowed than absorbed, an impression conveyed by the fact that Whitman also calls the sexual love of women "eternal" and the spiritual love of men "the last athletic reality." A somewhat confused effort, the poem is an early example of Whitman's tendency toward abstraction. In "Calamus," it may have served Whitman as a way to minimize or deflect criticism for the obvious homoerotic content of the sequence.

Alan Helms

Bibliography

Martin, Robert K. *The Homosexual Tradition in American Poetry.* Austin: U of Texas P, 1979.

Whitman, Walt. *Whitman's Manuscripts: "Leaves of Grass" (1860).* Ed. Fredson Bowers. Chicago: U of Chicago P, 1955.

See also "Calamus"; Sex and Sexuality

Ferries and Omnibuses

The cities around New York harbor developed public transportation early in the nineteenth century. Scheduled ferries traveled from Manhattan to the west bank of the Hudson and to the cities across the East River; stages and omnibuses plied the streets of the larger cities. By 1833 the ferries were double-ended steamboats, about 130 feet long, with side-mounted paddle wheels, a pilothouse at each end, and a single stack amidships. Cabins for passengers flanked gangways for vehicles; there was also an open upper deck. In the early 1850s at least seven lines ran scheduled crossings between Long Island and Manhattan; the Fulton Street Ferry took about ten minutes. The stages were coaches with lengthwise seats, drawn by a pair of horses. After 1831 they were supplemented, and eventually supplanted, by the omnibus, a longer vehicle seating about twelve, operating over fixed routes for fixed fares. On both, the driver rode on an exposed seat at the top.

In his journalism Whitman described the ferry passage several times, emphasizing the crowd, the harborscape, and the water traffic. He editorialized about the passengers' haste and impatience, which sometimes led to injuries or near drowning, and about smoking and chewing tobacco in the cabins. He wrote comparatively little about the stage service. Omnibus drivers were frequently accused of recklessness and cheating on fares, but Whitman attributed these practices to the cabs rather than to the omnibuses and spoke sympathetically of the drivers' exposed and monotonous work. In his articles Whitman usually figures not as passenger but as pedestrian, relishing the spectacle of his fellow walkers.

In *Specimen Days* Whitman extols the ferry and the omnibus as privileged points of view. The boat offers him a vantage point from which to survey the shows, panoramas, and prospects of New York harbor with its tides of water and of humanity: they provide "never-failing, living poems" (16). There he rides up in the pilot-house; on the omnibus he sits with the driver, listening to his yarns or shouting some passage of poetry out into the roar of Broadway. The view from the omnibus is not so much eyesight as temperament: the drivers were a class of "roughs" with whom the poet made friends and whose animal vitality, vernacular eloquence, and camaraderie "undoubtedly enter'd into the gestation of 'Leaves of Grass'" (18–19). Just so, in the only poems about city transport, "Crossing Brooklyn Ferry" capitalizes on the visual experience of the harbor, while "To Think of Time" describes the funeral of a driver, phrased in the jargon of his trade. It was while visiting sick and injured stage drivers in New York Hospital that Whitman first encountered wounded soldiers, whose similar virtues he would honor in *Drum-Taps* and later in *Specimen Days*.

James Dougherty

Bibliography

Brouwer, Norman. "'Cross from Shore to Shore': Whitman's Brooklyn Ferry." *Seaport* 26.1 (1992): 64–67.

Cudahy, Brian J. *Over and Back: The History of Ferryboats in New York Harbor.* New York: Fordham UP, 1990.

Stratton, Ezra M. *The World on Wheels.* 1878. New York: Blom, 1972.

Whitman, Walt. *Specimen Days.* Vol. 1 of *Prose Works 1892.* Ed. Floyd Stovall. New York: New York UP, 1963.

See also "Crossing Brooklyn Ferry"; New York City; Roughs; "To Think of Time"

Feudalism

Whitman's prose and poetry are infused with a democratic spirit. Indeed, virtually all of Whitman's prose works stress both the importance of creating a democratic state and the need for establishing a corresponding literary tradition to articulate the essence of a democratic people; *Leaves of Grass* (1855), of course, inaugurates just such a tradition. Yet prominent in even Whitman's most democratic works are repeated references to what Whitman terms "feudalism." While such references might at first appear incongruous, they in fact serve as a sophisticated rhetorical strategy. In short, Whitman employs references to feudalism as a touchstone against which to define democracy, the United States, and American literature.

Whitman used the term "feudalism" loosely and in a variety of contexts: historical, political, and literary. Whitman first of all saw feudalism as being "rooted in the long past" (Whitman 668). He repeatedly associated feudalism with the medieval world and with the Old World, which for Whitman translated as Asia and Europe (specifically the British Isles). Whitman, therefore, found feudalism to be at odds with the democratic ideal, in part, at least, because it "celebrate[d] man and his intellections and relativenesses as they have been," while he envisioned democracies such as that of the United States as breaking with the past to "sing [its people] all as they are and are to be" (668). For Whitman, in other words, democracy resided in the modern and would come to fruition in the future.

In addition to viewing feudalism in a historical milieu, Whitman also saw feudalism in a political context, namely as a system in which the disenfranchised masses labored for the benefit of an elite few, the aristocracy. While Whitman conceded that the feudal political system had had a glorious history, he again found it in conflict with the democratic ideal because it encouraged a caste system rather than the egalitarian one he desired for the United States. Therefore, despite feudalism's remarkable history, Whitman believed that feudalism had ultimately shown itself to be an inferior political system, and that because of "the law over all, and law of laws," that is, "the law of successions," it must necessarily give way to the superior political system, democracy (Whitman 381). Indeed, Whitman argued that such a political shift was an evolutionary given and asserted that the question was not "whether to hold on, attempting to lean back and monarchize, or to look forward and democratize," but instead "*how*, and in what degree and part, most prudently to democratize" (383).

In short, Whitman believed that the feudal system, as well as the culture and literature it so thoroughly permeated, had become enervated, that it had at last played itself out. When Whitman referred to feudal culture and its literature, his words became tinged with a sense of nostalgia and loss: "The odor of English social life in its highest range—a melancholy, affectionate, very manly, but dainty breed—pervading the pages like an invisible scent; the idleness, the traditions, the mannerisms, the stately *ennui;* the yearning of love, like a spinal marrow, inside of all; the costumes, brocade and satin; the old houses and furniture—solid oak, no mere veneering—the moldy secrets everywhere; the verdure, the ivy on the walls, the moat, the English landscape outside, the buzzing fly in the sun inside the window pane" (477). While Whitman clearly found the feudal culture and its literature in many ways beautiful, he ultimately considered it too overly refined and delicate to adequately express the vigor and roughness of the United States.

Early in his career Whitman repeatedly and adamantly criticized feudalism, asserting that it had nothing to offer the United States. Later, however, he tempered his criticism, acknowledging (at times grudgingly) that feudal literary tradition could at least offer American poets a foundation on which to build their own tradition. As Whitman explained, "The New World receives with joy the poems of the antique, with European feudalism's rich fund of epics, plays, ballads—seeks not in the least to deaden or displace those voices from our ear and area—holds them indeed as indispensable studies, influences, records, comparisons" (720). Whitman eventually went so far as to call on feudal poets, especially Shakespeare, to serve as muses for American poets. While he recognized that the feudal poets were "grown not for America, but rather for her foes, the feudal and the old," he at the same time realized that they could "breathe [their] breath of life into our New World's nostrils—not to enslave us, as now, but, for our needs, to breed a spirit like [their] own—perhaps, (dare we to say it?) to dominate, even destroy, what [they themselves] have left!" (407).

It was such an inspired race of poets that Whitman so desperately desired for the United States. He considered American poets, for the

F

most part, to be imitative of their feudal predecessors. He observed, for instance, that they had continued to offer poetry depicting "a parcel of dandies and ennuyees, dapper little gentlemen from abroad, who flood us with their thin sentiment of parlors, parasols, piano-songs, tinkling rhymes, the five-hundredth importation—or whimpering and crying about something, chasing one aborted conceit after another, and forever occupied in dyspeptic amours with dyspeptic women" (408). As Whitman at one point complained, "America has yet morally and artistically originated nothing" (395). For Whitman, such lack of originality was problematic, for as he noted, "the topmost proof of a race is its own born poetry" (474).

Consequently, Whitman called for native-born poets who could sing America, "fusing contributions, races, far localities, &c., together," and, in the process, give America its own distinctly democratic mythos (368). As Whitman concluded, "We see that almost everything that has been written, sung, or stated, of old, with reference to humanity under the feudal and oriental institutes, religions, and for other lands, needs to be re-written, re-sung, re-stated, in terms consistent with the institution of these States, and to come in range and obedient uniformity with them" (425). With *Leaves of Grass*, of course, he did just that.

Phyllis McBride

Bibliography

Furness, Clifton Joseph. "Walt Whitman's Estimate of Shakespeare." *Harvard Studies and Notes in Philology and Literature* 14 (1932): 1–33.
Marx, Leo, ed. *The Americanness of Walt Whitman*. Boston: Heath, 1960.
Miller, James E., Jr. *"Leaves of Grass": America's Lyric-Epic of Self and Democracy*. New York: Twayne, 1992.
Price, Kenneth M. *Whitman and Tradition: The Poet in His Century*. New Haven: Yale UP, 1990.
Scholnick, Robert J. "Toward a 'Wider Democratizing of Institutions': Whitman's *Democratic Vistas*." *American Transcendental Quarterly* 52 (1981): 287–302.
Stovall, Floyd. *The Foreground of "Leaves of Grass."* Charlottesville: UP of Virginia, 1974.
Whitman, Walt. *Prose Works 1892*. Ed. Floyd Stovall. Vol. 2. New York: New York UP, 1964.

See also AMERICAN CHARACTER; DEMOCRACY; *DEMOCRATIC VISTAS*; PREFACE TO *LEAVES OF GRASS*, 1855 EDITION; SHAKESPEARE, WILLIAM

"Fireman's Dream, The" (1844)

Whitman's incomplete novel "The Fireman's Dream: With the Story of His Strange Companion. A Tale of Fantasie" was first published in *Sunday Times & Noah's Weekly Messenger*, 31 March 1844. For publication history and text, see Bergman.

Like Whitman's other incomplete novel, "The Madman" (1843), this work appeared in apparently one installment, of two chapters, and ended with the words "To be continued." In chapter 1, a New York fireman, George Willis, spends his day off traveling to Hoboken (New Jersey) and chatting with some Native Americans. One tells George of the life of the forest. When George is injured later while at work, he becomes feverish. In a dream, walking through "unearthly scenes of tumult" (Bergman 10), he kills a fireman. Then in a wilderness of trees, he befriends a male Native American. In chapter 2 the dream continues with the Native American telling George his life story. The Native American was found by white pioneers when he was about seven. The Boanes raised him as their own, taught him English, and sent him to school, where he and Anthony Clark, nephew of the Boanes, excelled. The two boys became fast friends.

Whitman's use of dream narrative is noteworthy. Also noteworthy is his character with an upbringing almost directly opposite that of Natty Bumppo of *The Pioneers* (1823) and other James Fenimore Cooper novels, who is a white man raised by Native Americans. Whitman makes much of the dual forces at work in this Native American's character, even suggesting that the child, before being found, may have been raised by panthers. The first sentences of chapter 2 establish the duality: "I am white by education and an Indian by birth. Within my bosom reside two opposing elements" (Bergman 11). This duality may foreshadow Whitman's grotesque character Boddo in "The Half-Breed: A Tale of the Western Frontier" (1845).

Little critical attention has been given to "The Fireman's Dream."

Patrick McGuire

Bibliography

Bergman, Herbert. "A Hitherto Unknown Whitman Story and a Possible Early Poem." *Walt Whitman Review* 28 (1982): 3–15.

See also NATIVE AMERICANS (INDIANS); SHORT FICTION, WHITMAN'S

"First O Songs for a Prelude" (1865)

"First O Songs for a Prelude" appeared under the title "Drum-Taps" as the opening poem in Whitman's 1865 collection *Drum-Taps*. It retained its initial position when moved to the "Drum-Taps" cluster of *Leaves of Grass* in 1871 and subsequent editions, although it was prefaced in 1871 and 1876 by an untitled four-line epigraph. In 1881 the poem took its first line as its title and the epigraph reappeared in "The Wound-Dresser" (lines 4–6).

"Prelude" establishes the dominant symbol of "Drum-Taps" in its second line, with its call to "Lightly strike on the stretch'd tympanum." The entire poem celebrates the call to arms and the nervous, excited response of a democratic nation heeding that call. Whitman records the pageantry and energy of "Manhattan arming," responding "to the drum-taps prompt." The city is seized in a fervor of frenzied patriotism. In his litany of professionals laying down their work and taking up the challenge of war, only the mother demurs, and yet "not a word does she speak to detain him," making a noble sacrifice. "Prelude" is the celebration not of a professional army, but of the army of the Democracy rallying to the defense of a threatened Union. Within the cacophony of enthusiasm, however, there is a somber note of "determin'd arming"; these men and women know they shoulder tremendous responsibilities.

This poem has been read as autobiographical in nature, with several of the vignettes in the poem linked to actual occurrences in Whitman's life. His varied responses to the war are reflected by the changing tempo of the drum-taps throughout the group. In "Prelude," Whitman creates the constant and incessant "strike on the . . . tympanum" through his use of alliteration, homoeoteleuton (clauses successively ending with the same sounds), the rhythm of present participles capturing the arming in progress, and a one-sentence structure indicating the city's single continuous, relentless challenge that is inspired by its beat.

"Prelude" celebrates the glamorous veneer of war that Whitman had witnessed through military pomp and parade. He welcomes the Spirit of War, for he sees it as bringing new life to the land and energizing the potential of the common man. As the "Drum-Taps" poems progress, however, a darker, more ominous Spirit of War reveals its terrible power over the nation.

Sheree L. Gilbert

Bibliography

Cannon, Agnes Dicken. "Fervid Atmosphere and Typical Events: Autobiography in *Drum-Taps*." *Walt Whitman Review* 20 (1974): 79–96.

Davis, Robert Leigh. "Whitman's Tympanum: A Reading of *Drum-Taps*." *ATQ* 6 (1992): 163–175.

Hudson, Vaughan. "Melville's *Battle-Pieces* and Whitman's *Drum-Taps*: A Comparison." *Walt Whitman Review* 19 (1973): 81–92.

Kinney, Katherine. "Whitman's 'Word of the Modern' and the First Modern War." *Walt Whitman Quarterly Review* 7 (1989): 1–14.

McWilliams, John P., Jr. "'Drum-Taps' and *Battle-Pieces*: The Blossom of War." *American Quarterly* 23 (1971): 181–201.

Sullivan, Edward E., Jr. "Thematic Unfolding in Whitman's *Drum-Taps*." *Emerson Society Quarterly* 31.2 (1963): 42–45.

Whitman, Walt. *Walt Whitman's "Drum-Taps" (1865) and "Sequel to Drum-Taps" (1865–6): A Facsimile Reproduction.* Ed. F. DeWolfe Miller. Gainesville, Florida: Scholars' Facsimiles and Reprints, 1959.

See also "BEAT! BEAT! DRUMS!"; CIVIL WAR, THE; "DRUM-TAPS"

"For You O Democracy" (1860)

"For You O Democracy," written between 1859 and 1860, is a well-known "Calamus" poem originally printed in the 1860 edition of *Leaves of Grass* as the last three stanzas of "Calamus" number 5. Whitman broke up this fifteen-stanza, forty-two-line poem, rearranging the first twelve stanzas into the "Drum-Taps" piece "Over the Carnage Rose Prophetic a Voice" (1860). With its repetend added, "For

You O Democracy" took final shape in 1867 under the title "A Song" and took its present title in 1881.

Representative of Whitman's unifying program of "adhesiveness" (the phrenological term denoting for Whitman a physical-spiritual union), "For You O Democracy" has been called a dedicatory poem for the "Calamus" cluster. Echoing the eugenics of his time, Whitman proposes to "make the most splendid race the sun ever shone upon." This program involves the poet's "robust" "manly love," a spiritual breeding of the new democracy "anneal'd" into the "living union," proposed in *Democratic Vistas* (1871). As in the rest of "Calamus" and *Leaves of Grass,* the implications of "manly love" are complex. From Richard Maurice Bucke's defense of this feeling as strictly fraternal, to James Miller's insistence that it is a sublimated homoeroticism, to Betsy Erkkila's proposition that it involves a "homosexual republic," critics circumvent and circumscribe the question as their views dictate. With characteristic circumspection, Whitman will say only that the main message of "Calamus" is in its "political significance."

Because "For You O Democracy" is the climax of "Calamus" number 5, the later deletion of the first twelve stanzas has caused speculation. Roger Asselineau suggests that the suppression of such lines as "touch face to face" comes from an aging Whitman who would minimize erotic implications. Thomas Crawley finds the expression of "Calamus" number 5 intensified in the shorter piece, supporting James Miller's view that the poem was tightened up rather than censored.

"For You O Democracy" occurs in a stanzaic pattern with repetend, a scheme found in declarative pieces like "Pioneers! O Pioneers!" and "Eidólons." It is possible that Whitman adopted this more conventional form because of the rally-and-flag-waving nature of the patriotic verse. Yet this poem of "comrades" transcends all convention, all agreements to union by "lawyers" and "papers" ("Calamus" number 5, 1860 *Leaves*) as it incites an exuberant uprising of solidarity and love. To a nation on the verge of civil war, Whitman, fighting his own internal divisions, brings his preacher-on-a-stump oratory: "Come, I will make the continent indissoluble." Unlike any other poet before him, the poet of *Leaves of Grass* seizes his readers with loving force as he woos not only "comrades," but democracy "ma femme" with

"her" French echoes of "Liberté, fraternité, egalité!"

Carol M. Zapata-Whelan

Bibliography
Asselineau, Roger. *The Evolution of Walt Whitman: The Creation of a Book.* Trans. Roger Asselineau and Burton L. Cooper. Cambridge, Mass.: Harvard UP, 1962.

Crawley, Thomas Edward. *The Structure of "Leaves of Grass."* Austin: U of Texas P, 1970.

Erkkila, Betsy. *Whitman the Political Poet.* New York: Oxford UP, 1989.

Folsom, Ed, ed. *Walt Whitman: The Centennial Essays.* Iowa City: U of Iowa P, 1994.

Miller, James E., Jr. *A Critical Guide to "Leaves of Grass."* Chicago: U of Chicago P, 1957.

Whitman, Walt. *Leaves of Grass.* Ed. Sculley Bradley and Harold W. Blodgett. Norton Critical Edition. New York: Norton, 1973.

———. *Whitman's Manuscripts: "Leaves of Grass" (1860).* Ed. Fredson Bowers. Chicago: U of Chicago P, 1955.

See also "CALAMUS"; COMRADESHIP; "OVER THE CARNAGE ROSE PROPHETIC A VOICE"

Foreign Language Borrowings
Laying aside the contents of his poetry, Whitman once declared to Horace Traubel: "I sometimes think the Leaves is only a language experiment" (*Primer* viii). Indeed he loved words for their own sake and drew up lists of them. "Great is language," he exclaimed in 1855; "it is the mightiest of the sciences," and he added, "Great is the English speech . . . What speech is so great as the English?" ("Great Are the Myths," section 3). What he appreciated above all was that it had assimilated words from every language, rejecting none. The English language, Whitman said, is "[a]n enormous treasure-house, or range of treasure houses, arsenals, granary, chock full with so many contributions . . . from Spaniards, Italians and the French" (*Primer* 30). He wanted this process of assimilation to go on in America: "In a little while, in the United States, the English language, enriched with contributions from all languages, old and new, will be spoken by a hun-

dred millions of people" (*Primer* 2). Though he knew no other language than English and never visited a foreign country before his trip to Canada in 1880, he loved to pick up foreign words and parade them in his journalistic writings from 1848 on, i.e., from his stay in Louisiana on.

It was there that Whitman picked up French words and started using them in the New Orleans *Daily Crescent* for the sake of local color: "sang-froid," "chaqu'un à son gré" (for "chacun à son gré"), "sans culottes" (which he discussed humorously), "chapeau blanc," "marchande de fleurs," "tout à fait," "jolie grisette," "coiffeur," "distingué," "morceau of bijouterie" (a curious mongrel), "recherché," "embonpoint." It was there, too, that he found the word "Libertad" on Mexican coins (see "Turn O Libertad") and heard the word "camarada," which he thought was "camerado" under the influence of Walter Scott's novels. He was to use some of these words and many others in his writings when he returned to New York. There is already a sprinkling of French words in the first edition of *Leaves of Grass,* from "insouciance" in the Preface and "Faces," to "embouchure" in "Song of Myself," or "douceur" and "cache" in "The Sleepers." Whitman made increasing use of such borrowings in the later editions. He uses "délicatesse," for example, in "Spirit That Form'd This Scene," "Song of the Broad-Axe," "Not Youth Pertains to Me," and "By Blue Ontario's Shore," section 4 (he apparently liked the expressive sound of the word since he used it four times and dropped the accent the better to acclimatize it). The word "soirée" appears in "City of Orgies" and "aplomb" in "Song at Sunset" and "Me Imperturbe."

Another of Whitman's favorite borrowings was "ennui," which appears in "Song of Joys," "Ah Poverties, Wincings, and Sullen Retreats," and "As I Sit Writing Here." It becomes "ennuyés" in "The Sleepers." To it must be added "complaisance" in "A Song for Occupations," "coterie" in "Not Youth Pertains to Me," and "éclat" in "As I Walk These Broad Majestic Days." He misspelled "rondeur" as "rondure," which probably corresponded to his pronunciation. He loved the word which beautifully suggested the totality of the earth. He used it in "Passage to India," "Out of the Rolling Ocean," and "Song of the Exposition." For the same reason, he loved "ensemble," which evoked the immensity and the unity of the uni-

verse. "I will make poems, songs, thoughts, with reference to ensemble," he promised in "Starting from Paumanok" (section 12). He used it also in "Laws for Creations," "Song of the Exposition," "Song of the Universal," "Thou Mother with Thy Equal Brood" (section 6), and "By That Long Scan of Waves." (He needed such words to express his cosmic sense and suggest the infinity of space and time. He thus often resorted to the Greek work "Kosmos," which he deliberately spelt with a "k." "Kosmos" in Greek means order, harmony, beauty, *and* the universe.) "Feuillage" was particularly appropriate in a book entitled *Leaves of Grass,* and it appears even in the title of a poem, "Our Old Feuillage," and several times in the poem itself as well as in "Apostroph" and "Thoughts [Of these years . . .]" (section 2).

Another key word was "rapport," which is synonymous with spiritual or mystical connection as in "I think some divine rapport has equalized me with them," in "Salut au Monde!" (section 13), whose title is entirely in French. "Rapport" also occurs in "Cabin'd Ships at Sea," "By Blue Ontario's Shore" (section 3), "To Him That was Crucified," "Italian Music in Dakota," "The Sobbing of the Bells," "As I Draw to a Close," "You Tides with Ceaseless Swell," and "With Husky-Haughty Lips, O Sea." "Mélange" also provided Whitman with the word he needed to give a name to the mystical fusion and the cosmic unity in which he believed: "Melange mine own, the unseen and the seen" ("Starting from Paumanok," section 10). He liked the word "débris" (which he wrote like "melange" without an acute accent) since human activities, war in particular, leave many broken things for which there is no convenient word in English. He used it in "Song of Myself" (section 33), "As I Ebb'd with the Ocean of Life," "When Lilacs Last in the Dooryard Bloom'd," "Spain 1873–74," "Ashes of Soldiers," "A Voice from Death," and the 1860 *Leaves* poem "Debris." He also resorted to French military terms to describe Civil War scenes, especially in *Specimen Days:* "militaires," "sortie," and "reconnaissance" (which becomes "reconnoissance" in "A Song for Occupations" [section 3] and is then almost meaningless).

What chiefly drew Whitman to the French language was his sympathy for France, which he regarded as the champion of democracy in Europe, in the vanguard of revolutionary movements in 1789, 1830, and 1848. French was therefore in his eyes the language of popular dynamism. That is why he again and again called "Allons!" when he invited his reader to follow him on the open road of the future "through struggles and wars"; the word was a "call of battle" ("Song of the Open Road," section 14). He naturally borrowed the word "révolutionnaire," but spelled it without an accent and with one "n" only. He celebrated the French revolutionary poets like Béranger, whom he admired. He called them "chansonniers" ("France, The 18th Year of these States"). He considered himself one of them (see "The Centenarian's Story"). It was from French that he borrowed the word "en-masse." French was also for him the language of love. He spoke of his "amie" and "amies" in "Song of Myself." He addressed democracy as "ma femme" ("For You O Democracy," "France, The 18th Year of these States," and "Starting from Paumanok").

French words are so numerous in *Leaves of Grass* that it is difficult to draw up an exhaustive list. He must have borrowed them from many sources, for he uses an archaic form of "répondez" as the title of "Respondez!," while "trottoirs" (used in "Mannahatta," "Give Me the Splendid Silent Sun," and "You Felons on Trial in Courts") as well as "ateliers" ("Eidólons"), "detour" ("Song of the Universal"), "embouchure" ("Song of Myself" and "By Blue Ontario's Shore"), and "soiree" (without an accent; "City of Orgies" and "Faces") must have been memories of his stay in New Orleans. But where did he find "accoucheur" ("Song of Myself"), "eleve" ("To a Western Boy"), "emigré" ("Song of the Exposition"), "exalte" (with a grave instead of an acute accent; "Eidólons" and "To the East and to the West"), and "complaisance" ("A Song for Occupations")? He probably found such words in the magazines he read assiduously when he was a journalist in Brooklyn and New York. He picked a few in particular from the society reports of the New York *Aurora* in which French phrases were frequently used to give them *ton*. He was on the staff of the *Aurora* in 1842.

Since Whitman actually knew no French except a number of nouns and adjectives, he was bound to make mistakes—in spelling in particular. He thus spelt "savan" and "habitan" without the final "t," because he incorrectly deduced these forms from the then current plurals "savans" and "habitans." He treated "chef-d'oeuvre" in the plural as if it were an English compound word, adding an "s" to "oeuvre"

instead of "chef" ("Song of the Broad-Axe"). He also at times used some words inappropriately. He seems not to have grasped the exact meaning of "résumé" (which means "summary"), as when he exclaimed, "How plenteous! how spiritual! how resumé!" (without an accent on the first "e") in "Night on the Prairies," though he used it correctly in other contexts, e.g., "A Carol Closing Sixty-Nine." In the same way, "debouché" (with no accent on the first "e") is absolutely meaningless in the line, "On for your time, ye furious debouché" ("Last of Ebb, and Daylight Waning"). Whitman probably confused it with "debouching." The phrase "in arriere" (with no grave accent on the first "e"; "Starting from Paumanok" and "Our Old Feuillage") does not exist in French. The French phrase is "en arrière." His use of "luminé" in "As I Walk These Broad Majestic Days" and "Apostroph" is just as baffling. One even wonders what language the word belongs to. His description of God as a "reservoir" in "Passage to India" is quite unexpected and extremely bold. In the same poem, he even took liberties with the French language and coined the verb "eclaircise" from the French "éclaircir," a form which is neither French nor English.

Besides French and Spanish words, Whitman also resorted to Italian words which he picked up when he attended Italian operas in Manhattan. In "Proud Music of the Storm," after quoting hymn titles in German (Martin Luther's "Eine feste Burg ist unser Gott") and in Latin (Antonio Rossini's "Stabat Mater Dolorosa," "Agnus Dei," and "Gloria in Excelsis"), he accumulated Italian terms: "maestros" (it should be "maestri"), "soprani," "tenori," "bassi," "cantabile," "Paradiso," and "Italia." He also used "bravuras" when speaking of birds in "Song of Myself" and "scenas" (with English plurals), "tutti" in "That Music Always Round Me," and "finalè" in "The Base of All Metaphysics," "Song at Sunset," and "Now Finalè to the Shore." For no special reason, he preferred "ambulanza" to the banal "ambulance" in "Song of Myself" (section 33). In "Starting from Paumanok," he introduced himself in Italian as no "dolce affettuoso" (section 15).

Whitman borrowed words from modern languages, but also from old Greek ("eidōlon," which means "image, simulacrum") and from Latin, though he knew neither language. He nonetheless had access to the word "plenum" and to "afflatus," which he must have found in some magazine to mean "inspiration" in the most literal sense of the term ("Song of Myself," section 24).

No other American writer of his time made so many language borrowings as Whitman. He did so despite his great admiration for the English language and his rejection (in principle) of European influences. Yet his generous adoption of foreign words was consonant with his desire to incorporate all races and address all nations—and also with his love of rhetoric and high-sounding words.

Whitman's interest in foreign words appears not only in his published works, but also in a book on which he collaborated, but whose coauthorship he never recognized: *Rambles Among Words,* published under the name of his friend William Swinton in 1859. In the fifth volume of Whitman's *Notebooks and Unpublished Prose Manuscripts,* Edward Grier has reprinted the parts of this book which are most likely to have been written by Whitman (5:1624–1662). This includes in particular a list of French words, most of which were used in *Leaves of Grass.* He sometimes comments on them interestingly. He thus specifies that "debris" is "a symbolism from geology" and that "naïve" and "naïvety" are "most desirable words, with the French elusive charm and implying a combination of the ingenuous, candid, winning." As for "ensemble," it is "a noble word with immense vista" (*Notebooks* 5:1658–1660).

Whitman also loved American Indian words and commented on them lyrically in *An American Primer:* "All aboriginal names sound good. I was asking for something savage and luxuriant, and behold here are the aboriginal names" (18). But this is another subject.

For more precise references to the foreign words listed in this article, consult Edwin Harold Eby's concordance.

Roger Asselineau

Bibliography

Allen, Gay Wilson. *The New Walt Whitman Handbook.* 1975. New York: New York UP, 1986.

Asselineau, Roger. *The Evolution of Walt Whitman: The Creation of a Book.* Cambridge, Mass.: Harvard UP, 1962.

Eby, Edwin Harold, ed. *A Concordance of Walt Whitman's "Leaves of Grass" and Selected Prose Writings.* Seattle: U of Washington P, 1955.

Faner, Robert D. *Walt Whitman & Opera.* Carbondale: Southern Illinois UP, 1951.

Leonard, Douglas. "The Art of Walt Whitman's French in 'Song of Myself.'" *Walt Whitman Quarterly Review* 3.4 (1986): 24–27.

Matthiessen, F.O. *American Renaissance.* London: Oxford UP, 1941.

Pound, Louise. *Selected Writings.* Lincoln: U of Nebraska P, 1949.

———. "Walt Whitman and the French Language." *American Speech* 1 (1926): 421–430.

Whitman, Walt. *An American Primer.* Ed. Horace Traubel. Boston: Small, Maynard, 1904.

———. *Notebooks and Unpublished Prose Manuscripts.* Ed. Edward F. Grier. 6 vols. New York: New York UP, 1984.

———. *Walt Whitman of the New York Aurora.* Ed. Joseph Jay Rubin and Charles H. Brown. State College, Pa.: Bald Eagle, 1950.

See also AMERICAN PRIMER, AN; "AMERICA'S MIGHTIEST INHERITANCE"; DICTIONARIES; LANGUAGE; "SLANG IN AMERICA"; STYLE AND TECHNIQUE(S); SWINTON, WILLIAM

Forster, E.M. (1879–1970)

E.M. Forster, one of England's most important modern novelists, admired the poems of Walt Whitman and held humanist ideas analogous to those expressed by the American poet in his *Leaves of Grass* (1892). Like Whitman, Forster believed in bridging contraries to form a strong union. A central character in his fiction, for instance, pleads in *Howards End* (1910), "Only connect" (186). Similarly, Whitman declares throughout his work the necessity of connection between races, nations, religions, and ideas. As he says in his poem "Passage to India," he envisions "oceans to be cross'd, the distant brought near, / The lands to be welded together" (section 2).

Forster borrowed Whitman's title from that poem for his greatest novel, *A Passage to India* (1924), a work in which he explores the question of whether or not there can ever be a full reconciliation between an oppressed race and its oppressors. Both Whitman and Forster focus on the personal "passage" a person must travel to recognize truth, but Whitman's poem is decidedly more optimistic in tone since it concludes with a joyous assurance of the Soul's eventual connection with immortality. While *A Passage to India* also concludes with an assurance—that the British cannot ignore the legacy of colonialism—this recognition is not a reason for joy since it means connection between races is impossible.

Jim McWilliams

Bibliography

Allen, Gay Wilson. *The Solitary Singer: A Critical Biography of Walt Whitman.* 1955. Rev. ed. 1967. Chicago: U of Chicago P, 1985.

Beauman, Nicola. *E.M. Forster: A Biography.* New York: Knopf, 1994.

Beer, John. "The Undying Worm." *A Passage to India: A Casebook.* By E.M. Forster. Ed. Malcolm Bradbury. London: Macmillan, 1970. 186–215.

Forster, E.M. *Howards End.* 1910. New York: Vintage, 1921.

Furbank, P.N. *E.M. Forster: A Life.* San Diego: Harvest, 1981.

Trilling, Lionel. *E.M. Forster.* Norfolk, Conn.: New Directions, 1943.

See also BRITISH ISLES, WHITMAN IN THE; LEGACY, WHITMAN'S; "PASSAGE TO INDIA"

Fowler, Lorenzo Niles (1811–1896) and Orson Squire (1809–1887)

Walt Whitman's interest in phrenology led him on 16 July 1849 to the Phrenological Cabinet of Fowlers and Wells in New York City's Clinton Hall, where he sat for a phrenological examination. The Fowler brothers from Cohocton, New York, were practitioners of the science of mind which held that mental faculties are indicated by the skull's conformation and can be analyzed and improved. The Phrenological Depot established by O.S. and L.N. Fowler in 1842 offered casts of skulls, phrenological busts, and books, as well as phrenological examinations. With the admission of their brother-in-law, Samuel R. Wells, in 1844 the firm was restyled Fowlers and Wells.

Whitman's examination was made by Lorenzo Fowler, a skilled practitioner, and the written analysis, followed by a listing of faculties with their sizes, made a strong impression upon the subject. It was a perceptive reading that appraised Whitman as strong in "animal will" with large Amativeness, Self-Esteem, and Individuality. Whitman quoted from the analysis and published it several times. Phrenological themes and language appeared in his poetry.

In 1855 Fowlers and Wells advertised *Leaves of Grass* as for sale at their new Phrenological Depot at 308 Broadway. With the departure from the firm of Orson S. Fowler, occupied now with the octagonal house he had built in Fishkill, New York, and with his writings on phrenological subjects, the firm became Fowler and Wells. Its London agent, William Horsell, would play a part in establishing Whitman's English reputation. In October 1855 the *American Phrenological Journal,* published by Fowler and Wells, carried Whitman's unsigned review of *Leaves of Grass.* By November, Whitman became a staff writer for another Fowler and Wells periodical, *Life Illustrated,* his contributions including the series "New York Dissected."

The expanded second edition of *Leaves of Grass* was published anonymously by Fowler and Wells in August 1856. Stamped in gold on the spine of each volume appeared, without authorization, Emerson's words "I Greet You at the Beginning of a Great Career."

The book's unfavorable reception led the firm to withdraw their support of and relationship with the poet who, in turn, became disenchanted with the phrenologist-publishers. As for the Fowler brothers, through lectures, publications, and phrenological examinations during the decades that followed, each continued to popularize the belief that self-knowledge through phrenological analysis could lead to self-improvement. This they did without reference to Walt Whitman, the poet they had once perceptively analyzed and published without an imprimatur.

Madeleine B. Stern

Bibliography

Hungerford, Edward. "Walt Whitman and His Chart of Bumps." *American Literature* 2 (1931): 350–384.

Stern, Madeleine B. *Heads & Headlines: The Phrenological Fowlers.* Norman: U of Oklahoma P, 1971.

See also AMERICAN PHRENOLOGICAL JOURNAL; LIFE ILLUSTRATED; PHRENOLOGY; PSEUDOSCIENCE; WELLS, SAMUEL ROBERTS

France, Whitman in

The first French critic to review Whitman's work was Louis Étienne, whose "Walt Whitman, poète, philosophe et 'rowdy'" appeared 1 November 1861. Given the tradition of French poetry, it is not surprising that Étienne is harsh, centering his attack on Whitman's immorality and his outlandish sense of democratic ideals. It is ironic, however, that Whitman, who admired the French for their freedom in matters both sexual and political, was drubbed for such excesses in his own poetry. Fortunately, Étienne includes in his review a generous slice of Whitman lines, the first printed French translations that have surfaced. An earlier French review supposedly appeared in 1860, but the matter has been proved to have been a hoax. Henry Clapp, a New York Whitman enthusiast who began publishing the *Saturday Press* in late 1858, printed an anonymous article he claimed to have gleaned from something called *Bibliographie Impériale* announcing a forthcoming translation of *Leaves of Grass*. The preface to the book purportedly projected for Whitman a stellar reception among the French who, the anonymous reviewer claimed, have lacked excellence and originality in their indigenous verse. French poets are condemned for having had no confidence in their readership, a readership they have construed as stupid, incapable of appreciating obscure verse. The reviewer makes the astonishing claim that "a perfect poem should be completely incomprehensible" (qtd. in Greenspan 112). This is the wonder of Whitman: the more one reads him, the less one understands him. Such sentiments seem to twentieth-century readers either effusively grotesque or, on the other hand, bitterly satiric. But no periodical called *Bibliographie Impériale* ever existed in Paris, and the anonymous comments in the 1860 review should probably be attributed to the energy of Henry Clapp who was, after all, notorious for his championing of Whitman, so much so that the New York *Sunday Atlas* attributed the demise of his *Saturday Press* (some few weeks after the "French" review appeared) to the paper's "continual puffs of Walt Whitman's dirty '*Leaves of Grass*'" (qtd. in Greenspan 111). Whitman's early penchant for writing favorable reviews of his own poetry may have encouraged Clapp to do the same, or at least it indicates in mid-nineteenth-century America a whimsical attitude toward scholarly disinterestedness.

Seven years after the first article in France, an 1868 reference to the poet by Amédée Pichot appeared in the *Revue Britannique,* but it is scarcely more than a short sigh of exasperation that Whitman is difficult to understand. A more substantial article appeared in 1872 when Thérèse Bentzon, under the name Mme. Blanc, published "Un Poète américain—Walt Whitman: Muscle and Pluck Forever." She decries Whitman's attack on literary idealism and accuses him of confusing genius with brute force. In her attempt to champion social integrity, she reduces Whitman to a thug more interested in grubby reality than in the improvement of people's morals. She finds Whitman arrogant in his identification of the self with the universe, a spokesman to all generations, and she faults him for mixing body and spirit, not preserving the traditional dichotomy of body as evil and soul as good. She dislikes his poetics, his confusion of poetry with prose. However, in her favor she did reprint substantial excerpts from Whitman and thus brought him more mainstream than he had been before, in the golden years of his life. Moreover, her attack prompted Emile Blémont to publish three articles that same year in *Renaissance Littéraire et Artistique.* Blémont's first article is largely biographical, but the second and third treat of Whitman's philosophy, Blémont linking the poet to Hegel and the reconciliation of contraries. From this essential insight, Blémont is able to reach out and accept Whitman's individualism, his American esprit, and his appreciation of science. Blémont ignored the materialism in Whitman that had bothered Bentzon: Whitman is a leader of his people, a figure Blémont romanticizes into a kind of literary messiah. A poet himself, Blémont brought the French to respect Whitman more for his ideas than for his poetics.

In 1877 Henri Cochin attacked Whitman in *Le Correspondant,* arguing that American libertine democracy had produced an "egalitarian madness" (634) in Whitman that threatened all social institutions at home and abroad with an excessive democratic pride. He lambastes the 1855 portrait of the poet as vulgar and pretentious. Whitman is not only a materialist, but a man without faith. Like Bentzon, however, Cochin values Whitman's patriotism: *Drum-Taps* he finds beautifully evocative of Whitman's devotion and service during the Civil War.

French critics warmed slowly to Whitman. For example, in 1882 Léo Quesnel represents a curious blend of admiration and condemnation. He admits that Whitman is a great writer of poetic prose, thus echoing Bentzon, but he gives three reasons why Whitman will continue to meet resistance from French readership: first, Whitman suffers in translation; second, he avoids traditional forms of metrical verse; and third, his verses lack images, do not appeal to the ears, the eyes, the imagination. This latter criticism seems woefully misfounded; Quesnel, in his haste to censure Whitman's sense of metrics, overlooks the richness of his imagery.

Once the symbolist poets discovered Whitman, however, the critics soon followed. In 1886 Jules Laforgue published translations of "Inscriptions," "O Star of France," and "A Woman Waits for Me," and he planned a complete translation of *Leaves of Grass*. Unfortunately, Laforgue died in 1887, but not before his verses showed distinct signs of being influenced by Whitman's free-verse style. Then the championing of Whitman fell to two French poets born in America: Stuart Merrill and Francis Vielé-Griffin. The latter published translations of Whitman between 1888 and 1908. Thereafter, the first major critic to rally to the French poets' discoveries was Gabriel Sarrazin, who published an influential article on Whitman in 1888. In it, he champions Whitman's pioneering of a new kind of verse—median to prose and poetry, and akin to Hebrew metrics—and he accepts Whitman's pantheism as a poetic philosophy lying at the heart of his material and technique, a philosophy that was antithetical to that of earlier French critics. Sarrazin concludes his article with a laudatory portrait of Whitman, much of which he lifted from Bucke's biography of the poet and which set an impassioned tone for years to come in French appreciation of the poet's life. Whitman was highly appreciative of Sarrazin's article. Four years later, Whitman's death elicited half a dozen encomiums in the French press, indicating that the tide had forever turned in appreciation. The same year Henry Bérenger translated a highly influential piece by Havelock Ellis that appeared in *L'Ermitage* and afforded the French a reasoned critical evaluation of the poet.

With the turn of the century came the rise of the unanimists, led by Jules Romains, whose *La Vie unanime* (1908) shows definite influence of Whitman's poetry. That same year Léon Bazalgette published the first full-length French biography, *Walt Whitman: L'Homme et son oeuvre,* and one year later the first complete translation of *Leaves of Grass*. The biography is calm and deliberate, lacking much of the outlandish exuberance of earlier biographical pieces by the French, and endorses Whitman as much for being human as for being an important poet. We are given a picture of Whitman both as democratic and educated, two aspects of the poet that had raised concerns earlier: on the one hand the poet had been vilified as being too democratic, and on the other as being undereducated. In analyzing the soul of the poet, Bazalgette focuses on Whitman's reserve and his love of simple living, his appreciation of the individual above the law, and the acuteness of his poetic imagination. Whitman is thus a contradiction in society, but he refuses to explain himself, allowing his poetry and his very being to disarm critics. Bazalgette characterizes Whitman as "Oceanic, Adamic, Cosmic," a force that gathers all things into the "great All." The funeral rites in 1892 he terms pagan, but only because they were unconventional. Both the biography and the translation of poems brought André Gide into the Whitman fold, but only because he deplored Bazalgette's attempts to make Whitman heterosexual. In translating the poems, Bazalgette used "affection" to characterize homoerotic love and "amour" heterosexual love. Gide accused the translator of misrepresenting the poems and promised to publish a translation of his own, a book that eventually appeared in 1918 and remains today the finest French translation of Whitman. The attack by Gide did not prevent Bazalgette from publishing his critical analysis of *Leaves of Grass* in 1921: *Le Poème-évangile de Walt Whitman*.

In addition to the unanimists, the writers associated with the Abbaye movement rallied to Whitman early in the century: René Arcos, Charles Vildrac, Luc Durtain, and Georges Chennevière. For them Whitman represents a break with civilization and a return to the primitive. The group championed Bazalgette's critical works on Whitman and endorsed particularly the biographer's insistence that Whitman's life was as valuable to civilization as his poetry. For French poets, Whitman's political spirit continued to remain a valued contribution to literature, bringing to poetry a sense of revolution and freedom that the French have traditionally treasured more in their politics than in their poetics.

As Europe rolled toward World War I, French poets became more and more experimental. Occasionally they became outrageous in their assessment of Whitman. In 1913 Guillaume Apollinaire published an account of Whitman's funeral, supposedly derived from an eyewitness, detailing marching bands and an obnoxious crowd bordering on being orgiastic. Calmer voices among the "avant-garde" were Valery Larbaud, Blaise Cendrars, and Saint-John Perse, whose poetic rhythms show heavy reliance on the prosaic music of Whitman's meters.

In the aftermath of the war, France produced one of her major Whitman critics, Jean Catel, whose articles on the poet began appearing in 1923 and culminated with his major works: *Walt Whitman: La naissance du poète* (1929) and *Rythme et langage dans la 1re édition de "Leaves of Grass"* (1930). The first treats of Whitman's early years, beginning with his education and ending with the 1855 edition. Pucciani distrusts Catel's basic premises that Whitman's motivation was primarily a feeling of isolation and that his philosophical bases were more lyrical than real. Catel's failure to study effectively Whitman's fusion of the creative processes does not, however, detract from Catel's significant contribution to the study of Whitman as a complex personality. The second half of the biography is devoted to a study of the poetry itself. There Catel touches on Whitman's surrealism, sense of identity, concept of the soul, "I"-narrator, and sexuality. "Identity" he contrasts with "conformity," and the soul he sees as a force greater than the poet. The "I" is one unconscious mélange of contradiction, giving Whitman the ability to assume uncannily a female persona in the poetry. Catel's second book is limited to Whitman's poetics and represents the first work in any country to assess Whitman's life through a psychological interpretation of the poems. Whitman's poetic rhythm, Catel feels, is reflected in short bursts of words, often ungrammatical, and his punctuation follows an oral rather than written tradition. Catel groups Whitman's rhythms into "groupement binaire," "groupement ternaire," and "groupement en plus de trois," but the arrangement of these groups on the page is not important to a reader because, Catel argues, Whitman's is basically a spoken art. Somewhere between oratory and poetry, Whitman's art uses the direct action of the voice, which harks all the way back to earliest civilizations.

By the time of the Second World War, two important voices appeared in French studies of Whitman: Charles Cestre and Roger Asselineau. The former, the first chair of American literature at the Sorbonne, published articles on Whitman from 1930 to 1957 and is best remembered for his unraveling the 1860 Henry Clapp review hoax. Asselineau first published on Whitman in 1948 and remains today the single most important French critic of Whitman. In 1954 his *L'Évolution de Walt Whitman* appeared to great acclaim. Conceived as a continuation of Catel's study of the first edition of *Leaves of Grass,* the book departs from Catel in that Asselineau studies editions beyond that of 1855. The work is in two parts and was published in English translation separately as *The Creation of a Personality* (1960) and *The Creation of a Book* (1962). The biography volume has met with justified praise generally, and the study of themes in volume 2 has furthered Whitman studies on two continents. Among the traditional themes explored by Asselineau in the latter book are Whitman's mysticism, spiritual materialism, identity, pantheism, democracy, and sexuality. Concluding the book are three chapters devoted to analysis of style, language, and prosody. Asselineau's 1954 book received a front-page review in the *Figaro Littéraire,* which article led to renewed interest in Whitman in France. American critics have accused him, however, of overintellectualizing Whitman and ignoring Whitman's psyche. Asselineau himself admits that he gave little effort to explaining Whitman's lyricism. His subsequent translation of *Leaves of Grass* appeared in 1956 and was reprinted in 1972 and 1989.

George Klawitter

Bibliography

Allen, Gay Wilson, ed. *Walt Whitman Abroad.* Syracuse: Syracuse UP, 1955.

Allen, Gay Wilson, and Ed Folsom, eds. *Walt Whitman & the World.* Iowa City: U of Iowa P, 1995.

Asselineau, Roger. *L'Évolution de Walt Whitman.* Paris: Didier, 1954.

Bazalgette, Léon. *Le Poème-évangile de Walt Whitman.* Paris: Mercure de France, 1921.

——. *Walt Whitman: L'Homme et son oeuvre.* Paris: Societe du Mercure de France, 1908.

Bentzon, Thérèse. "Un Poète américain—Walt Whitman: 'Muscle and Pluck Forever.'" *Revue des Deux Mondes* 42 (1872): 565–582.

F

Blémont, Emile. "La Poésie en Angleterre et aux Etats-Unis." *Renaissance Litteraire et Artistique* 7 (1872): 54–56; 11 (1872): 86–87; 12 (1872): 90–91.

Catel, Jean. *Rythme et langage dans la 1re édition des "Leaves of Grass" (1855).* Montpellier: Causse, Graille et Castelnau, 1930.

———. *Walt Whitman: La naissance du poète.* Paris: Rieder, 1929.

Cestre, Charles. "Un intermède de la renommée de Walt Whitman en France." *Revue Anglo-Américaine* 13 (1935): 136–140.

Cochin, Henri. "Un Poète américain: Walt Whitman." *Le Correspondent* 25 November 1877: 634–635.

Erkkila, Betsy. *Walt Whitman Among the French: Poet and Myth.* Princeton: Princeton UP, 1980.

Étienne, Louis. "Walt Whitman, poète, philosophe et 'rowdy.'" *La Revue Européene* 1 Nov. 1861: 104–117.

Greenspan, Ezra. "The Earliest French Review of Walt Whitman." *Walt Whitman Quarterly Review* 6 (1989): 109–116.

Klawitter, George. "Early French Expectations of Walt Whitman." *Walt Whitman Review* 28 (1982): 54–63.

Pucciani, Oreste F. *The Literary Reputation of Walt Whitman in France.* New York: Garland, 1987.

Quesnel, Léo. "La Littérature aux Etats-Unis." *La Nouvelle Revue* 1 (1882): 121–154.

Sarrazin, Gabriel. "Poètes modernes de l'Amérique—Walt Whitman." *Nouvelle Revue* 52 (1888): 164–184.

See also APOLLINAIRE, GUILLAUME; ASSELINEAU, ROGER; BAZALGETTE, LÉON; CATEL, JEAN; CLAPP, HENRY; GIDE, ANDRÉ; INTERCULTURALITY; PSYCHOLOGICAL APPROACHES; SARRAZIN, GABRIEL

Franklin Evans (1842)

Walt Whitman's temperance novel, *Franklin Evans; or The Inebriate. A Tale of the Times,* was originally published in the *New World* (2.10, Extra Series, November 1842: 1–31). Reprinted as an "off-print from the *New World*" (Brasher 336), the 1843 edition appeared under the title: *Franklin Evans: Knowledge Is Power. The Merchant's Clerk, in New York; or the Career of a Young Man from the Country.* A third printing of the novel appeared in the Brooklyn *Daily Eagle* during the period that Whitman served as that paper's editor (March 1846–January 1848). Serialized episodes appeared in the *Eagle* from 16–30 November 1846. For this edition not only did Whitman change the title but he also edited the novel, making major deletions. Whitman's new title for this publication was *Fortunes of a Country-Boy; Incidents in Town—and His Adventures at the South.* Whitman also disguised his authorship of the novel by attributing it to "J.R.S." (Brasher 125). His reason for assigning the novel to a pseudonymous author is unknown. In addition to making radical revisions of the latter portion of the novel, Whitman deleted the introduction, conclusion, and chapter mottoes, as well as several incidents and embedded tales. In 1929, the original *New World* version of *Franklin Evans* was published in the *Uncollected Poetry and Prose of Walt Whitman* and by Random House as a book with an introduction by Emory Holloway.

In 1842 an advocate of the temperance movement, Park Benjamin, asked Whitman to write a "short novel for a worthy cause" (Winwar 73). In May of 1888, in a conversation with Horace Traubel, Whitman recalled that the request to write the novel came from "Parke Godwin and another somebody" (Traubel 93); however, biographers attribute the request to Benjamin, who was then editor of the *New World*. Because Benjamin offered a down payment of seventy-five dollars and a follow-up payment of fifty dollars if the publication sold, and because Whitman was "so hard up at the time" (Traubel 93), he agreed to attempt the task. Whitman claims to have completed the novel in three days; however, a noted twentieth-century biographer questions whether he could have written twenty thousand words per day even if he had been fortified with "gin cocktails" as he once claimed (Brasher 125). In order to assist and to speed up the writing of the novel, Whitman included some stories that he had previously written. Probably the stories of the Indian in chapter 2; "Little Jane," in chapter 14; and possibly the allegorical dream in chapter 21 had been written previously.

In the same 1888 conversation with Horace Traubel, Whitman called the novel "damned rot—rot of the worst sort" (Traubel 93). Contemporary biographers and critics seem to agree with Whitman's assessment. For

THE NEW WORLD.

PARK BENJAMIN,
EDITOR.

J. WINCHESTER,
PUBLISHER.

"No pent-up Utica contracts our powers; For the whole boundless continent is ours."

EXTRA SERIES.
OFFICE 30 ANN-STREET.
NUMBER 34

VOL. II....No. 10.
NEW-YORK, NOVEMBER, 1842.
PRICE 12½ CENTS.

Original Temperance Novel.

Entered according to Act of Congress, in the year 1842,
BY J. WINCHESTER,
In the Clerk's Office of the Southern District of New York.

FRANKLIN EVANS;

OR

THE INEBRIATE.

A TALE OF THE TIMES.

BY WALTER WHITMAN.

INTRODUCTORY.

THE story I am going to tell you, reader, will be somewhat aside from the ordinary track of the novelist. It will not abound, either with profound reflections, or sentimental remarks. Yet its moral—for I flatter myself it has one, and one which it were well to engrave on the heart of each person who scans its pages—will be taught by its own incidents, and the current of the narrative.

Whatever of romance there may be—I leave it to any who have, in the course of their every-day walks, heard the histories of intemperate men, whether the events of the tale, strange as some of them may appear, have not had their counterpart in real life. If you who live in the city should go out among your neighbors and investigate what is being transacted there, you might come to behold things far more improbable. In fact, the following chapters contain but the account of a young man, thrown by circumstances amid the vortex of dissipation—a country youth, who came to our great emporium to seek his fortune—and what befell him there. So it is a plain story; yet as the grandest truths are sometimes plain enough to enter into the minds of children—it may be that the delineation I shall give will do benefit, and that educated men and women may not find the hour they spend in its perusal, altogether wasted.

And I would ask your belief when I assert that, what you are going to read is not a work of fiction, as the term is used. I narrate occurrences that have had a far more substantial existence, than in my fancy. There will be those who, as their eyes turn past line after line, will have their memories carried to matters which they have heard of before, or taken a part in themselves, and which, they know, are real.

Can I hope, that my story will do good? I entertain that hope Issued in the cheap and popular form you see, and wafted by every mail to all parts of this vast republic; the facilities which its publisher possesses, giving him the power of diffusing it more widely than any other establishment in the United States; the mighty and deep public opinion which, as a tide bears a ship upon its bosom, ever welcomes anything favorable to the Temperance Reform; its being written *for the mass*, though the writer hopes, not without some claim upon the approval of the more fastidious; and, as much as anything else, the fact that it is as a pioneer in this department of literature—all these will give "THE INEBRIATE," I feel confident, a more than ordinary share of patronage.

For youth, what can be more invaluable? It teaches sobriety, that virtue which every mother and father prays nightly, may be resident in the characters of their sons. It wars against Intemperance, that evil spirit which has levelled so many fair human forms before its horrible advances. Without being presumptuous, I would remind those who believe in the wholesome doctrines of abstinence, how the earlier teachers of piety used parables and fables, as the fit instruments whereby they might convey to men the beauty of the system they professed. In the resemblance, how reasonable it is to suppose that you can impress a lesson upon him whom you would influence to sobriety, in no better way than letting him read such a story as this.

It is usual for writers, upon presenting their works to the public, to bespeak indulgence for faults and deficiences. I am but too well aware that the critical eye will see some such in the following pages; yet my book is not written for the critics, but for THE PEOPLE; and while I think it best to leave it to the reader's own decision whether I have succeeded, I cannot help remarking, that I have the fullest confidence in the verdict's being favorable.

And, to conclude, may I hope that he who purchases this volume, will give to its author, and to its publisher also, the credit of being influenced not altogether by views of the profit to come from it? Whatever of those views may enter into our minds, we are not without a strong desire that the principles here inculcated will strike deep, and grow again, and bring forth good fruit. A prudent, sober, and temperate course of life cannot be too strongly taught to old and young; to the young, because the future years are before them—to the old, because it is their business to prepare for death. And though, as before remarked, the writer has abstained from thrusting the moral upon the reader, by dry and abstract disquisitions—preferring the more pleasant and quite as profitable method of letting the reader draw it himself from the occurrences—it is hoped that the New and Popular Reform now in the course of progress over the land, will find no trifling help from a "TALE OF THE TIMES."

First printing of Franklin Evans, *Whitman's temperance novel. From* Walt Whitman: A Descriptive Bibliography, *by Joel Myerson, © 1993 by University of Pittsburgh Press.*

example, Gay Wilson Allen calls *Franklin Evans* a "melodramatic maudlin story" (59). Miller considers it "inept as a temperance plea and worthless as fiction" (19).

The temperance theme of the novel is apparent even in the first chapter, before the plot involving young Franklin Evans begins. As Evans sets out for New York, he and a companion enter a tavern. Evans has been acquainted with the tavern keeper prior to this meeting. He relates to readers that he can well remember when the tavern keeper's "eyes were not bleared" (Whitman, *Evans* 10). He adds that the tavern keeper now has "a face flushed with redness" and the appearance of a man "enfeebled by disease" (10). Evans draws the conclusion that alcoholic beverages have been the man's downfall. As the novel continues, Franklin Evans, as first-person narrator, relates the story in which strong drink causes his downfall. Predictably, by the end of his narrative, Franklin Evans concludes that "total abstinence" is the only safe course for him to follow (236).

Whitman's introduction to the novel sounds convincing. Of course, his journalistic experience helped him to write acceptable prose. By the time he came to write *Franklin Evans,* he had accumulated considerable experience in writing for newspapers, and Henry Seidel Canby says that Whitman was a "good journalist" (41). He was not, however, a fiction writer, even though *Franklin Evans* was advertised before publication as having been written by "one of the best Novelists of this country" (qtd. in Brasher 124). The avowed purpose of the novel was to "rescue Young Men from the demon of intemperance" (qtd. in Brasher 124). Although Whitman said that he "never cut a chip off that kind of timber again" (Traubel 93), he did start a second temperance novel, "The Madman." An opening chapter appeared in the New York *Washingtonian and Organ* on 28 January 1843. No additional chapters of the novel have survived.

The novel *Franklin Evans* does demonstrate Whitman's powers of observation and attention to detail. He says in the introduction that the novel will stir the memories of his readers, for they will know that the happenings are real. Whether he had experienced the happenings or had merely heard about them, he renders the scenes with elements of realism.

In the introduction to *Franklin Evans* Whitman writes that the novel "is not written

for the critics but for THE PEOPLE" (5). His statement serves as a harbinger of the role he later sought for himself in society, to be the poet of the people.

William G. Lulloff

Bibliography

Allen, Gay Wilson. *The Solitary Singer: A Critical Biography of Walt Whitman.* 1955. Rev. ed. 1967. Chicago: U of Chicago P, 1985.

Brasher, Thomas L., ed. *The Early Poems and the Fiction.* By Walt Whitman. New York: New York UP, 1963.

Canby, Henry Seidel. *Walt Whitman: An American.* Boston: Houghton Mifflin, 1943.

Miller, James E., Jr. *Walt Whitman.* New York: Twayne, 1962.

Traubel, Horace. *With Walt Whitman in Camden.* Vol. 1. Boston: Small, Maynard, 1906.

Whitman, Walt. *Franklin Evans.* 1842. New York: Random House, 1929.

———. *The Uncollected Poetry and Prose of Walt Whitman.* Ed. Emory Holloway. Vol. 2. Garden City, N.Y.: Doubleday, Page, 1921.

Winwar, Frances. *American Giant: Walt Whitman and His Times.* New York: Harper, 1941.

See also "CHILD AND THE PROFLIGATE, THE"; "DEATH OF WIND-FOOT, THE"; "LITTLE JANE"; "MADMAN, THE"; "REUBEN'S LAST WISH"; SHORT FICTION, WHITMAN'S; TEMPERANCE MOVEMENT

Free Inquirer

A "socialist and agnostic" newspaper (Mott 537) professing many liberal ideas of the day, the *Free Inquirer* (or *Free Enquirer*) was subscribed to by Walt Whitman's father, Walter Whitman, Sr. The impressionable young Whitman read it, absorbing its rhetoric and ideas.

The *Free Inquirer* was originally founded in 1825 by Robert Dale Owen as the *New-Harmony Gazette,* a journal that recorded the ideas of a small socialist community. As the *Free Inquirer,* it expanded its readership and purpose. Moving the paper to New York, Frances (Fanny) Wright, a radical public speaker and reformer, joined Owen as an editor during the years that the newspaper voiced support for the common laborer. Among the paper's topics were agnosticism, feminism, social politics, and liberal views on education. Published by well-known, fiery leaders, the *Free Inquirer* introduced a youthful Walt Whitman to radical thought.

Jennifer J. Stein

Bibliography
Mott, Frank Luther. *A History of American Magazines, 1741–1850*. Cambridge, Mass.: Harvard UP, 1938.
Perkins, A.J.G., and Theresa Woolfson. *Frances Wright, Free Enquirer: The Study of a Temperament*. Philadelphia: Porcupine, 1972.
Reynolds, David S. *Walt Whitman's America: A Cultural Biography*. New York: Knopf, 1995.

See also RADICALISM; WHITMAN, WALTER, SR.; WRIGHT, FRANCES (FANNY)

Free Soil Party

Organized at Buffalo, New York, on 9 August 1848, this political party was founded on the principle of opposing the extension of slavery into western territories. The Free Soil party was a significant force in American politics from 1848 until the birth of the Republican party in 1854 for the way in which it popularized antislavery sentiment and compelled the major parties to debate slavery as a national issue. Walt Whitman was an active member of the Free Soil party, representing his local party at the inaugural convention and editing a Free Soil newspaper.

Debate over the 1846 Wilmot Proviso, which prohibited slavery in the territory acquired from Mexico, led to the fragmentation of both the Democratic and Whig parties. The New York Democratic Barnburners, of which Whitman was a member, broke away from the party and in June 1848 nominated Martin Van Buren for president, adopting a Wilmot platform. Simultaneously, Conscience Whigs bolted their party. These elements, together with members of the abolitionist Liberty party, overcame significant differences to unite as a new party at a national convention in Buffalo, choosing as their motto "Free Soil, Free Speech, Free Labor, and Free Men" and nominating Van Buren for president. In contrast to abolitionists, who opposed slavery on moral grounds, most Free-Soilers opposed slavery because they felt that white laborers should not have to compete with—nor be "degraded" by—the presence of black slaves in the new territories. In fact, a plank to include black suffrage in the party platform was voted down. In representing antislavery as an issue of self-interest to whites, free-soilism made antislavery for the first time a viable political movement in the North.

Whitman served as one of fifteen Kings County delegates to the national convention in Buffalo and edited the Brooklyn *Freeman*, a short-lived Free Soil newspaper established in September 1848. The *Freeman*'s 9 September debut issue made clear that Whitman opposed the extension of slavery because he cared about the opportunities for white labor in the new territories, and not because he sympathized with slaves.

In the 1848 elections the Free Soil party claimed a fair degree of success, with twelve members elected to Congress and many more to state legislatures. More important, the party had succeeded in making antislavery the central issue in national politics. Free-soilism was dealt a heavy blow, however, by the 1850 Compromise, which Whitman and other Free-Soilers decried as a surrender of antislavery principles in the face of disunionist threats. By 1854, with the country having achieved an uneasy truce over slavery, the disorganized remnants of the Free Soil party became absorbed into the newly formed Republican party.

Martin Klammer

Bibliography
Foner, Eric. *Politics and Ideology in the Age of the Civil War*. New York: Oxford UP, 1980.
McPherson, James M. *Battle Cry of Freedom: The Civil War Era*. New York: Oxford UP, 1988.
Rubin, Joseph Jay. *The Historic Whitman*. University Park: Pennsylvania State UP, 1973.
Whitman, Walt. *The Gathering of the Forces*. Ed. Cleveland Rodgers and John Black. 2 vols. New York: Putnam, 1920.

See also BARNBURNERS AND LOCOFOCOS; BROOKLYN *FREEMAN*; BUFFALO FREE SOIL CONVENTION; COMPROMISE OF 1850; DEMOCRATIC PARTY; SLAVERY AND ABOLITIONISM; WILMOT PROVISO

F

Freedom

When with characteristic insight Emerson recognized "the wonderful gift of 'LEAVES OF GRASS'" in his letter of July 1855 to Whitman, it was the freedom of the poetry that spoke most powerfully to him. He responded to Whitman's "courage of treatment" and its effects on the reader, "namely, of fortifying and encouraging" (Whitman 729–730). Freedom is central to Whitman's vision of life—the artistic life, the individual life, and the life of the society.

As artist, Whitman demanded and demonstrated a new freedom in poetry. Breaking with tradition, he moved toward a more open, organic poetry (so-called free verse), allowing his thoughts and feelings to find expression in lines and stanzas of varying lengths. While his greatest poems exhibit the qualities of musical composition (fluidity, melody, recurring motifs), rhyme and meter went by the wayside. The line became the basic unit for Whitman—virtually all his lines are end-stopped—and this technique, which he derived from the Hebraic tradition, is in keeping with Whitman's sense of the poet as seer. The poet was also a creator, godlike in bringing—out of the divine imagination—new things into being. Each poem had its own form to find, and that form would emerge in the writing of the poem (Coleridge's "organic form"). Sensing new possibilities for poetry, Whitman married freedom of imagination to the courage of creative action, personifying what Rollo May called "the courage to create"—the artist exercising creative freedom and thereby living a fuller, more genuine life. Whitman's freer verse powerfully influenced the course of Western poetry, and he still remains its most impressive practitioner.

In his poetry's spontaneity, movement, and scope, Whitman sought to represent the life process itself, a process whose very essence is freedom. Besides openness of form, then, Whitman's freedom of language, subject matter, and tone infused energy and originality into American poetry. Whitman's words came from everywhere—opera, carpentry, science, city and country, other languages; if he couldn't find the word he wanted, he invented it. This freedom to employ nonpoetic language to enliven and communicate thoughts and feelings was paralleled by Whitman's determination to include people, topics, and experiences previously considered inappropriate or downright taboo. Consequently, the reader finds in Whitman's poems the downtrodden and denied (prostitute, drunkard, lunatic, slave, venerealee) along with the respected and attractive (president, deacon, bride). Desiring a poetry representative of actual life, Whitman acknowledged painful and repressed elements of mid-nineteenth-century America. The reader encounters dramatizations of slavery, the dead and dying of the Civil War (along with primitive surgical procedures), and, of course, human sexuality. Whitman celebrated the senses and invited the reader to do the same, rejoicing courageously in the libido and all its manifestations. And, to communicate this material so new to American poetry, Whitman broke poetic ground again by establishing a personal relationship between poet and audience by addressing the reader directly—as "reader" or "you"—sometimes asking questions to elicit responses, sometimes reaching out and hooking the reader around the waist or otherwise embracing him. Furthermore, Whitman's tone draws the reader in, as the poet speaks nonjudgmentally, tenderly, supportively, seductively, ecstatically, despairingly by turns. The "voice" in Whitman's poems is decidedly human, and it speaks in all the keys of life.

Even as he created a new poetry, Whitman's work revealed his hortatory purpose. The openness and inclusiveness of his verse encouraged the reader to live autonomously. Thus, *Leaves of Grass* was not only an example of artistic freedom; it was also a dramatization of a free life. As such, it invited the reader to examine and to liberate his life from fears and inhibitions that obstructed personal growth. In "Song of Myself" (sections 6, 7, 52) and "Crossing Brooklyn Ferry," for example, the poet raises the issue of death, explores its mystery and attempts to alleviate the reader's fears about it. In "Song of Myself" (sections 5, 24, 28, 29) and the "Children of Adam" poems, the speaker not only addresses sexuality (a courageous act in itself, considering Puritan and Victorian repressiveness), but he glorifies it, hymns it. Again, in "Song of Myself" (section 46), the "I" speaks in the voice of a counselor, friend, teacher, or parent regarding the courage to live. Not only does the speaker assure that all will be well, but he offers to accompany the reader part way, and at the poem's end, after his own death, to await the reader's arrival. Fear of death, fear of sexual desire, fear of life—all these Whitman addresses, as well as fear of the self in regard to denying or disowning unattractive personal qualities. Whitman portrays his own humanity by presenting his faults ("The wolf, the snake, the hog, not wanting in me" ["Crossing Brooklyn Ferry," section 6]). This is hardly boasting, but rather an attempt to model self-awareness and self-acceptance. Just as Whitman anticipates Freud regarding the unhealthiness of sexual repression, so too Whitman anticipates Jung regarding the shadow aspects of the psyche, aspects which must be acknowledged if the individual is to progress toward wholeness or integrity. Whitman understood that freedom becomes real only when translated into action. He dramatized, then, the courage necessary to do this in his art and in his life.

Ultimately, Whitman's vision of individual freedom (including artistic freedom) culminates in his hope for a truly democratic society. In such a culture, people are equal, unique, and free to become themselves. Yet, as much as Whitman celebrates the autonomous life, he unfailingly connects the individual to his community. Whitman's individual is no loner. Rather, he is one of the strands in a large living tapestry, one of the "leaves of grass." In Whitman's dream of America, all people are equal (men and women, poor and rich, black and white, professor and mechanic, Christian and non-Christian), all have maximum opportunity for self-development resulting in distinct and fully realized identities (individuation), and all share in the culture's life. Of all Whitman's poems, "Song of Myself" most fully expresses this vision. The catalogue sections (15 and 33) parade an extraordinary and representative variety of individuals going about their business in this new country. Each belongs. Each contributes to the picture. There is no hierarchy here.

Finally, then, Whitman's art and vision are expressions of hope and love—his hopes for America to achieve its potential as a truly democratic land, and his love for all people, starting with himself. Out of this healthy self-love, a person can love others, all others, by virtue of their common humanity. For Whitman, then, freedom is central to being. This tenet he embraced in his art, his sense of the individual life, and his dream for America.

Carl Martin Lindner

Bibliography

May, Rollo. *The Courage to Create*. New York: Norton, 1975.
Whitman, Walt. *Leaves of Grass: Compre-*
hensive Reader's Edition. Ed. Harold W. Blodgett and Sculley Bradley. New York: New York UP, 1965.

See also DEMOCRACY; EQUALITY; INDIVIDUALISM; PRIDE; SEX AND SEXUALITY; STYLE AND TECHNIQUE(S)

Freiligrath, Ferdinand (1810–1876)

Whitman's first German translator encountered Whitman's poetry in English exile. A revolutionary poet and personal friend of Karl Marx, Ferdinand Freiligrath was well known internationally as a translator of first-rate authors. He translated just ten poems from William M. Rossetti's *Poems by Walt Whitman* (1868), and his selection reflected German interest in the recently concluded Civil War. The poems appeared in the special weekly edition of the *Augsburger Allgemeine Zeitung,* one of Germany's leading dailies. None of the poems would have been particularly shocking to German readers, either aesthetically or thematically, because his translation smoothed Whitman's formal edges, thus adapting his poetry to conventional standards.

Freiligrath's introduction to Whitman is of greater significance because it was frequently reprinted. He emphasizes Whitman's formal experiments: "Are we really come to the point, when life, even in poetry, calls imperatively for new forms of expression? Has the age so much and such serious matter to say, that the old vessels no longer suffice for the new contents?" (qtd. in Grünzweig 14–15).

For the Whitman community and especially William O'Connor, Freiligrath's interest in Whitman was a source of great satisfaction. The article was translated and published in several American magazines. In a letter to Freiligrath, O'Connor recommended that he ignore Rossetti's incomplete edition and use the original which would enable him "to estimate the Poem in totality" (qtd. in Grünzweig 16). Although there are several incomplete translations of Whitman poems among Freiligrath's manuscripts, no more translations appeared in print.

Freiligrath is at the beginning of a long canon of leftist German admirers of Whitman. His brief interest in Whitman has had lasting effects by contributing to Whitman's construction as a political poet.

Walter Grünzweig

Bibliography

Freiligrath, Ferdinand. "Walt Whitman." *Augsburger Allgemeine Zeitung* (Wochenausgabe) 17 (1868): 257–259. Translations in 24 (1868): 369–371 and 25 (1868): 385ff.

Grünzweig, Walter. *Constructing the German Walt Whitman.* Iowa City: U of Iowa P, 1995.

Springer, Otto. "Walt Whitman and Ferdinand Freiligrath." *American-German Review* 11:2 (1944): 22–26, 38.

See also GERMAN-SPEAKING COUNTRIES, WHITMAN IN THE; ROSSETTI, WILLIAM MICHAEL

Fritzinger, Frederick Warren (1866–1899)

Whitman's nurse in his final illness, Frederick Warren Fritzinger, or "Warry," as he was known, was a sailor before coming to stay at 328 Mickle Street. He and his brother Henry (whose son was named Walter Whitman Fritzinger) had been raised by Mrs. Mary Davis, Whitman's Camden housekeeper, and Warry came to help her care for Whitman in October 1889. Whitman was very fond of him and spoke to J.W. Wallace of his good nature.

Fritzinger met Wallace and Dr. J. Johnston when they visited Camden and maintained contact with them after their return to Bolton, England. In a series of four letters written in 1891 and 1892, Fritzinger provided Wallace and Johnston with news of Whitman's last illness. The letters reveal a warm and affectionate caretaker. Whitman's final words, "Shift, Warry," were addressed to Fritzinger as a request to be turned in his bed.

Following Whitman's death, Fritzinger testified on behalf of Davis in her lawsuit brought against George Whitman for recovery of money she believed he owed her. He later married and worked as a clerk in a Camden shop. A photograph by Johnston taken at the Camden wharf in 1890 shows Fritzinger with Whitman.

Joann P. Krieg

Bibliography

Folsom, Ed. "'This Heart's Geography's Map': The Photographs of Walt Whitman." Special issue of *Walt Whitman Quarterly Review* 4.2–3 (1986–1987): 37.

Keller, Elizabeth Leavitt. *Walt Whitman in Mickle Street.* New York: Kennerley, 1921.

Walt Whitman, 1890, with nurse Warren Fritzinger. Courtesy of the Library of Congress.

Krieg, Joann P. "Letters from Warry." *Walt Whitman Quarterly Review* 11 (1994): 163–173.

See also DAVIS, MARY OAKES; HEALTH; JOHNSTON, DR. JOHN; MICKLE STREET HOUSE; WALLACE, JAMES WILLIAM

"From Far Dakota's Cañons" (1876)

"From Far Dakota's Cañons" was first published as "A Death Sonnet for Custer" in the New York *Tribune*, 10 July 1876, two weeks after General George Armstrong Custer's death. Whitman received ten dollars for the poem. It was intercalated in some copies of the Centennial edition of *Leaves of Grass* (1876) and added in its present position to the cluster "From Noon to Starry Night" in the 1881 edition, when it also took its present title. Aside from the change in title Whitman made no other revisions.

The poem celebrates the death of General Custer at the battle of the Little Bighorn (Custer's Last Stand), 25 June 1876, as the death of a hero during the Gilded Age, when national, political heroes were in short supply. The empathetic public note sounded by this poem is evinced by its drawing almost immediate praise (on 25 July) from John Hay, who had been Abraham Lincoln's private secretary. The poem's laudatory tone represents the typical view of Custer as a national hero—fighting at the front of his men for the honor of his country, dying a heroic death that gives credibility to the high ideals of his entire life, giving the most one can for his country and its ideals.

In keeping with his celebration of Custer, Whitman's characterization of North American Indians is slightly different in this poem than elsewhere. Whereas in "Song of Myself," for example, he implies an equality between the Indian and white man, in "Dakota's Cañons" he uses stereotypically derogatory words when referring to Indians and their actions: "dusky," "ambuscade," "craft." In this poem Whitman is very much the public poet who does not question national moral attitudes or actions against the Native Americans but who celebrates the standards of progress, westering, and Manifest Destiny.

Steven Olson

Bibliography

Erkkila, Betsy. *Whitman the Political Poet.* New York: Oxford UP, 1989.

Steensma, Robert C. "Whitman and General Custer." *Walt Whitman Review* 10 (1964): 41–42.

Whitman, Walt. *Leaves of Grass: Comprehensive Reader's Edition.* Ed. Harold W. Blodgett and Sculley Bradley. New York: New York UP, 1965.

See also "FROM NOON TO STARRY NIGHT"; NATIVE AMERICANS (INDIANS)

"From Noon to Starry Night" (1881)

"From Noon to Starry Night" first appeared as a cluster of twenty-two poems in the 1881 edition of *Leaves of Grass.* The cluster includes five poems new to this edition, and the others were gathered from collections that Whitman published from 1855 to 1876.

"From Noon to Starry Night" follows the cluster "Whispers of Heavenly Death" and immediately precedes the last section of *Leaves of Grass,* "Songs of Parting." Betsy Erkkila suggests that these final sections of *Leaves of Grass* progress from material to spiritual concerns and, by incorporating poems written at various times in Whitman's career, offer a sense of unity, closure, and grand design. This reading of "From Noon" is supported by the way in which the cluster's images and themes reconcile opposites.

Clearly the height and the end of a lifetime are implied in the essential images of noon and night. But so are these images indications of opposites, as is emphasized by the last three lines of the first poem, "Thou Orb Aloft Full-Dazzling." The next poem, "Faces," more obviously develops the notion of opposing forces. In this salient poem filled with powerful images, the poet poses the opposites of good and evil, base and noble, deific and satanic, old and young, male and female. Not only does he assert these opposites; he implies their correlations. After sketches of debased humanity in section 2 and noble humanity in section 4, section 3 suggests that these could be but surface differences, and despite the attempt of any person to hold a mask to the world, the poet will see behind it.

"The Mystic Trumpeter" introduces the opposite extents of time, beginning with a "prelude" that acknowledges the distant past and closing with the future. Between prelude and close, the poem treats the themes of love and war while it also intermingles images of day and night, light and dark, sun and stars. "To a Locomotive in Winter" reconciles the poetic Muse with modern science and technology whereas "Spirit That Form'd This Scene" compares the art of Whitman's poetry to the wildness of the Rocky Mountains. "Mannahatta" compares the pristine "aboriginal name" to Whitman's modern, thriving city. "All is Truth" reconciles truth and lies. While "A Riddle Song" supposedly has a two-word solution, it is riddled with opposing imagery of reality and illusion, public and private, solitude and city, babies and the dead, dawn and stars, beginning and ending, midnight and light. The poem is also an expression of the contradiction between poetry and the ineffable, and at the end of the cluster "A Clear Midnight" poetically sounds the theme of ineffability again. Two poems, "Excelsior" and "Ah Poverties, Wincings, and Sulky Retreats," are opposite to each other, "Excelsior" treating affirmative ideas and "Ah Poverties" treating negative ones.

F

Several poems examine political oppositions. "Thoughts" poses democracy against institutionalism. "Spain, 1873–74" and "Thick-Sprinkled Bunting" juxtapose Old World feudalism with the ideal of democracy. The political theme is most fully developed, however, in several poems about the Civil War of the United States. If Whitman's book of poems and the Civil War are in some sense one, "From Noon" fittingly reconciles war in general—and the Civil War in particular—with unity and the Union. Two poems express this reconciliation most clearly. Acknowledging that the "death-envelop'd march of peace as well as war goes on," "Weave in, My Hardy Life" implies that war is necessary for peace and the resulting democracy. Add to this idea the expression of "What Best I See in Thee," which states that General Ulysses S. Grant's greatness lies not in his successful battles nor presidency nor state visits to Europe and Asia, but in his embodying the dead "sovereigns," the common farmers and soldiers of democracy.

The last two poems of the cluster integrate culminating themes and images. "As I Walk These Broad Majestic Days" first juxtaposes war and peace, then devastation and production. It closes by positing an essential idealism but not discounting the profound effects of material existence. Finally, "A Clear Midnight" returns to the original imagery of the cluster's title.

While not all the poems in this cluster fit the pattern of opposition and reconciliation, these themes emerge as its focus—a fitting focus for a summary and conclusion of sorts to *Leaves of Grass*. Seen as a whole, the cluster is an amalgamation of opposing images and themes of life and poetry and creation, war and death and destruction.

Steven Olson

Bibliography

Erkkila, Betsy. *Whitman the Political Poet.* New York: Oxford UP, 1989.

Schwind, Jean. "Van Gogh's 'Starry Night' and Whitman: A Study in Source." *Walt Whitman Quarterly Review* 3.1 (1985): 1–15.

Whitman, Walt. *Leaves of Grass: Comprehensive Reader's Edition.* Ed. Harold W. Blodgett and Sculley Bradley. New York: New York UP, 1965.

See also "CLEAR MIDNIGHT, A"; "EXCELSIOR"; "FACES"; "MANNAHATTA"; "MYSTIC TRUMPETER, THE"; "SPIRIT THAT FORM'D THIS SCENE"; "THOU ORB ALOFT FULL-DAZZLING"; "TO A LOCOMOTIVE IN WINTER"

"From Pent-up Aching Rivers" (1860)

This poem was initially published in the third (1860) edition of *Leaves of Grass,* by Thayer and Eldridge, Boston, placed in the "Enfans d'Adam" poem cluster, and designated simply as number 2. The present title was assigned in 1867, when the poem cluster title was changed to "Children of Adam."

The poem begins by describing the aching need of the speaker for the creative and the procreative act and culminates in a description of that act. The opening section (lines 1–14) articulates the foreground to this "song of procreation": the long ache, the "hungry gnaw," and the search for suitable forms of expression. The speaker describes his determination to sing songs (poems) about the procreative act, the creation of "superb children." His search for an adequate means of expression finds its model in the natural world, which provides the speaker with myriad examples of fecundity. This second, shorter movement (lines 15–20) includes descriptions of those aspects of nature which inform the poem: "the wet of woods, the lapping of waves," "the pairing of birds," "the smell of apples." Line 19 contains an image reminiscent of Whitman's ocean poems, "Out of the Cradle Endlessly Rocking" and "As I Ebb'd with the Ocean of Life," both composed in the late 1850s. This line, the turning point of the poem, leads into the next movement as well. The sight of the "mad pushes of waves upon the land" provides the speaker with a figurative construct for the sexual act which follows in the third movement of the poem and serves as a transition to the focus on the human body.

The naked male swimmer of line twenty-two may be the speaker of the poem or a third figure, an example of the "perfect body." The following lines describe the "female form" and "what it arouses"—the abandonment of the sexual/procreative act. This section of the poem contains two parenthetical asides, both addressed to "you" in a much more intimate tone than the sections outside the parentheses. In a hushed voice, the speaker asks "you"—the reader/lover—to accompany him in this moment of sexual fulfillment. The metaphor of a vessel which has been taken over by a greater guiding force is used in lines 37–39; in this instance, however, it is the speaker who yields the vessel to the "master," in the interests of continuing with the "programme"/journey.

In the final movement of the poem (lines 40–57), sex is described as coming "from"—

from physical contact undenied and chronicled through these "act-poems" which celebrate the "act divine." The speaker/poet, in bed with one unwilling to let him go, leaves only for a "moment" (at dawn) in order to record these poems, then returns to the night and to the work of procreation.

Maire Mullins

Bibliography

Allen, Gay Wilson. *The New Walt Whitman Handbook*. 1975. New York: New York UP, 1986.

Killingsworth, M. Jimmie. *Whitman's Poetry of the Body: Sexuality, Politics, and the Text*. Chapel Hill: U of North Carolina P, 1989.

Miller, James E., Jr. *"Leaves of Grass": America's Lyric-Epic of Self and Democracy*. New York: Twayne, 1992.

Waskow, Howard J. *Whitman: Explorations in Form*. Chicago: U of Chicago P, 1966.

See also "CHILDREN OF ADAM"; HUMAN BODY; SEX AND SEXUALITY

Fuller, Margaret (1810–1850)

Sarah Margaret Fuller, essayist, literary critic, magazine editor, teacher, foreign correspondent, translator, and social commentator, was born at Cambridgeport, Massachusetts, on 23 May 1810. She was educated primarily at home and by her own choice of readings. She taught briefly in Boston (1836) and Providence (1837–1838). She returned to the Boston area in 1838, where she privately taught languages and literature, wrote, and edited *The Dial* (1840–1842). In 1844 she moved to New York to write for the New York *Tribune*. In 1846 she went to Europe, where she became involved in the revolution in Italy and where in 1847 she met Giovanni Angelo Ossoli, who became the father of her son, Angelo, born on 5 September 1848. Whether they married or not is open to question, but she did take his name before they sailed for New York in 1850. All three drowned (19 July) when their ship went aground off Fire Island, just south of Long Island, an event which Walt Whitman remembered with sadness the rest of his life. Her principal books were *Summer on the Lakes, in 1843* (1844); *Woman in the Nineteenth Century* (1845); and *Papers on Literature and Art* (1846).

Although Whitman never met Fuller nor corresponded with her, he was quite aware of and interested in her personality, ideas, concerns, and writings, and even more so after she moved to New York as a critic and fellow journalist for a paper which he read regularly. She had been the first woman participant in the Transcendental Club, first editor of its publication and strong contributor to it, and, of course, friend to one degree or another with all those involved in the ideas and endeavors of the transcendentalists. Fuller was also a forthright champion of equality and of women's rights and abilities (especially in her 1845 book). Whitman was generally sympathetic with these causes, as well as with transcendentalism and its various manifestations. The ideas about the relationship between man and nature in Fuller's 1844 book were also similar to his own. A case has been made for a direct influence of her dispatches to the *Tribune* about the revolution in Italy (with which Whitman was sympathetic) upon his poem "Resurgemus" (published in the *Tribune* on 21 June 1850).

However, it seems that Fuller's greatest impact on Whitman came from her ideas and challenges about American literature, what it was not yet, and what it could and should become, especially as expressed in her twenty-one-page essay "American Literature; Its Position in the Present Time, and Prospects for the Future" in her 1846 book. Whitman mentioned the book briefly but enthusiastically in the Brooklyn *Daily Eagle*, 9 November 1846, welcoming it "right heartily" (qtd. in Chevigny 507). More importantly, he removed from the book the forty pages on American literature, including the essay and her reviews of works by Nathaniel Hawthorne, Charles Brockden Brown, and Henry Wadsworth Longfellow, with his underlinings and marginal markings (primarily in the essay, but also some in the Longfellow review), and saved these pages for the rest of his life. From time to time in both print and conversation he mentioned, quoted, or paraphrased parts of the essay, particularly its first four pages. He especially noted its opening claim that there was not yet really an American literature because what was being written here was still too much dependent on European literature. He also noted Fuller's emphasis on "minds seizing upon life with unbroken power," "nationality and individuality," "frankness and expansion," and "abundant opportunity to develope a genius, wide and full as our rivers, . . . impassioned as our vast prairies" (Fuller 123) and her confidence that "such a genius is to rise and work in this hemisphere" (124). In her review of Longfellow he underlined various passages about poetry: poetry is "the fullest and therefore most completely natural expression of what is human" and is "for the delight of all who have ears to hear" (150); "the poets are the priests of Nature, though the greatest are also the prophets of the manhood of man"; "we need poets; men more awakened," with genuine vision and "expression spontaneous" (151). Clearly anyone who has read Whitman can see in these emphases at least parallels with, if not influence upon, his ideas, particularly about American culture and literature, as expressed in both his prose and poetry (particularly at those points where he actually cites Fuller). What he found must have given corroboration and encouragement, perhaps even direction and impetus, to his development as a poet in the years leading up to the 1855 publication of *Leaves of Grass*.

Julian Mason

Bibliography

Allen, Margaret Vanderhaar. *The Achievement of Margaret Fuller*. University Park: Pennsylvania State UP, 1979.

Capper, Charles. *Margaret Fuller: An American Romantic Life, The Private Years*. New York: Oxford UP, 1992.

Chevigny, Bell Gale. *The Woman and the Myth: Margaret Fuller's Life and Writings*. Rev. ed. Boston: Northeastern UP, 1994.

Fuller, S. Margaret. *Papers on Literature and Art*. Vol. 2. New York: Wiley and Putnam, 1846.

Myerson, Joel. *Margaret Fuller: An Annotated Secondary Bibliography*. New York: Burt Franklin, 1977.

———. *Margaret Fuller: A Descriptive Bibliography*. Pittsburgh: U of Pittsburgh P, 1978.

Reynolds, Larry J. *European Revolutions and the American Literary Renaissance*. New Haven: Yale UP, 1988.

Stern, Madeleine B. *The Life of Margaret Fuller*. 2nd ed. New York: Greenwood, 1991.

Stovall, Floyd. *The Foreground of "Leaves of Grass."* Charlottesville: UP of Virginia, 1974.

See also NEW YORK TRIBUNE; PREFACE TO LEAVES OF GRASS, 1855 EDITION; TRANSCENDENTALISM; WOMAN'S RIGHTS MOVEMENT AND WHITMAN, THE

Furness, Clifton Joseph (1898–1946)

Born on 30 April in Sheridan, Indiana, Clifton Joseph Furness received a B.A. from Northwestern University and attended Harvard University's Graduate School of Arts and Sciences from 1927 to 1932, earning an A.M. in education in 1928. He joined the faculty of the New England Conservatory of Music in 1929 and was Supervisor of Academic Studies at the time of his death.

Furness made significant contributions to Whitman studies. *Walt Whitman's Workshop* (1928) presented previously unpublished materials by Whitman on lecturing and oratory, antislavery notes, "The Eighteenth Presidency!," and intended introductions to American and English editions of *Leaves of Grass*. Furness also contributed to Clara Barrus's *Whitman and Burroughs, Comrades* (1931), and he wrote the introduction to the 1939 publication of *Leaves of Grass by Walt Whitman: Reproduced from the First Edition (1855)*. In a review of Frances Winwar's *American Giant* (1941), Furness faulted Winwar for overemphasizing Whitman's alleged affair in New Orleans and for sentimentalizing Whitman's family life. Prompted by his dissatisfaction with this and other biographies, Furness began his own "definitive" Whitman biography. He completed a manuscript, but it was rejected by at least a dozen publishers. After Furness's premature death, Gay Wilson Allen acquired the manuscript and notebooks of the biography and used them in writing *The Solitary Singer* (1955). Furness's unpublished biography of Whitman is now in the Fales Collection of the Bobst Library, New York University.

William A. Pannapacker

Bibliography

Allen, Gay Wilson. *The New Walt Whitman Handbook*. 1975. New York: New York UP, 1986.

Furness, Clifton J. Introduction. *Leaves of Grass by Walt Whitman: Reproduced from the First Edition (1855)*. New York: Columbia UP, 1939. v–xviii.

———. Rev. of *American Giant: Walt Whitman and His Times*, by Frances Winwar. *American Literature* 13 (1942): 423–432.

———, ed. *Walt Whitman's Workshop: A Collection of Unpublished Manuscripts*. Cambridge, Mass.: Harvard UP, 1928.

See also ALLEN, GAY WILSON; BIOGRAPHIES

G

Galaxy, The

The *Galaxy* was a New York monthly periodical founded and edited by William Conant Church and his brother Francis Pharcellus Church. The *Galaxy* began publication in 1866 and continued until 1878, when it was absorbed by the *Atlantic Monthly*. In December 1866 it published an important early critical essay on Whitman, John Burroughs's "Walt Whitman and His 'Drum-Taps,'" which Whitman's friend William O'Connor hailed as "the first article . . . that reveals real critical power and insight, and a proper reverence, upon the subject of Walt Whitman's poetry" (Whitman 296n). So pleased was Whitman with the essay that he wrote his mother three letters between 23 November and 4 December 1866, urging her to buy the magazine. In September 1867, the *Galaxy* published Whitman's poem, "A Carol of Harvest, for 1867," later titled "The Return of the Heroes."

On 7 September 1867 Whitman wrote to the elder Church that he had "in composition, an article (prose) of some length, the subject opportune. I shall probably name it 'Democracy.' It is partly provoked by, & in some respects a rejoinder to, Carlyle's *Shooting Niagara*" (Whitman 338). The *Galaxy* published the article in its December 1867 issue. Whitman later expanded "Democracy" into the book *Democratic Vistas*. In May 1868 the *Galaxy* also published Whitman's essay "Personalism," which was also incorporated into *Democratic Vistas*.

Whitman was evidently fond of the *Galaxy*. He wrote to O'Connor, "I have felt that the *Galaxy* folks have received and treated me with welcome warmth and respect" (Whitman 343). Years later, however, the relationship apparently soured, for Whitman complained to the *West Jersey Press* that his "offerings to *Scribner* are returned with insulting notes; the *Galaxy* the same" (qtd. in Grier 349).

John T. Matteson

Bibliography

Grier, Edward F. "Walt Whitman, *The Galaxy*, and Democratic Vistas." *American Literature* 23 (1951–1952): 332–350.

Reynolds, David S. *Walt Whitman's America: A Cultural Biography*. New York: Knopf, 1995.

Scholnick, Robert J. "'Culture' or Democracy: Whitman, Eugene Benson, and *The Galaxy*." *Walt Whitman Quarterly Review* 13 (1996): 189–198.

Whitman, Walt. *The Correspondence*. Ed. Edwin Haviland Miller. Vol. 1. New York: New York UP, 1961.

See also DEMOCRATIC VISTAS; "RETURN OF THE HEROES, THE"

García Lorca, Federico (1898–1936)

The Spanish poet and dramatist Federico García Lorca achieved early fame with books of poems such as *Gypsy Ballads* (1928), which combined folkloric elements with striking imagery and a dreamlike eroticism. A vivid and genial presence, he was immensely popular. Lorca was executed by right-wing elements at the beginning of the Spanish Civil War (1936–1939).

In 1929 and early 1930, Lorca was in the United States. Residing for the most part in New York, he met Hart Crane and read Whitman in Spanish translation. Lorca did his most audaciously innovative work at this time, and the eventual result was *Poet in New York* (1940), a shapeless jeremiad directed against urban materialism. The book's poems also contain references (often murky) to the poet's homo-erotic sentiments. In "Ode to Walt Whitman," Lorca exalts Whitman as a god of pastoral innocence and the antithesis of modern values. In this context, he favorably contrasts Whitman's notions of intimacy with those of modern homosexuals.

The surreal and splenetic qualities of "Ode to Walt Whitman" seem a far cry from *Leaves of Grass*. As has been the case with a number of Spanish-speaking writers, Lorca saw Whitman more as an inspirational figure than a source of technical novelties.

N.J. Mason-Browne

Bibliography

García Lorca, Federico. *Poet in New York.* Ed. Christopher Maurer. Trans. Greg Simon and Steven F. White. New York: Farrar, Straus and Giroux, 1988.

Gibson, Ian. *Federico García Lorca: 2. De Nueva York a Fuente Grande (1929–1936).* Barcelona: Grijalbo, 1987.

Walsh, John K. "The Social and Sexual Geography of *Poeta en Nueva York.*" *"Cuando yo me muera . . .": Essays in Memory of Federico García Lorca.* Ed. C. Brian Morris. Lanham, Md.: UP of America, 1988. 105–127.

See also LEGACY, WHITMAN'S; SPAIN AND SPANISH AMERICA, WHITMAN IN

Garland, Hamlin (1860–1940)

Best known for his realistic prose portrayals of the hardships of midwestern farm life, Hamlin Garland also is an important figure in the theory of American realism. His best-known works include *Main-Travelled Roads* (1891), *Crumbling Idols* (1894), *Rose of Dutcher's Coolly* (1895), and *Boy Life on the Prairie* (1899).

Garland's thoughts on the relationships between place, culture, democracy, and literature, dubbed "veritism" and summarized in his essay collection entitled *Crumbling Idols,* show signs of Whitman's influence. While developing his beliefs and talents, Garland championed Whitman in lectures and essays and planned to write a survey of American literature depicting Whitman as the fountainhead of future American writing. Garland wrote to Whitman in 1886, beginning a regular correspondence that led to a visit to Mickle Street in the autumn of 1888 and a tribute at the poet's seventieth birthday commemoration in 1889.

Whitman expressed interest in Garland's first letter, remarking to Horace Traubel upon the young writer's political vision and enthusiasm, but mostly his status as a Midwesterner. Both Whitman and Garland believed that a "true" American literary voice, free of eastern affectation, would emerge from the western states. Garland's enthusiasm for Whitman centered on the poet's patriotism, sympathy with working men and women, and faith in the destiny of the States. Although the two disagreed slightly on the frankness of late-century American literature, they agreed on the importance of the common person in literature. Garland was optimistic about the culture's possibilities, as was Whitman, though he saw himself more as a reporter than a prophet like Whitman.

In later years, Garland expressed some weariness with Whitman's optimistic and bombastic posture, but his enthusiasm for Whitman's ideas characterized much of his early work and led him to dub Whitman "the genius of democracy" (qtd. in Price 7).

Thomas K. Dean

Bibliography

Becknell, Thomas. "Hamlin Garland's Response to Whitman." *The Old Northwest* 7 (1981): 217–235.

Garland, Hamlin. *Hamlin Garland's Diaries.* Ed. Donald Pizer. San Marino, Calif.: The Huntington Library, 1968.

———. "'Let the Sunshine In.'" *The Rotarian* 55 (1939): 8–11.

Price, Kenneth M. "Hamlin Garland's 'The Evolution of American Thought': A Missing Link in the History of Whitman Criticism." *Walt Whitman Quarterly Review* 3.2 (1985): 1–20.

Price, Kenneth M., and Robert C. Leitz III. "The Uncollected Letters of Hamlin Garland to Walt Whitman." *Walt Whitman Quarterly Review* 5.3 (1988): 1–13.

Traubel, Horace. *With Walt Whitman in Camden.* 1908. Vol. 2. New York: Rowman and Littlefield, 1961.

See also REALISM; WEST, THE AMERICAN

German-speaking Countries, Whitman in the

Whitman's reception in the German-speaking countries is substantial, both statistically and in cultural significance. It is important for an understanding of Central European cultural development, as an intercultural phenomenon linking German and American cultures, and, by furnishing alternative readings and interpretations of Whitman, for Whitman scholarship in general. This entry deals with the critical and creative reception in the German-speaking *cultures* rather than academic studies at German-speaking universities (which tend to lack cultural specificity and fit into the main trends of Whitman scholarship in the United States).

Whereas Whitman's German reception has been the focus of several specialized studies since the 1930s (Harry Law-Robertson first investigates the phenomenon, but with a Nazi bias; Edward Allan McCormick and Monika Schaper analyze the translations from a new critical and a historical-contextual point of view respectively), a comprehensive study was undertaken only in the 1980s. A detailed comparative analysis of Whitman translations into German using the critical instruments of modern translation criticism is still lacking.

Since 1889 fifteen different book-length translations of Whitman's works have appeared, eight of which include major and representative selections from his oeuvre. Most of these appeared as widely distributed mass-market editions, making Whitman's works available to large audiences. In most cases the translators are significant personalities of literary and public standing (albeit mostly on the countercultural side) whose commitment proved favorable for Whitman's reception.

This intense interest in Whitman can be attributed to the popular German fascination with the New World. More specifically, Whitman's messianic image, as designed by W.D. O'Connor, and, later, Horace Traubel, seems to have held out a special promise to various groups in German, Austrian, and Swiss literary, cultural, and political worlds.

Whitman was first introduced into German in 1868 by Ferdinand Freiligrath, a revolutionary poet in exile in England. He read William M. Rossetti's Whitman edition and immediately understood the revolutionary potential of Whitman's aesthetics. Given the stifling authoritarianism in German and Austrian politics at that time, it is not surprising that the initial impetus for Whitman's German reception came from abroad.

This situation had hardly improved by the time the first book-length translation appeared in 1889, a collaborative product by the democratically inclined German-American researcher and educator Karl Knortz and the Irish-nationalist philologist Thomas William Rolleston. The book could only appear in Switzerland with a progressive publisher, J. Schabelitz, specializing in works by young German reformers and exiles. Knortz's involvement also points to a special market for Whitman editions in German: German-American readers, who, according to Knortz, were in dire need of the type of democratic education Whitman supposedly imparted. Whitman was personally acquainted with both translators and also wrote a dedication for his German readers in which he stressed that he would be "glad, very glad, to be accepted by the Germanic peoples" (trans. from *Grashalme* xii). The early German interest in Whitman was closely monitored and encouraged by Whitman and the Whitman community and thus established a pattern of interactive and intercultural reception which frequently makes it difficult to differentiate between source and target culture.

Whereas the early translations were mostly literal, thereby shocking German readers on account of Whitman's "formlessness," later translations became more stylized. The most popular translation, which has remained in print for ninety years and has always been available in inexpensive "pocket book" editions, is Johannes Schlaf's of 1907. Schlaf, a German writer with naturalist beginnings, is the single most significant personality in Whitman's German reception. With Horace Traubel as his correspondent and mentor, it is not surprising that it was he who introduced a cultist dimension into Whitman's German reception by focusing on the Good Gray Poet. Schlaf's translation further intensified the already strong aura and emotional (to some degree didactic) rhetoric of Whitman's poetry, creating a characteristic *Pathos* on which creative writers could draw.

If there is a "classic" translation of Whitman's poetry and prose, it is by Hans Reisiger, a first-rate translator and a friend of Thomas Mann. Mann, a Whitman devotee himself, endorsed the translation, calling it a "great, important, indeed holy gift . . . [for which] the German public . . . can not be grateful enough" (Allen and Folsom 201). Although the two-volume edition with gold-lettered spines forms the most comprehensive selection from Whitman's prose and poetry to date, it also has a specific focus. Reisiger's selection highlights the (homo)erotic tendencies in Whitman's poetry, for the first time including the "Children of Adam" and "Calamus" poems almost in their entirety. Its "classicity" is expressed more through its diction, which is less subdued and musical, stylistically reminiscent of such German authors as Goethe and Rilke.

Of the post–World War II translations, the largest and most ambitious is that of Erich Arendt, published in the German Democratic Republic in 1966. Emphasizing Whitman's social(ist) and in this sense revolutionary dimension, Arendt is faced with the twin task of escaping a *Pathos* which had become discredited by the rhetoric of German national-socialist propaganda and of presenting Whitman as a positive force in the construction of socialism. In this endeavor, he makes successful use of his experience in Latin America as an exile during the Nazi regime, where he was introduced to Whitman by friends, including Pablo Neruda.

Whitman always served as a special cultural bridge between the German Democratic Republic and the United States, and various Whitman translations were always available, even in a book market characterized by paper shortage and censorship. The first complete German edition of *Specimen Days* was published in the GDR in a translation by Götz Burghardt in 1985. The liberal and open-minded commentary by the editor, Eva Manske, foreshadows the ideological changes that occurred a few years after with the fall of the Berlin wall.

Even though new translations are still being published and older ones reprinted, the period of Whitman's greatest impact was between 1889 and 1933. Prior to 1889, there was no textual basis for Whitman's reception; after Hitler's takeover in Germany in 1933, Nazi rhetoric corrupted the potential of *Pathos* in German culture and thus also limited the impact of Whitman's poetry. The special situation of the German Democratic Republic excepted, Whitman's poetry, or rather its *Pathos*-laden German rendering, never really recovered from the fatal blow it was undeservedly dealt by Nazi propagandists and song writers, some of whom had been Whitmanites in their youth.

Whitman's impact on the modernization of German literature, and especially poetry, is enormous. In the 1890s, a first wave of writers, mostly belonging to the naturalist group, started to assimilate Whitman's poetic technique (rhymelessness, "free" rhythms, long lines, dynamic and protean lyrical personae) and themes (eroticism, urbanism, global vision) into their poetry and lyrical prose. Again, Johannes Schlaf, who claims that he managed to "overcome" the deterministic limitations of naturalism through his experience of Whitman, stands out. Schlaf, one of the most innovative and creative German writers (although often bypassed by German literary historians), used Whitman's techniques in long poems reminiscent of "Song of Myself" ("Frühling," 1894) and his themes in a series of novels exploring a "new humanity" based on "new developments in the human nervous system" (*Das dritte Reich*, 1900; *Die Suchenden*, 1902; *Peter Boies Freite*, 1903). These novels are the only significant examples of aestheticist literature in Germany and also point to an aestheticist dimension of Whitman's work frequently underestimated by American criticism. Two other significant German naturalists, Gerhart Hauptmann and Arno Holz, also expressed their fascination with Whitman, but only Holz creatively reworked Whitman's lyrical impulse into his poetry.

For a second group of writers in the subsequent generation, Whitman emerged as a lyrical and personal example. Without an understanding of the detailed cultural context of the period between 1910 and 1925, it is difficult to estimate Whitman's significant impact on this group. An artistic consequence of a profound crisis in the life and thinking of German-speaking Europeans around the turn of the century, expressionism was a direct reaction to the political and social effects of a rapid industrialization and urbanization. This crisis of sensibility led to the literary experimentation for which expressionist literature and art in Germany has become justly famous. With the achievements of expressionism, Germans joined worldwide modernist developments, and Whitman was a guiding figure.

German expressionism can be divided into two complementary groups. The "abstract" expressionists thematize the crisis, the "dissociation," and disintegration of the self. Among writers, this group includes Georg Trakl, Georg Heym, Gottfried Benn, and also Franz Kafka. While abstract expressionists were also interested in Whitman, especially for analytic reasons, a second group, referred to as "messianic" expressionists, more directly assimilated Whitman into their poetry. This group includes Johannes R. Becher, Ivan and Claire Goll, Ludwig Rubiner, Ernst Stadler, Ernst Toller, Armin T. Wegner, and Franz Werfel.

While expressionist poetry profited from Whitman's example, most German-speaking authors, while intent on following Whitman's grand example, found it difficult to deal with the lyrical and thematic consequences of Whitman's radical egalitarian vision. Frequently, a programmatic "farewell" to Whitman points to the antagonism between American egalitarian and Central European elitist cultures.

In the expressionist period, the tendency toward an intercultural, intra-European reception of Whitman that had started with Schlaf intensified. Immediately prior to World War I, the European Whitman movement assumed an international character strongly intertwined with the international development of the European avant-garde and its shared political (usually leftist and pacifist) assumptions.

As a testimony to the integrative force of expressionism as a cultural movement, Whitman's creative reception also spread to music. Swiss expressionist Othmar Schoeck's musical rendering of *Drum-Taps* (1915) is a formidable musical expression of the shock caused by the World War. Important German-speaking composers who set Whitman texts to music include Kurt Weill, Paul Hindemith, Franz Schreker, Ernst Toch, Ernst Hermann Meyer, Hans Werner Henze, and Gerd Kuhr. "When Lilacs Last in the Dooryard Bloom'd" and "The Mystic Trumpeter" are among the texts that most frequently inspired German composers.

Whereas Whitman's presence was most strongly felt in literature and the arts, there were also responses on other levels, frequently intertwined with poetic responses. Horace Traubel's leftist politics and the leftist political orientation of many expressionist poets have inspired a general leftist enthusiasm for Whitman. Typically, the various factions differ in their political construction of Whitman, even though they uniformly view him as the prophet of a new world order. Whereas Social Democrats recruit Whitman for their frequently opportunistic politics, wavering between revolutionary rhetoric and political compromise, communist and anarchist groups synthesize the radical consistency of the early Whitman and the messianic rhetoric of the later Whitman.

Their attitudes toward World War I are a characteristic example: Social Democrats, using Whitman's highly popularized Civil War image of the "wound dresser," stressed the necessity of getting involved in the war if only to minimize its fatal consequences. In this way, Whitman's example was used in order to justify the Social Democratic sellout of traditional pacifist policies by projecting a fantastic possibility of a beneficial participation in war. Leftist Social Democrats (the later communists) and anarchists, on the other hand, constructed a principled pacifist position by interpreting Whitman's war poetry and Civil War prose as antiwar documents.

Most factions agreed on Whitman's utopian vision, which they interpreted as socialist. This adoption led to the social-democratic Whitman editions by Max Hayek, which can still be found in many German trade union and party libraries, as well as the Whitman translation by the German-Jewish pacifist and anarchist Gustav Landauer; both were published shortly after the close of World War I. These versions of Whitman explain the strong interest in the poet on the part of German communists (fueled also by the intensive Soviet reception of the poet) and a limited resurgence of interest in the sixties (alongside a stronger interest in such poets as Allen Ginsberg).

On the other side of the political spectrum, rightist Whitman devotees are naturally scarce. It is interesting, however, that some of the propagandist poets of the Nazi regime started out as Whitmanites. The history of Nazi poetry and rhetoric shows a limited usefulness of Whitman's style, diction, and "aura."

The most interesting German assimilation of Whitman was in the area of sexual politics. In 1905 a wide-ranging public debate regarding Whitman's sexuality, involving Johannes Schlaf, Eduard Bertz (a novelist, philologist and self-declared sexual researcher), and others, split German Whitman devotees into two highly antagonistic factions. Bertz, in a 1905 article for a German journal for sexual research, attempted to prove Whitman was a nonactive homosexual. Bertz tried to enlist Whitman for what amounted to the first German homosexual movement, because it was important to point out famous and respected personalities who were homosexuals in order to convince the public of the social usefulness of homosexuals. (The political background was the 1899 petition to the German parliament to eliminate discriminatory legislation against homosexuals.) Schlaf, supported by Traubel, Ernest Crosby, H.B. Binns, and Léon Bazalgette, strongly denied Whitman's homosexuality. They estimated (probably correctly) that Whitman's significance in the German-speaking countries would drastically diminish if this pronouncement went unchallenged. Whereas Schlaf was successful in battling Bertz's claim—the discussion resurfaced some eight years later in France with Bertz, Bazalgette, and others as active participants—Whitman continued to play a role in German homosexuals' search for identity. Most prominently, this view can be traced in the essays and speeches of Thomas Mann, who links the development of German democracy to Whitman's homoeroticism.

Although the contemporary German gay movement may provide a focal point for Whitman's future German reception, a new, less *Pathos*-laden, more playful translation of *Leaves* will be needed. If such a translation were available, Whitman's poetry might once again become a significant force in German-speaking Europe as this region internationalizes as a result of European and Central European integration. There may also emerge an ecological reading of Whitman, although it would first have to undo the well-developed image of the poet of technology and progress. How such a postmodern German Whitman might look and sound remains to be seen.

Walter Grünzweig

Bibliography

Allen, Gay Wilson. *The New Walt Whitman Handbook*. 1975. New York: New York UP, 1986.

Allen, Gay Wilson, and Ed Folsom, eds. *Walt Whitman & the World*. Iowa City: U of Iowa P, 1995.

Bertz, Eduard. "Adulation and Paranoia: Eduard Bertz's Whitman Correspondence (1889–1914)." *Gissing Journal* 27.3 (1991): 1–20 and 27.4 (1991): 16–35.

———. "Walt Whitman: Ein Charakterbild." *Jahrbuch für sexuelle Zwischenstufen* 7 (1905): 153–287.

Grünzweig, Walter. *Constructing the German Walt Whitman*. Iowa City: U of Iowa P, 1995.

———. *Walt Whitmann: Die deutschsprachige Rezeption als interkulturelles Phänomen*. Munich: Fink, 1991.

Lang, Hans-Joachim. "Eduard Bertz vs. Johannes Schlaf: The Debate on Whitman's Homosexuality in Germany." *A Conversation in the Life of Leland R. Phelps. America and Germany: Literature, Art and Music*. Ed. Frank L. Borchardt and Marion C. Salinger. Durham, N.C.: Duke UP, 1987. 49–86.

Law-Robertson, Harry. *Walt Whitman in Deutschland*. Gießen: Munchow, 1935.

McCormick, Edward Allan. *Die sprachliche Eigenart von Walt Whitmans "Leaves of Grass" in deutscher Übertragung: Ein Beitrag zur Übersetzungskunst*. Bern: Haupt, 1953.

Martin, Robert K. "Walt Whitman and Thomas Mann." *Walt Whitman Quarterly Review* 4.1 (1986): 1–6.

Schaper, Monika. *Walt Whitmans "Leaves of Grass" in deutschen Übersetzungen: Eine rezeptionsgeschichtliche Untersuchung*. Bern: Lang, 1976.

Whitman, Walt. *Grashalme: Gedichte*. Trans. Karl Knortz and T.W. Rolleston. Zürich: Schabelitz, 1889.

See also BERTZ, EDUARD; FREILIGRATH, FERDINAND; INTERCULTURALITY; KNORTZ, KARL; ROLLESTON, THOMAS WILLIAM HAZEN

Gide, André (1869–1951)

André Gide was introduced to *Leaves of Grass* by his friend, the poet and critic Marcel Schwob, as early as 1893. He was above all interested in Whitman's homosexuality, for it corresponded to his own, which he justified and more and more loudly defended as normal in *Corydon* (1911–1924), invoking the example of Whitman. When Bazalgette's biography appeared, followed by his translation of *Leaves of Grass*, Gide criticized Bazalgette severely for misinterpreting "Calamus" and "heterosexualizing" Whitman's poems as well as for gratuitously inventing a heterosexual love affair in New Orleans. For this reason, he undertook to do a new translation of *Leaves of Grass* with the collaboration of some of his friends: Louis Fabulet, Jean Schlumberger, Francis Vielé-Griffin, and Valery Larbaud. Paul Claudel rejected his invitation on moral grounds. The translation was delayed by World War I and appeared in 1918 under the title of *Walt Whitman—Oeuvres choisies*. It was only a selection. "Song of Myself" in particular was represented by only one section (section 24). But it was definitely better than Balzagette's, which, as Gide pointed out, was too flat, and was literal rather than literary. Gide, who was a very scrupulous and sensitive artist, was also attracted to *Leaves of Grass* by its literary qualities. Being above all a prose writer, he approved of the revolution carried out by Whitman in the new medium he had invented halfway between prose and verse. He even experimented with Whitmanian free verse and published *Les Nourritures terrestres* (1897), in which he also created a Whitmanian character, Ménalque, a vagabond traveling on the open road, giving his young disciple, Nathanaël, lessons in life and fervor reminiscent of "Song of Myself" and "Song of the Open Road." His stylistic debt to Whitman is striking, and it is still important in *Les Nouvelles Nourritures* (1935), in which he no longer addressed Nathanaël, a name he now considered affected and plaintive, but his "camarade," Whitman's "camerado," in prose, rather than free verse. It was a call to manly action at a time when he was attracted by the voices of communist sirens. He now renounced dilettantism and sensuality and, like Whitman, dreamed of democratic vistas. His travel to Russia, however, disillusioned him (*Retour de l'URSS* 1936). He then realized the vanity of all such dreams.

Roger Asselineau

Bibliography

Allen, Gay Wilson. *The New Walt Whitman Handbook*. 1975. New York: New York UP, 1986.

Erkkila, Betsy. *Walt Whitman Among the French: Poet and Myth*. Princeton: Princeton UP, 1980.

Rhodes, S.A. "The Influence of Walt Whitman on André Gide." *Romanic Review* 31 (1940): 156–171.

See also BAZALGETTE, LÉON; FRANCE, WHITMAN IN; SEX AND SEXUALITY

Gilchrist, Anne Burrows (1828–1885)

Anne Burrows Gilchrist was born in London, the daughter of a prominent solicitor and, through her mother, the descendant of an old and distinguished family in Essex. A brilliant student, after completing the courses at a school for girls, she continued her education on her own, reading widely in science and philosophy. During the ten years of her marriage to Alexander Gilchrist, a young writer, in addition to having four children and acting as her husband's critic and amanuensis, she published five scientific essays and a book for children. After Alexander's death in 1861, with the help of his friends William Michael and Dante Gabriel Rossetti, Anne finished his biography of Blake, still a standard reference.

Anne Gilchrist is best known in American literature as the Englishwoman who fell passionately in love with Walt Whitman when she read *Leaves of Grass,* lent to her by William Rossetti in 1869. Undaunted by words and subject matter that shocked most Victorians, she recognized that this was a great work of art. Privately, she also responded to the poems by falling in love with the poet. She wrote a series of enthusiastic letters to Rossetti, who, realizing that this was exactly the kind of appreciative criticism that Whitman desperately needed, persuaded her to rewrite them for publication. "A Woman's Estimate of Walt Whitman" (changed to "An Englishwoman's Estimate of Walt Whitman" in 1887 by Herbert Gilchrist) was published anonymously in Boston in 1870. This brilliantly analytical essay, with its unqualified defense of Whitman, established Anne Gilchrist as one of the first great critics of *Leaves of Grass.*

To Anne's disappointment, Whitman sent his thanks to the anonymous writer through Rossetti. After a year, she wrote a long letter directly to the poet: introducing herself, confessing her love and her conviction that she was the ideal mate whom she believed "the tenderest lover" was seeking; and telling him that, when circumstances permitted, she planned to go to America to be near him. Walt's reply was cautious but kind. For six years they exchanged letters. Hers were frequent and ardent, his less frequent and friendly. However, Anne's belief that once they met Walt would return her love with equal ardor never waned. In 1876, although Walt tried to dissuade her, Anne came to Philadelphia bringing with her three of her children and her furniture, pictures, china, silver, and books.

Anne and Walt met in the hotel where the Gilchrists were staying until they found a house. For both, the meeting had an unexpected outcome. If Walt had been uneasy about meeting the woman who had wooed him for six years, his fears vanished when he met Anne Gilchrist. He was instantly taken with the charming Englishwoman and her attractive children, and felt wonderfully comfortable with them. For Anne, the encounter was both a blow and a revelation. From their first handclasp, it was clear that, although the poet was genuinely glad to see her, the responding fervor that she had hoped for was not there and never would be. It was the end of her romantic fantasy, but the beginning of a loving friendship that lasted all their lives.

The two years that the Gilchrists lived in Philadelphia was a happy period for Walt. He was an almost daily visitor at their house on North 22nd Street, entertaining his friends as freely as if it were his own, and sometimes living there in a room that was always kept ready for him. He was devoted to Anne's children: Beatrice, a medical student; Herbert, an artist; and Grace, who studied singing. For the only time in his life, Walt was the father figure in a family that included children and was presided over by, in his words, "a true wife & mother" (Whitman 91). What delighted him most, however, was the sparkle and depth of his conversations with Anne. They discussed art, science, literature, philosophy, politics, and personalities—always with spirit, if not always in agreement. "The best of her was her talk," Walt would tell Traubel in one of his tender reminiscences (Traubel 268). And to William Sloane Kennedy he wrote that with Anne "you did not have to abate the wing of your thought downward at all, in deference to any feminine narrowness of mind" (qtd. in Alcaro 178).

The Gilchrists left Philadelphia in April, 1878, and spent the following year in Concord, Boston, and New York. Anne became a celebrity. Wherever she went, the gracious friend of the Carlyles, Tennysons, Rossettis, and the Pre-Raphaelites—with her "fine presence" that Horace Scudder recalled with admiration (qtd. in Alcaro 195)—was lionized in literary circles. Anne and Walt met briefly in New York before the Gilchrists left America in 1879. Their parting was deeply emotional. After her return to England, Anne wrote "A Confession of Faith," a second essay on *Leaves of Grass;* edited a second edition of the *Life of Blake;* and wrote a biography of Mary Lamb, still in print. Walt remained a focal point in her life. Her letters—no longer passionate but reflecting a loving companionship—were frequent, and she worked tirelessly to raise funds for him. Anne died in 1885. Whitman's "Going Somewhere" was written for her: "My science-friend, my noblest woman-friend, / (Now buried in an English grave—and this a memory-leaf for her dear sake . . .)."

Marion Walker Alcaro

Bibliography

Alcaro, Marion Walker. *Walt Whitman's Mrs. G: A Biography of Anne Gilchrist.* Madison, N.J.: Fairleigh Dickinson UP, 1991.

Traubel, Horace. *With Walt Whitman in Camden.* Vol. 1. 1906. New York: Rowman and Littlefield, 1961.

Whitman, Walt. *The Correspondence.* Ed. Edwin Haviland Miller. Vol. 2. New York: New York UP, 1961.

See also GILCHRIST, HERBERT HARLAKENDEN; PHILADELPHIA, PENNSYLVANIA; ROSSETTI, WILLIAM MICHAEL

Gilchrist, Herbert Harlakenden (1857–1914)

Herbert Gilchrist, a painter, was born in London, son of Alexander and Anne Gilchrist. In 1876, when he accompanied his mother and sisters to America, he was a student at the Royal Academy of Arts. During the two years that the Gilchrists lived in Philadelphia, he continued painting on his own—for the most part, painting Whitman. However, in the winter that the Gilchrists spent in New York (1878–1879), he studied under William Merritt Chase.

Herbert's devotion to Whitman was the dominating force in his life. Like his mother's devotion to the poet, it began long before they met. When he was seventeen, Anne wrote to Walt that Herbert had read *Leaves of Grass* "quite through" with "a large measure of responsive delight" (qtd. in Alcaro 149). In America, Walt became the center of his existence. In Philadelphia, in addition to seeing the poet almost daily at the Gilchrists' house, Herbert often visited him in Camden and joined him at the Staffords' farm. There can be little doubt that Herbert was one of Walt's young lovers. When the Gilchrists returned to England (1879), like his mother, Herbert wrote regularly to Walt and helped collect funds for him. After Anne died in 1885, Herbert hastily compiled a biography, *Anne Gilchrist: Her Life and Writings* (1887), and returned to Philadelphia to paint Walt's portrait.

Herbert's powerful portrait of Whitman was warmly acclaimed in London. In Philadelphia its reception was less enthusiastic. Whitman preferred Eakins's portrait, claiming that Herbert had "prettified" him, given him "Italianate" curls (qtd. in Alcaro 175). However, Horace Traubel also recorded Walt's refusal to be too hard on it: "I love Herbert too much," Walt told Thomas Harned (Traubel 156). Herbert lived in Philadelphia for

328 Mickle street—
Camden New Jersey U S America
August 1 '85—

Dear Herbert Gilchrist yours of July 21 just rec'd, soliciting some definite word from me ab't an English or transatlantic "free will offering" — a proposed affectionate and voluntary gift to me from my friends there. I feel deeply. even for the prompting of it and should decidedly and gratefully accept any thing it produces. (My publisher David McKay, of Philadelphia, has just been over to pay the last half-annual royalty on my two Volumes Leaves of Grass and Specimen Days, which amounted to twenty-two dollars and six cents — this being the income to me from the sale of my books for the last six months)

Fearfully hot weather here. I have had a sunstroke which has made me weak and kept me indoors for the last twelve days, but I move around the house eat my rations fairly, write a little, and shall quite certainly soon resume my usual state of health. late times — (doubtless lower'd a slight notch or two, as I find that is the way things go on year after year.) Fortunately I have a good faithful young Jersey woman and friend, Mary Davis, who cooks for me, and vigilantly sees to me. Give my love to Wm M Rossetti and to all enquiring friends, known or unknown. you are at liberty to make any use of this letter you see fit. Walt Whitman

Walt Whitman letter to Herbert Gilchrist. From Walt Whitman: A Descriptive Bibliography, *by Joel Myerson,* © 1993 by University of Pittsburgh Press.

several years, visiting the ailing poet faithfully. He was a speaker at Walt's seventieth birthday celebration. After Whitman's death, Gilchrist returned to England. In 1914 he took his own life.

Marion Walker Alcaro

Bibliography

Alcaro, Marion Walker. *Walt Whitman's Mrs. G: A Biography of Anne Gilchrist.* Madison, N.J.: Fairleigh Dickinson UP, 1991.

Traubel, Horace. *With Walt Whitman in Camden.* Vol. 1. 1906. New York: Rowman and Littlefield, 1961.

See also GILCHRIST, ANNE BURROWS; PAINTERS AND PAINTING; PHILADELPHIA, PENNSYLVANIA

Gilder, Jeannette L. (1849–1916)

Jeannette Gilder, sister of Richard Watson Gilder, was an influential editor, journalist, and literary critic. She began her career as a reporter for the Newark *Register,* which her brother Richard had helped to found. Soon afterward, she went to work for the New York *Herald,* writing book reviews in her popular column, "Chats about Books," and eventually became the *Herald*'s review editor. Then in 1881 she and her brother Joseph founded the *Critic* (1881–1906), a highly influential literary magazine. The *Critic* is best known for its reviews of literature, music, and drama; its notices, many written by Gilder, were incisive, high-toned, and conservative and demonstrated a bias toward American authors. Indeed, some of the country's best talents were published in the magazine. A popular feature of the magazine was Gilder's "The Lounger," a kind of gossip column about artists and the literati.

As editor of the *Critic,* Gilder published Whitman's work, wrote articles about the poet, and published parts of his letters to keep the public informed of his activities and health. Moreover, the *Critic* published his series "How I Get Around at Sixty, and Take Notes" and a few of his poems. Most of Whitman's contributions, however, were in prose and included notes on Ralph Waldo Emerson; Alfred, Lord Tennyson; Edgar Allan Poe; Henry Wadsworth Longfellow; William Shakespeare; the Bible as poetry; and "Walt Whitman in Camden" (signed "George Selwyn").

In addition to her work with the *Critic,* Gilder was the New York correspondent for several newspapers; edited several books, including *Authors at Home* (1888); and wrote a novel, a couple of plays, and two volumes of her autobiography. In 1895 she established a literary brokerage, "Miss Gilder's Syndicate," and negotiated publication and dramatization rights for her clients.

Susan L. Roberson

Bibliography

Gilder, Jeannette L., and Joseph, eds. *Authors at Home: Personal and Biographical Sketches of Well-Known American Writers.* New York: Cassell, 1888.

Mott, Frank Luther. *A History of American Magazines, 1865–1885.* Cambridge, Mass.: Harvard UP, 1938.

Tutwiler, Julia R. "Jeannette L. Gilder." *Women Authors of Our Day in Their Homes.* Ed. Francis Whiting Halsey. New York: Pott, 1903.

See also GILDER, RICHARD WATSON

Gilder, Richard Watson (1844–1909)

Richard Watson Gilder was the managing editor and then editor of the *Century Illustrated Monthly Magazine.* Founded in 1870 as *Scribner's Monthly,* it was renamed the *Century* with a change in management in 1881. The *Century* was one of the nation's most esteemed periodicals, and as its editor Gilder was one of the most influential men in American letters. Indeed, the 1880s were called by his biographer, Herbert Smith, "the Gilder Age" (13).

Gilder began his career in journalism as a reporter for the Newark *Advertiser* (1868), and by 1870 he was associate editor at *Scribner's Monthly* and writing an opinion column, "The Old Cabinet," for the magazine. As editor of the *Century,* Gilder was instrumental in publishing works by some of America's best writers, among them Henry James, Mark Twain, William Dean Howells, and Walt Whitman. He also initiated a series on "Battles and Leaders of the Civil War," for which he asked Whitman to write a piece about his work as a volunteer nurse for the Union armies. "Army Hospitals and Cases" was published by *Century* four years later; meanwhile two short works, "Father Taylor and Oratory" and "Twilight," appeared in 1887. From 1887 until 1891, Whitman's work appeared once a year in *Century,* making Gilder the editor most receptive to Whitman.

Gilder first met Whitman in 1877 at a reception hosted by J.H. Johnston and befriended the poet when he had few social connections in New York City. From that time on, Gilder supported Whitman, publishing his work and participating in fund-raising benefits. Gilder started plans, seconded by John Burroughs, in 1878 for Whitman's first Lincoln lecture. With Edmund Clarence Stedman, Gilder insisted on including Whitman in a series on American poets despite the objections of *Scribner's* editor, Josiah Holland. Gilder admired Whitman's poetry and praised its "magnificent form" and spirit (qtd. in Smith 51).

Gilder was himself a prolific and popular poet, skilled at rhyme and meter and given to writing commemorative pieces. Obsessed with form, his work, as well as his attitude, remained largely genteel and conservative.

Susan L. Roberson

Bibliography

Gilder, Richard Watson. *Poems of Richard Watson Gilder.* Boston: Houghton Mifflin, 1908.

John, Arthur. *The Best Years of the Century: Richard Watson Gilder, Scribner's Monthly, and the Century Magazine, 1870–1909.* Urbana: U of Illinois P, 1981.

Mott, Frank Luther. *A History of American Magazines, 1865–1885.* Cambridge, Mass.: Harvard UP, 1938.

Smith, Herbert F. *Richard Watson Gilder.* New York: Twayne, 1970.

See also BURROUGHS, JOHN AND URSULA; JOHNSTON, JOHN H. AND ALMA CALDER; STEDMAN, EDMUND CLARENCE

Ginsberg, Allen (1926–1997)

Walt Whitman's enduring influence on American poetry can be seen in the work of Allen Ginsberg. The leading poet of the Beat generation of the 1950s, Ginsberg himself has testified to the importance of Whitman's prosody—his long, bardic free-verse line—in the discovery of his own poetic voice in "Howl" (1955). Whitman's explorations of open forms, in contrast to the orderly stanzas, received metrical patterns, and recurrent rhyme of much of the poetry of his day, provided Ginsberg with a model for his own poetic experiments.

Ginsberg's poetic practice in "Howl" draws upon Whitman's celebration of the American city in all its rich complexity. Ginsberg also follows Whitman's commitment to celebrating simultaneously what Whitman called the "simple separate person" and the "en-masse." Yet although Ginsberg sees Whitman as defining the role of the American poet as seer, revolutionary, and aesthetic rebel, the mid-twentieth-century poet's own poetic practice has been more critical of the shortcomings of American society than Whitman's was a century earlier.

Of particular importance to Ginsberg was his discovery, in Whitman, of a precursor poet with whose sexual openness and sexual orientation he could identify. His "A Supermarket in California" (1955) questions a materialistic world seemingly emptied of the soul which Whitman had insisted was concomitant with the body. The poem, imitating "Crossing Brooklyn Ferry" by using direct address, calls on Whitman as the poet's "dear father, graybeard, lonely old courage-teacher." "Love Poem on a Theme by Whitman" (1978) emphasizes Whitman's openness to sexual love and imitates his voyeurist qualities as a way to "rise up from the bed replenished."

Huck Gutman

Bibliography

Cherkovski, Neeli. *Whitman's Wild Children.* Venice: Lapis, 1988.

Merrill, Thomas F. *Allen Ginsberg.* New York: Twayne, 1969.

Schumacher, Michael. *Dharma Lion: A Critical Biography of Allen Ginsburg.* New York: St. Martin's, 1992.

See also KEROUAC, JACK; LEGACY, WHITMAN'S

"Give Me the Splendid Silent Sun" (1865)

First published in *Drum-Taps,* "Give Me the Splendid Silent Sun" remained almost unchanged through the later editions of *Leaves of Grass.* What little attention the poem has received concentrates on its even-handed celebrations of the "pastoral" world and of urban life. With its two opposing strophes, it is an equivocal poem, warring against itself, against the Copperheads (northern Democrats who supported the South), and against Whitman's own resources as a poet.

The 1865 *Drum-Taps,* like Whitman's earlier books, included poems of the countryside ("A Farm Picture" and "Pioneers! O Pioneers!") and of Manhattan ("First O Songs for a Prelude," "City of Ships," and "A Broadway Pageant"). In "Sun" the two are sharply contrasted. The farmer dwells with wife and child in a homey world; the city man moves through public spaces, watching people en masse, "new ones every day" (section 2). Whitman acknowledges the "primal sanities" of rural life, assigning to each a conventional epithet: "ripe and red" fruit, "odorous" and "beautiful" flowers (section 1). The city, on the other hand, is all ephemera, "shows" and "phantoms" (section 2), for which there are few ready-made descriptives. The country offers stability, quiet, and contentment; Manhattan, excitement, noise, and crowds.

Though this contrast seems to favor agrarian life, the poem endorses the city, ostensibly because it has enlisted in the war: one of its spectacles is the parade of embarking troops. "Sun," voicing Whitman's early bellicose Unionism, resembles "Song of the Banner at Daybreak" in its debate between a war party and a peace party. In linking the latter with a yearning for pastoral simplicity, and choosing a specifically western setting for the "peace" strophe, Whitman may be challenging the midwestern strength of the Copperheads (though, if the poem dates from 1862, he was striking early).

G

The second strophe subordinates the war and affirms Whitman's relish for the intense and varied pleasures of the street—"phantoms" though they be, and no less remote from the battlefield. Recognizing the urban illusion as well as the agrarian dream, "Sun" turns on the whole American panorama the skepticism of "Calamus" number 7, and thus joins "To a Certain Civilian" and "As I Lay with My Head in Your Lap Camerado" in extending the subversiveness of "Calamus" into this seemingly more conciliatory volume. Against the unreal city and the mythical farm, there are only the bivouac, the hospital, and the unconciliated poet with his doubts and his dirges.

James Dougherty

Bibliography

Dougherty, James. *Walt Whitman and the Citizen's Eye.* Baton Rouge: Louisiana State UP, 1993.

Everett, Graham. "A Reading of Walt Whitman's 'Give Me the Splendid Silent Sun.'" *West Hills Review* 8 (1988): 105–111.

Machor, James L. *Pastoral Cities.* Madison: U of Wisconsin P, 1987.

See also CITY, WHITMAN AND THE; DRUMTAPS; NATURE

Goethe, Johann Wolfgang von (1749–1832)

Johann Wolfgang von Goethe was a German dramatist, poet, and essayist who influenced many writers in Whitman's America through his leadership of the *Sturm und Drang* (Storm and Stress), an artistic movement of the 1770s which exalted freedom and nature. Although renowned in Europe for such works as *Faust* (1808) and *The Sorrows of Young Werther* (1774), Goethe influenced mid-nineteenth-century America primarily through two newly translated texts which put forward his theory of the importance of character in the life of the artist. The first, Margaret Fuller's translation of *Conversations with Eckermann* (1838), proved influential among the New England transcendentalists. The second, Parke Godwin's translation of Goethe's *Autobiography* (*Dichtung und Warheit*), would profoundly affect Whitman's development of his own artistic persona.

Whitman's first public exposition of Goethe came on 19 November 1846, when he reviewed the *Autobiography* for the Brooklyn *Daily Eagle.* He celebrated the simple directness of Goethe's approach to life and was especially impressed that Goethe managed to avoid overt moralizing. By relying on inference, Goethe allowed the reader to see how circumstance had imbued him with "character." Whitman was so taken by this history of the "soul and body's growth" that he dedicated three columns of the paper to extracts from it ("Incidents" 140).

In addition to his appropriation of the German poet's theory of character, Whitman also found in Goethe a source of nationalistic poetic theory, declaring in "A Backward Glance O'er Travel'd Roads" (1888) that new American poets had first and foremost to realize the lesson that Johann Gottfried Herder had taught the young Goethe so many years before: "[P]oetry is always . . . the result of a national spirit, and not the privilege of a polish'd and select few" (*Prose Works* 2:732).

In time, however, Whitman's enthusiasm for Goethe seems to have cooled. Although he had once declared Goethe to be "the first great critic" (*Notebooks* 5:1824), in his later prose criticism, such as the 1881 essay "Poetry To-day in America—Shakspere—The Future," Whitman dismisses Goethe's "Nature" as artificial (*Prose Works* 2:485), and in his "American National Literature," published ten years later, he ascribes Goethe's assertion that the poet could live by art alone to the "conventionality" of a court poet (2:665).

Phillip H. Round

Bibliography

Kaplan, Justin. *Walt Whitman: A Life.* New York: Simon and Schuster, 1980.

Stovall, Floyd. *The Foreground of "Leaves of Grass."* Charlottesville: UP of Virginia, 1974.

Whitman, Walt. "Incidents in the Life of a World-Famed Man." Rev. of "The Auto-Biography of Goethe." Brooklyn *Daily Eagle* 19 November 1846. Rpt. in *The Uncollected Poetry and Prose of Walt Whitman.* 1921. Ed. Emory Holloway. Vol. 1. Gloucester, Mass.: Peter Smith, 1972. 139–141.

———. *Notebooks and Unpublished Prose Manuscripts.* Ed. Edward F. Grier. 6 vols. New York: New York UP, 1984.

———. *Prose Works 1892.* Ed. Floyd Stovall. 2 vols. New York: New York UP, 1963–1964.

See also HERDER, JOHANN GOTTFRIED VON; INFLUENCES ON WHITMAN, PRINCIPAL

"Good-Bye my Fancy!" (1891)

The concluding poem of the Second Annex to the "authorized" 1891–1892 *Leaves of Grass,* "Good-Bye my Fancy!" was written near the end of Whitman's life and published by David McKay once before in the booklet of the same name in 1891. It also shares its name with a shorter poem early in the annex.

In eighteen lines Whitman's fancy, his poetic élan, discloses itself, becoming the guide to the aging body and the uncertain soul. This is a transition poem that redefines the relationship of the body and soul to the poetic faculty. In the first eight lines Whitman bids farewell. The length of the sentences increases as Whitman becomes despondent, and in the short middle stanza the pain of departure is measured by the intimacy of the established union. By the second line of the third stanza Whitman sees that the intensity and longevity of the relationship may allow them to "remain one." The tone becomes hopeful, the form follows the subject, and the stanza stretches into one long, complex sentence.

Halfway through the poem, at the point of separation, Whitman's fancy shows him the possibility of finding "the true songs." In "Out of the Cradle," Whitman discovers his fancy in the sea-whisper and bird's lament. "Good-Bye my Fancy!" describes a new journey of discovery, yet is still another metaphor of how corporeal life is only one aspect of the eternal. "Good-Bye my Fancy!" remains true to Whitman's earliest expressions of the relationship of the poet to his body and soul and is an appropriate conclusion to his life's work. See "Song of Myself," "Crossing Brooklyn Ferry," and "Passage to India" for developments of the relationship of Whitman to his fancy.

Karen Wolfe

Bibliography

Allen, Gay Wilson, and Charles T. Davis, eds. *Walt Whitman's Poems: Selections with Critical Aids.* New York: New York UP, 1955.

Whitman, Walt. *Leaves of Grass: Comprehensive Reader's Edition.* Ed. Harold W. Blodgett and Sculley Bradley. New York: New York UP, 1965.

See also "Good-Bye my Fancy" (Second Annex); "So Long!"

"Good-Bye my Fancy" (Second Annex) (1891)

This group of poems originally appeared in the book *Good-Bye My Fancy* (1891), Whitman's last miscellany of poetry and prose. In this collection the prose jottings are as interesting as the poems themselves, in their reflections on his poetry, his life, the condition of aging and illness, and death. The prose selections include "An Old Man's Rejoinder," defending once again his poetic vision and continuing to insist that he is rejected by all the great magazines; "Old Poets," a largely favorable appraisal of Longfellow, Whittier, Bryant, and Emerson; an essay on "American National Literature: Is There Any Such Thing—or Can There Ever Be?"; "Some Laggards Yet," collecting prose and verse fragments; and "Memoranda," a truly miscellaneous collection of short newspaper articles, journal entries, fragments of speeches, copies of letters, memories of the New York theater, etc.

A group of thirty-one poems from the book was later printed as "Good-Bye my Fancy . . . 2d Annex" to *Leaves of Grass* 1891–1892, the last edition published in Whitman's lifetime. ("Sands at Seventy" [1888] was then designated as the First Annex.) Of this "last cluster" Whitman wrote, "The clef is here changed to its lowest, and the little book is a lot of tremolos about old age, death, and faith. The physical just lingers, but almost vanishes. The book is garrulous, irascible (like old Lear) and has various breaks and even tricks to avoid monotony. It will have to be ciphered and ciphered out long—and is probably in some respects the most curious part of its author's baffling works" (Whitman 739–740).

Among the poems that Whitman chose to include in this annex are occasional poems on such subjects as the Paris Exposition, the burial of General Sheridan, and the Johnstown flood, and miscellaneous poems on various Whitman themes, the bulk of them on old age and death. Those dealing specifically with his aging, sickness, and confrontation with death reveal some interesting qualities about the man himself: his intellectual lucidity, his honesty, and his unwillingness to soft-pedal his medical disabilities or to try to avoid facing his unavoidable physical end. The poems speak directly and through standard metaphor—"A Twilight Song," "Sounds of the Winter," and "An Ended Day"—about time running out and death as a new beginning as well as the end of life.

G

Two poems demonstrate that Whitman had not lost his artistry: "To the Sun-Set Breeze" and "Unseen Buds." In the first of these, an unpretentious and even understated poem, we find again the sure touch of the master, whose confidence and assurance about the truth of what he believes keeps him from faltering or striking a false note. The poem was singled out two decades later by the young Ezra Pound, who wrote: "[I]f a man has written lines like Whitman's to the 'sunset breeze' one has to love him. I think we have not yet paid enough attention to the deliberate artistry of the man, not in details but in the large" (qtd. in Bergman 60).

In "Unseen Buds" Whitman uses a strange and unusual image: buds hidden under snow and ice with a latent potential to flower, which mysteriously suggest the idea of the universe as an eternal process of becoming. In the context of this group of late-in-life poems, "Unseen Buds" assumes a special significance, as Whitman moves away from an individual confrontation with death and places it on a truly cosmic scale. He becomes merely one of the many trillions of germinal presences which eternally and infinitely expand, grow, and die to make room for their successors, a view of death he had frequently expressed in his younger years.

There are two poems with the title "Good-Bye my Fancy," distinguished only by the exclamation point at the end of the one that closes the collection. This is a farewell to Whitman's other self, his poetic genius, which he had addressed throughout the course of his career, beginning with the opening stanzas of "Song of Myself."

Donald Barlow Stauffer

Bibliography

Bergman, Herbert. "Ezra Pound and Walt Whitman." *American Literature* 27 (1955): 56–61.

Fillard, Claudette. "Le vannier de Camden: Vieillesse, Poésie, et les Annexes de *Leaves of Grass*." *Études Anglaises* 45 (1992): 311–323.

Stauffer, Donald Barlow. "Walt Whitman and Old Age." *Walt Whitman Review* 24 (1978): 144–148.

Whitman, Walt. *Prose Works 1892*. Ed. Floyd Stovall. Vol. 2. New York: New York UP, 1964.

See also AGE AND AGING; DEATH; "SANDS AT SEVENTY" (FIRST ANNEX)

Gosse, Sir Edmund (1849–1928)

A popular British poet, critic, and literary biographer, Sir Edmund Gosse wrote more than sixty books between 1873 and 1928. He is best remembered for his personal memoir, *Father and Son* (1908).

In 1873 Gosse had sent Walt Whitman a copy of his own first book of poems, *On Viol and Flute* (1873), together with an effusive letter in which he declared himself to be "the new person drawn toward you . . . I draw only closer and closer to you" (Traubel 245). It was signed, "your sincere disciple" (246). Some years later, in the 1880s, Gosse was on a lecture tour in the United States and was able to visit with Whitman for several hours in his Camden home. By the time of the interview Gosse had apparently become much less enthusiastic about Whitman's poetry. In his essay about their interview, however, Gosse presented a clear and favorable picture of Whitman. He said that he had gone to see him as a "stiff necked unbeliever" but that he left with "a heart full of affection for the beautiful old man" (*Critical* 100, 106).

Gosse chose not to reveal much about their conversation. He devoted much of the essay to his theory that Whitman's poetry is "[l]iterature in the condition of protoplasm, an intellectual organism so simple that it takes the instant impression of whatever mood approaches it" (97). Gosse saw this as explaining why some readers liked Whitman while they were young but became less enthusiastic as they aged. The essay was not published during Whitman's lifetime. It first appeared in April of 1894 and was included by Gosse in his *Critical Kit-Kats* (1896). In a conversation with Horace Traubel in 1888 Whitman included Gosse in a list of several British critics who "seem to understand me" (Traubel 245), but in a letter to Richard Bucke in 1889 he characterized Gosse as "one of the amiable conventional wall-flowers of literature" (Whitman 392).

Gosse's last word on Whitman was not until 1927. In the last of his books, he concluded a review of John Bailey's new *Walt Whitman* by saying, "that is really the one subject of Walt Whitman, the masculinity of other men. . . . It is best not to inquire too closely about all this, but to accept Walt Whitman for what he gives . . . the undeniable beauty and originality of his strange unshackled rhapsody" (*Leaves and Fruit* 211).

Jerry F. King

Bibliography

Bailey, John. *Walt Whitman*. New York: Macmillan, 1926.

Barrus, Clara. *Whitman and Burroughs, Comrades*. Boston: Houghton Mifflin, 1931.

Gosse, Sir Edmund. *Critical Kit-Kats*. New York: Dodd, Mead, 1896.

———. *Leaves and Fruit*. London: Heinemann, 1927.

Thwaite, Ann. *Edmund Gosse, A Literary Landscape, 1849–1928*. London: Secker and Warburg, 1984.

Traubel, Horace. *With Walt Whitman in Camden*. Vol. 1. Boston: Small, Maynard, 1906.

Whitman, Walt. *The Correspondence*. Ed. Edwin Haviland Miller. Vol. 4. New York: New York UP, 1969.

Woolf, James D. *Edmund Gosse*. New York: Twayne, 1972.

See also BRITISH ISLES, WHITMAN IN THE

Gray, Fred (1834–1891)

One of the Bohemian regulars at Pfaff's, Gray lent the Fred Gray Association his name, although it remains unclear what purposes it might have had. Whitman and the good-humored, jolly Gray were close from before the Civil War; their principal connection seems to have been life at Pfaff's. The poet wrote Gray and Nathaniel Bloom an important and touching letter on 19 March 1863, in which he described the work he was doing in the hospitals, the suffering and loss he witnessed, and talked of life in Washington, including observations on Lincoln.

Son of the homeopathic physician John F. Gray, who lived opposite Madison Square, a few blocks west of the Herman Melvilles on East 26th Street, Fred Gray saw battle at Antietam and reported his experiences to Whitman in 1862. Gray rose to the rank of major and resigned the year the war ended. Following his father into medicine, he practiced in New York and Europe. Whitman had affection for the Gray family and visited them, but the connection apparently dissolved in the 1870s.

Donald Yannella

Bibliography

Howells, William Dean. *Literary Friends and Acquaintance*. New York: Harper, 1900.

Hyman, Martin D. "'Where the Drinkers and Laughers Meet': Pfaff's: Whitman's Literary Lair." *Seaport* 26 (1992): 56–61.

Lalor, Gene. "Whitman among the New York Literary Bohemians: 1859–1862." *Walt Whitman Review* 25 (1979): 131–145.

Parry, Albert. *Garrets and Pretenders: A History of Bohemianism in America*. 1933. New York: Dover, 1960.

Stansell, Christine. "Whitman at Pfaff's: Commercial Culture, Literary Life and New York Bohemia at Mid-Century." *Walt Whitman Quarterly Review* 10 (1993): 107–126.

See also PFAFF'S RESTAURANT

Great Plains and Prairies, The

Encompassing vast areas of Missouri, Illinois, Iowa, Kansas, and Nebraska, the great plains and prairies comprise an area of the United States that fascinated Walt Whitman. Although he traveled through parts of this region relatively late in his career, on a trip to Denver in 1879, Whitman incorporated the plains and prairies into much of his earlier poetry and prose. In *Democratic Vistas* (1871) he speculated that the nation's future capital could be "refounded" in its heartland.

Whitman records his firsthand observation of the great plains and prairies in *Specimen Days* (1882). There he writes that the vast stretches of buffalo grass and wild sage in the country's midlands are "North America's characteristic landscape," exceeding the beauty of Niagara Falls, Yosemite, and the upper Yellowstone (94). The "pure breath, primitiveness, boundless prodigality and amplitude" (95) of the prairies inspired several poems that appeared in *Leaves of Grass,* including "The Prairie States," "The Prairie-Grass Dividing," "Night on the Prairies," and "A Prairie Sunset."

Whitman not only absorbed the geographic landscape of the prairies into his work, but he also extolled the virtues of its inhabitants—pioneers, farmers, and presidents Abraham Lincoln and Ulysses S. Grant, both of whom came from great plains states. Whitman admired the freshness, spirit, and strong work ethic of the peoples in this region.

The great plains and prairies thus provided Whitman with an open and sunlit landscape— "with the far circle-line of the horizon all times of day" (*Specimen Days* 94). In his expansive vision of inland America he discovered an analogue for his own expansive consciousness and for his idealized conception of Americans living free of constraint.

Steven P. Schneider

Bibliography
Allen, Gay Wilson. *The Solitary Singer: A Critical Biography of Walt Whitman.* 1955. Rev. ed. 1967. Chicago: U of Chicago P, 1985.
Eitner, Walter H. *Walt Whitman's Western Jaunt.* Lawrence: Regents Press of Kansas, 1981.
Trachtenberg, Alan, ed. *Democratic Vistas: 1860–1880.* New York: George Braziller, 1970.
Whitman, Walt. *Specimen Days.* Boston: D.R. Godine, 1971.

See also "Prairie States, The"; "Prairie-Grass Dividing, The"; Travels, Whitman's; West, The American

Grey, Ellen

In his notebooks for 1856, Whitman mentions Ellen Grey, an actress for the Bowery Theater from approximately 1853–1854 and 1857–1860; she re-appeared in 1865. She married during her five-year absence from the stage, but other than her theater roles, little is known about her life.

In 1862, Whitman received a love letter from "Ellen Eyre," thought to be Grey's pseudonym. Scholars connect Grey to Eyre because of their similar names and Whitman's cryptic notations or conversational references to them. Since Whitman mentions Grey once and the connection to Eyre is slight, scholars cannot determine her impact on Whitman.

Martha A. Kalnin

Bibliography
Hollis, C. Carroll. "Whitman's 'Ellen Eyre.'" *Walt Whitman Newsletter* 2 (1956): 24–26.
Miller, Edwin Haviland. "Walt Whitman and Ellen Eyre." *American Literature* 33 (1961): 64–68.
Odell, George C.D. *Annals of the New York Stage.* 15 vols. New York: Columbia UP, 1927–1938.
Whitman, Walt. *Notebooks and Unpublished Prose Manuscripts.* Ed. Edward F. Grier. 6 vols. New York: New York UP, 1984.
Zweig, Paul. *Walt Whitman: The Making of the Poet.* New York: Basic Books, 1984.

See also Eyre, Ellen

Griswold, Rufus W. (1815–1857)

When asked her view of Whitman, Emily Dickinson famously replied that she had been told "he was disgraceful" (qtd. in Kaplan 26). The term is too pale to describe Rufus W. Griswold's anonymous estimate of the 1855 *Leaves* for the *Criterion,* a highly respectable—though short-lived—New York opinion weekly (1855–1856). Griswold had achieved fame as a literary anthologist (beginning with his 1842 compilation, *The Poets and Poetry of America*) and as Edgar Allan Poe's literary executor and biographer.

Griswold's training as an orthodox Baptist minister may explain why he begins his review by using *Leaves* to warn against New England liberal intellectuals. Its poems exemplify for him the despicable result to which Emersonian transcendentalism eventually leads. Claiming that even a single extract from the new book would spread contagion, Griswold goes on to indicate that his concern is not only with the poems' "reeking" ideas and the "obscenity" of their expression (27). More worrisome, more simply unacceptable, is their unrestrained eroticism, their "beastly sensuality that is fast rotting the healthy core of all the social virtues" (27). Griswold makes this allusion to prostitution fully explicit: the author, he writes, should be "placed in the same category" as a woman who "skulks along in the shadows of byways," the "slave of poverty, ignorance, and passion" (27).

Willis J. Buckingham

Bibliography
Bayless, Joy. *Rufus Wilmot Griswold: Poe's Literary Executor.* Nashville: Vanderbilt UP, 1943.
Griswold, Rufus W. Rev. of *Leaves of Grass, 1855 Edition. Walt Whitman: The Contemporary Reviews.* Ed. Kenneth M. Price. Cambridge: Cambridge UP, 1996. 26–27.
Kaplan, Justin. *Walt Whitman: A Life.* New York: Simon and Schuster, 1980.

See also Dana, Charles A.; Hale, Edward Everett; Norton, Charles Eliot; Sex and Sexuality

Gurowski, Count Adam de (1805–1866)

In spite of his aristocratic origins, Polish author and social and political commentator Adam Gurowski understood and identified with

American democracy and became an early and sincere admirer of Whitman. Gurowski was a naturally curious lover of intrigue, using his charm and intellect to insinuate himself into the company of the powerful and influential.

Arriving in New York (1849), Gurowski quickly became involved in American life, first meeting Whitman at Pfaff's restaurant. Gurowski moved to Washington (1861) and found work reading foreign newspapers and translating for the State Department, a job he lost because of his harsh criticism of Lincoln and Seward. Gurowski published his *Diary* in three volumes (1862, 1864, 1866). Full of gossip and outspoken opinions, the *Diary* was a great success. In it he referred to "the loftiest, the most original and genuine American hearts and minds. Such a one is the poet Walt Whitman" (Gurowski 3:187).

Whitman appreciated the count's publicly stated words of praise. He attended Gurowski's funeral, noting the presence of "all the big Radicals" (Whitman 275).

Frederick Hatch

Bibliography

Chittenden, L.E. *Recollections of President Lincoln and His Administration.* New York: Harper, 1891.

Fischer, LeRoy H. *Lincoln's Gadfly, Adam Gurowski.* Norman: U of Oklahoma P, 1964.

Gurowski, Adam. *Diary.* Vol. 1. Boston: Lee and Shepard, 1862; Vol. 2. New York: Carleton, 1864; Vol. 3. Washington: W.H. and O.H. Morrison, 1866.

Whitman, Walt. *The Correspondence.* Ed. Edwin Haviland Miller. Vol. 1. New York: New York UP, 1961.

See also WASHINGTON, D.C.

G

H

"Halcyon Days"

First published in the New York *Herald* on 29 January 1888, "Halcyon Days" is found in "Sands at Seventy," the First Annex to the 1891–1892 edition of *Leaves of Grass*.

In eight lines Whitman contrasts the usual great rewards in life ("successful" love, wealth, honor, fame) with what he sees as greater rewards "as life wanes," paralleling nature's quieter moods in the autumn or at day's end with the same condition in old age.

Since these days are "teeming" as well as being the "quietest, happiest days of all," and are "brooding" as well as being "blissful," they by no means suggest complete passivity and resignation. Although the language catches a dominant mood of affirmation, it avoids sentimentalizing old age. Whitman often uses a key word (key in choice, position, stress, or frequency) as he does here with "halcyon," well chosen for his purposes in meaning, sound, and rhythm.

Not all of Whitman's latter days were halcyon, however. He was wracked by illness and occasional doubts, as his letters, his old-age chronicler Horace Traubel, and several poems in the "Sands at Seventy" cluster attest, notably "As I Sit Writing Here," "Queries to My Seventieth Year," and "An Evening Lull." But in this cluster, as elsewhere, affirmative old-age poems strongly predominate.

David B. Baldwin

Bibliography

Schwiebert, John E. *The Frailest Leaves: Whitman's Poetic Technique and Style in the Short Poem*. New York: Lang, 1992.
Stauffer, Donald B. "Walt Whitman and Old Age." *Walt Whitman Review* 24 (1978): 144–148.
Whitman, Walt. *Leaves of Grass: Comprehensive Reader's Edition*. Ed. Harold W. Blodgett and Sculley Bradley. New York: New York UP, 1965.

See also AGE AND AGING; "AS I SIT WRITING HERE"; "SANDS AT SEVENTY" (FIRST ANNEX)

Hale, Edward Everett (1822–1909)

About Whitman's age and, according to William James, like him in his inborn spiritual and personal optimism, Edward Everett Hale wrote one of the first unqualified appreciations of *Leaves of Grass*. Already prominent in New England as an essayist and Unitarian minister, Hale would become nationally known as a clergyman, magazine editor, and prolific author. His works include fiction, sermons, travel writings, biography, and autobiography, chief among them a hugely popular patriotic short story, "The Man Without a Country" (1863).

Reviewing *Leaves of Grass* anonymously for the *North American Review,* Hale admires most its fresh and direct poetic voice. Its author, he writes admiringly, "has a horror of conventional language of any kind" (34). Most early commentators on *Leaves* find it *too* original, but for Hale the book's power inheres in its "simplicity," its absolute freedom from traditional, "strained," literary speech (35). Its second accomplishment lies in its vivid description: "sketches of life . . . so real that we wonder how they came on paper" (36). He concludes by observing that the poems' occasional "indelicacies" (36) are no more worrisome than those of Homer. His portrayal of Whitman as founder-poet and "American Homer" would become, as Timothy Morris points out, the dominant critical strategy leading to the poet's eventual canonization.

Willis J. Buckingham

Bibliography

Adams, John R. *Edward Everett Hale.* Boston: Twayne, 1977.

Hale, Edward Everett. Rev. of *Leaves of Grass,* 1855 Edition. *Walt Whitman: The Contemporary Reviews.* Ed. Kenneth M. Price. Cambridge: Cambridge UP, 1996. 34–36.

Holloway, Jean. *Edward Everett Hale: A Biography.* Austin: U of Texas P, 1956.

James, William. *The Varieties of Religious Experience.* 1902. Cambridge, Mass.: Harvard UP, 1985.

Morris, Timothy. *Becoming Canonical in American Poetry.* Urbana: U of Illinois P, 1995.

See also DANA, CHARLES A.; GRISWOLD, RUFUS W.; *NORTH AMERICAN REVIEW, THE;* NORTON, CHARLES ELIOT

"Half-Breed, The" (1845)

Whitman's novella "The Half-Breed: A Tale of the Western Frontier" was first published in *The Aristidean,* March 1845, as "Arrow-Tip" and reprinted with its current title in the Brooklyn *Daily Eagle,* 1–6, 8, 9 June 1846.

"The Half-Breed" is Whitman's second-longest piece of fiction; only the novel *Franklin Evans* (1842) is longer. Structurally, the novella shows some skill. Its nine chapters quietly build toward the climax, and much of the later action is dependent on character traits established early.

His characters may be improbable, but Whitman strives for some depth, especially in his depictions of Native Americans, whom he seems to take special care in humanizing. Arrow-Tip's teasing sense of humor leads to the confrontation that is his undoing. Accused first of theft and then murder, Arrow-Tip is as silent as Jesus, even as he is hanged. Boddo, the half-breed, is the story's villain, but he is evil because society has made him evil; ostracism has made him antisocial and vengeful. Folsom sees Arrow-Tip as anticipating Whitman's "friendly and flowing savage" in "Song of Myself" (section 39), and William Scheick uses Boddo's physical and moral deformities as evidence of Whitman's strong opposition to miscegenation.

In that light, the Native American of "The Fireman's Dream" (1844) may be viewed as Boddo's precursor.

"The Half-Breed," like the original version of "One Wicked Impulse!" (1845), may have been written as an implicit attack on capital punishment, although David Reynolds sees the story merely as sensationalism.

Whitman used the story to inaugurate a regular front-page literary feature in the Brooklyn *Daily Eagle.*

Patrick McGuire

Bibliography

Brasher, Thomas L. *Whitman as Editor of the Brooklyn Daily Eagle.* Detroit: Wayne State UP, 1970.

Folsom, Ed. *Walt Whitman's Native Representations.* Cambridge: Cambridge UP, 1994.

Reynolds, David S. *Walt Whitman's America: A Cultural Biography.* New York: Knopf, 1995.

Scheick, William J. "Whitman's Grotesque Half-Breed." *Walt Whitman Review* 23 (1977): 133–136.

Whitman, Walt. *The Early Poems and the Fiction.* Ed. Thomas L. Brasher. New York: New York UP, 1963.

See also FRANKLIN EVANS; "DEATH OF WIND-FOOT, THE"; "FIREMAN'S DREAM, THE"; NATIVE AMERICANS (INDIANS); SHORT FICTION, WHITMAN'S

"Hand-Mirror, A" (1860)

This twelve-line poem has received scant critical attention, but makes a significant contribution to the 1860 edition of *Leaves,* where it first appeared. Written between 1856 and 1859, "A Hand-Mirror" portrays a falling out of love with life and thus contrasts sharply with the "Calamus" poems, which also first appeared in the 1860 *Leaves.*

Of the critical responses, R.W.B. Lewis offers the most compelling, arguing that the intense self-loathing in the poem contributes to a subplot in this volume. While the "Calamus" poems celebrate life and all its pleasures, "A Hand-Mirror" and other similar poems explore types of death ranging from loss of sensations to loss of poetic creativity. For Lewis, this tension makes "A Hand-Mirror" itself significant. Harold Aspiz echoes Lewis's reading, arguing that the poem reveals a wasted body, one diminished by alcoholism, drug abuse, and venereal disease. (Whitman's variant, "venerealee," appears in the poem.) Aspiz rightly notes the wasting of the once beautiful body, the poet's unblinking gaze at this wasting, and the poisonous consequence of the man's misconduct against nature and himself. Like Lewis, Aspiz stresses the self-loathing that pervades the poem. Unlike Lewis and Aspiz, Betsy Erkkila stresses the public rather than the private emphasis in the poem. She argues that Whitman uses a divided-self theme, pointing out his concern over his public image. In her study, Erkkila shows Whitman's influence on French poets, indicating that "A Hand-Mirror" influenced Valery Larbaud's "Le Masque," a poem that also employs a mirror motif.

Because this poem portrays a man's self-loathing, it tends toward hyperbole. But the presence of excess merely affirms the excess that has ruined the man's life. Lewis comments on the painful difficulty of reading such a poem; still, the poem's excess may be the "fair costume" covering its disguised meaning: a guilt-ridden response to same-sex desire.

Jay Losey

Bibliography

Aspiz, Harold. *Walt Whitman and the Body Beautiful*. Urbana: U of Illinois P, 1980.

Erkkila, Betsy. *Walt Whitman Among the French: Poet and Myth*. Princeton: Princeton UP, 1980.

Lewis, R.W.B. *Trials of the Word: Essays in American Literature*. New Haven: Yale UP, 1965.

Whitman, Walt. *Leaves of Grass: A Textual Variorum of the Printed Poems*. Ed. Sculley Bradley, Harold W. Blodgett, Arthur Golden, and William White. Vol. 2. New York: New York UP, 1980.

See also "By the Roadside"; Leaves of Grass, 1860 Edition

Harlan, James W. (1820–1899)

On 30 June 1865 James Harlan, Secretary of the Interior, discharged Walt Whitman from his second-class clerkship in the Bureau of Indian Affairs. The facts surrounding Whitman's dismissal are ambiguous, though its results are certain: Harlan achieved a notoriety that initiated the decline of his political career, while Whitman's public stature began to grow.

Soon after taking office, Harlan, a former college president and Methodist minister, circulated a notice dated 30 May which expressed his intention of releasing all employees who performed perfunctory or unnecessary services, or whose "fidelity to duty" and "moral character" were questionable (qtd. in Allen 344). Most Whitman biographers conclude that Harlan dismissed Whitman on the sole grounds of his being the author of *Leaves of Grass*. J. Hubley Ashton, at the behest of Whitman's fiery, combative supporter, William Douglas O'Connor, held a personal interview with Harlan the following day. Ashton reports that Harlan, while snooping through the building after hours, discovered a copy of *Leaves of Grass* either on or in Whitman's desk. Since Whitman was in the process of editing poems for subsequent editions, Harlan found numerous underlined, amended, and marked-off passages. Curious, he carried it back to his office. Upon further reading, he declared the book obscene and its author immoral, discharging Whitman the next day.

Within twenty-four hours of Whitman's dismissal, Ashton secured for him a position in the Attorney General's Office. At the time, Whitman did not respond publicly to the affair, but later he would privately berate Harlan's "cowardly despicable act" (Traubel 477). Harlan afterward expressed regret concerning the incident, yet insisted that he fired Whitman for no reason other than that of forced economy. Whitman was often absent from his desk attending the sick and wounded soldiers, an activity which spoke volumes for his personal character but which also may have rendered his services dispensable. Most likely, Harlan dismissed Whitman for a combination of the reasons stated in his letter of 30 May.

The situation's apparent injustice galvanized support for Whitman and helped to form the beginnings of his literary following. O'Connor's spirited defense of Whitman's moral character, *The Good Gray Poet: A Vindication*, enhanced Whitman's public image, influencing a gradual change in the poet's public reception. Gay Wilson Allen notes that Harlan's actions may have caused Whitman to become less acquiescent in the face of prudish critics, and may even have led him to retain and strengthen specific, overtly sexual passages in the "Calamus" poems.

Joseph P. Hammond

Poet Stanley Kunitz reading at Whitman's tomb in Harleigh Cemetery, Camden, 31 May 1980. By permission, Walt Whitman Association. Photo courtesy of Geoffrey Sill.

Bibliography

Allen, Gay Wilson. *The Solitary Singer: A Critical Biography of Walt Whitman.* 1955. Rev. ed. 1967. Chicago: U of Chicago P, 1985.

Loving, Jerome. *Walt Whitman's Champion: William Douglas O'Connor.* College Station: Texas A&M UP, 1978.

Traubel, Horace. *With Walt Whitman in Camden.* Vol. 3. New York: Mitchell Kennerley, 1914.

See also ASHTON, J. HUBLEY; INDIAN AFFAIRS, BUREAU OF; O'CONNOR, WILLIAM DOUGLAS; *WALT WHITMAN'S BLUE BOOK*; WASHINGTON, D.C.

Harleigh Cemetery

Walt Whitman was buried on 30 March 1892, four days after his death. His funeral began with a viewing in the parlor of his home at 328 Mickle Street in Camden, followed by a procession of about a mile to the tomb that awaited him at Harleigh Cemetery, built for him by Reinhalter and Company of Philadelphia to his own specifications at a cost of about four thousand dollars. Whitman paid fifteen hundred dollars of that sum with money raised by friends to buy him a house in the country; the balance was paid by his literary executor, Thomas Harned.

The tomb occupies a twenty-by-thirty-foot plot set into a wooded hillside. Designed by Whitman to resemble the etching of "Death's Door" by William Blake, the tomb was constructed of massive blocks of unpolished Quincy granite. Three eighteen-inch-thick slabs form the sides and top, each weighing up to ten tons; a six-ton triangular capstone forms the pediment and anchors the six-inch-thick granite door that stands permanently ajar—perhaps because Whitman wanted his soul to remain free, but also because the door was too heavy to swing on its hinges. An iron gate protects the privacy of the tomb's seven inmates: Whitman, his mother Louisa Van Velsor Whitman, father Walter Whitman, brothers George W. and Edward Whitman, sister Hannah Whitman Heyde, and George's wife, Louisa Orr Whitman. An eighth vault remains empty.

Expensive though the tomb was, the plot at least was free. Whitman was offered his choice of plots in the new cemetery shortly after it was laid out in 1885. Like other "park lawn" cemeteries created after the Civil War, Harleigh was designed with curving drives, broad expanses of lawn, and artificial lakes. Such rural cemeteries were intended to supplant the crowded churchyard burial grounds that were considered both aesthetically displeasing and a source of urban pestilence. It was named "Harleigh" after the country place of Isaac Cooper, which was sold in 1838 to provide the grounds for Philadelphia's Laurel Hill cemetery, on which Harleigh was modeled. The architecture of its gatehouse resembles that of a country estate, and its selected varieties of trees and shrubs provide a sanctuary for scores of nesting birds. Whitman's tomb was therefore a key element in winning acceptance for a new concept for cemeteries, in which the dead become part of nature, rather than huddling behind city walls. He was eventually joined in Harleigh by some thirty-six thousand other souls, including his adherents Horace Traubel and Ella Reeve Omholt, better known as "Mother Bloor."

Geoffrey M. Sill

Bibliography

Greenberg, Gail. *A History of Harleigh Cemetery.* Camden County Historical Society Bulletin 36 (Fall/Winter 1983–84).

Kaplan, Justin. *Walt Whitman: A Life.* New York: Simon and Schuster, 1980.

See also BLAKE, WILLIAM; CAMDEN, NEW JERSEY; HARNED, THOMAS BIGGS; MICKLE STREET HOUSE

Harned, Thomas Biggs (1851–1921)

One of Whitman's three literary executors, Thomas Biggs Harned was a prosperous Philadelphia lawyer and a brother-in-law of Horace Traubel. His twenty-year acquaintance with Whitman involved nearly daily contact during the poet's final years. Harned's well-furnished Camden home was a social center where Whitman dined and drank richly, amused Harned's three children, and met prominent religious and political men. Harned funded the construction of Whitman's mausoleum and co-arranged his funeral, at which he participated as speaker and pallbearer. Later, Harned wrote the introduction to the definitive ten-volume Camden Edition of Whitman's works (1902). Some thought Harned's decision to publish *The Letters of Anne Gilchrist and Walt Whitman* (1918) in dubious taste.

Son of a Philadelphia wood carver, Harned quit school at age twelve to earn wages. After attending University of Pennsylvania Law School he practiced criminal law in Camden, then civil law in Philadelphia. At age twenty-two Harned met Whitman, and the two occasionally discussed news and the Shakespeare controversy, agreeing that the Stratford actor was not the author of the plays. In 1877 Harned married Augusta Anna Traubel, another Whitman admiree; her brother Horace's relationship with the poet developed at the Harned home, a frequent setting for Traubel's *With Walt Whitman in Camden.*

Harned's *Memoirs* (1920) document a quest for relevance, religious certainty, and social justice. A former Republican who ran unsuccessfully for the New Jersey state senate as an independent (1890), Harned was well read and interested in art and oratory. An abolitionist and Unitarian, Harned was greatly influenced by Rev. W.H. Furness. Whitman often cited Harned's honesty and directness, recognizing the heart of gold beneath his gruff exterior.

Dena Mattausch

Bibliography

Harned, Thomas Biggs. *Memoirs of Thomas B. Harned, Walt Whitman's Friend and Literary Executor.* Ed. Peter Van Egmond. Hartford: Transcendental Books, 1972.

Traubel, Horace. *With Walt Whitman in Camden.* 9 vols. Vol. 1. Boston: Small, Maynard, 1906; Vol. 2. New York: Appleton, 1908; Vol. 3. New York: Mitchell Kennerley, 1914; Vol. 4. Ed. Sculley Bradley. Philadelphia: U of Pennsylvania P, 1953; Vol. 5. Ed. Gertrude Traubel. Carbondale: Southern Illinois UP, 1964; Vol. 6. Ed. Gertrude Traubel and William White. Carbondale: Southern Illinois UP, 1982; Vol. 7. Ed. Jeanne Chapman and Robert MacIssac. Carbondale: Southern Illinois UP, 1992; Vols. 8–9. Ed. Jeanne Chapman and

H

Robert MacIssac. Oregon House, Calif.: W.L. Bentley, 1996.

See also BUCKE, RICHARD MAURICE; CAMDEN, NEW JERSEY; PHILADELPHIA, PENNSYLVANIA; TRAUBEL, HORACE L.

Harper's Monthly

Founded in New York in 1850 as *Harper's New Monthly Magazine, Harper's Monthly* initially published mostly British literature. It was much more widely circulated than the *Atlantic,* and in the late nineteenth century increasingly drew from American writers. Whitman published six poems in the periodical: "Song of the Redwood-Tree" (February 1874); "Prayer of Columbus" (March 1874); "Patroling Barnegat" (April 1881); "With Husky-Haughty Lips, O Sea!" (March 1884); "Of That Blithe Throat of Thine" (January 1885); and the posthumous "Death's Valley" (April 1892). In his later years Whitman believed, incorrectly, that *Harper's* had a standing editorial order to reject his poems. From comments by George Curtis on *Drum-Taps* to William Dean Howells's editorial on *November Boughs,* the magazine, on the whole, reviewed Whitman favorably (the exception being Henry Alden's criticism of *Leaves of Grass* as "a congeries of bizarre rhapsodies" (January 1882). Other notable *Harper's* articles include Curtis's contemplation on the future of Whitman's literary reputation "one hundred years from now" (July 1890) and Howells's reminiscence of meeting Whitman at Pfaff's (June 1895).

Scott L. Newstrom

Bibliography

Baker, Portia. "Walt Whitman's Relations with Some New York Magazines." *American Literature* 7 (1935): 274–301.

Giantvalley, Scott. "Additional Whitman Allusions in *Harper's Monthly.*" *Walt Whitman Quarterly Review* 5.3 (1988) 40–41.

Wells, Daniel A. "Whitman Allusions in *Harper's Monthly*: An Annotated List of Citations." *Walt Whitman Quarterly Review* 4.1 (1986): 16–23.

Whitman, Walt. *The Correspondence.* Ed. Edwin Haviland Miller. Vol. 3. New York: New York UP, 1964; Vol. 4. Ed. Edwin Haviland Miller. New York: New York UP, 1969.

See also "DEATH'S VALLEY"; HOWELLS, WILLIAM DEAN; "PATROLING BARNEGAT"; "PRAYER OF COLUMBUS"; "SONG OF THE REDWOOD-TREE"; "WITH HUSKY-HAUGHTY LIPS, O SEA!"

Harris, Frank (1856–1931)

Best known for his unreliable autobiography *My Life and Loves* (1922, 1934, 1963), with its exaggerated accounts of his lusty affairs, Harris was a formidable and controversial literary figure in England and America between the 1880s and the 1920s. As editor of many magazines, including the *Saturday Review* (1894–1898), he championed writers such as Shaw and Wilde. In *My Life and Loves,* he tells of hearing Whitman's 1877 Philadelphia lecture on Paine and being greatly impressed by Whitman's honesty and simplicity, going on to praise his courage for writing about sexuality. Among his other works, Harris published five volumes of *Contemporary Portraits* (1915–1927). In *Third Series* (1920) he says that "Prayer of Columbus" is Whitman's best poem, that his writing excels because it speaks to the soul via the language of the flesh, and that the poet was the greatest American—superior even to Lincoln.

Walter Graffin

Bibliography

Harris, Frank. *Contemporary Portraits.* Third Series. New York: the author, 1920.

———. *My Life and Loves.* 1922. Ed. John F. Gallagher. New York: Grove, 1963.

Pullar, Philippa. *Frank Harris: A Biography.* New York: Simon and Schuster, 1976.

See also HUMAN BODY; PAINE, THOMAS; "PRAYER OF COLUMBUS"

Harris, Thomas Lake (1823–1906)

Born in England, Thomas Lake Harris came to the United States as a young boy. Influenced by Swedenborgianism, Harris founded in New York an independent Christian spiritualist church that Whitman probably attended in the early 1850s. Around 1850, Harris began to go into trances. While in these mystical states, he would dictate long poems about celestial love. Harris's poems suggest that the human relationship with God is physical as well as spiritual.

Like Whitman's, they celebrate the sensual aspects of religious experience. Harris's followers practiced "open breathing," a process of inhaling the Divine Breath directly into the body, and a system of celibate marriage whereby each person was free to live with a heavenly "counterpart." Ascribing to the lungs a principal role in spiritual communion, Harris used in his poems words like "influx," "efflux," and "afflatus," which appear frequently in Whitman's poems. David S. Reynolds has recently suggested that poems by Harris like the four-thousand-line *An Epic of the Starry Heaven* (1854) may have helped to inspire Whitman's own erotic mysticism. This influence may be reflected in passages like the well-known section of "Song of Myself" in which the poet "loafes" with his soul on a transparent summer morning. Reynolds describes Harris as an "unappreciated figure in Whitman biography" (266).

John T. Matteson

Bibliography

Cuthbert, Arthur A. *The Life and World-Work of Thomas Lake Harris*. 1908. New York: AMS, 1975.

Harris, Thomas Lake. *An Epic of the Starry Heaven*. New York: Partridge and Brittan, 1854.

Reynolds, David S. *Walt Whitman's America: A Cultural Biography*. New York: Knopf, 1995.

See also MYSTICISM; SWEDENBORG, EMANUEL

Hartmann, C. Sadakichi (ca. 1867–1944)

Like the character he played in the 1924 film *The Thief of Bagdad*, Whitman enthusiast C. Sadakichi Hartmann played court magician to successive bohemian circles. Hartmann also produced a significant legacy as art historian and pioneer in the field of photographic criticism (sometimes aka Sidney Allan).

Son of a German diplomat and a Japanese woman, Hartmann studied widely in Europe before undertaking a career as an art critic and impresario in the United States. Having visited Whitman in Camden on several occasions beginning in 1884, experiences he would later publish as *Conversations with Walt Whitman* (1895), Hartmann in 1887 set about creating a Whitman Society in Boston. It collapsed due to Hartmann's high-handed tactics, opposition from Whitman confederates, and the poet's reluctance to be so commemorated. Resentments over his New York *Herald* account of conversations with Whitman (14 April 1889) further alienated him from the Whitman coterie.

As Greenwich Village's "King of Bohemia" and eventually as a colorful denizen of San Francisco and Hollywood circles, he continued, however, to reminisce about Whitman. Most remembered among his prolific writings are *A History of American Art* (1902) and essays for *Camera Work*.

John F. Roche

Bibliography

Hartmann, Sadakichi. *The Sadakichi Hartmann Papers*. Ed. Clifford Wurfel and John Batchelor. Riverside: U of California, Riverside Library, 1980.

———. *White Chrysanthemums: Literary Fragments and Pronouncements*. Ed. George Knox and Harry Lawton. New York: Herder, 1971.

———. *The Whitman-Hartmann Controversy: Including "Conversations with Walt Whitman" and Other Essays*. Ed. George Knox and Harry Lawton. Bern: Lang, 1976.

See also ASSOCIATIONS, CLUBS, FELLOWSHIPS, FOUNDATIONS, AND SOCIETIES

Hartshorne, William (1775–1859)

William Hartshorne grew up in Philadelphia but moved to Brooklyn around the close of the eighteenth century. He later became city printer for the city of Brooklyn.

In 1831 Hartshorne was printer for the *Long Island Patriot* when a twelve-year-old Walt Whitman became an apprentice for the paper. Whitman boarded with Hartshorne's granddaughter, and the older man took Whitman under his wing. Hartshorne initiated Whitman into the printing trade and showed him how to set his first page of type. He and Whitman often conversed, and Whitman loved to hear Hartshorne tell stories about meeting George Washington and Thomas Jefferson and about the early days of the republic and the American Revolution.

Although Whitman described him as small and rather fragile, Hartshorne lived to be eighty-four. Soon after Hartshorne died, Whitman wrote a tribute to him in the Brooklyn *Daily Eagle*. Hartshorne was described as a quiet,

H

kindly old man and was one of the most influential persons on Whitman's early years. Whitman said it was "impossible that he should ever have a biography—but he deserves one full as much as more eminent persons" (Whitman 246).

Brent L. Gibson

Bibliography

Allen, Gay Wilson. *The Solitary Singer: A Critical Biography of Walt Whitman.* 1955. Rev. ed. 1967. Chicago: U of Chicago P, 1985.

White, William. "A Tribute to William Hartshorne: Unrecorded Whitman." *American Literature* 42 (1971): 554–558.

Whitman, Walt. *The Uncollected Poetry and Prose of Walt Whitman.* Ed. Emory Holloway. Vol. 2. New York: Doubleday, Page, 1921.

See also BROOKLYN *DAILY EAGLE;* LONG ISLAND *PATRIOT;* PRINTING BUSINESS

"Hast Never Come to Thee an Hour" (1881)
"Hast Never Come to Thee an Hour" is one of the little, and little-known, poems written in the twilight time of Whitman's poetic career. The poem is located in the miscellaneous collection of poems called "By the Roadside," which Gay Wilson Allen describes as "merely samples of experiences and poetic inspirations along Whitman's highway of life" (150). "Hast Never," which is phrased in form of a question, speaks of a moment of inspiration, a "sudden gleam divine," which makes all of the "business aims" of life—"books, politics, art, amours"—like "bubbles" which, when burst, reveal that they consist of nothing that is really important. The pursuit of fame and fortune, Whitman is suggesting, at the twilight of his own career, results in "utter nothingness."

Ronald W. Knapp

Bibliography

Allen, Gay Wilson. *The New Walt Whitman Handbook.* 1975. New York: New York UP, 1986.

See also "BY THE ROADSIDE"

Health
There is a distinct contrast between Whitman's idealized notions of the human body as expressed in his literary work and the actual state of his health as it evolved over the course of his life. The many revisions of *Leaves of Grass* did not so much parallel his decline in health as reinforce his original conception of the natural human being as the divine reflection of the cosmos. Over time this idea as an essential theme of his work began to take precedence over others, serving as both his conception of America's unique characteristic as a people and the archetype of his own self-created myth for the model of healthy masculinity.

Whitman attributed his heartiness to his Dutch and English ancestry, particularly that of his mother's side. Although he attributed the collapse of his health to prolonged exposure to viruses and diseases while nursing dying soldiers during the Civil War, his inherent physical capacity to rebound from strokes was remarked upon with wonder by most of his friends and doctors. This capacity only added to his self-created myth as representative of the innate physical integrity and health of the American type. Late in life he was to admit that his family showed a marked tendency to paralysis, and the history of his bouts with illness and strokes that left him a semi-invalid for the remaining second half of his life tends to bear this out.

The first signs of serious health problems began during the war, when he started suffering extended periods characterized by sore throats, unexpected weight gain, bouts of dizziness, and at one point a loss of hearing. All of these were indications of hypertension and emotional stress brought on by his work in the hospitals. As time went on he complained of periods of increasing faintness, headaches, fatigue, and sore throats. In June 1864 he returned home to Brooklyn to recover his health and remained housebound a full month before eventually regaining his strength.

In the late 1860s Whitman's health began to sink again with a return of the same symptoms, including depression and head pains; in addition, he began to break out in sudden sweats diagnosed by doctors as symptoms of "hospital malaria" and "hospital poison" they believed had been absorbed into his system during the war. He recovered again, but in January 1873 suffered his first major stroke, which left him paralyzed. Some scholars have suggested the primary cause was a troubling emotional incident occurring in 1870 that sapped his energy, although the event has never been uncovered.

Whitman agreed to electric-battery shock therapy to try to bring about some recovery to his limbs, but there was little success. Only after a number of weeks was he able to sit upright. Although emotionally set back by the death of his mother during his convalescence, his health improved again, even though his left leg remained lame. By 1885 he found it increasingly difficult to walk, and three years later suffered a second paralytic stroke, which left him a semi-invalid needing regular care for the rest of his life. In spite of his debilitating maladies Whitman continued to maintain a belief in the healing power of nature and regularly asserted its primary significance as the crux of his philosophy.

Throughout his life Whitman was keenly aware of many types of unorthodox medical analyses and treatments, which ranged from homeopathy and hydropathy to phrenology, a science that claimed a connection between the shape of the skull and the innate characteristics of the individual. Whitman had visited the offices of the phrenologists Fowler and Wells in New York City many times, and it was they who distributed the first edition of *Leaves of Grass* as well as published the first review of the book; thus, his interest in all aspects related to the health of the individual clearly permeated his perception of the human experience.

Not completely sympathetic to the standard medical approaches of his day, Whitman felt that physicians were too quick to circumvent the natural healing processes of the body in favor of applying various emetics. He believed in a more holistic approach to health, advocating fresh air, exercise, and the full emotional and physical development of the self. He was considered by his medical friends to have a better-than-average knowledge of physiology and medicine, gained primarily by extensive reading of popular medical journals of the time, observation of doctors, and hospital experience during the war. In later years he admitted that had he been seeking a profession it would have been in the medical field as a doctor.

As a consequence, the health-imbued persona of mythic proportions he projected in his work fused with new and various aspects of his self-created image as healer in each newly revised edition of the work. Harold Aspiz believes the first three editions of *Leaves of Grass* illustrate a merger of what he terms the "fact and invention" of Whitman's self-portrayal as the self-endowed symbol of his own magnificent body. His image as "one of the roughs" in the first edition transforms in the second into a magnetic "folk-evangelist," in the third into a "reincarnated Adam" ready to bear healthy children, and in the fourth into the "healer-camerado." With each new edition, the body of the poet is used less and less as a metaphor for the physical vitality that was integral to his philosophy.

In addition, Aspiz shows that the editions after the Civil War reflect Whitman's marked attempt to gain a greater spiritual insight from his past. *Democratic Vistas*—his last major prose work—continued to emphasize the significance of a sound body as the basis for all virtues of the individual and the nation as a whole. His final essays derive little significance from the earlier image of himself as the physical example of the healthy American type, often taking on what Aspiz terms a "wistful" longing for his past health as he declined into old age.

Thomas Sanfilip

Bibliography

Allen, Gay Wilson. *The Solitary Singer: A Critical Biography of Walt Whitman.* 1955. Rev. ed. 1967. Chicago: U of Chicago P, 1985.

Aspiz, Harold. *Walt Whitman and the Body Beautiful.* Urbana: U of Illinois P, 1980.

Knapp, Bettina L. *Walt Whitman.* New York: Continuum, 1993.

Leon, Philip W. *Walt Whitman and Sir William Osler: A Poet and His Physician.* Toronto: ECW, 1995.

Traubel, Horace. *With Walt Whitman in Camden.* Vol. 2. New York: Appleton, 1908.

See also AGE AND AGING; CIVIL WAR NURSING; HUMAN BODY; PHRENOLOGY; PSEUDOSCIENCE

H

Hegel, Georg Wilhelm Friedrich (1770–1831)

Aside from some brief allusions scattered elsewhere, Whitman's references to Hegel are to be found in two prose pieces: "Carlyle from American Points of View," an entry in *Specimen Days & Collect* (1882), and "Sunday Evening Lectures," a manuscript fragment written probably around 1870. It is unclear whether Whitman ever read Hegel, even in translation, but textual evidence shows that Whitman borrowed from two texts containing summations of (as well as selections from) Hegel's philosophy—F.H. Hedge's *The Prose Writers of Germany* (1847) and Joseph Gostwick's *German Literature* (1854).

However superficial Whitman's understanding of Hegel was, the force of his interpretation of Hegel may be indicated by his statement in the "Lectures" that "Only Hegel is fit for America—is large enough and free enough" (*Notebooks* 6:2011). Hegel fits America because in Hegelian thinking the "varieties, contradictions and paradoxes of the world and of life . . . become a series of infinite radiations and waves of the one sealike universe of divine action and progress" (6:2011). In Hegel, the "contrarieties of material with spiritual, and of natural and artificial" appear as "radiations of one consistent and eternal purpose" (*Prose Works* 1:259). Under this Hegelian dialectical synthesis, even democratic contrarieties such as individual self and "en-masse," equality and singularity, are but polar terms in "the endless process of Creative thought" (1:259). America is a process and a progress, and so the only philosophy adequate to it is one that makes contradiction and the terms contradicted an essential part of life. Hegel has an all-inclusive vision, one casting anything excluded *and* the event of its exclusion as necessary to the development of Spirit, which for Whitman is equivalent to the progress of democracy. Hegel offers Whitman a system whereby "[o]ut of the dimness opposite equals advance," where there is "[a]lways a knit of identity," where Whitman can "find one side a balance and the antipodal side a balance" ("Song of Myself," sections 3, 22). In other words, Hegel's "catholic standard and faith" (*Prose Works* 1:259) Whitman interprets as a metaphysical analogue of his poetics of unity.

Mark Bauerlein

Bibliography

Fulghum, W.B., Jr. "Whitman's Debt to Joseph Gostwick." *American Literature* 12 (1941): 491–496.

Gostwick, Joseph. *German Literature.* Philadelphia: Lippincott, Grambo, 1854.

Hedge, Frederick Henry. *The Prose Writers of Germany.* Philadelphia: Carey and Hart, 1847.

Mary Eleanor, Sister. "Hedge's *Prose Writers of Germany* as a Source of Whitman's Knowledge of German Philosophy." *Modern Language Notes* 61 (1946): 381–388.

Whitman, Walt. *Leaves of Grass: Comprehensive Reader's Edition.* Ed. Harold W. Blodgett and Sculley Bradley. New York: New York UP, 1965.

———. *Notebooks and Unpublished Prose Manuscripts.* Ed. Edward F. Grier. 6 vols. New York: New York UP, 1984.

———. *Prose Works, 1892.* Ed. Floyd Stovall. 2 vols. New York: New York UP, 1963–1964.

See also CONTRADICTION; EVOLUTION

Heine, Heinrich (1797–1856)

Whitman considered Heinrich Heine one of the most significant writers of his time; he was the only German author Whitman discussed in great detail. He was aware of Heine as early as 1856 when he noted Heine's death and Charles Leland's translation of Heine's *Reisebilder* (1855). As late as 1888, he claimed that his admiration for Heine was "a constantly growing one" (*With Walt Whitman* 2:560).

Whitman seems to have been more interested in Heine's persona, as it emerges in his writings, than in his revolutionary politics. He identified with Heine's unconventional "improprieties" (*With Walt Whitman* 2:553) (presumably his liberal attitude toward sexuality) and the absence of bookishness in his works: "always warm, pulsing—his style pure, lofty, sweeping in its wild strength" (2:554).

Whitman's reading of Heine was guided by English-language criticism, especially by Matthew Arnold's essay on Heine (1863), which he mentions repeatedly as "the best thing Arnold ever did" and "the one thing of Arnold's that I unqualifiedly like" (*With Walt Whitman* 1:106). Arnold's essay stresses Heine's importance as a libertarian poet and designates him as the most important German successor of Goethe, thereby displacing the more politically conservative romantics who are normally considered to be in the mainstream tradition of German literature.

Whitman's emphasis on Heine's irony is his most perceptive critical judgment. He believed the ironical undercutting of the conventions of popular German romanticism to be Heine's original lyrical property, "a superb fusion of culture and native elemental genius" (*With Walt Whitman* 2:562). His critique of writers who unsuccessfully attempted to emulate Heine's lyrical mode also seems to explain the lack of Heine-esque traces in Whitman's own work. Russel A. Berman has compared the two authors in their political radicalism (especially in contrast with their more conservative predecessors, Goethe and Emerson) and in their efforts to develop an innovative, democratic literature by fusing diverse elements into a "postauratic public voice" (220). Whereas these analogies are not genetically related, they do point to the revolutionary year of 1848, which is important to both writers' works.

Walter Grünzweig

Bibliography

Berman, Russel A. "Poetry for the Republic: Heine and Whitman." *Heinrich Heine and the Occident: Multiple Identities, Multiple Receptions.* Ed. Peter Uwe Hohendahl and Sander L. Gilman. Lincoln: U of Nebraska P, 1991. 199–223.

Pochmann, Henry A. *German Culture in America: Philosophical and Literary Influences, 1600–1900.* 1957. Madison: U of Wisconsin P, 1961.

Traubel, Horace. *With Walt Whitman in Camden.* Vol. 1. Boston: Small, Maynard, 1906; Vol. 2. New York: Appleton, 1908.

See also LELAND, CHARLES GODFREY; REVOLUTIONS OF 1848

Herder, Johann Gottfried von (1744–1803)

Johann Gottfried Herder's name is conspicuously absent from Whitman's records. The sole significant reference appears in the conclusion of "A Backward Glance O'er Travel'd Roads" (1888): "what Herder taught to the young Goethe, that really great poetry is always (like the Homeric or Biblical canticles) the result of a national spirit, and not the privilege of a polish'd and select few" (Whitman 672). The widely held assumption that Whitman was closely familiar with Herder's writings is highly questionable.

Nevertheless, Herder was very much present in Whitman's culture. His scholarly, philosophical, and theological writings were widely available in translation, and American students studying at Göttingen brought Herderian thought into American scholarship. The foremost American exponent of Herder's conceptions of nation and national culture was George Bancroft, who applied them to the American search for identity and nationhood. Thus, Whitman may well have become acquainted with Herder by tapping mainstream American sources.

Whitman's reference accurately reflects Herder's double origin in the enlightenment and in a proto-romantic nationalism. Whereas Herder's writings are frequently critiqued as providing the philosophical basis for (German) nationalism, Whitman emphasizes the democratic quality of Herder's "national spirit," and his own attempts to write "songs" that appeal to the masses and are based on popular tradition can be considered in that tradition.

Walter Grünzweig

Bibliography

Bluestein, Gene. "The Advantages of Barbarism: Herder and Whitman's Nationalism." *Journal of the History of Ideas* 24.1 (1963): 115–126.

Mueller-Vollmer, Kurt. "Herder and the Formation of an American National Consciousness during the Early Republic." *Herder Today: Contributions from the International Herder Conference. Nov. 5–8, 1987, Stanford, California.* Ed. Mueller-Vollmer. New York: Gruyter, 1990. 415–430.

Pochmann, Henry A. *German Culture in America: Philosophical and Literary Influences, 1600–1900.* 1957. Madison: U of Wisconsin P, 1961.

Whitman, Walt. *Complete Poetry and Collected Prose.* Ed. Justin Kaplan. New York: Library of America, 1982.

See also GOETHE, JOHANN WOLFGANG VON

"Here the Frailest Leaves of Me" (1860)

"Here the Frailest Leaves of Me" was first published in the 1860 edition of *Leaves of Grass.* It was the forty-fourth of forty-five numbered poems in the "Calamus" cluster. When it was first published, it began with the line "Here my last words, and the most baffling." This line was dropped in 1871, and the poem remained that way in later editions.

Whitman commonly referred to his poems as leaves, and so in this poem, these leaves are his "Calamus" poems. They are his "frailest . . . and yet my strongest lasting." The "Calamus" poems were an exercise in self-definition, according to Robert K. Martin, and they were open expressions of Whitman's love for other men. Such expressions were dangerous in Whitman's day. These poems were vulnerable, as they could be attacked by hostile readers. As Alan Helms notes, "Frailest" reflected Whitman's cautiousness due to his fear of exposure. These poems were strong, however, because they were the honest songs of a bold and confident singer. For over one hundred years, these poems have survived as positive examples of homosexual desire.

Whitman admits in this poem, "I shade and hide my thoughts . . . yet they expose me." While Whitman does not reveal his secret in this poem, he does reveal the existence of a secret. By saying that he is hiding something, he is asking the reader to look for it. This search, therefore, is not intrusive but is welcomed by the poet.

Conrad M. Sienkiewicz

Bibliography

Cady, Joseph. "Not Happy in the Capitol: Homosexuality and the 'Calamus' Poems." *American Studies* 19.2 (1978): 5–22.

Helms, Alan. "'Hints . . . Faint Clews and Indirections': Whitman's Homosexual Disguises." *Walt Whitman: Here and Now.* Ed. Joann P. Krieg. Westport, Conn.: Greenwood, 1985. 61–67.

Killingsworth, M. Jimmie. "Sentimentality and Homosexuality in Whitman's 'Calamus.'" *ESQ* 29 (1983): 144–153.

Martin, Robert K. *The Homosexual Tradition in American Poetry.* Austin: U of Texas P, 1979.

Whitman, Walt. *Leaves of Grass: Comprehensive Reader's Edition.* Ed. Harold W. Blodgett and Sculley Bradley. New York: New York UP, 1965.

See also "Calamus"; Comradeship; Sex and Sexuality

Heroes and Heroines

A search for men and women Whitman saw in a heroic light yields fewer names than might be expected. Whitman admired many, with characteristic generosity of spirit, whether obscure or well known. But the usual idea of the heroic must be altered to accommodate his lifelong vision of humanity.

Historically the heroic has suggested behavior beyond the capacity of ordinary men and women. The classical hero was expected to accomplish superhuman feats for a far-reaching public cause and to be held in reverence by the public. Whitman did participate in some such hero worship common in the nineteenth century. He wrote poems about Christopher Columbus, Ulysses S. Grant, George Washington, Abraham Lincoln, certain opera singers. Yet he also wrote about more humble, obscure people such as the ox-tamer. These were the sorts of men and women whose fragmentary biographies are scattered liberally throughout *Leaves of Grass* in a treatment far from heroic. Even the public figures were treated in a way to stress their modest human traits.

Of the two genders, it was women that Whitman idealized and championed all his life. Women's maternal side commanded much of his attention, although not all. Frances Wright, the Scottish reformer, whose lectures stirred up stormy controversy, greatly appealed to him as a young man. But the root of his admiration for women, which could be seen as a kind of hero worship, was his mother. (For a negative view of his mother's influence, see Edwin Haviland Miller's work.) His father, apparently a dour and taciturn man, left little evident impression on Whitman. In his later years the traits of his mother that he singled out were the simplicity, reality, and "transparency" of her life. She "excelled in narrative," had great mimetic power, was "eloquent in the utterance of noble moral axioms" as well as being "very original in her manner, her style." Moreover, Whitman credited her with an enormous influence on his poetry: "Leaves of Grass is the flower of her temperament active in me" (*With Walt Whitman* 2:113–114). How close to the truth such a statement lies is impossible to say; there is probably a mixture of the nineteenth-century tendency to place women on a pedestal and the natural gratitude of a son for all the nurturing of an attentive mother. In any case Whitman's interest in women was less in their heroic aspect than in their nature as a largely untapped force (see *Democratic Vistas*). He went so far as to call *Leaves of Grass* "essentially a woman's book: the women do not know it, but every now and then a woman shows that she knows it: it speaks out the necessities, its cry is the cry of the right and wrong of the woman sex—of the woman first of all, of the facts of creation first of all—of the feminine: speaks out loud: warns, encourages, persuades, points the way" (*With Walt Whitman* 2:331).

Of the men that Whitman admired, heroes were few, common representatives many. One of the few public figures Whitman praised over a long period was Ralph Waldo Emerson: "I believe Emerson was greater by far than his books" (*With Walt Whitman* 6:23). He took the same approach to Abraham Lincoln, whom he never actually met, but on the Washington streets the two exchanged "bows, and very cordial ones" (*Prose Works* 1:60). When the time came to memorialize Lincoln, Whitman chose images, symbols, and figures that brought him down to a human level. "When Lilacs Last in the Dooryard Bloom'd" softened what might have been a heroic image. It scarcely mentions Lincoln at all till the end, when the poet refers to him as "the sweetest, wisest soul of all my days and lands" (section 16). It is unlikely that a conventional hero would expect to be called "sweet."

"Song of Myself" roams freely among Americans, their occupations, activities, relations, natures. No particular individual is lingered upon as heroic. Whitman had found a way of celebrating the human spirit differently: through his own persona, linking it to the reader's—"And what I assume you shall assume" (section 1). The attentive reader of "Song of Myself" can end the 52 sections as the poet's companion. Any need for the heroic will have been transformed into something more important to Whitman: the stimulation and enrichment of the reader's soul.

Whitman's dream of brotherhood and sisterhood was everywhere in *Leaves of Grass,* not least in the "Children of Adam" and "Calamus" sections. His own sexual orientation mattered little. He would celebrate the physical and erotic attributes of men and women with candor. Poet and reader are together imaginatively in a central human experience; the exceptional becomes the common, the universal.

The Civil War poems, "Drum-Taps," extend Whitman's effort to bond with the reader. Now the soldiers become, as it were, the readers, as Whitman is able in fact to reach out and touch those his emotional needs yearn for. His three years nursing in the Washington hospitals were surely heroic in humanitarian terms. It derived from the same impulse that created the war poems, which sought to ennoble the men of the conflict not in terms of heroics but of courage, loyalty, endurance, and suffering.

Though not a Christian, Whitman understood the example of Christ's suffering, as seen in "A Sight in Camp in the Daybreak Gray and Dim." In "To Him That was Crucified," he links himself completely to Christ in their common purpose: "till we saturate time and eras, that the men and women of races, ages to come, may prove brethren and lovers as we are." Whitman's vision for humanity was much closer to the Christian than to any classical or romantic view of the heroic.

If there is any thread running through Whitman's work, beyond that aura of freedom saturating it, it is that of the essentially equal worth and potential of all men and women. The search for heroes and heroines ends with any responding reader.

David B. Baldwin

Bibliography
Kummings, Donald D. "The Vernacular Hero in Whitman's 'Song of Myself.'" *Walt Whitman Review* 23 (1977): 23–34.
Miller, Edwin Haviland. *Walt Whitman's Poetry: A Psychological Journey.* New York: New York UP, 1969.
Traubel, Horace. *With Walt Whitman in Camden.* Vol. 2. New York: Appleton, 1908; Vol. 6. Ed. Gertrude Traubel and William White. Carbondale: Southern Illinois UP, 1982.
Whitman, Walt. *Leaves of Grass: Comprehensive Reader's Edition.* Ed. Harold W. Blodgett and Sculley Bradley. New York: New York UP, 1965.
———. *Prose Works 1892.* Ed. Floyd Stovall. 2 vols. New York: New York UP, 1963–1964.

See also COLUMBUS, CHRISTOPHER; EMERSON, RALPH WALDO; EPIC STRUCTURE; EQUALITY; LINCOLN, ABRAHAM; WASHINGTON, GEORGE; WHITMAN, LOUISA VAN VELSOR; WOMEN AS A THEME IN WHITMAN'S WRITING

Heyde, Charles Louis (1822–1892)
Charles L. Heyde, a French-born landscape painter, married Whitman's sister Hannah in 1852. He achieved local notoriety in Vermont as

a poet as well as a landscape painter. Late in her life, Hannah recalled having eloped with Heyde some thirteen years before their marriage. They lived in several Vermont communities before purchasing a house and settling in Burlington in 1865. By all accounts, their life together was stormy, and there are numerous references in the Whitman correspondence to the tensions that existed not only between Heyde and Hannah, but also between Heyde and every other member of the family. Even Walt disliked him, referring to him as "worse than bed bugs" (Whitman 135). The feeling was mutual, as evidenced by later reports that, when Whitman visited Hannah in Burlington in 1872 (when he was selected to deliver a commencement poem at Dartmouth), Heyde moved temporarily to his studio to avoid staying in the same house with him. Though relations thawed slightly toward the end of Whitman's life, Heyde was always more of an aggravation than an inspiration. Referring to Hannah as his "favorite sister" (qtd. in Molinoff 24), Whitman felt the pain of her unhappy relationship with particular intensity. It is likely that he also felt some responsibility for having introduced Heyde to Hannah in the first place, and his correspondence with his mother reflects an added dimension of concern due to the strain Hannah's unhappy marriage put on her. Heyde became increasingly delusional and despondent in his later years and was committed to the Vermont State Hospital at Waterbury in October 1892, one month before his death.

Steven Schroeder

Bibliography

Molinoff, Katherine. *Some Notes on Whitman's Family.* Brooklyn: Comet, 1941.
Whitman, Walt. *The Correspondence.* Ed. Edwin Haviland Miller. Vol. 1. New York: New York UP, 1961.

See also WHITMAN (HEYDE), HANNAH LOUISA

Heywood, Ezra H. (1829–1893)

Ezra Heywood, a radical proponent and propagandist for social and economic reform, became embroiled in a legal controversy surrounding the 1881 publication of *Leaves of Grass.* Though Heywood supported Whitman's cause, the poet met his assistance with ambivalence.

Early in 1882 the Boston district attorney, under pressure from Anthony Comstock, advised Whitman's publishers to suspend publication of *Leaves of Grass* on the grounds that it violated a federal antiobscenity law. Outraged by this attack on Whitman's poetry and the encroachment upon freedom of expression in general, Heywood openly defied legal authority by distributing through the mail two of the objectionable poems, "To a Common Prostitute" and "A Woman Waits for Me." The events surrounding Heywood's subsequent arrest and trial were viewed by Whitman with great interest and some reservation. He was eager to see his poetry stripped of its label as "obscene" literature, but was apprehensive about being associated with Heywood's radical free-love beliefs. Whitman remarked that upon a rare meeting with Heywood, "I treat him politely but that is all" (Whitman 157).

Ultimately, the judge presiding over Heywood's trial dismissed as evidence Whitman's poems and acquitted Heywood of all charges. As a result of Heywood's trial, the stigma of obscenity receded from public perception of Whitman's poetry.

Joseph P. Hammond

Bibliography

Blatt, Martin H. *Free Love and Anarchism: The Biography of Ezra Heywood.* Urbana: U of Illinois P, 1989.
Whitman, Walt. *The Correspondence.* Ed. Edwin Haviland Miller. Vol. 4. New York: New York UP, 1969.

See also COMSTOCK, ANTHONY; LEAVES OF GRASS, 1881–1882 EDITION; SOCIETY FOR THE SUPPRESSION OF VICE; STEVENS, OLIVER; "TO A COMMON PROSTITUTE"; "WOMAN WAITS FOR ME, A"

Hicks, Elias (1748–1830)

Elias Hicks was a popular and influential liberal Quaker minister. His followers became known as Hicksites during the 1827–1829 separation of Quakers into liberal and orthodox branches. Hicks explained his religious views and recorded his experiences as a minister in his *Journal* (1832).

Hicks, son of John and Martha Smith Hicks, was born in Hempstead, Long Island, New York. He educated himself by reading the Bible, Quaker journals and histories, and borrowed books, having received little formal education as a child. In 1771, Hicks married Jemima Seaman; soon thereafter, they made their permanent home in Jericho, Long Island.

From 1779 through 1829, the Quaker minister journeyed more than forty thousand miles to locations primarily in the Northeast; but he also made trips to Virginia (1797, 1801, 1819, 1828), to the northern shore of Lake Ontario, Canada (1803, 1810), and to Richmond, Indiana (1828). Hicks spoke outdoors and in meeting houses, barns, schools, homes, and taverns to overflowing crowds of Quakers and non-Quakers. He preached that people could experience salvation without the aid of ordained clergy. God dwells within every person, he explained, and reveals truths to each one by means of the Inner Light. Employing their free will, people could choose salvation by submitting to the will of God revealed to them, or they could choose sin by rejecting God's will to follow their "independent will" (Hicks 336).

Whitman believed in the Inner Light. In 1890, he told Horace Traubel, who recorded Whitman's conversations from 1888 until the poet's death, that he subscribed to Hicks's views of spirituality. Neither Whitman nor his parents were Quaker. However, Whitman's mother, Louisa Van Velsor Whitman, had often spoken to him about Hicks, and Whitman's father, Walter Whitman, admired Hicks. Moreover, Whitman's paternal grandfather, Jesse Whitman, and Hicks had been friendly as youths, and his maternal grandmother, Naomi Williams Van Velsor, had been born into a Quaker family and followed Quaker traditions. In November 1829, Whitman, at his father's invitation, went with his parents to Morrison's Hotel Ballroom in Brooklyn, where they heard Hicks speak about the Inner Light. Whitman was so impressed with Hicks's ideas and speaking ability that for decades he vowed to write about Hicks. He finally fulfilled this commitment with the publication of his *November Boughs* essay "Elias Hicks" (1888); he used Hicks's *Journal* as one source for the essay.

Christina Davey

Bibliography

Allen, Gay Wilson. *The Solitary Singer: A Critical Biography of Walt Whitman.* 1955. Rev. ed. 1967. Chicago: U of Chicago P, 1985.

Forbush, Bliss. *Elias Hicks: Quaker Liberal.* New York: Columbia UP, 1956.

Hicks, Elias. *Journal of the Life and Religious Labours of Elias Hicks. Written by Himself.* 1832. 5th ed. New York: Arno, 1969.

Templin, Lawrence. "The Quaker Influence on Walt Whitman." *American Literature* 42 (1970): 165–180.

Traubel, Horace. *With Walt Whitman in Camden.* Vol. 7. Ed. Jeanne Chapman and Robert MacIsaac. Carbondale: Southern Illinois UP, 1992.

Whitman, Walt. "Elias Hicks." *Prose Works 1892.* Ed. Floyd Stovall. Vol. 2. New York: New York UP, 1964. 626–653.

See also QUAKERS AND QUAKERISM; RELIGION; VAN VELSOR, NAOMI ("AMY") WILLIAMS

Higginson, Thomas Wentworth (1823–1911)

Thomas Wentworth Higginson was an unremitting critic of Whitman and *Leaves of Grass,* which he first read when he was on an ocean voyage—he attributed his seasickness to the poem. He wrote unfavorable reviews of every subsequent edition of the book.

Higginson is best known in American literary history for his relationship with Emily Dickinson and his editing of the only poems she published in her lifetime.

An antislavery reformer, advocate of women's rights, and radical Unitarian, Higginson was a Boston Brahmin who did not appreciate the merit of Whitman's book. A colonel in the Civil War commanding a South Carolina black regiment, Higginson later wrote extensively of the Harvard graduates who gave their lives in the war. He was critical of Whitman for not joining the Union Army while encouraging others to do so.

When, in 1886, a private relief bill was introduced in the Congress to give Whitman a twenty-five-dollar a month pension for his work nursing the wounded, Higginson opposed it and the matter was dropped. A physical culturist, Higginson also wrote of Whitman's depraved living as a reason for his failing health. Higginson's attitude was representative of Boston literary opinion on the undisciplined character of *Leaves of Grass.* The week after Whitman's funeral Higginson published anonymously in *The Nation* (7 April 1892) all of his old criticism of the poet as a depraved malingerer and author of a book Whitman should have burned.

W. Edward Harris

Bibliography

Barrus, Clara. *Whitman and Burroughs, Comrades.* Boston: Houghton Mifflin, 1931.

Burroughs, John. "Walt Whitman and His Recent Critics." *In Re Walt Whitman.* Ed Horace L. Traubel, Richard M. Bucke, and Thomas B. Harned. Philadelphia: McKay, 1893.

Erkkila, Betsy. *Whitman the Political Poet.* New York: Oxford UP, 1989.

Higginson, Thomas Wentworth. *Army Life in a Black Regiment.* 1869. East Lansing: Michigan State UP, 1960.

———. *Cheerful Yesterdays.* 1898. New York: Arno, 1968.

See also BOSTON, MASSACHUSETTS; DICKINSON, EMILY

Hindu Literature

There are numerous allusions to Hindu books, authors, and ideas scattered through Whitman's poems, prose writings, notebooks, and scrapbooks that indicate his general interest in India, its history and culture. Evidently Whitman shared the fascination of his century for India's mystical wisdom and sang of it in rapturous tones in "Passage to India." He wrote a brief explanatory comment on Emerson's "Brahma" in the Brooklyn *Daily Times* of 1857, which indicates his familiarity with the Hindu philosophical concept of Brahman or universal soul. But in none of these does Whitman exhibit more than a superficial acquaintance with Hindu philosophy, whereas his comments on the German thinkers—Immanuel Kant, Friedrich Schelling, and especially Georg Wilhelm Friedrich Hegel, in whom he evinced keen interest—are in comparison more extensive and reveal a more precise and detailed understanding of their key concepts.

While it appears that Whitman possessed some knowledge, direct or indirect, of Hindu philosophical literature, the extent of his indebtedness to that source is difficult to assess. We also do not know for certain when his interest in India began. Some of his early notebook entries suggest possible Hindu influence. What is puzzling is his denial to Thoreau in 1856 that he had read the Orientals and his later admission in "A Backward Glance O'er Travel'd Roads" (1888) of his having read "the ancient Hindoo poems" (meaning perhaps the epics *Ramayana* and *Mahabharata,* about which he had some knowledge) in preparation for *Leaves of Grass* (Whitman 569). In *The Roots of Whitman's Grass,* T.R. Rajasekharaiah examines a vast body of Indian philosophical literature—including periodical material, from some of which Whitman took clippings—that was in circulation during the period of the gestation of *Leaves of Grass* (1840s to 1855) and decides, on the strength of close parallels in thought and phrase, that Whitman owed more to these sources than he was willing to admit. Rajasekharaiah's study establishes a high probability that Whitman could not have escaped some, at least second-hand, knowledge of Hindu philosophy even before 1855, and that his affinities to it are perhaps more than merely accidental. Whitman mentions the Vedas by name, but no mention occurs of the *Bhagavad-Gita,* the most influential of the Hindu sacred books. He did own a copy of it, however, given to him by a friend in 1875. But he could have picked up a medley of Indian religious-philosophical ideas, including those of the Gita and the Upanishads, from scholarly expositions, from reviews in the *Dial* and other magazines, and above all from the writings of Ralph Waldo Emerson and Henry David Thoreau.

Some of the fundamental tenets of Whitman's poetic faith are no doubt strikingly similar to Hindu ideas, but one should be cautious in claiming for them exclusive resemblances, for they can be traced to many different sources, Eastern and Western. Such, for instance, are the ideas of soul, immortality, God, divine immanence, and so on. However, some discriminations are possible between the Indian and Western conceptions, both in regard to their underlying premises and thought structures and the experiential modes in which they are realized and expressed. Thus Whitman's conception of the soul and the egocentric perspective that dictates his ecstatic "Songs" are consistent with German and romantic idealistic philosophy. But in its structure and its mode of expression Whitman's soul is closer to the Vedantic Self in that it does not take the romantic route of humanizing/subjectivizing nature (pathetic fallacy), nor the German dialectical route of cultivating the opposition between the "I" and nature, but operates by the method of ego-magnification and by annulling the opposites through incorporation or identification. The God-like self portrayed in "Song of Myself" bears a close resemblance to the cosmic person of the Gita and the Self of the Upanishads both in form and spirit, although certain features of that vision—the unitive consciousness, the heightened perception of the phenomenal world, and above all the element of ecstasy—are also common to other expressions of mystical consciousness, including the theocentric type.

On the question of God, Hindu philosophy (especially the Gita) provides for both theistic and nontheistic approaches, and for both an immanent and a transcendent God. Whitman's early poetry is predominantly ego-centered rather than God-centered, equating the self with God and making it, rather than an immanent or pantheistic deity, the pervasive presence. This emphasis fits better into the Vedantic system of thought than into the Judeo-Christian or theistic Hindu molds. In his later poetry, Whitman addresses a deistic/pantheistic God (e.g., "Passage to India," "Prayer of Columbus"), whose description may recall the Brahman of the Upanishads or the Lord in the Gita. But it may equally be traced to Western sources, even though in "Passage" Whitman sees India as a generic symbol of man's spiritual quest.

A belief in the immortality of the soul is shared by many traditions, and Whitman could have found confirmation for that idea in more than one place. His conviction of a mystical identity or immaterial essence, however, "the Me myself" ("Song of Myself," section 4) beneath the phenomenal layers of consciousness, standing aloof like a spectator or detached participant in world action, belongs typically to the Vedanta and Samkhya systems expounded in the Gita, although it is not uncommon in other varieties of religious experience. Whitman's manner of presenting this experience—its declamatory flow and its paradoxical structure—is especially like the mystical effusions of the Upanishads and the Gita.

Similarly, on the question of the relative status of the spiritual and the real world, Whitman approximates the Vedantic position that the spirit or self alone is ultimately real and that the objective universe is only relatively (empirically) real and in that sense an illusion or maya—a thought that Whitman expresses in many places (see "Eidólons," Democratic Vistas). Whitman's adoration of life in all its forms presupposes a thought that is akin to the declaration of the Upanishads that all things are "honey for the self" because they are animated by the Self and are held dear to it. His celebration of sex may also be related to the Tantric worship of the human body as a conduit for divine energy.

The question of Whitman's actual borrowings from Hindu sources will perhaps never be settled. But these and other similarities in thought provide a legitimate ground for comparison. In addition, the Hindu philosophical models can serve as useful critical instruments: they can clarify and illuminate Whitman's meanings.

V.K. Chari

Bibliography

Allen, Gay Wilson. *The New Walt Whitman Handbook*. 1975. New York: New York UP, 1986.

Chari, V.K. *Whitman in the Light of Vedantic Mysticism*. Lincoln: U of Nebraska P, 1964.

Mercer, Dorothy F. Articles on Whitman and the Gita. *Vedanta and the West* 9 (1946) to 12 (1949).

Rajasekharaiah, T.R. *The Roots of Whitman's Grass*. Rutherford, N.J.: Fairleigh Dickinson UP, 1970.

Stovall, Floyd. *The Foreground of "Leaves of Grass."* Charlottesville: UP of Virginia, 1974.

Whitman, Walt. *Leaves of Grass: Comprehensive Reader's Edition*. Ed. Harold W. Blodgett and Sculley Bradley. New York: New York UP, 1965.

See also IMMORTALITY; MYSTICISM; REINCARNATION; RELIGION

Holloway, Emory (1885–1977)

Rufus Emory Holloway established himself as a Whitman scholar in 1921 when he published *The Uncollected Poetry and Prose of Walt Whitman*. His work on Whitman continued with the publication of *Whitman: An Interpretation in Narrative* in 1926, for which he won the Pulitzer Prize. This book established the importance of Whitman's journalism and prose to the emergence of *Leaves of Grass*. Holloway's biography was also stylistically innovative. It is characterized by a disjointed chronological structure, extended digressions into cultural history, and psychological analysis. Admitting that he was influenced by modernist narrative techniques, Holloway explained his style by asserting that "I have abbreviated the narrative by picking it up only where it has character, and where the abundance of records makes it possible, without invention, to tell an imaginative story" (*Interpretation* xi).

The strength of his Whitman scholarship earned Holloway a position on the faculty of

Queens College in New York City but he was also repeatedly compelled to justify his understanding of Whitman's homosexuality. In *Free and Lonesome Heart* (1960) Holloway argues that Whitman was bisexual and concludes that Whitman strove to imagine an androgynous position from which to live and write. Subsequent Whitman biographers such as Gay Wilson Allen, Justin Kaplan, and David S. Reynolds largely bypass Holloway's work, but by emphasizing the importance of Whitman's early career in journalism, they have also incorporated Holloway's research into the bedrock of Whitman scholarship.

T. Gregory Garvey

Bibliography

Holloway, Emory. *Whitman: An Interpretation in Narrative.* New York: Knopf, 1926.

———. *Free and Lonesome Heart: The Secret of Walt Whitman.* New York: Vantage, 1960.

Reynolds, David S. *Walt Whitman's America: A Cultural Biography.* New York: Knopf, 1995.

See also BIOGRAPHY; SCHOLARSHIP, TRENDS IN WHITMAN

Holmes, Oliver Wendell (1809–1894)

A renowned member of the New England literary caste, Oliver Wendell Holmes—physician, poet, novelist, and essayist—was ambivalent in his attitude toward Walt Whitman and *Leaves of Grass.*

When Emerson wanted to bring Whitman to a Saturday Club gathering, Holmes claimed to have no interest in meeting the "Brooklyn poet" (Allen 238). And in 1877, when asked about *Leaves of Grass* by Edward Carpenter, Holmes alluded to the erotica of Whitman's verse, stating, "it won't do" (qtd. in Masters 229–230).

Ironically, many of the characters in Holmes's novels appear to be sexually stimulated, such as Euthymia in *A Mortal Antipathy* (1885). However, Holmes's erotic fiction is supposedly antiseptic, since characters exemplify patients' neuroses documented from case studies.

Holmes, like Whitman, celebrated the political freedom of the nineteenth-century American who challenged tradition. In "Mechanism in Thought and Morals" (1870), Holmes defines the "moral universe" as that which "includes nothing but the exercise of choice" (qtd. in Small 117).

In his later years, Holmes gained new insight into *Leaves.* In *Over the Teacups* (1891) he speaks with great integrity about the aged poet: "[N]o man has ever asserted the surpassing dignity and importance of the American Citizen so boldly and freely as Mr. Whitman" (234).

Julie A. Rechel-White

Bibliography

Allen, Gay Wilson. *The Solitary Singer: A Critical Biography of Walt Whitman.* 1955. Rev. ed. 1967. Chicago: U of Chicago P, 1985.

Baker, Liva. *The Justice from Beacon Hill: The Life and Times of Oliver Wendell Holmes.* New York: HarperCollins, 1991.

Holmes, Oliver Wendell. *Over the Teacups.* Boston: Houghton Mifflin, 1891.

Masters, Edgar Lee. *Whitman.* New York: Biblo and Tannen, 1968.

Small, Miriam Rossiter. *Oliver Wendell Holmes.* New York: Twayne, 1962.

See also BRYANT, WILLIAM CULLEN; LONGFELLOW, HENRY WADSWORTH; LOWELL, JAMES RUSSELL; WHITTIER, JOHN GREENLEAF

Homer

According to Whitman, his first encounter with Homer came when, as a teenager, he read Buckley's prose translation on a Long Island beach (*Prose Works* 2:723; Floyd Stovall fixes this date later, at or around 1857). Although he knew Homer only in translation, Whitman reputedly liked to read the bard aloud either at the beach or in the city. Thoreau recounts that Whitman would "ride up and down Broadway all day on an omnibus, sitting beside the driver . . . and declaiming Homer at the top of his voice" (340). In his prose writings and notebooks, Whitman frequently places Homer alongside Shakespeare and the Bible as the highest examples of poetic vision. Typically, Whitman cites Homer as the ideal to which all modern poets should aspire and even exceed: "I have eulogized Homer, the sacred bards of Jewry, Eschylus, Juvenal, Shakspere . . . [but] I say there must, for future and democratic purposes, appear poets, (dare I to say so?) of higher class even than any of those" (*Prose Works* 2:420–421). That is, modern poets should not only achieve the same visionary power that Homer and the other sacred bards did, but they also must surpass the ancient bards just as American democracy surpasses older European civilizations.

Andrew Ladd

Bibliography

Thoreau, Henry David. "The Correspondence of Henry David Thoreau." *Whitman in His Own Time.* Ed. Joel Myerson. Detroit: Omnigraphics, 1991. 340–342.

Whitman, Walt. *Notebooks and Unpublished Prose Manuscripts.* Ed. Edward F. Grier. 6 vols. New York: New York UP, 1984.

———. *Prose Works, 1892.* 2 vols. Ed. Floyd Stovall. New York: New York UP, 1963–1964.

See also BIBLE, THE; SHAKESPEARE, WILLIAM

Hopkins, Gerard Manley (1844–1889)

An innovative English poet who has had great influence on twentieth-century poetry, Gerard Manley Hopkins was born in Stratford, near London. In 1866, while studying at Oxford, he became a convert to Roman Catholicism, and two years later entered the Jesuit order. His "terrible sonnets," begun in 1885 while a professor of Greek at University College, Dublin, reflect his unhappy stay in Ireland and his disappointment with himself as a priest and as a poet.

Attempts to show that Hopkins's poetry was influenced by Walt Whitman have as their source this passage from a letter Hopkins wrote to his friend Robert Bridges in 1882: "But first I may as well say what I should not otherwise have said, that I always knew in my heart Walt Whitman's mind to be more like my own than any other man's living. As he is a very great scoundrel this is not a pleasant confession" (qtd. in Hazen 41).

Hopkins read George Saintsbury's review of *Leaves of Grass* in 1874, and remembered it so well that he referred to it accurately in a letter to Bridges some eight years later. Hopkins also recalled reading Whitman in Bridges's library when he stayed with him in the summer of 1877 or 1878. Reacting to Bridges's suggestion that "The Leaden Echo and the Golden Echo" resembled Whitman, Hopkins protested in 1882 that he had not read more than "half a dozen" Whitman poems, yet went on to admit

that that might be enough "to influence another's style" (qtd. in Hazen 45). James Hazen contends that the "wilder beast from West" in Hopkins's sonnet "Andromeda" (1879) is a direct reference to Whitman, and William Darby Templeman finds echoes of Whitman in Hopkins's rhythm, alliteration, and diction. Indeed, in a letter to Bridges in 1887, Hopkins, who had just reworked an old sonnet called "Harry Ploughman" in which he celebrated the male form, wondered "if there is anything like it in Walt Whitman" (qtd. in Hazen 47).

Richard Raleigh

Bibliography

Hazen, James. "Whitman and Hopkins." *American Transcendental Quarterly* 12 (1971): 41–48.

Mariani, Paul L. *A Commentary on the Complete Poems of Gerard Manley Hopkins.* Ithaca, N.Y.: Cornell UP, 1970.

Martin, Robert Bernard. *Gerard Manley Hopkins.* New York: Putnam, 1991.

Olney, James. *The Language(s) of Poetry: Walt Whitman, Emily Dickinson, Gerard Manley Hopkins.* Athens: U of Georgia P, 1993.

Simkin, Stephen J. "'Extremes Meet': Hopkins and Walt Whitman." *Forum for Modern Language Studies* 30 (1994): 1–17.

Templeman, William Darby. "Hopkins and Whitman: Evidence of Influence and Echoes." *Philological Quarterly* 33 (1954): 48–65.

See also BRITISH ISLES, WHITMAN IN THE

Hotten, John Camden (1832–1873)

John Camden Hotten was born John William Hotten in London, the son of a carpenter. He was apprenticed to a bookseller at age fourteen and showed an aptitude for the business. In 1848 he went to America, where he stayed until 1856. Upon his return, Hotten went into the bookselling and publishing business. One of his specialties was American authors, and he published editions of Ambrose Bierce, Bret Harte, Nathaniel Hawthorne, Oliver Wendell Holmes, James Russell Lowell, and Artemus Ward, and he tried unsuccessfully to collect an edition of Ralph Waldo Emerson's writings. Hotten was also accustomed to controversial authors: he took over as publisher of A.C. Swinburne's *Poems and Ballads* after the original publisher withdrew following charges of obscenity. His fellow booksellers held him in low regard because of his personality, his many piracies and spurious "editions," and his connection to what was then considered pornographic literature.

Hotten published two books by Whitman—a selection from and a complete edition of *Leaves of Grass*. In 1867 he engaged William Michael Rossetti to edit a selection of Whitman's writings for twenty-five pounds, and the resulting *Poems by Walt Whitman* was published the following year. This 403-page selection from the 1867 *Leaves* was expurgated with Whitman's permission and assistance. Whitman had originally balked at a selected edition of *Leaves,* but faced with a choice between that or no edition at all, he chose the former. Moncure Daniel Conway, who was in London at the time, acted as Whitman's unofficial agent in dealing with Hotten and Rossetti. Hotten printed one thousand copies of the book, and when after his death his firm was taken over by Chatto and Windus, it was brought out in a new edition in 1886 and reprinted in 1901, 1910, 1926, and 1945.

In 1873, Hotten brought out five hundred copies of an unauthorized edition of the 1872 *Leaves of Grass,* which, technically, is the sixth edition of the title. It was a very accurate typefacsimile of Whitman's book, even down to the "Washington, D.C., 1872" imprint on the title page. Indeed, Hotten's name was nowhere to be found in the book. Hotten's anonymous piracy was no doubt due to British censorship laws, which held the publisher and not the distributor at fault in cases of selling obscene material, and which he probably thought he could avoid more easily by posing as the distributor of the book rather than as the publisher of it. As in the case of his earlier edition of Whitman's poems, Hotten paid Whitman no royalties for using his work.

Joel Myerson

Bibliography

Paley, Morton D. "John Camden Hotten and the First British Editions of Walt Whitman—'A Nice Milky Cocoa-Nut.'" *Publishing History* 6 (1979): 5–35.

Welland, Dennis. "John Camden Hotten and Emerson's Uncollected Essays." *Yearbook of English Studies* 6 (1976): 156–175.

See also BRITISH ISLES, WHITMAN IN THE; CONWAY, MONCURE DANIEL; ROSSETTI, WILLIAM MICHAEL

["Hours Continuing Long"] (1860)

Appearing only in the 1860 *Leaves* as "Calamus" number 9, ["Hours Continuing Long"] was originally the eighth in a series of twelve poems entitled "Live Oak with Moss" that Whitman copied into a small notebook in the spring of 1859. Whitman later referred to the series as "a Cluster of Sonnets" (qtd. in Helms 186). Though Whitman never published the series itself, all twelve of the poems of the series were reordered and included among the forty-five poems of the 1860 "Calamus."

Rarely does Whitman make it so clear that the object of his love is another man, or share his vulnerability and sense of abandonment so candidly, as in "Hours Continuing." Desperate because he saw the one he loved content without him, Whitman withdraws to isolated spots by day, and—unable to sleep at night—stifles plaintive cries while "speeding swiftly the country roads."

At one point he cries out "I am ashamed—but it is useless—I am what I am." Seeing echoes of Shakespeare's Sonnet 121 ("I am that I am") in the poem, Alan Helms nevertheless notes that Shakespeare's poem is affirmative and defiant, while Whitman's is defeatist, a casualty of homophobic oppression.

If the shame that Whitman spoke of was a result of the forbidden nature of his love, why was the similarly explicit companion poem "When I Heard at the Close of the Day" so joyful? Perhaps the shame sprang from the simple realization that another human being had such power to hurt him in love. In any case Whitman abandoned "Hours Continuing," along with two other "Calamus" poems, after the 1860 *Leaves,* no doubt as part of an effort to make *Leaves* more upbeat and less clearly homoerotic, and thus more acceptable to the general public.

Richard Raleigh

Bibliography

Allen, Gay Wilson, and Charles T. Davis. *Walt Whitman's Poems.* New York: New York UP, 1955.

Erkkila, Betsy. *Whitman the Political Poet.* New York: Oxford UP, 1989.

Helms, Alan. "Whitman's 'Live Oak with Moss.'" *The Continuing Presence of Walt Whitman.* Ed. Robert K. Martin. Iowa City: U of Iowa P, 1992. 185–205.

Killingsworth, M. Jimmie. *Whitman's Poetry of the Body: Sexuality, Politics, and the Text.* Chapel Hill: U of North Carolina P, 1989.

See also "Calamus"; "Live Oak with Moss"; Love; Sex and Sexuality; "When I Heard at the Close of the Day"

Howells, William Dean (1837–1920)

William Dean Howells early established and long maintained an ambivalent, grudging, and limited appreciation of Whitman. An advocate of realism, and inclined by training and taste to favor form and refinement in literature, Howells first criticized Whitman's poetry as too raw and barbaric, but he ultimately recognized Whitman as a fact of growing influence in literature and conceded that his poetry was vigorous and sometimes beautiful.

Howells's first review (1860) of a Whitman poem, "Bardic Symbols," complained that it was confusing because the poet discarded forms and laws. Later in 1860, in another review of *Leaves of Grass*, Howells sounded his distinctive note of ambivalence when he characterized Whitman as a bull in the china shop of poetry and, ironically, the critics as fretful "Misses Nancy" (1:12). For Howells, Whitman was both overrated and underrated. Although he disapproved of Whitman's excessive frankness, he found passages of great beauty in the poems and decided to leave the final judgment to posterity. The 1865 review of *Drum-Taps* granted pathos and "purity" to the collection (1:49), but concluded that its contents were only the stuff of poetry—embryonic poems—and that Whitman's rich possibilities were thwarted by his erroneous theories. The 1889 review of *November Boughs* was more kindly, perhaps because Howells realized that Whitman was near the end of his life. While Howells still denied that Whitman succeeded in freeing poetry from form, he admitted that Whitman dealt literary convention a permanent injury and produced a "new kind in literature" (2:108).

Howells was never comfortable with Whitman's poetry, but became broad-minded and gracious enough to concede potentialities for greatness in it that he could not grasp.

Lawrence I. Berkove

Bibliography

Cady, Edwin H. *The Realist at War: The Mature Years, 1885–1920, of William Dean Howells.* Syracuse, N.Y.: Syracuse UP, 1958.
———. *The Road to Realism: The Early Years, 1837–1885, of William Dean Howells.* Syracuse, N.Y.: Syracuse UP, 1956.
Howells, William Dean. *Selected Literary Criticism, Volume I: 1859–1885.* Ed. Ulrich Halfmann, Christopher K. Lohmann, Don L. Cook, and David J. Nordloh. Bloomington: Indiana UP, 1993.
———. *Selected Literary Criticism, Volume II: 1886–1897.* Ed. Donald Pizer, Christopher K. Lohmann, Don L. Cook, and David J. Nordloh. Bloomington: Indiana UP, 1993.
Madsen, Valden. "W.D. Howells's Formal Poetics and His Appraisals of Whitman and Emily Dickinson." *Walt Whitman Review* 23 (1977): 103–109.

See also Harper's Monthly; Realism

Hudson River

Despite its modest 315-mile length, the Hudson River is famous for its diverse surrounding landscapes. Slow-moving and salty with Atlantic water, the Hudson flows south through eastern New York from the Adirondack Mountains to New York Bay. Walt Whitman lived within sight of the Hudson for many years, but he made only three notable trips along the river. In 1848 he traveled to and from a short-lived newspaper job in New Orleans via the Hudson River, the Great Lakes, and the Mississippi. In 1878, Whitman, just beginning to travel again following his crippling 1873 stroke, visited the cottage of his friend John Burroughs about one hundred miles up the Hudson. He repeated this trip in 1879 and wrote of the area's salubrious influence.

Whitman considered the Hudson among the great American waterways. He mentions it three times in *Leaves of Grass*: "Song of the Answerer," "By Blue Ontario's Shore," and "Outlines for a Tomb." In these the river is listed alongside the Mississippi, Paumanok Sound, and the alien Thames. Whitman's Hudson prose is more descriptive. Early in the Preface to the 1855 *Leaves of Grass* Whitman calls the river "beautiful masculine Hudson" (Whitman 7). In *Specimen Days* (1882), he eulogizes the riverside train line, the fishermen's nets, and his favorite Hudson denizen, an eagle riding a storm over the river.

Whitman would also have seen the river as something of an American cultural phenomenon. In his day, a home on the Hudson was a status symbol, and a school of art, one of whose members Whitman publicly lauded, grew out of the river's distinctly American vistas.

Nathan C. Faries

Bibliography

Holloway, Emory. *Whitman: An Interpretation in Narrative*. New York: Knopf, 1926.

Howat, John K. *The Hudson River and Its Painters*. New York: Viking, 1972.

Whitman, Walt. *Complete Poetry and Collected Prose*. Ed. Justin Kaplan. New York: Library of America, 1982.

See also BURROUGHS, JOHN AND URSULA; RIVERBY

Hughes, Langston (1902–1967)

Important poet and essayist in the Harlem Renaissance and first noted for his *Weary Blues* (1926), Hughes claimed that Whitman was "America's greatest poet" and that *Leaves of Grass* was "the greatest expression of the real meaning of democracy" (qtd. in Hutchinson 17). In the 4 July 1953 Chicago *Defender*, Hughes called Whitman the "Lincoln of our Letters" (qtd. in Hutchinson 17).

Hughes's interest in Whitman included compiling three anthologies of his verse and including Whitman poems in his anthology *The Poetry of the Negro*. Hughes wrote a 1954 poem ("Old Walt") for the centennial of *Leaves of Grass* and repeatedly encouraged black writers to read Whitman. On his first trip to Africa, Hughes threw all his books overboard save his copy of *Leaves of Grass*.

One reason for Hughes's enthusiasm was Whitman's feelings of sympathy and stated claims of equality with black slaves. In a 1946 essay Hughes expressed his belief that, since Whitman had played with slave children in his youth, his sympathy for black Americans was both realistic and lifelong. This sympathy was the first step in Whitman's becoming the spokesman for "suppressed classes" all over the world (Hughes 8). According to Arnold Rampersad, Hughes's "I, Too, Sing America" is Whitmanian while departing from Whitman's celebratory chant.

Wesley A. Britton

Bibliography

Hughes, Langston. "The Ceaseless Rings of Walt Whitman." *I Hear the People Singing: Selected Poems of Walt Whitman*. Ed. Hughes. New York: International Publishers, 1946. 7–10.

Hutchinson, George B. "Langston Hughes and the 'Other' Whitman." *The Continuing Presence of Walt Whitman*. Ed. Robert K. Martin. Iowa City: U of Iowa P, 1992. 16–27.

Rampersad, Arnold. *The Life of Langston Hughes*. 2 vols. New York: Oxford UP, 1986.

See also LEGACY, WHITMAN'S

Hugo, Victor (1802–1885)

Novelist, dramatist, poet, Victor Hugo was the foremost French man of letters of the nineteenth century, best known for his *Nôtre Dame de Paris* (1831) and *Les Misérables* (1862). In the 1840s French romanticists like Hugo were enjoying a tremendous vogue in the literary circles in New York City, and Whitman as a Brooklyn editor and reviewer was aware of this new interest among the literary coterie. Hugo's plays were also enjoying successful performances on the New York stage. Whitman told Horace Traubel that "Hugo's immortal works were the dramas, the plays, the poems: least accessible, yet greatest of all—greater than the novels, stories, orations" (Traubel 522).

Whitman identified with the powerful way in which Hugo communicated with the masses, his attempt to give a literary voice to the real life of the people, the same kind of vital, poetic voice that Whitman was striving for in his own poetry. Hugo's *La Légende des siècles* (1859, 3rd series, 1883) was a favorite of Whitman, and he studied many different translations of this work. The haughty, sensual "I" of Hugo's poem, his epic catalogue of humanity, and his lyrical identification of man with the cosmos remind readers of that same dynamic energy in Whitman's "Song of Myself."

In the final decade of his life Whitman encouraged the comparisons that were being made between his poetry and that of Hugo. Indeed, what Hugo seemed to be doing for France in the way of new poetic techniques and themes of Liberty, Equality, and Fraternity, Whitman was doing for America.

Andy J. Moore

Bibliography

Erkkila, Betsy. *Walt Whitman Among the French: Poet and Myth*. Princeton: Princeton UP, 1980.

Greenberg, Wendy. "Hugo and Whitman: Poets of Totality." *Walt Whitman Review* 24 (1978): 32–36.

Lombard, Charles M. "Whitman and Hugo." *Walt Whitman Review* 19 (1973): 19–25.

Traubel, Horace. *With Walt Whitman in Camden.* 1908. Vol. 2. New York: Rowman and Littlefield, 1961.

See also ROMANTICISM

Human Body

In Whitman's poetry, the human body is a major theme—and much more. It is a prominent conceptual device; Whitman's use of body metaphors anticipates the work of twentieth-century cognitive linguists and language philosophers in the recognition of the body as the ground of human understanding to which all concepts ultimately relate. It is also a source of delight, on a footing with poetry itself, the seat of sexual pleasure and the sympathetic emotions which bind person to person. In this last sense the body is the heart of democratic politics, the common denominator in the experience of all men and women. In proclaiming himself in the 1855 *Leaves of Grass* to be the poet of the body as well as the poet of the soul, Whitman set out to elevate the status of physical existence as a theme and inspiration of modern poetry, fully exploiting the metaphorical possibilities of material life as well as advocating a complete realization of the body as a source of psychological, social, and political well-being.

The 1855 body-consciousness seemed to propel the poet beyond anything as simple as "interest" in the physiological processes of the body in health. He had expressed such an interest in his earliest poetry and prose, most notably in book reviews he wrote as a young journalist. But the 1855 versions of "Song of Myself," "The Sleepers," and "I Sing the Body Electric" take their very inspiration from the being and workings of the human body. In all of these poems, bodily health is at once a metaphor for spiritual, social, and political success and a literal topic set on equal footing with the more traditional topics of poetic expression. In "Body Electric" in particular, physical existence appears as a central element in the poet's project. The speaker proclaims, "The bodies of men and women engirth me, and I engirth them, / They will not let me off nor I them till I go with them and respond to them and love them." The bodies of the poet's "lovers" are set against "those who corrupted their own live bodies" and "those who defiled the living" bodies of others (section 1). The latter come under a special attack in twin sections of the poem dealing with what the social reformers of Whitman's day viewed as the two great evils of American society—slavery ("a man's body at auction" [section 7]) and prostitution ("a woman's body at auction" [section 8]). Neglecting one's own body, the poem implicitly argues, leads to the oppression of others' bodies, so that democratic consciousness ultimately depends upon care for and respect of the physical existence of every individual.

In "The Sleepers," the poet adopts the persona of the loving healer who attends the bodies of sleepers restless with illness and with dreams of unfulfilled sexuality. His sympathetic imagination arises from the common experience of bodily life that the poet shares with the subjects of his poem—and with his readers, who are invited to join in the examination and celebration of the physical. Far from being just a metaphor, the treatment of the body appears as the very foundation of all metaphorical communication. As the language philosophers George Lakoff and Mark Johnson suggest, every new concept a person learns has its grounding in—or may be traced to—a reference to the living body. The body is the starting place of all knowledge, a theme taken up directly in the cosmic drama of "Song of Myself," in which the poet treats "otherbeingness" in nature—the life of other people, as well as that of animals, trees, and even rocks in the crust of the earth—as sharing in the overall evolution of physical existence and as being tied to the individual human being through shared developmental processes. In one famous passage, the speaker of the poem marvels that "I incorporate gneiss and coal and long-threaded moss and fruits and grains and esculent roots, / And am stucco'd with quadrupeds and birds all over" (section 31). Such is the "knit of identity" (section 3), a trope that is simultaneously a metaphor for shared life and a metaphor for metaphor itself. Every metaphor knits an identity between unlike things. Whitman reveals material existence to be the starting place for all such identification and thus celebrates the body for its contribution to what he calls the "merge" ("Body Electric," section 5), the tendency toward the unification of individuals driven by the "procreant urge" of all life ("Song of Myself," section 3) to reproduce itself by interpenetrating with other life forms.

Whitman's attitude toward the body and his treatment of it did not remain static but changed over the several editions of *Leaves of Grass* as he added new poems and revised old ones. In the 1856 *Leaves,* Whitman was, if anything, more inclined to develop his celebration and exploration of physical life. In the poem eventually titled "Spontaneous Me," he again identified the poetic function with a physical one, this time with special emphasis on the male organs of sexual regeneration. In "Poem of Women," later titled "Unfolded Out of the Folds," he balanced the equation, presenting life as an evolving phenomenon unfolding upon the world much as a child emerges from the very folds of the mother's womb and vagina. In "Poem of Procreation," later "A Woman Waits for Me," the poet offers the vision of a future woman whose physical life is every bit as developed, as open, and as athletic as a man's.

By the 1860 edition, however, Whitman displayed a new trend toward developing his poems of spirituality and psychological drama and increasingly neglecting his poetry of the body. After his representation of the torn body of the nation and his own efforts at "wound-dressing" in the Civil War poems of *Drum-Taps,* he all but abandoned the celebration of physical existence. By that time, Ralph Waldo Emerson and other supporters had encouraged him to rethink his emphasis on the body because, they argued, it had cost him readers and interfered with his ambition to become the great poet of democracy. Moreover, he had lost much of his own physical vigor and, as a consequence, may have also lost some interest in being the poet of the body, though he never openly agreed to reduce, eliminate, or apologize for his work on sexuality and physical vitality in general, but instead defended it vigorously in essays like "A Memorandum at a Venture." Whatever the cause, however, the effect is clear: the poems written after 1865 are mainly soulful reflections on life from the vantage of an artistically distanced observer rather than the ardent celebrations of a lover of material life immersed in the very material of his being and song.

Early commentators on Whitman's poetry of the body, as well as critics and biographers well into the twentieth century, tended to understand the poems as a completely original gesture of a rebellious soul reacting to the strict demands of the Victorian Age. However, the image of the poetic rebel "singing the body" has been greatly modified by more recent scholarship under the influence of new developments in social history and a comparison of Whitman's work to contemporaneous writings outside the accepted literary canon (see Harold Aspiz; M. Jimmie Killingsworth, *Poetry of the Body;* and David S. Reynolds). Whitman drew upon a variety of scientific sources and from social reform literature in developing both the form and content of his treatment of physical life. He learned about evolution, for instance, from reading reviews of pre-Darwinian scientists like Jean Baptiste Lamarck and Robert Chambers. He borrowed the notion of "sexual electricity" from eclectic medical writers of the day, such as Edward H. Dixon and Orson S. Fowler, the founder of the phrenological firm Fowler and Wells, which served as the publisher and distributor of the second edition of *Leaves of Grass.* Phrenology encouraged Whitman in his notion that character could be "read" in a person's physical attributes and that moral character, as well as physical traits, could be transmitted from one generation to the next. From popular medical writing, Whitman picked up the theme of human perfectibility and wove eugenic themes into poems like "A Woman Waits for Me." Above all, it was the quirky physiology of nineteenth-century science writing that Whitman left behind when he shifted the emphasis of his own writing after the war. His farewell to the soap box and lecture hall of scientific reform is embodied in the 1860 poem "I Sit and Look Out" and in "When I Heard the Learn'd Astronomer," which first appeared in *Drum-Taps.*

Formalist and deconstructionist critics since the 1950s have looked with skepticism upon Whitman's assertions about the spontaneous connection between his poetry and the unmediated workings of nature and the body. But the poetry of the body continues to affect readers with a sense of immediacy and liveliness that is difficult to account for by reference to poetic conventions and semiotic processes. Much as Lawrence Buell suggests that we must retain a theory of referentiality (a way of linking poetry to its sources in lived experience) if we are to grasp the full significance of Henry David Thoreau's work and his tradition in the literature of the environmental imagination, so perhaps we must retain a sense of how language not only depicts but also grows out of bodily processes—an organic theory of art rooted in life—to fully appreciate Whitman's accomplishment in the poetry of the body.

M. Jimmie Killingsworth

Bibliography

Aspiz, Harold. *Walt Whitman and the Body Beautiful*. Urbana: U of Illinois P, 1980.

Beach, Christopher. *The Politics of Distinction: Whitman and the Discourses of Nineteenth-Century America*. U of California P, 1997.

Buell, Lawrence. *The Environmental Imagination: Thoreau, Nature Writing, and the Formation of American Culture*. Cambridge, Mass.: Harvard UP, 1995.

Johnson, Mark. *The Body in the Mind: The Bodily Basis of Meaning, Imagination, and Reason*. Chicago: U of Chicago P, 1987.

Killingsworth, M. Jimmie. *The Growth of "Leaves of Grass": The Organic Tradition in Whitman Studies*. Columbia, S.C.: Camden House, 1993.

———. *Whitman's Poetry of the Body: Sexuality, Politics, and the Text*. Chapel Hill: U of North Carolina P, 1989.

Lakoff, George, and Mark Johnson. *Metaphors We Live By*. Chicago: U of Chicago P, 1980.

Reynolds, David S. *Walt Whitman's America: A Cultural Biography*. New York: Knopf, 1995.

See also "I Sing the Body Electric"; Leaves of Grass, 1855 Edition; Leaves of Grass, 1856 Edition; Phrenology; Pseudoscience; Science; Sex and Sexuality; "Sleepers, The"; "Song of Myself"; Soul, The; "Spontaneous Me"; "Unfolded Out of the Folds"; "Woman Waits for Me, A"

Human Voice

Walt Whitman addresses the subject of human voice in his essay "The Perfect Human Voice" (1890). In his discussion of the voices of opera singers, preachers, and actors he calls for a close connection between the literal and metaphorical voice:

> To me the grand voice is mainly physiological—(by which I by no means ignore the mental help, but wish to keep the emphasis where it belongs.) Emerson says *manners* form the representative apex and vital charm and captivation of humanity: but he might as well have changed the typicality to voice. (*Prose Works* 2:674)

Regardless of the voice's association with elocution, drama, or opera, for Whitman the human voice itself is the most important:

> Of course there is much taught and written about elocution, the best reading, speaking, etc., but it finally settles down to *best* human vocalization. Beyond all other power and beauty there is something in the quality and power of the right voice (*timbre* the schools call it) that touches the soul, abysms. (2:674)

Whitman also specifies those whom he has known who possess the perfect human voice: Marietta Alboni, Elias Hicks, Father Taylor, Alessandro Bettini, Fanny Kemble, and Edwin Booth. For Whitman the "perfect physiological human voice" creates the best philosophy or poetry (2:674).

The direct reciprocation of speaking and talking is listening and hearing. Hardly ever differentiating between readers and auditors in *Leaves of Grass,* Whitman continually acknowledges the human voice through references to speaking and hearing. He incites his readers to listen to live words rather than reading dead print; they must participate as listeners in the experience of his poems. In "Song of Myself" Whitman presents "the origin of all poems" as something heard with the ear rather than read with the eye: "You shall no longer take things at second or third hand, nor look through the eyes of the dead, nor feed on the spectres in books, / You shall not look through my eyes either, nor take things from me, / You shall listen to all sides and filter them from your self" (section 2).

Whitman's poetry in *Leaves of Grass* is more a matter of saying and talking, a voice speaking with a tongue. In the opening lines of "Song of Myself" Whitman claims to be speaking with an individual "tongue." This is the tongue of a poet "in perfect health" who continues speaking "till death," and with this tongue, Whitman so speaks: "I permit to speak at every hazard, / Nature without check with original energy." The "original energy" with which he speaks is the energy of breath.

Origination of the spoken word takes place in the lungs, the throat, and the mouth. Whitman associates the spoken word of the human voice in his naming all of the poems, the entire book, *Leaves of Grass*. The poems, as grass, originate from the mouth—"from under the faint red roofs of mouths"—where Whitman's initiators of the spoken word—"so many uttering tongues"—are found ("Song of Myself," section 6).

Several Whitman critics and biographers provide negative appraisals of Whitman's own voice. Clifton Joseph Furness includes a letter from Harrison Smith Morris in his edition of Whitman papers. This letter suggests to later critics and biographers Edgar Lee Masters, F.O. Matthiessen, Henry Seidel Canby, and Arthur Briggs a "high-pitched" quality in Whitman's voice (*Workshop* 203). More than a dozen witnesses, however, who heard Whitman's voice provide more positive appraisals of it. In his biography of Whitman, Morris himself provides the following description of Whitman's voice, which contradicts his letter to Furness: "A voice of many soft vibrations that rippled now and then into human laughter, seldom loud, always measured and even hesitating for the right word, grave in season and never monotonous or complaining" (196). Amos Bronson Alcott, Dr. Richard Maurice Bucke, Hannibal Hamlin Garland, Thomas B. Harned, Frank Harris, William Dean Howells, Bertha Johnson, Dr. John Johnston, Stuart Merrill, William Douglas O'Connor, Sarah Payson (Fanny Fern), Helen Price, Horace Traubel, and Susan Hunter Walker all heard Whitman's voice and provide positive descriptions of it.

In fact, readers can determine the quality of Whitman's voice for themselves. As listeners, they can hear Whitman reading the first four lines of his six-line poem "America" (1888). Recorded first on a cylinder in 1890 (perhaps at the Victor Recording Studio in Philadelphia), owned once by the collector Roscoe Haley, broadcast in 1951 on NBC radio by Leon Pearson, and packaged by Audio-Text Cassettes and sold for classroom use in 1974, the Whitman recording is available today on acetate in the Belfer Audio Lab and Archives at Syracuse University, and is also available both on cassette tape from *The Walt Whitman Quarterly Review* at the University of Iowa and on CD-Rom from Rhino Records. When this writer listens to the recording, he hears a rich voice that is neither monotonous nor high-pitched.

In the final poem of "Messenger Leaves" in the 1860 edition of *Leaves of Grass,* "To You [Stranger, if you . . .]," which was later included in the "Inscriptions" cluster of the 1881 *Leaves,* Whitman presents two questions, that, as rhetorical questions, underscore the importance he must have placed on the human voice in his desire to speak to all his readers: "Stranger, if you passing meet me and desire to speak to me, why should you not speak to me? And why should I not speak to you?"

Larry D. Griffin

Bibliography

Morris, Harrison S. *Walt Whitman: A Brief Biography with Reminiscences.* Cambridge, Mass.: Harvard UP, 1929.

Whitman, Walt. "America." 1890. Rec. *Voices of the Poets: Readings by Great American Poets from Walt Whitman to Robert Frost.* American Literary Voices Audiotape. 14026. Center for Cassette Studies, 1974.

———. *Leaves of Grass: A Textual Variorum of the Printed Poems.* Ed. Sculley Bradley, Harold W. Blodgett, Arthur Golden, and William White. 3 vols. New York: New York UP, 1980.

———. *Prose Works 1892.* Ed. Floyd Stovall. 2 vols. New York: New York UP, 1963–1964.

———. *Walt Whitman's Workshop: A Collection of Unpublished Manuscripts.* Ed. Clifton Joseph Furness. Cambridge, Mass.: Harvard UP, 1928.

See also ACTORS AND ACTRESSES; "AMERICA [CENTRE OF EQUAL DAUGHTERS . . .]"; HICKS, ELIAS; OPERA AND OPERA SINGERS; ORATORY; TAYLOR, FATHER (EDWARD THOMPSON)

Humboldt, Alexander von (1769–1859)

Alexander von Humboldt was an internationally renowned Prussian naturalist whose work enjoyed broad popularity in the United States. Of considerable influence on Walt Whitman was Humboldt's highly ambitious work *Kosmos,* published in five volumes between 1845 and 1850. In *Kosmos* Humboldt sought "to depict in a single work the entire material universe, all that we know of the phenomena of heaven and earth" (Botting 257). In contrast to Darwinian theory, Humboldt described nature not in terms of chaos or conflict but as a harmoniously ordered system, as "one great whole animated by the breath of life" (Humboldt 1:24). Humboldt conceived nature not as morally neutral but as a reflection of the human spirit. He stressed simultaneously the endless variety of life and the ultimate unity of nature. Humboldt's naturalistic vision inscribed humankind at the center of creation, using science to affirm rather than question the place of humanity in the universe. Whitman, who referred to Humboldt in his notes in 1849, found the scientist's view highly appealing. Indeed, Whitman borrowed Humboldt's book title for his famous self-description in "Song of Myself": "Walt Whitman, a kosmos, of Manhattan the son" (section 24). Whitman also uses Humboldt's term as the title of his poem "Kosmos," in which he describes a person at one with the universe, "[w]ho includes diversity and is Nature, / Who is the amplitude of the earth, and the coarseness and sexuality of the earth."

John T. Matteson

Bibliography

Botting, Douglas. *Humboldt and the Cosmos.* New York: Harper and Row, 1973.

Humboldt, Alexander von. *Cosmos: A Sketch of a Physical Description of the Universe.* 1845. 4 vols. New York: Harper, 1858.

Reynolds, David S. *Walt Whitman's America: A Cultural Biography.* New York: Knopf, 1995.

See also SCIENCE

Humor

Is there such a thing as humor in Walt Whitman's work? Opinions differ. Constance Rourke included him in her inventory of *American Humor* (1931), but Jesse Bier in *The Rise and Fall of American Humor* (1968) made a case for his humorlessness and protested against Richard Chase's claim in *Walt Whitman Reconsidered* (1955) that on the whole "Song of Myself" is a comic (as well as a cosmic) poem whose comic effects often take the specific form of American humor. Whitman himself in 1889 declared to some of his Camden friends, "I pride myself on being a real humorist underneath everything else" (Traubel 49).

Humor is an elusive quality that defies definition. It mostly consists in discovering and expressing ludicrous or absurdly incongruous elements in ideas or situations, as, for example, in the case of a supposedly omniscient adult stumped by the very artless question of a child about one of the commonest things in the world, grass. It is on this that *Leaves of Grass* is built, since the major part of the book is an attempt indirectly to answer the child's question: "What

is the grass?" This awkward situation implies the true humorist's sense of the relativity of all values. What is important? What is not? No one can tell. This doubt applies to all religions and to time and space, which are mere illusions. Humor is thus a cosmic game between the "real" world of appearances and the ideal world of absolute truths. This is how Havelock Ellis defined it (with reference to Heinrich Heine) in *The New Spirit* (1890). This leads in particular to cosmic visions in which dimensions have no value: "My ties and ballasts leave me, my elbows rest in sea-gaps, / I skirt sierras, my palms cover continents . . ." ("Song of Myself," section 33). The poet is then turned into a sort of mystical Paul Bunyan or Western backwoodsman. Lyric poetry and the tall tale of the Southwest become almost identical in form and tone. "What widens within you Walt Whitman? . . . Within me latitude widens, longitude lengthens" ("Salut au Monde!," section 1). In chapter 16 of *Huckleberry Finn,* the drunken raftsmen whom Huck overhears in the middle of the Mississippi use exactly the same words. At such times, lyric poetry and humor lead to— or come from—the same exuberance. Whitman then used humor as a means of self-protection. When he grew grandiloquent, he laughed at himself in order not to be laughed at. He both celebrated himself and laughed at himself, his "gab," and his "loitering" ("Song of Myself," section 52).

As Sören Kierkegaard noted, humor, like realism, frequently results in prolixity, for humor and realism are very closely connected. Henri Bergson in *Le Rire* (1900) defined humor in contradistinction to irony as consisting in minutely describing things as they are while pretending to believe that they are as they should be, i.e., in describing the real as if it were the ideal. Now describing things as they are is precisely the essence of realism. Such a fusion of humor and prolix realism often occurs in *Leaves of Grass,* in particular in the "Song of the Exposition" when Whitman treats the Muse with utter disrespect and installs her in the middle of the kitchenware at the Fortieth Annual Exhibition in New York City.

At other times, Whitman's humor combines with irony and bitter invective (the kind of invective he indulged in in "The Eighteenth Presidency!"). He gives full vent to his indignation and despair in "A Boston Ballad (1854)" and above all with bitterness in "Respondez!" He did not like this mood, however, and dropped

"Respondez!" in 1881 and kept "A Boston Ballad (1854)" only at the insistence of his friend J.T. Trowbridge.

In general Whitman preferred to stand "Apart from the pulling and hauling . . . amused, complacent, compassionating, idle, unitary . . . Both in and out of the game and watching and wondering at it" ("Song of Myself," section 4). This is an excellent description of the humorist's attitude to his subject involving self-complacency and narcissism, for, as Freud has pointed out, "humor has something which liberates, like wit and comedy, but also something sublime and lofty. . . . This sublime element of course comes from the triumph of narcissism, from the invulnerability of the self which victoriously asserts itself" (qtd. in Breton 19–20). It is therefore inevitable that there should be humor in "Song of Myself," a Myself full of contradictions, torn between centripetal and centrifugal force, tortured by the incongruous contrasts of the human condition—both mortal and immortal, both finite and infinite (like Vladimir Mayakovsky's "cloud in trousers"), both "one's-self" and man "en-masse"—tempted at times to reach Mark Twain's despairing conclusion at the end of *The Mysterious Stranger*: "life itself is only a vision, a dream" (138). But Whitman never derides life and man to the point of nihilism, to what Thomas Carlyle called "descendentalism." He was saved from this by his transcendentalism. In his poetry man is not something to be laughed at, but, on the contrary, a miracle to be wondered at. Though we are "little plentiful manikins skipping around in collars and tail'd coats," walking with "dimes on the eyes" ("Song of Myself," section 42), man, in Whitman's eyes, is not a ludicrous and despicable biped, but an unfathomable mystery, "not contain'd between [his] hat and boots" (section 7).

In some forms of humor, there is an element of sympathy rather than scorn for the subject. William Makepeace Thackeray even defined eighteenth-century humor as "wit and love" (270). There is indeed more love than scorn in the humor of *Leaves of Grass*, even if Whitman occasionally made fun of "neuters and geldings" ("Song of Myself," section 23) or "learn'd and polite persons" ("Respondez!").

He is thus, together with Dylan Thomas and Paul Claudel, the best proof that lyricism and humor can coexist despite their apparent incompatibility. They are impelled by the same exuberance and lead to the same exaggerations.

Roger Asselineau

Bibliography

Asselineau, Roger. "Walt Whitman's Humor." *American Transcendental Quarterly* 22 (1974): 86–91.

Breton, André. Preface. *Anthologie de l'humour noir*. Paris: J.J. Pauvert, 1966. 11–22.

Clemens, Samuel L. *The Mysterious Stranger and Other Stories*. New York: Harper and Row, 1950.

Reynolds, David S. *Beneath the American Renaissance: The Subversive Imagination in the Age of Emerson and Melville*. New York: Knopf, 1988.

Tanner, James T.F. "Four Comic Themes in Walt Whitman's *Leaves of Grass*." *Studies in American Humor* ns 5 (1986): 62–71.

Thackeray, W.M. *The English Humourists, Charity and Humour, The Four Georges*. Ed. M.R. Ridley. London: Dent, 1968.

Traubel, Horace. *With Walt Whitman in Camden*. Vol. 4. Ed. Sculley Bradley. Philadelphia: U of Pennsylvania P, 1953.

Wallace, Ronald. *God Be With the Clown: Humor in American Poetry*. Columbia: U of Missouri P, 1984.

See also "BOSTON BALLAD (1854), A"; PARODIES; "RESPONDEZ!"; "SONG OF MYSELF"; "SONG OF THE EXPOSITION"

Huneker, James Gibbons (1857–1921)

Born in Philadelphia, the son of a printer and collector of prints, the younger Huneker was also encouraged in the arts by his Roman Catholic mother, an omnivorous reader. James left school in 1872, at the age of fifteen, taking with him a lifelong dislike for institutions and scholarship. He studied painting, worked in a foundry, and studied for the law, but finally returned to the piano, which he had studied as a child. Staking his future on music, he left for Paris, hoping to meet Franz Liszt and to enter the Conservatoire. A weak performance gained him admission only as an auditor, but he studied privately with George Mathias, a student of Frédéric Chopin. Following a year in Europe, during which he discovered the French impressionists, German philosophers, and Russian novelists, he returned to Philadelphia, where he continued music studies and wrote occasionally for newspapers and magazines. In 1886, at the age of thirty, he moved to New York and quickly became a respected daily columnist and popular critic and writer. By 1900, Huneker was one of the nation's most read and respected critics. By his death in 1921, he had published twenty books of criticism, fiction, and autobiography. In the words of H.L. Mencken, "no other critic of his generation had a tenth of his influence. Almost single-handed he overthrew the aesthetic theory that had flourished in the United States since the death of Poe" (qtd. in Bachinger 36).

Huneker's connection with Whitman began in 1878 when, impressed by *Leaves of Grass,* the young man called on Whitman in Camden. The future critic occasionally met Whitman outside Philadelphia's Academy of Music after a concert and escorted him to the Camden ferry streetcar. In 1887, Huneker publicly praised Whitman's frankness, and on 31 May 1891 he listed Whitman among the great personalities then living in America. On 1 November 1891, in a long, complimentary article in the *Recorder,* Huneker condemned America's neglect of Whitman, concluding that Whitman was "one of the greatest natural forces in American literature" (qtd. in Schwab, "Criticism" 66). By 13 July 1898, however, Huneker had developed some reservations. Although he continued to praise some poems as "the finest things America has given to the nations," he now also saw "slush, trash, nonsense, obscurity, morbid eroticism, vulgarity and preposterous mouthing" (qtd. in Schwab, "Criticism" 67). Huneker may, in fact, have been the first American critic to refer openly to Whitman's homosexual leaning. In this respect, he helped to focus attention on an aspect of Whitman which later critics have not been able to ignore.

James E. Barcus, Jr.

Bibliography

Bachinger, Katrina. "Years of Ferment: American Literary Criticism Enters the Twentieth Century." *American Studies International* 20.4 (1982): 31–45.

Schwab, Arnold T. *James Gibbons Huneker: Critic of the Seven Arts.* Stanford, Calif.: Stanford UP, 1963.

———. "James Huneker on Whitman: A Newly Discovered Essay." *American Literature* 38 (1966): 208–218.

———. "James Huneker's Criticism of American Literature." *American Literature* 29 (1957): 64–78.

See also Critics, Whitman's; Scholarship, Trends in Whitman

Hunkers

During the 1840s, a schism developed within the New York Democratic party over the issues of the day. The conservative Hunkers (so named by their antagonists because they were alleged to "hunger," "hanker," or "hunker" for office) favored state-supported internal improvements and opposed antislavery agitation, while their chief opponents, the more radical Barnburners (alluding to the farmer who burned down his barn to get rid of the rats) opposed the extension of slavery into the new territories. When, in 1847, the Hunker-controlled Democratic National Convention ignored the Wilmot Proviso (a resolution against the extension of slavery to free territory), the Barnburners bolted the party, united with the Free Soil party, and nominated Martin Van Buren for president.

Walt Whitman, who over the course of his career in journalism worked for several Democratic newspapers, aligned himself first with the liberal Barnburners and then later with the Free-Soilers. In a series of editorials written while he served as editor of the Brooklyn *Daily Eagle,* Whitman celebrated white free labor and urged the Democratic party to take a free-soil stance. Throughout 1847, as Whitman presented his pro-Wilmot arguments, his employer, Isaac Van Anden, a Hunker Democrat, patiently tolerated his liberal views, but this patience apparently waned by the end of the year, and as the Hunkers consolidated their control of the New York party machine, Whitman found himself dismissed as editor of the *Eagle.*

Although Whitman went on to work for other free-soil papers, the divisions within the party cost the Democrats the 1848 presidential election, and during the 1850s, many Barnburners decided to return to the party while others joined the newly formed Republican party. Meanwhile, the Hunkers divided into the "Hards," who opposed reunion with the Barnburners, and "Softs," who desired a reconciliation. Thus, the term "Hunker" became obsolete.

Charles B. Green

Bibliography

Allen, Gay Wilson. *The Solitary Singer: A Critical Biography of Walt Whitman.* 1955. Rev. ed. 1967. Chicago: U of Chicago P, 1985.

Foner, Eric. *Politics and Ideology in the Age of the Civil War.* New York: Oxford UP, 1980.

Klammer, Martin. *Whitman, Slavery, and the Emergence of "Leaves of Grass."* University Park: Pennsylvania State UP, 1995.

See also Barnburners and Locofocos; Brooklyn *Daily Eagle*; Democratic Party; Free Soil Party; Political Views; Republican Party; Wilmot Proviso

I

"I Dream'd in a Dream" (1860)

This is one of the poems in the "Calamus" cluster, which was written, as Whitman noted in the first poem in the collection, "to celebrate the need of comrades." The poems in the "Calamus" collection were written to celebrate the love of man for man—"Adhesiveness"—as the poems in the "Children of Adam" cluster were written to celebrate the love of man for woman—"Amativeness." The "Calamus" poems move from the intensely personal and individual to the social and, ultimately, to the universal.

"I Dream'd in a Dream" is an example of the universal nature of the "Calamus" ideal. Whitman felt that men must love other men with the same passion as that with which they love women, writes Henry Seidel Canby in *Walt Whitman: An American,* or there can be "no comradeship strong enough to hold together an ideal democracy" (201). Richard Chase, in *Walt Whitman Reconsidered,* adds that the "Calamus" poems, "by some mysterious yet sublime seductions," enable the reader to see, beyond death, what Whitman calls the "city of Friends" (119). David Kuebrich, in *Minor Prophecy,* links the "Calamus" theme in "I Dream'd" to Christian teachings about "The Brotherhood of Man" and relates this to the message of contemporary preachers like Lyman Beecher. Gay Wilson Allen, in *The Solitary Singer,* believes that Whitman was able to "transcend his personal suffering," which was generated by the poet's "unsatisfied homoerotic yearnings," by generalizing them in a dream of "'a city where all the men were like brothers'" (225).

The world envisioned in "I Dream'd" is one in which "Robust love" between men would bring an end to war and lead to a just and democratic social order.

Ronald W. Knapp

Bibliography

Allen, Gay Wilson. *The Solitary Singer: A Critical Biography of Walt Whitman.* 1955. Rev. ed. 1967. Chicago: U of Chicago P, 1985.

Canby, Henry Seidel. *Walt Whitman: An American.* Boston: Houghton Mifflin, 1943.

Cavitch, David. *My Soul and I: The Inner Life of Walt Whitman.* Boston: Beacon, 1985.

Chase, Richard. *Walt Whitman Reconsidered.* New York: William Sloane Associates, 1955.

Kuebrich, David. *Minor Prophecy: Walt Whitman's New American Religion.* Bloomington: Indiana UP, 1989.

See also "CALAMUS"; COMRADESHIP

"I Hear America Singing" (1860)

"I Hear America Singing" appeared first in the 1860 (third) edition of *Leaves of Grass* as number 20 in "Chants Democratic" with the first line "American mouth-songs!" and an awkward final stanza, both of which Whitman wisely deleted for the next version of the poem in "The Answerer" cluster of 1871. His revision of the first line to "I Hear America singing, the varied carols I hear" (1871) provided what would become its title in his final placement of the poem in "Inscriptions" (1881).

When this poem first appeared in the 1860 edition, Whitman placed it between "I was Looking a Long While" and "As I Walk These Broad Majestic Days." In this context, "I Hear" found a place in Whitman's announcement of the great theme of freedom and in his early invention of new literary techniques. In its "Inscriptions" surroundings, this poem is thematically related to "To Thee Old Cause" (1871), "America" (1888), "Thou Mother with Thy Equal Brood" (1872), and the prophetic nationalism of "To-day and Thee" (1888).

The idea of "America" in "I Hear" is that of the poem "America" (1888), conceived of as the Mother, source of the themes of freedom, law, and love expressed by her children. These children are the daughters and sons who find voice in "I Hear." The songs they sing are those described in "Starting from Paumanok" (1860): the poems of materials that are the most spiritual poems. To the expanding and rhapsodic ego discovering the universal immanent in each particular, Whitman found appropriate the catalogue of parallelisms contained in a thematic envelope. But in "I Hear" the abbreviated exploration of this method restricts expansion.

Isadora Duncan, calling herself "the spiritual daughter of Walt Whitman" (39), was inspired by this poem and sought commensurate dance and music. Critical response notes this poem's nonmusicality, its vagueness, sentimentality, and folksy nationalism, yet places the poem in the category of dilation, transport, and amazement. "I Hear" is the exploration of a method, not a full literary development of it; the poet is still in his workshop, but the themes, materials, and method are all in plain view.

Charles W. Mignon

Bibliography

Allen, Gay Wilson. *Walt Whitman Handbook*. 1946. New York: Hendricks House, 1962.

Bradley, Sculley, Harold W. Blodgett, Arthur Golden, and William White. Introduction. *Leaves of Grass: A Textual Variorum of the Printed Poems*. Ed. Bradley, Blodgett, Golden, and White. Vol. 1. New York: New York UP, 1980. xv–xxv.

Duncan, Isadora. *My Life*. London: Victor Gollancz, 1928.

Miller, James E., Jr. *A Critical Guide to "Leaves of Grass."* Chicago: U of Chicago P, 1957.

Stovall, Floyd. Introduction. *Walt Whitman: Representative Selections*. 1939. Ed. Stovall. Rev. ed. New York: Hill and Wang, 1961. xi–lii.

Vanderbilt, Kermit. "'I Hear America Singing': Whitman and Democratic Culture." *Walt Whitman Review* 21 (1975): 22–28.

See also "AMERICA [CENTRE OF EQUAL DAUGHTERS . . .]"; "INSCRIPTIONS"; "THOU MOTHER WITH THY EQUAL BROOD"; "TO THEE OLD CAUSE"

"I Hear It was Charged against Me" (1860)

This poem appeared first as number 24 in the 1860 "Calamus" cluster. In later editions it remained in essentially the same position, with just one word changed ("was" replacing "is" in the first line in 1867).

The first three lines state a criticism (that Whitman opposes and undermines society) and answer it by categorically denying the charge's validity (he has nothing whatever to do with society's institutions). The last four lines then go beyond the negative by declaring what, in fact, the poet aims at: "the institution of the dear love of comrades." Versions of this theme appear throughout "Calamus": that love of comrades is more real, essential, or precious than anything else. In particular, the similarly titled "When I Heard at the Close of the Day" mirrors this poem, for it responds to the opposite situation ("plaudits in the capitol") with the same answer. Whether praise or blame is offered, nothing compares to the love of comrades.

Structurally the poem relies on prepositions. The poet is neither "for" nor "against" existing institutions, but will establish the love of comrades "in" (repeated) and "above" and "without" (i.e., outside) them. In a familiar Whitman pattern, elaborated prepositional phrases delay expected sentence completion until the last line of the poem, giving it climactic emphasis.

The poem might be read as a dialectic: thesis (the charge) and antithesis (its denial) are followed by synthesis (love of comrades as a wholly different kind of "institution" he will "establish"). Critics have explored this concluding noninstitutional institution as a dramatic tension, a paradox, a self-contradiction, etc. It seems clear that the poem derives vitality from both denying and confirming the "charge" made. In the end, Whitman's floating comradely love-feast is probably far more radical and threatening to established mores than anything charged by his detractors. At the same time, Whitman conceives this radically unsettling love as the invisible bond that will cement the New World democracy into a unity. The democratic uses of brotherhood hinted at in this poem are expanded elsewhere, for instance in the "Calamus" poem "For You O Democracy."

David Oates

Bibliography

Cady, Joseph. "Not Happy in the Capitol: Homosexuality in the 'Calamus' Poems." *American Studies* 19.2 (1978): 5–22.

Erkkila, Betsy. *Whitman the Political Poet.* New York: Oxford UP, 1989.

Larson, Kerry C. *Whitman's Drama of Consensus.* Chicago: U of Chicago P, 1988.

Nathanson, Tenney. *Whitman's Presence: Body, Voice, and Writing in "Leaves of Grass."* New York: New York UP, 1992.

Whitman, Walt. *Leaves of Grass: Comprehensive Reader's Edition.* Ed. Harold W. Blodgett and Sculley Bradley. New York: New York UP, 1965.

See also "CALAMUS"; COMRADESHIP; "FOR YOU O DEMOCRACY"; "WHEN I HEARD AT THE CLOSE OF THE DAY"

"I Heard You Solemn-Sweet Pipes of the Organ" (1861)

This poem was first published in the New York *Leader* (12 October 1861) under the title "Little Bells Last Night." When it appeared in *Sequel to Drum-Taps* (1865–1866), it acquired the current title and lost four of the original nine lines—the first three, which were filled with contemporary martial allusions, and the seventh, which was addressed to a female harpist; thereafter the poem stayed at five lines. (The original is available in Gay Wilson Allen, *The Solitary Singer.*) After appearing in *Leaves* in 1867, the poem was transferred to the "Children of Adam" cluster in 1871, thereby emphasizing the sexual content of the poem. Perhaps surprisingly, given the removal of the female harpist and the lack of gender specificity in the last line, the poem has no history in "Calamus."

Sacrificed in Whitman's excisions were "beating" and "drums," which prefigured "heart" and "ear" in the last two lines, and the epithet "round-lipp'd" (for cannons), which subtly initiated the sensual intimacy of the poem's conclusion. Whitman may have considered the original seventh line repetitive of the human voice (Italian tenor) and of musical instrumentation (church organ). He simplified the punctuation of the first version considerably for *Leaves,* dropping most commas and changing dashes and semicolons to commas. Because of a dropped comma in line five, "still" could now be read as an adverb modifying "ringing," whereas its original punctuation makes clear it is an adjective modifying "all."

Four categories of sound constitute the subject of the poem, in apparently ascending order of importance: artificial, instrumental music; the music of nature; the singing human voice; the audible pulse of human love. The last line's image of "little bells last night," though the emotional crescendo, circles the poem back to the first category of sound, effecting both closure and the suffusion of the physical with the spiritual ("bells" recalls "church"). A tone of intimacy is achieved by the use of apostrophe in all lines but the middle one. Appropriate for a poem about music, the sound effects are multiple, striking, and subtle (e.g., the play between "morn" and "mourn" in lines one and two and the lulling repetition of the letter "l" in five out of the eight syllables in "all was still ringing little bells").

The combination here of two subjects greatly important to Whitman, music and personal love, and his consummate handling of them in such a short space, gives this poem significance far beyond its size.

Philip Dacey

Bibliography

Allen, Gay Wilson. *The Solitary Singer: A Critical Biography of Walt Whitman.* 1955. Rev. ed. 1967. Chicago: U of Chicago P, 1985.

Coberly, James H. "Whitman's *Children of Adam* Poems." *Emerson Society Quarterly* 22 (1961): 5–8.

Crawley, Thomas Edward. *The Structure of "Leaves of Grass."* Austin: U of Texas P, 1970.

Faner, Robert D. *Walt Whitman & Opera.* Carbondale: Southern Illinois UP, 1951.

Miller, James E., Jr. *A Critical Guide to "Leaves of Grass."* Chicago: U of Chicago P, 1957.

Pound, Louise. "Walt Whitman and the French Language." *American Speech* 1 (1926): 421–430.

Schwiebert, John E. *The Frailest Leaves: Whitman's Poetic Technique and Style in the Short Poem.* New York: Lang, 1992.

Wright, James. "The Delicacy of Walt Whitman." *The Presence of Walt Whitman: Selected Papers from the English Institute.* Ed. R.W.B. Lewis. New York: Columbia UP, 1962. 164–188.

See also "Children of Adam"; Love; Music, Whitman and

"I Saw in Louisiana a Live-Oak Growing" (1860)

This poem was originally published as number 20 in the "Calamus" cluster of the 1860 *Leaves of Grass*. Its text remained the same in all succeeding editions, except for minor alterations in punctuation. It took its first line as its title from 1867 onward.

Whitman's manuscripts show that this poem began as the second in a twelve-poem sequence prospectively entitled "Live Oak with Moss," in which the live-oak serves as the primary botanic symbol of male same-sex attachments; its accompanying poems stress both the desire to withdraw from conventional society into a protected homosexual subculture and the pain of unrequited homoerotic longings. However, Whitman later chose the more phallic calamus root as his main symbol for "adhesiveness" and added thirty-three poems—many of which unambivalently celebrate "the need of comrades" ("In Paths Untrodden")—to form "Calamus."

Because of this revision in Whitman's original conception, "Calamus" vacillates between the urge to flee society and the project of elevating "adhesiveness" into a redemptive social paradigm. In poems such as "When I Heard at the Close of the Day" (1860), "Of the Terrible Doubt of Appearances" (1860), and "Recorders Ages Hence" (1860), Whitman abjures his public, poetic vocation in favor of a private, romantic life which forgoes poetry altogether. "I Saw in Louisiana a Live-Oak Growing," in Kerry Larson's estimation, is more successful at balancing these two alternatives without devaluing either.

"Louisiana Live-Oak" encapsulates this conflict of desires as a tension between homoerotic emotions unrepresentable in poetry and Whitman's stance of poetic self-sufficiency. Byrne Fone has shown that the need for affection and the impossibility of solitude which "Louisiana Live-Oak" ultimately assert are pervasive themes in Whitman's early, pre-*Leaves* poetry. By contrast, Michael Moon argues that Whitman recognizes in the live-oak's ability to "utter joyous leaves" while "standing alone" a reflected image of his own poetic practice. But the poet's subsequent avowal of desire for his "own dear friends" and his reiterated denial that he could "utter joyous leaves" while remaining solitary mask his anxiety that he has written and might

continue to write poems out of frustrated desire, as he does in "Sometimes with One I Love" (1860) and the eventually rejected "Calamus" number 9—["Hours Continuing Long"] (1860).

Carl Smeller

Bibliography

Fone, Byrne R.S. *Masculine Landscapes: Walt Whitman and the Homoerotic Text.* Carbondale: Southern Illinois UP, 1992.

Larson, Kerry C. *Whitman's Drama of Consensus.* Chicago: U of Chicago P, 1988.

Moon, Michael. *Disseminating Whitman: Revision and Corporeality in "Leaves of Grass."* Cambridge, Mass.: Harvard UP, 1991.

Whitman, Walt. *Complete Poetry and Collected Prose.* Ed. Justin Kaplan. New York: Library of America, 1982.

———. *Whitman's Manuscripts: "Leaves of Grass" (1860).* Ed. Fredson Bowers. Chicago: U of Chicago P, 1955.

See also "Calamus"; Comradeship; "Live Oak with Moss"

"I Sing the Body Electric" (1855)

"I Sing the Body Electric" was one of the twelve poems which comprised the first edition of *Leaves of Grass* (1855). As with the other poems in that edition, it appeared without a title. The poem's first line, later changed, was, "The bodies of men and women engirth me, and I engirth them," at the outset announcing itself as a poem about the human body. After revision and the addition of what is now the final section of the poem, it appeared as "Poem of the Body" in the 1856 *Leaves*. In the 1867 edition it appeared in its present nine-section version, with its present title, as part of the "Children of Adam" sequence.

Unlike many of the other poems in the first edition of *Leaves,* "I Sing the Body Electric" has received relatively little critical attention. Some critics have felt that it is obvious and repetitive; others have found it lacking in the deeper mysteries characteristic of Whitman's major works. Many have criticized the final section, an extensive catalogue of the human body. Tenney Nathanson is typical when he says that the catalogue is "a struggle against alienation. It is a struggle the poet seems to lose. What ought to be a ritual of repossession . . . comes to seem instead like an obsessive enumeration" (288).

But despite these critical caveats, "I Sing the Body Electric" remains a magnificent poem of Whitman's early period. Whitman was in his mid-thirties when he first turned to poetry, uncertain of himself yet determined to celebrate the glories of existence. He explored the mysteries of identity in "Song of Myself," of childhood in "There was a Child Went Forth," of the rivers of subconscious desire in "The Sleepers." In "I Sing the Body Electric" Whitman records his delight—and delight is too weak a term—at the wondrous qualities of the human body. "If any thing is sacred the human body is sacred" (section 8), he writes, "And if the body were not the soul, what is the soul?" (section 1). The reader encounters in "Body Electric" Whitman's profound love of bodily flesh. Always a central element in Whitman's ecstatic imagination, the body is here both ostensible and central subject of the poem.

Almost at the outset Whitman acknowledges that many have doubts about the body—doubts originating in the enduring Christian notion that the body is different from the soul, and is the seat of the soul's corruption. Similar doubts will also surface in "Crossing Brooklyn Ferry" (1856) and "Out of the Cradle" (1860). "Body Electric," however, is not a poem of doubt but a response to those who doubt the body. It is a paean of praise to the wonders of the sensual body.

Section 2 asks the reader to consider the perfection of the body, devolving into a stream of images in which the poet looks at bodies with the gaze of sensual desire: the "swimmer naked in the swimming-bath," the "embrace of love and resistance" of two young boy wrestlers, the "play of masculine muscle" of marching firemen. The poet is attracted to all of these bodies, especially those of virile men, and sheds the rigid contours of his identity so that he can become close to them: "I loosen myself, pass freely, am at the mother's breast with the little child, / Swim with the swimmers, wrestle with the wrestlers, march in line with the firemen."

In section 3 the poet gazes with love and affection at the body of a patriarchal farmer, an idealized figure quite at odds with Whitman's own father as described in "There was a Child Went Forth." Paul Zweig argues persuasively that the old man "stands for the self Whitman was even then making in his poems and in his person" (196). By section 4 the poet is convinced that nothing is more satisfying than to admire the bodies of men and women: "I do not ask any more delight, I swim in it as a sea."

Whitman then proceeds, in the following two sections, to describe the bodies of women and the bodies of men. It is usual for Whitman to idealize the erotic attraction of women, something he does when he speaks of their "divine nimbus" and their function as "the bath of birth." But he also presents women as exceedingly sexual, for "mad filaments, ungovernable shoots" of erotic attraction play out of their bodies. The poet, describing himself as "ungovernable," gives way, and reaches the heights of sexual climax in the lines which begin "Ebb stung" and end with "delirious juice."

Concentration on the body of a woman occasions a parallel concentration on the body of a man. But here a new note emerges, one which is likewise a constituent element of "Song of Myself." Whitman finds a link, an identity, between the erotic body and the body politic. For if "the man's body is sacred and the woman's body is sacred," then all bodies are sacred—even those which belong to the "dull-faced immigrants just landed on the wharf." Every single body has its place in the great democratic procession. Other-directed, Whitman is in sections 6–8 less prone to egotism than in any other major early work; he speaks to himself as well as the reader when he chides, "Do you think matter has cohered together from its diffuse float, and the soil is on the surface, and water runs and vegetation sprouts, / For you only, and not for him and her?"

The poet continues to assert this democratic viewpoint in sections 7 and 8, in which his gaze is focused on a male slave and a female slave on the auction platform. His is an antislavery argument, an argument derived perhaps from his Quaker background: "Within there runs blood, / The same old blood! The same red-running blood!" The political content of these sections is discussed by Betsy Erkkila, who notes that in writing about slaves and bodies-as-property Whitman provides an "ominous political prophecy [because] the body electric is also black" (125). Some critics are disconcerted that as Whitman moves from the body itself to the political importance of the body, he switches rhetorical modes, from the narrative rhapsodic to what Edwin Miller correctly assesses as the "forthrightly satirical" (133). A contemporary analogue of such mixed modalities is *Moby-Dick,* published four years earlier.

Section 8 concludes with the curious questions about concealment, defilement, degradation with which the poem began. These lines reinforce the possibility that the poet's song arises not solely from a need to celebrate the human body, but also from a need to come to terms with his own ambivalence over his sexual appetites. "Body Electric" prefigures much of Whitman's later work by raising the possibility that the poet's bodily celebration is a complex mechanism of defense and self-argument which makes manageable the unruly emotions which arise in his psyche. Seen from this perspective, the poem is an assertion by the poet, to himself, that the sexual hungers which gnaw at him—hungers that we today recognize as an attraction to men—are legitimate because the body is so electric, so filled with a vital energy that attracts and a galvanic current that flows.

Whether simple celebration or complex self-assertion, the final section, added in the 1856 edition of *Leaves,* "makes sense as the climax of the poem," as Howard Waskow says (86). It catalogues the glories of the body, moving from head to toe and from outer surfaces to inner organs and processes.

Whitman's erotic specificity in the catalogue, and in the entire poem, has often discomfited readers. Yet despite exhortations to modify the poem, he did not. Nowhere is the poet's commitment to the importance of celebrating the body in erotic terms clearer than in the long conversation which took place between Whitman and Ralph Waldo Emerson in 1860. For two hours the two men walked the streets of Boston, Emerson arguing that *Leaves of Grass* would find the large audience it deserved only if Whitman cut some of the most sexual and bodily passages from "Body Electric" and other poems in the "Children of Adam" section. "[H]e was the talker and I the listener. It was an argument-statement, reconnoitring, review, attack, and pressing home . . . of all that could be said against that part (and a main part) in the construction of my poems . . . each point of E.'s statement was unanswerable, no judge's charge ever more complete or convincing, I could never hear the points better put—and then I felt down in my soul the clear and unmistakable conviction to disobey all, and pursue my own way" (Whitman 281).

Huck Gutman

Bibliography

Coskren, Robert. "A Reading of Whitman's 'I Sing the Body Electric.'" *Walt Whitman Review* 22 (1976): 125–132.

Erkkila, Betsy. *Whitman the Political Poet.* New York: Oxford UP, 1989.

Fone, Byrne R.S. *Masculine Landscapes: Walt Whitman and the Homoerotic Text.* Carbondale: Southern Illinois UP, 1992.

Miller, Edwin Haviland. *Walt Whitman's Poetry: A Psychological Journey.* New York: New York UP, 1968.

Nathanson, Tenney. *Whitman's Presence: Body, Voice, and Writing in "Leaves of Grass."* New York: New York UP, 1992.

Waskow, Howard J. *Whitman: Explorations in Form.* Chicago: U of Chicago P, 1966.

Whitman, Walt. *Prose Works 1892.* Ed. Floyd Stovall. Vol. 1. New York: New York UP, 1963.

Zweig, Paul. *Walt Whitman: The Making of the Poet.* New York: Basic Books, 1984.

See also "CHILDREN OF ADAM"; HUMAN BODY; *LEAVES OF GRASS,* 1855 EDITION; SEX AND SEXUALITY; SOUL, THE

"I Sit and Look Out" (1860)

First published in the 1860 edition of *Leaves of Grass,* this ten-line lyric shows Whitman in his imagination surveying certain illustrative tragic or difficult scenes the world over. With rare understatement, he conveys his grief that such negative conditions abide and his dismay that he is helpless in the face of them.

Eight of the lines begin with "I," but the effect is less to call attention to the writer than to locate the observer, not otherwise described. Sitting passively somewhere, he is simply the viewer and the listener (a role common for Whitman but in a more affirmative mood). The reader is drawn to identify with this abstracted "I." The later particular images are given a sharper focus after the general first-line orientation: "I sit and look out upon all the sorrows of the world, and upon all oppression and shame." After a collection of instances, the poem at the end circles back to its opening thrust: "All these—all the meanness and agony without end I sitting look out upon, / See, hear, and am silent." Keeping silent establishes the dignity of the viewer, whose responses remain understood although hidden.

The instances themselves seem random: a young man at anguish over some wrongdoing, a mother's being neglected, a wife's being abused, someone in love's agonies; more widely, the "workings of battle, pestilence, tyranny," famine at sea, and finally the treatment of the weak by "arrogant persons." But taken together these images illustrate the nature of Whitman's concerns.

In this powerful lyric, then, he is dramatizing the fact that he sees the world as it is in its worst condition, that he is pained by what he sees, but that he has no choice but to accept it. The reader participates in that viewpoint.

David B. Baldwin

Bibliography
Miller, James E., Jr. *A Critical Guide to "Leaves of Grass."* Chicago: U of Chicago P, 1957.

Whitman, Walt. *Leaves of Grass: Comprehensive Reader's Edition.* Ed. Harold W. Blodgett and Sculley Bradley. New York: New York UP, 1965.

See also "By the Roadside";"Me Imperturbe"; "Song of Joys, A"; "Song of Prudence"; Stoicism

"I Was Looking a Long While" (1860)
Although Walt Whitman began working on it as early as 1856 or 1857, this ten-line poem was not published until the 1860 edition of *Leaves of Grass,* when it appeared as "Chants Democratic" number 19. Whitman subsequently gave the poem its current title in 1867, and later made a handful of minor revisions before considering "I Was Looking a Long While" finished in 1881.

As he does in so much of his work, Whitman pays homage in this poem to the "average man of to-day," arguing that the key to a brilliant future for humanity lies not with "fables in the libraries" but with a modern democracy in which all people live life to the fullest through a free exchange of ideas. He suggests that since the present is so wonderful, even though the past seemed to promise little, the future must be even better than the present.

"I Was Looking a Long While" is certainly a minor poem, and as such it has not attracted much critical commentary. Indeed, Whitman explains his belief in a positive future for humanity in greater detail, and with considerably more artistry, in poems such as "Passage to India." Still, it is difficult indeed not to be impressed by Whitman's sense of optimism in this short poem.

Jim McWilliams

Bibliography
Allen, Gay Wilson. *The Solitary Singer: A Critical Biography of Walt Whitman.* 1955. Rev. ed. 1967. Chicago: U of Chicago P, 1985.

Miller, James E., Jr. *A Critical Guide to "Leaves of Grass."* Chicago: U of Chicago P, 1957.

Whitman, Walt. *Leaves of Grass: Comprehensive Reader's Edition.* Ed. Harold W. Blodgett and Sculley Bradley. New York: New York UP, 1965.

———. *Whitman's Manuscripts: "Leaves of Grass" (1860).* Ed. Fredson Bowers. Chicago: U of Chicago P, 1955.

See also "Autumn Rivulets"; Optimism

Immigrants
Ever the humanitarian, ever the Singer of Democracy, Walt Whitman defended—even promoted—immigration and descried the plight of immigrants and the discrimination these "poor creatures" often suffered. Indeed, he could not understand how anyone with a heart could feel less than compassionate for the needy ones coming from Europe's closed society to America's plentiful storehouse. Immigration and free trade, he felt, would serve to break down barriers between peoples. He even wanted the nation's presses to cease using the word "foreigners."

As the young (age 22) editor of the New York *Aurora,* Whitman welcomed immigrants, though he did warn them not to try to enforce upon the developing democratic nation their old, outmoded ideas and practices. Believing as he did in the genius and greatness of America, he exclaimed, "Restrict nothing—keep everything open: to Italy, to China, to anybody" (*With Walt Whitman* 1:113). In "Salut au Monde!" he greeted the continentals of Asia, Africa, Europe, and Australia, as well as those on the many islands of the archipelagos, with warm affection: "Health to you! good will to you all, from me and America sent!" (section 11). In the Preface to *As a Strong Bird on Pinions Free* America was to him "the modern composite Nation, formed from all, with room for all, welcoming all immigrants" (*Comprehensive* 741).

Whitman was not patient with prejudiced people. He openly opposed the Native American party (the "Know-Nothings") when it venomously argued against "foreigners," especially Irish and German immigrants. The party proposed to deny citizenship to all aliens and even went so far as to recommend an end to all immigration for fear that immigrants would become a threat to the republic and western settlement. Taking the contrary position, as he also did with the proposals for restricted trade and the introduction of slavery in new territories, Whitman considered the outlawing of immigration a social evil. He saw the masses of immigrants as supplying the increasing need for laborers as westward expansion continued to draw multitudes from the industrialized eastern areas. But he did not stop there. He wanted many of these newcomers themselves to travel on to the far West and there take advantage of the riches ready for the taking by industrious, deserving men and women of sturdy stock such as he found the immigrants to be. That most did not, he observed, was because many of the "poor things" had exhausted all their means on passage—a problem that could, and should, be remedied by organized means to speed them on their way. This suggestion, he maintained, not only was economically advantageous but also was demanded by necessity and benevolence.

As editor of the Brooklyn *Daily Eagle*, he sternly countered the malicious gossip that certain authorities in Europe were exporting their paupers and criminals to the United States. He labeled as "legislative nonsense," "utterly ridiculous, impracticable—and, moreover, unnecessary" (*Gathering* 1:160) a bill introduced by Mr. Seaman, the Whig-Native representative in Congress, to outlaw the importation of paupers and criminals into the country. To rebut the gossip and its consequent legislative proposal, he reasoned that such undesirables would certainly not be deterred by the required oath that they were not paupers or criminals. Moreover, he wrote, to think that sick and infirm denizens of poorhouses, who had been sent there because they could not work, would survive the rigors of a long, exhausting ocean voyage was ludicrous. However, even if there were a basis for thinking Europe was transporting its unwelcome citizens to the United States—a suggestion he repudiated—the bill lacked merit, for he welcomed to the growing nation those hardy souls stout enough to survive the journey. Years later he told friends that without exception "America must welcome all" (*With Walt Whitman* 2:34), regardless of their national origin, their financial condition, or their legal status, for America must become an asylum for any who choose to come.

Nowhere is Whitman's admiration for immigrants and his sympathy for their condition more apparent than in an unpublished manuscript titled "Wants," that is, Want Ads. He was struck by the sturdiness of the men and the "patience, honesty, and good nature" (*Notebooks* 1:89) of the women. Yet he was touched by the sad state of affairs out of which they had little hope of rising. Their ability to accept their condition with determination and good humor may well account for his unwavering defense of his country's open arms to the thousands of immigrants that arrived daily on its shores.

Maverick Marvin Harris

Bibliography

Gohdes, Clarence, and Rollo G. Silver, eds. *Faint Clews & Indirections: Manuscripts of Walt Whitman and His Family.* Durham, N.C.: Duke UP, 1949.

Traubel, Horace. *With Walt Whitman in Camden.* Vol. 1. Boston: Small, Maynard, 1906; Vol. 2. New York: Appleton, 1908.

Whitman, Walt. *The Gathering of the Forces.* Ed. Cleveland Rodgers and John Black. 2 vols. New York: Putnam, 1920.

———. *Leaves of Grass: Comprehensive Reader's Edition.* Ed. Harold W. Blodgett and Sculley Bradley. New York: New York UP, 1965.

———. *Notebooks and Unpublished Prose Manuscripts.* Ed. Edward F. Grier. 6 vols. New York: New York UP, 1984.

———. *Walt Whitman of the New York Aurora.* Ed. Joseph Jay Rubin and Charles H. Brown. State College, Pa.: Bald Eagle, 1950.

See also AMERICAN CHARACTER; BROOKLYN *DAILY EAGLE*; NEW YORK *AURORA*; "SALUT AU MONDE!"

Immortality

To understand Whitman's achievement, it is important to acknowledge the extent to which his poetry is a thanatopsis. Death constitutes either the central theme or a crucial motif in all of his major poems and many of the poetic sequences. Yet critics are far from agreement regarding Whitman's views on death. At the risk of oversimplification, it may be said that current scholarship presents four viewpoints: first, that Whitman always affirmed personal immortality; second, that throughout his career he did not believe in immortality; third, that he at first affirmed it and then denied it in the late 1850s and 1860s in response to a crisis of faith precipitated by his new awareness of his homosexuality; and fourth, that beginning in the 1870s he imposed a theme of immortality on *Leaves* as part of a new emphasis on religion to compensate for the failure of his political vision or to camouflage his earlier celebration of homosexuality. The following essay argues that Whitman consistently asserted a belief in immortality and that, in fact, influenced by early nineteenth-century evolutionary theory, he formulated a new understanding of immortality as an ongoing process of development.

Whitman's writings on death consist of two types of utterances. One is a rational discourse which asserts a belief in immortality to the reader's intellect as a simple statement of fact. The second, a much more complex form of communication, is a mystical language which alludes to meanings which are, although ineffable, nevertheless capable of being grasped by the reader in epiphanic moments of spiritual realization. In considering the dynamics of this second type of utterance, one finds that Whitman's poetic makes several demands upon the reader that are rather commonplace in theologies of mystical formation: for example, a rejection of worldly values and commitment to one's spiritual development; a recognition of the importance of love and a striving to achieve a loving attitude toward other humans and the rest of creation; and the experiencing of the beauty and sublimity of nature. Whitman's mystical communication on immortality requires ideal readers who will pursue their spiritual advancement and, influenced by the power of love and certain calming aspects of nature such as the sea and starry nights, achieve a sense of profound psychological serenity and well-being. To readers who attain this state of heightened consciousness, Whitman subtly imposes his suggestions of spiritual meaning in an effort to convince them that they are, in this special moment, participating in the spirit of a providential, loving God whom they will know more fully in the afterlife.

Whitman's intellectual affirmations of immortality are consistently present in his writings throughout his career. The 1855 "Song of Myself" asserts that it is "lucky to die" (section 7) and that "[t]he smallest sprout shows there is really no death" (section 6). One of Whitman's anonymous reviews for the first edition points out that the author "recognizes no annihilation, or death, or loss of identity" (39). In the 1860 *Leaves* he speaks of the "joy of death" and the "beautiful touch of Death, soothing and be-numbing a few moments, for reasons," and he goes on to affirm that his soul or "real body" is "doubtless left to me for other spheres" ("Song of Joys"). Similarly "Starting from Paumanok," also of 1860, asserts that the "real body" will "elude the hands of the corpse-cleaners, and pass to fitting spheres" (section 13). The Civil War poem of 1865–1866 "How Solemn as One by One" proclaims "The soul!" which "the bullet could never kill . . . Nor the bayonet stab." A belief in immortality was so important to Whitman that in the 1876 Preface he proposed that a crucial criterion for evaluating either a poem or a culture is "what it thinks of Death," and he insisted that it was the "idea of immortality, above all other ideas" that was to "vivify, and give crowning religious stamp, to democracy in the New World" (*Prose Works* 2:465–466n). In 1881, as he brooded over the death of Thomas Carlyle, Whitman asked himself if it were possible that he "remains an identity still?" and he answered, "I have no doubt of it" (*Prose Works* 1:253). In his final years, he insisted emphatically to Traubel that when he spoke of immortality he meant "identity—the survival of the personal soul—your survival, my survival" (Traubel 149).

Whitman's belief in immortality undoubtedly had its genesis in the fact that he matured in a Christian culture that affirmed the immortality of the soul. Later, however, as he developed his own religious vision, he, like other contemporary religious visionaries, such as Joseph Smith and the noted spiritualist Andrew Jackson Davis, developed a new understanding of the idea of immortality from the culture's widespread belief in progress and the advent of evolutionary science. Believing that both history and nineteenth-century evolutionary thought indicated that the universe was infused with a divinely ordained principle of progressive advancement, Whitman extended this idea of ongoing amelioration to the soul after its human death. Viewed from Whitman's transcendentalist perspective, the signs of progress in nature and history were more than natural facts; they were also "eidólons" or religious symbols, and as symbols they were the "needed emblem" of the "progress of the souls of men and women along the grand roads of the universe" ("Song of the Open Road," section 13). The highways for souls were grand because there were no dead ends; the progress of the soul was a "perpetual journey" ("Song of Myself," section 46), a "journey ever continued" ("Thoughts [Of ownership . . .]"), an "endless march" ("Going Somewhere"). Apart from affirming its ongoing existence and development until it meets with God or becomes a god itself, Whitman remains intentionally vague about the soul's posthuman existence, merely stating that it passes to "other spheres" or "fitting spheres" ("By Blue Ontario's Shore," section 5; "Starting from Paumanok," section 13; "A Song of Joys"; "The World below the Brine").

It is not generally recognized that "Song of Myself," in which Whitman presents himself as the prophet of a new religion, culminates with a presentation of this understanding of immortality as ongoing process. In the 1855 edition, after briefly tracing his evolution from the "huge first Nothing" at the beginning of the creation up to human existence (section 44), Whitman then looks out at night upon the immensity of the star-filled universe: "the far-sprinkled systems" that "edge but the rim of the farther systems" (section 45). Gazing upon the "crowded heaven," he asks his ever yearning spirit whether it will be "filled and satisfied" when we become "the enfolders of those orbs," and his soul replies, "No, we but level that lift to pass and continue beyond" (section 46). In the midst of these lines, Whitman explicitly assures his readers of their immortality and ongoing development: "Our rendezvous is fitly appointed. . . . God will be there and wait till we come" (section 45). Later, in 1867, he reinforces this message by expanding the second half of the line: "The Lord will be there, and wait till I come, on perfect terms; / (The great Camerado, the lover true for whom I pine, will be there.)"

In contrast to these intellectual assertions, Whitman's mystical affirmations of immortality attempt to lead the spiritually prepared reader to a profound sense of calm well-being which constitutes itself in the consciousness of the subject as having a special reality or power. Whitman then interprets this elevated state of consciousness as an experience of a transcendent spiritual reality (or divinity) which the soul will know more fully in the afterlife. The calmness of spirit induced by a sense of being loved was, for Whitman, the strongest mystical anticipation of the afterlife. For example, a letter to his Australian friend and disciple Bernard O'Dowd concludes with "love & best respects" and asserts that this "pure sentiment" may be the "best proof of immortality" (*Correspondence* 5:168). Thus in Whitman's mystical poetry on death it is important to note that when

his poetic persona assumes a mystical state of consciousness, concepts such as reality, God, love, and death become virtually synonymous.

The second entry in "Calamus," "Scented Herbage of My Breast," a largely misinterpreted poem, is crucial to grasping Whitman's mystical understanding of the relationship between love and death. In the opening "Calamus" poem and the first half of "Scented Herbage," Whitman announces that the calamus grass is a religious symbol that has "talk'd to" his soul. Then in the second part of "Scented Herbage," he interprets the calamus as symbol of the comradeship that is the best proof of immortality. He experiences a mystical state of consciousness that quiets and elevates his soul ("how calm, how solemn it grows to ascend to the atmosphere of lovers"), giving him a sense of participating in a more real spiritual order: the "real reality" which transcends the natural world. In comparison to this sacred experience, the ordinary world of secular experience seems mere illusion: a "mask of materials" or "show of appearance." Because Whitman interprets this love as a mystical prolepsis of the spiritual existence he will know after death when his soul participates more fully in the spirit of a loving divinity, he can assert that he has the necessary spiritual insight to deliver his readers from the terror of death: "Through me shall the words be said to make death exhilarating." Death will be a fuller experience of the love the soul has known in this life; thus Whitman asserts that love and death mean "precisely the same" or are "folded inseparably together."

Whitman's most celebrated poems on death, "Out of the Cradle Endlessly Rocking" and "When Lilacs Last in the Dooryard Bloom'd" (spanning a period from 1858 to 1867), work to bring the reader to a mystical state in a manner similar to "Scented Herbage." However, instead of drawing upon the experience of human love, they instead appeal to certain aspects of nature that Whitman experienced as instilling the soul with a sense of spiritual serenity and transcendence. Key among these were not only the stars (already discussed as a symbol of immortality in "Song of Myself") but also the night, the sea and other bodies of water, and the nocturnal warbling of the hermit thrush. Whitman's sense of the night as conveying an ineffable sense of a more real spiritual realm is succinctly encapsulated in an 1876 note which describes the night as presenting "such suggestions to the soul of space, of mystery, of spirituality, of the ideal—without words, without touch, yet beyond all words" (*Notebooks* 3:1093). Like the night, the sea was also a prime symbol of the spiritual, and Whitman frequently used it to symbolize the transcendent God from which the creation came and to which souls returned in their posthuman existence. For Whitman, the hermit thrush was virtually a spiritual entity; its habitat was "the solemn primal woods & of nature pure and holy" and its song was a "hymn / real, serious sweet" (*Notebooks* 2:766).

This symbolism of immortality and a transcendent spiritual realm must be kept in mind when interpreting Whitman's two great poems on death. In "Out of the Cradle," Whitman, as both boy and poet, anguishes over the inevitable frustration of human love, but then experiences the soothing effect of the sea's rhythmic "whispering" and "laving" waves under the star-filled heavens. This induces a state of calm and reassurance that is interpreted as a mystical anticipation of the afterlife. Thus the God of "Out of the Cradle" is a "fierce old mother" who sternly demands the death of her creatures but also a loving mother who speaks through her creation to convince the soul that death leads to an afterlife in which the soul's yearning for love is satisfied by a God of love (the "Great Camerado, the lover true" of "Song of Myself," section 45). The concluding movement of the "Lilacs" elegy works to create a similar calming effect and employs many of the same symbols. After presenting a tranquil evening scene of a recovered nation of productive farmers and workers, it then, with the coming of darkness, culminates in the liquid aria of the hermit thrush that blesses the entire creation, giving final emphasis to the star-filled night and the "*ocean shore and husky whispering wave*" (section 14).

In addition to using symbol and mood to establish a mystical sense of immortality in these poems, Whitman also carefully links these passages of repose with other parts of *Leaves* that do contain explicit assertions of immortality. For instance, in "Out of the Cradle," the sea's final, emphatic whispering of "death" connects this poem to the suggestions of immortality associated with "death" in "Scented Herbage." Similarly, the source of the poet's "unsatisfied love," the "unknown want" of "Out of the Cradle," is clarified by Whitman's later addition in 1871 of the couplet in "Songs of Parting" which tells the soul that after death it will be free to "sail" out into the divine sea to "seek and find" the "untold want" that life "ne'er grant-

ed" ("The Untold Want"). In "Lilacs," the lilac becomes a symbol of immortality by being described as "blooming perennial" (section 1) and "tall-growing" with "delicate" blossoms and "perfume strong" (section 3), thus becoming an analogue to the "perennial," "tall," "delicate," and "[s]cented" calamus grass of "Scented Herbage" which is, in turn, associated with the grass of "Song of Myself," which "shows there is really no death" (section 6).

Turning from Whitman's writings to a consideration of the critical discussion of his views on immortality, it seems fair to conclude that there is clearly no basis for either the position that Whitman never believed in immortality or that he only developed this belief in the later editions. Nor is there any consistent evidence for arguing that Whitman expressed no belief in immortality in the new poems of the late 1850s and 1860s. The one issue for which there is some ground for disagreement is whether "Out of the Cradle" and "Lilacs" affirm immortality. The strongest negative evidence is the absence of overt assertions of the soul's transcendence. However, if the reader is sensitive to the mystical dimensions of Whitman's poetry and places these poems within the larger context of *Leaves,* the evidence for reading them as attempting to bring the reader to an existential sense of immortality is compelling.

David Kuebrich

Bibliography

Allen, Gay Wilson. *The Solitary Singer: A Critical Biography of Walt Whitman.* 1955. Rev. ed. 1967. Chicago: U of Chicago P, 1985.

Erkkila, Betsy. *Whitman the Political Poet.* New York: Oxford UP, 1989.

Griffith, Clark. "Sex and Death: The Significance of Whitman's 'Calamus' Themes." *Philological Quarterly* 39 (1960): 18–38.

Helms, Alan. "Whitman Revised." *Études Anglaises* 37 (1984): 247–271.

Kuebrich, David. *Minor Prophecy: Walt Whitman's New American Religion.* Bloomington: Indiana UP, 1989.

Miller, Edwin Haviland. *Walt Whitman's Poetry: A Psychological Journey.* Boston: Houghton Mifflin, 1968.

Miller, James E., Jr. *A Critical Guide to "Leaves of Grass."* Chicago: U of Chicago P, 1957.

Traubel, Horace. *With Walt Whitman in Camden.* Vol. 1. Boston: Small, Maynard, 1906.

Whicher, Stephen. "Whitman's Awakening to Death: Toward a Biographical Reading of 'Out of the Cradle Endlessly Rocking.'" *Studies in Romanticism* 1 (1961): 9–28.

Whitman, Walt. *The Correspondence*. Ed. Edwin Haviland Miller. 6 vols. New York: New York UP, 1961–1977.

———. *Notebooks and Unpublished Prose Manuscripts*. Ed. Edward F. Grier. 6 vols. New York: New York UP, 1984.

———. *Prose Works 1892*. Ed. Floyd Stovall. 2 vols. New York: New York UP, 1963–1964.

———. "Whitman's Anonymous Self-reviews 1855–6." *Walt Whitman: The Critical Heritage*. Ed. Milton Hindus. London: Routledge and Kegan Paul, 1971. 34–41.

See also COMRADESHIP; DEATH; EVOLUTION; METAPHYSICS; PANTHEISM; RELIGION; SEA, THE; SOUL, THE

Imperialism

Whitman's acclaim as poet of egalitarianism, humanitarian progress, and democracy has tended to obscure his involvement in movements and beliefs which are embarrassing to some of his admirers in the second half of the twentieth century. Imperialism is a characteristic case. Much of Whitman's poetry is informed by a commitment to manifest destiny, westward expansion and imperialism. This seeming paradox may be explained in terms of the ambivalence of the culture of which Whitman was a part.

In *Walt Whitman: Racista, Imperialista, Antimexicano*, Mauricio González de la Garza characterized Whitman as an "hombre contradictorio" who displayed "el sentimiento del internacionalismo" in his poetry while expressing regrettable imperialist attitudes in his early journalistic prose (de la Garza 9f). The examples de la Garza provides actually relate to Whitman's expansionism, which is limited to neighboring countries and territories. The victims of expansionism were mainly Mexicans and, as Ed Folsom stresses, Native Americans, toward whom Whitman also had a strongly ambivalent attitude. Imperialism, on the other hand, refers to hemispherical, even globalized, developments and strategies. In Whitman's texts, both are linked in the same large and contradictory cultural narratives that inform the author's vision of America. The rhetoric of manifest destiny is applied on a global scale: "It seems as if the Almighty had spread before this nation charts of imperial destinies, dazzling as the sun" (*Complete* 990).

Although Whitman's poetry is probably just as expansionist and/or imperialist as his prose, the conflict between the noble internationalist and the imperialist is adequately assessed by de la Garza. For Whitman, who desired a "mutual benevolence of all humanity, the solidarity of the world" (*Grashalme* xii), empire is frequently a requirement for a productive development and coexistence. To him, "the existence of the true American continental solidarity . . . wholly depends on a compacted imperial ensemble" (*Complete* 1050). American "individuality" would "flourish best under imperial republican forms" (*Complete* 959).

In early nineteenth-century American political discourse, empire at times represented the democratic counterpart to dynastical European monarchism, and Whitman may well have employed that rhetoric. Yet, like later critics such as Mark Twain, he also seems aware of the problematical implications of imperialism, for he suggests the problems caused by an "empire of empires": "But behold the cost. . . . Thought you greatness was to ripen for you like a pear? If you would have greatness, know that you must conquer it through ages, centuries—must pay for it with a proportionate price" (*Complete* 990).

In order to critique Whitman's poetry from the anti-imperialist angle, it is not necessary to refer to explicit lines such as the one in "A Broadway Pageant": "I chant the new empire grander than any before, as in a vision it comes to me" (section 2). The celebrated catalogues of *Leaves* seem to project an inclusive universalism, with hundreds of lines representing the colorful conglomerate of world cultures. However, these lines, each representing one such culture, rather resemble homogenized computer entries, highlighting one peculiar aspect of each much in the way modern tourism markets foreign countries. In their utilitarian compactness, these catalogues erase cultural differences and, through their very form, subject non-Western (or even non-Anglo-Saxon) cultures to Western standards. Even in "Salut au Monde!," Whitman's most successful and (given its global reception) most credible international(ist) poem, the vision of the lyrical persona forces Western technology on the whole world: "I see the tracks of the railroads of the earth, / I see them in Great Britain, I see them in Europe, / I see them in Asia and in Africa" (section 5). While the railroad tracks seem to equalize all continents and bring them together, they also standardize them on Western terms following a Western logic.

In one of Whitman's best-known poems, "Passage to India," the dialogue of the lyrical persona with his soul, though frequently a liberating experience in Whitman's poems, betrays the poem's imperialist impulse: "Passage to India! / Lo, soul, seest thou not God's purpose from the first? / The earth to be spann'd, connected by network" (section 2). Again, manifest destiny is extended globally, controlled by a universal "network." The explorer Vasco da Gama, uncritically introduced into the text, explicitly represents the colonialist and imperialist impetus of Western culture. Whitman envisions the world as "Doubts to be solv'd, the map incognita, blanks to be fill'd" (section 6). It is on *Western* maps, iconic texts of imperialism, where any territory not under Western domination appears as "blank," waiting to be opened up to world trade.

What is curious is not so much the existence of imperialist thinking in Whitman's poetry but its complex lyrical representation which, by fusing industrial, technological, logistical, and imperial images as early as 1871, already anticipates the Marxist-Leninist interpretation of imperialism as an ideology brought about by the development of monopoly capitalism.

Whitman's personae, seemingly celebrating the progress of the race, frequently celebrate the progress of Americanism in imperialist terms. Speaking prophetically to the world and using an enlightened rhetoric, they oftentimes identify the cause of America with that of humankind in general. Proceeding from his idea of America as a "composite" nation containing in itself all elements of humanity, Whitman develops a theory that America is by definition the one country that can serve as a model for all others. Thus, because imperialism is actually mandated in the interest of humanity, the imperialist charge would probably not have bothered him much. Emanating from progressive America, American imperialism would have appeared to him as benign, productive, and serving the common good.

While this naiveté may be shocking to those desiring a politically correct literature, imperialism was probably not a decisive moral issue for Whitman. In spite of an occasional uneasiness, he would have been unaware of the imperialism implicit in his globalist rhetoric.

Walter Grünzweig

Bibliography

Erkkila, Betsy. *Whitman the Political Poet.* New York: Oxford UP, 1989.

Folsom, Ed. *Walt Whitman's Native Representations.* Cambridge: Cambridge UP, 1994.

González de la Garza, Mauricio. *Walt Whitman: Racista, Imperialista, Antimexicano.* México: Colección Málaga, 1971.

Grünzweig, Walter. "'For America—For All the Earth': Walt Whitman as an International(ist) Poet." *Breaking Bounds: Whitman and American Cultural Studies.* Ed. Betsy Erkkila and Jay Grossman. New York: Oxford UP, 1996. 238–250.

———. "Noble Ethics and Loving Aggressiveness: The Imperialist Walt Whitman." *An American Empire: Expansionist Cultures and Policies, 1881–1917.* Ed. Serge Ricard. Aix-en-Provence: Université de Provence, 1990. 151–165.

Whitman, Walt. *Complete Poetry and Collected Prose.* Ed. Justin Kaplan. New York: Library of America, 1982.

———. *Grashalme: Gedichte.* Trans. Karl Knortz and T.W. Rolleston. Zürich: Schabelitz, 1889.

See also "BROADWAY PAGEANT, A"; INTERCULTURALITY; MEXICAN WAR, THE; NATIVE AMERICANS (INDIANS); "PASSAGE TO INDIA"; "SALUT AU MONDE!"

"In Paths Untrodden" (1860)

The initial poem of the "Calamus" sequence has remained remarkably little changed since its first appearance in 1860. The manuscripts indicate, however, that Whitman began this poem without the central symbol of the "calamus." What was present from its inception was the idea of change or conversion. The six original lines stress the opposition between a past self that conformed to conventional expectations and a new life not publicly known. By escaping from the old life of conventional morality and social organization, the speaker realizes the possibility of celebrating "the love of comrades" (later revised to the "need" of comrades).

The first published version reflects Whitman's discovery of the "calamus" as a central figure for male sexuality and for his art. The added first two lines provide a physical and symbolic setting for reawakening. The poet must move toward the marginal in order to find the freedom to be himself. Whitman stresses his need to go beyond the conventional, to find in seclusion an ability to speak that he is not capable of elsewhere. The sylvan setting of the pond joins imagery of baptism and renewal with the erotic, allowing for "athletic love," or male homosexuality. In a line added in 1860 Whitman speaks of the burden of speech as "the secret of my nights and days," giving a personal urgency to a generalized claim of freedom from convention.

Whitman thus introduces the first "Calamus" poem as a text of "coming out," both literal and metaphorical, as the discovery of the self and its expression. Whitman announces his purpose in this sequence of poems as singing "manly attachment," creating a body of work that will record the joys and sorrows of his desires under the pressure of social disapproval. That the "calamus" is a figure for the male genitals is clear from "Song of Myself"; hence the love evoked is seen as both physical and metaphysical. His mission is to provide models for an as yet uncreated love. As in the first poem, the task becomes one of drawing on whatever literary tradition of male homosexuality was available to him (Greek and Roman pastoral in this case) while at the same time making it over into a democratic discourse.

Despite the striking sexual imagery and firmly stated intent, many critics have followed James E. Miller's lead in seeing the poem largely in terms of a generalized dissent or skepticism. Edwin Miller acknowledges the poem's sexuality but dismisses it as narcissistic and regressive. Following Martin in seeing the text as announcing a homosexual identity, Fone locates its discourse in the context of Victorian sexology. Whitman's text serves as a confession that establishes a self.

Robert K. Martin

Bibliography

Fone, Byrne R.S. *Masculine Landscapes: Walt Whitman and the Homoerotic Text.* Carbondale: Southern Illinois UP, 1992.
Martin, Robert K. *The Homosexual Tradition in American Poetry.* Austin: U of Texas P, 1979.
Miller, Edwin Haviland. *Walt Whitman's Poetry: A Psychological Journey.* Boston: Houghton Mifflin, 1968.
Miller, James E., Jr. *A Critical Guide to "Leaves of Grass."* Chicago: U of Chicago P, 1957.

See also "CALAMUS"; SEX AND SEXUALITY

India, Whitman in

Whitman's reputation in India has been due mainly to the affinities that Indian readers have felt between his ideas and the Hindu philosophical teachings. He has been admired for his bold, prophetic voice, for his all-embracing sympathies, and above all for his ecstatic celebration of the Self, in which Indian readers could readily recognize resemblances to the sublime utterances of the Gita and the Upanishads. But whether these resemblances are a pure coincidence or whether they point to actual indebtedness on Whitman's part to Indian sources remains uncertain in spite of the most laborious research. Whatever the case may be, Indian readers have over the years come to see in Whitman's poems the quintessential spirit of Indian philosophy.

It was, however, the American orientalists who first detected Indian elements in Whitman's thought. Indian interest in Whitman came later, toward the turn of the century, due to contacts with American intellectuals and due also to the new enthusiasm for Indian philosophical systems such as Vedanta, Samkhya, and Yoga, generated by the activities of the Vedanta missionaries headed by Swamy Vivekananda in the 1890s. Later Indian scholarship on the subject also followed important investigations by American scholars; it was in fact spurred by them.

The very first individuals to observe Indian elements in Whitman were the poet's own friends and admirers. We learn from Frank B. Sanborn's account in "Reminiscent of Whitman" (*The Conservator*, May 1897) that Emerson described *Leaves of Grass* as "a remarkable mixture of Bhagvat Ghita [*sic*] and the *New York Herald*" (qtd. in Rajasekharaiah 21). In a letter to Harrison Blake, 6–7 December 1856, Henry David Thoreau called the poems "[w]onderfully like the Orientals" (qtd. in Allen 260). Edward Carpenter, in *Days with Walt Whitman* (1906), cited many parallels from the Upanishads, the Gita, and the Buddhist scriptures. William Norman Guthrie, in *Walt Whitman the Camden Sage* (1897), thought that the study of the Gita was indispensable for a correct understanding of Whitman's poems. More recently, Malcolm Cowley, in the introduction to his edition of the 1855 poems, claimed that most of Whitman's mystical ideas belonged to the mainstream of Indian philosophy. The first systematic and full-scale attempt at a comparative study of Whitman and Indian thought is, however, Dorothy F. Mercer's University of

California dissertation "*Leaves of Grass* and the Bhagavad Gita: A Comparative Study" (1933), published in part as a series of articles in *Vedanta and the West* (1946–1949), in which she examined parallel ideas such as God, Self, Love, and Yoga.

One of the first Indians to be impressed with Whitman's spirituality was Swamy Vivekananda (1862–1902). We learn from Romain Rolland's account of him in *Prophets of the New India* that Vivekananda called Whitman "the Sannyasin [monk] of America" (348 ff.). Rabindranath Tagore was equally struck by Whitman's mysticism and said that "No American has caught the Oriental spirit of mysticism as well as he" (qtd. in Holloway 156). The noted philosopher and Indologist Anand K. Coomaraswamy, in *Buddha and the Gospel of Buddhism* (1916), found in the lines of "Song of Myself" modern equivalents of the spiritual values of the Buddhist and Hindu religions. Subsequent studies of Whitman by Indian scholars, both books and articles, consistently followed the mystic line, bringing further substantiation to the established view of Whitman as a mystical poet. The concern of many of these studies is not, however, to discover resemblances in a purely comparatist spirit, but to use the Indian philosophical concepts as critical tools to explain Whitman's meanings. Thus V.K. Chari's *Whitman in the Light of Vedantic Mysticism* uses the Vedantic concept of the Self to interpret Whitman's cosmic dynamism and other aspects of his thought. O.K. Nambiar in *Walt Whitman and Yoga* applies the principles of the Yoga philosophy to explicate enigmatic passages in "Song of Myself," especially section 5. Indian philosophies have generally regarded sex as a sacred function and a manifestation of divine energy, capable, if properly tapped, of helping us to transcend the narrow limits of ego-consciousness; thus scholars have tried to justify Whitman's sexuality in that light.

While most comparative studies of Whitman evade the question of Whitman's debt to Hindu literature, T.R. Rajasekharaiah in *The Roots of Whitman's Grass* is convinced that Whitman borrowed all of his basic philosophical ideas from Hindu sources, but that he deliberately tried to suppress all evidence of his borrowings. Rajasekharaiah's study is valuable, not as a source study, because it does not take us much beyond the realm of probability, but for the many, hitherto unsuspected, parallels it discovers in thought, image, and language.

Indian studies of Whitman have focused almost exclusively on his mysticism and paid little attention to the ideological aspects of his writings. They have been inclined to view his ideology as a natural corollary to his mystical vision. Two scholars, Kshitindranath Tagore and R.K. Dasgupta, however, have struck a different note and seen Whitman's value as a prophet of democracy rather than as a mystic. Some recent studies, including Chari's essay "Whitman Criticism in the Light of Indian Poetics," focus on critical and aesthetic matters, perhaps indicating a shift in interest.

Whitman has left no significant mark on the course of modern Indian literatures for the obvious reason that there were no translations of his poems into any of the Indian languages until recently. Hence interest in him has been confined to English-educated scholars and literati. However, an interesting study by V. Sachithanandan, *Whitman and Bharati,* reveals the high admiration that the Tamil national poet Bharati (1880–1921) felt for Whitman. Bharati, who had an English education, was inspired not only by Whitman's mysticism but by the American nationalistic fervor that prompted him to write some of his patriotic songs. Whitman's prosodic freedom influenced Bharati in his attempts to free Tamil poetry from the tyranny of literary conventions. He wrote a poem entitled "Nan" ("I") in free verse, apparently in imitation of Whitman. Rabindranath Tagore also noticed Whitman's significance for a new poetry and probably followed his example in structuring the English version he wrote of his *Gitanjali.*

Indian response to Whitman has been remarkably enthusiastic throughout. The consistent aim of the Indian studies has been to vindicate the poet's vision of man and his cosmos, and to see all facets of his poetic personality as an expression of that unifying vision.

V.K. Chari

Bibliography

Allen, Gay Wilson. *The New Walt Whitman Handbook.* New York: New York UP, 1975.

Allen, Gay Wilson, and Ed Folsom, eds. *Walt Whitman & the World.* Iowa City: U of Iowa P, 1995.

Chari, V.K. "Whitman Criticism in the Light of Indian Poetics." *Walt Whitman: The Centennial Essays.* Ed. Ed Folsom. Iowa City: U of Iowa P, 1994. 240–250.

———. *Whitman in the Light of Vedantic Mysticism.* Lincoln: U of Nebraska P, 1964.

Dasgupta, R.K. "Indian Response to Walt Whitman." *Revue de Littérature Comparée* 47 (1973): 58–70.

Holloway, Emory. *Walt Whitman: An Interpretation in Narrative.* New York: Knopf, 1926.

Mercer, Dorothy F. Articles on Whitman and the Gita. *Vedanta and the West* 9 (1946) to 12 (1949).

Mishra, R.S. "Whitman's Sex: A Reading of 'Children of Adam.'" *Calamus* 23 (1983): 19–25.

Nambiar, O.K. *Walt Whitman and Yoga.* Bangalore: Jeevan Publications, 1966.

Rajasekharaiah, T.R. *The Roots of Whitman's Grass.* Rutherford: Fairleigh Dickinson UP, 1970.

Rolland, Romain. *Prophets of the New India.* New York: Boni, 1930.

Sachithanandan, V. *Walt Whitman and Bharati: A Comparative Study.* Madras: Macmillan, 1978.

Tagore, Kshitindranath. "Walt Whitman." Trans. from Bengali by R.K. Dasgupta. *Walt Whitman Review* 19 (1973): 3–11.

Whitman, Walt. *Walt Whitman's "Leaves of Grass": The First (1855) Edition.* Ed. Malcolm Cowley. New York: Viking, 1959.

See also: HINDU LITERATURE; INTERCULTURALITY; MYSTICISM

Indian Affairs, Bureau of

On 1 January 1865 Whitman was hired as a clerk at the Bureau of Indian Affairs, a governmental agency within the Department of Interior. Six months later, the newly appointed Secretary of Interior, James Harlan, a former Methodist minister and senator from Iowa, fired Whitman upon discovering he was the author of *Leaves of Grass,* a book Harlan knew by reputation as immoral and pornographic. The incident caused considerable stir within the administration as prominent supporters of Whitman came to his defense, eventually securing him a position in the Attorney General's Office.

Upon deciding in 1862 to stay in Washington, Whitman had initially secured a position in the paymaster's office as a clerk, but was dissatisfied. To secure a better position, he sought help from several influential friends, including Ralph Waldo Emerson, who wrote a recommendation on his behalf. After receiving the Department of Interior appointment, Whitman, from all accounts and from his letters home, was delighted for a number of reasons. First, he was fascinated by the visiting delegations of American Indians from the plains tribes. It was even reported that he would sometimes visit them in the evenings in their hotel rooms and speak with them via an interpreter. Secondly, he enjoyed the more relaxed atmosphere of the office, which allowed greater flexibility in his schedule so that he could visit the nearby field hospitals to help with the wounded. He wrote in a letter to his brother Jeff that though he was supposed to work from nine to four, he almost never arrived as early as nine and only stayed until four if he wanted. Finally, he was delighted with the per annum pay of twelve hundred dollars, a considerably higher sum than his previous position, which he needed both to support himself in Washington and to send home to his mother and younger siblings.

The job, which primarily consisted of copying out reports made by BIA officials, was suited to Whitman's needs at the time, and he was well liked by his immediate superior William P. Dole, who promoted him to a second-class clerkship on 11 May 1865, just a few days prior to his dismissal.

Edward W. Huffstetler

Bibliography

Allen, Gay Wilson. *The Solitary Singer: A Critical Biography of Walt Whitman.* 1955. Rev. ed. 1967. Chicago: U of Chicago P, 1985.

Asselineau, Roger. *The Evolution of Walt Whitman.* 2 vols. Cambridge, Mass.: Harvard UP, 1960–1962.

Kaplan, Justin. *Walt Whitman: A Life.* New York: Simon and Schuster, 1980.

Schyberg, Frederik. *Walt Whitman.* Trans. Evie Allison Allen. New York: Columbia UP, 1951.

See also ATTORNEY GENERAL'S OFFICE, UNITED STATES; CIVIL WAR, THE; HARLAN, JAMES W.; NATIVE AMERICANS (INDIANS); O'CONNOR, WILLIAM DOUGLAS; WASHINGTON, D.C.

Individualism

Walt Whitman approached individualism from a distinctively post-Revolutionary American viewpoint. In notes published in *Walt Whitman's Workshop,* he compared himself to Washington, who "made free the body of America" (35). Through his own poetry, Whitman says in an 1855 review of his own work published in *Rivulets of Prose,* "The interior American republic shall also be declared free and independent" (1). He hoped to foster the psychic redefinition required under a new social contract through his poetry of self-affirmation.

Like Ralph Waldo Emerson, Whitman decried the continuing power of British cultural models over nineteenth-century American literature, aesthetic standards, and social assumptions and practices. Alarmed at the continuing influence of "feudalism, caste, the ecclesiastic traditions," as described in *Democratic Vistas* (*Prose Works* 2:364), he feared the power of inherited cultural influences to undermine the basic assumption of a democracy—that citizens can and must be self-governing, i.e., self-regulating. A functioning democracy must "train communities through all their grades, beginning with individuals and ending there again, to rule themselves," he says in *Vistas* (380).

Whitman believed that cultural models must be revised to promote self-regulation. A "democratic literature," he says in *Vistas,* must "bring forth, cultivate, brace, and strengthen" the "perennial regulation, control, and oversight, by self-suppliance" of "individuals and society" (421). Whitman early concluded that the best way to "cultivate" self-regulation is through self-realization, and he determined to supply a prototype of the fully-realized self-regulating democratic citizen in his own poetry: "I am satisfied with Leaves of Grass . . . as expressing what was intended, namely, to express . . . *One's-Self* & also . . . to map out . . . for American use, a gigantic embryo or skeleton of Personality, fit for the West, for native models," he wrote to William D. O'Connor in 1865 (*Correspondence* 1:247).

Whitman used himself and his observations of his own culture to construct the map, these being the materials that he knew best and representing the lowest common denominator available to everyone. In the 1855 Preface to *Leaves,* he explores in prose his concerns that a cultural model based on aristocratic exclusions would undermine the inclusiveness required in a democracy. In his poetry, especially "Song of Myself," he seeks to repair the ravages of exclusionary models on the cultural psyche. In *Vistas* Whitman discusses "democracy's rule" that all citizens must "be placed, in each and in the whole, on one broad, primary, universal common platform" (380).

Like Emerson and others of the period, Whitman believed that this common platform is provided by nature. The "lesson of Nature," he says in *Vistas,* is the "quality of BEING, in the object's self, according to its own central idea and purpose, and of growing therefrom and thereto—not criticism by other standards" (394). Like Emerson, Whitman believed that it is not only possible but also safe to construct new cultural models from nature because modern scientific discoveries show nature to be essentially self-regulating. In the 1872 Preface to *As a Strong Bird on Pinions Free,* he calls for "an *imaginative* New World, the correspondent and

Walt Whitman, ca. 1860. By permission, Beeghly Library, Ohio Wesleyan University.

counterpart to the current Scientific and Political New Worlds" (*Prose Works* 2:461). "These States," he says in *Vistas,* need "forms of lasting power and practicality . . . rivaling the operations of the physical kosmos" to undergird "the democratic republican principle, and the theory of development and perfection by voluntary standards" (362). In the 1855 Preface, Whitman praises the outer embodiment of an inner coherence in the perfect and satisfying natural forms of lilacs and oranges, and he recommends these as models for a democratic aesthetics.

Because democracy requires a cultural model that will entice rather than coerce, a democratic aesthetic is particularly necessary: "a great original literature is surely to become the justification and reliance . . . of American democracy," Whitman says in *Vistas* (366). An aesthetic construct is itself a model of self-regulation because it derives meaning from sensory data through an internally coherent system. In the 1855 Preface, Whitman calls the democratic poet "the equable man" (*Comprehensive* 712) and "the president of regulation" (714) and adds that in a successful democracy "[t]heir Presidents shall not be their common referee so much as their poets shall" (712). The aesthetic paradigm of self-regulation is the most accessible as well as the most seductive one available to a democratic culture since it is ultimately pleasurable and encourages development, as Whitman says in *Vistas,* by "voluntary standards" (362) and "not repression alone, and not authority alone" (379). Since language is at the center of human consciousness, the struggle with language in the creation of poetry is the closest approximation to the struggle with experience in the creation of a self; Whitman therefore determined that the reader must be a partner in the creation of "Song of Myself." Reading must not be "a half-sleep" but a "gymnast's struggle"; "the reader is to do something for himself," he says in *Vistas* (424–425).

In "Song of Myself," Whitman quickly draws the reader into the drama of self-creation: "every atom belonging to me as good belongs to you" (section 1). This interior adventure is driven by an erotic attraction between pairs of opposites: body and soul, earth and sun, reader and bard, self and community. The "atoms" shared by reader and bard provide a metaphysical basis for a democratic communal identity. All are equally capable of self-realization: "there is in the possession of . . . each single individual,

something so transcendent, so incapable of gradations, (like life,) that . . . it places all beings on a common level," he says in *Vistas* (380). This capacity for selfhood is necessarily located first in the body or the physical world, and the affirmation of the body becomes the basis for all subsequent unfoldings in "Song of Myself."

The earliest known fragments of the poetry that became *Leaves* refer to a slave auction such as Whitman must have witnessed in New Orleans in 1848. Later incorporated in sections 7 and 8 of "I Sing the Body Electric," these fragmentary celebrations of the sanctity of the body show Whitman's concern in pre–Civil War America to heal the ancient rift between body and soul—extending at least as far back as Plato—that allowed bodies to be sold at auction, to be humiliated by ridiculous fashions and ascetic religious practices, and to be suppressed as vehicles of rampant sexual energy and physical corruption. The necessity of affirming the body in an authentic democratic cultural model also supplied the erotic dynamic of Whitman's epic of self-creation.

Asserting that "there are in things two elements fused though antagonistic," Whitman defined these elements as sexual opposites: "the Soul of the Universe is the Male and genital master and the impregnating and animating spirit—Physical matter is Female and Mother." These elements are also metaphysical opposites: the "bodily element . . . has in itself the quality of corruption and decease; . . . the Soul . . . goes on . . . enduring forever and ever," according to notes in *Workshop* (49). It is the necessary union of these mythic opposites—"Out of the dimness opposite equals advance, always substance and increase, always sex" (section 3)—that produces the evolving consciousness in "Song of Myself" as well as the developmental crises of that evolution.

In addition, the interaction of these primal forces induces self-regulation because their "antagonistic" pull on each other keeps either from self-destructive excess. In the process of self-creation, the body individualizes the self and provides a center through which experiences are processed: "the unseen is proved by the seen, / Till that becomes unseen and receives proof in its turn" ("Song of Myself," section 3). The soul leads the self inevitably outward to encompass wider and wider realms of experience: "And I know that the hand of God is the promise of my own, / And I know that the spirit of God is the brother of my own" (section 5).

These mythic progenitors of the re-created self are dimensions of another pair of generative forces in this work—the earth and the sun: "Stop this day and night with me and you shall possess the origin of all poems, / You shall possess the good of the earth and sun" (section 2). The evolution of the self in the poem is marked by a changing relationship to earth and sun. The self moves from "the song of me rising from bed and meeting the sun" in section 2 to an oedipal rivalry in sections 24 and 25 after the powers of the self have been more fully explored: "Dazzling and tremendous how quick the sun-rise would kill me, / If I could not now and always send sun-rise out of me." After a final cataclysmic transition in section 28, the self moves decisively from private consciousness to culture hero and announces in section 40: "Flaunt of the sunshine I need not your bask—lie over! / . . . Earth! you seem to look for something at my hands, / Say, old top-knot, what do you want?"

The self's relationship to the symbolic "leaves of grass" progresses similarly from "guesses" as to the meaning of the grass in section 6 to perceptions of the universality of the individual experience in section 17: "This is the grass that grows wherever the land is and the water is, / This is the common air that bathes the globe." After the decisive transition in section 28, the expanded meaning of the self and the grass develops into a credo in section 31: "I believe a leaf of grass is no less than the journey-work of the stars." At this point, the cosmic significance of the fully realized self becomes the basis for a democratic community. In *Vistas* Whitman says that his poetry is not about "that half only, individualism, which isolates" but also about "another half, which is adhesiveness or love, that fuses, ties and aggregates, making the races comrades, and fraternizing all" (381).

The individual consciousness created through the union of body and soul, an experience available to everyone, produces a prototypical personality that is spiritually prepared for union with other similar personalities. The universality of the soul provides a basis for the union, and the "corruption and decease" of the body make the union desirable and necessary. Recognizing that the individual eventually perishes though the community lives on, the isolated private self in the transitional section 11 of "Song of Myself"—the "handsome" woman created by the sensory experiences of the body—longs for existential redefinition through regenerative participation in the comradeship of the twenty-eight young men afloat in the rivers of time. Whitman explored more fully the creation of the individual personality through the union of mythic opposites in "Children of Adam" and the creation of the democratic community through the union of similar human selves in "Calamus." Whitman summarized the relationship of these forces in the short poem introducing *Leaves,* "One's-Self I Sing."

The most common criticism of the individualism in Whitman's poetry is that it is narcissistic, egotistical, anarchic, and even pathological in origin. However, Whitman insisted in his prose, from the earliest days of his creative life to his last, that his poetry was about democratic reconstruction—as he puts it in *Vistas,* "the grand experiment of development . . . the forming of a full-grown man or woman" (380). He was convinced that "To ballast the State is also secured, and in our times is to be secured, in no other way" (380).

Margaret H. Duggar

Bibliography

Anderson, Quentin. *The Imperial Self: An Essay in American Literary and Cultural History.* New York: Knopf, 1971.

Erkkila, Betsy. *Whitman the Political Poet.* New York: Oxford UP, 1989.

Larson, Kerry C. *Whitman's Drama of Consensus.* Chicago: U of Chicago P, 1988.

Thomas, M. Wynn. *The Lunar Light of Whitman's Poetry.* Cambridge, Mass.: Harvard UP, 1987.

Whitman, Walt. *The Correspondence.* Ed. Edwin Haviland Miller. 6 vols. New York: New York UP, 1961–1977.

———. *Leaves of Grass: Comprehensive Reader's Edition.* Ed. Harold W. Blodgett and Sculley Bradley. New York: New York UP, 1965.

———. *Prose Works 1892.* Ed. Floyd Stovall. 2 vols. New York: New York UP, 1963–1964.

———. *Rivulets of Prose: Critical Essays by Walt Whitman.* Ed. Carolyn Wells and Alfred F. Goldsmith. New York: Greenberg, 1928.

———. *Walt Whitman's Workshop: A Collection of Unpublished Manuscripts.* Ed. Clifton Joseph Furness. Cambridge, Mass.: Harvard UP, 1928.

See also DEMOCRACY; *DEMOCRATIC VISTAS;* EQUALITY; FEUDALISM; FREEDOM; HUMAN BODY; PREFACE TO *LEAVES OF GRASS,* 1855 EDITION; PRIDE; "SONG OF MYSELF"; SOUL, THE

Influences on Whitman, Principal

"I contain multitudes," announces the speaker in Whitman's "Song of Myself" (section 51), and any attempt to provide even a basic catalogue of the principal influences upon the poet only confirms his famous boast. The great number of those influences and their wide range—literature, music, painting, photography, science, religion, politics, philosophy, to name only a few—obliges one before surveying each influence individually to speculate on just why the scope of influences is so much greater for Whitman than for most poets. At least part of the answer lies in Whitman's quest to express the totality of existence, to encompass poetically the entire sum of human experience past and present, to write, as he proposed, a new Bible which, like its predecessor and model, would cover mankind's origins and destiny, would express literally and metaphorically the purpose and meaning of life, and would in the process offer a unifying vision of being. Consequently, while Whitman would draw inspiration from many places, the most profound influences on him were those which offered precisely this sort of totalizing vision: religion and philosophy.

The first significant religious influence on Whitman was the deism he acquired at home as a boy. Whitman's father had long been a follower of Thomas Paine, whose *Age of Reason* young Walt read, and Frances Wright, whom Walt heard lecture. The effect of his early exposure to deism or freethinking would usefully ensure that his emotional and intellectual development would not be narrowly circumscribed by any single creed, while at the same time deism's relatively cosmopolitan and generous willingness to allow for a degree of value in a variety of religious practices almost certainly encouraged the development of the broad and sympathetic embrace of diverse faiths which would be characteristic of Whitman's maturity. Moreover, it is likely that deism's sense of a benign creator and a providential, rational design underlying the universe helped to set early on the course of Whitman's holistic and optimistic perspective on the world.

Besides deism, Quakerism, specifically the controversial offshoot of orthodox Quakerism led by Elias Hicks, exerted considerable influence on the Whitman household. Hicks, who had been an acquaintance of both Whitman's grandfather and father, espoused a particularly liberal version of Quakerism, intensely anti-institutional and placing a greatly increased emphasis on the authority of the Inner Light. Additionally, Hicks's strong sense of divinity present in all aspects of nature bears an interesting resemblance to Whitman's own later sense of spirit at work in the natural world.

A large part of the power Hicks exerted over the imagination of the boy Whitman resulted from the rhetorical style of his sermons. Hicks's rhythmic biblical style bears enough of a resemblance to Whitman's poetic style to suggest at least a degree of influence also. Indeed, Whitman came to maturity during a particularly rich period of American religious oratory. In the wake of the Second Great Awakening, Protestant pulpit style, particularly that of evangelicals, became freer and more varied and played upon a much broader emotional range. In the construction of his own style, Whitman paid considerable attention to the oratory of influential ministers like Henry Ward Beecher. Aside from Beecher, perhaps the most famous preacher to influence Whitman was Edward Thompson Taylor of Seamen's Bethel Chapel, whose vivid style, rich with the language and imagery of the sea, also caught the attention of Ralph Waldo Emerson and Herman Melville. Taylor's use of the common, practical details of sea life to illustrate spiritual truths suggests Whitman's own use of everyday life to express his own spiritual vision.

A further and perhaps more crucial influence on Whitman's desire to reveal the spiritual significance of the everyday world was the theology of Emanuel Swedenborg. The great seventeenth-century Swedish scientist and mystic developed an elaborate cosmology, the most influential aspect of which consisted of his assigning specific moral and spiritual meanings to the various phenomena and entities of the natural world. This doctrine of correspondence, as it was called, insists that the microcosm reflects the macrocosm and that both are subject to interpretation as symbols. Swedenborg's version of the common mystical equation of communion with the divine as a type of sexual bond encouraged or gave support to Whitman's own conception of God as a "loving bed-fellow" or the "Great Camerado."

To these diverse Christian influences must also be added the various occult practices that became immensely popular in America during Whitman's lifetime. After the famous Hydesville rappings of 1848, different varieties of séances such as spirit-rapping flourished and spread throughout the century. Mesmerism, a popular form of hypnotism that began in late eighteenth-century Europe, enjoyed a new popularity in 1830s America, where it took on an additional dimension of spiritual healing. Mesmerists maintained that all things were animated by an electric fluid or, as it was sometimes called, an animal magnetism. Whitman's own vatic pose often resembles that of the trance-mediums of his day.

Finally, although Whitman was less directly influenced by European religious thought than almost any other major figure of American romanticism, mention should be made of the increasingly important role Georg Wilhelm Friedrich Hegel came to occupy in Whitman's thinking after the Civil War. The chief intellectual contribution made by Hegel's philosophy was the deferred, almost religious expectation of an eventual reconciliation of diverse aspects of experience. This deferral allowed Whitman to reconcile his conception of national unity underlying the multiple and increasingly conflicting elements of national life as the century progressed. Through the Hegelian model of development Whitman could retain the hopeful democratic vision of his prewar writings simply by placing his confident celebratory perspective into a utopian future. In fact, Hegel had served Emerson in much the same way as his vision of contemporary society's possibilities increasingly darkened during the 1850s.

Although Whitman's interest in Hegel does not appear to have a direct relationship with Emerson's, in many other respects, Emerson, as is well known, exerted a significant degree of influence on Whitman. Whitman had been exposed to Emerson's thinking as early as 1842, when Emerson lectured in New York, and it appears that Whitman heard at least his lecture on poetry. Whitman continued to show an interest in Emerson's thinking up to and after Emerson's famous and rather brave letter complimenting Whitman on the first edition of *Leaves* (1855). But perhaps as a result of Emerson's increasing reservations about Whitman's verse, Whitman began in his later years to downplay both his early knowledge of Emerson's thought and the degree of his influence. A few modern commentators have given support to this later view of Whitman's, greatly circumscribing Emerson's influence in favor of the far better known ideas of popular new religions and spiritual movements. Yet no reader can deny the powerful resemblance Whitman's conception of the poet as spokesman and shaman

for the nation and its people bears to the prophetic and representative role of the bard as described in Emerson's essay "The Poet."

However, understanding just why such a conception of the poet's role should have held such appeal requires turning to the social and political context of Whitman's writing. Whitman's persona took form in response not just to the American political scene of his early maturity, but also retrospectively to the memory of the revolutionary generation and prospectively to likely results of increasing sectional conflict.

Whitman grew up hearing stories about his own family's involvement in the Revolutionary War. Of all the various confrontations with British forces in and about New York, the battle of Brooklyn was particularly meaningful for Whitman, who had even lost a granduncle in the battle. This heroic defeat for Washington's army came to be emblematic for Whitman of patriotic sacrifice and heroic resistance to injustice. Indeed many of his poetic references to the battle anticipate the images of blood sacrifice and cleansing death found in his Civil War writings. The Revolutionary War stood for the national unity he saw threatened in antebellum America; the great leaders of that era, the founding fathers, came to represent the ideal of a selfless and principled leadership. One of the heroes of the revolutionary generation, Thomas Paine, had been a particular hero of Whitman's father, who handed on his admiration for the freethinker and radical to his son Walt. Paine's combination of patriotic fervor, opposition to religious superstition, and firm belief in radical democracy crucially shaped Whitman's own understanding of America.

Whitman's upbringing initiated him into the world and values of working-class democratic life. This allegiance was confirmed by the long line of Democratic papers he wrote for in the early part of his life. The actual goals and values of the Democratic party during this period are complex, shifting, and often contradictory. Happily, however, the actual program of the party is less important in understanding Whitman than the image the party cultivated for itself in the national mind. The Democratic party represented itself as the party of the common man; it claimed to stand up for the rights and interests of working people against entrenched power and accumulated wealth. It was strongly nationalist, friendly to foreign democratic revolutions, and pro-expansion (the term "manifest destiny" had been popularized by a

Democratic journal). As a journalist for a Democratic paper, Whitman's conception of himself as a writer became closely associated in his mind with his role as the representative and bard of all Americans, without regard to social status. But it was the actions of this same Democratic party which ultimately disillusioned Whitman with party politics entirely and led him to a deeper sense of the poet's role as the only true representative of the nation.

As part of its intense nationalism, the Democratic party was unwilling to countenance antislavery sentiment and the threat it posed to national unity. Whitman's moral opposition to the institution of slavery increasingly drove him away from the Democratic party. From the Fugitive Slave Law of 1850, through the election of 1852, to the extension of slavery in the Kansas-Nebraska Act of 1854, Whitman moved farther and farther away from the Democrats and ultimately from party politics in general. The outcome of this disillusionment was that Whitman the political journalist gradually shifted his allegiance from the people's representatives in Washington to the moral authority of the people themselves. The failure of the nation's political representatives to provide adequate moral leadership prompted Whitman to become a sort of representative himself and to provide the kind of moral direction he sees as missing in national life.

Besides reinforcing his democratic leanings, Whitman's work as a journalist ensured that he would be exposed to the popular press of his day. Prior to his newspaper work he had shown enthusiasm for the novels of Sir Walter Scott and James Fenimore Cooper, but by the time he began to write his early fiction he was clearly far more influenced by the sentimental and sensationalistic fiction of his day. What is most interesting about his use of these popular genres, however, is his attempt to draw simultaneously on both the violent and romantic aspects of sensationalism and on the moral, pious, and didactic elements of sentimental writing. Although as Whitman matured as a writer he would leave the more extreme aspects of sensationalism behind, various episodes and images from both sensationalism and sentimentalism persist throughout *Leaves*. Arguably, the influence of these popular modes greatly adds to the astonishing range of subject and tone in Whitman's best work.

Of equal importance in shaping Whitman's emotionally charged style and images are the fine arts, particularly painting, early photography, theater, and music.

American painting in Whitman's formative years was almost exclusively realist with a certain amount of romantic idealization. Nature paintings, those of the luminists, for example, used a beautiful but exaggerated light to restore to the viewer a sense of wonder before the natural world. Genre paintings similarly romanticized everyday life in order to bring out a certain democratic poetry of the commonplace. Both types of painting were comfortingly realistic and uncritical; they were designed for a popular mass audience, which quickly took them to heart. This desire for a popular art both realistic and transcendent was congenial to Whitman's own developing conception of art. Whitman also quickly developed an interest in the new art of photography and particularly admired its ability to offer an honest, unvarnished representation of life. He saw in both popular painting and photography an opportunity to refine and uplift the perception of the public, an aspiration he held for his own poetry.

An even more forceful image of the effect of art on its public was to be found in the playhouses of his day, where lively audiences engaged in a host of exchanges with the performers and each other. Whitman's favorite actors were those like Junius Brutus Booth, the father of John Wilkes and Edwin Booth, whose extravagant, vehement style drove naturally vociferous audiences to even greater extremes of response. All of Whitman's exposure to theater, both audiences and actors, from sensational melodrama to Shakespeare, intensified his own theatricality, both in the dramatic aspects of *Leaves* and perhaps more tellingly in the construction of his own rather theatrical persona as "America's bard."

The comprehensiveness of the theatrical experience—its use of words, images, movement, extreme emotional states—was at the heart of Whitman's other great theater-going experience, grand opera. The great bel canto stylists like Giulia Grisi and Marietta Alboni were dramatic incarnations of the poet, spellbinding audiences with their voices, transfixing the present moment with sublimity. Prior to his infatuation with opera, Whitman had shown interest in American popular music: various singing families like the Hutchinsons, minstrel singers and songwriters, especially Stephen Foster. Whitman's ability to incorporate such diverse musical influences in his poetry once again bespeaks the wide range of his vision and his urgent desire to offer an image of the whole of his culture.

Ironically, poetic influences on Whitman are perhaps less important than any of the aforementioned subjects. Even in terms of literary style, prose writers, polemicists, and preachers had a greater impact on him than any poets. Scott's *Border Minstrelsy* was an early favorite of Whitman's, as was McDonald Clarke, the so-called Mad Poet of Broadway, whose defiance of social convention and curious, often maudlin, verse shaped Whitman's early sense of the possibilities of poetry. Part of the reason Whitman's poetry was so little influenced by that of other poets is to be found in its unusual style. Those who influenced him most directly were primarily prose-poets like the eighteenth-century Scots poet James Macpherson, whose pseudo-ancient poems, published under the name of "Ossian," Whitman found to be powerful but also a bit windy. The most popular American prose poetry before Whitman was written by Martin Farquhar Tupper. In addition to the remarkable similarity of his style to Whitman's, Tupper also anticipated Whitman's exaltation of the events and details of everyday life and nature.

The rather paradoxical conclusion one draws from an overview of the principal influences on Whitman is that in large part it is precisely because of the vast number of these influences that Whitman is so startlingly original. Whitman's attempt to represent the fullness of life, the totality of experience, not only benefited from but actually required the incorporation of many disparate voices into his work.

Sam Worley

Bibliography

Allen, Gay Wilson. *The Solitary Singer: A Critical Biography of Walt Whitman.* 1955. Rev. ed. 1967. Chicago: U of Chicago P, 1985.

Aspiz, Harold. *Walt Whitman and the Body Beautiful.* Urbana: U of Illinois P, 1980.

Asselineau, Roger. *The Evolution of Walt Whitman.* 2 vols. Cambridge, Mass.: Harvard UP, 1960–1962.

Reynolds, David S. *Walt Whitman's America: A Cultural Biography.* New York: Knopf, 1995.

Stovall, Floyd. *The Foreground of "Leaves of Grass."* Charlottesville: UP of Virginia, 1974.

Zweig, Paul. *Walt Whitman: The Making of the Poet.* New York: Basic Books, 1984.

See also ACTORS AND ACTRESSES; AMERICAN REVOLUTION, THE; BIBLE, THE; EMERSON, RALPH WALDO; JOURNALISM, WHITMAN'S; MACPHERSON, JAMES ("OSSIAN"); METAPHYSICS; MUSIC, WHITMAN AND; OPERA AND OPERA SINGERS; ORATORY; PAINTERS AND PAINTING; PHOTOGRAPHS AND PHOTOGRAPHERS; POLITICAL VIEWS; POPULAR CULTURE, WHITMAN AND; PSEUDOSCIENCE; QUAKERS AND QUAKERISM; READING, WHITMAN'S; RELIGION; ROMANTICISM; SCIENCE; SWEDENBORG, EMANUEL; TUPPER, MARTIN FARQUHAR; WRIGHT, FRANCES (FANNY)

Ingersoll, Robert Green (1833–1899)

Robert Green Ingersoll was a colonel in the Civil War, Attorney General of Illinois (1867–1869), and best known as a public speaker. A remarkable orator, Ingersoll could command the attention of audiences who basically opposed his political and social views. He was a leading spokesman for the Republican party in the elections of 1876, 1880, and 1884. In spite of his services to the party he was, because of his religious views, never promoted to national office.

Enormously popular as a lecturer, commanding huge fees (up to thirty-five hundred dollars), he spoke on topics critical of the Bible and the Christian religion. He exposed the orthodox superstitions of the time and can be said to have introduced and popularized German "higher criticism" in the United States. Among his speeches, *Some Mistakes of Moses* was given hundreds of times to enthusiastic audiences.

Ingersoll was a great supporter of Whitman and recognized in him an affinity for humanistic philosophy centered on life in this world, saying, "He was, above all I have known, the poet of humanity, or sympathy" ("Spoken" 159). He gave the eulogy at Whitman's funeral in Harleigh Cemetery in Camden on 30 March 1892, saying, "He was the poet of that divine democracy which gives equal rights to all the sons and daughters of men" ("Spoken" 159) and that he preached "the gospel of humanity—the greatest gospel which can be preached" ("Spoken" 161).

W. Edward Harris

Bibliography

Ingersoll, Robert Green. *The Letters of Robert G. Ingersoll.* Ed. Eva Ingersoll Wakefield. New York: Philosophical Library, 1951.

———. *Liberty in Literature: Testimonial to Walt Whitman*. New York: Truth Seeker, 1892.

———. *The Philosophy of Ingersoll*. San Francisco: P. Elder, 1906.

———. *Some Mistakes of Moses*. New York: Truth Seeker, 1882.

———. "[Spoken at Whitman's Funeral]." *Critical Essays on Walt Whitman*. Ed. James Woodress. Boston: Hall, 1983. 159–161.

Larson, Orvin Prentiss. *American Infidel: Robert Green Ingersoll*. New York: Citadel, 1962.

See also BIBLE, THE; RELIGION

"Inscriptions" (1871)

"Inscriptions" is the name given to the first cluster in *Leaves of Grass*, beginning with the 1871 edition. A single poem called "Inscription" leads off the 1867 edition. By 1871 this poem appears as "One's-Self I Sing" and is one of nine in the "Inscriptions" cluster. ("One's-Self I Sing" remains the inaugural poem in all the later editions.) In the 1881 and Deathbed editions, "Inscriptions" expands to twenty-four poems. "As I Ponder'd in Silence" and "In Cabin'd Ships at Sea" debut in 1871; the vapid and unnecessary "Thou Reader" is the only new poem in 1881. Best known are "One's-Self I Sing," "When I Read the Book," "Me Imperturbe," "I Hear America Singing," and "Poets to Come."

Less coherent than other clusters in *Leaves of Grass* and consisting in great part of edited and transposed versions of earlier works, "Inscriptions" is an extreme but illustrative product of Whitman's habitual shuffling of his verse. The poems run from two lines ("Thou Reader") to eighty-four ("Eidólons") and range widely in quality and tone. Important themes such as war and voyaging seem obliquely related at best. As an overture, the cluster sounds many motifs but fails to establish a dominant mood. As an entryway to a man's life work, the section's arrangement is, as Gay Wilson Allen notes, vague and unsystematic. Not surprisingly, the poems have more often been quoted singly than interpreted as a group.

"Inscriptions" nevertheless represents Whitman's last answer to a problem that had tormented him since the 1855 edition and the drastic revisions of 1856—how to introduce to the general reader a verse form and content so unfamiliar and revolutionary. Also, whenever Whitman seems egregiously multiple and inconsistent, it is wise to inquire after his motives. Serious, detailed consideration of this introductory motion remains one of the unfulfilled tasks of Whitman criticism. Patterns are visible in "Inscriptions." Sometimes the poems follow a point-counterpoint ordering. The celebratory Self of the first poem elicits the haunting, accusatory Other of the second ("As I Ponder'd in Silence"). The joyous and Arcadian "I Hear America Singing" yields to the war imagery of "What Place is Besieged?"; then the pendulum swings back with "Still though the One I Sing," the title acknowledging its place in sequence. "One, yet of contradictions made" is what he truly forms, sings the second line. It is a felicitous image, soon to be repeated; Whitman's self, his leaves, and especially his "Inscriptions," contain multitudes and contradictions.

When Whitman speaks of the transmutation of many materials, "changing, crumbling, re-cohering" ("Eidólons"), he describes his work process and the undirected, nonlinear, and creative reading experience *Leaves of Grass* offers. Whitman's One is always fractious, seething, combinatory. The totalities of man and book are conjectural, never fixed; the whole cannot be known in any complete or homogenous way while it lives, necessarily, in the flux of its parts. In "When I Read the Book" the dispute with the axioms of traditional biography is telling. Whitman cannot convey any hard truth of his being, only "diffused faint clews and indirections." "Inscriptions" does the same for *Leaves of Grass*. Where a standard introduction would give directions to what comes next, "Inscriptions" faithfully gives many "indirections," from Whitman's many aspects, for the readers' many aspects, to the many paths through the subsequent leaves. The book may be a biography in one mood, "the history of the future" in another, a substantial reality to this reader, an eidólon to that.

Thus the structure of "Inscriptions" indicates the manifold, closure-resistant sense of possibility at the heart of *Leaves of Grass* by embodying it formally. One inscription could imply a single, authorized line of sight into the prospect of the text. A governing sentiment might petrify the many leaves into a monolithic monument, its univocal significance captured in an epigraph that is also, inconsolably, an epitaph. But a series of disparate declarations does the courteous work of opening one door after another, and letting the reader choose. "Inscriptions" incarnates and glosses Whitman's sense of freedom, openness, and respect. (Today's diminished language for this "interactivity" would come from the world of information technology: at its initial interface *Leaves of Grass* offers a spread of hypertextual alternatives, with more promised.) "Inscriptions" also foreshadows the experience of Whitman's longer poems, with their variety in stanza and rhythm, and their labyrinthine relations of thematic development, digression, and multiple listing.

There are timidities; certain topics and intensities are not forthrightly introduced. Neither the heated physicality nor the spiritual agonizing so central to *Leaves of Grass* is presaged in "Inscriptions." Whitman wants his readers committed to the crossing before buffeting them midstream with destabilizing forces. And why twenty-four inscriptions? It is happenstance, most likely, though the number evokes the diurnal round through daylight, darkness, dawn. Whitman usually avoids symmetrical and simplistic organizational schemes, but hinting that *Leaves of Grass* could be experienced as a latter Book of Hours, a modern and secular cycle of chant, meditation, and prayer, has a certain Whitmanian flair. "As a wheel on its axis turns, this book unwitting to itself, / Around the idea of thee," he inscribes in "To Thee Old Cause." The old cause, in the beginnings of the book as in its ends, is ever the progressive illumination of Self and Humanity.

Robert Johnstone

Bibliography

Allen, Gay Wilson. *The New Walt Whitman Handbook*. 1975. New York: New York UP, 1986.
Asselineau, Roger. *The Evolution of Walt Whitman: The Creation of a Book*. Trans. Roger Asselineau and Burton L. Cooper. Cambridge, Mass.: Harvard UP, 1962.
Whitman, Walt. *Complete Poetry and Collected Prose*. Ed. Justin Kaplan. New York: Library of America, 1982.
———. *Leaves of Grass: Comprehensive Reader's Edition*. Ed. Harold W. Blodgett and Sculley Bradley. New York: New York UP, 1965.

See also "As I Ponder'd in Silence"; "Eidólons"; Freedom; "I Hear America Singing"; "Me Imperturbe"; "One's-Self I Sing"; "Poets to Come"; "To Thee Old Cause"; "When I Read the Book"

Interculturality

Walt Whitman saw himself as an international poet and carefully mapped out his reputation abroad. Insofar as this internationality is collaborative rather than antagonistic and generally cultural rather than specifically political, it can be referred to as intercultural. This interculturality is located on the textual level, on the level of the communication between the author (or his associates) and his readers abroad, and informs the interactive relationships among Whitmanites of many countries. In this way, interculturality has become a special feature of Whitman's reception.

Whitman's hope to create "new formulas, international poems" amounted to a new program in American literature. In his introduction to the first German edition of *Leaves* in 1889, he claimed that "I did not only have my own country in mind when composing my work. I wanted to take the first step towards bringing into life a cycle of international poems." This hope coincided with his view of the role of the United States as furthering "mutual benevolence of all humanity, the solidarity of the world" (trans. from *Grashalme* xii). Whitman had a sense of poetry as a new vehicle for international relations, "an internationality of poems and poets, binding the lands of the earth closer than all treaties and diplomacy" (*Complete* 1049), setting an open democratic poetry against the secret treaties and diplomacy of the reactionary European powers of his period.

Thus, the foremost *American* poet of his time also emerges as a programmatically internationalist author; this is a paradox Whitman explains by referring to the special nature of American culture. As a "composite" culture, it has per se an intercultural quality—"on our shores the crowning resultant of those distillations, decantations, compactions of humanity" (*Complete* 1075).

Based on this theory, Whitman developed an intercultural poetics which manifests itself most prominently in his lyrical catalogues. There is hardly a geographical or cultural space in the atlas not addressed by Whitman's poetry. His interculturalist poetics thus seems to be based on universality and inclusiveness.

His poetry also reflects another basic theme of interculturalist research of the late twentieth century: Whitman never looks at foreign cultures as exotic artifacts, but emphasizes the relationship between self and other, between America and the lyrical globe he projects. In his most famous and most explicitly international poem, "Salut au Monde!," the speaker states in conclusion: "Toward you all, in America's name, / I raise high the perpendicular hand, I make the signal" (section 13).

Yet another tenet of interculturalism is its emphasis on regional and local cultures rather than on (national) states which are deemed oppressive. Whitman's intercultural poetics provide for recognition of the periphery as well as the center. In fact, he prefers to identify groups of individuals through regions and landscapes, as inhabitants of cities, rather than presenting them as belonging to national states and cultures.

However, Whitman's globalist poetry is at times also quite Eurocentric. In spite of the egalitarian form of the catalogues, there is a hidden hierarchy which puts (Anglo-)American culture first. The celebration of discovery and expansion (e.g., in "Years of the Modern" and "Passage to India") furthermore links Whitman with imperialist conceptions in international relations.

Starting in the late 1860s, Whitman and his friends took a personal interest in his reception abroad. The object was to project the image of Whitman as Good Gray Poet and prophet of a global democracy. Whitmanites abroad were furnished with material meant to steer their activities in the desired direction. The first attempt to establish an international Whitman Society was undertaken during Whitman's lifetime, by a German-Japanese-American artist, Sadakichi Hartmann. Whereas this project failed for financial reasons, Horace Traubel's organization, Walt Whitman Fellowship International, was very successful in bringing such Whitmanites as the French Whitman translator Léon Bazalgette, the eminent Polish-German-American cultural critic Amelia von Ende, and the German-Scottish anarchist poet John Henry Mackay into the inner circle.

Some European Whitmanites wanted to establish a special organization in Europe. Léon Bazalgette and Germany's foremost Whitman supporter, Johannes Schlaf, repeatedly discussed the creation of a Whitman society in Europe modeled after the Fellowship. Individuals involved in this discussion were Stefan Zweig, Emile Verhaeren, Romain Rolland, Francis Viélé-Griffin, Jules Romains, and others. Increasing tensions among Europeans in the foreground to World War I apparently prevented the realization of this project.

The manifold contacts among Whitman devotees from different cultures form an intercultural network of impressive complexity. Whitman appears prominently in Stefan Zweig's and Hermann Hesse's correspondence with Romain Rolland. A pacifist selection of Civil War poetry and prose appeared in Switzerland in 1919 edited by René Schickele, an Alsatian expressionist, with translations by the Franco-German poet Ivan Goll and the German-Jewish writer and translator Gustav Landauer.

Among Slavic nations, enthusiasm for Whitman developed in collaboration with Central and Western Europeans. Johannes Schlaf's German translation was the basis for much of Whitman's reception in the Czech lands and other Slavic nations. Emanuel Lesehrad's Czech translation was inspired by an early German Whitmanite, Alfred Mombert.

The intercultural network continued to exist far into the twentieth century. Exiled Western communist writers learned about Whitman in Russia, where the first Soviet commissar of culture, Anatoly Lunacharsky, had firmly established a Soviet tradition of Whitman reception. Erich Arendt, author of a representative Whitman translation in the German Democratic Republic, fled from Hitler to South America and encountered Whitman through Pablo Neruda. In 1955 the International Peace Council, often described as a Communist Front organization, staged an international celebration for the centennial of *Leaves*.

Thus Whitman's intercultural poetics and poetry have inspired an intercultural reception. Reception processes in individual cultures did not occur in isolation from each other but amount to a highly interactive, dynamic process. Betsy Erkkila has appropriately spoken of a "new trend toward an international community of art" (237) with Whitman as a focal point and has called for a "different and more cosmopolitan image of the American poet" (5).

Walter Grünzweig

Bibliography

Allen, Gay Wilson, and Ed Folsom, eds. *Walt Whitman & the World*. Iowa City: U of Iowa P, 1995.

Erkkila, Betsy. *Walt Whitman Among the French: Poet and Myth*. Princeton: Princeton UP, 1980.

Grünzweig, Walter. "'Collaborators in the Great Cause of Liberty and Fellowship': Whitmania as an Intercultural Phenomenon." *Walt Whitman Quarterly Review* 5.4 (1988): 16–26.

———. *Constructing the German Walt Whitman.* Iowa City: U of Iowa P, 1995.

———. "'For America—For All the Earth': Walt Whitman as an International(ist) Poet." *Breaking Bounds: Walt Whitman and American Cultural Studies.* Ed. Betsy Erkkila and Jay Grossman. New York: Oxford UP, 1996. 238–250.

Whitman, Walt. *Complete Poetry and Collected Prose.* Ed. Justin Kaplan. New York: Library of America, 1982.

———. *Grashalme: Gedichte.* Trans. Karl Knortz and T.W. Rolleston. Zürich: Schabelitz, 1889.

See also AFRICA, WHITMAN IN; ASSOCIATIONS, CLUBS, FELLOWSHIPS, FOUNDATIONS, AND SOCIETIES; AUSTRALIA AND NEW ZEALAND, WHITMAN IN; BRITISH ISLES, WHITMAN IN THE; CANADA, WHITMAN'S RECEPTION IN; CHINA, WHITMAN IN; FRANCE, WHITMAN IN; GERMAN-SPEAKING COUNTRIES, WHITMAN IN THE; IMPERIALISM; INDIA, WHITMAN IN; IRELAND, WHITMAN IN; ISRAEL, WHITMAN IN; ITALY, WHITMAN IN; JAPAN, WHITMAN IN; LEGACY, WHITMAN'S; PORTUGAL AND BRAZIL, WHITMAN IN; RUSSIA AND OTHER SLAVIC COUNTRIES, WHITMAN IN; "SALUT AU MONDE!"; SCANDINAVIA, WHITMAN IN; SPAIN AND SPANISH AMERICA, WHITMAN IN

Internet, Whitman on the

When Walt Whitman hymned praises of the body electric, he sang of more than he knew. Although the electronic network known as the Internet is not yet thirty years old, it already features hundreds of addresses at which information on Whitman can be found. At present, many of these addresses, or websites, are ephemeral in nature and of limited value to the serious student. Some, however, have an air of permanence and provide entrance to literary riches. An example of the latter is the Walt Whitman Home Page of the Library of Congress (http://lcweb2.loc.gov/wwhome.html). Stored here is information about the library's (and the country's) unparalleled collection of Whitman materials, some ninety-eight thousand manuscripts and books. Here, too, available in digital format, are four small notebooks and a cardboard butterfly that disappeared from the library's archives during World War II

but which were recovered some forty years later, on 24 February 1995. Exciting it is, indeed, for student and scholar alike, to view in these notebooks Whitman's early pencil drafts of his poetry or his on-the-spot reflections concerning dying soldiers in the Civil War hospitals.

No doubt destined to become, in the years ahead, the foremost Whitman resource on the Internet is the Walt Whitman Hypertext Archive (http://jefferson.village.Virginia.EDU.whitman/), now being constructed by project directors Ed Folsom and Kenneth M. Price. Jointly sponsored by the College of William and Mary, the University of Iowa, and the Institute for Advanced Technology in the Humanities, the archive is a structured database which, in due course, will hold digitized images of Whitman's works (including first editions of *Leaves of Grass*), manuscripts, notebooks, letters, and reviews of his various books. Accompanying these materials will be a Whitman biography, photographs of the poet, commentary on his work, and a search engine that facilitates finding documents in the database. Finally, the archive will contain "teaching units," electronic files that consist of images, questions, and suggestions relevant to the exploration of various topics of study.

At some point, the Internet may become an essential tool in the discussion of Whitman in the classroom. In time, it may hold out a research potential unimaginable to scholars of earlier eras.

Donald D. Kummings

Bibliography

Clark, Michael. *Cultural Treasures of the Internet.* 2nd ed. Upper Saddle River, New Jersey: Prentice Hall, 1997.

Fineberg, Gail. "Whitman on the Web: Four Recovered Notebooks to Be Digitized." *Library of Congress Information Bulletin* 54.7 (1995): 139–144.

Green, Charles B. "Walt Whitman on the Web." *Walt Whitman Quarterly Review* 15 (1997): 44–51.

Stull, Andrew T. *English on the Internet: A Student's Guide.* Adapted for English by Barbara Johnson. Upper Saddle River, New Jersey: Prentice Hall, 1997.

See also COLLECTORS AND COLLECTIONS, WHITMAN; MEDIA INTERPRETATIONS OF WHITMAN'S LIFE AND WORKS; *NOTEBOOKS AND UNPUBLISHED PROSE MANUSCRIPTS;* TEACHING OF WHITMAN'S WORKS

Ireland, Whitman in

Although Walt Whitman never realized his plan to visit Ireland, his presence was significant in Dublin literary circles during his lifetime and beyond. As a nationalist poet who also claimed a cosmopolitan scope, as a respecter of native traditions who was at the same time a bold literary experimenter, Whitman provided a model for Irish writers of opposing literary creeds and political purposes.

Whitman's poetic project deeply influenced the Irish Literary Revival, the movement fathered by Standish O'Grady (1846–1928) to generate a national literature and culture. Known to don a floppy Whitmanesque hat and sprinkle his discourse with "Calamus" quotes, O'Grady's self-construction as bard of his country included imitating Whitman's epic, energetic style and proclaiming comradeship with workers on the land. Mapping a Gaelic project onto Whitman's cultural nativism, the minstrel of Ireland believed with his American counterpart that the essential character of a people inheres in its language, songs, and stories. O'Grady popularized ancient Celtic legends, raised Ireland's consciousness about its mythic past, and was joined in this cultural crusade by fellow Whitmanites W.B. Yeats (who in his letters called Whitman "the greatest teacher of these decades" [9]) and Lady Augusta Gregory (1852–1932).

To the embattled Irish, Whitman's voice fulfilled the best intentions of a nationalist spirit. His metaphysic of wholeness and image of an undivided society particularly appealed to cultural nationalists, most of whom were Protestants facing a turbulent political present, but whose work envisioned a prelapsarian Ireland free from sectarian strife. This Whitmanesque turn to culture was meant as a corrective to a sterile political Irish nationalism (from which such writers would have much to lose). Whitman's sympathy with the aggressively nationalist Fenian Brotherhood, to which "Old Ireland" refers, and his declared support for a free Ireland, suggests that cultural nationalists followed him when it suited them. O'Grady expressed his aversion to the democratic fervor of *Leaves of Grass* and envisioned for Ireland instead a feudal society of born-again Celtic chiefs. Like Whitman, however, cultural nationalists baptized the language of daily social intercourse as poetry, and called the nation to look to native folk traditions to rediscover its identity.

Whitman's chief liaison officer and greatest promoter in Ireland was far from the camp of cultural nationalists. Edward Dowden, professor of English at Trinity College from 1867 to 1913 and a frequent correspondent of Whitman's, introduced *Leaves of Grass* to his students (including *Dracula* author Bram Stoker, who as a student wrote Whitman an embarrassing love letter and later visited him in Camden; and T.W. Rolleston, who went on to translate Whitman into German and was the first to connect the American with German idealism). Dowden sought Whitman converts (including J.B. Yeats, father of the poet) throughout Ireland, and his public lectures and subscriptions established the poet in Dublin literary circles. It was Dowden who invited Whitman to Ireland and began preparations for his visit, informing him that there were "Whitmanites" connected with "three principal Dublin newspapers" and assuring him that he had "many readers" (*Letters* 62) in Ireland (though *Leaves of Grass* was later removed from the Trinity library). His seminal article on Whitman, which acclaimed him as the poet of democracy, took over a year to get into print, rejected by several British reviews for being too "dangerous."

Far from dangerous and revolutionary, Dowden's criticism took a purely scholarly interest in Whitman, coolly analyzing the character of democratic poetry. Bitterly opposed to Home Rule for Ireland, Dowden did not share Whitman's concept of democracy. A true Irish Victorian, the professor admired the poet for celebrating the Spirit of the Age—human progress, evolution, scientific law, and universal culture. Clearly, writers like O'Grady and Yeats had reasons for promoting Whitman that were different from those of Dowden, who sneered at the parochialism of the literary revival and declared that his position was "cosmopolitan and imperial" rather than "provincial" (qtd. in Blodgett 44). In his rejection of the Irish renaissance as so much "intellectual brogue" (*Transcripts* 19), Dowden failed to recognize in Ireland what he applauded in America—the birth of a new literature. Though Whitman thought Dowden "bitten with the frost of the literary clique" (qtd. in Blodgett 45), he was forever grateful to the critic for promoting his reputation abroad—a recognition that ricocheted back across the Atlantic to improve his reception at home.

Oscar Wilde's (1854–1900) first exposure to Whitman was from his mother, fervent nationalist Lady Wilde, who read to him from an early edition of *Leaves of Grass*. Wilde admired the poet throughout his life, beginning with his student days at Oxford, where he carried *Leaves of Grass* with him, and where he defended the poet in response to an exam question asking how Aristotle would evaluate Whitman. Whitman appealed to Wilde less as a poet than as a prophet and personality; Oscar recognized himself in Walt's personal and literary experiment, in his self-construction and self-promotion. The Irish dandy visited the American rough twice in Camden in 1882, and later acclaimed him as the herald of a new era and a factor in the spiritual evolution of humanity.

George Moore's (1852–1933) *Hail and Farewell,* which explores the relation between autobiography and nation, also appreciated Whitman's "unashamed" self as just what Dublin—where "everyone is afraid to confess himself"—needed (652). Joyce scholars point to *Finnegans Wake* for traces of Whitman, or, as the *Wake* calls him, "old Whiteman," whose cataloguing style and capacity to merge with the universe "foredreamed" Joyce's novel.

Whitman once wrote in a letter to Dowden that he always took "real comfort" in his many "friends in Ireland" (134). Writers in an Irish nation struggling to be born often took comfort in and cues from the poet of that other newborn nation across the Atlantic.

Willa Murphy

Bibliography
Allen, Gay Wilson, and Ed Folsom, eds. *Walt Whitman & the World*. Iowa City: U of Iowa P, 1995.
Blodgett, Harold W. *Walt Whitman in England*. Ithaca, N.Y.: Cornell UP, 1934.
Brown, Terence. *Ireland's Literature*. Dublin: Lilliput, 1988.
Dowden, Edward. *Letters of Edward Dowden and His Correspondents*. London: Dent, 1914.
———. *Transcripts and Studies*. 2nd ed. London: K. Paul, Trench, Trubner, 1896.
Fleck, Richard F. "A Note on Whitman in Ireland." *Walt Whitman Review* 21 (1975): 160–162.
Howarth, Herbert. "Whitman and the Irish Writers." *Comparative Literature: Proceedings of the Second Congress of the International Comparative Literature Association*. Ed. Werner P. Friedrich. UNCSCL 24. Chapel Hill: U of North Carolina P, 1959. 479–488.
Marcus, Philip. *Standish O'Grady*. Lewisburg, Pa.: Bucknell UP, 1970.
Miller, Edwin Haviland, ed. *A Century of Whitman Criticism*. Bloomington: Indiana UP, 1969.
Moore, George. *Hail and Farewell*. Ed. Richard Allen Cave. Gerrards Cross, England: Colin Smyth, 1985.
Traubel, Horace. *With Walt Whitman in Camden*. Ed. Sculley Bradley. Vol. 4. Philadelphia: U of Pennsylvania P, 1953.
Whitman, Walt. *The Correspondence*. Ed. Edwin Haviland Miller. Vol. 2. New York: New York UP, 1961.
Yeats, William Butler. *The Collected Letters of W.B. Yeats*. Ed. John Kelly. Vol. 1. Oxford: Clarendon, 1986.

See also BRITISH ISLES, WHITMAN IN THE; DOWDEN, EDWARD; INTERCULTURALITY; JOYCE, JAMES; WILDE, OSCAR

Israel, Whitman in

Whitman's presence in Israel has been previously acknowledged by Gay Wilson Allen and by Ezra Greenspan, who both note that the poet was already admired by Hebrew poets and critics in the 1920s. A close consideration can demarcate three areas of response to Whitman in Israel: literary, critical, and cultural. Whitman's reception in this country can therefore be considered an interesting example of his function as both poet and icon.

The best-known literary response is that of Uri Zvi Greenberg (1895–1981), one of Israel's leading poets. Greenberg himself points to such a connection in several of his earlier manifestos. Thus, for example, in 1928 he declares, "Arise, the Hebrew Walt Whitman, Arise!" (qtd. in Goodblatt 238). This statement connects Whitman, adopted by the German expressionists as their precursor, to Greenberg, a primary importer of expressionism into Yiddish and Hebrew poetry. Cutting across languages and cultures, two Israeli critics have paid close attention to this connection. Benjamin Hrushovski discerns an unconventional rhythmic structure, combining regular metrics with syntactic and semantic units, in three expressionist poets: the Hebrew Greenberg, the Russian Vladimir Mayakovsky (1894–1930), and the American Whitman. Chanita Goodblatt focuses on an extended rhetorical comparison between Whitman and Greenberg, designed to emphasize a shared conception of poetry that challenges the monologic nature of the poetic text and stresses instead one that is publicistic and multivoiced.

Simon Halkin has nurtured the varied critical and cultural responses to Whitman in Israel, by translating Whitman into Hebrew and by composing a seminal Hebrew introduction for the Israeli reader. In 1952 he produced the most extensive Hebrew translation of *Leaves of Grass,* reprinted and enlarged in 1984 to contain over 500 pages. This and the accompanying publication of Halkin's Hebrew introduction (1952) comprised a double contribution to Whitman studies. Thus in the first chapter he adumbrates the critical change that has, in the meantime, occurred in Whitman studies during the last forty years. While reviewing the situation of Whitman studies in 1952, Halkin criticizes the problematic nature of the critical approach to Whitman's works that at that time was primarily characterized by the attempt to use biographical information to explain the literary corpus. The following three chapters present and explain the poet and his works to the Israeli reader, placing Whitman within American culture and experience, as well as discussing three basic characteristics of his poetry: his love of the world of the senses; his love for and belief in humanity; and his love for America and his belief in her mission in human history.

Two other Israeli critics have raised central issues regarding Whitman's poetry. Sholom J. Kahn confronts the poet's sense of evil, explaining that its limitations lie primarily in Whitman's attempt to remain ethically neutral. In other words, for him suffering is caused by a purely natural evil to which no reason or guilt can be ascribed. Zephyra Porat confronts Whitman's crises of faith in himself, as revealed in the poem "As I Ebb'd with the Ocean of Life" (1860). She reformulates the psychological concept of the Oedipal conflict as comprising for Whitman one between pride (self-love) and love of what is external to him, as well as pointing out the various ways in which the poem affords him a way to resolve this conflict.

This varied critical response to Whitman in Israel is accompanied by a varied cultural one as well. He has become part of the canon of general English studies. Two of his poems ("O Captain! My Captain!" and "A Noiseless Patient Spider") are included in the standard syllabus for the English Matriculation Examination in Israeli high schools. What is more, Whitman has come to be seen as a cultural icon, used by different groups in contemporary Israeli culture to express their ideologies. Upon publication of Halkin's translation, the literary section *Masa* in the newspaper *Davar* (the official organ of the Labor Federation) printed a Hebrew translation of Mirsky's socialist evaluation of Whitman's poetry. As socialist values were very much evident then in Israel, such an act exhibits a willingness to give voice to this ideological interpretation of Whitman. There is also Zoltin's recent article, which appeared in a special interest section on homosexuality in the weekend magazine of *Davar.* At a time when homosexuality is being debated in Israel, Whitman is represented as the figure of an embattled national poet, because of the explicit expression in his writings of homosexual feelings. Finally, the newspaper *Ha'arets* (11 October 95) printed Whitman's poem on Lincoln's assassination, "O Captain! My Captain!," as a tribute to Yitzhak Rabin's memory after his assassination. One can suggest that this is a reworking through Whitman of America's response to a presidential murder, within the context of an upheaval in Israeli society. It can indeed be said that in this country Whitman's presence is strongly felt on many levels.

Chanita Goodblatt

Bibliography

Allen, Gay Wilson. "Whitman in Israel." *Walt Whitman Abroad.* Ed. Gay Wilson Allen. Syracuse, N.Y.: Syracuse UP, 1955. 235–236, 280.

———. "Whitman in Other Countries: Japan, Israel, China." *The New Walt Whitman Handbook.* New York: New York UP, 1975. 323–327.

Goodblatt, Chanita. "Walt Whitman and Uri Zvi Greenberg: Voice and Dialogue, Apostrophe and Discourse." *Prooftexts* 13 (1993): 237–251.

Greenspan, Ezra. "Whitman in Israel." *Walt Whitman & the World.* Ed. Gay Wilson Allen and Ed Folsom. Iowa City: U of Iowa P, 1995. 386–395.

Halkin, Simon. *Walt Whitman: The Poet's Life and Work: An Essay* (in Hebrew). Tel Aviv: Hakibbutz Hame'uhad, 1952.

Hrushovski, Benjamin. *The Theory and Practice of Rhythm in the Expressionist Poetry of U.Z. Greenberg* (in Hebrew). Tel Aviv: Hakibbutz Hame'uhad, 1978.

Kahn, Sholom J. "Whitman's Sense of Evil: Criticisms." *Walt Whitman Abroad.* Ed.

Gay Wilson Allen. Syracuse, N.Y.: Syracuse UP, 1955. 236–254.

Mirsky, D.S. "Walt Whitman: Poet of American Democracy" (in Hebrew). Trans. editorial staff. Parts 1 and 2. *Masa* 8 (29 May 1952): 4–5; 9 (12 June 1952): 3, 8, 9, 11.

Porat, Zephyra. "What is Yours is Mine, My Father: On One Poem by Walt Whitman." *Prometheus Among the Cannibals: Studies in the Question of Rebellion in Literature* (in Hebrew). Tel Aviv: Am Oved, 1976. 46–59.

Whitman, Walt. *Leaves of Grass* (in Hebrew). Collected and translated by Simon Halkin. Tel Aviv: Hakibbutz Hame'uhad, 1984.

Zoltin, Lior. "Resist Much, Obey Little" (in Hebrew). *Davar Hashavua* 39 (1994): 20–21.

See also INTERCULTURALITY; LEGACY, WHITMAN'S

"Italian Music in Dakota" (1881)

Written after Whitman's western excursion in 1879, "Italian Music in Dakota" appeared for the first time in the 1881 *Leaves*. Though his tour did not include the Dakotas, Whitman no doubt heard the Seventeenth Regimental Band—described in a caption as "the finest Regimental Band I ever heard"—in an appearance in the western region.

In seventeen lines Whitman captures the effect of hearing music of Italian opera in the natural setting of the American West. For him the effect amounts to the blessing of nature on the art form he most loved. Originally disdainful of European music, especially opera, in a democratic nation, Whitman had succumbed to Italian opera by 1855 and later declared it one of the sources for *Leaves*. "Italian Music" contains specific references to bel canto works, Vincenzo Bellini's *La Sonnambula* (1831) and *Norma* (1831) and Gaetano Donizetti's *Poliuto* (1838), which were favorites of Whitman in the 1840s when he attended opera in Manhattan. When played by the regimental band in the western wilderness, rather than in a city opera house, the operatic harmonies seem to the poet to acquire new and more subtle meaning, and nature, in its wild state, appears to acknowledge an affinity with this music, which produces a complete harmony. In essence, the poem epitomizes Whitman's many references to music, in that it reconciles and dispels apparent disparities.

Joann P. Krieg

Bibliography

Faner, Robert D. *Walt Whitman & Opera*. Carbondale: Southern Illinois UP, 1951.

See also OPERA AND OPERA SINGERS; WEST, THE AMERICAN

Italy, Whitman in

The first translation of Whitman into Italian appeared in 1887 by Luigi Gamberale. This small selection contained forty-eight poems and was published under the title *Canti Scelti*. In 1890 a new edition was published with the addition of seventy-one more poems. In 1907 a complete translation was completed by Gamberale and published as *Foglie d'erba e Prose*. In 1950 a complete edition of *Leaves of Grass*—which also included *Specimen Days,* the 1855 Preface, and "A Backward Glance O'er Traveled Roads" translated by Enzo Giachino and dedicated to Cesare Pavese—was published by Giulia Einuadi of Turin. This edition is considered the most complete in any foreign language edition to date.

In 1879 the first critical appraisal of Whitman was published by the Italian critic Enrico Nencioni in the newspaper *Il Fanfulla della Domenica,* followed by three more articles written in 1881, 1883, and 1884. In his 1881 article he praised Whitman as being impressive even in his faults, a needed antidote to the narrow scope of the boudoir literature of the time. Nencioni's article caught the attention of the Italian poet Giosuè Carducci, who became interested in Whitman's work. He considered Whitman on equal footing with Homer, Shakespeare, and Dante, and described him enthusiastically as "immediate and original" (qtd. in Miller 29). Nencioni's 1883 article caught the interest of Gabriele D'Annunzio, who was said to have drawn inspiration from *Leaves of Grass* for his poetic work *Laus Vitae*. In a final essay on Whitman published in 1891, Nencioni believed Whitman had the largest grasp of humanitarianism and democracy out of all previous advocates such as Percy Bysshe Shelley, Robert Burns, Friedrich von Schiller, Guiseppe Mazzini, and others. For him, Whitman was in the same class with Thomas Carlyle, Jules Michelet, and Victor Hugo as one of the four greatest poetical imaginations of the time.

The earliest and most astute critical evaluation of Whitman's poetic technique was by

Pasquale Jannaccone, a scholar familiar with primitive forms of Greek and Latin poetry. In 1898 he published a study of Whitman's poetic technique under the title *La Poesia di Walt Whitman e L'Evoluzione della Forme Ritmiche*. Jannaccone saw Whitman's poetry more as a revival of older, more ancient poetic forms than as the evolution of any new poetic techniques. In his view these archaic poetic forms provided a rationale and aesthetic framework for the meter of his language and his organic rhythms, along with what he considered Whitman's reluctance to be limited by conventional poetic forms.

Giovanni Papini, the critic and essayist, claimed his discovery of Whitman was one of the most important of his early years. He felt Whitman was a precursor to Fyodor Dostoevsky and Leo Tolstoy, and had the same Dionysiac passion as Friedrich Nietzsche. He believed Whitman's work had the power to purge Italians of their dilettantism and return them again to some degree of primality whereby they would be able to rediscover the roots of real poetry reborn again from an earlier "barbarism" (Papini).

Cesare Pavese, the Italian novelist, published in 1933 what is still considered in Italy the most perceptive evaluation of Whitman written by an Italian. He believed that by sheer force of will Whitman had clarified and liberated the accepted poetic form of his time in order to realize his self-assumed mission to make *Leaves of Grass* the definitive expression of America. Although he thought Whitman unsuccessful in this attempt, he believed the poet had successfully created a "poetry of the discovery of a world new in history and of the singing of it" (Pavese 193), a unique poetry made out of deliberate design. In addition, he thought Whitman's originality had been minimized by commentators reducing the significance of *Leaves of Grass* to the "Calamus" poems. He contended this misguided assessment tended to negate Whitman's mature accomplishment as a poet evident in the songs of the first and second editions of the work. Whitman's artistic intentions, he contends, can be argued to have been "worked consciously and with a certain critical sense" (193).

According to Eugenio Montale, there has been no direct influence of Whitman on twentieth-century Italian poetry other than on Dino Campana and his *Canti Orfici*, published in 1914. Considered the most important poetic work produced this century in Italy, it showed Whitman's influence in both language and persona. Campana attributed great significance to Whitman's concept of freedom and liberation, attaching at the end of *Canti Orfici* probably the first and only quotation from *Leaves of Grass* appended to a poetic work by an Italian poet. If there has been any influence by Whitman on Italian poetry since then, Montale asserts, it has been under the surface and adjusted to the nature of Italian language and tradition, contributing "not a free verse, but a more liberated verse" (Montale 188).

With the rise in fascism in Italy, critical writing on Whitman declined until after the end of World War II. A number of prominent Italian critics then turned their attention to analyzing him. Mario Paz compared him to Proust, seeing his poetry as born out of an infantile psyche, but having more basic freshness and purity. Carlo Bo described *Leaves of Grass* as a single discourse alive to the whole panoply of human emotions. Glauco Cambon contends Whitman was the major player in creating a new tradition of American poetry. He disagrees with psychosexual interpretations of Whitman, finding them "a little too decadent," asserting instead that his authentic self-discovery was a recognition of Adamic innocence and "the paradise of the liberated senses" (qtd. in Miller 30).

Thomas Sanfilip

Bibliography

Allen, Gay Wilson, and Ed Folsom, eds. *Walt Whitman & the World*. Iowa City: U of Iowa P, 1995.

Campana, Dino. *Orphic Songs and Other Poems*. Trans. Luigi Bonaffini. New York: Lang, 1991.

Jannaccone, Pasquale. *Walt Whitman's Poetry and the Evolution of Rhythmic Forms* and *Walt Whitman's Thought and Art*. Trans. Peter Mitilineos. Washington, D.C.: NCR Microcard Editions, 1973.

McCain, Rea. "Walt Whitman in Italy." *Italica* 20 (1943): 4–16.

Miller, James E., Jr. "Whitman in Italy." *Walt Whitman Review* 5 (1959): 28–30.

Montale, Eugenio. *The Second Life of Art: Selected Essays of Eugenio Montale*. Ed. and trans. Jonathan Galassi. New York: Ecco, 1982.

Papini, Giovanni. "Whitman." Trans. Roger Asselineau. *Walt Whitman Abroad*. Ed. Gay Wilson Allen. Syracuse: Syracuse UP, 1955. 189.

Pavese, Cesare. "Whitman—Poetry of Poetry Writing." Trans. Roger Asselineau. *Walt Whitman Abroad*. Ed. Gay Wilson Allen. Syracuse: Syracuse UP, 1955. 189–198.

Raffaniello, William. "Pasquale Jannaccone and 'The Last Invocation.'" *Walt Whitman Review* 14 (1968): 41–45.

See also INTERCULTURALITY

I

J

Jackson, Andrew (1767–1845)

The president of the United States from 1828 to 1836, Andrew Jackson furnished Walt Whitman with an important link between antebellum culture and the nation's revolutionary past. As a boy growing up in South Carolina, Jackson had participated in the American Revolution (1780–1781), during which he was captured and held as a prisoner of war. Jackson led American troops against both the British and the Creek Indians during the War of 1812. Although it proved to have little consequence in the outcome of the conflict, the general's victory at the battle of New Orleans (1815) made him a hero of national stature. Jackson nearly won the presidency in 1824, but as no candidate received a majority of electoral votes, the election was thrown into the House of Representatives, which decided in favor of John Quincy Adams. The controversies surrounding the election helped solidify Jackson's reputation as a "man of the people," and in 1828 he defeated Adams with an unprecedented percentage of the popular vote. To admirers such as Walt Whitman, Jackson's presidency was most distinguished by his attack on the Second National Bank, an institution he successfully portrayed as an aristocratic monopoly.

As Sean Wilentz has observed, Jackson's association with democratic politics inspired a generation of artisan-laborers, and Whitman was not alone in seeing "Old Hickory" as an emblem of civic virtue. In his editorials for the Brooklyn *Daily Eagle*, Whitman frequently championed Jackson as the patron saint of the Democratic party, ranking him above even George Washington and Thomas Jefferson in his trinity of national heroes. Whitman's respect for individual rights and his egalitarian vision were prevalent throughout the Age of Jackson. At the center of this sociopolitical movement was a faith in the people as the source of national renewal.

Whitman found Jackson's democratic personality extremely suggestive, and David Reynolds has questioned whether Whitman learned to imitate Jackson's peculiar combination of egalitarian despotism. The president had visited Brooklyn in 1832 when Whitman was thirteen years old, and in an 1846 editorial, he fondly recalled the crowd's excited reception of the "hero and the Sage" (Whitman 179). Whitman saw in Jackson a "truly sublime being" whose infamous will merely reflected his devotion to the public good (qtd. in Brasher 101). Despite his eventual disenchantment with American politics, Whitman always spoke of the president with extraordinary respect. Jackson was "true gold," he told Horace Traubel in Camden, "the genuine ore in the rough" (*With Walt Whitman* 3:30).

David Haven Blake

Bibliography

Brasher, Thomas L. *Whitman as Editor of the Brooklyn Daily Eagle*. Detroit: Wayne State UP, 1970.

Reynolds, David S. *Walt Whitman's America: A Cultural Biography*. New York: Knopf, 1995.

Schlesinger, Arthur M., Jr. *The Age of Jackson*. Boston: Little, Brown, 1946.

Traubel, Horace. *With Walt Whitman in Camden*. Vol. 1. Boston: Small, Maynard, 1906; Vol. 3. New York: Mitchell Kinnerley, 1914.

Watson, Harry L. *Liberty and Power: The Politics of Jacksonian America*. New York: Hill and Wang, 1990.

Whitman, Walt. *The Gathering of the Forces*. Ed. Cleveland Rodgers and John Black. Vol. 2. New York: Putnam, 1920.

Wilentz, Sean. *Chants Democratic: New York City & the Rise of the American Working Class, 1788–1850*. New York: Oxford UP, 1984.

See also BROOKLYN, NEW YORK; POLITICAL VIEWS; PRESIDENTS, UNITED STATES

James, Henry (1843–1916)

American writer of novels, short stories, and literary criticism, Henry James stands among the most important cultural figures of the nineteenth century. Known by the formidable, if affectionate, sobriquet "the Master," James's probing wit, analytical acumen, and unflinching honesty impelled him to dissect those writers he reviewed—including Whitman—with merciless precision. James spent much of his life abroad, cultivating the friendships of such European masters as Gustave Flaubert, Ivan Turgenev, and Guy de Maupassant. He adopted the careful narrative craftsmanship of these authors in his own fiction, which evolved from the readily accessible and popular *Daisy Miller* (1879) to the extraordinarily complex and dense *The Golden Bowl* (1904).

When he came to review Whitman's work, James, not surprisingly, betrayed impatience with the poet whose "barbaric yawp" seemed to drown out more subtle and intricate questions of craft. In an 1865 review of *Drum-Taps,* at the upstart age of twenty-two, James cuttingly pronounced this volume to be "an offense against art" (113) that makes for "melancholy reading" (110). Later, however, the spleen had drained off James's tone. In his 1898 review of *Calamus,* he wrote with affection and appreciation for the "beauty of the natural" in this "audible New Jersey voice" that relates "many odd and pleasant human harmonies" (260). And in a letter of 1903 James repented of the "gross impudence of youth" that compelled him to perpetrate the "little atrocity" of his 1865 review on Whitman (*Selected Letters* 348). In her autobiography *A Backward Glance* (1933), Edith Wharton narrates an evening when James read aloud from Whitman's poetry "in a mood of subdued ecstasy" while they all "sat rapt"

(186). During the ensuing discussion, James declared Whitman a "very great genius!" James's shifting assessment of Whitman over the course of forty-five years forms a not inaccurate model for Whitman's larger reception: from invective to acceptance, from grudging admiration to buoyant celebration.

Renée Dye

Bibliography

Edel, Leon. *Henry James.* 5 vols. Philadelphia: Lippincott, 1953–1972.

James, Henry. "Henry James on Whitman. 1865." *Walt Whitman: The Critical Heritage.* Ed. Milton Hindus. New York: Barnes and Noble, 1971. 110–114.

———. "Henry James on Whitman. 1898." *Walt Whitman: The Critical Heritage.* Ed. Milton Hindus. New York: Barnes and Noble, 1971. 259–260.

———. *Henry James: Selected Letters.* Ed. Leon Edel. Cambridge, Mass.: Harvard UP, 1987.

Wharton, Edith. *A Backward Glance.* 1933. New York: Scribner's, 1988.

Whitman, Walt. *Calamus: A Series of Letters Written during the Years 1868–1880 by Walt Whitman to a Young Friend (Peter Doyle).* Ed. Richard Maurice Bucke. London: Putnam, 1898.

See also CRITICS, WHITMAN'S; WHARTON, EDITH

James, William (1842–1910)

It is certain that William James, the American philosopher-psychologist and brother of Henry James, read and appreciated the works of Walt Whitman and that he interpreted them with remarkable critical acumen, for he refers to and quotes Whitman in "Is Life Worth Living?," "On a Certain Blindness in Human Beings," *The Sentiment of Rationality* (1905), *The Will to Believe* (1897), *Human Immortality* (1898), *Pragmatism* (1907), and *The Varieties of Religious Experience* (1902). Furthermore, it is known that James reacted strongly against the opinion of George Santayana (1863–1952), whose book *Interpretations of Poetry and Religion* (1900) discussed Whitman's "barbarism." In general, Whitman symbolized for James the emancipated and sympathetically tolerant human figure.

James owed much of his knowledge of Whitman's life and works to Richard Maurice

Bucke, the Canadian psychiatrist and personal friend of Whitman whose book *Cosmic Consciousness,* published in 1901, just a year before James's own *Varieties of Religious Experience,* furnished much valuable information for the latter book. In his various and random comments on Whitman, James quotes *Specimen Days,* "Song of Myself," "Crossing Brooklyn Ferry," and "To You [Whoever you are . . .]" (a poem he particularly admired). Gay Wilson Allen suggests that Whitman, in "By Blue Ontario's Shore," curiously anticipates William James in his *Pluralistic Universe* (1919).

James T.F. Tanner

Bibliography

Allen, Gay Wilson. *The Solitary Singer: A Critical Biography of Walt Whitman.* 1955. Rev. ed. 1967. Chicago: U of Chicago P, 1985.

———. *William James: A Biography.* New York: Viking, 1967.

Bucke, Richard Maurice, ed. *Cosmic Consciousness: A Study in the Evolution of the Human Mind.* Philadelphia: Innes, 1901.

James, William. *Pragmatism and Other Essays.* 1907. New York: Washington Square, 1963.

———. *Talks to Teachers on Psychology.* New York: Holt, 1899.

———. *The Varieties of Religious Experience.* 1902. New York: New American Library, 1958.

———. *The Will to Believe and Other Essays in Popular Philosophy, and Human Immortality.* New York: Dover, 1956.

Matthiessen, F.O. *The James Family: A Group Biography.* 3rd ed. New York: Knopf, 1961.

Perry, Ralph Barton. *The Thought and Character of William James.* 2 vols. Boston: Little, Brown, 1935.

Tanner, James T.F. "Walt Whitman and William James." *Calamus: Walt Whitman Quarterly International* 2 (1970): 6–23.

See also BUCKE, RICHARD MAURICE; COSMIC CONSCIOUSNESS; SANTAYANA, GEORGE

Japan, Whitman in

Whitman's observation of the "swart-cheek'd two-sworded envoys" riding through Manhattan on 16 June 1860 ("A Broadway Pageant," section 1) was the first and last personal contact the poet ever had with the faraway "Niphon," which gave him an impetus later to write "Passage to India." Yet the American poet and his writings made a deeper and more enduring impact, over the course of a century, on Japanese writers and scholars. At the time of the Meiji Restoration (1868), political leaders and educators in Japan looked up to "the sacred land of liberty" as a model on which to modernize the country emerging from a three-hundred-year isolation from the Western world. A history of modern Japan, then, is to a great extent that of Western influence and absorption into its traditional culture. And Whitman with his yawp exhorting "Libertad!" seems to embody the very spirit of "the sacred land of liberty" for people in Japan then and now.

Whitman's reception in Japan falls roughly into two stages—the first covering a good part of the Meiji era (1868–1912) through the Taisho period (1912–1925) and the second dating from after the end of World War II in 1945—with a certain lapse in between.

At the beginning, however, American democratic thoughts and radical individualism were introduced and absorbed in political/social spheres rather than in literary writings. The names of Benjamin Franklin and Thomas Jefferson, or Henry Wadsworth Longfellow and Ralph Waldo Emerson, outshone that of Whitman until his death in 1892. Coincidentally, that very year Soseki Natsume, then a student at Tokyo University, published in a philosophical journal an essay entitled "On the Poetry of Walt Whitman—an Egalitarian Poet." Soseki read Whitman in the Canterbury Poets Series of *Poems of Walt Whitman* (1886), and introduced "the representative poet of egalitarianism." The article was a rehash of Edward Dowden's "The Poetry of Democracy: Walt Whitman" in *Studies in Literature, 1789–1877.* Thus, Whitman first came to be known to Japanese audiences via British scholarship.

From then through the years of Taisho democracy (1912–1925) Whitman and his belief in the absolute freedom of the individual man and woman enjoyed enthusiastic reception. Writers of the Shirakaba School, founded in 1910, discovered their kindred spirit in the poet, wrote introductory essays and articles on him, and made various translations of his poems as well as prose works such as *Democratic Vistas* and *Specimen Days.*

Kanzo Uchimura, an influential Christian educator, used to give lectures on Whitman before the publication of his *Walt Whitman the Poet* (1909) and *The Poet of Common People* (1914). Indeed it is Uchimura's "Monday lectures" that first introduced Whitman to Takeo Arishima around 1898. This most important writer of the Shirakaba School later became a devotee of Whitman and his democratic ideas.

Arishima's interest in Whitman surfaced during his sojourn in America (1903–1906); after his return, Arishima wrote prolifically on Whitman. He also published translations of Whitman's poetical works (1921, 1923), which were revised and went through many printings. His translation of *Leaves of Grass,* despite its flaws, is still the best of its kind. Furthermore, Whitman's belief in the absolute freedom of an individual human being was transformed into Whitmanesque characters in Arishima's own novels such as *A Certain Woman* (1911–1913) and *The Maze* (1918). In this first phase of Whitman's reception, it was writers and poets or educators who were interested in the poet and his writings rather than scholars in academe.

The second stage of Whitman's reception begins after the end of the Second World War, when American democracy was reintroduced. American literature then became an independent discipline apart from English literature at many colleges and universities. The founding of a Walt Whitman Society in 1964 indicates Japanese scholars' interest in and commitment to Whitman. The society, with a membership of about eighty, has been instrumental in organizing annual conferences and literary events related to the poet. Its newsletter, published annually, provides updated information on Whitman scholarship, foreign and Japanese.

Of various scholarly achievements the most valuable work to date is Shunsuke Kamei's *Kindai Bungaku ni okeru Hoitoman no Unmei* (*The Fate of Whitman in Modern Literature*) (1970), which won the prestigious Gakushiin sho (the Japan Academy Prize). Kamei's voluminous book of 648 pages consists of two parts: the first part deals with Whitman in modern European literature; the second examines Whitman's reception in modern Japanese literature, which serves as a magnetic field where Whitman both attracted and repelled the serious writers and thinkers of modern Japan. A few other scholarly accomplishments are *Whitman and Dickinson: Cultural Symbols in Their Writings* (1981), by Tamaaki Yamakawa et al., and

Minoru Hirooka's *Walt Whitman and Contemporary American Poets* (1987). Each of these works examines Whitman in relation to his time and to later American poets.

In Japan today scholars find a renewed interest in the feminist Whitman. Kuniko Yoshizaki's critical biography *Walt Whitman in Our Time* (1992) presents Whitman the feminist thinker. Yoshizaki's book uses much of Gay Wilson Allen's *The Solitary Singer* (1955), while it emphasizes Whitman's all-inclusive soul that sings "the Female equally with the Male" ("One's-Self I Sing"). Her thesis that Whitman is the first American poet of feminism who wrote for the liberation of woman's soul and body is only too valid. In addition, the 1995 convention of the American Literature Association of Japan, held in Kyoto, featured a symposium on "Whitman and Feminist Criticism."

On the occasion of his retirement from Tokyo University, March 1995, Professor Kamei gave his private Walt Whitman collection to the Gifu Women's University Library, with a catalogue prepared by himself. The chronologically arranged list of some six hundred items of Whitman's writings, bibliographies, books, translations, magazines, and newspapers is in itself an excellent survey of Whitman's reception and influence in Japan over the period of a century since his first introduction in 1892. It is an invaluable collection, together with the Nagamuna Collection of similar scope and interest, located at Konan University in Kobe.

The secret of Whitman's continued popularity among scholars and devotees in Japan lies in his democratic idealism and also in what Richard Maurice Bucke termed as the "cosmic consciousness" which Whitman shared with mystics West (e.g., Blake) and East (e.g., Zen Buddhists).

Keiko Beppu

Bibliography

Allen, Gay Wilson, and Ed Folsom, eds. *Walt Whitman & the World.* Iowa City: U of Iowa P, 1995.

Kamei, Shunsuke. *The Kamei Collection: A Catalogue* (March 1995).

———. *Kindai Bungaku ni okeru Hoitoman no Unmei* [*The Fate of Walt Whitman in Modern Literature*]. Tokyo: Kenkyusha, 1970.

———. "The Walt Whitman Collection." *Eigo Seinen* [*The Rising Generation*] (March 1995): 12–13.

———. "Whitman in Japan." *Eigo Seinen* [*The Rising Generation*] Walt Whitman

Special Number (1969): 29–36.

Kato, Shuichi. *A History of Japanese Literature*. Trans. Don Sanderson. Vol. 3. Tokyo: Kodansha International, 1979.

Sadoya, Shigenobu. *Walt Whitman in Japan: His Influence in Modern Japan*. Bulletin No. 9. Fukuoka: Research Institute, Seinan Gakuin University, 1969.

Yoshizaki, Kuniko. *Hoitoman: Jidai to tomoni Ikiru* [*Walt Whitman in Our Time*]. Tokyo: Kaibunsha, 1992.

See also "BROADWAY PAGEANT, A"; INTERCULTURALITY

Jarrell, Randall (1914–1965)

The distinguished career of Randall Jarrell, Tennessee-born author, educator, editor, and critic, centers on the poetry he wrote during World War II. Throughout his career Jarrell championed Whitman's use of language, form, and epic scope, finding his style "beautifully witty" (*Poetry* 103) while admitting Whitman had tedious passages. In letters written in late 1951, Jarrell instructed friends to put flowers at Whitman's birthplace, saying, "Whitman is a wonderful poet at his best" (*Letters* 288) and praising "Song of Myself" and "The Sleepers."

In "The Age of Criticism" (1952) Jarrell praises Whitman as a poet defying the analytical approach of the New Critics, quoting his favorite Whitman lines: "I am the man, I suffered, I was there" ("Song of Myself," section 33). In *Poetry and the Age* (1953), Jarrell evaluates Whitman's then minor reputation and finds him crude and awkward, but with "the most comprehensive soul" (*Poetry* 115), a poet who could not resist the truth. Whitman, Jarrell asserts, should not be dismissed or patronized by critics and should be considered alongside Herman Melville and Emily Dickinson. He admired "Out of the Cradle" which was later compared to his own "The Bronze David of Donatello."

Wesley A. Britton

Bibliography

Jarrell, Randall. *Poetry and the Age*. New York: Vintage, 1953.

———. *Randall Jarrell's Letters: An Autobiographical and Literary Selection*. Ed. Mary Jarrell. Boston: Houghton Mifflin, 1985.

See also CRITICS, WHITMAN'S

Jefferson, Thomas (1743–1826)

The third president of the United States (1800–1808), Thomas Jefferson epitomized the Enlightenment man in America. A graceful writer, an adept politician, a formidable intellectual, and a talented architect, Jefferson bequeathed to the new nation a weighty legacy of achievements. He drafted the Declaration of Independence (1776), he founded the University of Virginia, and his library—over ten thousand volumes—formed the original collection of the Library of Congress. During the vitriolic debates over the National Bank, Jefferson emerged as the champion of strong state and individual rights at the expense of a powerful federal government. His vision of America featured a hardy and self-sufficient yeomanry, whom he proclaimed "the chosen people of the earth," secure in their rural enclaves from the corruption of cities and governments.

Whitman considered Jefferson the most authentic democratic statesman the young country had yet produced. In conversation with Horace Traubel in 1888, Whitman described Elias Hicks as "the only real democrat among all religious teachers: the democrat in religion as Jefferson was the democrat in politics" (*With Walt Whitman* 2:36). On another occasion Whitman agreed that Jefferson was "greatest of the great: that names him: it belongs to him: he is entitled to it" (*With Walt Whitman* 3:229). Jefferson was "entitled" to the epithet for his unwavering devotion to the premier principle of democracy: the entitlement of all persons to their "inalienable rights." In "Song of Myself," Whitman's tender cataloguing of all the inhabitants of the United States—slave and free, immigrant and native, young and old, rich and poor—embodies poetically the abstract creed of natural equality penned by Jefferson and preached by Hicks, the poet's two representative democrats.

Renée Dye

Bibliography

Malone, Dumas. *Jefferson and His Time*. 6 vols. Boston: Little, Brown, 1948–1981.

Randall, Willard Sterne. *Thomas Jefferson: A Life*. New York: Holt, 1993.

Traubel, Horace. *With Walt Whitman in Camden*. Vol. 2. New York: Appleton, 1908; Vol. 3. New York: Mitchell Kennerley, 1914.

See also AMERICAN REVOLUTION, THE; DEMOCRACY; HICKS, ELIAS; PRESIDENTS, UNITED STATES

Johnston, Dr. John (d. 1918)

John Johnston, an English physician, was a Walt Whitman enthusiast; a member of Bolton "College"; a visitor, correspondent, and photographer of Whitman; and coauthor of a book with Bolton College founder James William Wallace (1853–1926) about their separate visits to the poet.

Johnston attended the Monday night meetings at the house of Wallace's father on Eagle Street in Bolton, England. Known locally as the "Eagle Street College" and abroad as Bolton College, this primarily working-class group of men included few educated professionals. The nomenclature "College" shows their humor. Anything but a college, the group held their loosely organized weekly gatherings for discussion of local interest topics, politics, and spiritual matters. In spiritual matters, Bolton College members, several of whom were Whitman students and admirers, followed the ideas of Dr. Richard Maurice Bucke, especially those about cosmic consciousness.

On behalf of Bolton College, Johnston and Wallace started corresponding with Whitman in 1887. Whitman wrote them more than 120 letters and postcards and sent Bolton College books and other gifts. Today the Metropolitan Library in Bolton houses the Whitman gifts.

In 1890 Johnston visited Whitman in Camden, where he photographed the poet and other members of the household. He then visited Andrew H. Rome in New York. Johnston also interviewed John Y. Baulsir, a Fulton Ferry deckhand. On Long Island, he spent the night at Henry Jarvis's home (the Whitman Birthplace), interviewed former Whitman student Sanford Brown, and visited painter Herbert Harlakenden Gilchrist. Johnston then traveled to West Park, New York, where he visited John Burroughs.

Larry D. Griffin

Bibliography

Bucke, Richard Maurice. *Cosmic Consciousness: A Study in the Evolution of the Human Mind.* Philadelphia: Innes, 1901.
———. *Walt Whitman.* Philadelphia: McKay, 1883.
Hamer, Harold. *A Catalogue of Works by and Relating to Whitman in the Reference Library, Bolton.* Bolton, England: Libraries Committee, 1955.
Johnston, John, and James William Wallace. *Visits to Walt Whitman in 1890–1891 by Two Lancashire Friends.* London: Allen and Unwin, 1917.
Salveson, Paul. *Loving Comrades: Lancashire's Links to Walt Whitman.* Bolton, England: Worker's Educational Association, 1984.

See also BOLTON (ENGLAND) "EAGLE STREET COLLEGE"; BRITISH ISLES, WHITMAN IN THE; BUCKE, RICHARD MAURICE; CAMDEN, NEW JERSEY; WALLACE, JAMES WILLIAM

Johnston, John H. (1837–1919) and Alma Calder

J.H. Johnston was a New York jeweler who befriended Whitman and provided personal and financial support for the aging poet. Johnston often opened his house to Whitman. During a month-long visit in February 1877, Whitman was introduced to a variety of people, among them Richard Watson Gilder. Whitman's visit was marred, however, by the sudden illness and death of Johnston's first wife on the day he planned to leave. After Johnston's marriage to his second wife, Alma Calder Johnston, Whitman returned in June 1878 to visit the Johnston home, now on upper Fifth Avenue. During August 1881, Whitman stayed with the Johnstons at their summer home at Mott Haven on the Harlem River to finish editing his new *Leaves of Grass.* Whitman apparently felt at home with the Johnstons, whose children referred to him affectionately as "Uncle Walt."

Johnston was also instrumental in organizing fund raisers for Whitman's benefit. He was the chief organizer of the 1887 benefit for Whitman in conjunction with the Lincoln lecture at Madison Square Theater. In October 1890 Johnston arranged the benefit lecture by Robert G. Ingersoll in Philadelphia, which realized $870. Whitman trusted Johnston's financial acumen, finding him to be acute in business matters.

Alma Calder Johnston's literary endeavors include a recollection of Whitman (1917) and a story, *Miriam's Heritage* (1878).

J.H. Johnston, the jeweler, is not to be confused with Dr. John Johnston, an English medical doctor and admirer of Whitman.

Susan L. Roberson

Bibliography

Johnston, Alma Calder. "Personal Memories of Walt Whitman." *Whitman in His Own Time: A Biographical Chronicle of His Life, Drawn from Recollections,*

Memoirs, and Interviews by Friends and Associates. Ed. Joel Myerson. Detroit: Omnigraphics, 1991. 260–273.

See also GILDER, RICHARD WATSON; INGERSOLL, ROBERT GREEN

Jordan, June (1936–)

The poet and essayist June Jordan is part of the generation of powerful black feminist voices that emerged in the 1960s and 1970s. With the publication of *Some Changes* in 1971, it was clear that Jordan's passionate, committed, conversational, jazzy poetry owed something to Whitman, probably via Langston Hughes. The Whitman connection was made clearer in *Passion* (1980), a book of poems written in the 1970s and prefaced by Jordan's important essay called "For the Sake of a People's Poetry: Walt Whitman and the Rest of Us." Here Jordan offers a revisionist reading of Whitman as "the one white father who shares the systematic disadvantages of his heterogeneous offspring" (*Passion* x), the one "white father" who could effectively serve as a model for the diverse and marginalized poets who arose to challenge the canonical status quo.

Jordan proclaims her own descent from Whitman—"I too am a descendant of Walt Whitman" (*Passion* xxiv)—and assigns "Black and Third World poets" the central place "within the Whitman tradition," a tradition she defines as one promulgating an "egalitarian sensibility" (*Passion* xv). Just as Hughes echoed Whitman when he wrote "I, too, sing America" (Hughes 46), so Jordan echoes Hughes as well as Whitman as she unites black, feminist, and other marginalized voices in saying "we, too, go on singing this America" (*Passion* xxvi). Her spirited assessment is an important document in casting Whitman as the poet of radical democracy who celebrates America's diversities.

Ed Folsom

Bibliography

Hughes, Langston. *The Collected Poems of Langston Hughes*. Ed. Arnold Rampersad. New York: Knopf, 1994.
Jordan, June. *Civil Wars: Selected Essays, 1964–1980*. Boston: Beacon, 1981.
———. *Passion: New Poems, 1977–1980*. Boston: Beacon, 1980.

See also HUGHES, LANGSTON; LEGACY, WHITMAN'S

Journalism, Whitman's

Biographers have always recognized Whitman's career in journalism as a prominent feature of his life and his development as the "poet of democracy." First through printing and then through news writing and newspaper editing, Whitman discovered the power of the written word in an age of increasing literacy. It was through journalism that Whitman first discovered himself to be a writer, first joined the public "conversation" on matters literary and political, and first established himself as a professional figure in an era when professionalism was on the rise.

Whitman's career in journalism was an outgrowth of his apprenticeship in the printing craft, which he began in 1831 at the age of twelve, working at the hand-press of the *Long Island Patriot*. The special combination of craftsman's pride, working people's democracy, and impassioned writing inspired by social and political affairs was as much a part of the journalist's environment of this time as it would be of *Leaves of Grass* later, though his earliest writing tended to be conventionally introspective, impressionistic, and, not surprisingly, caught up with the psychological problems of the adolescent ego. By the time Whitman graduated to journeyman printer in 1835, he was already publishing short pieces in various papers, not only routine features and news but also reviews, essays, and poems. When bad economic times left him out of work as a printer and journalist in 1836, he turned to schoolteaching, but continued to write and seek publication. By 1838, Whitman was back to regular work in journalism, this time as the founding editor and publisher of a weekly, the *Long Islander*. No files of this paper survive, but a few pieces were reprinted in the *Long Island Democrat* and thus come down to us as the earliest examples of Whitman's published work. Also dating from this time, but probably written earlier, is a series of ten essays "From the Desk of a Schoolmaster" entitled "Sun-Down Papers." The *Long Islander* did not thrive financially under Whitman's management, and when his backer sold it, he went to work for the *Democrat*. Then, completing the pattern that dominated his early career, he drifted back to schoolteaching and finally moved to New York to find work as a printer. During the early 1840s, he contributed reviews and essays to papers and literary journals and also began to write fiction. In critical notices and reviews, he vigorously joined the rush to define and defend a democratic ideal of literature that then consumed the pages of periodicals like the *United States Review* and the *New World*.

In 1842, Whitman produced a sizable body of work and served as chief editor for a single paper, the New York *Aurora*. In this role we see him for the first time writing hotly on local political topics such as the Catholic-Protestant disputes in the streets of New York and the associated stirrings of the anti-immigrant Nativist movement. Like most journalists of his day, Whitman was not above name-calling and rabble-rousing and may well have lost his editorial post because of his refusal to tone down the editorials published in the paper. His difficulty in keeping to a schedule may have also contributed. Loafing and inviting his soul may later have served him well as a method of poetic composition, but did not suffice for newspaper work with its tight production schedules. For whatever reason, Whitman left the *Aurora* after a few months and for the next three years supported himself by writing prose fiction, including the temperance novel *Franklin Evans*, as well as piecework for a number of New York papers, including the *Tattler, Sunday Times, Statesman, Plebeian, Sun, Democrat,* and *Mirror*.

Whitman returned to Brooklyn in 1845, where for a while he served as a kind of cultural reporter for the *Star,* writing on such topics as music, theater, education, and books. When the editor of the leading Brooklyn paper, the *Daily Eagle,* died, Whitman was hired to fill the post. He remained with the *Eagle* for two years, writing on a variety of topics, which Thomas Brasher in a book-long study of Whitman's work at the *Eagle* divides into three large categories: the political and economic scene, including editorials and features on such topics as nationalism, the West, the Old World versus the New, party politics, and the question of immigration; the social scene, including treatments of crime and punishment, temperance, slavery, and health issues; and literature and the arts, including reviews of plays and operas, as well as discussions of music, ballet, architecture, painting, and sculpture. Whitman's writings for the *Eagle* are enough to fill the two large volumes of *The Gathering of the Forces,* and this is only a selection of the editor's total output. The range and volume of Whitman's writing as a newspaper editor provided a more than adequate preparation for the poet who would

boast in his most famous poem that he "contains multitudes," and it gave him a medium in which to try on different personae and otherwise experiment with the democratic discourse of self-assertion. He took pleasure and pride in the power of the daily paper to foster special ties between author and audience. "There is a curious kind of sympathy (haven't you ever thought of it before?) that arises in the mind of a newspaper conductor with the public he serves. . . . Daily communion creates a sort of brotherhood and sisterhood between the two parties," Whitman wrote (qtd. in Brasher 6), foreshadowing *Leaves of Grass* in theme and style (notice the use of parenthetical direct address of the reader). Despite such occasional flashes, however, Brasher concludes, as do most scholars and critics, that the great mass of Whitman's writing for the *Eagle* is the work of a literary apprentice who had yet to find his own voice. In general, Whitman's literary criticism and cultural pronouncements tended to be conventional and predictable, the labor of a busy journalist with precious little time to refine and reflect upon his style and subject matter. His political editorials, especially at the beginning of his tenure, show him to be a party man writing for a party paper, defending the Democrats against the powerful Whig papers across the river in New York, even supporting excesses such as the Mexican War, which had greatly offended Ralph Waldo Emerson, James Russell Lowell, and other liberal writers. Ultimately, though, Whitman may have lost his job at the *Eagle* because he was unable to sustain the hard party line his publishers demanded. In *Specimen Days,* he would recall, "The troubles in the Democratic party broke forth . . . and I split off with the radicals, which led to rows with the boss and 'the party,' and I lost my place" (*Prose Works* 1:288).

In the next post he took as a journalist, traveling south with his younger brother Jeff to work for the New Orleans *Crescent,* he avoided politics almost entirely, reporting on cultural events, reviewing books, and writing feature essays. He capitalized on his trip south in "Excerpts from a Traveller's Note Book," published in several installments soon after his arrival in New Orleans; he warmed up for the famous catalogues that would appear in *Leaves of Grass* with impressionistic essays of characters and places around the city; and he used the occasion of controversy over a performance by the "model artists," who used human groupings to portray famous scenes from art and history, to defend the fundamental purity of celebrating the human body in art. Working for a paper that accepted advertising from slave traders and in every way catered to a slave-owning population, Whitman must have felt his status as a political outsider. This may have contributed to the decline of his political muse and even his rather early departure from his only southern post, which was also hastened by his own homesickness and that of his brother. He lasted only two months with the New Orleans paper.

By the end of 1848, he was back in Brooklyn, publishing the *Freeman,* a weekly devoted to the free-soil ideal. In his first editorial, he wrote of Thomas Jefferson, "How he hated slavery! He hated it in all its forms—over the mind as well as the body of man" (qtd. in Kaplan 145). In the charged and changeable political atmosphere of the day, he could keep the *Freeman* going only a year, after which time he again took up the life of a freelance journalist, contributing travel letters and man-on-the-street essays to a number of New York and Brooklyn papers. He would continue to produce this kind of work right through the time of the first two editions of *Leaves of Grass* in 1855 and 1856. Notable among these pieces were those published in *Life Illustrated* under the sponsorship of the phrenologists Fowler and Wells, who also published the second edition of *Leaves.*

Feeling the pinch of tight finances after focusing his efforts on producing the first two editions of his poems, Whitman gave full-time journalism one last try in 1857, accepting an editorial position on the Brooklyn *Daily Times.* Despite having become the controversial author of *Leaves of Grass,* Whitman cultivated a persona in the *Times* that remained a largely conventional one. He replicated his earlier stance, which Jerome Loving has called "the pose of the journalist as moral paragon" (60), taking charge of his readership's public education, moderating local disputes such as the treatment of slavery in the churches, and chiding the "ultra-abolitionists" and radical advocates of social programs like women's rights even as he resisted the extension of slavery and pondered the position of women in a society that offered few options for the unmarried. Yet we can see a slightly greater independence in Whitman the editor in this later period. He was no longer a party man, for example, arguing at one point that an overweening commitment to political parties had led to corruption and naiveté in American politics, local and national. He seems a bit more willing to take on controversial stances—favorably reviewing W.W. Sanger's *History of Prostitution,* for instance, which argued for controlled legalization—and he stretched the limits of sensationalistic news reporting with regular stories of rape, murder, and incest, and even one account of a homosexual rape. In all, he portrayed a "detached yet sympathetic spirit," in the words of Emory Holloway (*I Sit* 24), a recognizable, if watered-down, version of the speaker in "Song of Myself," both "in and out of the game" (section 4). Why Whitman left the *Daily Times* in June 1859 is not clear, though it has been suggested by various commentators that he offended the church people of the town, either with his stance on slavery or with his liberal attitude toward sexuality, even the attenuated version he developed for his newspaper audience. Though he never again worked formally for a single paper, Whitman kept his journalistic connections alive throughout his life, publishing poems, essays, and sketches in various papers and journals.

Much work remains to be done on Whitman's journalism. Though selections appear in the various collections listed in the following bibliography, no complete collection of extant work, comparable to Floyd Stovall's edition of the prose works, exists. (Whether some of his freelance works should be characterized as literary journalism or prose nonfiction in fact remains an unsettled question.) Nor has any biographer or critic fully accounted for the continuities and discontinuities between Whitman the poet and Whitman the journalist, though the differences have fascinated scholars since Whitman's own day. The significance of journalism in Whitman's overall development is at least partly clear, however. Newspaper work provided Whitman with a way of earning an income through writing in an age where the dominance of crafts was giving way to professionalism. It also gave him room to experiment—though in a closely controlled environment—with the rhetoric of democratic discourse, in which an ordinary citizen, the journalist, takes on the task of informing, educating, and exhorting a large and active readership composed of fellow citizens.

M. Jimmie Killingsworth

Bibliography

Brasher, Thomas L. *Whitman as Editor of the Brooklyn Daily Eagle*. Detroit: Wayne State UP, 1970.

Kaplan, Justin. *Walt Whitman: A Life*. New York: Simon and Schuster, 1980.

Loving, Jerome. *Emerson, Whitman, and the American Muse*. Chapel Hill: U of North Carolina P, 1982.

Reynolds, David S. *Walt Whitman's America: A Cultural Biography*. New York: Knopf, 1995.

Whitman, Walt. *The Gathering of the Forces*. 2 vols. Cleveland Rodgers and John Black. New York: Putnam, 1920.

———. *I Sit and Look Out: Editorials from the Brooklyn Daily Times*. Ed. Emory Holloway and Vernolian Schwarz. New York: Columbia UP, 1932.

———. *Prose Works 1892*. Ed. Floyd Stovall. 2 vols. New York: New York UP, 1963–1964.

———. *The Uncollected Poetry and Prose of Walt Whitman*. 2 Vols. Ed. Emory Holloway. Garden City, N.Y.: Doubleday, Page, 1921.

———. *Walt Whitman of the New York Aurora*. Ed. Joseph Jay Rubin and Charles H. Brown. State College, Pa.: Bald Eagle, 1950.

See also Brooklyn Daily Eagle; Brooklyn Daily Times; Brooklyn Freeman; Life Illustrated; Long Island Democrat; Long Island Patriot; Long Island Star; Long Islander; New Orleans Crescent; New World, The (New York); New York Aurora; Political Views; Printing Business

Journeying

Whitman's poetry affirms travel. His "perpetual journey" is life itself; the evolution of man and the procession of the universe are journeys. In "Song of the Open Road," for example, Whitman asserts his belief in a cosmic evolution, never reaching a culminating perfection, but always ascending: "To know the universe itself as a road, as many roads, as roads for traveling souls . . . Forever alive, forever forward . . . I know not where they go, / But I know that they go toward the best—toward something great" (section 13). The "open" road is unlimited and unrestricted, and the procession toward perfection is ceaseless because there is no death, only change.

Whitman's hardy, tan-faced journeyer in casual clothes and sturdy shoes is undisturbed by civilization. Divinely free and joyously content, he shouts his barbaric yawp to the world. Although he identifies with others and seeks comrades along the way, he travels essentially alone and he insists that each person journey alone as well. Whitman's ideal image of the democratic man was Abraham Lincoln. He applauded Lincoln for going down his own lonely road, refusing guides, ignoring warnings, and worrying only about keeping appointments with himself. Whitman encourages his fellow man to break from the crowd, to discover his own path, and to journey forth independently. "Not I, not any one else can travel it for you, / You must travel it for yourself" ("Song of Myself," section 46). According to Paul Zweig, "Song of Myself" is most "probably the finest enactment in all literature of the adventure of self-making, akin to such great quest poems as *The Epic of Gilgamesh* and *The Divine Comedy*" (18). Whitman's protagonist travels forth into the material world: "There was a child went forth every day, / And the first object he look'd upon, that object he became, / And that object became part of him for the day or a certain part of the day, / Or for many years or stretching cycles of years" ("There was a Child Went Forth"). His persona becomes the reality of his perception. His life-journey is a continual process of becoming.

For Whitman, the road is the most important feature of the outer world because it represents endless becoming of reality, expansive hope, and restlessness. As the background for comradeship, the road provides the possibility for travelers to share their participation in the journey of ongoing life. Whitman's protagonist offers his fellow man "no chair, nor church nor philosophy" ("Song of Myself," section 46). With his arm about his comrade's waist, he leads his comrade to a knoll, to the water's edge, or to the marshlands where the calamus plants grow. There his followers are able to perceive the fragmented particulars in relation to the whole. And they discover that love is the great cosmic unifier, connecting polarities, arousing joy.

Because the journey is imaginative, Whitman's protagonist can identify with the lives of others. He enters vicariously the life of the athlete, mechanic, trapper, slave, half-breed, and prostitute. He wanders into past and future time periods. "Space and Time! now I see it is true, what I guess'd at . . . My ties and ballasts leave me . . ." ("Song of Myself," section 33). Whitman uses the extended catalogue to convey the majesty, the expansiveness of the land, and the diversity of its people. The cumulative effect of the lists is a sensory bombardment of sights and sounds of American city and country life, emphasizing both the harmonious unity in variety and the singularity of the particular. For example, in his cosmic flight in "Song of Myself," Whitman's protagonist enlarges into a divine being by becoming one with the succession of men and women he encounters, with the evolution of the stars, and with the origin of life. He no longer is the individual man but feels a sense of oneness with all. Nothing is so tiny or so immense that it is unable to be incorporated into his expanding self.

Whitman's expansive journey included the revolutionizing of American poetry. He used rhymeless and expansive lines, repetitions, parallelism, varied rhythm and stress, and regional dialects in his attempt to express his highly flexible and all-inclusive philosophy. He wanted to be easily read, a poet of the common people. His earliest writings especially contain words particular to the United States, words such as "quahaug," "prairie-dog," "chickadee," "congressman," and "quadroon." He was particularly attracted to the idiom of the frontier. "I like limber, lasting, fierce words," he wrote in *An American Primer* (21). But it wasn't the words themselves that excited him. It was their ability to condense actual experience. In "Slang in America," Whitman defines slang as the "lawless germinal element, below all words and sentences, and behind all poetry" (572). As David Reynolds shows in *Beneath the American Renaissance,* Whitman used this antiauthoritarian rhetoric to appeal to the common people as well as to revolt against America's ruling class. For Whitman, poetry had the power to unify the fragmented nation by using language that gave vent to the full diversity of the United States and at the same time incorporating words that would dissolve boundaries and realize the country's potential.

Although the general thrust of the "perpetual journey" is ascension, the forward movement is frequently interrupted. Whitman's expanding traveler will at times momentarily retract. He will descend into darkness, become fragmented or dissipated, later to progress again, rejuvenated. Whitman emphasizes this forward/retreat movement of his traveler with the shrinking and lengthening of his lines and the alternation of rising and falling rhythms.

Whitman's poems refer to the poetic self's perception which unites him to the thing he sees. Whitman tries to include his reader in an odyssey similar to the expanding journey his poetic ego takes. When Whitman writes, "It is you talking just as much as myself, I act as the tongue of you" ("Song of Myself," section 47), he attempts to remove the distinction between the poet, the reader, and the poem. His development of the theme of "camerados" furthers the poet's attempted union with the reader. In "So Long!" he emphasizes this identification: "Camerado, this is no book, / Who touches this touches a man."

Whitman attempts to break the barriers between poet and reader, allowing the reader to merge vicariously with the poet and share in his expanding perception. Through the primal energy of the words, he encourages the reader to take part in his imaginative journey of self-making.

Deborah Dietrich

Bibliography

Allen, Gay Wilson. "Walt Whitman's Long Journey Motif." *Journal of English and Germanic Philology* 38 (1939): 76–95.

Asselineau, Roger. "Walt Whitman: From Paumanok to More Than America." *Studies in American Literature in Honor of Robert Dunn Faner, 1906–1967.* Ed. Robert Partlow. Supplement to *Papers on Language and Literature 5* (1969): 18–39.

Lewis, R.W.B. "Always Going Out and Coming In." *Walt Whitman.* Ed. Harold Bloom. New York: Chelsea House Publishers, 1985. 99–125.

Reynolds, David S. *Beneath the American Renaissance.* New York: Knopf, 1988.

Trachtenberg, Alan. "Whitman's Visionary Politics." *Walt Whitman of Mickle Street: A Centennial Collection.* Ed. Geoffrey M. Sill. Knoxville: U of Tennessee P, 1994. 94–108.

Whitman, Walt. *An American Primer.* Ed. Horace Traubel. 1904. Stevens Point: Holy Cow!, 1987.

———. "Slang in America." *Prose Works 1892.* Ed. Floyd Stovall. Vol. 2. New York: New York UP, 1964. 572–577.

Zweig, Paul. *Walt Whitman: The Making of the Poet.* New York: Basic Books, 1984.

See also CATALOGUES; COMRADESHIP; EVOLUTION; "SONG OF MYSELF"; "SONG OF THE OPEN ROAD"

Joyce, James (1882–1941)

James Joyce, Irish poet and novelist, was born in Dublin and educated at Irish Jesuit colleges. Unhappy with the intellectual atmosphere in Dublin, he left Ireland in 1902 determined to pursue a literary career. He first wrote a collection of short stories entitled *Dubliners* (1914), followed this with *A Portrait of the Artist as a Young Man* (1916), and catapulted onto the literary scene with his second novel, *Ulysses* (1922), a tour de force of the early modernist period. He has profoundly influenced twentieth-century fiction since then. Other important works include two volumes of poetry and *Finnegans Wake* (1939).

Ulysses and *Finnegans Wake* reverberate with lines from Whitman's poetry. In *Ulysses* readers find these echoes and phrases from "Song of Myself": "I have heard the melodious harp / On the streets of Cork playing to us . . ."; "I see everything, I sympathise with everything . . ."; "the yankee yawp"; "Do I contradict myself? . . . then I contradict myself" (*Ulysses* 18). In *Finnegans Wake* Whitman is referred to as "old Whiteman self" (*Wake* 263) and "the soul of everyelsesbody rolled into its olesoleself" (*Wake* 329). Joyce's character Leopold Bloom in *Ulysses* also reveals a fascinating parallel to the mystical speaker in "Song of Myself." Both are representative of an Everyman responding to the creative energy of the universe, identifying completely with all life, flowing freely through time and space. Joyce's brother Stanislaus records that the title of an early collection of Joyce lyrics, *Shine and Dark,* was borrowed from Whitman's line in "Song of Myself," "Earth of shine and dark mottling the tide of the river" (section 21).

Biographers reveal that Joyce had a portrait of Whitman and copies of *Leaves of Grass* and *Democratic Vistas* in his library. Joyce seemed to have found a kindred spirit in Whitman's democratic themes and free flow of language.

Andy J. Moore

Bibliography

Chase, Richard. *Walt Whitman Reconsidered.* New York: William Sloane, 1955.

Ellmann, Richard. *James Joyce.* New York: Oxford UP, 1959.

Joyce, James. *Finnegans Wake.* 1939. New York: Penguin, 1976.

———. *Ulysses.* 1922. New York: Modern Library, 1946.

Joyce, Stanislaus. *My Brother's Keeper: James Joyce's Early Years.* Ed. Richard Ellmann. New York: Viking, 1958.

Summerhayes, Don. "Joyce's *Ulysses* and Whitman's 'Self': A Query." *Wisconsin Studies in Contemporary Literature* 4 (1963): 216–224.

See also BRITISH ISLES, WHITMAN IN THE; IRELAND, WHITMAN IN; LEGACY, WHITMAN'S

K

Keller, Elizabeth Leavitt (b. 1839)

A professional nurse, Keller was employed to care for Whitman (1892), along with his personal nurse, Warren Fritzinger, during the last months of his life.

Born in Buffalo, New York, she married William Keller in 1858 and was widowed seven years later. She was educated at the Women's Hospital in Philadelphia.

Keller's book *Walt Whitman in Mickle Street,* ostensibly based on her observations of the poet's home life, is primarily a vindication of Whitman's housekeeper, Mary O. Davis, and her claim against Whitman's estate for services rendered from 1885 to his death. Keller testified for Davis in a suit tried in April 1894, which Davis won. Keller also wrote an article for *Putnam's Monthly,* "Walt Whitman: The Last Phase" (1909), most of which came from her book.

Patricia J. Tyrer

Bibliography

Keller, Elizabeth Leavitt. *Walt Whitman in Mickle Street.* New York: Mitchell Kennerley, 1921.

See also DAVIS, MARY OAKES; FRITZINGER, FREDERICK WARREN; HEALTH; MICKLE STREET HOUSE

Kennedy, William Sloane (1850–1929)

Biographer, editor, and critic, William Sloane Kennedy was one of Whitman's most devoted friends and admirers. Born in Brecksville, Ohio, to Rev. William Sloane Kennedy and the daughter of a minister, Sarah Eliza Woodruff, Kennedy attended Yale, graduating in 1875. He left Harvard Divinity School in 1880 without taking his degree, deciding instead to pursue a literary career. Kennedy first met Whitman in Philadelphia in 1880 while working on the staff of the *American.* He soon became a frequent correspondent and visitor to Whitman's Camden, New Jersey, home, a constant contributor of small gifts, and the author of several essays and newspaper articles in praise of Whitman. Kennedy also dedicated himself to writing, over a period of many years, a book-length study of the poet. Although Whitman at times expressed reservations about this work-in-progress (see Traubel 165), he appreciated Kennedy's devotion, calling him a "loyal guardsman" (Traubel 382). Whitman moreover supplied much editorial comment to Kennedy's work, which did not appear in print until after the poet's death in 1892. In 1896 Kennedy published *Reminiscences of Walt Whitman with Extracts from His Letters and Remarks on His Writings.* He then edited *Walt Whitman's Diary in Canada* (1904) and in 1926 published *The Fight of a Book for the World: A Companion Volume to "Leaves of Grass,"* which he considered to be his most important work. Kennedy drowned while taking his daily swim in Lewis Bay near his home in West Yarmouth, Massachusetts, on 4 August 1929.

Katherine Reagan

Bibliography

Kennedy, William Sloane. *The Fight of a Book for the World.* West Yarmouth, Mass.: Stonecroft, 1926.
———. *Reminiscences of Walt Whitman.* London: Alexander Gardner, 1896.

Traubel, Horace. *With Walt Whitman in Camden.* Vol. 1. 1906. New York: Rowman and Littlefield, 1961.

Whitman, Walt. *Walt Whitman's Diary in Canada.* Ed. William Sloane Kennedy. Boston: Small, Maynard, 1904.

See also PHILADELPHIA, PENNSYLVANIA

Kerouac, Jack (1922–1969)

Prolific writer of verse and rhapsodic, spontaneous "bop" musical prose in the 1950s and 1960s, Kerouac, like fellow Beat generation writer Allen Ginsberg, repeatedly claimed that his work was in Whitman's direct lineage. Kerouac couched his aesthetic in a jazzy and distinctively Whitmanian idiom, arguing that "the best writing is always the most painful personal wrung-out tossed from cradle warm protective mind—tap from yourself the song of yourself, *blow!—now!*—your way is your only way" ("Essentials" 73).

Gaining perspective from Whitman in high school and at Columbia University, Kerouac frequently spoke directly to the older poet as his muse, as in his popular *On the Road* (1955). He alluded to Whitman in such poems as "Berkeley Song in F Minor" and "Long Island Chinese Poem Rain." In the "168th Chorus" of *Mexico City Blues* he declared that "Whitman examined grass / and concluded / It to be the genesis / & juice, of pretty girls" (168).

In his correspondence, Kerouac often praised his forebear, as in an October 1954 letter to Alfred Kazin that observes that Whitman's poetry "is the biggest in the world because there could never have been a Whitman in Europe and the Whitman of Africa is yet to come" (*Selected Letters* 451).

Wesley A. Britton

Bibliography

Kerouac, Jack. "Essentials of Spontaneous Prose." *Evergreen Review* 2.5 (1958): 72–73.

———. *Jack Kerouac: Selected Letters, 1940–1956.* Ed. Ann Charters. New York: Viking, 1995.

———. *Mexico City Blues.* New York: Grove, 1959.

See also GINSBERG, ALLEN; LEGACY, WHITMAN'S; "SONG OF THE OPEN ROAD"

Kinnell, Galway (1927–)

Galway Kinnell is a poet whose work has been significantly influenced by Whitman. His major books, *Body Rags* (1968), *The Book of Nightmares* (1971), *The Avenue Bearing the Initial of Christ into the New World: Poems 1946–64* (1974), *Mortal Acts, Mortal Words* (1980), *The Past* (1985), and *Imperfect Thirst* (1994) often invoke, echo, and debate Whitman. In addition, Kinnell has written penetrating essays about Whitman and has edited a collection of Whitman's poetry (*The Essential Walt Whitman* [1987]).

Kinnell's response to Whitman is complex and multifaceted. He talks back to Whitman in illuminating ways, arguing with him even as he affirms key aspects of his poetics and central ideas. Kinnell has often expressed his admiration for what he calls the "mystic music" of Whitman's voice ("Indicative Words" 216), and he claims to have modeled his own free verse on Whitman's practice of writing "in what could only be called the rhythm of what's being said" (*Walking* 47). He admires Whitman's "mystically physical" nature (*Walking* 21) and credits him as the inspiration for his own melding of the intensely physical and the hard-won spiritual in *The Book of Nightmares*. He admires and follows Whitman's descendent (instead of transcendent) gaze, "a motion from the conventionally highest downward toward union with the most ordinary and the least, the conventionally lowest, the common things of the world" ("Indicative Words" 224).

What Kinnell finds most problematic about Whitman is his refusal to reveal "his troubled side" ("Indicative Words" 220), his tendency to absorb but not to struggle with death and evil. When Kinnell directly evokes Whitman in his poetry, then, the occasion often turns parodic (as in his echoing of "I Hear America Singing" in "Vapor Trail Reflected in the Frog Pond") or sarcastic (as in "The Avenue Bearing the Initial of Christ into the New World," when a character, about to die, comes across a Whitman passage about death and mutters "Oi! / What shit!" [*Avenue* 114]).

Kinnell's admiration for and understanding of Whitman are immense, however, and he is one of the few major contemporary American poets who has worked to develop Whitman's poetics and adapt them to a dramatically changed American culture.

Ed Folsom

Bibliography

Kinnell, Galway. *The Avenue Bearing the Initial of Christ into the New World: Poems 1946–64*. Boston: Houghton Mifflin, 1974.

———. *Walking Down the Stairs: Selections from Interviews*. Ann Arbor: U of Michigan P, 1978.

———. "Whitman's Indicative Words." *Walt Whitman: The Measure of His Song*. Ed. Jim Perlman, Ed Folsom, and Dan Campion. Minneapolis: Holy Cow!, 1981. 215–227.

Tuten, Nancy Lewis. "The Language of Sexuality: Walt Whitman and Galway Kinnell." *Walt Whitman Quarterly Review* 9 (1992): 134–141.

Zimmerman, Lee. *Intricate and Simple Things: The Poetry of Galway Kinnell*. Urbana: U of Illinois P, 1987.

See also LEGACY, WHITMAN'S

Knortz, Karl (1841–1918)

Karl Knortz was born in Garbenheim, Germany, and emigrated to the United States in 1863, where he lived in the Midwest and in the New York City area. An educator, editor, and cultural historian, he attempted to interpret American culture for German-speaking Europeans and for German-Americans; he considered both groups backward and unacquainted with the American democratic process.

Whitman's works were a vehicle for Knortz's pedagogical program. In 1882, probably the year he started his correspondence with Whitman, Knortz wrote a lengthy essay on Whitman for a German-American newspaper which later appeared, in an extended version, as a monograph both in the United States (1886) and in Germany (1899). Whereas he celebrates Whitman's ideas—his democratic principles, his championship of science, and his liberal attitude toward sexuality and the human body—Knortz's criticism of Whitman's language as dark and confusing reveals a lack of understanding of Whitman's revolutionary aesthetics.

Together with Thomas William Hazen Rolleston, Knortz was coauthor of the first book-length translation of Whitman's poetry.

Although Rolleston contributed the major portion of the translated poetry, it was Knortz who convinced Jakob Schabelitz, his liberal Swiss publisher, to publish *Leaves* as *Grashalme* in 1889. Whereas Rolleston wanted the translation to be as shocking to German readers as the original was to Americans, Knortz, in accordance with his enlightened pedagogical principles, wanted the text as smooth and unambiguous as possible. Fortunately for Whitman's reception in German, Rolleston's view prevailed.

Knortz continued to propagate Whitman's work, for example in his excellent history of North American literature published in Germany in 1891. A curious later book with a strongly anticapitalist rhetoric, entitled *Walt Whitman und seine Nachahmer: Ein Beitrag zur Literatur der Edelurninge* (Walt Whitman and His Imitators: On the Literature of the Noble Urnings, 1911), identified Whitman's works as creations of a sexually inactive ("noble") homosexual and referred to Whitmanites such as Horace Traubel, Edward Carpenter, and Ernest Crosby as Whitman's followers.

Walter Grünzweig

Bibliography

Frenz, Horst. "Karl Knortz: Interpreter of American Literature and Culture." *American-German Review* 13 (1946): 27–30.

———. "Walt Whitman's Letters to Karl Knortz." *American Literature* 20 (1948): 155–163.

Grünzweig, Walter. *Constructing the German Walt Whitman*. Iowa City: U of Iowa P, 1995.

Knortz, Karl. *Walt Whitman und seine Nachahmer: Ein Beitrag zur Literatur der Edelurninge*. Leipzig: Heichen, 1911.

———. *Walt Whitman: Vortrag gehalten im Deutschen Gesellig-Wissenschaftlichen Verein von New York*. New York: Bartsch, 1886.

Whitman, Walt. *Grashalme: Gedichte*. Trans. Karl Knortz and T.W. Rolleston. Zurich: Schabelitz, 1889.

See also GERMAN-SPEAKING COUNTRIES, WHITMAN IN THE; ROLLESTON, THOMAS WILLIAM HAZEN

L

"L. of G.'s Purport" (1891)

First published in the last section of *Leaves of Grass* supervised by the author ("Good-Bye my Fancy" [1891–1892]), this twelve-line lyric was apparently fashioned from three topics, each explored earlier in a separate poem: the aim of *Leaves of Grass,* the way it grew, and the approach of Whitman's death.

Of these, the most valuable to examine is the first because it is the most complex and controversial. That he included his concern for his own death, which could not have been more than months away, shows his lifelong ability to link the most abstract and universal to the most personal. His explaining how *Leaves of Grass* grew was a common topic in his writing.

The first two lines throw light on the less coherent issue of Whitman's purpose, although it is an issue he often addressed: "Not to exclude or demarcate, or pick out evils from their formidable masses (even to expose them,) / But add, fuse, complete, extend—and celebrate the immortal and the good." The surprising first line, giving a major role to evil, put against the second, marks Whitman's tendency to be Manichean, seeing life as a contest between good and evil. The first line, moreover, justifies his not having stressed the evil in *Leaves of Grass,* although several poems and many parts of poems, such as section 6 of the otherwise benign "Crossing Brooklyn Ferry," express the power of evil felt within or outside the writer. No aspect of Whitman more clearly sets him apart from Emerson and the Concord group, nor binds him closer to common humanity. The second line, declaring a purposeful championing of what is good and what is immortal, implies this as a constant aim of his work from the first. Within

the text there is ample reason to take him at his word.

However, the next lines shift the focus away from a moral toward a philosophical perspective: "Haughty this song, its words and scope, / To span vast realms of space and time, / Evolution—the cumulative—growths and generations." Many readers have seen Whitman as an evolutionist. Whitman saw himself that way, but in other than biological terms, as is suggested by these words: "'Leaves of Grass' and evolution are one. . . . We can't know what we are bound to—but bound to something? We can't doubt it—no, can't" (Traubel 458). Close parallels have been noted between the thought of the Jesuit priest and scientist Teilhard de Chardin and, especially, Whitman's "Song of Myself." Teilhard de Chardin saw humankind as slowly moving toward greater intellectual and emotional consciousness. By way of his poems, Whitman intuitively sought for stronger links among all through greater awareness, stronger identities, and a reaching out to others in recognition and love. Although the priest's Christian commitment and Whitman's Manichean tendencies prevent identical outlooks, their belief in the world's progressive psychic growth binds them closely.

This highly compressed lyric gives evidence that Whitman held to the end to his views about the role of poetry and the nature of the world.

David B. Baldwin

Bibliography

Allen, Gay Wilson. *The New Walt Whitman Handbook.* 1975. New York: New York UP, 1986.

Moore, William L. "L. of G.'s Purport: Evolution—The Cumulative." *1980: "Leaves* of Grass" at 125: Eight Essays. Ed. William White. Supplement to the *Walt Whitman Review*. Detroit: Wayne State UP, 1980. 45–57.

Traubel, Horace. *With Walt Whitman in Camden*. Ed. Jeanne Chapman and Robert MacIsaac. Vol. 7. Carbondale: Southern Illinois UP, 1992.

Whitman, Walt. *Leaves of Grass: Comprehensive Reader's Edition*. Ed. Harold W. Blodgett and Sculley Bradley. New York: New York UP, 1965.

See also EVIL; EVOLUTION; "GOOD-BYE MY FANCY" (SECOND ANNEX)

Labor and Laboring Classes

In the famous daguerreotype frontispiece to the first edition of *Leaves of Grass* (1855), Walt Whitman chose to appear in the guise of a workingman. In so doing, he both signaled his intention to give the mechanics, laborers, and artisans of America "a voice in literature" (Traubel 143) and proudly proclaimed his own social origins in working-class Brooklyn, New York. He did not again use that picture as frontispiece until 1881. By then the socioeconomic condition of the American laborer had changed profoundly, in ways Whitman's poetry was ill equipped to handle, since it had been specifically evolved to embody an earlier period's dreams of labor.

Whitman was born into an ordinary working family in a year (1819) that saw the first of a series of economic depressions which were to affect the laboring class over the following decades. These slumps were symptoms of a new phase of capitalist development leading to the gradual transformation of the skilled artisan class, to which Whitman's family belonged, into either unskilled, wage-earning laborers or small entrepreneurs. Politicized and radicalized by the threat of change, the workers responded by voting Jackson president in 1828. In spite of its populist rhetoric, however, Jacksonianism failed to arrest, let alone reverse, the effective decline in the social, political, and economic power of the average workingman. Consequently the Democratic party developed a radical "locofoco" wing, consisting of a broad front of campaigners, agitators, and reformers. Simultaneously, embryonic working-class movements appeared in the mid-1830s, only to fizzle out because of deteriorating economic circumstances.

All his life, Whitman continued proudly to label himself a Jacksonian Democrat, a Jeffersonian republican, and a locofoco. He also continued to revere the radical figures to whose work he had been introduced by his carpenter-cum-house-builder father. These included Tom Paine, Fanny Wright, Robert Dale Owen, and William Leggett, all of whom preached that gospel of social, economic, and political egalitarianism which, as Joseph Jay Rubin has shown, permeated both the journalistic writings of Whitman during the 1840s and the poetry of *Leaves of Grass* (1855). As an influential journalist and editor virtually throughout the 1840s, Whitman steadily, sometimes fiercely, supported the radical Democratic agenda and aligned himself with the interests of labor on such key issues of the day as temperance, business monopolies, paper money, banks, social conditions, the exploitation of female labor—and slavery.

In this latter connection he began, as Martin Klammer has pointed out, by adopting (in *Franklin Evans* [1842]) the prevailing antislavery and anti-black philosophy characteristic of white labor. By 1848 he was wholly committed to the Free Soil politics of those who wanted to keep the new Western territories free of slave labor, and he joined other radicals at this time in breaking away from a Democratic party that was prepared to compromise with Southern interests on this issue. Here again, his main concern was to protect the status and the rights of white labor (male and female), which would, or so he dreamed, bring a new egalitarian America into being in the West. But as Klammer has demonstrated, Whitman's sympathy with blacks increased appreciably over the next few years, until in "Song of Myself" (1855) he showed himself capable of empathizing with slaves and of portraying a black man as a magnificent representative of American labor.

Scholars are divided over whether Whitman's labor politics was confined to his journalism or whether it also significantly influenced his poetry. M. Wynn Thomas and Betsy Erkkila have argued that the early poetry is not an escape from but a continuation of politics by other means. They point to such features of *Leaves of Grass* as its sweepingly egalitarian social and spiritual philosophy and the Bowery b'hoy swagger of "Song of Myself." In the same poem, Whitman's early artisanal background is reflected in his depiction of an idealized world of self-sufficient workers contentedly constituting a harmonious community of spontaneously cooperative labor—an artisanal dream from the past, masquerading as a vision of the present, which is reaffirmed in his rousing hymn to labor, "A Song for Occupations" (1855). Here, as in his prose work "The Primer of Words" (1850s, later published as *An American Primer*), Whitman demonstrates a fascination with the multiplicity of terms for the new occupations spawned by a dynamic capitalist economy. On the other hand, although he was undoubtedly excited by the energy of change, Whitman's poetic imagination tended to treat the contemporary scene as if it were the fulfillment of the labor dreams of a departed age. Indeed, Thomas has ventured so far as to argue that once Whitman's America had, after the Civil War, altered so much as to render such a feat of imaginative adaptation and reconstruction impossible, he was left permanently disabled as a poet.

If Whitman's labor politics is at most an implicit feature of the 1855 *Leaves,* it is explicitly avowed in his unpublished pamphlet "The Eighteenth Presidency!" (1856). From start to finish, this is an impassioned revolutionary appeal to "workmen and workwomen" to come into their own, to seize the political initiative, to dismiss their morally bankrupt rulers, and to establish a new ideal commonwealth. Steeped though it was in 1830s artisanal ideology, the pamphlet was simultaneously a reaction to the quagmire politics of its time and unconsciously prophetic of Whitman's future attachment to Lincoln, whom he was eventually to see as an artisanlike figure come from the West to save the democratic Union. (The great elegy "When Lilacs Last in the Dooryard Bloom'd" [1865] gives repeated symbolic expression to this vision.) Whitman's enthusiastic response to the outbreak of the Civil War was largely due to his belief that at last Northern workingmen had risen up not only against the Southern slave owners but also against the Northern business, financial, and political bosses who were their counterparts and allies.

Believing the Northern armies to consist mainly of workingmen, Whitman blamed not them but the un-American elite of the officer class for early military setbacks. The two years he subsequently spent visiting sick soldiers in the Washington hospitals left him utterly convinced, as is apparent in *Drum-Taps* (1865), *Memoranda During the War* (1875–1876), and *Specimen Days* (1882), that the authentic America was to be found among such noble representatives of the laboring masses. His attachment to them, and to the cause of labor, also undoubtedly owed something to his homoerotic attraction to workingmen, which found expression in a cult of comradeship already apparent in the prewar "Calamus" poems (1860 *Leaves of Grass*). However, with the end of the war came disappointment of Whitman's hopes that the returning troops would transform society into a new artisanal republic. Instead, America emerged from the war as a modern, ruthlessly competitive, industrialized economy. In *Democratic Vistas* (1871) Whitman rails against the new mania for wealth and deplores the increasingly marked class divisions within postwar society, but he also reaffirms (albeit in poignantly unconvincing terms) his faith in the eventual evolution of America into a genuine democratic community of prosperous working people. The same year (1871) he published a new edition of *Leaves of Grass* that contained a section, "Songs of Insurrection," specifically designed to arouse resistance to "the more and more insidious grip of capital" (*Workshop* 229). To some editions of his 1871 collection he also added two annexes, *Passage to India* and *After All, Not to Create Only* (later "Song of the Exposition"). In both annexes, but by different means, he sought to celebrate the extraordinary technological advances of his times in terms consistent with his unreconstructed belief in the dignity and the rights of labor.

The increasingly bitter struggles between all-powerful capital and a newly proletarianized, ethnically mixed labor force that marked the Gilded Age left Whitman depressed and ideologically baffled, as is evident from his confused reaction to the Chicago Haymarket riots (1886). Following the great railroad strike of 1877 he wrote an anguished note on "The Tramp and Strike Questions" (1878), warning of the "unjust division of wealth-products, and the hoggish monopoly of a few, rolling in superfluity, against the vast bulk of the work-people, living in squalor" (*Prose Works* 2:528). But he could not accept the remedies offered by the developing politics of organized labor movements. To the end, his vision of a Union of egalitarian, democratic states was incompatible with the new labor unions, which he saw as socially divisive and as a betrayal of those ideals of artisanal radicalism with which he had been indelibly imbued in his youth.

M. Wynn Thomas

Bibliography

Erkkila, Betsy. *Whitman the Political Poet.* New York: Oxford UP, 1989.

Hodges, Graham. "Muscle and Pluck: Walt Whitman's Working-Class Ties." *Seaport* 26 (1992): 32–37.

Klammer, Martin. *Whitman, Slavery, and the Emergence of "Leaves of Grass."* University Park: Pennsylvania State UP, 1995.

Rubin, Joseph Jay. *The Historic Whitman.* University Park: Pennsylvania State UP, 1973.

Shulman, Robert. *Social Criticism & Nineteenth-Century American Fictions.* Columbia: U of Missouri P, 1987.

Thomas, M. Wynn. *The Lunar Light of Whitman's Poetry.* Cambridge, Mass.: Harvard UP, 1987.

———. "Whitman and the Dreams of Labor." *Walt Whitman: The Centennial Essays.* Ed. Ed Folsom. Iowa City: U of Iowa P, 1994. 133–152.

Trachtenberg, Alan. *The Incorporation of America.* New York: Hill and Wang, 1982.

Traubel, Horace. *With Walt Whitman in Camden.* Vol. 2. New York: Appleton, 1908.

Whitman, Walt. *The Gathering of the Forces.* Ed. Cleveland Rodgers and John Black. 2 vols. New York: Putnam, 1920.

———. *I Sit and Look Out: Editorials from the Brooklyn Daily Times.* Ed. Emory Holloway and Vernolian Schwarz. New York: Columbia UP, 1932.

———. *Prose Works 1892.* Ed. Floyd Stovall. 2 vols. New York: New York UP, 1963–1964.

———. *The Uncollected Poetry and Prose of Walt Whitman.* Ed. Emory Holloway. 2 vols. Garden City, N.Y.: Doubleday, Page, 1921.

———. *Walt Whitman's Workshop: A Collection of Unpublished Manuscripts.* Ed. Clifton Joseph Furness. Cambridge, Mass.: Harvard UP, 1928.

Wilentz, Sean. *Chants Democratic: New York City & the Rise of the American Working Class, 1788–1850.* New York: Oxford UP, 1984.

See also BARNBURNERS AND LOCOFOCOS; CIVIL WAR, THE; DEMOCRATIC PARTY; *DEMOCRATIC VISTAS;* "EIGHTEENTH PRESIDENCY!, THE"; EQUALITY; FREE SOIL PARTY; JACKSON, ANDREW; JEFFERSON, THOMAS; JOURNALISM, WHITMAN'S; POLITICAL VIEWS; "SONG FOR OCCUPATIONS, A"; "TRAMP AND STRIKE QUESTIONS, THE"

Lafayette, Marquis de (1757–1834)

In 1825 the marquis de Lafayette, the colonists' friend during the Revolutionary War and participant in the surrender of Cornwallis after the battle of Yorktown, made a return visit to the young nation as its honored guest. Ushered from city to city to review the progress of the young American republic, he was greeted everywhere by enthusiastic crowds. When the honored general came to Brooklyn to lay the cornerstone of the Apprentices' Library, school was let out so that the children might view this auspicious event. One of those children was five-year-old Walt Whitman, who, as he recorded in "My First Reading.—Lafayette" in *Specimen Days* (1882), was embraced and kissed by Lafayette himself as he helped lift children away from a dangerous excavation to safer viewing spots. Whitman never forgot the experience and liked to think that the "old Republican" had dedicated him to the cause of liberty and democracy.

Maverick Marvin Harris

Bibliography

Burroughs, John. *Notes on Walt Whitman.* New York: American News, 1867.

Fausset, Hugh I'Anson. *Walt Whitman: Poet of Democracy.* New Haven: Yale UP, 1942.

O'Connor, William Douglas. *The Good Gray Poet: A Vindication.* New York: Bunce and Huntington, 1866.

Whitman, Walt. "My First Reading—Lafayette." *Specimen Days.* Vol. 1 of *Prose Works 1892.* Ed. Floyd Stovall. New York: New York UP, 1963. 13.

Winwar, Frances. *American Giant: Walt Whitman and His Times.* New York: Harper, 1941.

See also AMERICAN REVOLUTION, THE

Lamarck, Jean Baptiste (1744–1829)

Jean Baptiste Lamarck, an important figure in the development of pre-Darwinian evolutionary theory, exerted considerable influence on American writers prior to Charles Darwin's *Origin of Species* (1859). Ralph Waldo Emerson, for example, in his *Journals,* mentions Lamarck with respect. The fact that Walt Whitman was clearly an evolutionist in the first edition of *Leaves of Grass,* published four years before Darwin's work, prompts some scholars to point to Lamarck's influence on Whitman's evolutionary thought. It is important to remember that the phrenologists (influential for the early Whitman) knew of Lamarck's work and applied it regularly in their practice. A study of Whitman's Lamarckianism would likely link him to writers like Friedrich Nietzsche (the Superman theory), Thomas Carlyle, Henri Bergson, George Bernard Shaw, and others. The writings of Herbert Spencer (1820–1903) made Lamarck's views popularly known during the nineteenth century.

Lamarck believed that complex organisms were developed from pre-existent simpler forms, and based his theories on four "laws": (1) Life by its proper forces tends continually to increase the volume of every body possessing it, and to enlarge its parts up to a limit which it brings about; (2) The production of a new organ in an animal body results from a supervention of a new want continuing to make itself felt, and a new movement which this want gives birth to and encourages; (3) The development of organs and their force of action are constantly in ratio to the employment of these organs; (4) All which has been acquired, laid down, or changed in the organization of individuals in the course of their life is conserved by generation and transmitted to the new individuals that proceed from those which have undergone these changes.

Readers of *Leaves of Grass* will readily see that Lamarckianism fits Whitman's moral and spiritual scheme admirably. For Whitman, man himself reflects the dominant manifestation of the life-force; man is therefore always imperfect, yet forever striving for perfection; society, made up of men, is imperfect, yet forever climbing toward a perfect state; all the universe is a growing organism, proceeding from all that preceded it and contributing to all that will follow it; all life is made of the same stuff and is continually propelled to higher momentum, compelled to move and change; all forms of life are in communion with one another; man, as leader of the process of becoming, must exercise his imagination, conceive new wants, and guard his freedom, which—although it ascribes harsher and harsher responsibilities—is the prerequisite to progress. In the social realm, Lamarckianism promises that what one generation struggles for and achieves may be transmitted to the next generation and all others which follow it.

James T.F. Tanner

Bibliography

Allen, Gay Wilson. *The Solitary Singer: A Critical Biography of Walt Whitman.* 1955. Rev. ed. 1967. Chicago: U of Chicago P, 1985.

Aspiz, Harold. *Walt Whitman and the Body Beautiful.* Urbana: U of Illinois P, 1980.

Beaver, Joseph. *Walt Whitman: Poet of Science.* Morningside Heights, N.Y.: King's Crown, 1951.

Conner, Frederick William. *Cosmic Optimism: A Study of the Interpretation of Evolution by American Poets.* Gainesville: U of Florida P, 1949.

Reynolds, David S. *Walt Whitman's America: A Cultural Biography.* New York: Knopf, 1995.

Tanner, James T.F. "The Lamarckian Theory of Progress in *Leaves of Grass.*" *Walt Whitman Review* 9 (1963): 3–11.

See also DARWIN, CHARLES; EVOLUTION; PHRENOLOGY

Language

First as a teacher, then as a journalist, and ultimately as a poet, Walt Whitman knew that he was in the language business. His early writings display the journalist's sense of intrigue at occasional odd words or unusual names, but during the 1850s he began a more intensive study of language in general and the English language in particular. That study resulted in a few published pieces on language, but Whitman accumulated a collection of material which indicates that philological matters were more than a hobby for him.

The English language is celebrated in the Preface to the first edition of *Leaves of Grass* (1855). Near the conclusion of the Preface, in which he catalogues what is most important for the poet who would speak for the country, Whitman writes that the English language "befriends the grand American expression" (*Comprehensive* 727). The language of *Leaves* drew immediate attention to the book, with some praising its freshness and others put off by its slang, its perceived indecency, or simply its idiosyncrasies, such as Whitman's spelling, e.g., "loafe" or "kosmos."

It was not long after the first edition of *Leaves* and just before the publication of the second that Whitman's first essay devoted exclusively to language, "America's Mightiest Inheritance" (1856), appeared in *Life Illustrated.* At the time, he was flush with his new poetic identity, and his language study was closely aligned to his sense of self. In the essay, Whitman recounts the historic roots of English, connecting it to the languages of Europe and Asia, to show that, like civilization itself, language has moved from East to West, culminating in the perfect summation: the English language in America. He singles out for special praise "language-searchers," historical philologists, "a modern corps, to whom history is to be more indebted than any of the rest" ("Inheritance" 57). Some of the information in the essay is based on a school text, *A Hand-book of the Engrafted Words of the English Language* (1854). The chief point of this text and of Whitman in "Inheritance" is that the English language is "a composite one, differing from all others" ("Inheritance" 56). At the conclusion of the essay, he adds a short section, entitled "Appendant for Working-People, Young Men and Women, and for Boys and Girls," which encourages healthy, full-voiced pronunciation of words and which ends with a list of *"A few Foreign Words, mostly French, put down suggestively."* The foreign vocabulary and pronunciation suggestions appear drawn from contemporary dictionaries, and the list includes several French terms that find their way into *Leaves,* such as "ensemble" and "allons."

Whitman saw it as part of his poetic identity that he should continue the process of English language borrowing and incorporating words of other languages, especially French and Spanish, the two other major colonial languages that share the New World with English. See, for example, two of his favorite terms for his readers, "eleve" (French) and "camerado" (Spanish). There is no evidence that Whitman could actually read or speak any language other than English. His brief residence in New Orleans (1848) gave him firsthand contact with spoken French, but he never mastered the language. He did, however, have a strong appreciation for the role of French in the development of English, and his research materials include essays, dating from the late 1840s, on Geoffrey Chaucer and the French elements in that poet's language. The contents of "Inheritance" and the manuscript pages and notebooks that date from the time of its publication indicate that his probing the nature of language is inextricably linked to his stance and outlook as he undertook the *Leaves* project.

The manuscripts demonstrating Whitman's language study include collections of loose notes, clippings from newspapers and magazines (sometimes annotated), and some notebooks, the largest of which is entitled "Words."

It is made up of 176 sheets of paper, among which he stuffed further clippings. Like many of the Whitman language-related manuscripts, it is part of the Feinberg Collection in the United States Library of Congress. In "Words" he recorded his reading notes from dictionary introductions, textbooks, journalism, and even some more scientific sources. He took notes on place names, foreign words, slang expressions, idioms, neologisms, phonetic spelling, grammatical gender, syntax, the history of the English language, and many other linguistic topics.

Whitman left clues in his notes to the sources of his information about language. Among the "language searchers" he had read were Maximilian Schele de Vere, Wilhelm von Humboldt, and Christian C.J. Bunsen, as well as more general sources, such as school textbooks and popular journalism. He took notes on place names from Samuel Griswold Goodrich's *Geography* (1855) and later used the material in such poems as "O Magnet-South." In his notebooks, Whitman mentions the great American lexicographers, Noah Webster and Joseph Worcester, and some of his notations indicate that he entertained the idea of someday producing a "perfect dictionary" ("Inheritance" 59) of the American language that would be richer and more inclusive than any produced so far.

A large set of notes, dating from this same era, was published by Horace Traubel, one of his literary executors, under the title *An American Primer* (1904). Whitman apparently considered the idea of imitating his mentor Ralph Waldo Emerson by embarking on a series of lectures, and language seems to have been a topic about which he had something important to say. Whitman expresses strong preferences in the *Primer* for the proper choice of words to name American places. He strongly favors American Indian names and dislikes transplanted European names.

Other Whitman language notes contain definitions of words, pronunciation and etymological notations, explanations of linguistic terms, snatches of historical and mythological information, literary history, and observations on social issues, including the place of women in the history of culture and examples of customs of various races, professions, and eras. Interspersed among the language notes, also, appear tentative notes for later poems, such as "Song of the Answerer" and "There was a Child Went Forth" (*Daybooks* 3:775). The notes abound with plans for projects and instances where

Whitman seems to be thinking through the possibilities of something he has just read or heard.

The probability that Whitman was the coauthor or ghostwriter of *Rambles Among Words,* published in 1859 by his friend William Swinton, was first put forth and convincingly argued by C. Carroll Hollis (1959). (Swinton, a journalist, would go on to become a professor at the University of California and the author of many school textbooks.) Hollis's theory is based on evidence that the two men knew one another and discussed language matters, the Whitman-like style in certain sections of *Rambles,* and correspondences between the contents of the book and many of Whitman's published and unpublished observations on language. That Whitman had a hand in *Rambles* has been accepted by many and developed further by James Perrin Warren (1984), but the extent or exact nature of the Swinton-Whitman collaboration are still matters of discussion among scholars.

Although most of Whitman's language research seems to have been accomplished before 1860, he continued for most of his life to save and annotate clippings from newspapers on language matters, including early notices of the massive scholarly effort to produce what is now known as the *Oxford English Dictionary.* The final article he wrote on language, "Slang in America" (1885), is a compilation of notes and thoughts on language, especially the vernacular, the language of the people. Whitman published it after it was clear to him that his research and note taking would result in no other major work. The essay includes discussion of how languages change through time, the nature of American English, and American naming practices of people, places, and institutions. "Slang in America" borrows etymologies from Ralph Waldo Emerson's essay *Nature,* two of which ("supercilious" and "transgression") also occur in *Rambles.*

Whitman's language study affected his writing, both poetry and prose, in both important ways and small ways. He asserted a broad and nontraditional poetic vocabulary based on philosophic and philological principles. His characteristic use of an apostrophe in the final syllable of past participles (e.g., "view'd" or "consider'd") was based on his readings in language and pronunciation. His use of the models of platform oratory and grand opera for his poetic utterances is intertwined with his interest in language, and these models contribute to the unique style of his poetic diction, as in his characteristic use of present participles or his direct address to the reader and use of the pronouns "I" and "you."

In his foreword to the *Primer,* Traubel says that Whitman offered the possibility that *Leaves* was, after all, "only a language experiment" (viii). This statement has captivated readers of Whitman ever since because, for anyone approaching *Leaves,* it is immediately apparent that in style and inclusiveness of language the poetry is unique. That striking quality of language is just as much the result of the conscious choice of the poet as are his bold approach to unconventional topics and his transcendental appreciation of life and nature. "Words are signs of natural facts," says Emerson in *Nature* (20), at the beginning of his explanation of the way in which language grows from nature and leads to a full appreciation of the transcendent, because "Nature is the symbol of spirit" (20). Whitman's interest in language is germinal and basic to his poetic practice and inspiration.

Michael R. Dressman

Bibliography

Bauerlein, Mark. *Whitman and the American Idiom.* Baton Rouge: Louisiana State UP, 1991.

Dressman, Michael R. "Walt Whitman's Plans for the Perfect Dictionary." *Studies in the American Renaissance 1979.* Ed. Joel Myerson. Boston: Twayne, 1979. 457–474.

Emerson, Ralph Waldo. "Nature." *Essays & Lectures.* Ed. Joel Porte. New York: Library of America, 1983. 7–49.

Folsom, Ed. *Walt Whitman's Native Representations.* Cambridge: Cambridge UP, 1994.

Hollis, C. Carroll. *Language and Style in "Leaves of Grass."* Baton Rouge: Louisiana State UP, 1983.

———. "Whitman and Swinton: A Co-operative Friendship." *American Literature* 30 (1959): 425–449.

Kramer, Michael P. "'A Tongue According': Whitman and the Literature of Language Study." *Imagining Language in America: From the Revolution to the Civil War.* By Kramer. Princeton: Princeton UP, 1992. 90–115.

Nathanson, Tenney. *Whitman's Presence: Body, Voice, and Writing in "Leaves of Grass."* New York: New York UP, 1992.

Southard, Sherry G. "Whitman and Language: An Annotated Bibliography." *Walt Whitman Quarterly Review* 2.2 (1984): 31–49.

Warren, James Perrin. *Walt Whitman's Language Experiment.* University Park: Pennsylvania State UP, 1990.

―――. "Whitman as Ghostwriter: The Case of *Rambles Among Words.*" *Walt Whitman Quarterly Review* 2.2 (1984): 22–30.

Whitman, Walt. *An American Primer.* Ed. Horace Traubel. 1904. Stevens Point, Wis.: Holy Cow!, 1987.

―――. "America's Mightiest Inheritance." *New York Dissected.* Ed. Emory Holloway and Ralph Adimari. New York: Rufus Rockwell Wilson, 1936. 55–65.

―――. *Daybooks and Notebooks.* Ed. William White. 3 vols. New York: New York UP, 1978.

―――. *Leaves of Grass: Comprehensive Reader's Edition.* Ed. Harold Blodgett and Sculley Bradley. New York: New York UP, 1965.

See also AMERICAN PRIMER, AN; "AMERICA'S MIGHTIEST INHERITANCE"; DICTIONARIES; FOREIGN LANGUAGE BORROWINGS; PLACE NAMES; SLANG; "SLANG IN AMERICA"; STYLE AND TECHNIQUE(S); SWINTON, WILLIAM

Lanier, Sidney (1842–1881)

Sidney Lanier was a poet, musician, and literary theoretician who sought to emphasize the relationship between poetry and music. He is today remembered for a few notable poems which embody the theories he advanced in *The Science of English Verse* (1880).

Whitman criticized Lanier's poetry primarily for favoring the sound of words rather than the sense. When Lanier first carefully read *Leaves of Grass* in 1878, he promptly wrote Whitman a letter opposing his views on artistic form but nevertheless praising *Leaves* for being a strikingly beautiful "modern song" (qtd. in Starke 307). Lanier regarded the poetry of *Leaves* as being rhythmic, despite Whitman's beliefs. In lectures written in 1881, Lanier continued to take exception to Whitman's artistic principles and also disagreed with him on what constituted true democracy, yet again lauded his poetry for its "bigness and naïvety" and singled out "My Captain, O my Captain" [*sic*] as "surely one of the most tender and beautiful poems in any language" (Lanier 39).

Both Lanier and Whitman were significant experimenters in poetic technique. Lanier's conception of melody in poetry was conventional, Whitman's revolutionary, but both achieved it on their own terms.

Lawrence I. Berkove

Bibliography

Brooks, Van Wyck. *The Times of Melville and Whitman.* New York: Dutton, 1947.

Faner, Robert D. *Walt Whitman & Opera.* Carbondale: Southern Illinois UP, 1951.

Lanier, Sidney. *The English Novel.* Vol. 4 of *Centennial Edition of the Works of Sidney Lanier.* Ed. Clarence Gohdes and Kemp Malone. Baltimore: Johns Hopkins, 1945.

Starke, Aubrey Harrison. *Sidney Lanier: A Biographical and Critical Study.* 1933. New York: Russell and Russell, 1964.

See also PROSODY; STYLE AND TECHNIQUE(S)

"Last Loyalist, The" (1842)

This short story was first published as "The Child-Ghost; a Story of the Last Loyalist" in *United States Magazine and Democratic Review,* May 1842. After revisions—mostly cutting—it appeared as "The Last Loyalist" in *Specimen Days & Collect* (1882). For publication details and revisions, see Thomas L. Brasher's edition of *The Early Poems and the Fiction.*

This ghost story has a historical setting. The evil Vanhome is a loyalist during the American Revolutionary War. Before the war, his brother's orphan becomes his ward and dies within two years. During the war, Vanhome joins the British military and earns a reputation for cruelty to enemy soldiers and civilians alike. Near the war's end, he visits the family estate, which is soon to be confiscated by the new American government. While there, he encounters the Gills, an old poverty-stricken couple who have become tenants on the estate. Unaware who his visitor is, old man Gills talks about the previous owner—Vanhome himself, a man who beat to death the little boy under his care. Vanhome is given for the night the very room the boy died in. The ghost of the boy comes and terrifies him so that he flees to the last British ship embarking from America.

Like Lugare in "Death in the School-Room (a Fact)" (1841), Vanhome is a sadistic man, and he is like Adam Covert in "One Wicked Impulse!" (1845) in that he allows his own greed to interfere with his duties to his ward. But "The Last Loyalist" seems to offer a compromise to the solutions of those two stories. Lugare is meted no punishment, and Covert is killed. Vanhome lives, having been terrified, humiliated, and exiled.

This work has received little critical attention.

Patrick McGuire

Bibliography

Whitman, Walt. *The Early Poems and the Fiction.* Ed. Thomas L. Brasher. New York: New York UP, 1963.

See also AMERICAN REVOLUTION, THE; "DEATH IN THE SCHOOL-ROOM (A FACT)"; "ONE WICKED IMPULSE!"; SHORT FICTION, WHITMAN'S

"Last of the Sacred Army, The" (1842)

This short story first appeared in *United States Magazine and Democratic Review* in March 1842. For publication history, see Thomas L. Brasher's edition of *The Early Poems and the Fiction.* Brasher notes that the dream sequence in chapter 20 of *Franklin Evans; or The Inebriate. A Tale of the Times* (1842) is an altered version of this story.

The story is a dream narrative in which the narrator watches an old soldier of the Revolutionary War being honored for having been one of Washington's men. Washington is spoken of with a religious awe, and a medallion he had given the old soldier is treated like a holy relic.

Reynolds cites this story as an example of Whitman's jingoism and connects it to Whitman's patriotic poems like "The Centenarian's Story" (1865). But the structural irony of the piece may allow for an alternative reading. Before his dream, the narrator speaks of the coming obsolescence of war; taking hold is a new philosophy, "teaching how evil it is to hew down and slay ranks of fellowmen" (95). What occurs in the dream, however, inculcates the old philosophy that makes heroes, even gods, of warriors.

Robert Abrams, calling this dream narrative a precursor of "The Sleepers" (1855), sees it as an utter failure because Whitman had not yet allowed art to speak honestly. Justin Kaplan sees Nathaniel Hawthorne's "The Gray Champion" (1835) as Whitman's original source.

Patrick McGuire

Bibliography

Abrams, Robert E. "An Early Precursor of 'The Sleepers': Whitman's 'The Last of the Sacred Army.'" *Walt Whitman Review* 22 (1976): 122–125.

Kaplan, Justin. *Walt Whitman: A Life.* New York: Simon and Schuster, 1980.

Reynolds, David S. *Walt Whitman's America: A Cultural Biography.* New York: Knopf, 1995.

Whitman, Walt. *The Early Poems and the Fiction.* Ed. Thomas L. Brasher. New York: New York UP, 1963.

See also AMERICAN REVOLUTION, THE; "CENTENARIAN'S STORY, THE"; *FRANKLIN EVANS*; SHORT FICTION, WHITMAN'S; "SLEEPERS, THE"

Lawrence, D.H. (1885–1930)

Like that of other critics, such as Ezra Pound and T.S. Eliot, D.H. Lawrence's assessment of Walt Whitman was ambivalent. Finally, though, no one had a sense of closer kinship with Whitman or praised him more extravagantly than Lawrence did in two versions of his essay "Whitman"—a 1918 text published much later in *The Symbolic Meaning* (1962), and the later, better-known, more balanced evaluation published in *Studies in Classic American Literature* (1923).

In the earlier version, Lawrence, with his insistence on the primacy of the present and the spontaneous physical self, celebrated Whitman above all other writers. Despite the weaknesses he found in Whitman, he saw that "Whitman, at his best, is purely himself. His verse springs sheer from the spontaneous sources of his being. Hence its lovely, lovely form and rhythm. . . . The whole soul speaks at once, and is too pure for mechanical assistance of rhyme and measure. The perfect utterance of a concentrated spontaneous soul. The unforgettable loveliness of Whitman's line!" (*Symbolic* 264).

Lawrence tempers his adulation in the later text of "Whitman." For example, he pokes fun at Whitman's dissolution of self by merging with everything, a process Lawrence finds a kind of death: "Walt's great poems are really huge fat tomb-plants, great rank graveyard growths," he mocks (*Studies* 245). Still, Lawrence finds Whitman's artistic salvation in his feeling for death: "Whitman would not have been the great poet he is if he had not taken the last steps and looked over into death" (252). But he was indeed great, Lawrence asserts, "the one pioneer" in American and European literature among "mere innovators" (253).

Alan Shucard

Bibliography

Delavenay, Emile. *D.H. Lawrence: The Man and His Work. The Formative Years: 1885–1919.* Trans. Katharine M. Delavenay. Carbondale: Southern Illinois UP, 1972.

Lawrence, D.H. *Studies in Classic American Literature.* New York: Seltzer, 1923.

———. *The Symbolic Meaning: The Uncollected Versions of Studies in Classic American Literature.* Ed. Armin Arnold. Arundel: Centaur, 1962.

Trail, George Y. "Lawrence's Whitman." *The D.H. Lawrence Review* 14 (1981): 172–190.

See also BRITISH ISLES, WHITMAN IN THE; LEGACY, WHITMAN'S; SPONTANEITY

Lawrence, Kansas

Whitman visited Lawrence once, for the Kansas Quarter Centennial Celebration (1879). During his three days there, he was a guest of Mayor John P. Usher, who had been Interior Secretary under Abraham Lincoln. In *Specimen Days,* he described Lawrence and Topeka as "large, bustling, half-rural, handsome cities" (207). He attended the celebration on 15 September but was absent the next day, when he had been scheduled (without his prior knowledge) to present a poem written for the occasion. He recalled that he had such a good time with "the Usher boys," John and Linton, that he just let the hours slip away. This was Whitman's only journey west of the Mississippi, carrying him as far as Colorado and the Rocky Mountains, and it gave him an opportunity to experience a region that had long been vividly alive in his imagination: "I have found the law of my own poems," he wrote (210). The Quarter Centennial commemorated the origins of Kansas and Lawrence in the struggle that followed enactment of the Kansas-Nebraska Bill (1854). That bill precipitated a contest between proslavery and antislavery forces to see who could move more settlers into the territory before the issue of slavery was decided. Lawrence was settled with the support of an antislavery "Emigrant Aid Society" organized in Boston and was named for one of its most prominent supporters; it was the de facto capital of the free-state movement in Kansas from 1854 until Topeka was selected as capital in 1861. Lawrence continued as an important symbol of that movement during the Civil War. Located only forty miles from the Missouri border, it was a prime target for proslavery forces active in Missouri before and during the war. Its history from 1854 to the time of Whitman's visit was a crucible for the struggle that played such a central role in shaping his work, including his editorial involvement with the Free Soil press.

Steven Schroeder

Bibliography

Eitner, Walter H. *Walt Whitman's Western Jaunt.* Lawrence, Kans.: Regents Press of Kansas, 1981.

Whitman, Walt. *Specimen Days.* Vol. 1 of *Prose Works 1892.* Ed. Floyd Stovall. New York: New York UP, 1963.

See also TRAVELS, WHITMAN'S; WEST, THE AMERICAN

Leaves of Grass

Widely considered the cornerstone of modern poetry, Whitman's book of poems in all its transformations may be the most radically original book of important poetry. In the first poem of the first edition, Whitman sings of "Myself." With the gradual success that came during the last thirty-six years of his life, for better and for worse, the book established the poet's self as the central topic and process of poetry.

The poet insists he is inseparable from his poems, that he is his poems, that he creates himself by writing poems, and that his readers and he become part of each other when the poems are read. Egotistical, defiant of manners and conventions, a loner, disingenuous, tactless, the obvious flaws of his persona failed to put off a host of partisans who devoted themselves to Walt with intense loyalty that carried on beyond his lifetime. By his death in 1892 *Leaves of Grass* was finding some acceptance in the literary establishment. A century later it seems the preeminent book of American poetry, the book that defines American poetry.

Simultaneously obscure and exhilarating, *Leaves of Grass* has never been an easy book for readers. Long unmetrical lines define their own rhythms as they go along. The poems are Homerically digressive, often seeming aimless to the point of incoherence. The meanings of the poems seem inseparable from the process by which they are made. Words, phrases, and images that fill the lines arise in a poet's whim that wanders wherever the eye looks next. In making the poems, the poet seems to drift regressively into his deepest self—beyond the reach of conventions, logic, or inhibitions.

First lines announce a poem's topic, and then the poet names objects, images, impressions that occur to him in connection with the topic. By naming things, the poet creates his connection to the topic and also creates a context which defines the topic for him. He demands that readers suspend all preconceptions about the world, about language, about poetry, and even about themselves. Those who can let themselves flow along in the poet's flood of good-humored energy may escape the puzzlements. Like the poet they must be able and willing to tolerate a vast degree of disorder and be confident that when the need arises, they can step back into the world of other people and ordinary discourse.

Whitman's poems do not describe actual or psychological events; they *are* the events. The poet made himself from line to line and poem to poem. So the book grew. In 1855 there were a dozen poems, including "Song of Myself." Fourteen months later there were thirty-two poems, which he printed as the second *Leaves of Grass*. Eight months later he wrote a friend that he had written sixty-eight new poems and was about to publish a third edition of a hundred poems. Instead, there was a delay of about eighteen months when Whitman apparently wrote little. There was almost certainly an emotional crisis, possibly involving an affair with an actual lover. The act of writing the "Calamus" poems, poems about the love of comrades, seems deeply involved with the crisis.

When the third *Leaves of Grass* finally appeared (1860), it contained 156 poems, including nearly all Whitman's best poems. Although he would write nearly 250 more poems, only a few more would involve the deeply regressive journeys to the sources of poetry that produced works like "Song of Myself," "The Sleepers," "There was a Child Went Forth," "Crossing Brooklyn Ferry," or "Song of the Broad-Axe." In his first five years as a poet Whitman created a style and a voice, and all but a handful of the great poems he would ever write. It was truly a miraculous event of poetic fecundity. After 1860 Whitman almost ceased to undertake the very deep regressive journeys which had produced his first great flowering.

The new poems written after the crisis, especially "Out of the Cradle," and "As I Ebb'd

with the Ocean of Life," differed from most previous *Leaves of Grass* poems in often having distinct beginnings, middles, and ends; they reflected a new need for conscious order and structure. The poet became increasingly able to turn away from his almost exclusive preoccupation with the self, turning to the Not Me and to circumstances. He now wrote impressionistic sketches of Civil War scenes, *Drum-Taps*, sketches that work in words as impressionist paintings work in colors. The eye that records the war scenes is more attuned to otherness than the voice that speaks the earlier poems of *Leaves of Grass*. The new receptiveness to the Not Me reaches its height in the superb elegy to Abraham Lincoln, "When Lilacs Last in the Dooryard Bloom'd," but it continues to be present in numerous brief lyrics. Two more major poems remained to be written: "Passage to India" (1871) and "Prayer of Columbus" (1874).

In the 1867 edition, Whitman began the restless sorting, organizing, and classifying of poems that would occupy him for the rest of his life. Apparently he sought an external, conscious structure to answer critics who said his work was formless or obscure. Through revisions, Whitman also tried to ameliorate the extremity of the early poems, some revisions being so severe that no more than a line or two of the original poem remained. The revisions, too, seemed a gesture in the direction of being more sociable, less the loner. Gay Wilson Allen calls the fourth the "Workshop Edition," and judges it the most "chaotic" of them all (118). Whitman's critical vigor was not in harmony with his creative achievements.

Through the remaining five editions (of 1871–1872, 1876, 1881–1882, 1889, and 1891–1892) Whitman continued to seek outward structure and order. Scholars have devised numerous descriptions of whatever plan they perceive, but the plurality of descriptions suggests that, like the poems themselves, Whitman's scheme for giving order to his book requires the active engagement of the reader—and even then, nothing is clear. It is conservative and perhaps least unsatisfactory to posit that changes in the book and poems reflect changes in its author as he passed through life's various changes.

When the meaning of the poems seems inseparable from the process of their creation, particular problems arise concerning questions of preferred texts. Which version of *Leaves of*

Grass is best and should be recommended to readers may be a question that cannot be answered to everyone's satisfaction. In 1995 only the first and last editions were in print. Many scholars (including Roy Harvey Pearce, Edwin Miller, Leslie Fiedler, and David Cavitch) have argued that the poems should be read in early printed versions. Cornell University Press heroically kept the 1860 edition in print for decades and dropped it only recently. Perhaps someone else will pick it up. When the poet's journey is everything and arriving is little, the journey should not be concealed.

Stephen A. Black

Bibliography

Allen, Gay Wilson. *The New Walt Whitman Handbook.* New York: New York UP, 1975.

Black, Stephen A. *Whitman's Journeys into Chaos: A Psychoanalytic Study of the Poetic Process.* Princeton: Princeton UP, 1975.

Cavitch, David. *My Soul and I: The Inner Life of Walt Whitman.* Boston: Beacon, 1985.

Feehan, Michael. "Multiple Editorial Horizons of *Leaves of Grass.*" *Resources for American Literary Study* 20 (1994): 213–230.

Fiedler, Leslie. Introduction. *Whitman.* The Laurel Poetry Series. New York: Dell, 1959. 7–22.

Miller, Edwin Haviland. Introduction. *Whitman's "Leaves of Grass": Selections.* New York: Appleton-Century-Crofts, 1970. vii–x.

Pearce, Roy Harvey. Introduction. *Leaves of Grass by Walt Whitman: Facsimile Edition of the 1860 Text.* Ithaca, N.Y.: Cornell UP, 1961. vii–li.

Warren, James Perrin. "The 'Paths to the House': Cluster Arrangements in *Leaves of Grass,* 1860–1881." *ESQ* 30 (1984): 51–70.

See also LEAVES OF GRASS, 1855 EDITION; LEAVES OF GRASS, 1856 EDITION; LEAVES OF GRASS, 1860 EDITION; LEAVES OF GRASS, 1867 EDITION; LEAVES OF GRASS, 1871–1872 EDITION; LEAVES OF GRASS, 1876, AUTHOR'S EDITION; LEAVES OF GRASS, 1881–1882 EDITION; LEAVES OF GRASS, 1891–1892, DEATHBED EDITION; LEAVES OF GRASS, VARIORUM EDITION

Leaves of Grass, 1855 Edition

The importance of the first edition of *Leaves of Grass* to American literary history is impossible to exaggerate. The slender volume introduced the poet who, celebrating the nation by celebrating himself, has since remained at the heart of America's cultural memory because in the world of his imagination Americans have learned to recognize and possibly understand their own. As *Leaves of Grass* grew through its five subsequent versions in eight editions into a hefty book of 389 poems, it gained much in variety and complexity, but Whitman's distinctive voice was never stronger, his vision never clearer, and his design never firmer than in the twelve poems of the first edition.

The first *Leaves of Grass* was put on sale in two stores, one in New York and another in Brooklyn, on 6 July 1855. Printed in the shop of the brothers James and Thomas Rome of Brooklyn, the quarto-size volume was designed and published by Whitman himself, who is also believed to have set in type some ten of its ninety-five pages. As William White has shown, 795 copies were printed in all, 200 of which were bound in cloth, the rest in cheaper material. Very few copies of the first edition have survived into the 1990s, and today it is one of the rarest and most valuable American books (four facsimile editions are listed in the bibliography below).

The text begins with a ten-page statement in prose, untitled here and later known generally as the 1855 Preface. This is followed by twelve poems on eighty-five pages, the first six entitled "Leaves of Grass" and the remaining six untitled (listed here in order of appearance, they will be referred to in this entry under the title Whitman gave them in the 1891–1892 edition of *Leaves*): "Song of Myself," "A Song for Occupations," "To Think of Time," "The Sleepers," "I Sing the Body Electric," "Faces," "Song of the Answerer," "Europe, The 72d and 73d Years of These States," "A Boston Ballad (1854)," "There was a Child Went Forth," "Who Learns My Lesson Complete," and "Great Are the Myths." Whitman worked on the Preface while the book was being printed and wrote most of the poems in 1854 and 1855, although some lines that eventually found their way into the volume occur in his "green notebook" as early as 1847. The manuscript of the book is lost. As Whitman told Horace Traubel decades later, he left it with the Rome brothers, and in 1858 it "was used to kindle the fire or feed the rag man" (Traubel 92).

Walt Whitman, frontispiece, first (1855) edition of Leaves of Grass. By permission, Beeghly Library, Ohio Wesleyan University.

Title page of 1855 Leaves of Grass. From Walt Whitman: A Descriptive Bibliography, by Joel Myerson, © 1993 by University of Pittsburgh Press.

The physical design of the book is unusual. Spread over the dark green covers and sprouting from the words "Leaves of Grass" embossed in gold in the center, patterns of vines, tendrils, and tufts of grass announce the spirit of organicism and give visual confirmation to the words' suggestion that the contents have grown like grass. These words are the only title to appear in the book, in bold big letters on the title page, in somewhat smaller characters at the head of the first six poems, and as a modest refrain at the top of each page. On the frontispiece is a portrait of a bearded young man. The collar of his shirt open, a wide-brimmed hat at a jaunty angle on his head, one hand in his pocket and the other one on his hip, he stares down the onlooker.

The portrait represents Whitman, of course; it is a stipple engraving by Samuel Hollyer of a photograph (often referred to as "the carpenter portrait") taken a year earlier by the painter-photographer Gabriel Harrison. The young man, however, is not identified, just as no author's name is given on the title page; there is no reason to associate with portrait or text the Walter Whitman who, according to the small print at the bottom of the back of the title page, registered the book in the U.S. District Court in the Southern District of New York on 15 May 1855. One effect of the arrangement is that the identity of the person speaking the poems emerges from the poems themselves and is not confused with any actual individual. So successful in this respect was Whitman's layout that even after hearing the speaker of "Song of Myself" identify himself as "Walt Whitman, an American, one of the roughs, a kosmos," an astute reader like Ralph Waldo Emerson could not "trust the name as real & available for a post-office" (*Correspondence* 1:41).

That identity, rather than any argument, is the true significance of the volume; that is what it means. The topics and themes taken up by the poems are components of the speaker's personality, and the order in which they are arranged does not so much advance propositions leading toward a reasoned conclusion as it discloses the dynamism through which that personality is constituted. The key to that personality is the speaker's intuitive certainty that by being himself and himself alone he is everyone else and that, beyond all apparent conflicts, differences, and contradictions, he and America, thus people and land, are one, for each receives identity from the other as they respond to one another—"tally," as Whitman often puts it—in profound harmony. The speaker of the first *Leaves* does not justify or explain his vision but bears witness to it; as the Preface has it, "he is no arguer . . . he is judgment" (1855 *Leaves* v).

To articulate this sense of the self or, as Whitman phrased it thirty-three years later in "A Backward Glance," "to put *a Person . . .* freely, fully and truly on record" (*Prose Works* 2:731) is the volume's program, as it will, indeed, remain the program of *Leaves of Grass* throughout all its subsequent versions. In the first edition, it is announced in the Preface, enacted in "Song of Myself," and elaborated in the other eleven poems.

The theory of poetry emerging from the Preface, that the poet is the prophet of his land because "the others are as good as he, only he sees it and they do not" (v), is clearly indebted to Emerson's essay "The Poet"; it is small wonder that Emerson responded to it enthusiastically. The Preface also points to what proves to be a substantial difference between the later editions and the first one. As it describes, exuberantly and at length, the speaker's undertaking and catalogues his raw materials (defiantly testing the limits of conventional prose all the while), this introduction avoids the first-person singular with an almost pedantic rigor that is in startling contrast with the carefree unrestraint of the rest. The absence of "I" throughout the piece is a reminder that its words are spoken about, but not by, "the greatest poet," because at the outset of the first *Leaves* this program is also "the direct trial of him who would be the greatest poet"(xi). He must find the voice, the language—Whitman spoke of *Leaves of Grass* as "only a language-experiment" (*American Primer* 4)—that will communicate his vision to those who are blind to its truth even as they embody and live it. If the experiment succeeds, if the speaker passes his trial, he will have become "the greatest poet."

In none of the later editions will Whitman have to face this challenge, for "Song of Myself" follows, and by the time it reaches its end the trial is over: the poetic self named Walt Whitman is born. In all its editions, not just the first one, *Leaves of Grass* is dominated by this presence emerging from "Song of Myself," Whitman's greatest poem and one of the truly great poems in the language. It is as if the rest of the poems had been written by the poet who *is* "Song of Myself" (as a matter of fact, in the four editions between 1860 and 1876 the poem was titled simply "Walt Whitman"). As for the world beyond *Leaves of Grass,* the Whitman it has known is the person it met in the 1855 version of "Song of Myself."

How that "hankering, gross, mystical, nude" (section 20) poet comes to life in the poem's 1,336 lines is beyond the scope of this essay. Inventive and illuminating accounts abound, and by their very diversity they prove not that it is indeterminate but that it is inexhaustible. However construed, the poem discloses the private world of its protagonist, the "I" so conspicuously missing from the Preface, as he "invite[s his] soul" and "observ[es] a spear of summer grass" (section 1). The soul is what senses the self in the other and the other in the self; its presence allows the private world to "tally" with the whole world without losing any of its own integrity. It is an irresistibly attractive, various world of delicacy, strength, and joyous acceptance. It is also a world where the vision often darkens and moments of weakness, guilt, pain, and mortal fear must be confronted. (Whitman's romance with death begins only with the third edition, in 1860.) That in this exuberant yet anxious world of contrasts and tensions Americans—indeed, Americans of the globe—can recognize their own (or perhaps see it for the first time) is what gives the poem its rank in the literature of the United States and explains the continuing and sometimes anxious fascination it has held for its readers.

In the 1855 edition, the power of "Song of Myself" is at its least controlled or self-consciously "poetic," and the versatility and wit of its language are at their freshest and most exhilarating. The "-ed" of the past tense is not yet replaced by the later editions' "-d"; four points of suspension are the only punctuation within a line; and beyond double spaces grouping lines into stanzas, no subdivisions of the sort that appear in later editions interrupt the onrush of words. Thus the reader's sense is reinforced that for all the variety and multiplicity of the images, moods, and episodes that make it up, the poem is a single, unified experience just as its subject, the Whitman presence, is one, for all its multifariousness. The diction is also freer and the verse more supple in 1855 than later. In the first edition, the speaker "cocks [his] hat as [he] please[s]" instead of wearing it, as in later editions; he is "a rough" in the 1855 edition and "of Manhattan the son" in the 1891–1892 edition (section 24); his slang is more pungent ("Washes and razors for foofoos") than in later versions, and when the occasion arises he will even curse—"O Christ! My fit is mastering me!" The line that by 1881 becomes "And mossy scabs of the worm fence, heap'd stones, elder, mullein and poke-weed" (section 5) breathes much more easily in 1855: "And mossy scabs of wormfence, and heaped stones, and elder and mullen and pokeweed." Although "Song of Myself" has remained throughout all editions substantially what it was in 1855, Whitman kept coming back to its text until 1881, weeding and pruning even when he might have left the leaves of grass as they had grown.

An important difference between "Song of Myself" and the eleven poems that follow it is that the latter are structurally closed and thus formally less innovative than the former with its essentially open, loose structure. These eleven poems have often been referred to as "cuttings" from the long poem, passages that for one reason or another Whitman chose not to include in it yet would not discard altogether. The assumption seems to underrate both Whitman's sense of organization and the structural unity achieved in the volume. To be sure, the topical anger of the two political poems, "Europe, The 72d and 73d Years of These States" and "A Boston Ballad (1854)," would be hard to fit into "Song of Myself," and the omission of the slight "Who Learns My Lesson Complete" would probably not have made much difference to the book, nor is there good reason to regret that Whitman decided to leave out "Great Are the Myths" from later editions altogether. Some of the other poems, however, like "I Sing the Body Electric" or "There was a Child Went Forth," are Whitman at his best, and the sequence as a whole is indispensable, for it concludes the business that "Song of Myself" has left unfinished.

The tenor of "Song of Myself" is robustly optimistic and self-confident, yet its protagonist is "somehow . . . stunn'd" (section 38) time and again by moments of anxiety, even terror, and haunted by powerful images of frustration, violence, and death. He can extricate himself from each of these episodes but cannot shake them off completely. To discover and thereby confront and overcome the forces that stun him, he must probe the depths of his self: this process is the primary burden of the so-called "cuttings." The climax of the drama occurs in another great poem in the volume: "The Sleep-

ers." In the dream-vision of "The Sleepers" the "I" moves through several increasingly intense nightmare-episodes until he finds in himself the murderous impulse which may precipitate his fits of existential anxiety and sexual guilt: "My tap is death." Once he has discovered and admitted to himself that, with all his affection and goodwill, he also has anger enough to kill, his nightmare is over, and his trance becomes a reinvigorating dream of harmony and "summer softness" (section 7) as he joins the other sleepers, and "they flow hand in hand over the whole earth" (section 8). This drama is possible only in the 1855 text of "The Sleepers"; Whitman's later revisions have radically altered the poem's shape and character. In this original version, however, it is at the very heart of *Leaves of Grass*, forming, with "Song of Myself," what Justin Kaplan calls the matrix of the work.

"The Sleepers" stands in the exact middle of the first of the two clusters of poems—the one titled and the other untitled—that make up the "cuttings." In the order in which they appear the other four poems in the first cluster frame and center the climactic moment in "The Sleepers." The processional movement induced by the grand catalogue that is "A Song for Occupations" continues through the funeral march in "To Think of Time," slows down as it gathers strength in "The Sleepers," and speeds up again once the moment of high drama is past. After two other lists, in "I Sing the Body Electric" and "Faces," the procession comes to rest in the latter poem with the discovery of the face of "the justified mother of men" (section 5).

In the untitled cluster, the last six poems in the volume, a similar pattern, though much fainter, less pronounced, can be discerned. These poems frame "There was a Child Went Forth" as the titled cluster frames "The Sleepers," and if the parallel can be sustained, they make the "mean, angered, unjust" father's "blow" and "quick, loud word" of "There was a Child" as conspicuous as the speaker's deadly "tap" is made in "The Sleepers." As the first sequence ends reaching the mother, the second one, and with it the entire book, concludes discovering death: "Sure as the stars return again after they merge in the light, death is great as life" ("Great Are the Myths"). In another four years, in the magnificent conclusion of "Out of the Cradle Endlessly Rocking," the two images will be fused.

On the morrow of the publication of the first *Leaves* Whitman definitely did not wake to find himself famous. Though no reliable records have survived, probably very few copies of the book were sold. Few reviews appeared, some of them discerning and sympathetic, but most of them somewhat bewildered by the new work and also offended by the sexual frankness of some of its passages. A handful of unsigned reviews also appeared, which praised the volume in extravagant terms and in what must have appeared rather extravagant prose. These were written by the poet himself, who used his connections among the newspaper editors of New York to get them published. Apparently, they did not help sales much.

Thus, nothing in the public response gave Whitman any encouragement to continue his "experiment." The majority of the readers who happened to have come upon the book seem to have been simply indifferent. But Whitman had also had the good sense to send out a few complimentary copies. Although the Quaker poet John Greenleaf Whittier reportedly threw one of these into the fire, another copy reached Emerson. A few weeks after the book's publication, Emerson acknowledged the gift in a letter in which he greeted the poet "at the beginning of a great career" and declared that he found "incomparable things said incomparably well" in Leaves of Grass (Correspondence 1:41). The praise from the author of "Self-Reliance" and "The Poet" was enough to outweigh the indifference or hostility of all other readers and to start Whitman on his plans for the 1856 edition.

With the publication of this new edition, the first one all but disappeared. When Malcolm Cowley reprinted it in paperback in 1959, he had to introduce it as "the buried masterpiece of American writing" (Cowley x). Until then, the text was not easily available and, except in Jean Catel's French study in 1930, received little scholarly or critical attention. That the situation has radically changed is a result, to a large extent, of Gay Wilson Allen's influence. Even before Cowley, Allen gave the first edition its due both in his handbook in 1946 and in his exemplary biography of Whitman, The Solitary Singer, in 1955. No serious study of Whitman has appeared since in which the 1855 text is not extensively discussed and its significance in Whitman's achievement not recognized. It has also been examined on its own in a book-length study and in a large number of critical articles, and two of its major poems, "Song of Myself" and "The Sleepers," are probably more often studied now in their first version than in their last. E.H. Miller's mosaic of interpretations of "Song of Myself," for example, dedicated to the "nearly 300" scholars from whose work the mosaic has been assembled, is accompanied by the 1855 text of the poem, and in the Library of America edition of Leaves of Grass both the 1855 and 1892 texts are given in their entirety.

Changes in critical perspectives and preoccupations are reflected, of course, in the responses to the first Leaves as well. The New Critical formalism of the sixties and early seventies has been long replaced by postmodern approaches, and these, too, will undoubtedly evolve and change; meanwhile, the fascination with the 1855 edition continues, and the book is unlikely to become a buried masterpiece again.

Ivan Marki

Bibliography

Allen, Gay Wilson. *The Solitary Singer: A Critical Biography of Walt Whitman.* 1955. Rev. ed. 1967. Chicago: U of Chicago P, 1985.

Catel, Jean. *Rythme et langage dans la 1re édition des "Leaves of Grass" (1855).* Montpellier: Causse, Graille et Castelnau, 1930.

Cowley, Malcolm. Introduction. *Walt Whitman's "Leaves of Grass": The First (1855) Edition.* Ed. Cowley. New York: Viking, 1959. vii–xxxvii.

Hutchinson, George B. *The Ecstatic Whitman: Literary Shamanism & the Crisis of the Union.* Columbus: Ohio State UP, 1986.

Kaplan, Justin. *Walt Whitman: A Life.* New York: Simon and Schuster, 1980.

Marki, Ivan. *The Trial of the Poet: An Interpretation of the First Edition of "Leaves of Grass."* New York: Columbia UP, 1976.

Miller, Edwin Haviland. *Walt Whitman's "Song of Myself": A Mosaic of Interpretations.* Iowa City: U of Iowa P, 1989.

Traubel, Horace. *With Walt Whitman in Camden.* Vol. 1. Boston: Small, Maynard, 1906.

White, William. "The First (1855) *Leaves of Grass:* How Many Copies?" *Papers of the Bibliographical Society of America* 57 (1963): 352–354.

Whitman, Walt. *An American Primer.* Ed. Horace Traubel. Boston: Small, Maynard, 1904.

———. *The Correspondence.* Ed. Edwin Haviland Miller. 6 vols. New York: New York UP, 1961–1977.

———. *Prose Works 1892.* Ed. Floyd Stovall. 2 vols. New York: New York UP, 1963–1964.

Facsimile Editions of Leaves of Grass (1855)

Whitman, Walt. *Leaves of Grass.* 1855. New York: Library of American Poets/Collectors Reprints, 1992.

———. *Leaves of Grass: A Facsimile of the First Edition.* Ed. Richard Bridgman. San Francisco: Chandler Publishing, 1968.

———. *Leaves of Grass: A Facsimile of the First Edition Published by Whitman in Brooklyn in 1855.* New York: Eakins, 1966.

———. *Leaves of Grass: Facsimile of the 1855 Edition.* Ed. Clifton J. Furness. New York: Columbia UP, 1939.

See also "Boston Ballad (1854), A"; Emerson, Ralph Waldo; "Europe, the 72d and 73d Years of These States"; "Faces"; "I Sing the Body Electric"; Language; *Leaves of Grass*; Poetic Theory; Preface to *Leaves of Grass*, 1855 Edition; Self-Reviews of the 1855 *Leaves*, Whitman's Anonymous; "Sleepers, The"; "Song for Occupations, A"; "Song of Myself"; "Song of the Answerer"; Style and Technique(s); "There was a Child Went Forth"; "To Think of Time"; "Who Learns My Lesson Complete"

Leaves of Grass, 1856 Edition

Registered for copyright on 11 September 1856, the second edition of *Leaves of Grass* resulted from the continued surge of creativity that produced the first edition. The title page does not bear the author's name, but the verso page copyright is assigned to Walt Whitman (see Walter Whitman in the first edition). The little volume is bound in olive-green cloth; its front cover is blindstamped with leaves and berries and goldstamped "Leaves of Grass"; its back cover (without goldstamping) is identical. The spine is goldstamped with the title, leaf designs, and "I Greet You at the / Beginning of A / Great Career / R.W. Emerson." Unlike the slim, outsized format of the first edition, this thick, squat volume measures approximately $6^{2}/_{3}$ by $3^{3}/_{16}$ inches and looks "like a fat hymn book" (Allen, Introduction xvi). The poems are set in well-leaded ten-point type, so that Whitman's characteristically long lines tend to overflow, sometimes three or four times. The New York *Tribune* advertised the one-dollar volume as "handy for pocket, table, or shelf" (Stern 121), so that when Whitman (in "Whoever You are

L

Holding Me Now in Hand") challenges the reader to "carry me" "beneath your clothing," in breast or hip pocket, he imagines this volume as the embodiment of himself.

The volume's frontispiece is a photograph of Whitman in the "carpenter" pose. Its thirty-two numbered poems, including all twelve carried over from the first edition, are for the first time given titles. They are followed by "Leaves-Droppings," consisting of Ralph Waldo Emerson's encouraging but private 21 July 1855 letter of praise (previously reprinted in the 10 October 1855 New York *Tribune* and tipped into some late issues of the first edition); Whitman's "dear Friend and Master" reply, in effect, a prose essay; and "Opinions, 1855–6"—nine favorable and unfavorable reviews, including two anonymous self-reviews.

Despite its artistic merit, the volume was Whitman's greatest publishing failure. Its factual but unacknowledged publishers were Fowler and Wells, distributors of books and periodicals on phrenology, health reforms, and occasionally, belles lettres, to whose weekly *Life Illustrated* Whitman was then a contributor. Although reluctant to print the work, the firm advertised on 16 August in the same periodical that it was the principal distributor for this "neat pocket volume" in a stereotyped edition of one thousand copies: "The author is still his own publisher, and Messrs. Fowler and Wells will again be his agents for the sale of the work" (qtd. in Stern 119). Despite Whitman's boast to Emerson that "these thirty-two Poems I stereotype to print several thousand copies of" (*Comprehensive* 730), sales were even poorer than those for the first edition; copies are now quite rare. Readers were embarrassed by such overtly sexual poems as "Spontaneous Me" and "A Woman Waits for Me," by the author's self-promotion, and by his unauthorized appropriation of Emerson's letter. Thus *The Christian Examiner* attacked the "foul work" ("Impious" 62) for its "pantheism and libidinousness" and its "self-applause" (63). Relations soured between poet and publisher. In 1857, when Whitman had a hundred poems ready for the press, he declared that "Fowler & Wells are bad persons for me.—They retard my book very much" (*Correspondence* 1:44).

This edition is more programmatic than its predecessor. In a notebook jotting, Whitman defines the "Idea to pervade" the book as "Eligibility—I, you, any one . . . any being, no matter who" (*Notebook* 8). And in a characteristic mixture of semi-mystic populism and personal hauteur, he positions himself as the spokesman-poet of the American masses, telling Emerson that "A profound person can easily know more of the people than they know of themselves" (*Comprehensive* 733). His letter to Emerson—in effect an essay explaining his poetic intentions to the literary establishment in the critical 1856 election year—asserts that his poems are intended to unify the nation, "for the union of the parts of the body is not more necessary to this life than the union of These States is to their life" (*Comprehensive* 733). He proposes a new literature for America to inspire a free, democratic youth, aware of their singularity and their sexuality and destined to overcome personal and national corruption.

Like the authors of Fowler and Wells's manuals of reform and personal advice—many of whose ideas are interwoven into Whitman's poems—the persona often appears as a fatherly or brotherly counselor in matters physical, personal, or spiritual. At times his prescriptive tone borders on the prosaic, even the banal, and dilutes the intensity of some of the new poems. But Whitman was attempting to enlarge the poet-reader relationship by projecting himself as typifying "the general human personality" (qtd. in Bucke 63). And Whitman's contemporaries often found this hortatory tone to be congenial. Of this edition, Henry David Thoreau (while troubled by the edition's sensuality and its mixture of poetic wonders with "a thousand of brick") declared: "I do not believe that all the sermons, so-called, that have been preached in this land put together are equal to it for preaching" (Thoreau 68).

With the 1856 edition Whitman began his lifelong practice of adding new poems, reworking previously published poems, and reordering poems into different groupings. Thus the dozen poems of the first edition are here distributed in the following sequence: 1, 4, 32, 26, 7, 27, 19, 16, 22, 25, 29, and 6, beginning with "Song of Myself," here called "Poem of Walt Whitman, an American." He added, deleted, and combined lines. For example, he deleted the two-line curse against those who defile the human body at the end of the 1855 "I Sing the Body Electric" and added a thirty-six-line quasi-anatomical catalogue. He also began the

practice of removing overused conjunctions and abandoned the idiosyncratic but rhetorically effective combination of dots, dashes, and conventional punctuation of the first edition in favor of a more standardized system.

The 1856 edition is more than an update; it is, in effect, a new work. Despite some poetic lapses, it is probably the most effectively designed of the six editions, and it is poetically dazzling. Its most impressive cluster of new poems, numbered 8 through 13, includes the following: The massive "By Blue Ontario's Shore," largely cannibalized from the 1855 prose Preface, is a paean to the present and future greatness of Americans ("It is I who am great, or to be great—it is you, or any one" [section 15]) and to the superb Whitman persona, the "equable," profound interpreter of the world and its symbols. "This Compost" evokes the persona's emotional interplay between his fear of death and his faith in the perpetuation of life. The short poem "To You [Whoever you are . . .]" is the persona's comradely outreach to his downtrodden fellows. "Crossing Brooklyn Ferry," with its stunning coloration and its musical and philosophical subtleties—the undisputed masterpiece of the second edition—pictures a deathless, empathic Whitman persona whose presence becomes palpable to generations of readers. "Song of the Open Road" presents the dynamic persona as a reader of the world's symbols proposing to lead the American masses out of their cramped existences into a continuum of transcendental selfhood. The group concludes with the sexually provocative "A Woman Waits for Me."

Memorable new poems in this edition also include "Salut au Monde!," an inspired visionary catalogue of the persona's fellow beings throughout the world; "Song of the Broad-Axe," whose variations on the axe motif herald the emergence from tyranny of a new breed of individualistic Americans; "Song of Prudence," also largely derived from the 1855 Preface; the uniquely ironic "Respondez!"; "On the Beach at Night Alone," which, in its original version, testifies to Whitman's agonized struggle to comprehend death; and, the penultimate poem in the collection, "A Song of the Rolling Earth," with its image of the Whitman persona interpreting the world of beauty, language, and Emersonian compensation. The edition concludes with the 1855 funereal poem "To Think of Time," which intones a somewhat troubled faith in the immortality of the poet and his work. (All poems have been listed by their customary, rather than 1856, titles.)

Despite its relative obscurity, the second edition has not been without admirers. The poet Edgar Lee Masters praised it; the French critic Léon Bazalgette commended its "tremendous beauty" and its "passion, superabundance, torrential violence" (qtd. in Giantvalley 395, 291); and Gay Wilson Allen emphasized its "solid merits . . . literary, bibliographical, and biographical" (Introduction xii). Whitman had set himself the highest goal for this edition—to create an exemplary persona who combined the merits of his idealized self with the best elements in men and women: "I must combine the tolerance and sympathetic manliness of Jean Paul [Richter] with the strength of Homer and the perfect *reason* of Shakespeare" (*Notebook* 6). The volume provides valuable insights into a troubled genius whose public voice (in this most political of editions) and private (confessional) voice achieve a remarkable degree of blending. A study of this singular masterpiece will reward amateur and scholar alike.

Harold Aspiz

Bibliography

Allen, Gay Wilson. Introduction. *Leaves of Grass: Facsimile of the 1856 Edition*. By Walt Whitman. Norwood, Pa.: Norwood Editions, 1976. xi–xxi.

———. *The New Walt Whitman Handbook*. 1975. New York: New York UP, 1986.

———. *The Solitary Singer: A Critical Biography of Walt Whitman*. New York: Macmillan, 1955.

Bucke, Richard Maurice. *Walt Whitman*. Philadelphia: McKay, 1883.

Erkkila, Betsy. *Whitman the Political Poet*. New York: Oxford UP, 1989.

Giantvalley, Scott. *Walt Whitman, 1838–1939: A Reference Guide*. Boston: Hall, 1981.

Goodson, Lester. "The Second *Leaves of Grass* (1856): A Re-Evaluation." *Papers on Walt Whitman*. The University of Tulsa Monograph Series 11. Ed. Lester F. Zimmerman and Winston Weathers. Tulsa: U of Tulsa P, 1970. 26–34.

"Impious and Obscene." *Walt Whitman: The Critical Heritage*. Ed. Milton Hindus. New York: Barnes and Noble, 1971. 62–64.

Myerson, Joel. *Walt Whitman: A Descriptive Bibliography*. Pittsburgh: U of Pittsburgh P, 1993.

Stern, Madeleine B. *Heads & Headlines: The Phrenological Fowlers*. Norman: U of Oklahoma P, 1971.

Thoreau, Henry David. "Thoreau on Whitman." *Walt Whitman: The Critical Heritage*. Ed. Milton Hindus. New York: Barnes and Noble, 1971. 67–68.

Whitman, Walt. *Leaves of Grass*. 1856. Facsimile Edition. Ann Arbor: Microfilm International, 1980.

———. *Leaves of Grass: Comprehensive Reader's Edition*. Ed. Harold W. Blodgett and Sculley Bradley. New York: New York UP, 1965.

———. *The Correspondence*. Ed. Edwin Haviland Miller. 6 vols. New York: New York UP, 1961–1977.

———. *Leaves of Grass: A Textual Variorum of the Printed Poems*. Ed. Sculley Bradley, Harold W. Blodgett, Arthur Golden, and William White. Vol. 1. New York: New York UP, 1980.

———. *Walt Whitman: An 1855–56 Notebook Toward the Second Edition of "Leaves of Grass."* Ed. Harold W. Blodgett. Carbondale: Southern Illinois UP, 1959.

See also "By Blue Ontario's Shore"; "Crossing Brooklyn Ferry"; Fowler, Lorenzo Niles and Orson Squire; *Leaves of Grass*; *Leaves of Grass*, 1855 Edition; "Leaves-Droppings"; "Letter to Ralph Waldo Emerson"; "On the Beach at Night Alone"; "Respondez!"; "Salut au Monde!"; "Song of Prudence"; "Song of the Broad-Axe"; "Song of the Open Road"; "Song of the Rolling Earth, A"; "Spontaneous Me"; "This Compost"; "To You [Whoever you are . . .]"; Wells, Samuel Roberts; "Woman Waits for Me, A"

Walt Whitman, frontispiece, third (1860) edition of Leaves of Grass. *Courtesy of the Library of Congress.*

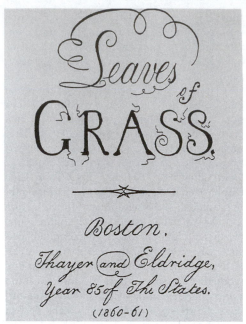

Title page of 1860 Leaves of Grass. *From* Walt Whitman: A Descriptive Bibliography, *by Joel Myerson,* © 1993 by University of Pittsburgh Press.

Leaves of Grass, 1860 Edition

In 1856, not long after the publication of the second edition of *Leaves of Grass,* Walt Whitman began planning a third edition. By June 1857, in an explosion of poetic production, he wrote about sixty-eight new poems and was seeking a publisher to bring out a new edition of *Leaves of Grass.* During the next two years, Whitman failed to locate a publisher. Yet he did ask the Rome brothers to typeset and print page proofs of the new poems; as he revised, Whitman liked to see printed versions of the poems and think about readers looking at the printed page. In February 1860 Whitman received an unexpected letter from Boston publisher Thayer and Eldridge, enthusiastically offering to publish his poems. A contract was quickly negotiated, and by 5 March Whitman had arrived in Boston to meet personally with his new publishers and to oversee the printing. Thayer and Eldridge announced the publication of the new edition in April, and the book appeared in May 1860. Although no one knows precisely how many copies of *Leaves of Grass* Thayer and Eldridge printed before the firm went bankrupt in 1861, Whitman biographers and bibliographers estimate two thousand

(two printings of one thousand copies) to five thousand (the estimate of Whitman's friend, John Burroughs)—a significant increase over the first two editions. There were also a number of pirated copies. In 1879 Richard Worthington purchased the electrotype plates and began printing and marketing unauthorized copies.

The 1860 edition of *Leaves of Grass* was 456 pages long and appeared in a variety of different-colored cloth bindings—orange, green, and brown—many embossed with decorative designs. The book's pages were well printed in a clear ten-point type on heavy white paper and elaborately decorated with line drawings around titles and the beginning and end of poems. The title page and the poem titles appear in various fonts and sizes, and some—like the scriptlike typography of the title page—are fancy. Scattered throughout the volume are small illustrations of a butterfly perched on a human finger, a sunrise, and a globe resting on a cloud and revealing the western hemisphere. The frontispiece is an engraving by Stephen Alonzo Schoff from an oil painting portrait by Charles Hine; it depicts Whitman not as a working-class rough as in the 1855 frontispiece but as a well-coiffured and genteel romantic poet wearing a large, loose silk cravat. In its advertisements, Thayer and Eldridge highlighted the book's elegant design.

To the thirty-two poems of the second edition, Whitman added a total of 146 new poems, the single largest augmentation of *Leaves of Grass* in its thirty-seven-year growth from 1855 to 1891–1892. He altered earlier poems and revised their titles. And for the first time he placed some of the poems in the distinctive, thematic, titled groupings that he called "clusters." The 1860 edition includes seven clusters: "Chants Democratic and Native American" (a group of twenty-one numbered poems prefaced by an introductory poem titled "Apostroph"), "Leaves of Grass" (which contains twenty-one numbered poems), "Enfans d'Adam" (fifteen numbered poems), "Calamus" (forty-five numbered poems), "Messenger Leaves" (fifteen short titled poems), "Thoughts" (seven short numbered poems), "Says" (eight short numbered poems), and "Debris" (seventeen short unnumbered and untitled poetic fragments). "Enfans d'Adam" (later called "Children of Adam") and "Calamus" possess the most thematic coherence as groupings. Whitman retained these two clusters in future editions, dropping the other five arrangements. There are also twenty-six individual, unclustered poems—several of them important, such as "Walt Whitman" (from the 1855 edition, later called "Song of Myself") and "A Word Out of The Sea" (new to *Leaves of Grass* in 1860, later titled "Out of the Cradle Endlessly Rocking").

The clusters and the carefully chosen titles in the third edition indicate an increased attentiveness to organization and structure. The 1860 *Leaves of Grass* begins with "Proto-Leaf" (later called "Starting from Paumanok"), a prefatory poem that announces the poet's intentions and major themes, a poem that deliberately marks the beginning of the book, just as *So long!* concludes the book. Because of these structural revisions, Whitman considered the third edition complete, although future editions indicate that he later changed his mind.

While planning this edition and writing poems for it, Whitman saw his project as "*The Great Construction* of the *New Bible*" (*Notebooks* 1:353). In some respects the 1860 edition of *Leaves of Grass* looks like a Bible. It groups poems into clusters, numbers (rather than titles) the clustered poems, and individually numbers stanzas in a way that resembles the book, chapter, and numbered verse divisions of the Bible. This Bible-like appearance amplifies the 1860 edition's increased thematic emphasis on religion. In "Proto-Leaf," the program poem that begins the third edition, the poet invites his comrade to share with him "two greatnesses" (love and democracy) and also "a third one, rising inclusive and more resplendent"—"the greatness of Religion."

Love is the theme of the two most important, most coherent, and most famous clusters. Whitman conceived of "Enfans d'Adam" as a cluster about "the amative love of woman" (*Notebooks* 1:412), phrenological jargon for sexual love between women and men. These poems celebrate procreative sex and the innocence, beauty, and sacredness of the human body. Although Ralph Waldo Emerson urged him to delete these poems, Whitman retained them and their bold, erotic language. Moralistic critics and public officials condemned the "Enfans d'Adam" poems as obscene, while other readers—many of them women—expressed admiration.

The companion cluster, "Calamus," focuses on love between men, what Whitman called comradeship or "adhesiveness," the phrenological term for "manly love" (*Notebooks* 1:413). The cluster's introductory poem (later titled "In Paths Untrodden") announces the theme of "manly attachment," and the cluster explores that theme in poems that are sometimes joyful and content and sometimes suspicious, anxious, and yearning. The origin of "Calamus" is a series of twelve poems originally titled "Live Oak with Moss," a series that biographers and critics see as Whitman's story about or poetic response to an unhappy romantic relationship in the late 1850s, a narrative about love and lost love. While the "Calamus" pieces are clearly personal, intimate, often erotic love poems, Whitman insisted that they were political. And indeed they are, for in them Whitman imagines homoerotic affection as the basis for the Union and democracy. The politics imagined here are an expression of faith in a spiritualized comradeship. Hence, "Calamus" is an important example of the merger of the third edition's major themes (love, democracy, religion).

L

More overtly, but perhaps less convincing, political poems are found in this edition's largest cluster, "Chants Democratic and Native American." In it Whitman celebrates democratic America with a nationalistic fervor that can at times sound shrill, especially given the approaching crisis—the bloody, four-year-long Civil War that threatened to dissolve the United States. Whitman's response to this threat in "Chants Democratic"—"O a curse on him that would dissever this Union for any reason whatever!" ("Apostroph") barely masks a deeper anxiety about the impending crisis.

Whitman's scarcely contained dread about national divisions and the sometimes suspicious or despairing poems in "Calamus" mark an important distinguishing characteristic of the third edition—its dark mood. In contrast to the confident, self-reliant persona of the 1855 edition or the 1856 "Song of the Open Road," the disconsolate speaker in the 1860 edition expresses melancholy, woe, and painful uncertainty about personal identity, national destiny, and metaphysical order. In the first poem from the "Leaves of Grass" cluster (originally published in the *Atlantic Monthly* [April 1860] as "Bardic Symbols" and later titled "As I Ebb'd with the Ocean of Life"), the poet walks along the desolate ocean shore, examining the debris from the sea and identifying with the washed-up fragments. He yearns for nurturing from a maternal father figure, but to no avail. The poem ends with an address to the cosmos, an apparently deaf "You, up there," and an acknowledgment that like the sea debris, "we too lie in drifts at your feet." Self-doubt converges with skepticism about the order, benevolence, and responsiveness of the natural and metaphysical universe.

A melancholic tone also characterizes "A Word Out of the Sea" (first published in *Saturday Press* [24 December 1859] as "A Child's Reminiscence," later called "Out of the Cradle Endlessly Rocking"), a poem about a childhood encounter with death. Like "Leaves of Grass" number 1 ("As I Ebb'd"), this poem is set on the Long Island shore. The poet remembers observing as a child a pair of mockingbirds and listening to their songs. When the she-bird disappears, the solitary he-bird sings a wild, despairing song. But, unlike the nearly nihilist "Leaves of Grass" number 1, in which the isolated poet sees himself in the washed-up

sea debris, "A Word Out of the Sea" has the boy identify with the solitary bird and take inspiration in the bird's sad, desperate song. Moreover, the ocean is no longer representative of the enormous, unresponsive universe, but of death—a cool, inviting, erotic merge with the universe. "A Word Out of the Sea" is certainly a dark poem, full of the desperation, yearning, melancholy, and doubt that characterize the 1860 edition. Yet, the focus on death here is notably religious; it leads to a reconciliation with death and the spiritual, maternal cosmos.

In addition to selling far more copies than previous editions, the well-advertised 1860 *Leaves of Grass* received more attention and critical acclaim than the first two. There are thirty-two known contemporary reviews of the third edition, and most of them are positive or mixed. Only eight reviews were mostly negative. Women readers and critics (such as Juliette H. Beach, Mary A. Chilton, and the renowned African-American actress and poet Adah Isaacs Menken) greeted this edition with exceptional enthusiasm, defending it against the hostile sometimes vicious judgments of male critics who disapproved of the candid, erotic passages in "Enfans d'Adam."

The significance of the 1860 edition of *Leaves of Grass* tends to be paradoxical. Although the poems often express grief over romantic and professional failures, the book's new sense of structure, the sizable increase in poems, its wider readership and critical praise made it one of Whitman's most successful books. Although the poems seem more intimate and personal than previous Whitman poems, the third edition is also a deliberate intervention into public life, an attempt to realize American democratic ideals and save the Union. And while it expresses a strong faith in comradeship as the means for realizing democracy, the 1860 edition also reveals a darker Whitman, suspicious, uncertain, and lonely: "Here the frailest leaves of me, and yet my strongest-lasting" ("Calamus" number 44).

Gregory Eiselein

Bibliography
Allen, Gay Wilson. *The New Walt Whitman Handbook.* 1975. New York: New York UP, 1986.
———. *The Solitary Singer: A Critical Bi-*

ography of *Walt Whitman*. New York: Macmillan, 1955.

Erkkila, Betsy. *Whitman the Political Poet*. New York: Oxford UP, 1989.

Graham, Rosemary. "Solving 'All the Problems of Freedom': The Case of the 1860 *Leaves of Grass*." *American Transcendental Quarterly* 7 (1993): 5–23.

Moon, Michael. *Disseminating Whitman: Revision and Corporeality in "Leaves of Grass."* Cambridge, Mass.: Harvard UP, 1991.

Myerson, Joel. *Walt Whitman: A Descriptive Bibliography*. Pittsburgh: U of Pittsburgh P, 1993.

Warren, James Perrin. *Walt Whitman's Language Experiment*. University Park: Pennsylvania State UP, 1990.

Whitman, Walt. *Leaves of Grass: Facsimile Edition of the 1860 Text*. Ed. Roy Harvey Pearce. Ithaca, N.Y.: Cornell UP, 1961.

———. *Leaves of Grass: A Textual Variorum of the Printed Poems*. Ed. Sculley Bradley, Harold W. Blodgett, Arthur Golden, and William White. 3 vols. New York: New York UP, 1980.

———. *Notebooks and Unpublished Prose Manuscripts*. Ed. Edward F. Grier. 6 vols. New York: New York UP, 1984.

———. *Walt Whitman's Blue Book*. Ed. Arthur Golden. New York: New York Public Library, 1968.

———. *Whitman's Manuscripts: "Leaves of Grass" (1860)*. Ed. Fredson Bowers. Chicago: U of Chicago P, 1955.

See also "As I Ebb'd with the Ocean of Life"; Boston, Massachusetts; "Calamus"; "Children of Adam"; Comradeship; Leaves of Grass; Leaves of Grass Imprints; "Live Oak with Moss"; "Out of the Cradle Endlessly Rocking"; Sex and Sexuality; "So Long!"; "Starting from Paumanok"; Thayer and Eldridge; Walt Whitman's Blue Book

Leaves of Grass, 1867 Edition

The fourth (1867) edition of *Leaves of Grass* was actually published in November 1866 as the third installment of Whitman's Reconstruction project. Following closely on *Drum-Taps* (1865) and the *Sequel to Drum-Taps* (1865–1866), the first of at least four different formats of the text were available from the presses of a New York printer, William E. Chapin. In various permutations, Whitman circulated this fourth edition as four separately paginated books stitched together between two covers: a vastly reedited version of the 1860 *Leaves*, a reissue of *Drum-Taps*, a reissue of the *Sequel to Drum-Taps*, and a striking coda called *Songs Before Parting*. This most chaotic of all six editions of *Leaves* contains only six new poems ("Inscription" [later "One's-Self I Sing" and "Small the Theme of My Chant"], "The Runner," "Leaves of Grass" number 2 [later "Tears"], "Leaves of Grass" number 3 [later "Aboard at a Ship's Helm"], "When I Read the Book," and "The City Dead-House"), but its significance lies in its intriguing raggedness, which is embedded in the social upheaval in the immediate aftermath of the Civil War.

The 1867 *Leaves* has been designated the "workshop" edition, and as such has been relegated to the status of a curiosity in the ongoing evolution of *Leaves of Grass*. However, as a text that circulated in the midst of an unsettled cultural "workshop" that was reconstituting the ruins of postwar America, this edition provides a fertile site in representing the incipient nationalist ideology that intensified in the years following Appomattox. On publication, the scant critical attention devoted to this edition underscored Whitman's nationalism and his exuberant democratic instinct. The images of a coherent Union proliferate throughout all parts of the 1867 edition, but the physical "dismemberment" of the book mirrors not only the fracturing of the North from the South, but also bears the same stress marks as the contentious rhetoric across America concerned with reinstating rebel states and racial differences between whites and newly emancipated slaves. For instance, with the legislative tide turning toward the ratification of the Fourteenth Amendment in 1868, which guaranteed African Americans citizenship on a national scale, Whitman's poetics sought at every turn to reinforce the fragile coalition between sectional and racial factions. Through several strategic revisions of his antebellum poems, along with his new

1867 insertions, Whitman urgently accented democratic nationality, while carefully superintending his earlier images of cultural diversity on the Union landscape.

For the first time, the 1867 *Leaves* opened with the poem "Inscription," which would thereafter introduce the work to subsequent readers. It has been suggested that "Inscription" contains in its six verses the skeletal purpose of the final edition of *Leaves of Grass*. The dominant image of "ONE'S-SELF" as the subject of the chant "for the use of the New World," quickly becomes an exchange between the individual self and the collective self: after announcing "Man's physiology complete," the speaker continues to exert a larger scheme, which moves from "One's-Self" to "En-Masse." In a single line, the slippage in the movement from the isolated individual to the collective body politic underwrites Whitman's commitment to sing of his historical position in postwar America. The image of "One's-Self" has been conventionally read as a call for the sovereignty of the individual, the irreducible agent of democracy. But the egotistical sublime fails to account for the movement from "single" to "unitary" (collective) self.

Several revisions of earlier poems in the rearranged 1867 version of *Leaves* help the reader to map out the increasing emphasis the poet places on collective identity. In the second poem of this edition, "Starting from Paumanok," Whitman modifies the autobiographical references in the 1860 version and gives the poetic persona a continental identity. The federalizing spirit that was emanating from Washington, in its legislative attempts to reconstruct the Union, finds an echo in "Paumanok" through the embrace of diverse geographical sites. Also, there is an echo of Whitman's elegy, "When Lilacs Last in the Dooryard Bloom'd," where the "hermit thrush" moves the speaker to inaugurate a "New World" out of the ashes of the war. In addition, the renovated world that Whitman was inaugurating had already begun its reversal of the effects of the war, through the 1865 abolition of slavery, and therefore, the "Paumanok" speaker can reincorporate the ex-Rebel states as potential readers of *Leaves*. There is an explicit mention of the racial politics of 1866 when Whitman cites the "comity clause" of the Constitution (Article 4, Section 2) in section 6. This clause entitles all citizens of an individual state to the privileges and immunities of every other state. Abolitionists had

since the 1840s widened the scope of the comity clause to include free blacks and slaves under these protections. In July 1868, with the ratification of the Fourteenth Amendment, Whitman's 1866 "Paumanok" text intersects with this understanding of that constitutional diction as applying to the renovated concept of national citizenship. After 1868, the federal government had the right to preside over the states' conduct in the forum of civil liberties, beyond local and regional custom, especially in relation to ex-slaves as they laid claim to authentic status as descendants of the Constitution. In the 1867 *Leaves*, Whitman debuted the poem "Tears," which offers the enigmatic spectacle of a weeping "muffled" figure on a "white" shore. Given the color coding ("white"/"shade") and the undeniable remorse expressed in this text, "Tears" may well have resonated with the concurrent debates over the incorporation of African Americans into the national family. Therefore, when read as a cultural text, Whitman's antebellum frankness in depicting blacks (most famously, in "Song of Myself," speaking in the voice of the slave) has receded into indeterminacy. But the sentimental "lump" suddenly takes on a threatening persona and wills a strong storm to engulf the "white" shore. Thus, read allegorically, the text has enacted the race hatred that greeted ex-slaves at every turn in their bid for postwar equality. Whitman's poem points threateningly to the result of such hatred if the cultural inequalities between races persisted indefinitely.

Whitman's texts of social solidarity, the "Calamus" cluster, comprise the longest cluster of poems in the 1867 *Leaves,* and the poet has moved them closer to the front of the volume. Along with the "Children of Adam" cluster, these two groupings, centered on social relations, are the least destabilized of any clusters from the 1860 edition. The growing coherence of a popular awareness of national identity may have pushed Whitman to foreground these "Calamus" poems, which represent comradeship among strangers from diverse backgrounds, as opposed to local, ethnic, and even racial allegiances. Whitman seems to have learned this lesson in his wartime hospital visits to thousands of wounded veterans from the four corners of the Union (witness his intercalation of *Drum-Taps* and *Sequel to Drum-Taps* in the 1867 edition). The poet also deleted three of the most privatized confessions which had appeared in the "Calamus" cluster of the 1860 edition, and thereby enabled the cluster to be read better as a manifesto of public solidarity among citizens. Rather than the pull of local family ties, then, in the 1867 "Calamus," it can be argued that Whitman was announcing a model of national solidarity built on affiliations between strangers enlisted in the quest for a revivified Union.

In this moment of an explosion of discourse on civil rights, Whitman registered his regret over the continued insistence that marginalized citizens could be discarded through social exclusion in the new poem, "The City Dead-House." At the heart of this text, the issue of disposable persons in a flawed democracy is argued with as much rhetorical force as it was by the Radical Republicans in the houses of Congress, on behalf of African Americans; only Whitman's marginal figure is a dead prostitute lying within sight of the United States Capitol. Socially outcast, the body of the prostitute requires the intervention of the poet's speaker in order that she may be represented visibly, in a democracy in which many are invisible. If persons were rotting on the pavement within sight of the Capitol, this compelling poem enacts a recovery of the rightful place of human solidarity among strangers. Another of the new 1867 compositions, "The Runner," could be read as an allegorical snapshot which represents the athletic determination required to bring coherence to a postwar Union weakened by sectionalism and racism. Without such athletic vigilance, the inherent danger to the Union lay in its static attachment to a failed social compact that had come undone in the firing on Fort Sumter. In "Aboard at a Ship's Helm," another of the new compositions of the 1867 *Leaves,* Whitman's figure of the "ship of state" avoids wreckage on the shore of history only through the alarm-bell aboard which warned of continued social divisions. Only by engaging in an egalitarian revision of social relations, to become more inclusive rather than exclusive, would the Union avoid another cataclysm like the Civil War, only this time along the racial divide rather than the sectional divide.

With the legislative tide turning toward "equal protection" for black and white citizens, Whitman coerced several poems from previous editions of *Leaves* into a new book, appended to the end of the 1867 edition. Called *Songs Before Parting,* this coda resonates with the same federalizing motifs that were rife in public debate as the Fourteenth Amendment made its rough passage to its port in the Constitution. Obviously, these songs represent Whitman's desire for the prevention of "parting" the newly recovered Union, but they were also written "before" the 1861 "parting" of the South from the North. In 1867, these songs can be reheard in the context of the "parts" becoming united again. To reinforce such a representation of national unity, Whitman opens these songs with "As I sat Alone by Blue Ontario's Shore," which announces that a nation is emerging from its lines. The poem is divided into two voices: alongside the exuberant call for the formation of national identity there is a parenthetical voice which sounds portentous warnings concerning the racial and sectional strife of the Union, still caught in the "throes" of giving birth to democracy. By extending eligibility to "all" persons desirous of equality, the poem reminds the reader that Whitman had not abandoned his dream of a "Radical Democracy." The representative who stands in for the people becomes the "bard" who can still be the agent for democratic change.

Therefore, Whitman offered *Songs Before Parting* as the incipient representation of a national compact, in which images of federal affiliation were enlisted to perform the cultural work of enlarging national consciousness and racial sympathy and the dismantling of sectional malice, which sought a return to antebellum black subjugation. America would be reconstructed at some deferred future moment, for these "Songs" never tire of their gestures toward the "great Idea" of democratic equality. When the political foundation of America recovered the "inalienable rights" promised in the Declaration of Independence, then the temporary aberrations of social divisions would cease, not before. The end of democracy is always a beginning, in a circular movement between resistance and surrender to empathy to strangers in our midst. Whitman's announcement of a nation, which was the reconstructive purpose of this cluster, is represented by any desire for "libertad," the poet's curious expression for liberty, from whatever point of origin in the field of social relations. The 1867 *Leaves* announces, in newly added lines to "On the Beach at Night Alone," that "A VAST SIMILITUDE" conjoins all races (and sections) within the borders of the United States. In 1867, such an "interlocking" required Whitman's intervention with a radically altered *Leaves of Grass,* always on the verge of dissolution in its disarray, and yet always shoring up the productivity of reconstructive solidarity, active in binding together factions at multiple points in the disquieting months after Appomattox.

Luke Mancuso

Bibliography

Allen, Gay Wilson. *The New Walt Whitman Handbook.* 1975. New York: New York UP, 1986.

Erkkila, Betsy. *Whitman the Political Poet.* New York: Oxford UP, 1989.

Mancuso, Luke. "'The Strange Sad War Revolving': Reconstituting Walt Whitman's Reconstruction Texts in the Legislative Workshop, 1865–1876." Diss. U of Iowa, 1994.

Moon, Michael. *Disseminating Whitman: Revision and Corporeality in "Leaves of Grass."* Cambridge, Mass.: Harvard UP, 1991.

Whitman, Walt. *Walt Whitman's Blue Book.* Ed. Arthur Golden. 2 vols. New York: New York Public Library, 1968.

See also "City Dead-House, The"; *Drum-Taps*; *Leaves of Grass*; "One's-Self I Sing"; Reconstruction; *Sequel to Drum-Taps*; *Walt Whitman's Blue Book*; "When I Read the Book"; "When Lilacs Last in the Dooryard Bloom'd"

Leaves of Grass, 1871–1872 Edition

As early as the summer of 1869, Walt Whitman had been preoccupied with a revised edition of *Leaves of Grass* to follow the publication of the fourth (1867) edition. When the poet escaped the summer heat of Washington, D.C., to return to New York in July 1870, having secured a substitute in his clerkship at the Attorney General's Office, he was determined to publish the fifth edition with J.S. Redfield of New York. By the winter of 1870–1871, the fifth edition of *Leaves* was on sale in New York, Boston, Philadelphia, and Washington. Despite this signal moment, Whitman was virtually ignored by the critics, though the handful of reviewers noted his universality and his personal incarnation of American democracy. The complicated publishing history of the fifth edition includes at least three rearrangements of the book, perhaps signaling his displeasure over the absence of an audible response from the public to what, for him, was a major publishing event. In any case, Whitman reissued *Leaves* with the *Passage to India* annex, adding 120 pages with seventy-four poems, twenty-four of which were new texts, while the others were culled from earlier editions of his work. In 1872, this bifurcated edition was reissued, directly from Washington, D.C., dated 1872 but copyrighted in 1870. Still another issue of the book contained the *Passage to India* annex, with separate pagination, as well as the additional supplement *After All, Not to Create Only* (later "Song of the Exposition"), with twenty-four additional pages, also published as a separate pamphlet with separate pagination. In short, the fifth edition of *Leaves* contained in its format three separate books of poetry, as well as the related publication of a pamphlet called *As a Strong Bird on Pinions Free, and Other Poems* in 1872. The latter *As a Strong Bird* booklet also contained the significant prose Preface, now known as the 1872 Preface.

This convoluted series of editions adds up to a massive displacement of Whitman's work as the reading public had known it up to that time; in effect, Whitman was pointing to a reassessment of how his evolving project would speak to postwar America, at the moment when he was announcing a companion volume to *Leaves* which he labeled a book of "*democratic nationality*" (Whitman 1005). The most significant innovation of the 1871–1872 *Leaves*, aside from the obvious fact that Whitman took nearly a third of his published poems and shifted them into the *Passage to India* annex, amounts to the poet's dispersal of the *Drum-Taps* collection throughout the body of *Leaves*. Thus, while *Drum-Taps* appeared as a part of *Leaves* for the first time in this fifth edition, the Civil War texts have been scattered and re-edited into three clusters: "Drum-Taps," "Marches Now the War is Over," and "Bathed in War's Perfume." This textual multiplication underscores Whitman's assertion that he owed the existence of *Leaves* to the creative energy he found in war itself.

The cluster "Marches now the War is Over" enlisted images of nationalism in the pursuit of civil restoration immediately after the war years. One of the poems that points the way for the reconstruction of the social order, "Pioneers! O Pioneers!," reinforces this containment of social disruption in its traditional form, complete with trochaic meter and conventional stanzaic patterns. While the title echoes the westward migration, the word "pioneer" traces its etymological roots back to include "foot soldier," and

Walt Whitman, ca. 1870, taken by G. Frank Pearsall. By permission, Beeghly Library, Ohio Wesleyan University.

thus connotes an imagistic parallel to the martial images of the war troops. Thus, while the "Pioneers!" text points backward as an echo chamber of the war memory, the poem also points forward to the reconstructive energies of creating a future that will recast soldiers as pioneers. Clearly, Whitman's pioneers were moving forward, as originators of a new social order, in order to prepare the way for an inclusive, socially diverse citizenry fit for Reconstruction America. Whitman's "foot soldiers," like his conventional poetic "feet," were stepping into the postwar urge for forging a future out of social solidarity. Such solidarity stressed the extension of democratic identity beyond the neighborhoods, towns, and states which had contributed self-understanding to Americans before the Civil War. Such provincial identity had to include national allegiance as well, which was one of the high-profile controversies in the extension of civil liberties to African Americans through the ratification of the Fifteenth Amendment in 1870 (enfranchising African-American males). An earlier poem, "Respondez!," also makes its debut in this cluster of war marches. In "Respondez!" Whitman appeals for a "new distribution of roles" in the social relations of the United States. Like "Pioneers!" this march enables readers to unmoor themselves from the outmoded past in order to be empowered to rewrite their social roles on a more egalitarian basis than had been the case in antebellum America.

The dominant image of the second Civil War cluster, "Bathed in War's Perfume," constitutes Whitman's metonymic representation of the United States in the flag, the "Stars and Stripes." In fact, the "delicate flag" embodies the referent of the title, which is washed in the aroma of the Civil War. The most significant text that appears in this cluster of poems made its debut in the 1871–1872 Leaves as the first attempt by Whitman to address explicitly the subject of African Americans since the 1855 edition of Leaves spoke, in "Song of Myself" and in "The Sleepers," in the voice of the slave. "Ethiopia Saluting the Colors" centers on the bewildered confrontation between a "dusky" African-American woman and a soldier in Sherman's army during the Civil War. Situated in a poetic cluster of "flag" poems, the affront of the African-American woman's salute to the Stars and Stripes takes on pointed significance in the soldier's inability to recognize her selfhood except as a "hardly human" object. Sherman's

underling calls her only "Ethiopia," and thus strips her of any legitimate identity within the boundaries of American civil liberties, despite the newly minted Civil War amendments to the Constitution which ratified African-American citizenship for the first time. In effect, the black woman reaches out to the flag in a gesture of inclusion, interracial comradeship, and political citizenship; the soldier's inability to recognize her finds its analogue in the historical agitation in 1871–1872 over the inability of the white majority to cede its social authority over African Americans.

Curiously, the 1871–1872 Leaves struggles with this question of liberation from domination in a cluster of poems that appeared only in this edition, called "Songs of Insurrection." The insurrection of African-American struggles for recognition, as well as the revolt of Southern whites against federal interference with their local racist customs, lends this cluster a material value in its historical context. In his textual production, Whitman came closest to overcoming the incessant struggles for power that marked his moment. In the syntax of his Reconstruction poems, he enacted a model of the poet as the legislator of social solidarity across lines of racial and sectional fighting. Hence, in 1871, Whitman accented the federalization of America, represented in this pastiche of mainly earlier "Insurrection" poems, now given a new thematic identity in a turbulent postwar setting. This cluster recognizes that "democratic nationality" might be deferred, but could not be defeated.

Whitman's construction of a book of "democratic nationality" took more coherent form in the first annex to the 1871–1872 Leaves, namely Passage to India, which contained seventy-five poems, mostly lifted from earlier editions but including twenty-three new texts. The poet's centralizing imagery takes on an added urgency here, just as the national Capitol sought to federalize civil liberties for African Americans. Whitman deemphasizes the autonomous sovereignty of the individual in favor of a composite image of national identity, which finds an allegorical echo in the two dominant images of this annex: voyaging ships and death. Each of these images has a dual significance, at once both literal and allegorical. Whitman's willingness to abandon the shoreline, evident in the Passage cluster called "Sea-Shore Memories," opened a newer ocean-going preoccupation for a poet who had heretofore stood on the shore.

Such a departure pointed to Whitman's willingness to hazard uncertain future destinations, as well as to suggest that the "Ship of State" had to unmoor itself from older models of self-understanding in favor of an accent on centralized notions of democratic nationality. Of course, the most recognizable image of the "Ship of State" had been published in the popular 1865–1866 text, "O Captain! My Captain!," which Whitman reprinted in *Passage to India* in the cluster called "President Lincoln's Burial Hymn." In addition, the death that Whitman was dispersing in *Passage* included both the actual deaths of Civil War soldiers on the battlefields, and the death of the antebellum notions of local self-understanding, in favor of the dissolution of outmoded social relations unsuited to the new demands of postwar America. Such a dissolving of the crippled inheritance of the political past, broken by the Civil War, signaled the desire to set out on the open road of reconstructing America.

Again and again, the twenty-three new texts in the *Passage to India* annex return to the preoccupation with letting go of the past, in order to stretch out toward the possibilities for unprecedented social solidarity in the future. Significantly, the "Passage to India" text has landed on the shores of America, and not the shores of India. As a prototype of the Western migration to the New World, Columbus inaugurates the historical narrative which would culminate in Whitman's dream of a reconstructed America. Like Columbus, the text is grounded in a transcontinental passage across the United States in order to arrive at the Pacific shoreline. After such a continental passage, the social solidarity of Whitman's Reconstruction project would be accomplished through the departure of the "Ship of State" from the shores of racism and sectionalism. Syntactically, Whitman repeatedly collapses plural images into singular ones (for example, "ourselves" into "all"). In such new clusters as "Whispers of Heavenly Death," the poet continually positions the national Soul as surpassing the possibility of its dissolution. Read allegorically, a new composition called "A Noiseless Patient Spider" casts the agency for social reform into the future. The spider represents a compelling emblem for the Reconstruction poet, though apparently isolated and casting filaments into an unpromising future, who will continue to desire to connect the present social turmoil to the unwritten national future.

The second annex appended to the 1871–1872 *Leaves* extends Whitman's desire to construct a book of "democratic nationality" in its celebration of the technological ingenuity of American industry. *After All, Not to Create Only* (later "Song of the Exposition") was recited by Whitman himself at the fortieth annual exhibition of the American Institute in New York on 7 September 1871 and was issued in pamphlet form by the Robert Brothers of Boston. The text provides a kind of coda to the poem "Passage to India," insofar as Columbus's abrupt landing in 1492 on the shores of America had provided the opportunity for the muse of invention to import the cultural artifacts of the Old World, in order to imprint them on native genius. By 1871, Whitman represented industrial products as agents of rehabilitation from the trauma of the cultural vertigo induced by the Civil War. Whitman extols the centralizing image of national identity in the imperial Union, for he celebrates "Our freedom all in Thee!" (section 9). Once again, Whitman is stylistically enacting his centralizing strategy by the movement from the plural ("Our") to the singular ("Thee"). As the newly appointed arbiter of civil liberties, the federal government represents an absolute Union ideology, and Whitman, as a representative poet, seeks to further the consolidation of national energy with an enthusiasm that has hardly been noticed by either Whitman's readers or his critics. Perhaps, the strange critical silence surrounding the contemporary reception of this fifth edition of *Leaves of Grass* can be read as an (unconscious) resistance of Whitman's egalitarian solidarity against the white majority, who were resisting the widening of liberties for marginalized minorities. Indeed, Whitman qualifies as an "unacknowledged legislator" of the world of Reconstruction culture. Most Americans were not ready to admit that the dismemberment of discrimination through federal surveillance of civil rights was a justifiable intervention in the evolution of an interracial democracy.

Luke Mancuso

Bibliography

Allen, Gay Wilson. *The New Walt Whitman Handbook*. 1975. New York: New York UP, 1986.

Erkkila, Betsy. *Whitman the Political Poet*. New York: Oxford UP, 1989.

Mancuso, Luke. "'The Strange Sad War Revolving': Reconstituting Walt Whitman's Reconstruction Texts in the Legislative Workshop, 1865–1876." Diss. U of Iowa, 1994.

Szczesuil, Anthony. "The Maturing Vision of Walt Whitman's 1871 Version of *Drum-Taps*." *Walt Whitman Quarterly Review* 10 (1993): 127–141.

Whitman, Walt. *Complete Poetry and Collected Prose*. Ed. Justin Kaplan. New York: Library of America, 1982.

See also "Drum-Taps"; "Ethiopia Saluting the Colors"; "Inscriptions"; *Leaves of Grass;* "Noiseless Patient Spider, A"; "Passage to India"; Preface to *As a Strong Bird on Pinions Free;* Reconstruction; *Sequel to Drum-Taps;* "Song of the Exposition"; "Songs of Parting"; "Whispers of Heavenly Death" (cluster)

Leaves of Grass, 1876, Author's Edition

The 1876, or Centennial, edition of *Leaves of Grass* is technically not a new edition, because it was printed from the 1871 plates, yet Whitman made a number of innovations in this printing, both by splitting off previously annexed and new material into a companion volume, *Two Rivulets,* and through alterations in the title page and intercalations in the text.

The 1876 Author's edition of *Leaves of Grass* mirrors Whitman's and the nation's struggle to define themselves in the aftermath of the Civil War. It is a well-known fact that Whitman never wavered from his initial concept of regarding poetry as a living, breathing organism: "Who touches this [book] touches a man" ("So Long!"). Yet by 1876, his role, mission, and imaginative form and method have shifted toward a poetics of accommodation during a period of Reconstruction. The poet's complex aim is to reflect his conflicting but not self-canceling responses—to the war in the face of peace, to life in the midst of death, to the body straddled between the soul and the Eternal Soul, and to America moving in and out of time.

Much had happened to Whitman since the last, 1871–1872, *Leaves* was published. In 1873, he had a stroke, his mother died, and he unceremoniously exited Washington for Camden, which left him separated from his intimate friend, Peter Doyle. Given all these psychic traumas, Whitman channels his poetic energies differently and says as much in a Camden newspaper in 1876: "he *soars* more and *sings* less than ever" (Whitman, "Literature"). By shifting into a poetics of "sight over sound," he experiments with displaying himself on the page in as many ways as the visual and tactile mediums permit. Stated in more specific printerly terms: his 1876 *Leaves* carries more "sock" than "kiss" (Lieberman 40).

Whitman's use of the visible mediums of print and photo to "talk to" (his rhetorical strategy in the 1876 *Leaves*) the verbal medium of poetry dramatizes his sense of the work as a living form, a human personality. To enrich the texture and give physical density, *Leaves* contains a number of graphic firsts.

Whitman himself, for example, pastes "intercalations" (paper scraps of poems, titles, and parts of a table of contents page) onto a finished text (*Leaves of Grass.* Author's Edition, With Portraits and Intercalations). He also mixes different type sizes and typefaces for the two S's in the word **GRASS** on a title page (*Leaves of Grass.* Author's Edition, With Portraits from Life). He places an epigraph poem on a title page and personally autographs it. He inserts two "Portraits" into the text by having them face their companion verses. He adds the imprint "Author's Edition" on the title page.

These striking firsts more than compensate for the small number of new poems (five) contained in the 1876 *Leaves:* four intercalated poems and the title page's "Come, said my Soul," revised from its first appearance in the 1874 Christmas issue of the New York *Daily Graphic.*

Approaching his verse through typography and photography offer alternative ways to examine his poetic composition and compelling evidence that the 1876 *Leaves* is a text to be reckoned with. And this method is provocative enough to reinvigorate the poet of the 1870s along with his image-in-verse experiment.

Frances E. Keuling-Stout

Bibliography
Allen, Gay Wilson. *The New Walt Whitman Handbook*. 1975. New York: New York UP, 1986.

Benton, Megan and Paul. "Typographic Yawp: *Leaves of Grass*, 1855–1992." *Bookways: A Quarterly for the Book Arts* 13 & 14 (1994–1995): 22–31.

Lieberman, J.B. *Types of Typefaces: And How to Recognize Them*. New York: Sterling, 1967.

Myerson, Joel. *Walt Whitman: A Descriptive Bibliography.* Pittsburgh: U of Pittsburgh P, 1993.

Whitman, Walt. *Leaves of Grass.* Author's Edition, With Portraits and Intercalations. Camden, N.J.: Author's Edition, 1876.

———. *Leaves of Grass*. Author's Edition, With Portraits from Life. Camden, N.J.: Author's Edition, 1876.

———. *Leaves of Grass: A Textual Variorum of the Printed Poems*. Ed. Sculley Bradley, Harold W. Blodgett, Arthur Golden, and William White. 3 vols. New York: New York UP, 1980.

———. "Literature/Walt Whitman's Works, 1876 Edition." Camden *New Republic* 11 Mar. 1876: 2.

See also CAMDEN, NEW JERSEY; DOYLE, PETER; LEAVES OF GRASS, 1871–1872 EDITION; LEAVES OF GRASS, 1881–1882 EDITION; PHOTOGRAPHS AND PHOTOGRAPHERS; PREFACE TO *TWO RIVULETS*; PRINTING BUSINESS; RECONSTRUCTION; *TWO RIVULETS*, AUTHOR'S EDITION

Leaves of Grass, 1881–1882 Edition

Walt Whitman recognized that the timing of the 1881–1882 edition of *Leaves of Grass* was fortunate because it was a chance to consolidate and unify his work late in his career. He could achieve "the consecutiveness and *ensemble*" he had always wanted, he told his friend John Burroughs (*Correspondence* 3:231). To accomplish this goal, Whitman regrouped many poems in five new subtitled sections or clusters, a formal device with which he had long been experimenting. Generally recognized as the definitive edition of his poems, this edition was published in Boston by James R. Osgood and Company in October 1881. It was the seventh edition, counting a pirated typesetting distributed in England. Other than adding supplements of later poems, Whitman did not change the design of the volume in the final decade of his life. The last of fifteen printings of the edition occurred in 1892, the year of Whitman's death.

The Osgood edition is notable both for its legacy of clustering and because for the first time Whitman's book was being distributed by a mainstream publisher; Osgood's authors included Henry James, William Dean Howells, and Mark Twain. Whitman's book sold more than fifteen hundred copies before the publisher withdrew it after a district attorney objected to the sexual content and threatened to prosecute the company for selling obscene literature. The poet soon arranged to resume printing with Philadelphia publishers—first Rees Welsh, then David McKay when McKay acquired *Leaves* and other nonlegal titles from Welsh, who specialized in law

books. Spurred by publicity, Philadelphia sales eventually surpassed six thousand copies, earning Whitman more than one thousand dollars in royalties by December 1882.

In the summer of 1881, Whitman spent three weeks revising his book in New York City, then oversaw publishing details for two months in Boston. He cut thirty-nine poems in their entirety, added seventeen new ones, and modified hundreds of lines, but many of the changes were minor adjustments of punctuation. For his final edition of *Leaves* Whitman focused his editorial efforts on regrouping poems to create the sequence and unity of dramatic effects he had in mind.

Whitman's remarks are sketchy about the formal device of clustering, but the evidence supports James E. Miller's conclusion that Whitman envisioned the overall organization of his poems in dramatic terms, with a protagonist and a narrative divided into acts. In his preface for the Centennial edition, whose structure was transitional toward the final arrangement of the poems, Whitman explains the function of the *Passage to India* annex in this way: "As in some ancient legend-play," these poems serve "to close the plot and the hero's career" (*Comprehensive* 745). In the same preface, Whitman also makes a distinction between the spiritual poems—his thoughts "on Death, Immortality, and a free entrance into the Spiritual world" (746)—and the political poems that presumably advance the career of his protagonist, which may be understood as the poet's conflation of a poet figure and the American people, struggling to achieve the ideals of the Revolution.

Whitman published the "two altogether distinct veins" (746) of his poetry—spiritual and political—in separate volumes for his Centennial printing. Spiritual poems—combined with prose works in a second volume, *Two Rivulets*—were understandably ascendant in Whitman's final arrangement of his poems. He was mindful of the transience of his own life "at the eleventh hour, under grave illness" (744), he explained, having suffered a paralytic stroke and the loss of his mother, who had died three years earlier. In spiritual poetry, Whitman offered elaborate poetic visions of immortality, post-Christian in imagery, yet largely compatible with Christian hopes.

In the final arrangement of his poems, Whitman reintegrated the spiritual poems from the second volume of his 1876 printing back into a single volume of *Leaves of Grass*. Critics differ over whether this reintegration succeeds or fails. Those who presume that the primary literary intention of the text was putting the imaginative life of a poet into a sequence of poems tend to discern miscellaneous instead of purposeful regroupings in the 1881–1882 edition. Harold Blodgett and Sculley Bradley complain that "Autumn Rivulets" lacks a common theme or progression of ideas, James E. Miller, Jr., finds only a casual thematic unity in "By the Roadside," and Gay Wilson Allen concludes that Whitman erred when he did not arrange poems according to the chronology of their composition or his autobiography. Assuming that Whit-

man used clusters to deal with the tension between the private origin of lyrics and the public setting he established for his poems, however, James Perrin Warren concludes that clustering in the 1881–1882 edition succeeds. Critics who read the literary intention of *Leaves* from historical perspectives also are favorable about Whitman's final design.

Starting with the observation by editors of the Variorum edition that Whitman seemed to have rejected nearly one of ten poems not for aesthetic reasons, but because the poems did not fit

Walt Whitman, ca. 1880, taken by Bartlett F. Kenny. Courtesy of the Library of Congress.

his plan for the book and drawing upon historical criticism by Betsy Erkkila and M. Wynn Thomas, Mary Virginia Stark offered the first extensive explications of new clusters in the 1881–1882 edition. Stark concludes that in his final design Whitman groups poems to create the dramatic effect of rising action, crisis, and resolution common in the narratives of Western literary culture. He portrays the aspirations of his protagonist-speaker under cluster subtitles from earlier editions—"Children of Adam" and "Calamus"—and in unclustered political poems like "Song of Myself," other "Songs," and "Crossing Brooklyn Ferry." These poems are all placed before the "Drum-Taps" cluster of Civil War poems Whitman called pivotal.

Stark observes a foreboding and intensifying somberness in the three new clusters placed before the crisis Civil War poems in the 1881–1882 edition. The "Birds of Passage" cluster opens with "Song of the Universal," in which images of hope are surrounded by images of peril and defeat: "From imperfection's murkiest cloud, / Darts always forth one ray of perfect light" (section 3). The "Sea-Drift" cluster expands war imagery and amplifies the somber tone presaging the crisis of civil war. The third new cluster, "By the Roadside," opens with the harshly satirical "A Boston Ballad (1854)" and closes with scathing lines about the last three prewar "presidentiads"—"scum floating atop of the waters . . . bats and night-dogs askant in the capitol," while "these States sleep" ("To the States"). The roadside metaphor suggests the journey of American promise is being thwarted or delayed.

Following the crisis Civil War poems in the "Drum-Taps" and "Memories of President Lincoln" groupings comes the fourth new cluster, the healing poems of "Autumn Rivulets"—"songs of continued years," as Whitman calls them in the first poem of the cluster ("As Consequent, Etc."), and of peace and hope born by the "rivulets" swelled by the storm of the war.

Spiritual poems in the last new cluster—"From Noon to Starry Night"—provide comforting resolution for the conflicts and suffering of the tragic narrative, leading to "Songs of Parting," the grouping with which Whitman had ended each edition since he began experimenting with cluster arrangements in 1860. In all of the new clusters Stark discerns structural parallels to Shakespeare's tragedies about Britain and episodes of crisis in the history of Israel from the Bible—literary models for Whitman's work. Penultimate poems, first poems, repeated metaphors, and allusions also

unify the clusters in relation to the Civil War and *Leaves of Grass* as a whole, Stark has shown.

Even granting the coherence of Whitman's final design, the superior literary standing of prewar poems and clusters will probably endure. However, instead of blaming the abstractness of postwar poems and programmatic clusters in the 1881–1882 edition on a waning of poetic powers—a subtle form of ageism—critics can recognize the logic of the volume as Whitman designed it, acknowledging that twentieth-century readers have admired Whitman's achievement as a lyric poet more than the larger communal and national purposes he envisioned for his work.

Dennis K. Renner

L

Bibliography

Allen, Gay Wilson. *The New Walt Whitman Handbook*. 1975. New York: New York UP, 1986.

———. *The Solitary Singer: A Critical Biography of Walt Whitman*. 1955. Rev. ed. 1967. Chicago: U of Chicago P, 1985.

Bradley, Sculley, Harold W. Blodgett, Arthur Golden, and William White. Introduction. *Leaves of Grass: A Textual Variorum of the Printed Poems*. Ed. Bradley, Blodgett, Golden, and White. Vol. 1. New York: New York UP, 1980. xv–xxv.

Crawley, Thomas Edward. *The Structure of "Leaves of Grass."* Austin: U of Texas P, 1970.

Miller, James E., Jr. *A Critical Guide to "Leaves of Grass."* Chicago: U of Chicago P, 1957.

Stark, Mary Virginia. "Clustered Meaning in Walt Whitman's *Leaves of Grass*." Diss. U of Iowa, 1990.

Warren, James Perrin. "The 'Paths to the House': Cluster Arrangements in *Leaves of Grass*, 1860–1881." *ESQ* 30 (1984): 51–70.

Whitman, Walt. *The Correspondence.* Ed. Edwin Haviland Miller. 6 vols. New York: New York UP, 1961–1977.

———. *Leaves of Grass: Comprehensive Reader's Edition.* Ed. Harold W. Blodgett and Sculley Bradley. New York: New York UP, 1965.

See also "Autumn Rivulets"; "Birds of Passage"; Boston, Massachusetts; "By the Roadside"; Comstock, Anthony; "From Noon to Starry Night"; *Leaves of Grass; Leaves of Grass, 1891–1892, Deathbed Edition; McKay, David; Osgood, James R.; "Sea-Drift"; Society for the Suppression of Vice; Stevens, Oliver

Leaves of Grass, 1891–1892, Deathbed Edition

Copyrighted in 1891, published in 1892, the 1891–1892 so-called Deathbed edition of *Leaves of Grass* is, strictly speaking, not an edition at all, but an *impression;* nor does the epithet "deathbed" pertain accurately to the text that has come to be so identified.

While the 1891–1892 volume was the ninth published during Whitman's lifetime to be entitled *Leaves of Grass,* and is therefore sometimes referred to as the ninth edition, it does not qualify as an edition according to generally accepted modern standards, since it contained no significant new material. The authentic editions of *Leaves of Grass* that Whitman compiled would be those of 1855, 1856, 1860, 1867, 1871, and 1881. With twenty-three minor revisions, pages 3–382 of the 1891–1892 *Leaves of Grass* reprint the 1881 text from the plates of James R. Osgood, the Boston publisher; the revisions include corrections of misspellings, changes of punctuation, and other alterations of the Osgood text that Whitman made for the 1882 and 1889 publications of *Leaves of Grass* and for the *Complete Poems & Prose* of 1888.

In the 1881 edition—the seventh publication of *Leaves of Grass* and the sixth (and last) true edition—the 293 poems, seventeen of them new, were given their final order and arrange-

Walt Whitman, 1891, about ten months before his death. By permission, Rare Books Division, New York Public Library.

Leaves of Grass

Including

SANDS AT SEVENTY ... *1st Annex,*

GOOD-BYE MY FANCY ... *2d Annex,*

A BACKWARD GLANCE O'ER TRAVEL'D ROADS,

and Portrait from Life.

COME, said my Soul,
Such verses for my Body let us write, (for we are one,)
That should I after death invisibly return,
Or, long, long hence, in other spheres,
There to some group of mates the chants resuming,
(Tallying Earth's soil, trees, winds, tumultuous waves,)
Ever with pleas'd smile I may keep on,
Ever and ever yet the verses owning—as, first, I here and now,
Signing for Soul and Body, set to them my name,

Walt Whitman

PHILADELPHIA
DAVID McKAY, PUBLISHER
23 SOUTH NINTH STREET
1891-'2

Title page of 1891–1892 Leaves of Grass. *From* Walt Whitman: A Descriptive Bibliography, *by Joel Myerson,*
© *1993 by University of Pittsburgh Press.*

ment. The "clusters," as Whitman called his special groupings of poems under various titles, would now remain unchanged, having gone through extensive revision since their first appearance in the 1860 *Leaves;* and the twenty-five poems standing prominently outside the clusters were given their final placements. Although one additional poem, "Come, said my Soul," would later be restored to the *Leaves* as epigraph, it would appear on the title page, reclaiming a position it had first occupied in the impression of 1876.

In 1881 the poems of *Leaves of Grass* had achieved their final design. The plates for the 1881 edition were used in all subsequent publications of *Leaves of Grass* during Whitman's lifetime, as well as for the edition of 1897; thus no poem written after 1881 appears in *Leaves of Grass* proper. Whitman continued to write, however, and additional poems were published in two volumes, the poems of which were later to be included in the 1891–1892 *Leaves of Grass* as annexes rather than being integrated into the total structure.

The first annex was printed initially in the varied collection entitled *November Boughs,* published in 1888 by David McKay in Philadelphia. In its 140 pages the volume included a long prefatory essay entitled "A Backward Glance O'er Travel'd Roads" and sixty-four new poems, all short, as well as a collection of prose works. *November Boughs* appeared in its entirety as part of the *Complete Poems & Prose* of 1888; and then, under the title "Sands at Seventy," the poems of *November Boughs* were annexed first to the 1888 and 1889 impressions of *Leaves of Grass,* and finally to the 1891–1892 impression as pages [383]–404. "A Backward Glance O'er Travel'd Roads" was published in the 1889 *Leaves of Grass* and then was made the concluding text of the 1891–1892 volume as pages [423]–438. Between the poems and the essay, filling pages 405–422, appeared the second annex, "Good-Bye my Fancy," a collection of thirty-one short poems taken from the gathering of prose and poetry published under that title by McKay in 1891.

A posthumous gathering of poetry, "Old Age Echoes," edited by Horace Traubel, with the title supplied by Whitman, was included in the 1897 text of *Leaves of Grass* published by Small, Maynard and Company of Boston. In addition to its thirteen short poems it contained Traubel's preface, "An Executor's Diary Note, 1891," consisting mostly of Whitman's responses to two questions that Traubel, one of Whitman's literary executors, had asked him about the disposition of poems written after publication of the forthcoming 1891–1892 *Leaves of Grass.* Whitman is reported to have said, in part, "So far as you may have anything to do with it I place upon you the injunction that whatever may be added to the *Leaves* shall be supplementary, avowed as such, leaving the book complete as I left it, consecutive to the point I left off, marking always an unmistakable, deep down, unobliterable division line. In the long run the world will do as it pleases with the book. I am determined to have the world know what I was pleased to do" (*Comprehensive* 575). Not generally recognized as part of the *Leaves of Grass* canon, "Old Age Echoes" appears in some, but not all, volumes of Whitman's "complete poetry."

As the *Textual Variorum of the Printed Poems* indicates, the 1891–1892 *Leaves of Grass* appeared in two distinct versions before the final publication by David McKay in the spring of 1892. While both included the annexes and other additional materials, there were differences in the texts of the poems of *Leaves of Grass.* One version, assembled in December of 1891, was a paperbound volume that contained unbound sheets of the 1889 impression; "rude, flimsy cover," was Whitman's comment about it in a letter to Dr. Richard Maurice Bucke dated 6 December 1891, "but good paper, print & stitching" (*Correspondence* 5:270). These sheets incorporated the various minor corrections that Whitman had been making over the years to the plates of the 1881 edition, and the corrected plates of 1881 were used for the 1889 impression as well as for that of 1891–1892. Therefore, while the 1881 *Leaves of Grass* established the order, arrangement, and essential texts of the poems, the Deathbed edition was not, as is sometimes stated, simply a reprinting, with additional materials, of the 1881 *Leaves,* since Whitman later made a number of revisions to that volume—minor, to be sure, but revisions nonetheless.

A second version was bound in December of 1891 for presentation to friends in time for Christmas; it contained uncorrected sheets of the 1888 *Leaves of Grass,* sheets incorporating only the few minor changes made for the 1882 impression. The presentation copies were bound in heavy paper, with plain covers in gray or dark brown, and on the spine only a pasted label, showing the author's name and the title.

The production of the assembled volumes was a makeshift job, done in some haste so that Whitman might have a copy of the final *Leaves* before his death, and it came not a moment too soon. In the same letter of December 6 to Dr. Bucke, Whitman remarked on his physical condition—"Bad days & nights with me, no hour without its suffering"—and expressed satisfaction over the completion of his long labors: "L. of G. *at last complete*—after 33 y'rs of hackling at it, all times & moods of my life, fair weather & foul, all parts of the land, and peace & war, young & old—the wonder to me that I have carried it on to accomplish as essentially as it is, tho' I see well enough its numerous deficiencies & faults" (*Correspondence* 5:270). On December 17 Whitman came down with a chill and had to be helped to bed. He was found the next day to have congestion in the right lung; his physicians sensed that the end was near. Despite an improvement in January, Whitman did little more than endure, often in considerable pain, until his death on 26 March 1892.

While the 1891–1892 *Leaves of Grass* has come to be known as the Deathbed edition, that epithet would most properly be applied to the paperbound texts of 1891 rather than to the hardbound *Leaves* that would be published in the spring of 1892; still, it should be noted that the "deathbed" epithet, while romantically appealing, is in any case not wholly accurate, since compilation of the authorized text had been completed at least some weeks before the author's final illness (although he was assuredly in very poor health at the time). As early as 1 December 1891, Whitman noted in a letter to Dr. Bucke, "no books last edn L of G yet f'm binder, but expect them every day" (*Correspondence* 5:268). Bucke received his copy by 8 December; on 10 December Whitman wrote again to say that he was awaiting additional copies with heavier paper covers, one of which he would send to Bucke, and commented, "As I now consider it *finished* as I propose & laid out—even its deficiencies are provided for, or plainly hinted at—to me its best points are an unmistakable *atmosphere* and with any maturity or stamina or the like *its being in process* (or evolution) qualities f'm first to last" (*Correspondence* 5:271).

Actual publication of the 1891–1892 *Leaves of Grass* took place several months into 1892. Issued by David McKay, the book had plain covers, a hardbound cloth binding of dark green, and on the spine gold-stamped lettering bearing

the title and the names of author and publisher. The final text of *Leaves of Grass* that Whitman authorized, then, began with the epigraphic poem "Come, said my Soul" on the recto of the title page, and on the verso it presented Whitman's definitive statement of preference for the 1891–1892 text. "As there are now several editions of L. of G.," he wrote, "different texts and dates, I wish to say that I prefer and recommend this present one, complete, for future printings, if there should be any; a copy and fac-simile, indeed, of the text of these 438 pages. The subsequent adjusting interval which is so important to form'd and launch'd work, books especially, has pass'd; and waiting till fully after that, I have given (pages 423–438) my concluding words" (*Variorum* 1:xxv). Whitman's statement was followed by the 1889 text of the poems of *Leaves of Grass;* the two annexes, "Sands at Seventy" and "Good-Bye my Fancy"; and finally the essay "A Backward Glance O'er Travel'd Roads" with its closing words—"the strongest and sweetest songs yet remain to be sung"—bringing the book to an end (*Comprehensive* 574). The total number of poems is 389.

The question inevitably arises, since the poems are not in chronological order of composition, What does the structure *mean*? Various attempts have been made to find a coherent principle of organization, but none has proven definitive. Whitman himself compared the growth of *Leaves of Grass* to the successive growth of a tree, but a tree follows chronological order, while Whitman did not. It could, however, be said in general that the 1891–1892 *Leaves of Grass* demonstrates, at least in broad outline, a recognizable thematic structure.

The book begins with a prelude introducing major and minor themes to follow; this section includes the prefatory poem "Come, said my Soul" and the short poems gathered in the "Inscriptions" cluster. It then turns to varied explorations of human life in "Starting from Paumanok," "Song of Myself," and the "Children of Adam" and "Calamus" clusters, poems largely youthful in their passions, their sorrows, their expectations, and their energies. The dominant poem is of course "Song of Myself," with its celebrations both of human physicality and of a transcendent universe.

The book proceeds to move outward from personal experience to public, as it explores the mature poet's perceptions of human experience, beginning with poems significantly entitled

"Salut au Monde!" and "Song of the Open Road." The central poem of this section is "Crossing Brooklyn Ferry," in which the poet looks out beyond himself to the lives of people present and future. The tone then darkens as the book turns to poems expressing mature awareness of loss, poems imbued with the inherent sadness of humanity. This section includes such "Songs of Experience" as "Out of the Cradle Endlessly Rocking" and "As I Ebb'd with the Ocean of Life" in the "Sea-Drift" cluster; it also includes poems of a philosophical and meditative nature, such as "On the Beach at Night" and "On the Beach at Night Alone."

Following the brief poems of "By the Roadside," poems that, as the title suggests, are vignettes of passing life, *Leaves* then turns to the life of a nation with the two wartime sections, "Drum-Taps" and "Memories of President Lincoln." Following the carnage of war, the concluding sections of *Leaves of Grass* are distinctly elegiac, taking us into advancing age and the approach of death, as in the dominant poem, "Passage to India." The titles of the clusters themselves tell a story: "Autumn Rivulets"; "Whispers of Heavenly Death"; "From Noon to Starry Night"; and "Songs of Parting."

In sum, *Leaves of Grass* takes its readers through the course of a human life, from birth to death. Significantly, the first lines of "Starting from Paumanok," the initial major poem following the brief introductory poems of "Inscriptions," speak of origins—"Starting from fish-shape Paumanok where I was born / Well-begotten, and rais'd by a perfect mother"—and the concluding lines of the final poem, "So Long!," in the "Songs of Parting" cluster, are spoken as from the grave: "Remember my words, I may again return, / I love you, I depart from materials, / I am as one disembodied, triumphant, dead." In between the two poems, *Leaves of Grass* ranges widely through the stages and circumstances of human life.

Beyond this general framework, however, there seems to be no clear plan; and even the broad scheme outlined above is subject to dispute, for many placements of poems may seem arbitrary rather than purposeful, as appropriate to one place as to another—indeed, a significant number of poems had already *been* in other places, since the arrangements of poems within and without the clusters had been so frequently revised over the course of more than twenty years.

Thus the structure of *Leaves of Grass* will always be open to differing perceptions. That is

as it should be, for Whitman was not writing according to a strict blueprint, but according to his own spontaneous nature and lyric sensibility. *Leaves of Grass* may have the cumulative force of epic, but its components have the vitality and the variety of lyric.

Perhaps Whitman's summarizing comment in "A Backward Glance O'er Travel'd Roads" deserves the final say. "*Leaves of Grass*," he insisted, "has mainly been the outcropping of my own emotional and other personal nature—an attempt, from first to last, to put a *Person*, a human being (myself, in the latter half of the Nineteenth Century, in America,) freely, fully and truly on record" (*Comprehensive* 573–574). While Whitman made a number of assertions about the nature of his book, some of them highly ambitious, some of them conflicting, this modest statement, taken with due regard for Whitman's characteristic reticence about precise details of his life as well as for the force of his artistic creativity, suggests at the very least a possible route into the large landscape of *Leaves of Grass*.

R. W. French

Bibliography

Allen, Gay Wilson. *The New Walt Whitman Handbook*. 1975. New York: New York UP, 1986.

———. *A Reader's Guide to Walt Whitman*. New York: Farrar, Straus and Giroux, 1970.

Bowers, Fredson. *Principles of Bibliographical Description*. Princeton: Princeton UP, 1949.

Crawley, Thomas Edward. *The Structure of "Leaves of Grass."* Austin: U of Texas P, 1970.

Miller, James E., Jr. *A Critical Guide to "Leaves of Grass."* Chicago: U of Chicago P, 1957.

———. *"Leaves of Grass": America's Lyric-Epic of Self and Democracy*. New York: Twayne, 1992.

———. *Walt Whitman*. Updated ed. 1962. Boston: Twayne, 1990.

Whitman, Walt. *The Correspondence*. Ed. Edwin Haviland Miller. 6 vols. New York: New York UP, 1961–1977.

———. *Leaves of Grass: A Textual Variorum of the Printed Poems*. Ed. Sculley Bradley, Harold W. Blodgett, Arthur Golden, and William White. 3 vols. New York: New York UP, 1980.

———. *Leaves of Grass: Comprehensive Reader's Edition*. Ed. Harold W. Blodgett and Sculley Bradley. New York: New York UP, 1965.

See also "Autumn Rivulets"; "Backward Glance O'er Travel'd Roads, A"; "Birds of Passage"; Bucke, Richard Maurice; "By the Roadside"; "Calamus"; "Children of Adam"; "Crossing Brooklyn Ferry"; "Drum-Taps"; "From Noon to Starry Night"; "Good-Bye my Fancy" (Second Annex); "Inscriptions"; *Leaves of Grass*; McKay, David; "Memories of President Lincoln"; *November Boughs*; "Sands at Seventy" (First Annex); "Sea Drift"; "Song of Myself"; "Songs of Parting"; "Starting from Paumanok"; "Whispers of Heavenly Death" (cluster)

Leaves of Grass Imprints (1860)

In 1860 Thayer and Eldridge of Boston agreed to publish the third edition of *Leaves of Grass*. In response to Walt Whitman's desire to market himself and his work energetically, the publishing firm simultaneously released a sixty-four-page pamphlet of advertisements called *Leaves of Grass Imprints*. The imprints were available at no cost to prospective buyers, and the company used them as a unique promotion device. The pamphlet was made up of twenty-five reviews of *Leaves of Grass* since its 1855 publication. These included Whitman's assessments of his own work.

Throughout his career Whitman was a conscientious overseer of both his poetry and its critical reception. As enthusiastic in marketing as he was in writing poetry, Whitman had developed a reputation for professionalism early in his career. The Rome brothers, owners of a print shop specializing in legal documents, set the 1855 edition of *Leaves of Grass*, with Walt Whitman serving as a careful consultant and editor. In fact, the poet himself set approximately ten pages of type.

Unlike Herman Melville and other of his contemporaries, Whitman was not shy about selling himself, and he had throughout his career meticulously collected reviews of his work. It made no difference to him if the reviews were positive or negative, since he considered them all publicity. He also wrote numerous self-critiques. Several of Whitman's biographers express surprise that his collection of reviews included even a particularly harsh moral attack by William Swinton in the New York *Times*. Swinton attacked Whitman for being self-serving in writing reviews of his own work.

Fortunately, Thayer and Eldridge shared Whitman's zeal for self-promotion and calcu-lated advertising. For prospective buyers, *Leaves of Grass Imprints* served as a convenient overview of Whitman's style and subject matter. For Thayer and Eldridge, it served as testimony of their intent to make the new volume a success. For Whitman and literary historians, it was a collection of reviews summarizing his critical reception from 1855 to 1860. Largely because of Whitman's involvement in the project, *Imprints* remains the best documentation of how Whitman was received by the American public prior to the third edition.

Jan Whitt

Bibliography
Greenspan, Ezra. *Walt Whitman and the American Reader.* Cambridge: Cambridge UP, 1990.

Zweig, Paul. *Walt Whitman: The Making of the Poet.* New York: Basic Books, 1984.

See also Leaves of Grass, 1860 Edition; Self-Reviews of the 1855 Leaves, Whitman's Anonymous; Thayer and Eldridge

Leaves of Grass, Variorum Edition

The textual history of *Leaves of Grass* is very complicated. Over the span of a thirty-seven-year career, Whitman issued six separate editions in 1855, 1856, 1860, 1867, 1871, and 1881. Thereafter, using the corrected plates of the final 1881 edition for later impressions of *Leaves of Grass*, Whitman added the supplementary annexes "Sands at Seventy" (1888) and "Good-Bye my Fancy" (1891–1892) to make up the so-called Deathbed edition of 1891–1892, to which Whitman gave his final approval.

Beginning with the second (1856) edition, Whitman not only added new poems to succeeding editions, but also made it his practice to revise previously published poems, by adding or deleting lines, phrases, and words. Occasionally, he shifted lines from one poem to another, or used lines from a rejected poem to form a separate poem, and the like. Along the way there were further refinements. The twelve poems of the first (1855) edition were untitled and without stanza numbers. In subsequent editions, he structured the poems with separately numbered stanzas. In other instances, individual poems that were numbered under cluster headings were later given titles. And throughout, he altered titles, so that, for example, the untitled opening 1855 poem was in 1856 titled "Poem of Walt Whitman, an American" and from 1860 to 1871 titled simply "Walt Whitman," before he finally settled in 1881 on the familiar "Song of Myself."

With the third (1860) edition, Whitman began his practice of grouping both previously published and new poems thematically. Among others, he formed such separate "clusters," as he termed them, as "Enfans d'Adam" (later "Children of Adam"), "Calamus," and the nationalistic "Chants Democratic and Native American," whose distinctive title was dropped after 1860, with the poems distributed. Additionally, over the years Whitman issued separately such collections as *Drum-Taps* (1865), *Sequel to Drum-Taps* (1865–1866), and the 120-page *Passage to India* (1871), of which twenty-four poems were new, including the title poem. These separately paginated volumes were then bound-in with editions of *Leaves of Grass* closest to their respective dates of publication. In 1881 these poems appeared as an integral part of the *Leaves of Grass* canon.

For the reader to understand how *Leaves of Grass* grew from edition to edition, some sense had to be made of these often bewildering textual permutations. Indeed, one of Whitman's publishers, David McKay, was the first to recognize the importance of variant readings in assessing the development of Whitman as a poet by issuing in 1900 a single-volume *Leaves of Grass* which also stated on the title page, "including a facsimile autobiography, variorum readings of the poems, and a department of gathered leaves." Although McKay was able to alert the reader through variants and selected manuscript citations to the "growing as well as the grown Whitman," this edition proved to be a well-meaning but inadequate affair, compounded by his puzzling choice of the 1871 edition—not the 1891–1892 Deathbed edition—as copy-text. The variant readings are for editions up to 1867, with notes on additions to 1871. The variants are incomplete and contain errors.

Two years later, Oscar Lovell Triggs, in the third volume of the *Complete Writings of Walt Whitman* (1902), offered a more ambitious attempt at providing "Variant Readings," along with selected manuscript selections.

Triggs's textual variants were more comprehensive than McKay's, but were similarly marred by omissions and at times errors. Also lacking was a comprehensive supporting apparatus. In 1924 Emory Holloway reprinted Triggs's variorum text in his *"Inclusive Edition"* of *Leaves of Grass,* cautioning that while these readings were taken verbatim from Triggs, where "omissions or inaccuracies have been noted, corrections or additions have been made" (540).

In 1955, the centenary of the first edition of *Leaves of Grass,* New York University Press announced the new *Collected Writings of Walt Whitman,* under the general editorship of Gay Wilson Allen and Sculley Bradley. Bradley and Harold W. Blodgett were to edit the variorum text. In 1965 they edited a preliminary one-volume text of *Leaves of Grass,* the *Comprehensive Reader's Edition* (available as a Norton paperback). After a number of delays, William White and Arthur Golden were brought in to complete the textual variorum. In 1980 a three-volume *Textual Variorum of the Printed Poems: 1855–1891* appeared, with manuscript variants to follow.

With the 1891–1892 Deathbed edition as copy-text, the *Variorum* offers the reader an overview of all the variants appearing over the six separate editions of *Leaves,* the annexes, and a fresh editing of the posthumous "Old Age Echoes." As such, the *Variorum* provides both a textual and historical perspective of the growth of *Leaves,* with the successive variants enabling the reader to reconstruct a given (or rejected) poem as it appeared in any specific earlier edition, beginning with the 1855. Additionally, facsimiles of title pages and tables of contents of the editions are provided. Also included are such separate sections as "Cluster Arrangements in *Leaves of Grass,*" "Collated Editions, Supplements, Annexes, and Impressions of *Leaves of Grass,*" "A List of Variant Readings within Editions of, and Annexes to, *Leaves of Grass,*" as well as "A Chronology of Whitman's Life and Work."

The *Variorum* shows that Whitman finally excluded nearly one of ten poems from 1855 to 1881. The *Variorum* makes available for the first time an account of all the printed *Leaves of Grass* variants, with the manuscript variants to follow.

Arthur Golden

Bibliography

Allen, Gay Wilson. "Editing *The Writings of Walt Whitman.*" *Arts and Sciences* 1.2 (1962–1963): 7–12.

———. "The Growth of *Leaves of Grass.*" *The New Walt Whitman Handbook.* By Allen. New York: New York UP, 1975. 67–160.

Bradley, Sculley. "The Problem of a Variorum Edition of Whitman's *Leaves of Grass.*" *English Institute Annual: 1941.* Ed. Rudolph Kirk. New York: Columbia UP, 1942. 129–157.

Folsom, Ed. "The Whitman Project: A Review Essay." *Philological Quarterly* 61 (1982): 369–383.

Myerson, Joel. *Walt Whitman: A Descriptive Bibliography.* Pittsburgh: U of Pittsburgh P, 1993.

Triggs, Oscar Lovell, ed. "Variorum Readings of *Leaves of Grass.*" *The Complete Writings of Walt Whitman.* Ed. Richard Maurice Bucke, Thomas B. Harned, and Horace L. Traubel. Vol. 3. New York: Putnam, 1902. 83–255.

White, William. "Editions of *Leaves of Grass:* How Many?" *Walt Whitman Review* 19 (1973): 111–114.

Whitman, Walt. *Leaves of Grass.* Ed. David McKay. Philadelphia: McKay, 1900.

———. *Leaves of Grass: Inclusive Edition.* Ed. Emory Holloway. Garden City: Doubleday, 1924.

———. *Leaves of Grass: A Textual Variorum of the Printed Poems.* Ed. Sculley Bradley, Harold W. Blodgett, Arthur Golden, and William White. 3 vols. New York: New York UP, 1980.

———. *The Walt Whitman Archive: A Facsimile of the Poet's Manuscripts.* 3 vols. 6 parts. Ed. Joel Myerson. New York: Garland, 1993.

———. *Walt Whitman's Blue Book.* Ed. Arthur Golden. 2 vols. New York: New York Public Library, 1968.

———. *Whitman's Manuscripts: "Leaves of Grass" (1860).* Ed. Fredson Bowers. Chicago: U of Chicago P, 1955.

See also HOLLOWAY, EMORY; LEAVES OF GRASS (ALL EDITIONS); MCKAY, DAVID; TRIGGS, OSCAR LOVELL

"Leaves-Droppings" (1856)

As an appendix to the second (1856) edition of *Leaves of Grass,* Whitman published "Leaves-Droppings" (perhaps a pun on "eavesdropping"), primarily a collection of critical responses to the first (1855) edition. The first section, entitled "Correspondence," consists of Emerson's famous letter to Whitman, heralding *Leaves of Grass* as "the most extraordinary piece of wit and wisdom that America has yet contributed" (*Comprehensive* 729), followed by Whitman's 3,800-word reply to his "Master." Ralph Waldo Emerson was angry and embarrassed, and the literary world in general was offended, because the letter, a private note that did not express Emerson's considerable reservations about the poetry, was published without his permission. Whitman's epistolary reply to Emerson is essentially an announcement of his literary ambitions and the American poetics he had first (and more successfully) elaborated in the 1855 Preface. The letter also baldly exaggerates the popular success of the first edition and predicts the steady growth of the poet's popularity and importance in future years.

The second section of "Leaves-Droppings," entitled "Opinions. 1855–6," reprints nine reviews of the 1855 *Leaves* that had originally appeared in (1) the London *Weekly Dispatch,* (2) the Brooklyn *Daily Times,* (3) the *Christian Spiritualist,* (4) *Putnam's Monthly,* (5) the *American Phrenological Journal,* (6) the *Critic,* (7) the *Examiner,* (8) the London *Leader,* and (9) the Boston *Intelligencer.* This collection nearly equaled the "Correspondence" in generating controversy, since two of the reviews (numbers 2 and 5) were written (though unsigned) by Whitman himself. Moreover, he did not shy away from including puzzled, mixed, or even flatly negative reviews in this collection, further showcasing the controversial nature of his poetry.

"Leaves-Droppings" illustrates the shamelessness and skill with which Whitman promoted *Leaves of Grass* early in his career, gaining himself a degree of useful notoriety and establishing himself as a literary outsider. "Leaves-Droppings" has never been reprinted in its entirety, but the "Correspondence" appears in *Leaves of Grass: Comprehensive Reader's Edition,* and the reviews have been reprinted individually in Milton Hindus's *Walt Whitman: The Critical Heritage.*

John Rietz

Bibliography

Hindus, Milton, ed. *Walt Whitman: The Critical Heritage*. New York: Barnes and Noble, 1971.

Kaplan, Justin. *Walt Whitman: A Life*. New York: Simon and Schuster, 1980.

Traubel, Horace. *With Walt Whitman in Camden*. Vol. 3. New York: Mitchell Kennerley, 1914.

Whitman, Walt. *Leaves of Grass*. Brooklyn: Fowler and Wells, 1856.

———. *Leaves of Grass: Comprehensive Reader's Edition*. Ed. Harold W. Blodgett and Sculley Bradley. New York: New York UP, 1965.

See also EMERSON, RALPH WALDO; LEAVES OF GRASS, 1855 EDITION; LEAVES OF GRASS, 1856 EDITION; LEAVES OF GRASS IMPRINTS; "LETTER TO RALPH WALDO EMERSON"; SELF-REVIEWS OF THE 1855 LEAVES, WHITMAN'S ANONYMOUS

Leech, Abraham Paul (1815–1886)

Leech was rescued from oblivion in 1985, with the recovery of nine Whitman letters he had received between 1840–1841. The letters were purchased at auction by the Library of Congress. Leech's personal eighteen-page notebook, the drafts of two letters to Whitman, and miscellaneous genealogical material rounded out the sale.

A bookkeeper by profession, Leech appears to have met Whitman in 1840 in Jamaica, Long Island, where he lived most of his life. His notebook records local marriages, births, deaths, and (Presbyterian) church and temperance meetings. The letter drafts show a pleasant, if ordinary, person of 25, who mainly provided Whitman with local gossip. Though Whitman was an ardent Democrat, Leech handled his advocacy of Whig politics without strain.

Of the nine letters, six predate the earliest letter in the *Correspondence* and all predate the two extant 1842 letters. They were written from July 1840, when Whitman was teaching school in Woodbury, Long Island, to late 1841, from New York City, and as such shed new light on Whitman's early years. Whitman's letters portray a generally frustrated young man with literary aspirations, chafing at the onerous rural teaching and boarding routine in "Purgatory Fields," as he termed Woodbury. His ordeal ended when he left teaching for a journalism career in New York City. After 1842 Leech

appears to have dropped out of Whitman's life, but for a period of some two years he had provided him with a convenient sounding board for his views on local politics, farmers, Woodbury, and the like. The letters offer the reader an invaluable firsthand account of this early period of Whitman's life.

Arthur Golden

Bibliography

Golden, Arthur. "Nine Early Whitman Letters, 1840–1841." *American Literature* 58 (1986): 342–360.

Miller, Edwin Haviland, ed. *The Correspondence of Walt Whitman: A Second Supplement with a Revised Calendar of Letters Written to Whitman*. Spec. Double Issue of *Walt Whitman Quarterly Review*, 8.3–4 (1991): 1–106.

Whitman, Walt. *The Correspondence*. Ed. Edwin Haviland Miller. Vol. 1. New York: New York UP, 1961.

See also LONG ISLAND, NEW YORK

Legacy, Whitman's

Walt Whitman once remarked to Horace Traubel that James Fenimore Cooper's Natty Bumppo was "a *Leaves of Grass* man" (Traubel 62), presumably because Whitman recognized affinities between his own and Cooper's work. Many subsequent authors, like Cooper before them, bear resemblances to Whitman, but the affinities are not necessarily derivative. Most are probably circumstantial in origin—commonplace literary responses to similar situations and themes instead of evidence of literary influence, a cautionary distinction Wellek and Warren mention in their discussion of influence and literary history in *Theory of Literature*.

Nonetheless, in progressive narratives of literary descent most scholars credit Whitman with several innovations: he opened the full range of rhythmic possibilities beyond traditional metrics and rhyme, expanded the subject of human experience for literature to include sex and explore the unconscious, and liberated the imagination for a realm of symbolic meaning needed for the post-Enlightenment cultural situation in which traditional repositories of meaning in religion have appeared archaic or have been eclipsed by philosophical critique. Whitman displayed his forward-looking adaptations in the aptly chosen hybrid genre of the

American long poem, which in its brief lyric passages sometimes advanced the precision of imagery and in its larger structure decentered narrative, introducing sophisticated techniques of spatial form that Joseph Frank later discerned in mature works of literary modernism. Whitman advanced poetics, in this common assessment, despite embarrassing impurities and political sentiments.

The political Whitman, of less interest than the poetical one in the United States, has attracted more international attention. The struggles from monarchical regimes to modern nation-states in Europe and from colonial to postcolonial regimes in the Third World have been accompanied by the same political turmoil Whitman encountered as an aspiring poet in the first new nation. His poetry has seemed revolutionary to writers working from within regimes inhospitable to yearnings for liberty and social justice. In this sense Whitman succeeded in his project to theorize democratic alternatives to the literatures of feudalism.

In American literary history, however, Whitman has been recognized less as a democratic theorist than as a precursor for later poets who refined their own sense of the literary vocation by creating an image of Whitman that would serve their own poetic agenda. More than one hundred literary responses to Whitman have been anthologized from among the many writers who have felt the need to explain their relationship to this original American poet. Generalizing about the nature of Whitman's legacy from such evidence is complicated by the fact that the precedents he established are refracted through several loops of literary descent—internationalist refractions in Ezra Pound and T.S. Eliot, nativist versions in William Carlos Williams and Hart Crane, and refractions from abroad in poetry and criticism by the French symbolists and D.H. Lawrence.

Instead of assessing influence from the labyrinth of parallels, echoes, and other textual resemblances and from arguments among poets as though poets floated in a stream of literary art free from the constraints of social and economic systems, literary historians have begun to refocus on such factors as how poets gain access to audiences and the resources of publishing and how gatekeepers in the institutions of literary culture perform their roles.

This approach leads to efforts to identify Whitman's role in developments that would seem less likely or impossible without his presence, beginning with the convergence of a remarkable combination of subversive elements in his background—his culturally disadvantaged boyhood and early contact with Jeffersonian political theory, his grounding in the competencies necessary for democratic publishing, and his motives for promoting a new literary style. This background and his poetic brilliance empowered Whitman's forty-year campaign to gain at least marginal visibility for a style of indigenous literary art different from mainstream poetry by Henry Wadsworth Longfellow and other Fireside poets.

Whitman's access to the publishing world, made possible by cheaper newspapers and the market for temperance fiction, gave him the power to print and promote his own books, which in turn made him available for appropriation by George Santayana. The Harvard philosophy professor picked an opportune moment—an address in California in which he critiqued Calvinism and its secular philosophical tradition—to declare that Walt Whitman was probably the only poet to escape this "genteel tradition." His poems were "unpalatable for educated Americans" but contained seeds for "the growth of a noble moral imagination" (Santayana 52–53).

Santayana's backhanded endorsement brought Whitman enough respectability for appropriation by younger poets, several of whom—notably Eliot and Stevens—studied with Santayana at Harvard. Many essays about Whitman began appearing in the "little magazines," including *Poetry* and *The Little Review,* promoting what became the tradition of American literary modernism. Thus Whitman's innovations—though not his political theory—became associated with the poetic tradition that would dominate the realm of academic literary culture for the next forty years.

Whitman's poetry also seems to have had an impact on the course of American literary history by accelerating the acceptance of complex gender relationships and sexuality in literature. A decisive development occurred when Whitman circumvented the restrictions on sexual content by refusing to accept deletions to avoid a Boston obscenity charge. Instead, he found an alternative Philadelphia publisher, and the message from the flurry of sales provoked by the controversy was not lost on the growing publishing industry. Until then portrayals of sexuality were limited to physical attraction and courtship ending in marriage. Even though ta-

L

boos were still strong, the market for expanding sexual and gender themes now seemed more promising.

Hamlin Garland's novel *Rose of Dutcher's Coolly* (1895) and Kate Chopin's *The Awakening* (1899) were among the first novels to follow Whitman's precedents—portraying human sexuality more openly, democratizing relationships between men and women, and questioning gender roles. Even the British novelist E.M. Forster had Whitman's precedent in mind in portraying gender relationships in *A Room with a View* (1908), a novel with homosexual themes and a heroine who escapes conventional subordination in marriage by achieving companionship and equality.

These two developments—Whitman's appropriation by modernist poets and his contribution to progress in gender portrayals—are examples from Kenneth Price's effort to reformulate Whitman's legacy. Whitman is also sometimes credited with having established a tradition of writing about common occupations and ordinary people, continued by proletariat poets who thought of themselves as working in Whitman's shadow—Edgar Lee Masters, Vachel Lindsay, and Carl Sandburg. Although they sometimes adopted the form of Whitmanesque free verse and Sandburg expanded coverage of urban life, these poets were working with proven subjects for popular poetry used earlier by the Fireside poets.

The more innovative line of descent—literary modernism—produced significant resemblances, but not the affinities Whitman probably had in mind. Even the closest inheritors of Whitman's poetic stance toward his country and compatriots, Hart Crane and William Carlos Williams, differed from Whitman in significant ways.

Crane's memorable image of the poet in "Chaplinesque"—as someone sheltering human feelings in language like a kitten in a coat pocket—misses the assertiveness of Whitman's poet-figure. This is not the expansive and defiant poet of action dominating Whitman's poems. In *Paterson* Williams's analogue for the poet—the figure of a dog sniffing local trees and digging in indigenous earth—argues well against the alternative of the Anglo-European literary tradition embraced by Eliot, but a sniffing dog is hardly Whitmanesque.

Crane, wishing to counter the negations of Eliot's poetry, embraced the image of Whitman as a mystic, not as a political poet. Williams,

looking for resources to oppose Puritanism, embraced Whitman's image as a poet of immediate experience, and he admired Whitman's metrical innovations, but in his book-length quest for a usable past, *In the American Grain,* Williams turns to Edgar Allan Poe, not Whitman, as the "anchor" for American literature (226).

Such distinctions are not meant to devalue the achievements of Crane and Williams but to recognize significant features of Whitman's precedent they did not adopt. As modernist poets, both Crane and Williams emphasize the individual imagination, whereas Whitman contextualizes the imagination in a political community—a diverse, evolving aggregate of individuals pursuing the promise of the American Revolution, contested, uncertain, and at times implausible as that promise has always been. That this promise still resonates in American life was demonstrated by its reverberations in the political rhetoric of Martin Luther King, but the extent to which twentieth-century American poets have followed Whitman's poetic use of the Revolutionary heritage has not been studied as thoroughly as his legacy for modernist poets.

Modernist appropriations of Whitman have dominated assessments of his legacy to twentieth-century literary history, but a weak alternative lineage has been traced from the early Emerson through Whitman and into the twentieth century through writers for the *Seven Arts Magazine.* Alfred Kazin has called Whitman the "chief actor" in this "green" American tradition of cultural organicism, whose inheritors were Isadora Duncan in dance, Louis Sullivan and through him Frank Lloyd Wright in architecture, and Alfred Stieglitz and Robert Henri in photography and painting (342–343). Critics have associated the poets Crane, Williams, Charles Olson, and Gary Snyder with this tradition.

During the 1950s and 1960s, a coterie of poets—the Beats—returned to Whitman's precedent for social criticism, lamenting the lost America he celebrated in his poems and echoing the rage of prophetic passages of pre-Civil War editions of *Leaves of Grass.* They replaced Whitman's targets of attack, the evils of slave expansion and disunion, with the new evils of corporate greed and American militarism.

Just as Cooper's novels carried images of the United States abroad, *Leaves of Grass* has been read internationally as a representative democratic text. Within years of Whitman's death, an anthology editor in Great Britain had included Whitman, annotating his poems with glosses about democratic literature from Alexis de Tocqueville, to help distinguish Whitman from conservative English literary works. Authorities in Czarist Russia censored Whitman's poetry as decadent and subversive. Readers abroad have sometimes enacted their understandings of *Leaves of Grass* in political programs that have risked and on occasion resulted in imprisonment or execution. Many countries have at least one poet who is Whitmanesque, although this legacy may not be a direct literary influence. Rather, the editors of *Walt Whitman and the World,* a collection of reception studies and tributes to the poet from abroad, view their anthology as a step toward a history of intercultural exchanges.

In his own country, poets from diverse ethnic and racial backgrounds have often sensed in Whitman a democratic inclusiveness and an encouragement for political struggles with which they identify. Authors associated with the Harlem Renaissance, for example, have mentioned Whitman as a precursor for their use of folk elements in literature.

Whitman's literary inheritors look over their shoulders at how this American poet answered fundamental questions: What is the relationship between poetry and political experience? Who is the audience for poetry? What language is appropriate? The American long poem is flexible in accommodating diverse and contentious responses to such questions, but not all of Whitman's answers have had equal access to the realms of discourse in literary criticism. As Sherry Ceniza has shown, by 1860 women who responded from heterosexual perspectives were struggling to explain what Whitman had achieved by trying to neutralize the language of gender definition in his poetry. Clearly, he had been informed by protofeminist critiques of the institution of marriage published in the small journals of New York, but critics who worked to expand the audience for *Leaves of Grass* from this perspective were largely silenced and, with them, an important Whitman legacy. Recently, critics from gay and lesbian perspectives have used Whitman's poems more freely for the politics of gender identity.

Whitman's answer to questions about the relationship between poetry and politics has often been rejected or silenced, but signs of renewed interest in this legacy have begun to appear. Nationality, like class, may be a stage in identity formation through which human beings in modern societies pass on the way to a more universal identity, as Jay Parini has observed. This seems close to Whitman's internationalist theory of American culture; however, in literary criticism the cosmopolitanism of the intelligentsia and the presumption that nationalisms are expressions of false consciousness or that they risk the perversions that developed in Nazi Germany have tended to silence the legacy of Whitman's thinking about national culture.

Whether in the Balkans, in the fractious republics of the former Soviet Union, or in the increasingly fragmented mosaic of mass-mediated and diverse gender, class, and ethnic "republics" in the United States, peaceful and constructive integration amid diversity has proven difficult to achieve. Imagining social bonds to sustain integration in a rights-based, pluralistic democratic regime was a fundamental goal of Whitman's political poetic. Like Lincoln, Whitman was positioned in the second and perhaps last generation of Americans trying to enact the founding principles of a new American polity, as historian of federalism Samuel Beer has observed. As a "master of the sociological imagination," Whitman displays a useful vision of social integration in America in the composite experience of his poet-figure (Beer 377). The philosopher George Kateb has also reopened a lineage to Whitman's political theory. As "a great philosopher of democracy," Whitman provides reflections on the nature of persons and the forms and motives for democratic acceptance of difference (Kateb 545). One legacy from Whitman as poet-critic is too rarely accepted in the appropriations of his work for the culture wars of academic discourse—his resistance to exclusivity.

Dennis K. Renner

Bibliography

Allen, Gay Wilson, and Ed Folsom, eds. *Walt Whitman & the World.* Iowa City: U of Iowa P, 1995.

Beer, Samuel H. "Liberty and Union: Walt Whitman's Idea of the Nation." *Political Theory* 12 (1984): 361–386.

Bohan, Ruth L. "'I Sing the Body Electric': Isadora Duncan, Whitman, and the Dance." *The Cambridge Companion to Walt Whitman.* Ed. Ezra Greenspan. Cambridge: Cambridge UP, 1995. 166–193.

L

Ceniza, Sherry. "'Being a Woman . . . I Wish to Give My Own View': Some Nineteenth-Century Women's Responses to the 1860 *Leaves of Grass*." *The Cambridge Companion to Walt Whitman*. Ed. Ezra Greenspan. Cambridge: Cambridge UP, 1995. 110–134.

Folsom, Ed. "Talking Back to Walt Whitman: An Introduction." *Walt Whitman: The Measure of His Song*. Ed. Jim Perlman, Ed Folsom, and Dan Campion. Minneapolis: Holy Cow!, 1981. xxi–liii.

Greasley, Philip Alan. "American Vernacular Poetry: Studies in Whitman, Sandburg, Anderson, Masters, and Lindsay." Diss. Michigan State U, 1975.

Grünzweig, Walter. "'For America—for All the Earth': Walt Whitman as an International(ist) Poet." *Breaking Bounds: Whitman and American Cultural Studies*. Ed. Betsy Erkkila and Jay Grossman. New York: Oxford UP, 1996. 238–250.

Hutchinson, George B. "The Whitman Legacy and the Harlem Renaissance." *Walt Whitman: The Centennial Essays*. Ed. Ed Folsom. Iowa City: U of Iowa P, 1994. 201–216.

Jordan, June. "For the Sake of a People's Poetry: Walt Whitman and the Rest of Us." *Walt Whitman: The Measure of His Song*. Ed. Jim Perlman, Ed Folsom, and Dan Campion. Minneapolis: Holy Cow!, 1981. 343–352.

Kateb, George. "Walt Whitman and the Culture of Democracy." *Political Theory* 18 (1990): 545–571.

Kazin, Alfred. "Sherman Paul and the Romance with America." *The Green American Tradition: Essays and Poems for Sherman Paul*. Ed. H. Daniel Peck. Baton Rouge: Louisiana State UP, 1989. 341–345.

Miller, James E., Jr. *The American Quest for a Supreme Fiction: Whitman's Legacy in the Personal Epic*. Chicago: U of Chicago P, 1979.

Musgrove, Sidney. *T.S. Eliot and Walt Whitman*. Wellington: New Zealand UP, 1952.

Parini, Jay, and Brett C. Miller, eds. *The Columbia History of American Poetry*. New York: Columbia UP, 1993.

Perkins, David. *A History of Modern Poetry: Modernism and After*. Cambridge, Mass.: Harvard UP, 1987.

Price, Kenneth M. *Whitman and Tradition: The Poet in His Century*. New Haven: Yale UP, 1990.

Santayana, George. *The Genteel Tradition: Nine Essays*. Ed. Douglas L. Wilson. Cambridge, Mass.: Harvard UP, 1967.

Tapscott, Stephen. *American Beauty: William Carlos Williams and the Modernist Whitman*. New York: Columbia UP, 1984.

Trachtenberg, Alan. "Walt Whitman: Precipitant of the Modern." *The Cambridge Companion to Walt Whitman*. Ed. Ezra Greenspan. Cambridge: Cambridge UP, 1995. 194–207.

Traubel, Horace. *With Walt Whitman in Camden*. Vol. 4. Ed. Sculley Bradley. Philadelphia: U of Pennsylvania P, 1953.

Waggoner, Hyatt H. *American Poets from the Puritans to the Present*. Boston: Houghton Mifflin, 1968.

———. *American Visionary Poetry*. Baton Rouge: Louisiana State UP, 1982.

See also ANDERSON, SHERWOOD; BERRYMAN, JOHN; BORGES, JORGE LUIS; CATHER, WILLA; CHOPIN, KATE; CRANE, HART; CREELEY, ROBERT; DEMOCRACY; DOS PASSOS, JOHN; DUNCAN, ROBERT; ELIOT, T.S.; EVERSON, WILLIAM; FORSTER, E.M.; GARCÍA LORCA, FEDERICO; GARLAND, HAMLIN; GIDE, ANDRÉ; GINSBERG, ALLEN; HUGHES, LANGSTON; INTERCULTURALITY; JARRELL, RANDALL; JORDAN, JUNE; JOYCE, JAMES; KEROUAC, JACK; KINNELL, GALWAY; LAWRENCE, D.H.; MASTERS, EDGAR LEE; MILLER, HENRY; MUSIC, WHITMAN'S INFLUENCE ON; NERUDA, PABLO; PESSOA, FERNANDO; POUND, EZRA; RUKEYSER, MURIEL; SANDBURG, CARL; SIMPSON, LOUIS; STEVENS, WALLACE; WHARTON, EDITH; WILLIAMS, WILLIAM CARLOS; WRIGHT, JAMES

"Legend of Life and Love, A" (1842)

This short story initially appeared in *United States Magazine and Democratic Review*, July 1842. For publication history and revisions, see Brasher's edition of *The Early Poems and the Fiction*.

There is a simple message to this story of two brothers, orphans whose last remaining relative, a grandfather, gives them advice on his deathbed. Basically the advice is a statement of pessimism about human beings: avoid love, avoid trust, avoid getting involved. The young men go their own ways. One brother, Mark, follows the advice to the letter; the other, Nathan, does not. After seventy years they meet each other and tell their stories. Hearing of Nathan's wife, children, and grandchildren, Mark realizes, in Nathan's words, "the world has misery—but it is a pleasant world still" (Whitman 119).

Allen sees the grandfather in this story as a variation on the cruel father theme that plays through several of Whitman's short stories. Related to this theme is another motif that figures in much of Whitman's fiction: the separation of brothers. Both themes, for example, appear in "Wild Frank's Return" (1841) and "Bervance: or, Father and Son" (1841).

Patrick McGuire

Bibliography

Allen, Gay Wilson. *The Solitary Singer: A Critical Biography of Walt Whitman.* 1955. Rev. ed. 1967. Chicago: U of Chicago P, 1985.

Whitman, Walt. *The Early Poems and the Fiction.* Ed. Thomas L. Brasher. New York: New York UP, 1963.

See also "BERVANCE: OR, FATHER AND SON"; SHORT FICTION, WHITMAN'S; "WILD FRANK'S RETURN"

Leggett, William L. (1801–1839)

William Leggett, poet and journalist, stirred the hearts of many New Yorkers during his mercurial career. After a United States Navy court-martial in 1825, he began writing verse and fiction. But his most important work was his journalism, particularly at the New York *Evening Post,* where he worked from 1829 to 1836 under William Cullen Bryant. While Bryant was in Europe in 1834 and 1835, Leggett poured out vitriol against the political chicanery he saw about him, saving most of his abuse for champions of banks and corporations. Instead, he advocated free trade, increased suffrage, and the general principles of Jacksonian democracy, although in 1835 he led the Locofoco revolt from the local Democrats. He also aroused controversy for supporting the rights of abolitionists. From 1836 to 1837, Leggett edited his own paper, the *Plaindealer,* but his health failed, and he died in 1839. Many considered him a Democratic martyr, and

Bryant and John Greenleaf Whittier paid eloquent homage to him.

It is likely Leggett influenced Whitman profoundly, both for his fusion of literature and public life and his relentless individualism. Whitman called him "the glorious Leggett" (Brooklyn *Daily Eagle,* 3 November 1847), and remembered seeing him at the theater in "The Old Bowery." Even at the end of his life, Whitman remembered the old radical fondly, remarking to Horace Traubel that Leggett was "one of the best of 'em" (Traubel 191) at penetrating the legal sophistry of political writing.

Ted Widmer

Bibliography

[Bryant, William Cullen.] "William Leggett." *United States Magazine and Democratic Review* 6 (1839): 17–28.

Leggett, William. *A Collection of the Political Writings of William Leggett.* Ed. Theodore Sedgwick, Jr. New York: Taylor and Dodd, 1840.

———. *Democratick Editorials: Essays in Jacksonian Political Economy.* Ed. Lawrence H. White. Indianapolis: Liberty, 1984.

Meyers, Marvin. *The Jacksonian Persuasion: Politics and Belief.* 1957. New York: Vintage, 1960.

Traubel, Horace. *With Walt Whitman in Camden.* Vol. 2. 1908. New York: Rowman and Littlefield, 1961.

See also BARNBURNERS AND LOCOFOCOS; BRYANT, WILLIAM CULLEN; DEMOCRATIC PARTY; NEW YORK *EVENING POST*

Leland, Charles Godfrey (1824–1903)

Charles Godfrey Leland was born in Philadelphia on 15 August 1824. He graduated from Princeton University in 1845 and spent the next three years in Europe, studying at Heidelberg and Munich. Upon returning to Philadelphia, he studied law and practiced briefly beginning in 1851 before turning to a career as a writer and journalist. During his lifetime, he was best known for his playful and popular "Hans Breitmann" poems which, in their cleverly twisted Anglo-German dialect, displayed Leland's considerable linguistic skills. Those skills were also evident in his translation of Heinrich Heine's *Pictures of Travel* and *Book of Songs* (1855) and in his studies of Romany, Etruscan, Shelta, and other equally obscure languages and dialects. Leland's role in founding an industrial arts school in Philadelphia (1881) is evidence of his practical commitment to popular education. His connection with Whitman came first by way of his brother Henry, whom Whitman recalled fondly as an early supporter, and by way of his translation of Heine's *Pictures,* which Whitman read in 1856. More directly, the connection was established in Whitman's later years when Leland's frequent visits to "Gypsy" communities in Camden included visits with Whitman. It is unlikely that Leland directly influenced Whitman's writing (except, perhaps, by way of the Heine translation), but they were drawn together by common interests in common folk, and their ways of expressing those interests is mutually illuminating.

Steven Schroeder

Bibliography

Leland, Charles Godfrey. *Memoirs.* 2 vols. London: William Heinemann, 1893.

Pennell, Elizabeth Robins. *Charles Godfrey Leland: A Biography.* 2 vols. Boston and New York: Houghton Mifflin, 1906.

See also HEINE, HEINRICH; LELAND, HENRY PERRY; PHILADELPHIA, PENNSYLVANIA

Leland, Henry Perry (1828–1868)

Leland was an early supporter of Whitman, and Whitman credited Leland with providing him renewed inspiration during a period of despair by sending an encouraging personal letter of support.

The younger brother of Charles G. Leland, Henry Leland was also a writer. His works include *Americans in Rome, Grey-Bay Mare and Other Humorous American Sketches,* and he is the supposed author of *Americans in Paris.* Fatally wounded in the Civil War, he died five years later.

Leland's article "Walt Whitman" in the *Saturday Press* (1860) was an enthusiastic endorsement of the poet which urged readers to discover Whitman.

Patricia J. Tyrer

Bibliography

Leland, Charles Godfrey. *Memoirs.* 2 vols. London: William Heinemann, 1893.

Stovall, Floyd. *The Foreground of "Leaves of Grass."* Charlottesville: UP of Virginia, 1974.

See also LELAND, CHARLES GODFREY; SATURDAY PRESS

"Letter to Ralph Waldo Emerson" (1856)

Though Whitman placed it in the appendix of the second edition of *Leaves of Grass* (1856), alongside the famous letter Emerson wrote him a year earlier, the "Letter to Ralph Waldo Emerson" could just as well serve as the preface to the second edition, for it is a statement of Whitman's objectives as a poet.

Addressing Emerson as "dear Friend and Master" (Whitman 1326), Whitman presents the thirty-two poems of the 1856 *Leaves* to him as his response to Emerson's gracious, and until then unanswered, letter. Allowing that he much enjoys "making poems," Whitman rejoices in the fact that the United States is founding a literature "swiftly, on limitless foundations" (1327). Saying that "that huge English flow" has done much good in the United States, he calls for new great masters to comprehend new arts, and urges Americans to "strangle the singers who will not sing you loud and strong" (1328).

Whitman marvels at the "nourishments" (1329) to literature available in the United States, the progress of popular reading and writing in the past fifty years, the thousands of authors and editors, the twenty-one giant steam presses (of twenty-four in the world), and the some twelve thousand shops for dispensing books and newspapers.

Echoing Emerson in "The American Scholar," Whitman calls for a native literature, saying that the "genius of all foreign literature is clipped and cut small" and is, when viewed from the American perspective, "haggard, dwarfed, ludicrous" (1330).

In long, cascading sentences, Whitman celebrates the American poets "walking freely out from the old traditions" (1333) and sees poetry even in the scientific advances, "those splendid resistless black poems, the steam-ships of the sea-board states, and those other resistless splendid poems, the locomotives" (1334). Calling for an end to censorship, Whitman says that the courageous soul may be proved by faith in sex. Suggesting that a degree of agitation and turbulence is good for America, he admits: "As for me, I love screaming, wrestling, boiling-hot days" (1336).

Concluding the letter, Whitman calls Emerson "the original true Captain who put to sea" and assures him of his loyalty and that of "all the young men" (1336).

Henry Bryan Binns finds the "Letter" disagreeable to read, filled with careless, egotistical, naive, and exaggerated remarks. Sculley Bradley and Harold Blodgett question Whitman's claim at the beginning of the letter that a thousand copies of the first edition of *Leaves* (1855) "readily sold" (1326), and that "several thousand copies" (1327) of the second edition (1856) were printed; they suggest instead that very few copies of the first edition were sold, and that the rarity of the second edition would seem to indicate that it is unlikely that several thousand copies were run off.

Gay Wilson Allen feels that Whitman sometimes let his dreams outrun his judgment in the letter, and that he sometimes displayed erratic judgment. As to the reference in the beginning and end of the letter to Emerson as "Master," Bradley and Blodgett maintain that in the nineteenth century that word, as applied to a teacher, writer, or artist, did not suggest servility.

Richard Raleigh

Bibliography

Allen, Gay Wilson. *The Solitary Singer: A Critical Biography of Walt Whitman.* 1955. Rev. ed. 1967. Chicago: U of Chicago P, 1985.

Binns, Henry Bryan. *A Life of Walt Whitman.* 1905. New York: Haskell House, 1969.

Loving, Jerome. *Emerson, Whitman, and the American Muse.* Chapel Hill: U of North Carolina P, 1982.

Price, Kenneth M. "Whitman on Emerson: New Light on the 1856 Open Letter." *American Literature* 56 (1984): 83–87.

Whitman, Walt. *Complete Poetry and Collected Prose.* Ed. Justin Kaplan. New York: Library of America, 1982.

See also EMERSON, RALPH WALDO; LEAVES OF GRASS, 1856 EDITION; PREFACE TO LEAVES OF GRASS, 1855 EDITION

Libraries (New York)

The earliest libraries in New York City existed as private collections, some of substantial holdings by the eighteenth century. With the exception of a small deposit of books in Trinity Church, recorded in 1698 and considered the first known nonprofit library, there were few

library enterprises in the eighteenth century. The first library of significance was founded in 1754, when a period of cultural awakening led to the establishment of the New York Society Library, an institution modeled after Benjamin Franklin's Library Company of Philadelphia. The New York Society Library originally operated as a subscription, or social, library which charged a fee for its use and for many years was an enclave for the city's elite. Many of its first directors were also involved in the founding of King's College in 1754, which would later become Columbia University. The college's library, which reached ninth in holdings among American libraries by 1876, was established in 1757. In 1763 the bookseller Garret Noel opened a for-profit lending library and reading room, the first of its kind in the city, the third in the colonies, and from 1797 to 1804, the finest mercantile lending library in North America was operated by Hocquet Caritat of New York City. During the late eighteenth and early nineteenth centuries, specialized libraries began to surface around the city, notably at the New-York Historical Society, Union Theological Seminary, New York Hospital, and the New York Academy of Medicine.

As additional libraries continued to appear throughout the city during the nineteenth century, there can be little doubt that Walt Whitman made use of the increasing availability of books. The circulating library in the village of Jamaica, for example, where Whitman lived while working for the *Long Island Democrat,* contained four hundred volumes in 1838. One of several libraries established for the education and moral improvement of urban workers, the Mercantile Library was probably the best known of its time. It was established in 1821 with seven hundred volumes, and clerks could subscribe by paying an initiation fee of one to two dollars for full use of the reading room and the library. Between 1830 and 1854 it was housed in Clinton Hall at the corner of Nassau and Beekman Streets, a short distance from the boarding houses that Whitman lived in during the years 1842–1844. By 1857 it had holdings of over forty thousand volumes and was later transformed into a general subscription library. Another library within easy reach for Whitman, the Apprentices' Library, was established by the General Society of Mechanics and Tradesmen in 1820 as a free institution reserved for the exclusive use of apprentices. By 1857 it had developed a significant collection of general literature numbering some fourteen thousand volumes. The first privately endowed, independent, free public reference library in the United States was also available to Whitman. The Astor Library, considered the best research library in New York at the time, was established in 1848 and by 1864 it contained over one hundred thousand volumes. Other libraries that Whitman could have accessed include the Harlem Library (1825), the Washington Heights Library (1825), the Brooklyn Apprentices' Library (1820s), and several libraries in Queens.

Between the 1870s and 1890s many of the privately endowed free lending libraries began to receive municipal appropriations under New York state law and were eventually converted into free public libraries. The founding of the New York Public Library in 1895, a merger of the Astor Library, the Lenox Library, and the Tilden Trust, created the impetus for establishing a system of public libraries in New York City, and shortly after the city was consolidated in 1898 it agreed to build and maintain a central building in Manhattan for the institution. These events culminated in the establishment of three public library systems: the Brooklyn Public Library, the Queens Borough Public Library, and the New York Public Library. The establishment of the New York Public Library, combined with a gift of funds from philanthropist Andrew Carnegie, became a catalyst for the absorption of most of the city's free lending libraries and for the construction of new branch library buildings throughout the city. The municipality, in turn, agreed to provide annual maintenance for a public library service, and public libraries in New York City thus became permanently established as essential public services. Whitman, of course, left New York City in the early 1860s and so would not have used the libraries that emerged later in the century.

Charles B. Green

Bibliography

Jackson, Kenneth T., ed. *Encyclopedia of New York City.* New Haven: Yale UP, 1995.
Keep, Austin Baxter. *The Library in Colonial New York.* New York: Ben Franklin, 1970.
Rajasekharaiah, T.R. *The Roots of Whitman's Grass.* Rutherford: Fairleigh Dickinson UP, 1970.
Stovall, Floyd. *The Foreground of "Leaves of Grass."* Charlottesville: UP of Virginia, 1974.

See also NEW YORK CITY

Liebig, Justus (1803–1873)

A Prussian scientist and a pioneer of laboratory education, Justus Liebig was an influential theorist in the field of organic chemistry. When the American edition of Liebig's *Chemistry in its Application to Agriculture and Physiology* appeared in 1847, it made a strong impression on Whitman, who gave it a glowing review in the 28 June 1847 Brooklyn *Daily Eagle.* Liebig was especially interested in the cyclical patterns of nature and the ways in which dead matter is converted into new life. When an organism decomposes, Liebig argued, its atoms recombine into different compounds, leading "to the production of a compound which did not before exist in [the body]" (227). In this process, whatever diseases the body had were destroyed. Liebig saw this process as a type of natural resurrection. David S. Reynolds has recently observed echoes of Liebig's theory in Whitman's metaphors for regeneration in "Song of Myself." Reynolds cites the following passage as an example: "Tenderly will I use you curling grass, / It may be you transpire from the breasts of young men, . . . The smallest sprout shows there is really no death" (section 6). Liebig's influence can also be traced in the shorter poem "This Compost." Reynolds also suggests that Liebig's broad definition of "leaves" as comprising the "green parts of all plants" may have had bearing on Whitman's decision to call his collection *Leaves of Grass* (241).

John T. Matteson

Bibliography

Liebig, Justus. *Organic Chemistry in Its Application to Agriculture and Physiology.* London: Taylor and Walton, 1840.
Reynolds, David S. *Walt Whitman's America: A Cultural Biography.* New York: Knopf, 1995.

See also DEATH; IMMORTALITY; SCIENCE; "THIS COMPOST"

Life Illustrated

A miscellany of literature, agriculture, photography, mechanics, reform movements, and other topics, *Life Illustrated* was a weekly four-page folio printed in New York by Fowler and Wells from 1854 until it merged in 1861 with the *American Phrenological Journal,* another Fowler and Wells publication, to become the *American Phrenological Journal* and *Life Illustrated,* which continued until 1869.

Life Illustrated provided publicity and support for the first two editions of *Leaves of Grass.* Fowler and Wells sold the first edition (July 1855) in their shop at 308 Broadway, and one of the first reviews of *Leaves* appeared in *Life Illustrated* (28 July 1855). They published Ralph Waldo Emerson's letter to Whitman of 21 July, "I greet you at the beginning of a great career" (20 October); they responded to Rufus Griswold's criticisms in the *Criterion* with the "Annihilation of Walt Whitman" (15 December); and they reprinted favorable material from other periodicals such as Fanny Fern's review in the New York *Ledger* (17 May 1856) and an unsigned review in the London *Leader* (19 July 1856).

Meanwhile, Whitman resumed his journalistic career at *Life Illustrated* from November 1855 to August 1856. His publications covered a range of topics: "The Opera" (10 November); "The Egyptian Museum" (8 December); "Christmas at 'Grace'" (26 January); "America's Mightiest Inheritance [The English Language]" (12 April); "Decent Homes for Working-Men" (12 April); and "Voltaire" (10 May). He also published a series of articles in *Life Illustrated* called "New York Dissected," which included "The Fourth of July" (12 July); "Wicked Architecture" (19 July); "The Slave Trade" (2 August); "Broadway" (9 August); and "Street Yarn" (16 August).

In 1856 Fowler and Wells agreed to finance the second edition of *Leaves of Grass.* An article in *Life Illustrated* (16 August) proclaims the popularity of the first edition and announces the advent of a second edition with "amendments and additions," including Emerson's famous greeting on the spine. Nevertheless, Whitman was dissatisfied with Fowler and Wells as publishers, and his relationship with them soon dissolved, along with his connection to *Life Illustrated.*

William A. Pannapacker

Bibliography

Allen, Gay Wilson. *The Solitary Singer: A Critical Biography of Walt Whitman.* 1955. Rev. ed. 1967. Chicago: U of Chicago P, 1985.

Mott, Frank Luther. *A History of American Magazines.* 5 vols. Cambridge, Mass.: Harvard UP, 1938–1968.

Whitman, Walt. *New York Dissected.* Ed. Emory Holloway and Ralph Adimari. New York: Rufus Rockwell Wilson, 1936.

See also AMERICAN PHRENOLOGICAL JOURNAL; FOWLER, LORENZO NILES AND ORSON SQUIRE; JOURNALISM, WHITMAN'S; LEAVES OF GRASS, 1855 EDITION; LEAVES OF GRASS, 1856 EDITION; WELLS, SAMUEL ROBERTS

Lincoln, Abraham (1809–1865)

Abraham Lincoln was the sixteenth president of the United States (1861–1865). Walt Whitman and Abraham Lincoln are often linked as kindred spirits for their commitment to democratic ideals, the preservation of the Union, and the greatness of the common folk. Lincoln's two inaugural addresses (1861, 1865) and his "Gettysburg Address" (1863), along with Whitman's *Drum-Taps* (1865), are among the most significant literary products of the Civil War. Whitman's poems, "O Captain! My Captain!" and "When Lilacs Last in the Dooryard Bloom'd," published as a sequel to *Drum-Taps* in 1865, became the most admired poetic tributes to the assassinated president. After the Civil War, Whitman was increasingly identified with Lincoln because of numerous newspaper and magazine articles, *Memoranda During the War* (1875–1876), *Specimen Days & Collect* (1882), and his lecture "Death of Abraham Lincoln" (1879). "Lincoln," Whitman said, "is particularly my man" (qtd. in Barton 170).

Lincoln probably knew little about Whitman. There is an account of Lincoln reading *Leaves of Grass* in his Springfield law office, and the president is reported to have seen Whitman in Washington, D.C., and said, "Well, he looks like a man!" (qtd. in Barton 96). William Barton, in his study of the two men, shows that these events are probably fabrications. Yet there were political, rhetorical, and biographical similarities that supported an association of Whitman with Lincoln. As Whitman observed, they were "afloat in the same stream" and "rooted in the same ground" (qtd. in Barton 170). Both opposed the expansion of slavery, but they were not abolitionists. Both were committed to free labor and territorial expansion, but the preservation of the Union was paramount. Both revered the heroes of the American Revolution, particularly Washington; neither adhered to any religious sect. They shared working-class origins, and each adopted the rhetoric of Jacksonian populism. Their literary styles were both influenced by the Bible, William Shakespeare, Thomas Paine, and Robert Burns; both also tapped the vitality of American vernacular speech, political oratory, and drama. Lincoln even seems an incarnation of the poet-redeemer described in the 1855 Preface to Whitman's *Leaves of Grass,* and Whitman himself would later imply that they were comparable types: "Lincoln gets almost nearer me than anybody else" (*With Walt Whitman* 1:38).

In 1856 Whitman describes his ideal president as a "heroic, shrewd, fully-inform'd, healthy-bodied, middle-aged, beard-faced American blacksmith or boatman" emerging from the West (*Prose Works* 2:535). But Whitman was not initially enthusiastic about Lincoln; his admiration grew from personal exposure. When Lincoln visited New York en route to Washington in 1861, his striking appearance and unpretentious dignity made a lasting first impression on Whitman. While living in Washington from 1862 to 1865, Whitman observed the president regularly and came to trust the "supernatural tact" and "idiomatic Western genius" of his "captain" (*Correspondence* 1:83). He admired the president's plainness, his homespun humor; he often contemplated Lincoln's face, "the peculiar color, the lines of it, the eyes, mouth, expression" (*Prose Works* 1:100). No portrait, he repeatedly said, had ever captured Lincoln's "goodness, tenderness, sadness, and canny shrewdness" (*Prose Works* 1:92). In 1863 Whitman writes, "I love the President personally," and the poems of *Drum-Taps* soon echoed the themes of Lincoln's speeches (*Notebooks* 2:539).

Whitman was deeply moved by Lincoln's death on Good Friday, 14 April 1865. It was a personal tragedy, but it also seemed like the culminating sacrifice of an epic poem. *Drum-Taps* was incomplete without some concluding tribute to Lincoln. Whitman eventually added four poems: "O Captain! My Captain!," "When Lilacs Last in the Dooryard Bloom'd," "Hush'd be the Camps To-day," and "This Dust was Once the Man." "O Captain!" describes the poet's grief for the Union's fallen helmsman in uncharacteristically conventional verse. "Lilacs," on the other hand, is a complex threnody that moves from personal loss to a contemplation of mortality in general. Without specifically mentioning Lincoln, it transforms his assassination into a redemptive martyrdom that restores the poet's lost voice and binds up the shattered Union.

In later years, Whitman was divided between a ritualized commitment to Lincoln's memory, stated at the outset of "Lilacs," and increasingly self-serving demonstrations of civic piety. The Lincoln poems, particularly "O Captain!," were received indulgently; they helped to make the controversial author of *Leaves* more acceptable to genteel readers. With the aid of supporters like William D. O'Connor, Whitman promoted himself as an authority on Lincoln, a comparable type, and even the object of Lincoln's admiration. Whitman's lecture on the assassination at Ford's Theater, "Death of Abraham Lincoln," was an annual rite between 1879 and 1890 in which Lincoln became America's mythical "Martyr Chief," and Whitman became the Good Gray Poet (*Prose Works* 2:509). Whitman thought "O Captain!" to be one of his weaker poems and often tired of reading it. "Damn My Captain," he said, "I'm almost sorry I ever wrote the poem" (*With Walt Whitman* 2:304). Nevertheless, he almost always concluded his lectures with an emotional reading of "O Captain!" Like Washington, Lincoln had entered the American civil religion, and Whitman submitted to demands for a conventional elegist. It was a profitable venture, for it kept Whitman before the public long enough to reveal the value of his other works.

William A. Pannapacker

Bibliography

Barton, William E. *Abraham Lincoln and Walt Whitman.* Indianapolis: Bobbs-Merrill, 1928.

Coyle, William, ed. *The Poet and the President: Whitman's Lincoln Poems.* New York: Odyssey, 1962.

Grossman, Allan. "The Poetics of Union in Whitman and Lincoln: An Inquiry Toward the Relationship of Art and Policy." *The American Renaissance Reconsidered.* Ed. Walter Benn Michaels and Donald E. Pease. Baltimore: Johns Hopkins UP, 1985. 183–208.

Lincoln, Abraham. *The Collected Works of Abraham Lincoln.* Ed. Roy P. Basler. 9 vols. New Brunswick: Rutgers UP, 1953–1955.

Traubel, Horace. *With Walt Whitman in Camden.* Vol. 1. Boston: Small, Maynard, 1906; Vol. 2. New York: D. Appleton, 1908.

Whitman, Walt. *The Correspondence.* Ed. Edwin Haviland Miller. 6 vols. New York: New York UP, 1961–1977.

———. *Notebooks and Unpublished Prose Manuscripts.* Ed. Edward F. Grier. 6 vols. New York: New York UP, 1984.

———. *Prose Works 1892.* Ed. Floyd Stovall. 2 vols. New York: New York UP, 1963–1964.

See also CIVIL WAR, THE; "DEATH OF ABRAHAM LINCOLN"; LINCOLN'S DEATH; "MEMORIES OF PRESIDENT LINCOLN"; "O CAPTAIN! MY CAPTAIN!"; PRESIDENTS, UNITED STATES; "WHEN LILACS LAST IN THE DOORYARD BLOOM'D"

Lincoln's Death

The death of Abraham Lincoln had a profound impact on Walt Whitman and his writing. It is the subject of one of his most highly regarded and critically examined pieces, "When Lilacs Last in the Dooryard Bloom'd" (1865–1866) and one of his best-known poems, "O Captain! My Captain!" (1865–1866). Whitman also delivered (sporadically) annual public lectures commemorating Lincoln's death beginning in April 1879. Although the two never met, Whitman and Lincoln, both deeply committed to the Union, remain intertwined in Whitman's writing and in American mythology.

Whitman intensely admired Lincoln from the late 1850s onward, remarking at one point, "After my dear, dear mother, I guess Lincoln gets almost nearer me than anybody else" (Traubel 38). On the Friday of 14 April 1865, when John Wilkes Booth shot Lincoln at Ford's Theater in Washington, D.C., Whitman was in New York and read about the assassination in the daily newspapers and extras.

His first poem responding to Lincoln's death came only a couple of days later when he added to *Drum-Taps* (1865), already in press, a short piece titled "Hush'd be the Camps To-day" (1865). Although it ends solemnly with "the heavy hearts of soldiers," this public commemoration of Lincoln's funeral—spoken to the poet by and for Union soldiers—asks us to "celebrate" his death, as it remembers "the love we bore him." "Hush'd be the Camps To-day" is not one of Whitman's best-known poems, but it is significant not merely because it was his first poetic word on Lincoln's death, but also because it exemplifies the primary features that generally characterize Whitman's poetic treatment of Lincoln's death: as in "Lilacs," the poem mourns for the dead but celebrates death; it identifies Lincoln's death with the coming of peace; and it remembers Lincoln not because he was a great leader or conqueror but because he was well loved. The poem also associates Lincoln with the war's ordinary soldiers, an association that prefigures "Lilacs" and its treatment of Lincoln's death as a metonymy for all the war dead.

"Hush'd be the Camps To-day" and the other Lincoln poems ("Lilacs," "O Captain!," and "This Dust was Once the Man" [1871]) never mention Lincoln by name. As some critics have noted, Whitman had no need in the postbellum era to refer directly to Lincoln because his readers would easily recognize these poems as elegies for President Lincoln. Later, after the immediacy of Lincoln's death had faded into historical memory, Whitman identified the subject of these poems by grouping the four of them together, first in a cluster titled "President Lincoln's Burial Hymn" in an annex to *Passage to India* (1871) and later in the "Memories of President Lincoln" cluster in the 1881 edition of *Leaves of Grass*. Other critics believe that the lack of direct reference to Lincoln indicates the poet's attempt to address universal themes.

Whitman does, of course, use Lincoln's death to talk about subjects beyond the events at Ford's Theater, including the subject of death itself. In "Lilacs," Whitman reconciles himself and the nation to Lincoln's death and death in general by fashioning the historical fact of the assassination and burial into a spiritual embrace of death in which death becomes both a personal and a national regeneration and cleansing. The treatment of Lincoln's death in "Lilacs" is famous for its symbolism and its formal, musical qualities. Indeed the poem relentlessly transforms its historical content into symbols. Lincoln as a person disappears only to reappear as a "western fallen star" and as the evoked metonymic associations of the poem's other symbols and images—coffin, lilacs, cloud, and the hermit thrush's song.

Whitman's handling of Lincoln's death in the lectures diametrically reverses the musical, ethereal, often abstract, heavily symbolized style of "Lilacs." In his lecture on the "Death of Abraham Lincoln" (1879), Whitman depicts the scene of the murder with dramatic immediacy, as if he were an eyewitness. The narration is suspenseful, detailed, and focuses on specifics (sometimes minutiae). Although Whitman was not an eyewitness, his close companion, Peter Doyle, was at Ford's Theater, and Whitman made impressive use of Doyle's story in his imaginative retelling. In the lecture, the president's murder is not a bizarre denouement to an inevitable war but rather the culmination of and solution to all the historic, national conflicts of the Civil War era. Lincoln's death becomes a metaphor for the bloody war itself and the climax of a lofty tragic drama that redeems the Union. Whitman's lecture turns Lincoln's assassination into the ceremonial sacrifice that gives new life to the nation.

Whitman's Lincoln possessed an undeniably heroic stature. Whitman called him "the grandest figure yet, on all the crowded canvas of the Nineteenth Century" (*Prose Works* 2:604). Still, the poet did not merely apotheosize the dead president; he also transformed Lincoln and his death into a symbolic referent for thoughts on the war, comradeship, democracy, union, and death. Perhaps best exemplified by the "Lilacs" elegy, Lincoln's death became the event around which Whitman twined so sadly and beautifully his understanding of death's affiliation with love.

Gregory Eiselein

Bibliography

Allen, Gay Wilson. *The Solitary Singer: A Critical Biography of Walt Whitman.* 1955. Rev. ed. 1967. Chicago: U of Chicago P, 1985.

Erkkila, Betsy. *Whitman the Political Poet.* New York: Oxford UP, 1989.

Larson, Kerry C. *Whitman's Drama of Consensus.* Chicago: U of Chicago P, 1988.

Reynolds, David S. *Walt Whitman's America: A Cultural Biography.* New York: Knopf, 1995.

Traubel, Horace. *With Walt Whitman in Camden.* Vol. 1. Boston: Small, Maynard, 1906.

Whitman, Walt. *Leaves of Grass: Comprehensive Reader's Edition.* Ed. Harold W. Blodgett and Sculley Bradley. New York: New York UP, 1965.

———. *Memoranda During the War & Death of Abraham Lincoln.* Ed. Roy P. Basler. Bloomington: Indiana UP, 1962.

———. *Prose Works 1892.* Ed. Floyd Stovall. 2 vols. New York: New York UP, 1963–1964.

———. *Walt Whitman's "Drum-Taps" (1865) and "Sequel to Drum-Taps" (1865–6): A Facsimile Reproduction.* Ed. F. DeWolfe Miller. Gainesville: Scholars' Facsimiles and Reprints, 1959.

See also "DEATH OF ABRAHAM LINCOLN"; LINCOLN, ABRAHAM; "MEMORIES OF PRESIDENT LINCOLN"; "O CAPTAIN! MY CAPTAIN!"; "WHEN LILACS LAST IN THE DOORYARD BLOOM'D"

"Lingave's Temptation"

First publication data for "Lingave's Temptation" is unknown. A clipping of the tale, obviously from a periodical, is in the Feinberg Collection with Whitman's handwritten revisions. The revised story was printed in *Specimen Days & Collect* (1882). For publication particulars and revisions, see Brasher's edition of *The Early Poems and the Fiction.*

This tale is unique in Whitman's fiction; its hero is a poet, "a master of elegant diction, of fine taste, in style passionate yet pure, and of the delicate imagery that belongs to the children of song" (Whitman 333). Lingave's temptation is that, while bitterly unhappy about being poor, he is offered a position using his talents in the cause of some repulsive economic scheme. Lingave overcomes the temptation and plods on in his poverty as before.

The story contains some noteworthy observations about the poet's psyche. Lingave, like Archibald in "The Shadow and the Light of a Young Man's Soul," is given to angry reflection, but the poet is easily drawn from his envy by the simple joys around him.

Parts of the story, written in a kind of editorial "we," are addressed to Lingave: "O, Lingave, be more of a man!" (331). This direct address is followed by a paragraph about us and them. It is "our circle of understanding" versus them, their possessions, and the "lowly flights of their crippled wings" (332).

It is possible to infer that Lingave's rejection of work that would compromise his talent is in effect parallel to Whitman's own dissatisfaction with much of the writing he had done throughout the 1840s.

The story has received little critical attention.

Patrick McGuire

Bibliography

Whitman, Walt. *The Early Poems and the Fiction.* Ed. Thomas L. Brasher. New York: New York UP, 1963.

See also "SHADOW AND THE LIGHT OF A YOUNG MAN'S SOUL, THE"; SHORT FICTION, WHITMAN'S

Literariness

Walt Whitman hated "Literary Literature" (*Notebooks* 4:1594) and he wrote condemning literariness. "No one will get at my verses who insists upon viewing them as a literary performance, or attempt at such performance, or as aiming mainly toward art or aestheticism," he emphasized in "A Backward Glance O'er Travel'd Roads," his prose epilogue to *Leaves of Grass* (*Comprehensive* 574). "I am not literary, my books are not literature," he proclaimed to Horace Traubel (*With Walt Whitman* 2:460). Whitman detested not only artificial, polite, decorous parlor verse, but all literature and literary analysis which emphasized performance rather than persuasion.

Whitman was a rhetorician. His purpose was to reach people, to "filter and fibre" their blood, to use his "New Bible" to help create the physically perfected and spiritually dilated individuals of an evolved society, the Religious Democracy. "The whole drift of my books is to form a new race of fuller & athletic yet unknown characters, men & women, for the United States to come. I do not write to amuse or furnish fine poetry, so-called . . ." he wrote in 1869 (*Notebooks* 4:1508). As a rhetorician, Whitman emphasized message, not form. "I do not value literature as a profession," he told Traubel. "I feel about literature what Grant did about war. He hated war. I hate literature . . . it is a means to an end, that is all there is to it: I never attribute any other significance to it" (*With Walt Whitman* 1:58). "I don't value the poetry in what I have written so much as the teaching; the poetry is only a horse for the other to ride," he told an unsympathetic critic (qtd. in Thayer 678). From Whitman's perspective, literariness, literary analysis, the "tendency permitted to Literature . . . to magnify & intensify its own technism" (*Notebooks* 4:1603) not only provided inappropriate criteria for assessing his work but was also a tool used by literary professionals to distort his message and frustrate his purposes. Focus on literariness undermined persuasiveness. Thus he wrote and spoke harshly of the advocates of art for art's sake and of literary professionals—the "disciples of finesse" and the "protagonists of filigree" (*With Walt Whitman* 2:529). "Literature," he declared, "is big only in one way—when used as an aid in the growth of the humanities—a furthering of the cause of the masses—a means whereby men may be revealed to each other as brothers" (*With Walt Whitman* 1:283).

Alas, however, literary professionalism, fortified in the twentieth century by an academic sinecure, fully absorbed Whitman and his works into literary literature. It was a fate which he expected and feared with good reason. To keep Whitman salient while the Pound–Eliot–New Criticism crowd were in control, his apologists set aside his rhetorical purposes as irrelevant, or embarrassing, while shifting focus to his literary performance. Assistant professors earning tenure by conducting partitive studies of "Song of Myself" to prove his "craftsmanship" were not the responses Whitman intended! Louis H. Sullivan's architecture, Clarence S. Darrow's social commitment, and Hamlin Garland's provocative writings were. In an era in which deconstruction of the Bible as literature is common, however, it is not surprising that only "our" Whitman the poet rather than Whitman the persuader of personalism survives.

In the nineteenth and early twentieth centuries many men and women did respond appropriately to the supraliterary rhetorical dimensions of *Leaves of Grass*. Sullivan, Darrow, Garland, and others similarly influenced had an advantage, however. They read the works that Whitman personally honed page by page to his purposes. Today's readers experience *Leaves of Grass* in editions that are anthologized, introduced, reorganized, shortened, elongated, footnoted, endnoted, edited, and generally overwhelmed with the paraphernalia of literary literature. Whitman's horse is corralled by literariness. Yet, had Whitman been a less skilled writer, and perhaps a better organizer, and Mary Baker Eddy a better writer and less skilled organizer, the places of the two contemporaries in American culture might easily have been reversed.

John Lee Jellicorse

Bibliography

Jellicorse, John Lee. "Whitman and Modern Literary Criticism." *Whitman in Our Season*. Ed. B. Bernard Cohen. Hartford: Transcendental Books, 1971. 4–11.

Thayer, William Roscoe. "Personal Recollections of Walt Whitman." *Scribner's Magazine* 65 (1919): 674–687. Rpt. in *Whitman in His Own Time*. Ed. Joel Myerson. Detroit: Omnigraphics, 1991. 283–308.

Traubel, Horace. *With Walt Whitman in Camden*. Vol. 1. Boston: Small, Maynard, 1906; Vol. 2. New York: Appleton, 1908; Vol. 4. Ed. Sculley Bradley. Philadelphia: U of Pennsylvania P, 1953.

Whitman, Walt. *Leaves of Grass: Comprehensive Reader's Edition*. Ed. Harold W. Blodgett and Sculley Bradley. New York: New York UP, 1965.
———. *Notebooks and Unpublished Prose Manuscripts*. Ed. Edward F. Grier. 6 vols. New York: New York UP, 1984.

See also AMERICAN CHARACTER; POETIC THEORY; RELIGION; RHETORICAL THEORY AND PRACTICE

Literature

Walt Whitman's conception of literature grew, in part, from his larger theory of American democracy. He insisted that we would become a great democratic nation only if America developed its own national literature. In the 1876 Preface to the Centennial edition of *Leaves of Grass* he wrote that "the true growth-characteristics of the democracy of the New World are henceforth to radiate in superior literary, artistic and religious expressions" (Whitman 465). And in *Democratic Vistas* he wrote that "what finally and only is to make of our western world a nationality superior to any hitherto known, and outtopping the past, must be vigorous, yet unsuspected Literatures, perfect personalities and sociologies, original, transcendental, and expressing . . . democracy and the modern" (364). No person, in Whitman's opinion, was better suited for this challenge than the well-trained poet of America.

In fact his definition of the poet in the 1855 Preface is a foreshadowing of what would become one of the most convincing aspects of Whitman's democratic theory, the need for a national literature. In the Preface he wrote that the poet "is a seer—he is individual—he is complete in himself—the others are as good as he, only he sees it, and they do not. He is not one of the chorus—he does not stop for any regulation—he is the president of regulation. What the eyesight does to the rest, he does to the rest" (438). It is quite probable, in fact, that he was defining himself, since the rhetoric of his definition sounds suspiciously like the rhetoric found in "Song of Myself," where he proclaimed himself to be the great "seer."

Establishing himself, then, as the spiritual leader of America, Whitman took on a messianic voice in his pledge to fight for equality and freedom for the people. He was the great savior, come to grant salvation to the American

common man: "The priest departs, the divine literatus comes" (365). And as the great poetic prophet, Whitman preached the importance of establishing a sound, national literature. In *Vistas* he announces that "Above all previous lands, a great original literature is surely to become the justification and reliance, (in some respects the sole reliance,) of American democracy" (366). He believed that literature was the great penetrator, able to shape the individual as well as the masses. Moreover, Whitman saw literature in America as powerful enough to cause changes and growth in a society destined to lead the world.

Whitman also acknowledged the historical shortcomings of literature and pointed to the effects of such failures on nineteenth-century America. He contended that "Literature, strictly consider'd, has never recognized the People, and, whatever may be said, does not to-day. Speaking generally, the tendencies of literature, as hitherto pursued, have been to make mostly critical and querulous men. It seems as if, so far, there were some natural repugnance between a literary and professional life, and the rude rank spirit of the democracies" (376). It was Whitman's goal to create a literature for America that would recognize the people, a literature that would add strength to his democratic theory.

The one redeeming factor about the prospects for a national literature is that Whitman saw in it a growth process that paralleled the growth of the individual, society, and language, three components that, combined with a literature for America, would all but ensure the future stability and advancement of our country. Whitman believed that "first-class literature does not shine by any luminosity of its own; nor do its poems. They grow of circumstances, and are evolutionary" (717). And in "American National Literature," he pleaded with the reader to see the simplicity of his argument: "[F]irst, that the highest developments of the New World and Democracy, and probably the best society of the civilized world all over, are to be only reached and spinally nourish'd (in my notion) by a new evolutionary sense and treatment; and, secondly, that the evolution-principle, which is the greatest law through nature, and of course in these States, has now reach'd us markedly for and in our literature" (667). Literature, because it grows from the same "evolution-principle" as those whose lives it affects, became the great tool which the poet would use to help shape and perfect America's future. It is the poet, after all, who "does not moralize or make applications of morals—he knows the soul" (443). As the great spiritual eye, it was also the poet, according to Whitman, who understood that "the real poems of the present, ever solidifying and expanding into the future, must vocalize the vastness and splendor and reality with which scientism has invested man and the universe . . . and must henceforth launch humanity into new orbits, consonant with that vastness, splendor, and reality . . . like new systems of orbs, balanced upon themselves, revolving in limitless space, more subtle than the stars" (472). The poet, seeing both past and future with his spiritual eye, became, for Whitman, the spokesperson who would "vocalize the vastness and splendor of reality" of nineteenth-century America.

Robert W. Barnett

Bibliography

Reynolds, David S. "Whitman's America: A Revaluation of the Cultural Backgrounds of *Leaves of Grass*." *The Mickle Street Review* 9.2 (1988): 5–17.

Scholnick, Robert J. "Of War Times and Poetry and Democracy: A Final Visit With Whitman." *Walt Whitman Review* 28 (1982): 32–34.

Whitman, Walt. *Prose Works 1892*. Ed. Floyd Stovall. Vol. 2. New York: New York UP, 1964.

See also DEMOCRACY; DEMOCRATIC VISTAS; FEUDALISM; POETIC THEORY; PREFACE TO LEAVES OF GRASS, 1855 EDITION

"Little Jane" (1842)

This short story and "The Death of Wind-Foot" initially appeared as embedded tales in Whitman's temperance novel, *Franklin Evans* (1842). It appeared separately with its title in the Brooklyn *Daily Eagle,* 7 December 1846. For publication history and revisions, see Brasher's edition of *The Early Poems and the Fiction.*

A young fellow, Mike, is riotously drinking with his friends. An elder brother comes to warn him that their little sister, Jane, is nearing death. Mike scoffs that for three years now such warnings have taken him from his partying, and she is still alive. The elder brother goes home alone, and Mike returns to the tavern, but his heart is laden with guilt. At home, little Jane dispenses keepsakes to her parents and siblings. The last one is reserved for Mike; it is a religious story for children, which Jane's mother had given her. Finally, Mike comes home and the children's stern father wishes him barred from Jane's sickbed. But the little girl summons Mike and, with her dying breath, gives him the religious storybook. Mike thereafter is a reformed man.

This temperance tale easily parallels "Reuben's Last Wish" (1842), in which an intemperate father reforms when he is given an embroidered pledge as the last act of his dying son.

As a story, "Little Jane" is slight, but it contains some typical themes of Whitman's fiction: tension between father and son, enmity between brothers, reformation of a drunkard through a child's act. Also, Whitman quite openly expresses some interesting ideas about death and children. For example, "Children . . . increase in beauty as their illness deepens" and "a solemn kind of loveliness . . . surrounds a sick child" (198).

The story has received little critical attention.

Patrick McGuire

Bibliography

Whitman, Walt. *The Early Poems and the Fiction*. Ed. Thomas L. Brasher. New York: New York UP, 1963.

See also FRANKLIN EVANS; "REUBEN'S LAST WISH"; SHORT FICTION, WHITMAN'S

"Little Sleighers, The" (1844)

"The Little Sleighers. A Sketch of a Winter Morning on the Battery" first appeared in *Columbian Magazine*, September 1844. For publication particulars, see Brasher's edition of *The Early Poems and the Fiction.*

This sketch is ostensibly about that section of Manhattan called the Battery and the bitterly cold wind. But description of these gives way easily to a meditation on the joys of childhood, as manifest in the happy antics of the children on their sleds whom the speaker encounters on a noontime walk through the Battery. Like the bachelor-speaker of "My Boys and Girls," the speaker here knows that the way to keep his heart fresh and outlook young is to mix with those who are "fresh" and "youthful" (255). He comments favorably on the custom of covering the corpses of children with flowers, for flowers, which fade quickly, are fitting emblems of children. Childhood here, as in "My Boys and Girls," calls up other reminders of the sorrows of the world and especially of death. Of these young sleighers, the speaker concludes, "All, all will repose at last" (256).

The speaker undermines the starkness of this vision by accusing himself of having become a "sombre moralist." He calls these dark thoughts his "mottled reveries" and would rather carry home with him the gleeful music of the children's voices (256).

Critical attention to the sketch has been limited to cursory descriptions of the piece.

Patrick McGuire

Bibliography

Allen, Gay Wilson. *The Solitary Singer: A Critical Biography of Walt Whitman.* 1955. Rev. ed. 1967. Chicago: U of Chicago P, 1985.

Callow, Philip. *From Noon To Starry Night: A Life of Walt Whitman.* Chicago: Ivan R. Dee, 1992.

Whitman, Walt. *The Early Poems and the Fiction.* Ed. Thomas L. Brasher. New York: New York UP, 1963.

See also "MY BOYS AND GIRLS"; SHORT FICTION, WHITMAN'S

"Live Oak with Moss" (1953–1954)

According to Fredson Bowers, this important sequence of twelve love poems was probably composed shortly before the spring of 1859. Whitman included all twelve poems in the first publication of "Calamus" in the 1860 *Leaves of Grass,* but he rearranged and absorbed them into the longer sequence, thereby obliterating their identity as a discreet work. (In published form, the poems became "Calamus" numbers 14, 20, 11, 23, 8, 32, 10, 9, 34, 43, 36, and 42.) Whitman never published "Live Oak with Moss," and no one even knew of its existence until Bowers discovered it in the early 1950s while working on the Valentine-Barrett manuscripts now at the University of Virginia (Whitman's holographs for most of the new poems in the 1860 edition). Bowers found that twelve poems among the manuscripts, clearly fair copies of lost originals, had originally composed a little notebook; the poems were written on identical paper and numbered in consecutive Roman numerals, and they formed a coherent narrative of a love affair with a man. Bowers published his discovery almost a century after Whitman composed the sequence.

"Live Oak" tells the story of the speaker's infatuation with a male lover, his abandonment, and his accommodation to his loss. The first poem is an ecstatic declaration of love, followed by "I Saw in Louisiana a Live-Oak Growing," the poem that provides the title of the sequence. The lovers are united in the third poem, "When I Heard at the Close of the Day." In the fifth poem, the speaker announces that he can no longer sing "the songs of the New World," for his lover "withdraws me from all but love." In the seventh he asks "bards of ages hence" to remember him not as a poet, but as "the tenderest lover," who was proud only of "the measureless ocean of love within him." In the next poem, one of the most despairing Whitman ever wrote, the speaker has been abandoned, and the remaining four poems recount his accommodation to his loss. The sequence concludes with an address to "the young man" who would become "eleve of mine," presumably learning from the speaker what he himself has learned from his unhappy experience. Having begun the sequence as an ardent lover, he ends it as a paternal teacher, rather like the Good Gray Poet that Whitman was soon to become.

"Live Oak" appears to be Whitman's attempt at a sonnet sequence, and in fact he refers to "A Cluster of Poems, Sonnets" on the back of a separate manuscript of the title poem. Although several of the poems approach the sonnet's length and employ its formal "turn," they are sonnets only in the loosest sense of the word. Whitman's principal influence is William Shakespeare, since Shakespeare provided him not only with a model for writing a sonnet sequence but also sanction for writing about homosexual love. In "Live Oak" number 8 Whitman echoes Shakespeare's Sonnet 121 ("I am that I am") when he writes "I am what I am."

That "Live Oak" had a special significance for Whitman is proved by his having copied the poems in the little notebook that Bowers discovered, but why he never published them or even mentioned them remains a mystery. He may have felt that the subject of the sequence was too sensitive, or that the sequence was too autobiographically revealing. (Charley Shively has identified the lover of "Live Oak" and "Calamus" as Fred Vaughan, a young man who lived with Whitman and his family in Brooklyn in the late 1850s.) In any case the sequence contains some of Whitman's best writing in the short lyric, including the title poem and "When I Heard at the Close of the Day," often called one of the most beautiful love poems in English. Among the most personally revealing of the poems, numbers 5 and 8 also show Whitman's talents to advantage, but they are less well-known than they deserve to be since Whitman suppressed them after 1860; they therefore do not appear in most indexes of his poetry. (The interested reader should consult the 1860 edition, where these poems appear as "Calamus" numbers 8 and 9.)

It is hard to overestimate the importance of "Live Oak," both as a discrete sequence and as a central document in Whitman's life and work. For one thing, it gives us the most extended treatment of male homosexual love in all of his poetry; for another, insofar as it appears to be autobiographical, it shows Whitman's dawning awareness of the cost of expressing his homosexuality, and it may thus explain why he avoids the subjects of personal love and sexuality after the 1860 edition. It formed the nucleus of "Calamus," and it gave Whitman the idea of the "cluster," a formal feature that plays an essential role in his arrangement of all subsequent editions of *Leaves of Grass*. It also helps explain the depression attended by self-doubt and self-loathing that Whitman experienced in the late 1850s (his "slough") and that features prominently in "As I Ebb'd with the Ocean of Life" and other poems first published in 1860. That such a central work has been so little discussed is probably a result of the homophobia that until recently characterized the scholarly and critical response to Whitman's work.

Alan Helms

Bibliography

Bowers, Fredson. "Whitman's Manuscripts for the Original 'Calamus' Poems." *Studies in Bibliography* 6 (1953): 257–265.

Helms, Alan. "Whitman's 'Live Oak with Moss.'" *The Continuing Presence of Walt Whitman*. Ed. Robert K. Martin. Iowa City: U of Iowa P, 1992. 185–205.

Kaplan, Justin. *Walt Whitman: A Life*. New York: Simon and Schuster, 1980.

Kearney, Martin F. "Whitman's 'Live Oak with Moss': Stepping Back to Sere." *Innisfre* 7 (1987): 40–49.

Shively, Charley. *Calamus Lovers: Walt Whitman's Working Class Camerados*. San Francisco: Gay Sunshine, 1987.

Whitman, Walt. *Whitman's Manuscripts:*

"Leaves of Grass" (1860). Ed. Fredson Bowers. Chicago: U of Chicago P, 1955.

Zweig, Paul. *Walt Whitman: The Making of the Poet*. New York: Basic Books, 1984.

See also "CALAMUS"; ["HOURS CONTINUING LONG"]; "I SAW IN LOUISIANA A LIVE-OAK GROWING"; *LEAVES OF GRASS, 1860 EDITION*; ["LONG I THOUGHT THAT KNOWLEDGE ALONE WOULD SUFFICE"]; SEX AND SEXUALITY; VAUGHAN, FREDERICK B.; "WHEN I HEARD AT THE CLOSE OF THE DAY"

"Lo, Victress on the Peaks" (1865–1866)

First published in *Sequel to Drum-Taps* (1865–1866), this poem was revised, grouped under "Bathed in War's Perfume" in the 1871 and 1876 editions, and then placed in the "Drum-Taps" cluster in 1881.

"Libertad" (Spanish for "liberty") is Whitman's name for a goddess-like personification of American independence. The "chanting" poet of America offers "psalms of the dead" to Libertad. However, the Civil War was the world's vain conspiracy to prevent Libertad from creating the American Dream. By addressing Libertad as "Victress," Whitman passionately assures her that she has thwarted all enemies, triumphing "with the dazzling sun around thee."

The poem expresses Whitman's common theme of recalling the tragedy of the war's dead while looking forward to a better future. Written in irregular form, it begins with the exultant six-syllable title line, swells to lines as long as twenty syllables, then recedes to the somber five-syllable closing. This structure, suggesting the ebb and flow of Libertad throughout history, warns that the Victress must be eternally vigilant.

Matthew Ignoffo

Bibliography

Bensko, John. "Narrating Position and Force in Whitman's *Drum-Taps*." *Walt Whitman Centennial International Symposium*. Ed. Manuel Villar Raso, Miguel Martinez Lopez, and Rosa Morillas Sanchez. Granada: Universidad de Granada, 1992. 33–43.

Burrison, William. "Whitman's *Drum-Taps* Reviewed: The Good, Gray, Tender Mother-Man and the Fierce, Red, Convulsive Rhythm of War." *Walt Whitman: Here and Now*. Ed. Joann P. Krieg. Westport, Conn.: Greenwood, 1985. 157–169.

Ignoffo, Matthew. *What the War Did to Whitman*. New York: Vantage, 1975.

Whitman, Walt. *Leaves of Grass: Comprehensive Reader's Edition*. Ed. Harold W. Blodgett and Sculley Bradley. New York: New York UP, 1965.

See also CIVIL WAR, THE; "DRUM-TAPS"; SEQUEL TO DRUM-TAPS

London, Ontario, Canada

Walt Whitman spent the summer of 1880 at the home of his friend and biographer, Dr. Richard Maurice Bucke, who was at that time the superintendent of the London Asylum for the Insane, located two miles outside of the city.

Although its population today is 161,000, at the time of Whitman's visit London was a small town of 19,941. Nonetheless, London could boast of two newspapers, and both reported Whitman's arrival with Bucke, who had accompanied him from Camden. Bucke had already aroused local curiosity about Whitman by proclaiming him the prophet of a new moral state during a lecture to the local teachers' association. This led to a flurry of letters to the London newspapers in March 1880 "criticising both Bucke and Whitman" (Rechnitzer 78). In interviews with the London *Free Press* and London *Advertiser* Whitman discussed his work in the hospitals during the Civil War. He also spoke about *Leaves of Grass,* in particular about the difference between the "strong and rank" (qtd. in Rechnitzer 78) nature to which he gave voice and the work of other poets.

Except for their trips to Sarnia, Toronto, and the Thousand Islands in Ontario, and to Montreal and the Saguenay River in Quebec, Whitman spent most of the summer quietly at the Bucke residence on the asylum grounds. Whitman's *Diary in Canada* and *Specimen Days* record his observations of nature and his enjoyment of the quiet countryside. He was immediately impressed with the "long stretch'd sunsets" and "lingering, lingering twilights" of the north (*Daybooks* 3:612) and wrote frequently of local birds and flowers. He noted the great numbers of "big, tame" robins (3:620) and of the "free swallow dance" he observed over a lawn (3:622), adding that he had never "heard singing wrens . . . to such advantage" (3:620). He wrote enthusiastically as well about the tall delphiniums, scarlet peonies, and wild tansy.

Bucke's enlightened treatment of his patients interested Whitman, and he recorded his favorable impressions. He called the London Asylum one of "the most advanced, perfected, and kindly and rationally carried on, of all its kind in America" (*Specimen Days* 239). During one visit "those crazed faces" of the inmates impressed Whitman, not because they were "repulsive or hideous" but for the "common humanity," the "woes and sad happenings of life and death" he saw reflected in them (238).

Whitman said very little about the local people he met, but did note that Londoners seemed very temperate and clean: "I have seen no drunken man (nor drunken woman)—have run across no besotted or low or filthy quarters of the town either" (qtd. in Dunbabin). Bucke has recorded Whitman's interaction with the children at a picnic for London's poor: "During the day I lost sight of my friend for perhaps an hour, and when I found him again he was sitting in a quiet nook by the river side, with a rosy-faced child of four or five years old, tired out and sound asleep in his lap" (*Walt Whitman* 55).

Most of the information about Whitman's character, personality, and habits that Bucke reports in his biography were the results of his observations of Whitman during that summer. Bucke's admiration and respect for Whitman continued to grow during that period, and their lifelong friendship was firmly established. However, both Peter Rechnitzer's recent study and the Canadian film *Beautiful Dreamers,* which depicts Whitman's relationship with Bucke during that summer in London, suggest that Mrs. Bucke did not entirely share her husband's enthusiasm for Whitman and vetoed a second visit planned for the summer of 1882. Nonetheless, to the end of his life in London, Bucke continued to champion Whitman's work and to herald him as a prophet of "cosmic consciousness."

Lorelei Cederstrom

Bibliography

Beautiful Dreamers. Dir. John Kent Harrison. Prod. Micheal Maclear. A National Film Board of Canada Production. With Colm Feore and Rip Torn. 108 minutes. 1992.

Bucke, Richard Maurice. *Cosmic Consciousness: A Study in the Evolution of the Human Mind*. 1901. New York: Dutton, 1969.

———. *Walt Whitman*. 1883. New York: Johnson Reprint, 1970.

Dunbabin, Thomas. "Walt Whitman Found London 'A Great Place for Birds.'" London (Ontario) *Free Press* 3 Feb. 1962.

Lynch, Michael. "Walt Whitman in Ontario." *The Continuing Presence of Walt Whitman: The Life After the Life.* Ed. Robert K. Martin. Iowa City: U of Iowa P, 1992. 141–151.

Rechnitzer, Peter A. *R.M. Bucke: Journey to Cosmic Consciousness.* Canadian Medical Lives 12. Toronto: Fitzhenry and Whiteside, 1994.

Whitman, Walt. *The Correspondence.* Vol. 3. Edwin Haviland Miller. New York: New York UP, 1964.

———. *Daybooks and Notebooks.* Ed. William White. 3 vols. New York: New York UP, 1978.

———. *Specimen Days.* Vol. 1 of *Prose Works 1892.* Ed. Floyd Stovall. New York: New York UP, 1963.

See also BUCKE, RICHARD MAURICE; CANADA, WHITMAN'S RECEPTION IN; CANADA, WHITMAN'S VISIT TO; COSMIC CONSCIOUSNESS

["Long I Thought That Knowledge Alone Would Suffice"] (1860)

This twelve-line poem appeared only in the 1860 *Leaves of Grass* "Calamus" cluster as number 8 and was excluded from the subsequent 1867 edition. Previously, it was number 5 in the unpublished "Live Oak with Moss" cluster, ostensibly chronicling an unhappy love affair with a man. The conflict this elegiac poem dramatizes is that between the speaker's desire to be America's poet and his proscribed desires. The conflict's resolution in the poem is that the speaker "can be [the country's] singer of songs no longer . . . I will go with him I love." The poem addresses what Alan Helms calls the intrusions of the "capitol," the claims of which conflict with the claims of the lover (189). In the first four lines of the poem, the speaker recounts his previous poetic obsessions with knowledge, the land, and heroes, and his desire to sing about them all. Lines 5–10 are a warning to "The States" that the speaker will cease singing for them, with the reason given in the last two lines, that the speaker may be with his lover. Admittedly, the language of the poem parallels that of contemporary male-male friendship, but in it the poet rejects a heterosexual male ideal of productivity.

Sculley Bradley and Harold Blodgett link this poem with "Once I Pass'd through a Populous City"; both in manuscript form refer to the beloved as a man, though "Once I Pass'd" was revised to refer to a woman. It is also linked to two other excised "Calamus" poems, ["Who Is Now Reading This?"] (number 16), and ["Hours Continuing Long"] (number 9), each of which is linked to confusion over sexual difference. Various reasons have been given for this poem's exclusion from *Leaves*. M. Jimmie Killingsworth argues that these poems, with their awareness of an unconventional same-sex relationship, clashed with "Drum-Taps," in which Whitman strategically deployed the "soldier-comrade" as a veiled strategy of homosexual self-disclosure. He argues that if the three "Calamus" poems had appeared in the 1867 edition they would have betrayed the hidden underpinnings of "Drum-Taps." Kerry Larson, seeing the lover as a mere pretext for Whitman's proposed withdrawal from poetry, argues that the poem concerns Whitman's realization that his poetry has not facilitated national consensus. Considering the other excised poems this poem keeps company with, the argument that this poem's homoeroticism is incompatible with "Drum-Taps" is most plausible.

Because Whitman excised this poem early on, it has received little attention and has not been part of the canon. Additionally, some critics have found it flawed in its confused address between the public and the private and therefore its loss no misfortune. But its removal does provide a fascinating study of motives.

Alan Kozlowski

Bibliography

Helms, Alan. "Whitman's 'Live Oak with Moss.'" *The Continuing Presence of Walt Whitman: The Life after the Life.* Ed. Robert K. Martin. Iowa City: U of Iowa P, 1992. 185–205.

Killingsworth, M. Jimmie. *Whitman's Poetry of the Body: Sexuality, Politics, and the Text.* Chapel Hill: U of North Carolina P, 1989.

Larson, Kerry C. *Whitman's Drama of Consensus.* Chicago: U of Chicago P, 1988.

Whitman, Walt. *Leaves of Grass: Comprehensive Reader's Edition.* Ed. Harold W. Blodgett and Sculley Bradley. New York: New York UP, 1965.

———. *Whitman's Manuscripts: "Leaves of Grass" (1860).* Ed. Fredson Bowers. Chicago: U of Chicago P, 1955.

See also "CALAMUS"; ["HOURS CONTINUING LONG"]; "LIVE OAK WITH MOSS"; SEX AND SEXUALITY

Long Island Democrat

"Yes: I would write a book!" (qtd. in Reynolds 64). Whitman's exclamation in the 29 September 1840 edition of the *Long Island Democrat* was perhaps the first sign of the budding *Leaves of Grass*. The *Democrat,* a weekly newspaper founded by James J. Brenton in 1835, provided Whitman with one of the earliest opportunities to see his poetry in print; not only had Brenton copied a poem from Whitman's own *Long Islander* in 1838, but he published ten more of his poems, plus six of Whitman's "Sun Down Papers—From the Desk of a Schoolmaster," after Whitman began working for him in August 1839.

After selling the *Long Islander,* Whitman prevailed upon the *Democrat*'s editor to take him on as helper. Brenton, already an admirer of Whitman's journalistic skills, easily conceded; Whitman then settled in Jamaica, to work for Brenton and live in his home. The room and board he received probably constituted a large portion of the compensation for writing and setting type. Whether because of Whitman's dissatisfaction concerning his wages, or Mrs. Brenton's unfavorable opinion of the "inordinately indolent" (qtd. in Holloway xxxiii n) young man, Whitman returned to schoolteaching in December. Nevertheless, the *Democrat* continued to publish his writings, and Brenton congratulated Whitman through the *Democrat* whenever Whitman obtained a new editorial position.

Brenton fanned Whitman's political interests, and his influence probably secured Whitman's appointment as an electioneer for the Van Buren campaign. The *Democrat*'s denouncement of a September 1840 Whig rally was supported by its former employee, who wrote spirited letters to the *Democrat* denouncing the Whig advocate, Charles King.

Karen Karbiener

Bibliography

Allen, Gay Wilson. *The Solitary Singer: A Critical Biography of Walt Whitman.* 1955. Rev. ed. 1967. Chicago: U of Chicago P, 1985.

Holloway, Emory. Introduction. *The Uncollected Poetry and Prose of Walt Whitman.* Vol. 1. Ed. Holloway. Garden City, N.Y.: Doubleday, Page, 1921. xxiii–xcii.

Reynolds, David S. *Walt Whitman's America: A Cultural Biography.* New York: Knopf, 1995.

Rubin, Joseph Jay. *The Historic Whitman.* University Park: Pennsylvania State UP, 1973.

White, William. *Walt Whitman's Journalism: A Bibliography.* Detroit: Wayne State UP, 1969.

See also DEMOCRATIC PARTY; JOURNALISM, WHITMAN'S; *LONG ISLANDER;* PRE-*LEAVES* POEMS

Long Island, New York

In *Specimen Days* (1882) Whitman says of the region where he was born, "the successive growth-stages of my infancy, childhood, youth and manhood were all pass'd on Long Island, which I sometimes feel as if I had incorporated" (10). Such a statement, from a poet whose work is so concentrated on the corporeal self, can hardly be ignored or its import slighted. In fact, examination of his life and work reveals the extent to which the feeling is substantiated.

Both the Whitman and Van Velsor families had roots in Long Island, his father's side having been there for some five generations. While the Whitmans were spread throughout the West Hills region, it may well have been his mother's birthplace, the Van Velsor farm in nearby Cold Spring, that is the remembered childhood site of "There was a Child Went Forth." Something of the everyday life of the two families, and of the influence on them of their island habitat, can be gleaned from the poem and from the remembrances Whitman set down in *Specimen Days*.

Whitman always referred to Long Island by its aboriginal name, "Paumanok," and was familiar with its geographical contours as they existed prior to the 1898 consolidation, when the westernmost portion of the island became part of the city of New York. In Whitman's time Long Island stretched eastward from Brooklyn to Montauk Point. Though his family left West Hills for Brooklyn when he was four years old, Whitman spent much of his boyhood in the eastern regions of the island, sailing, fishing (ice fishing in winter), clamming, and bathing. Scenes from these and other island activities are scattered throughout his poetry and always suggest a great sense of happiness.

In young manhood, both before and after his employment on newspapers in Queens and Brooklyn, Whitman was for a time less happily engaged in schoolteaching in various Long Island communities. In letters written from Woodbury in 1841, the twenty-one-year-old described his days as a schoolteacher boarding in the homes of his pupils as a kind of damnation, though in old age he remembered them as among his best experiences. In 1839 he had started his own newspaper in Huntington, *The Long Islander,* which he sold a year later. Manhattan claimed him, but Whitman returned to Long Island regularly to visit friends and relatives (his sister Mary lived in Greenport) and to enjoy its natural setting.

It is this setting that permeates *Leaves of Grass,* especially the presence of the sea, which inspired in Whitman a great sense of the ebb and flow of all of life and stirred him to visions of himself as setting forth on a great voyage of poetic discovery with his soul his only companion. The solitary nature of the voyage is made clear on Paumanok's shore in "Out of the Cradle," where the rhythm of the sea informs a myth about the making of a poet. In "Starting from Paumanok" the voyage to the "New World" of poetic expression begins on Long Island's shores. The voyage itself appears again and again, in the narrative style of "Old Salt Kossabone" and "O Captain! My Captain!," in the declamations of "Passage to India," and in the reveries of "Prayer of Columbus" and many of the "Songs of Parting."

The experience of having been born and of having lived so many of his formative years on an island seems to have been the shaping power of Whitman's life and work. The fascination he felt for the sea and its repetitive approach to the land is revealed in "Sea-Shore Fancies" in *Specimen Days,* where he tells of a boyhood fancy of writing about the seashore as a meeting place of sea and land, where the two met and fused. Rather than having produced it as a single piece, however, he claims to have allowed this fancy to remain "an invisible *influence*" in his composition, where the vision of fused natural powers is "indirectly" revealed in the rhythms and themes of the works (*Specimen Days* 139). Though it is not precisely a seashore vision, "Crossing Brooklyn Ferry" clearly expresses this fusion, extending it to a greater dimension so that the "invisible influence" overflows the bounds of time and space.

Other aspects of nature as found on Long Island appear in the poems—sea gulls, lilac bushes, mockingbirds—as do aspects of the life of the people there. The island itself appears in "As I Ebb'd with the Ocean of Life," where it is the father land, the place on which he has been tossed by the great ocean of life out of the fierce mother, the sea. Again, the island seems to be a microcosm of earth, the "vast Rondure, swimming in space" in section 5 of "Passage to India."

Whitman brought his ailing father back to West Hills two years before the father's death and returned again in 1881. On the latter visit he contemplated the burial places of both sides of his family, commenting in *Specimen Days* on the many "ancient graveyards" on Long Island and how his whole family history, three centuries, was told there (6).

In 1890 Dr. John Johnston, one of Whitman's admirers from Bolton, England, visited Whitman in Camden and then made a pilgrimage to Long Island, viewing the places associated with the poet's family and his early life. He also visited Herbert Gilchrist, the artist son of Whitman's close friend, Mrs. Anne Gilchrist. The young Englishman (perhaps as a result of the poet's glowing remembrances of Long Island) had settled in Centerport. The following year J.W. Wallace, another of the Bolton admirers, also made the Long Island pilgrimage to see the place where Whitman was born.

Though Whitman chose to be buried outside Camden, New Jersey, his memory is honored on Long Island, where a high school, shopping mall, movie theater, and various small businesses bear his name. His birthplace in West Hills is a New York State Historic Site, and the newspaper he started, *The Long Islander,* is still published in Huntington. Brooklyn College, part of the City University of New York, has its Whitman Hall, and from time to time some fragment of the poet's presence on Long Island comes to light, such as the holograph version of "Thou Vast Rondure Swimming in Space," which surfaced in the 1980s among the contents of an old Long Island house about to be demolished. All are reminders of the poet's life and work, the going forth, "Starting from Paumanok."

Joann P. Krieg

Bibliography

Allen, Gay Wilson. *The Solitary Singer: A Critical Biography of Walt Whitman.* 1955. Rev. ed. 1967. Chicago: U of Chicago P, 1985.

Berbrich, Joan D. "Walt Whitman." *Three Voices from Paumanok: The Influence of Long Island on James Fenimore Cooper, William Cullen Bryant, and Walt Whitman.* Empire State Historical Publications Series, No. 81. Port Washington, New York: Ira J. Friedman, 1969. 109–196.

L

Funnell, Bertha H. *Walt Whitman on Long Island*. Empire State Historical Publications Series, No. 91. Port Washington, New York: Kennikat, Ira J. Friedman Division, 1971.

Johnston, J., and J.W. Wallace. *Visits to Walt Whitman in 1890–1891*. 1917. New York: Haskell House, 1970.

Whitman, Walt. *Leaves of Grass: Comprehensive Reader's Edition*. Ed. Harold W. Blodgett and Sculley Bradley. New York: New York UP, 1965.

———. *Specimen Days*. Vol. 1 of *Prose Works 1892*. Ed. Floyd Stovall. New York: New York UP, 1963.

See also BIRTHPLACE, WALT WHITMAN'S; LONG ISLANDER; "OUT OF THE CRADLE ENDLESSLY ROCKING"; SEA, THE; SPECIMEN DAYS; "STARTING FROM PAUMANOK"; "THERE WAS A CHILD WENT FORTH"

Long Island Patriot

Founded in 1821 by Tammany Democrats, the *Long Island Patriot* was almost as young as Whitman was when he began work there as a printer's apprentice in 1831. The four-page weekly listed Whitman's father among its five hundred subscribers; perhaps Whitman Senior himself had sought employment for his son in its Fulton Street office, about ten blocks from their Brooklyn home.

Though Whitman only worked at the "Pat" for about a year, this introduction to the world of journalism strongly affected his own literary output. Not only did he learn much about typography—information that he later applied to the layout and printing of *Leaves of Grass*—but he also sampled his first taste of authorship in writing "sentimental bits" (*Specimen Days* 286–287).

Whitman and the other apprentices, including future Brooklyn Democratic leader Henry Murphy, boarded with the granddaughter of editor Samuel E. Clements. A flamboyant dresser and daring horseman, Clements sometimes took his young employees on breathless buggy rides around New Lots, Flatlands, and Bushwick; he was eventually forced to flee Brooklyn because of his involvement in a plot to exhume Elias Hicks's body and take a plaster cast of the head and face. Despite Clements's charisma and powerful position, Whitman was more deeply impressed by the *Patriot*'s foreman

printer, William Hartshorne. Born during Revolutionary times, Hartshorne enthralled his young pupil with accounts of early American notable figures and events. Whitman later memorialized this "most worthy member of the craft preservative of all crafts" (*Uncollected* 2:245) by writing a tribute to him in the Brooklyn *Daily Eagle*.

Karen Karbiener

Bibliography

Allen, Gay Wilson. *The Solitary Singer: A Critical Biography of Walt Whitman*. 1955. Rev. ed. 1967. Chicago: U of Chicago P, 1985.

Kaplan, Justin. *Walt Whitman: A Life*. New York: Simon and Schuster, 1980.

White, William. "A Tribute to William Hartshorne: Unrecorded Whitman." *American Literature* 42 (1971): 554–558.

Whitman, Walt. *Specimen Days*. Vol. 1 of *Prose Works 1892*. Ed. Floyd Stovall. New York: New York UP, 1963.

———. *The Uncollected Poetry and Prose of Walt Whitman*. Ed. Emory Holloway. 2 vols. 1921. Gloucester, Mass.: Peter Smith, 1972.

See also HARTSHORNE, WILLIAM; JOURNALISM, WHITMAN'S; PRINTING BUSINESS

Long Island Star

As the *Long Island Patriot* was the organ of the Jacksonian party in Brooklyn, the *Long Island Star* was the opposing Whig newspaper. According to Whitman in "Brooklyniana," the *Star* was first issued in 1808 or 1809 and contained little more than news scraps, jokes, and notices of hired slaves; by the time Whitman was hired as a printer's devil in 1832, it was an ambitious four-page weekly. His employment there served him as trade school, and he left as a journeyman printer at sixteen.

Colonel Alden Spooner, the editor and publisher of the *Long Island Star* during Whitman's apprenticeship, was a successful businessman, an active civic leader, and a prominent citizen of Brooklyn. He clearly had grand plans for his newspaper as well. Intending it to be much more than simply a political mouthpiece, Spooner gave prominence to science, art, and ideas in the *Star*, and even provided space for the writings of local authors.

Whitman must have been impressed by Spooner's interest in literature, as well as his strong opinions; for example, Spooner's involvement in the temperance movement probably influenced Whitman's decision to abstain from spirits and to write a temperance novel, *Franklin Evans* (1842).

When Whitman addressed a Democratic rally in City Hall Park in 1841, the *Star* mocked its former employee for presuming to teach politics to "those big children of Tammany Hall" (qtd. in Kaplan 97), and recommended that he come back and finish his apprenticeship. Four years later, Whitman did in fact reapply for work at the *Star*, now a daily run by Alden's son and known as the Brooklyn *Evening Star*. Edwin Spooner strongly disapproved of Whitman's political views, but he also realized that few, if any, Brooklyn journalists could match Whitman's record of editing several metropolitan dailies. Spooner thus engaged Whitman to write about fifty articles over the next five months. These informal editorials centered on Whitman's favorite subjects of the time: education, music, theater, temperance, and manners. In March 1846 Whitman gave up writing opinion pieces for the *Star* and assumed the editorship of one of its rivals, the Brooklyn *Daily Eagle*.

Karen Karbiener

Bibliography

Allen, Gay Wilson. *The Solitary Singer: A Critical Biography of Walt Whitman.* 1955. Rev. ed. 1967. Chicago: U of Chicago P, 1985.

Kaplan, Justin. *Walt Whitman: A Life.* New York: Simon and Schuster, 1980.

Rubin, Joseph Jay. *The Historic Whitman.* University Park: Pennsylvania State UP, 1973.

White, William. *Walt Whitman's Journalism: A Bibliography.* Detroit: Wayne State UP, 1969.

Whitman, Walt. *The Uncollected Poetry and Prose of Walt Whitman.* Ed. Emory Holloway. Vol. 2. 1921. Gloucester, Mass.: Peter Smith, 1972.

See also JOURNALISM, WHITMAN'S; LONG ISLAND PATRIOT; PRINTING BUSINESS; WHIGS

Long Islander

Described by Whitman as his "first real venture" (*Specimen Days* 287), this weekly newspaper was founded by him in 1838 in Huntington, the area in which he grew up. Whitman had been teaching school for three years and was clearly eager to return to journalism. Although the *Long Islander* is still in print today, Whitman's involvement in his project was short-lived: he sold the paper within ten months. He later claimed his restlessness had kept him from establishing permanent residence on Long Island, but a note in the *Hempstead Inquirer* of 20 July 1839 suggests that Huntington residents had not evinced a "desire to support a newspaper among themselves" (qtd. in Funnell 50). Of course, Whitman also may have grown tired of the too regular and time-consuming work.

Whitman set up shop in a small building about half a block west of the *Long Islander*'s present home, bringing a press and an assortment of types. Upstairs he fashioned his frugal sleeping quarters; downstairs he performed his duties as editor, compositor, pressman, and printer's devil. In the evenings, the boys of the village gathered in the printing room to hear him read stories or some of his own poetry: "yawps" (qtd. in Funnell 46), as he then called his verses.

As the *Long Island Star* had warned the nineteen-year-old editor, a country newspaper was a dubious business venture. Expenses accumulated because subscribers and advertisers often paid in potatoes and cordwood instead of cash. Whitman also found it necessary to buy a horse and establish a weekly thirty-mile paper route through Babylon, Smithtown, and Commack. Despite the rough roads and the time commitment—the journey took a full day and night each week—Whitman later declared, "I never had happier jaunts" (287).

Though there is no extant copy of Whitman's *Long Islander*, some of its content is available because newspapers of the time customarily borrowed articles from one another. On 8 August 1838, for example, the *Long Island Democrat* reproduced Whitman's article "Effects of Lightning" from the *Long Islander*; this remains his earliest extant writing. Whitman's poem "Our Future Lot," appearing in the *Democrat* on 31 October 1838, was also copied "from the *Long Islander*."

In his later years, Whitman showed a sentimental fondness for the *Long Islander*. He reminisced about the newspaper's beginnings in *Specimen Days*, and he proudly showed his Camden visitors a copy of the newspaper he had founded as a boy. Richard Maurice Bucke reported that he and Whitman stopped in the offices of the *Long Islander* when they visited Huntington in 1881. Sinking into the editor's chair, Whitman took time to contemplate the changes that had come about since he had left.

The *Long Islander* rarely mentioned its founder until George Shepard, the third publisher after Whitman, wrote a scathing review of *Leaves of Grass*. As Whitman gained literary prestige, the *Long Islander* took more positive notice of Whitman's work; since 1959, the newspaper has published an annual "Walt Whitman Page" or "Supplement" to commemorate the poet's birthday.

Karen Karbiener

Bibliography

Funnell, Bertha H. *Walt Whitman on Long Island*. Port Washington, N.Y.: Kennikat, 1971.

Kaplan, Justin. *Walt Whitman: A Life*. New York: Simon and Schuster, 1980.

White, William. *Walt Whitman's Journalism: A Bibliography*. Detroit: Wayne State UP, 1969.

Whitman, Walt. *Specimen Days*. Vol. 1 of *Prose Works 1892*. Ed. Floyd Stovall. New York: New York UP, 1963.

———. *The Uncollected Poetry and Prose of Walt Whitman*. 1921. Ed. Emory Holloway. 2 vols. Gloucester, Mass.: Peter Smith, 1972.

See also Journalism, Whitman's; Long Island Democrat; Long Island, New York; Long Island Patriot; Long Island Star

---

"Long, Too Long America" (1865)

Walt Whitman wrote this five-line poem for the first publication of *Drum-Taps* (1865). When Whitman arranged the 1881 edition of *Leaves of Grass*, he placed "Long, Too Long America" at the exact center of the "Drum-Taps" section, preceded by twenty-three Civil War poems and followed by twenty-three others.

"Long, Too Long" merges the militant themes of the early Civil War poems with the peace and reconciliation themes of later ones. Whitman continues to accept the need to pursue the war, despite the horrors he has seen in his hospital experiences, but he hopes the land can "learn from crises of anguish, advancing, grappling with direst fate and recoiling not," and now "show to the world what your children en-masse really are."

"Long, Too Long America" deals less than some of Whitman's Civil War poems with personal losses and tragedies. It deals more directly with Whitman's prewar visions of America, as candidly stated in the otherwise enigmatic last line, and he dares to hope that this land can emerge stronger than before the war; this is because up until then America had "learned from joys and prosperity only."

Whitman made only one change in this poem after its first publication. That was in 1881, to change the title and the first line so that they name "America"; originally these references had been to "O Land."

During the 1960s this poem gained popularity and was read or recited at many anti-Vietnam war meetings.

Jerry F. King

Bibliography

Coyle, William, ed. *The Poet and the President: Whitman's Lincoln Poems*. New York: Odyssey, 1962.

Hindus, Milton, ed. *"Leaves of Grass" One Hundred Years After*. Stanford, Calif.: Stanford UP, 1955.

Miller, James E., Jr. *A Critical Guide to "Leaves of Grass."* Chicago: U of Chicago P, 1957.

Perry, Bliss. *Walt Whitman: His Life and Work*. New York: Houghton Mifflin, 1906.

See also Civil War, The; "Drum-Taps"

Longaker, Dr. Daniel (1858–1949)

Philadelphia physician Daniel Longaker treated Whitman during his final illness. He, as well as Dr. Alexander McAlister of Camden, were Whitman's main doctors. Neither presented bills for his services. Longaker earned his medical degree from the University of Pennsylvania in 1881 and was a pioneer in obstetrics; he is credited with being one of the first in Philadelphia to perform a caesarean section in a patient's home. He served on the staff of Lying-In Hospital and Jewish Maternity Hospital and for several years was Chief of Obstetrics at Kensington Hospital for Women.

Early in 1891, Whitman's friend Horace Traubel asked Longaker to serve as Whitman's doctor. He and Whitman were most likely drawn to Longaker's liberal sympathies. After Longaker's death, for example, a newspaper revealed that his daughter had had him institutionalized because he gave money to leftist groups such as the Joint Anti-Fascist Refugee Committee. Longaker attributed Whitman's illness to the emotional strain of Civil War hospital work and to blood poisoning acquired from gangrenous wounds of patients Whitman had nursed. Longaker paid frequent visits and provided various medications, which Whitman's nurse, Elizabeth Leavitt Keller, describes as minimal, designed to alleviate acute or persistent pain. Whitman assisted in his own treatment by detailing his condition to Longaker orally and in letters. Longaker enjoyed talking with Whitman about human nature and reflects that Whitman responded as well to their conversations as he did to medical remedies. Whitman's condition worsened on 17 December 1891, when a fever, accompanied by chills and respiratory problems, incapacitated him. He partially recovered but died on 26 March 1892, too suddenly for Longaker to be called. He was attended by Dr. McAlister, his housekeeper Mary Oakes Davis, nurse Warren Fritzinger, and friends Thomas B. Harned and Horace Traubel.

Longaker and Whitman's other doctors vastly underestimated their patient's condition, perhaps because Whitman complained relatively little and seemed to accept his imminent death. An autopsy, performed by Professor Henry W. Cattell, demonstrator of Gross Morbid Anatomy at the University of Pennsylvania, which Longaker attended, revealed serious maladies—abscesses, tubercles, a large gallstone, deteriorated lungs and liver, and an enlarged prostate. Gay Wilson Allen and David Reynolds provide useful summaries of Longaker's treatment of Whitman, but Emory Holloway misspells Longaker's and McAlister's names.

Carol J. Singley

Bibliography

Allen, Gay Wilson. *The Solitary Singer: A Critical Biography of Walt Whitman.* 1955. Rev. ed. 1967. Chicago: U of Chicago P, 1985.

Holloway, Emory. *Whitman: An Interpretation in Narrative.* New York: Knopf, 1926.

Keller, Elizabeth Leavitt. *Walt Whitman in Mickle Street.* New York: Kennerley, 1921.

"Longaker, Daniel." Alumni Records File. University of Pennsylvania Archives. Philadelphia, Pa.

Longaker, Daniel. "The Last Sickness and the Death of Walt Whitman." *In Re Walt Whitman.* Ed. Horace L. Traubel, Richard Maurice Bucke, and Thomas B. Harned. Philadelphia: David McKay, 1893. 393–411. Rpt. in *Whitman in His Own Time: A Biographical Chronicle of His Life, Drawn from Recollections, Memoirs, and Interviews by Friends and Associates.* Ed. Joel Myerson. Detroit: Omnigraphics, 1991. 90–108.

Reynolds, David S. *Walt Whitman's America: A Cultural Biography.* New York: Knopf, 1995.

Whitman, Walt. *The Correspondence.* Ed. Edwin Haviland Miller. Vol. 5. New York: New York UP, 1969.

See also DAVIS, MARY OAKES; FRITZINGER, FREDERICK WARREN; HARNED, THOMAS BIGGS; HEALTH; KELLER, ELIZABETH LEAVITT; MICKLE STREET HOUSE ; TRAUBEL, HORACE L.

Longfellow, Henry Wadsworth (1807–1882)

Author of "Evangeline" (1847) and "Hiawatha" (1855), Henry Wadsworth Longfellow, one of the most well-received poets of his time, was publicly challenged by Walt Whitman for the title "excelsior" (more lofty; higher) poet of America.

On 12 October 1846, in the Brooklyn *Daily Eagle*, Whitman reviewed *The Poems of Henry Wadsworth Longfellow* (1846), in which Longfellow's poem "Excelsior" appeared. Whitman wrote, "this Handsome fifty cent edition" contained "beautiful thoughts in beautiful words," and equated Longfellow with the pinnacle of romantic poetry. However, Whitman's estimation of Longfellow plummeted in the 1860s; while Whitman was in Washington writing about the sacrificial deaths of American soldiers, Longfellow continued with sentimental verse, as found in "Excelsior." Longfellow's book *Ballads and Other Poems*, in which "Excelsior" appeared, had been reprinted nine times since 1842. Consequently, in 1867 Whitman invoked Longfellow's work by selecting "Excelsior" as the permanent title for one of his poems in *Leaves of Grass*.

Enraged by Longfellow's "beautiful words" that ignored the war, Whitman, with his new title "Excelsior," indicted Longfellow as the "him" in the following line which first appeared in the 1856 edition of *Leaves of Grass* and was not removed until 1882: "And who has projected beautiful words through the longest time? By God! I will outvie him! I will say such words, they shall stretch through longer time!" (1856 *Leaves*).

By 1876, Whitman's attitude toward Longfellow softened with their first recorded personal encounter. Although Whitman's reputation was growing, Longfellow was still publicly known as the greater of the two poets. Recognizing that the famous poet's visit was an important acknowledgment of his work, Whitman in turn publicly acknowledged Longfellow in "My Tribute to Four Poets," as well as documenting their second meeting, which took place on 16 April 1881. However, it was their third meeting, which Whitman speaks of in his letters to John Burroughs and Alma Calder Johnston (both 24 September 1881), that marked a complete reconciliation on the part of Whitman. After meeting with Longfellow for the third and final time, Whitman deleted from his "Excelsior" at the last moment—while the 1881 edition of *Leaves* was being plate-cast—the antagonistic line that indicted Longfellow and his "beautiful" words.

Whitman, who at first idolized Longfellow and then publicly swore to "outvie" his idol, later, in his maturation, reconciled with Longfellow and his work.

Julie A. Rechel-White

Bibliography

Arvin, Newton. *Longfellow: His Life and Work*. Boston: Little, Brown, 1963.
Fletcher, Angus. "Whitman and Longfellow: Two Types of the American Poet." *Raritan* 10 (1991): 131–145.
Longfellow, Henry Wadsworth. *Ballads and Other Poems*. Cambridge, Mass.: J. Owen, 1842.
———. *The Poems of Henry Wadsworth Longfellow*. New York: Harper, 1846.
Price, Kenneth M. *Whitman and Tradition: The Poet in His Century*. New Haven: Yale UP, 1990.
Rechel-White, Julie A. "Longfellow's Influence on Whitman's 'Rise' from Manhattan Island." *ATQ* 6 (1992): 121–129.
Whitman, Walt. *The Correspondence*. Ed. Edwin Haviland Miller. Vol. 3. New York: New York UP, 1964.
———. "The Literary World." Brooklyn *Daily Eagle* 12 Oct. 1846.

See also BRYANT, WILLIAM CULLEN; "EXCELSIOR"; HOLMES, OLIVER WENDELL; LOWELL, JAMES RUSSELL; WHITTIER, JOHN GREENLEAF

Love

In "There was a Child Went Forth," Whitman's "yearning and swelling heart" fed an "[a]ffection that will not be gainsay'd" for a mother "with mild words" and an "anger'd, unjust" father. Walter Whitman, Sr., was so often incapacitated by depression or alcoholism that Walt acted as a substitute father to his brothers and sisters, as he suggests in an early story, "My Boys and Girls." Even when Louisa Whitman's "very good but very strange boy" (qtd. in Perry 19) grew to manhood and buried his father, he acknowledged in "As I Ebb'd with the Ocean of Life" that he was still crying out for his father's withheld embrace and loving kiss.

The poet also continued to hunger for his mother's acceptance of his renegade sexuality, recreating her in "Song of the Broad-Axe" as "the best belov'd" who is "less guarded than ever, yet more guarded. . . . Oaths, quarrels, hiccupp'd songs, smutty expressions . . . do not offend her" (section 11). In reality, in 1856, when those lines were written, Moncure Conway had in fact detected a guarded expression in Louisa's eyes when he dropped in for his interview and found two impressions in Walt's unmade bed. In 1856 Fred Vaughan was living in the Whitman household. Despite her foreboding, however, Louisa supported her son by describing her own same-gender attraction to an Indian squaw, as recorded in "The Sleepers."

As the adult child of an alcoholic, Whitman's formative experiences of love "became part of him . . . for many years" ("There was a Child Went Forth") and conditioned his frustrations in securing lifelong love, creating the "bitterest envy" described in "When I Peruse the Conquer'd Fame." When he confessed in "Calamus" number 16 that he was puzzled at himself, or in "Calamus" number 9 that "I am ashamed—but it is useless—I am what I am" (1860 *Leaves*), he was concerned with his self-defeating behavior. In "Are You the New Person Drawn toward Me?" he warned prospective lovers that the fault lay within himself: "Do you think the friendship of me would be unalloy'd satisfaction?"

Whitman's major lovers—Fred Vaughan, Peter Doyle, and Harry Stafford—were cut from much the same depressive, journeyman mold as Whitman Senior. Whitman caroused with Vaughan at Pfaff's tavern and with Doyle in its Washington equivalents, enabling their addictions and thereby perpetuating his hold over them. He rationalized his attraction to these roughs by arguing that his superabundance of personal magnetism could cheer them up. In reality, his relationships were generally marked by stormy scenes, jealousies, infidelities, betrayals, and eventual abandonment. However, he viewed Horace Traubel (who broke the journeyman mold) as his final, steadfast lover, in every sense except the physical.

In "Song of the Open Road," we find another problem that a man like Fred Vaughan encountered in trying to love Walt Whitman: Whitman's demand to come out of the "dark confinement" (section 13) and walk along the "open road." "I nourish active rebellion," Whitman challenges (section 14); "Camerado, I give you my hand! . . . will you come travel with me?" (section 15). As he boldly "saunter'd the streets," Whitman "curv'd with his arm the shoulder of his friend" ("Recorders Ages Hence") and had intended in "Calamus" number 8 to "go with him I love" (1860 *Leaves*), but even for Whitman, the decision to publicly "tell the secret of my nights and days" ("In Paths Untrodden") was so frightening that he compared himself to Jesus in the garden sweating blood ("Trickle Drops"). All too soon he saw Vaughan "content himself without me" ("Calamus" number 9, 1860 *Leaves*). Vaughan's escape from the "ironical smiles and mockings" along the open road ("Song of the Open Road," section 11) was to impregnate his girlfriend Frances and thereby trap himself into marriage.

Because of these well-known failures, critics have seldom grasped how Whitman's loving relationships were paradoxically successful in giving him a crucial measure of the love he craved, as he stated in "Calamus" number 39 (1860 *Leaves*): "Doubtless I could not have perceived the universe, or written one of my poems, if I had not freely given myself to comrades, to love." Doyle was his lover for roughly ten years. Vaughan regretted his desertion and never stopped thinking of Walt. But Traubel was with him at his deathbed. All of these men spoke of Whitman's persistent spiritual presence in their lives.

"Song of Myself" is the poem in which Whitman explicitly links his experience of God to his loving bedfellow (section 3). Perhaps he was thinking of Vaughan when he wrote, "This the far-off depth and height reflecting my own face, / This the thoughtful merge of myself, and the outlet again" (section 19). Once he saw the Self reflected in his lover's eyes, his tentative celebrations of it were utterly justified to his own heart. As a transcendentalist, Whitman believed that this epiphany, "the origin of all poems" (section 2), like the "damp of the night" drove deeper into the soul than any sermons or logic (section 30). His conviction is dramatized in section 5 of "Song of Myself," which begins when he loafs with his soul on the grass and ends in his encounter with the fullness of the Godhead, which Elias Hicks said resided in every blade of grass.

The deep affirmation he found with his soul alleviated shadows of shame and self-doubt and thereby unlocked his native affinity with creation. In section 5 of "Song of Myself" he attests to his restored sense of brotherhood with men and women, and in section 6 he compares this essential commonality with the grass: "Growing among black folks as among white . . . I give them the same, I receive them the same." Whitman's frequent sympathy for "shunn'd persons" ("Native Moments"), as well as his social and geographical catalogues, are an attempt to communicate this feeling.

Love, then, the "kelson of creation" ("Song of Myself," section 5), is the unifying "purport" of *Leaves of Grass* and Whitman's entire career. Since Whitman perceived that all America's "experience, cautions, majorities, ridicule, / And the threat of what is call'd hell" were actively arrayed against men like himself, he vows that his words would remain always "weapons full of danger, full of death," and that he would "confront peace, security, and all the settled laws, to unsettle them" ("As I Lay with My Head in Your Lap Camerado"). America's acceptance of his dream of a "new city of Friends" ("I Dream'd in a Dream"), where other men and women would be free to share his transcendent experience of love, was the next great test of the young American democracy.

Mitch Gould

Bibliography

Perry, Bliss. *Walt Whitman: His Life and Work*. Boston: Houghton Mifflin, 1906.

Shively, Charley. *Calamus Lovers: Walt Whitman's Working Class Camerados*. San Francisco: Gay Sunshine, 1987.

Whitman, Walt. *Whitman's Manuscripts: "Leaves of Grass" (1860)*. Ed. Fredson Bowers. Chicago: U of Chicago P, 1955.

See also COMRADESHIP; DOYLE, PETER; SEX AND SEXUALITY; STAFFORD, HARRY L.; TRAUBEL, HORACE L.; VAUGHAN, FREDERICK B.

"Love of Eris: A Spirit Record, The" (1844)

"The Love of Eris: A Spirit Record" first appeared in *Columbian Magazine*, March 1844, under the title "Eris: A Spirit Record." It was reprinted with the current title and other slight revisions in the Brooklyn *Daily Eagle*, 18 August 1846. For publication history and revisions, see Brasher's edition of *The Early Poems and the Fiction*.

The story is slight. A guardian angel, Dai, falls in love with his charge, Eris. She is betrothed. When the angel reveals himself to Eris, she dies. For being false to his mission, the angel is blinded and made to wander through heaven, calling out the name of his beloved. Eris's fiancé, meanwhile, languishes and longs for death.

The story contains an avowal of belief in angels and invisible spirits, but the moral at the end implicitly establishes a priority about such things. "The pure love of two human beings is a sacred thing, which the immortal themselves must dare not to cross" (Whitman 247).

Justin Kaplan, placing this story in line with those about sons and fathers, notes that Eris, spelled backwards, is "sire." Gay Wilson Allen notes that this story is in the manner of Edgar Allan Poe, but further sees the cosmic loneliness of Eris as a foreshadowing of elements in lines from Whitman's hospital notebook (1862–1863) which are the germ of the 1868 poem "A Noiseless Patient Spider."

Patrick McGuire

Bibliography

Allen, Gay Wilson. *The Solitary Singer: A Critical Biography of Walt Whitman*. 1955. Rev. ed. 1967. Chicago: U of Chicago P, 1985.

Kaplan, Justin. *Walt Whitman: A Life*. New York: Simon and Schuster, 1980.

Whitman, Walt. *The Early Poems and the Fiction*. Ed. Thomas L. Brasher. New York: New York UP, 1963.

See also SHORT FICTION, WHITMAN'S

Lowell, James Russell (1819–1891)

Poet, editor, educator, and diplomat, Lowell was born in Cambridge, Massachusetts, and graduated from Harvard University (1838, LL.B. 1840, M.A. 1841). He was editor of *The Pioneer* (1843), the *Atlantic Monthly* (1857–1861), coeditor with Charles Eliot Norton of the *North American Review* (1864–1872), Smith Professor of Modern Languages, Harvard (1855–1886), U.S. minister to Spain (1877–1880) and to England (1880–1885). Lowell's literary works include *A Year's Life* (1841), *The Biglow Papers* (1848, 1867), *The Vision of Sir Launfal* (1848), *A Fable for Critics* (1848), and "Ode Recited at the Harvard Commemoration" (1865). Walt Whitman told his biographer, Horace Traubel, that James Russell Lowell was his bitterest enemy: "'Lowell never even tolerated me as a man: he not only objected to my book: he objected to me'" (*With Walt Whitman* 4:74).

Lowell's letters and reported conversations suggest that he helped to block Whitman's acceptance by the New England literary establishment. Although Norton admired the first *Leaves of Grass* in 1855, Lowell disapproved of it: "When a man aims at originality he acknowledges himself consciously unoriginal" (*Letters* 1:242). In 1863 Lowell pronounced *Leaves* "a solemn humbug" and promised to "keep it out of the way of the students" (*New Letters* 115–116). Lowell was also among those who persuaded Ralph Waldo Emerson not to invite Whitman to Boston's Saturday Club in 1860, and, in later years, Lowell may have discouraged foreign guests from visiting Whitman in Camden. On the other hand, Lowell published an edited version of Whitman's "Bardic Symbols" in the *Atlantic* in April 1860, and he insisted on contributing to a Whitman benefit at the Madison Square Theater in 1887. At the end of Whitman's performance at this benefit Lowell is said to have exclaimed, "This has been one of the most impressive hours of my life!" (Johnston 157).

A Brahmin, a maker of rhymed verse, a professor, a politician—Lowell seemed the antithesis of everything Whitman claimed to represent: "Lowell is one kind: I'm another," he said (*With Walt Whitman* 4:74). They were also nearly exact contemporaries, and Whitman's "O Captain! My Captain!" rivaled Lowell's "Commemoration Ode" as a tribute to Abraham Lincoln. This often caused their juxtapositioning in literary histories, anthologies, and college courses. Efforts to commemorate one competed with efforts to commemorate the other. In 1892 Traubel presented Lowell as a foil for Whitman: "One man contributes preservation; another movement. One is conservative; another dynamic" ("Lowell—Whitman" 22). Despite Lowell's complexities, subsequent comparisons have often promoted Whitman as a neglected genius struggling against the genteel conservatism Lowell came to embody.

William A. Pannapacker

Bibliography

Duberman, Martin. *James Russell Lowell*. Boston: Houghton Mifflin, 1966.

Johnston, J.H. "In Re Walt Whitman." *Walt Whitman as Man, Poet and Friend*. Ed. Charles N. Elliot. Boston: Richard G. Badger, 1915. 147–174.

Lowell, James Russell. *Letters of James Russell Lowell*. Ed. Charles Eliot Norton. 2 vols. New York: Harper, 1894.

———. *New Letters of James Russell Lowell*. Ed. M.A. De Wolfe Howe. New York: Harper, 1932.

———. *The Writings of James Russell Lowell*. 10 vols. Boston: Houghton Mifflin, 1890.

Traubel, Horace. "Lowell—Whitman: A Contrast." *Poet-Lore* 4 (1892): 22–31.

———. *With Walt Whitman in Camden*. Ed. Sculley Bradley. Vol. 4. Philadelphia: U of Pennsylvania P, 1953.

See also ATLANTIC MONTHLY, THE; BRYANT, WILLIAM CULLEN; HOLMES, OLIVER WENDELL; LONGFELLOW, HENRY WADSWORTH; NORTH AMERICAN REVIEW, THE; NORTON, CHARLES ELIOT; TRAUBEL, HORACE L.; WHITTIER, JOHN GREENLEAF

Lucretius (Titus Lucretius Carus) (ca. 94–50 B.C.)

Lucretius was a Latin poet and philosopher, an exponent of the ideas of Epicurus concerning the nature and purpose of life. He is the author of a single long poem, *De rerum natura (On the Nature of Things)*. Even in translation it has powerful poetic imagery and a capacity to move the reader. The poem was a powerful influence on Whitman who, in the 1830s, outlined it section by section.

The poem is a statement of the materialist theory of Epicurus, arguing that no thing is either created out of nothing or reducible to nothing. The atoms persist, forming and reforming over time in a majestic unfolding of life. Change is the nature of things but all the changes are wonderful and beautiful.

In section 52 of "Song of Myself" we can see the Lucretian influence in the lines "I bequeath myself to the dirt to grow from the grass I love, / If you want me again look for me under your boot-soles."

Lucretius celebrates the Epicurean doctrine of maximizing pleasure and minimizing pain. He argues that this can only be accomplished by knowing the proper nature of life by philosophy which can overcome the fear of death and the gods. Whitman asserts a lack of fear of death and a humanist philosophy of life.

Lucretius's text is not just a philosophical argument but a poetic work of the highest order. We have here an example of one great poet inspiring another over many hundreds of years.

W. Edward Harris

Bibliography

Allen, Gay Wilson. *The Solitary Singer: A Critical Biography of Walt Whitman*. 1955. Rev. ed. 1967. Chicago: U of Chicago P, 1985.

Lucretius, Carus Titus. *The Nature of Things*. Trans. Frank O. Copley. New York: Norton, 1977.

See also EPICTETUS; EPICURUS; HARRIS, THOMAS LAKE; WRIGHT, FRANCES (FANNY)

M

McKay, David (1860–1918)

David McKay was born in Dysart, Scotland, and emigrated to America in 1871. He entered the employ of J.B. Lippincott of Philadelphia in 1873, working as a bookseller. In 1881, Rees Welsh convinced McKay to take over his bookselling business, which McKay did. In the following year, McKay took a few hundred dollars of his own and about twenty-five hundred he borrowed and bought both of Welsh's bookselling and publishing businesses, changing the name of the firm to indicate the new owner. The business prospered: McKay sold the bookselling division in 1896 and enlarged his firm by buying a number of smaller ones, including Street and Smith's line of juveniles. At his death, he left a wife and five children.

After the 1881 edition of *Leaves of Grass* was declared "obscene literature" by the district attorney of Massachusetts, and Whitman refused to delete the offending passages, the publisher, James R. Osgood of Boston, withdrew and sold the plates and stock to Whitman on 17 May 1882. On 5 June, McKay wrote Whitman on behalf of Rees Welsh and offered to publish the book. A contract was signed on 22 July and a new edition of *Leaves* was published on 17 or 18 July, rapidly going through five printings under the Rees Welsh imprint. McKay "formally bo't out and assumed" Rees Welsh's business in October (Whitman 314), and thereafter was Whitman's American publisher. McKay also took over the publication of *Specimen Days & Collect* from Rees Welsh after one printing, and later published *November Boughs* (1888), *Good-Bye My Fancy* (1891), and *Gems from Walt Whitman* (1889) on his own. After Whitman's death, McKay published Whitman's *Complete Prose Works* (1892). McKay's contract with Whitman contained one unusual clause: Whitman was allowed to sell copies of his works on his own and keep the profits, which he did, most notably with sales of the *Complete Poems & Prose* (1888) volume to Britain.

Joel Myerson

Bibliography

"David McKay, 1860–1918." *Publishers Weekly* 30 Nov. 1918: 1799.

Myerson, Joel. *Walt Whitman: A Descriptive Bibliography*. Pittsburgh: U of Pittsburgh P, 1993.

Whitman, Walt. *The Correspondence*. Ed. Edwin Haviland Miller. Vol. 3. New York: New York UP, 1964.

See also LEAVES OF GRASS, 1881–1882 EDITION; OSGOOD, JAMES R.; PHILADELPHIA, PENNSYLVANIA

Macpherson, James ("Ossian") (1736–1796)

Macpherson's "Poems of Ossian" (1760–1763) was a popular epic "translation" of ancient cycle poems written in a medieval Scottish Gaelic dialect. The authenticity of the poems was a hotly debated issue during Macpherson's own time (his most famous detractor being Samuel Johnson), but it was not until after his death that scholars finally concluded that the poems were indeed forgeries. Nevertheless, Macpherson's rhapsodic poetry, his nationalistic fervor, and his original, evocative language heavily influenced major romantic writers in nineteenth-century Europe and America, including William

Blake, Sir Walter Scott, Lord Byron, Ralph Waldo Emerson, Henry David Thoreau, and Walt Whitman. Whitman himself was fond of placing the Ossianic poems alongside the most cherished books of his youth—Homer, Shakespeare, and the Bible (*Prose Works* 2:722)—and he often ranked the bona fide Ossian among the greatest primitive poets of antiquity. Whitman, as John Townsend Trowbridge attests, was particularly fond of the bardic quality of Macpherson's poetry: "he liked to get off alone by the seashore, read Homer and Ossian with the salt air on his cheeks, and shout their winged words to the winds and waves" (172). Although Whitman once resolved never to "fall into the Ossianic, by any chance" (*Notebooks* 5:1806), the influence of Macpherson's poetry on Whitman's cannot be discounted.

Andrew Ladd

Bibliography

Trowbridge, John Townsend. "Reminiscences of Walt Whitman." *Whitman in His Own Time.* Ed. Joel Myerson. Detroit: Omnigraphics, 1991. 169–191.

Whitman, Walt. *Notebooks and Unpublished Prose Manuscripts.* Ed. Edward F. Grier. 6 vols. New York: New York UP, 1984.

———. *Prose Works 1892.* Ed. Floyd Stovall. 2 vols. New York: New York UP, 1963–1964.

See also INFLUENCES ON WHITMAN, PRINCIPAL

"Madman, The" (1843)

This fragment of a novel appeared in the *Washingtonian and Organ,* 28 January 1843. It consists of an unnumbered first chapter and a second chapter which ends with the words "(To be continued)." No other parts of the novel have been uncovered. For further information see Brasher's edition of *The Early Poems and the Fiction.*

The fragment begins with a description of a crowded dining hall. Emphasis is put on the haste with which people are eating and of the honesty of the diners, who tally their own bills and pay as they leave. This honesty stands in opposition to what "foreign slanderers" have said about "our national integrity" (Whitman 240). Then two characters are introduced. Richard Arden, though poor, is a man of good taste. He eats slowly. He is a philosopher. Pierre Barcoure is a descendant of French radicals. He scorns religious superstitions and abhors religious fanaticism, but allows that each religion holds some excellence. Barcoure is called "an infidel" (243). The fragment draws to its end with Richard and Pierre becoming fast friends.

The final paragraph is an apostrophe against friendships that are "rivetted by intimacy in scenes of dissipation" (243). The intensity of this final paragraph and other references to "ardent liquors" (240) indicate the probable didactic purpose of the novel. Its appearance in a temperance newspaper suggests the same purpose.

Reynolds sees "The Madman" as another attempt by Whitman to appeal to the American masses. Kaplan, following Brasher, suggests that this story undermines Whitman's recollections about abandoning work in the manner of *Franklin Evans; or The Inebriate. A Tale of the Times* (1842).

Patrick McGuire

Bibliography

Kaplan, Justin. *Walt Whitman: A Life.* New York: Simon and Schuster, 1980.

Reynolds, David S. *Walt Whitman's America: A Cultural Biography.* New York: Knopf, 1995.

Whitman, Walt. *The Early Poems and the Fiction.* Ed. Thomas L. Brasher. New York: New York UP, 1963.

See also FRANKLIN EVANS; POPULAR CULTURE, WHITMAN AND; SHORT FICTION, WHITMAN'S; TEMPERANCE MOVEMENT

"Mannahatta [I was asking . . .]" (1860)

Walt Whitman's poem "Mannahatta," beginning "I was asking . . .," is one of two lyrics bearing this title. It was first published in the third edition of *Leaves of Grass* (1860). Subsequently, it was published in *Leaves* (1867), incorporated in a "Leaves" group in 1871, and placed in its present cluster, "From Noon to Starry Night," in 1881. Whitman's original poem included significant closing lines that were deleted after 1871. The earlier conclusion calls "Mannahatta" "The free city! no slaves! no owners of slaves" (1871 *Leaves*). Additionally, Whitman lauds the women of New York, saying he is mad to be with them and promising he will return after death to be with them. Whitman also extols the young men, saying, "I swear / I cannot live happy, without I often / go talk, walk, eat, drink, sleep, with them!" (1871 *Leaves*).

In the opening line of the poem Whitman asks for "something specific and perfect for my city." He recalls the "aboriginal name." In his *An American Primer* Whitman talks about various naming words and asks, "What is there in the best aboriginal name?" (19). In an 1889 conversation with Horace Traubel about the word "Mannahatta," Whitman attempted to answer the question. Whitman told Traubel that Dr. Daniel Garrison Brinton once reported in *Folk-Lore* that an Indian had said that "Mannahatta" meant a place to buy bows and arrows. Whitman felt that the definition was "improbable." From his memories of other comments of "authorities" he conjectured that the word meant "a point of land surrounded by rushing, tempestuous, demonic waters" (Traubel 56).

In addition to Whitman's use of the word "Mannahatta" as a title for his poem in 1860, and as a naming word in "Me Imperturbe" (1860), his brother, Thomas Jefferson Whitman (Jeff), and Jeff's wife, Martha, named their first born daughter "Mannahatta." Biographer David Reynolds concludes that "Hattie" was "poetically named" (375).

The poem "Mannahatta," sans the flamboyant references both to men and to women, remains a tribute to Whitman's city. From the "water bays, superb," and the "flowing sea-currents" to the "down-town streets" and "carts hauling goods," Whitman seems transfixed.

William G. Lulloff

Bibliography

Reynolds, David S. *Walt Whitman's America: A Cultural Biography*. New York: Knopf, 1995.
Traubel, Horace. *With Walt Whitman in Camden*. Ed. Gertrude Traubel and William White. Vol. 6. Carbondale: Southern Illinois UP, 1982.
Whitman, Walt. *An American Primer*. Ed. Horace Traubel. 1904. Stevens Point, Wis.: Holy Cow!, 1987.
———. *Leaves of Grass: Comprehensive Reader's Edition*. Ed. Harold W. Blodgett and Sculley Bradley. New York: New York UP, 1965.

See also CITY, WHITMAN AND THE; NEW YORK CITY; PLACE NAMES

M

"March in the Ranks Hard-Prest, and the Road Unknown, A" (1865)

Written during the Civil War, "A March in the Ranks Hard-Prest, and the Road Unknown" was first published in *Drum-Taps* (1865). It was incorporated into the body of *Leaves of Grass* in 1871 as part of the "Drum-Taps" cluster, where it remained through subsequent editions. Whitman bases the poem on an account of the battle of White Oaks Church as related to him by a soldier in one of the hospital wards. With its attention to raw and horrific detail, the poem exemplifies Whitman's realistic, reportorial style of war poetry at its best.

Retreating after battle in the middle of the night, the speaker and the "remnant" of the army to which he belongs come upon "a dim-lighted building" (a church), functioning as an impromptu hospital. They encounter bloody forms of dead and wounded soldiers, among them a lad "shot in the abdomen" and with a face "white as a lily." The speaker moves to stanch the young man's wound; as the lad dies the speaker and his comrades are summoned to resume their retreat.

The poem conveys a nearly overwhelming sense of disorientation and confusion. Rather than moving toward some determinate goal, the speaker and troops are in much the same position at the poem's end as they were at the beginning—in haste and darkness, "the unknown road still marching." The poem's twenty-five lines are composed of a single sentence that weaves through a bewildering maze of images: "Faces, varieties, postures beyond description . . . Surgeons operating, attendants holding lights, the smell of ether, the odor of blood," and so on. While this layered sequence of images suggests the familiar Whitmanesque catalogue, the effect differs strikingly from that of earlier Whitman catalogues: rather than conveying feelings of oneness and connection, it is a catalogue of lurid shapes, discombobulated forms, anatomical smells and fragments, and random cries, shouts, and screams. Nevertheless, here—as in even the grimmest and most disturbing of the "Drum-Taps" poems—a symbol of hope appears, as the "lily" face of the lad suggestively illumines the chaos and darkness of the scene.

John E. Schwiebert

Bibliography

Erkkila, Betsy. *Whitman the Political Poet*. New York: Oxford UP, 1989.
Glicksberg, Charles I., ed. *Walt Whitman and the Civil War*. Philadelphia: U of Pennsylvania P, 1933.

Schwiebert, John E. *The Frailest Leaves: Whitman's Poetic Technique and Style in the Short Poem.* New York: Lang, 1992.

See also CIVIL WAR, THE; "DRUM-TAPS"; *DRUM-TAPS*

Masters, Edgar Lee (1868?–1950)

A midwestern lawyer who took on literature as an avocation, Masters gained fast fame for his popular *Spoon River Anthology* (1915), for which John Cowper Powys hailed him as "the natural child of Walt Whitman" (qtd. in Primeau 94). His initial success was followed by a prolific series of poems, novels, and plays.

In his 1936 autobiography, Masters wrote, "What had enthralled me with Whitman from my days with Anne in Lewistown was his conception of America as the field of a new art and music in which the people would be celebrated instead of kings; and the liberty of Jefferson should be sung until it permeated the entire popular heart" (*Across* 336). In his 1937 *Whitman*, Masters called Whitman "a tribal prophet and poet" (306) who knew that poetry "must come out of the earth" (307). Whitman, writes Masters, "[s]piritually . . . placed himself at the center of America . . . as Jefferson did, through his heredity, environment and native genius" (8). The greatness of Whitman, he continues, lay in the fact that by the time of the first edition of *Leaves of Grass* in 1855 he had acquired his prophetical powers concerning his country—had "the prospect before his eyes of what American poetry could and should be" (76). Masters liked Whitman's celebration of a future America with democratic art in which Whitman would act as a new Hesiod. According to Masters, a new Homer, ostensibly Masters himself, would follow in the Whitmanian future.

Wesley A. Britton

Bibliography
Burgess, Charles E. "Masters and Whitman: A Second Look." *Walt Whitman Review* 17 (1971): 25–27.
Primeau, Ronald. *Beyond Spoon River: The Legacy of Edgar Lee Masters.* Austin: U of Texas P, 1981.
Masters, Edgar Lee. *Across Spoon River: An Autobiography.* New York: Farrar and Rinehart, 1936.
———. *Whitman.* New York: Scribner's, 1937.

See also BIOGRAPHIES; LEGACY, WHITMAN'S

Mathews, Cornelius (ca. 1817–1889)

One of the most visible and contentious members of New York's Young America nationalist movement, Cornelius Mathews was, like Whitman, an active journalist during the early 1840s and through the early 1850s. Mathews was a journalistic writer and periodical editor throughout his long career and wrote across the genres: fiction, sketches, poetry, and plays. He was near the center of the Duyckinck Circle, which helped create Young America, and with Whitman contributed to the movement's most noted outlet, the *United States Magazine and Democratic Review,* edited by John L. O'Sullivan. They were dedicated to Locofoco political radicalism and literary nationalism.

There is good reason to believe that Whitman and Mathews were acquainted both because of their ideological sympathies and because, as active journalists, they would have frequented and at times occupied office space in New York's printing, publishing, and book-selling district on Nassau Street north of Wall. Mathews was a serious author trying to reach a mass audience created by the advances in printing technology beginning in the 1830s and encouraged by Jacksonian democracy's promotion of the common man. He became active in the Know-Nothing party, which assaulted recently arrived Irish Catholics, among other groups, as Whitman himself had in his 1842 *Aurora* pieces. Mathews addressed New York City Nativists—he was vice president of the organization, according to the 5 June 1855 *Tribune*—a month before the first appearance of *Leaves.* But while Whitman might have flirted with Nativism even earlier than the high point of its popularity, he was ultimately inclusive in his democratic sympathies while Mathews was exclusive, holding, it appears, a jingoistic version of democracy, though not as conservative as depicted by his biographer Stein. Pritchard is perhaps right in suggesting that Mathews's *Poems on Man* (1842)—one of his many celebrations of American Republicanism—anticipates *Leaves* in purpose and spirit, but it is far inferior in vision and execution.

Donald Yannella

Bibliography
Chielens, Edward E., ed. *American Literary Magazines: The Eighteenth and Nineteenth Centuries.* New York: Greenwood, 1986.
Pritchard, John Paul. *Criticism in America.* Norman: U of Oklahoma P, 1956.

Stafford, John. *The Literary Criticism of "Young America": A Study in the Relationship of Politics and Literature.* Berkeley: U of California P, 1952.

Stein, Allen F. *Cornelius Mathews.* New York: Twayne, 1974.

Yannella, Donald. "Cornelius Mathews." *American Literary Critics and Scholars, 1850–1880.* Vol. 64 of *Dictionary of Literary Biography.* Ed. John W. Rathbun and Monica M. Grecu. Detroit: Gale, 1988. 178–182.

See also BARNBURNERS AND LOCOFOCOS; DEMOCRATIC REVIEW; DUYCKINCK, EVERT AUGUSTUS; YOUNG AMERICA MOVEMENT

Matthiessen, F.O. (1902–1950)

Harvard Professor of English from 1929 to his death in 1950, Francis Otto Matthiessen helped pioneer the scholarly study of American literature through his six book-length critical studies, numerous articles and reviews, and his efforts in establishing the program in American Civilization at Harvard in 1937. His most influential book, *American Renaissance* (1941), details the shared "devotion to the possibilities of democracy" enunciated in the writings of Ralph Waldo Emerson, Henry David Thoreau, Nathaniel Hawthorne, Herman Melville, and Walt Whitman through a deft interweaving of textual analysis and historical background (ix).

Matthiessen's chapters on Whitman follow his discussion of the "transcendental affirmation" of Emerson and Thoreau and its "counterstatement" by the "tragic writers" Hawthorne and Melville (179). Ever sensitive to Whitman's manipulations of language and poetic form, Matthiessen explores *Leaves of Grass* as, in Whitman's own words, "only a language experiment" (qtd. in Traubel viii). Matthiessen chronicles Whitman's exuberant culling from the "language of the street," which he considered the most vital of languages, to produce the poet's alternately acclaimed and reviled style. Matthiessen moves agilely from close readings of passages to broad cultural considerations and back again to consider also Whitman's debt to Quakerism, particularly Elias Hicks, as well as his enchantment with sermonic oratory, embodied in his tribute to Father Taylor. Matthiessen adroitly likens Whitman's poetic landscapes to the paintings of W.S. Mount, his realism to that of the artists Jean François Millet and Thomas

Eakins. And he traces out the influence of Whitman's free-verse rhythms on Gerard Manley Hopkins's innovative sprung rhythm. Yet Matthiessen emerges ultimately ambivalent about Whitman's artistic accomplishments. Whitman's "inordinate and grotesque failures," he insists, "throw into clearer light his rare successes" (526). Nevertheless, Matthiessen's analysis of Whitman has proved insightful and provocative, and *American Renaissance* remains today a critical force in Whitman studies.

Renée Dye

Bibliography

Cain, William E. *F.O. Matthiessen and the Politics of Criticism.* Madison: U of Wisconsin P, 1988.

Gunn, Giles B. *F.O. Matthiessen: The Critical Achievement.* Seattle: U of Washington P, 1975.

Matthiessen, F.O. *American Renaissance: Art and Expression in the Age of Emerson and Whitman.* New York: Oxford UP, 1941.

Stern, Frederick C. *F.O. Matthiessen: Christian Socialist as Critic.* Chapel Hill: U of North Carolina P, 1981.

Traubel, Horace. Foreword. *An American Primer.* By Walt Whitman. 1904. Stevens Point, Wis.: Holy Cow!, 1987. v–ix.

See also SCHOLARSHIP, TRENDS IN WHITMAN

"Me Imperturbe" (1860)

This poem first appeared in *Leaves of Grass* in 1860 as number eighteen of "Chants Democratic." In 1867 it acquired its present title and in 1881 was transferred to the "Inscriptions" cluster.

Whitman's use of French in the title and opening line exemplifies a practice both typical and controversial: his visit to New Orleans in 1848 apparently stimulated a long-lasting interest in the language, yet his emphatic Americanness renders his frequent employment of French anomalous. Softening the anomaly, however, may be the fact that Whitman, never in France and never a formal student of French, felt relatively unconstrained by the requirements of that language's conventional usage. For example, "imperturbe," used adjectivally, is neologistic, a hybrid of "imperturbable," the adjective, and "perturbe," the verb. Also, many of his "French" words (though not "imperturbe") appeared in

M

contemporary editions of Webster's dictionary and were already undergoing domestication. A third language is actually present in the poem, as "Mannahatta," a word used many times by Whitman, is an Algonquin Indian name for New York and means "large island."

The two words of the title can be read as a microcosm of the poem's structure, which contrasts the human animal, given to foibles and capable of saying "me," with nature, a system self-balanced and ultimately imperturbable. The poem's subtly handled syntax, which never settles into grammatical closure, reflects that contrast: Whitman's apparent claims of imperturbability in the opening four lines are revealed in lines 7 and 8 to be more a matter of wishing than the initial tone indicates; the optative gesture, "O to be," carries the weight of aspiration and prayer. The poem can be seen, therefore, as an important part of the process of Whitman's self-creation, both literary and otherwise; only a man given to perturbations in his personal life might hanker so intensely for imperturbability.

The primary emphasis on the personal in this poem should not obscure the force of lines 5 and 6, which broaden the poem to a prayer for the nation and thus the list of exigencies in line 4, including "poverty" and "crimes," to the status of a less than flattering national portrait with which "we imperturbe," the citizens, must learn to live.

Finally, a note on "me" rather than "I," the latter of which would seem to be more appropriate grammatically throughout the poem: the use of the objective form has the effect of making the self more passive and receptive, a target, as it were, for various agencies. This role of the sufferer, of course, was one from which Whitman did not shy: "I am the man, I suffer'd, I was there" ("Song of Myself," section 33).

Philip Dacey

Bibliography

Allen, Gay Wilson, and Charles T. Davis, eds. *Walt Whitman's Poems*. New York: New York UP, 1955.

Erkkila, Betsy. *Whitman the Political Poet*. New York: Oxford UP, 1989.

Francis, K.H. "Walt Whitman's French." *Modern Language Review* 51 (1956): 493–506.

Kahn, Sholom J. "Whitman's Stoicism." *Scripta Hierosolymitana* 9 (1962): 146–175.

Pound, Louise. "Walt Whitman and the French Language." *American Speech* 1 (1926): 421–430.

Rajasekharaiah, T.R. *The Roots of Whitman's Grass*. Rutherford, N.J.: Fairleigh Dickinson UP, 1970.

Schyberg, Frederik. *Walt Whitman*. Trans. Evie Allison Allen. 1951. New York: AMS, 1966.

Thurin, Erik Ingvar. *Whitman Between Impressionism and Expressionism: Language of the Body, Language of the Soul*. Lewisburg, Pa.: Bucknell UP, 1995.

See also FOREIGN LANGUAGE BORROWINGS; "INSCRIPTIONS"; STOICISM

Media Interpretations of Whitman's Life and Works

Whitman's verse and biography are subjects captured on film, television, CD-ROM, and recording media for both educational and entertainment purposes. Musical composers, both classical and popular, have set his verse in a variety of languages, and many actors have lent their voices to Whitman's words. Below is a listing and analysis of these efforts, emphasizing the most important and useful projects to date.

Movies

Hemdale Films's *Beautiful Dreamers* (1992, directed by John Kent Harrison) starred Rip Torn as Whitman visiting Dr. Richard Maurice Bucke at an insane asylum in London, Ontario. Set in 1880, the film explores Bucke's use of Whitman's ideas and poetry in what would become modern occupational therapy. (Available on video.)

The 1994 sixteen-minute film *Yonnondio*, inspired by Whitman's poem, consists of readings, music, and visual imagery blended by Ali Mohamed Selim into a montage of mankind. Peter Buffett's musical score merges various voices, emphasizing the film's themes of hope, joy, compassion, forgiveness, and understanding. (Available on video.)

Whitman is frequently quoted in director Peter Weir's *Dead Poets Society* (1989), is the subject of a question in Robert Redford's *Quiz Show* (1994), and is alluded to in *Little Women* (1994, directed by Gillian Anderson). He figures notably in *Fame* (1980, directed by Alan Parker), *Bull Durham* (1988, directed by Ron Shelton), *The Road Scholar* (1992, directed by Roger Weisberg), and *With Honors* (1994, directed by Alek Keshishian). In the documentary *The Road Scholar*, poet Andrei Codrescu visits Whitman's home in Camden, New Jersey.

Television

Whitman's verse has been quoted in both educational and entertainment shows, such as the 1960s series *Room 222,* set in the Walt Whitman High School. The CBS series *American Parade* produced *Song of Myself* (first broadcast 9 March 1976), starring Rip Torn as Whitman and Brad Davis as Peter Doyle. Many episodes of the CBS series *Northern Exposure* featured disc jockey Chris Stevens reading passages and discussing "my mentor, Walt Whitman," on fictional KBER radio. The 28 January 1995 episode of *Dr. Quinn, Medicine Woman* included two characters discussing seeing Whitman at a New York Lyceum. Whitman is one of many contemporary voices in Ken Burns's PBS miniseries *The Civil War* (1990) and his subsequent series, *Baseball* (1994).

The best video is a 1988 episode of PBS's *Voices and Visions* series entitled *Walt Whitman,* produced by the New York Center for Visual History. Directed by Jack Smithie for the South Carolina Educational Television Network, the hour blends biography, literary criticism, and modern responses to Whitman, most notably by Allen Ginsberg, Galway Kinnell, and Donald Hall.

Educational Video, Film, and CD ROM

Educational filmmakers have repeatedly explored Whitman's relationship with the Civil War. WITF, a Hershey, Pennsylvania PBS affiliate, produced the thirty-minute *Walt Whitman and the Civil War* (1976) featuring the First Poetry Quartet. Churchill Media's *Walt Whitman's Civil War* (1972) is a fifteen-minute color discussion. Films for the Humanities' twelve-minute "Walt Whitman: American Poet," from the "Against the Odds" series (1988), is a well-produced introduction discussing Whitman's place in literary history and his reactions to the Civil War, using period photography, animations, and modern film footage.

The bizarre, fanciful *Walt Whitman: Endlessly Rocking* (1986) is a twenty-one-minute film (or video) showing Whitman teaching students to read "Out of the Cradle" by way of rap (Syracuse University Classroom Films). *American Bard* (1981) features a reading by poet William Everson from his book *American Bard* (1981), a setting of the 1855 Preface as a poem.

The "Time, Life, and Works of Whitman" (1995) is a CD-ROM educational tool combining visuals with lengthy passages from Whitman's verse and emphasizing his important themes (Filmic Archives).

Other educational media: *Poems of Walt Whitman,* readings of Whitman poems, McGraw-Hill, Lumin Films, 16 mm; *Walt Whitman* discusses Whitman's poetic language, Films for the Humanities and Sciences, 1988, twelve minutes, color; *Walt Whitman,* Poetry by Americans Series, biography, with poetry narrated by Efrem Zimbalist, Jr., AIMS Media, 1972, color; *Frost and Whitman* features excerpts from the two poets' works performed by Will Geer, New York State Education Dept., 1965, thirty minutes, b/w.; *Walt Whitman: Poet for a New Age* explores Whitman and democracy, mystical truths, mortality, primacy of the personality and love, Encyclopaedia Britannica Educational Corporation, 1971, thirty minutes, color (award-winning program); *Walt Whitman: The Centennial* presents a discussion of Whitman's life and work by Milton Kessler, Streetlight Productions, 1992, fifty-six minutes.

Music

One frequently recorded setting is Paul Hindemith's 1948 "When Lilacs Last in the Dooryard Bloom'd; A Requiem for Those We Love" in both English and German. "Lilacs" has been set as a cantata by Roger Sessions (1974), Frank Shallenberg (1967), and George Crumb ("Apparition," 1980). Karl Amadeus Hartmann composed "Symphonie: Versuch Eines Requiems nach Worten von Walt Whitman" in German (1957), and Per Norgard's "Den Himmelske og den Jordiske Kaerlighed [Sacred and Profane Love]" is sung in Danish (1978). Harry T. Burleigh used the words from "Ethiopia Saluting the Colors" in his collection of spirituals entitled *Deep River,* and Ralph Vaughan Williams used Whitman as an inspiration for "Toward the Unknown Region" (1907), "A Sea Symphony" (1909), and "Darest Thou Now O Soul" (1925). Charles Wuorinen's "Unseen Leaves for Oboe, Soprano, and Electronic Tape" (1977) set the stage for future experimental multimedia uses of Whitman's text, such as Anita Kerr's 1988 *In the Soul* (Gaia Records), which set Whitman's verse to original synthesizer music.

In 1995 playwright Alan Brody and composer Peter Child, both MIT professors, staged a Boston production of their dramatic oratorio "Reckoning Time: Song of Walt Whitman." The chorale takes place in the moment between Whitman's last breath of inspiration and his last exhalation, with dialogues between Whitman and Peter Doyle. Whitman encounters four ships representing four periods of his life with lyrics taken from "Starting from Paumanok," "Crossing Brooklyn Ferry," and "Passage to India." Allen Ginsberg, who partially inspired the work, appears in the production, beckoning Whitman onto the fourth ship of immortality.

Various musicians and actors have also responded to Whitman. Folk singer Joan Baez used Whitman materials in her "I Saw the Vision of Armies" on her *Baptism: A Journey Through Our Time* (Vanguard, 1968), and the Gregg Smith Singers sang Whitman on *An American Triptych* (1965). Actor John Carradine performed "Poets to Come" with a jazz setting for vol. 1 of *An Anthology of Poetry and Jazz* (World Pacific), as did actor Stacy Keach with "Low, Body and Soul" on *Earth Day* (Caedmon). Former Fleetwood Mac guitarist Lindsey Buckingham released a solo CD in 1992, "Out of The Cradle" which included a booklet of facsimile excerpts from "Out of the Cradle Endlessly Rocking." In 1983, Irish singer Van Morrison invoked Whitman in his song "Rave on John Donne," recorded on the album *Inarticulate Speech of the Heart.*

Many other musical settings are readily available in CD, LP, or cassette formats, many performed by more than one artist. Others are published only as scores.

Spoken Word Recordings

Cassettes, record albums, and CDs of readings from Whitman and lectures about him are available from a variety of sources. The Library of Congress recorded the significant 1955 *Leaves of Grass* Centennial Series, including Gay Wilson Allen's "Whitman, the Man," David Daiches's "Whitman, the Philosopher," and Mark Van Doren's "Whitman the Poet." Poet Robert Duncan's 1979 lecture, "Whitman's line . . . ," for the 80 Langdon Street talk series is available on tape, as is his lecture on Whitman's homosexuality on "Poetry Reading" which includes Allen Ginsberg reading Whitman's verse (1970).

Ginsberg's own poetry album, *Howl and Other Poems* (1959, Fantasy Records), includes his reading of "A Supermarket in California," an imaginative meeting between Ginsberg and his ghost-mentor, Whitman. Whitman is also invoked in Ginsberg's "Ode to Failure," read with musical background on the 1989 CD *The Lion for Real* (Island).

Alexander Scourby, the most famous voice on spoken word records, has been a frequently used reader of Whitman's verse. He is featured on the 1961 *An Introduction to Great Poetry* (Pan-Harmonic Musical Educational Society). Louis Untermeyer's script cites Whitman as an example of a free-verse poet celebrating the "divine average" in "I Hear America Singing." Scourby, and Nancy Wickwire read *Enjoying Poetry: 19th Century American Poets* (1966), an album including Whitman and others (Listening Library). Scourby reads Whitman's verse in *Golden Treasury of American Verse* (Spoken Arts), *Treasury of Great Poetry* (Listening Library), and several editions of *Treasury of Walt Whitman: Leaves of Grass,* a two-record or cassette set featuring selected poems (Musical Heritage Society/Spoken Arts).

Jeff Riggenbach read the abridged *Specimen Days Journal* on two cassettes (Audio Scholar), a spoken word Whitman autobiography describing his life as nurse, poet, and philosopher during the Civil War and subsequent years.

Numerous other recordings are listed in the Hoffman index.

Filmstrips

Among filmstrips available are the following: *The Living Tradition: Ginsberg on Whitman,* featuring Beat poet Allen Ginsberg discussing Whitman's life and literature, 1980, one filmstrip, two cassettes, teacher's guide, forty-eight minutes (also on videocassette); *The Civil War,* filmstrip 2, unit 6, edited by Reginald Gibbon, discusses Whitman's relationship to the war both personally and philosophically, Films for the Humanities, 1978; *Whitman: The American Singer,* written and produced by Thomas S. Klise, critical assessment of Whitman's literary standing with biographical notes, 1971 (also on videocassette); *Walt Whitman's Civil War,* Will Geer as Whitman, Magus Films, 1969, sound/filmstrip; and *Walt Whitman: Poet for a New Age,* Encyclopedia Britannica Films, 1971, sound/filmstrip.

Wesley A. Britton

Bibliography

Bowker's Complete Video Directory: 1994. Vol. 3: Education Titles S-Z. New Providence, N.J.: Bowker, 1994. Annotated listings with rental information on selected Whitman videos.

Hoffman, Herbert H., and Rita Ludwing Hoffman. *International Index to Recorded Poetry.* New York: Wilson, 1983.

Kummings, Donald D., ed. *Approaches to Teaching Whitman's "Leaves of Grass."* New York: MLA, 1990. List and discussion of available audio-visual tools for the classroom, including photographs, filmstrips, films, and music: 20–22, 186–187.

Padgett, Ron. "Whitman Resources." *Teachers and Writers Guide to Walt Whitman.* New York: Teachers and Writers Collaborative, 1991. 197–206. Annotated listing of selected educational tools.

UCAL Melvyl On-line catalogue. Detailed listings of videos and 111 musical settings and lecture media, including all known recordings and formats.

See also "AMERICA [CENTRE OF EQUAL DAUGHTERS . . .]"; INTERNET, WHITMAN ON THE; MUSIC, WHITMAN'S INFLUENCE ON; PHOTOGRAPHS AND PHOTOGRAPHERS

Memoranda During the War (1875–1876)

"My idea is a book of the time, worthy the time" (*Correspondence* 1:171), Whitman wrote to the Boston publisher James Redpath in October 1863, proposing a Civil War narrative he planned to title "Memoranda of a Year." Redpath turned down the offer and Whitman's Civil War autobiography would be another ten years in the making. In 1874 Whitman published a version of his original project, now entitled "'Tis But Ten Years Since," in six articles for the New York *Weekly Graphic*. A year later he collected and republished the *Weekly Graphic* articles as *Memoranda During the War* in a private printing of less than one hundred copies. In 1876 Whitman republished *Memoranda During the War* as a section of *Two Rivulets,* the second volume of the Centennial edition of his work, and then again as a section of *Specimen Days & Collect* (1882).

Much had happened in the ten years since the war. Published three years after the Crédit Mobilier scandal of the Grant administration, two years after the "salary grab" of 1873, and in the midst of the worst economic depression in American history, *Memoranda During the War* is indeed "a book of the time," as Whitman knew. But it is a book as implicated in the cultural contexts of the Gilded Age as in the Civil War itself. The America emerging from the ashes of war frankly baffled the poet. Whitman's dream of a democratic republic of free labor was overwhelmed by the emergence of an industrialized power-state, what he called the "leviathan" of postwar America. That America, in Whitman's eyes, was despotic, stratified, hypocritical, and corrupt—even less committed to the possibilities of popular democracy, even less interested in the destiny of the common people than American culture before the war. The nation had become a huge body, Whitman wrote in *Democratic Vistas* (1871), "with little or no soul" (*Prose Works* 2:370).

Memoranda responds to that diminishment. As Betsy Erkkila argues in *Whitman the Political Poet*, the book is an anthology of republican virtue, a case study of democratic idealism implicitly attacking the business ethos of the Gilded Age. The central issue in *Memoranda* is not politics but character. Whitman is largely silent on the major public issues of the era: slavery, emancipation, Reconstruction, suffrage. Mythologizing the war as a demonstration of what he terms "the latent Personal Character and eligibilities of These States" (*Memoranda* 4), Whitman subordinates political issues to brief, intimate portraits of common courage and self-sacrifice. He has little to say about battles, generals, tactics or turning-points. His heroes are not Ulysses S. Grant and Robert E. Lee, but Calvin Harlowe and Thomas Haley. And his focus is almost exclusively on the suffering of common soldiers. His titles signal that emphasis: "Two Brooklyn Boys," "A New York Soldier," "A Secesh Brave," "Bad Wounds, the Young." Facing a spectacle of postwar greed and political scandal, Whitman returns to the hospitals and battlefields of the Civil War with a sense almost of relief. There he finds the latent character of the American people—in a Massachusetts soldier returning from Andersonville, in an Armory Square nurse sitting at the bedside of a dying patient, in a middle-aged Southerner comforting the wounded at Chancellorsville.

This is the "interior history" of Whitman's Civil War, the "soul" bargained away by Gilded Age America. Whitman summons that soul in the pages of his text. "They summon up," he begins, "even in this silent and vacant room as I write, not only the sinewy regiments and brigades, marching or in camp, but the countless phantoms of those who fell . . ." (*Memoranda* 3). If the *Memoranda* is a jeremiad in the tradition of Ralph Waldo Emerson and Henry David Thoreau, it is also a kind of romance. Like Nathaniel Hawthorne and Edgar Allan

M

Poe, Whitman resurrects the dead. He stirs the ghosts of a recent past—'tis but ten years since—and restores the reality of past suffering to a postwar America all too willing to forget. The Civil War hospital is Whitman's House of Pain, his House of the Seven Gables, and he conjures the phantoms of the dead to connect the present age to the living history of its own war, a war "in danger," Whitman feared, "of being totally forgotten" (*Memoranda* 5).

Robert Leigh Davis

Bibliography

Aaron, Daniel. *The Unwritten War: American Writers and the Civil War.* 1973. Madison: U of Wisconsin P, 1987.

Erkkila, Betsy. *Whitman the Political Poet.* New York: Oxford UP, 1989.

Sweet, Timothy. *Traces of War: Poetry, Photography, and the Crisis of the Union.* Baltimore: Johns Hopkins UP, 1990.

Thomas, M. Wynn. *The Lunar Light of Whitman's Poetry.* Cambridge, Mass.: Harvard UP, 1987.

Whitman, Walt. *The Correspondence.* Ed. Edwin Haviland Miller. 6 vols. New York: New York UP, 1961–1977.

———. *Memoranda During the War & Death of Abraham Lincoln.* Ed. Roy P. Basler. Bloomington: Indiana UP, 1962.

———. *Prose Works 1892.* Ed. Floyd Stovall. 2 vols. New York: New York UP, 1963–1964.

See also CIVIL WAR, THE; CIVIL WAR NURSING; LABOR AND LABORING CLASSES; SPECIMEN DAYS; TWO RIVULETS, AUTHOR'S EDITION

"Memories of President Lincoln" (1881–1882)

"I love the President personally," Walt Whitman wrote in his diary (*Complete* 272), impressed with the statesman's high moral and spiritual character and unconquerable steadiness. He first sighted Abraham Lincoln in February 1861—when the president-elect arrived in New York on his way to his inauguration—and observed him often in Washington during the war years but he never personally met him. Lincoln, a westerner, came to be the "Redeemer President of These States" Whitman had been looking for (*Complete* 259). From the moment of his election to the nineteenth term of the presidency (1861–1865), the doubting poet was drawn to him. Their positions on slavery and disunion were alike. Beginning with Lincoln's resolution to overcome the Union's disastrous defeat in the first battle of Bull Run (21 July 1861), Whitman's esteem for him grew. Both had similar views and hopes for democracy in America and abroad.

Whitman grouped his four elegies on the death of Lincoln in *Leaves of Grass* (1881–1882) under the title "Memories of President Lincoln" (originally entitled "President Lincoln's Burial Hymn"). To emphasize a symbolic representation of the American people, Whitman did not use Lincoln's name in any of the poems. "When Lilacs Last in the Dooryard Bloom'd" (1865–1866) expresses a most profound, noble, personal grief and despair at the loss of this "powerful western fallen star" (section 2). The nation unites in mourning (indicative of the centrality of Whitman's nationalism) as the funeral train travels across a portion of rural and urban America amidst the blue and gray soldiers who died. The poet places a sprig of lilacs on the president's coffin to express affection. But Whitman also grieves publicly and longs to deck the coffins of all the dead with lilacs. Further, the pictures "of farms" and "workshops" (section 11) he hangs in the burial house of a democratic president reflect democratic America. Though still gripped by sorrow, he prepares to turn toward the hermit bird's song, which sings of death as a *"strong deliveress"* from suffering (section 14). This enables him to reconcile himself to Lincoln's physical death and to all death. He is now able to envisage the "battle-corpses, myriads of them" (section 15) whom he "loved so well" (section 16) and who are forever enshrined in his—and civic—memory and as a significant theme of the dirge.

In "O Captain! My Captain!" (1865–1866), his most popular poem, written soon after "Lilacs," the wailing Whitman dealt with Lincoln's death differently. The president is described as the fallen captain of the ship of state he had steered to victory. Gazing at the "bleeding, pale" body of Lincoln, the poet memorializes him as the nation's martyr chief as he is universally mourned. Whitman repeatedly recited this patriotic ballad at the end of his memorial lectures—meant for the entire nation—given on the "Death of Abraham Lincoln" from 1879 to 1890.

Whitman immediately commemorated the occasion of Lincoln's funeral procession in Washington (which he witnessed) with his short poem "Hush'd be the Camps To-day" (4 May 1865). Spokesman for the silent, grieving, and meditative soldiers, Whitman celebrates "our commander's death" as a release from "life's stormy conflicts," ending on a note of finality as "they envault the coffin there."

His final four-line epitaph "This Dust was Once the Man" (1871–1872) honors Lincoln as the "gentle, plain, just and resolute" man who with "cautious hand" preserved the Union.

Whitman's judgment of Lincoln was correct and discerning. Now, a little over a century and a quarter since Lincoln's death, the publication of books on Lincoln still recalls his greatness as president. When, for instance, former Governor Mario M. Cuomo of New York was asked by a delegation of teachers from Poland's Solidarity Union to suggest published material on democracy, he chose Lincoln (see *Lincoln on Democracy,* edited by Mario M. Cuomo [1990]).

Bernard Hirschhorn

Bibliography

Coyle, William, ed. *The Poet and the President: Whitman's Lincoln Poems.* New York: Odyssey, 1962.

Donald, David Herbert. *Lincoln.* New York: Simon and Schuster, 1995.

Erkkila, Betsy. *Whitman the Political Poet.* New York: Oxford UP, 1989.

Kaplan, Justin. *Walt Whitman: A Life.* New York: Simon and Schuster, 1980.

Miller, James E., Jr. "'Lilacs': Grief and Reconciliation." *A Critical Guide to "Leaves of Grass."* By Miller. Chicago: U of Chicago P, 1957. 111–119.

Whitman, Walt. "Abraham Lincoln." *Complete Poetry and Collected Prose.* Ed. Justin Kaplan. New York: Library of America, 1982. 1196–1199.

———. "Death of Abraham Lincoln." *Complete Poetry and Collected Prose.* Ed. Justin Kaplan. New York: Library of America, 1982. 1036–1047.

———. *Memories of President Lincoln and Other Lyrics of the War.* Portland, Maine: Thomas B. Mosher, 1906.

———. "Walt Whitman on Abraham Lincoln." Rpt. from Whitman's lecture on Abraham Lincoln's death. *Semi-Weekly Tribune* 18 Apr. 1879. (A copy is in the collection of the Easthampton Free Library, Easthampton, Long Island, N.Y.)

See also CIVIL WAR, THE; "DEATH OF ABRAHAM LINCOLN"; LINCOLN, ABRAHAM; LINCOLN'S DEATH; "O CAPTAIN! MY CAPTAIN!"; "WHEN LILACS LAST IN THE DOORYARD BLOOM'D"

Menken, Adah Isaacs (ca. 1835–1868)

Born Dolores Adios in New Orleans in straitened circumstances, possibly to a Jewish family, the woman later to be known as Adah Menken performed from an early age as an actress, musician, artist's model, and dancer in opera houses and circuses up and down the Mississippi Valley, the Midwest, and in Texas. Although lacking formal education and, as an actress, consigned to the Victorian demimonde, Menken was a serious artist and published poetry and essays in local newspapers. A marriage to a Jewish musician, Alexander Menken, ended in divorce. She arrived in New York in 1858 and, aided by a second marriage to the popular prizefighter John Heenan, became something of a celebrity on the Bowery theater circuit. In 1860 she created what was to become an international sensation in the melodrama *Mazeppa.* Menken played a deposed prince. In one daring scene, dressed in a tight flesh-colored costume which simulated male nudity, she rode a "fiery untamed steed" across the stage. During her New York sojourn Menken was, along with her friend Ada Clare, one of a handful of women to ignore conventions of female propriety and frequent the bohemian saloon Pfaff's; she met Whitman there along with the drama critics and writers she cultivated. A poet herself, she was moved by his gifts; he, in turn, saw the group of women of which she was a part as some of his greatest supporters at a low point in his career. Menken took up residence in Europe in the 1860s, befriending literary notables in Paris and London, including Swinburne, Dickens, and Dumas *père.* She continued to write poetry, some of it Whitmanian free verse. She died of unidentified causes, attended by a rabbi.

Christine Stansell

Bibliography

Falk, Bernard. *The Naked Lady: A Biography of Adah Isaacs Menken.* London: Hutchinson, 1934.

Northcott, Richard. *Adah Isaacs Menken: An Illustrated Biography.* London: Press Printers, 1921.

See also ACTORS AND ACTRESSES; CLARE, ADA (JANE MCELHENEY); PFAFF'S RESTAURANT

Metaphysics

In "Starting from Paumanok" (1860), Walt Whitman proclaimed his intention to "inaugurate a religion" (section 7), and ever since scholars have debated the precise nature of Whitman's metaphysics. Influenced from early childhood by the Quaker religion of his parents and by the preaching of Elias Hicks, Whitman rejected dogma in favor of his own free-ranging exploration of spirituality.

Whitman acquired a romantic pantheism from German and English sources, according to Gay Wilson Allen, as well as from Ralph Waldo Emerson. Although T.R. Rajasekharaiah and V.K. Chari attempt to identify some Eastern sources of Whitman's metaphysics, more probably the poet was influenced by popular philosophical works of his own age, namely, Frances Wright's *A Few Days in Athens* and Count Volney's *Ruins*. Both books helped create Whitman's philosophy, offering an Epicureanism that he readily assimilated. Critics have underestimated the impact these works had on Whitman's conception of metaphysics, George Hutchinson believes, in particular on the creation of his eclectic spirituality. After reading Wright's book, Whitman studied Lucretius's *De Rerum Natura (On the Nature of Things)*, a massive, didactic poem intended to explain Epicureanism. Although Whitman disliked systems and never embraced Epicureanism in its entirety, one can see in his poems evidence of an acceptance of its main tenet, the unity of body and soul.

The most eloquent expression of this belief is "Sun-Down Poem" (1856), later renamed "Crossing Brooklyn Ferry," which appeared in the second edition of *Leaves of Grass*. In this poem Whitman conflates time, space, and the individual souls of the ferry passengers into an eternal unity. Whitman expresses this unity in many of his greatest poems by blending the material and the spiritual. In "Song of Myself," for example, the poet sees "God in every object" (section 48), and even though he admits not understanding God, he has faith that the spirit of life continues because the matter of nature is inexhaustible. Whitman concludes the poem by asserting the unity of spirit and matter and by exhorting the reader to search for the poet in the grass under his "boot-soles" (section 52). The implied connection between body and soul, reader and poet, and more generally between one person and another, provides the heart of Whitman's metaphysics. In "The Base of All Metaphysics" (1871), Whitman asserts that the "attraction of friend to friend" underlies all the world's systems of philosophy.

Many critics have questioned, however, whether Whitman was ever really able to resolve in his own mind the question of the body-versus-soul dichotomy. Roger Asselineau, for example, argues that Whitman had settled on such unity before the appearance of the 1855 edition of *Leaves of Grass,* but that his attitude gradually changed in favor of the spiritual part of his belief as his body grew infirm. As early as 1867, following his experiences visiting wounded soldiers during the Civil War, and with his own physical condition becoming problematic, Whitman began to stress a spiritual longing that would offer escape from corporeal bounds. James Warren sees the change even earlier, with the appearance of the 1860 edition of *Leaves of Grass*. In that version Whitman inaugurates his religion by moving "Starting from Paumanok" to the initial position. David Kuebrich, perhaps the first modern critic to take Whitman's religion seriously, provides an interesting counter-current to those who discuss the phases of Whitman's development by asserting that the poet's metaphysics provided from the very beginning the core of his poetic endeavor.

Still, there is evidence that, as he grew older, Whitman was not satisfied with some of the implications of his earlier work, in particular the idea that no individual identity would survive the death of the body. Michael Moon, in his fine work with the first four versions of *Leaves of Grass,* finds evidence of a shifting perspective. Moon and Hutchinson agree that Whitman grew increasingly preoccupied with the mortality of the flesh and with the immortality of the soul. Certainly, Whitman did become more concerned with what his religion might mean for him after death. In the Preface to the 1876 edition of *Leaves of Grass,* for example, Whitman speaks soberly of the "eleventh hour" of his life, acknowledging that many of the poems are somber enough that the book might be titled "Death's book" (Whitman 744). In his later poems, and in revisions of earlier ones, Whitman stresses the belief that a discrete individual will survive the death of the body. Fittingly, 1892, the year of Whitman's death, witnessed the poem "Good-Bye my Fancy!," in which the poet exults to his soul "Good-bye—and hail!," again presenting death as both cessation and commencement. While Whitman's metaphysics do seem to engage more spiritual realms as he grows older, the physical continues to be implicated in the spiritual even in his later work. Against a backdrop of fluctuation, a continuity in Whitman's thought emerges, and with "Good-Bye my Fancy!" he ends his career still asserting that body and soul are "blended into one."

Joe Boyd Fulton

Bibliography

Allen, Gay Wilson. *The Solitary Singer: A Critical Biography of Walt Whitman.* 1955. Rev. ed. 1967. Chicago: U of Chicago P, 1985.

Asselineau, Roger. *The Evolution of Walt Whitman: The Creation of a Book.* Trans. Roger Asselineau and Burton L. Cooper. Cambridge, Mass.: Harvard UP, 1962.

Chari, V.K. *Whitman in the Light of Vedantic Mysticism.* Lincoln: U of Nebraska P, 1964.

Hutchinson, George B. *The Ecstatic Whitman: Literary Shamanism & the Crisis of the Union.* Columbus: Ohio State UP, 1986.

Kuebrich, David. *Minor Prophecy: Walt Whitman's New American Religion.* Bloomington: Indiana UP, 1989.

Moon, Michael. *Disseminating Whitman: Revision and Corporeality in "Leaves of Grass."* Cambridge, Mass.: Harvard UP, 1991.

Rajasekharaiah, T.R. *The Roots of Whitman's Grass.* Rutherford, N.J.: Fairleigh Dickinson UP, 1970.

Warren, James Perrin. *Walt Whitman's Language Experiment.* University Park: Pennsylvania State UP, 1990.

Whitman, Walt. *Leaves of Grass: Comprehensive Reader's Edition.* Ed. Harold W. Blodgett and Sculley Bradley. New York: New York UP, 1965.

See also "Base of All Metaphysics, The"; Epicurus; Human Body; Lucretius; Mysticism; Religion; Soul, The; Volney, Constantin; Wright, Frances (Fanny)

Mexican War, The

War with Mexico intensified the division between defenders and opponents of slavery. Revolting against Spain, Mexico abolished slavery in 1813, but in 1821 they allowed immigrants to bring slaves into Texas. When Mexico reasserted abolition in 1829, North American slave owners in the United States and in Texas interpreted this as an act of war. In 1836, Texas declared independence; war between Texas and Mexico then began.

Santa Anna proclaimed combatant Texans to be outlaws subject to death on capture. Aware of this policy, every defender at the Alamo died fighting. A few days later, 27 March 1836, at Goliad, the Mexicans, after taking prisoners, shot 342 (Whitman counted 412). Section 34 of "Song of Myself" memorializes the "Goliad Massacre." The narrator passes over the better-known site: "I tell not the fall of Alamo / Not one escaped to tell the fall of Alamo." The grim story of Goliad follows: "A youth not seventeen years old seiz'd his assassin till two more came to release him, / The three were all torn and cover'd with the boy's blood."

Whitman enthusiastically supported the wars against Mexico—fought by Texas, 1836–1845, and by the United States, 1845–1848. He believed in North America's manifest destiny to incorporate Texas, Arizona, Santa Fe, Nevada, California, Oregon, Cuba, and perhaps the Yucatan; however, he opposed annexing all Mexico, Central America, Venezuela, and Ecuador. These "weak and imbecile powers" needed first "to respect us, and when they are so far civilized and educated . . . it will be time enough to think of annexation" (*I Sit* 162).

With his Quaker background, however, Whitman became uncomfortable with the Mexican War. Initially thrilled, he asked, "What has miserable, inefficient Mexico—with her superstition, her burlesque upon freedom, her actual tyranny by the few over the many—what has she to do with the great mission of peopling the New World with a noble race?" (*Gathering* 1:247). Soon, however, Whitman supported the Wilmot Proviso that would exclude slavery from conquered territories and called for an end to the war. Those like Whitman who could not support the extension of slavery founded the Free Soil Party: "Free soil, free speech, free labor and free men." "Free men" included only the "white workingmen . . . mechanics, farmers and operatives"; slaves would not be emancipated; nor could dark-skinned Mexicans be incorporated into the union (*Gathering* 1:208).

Fired from the Brooklyn *Daily Eagle* because he supported free soil, Whitman worked in New Orleans from January to May 1848. The city was the gateway to Mexico; Whitman recalled "the crowds of soldiers, the gay young officers, going or coming, the receipt of important news, the many discussions, the returning wounded, and so on" (*Prose Works* 2:605). In the *Crescent,* he described General Zachary Taylor at the theater. From the returning soldiers, Whitman may have gathered the Spanish word *camarada,* which he masculinized and anglicized as "camerado." The term comes from the Spanish *cama; camarada* means "someone who studies, eats or lives with another," but literally translates as "bedmate." *La camarada* formed the smallest Spanish military unit.

In later poems, journals, letters, and reminiscences, Whitman seldom mentioned the Mexican War and rejected his anti-Mexican rhetoric. In 1864, he confessed that Mexico was "the only one to whom we have ever really done wrong" (*Prose Works* 1:93). In 1883, celebrating the 333rd anniversary of Santa Fe, he wrote: "To that composite American identity of the future, Spanish character will supply some of the most needed parts." American identity must include Spanish as well as "our aboriginal or Indian population—the Aztec in the South, and many a tribe in the North and West" (*Prose Works* 2:553).

Charley Shively

Bibliography

Davenport, Harbert. "Goliad Massacre." *The Handbook of Texas.* Ed. Walter Prescott Webb. Vol. 1. Austin: Texas State Historical Association, 1952–1976. 704–705.

González de la Garza, Mauricio. *Walt Whitman: Racista, Imperialista, Antimexicano.* Mexico City: Málaga, 1971.

Whitman, Walt. *The Gathering of the Forces.* Ed. Cleveland Rodgers and John Black. 2 vols. New York: Putnam, 1920.

———. *I Sit and Look Out: Editorials from the Brooklyn Daily Times.* Ed. Emory Holloway and Vernolian Schwarz. New York: Columbia UP, 1932.

———. *Prose Works 1892.* Ed. Floyd Stovall. 2 vols. New York: New York UP, 1963–1964.

See also BROOKLYN, NEW YORK; FREE SOIL PARTY; IMPERIALISM; RACIAL ATTITUDES; SLAVERY AND ABOLITIONISM; WILMOT PROVISO

Michelet, Jules (1798–1874)

Jules Michelet was a French romantic historian who, in his most celebrated multivolume work, *Histoire de France* (1833–1867), approached the past from the perspective of the present as part of an ongoing struggle of the people for liberty against tyranny, oppression, and fate. As editor of the Brooklyn *Daily Eagle,* 1846–1848, Whitman reviewed the work of several French romantic writers and historians, including a translation of Michelet's *History of France.* Whitman may also have read an 1846 translation of Michelet's *The People* (1846). Michelet's messianic and prose-poetic vision of the nationalist historian as the "voice of the people" appears to have had some impact on Whitman's own attempt to invent an American poet and a democratic poetry that embodies the simultaneously national and international aspirations of the people through time. While the many parallels between Michelet's historian of the people and Whitman's democratic poet may be the result of their shared intellectual heritage in the enlightenment and revolutionary periods in France and America, in at least one instance Whitman lifted an entire passage from an 1869 translation of Michelet's *The Bird* (1856) and rearranged it as verse in his 1876 poem "To the Man-of-War-Bird." Against what he considered to be the more conservative pro-monarchist politics of the British romantics, Whitman identified with and drew upon the works of several French enlightenment and romantic writers, including (along with Michelet) Voltaire, Constantin Volney, Jean-Jacques Rousseau, George Sand, and Victor Hugo. Perhaps more important than the work of identifying Michelet or some other French writer as the source of this or that passage in Whitman, however, is the need to rethink the tendency of past critics to emphasize the national and specifically American origins of Whitman's work. What the literary and cultural exchanges between Whitman, Michelet, and other French writers suggest, finally, is the need for a more transnational and ultimately global approach both to Whitman and to the study of American literature and culture more generally.

Betsy Erkkila

Bibliography

Allen, Gay Wilson. *The New Walt Whitman Handbook.* 1975. New York: New York UP, 1986.

Barthes, Roland, ed. *Michelet*. 1975. Trans. Richard Howard. New York: Hill and Wang, 1987.

Erkkila, Betsy. *Walt Whitman Among the French: Poet and Myth*. Princeton: Princeton UP, 1980.

Haac, Oscar A. *Jules Michelet*. Boston: Twayne, 1982.

Kippur, Stephen A. *Jules Michelet: A Study of Mind and Sensibility*. Albany: State U of New York P, 1981.

Mitzman, Arthur. *Michelet: Rebirth and Romanticism in Nineteenth-Century France*. New Haven: Yale UP, 1990.

See also HUGO, VICTOR; SAND, GEORGE; VOLNEY, CONSTANTIN

Mickle Street House (Camden, New Jersey)

On his sixty-fifth birthday, 26 March 1884, Walt Whitman moved into the only home he ever owned. His brother George had recently retired and moved his family to a farm twelve miles outside of Camden, but Walt had come to like the city and refused to leave. With a savings fund of $1,250, earned through royalties from the 1882 edition of *Leaves of Grass,* and a loan of five hundred dollars from George W. Childs,

M

he purchased a humble two-story frame house that was for sale on nearby Mickle Street. The house had many deficiencies—it had no furnace, needed repairs, was close to the railroad yards and the ferry terminals, and seemed overpriced to his brother George. But Walt liked it, and on 20 April 1884 he wrote to Anne Gilchrist, "I have moved into a little old shanty of my own . . . am much more contented" (Whitman 368).

The house that Whitman bought had probably been constructed around 1847 by Adam Hare on a lot that was laid out by Edward Sharp in 1820. The house passed to Rebecca Jane Hare in 1873, who sold it to Whitman in 1884. When Whitman died in 1892, he left the house to his brother Edward, and gave his housekeeper, Mrs. Mary Oakes Davis, the right to live there as a tenant for the rest of her life. Edward's death in that same year, however, left the house in the hands of George, who evicted Mrs. Davis because of a claim she had made against the estate. The house passed to Walt's niece Jessie Whitman of St. Louis on George's death, and Jessie sold it to the city of Camden for restoration as a memorial to the poet in 1921.

The efforts to preserve Whitman's house had begun almost immediately after his death. Though the house number had recently been

Whitman's house (shortest on the block), Mickle Street, Camden, New Jersey. By permission, Walt Whitman Association.

changed from 328 to 330 Mickle Street, the address was still spoken with reverence by Whitman's admirers around the world. A campaign organized by Horace Traubel in 1892 was not successful, but a second effort led by J. David and Juliet Lit Stern in 1920 led to its purchase. The Walt Whitman Foundation was established to administer the house, with Whitman's physician, Dr. Alexander McAlister, as its first chairman. The foundation furnished the house with artifacts collected from the neighborhood, including Whitman's rocking chairs, his deathbed, and other furniture that had belonged to Mrs. Davis. The house was acquired by the state of New Jersey in 1946, and the foundation was reincorporated as the Walt Whitman Association in 1965. The association led efforts to restore the neighboring buildings at 326 and 328 Mickle Boulevard for use as library and exhibit space. The Walt Whitman Library, comprising chiefly rare editions of Whitman's works and based on collections by Mr. Charles Feinberg and Colonel Richard Gimbel, was dedicated in October 1984 and is open for supervised use by visitors and scholars.

Geoffrey M. Sill

Bibliography

Allen, Gay Wilson. *The Solitary Singer: A Critical Biography of Walt Whitman.* 1955. Rev. ed. 1967. Chicago: U of Chicago P, 1985.

Carpenter, George Rice. *Walt Whitman.* New York: Macmillan, 1909.

Sill, Geoffrey M. "A Thumbnail History of the Walt Whitman Library." *The Mickle Street Review* 9 Part 1 (1987): iii–v.

Stern, J. David. *Memoirs of a Maverick Publisher.* New York: Simon and Schuster, 1962.

Whitman, Walt. *The Correspondence.* Ed. Edwin Haviland Miller. Vol. 3. New York: New York UP, 1964.

Winterich, Douglas, Curator of the Walt Whitman House. Personal Interview. 17 Feb. 1995.

See also ASSOCIATIONS, CLUBS, FELLOWSHIPS, FOUNDATIONS AND SOCIETIES; CAMDEN, NEW JERSEY; COLLECTORS AND COLLECTIONS, WHITMAN; DAVIS, MARY OAKES; HARLEIGH CEMETERY; WHITMAN, GEORGE WASHINGTON

Miller, Edwin Haviland (1918–)

One of the most eminent Whitman scholars in the latter half of the twentieth century, E.H. Miller began his work on the poet by identifying and locating his letters. In 1957, with his wife Rosalind S. Miller, he issued a checklist of Whitman's correspondence. This book amounted to spadework that resulted in five volumes of *The Correspondence of Walt Whitman* (1961–1969), which were among the inaugural publications in the monumental *Collected Writings of Walt Whitman* (New York University Press, 1961–1984). In 1977 Miller added to the *Collected Writings* a sixth volume of letters: *A Supplement with a Composite Index.* Years later he would revisit the correspondence, publishing *Selected Letters of Walt Whitman* (University of Iowa Press, 1990) and "The Correspondence of Walt Whitman: A Second Supplement with an Updated Calendar of Letters Written to Whitman" (*Walt Whitman Quarterly Review,* Special Double Issue, 1991). Reviewers have expressed only the highest praise for Miller's editorship, finding his judgment beyond reproach, his mastery of detail extraordinary.

Born in Johnstown, Pennsylvania, and educated at Lehigh (A.B., 1940), Pennsylvania State (A.M., 1942), and Harvard (Ph.D., 1951), Miller taught at Penn State (1940–1942; 1945–1946) and Simmons College in Boston (1947–1961) before spending twenty-five years at New York University (1961–1986). Along with his work on the correspondence, Miller has edited *A Century of Whitman Criticism* (1969) and *The Artistic Legacy of Walt Whitman* (1970). He has authored *Walt Whitman's Poetry: A Psychological Journey* (1968) and *Walt Whitman's "Song of Myself": A Mosaic of Interpretations* (1989). *Walt Whitman's Poetry* is a celebrated example of psychoanalytic criticism. It reflects Miller's profound interest in connections between literature and psychology, as do his two biographies: *Melville* (1975) and *Salem Is My Dwelling Place: A Life of Nathaniel Hawthorne* (1991).

Donald D. Kummings

Bibliography

Killingsworth, M. Jimmie. *The Growth of "Leaves of Grass": The Organic Tradition in Whitman Studies.* Columbia, S.C.: Camden House, 1993.

See also COLLECTED WRITINGS OF WALT WHITMAN, THE; CORRESPONDENCE OF WALT WHITMAN, THE; PSYCHOLOGICAL APPROACHES

Miller, Henry (1891–1980)

Miller, a writer best known for works that explore sexuality and personal freedom through an innovative American autobiographical romanticism, expressed a lifelong admiration for and identification with Walt Whitman. Miller's earliest, and perhaps strongest, connection to Whitman derives from their shared origin in Brooklyn, New York. At various points in his life, moreover, Miller saw distinct parallels between his progress as a writer and Whitman's development. Early in his career, for example, when Miller's writing career floundered, he drew sustenance from the knowledge that Whitman also experienced early rejection. Also like Whitman, Miller printed his own earliest work and sold it door to door.

However, Miller's identification with Whitman transcended these similarities of life experience. Miller frequently referred to Whitman as one of the few American writers whose work had a discernible influence on his own writing. Miller was especially attracted to the generally unfettered self—free, wild, sexual, and emotional—that Whitman constructed in his poetry. Moreover, Miller admired Whitman's strategy of using his work to present the reader with himself: "who touches this [book] touches a man" ("So Long!"). Following Whitman's lead, Miller crafted his first book—*Tropic of Cancer*—as a fictional narrative that used an autobiographical self to explore the meaning of being "Henry Miller" in the early twentieth century.

Miller's essay "Walt Whitman" (1957) offers further insight into the connection Miller made between himself and Whitman. Miller's tribute to Whitman focuses on the poet's status as a "seer" (115). Noting that Whitman was never "understood . . . or accepted" by America and rejecting the notion that Whitman's "outlook" (116) is American, Miller instead lauds Whitman's "all-embracing" (115) vision, his worldliness, and his "unique view of [the] emancipated individual" (116). Miller, moreover, characterizes Whitman as an anarchist, a "pure phenomenon," a man who "does not know the meaning of hate, fear, envy, jealousy, rivalry" (117).

Jon Panish

Bibliography

Ferguson, Robert. *Henry Miller: A Life.* New York: Norton, 1991.

Gottesman, Ronald, ed. *Critical Essays on Henry Miller.* New York: Hall, 1992.

McCarthy, Harold T. "Henry Miller's Democratic Vistas." *American Quarterly* 23 (1971): 221–235.

Martin, Jay. *Always Merry and Bright: The Life of Henry Miller.* New York: Penguin, 1978.

Miller, Henry. *Tropic of Cancer.* New York: Grove, 1961.

———. "Walt Whitman." *Walt Whitman: The Measure of His Song.* Ed. Jim Perlman, Ed Folsom, and Dan Campion. Minneapolis: Holy Cow!, 1981. 115–117.

See also LEGACY, WHITMAN'S

Miller, James Edwin, Jr. (1920–)

Among the most distinguished Whitman scholars of the last four decades, James E. Miller, Jr., came to prominence in the late 1950s and early 1960s. In an era when Whitman's poetry was widely regarded as undisciplined, formless, devoid of conscious artistry, Miller published *A Critical Guide to "Leaves of Grass"* (1957) and *Walt Whitman* (1962; rev. ed., 1990), two books that persuasively demonstrated the poet's technical excellence. In an age when Whitman's work was snubbed by the ruling sensibilities, in particular by T.S. Eliot and the American New Critics, Miller, assisted by Bernice Slote and Karl Shapiro, challenged the status quo with a polemical collection of essays entitled *Start with the Sun: Studies in the Whitman Tradition* (1960; initially subtitled *Studies in Cosmic Poetry*). At a time when good and ample collections of Whitman's writings were relatively scarce, Miller put together the Houghton Mifflin-Riverside Edition of *Walt Whitman: Complete Poetry and Selected Prose* (1959).

Born in Bartlesville, Oklahoma, and educated at the University of Oklahoma (B.A., 1942) and University of Chicago (M.A., 1947; Ph.D., 1949), Miller taught at various institutions, such as Michigan, Nebraska, and Hawaii, but spent most of his career at the University of Chicago (1962–1990). Following his auspicious debut, Miller went on to publish other important works on Whitman, notably *The American Quest for a Supreme Fiction: Whitman's Legacy*

M

in the *Personal Epic* (1979). He also published studies of other American authors, including Herman Melville, F. Scott Fitzgerald, Henry James, and T.S. Eliot. It is his work on Whitman, however, that most commands attention, for it unquestionably contributed to the mid-century rehabilitation of the poet's reputation. Moreover, it bequeathed to the lexicon of Whitman studies certain highly useful and now familiar terms: "inverted mystical experience," "personal epic," and "omnisexuality."

Donald D. Kummings

Bibliography

Miller, James E., Jr. "Whitman Then and Now: A Reminiscence." *Walt Whitman Quarterly Review* 8 (1990): 92–101.

See also SCHOLARSHIP, TRENDS IN WHITMAN

Miller, Joaquin (1837–1913)

Joaquin Miller is the pseudonym of Cincinnatus Hiner. He was a minor but colorful poet whose romantic verse, plays, and prose mainly glorified the West. His most important works are *Songs of the Sierras* (1871) and *Life Amongst the Modocs* (1873).

Although Miller and Whitman were personally acquainted, read each other's works, and briefly corresponded, they were both on the peripheries of the other's circle. There appears to be no influence of Miller on Whitman and only superficial influence in the other direction. Miller wrote "To Walt Whitman" (1877) and included him in the elegy "The Passing of Tennyson" (1896) as one in a procession of recently deceased great poets.

The bulk of Miller's poetry was written in tetrameter, an indication of how little impact Whitman's style had on him. The sweep and grandeur of Whitman's subject matter, his romantic idealism, and his personal example of standing out as an individual were likely the qualities which appealed to Miller. The mild interest that the two poets had in each other derived more from their professional relationship than from a sharing of principles.

Lawrence I. Berkove

Bibliography

Brooks, Van Wyck. *The Times of Melville and Whitman*. New York: Dutton, 1947.

Frost, O.W. *Joaquin Miller*. New York: Twayne, 1967.

Miller, Joaquin. *The Poetical Works of Joaquin Miller*. Ed. Stuart P. Sherman. New York: Putnam, 1923.

See also WEST, THE AMERICAN

Millet, Jean-François (1814–1875)

Walt Whitman had seen reproductions of some of Millet's paintings in magazines at an early date, but discovered his actual works during a short stay in Boston, when he visited the Millet collection of Quincy Shaw (now in the Boston Museum of Fine Arts) on 18 April 1881. He has described his experience in *Specimen Days:* "Two rapt hours . . . I stood long and long before 'the Sower.' . . . I shall never forget the simple evening scene, 'Watering the Cow'" (Whitman 267–268). He considered these paintings "perfect as pictures" and "with that last impalpable ethic purpose from the artist (most likely unconscious to himself) which I am always looking for" (268). He wondered: "Will America ever have such an artist out of her own gestation, body, soul?" (269). The peasants painted by Millet helped him to understand the violence of the French Revolution, caused by the "abject poverty" to which they were condemned (268). He never ceased afterward to admire Millet and discuss him with Horace Traubel and his friends.

"The Leaves are really only Millet in another form," he said to Harned; "they are the Millet that Walt Whitman has succeeded in putting into words" (*With Walt Whitman* 1:7). Whitman preferred Millet to Thomas Eakins: "We need a Millet in portraiture—a man who sees the spirit but does not make too much of it—one who sees the flesh but does not make a man all flesh. . . . Eakins almost achieves this balance . . . not quite . . . Eakins errs just a little . . . in the direction of the flesh" (*With Walt Whitman* 1:131). He particularly approved of Wyatt Eaton's article, "Recollections of Jean-François Millet," in *Century Magazine,* especially the sentence, "One must be able to make use of the trivial for the expression of the sublime" (92), which very aptly described his own art.

"Millet is my painter," Whitman said; "he belongs to me: I have written Walt Whitman all over him" (*With Walt Whitman* 1:63). No wonder Richard Maurice Bucke found eleven points the painter and the poet had in common. (He drew up the list for the *Conservator.*) Indeed

Whitman again and again emphasized the similarity himself. He thought they shared above all the same implicit transcendentalism: "The thing that first and always interested me in Millet's pictures was the untold something behind all that was depicted—an essence, a suggestion, an indication leading off into the immortal mysteries" (*With Walt Whitman* 2:407).

Roger Asselineau

Bibliography

Asselineau, Roger. "Whitman et Millet." *Quinzaine Littéraire* 16 (1975): 18.

Eaton, Wyatt. "Recollections of Jean-François Millet." *Century Magazine* 38 (1889): 90–104.

Merwin, Henry Childs. "Millet and Walt Whitman." *Atlantic Monthly* 79 (1897): 719–720.

Traubel, Horace. *With Walt Whitman in Camden.* Vol. 1. Boston: Small, Maynard, 1906; Vol. 2. New York: Appleton, 1908.

Whitman, Walt. *Specimen Days.* Vol. 1 of *Prose Works 1892.* New York: New York UP, 1963.

See also EAKINS, THOMAS; PAINTERS AND PAINTING

"Miracles" (1856)

First published as "Poem of Perfect Miracles," "Miracles" received its shortened title in 1867 and took its final form, shortened by eleven lines, in 1881, as a part of the "Autumn Rivulets" cluster. The poem opens with a question, "Why, who makes much of a miracle?" and offers in response a catalogue of sights and actions, for all of which the poet claims miraculous status. Readers of Whitman's poetry will recognize in this catalogue a number of images and activities that figure importantly in other, better-known poems: walking Manhattan streets, wading along a shore, sleeping with another, observing strangers, watching animals graze. The images lack the bracing imaginative freshness of similar passages in "Song of Myself," yet "Miracles" has a plain sort of beauty, and its images succinctly call forth a variety of spheres and complements: things urban and rural; indoors and out; human and animal; day and night; water, land, and sky. The catalogue closes with the fundamental transcendental intuition of the unity of the whole and the part. After a reassertion of the miraculousness of all things ("Every cubic inch of space is a miracle"), the poem ends with a sort of coda—a brief series of images associated with the sea and a variation of the opening question, which brings the poem full circle.

Miracles have often been looked to as proof of divine status or power, and the debate regarding the authenticity of biblical miracles already had a long history when Whitman wrote. His response was not to debunk such exceptional events but rather to disregard them. Arguments about their actuality were beside the point, since to him the natural was more interesting and important than the supernatural, and the common (commonplace, common man) was fully miraculous and sufficiently divine.

Howard Nelson

Bibliography

Gatta, John, Jr. "Making Something of Whitman's 'Miracles.'" *ESQ* 27 (1981): 222–229.

See also CATALOGUES; "SONG OF MYSELF"

Mississippi River

Whitman spent time during two three-month periods of his life in close proximity to the Mississippi. Much of what he observed found its way into *Leaves of Grass* and *Collected Prose Works.* In *Specimen Days* he calls the river "the most important stream on the globe" (*Complete* 865).

In 1848, Walt (with his brother Jeff) traveled to New Orleans to work on the *Crescent* as assistant editor. During their stay, from 25 February until 27 May, Whitman made daily visits to the river to observe the commerce and activity. He delighted in making "acquaintances among the captains, boatmen, or other characters" (*Complete* 1201) and featured them in sketches he wrote for the *Crescent.*

It was not until thirty-one years later that Whitman again saw the Mississippi. Having been invited to participate in the Kansas Quarter Centennial, he continued on to Denver and became ill on the return trip. Walt stayed from 27 September 1879 until 4 January 1880 with his brother Jeff, who lived in St. Louis. While there he visited the river as frequently as his health would allow, "every night lately" (*Complete* 871) as he records at the end of October.

The influence of this last trip is evident in several new short poems featuring the Mississippi in the 1881 edition of *Leaves*. Whitman calls it "the fresh free giver the mother" in the revised version of "Thoughts" from "Songs of Parting."

Jack Field

Bibliography

Allen, Gay Wilson. *The Solitary Singer: A Critical Biography of Walt Whitman.* 1955. Rev. ed. 1967. Chicago: U of Chicago P, 1985.

Whitman, Walt. *Complete Poetry and Collected Prose.* Ed. Justin Kaplan. New York: Library of America, 1982.

———. *The Uncollected Poetry and Prose of Walt Whitman.* 1921. Ed. Emory Holloway. 2 vols. New York: Peter Smith, 1932.

See also NEW ORLEANS CRESCENT; NEW ORLEANS, LOUISIANA; ST. LOUIS, MISSOURI; TRAVELS, WHITMAN'S; WHITMAN, THOMAS JEFFERSON

Mitchel, O.M. (Ormsby Macknight) (1809–1862)

After employment as a professor of mathematics and a lawyer, O.M. Mitchel found his calling when he was appointed professor of mathematics, philosophy, and astronomy at Cincinnati College (1836). Astronomy became Mitchel's central field of inquiry, and he helped found the Cincinnati Astronomical Society in 1842. Two years later, this society erected an observatory partly funded by donations from the audiences of Mitchel's public lectures on astronomy. Mitchel functioned as director of the observatory, and to gain financial support he published *Sidereal Messenger* (1846–1848), the first magazine on astronomy directed toward a popular audience. Mitchel worked to create public interest in the astronomical discoveries of his day until his participation in the Civil War brought him a fatal case of yellow fever in 1861.

Walt Whitman may have attended Mitchel's lectures at the Brooklyn Tabernacle in December of 1847. If not present at the lectures, Whitman was certainly familiar with the published transcripts of the lectures, *A Course of Six Lectures on Astronomy* (1848). Whitman was impressed by Mitchel and published an editorial in the 20 March 1847 Brooklyn *Daily Eagle* commending Mitchel's work on establishing observatories. Mitchel's lectures are a probable source not only for many of the astronomical details in Whitman's writings, but also for the imagery Whitman uses to describe the solar system.

Timothy Stifel

Bibliography

Beaver, Joseph. *Walt Whitman: Poet of Science.* Morningside Heights, N.Y.: King's Crown, 1951.

Whitman, Walt. *The Gathering of the Forces.* Ed. Cleveland Rodgers and John Black. 2 vols. New York: Putnam, 1920.

See also SCIENCE

Mitchell, Silas Weir (1829–1914)

This Philadelphia physician, neurologist, novelist, and poet assisted Whitman medically and financially from the late 1870s onward. Mitchell was the first to diagnose the psychosomatic nature of Whitman's complaints.

Mitchell published widely on rattlesnake venom, nerve wounds, and nervous diseases, but he is remembered as the inventor of the "rest cure" as a treatment for nervous prostration or neurasthenia. He was also the author of a dozen novels and several volumes of verse.

Whitman consulted Mitchell twice in 1878 with symptoms of rheumatism and prostration, apparently a relapse from the paralytic stroke he sustained in 1873. Mitchell examined Whitman on 13 and 18 April 1878, attributing his earlier paralysis to a ruptured blood vessel in the brain, and finding no heart ailment. He blamed Whitman's spells on "habit," perhaps brought on by the stress of his upcoming Lincoln lecture, and prescribed mountain air and outdoor activity. After the visits, Whitman improved.

Mitchell charged Whitman no fee for his services and those of his son, physician John Kearsley Mitchell, who also treated Whitman. Mitchell donated one hundred dollars for his tickets to Whitman's April 1886 Philadelphia lecture on Lincoln, occupying a box with his wife and several guests. Mitchell also supported Whitman by giving him fifteen dollars a month for over two years.

Jennifer A. Hynes

Bibliography

Allen, Gay Wilson. *The Solitary Singer: A Critical Biography of Walt Whitman.* 1955. Rev. ed. 1967. Chicago: U of Chicago P, 1985.

Brown, Charles Reynolds. "Silas Weir Mitchell: Wise and Kind in the Art of Healing." *They Were Giants.* 1934. Essay Index Reprint Series. Freeport, N.Y.: Books for Libraries, 1968. 129–147.

Burr, Anna Robeson. *Weir Mitchell: His Life and Letters.* New York: Duffield, 1919.

Earnest, Ernest. *S. Weir Mitchell: Novelist and Physician.* Philadelphia: U of Pennsylvania P, 1950.

Whitman, Walt. *The Correspondence of Walt Whitman.* Ed. Edwin Haviland Miller. 6 vols. New York: New York UP, 1961–1977.

See also Drinkard, Dr. William B.; Health; Longaker, Dr. Daniel; Osler, Dr. William

Molinoff, Katherine

Katherine Molinoff is the author of several privately printed pamphlets about Whitman, including *Some Notes on Whitman's Family* (1941), *Whitman's Teaching at Smithtown, 1837–38* (1942), and *Walt Whitman at Southold* (1966). She is the editor of *An Unpublished Whitman Manuscript: The Record Book of the Smithtown Debating Society, 1837–1838* (1941). These pamphlets present revealing and, in some cases, controversial information about the Whitman family and Whitman's life and work as a teacher in the Long Island countryside between 1838 and 1841. Against the idealized image of his family perpetuated by Whitman and his early biographers, *Some Notes on Whitman's Family* presents documents revealing that Whitman's youngest brother, Eddy, was mentally retarded, his brother Andrew was a drunkard, his sister Hannah was driven to psychopathic behavior by an abusive husband, and his oldest brother, Jesse, died in an insane asylum. In *Walt Whitman at Southold,* Molinoff presents notes from the Southold town historian Wayland Jefferson (based on oral testimony) suggesting that while Whitman was teaching in Southold between late fall and early winter 1840–1841 he was denounced from the pulpit as a sodomite and tarred, feathered, and run out of town by a local mob. The school where he putatively taught was renamed "the School of Sodom." There is no documentary evidence that Whitman ever taught at Southold or that such an event occurred. But while biographers have generally treated the Southold story as apocryphal, Molinoff's pamphlet suggests that as early as 1840–1841, in the period immediately preceding Whitman's publication of such homoerotically nuanced stories as "The Child's Champion" (1841) and *Franklin Evans* (1842), Whitman may have experienced a deep physical and emotional attachment to a young man which led to his being persecuted by the townspeople of Southold.

Betsy Erkkila

Bibliography

Molinoff, Katherine. *Some Notes on Whitman's Family.* Brooklyn, N.Y.: Comet, 1941.

———. *Walt Whitman at Southold.* Brookville, N.Y.: C.W. Post College of Long Island University, 1966.

———. *Whitman's Teaching at Smithtown, 1837–38.* Brooklyn, N.Y.: Comet, 1942.

———, ed. *An Unpublished Whitman Manuscript: The Record Book of the Smithtown Debating Society, 1837–1838.* Brooklyn, N.Y.: Comet, 1941.

Reynolds, David S. *Walt Whitman's America: A Cultural Biography.* New York: Knopf, 1995.

See also "Child and the Profligate, The"; *Franklin Evans;* Long Island, New York; Whitman, Andrew Jackson; Whitman, Edward; Whitman (Heyde), Hannah Louisa; Whitman, Jesse (brother)

Motherhood

This is a topic with which Whitman was strongly identified, for complex reasons. First and foremost, Whitman was deeply devoted to his own mother, nee Louisa Van Velsor, whom he considered the ideal woman, though he made it clear that he turned to her for emotional support rather than for intellectual instruction. Abstracting from his own biographical experience, Whitman then looked to the institution of motherhood to restore those collective spiritual values which might reintegrate the tormented American psyche—deeply threatened, as he knew it to be, by the harsh competitions of nineteenth-century life. As a son, as a social strategist engaged in the recuperation of a usable past, and as a literary artist wording the future, Whitman associated the perfectly nurturant practices of the mythologized mother—both his imaginary mother and any man's mother, the mother created by individual desire and by national fantasy—with the apolitical evenhandedness he attributed, in certain moods, to nature herself.

Psychobiographical critics intent on demonstrating that Whitman's career was driven by sexual angst have amply demonstrated that Whitman's mother Louisa was not without her faults, but the pendulum is now swinging back in the other direction. For the fact remains that despite her limitations, some of them the product of exceptionally cramped material circumstances, Louisa had a circle of staunch admirers, among whom Whitman was first and foremost. Ironically, however, Whitman's use of the figural mother has provoked intense critical controversy, in part because of his inability and/or unwillingness to develop his curiously insistent maternal tropes into a sustained psychosexual narrative. Negotiating between his own highly individualized homoerotic or homosexual experience, his faith in fervent comradeship, and the coercive heterosexism of his maternalizing poetic project, Whitman vehemently endorsed the social serviceability of female (hetero)sexuality. Consequently, whereas the poet seemingly deployed the figure of the biologically and spiritually powerful mother to symbolize a generous and enduring community organized by the drive to connect rather than fragmented by the will to compete, his maternal ideology arguably limits his feminism. More particularly, in extolling the preeminence of maternal power, Whitman has seemed to some astute readers to be reinscribing women within a traditional discourse of female inferiority in which reproductive superiority is not political, economic, intellectual, or even erotic equality. Thus, though not an advocate of the so-called Cult of True Womanhood, which sought to confine white, middle-class women within their privileged and protected domestic circles, Whitman did not fully extricate himself from the linguistic snares of an elitist, sexist vocabulary that he also aggressively and effectively dismantled.

Resisting the genteel cult of domesticity and the sexual division of labor it justified, in the 1855 *Leaves* the buoyant, early Whitman unanxiously noted the presence of women workers such as "[t]he spinning-girl [who] retreats and advances to the hum of the big wheel." Refusing to specify whether this productivity occurs in the home or in the factory, Whitman carves out a more fluid liminal space which obscures the distinction between public and private spheres. (This wonderful figure occurs in section 15 of "Song of Myself," the first extended catalogue section of this career-defining poem.) Yet even in "Song of Myself," after seemingly casual permutations, Whitman's visionary grace eventuates in such famously strident, famously gendered exclamations as the following: "I am the poet of the woman the same as the man, / And I say it is as great to be a woman as to be a man, / And I say there is nothing greater than the mother of men" ("Song of Myself," section 21). Consequently, though many readers both in Whitman's time and in our own have praised his poetic project as a bold experiment in sexual democracy, others have been more resistant to his message(s). For example, the ideology of "divine maternity" enunciated in *Democratic Vistas* (1871) proclaims the potential if not actual superiority of women to men, in what Whitman denominates "loftiest spheres." Woman's reproductive capacity becomes the key to the future of the race, and the female body is from this perspective wholly identified with its physical fecundity. Interestingly, needy readers such as the intellectual Englishwoman Anne Gilchrist, herself a widowed mother, found some form of personal salvation in this line of argument, which she interpreted as a critique of the misogynist Victorian practices that had reduced her to personal despair. The nineteenth-century feminist reformer Elizabeth Cady Stanton, on the other hand, was not persuaded. "He speaks," she observed in her 1883 diary, "as if the female must be forced to the creative act, apparently ignorant of the great natural fact that a healthy woman has as much passion as a man, that she needs nothing stronger than the law of attraction to draw her to the male" (210). Whereas for Gilchrist Whitman's vision of a human community in which women might reclaim their self-pride not in spite of but because of their bodies was powerfully persuasive, Stanton implicitly rejected Whitman's understanding of female eroticism, objecting more particularly to the poem "A Woman Waits for Me," published originally in 1856 as "Poem of Procreation," in which Whitman strained to justify heterosexual desire as a social good.

Whitman's depiction of the female figure spinning her cloth in "Song of Myself" was perhaps prophetic. Retreating and advancing to the hum of the big wheel, she is neither child nor woman, neither firmly ensconced in a factory nor obviously confined to her home, neither urban nor rural, neither married nor unmarried, neither maternal nor nonmaternal, neither worker nor artist, neither producer nor dreamer; as a liminal figure, she exemplifies the social, psychological, and sexual fluidity valued by Whitman in his visionary mode. Yet Whitman, like other men and women responding to the extraordinary social, economic, and political transformations which led up to the American Civil War, was often confused by what he saw. In the wake of this confusion, he turned back to an earlier time when the word "mother," however contextually vague, might represent the gratification of a perhaps universal desire for peace. In so doing, he tended to collapse the difference between women and between different subjective experiences of mothering. For many compelling reasons, he turned to the mothers of America to realize one of the myths of America: the myth of universal democracy, spun out of the historically decontextualized female form.

Vivian R. Pollak

Bibliography

Allen, Gay Wilson. *The Solitary Singer: A Critical Biography of Walt Whitman*. 1955. Rev. ed. 1967. Chicago: U of Chicago P, 1985.

Black, Stephen A. *Whitman's Journeys into Chaos*. Princeton: Princeton UP, 1975.

Cavitch, David. *My Soul and I: The Inner Life of Walt Whitman*. Boston: Beacon, 1985.

Erkkila, Betsy. *Whitman the Political Poet*. New York: Oxford UP, 1989.

Gilchrist, Anne. *Anne Gilchrist: Her Life and Writings*. Ed. Herbert Harlakenden Gilchrist. London: T. Fisher Unwin, 1887.

Kaplan, Justin. *Walt Whitman: A Life*. New York: Simon and Schuster, 1980.

Killingsworth, M. Jimmie. *Whitman's Poetry of the Body: Sexuality, Politics, and the Text*. Chapel Hill: U of North Carolina P, 1989.

Moon, Michael, and Eve Kosofsky Sedgwick. "Confusion of Tongues." *Breaking Bounds: Whitman and American Cultural Studies*. Ed. Betsy Erkkila and Jay Grossman. New York: Oxford UP, 1996. 23–29.

Pollak, Vivian R. "'In Loftiest Spheres': Whitman's Visionary Feminism." *Breaking Bounds: Whitman and American Cultural Studies*. Ed. Betsy Erkkila and Jay Grossman. New York: Oxford UP, 1996. 92–111.

Ryan, Mary. *The Empire of the Mother: American Writing about Domesticity 1830–1860*. New York: Haworth, 1982.

Stanton, Elizabeth Cady. *Elizabeth Cady Stanton as Revealed in Her Letters, Diary and Reminiscences*. Ed. Theodore Stanton and Harriot Stanton Blatch. Vol. 2. New York: Harper, 1922.

Welter, Barbara. "The Cult of True Womanhood: 1820–1860." *American Quarterly* 18 (1966): 151–174.

See also GILCHRIST, ANNE BURROWS; HUMAN BODY; PSYCHOLOGICAL APPROACHES; WHITMAN, LOUISA VAN VELSOR; "WOMAN WAITS FOR ME, A"; WOMAN'S RIGHTS MOVEMENT AND WHITMAN, THE; WOMEN AS A THEME IN WHITMAN'S WRITING

Music, Whitman and

Few poets have surpassed Whitman in his use of music as a primary source of inspiration. His love of music and the expressive power of the human voice began in the cradle. His mother, Louisa Van Velsor Whitman, of Dutch descent and Quaker faith, was fond of singing folk songs and telling stories to her large family. Thus little Walt, who was her favorite, the second of nine children, was bonded to music early in life.

By the time he had written the first edition of *Leaves of Grass* in 1855, he was acquainted not only with the sentimental ballads, folk songs, and hymns popular in his time, but with the music of Handel, Haydn, Mozart, Beethoven, Rossini, Bellini, Donizetti, Verdi, Auber, Meyerbeer, Weber, Mendelssohn, and Gounod as well. Musical terms are used in abundance throughout his poetry. The larger forms of opera, oratorio, symphony, chamber and instrumental music, as well as solo arias, influence the structure, style, and design of the longer as well as some of the shorter poems. His orchestral "Proud Music of the Storm" celebrates all the passionate chants of life.

His reviews of the music that he heard in the concert halls and theaters in New York and Brooklyn provide much information about the history of American music during the middle of the nineteenth century. As a journalist during the early 1840s he listened to Mendelssohn's oratorio *St. Paul,* and experienced the virtuoso playing of the French violinist Henry Vieuxtemps and the Norwegian violinist Ole Bull. But he was mainly attracted to the simple "heart-music" sung by the family trios and quartets of groups like the Hutchinson family of New Hampshire, the Cheney children from Vermont, the Alleghenians, the Harmoneons, and Father Kemp's Old Folks. He preferred sentimental ballads like "My Mother's Bible," "The Soldier's Farewell," and the "Lament of the Irish Emigrant," with their easy unison melodies and simple harmonies.

When he first attended the operas of Bellini, Donizetti, and Verdi, he complained about "the trills, the agonized squalls, the lackadaisical drawlings, the sharp ear-piercing shrieks, the gurgling death-rattles" (qtd. in Brasher 109). He was slow to appreciate grand opera, but when he did, he became passionately fond of it. He was to maintain, later in life, that the dramatic overtures, the passionate cantabile arias, the eloquent sobbing recitatives, were among the shaping forces of his free-verse style of poetry. From the middle 1840s on, whenever opera companies from London, Paris, Milan, Havana, and New Orleans appeared in the New York theaters, Whitman was present. His love for "heart-singing" gave way to his love for "art-singing": "I hear the chorus, it is grand opera, / Ah this indeed is music—this suits me" ("Song of Myself," section 26).

As a journalist and "music critic" of twenty-eight, he wrote about opera singers with considerable sensitivity. He describes the singing of the English soprano Anna Bishop, in Donizetti's *Linda di Chamounix,* in a most enthusiastic manner. He assures his readers of the Brooklyn *Daily Eagle* that her performance on 5 August 1847 was exceptional:

Her voice is the purest soprano—and of as silvery clearness as ever came from the human throat—rich but not massive—and of such flexibility that one is almost appalled at the way the most difficult passages are not only gone over with ease, but actually dallied with, and their difficulty redoubled. They put one in mind of the gyrations of a bird in the air. (*Gathering* 2:351–352)

He was even more effusive where the Italian contralto Marietta Alboni was concerned. During the 1852–1853 season the Italian prima donna gave a dozen concerts, including a performance of Rossini's *Stabat Mater.* Her singing gave Whitman "indescribable delight," for he considered her to be "the greatest of them all . . . Her singing, her method, gave the foundation, the start . . . to all my poetic literary efforts" (*Prose Works* 1:235n). Were it not for opera, he maintained, "I could never have written *Leaves of Grass*" (qtd. in Trowbridge 166).

A list of the vocal compositions heard by the poet-journalist between 1840 and 1860 is impressive. It includes twenty-five operas and three oratorios, plus Rossini's *Stabat Mater.* His poem "Proud Music of the Storm" makes mention of Haydn's and Beethoven's symphonies, as well as music by Handel and a hymn by Martin Luther. He singles out scenes from numerous operas for inclusion in his poems. Most of the music known to Whitman continues to be performed in the opera houses and concert halls of the world. According to Robert D. Faner, Whitman's favorite operas appear to have been "Donizetti's *Lucrezia Borgia* and *La Favorita;* Bellini's *Norma;* and Verdi's *Ernani*" (49). The human voice, Whitman felt, was a divine instrument and music itself the great "combiner, nothing more spiritual, nothing more sensuous, a god, yet completely human" (*Prose Works* 2:367).

Although Whitman was not a composer, he dreamed of writing an American opera. His notes to himself about doing so are somewhat humorous and simplistic, but they move in the direction of the musical theater in the twentieth century:

American Opera—put three banjos (or more?) in the orchestra—and let them accompany (at times exclusively), the songs of the baritone or tenor—Let a considerable part of the performance be instrumental—by the orchestra only—Let a few words go a great ways—the plot not complicated but simple—Always one leading idea—as Friendship, Courage, Gratitude, Love,—always a distinct meaning. . . . In the American opera the story and libretto must be the *body* of the performance. (*Workshop* 201–202)

Music for Whitman was possessed of mystical and spiritual powers. As Charmenz S. Lenhart has observed, it "was the only art Whitman acknowledged to be greater than poetry" (168–169). In his poem "Poets to Come" Whitman calls for a new brood of musicians, "greater than before known." Had he lived beyond his century, he would have encountered the new brood, perhaps not greater than before, but certainly inspired by his poetry to create hundreds of songs, choral compositions, cantatas, oratorios, symphonies, and chamber music of significance. Among twentieth-century composers inspired by his rhapsodic word-music are Ralph Vaughan Williams, Frederick Delius, Gustav Holst, Paul Hindemith, Roger Sessions, Ernest Bloch, Charles Ives, Roy Harris, William Schuman, Carl Ruggles, and George Kleinsinger. Within the past several years, compositions by Lukas Foss, John Adams, and Robert Strassburg have increased the repertoire of Whitman music. As of January 1994, over five hundred composers have made settings of *Leaves of Grass.*

Robert Strassburg

Bibliography

Berndt, Fredrick. *A List of Composers of "Whitman Music."* 7th ed. San Francisco: Walt Whitman Music Library, 1991.

Brasher, Thomas L. "Whitman's Conversion to Opera." *Walt Whitman Newsletter* 4 (1958): 109–110.

Faner, Robert D. *Walt Whitman & Opera.* Carbondale: Southern Illinois UP, 1951.

Hovland, Michael. *Musical Settings of American Poetry: A Bibliography.* New York: Greenwood, 1986.

Kaplan, Justin. *Walt Whitman: A Life.* New York: Simon and Schuster, 1980.

Lenhart, Charmenz S. *Musical Influence on American Poetry.* Athens: U of Georgia P, 1956.

Strassburg, Robert. *Walt Whitman's "Leaves of Grass": An Introduction to the Poetry and Word-Music of America's Poet of Hope.* Los Angeles: University Square, 1992.

Trowbridge, John Townsend. "Reminiscences of Walt Whitman." *Atlantic Monthly* 89 (1902): 163–175.

Whitman, Walt. *The Gathering of the Forces.* Ed. Cleveland Rodgers and John Black. 2 vols. New York: Putnam, 1920.

———. *Leaves of Grass.* Ed. Sculley Bradley and Harold W. Blodgett. Norton Critical Edition. New York: Norton, 1973.

———. *Prose Works 1892.* Ed. Floyd Stovall. 2 vols. New York: New York UP, 1963–1964.

———. *Walt Whitman's Workshop: A Collection of Unpublished Manuscripts.* Ed. Clifton Joseph Furness. Cambridge, Mass.: Harvard UP, 1928.

See also HUMAN VOICE; MUSIC, WHITMAN'S INFLUENCE ON; "MYSTIC TRUMPETER, THE"; OPERA AND OPERA SINGERS; "PROUD MUSIC OF THE STORM"; "THAT MUSIC ALWAYS ROUND ME"; THEATERS AND OPERA HOUSES

Music, Whitman's Influence on

Robert Faner's book, *Walt Whitman & Opera*, traces the poet's infatuation with works of the lyric stage. But the interest here is in the use that has been made by composers both at home and abroad of Walt Whitman's poetry, either as a specific text for a musical setting or as an inspiration for an orchestral work. Therefore, this entry will try to estimate the extent of and the reasons for the textual choices that have been made.

Michael Hovland lists 539 separate works which use Whitman's poems in one way or another. Contrast this with 1,223 entries for Henry Wadsworth Longfellow. While he may exceed Whitman, most of those settings were made in the nineteenth century, whereas Whitman's attractiveness continues to grow. In Fredrick Berndt's more recent estimation, about five hundred composers have written about twelve hundred works rooted, in some way, in Whitman. What constitutes a "setting" may vary. For instance, probably the earliest and the first American use of Whitman was by Frederic Louis Ritter, "A dirge for two veterans," an 1880 composition for piano, to accompany a recitation of the poem (Wannamaker 27–28). In other settings, as will be seen, Whitman himself may be the subject of a musical composition, or a poem may inspire a purely orchestral work. But, by and large, interest here centers on the use made by composers of the texts of particular Whitman poems.

As with the poetry itself, early interest in setting the poems to music came in Britain. Before and after the turn of the century, composers of the "English Musical Renaissance" (Charles Wood, Samuel Coleridge-Taylor, Charles Villiers Stanford, Frederick Delius, Gustav Holst, Cyril Scott, Hamilton Harty, and

Ralph Vaughan Williams) all made settings of Whitman poems. Stanford, Wood, and Scott, for instance, set, respectively, sections of "When Lilacs Last in the Dooryard Bloom'd" (hereafter "Lilacs"), "Ethiopia Saluting the Colors," and "O Captain! My Captain!" in the years 1884–1904. Gustav Holst produced a "Walt Whitman Overture" in 1899. But by far the most important early works were those of Frederick Delius, whose *Sea-Drift,* using lines from "Out of the Cradle Endlessly Rocking," was written in 1903–1904 and Ralph Vaughan Williams, whose "Sea Symphony" appeared in 1909. Vaughan Williams also used three poems from "Sea-Drift": "Song for All Seas, All Ships," "On the Beach at Night Alone," and "After the Sea-Ship." Words for the last movement were drawn from "Passage to India." Delius returned to Whitman at the end of his life, producing "Songs of Farewell" (1930) and *Idyll,* "I once passed through a populous city" (1932).

While there was some early interest in Whitman in the United States, major composers began to turn to him as early as the 1920s, with the greatest attention coming in the 1930s and 1940s. The range is impressive. Charles Ives's only setting of Whitman, a part of section 20 from "Song of Myself," was written in 1921 and appeared in Ives's 1933 *Collection of 34 Songs.* Howard Hanson drew on Whitman throughout his career: from "Songs from Drum Taps" (1935) to the Seventh Symphony, "A Sea Symphony" (1977). Merely to list a few of the more important composers and some selected works may give an idea of the scope: Otto Luening, lines from "A Song for Occupations" in an a cappella version (1966); William Schuman, "Pioneers!," an a cappella choral octet, based on "Pioneers! O Pioneers!" (1938); Norman Dello Joio, several choral works ranging from "Vigil Strange" for chorus and piano four hands (1941) to "As of a Dream," a modern masque for solo voices, chorus, narrator, dancers, and orchestra (1978); Vincent Persichetti, "Celebrations" (a choral work for wind ensemble), using a number of Whitman poems (1966); Philip Glass, three settings for chorus a cappella, included in the Contemporary Music Project for Creativity in Music Education under the auspices of the Music Educators National Conference in 1968. Four other composers, Hindemith, Sessions, Rorem, and Adams, may be examined in greater detail.

While both Roger Sessions (1896–1985)

and Paul Hindemith (1896–1963) set "Lilacs," Hindemith's is probably the better known. It was done on a commission from Robert Shaw's Collegiate Chorale, first presented in 1946, and perceived at the time as an elegy for Franklin Roosevelt. The hour-long cantata has been most recently performed in January 1995, by Robert Shaw once again. Hindemith, a refugee from the Nazis, brought with him a Bachian formalism which results in something of a mismatch between Whitman's ecstatic poetic vision and the rather prosaic setting of the composer. For some, the stylistic disjunction makes it less successful than a work like Delius's *Sea-Drift.* But Ned Rorem says that it remained for composers from Europe like Hindemith and Kurt Weill to show the way toward a broader and more touching representation.

Sessions composed his cantata for chorus, with soprano, contralto, and baritone soloists and orchestra in 1970, at the age of seventy-four, and it was one of his more important successes. Sessions's style had always closely matched that of Whitman, and in "Lilacs" he followed the spontaneous, free-flowing rise and fall of the verse. That two such different composers as Hindemith and Sessions were attracted to the same work of Whitman perhaps suggests the breadth of Whitman's appeal and the infinite variety of response it inspires.

Two other stylistically different composers, Ned Rorem (1923–) and John Adams (1947–), have also been inspired by Whitman. Like other composers, Rorem has been attracted to Whitman throughout his life. Single songs, written in 1957, were later collected into "Five Poems of Walt Whitman" in 1970. In 1971 he published another song cycle, "War Scenes," and in 1982, "Three Calamus Poems." In addition, he used Whitman's "The Dalliance of the Eagles" as a "program" for his brief but powerful orchestral piece "Eagles," premiered by the Philadelphia Orchestra in 1958. Like Rorem, John Adams was attracted to Whitman's poems about the Civil War, and he uses Whitman's "The Wound-Dresser" as the basis of a piece for solo voice and orchestra. While he was writing the piece, Adams says, his father was dying of Alzheimer's disease and his mother was nursing him. The theme of caring for the sick has an immediate application (noted by several critics) in the age of AIDS.

In a more direct relationship to the AIDS crisis, Whitman is used symbolically by Perry Brass, whose poem "Walt Whitman in 1989" is the basis of a brief song set by composer Chris DeBlasio. The work is included in "The AIDS Quilt Song Book" recording and follows the recitative and aria form. Once again, as in the Adams work, Whitman's role as nurse is exploited. However, the war in this case is that against bigotry and hatred.

Whitman's attraction for composers may well be due to his own fluidity and musicality. He called many of his poems "Songs" and developed his poetic ideas thematically, almost symphonically, with repetitions calculated as a composer might. For instance, in "Crossing Brooklyn Ferry" Whitman's images of the gulls, the waves, and the flow of the river—contrasted with the crossing of the ferryboat—develop in their repetition and recurrence a fitting poetic setting of the poignant themes of time and timelessness. The poem as set by Virgil Thomson in 1960 for chorus and piano represents his only use of Whitman.

Perhaps the most ambitious setting of all is a fairly complete version of "Song of Myself" for "Narrator, Soprano, chorus and a brass/percussion ensemble" by Robert L. Sanders. This work has had at least one performance, lasting nearly three hours on 19 April 1970. While it may not seem so, Sanders, as do many composers, takes from the poem what he can use, adapting the text rather than following it slavishly. Ned Rorem attributes Whitman's popularity among composers to his immediacy, the involvement that Whitman demands of his reader. Rorem also notes that part of the importance of Whitman for composers in the 1930s and 1940s was his very Americanness. Certainly, the most prominent representative of that nationalistic idiom was Roy Harris (1898–1979). Like Aaron Copland, Harris drew on folk tunes and popular dance rhythms, as well as using a national figure like Abraham Lincoln. But unlike Copland, Harris was attracted to Whitman. He used Whitman poems as early as his "Song Cycle on words of Walt Whitman," for women's voices and two pianos (1927), and continued to use them in compositions such as "Symphony for Voices" (1935), "The Walt Whitman Triptych" (1940), and the cantata for baritone and orchestra, "Give me the Splendid, Silent Sun" (1955). In all, Harris used Whitman in at least nine separate works, most of which reflect his devotion to American ideals.

At present, there are no major books which deal definitively with the topic. Michael Hovland's *Musical Settings of American Poetry* is a bibliography which lists the writings of ninety-nine American authors, including approximately fifty-eight hundred settings, twenty-one hundred composers, and twenty-four hundred titles of literary works. A work of such scope may perhaps be forgiven for lapses here and there in the Whitman section. John Samuel Wannamaker's unpublished doctoral dissertation is another extensive work and a mine of information. Brooks Toliver's article on Debussy and Whitman raises some intriguing questions without providing definitive answers. Two forthcoming works offer promise. One is Fredrick Berndt's "Most Jubilant Song" (still in manuscript), which no doubt will reflect the author's many years of interest in the relationship between music and Whitman. The other is a recording by baritone Thomas Hampson of hitherto unknown or forgotten songs using Whitman texts. Such a project bespeaks the continuing interest in Whitman and the music he has inspired.

Lyman L. Leathers

Bibliography

Berndt, Fredrick, ed. *The Bulletin of the Walt Whitman Music Library*. San Francisco: Walt Whitman Music Library, 1993.

Faner, Robert. *Walt Whitman & Opera*. Carbondale: Southern Illinois UP, 1951.

Hitchcock, H. Wiley, and Stanley Sadie. *New Grove Dictionary of American Music*. London: Macmillan, 1986.

Hovland, Michael. *Musical Settings of American Poetry: A Bibliography*. New York: Greenwood, 1986.

Miller, Edwin Haviland, ed. *The Artistic Legacy of Walt Whitman*. New York: New York UP, 1970.

Neilson, Kenneth P. *The World of Walt Whitman Music: A Bibliographical Study*. Hollis, N.Y.: Kenneth P. Neilson, 1963.

Taruskin, Richard. "In Search of the 'Good' Hindemith Legacy." New York *Times* 8 Jan. 1995: H–25, 30, 31.

Toliver, Brooks. "*Leaves of Grass* in Claude Debussy's Prose." *Walt Whitman Quarterly Review* 11 (1993): 67–81.

Wannamaker, John Samuel. "The Musical Settings of the Poetry of Walt Whitman: A Study of Theme, Structure, and Prosody." Diss. U of Minnesota, 1972.

See also "CALAMUS"; "DRUM-TAPS"; "MEMORIES OF PRESIDENT LINCOLN"; MUSIC, WHITMAN AND; OPERA AND OPERA SINGERS; "SEA-DRIFT"; "SONG OF MYSELF"

M

"My Boys and Girls" (1844)

While this sketch first appeared in *The Rover,* 20 April 1844, biographers suppose that it was written as early as 1835. For publication and biographical comments, see Thomas Brasher's edition of *The Early Poems and the Fiction.*

This sketch is viewed as a small exercise in autobiography. It is a listing in paragraphs of children that the bachelor-speaker looks upon as his own. He describes the children and their fun, but he also laments their growth into the world of sin and pain. David Reynolds reads the sketch as Whitman's attempt to keep himself and his siblings frozen in childhood.

There is some humorous play in the sketch. Three children, like Whitman's brothers, have the names of United States presidents. "Strange paradox!" (Whitman 248)—Andrew Jackson is considerably older than Thomas Jefferson and George Washington. Other children are referred to by their initials, as if to preserve a secret. Other humor is derived from the idea of a bachelor being a father.

In a notable paragraph, there is some stylistic and thematic foreshadowing of Whitman's later work. Specifically, Whitman lists the world's ills, using the parallelism of much of his later poetry. Also, the description of a child's burial includes the overwhelming scent of apple blossoms, which gives "a deadlier sickness in our souls" (249) and thereby anticipates "When Lilacs Last in the Dooryard Bloom'd" (1865). Kaplan ties this paragraph as well to the homoeroticism of "Calamus." Callow sees an anticipation of "There was a Child Went Forth" (1855) in the entire sketch.

Patrick McGuire

Bibliography

Allen, Gay Wilson. *The Solitary Singer: A Critical Biography of Walt Whitman.* 1955. Rev. ed. 1967. Chicago: U of Chicago P, 1985.

Callow, Philip. *From Noon to Starry Night: A Life of Walt Whitman.* Chicago: Ivan R. Dee, 1992.

Kaplan, Justin. *Walt Whitman: A Life.* New York: Simon and Schuster, 1980.

Reynolds, David S. *Walt Whitman's America: A Cultural Biography.* New York: Knopf, 1995.

Whitman, Walt. *The Early Poems and the Fiction.* Ed. Thomas L. Brasher. New York: New York UP, 1963.

See also "Little Sleighers, The"; Short Fiction, Whitman's; Whitman, Andrew Jackson; Whitman, George Washington; Whitman, Thomas Jefferson

"My Picture-Gallery" (1880)

First published in *The American* in 1880 and incorporated into *Leaves of Grass* in 1881, "My Picture-Gallery" is a (revised) six-line excerpt from a much earlier and longer poem entitled "Pictures" (1925), which Whitman never published. An important pre-*Leaves* exercise from the early 1850s, "Pictures" shows Whitman experimenting with many of the elements that were to become his hallmarks: the rejection of European literary models (it appears to be a response to Alfred, Lord Tennyson's "Palace of Art" [1842]); the catalogues of (mostly visual) images of daily life; the poet-speaker as container of those images; the loose, free-associational structure; the sprawling lines; the ecstatic tone.

"My Picture-Gallery," which originally served to set up the 115-line catalogue of "Pictures," is a riddle poem in which the speaker's head is presented as "a little house," a gallery displaying the images that follow. That conceit reflects a number of Whitman's preoccupations during the gestation of *Leaves of Grass* in the early 1850s, when he frequented the various galleries along Broadway. The archaeological and artistic galleries are represented in the catalogues of ancient treasures and carefully composed historical and allegorical images, but Whitman's "little house" is most closely modeled after the daguerreotype gallery, with its precise, unadorned reflections of the visible world. Whitman undoubtedly also had in mind Orson Fowler's phrenological gallery, with its charts, in turn, depicting the human head as a symbolic gallery.

But if the poet's head is depicted as a photographic gallery displaying images, it simultaneously stands for the camera recording them. Moreover, "My Picture-Gallery" closes with the image of "cicerone himself, / With finger rais'd," suggesting that the poet also serves as a guide to the show. With the catalogue of "Pictures" excised, the emphasis of "My Picture-Gallery" is shifted away from the world as observed and onto the complex role of the poet, who is simultaneously collector, container, and presenter of "all the shows of the world."

John Rietz

Bibliography

Holloway, Emory. "Whitman's Embryonic Verse." *Southwest Review* 10 (1925): 28–40.

Kaplan, Justin. *Walt Whitman: A Life.* New York: Simon and Schuster, 1980.

Price, Kenneth M. *Whitman and Tradition: The Poet in His Century.* New Haven: Yale UP, 1990.

Soule, George H., Jr. "Walt Whitman's 'Pictures': An Alternative to Tennyson's 'Palace of Art.'" *ESQ* 22 (1976): 39–47.

Zweig, Paul. *Walt Whitman: The Making of the Poet.* New York: Basic Books, 1984.

See also ART AND DAGUERREOTYPE GALLERIES; "AUTUMN RIVULETS"; FOWLER, LORENZO NILES AND ORSON SQUIRE; PHOTOGRAPHS AND PHOTOGRAPHERS; PHRENOLOGY; PRE-*Leaves* POEMS; TENNYSON, ALFRED, LORD

"Myself and Mine" (1860)

In the 1860 *Leaves* "Myself and Mine" was the tenth poem of the "Leaves of Grass" cluster. It was second in another cluster named "Leaves of Grass" in the 1867 edition. In the editions of 1871–1872 and 1876, it was included in the "Passage to India" poems with its present title. The two original opening lines were an immediate call to action. "It is ended—I dally no more, / After to-day I inure myself to run, leap, swim, wrestle, fight" (1860 *Leaves*). Whitman deleted them in 1867. At the same time, he dropped the two lines (before the present line 26) which confessed "the evil I really am" (1860 *Leaves*).

In its declaration of personal intent, "Myself and Mine" is similar to the "Inscriptions" poems. The poet has accepted his vocation and he acknowledges his relation to the materials of poetry. Whereas in 1847 he had written in the Brooklyn *Daily Eagle* that the most elevated office on earth was the presidency, now he feels that the brilliance of the United States resides not in the lawmakers, but in the common people. As a poet, he will extol the masses and praise "no eminent man." He will make poems out of the fiber of his age and will chisel them "with free stroke." Whitman assumes for the reader what he assumes for himself: "I charge you to leave all free, as I have left all free."

Advocating civil disobedience, he declares his independence in thinking and acting: "Let me have my own way, / Let others promulge the laws, I will make no account of the laws, / Let others praise eminent men and hold up peace, I hold up / agitation and conflict."

Half-tauntingly, he calls for an answer to the question, "Who are you? and what are you secretly guilty of all your life?" He then forbids any justification for guilty acts or any interpretations of his works. "I charge you forever reject those who expound me, for I cannot expound myself." Even the poet's language has its limitations. His words merely provoke and throw off possibilities of vision and vista.

In the opening line of the poem the "myself" is the shifting unity of body and soul, which for Whitman is the poem. As he says of his poetry in "So Long!"—"Camerado, this is no book, / Who touches this touches a man"—Whitman's poetry calls for the reader's collaboration. He asks the reader to commit his "self." This interrelatedness among poet, reader, and poetic text, which Whitman called a "gymnast's struggle," makes for ever changing and inexhaustible interpretations. Therefore, no system of thought or school can be imposed on it. In "Myself and Mine" Whitman demands his freedom, refusing to be isolated, defined, and reduced to a single meaning.

Deborah Dietrich

Bibliography

Bloom, Harold, ed. *Modern Critical Views: Walt Whitman.* New York: Chelsea House, 1985.

Duffey, Bernard. *Poetry in America: Expression and Its Values in the Times of Bryant, Whitman, and Pound.* Durham: Duke UP, 1978.

Pearce, Roy Harvey. "Whitman Justified: The Poet in 1860." *Whitman: A Collection of Critical Essays.* Ed. Roy Harvey Pearce. Englewood Cliffs, N.J.: Prentice-Hall, 1962. 37–59.

Trachtenberg, Alan. "Whitman's Visionary Politics." *Walt Whitman of Mickle Street: A Centennial Collection.* Ed. Geoffrey M. Sill. Knoxville: U of Tennessee P, 1994. 94–108.

See also "BIRDS OF PASSAGE"; *LEAVES OF GRASS,* 1860 EDITION

"Mystic Trumpeter, The" (1872)

First published in *The Kansas Magazine* in February 1872, this poem was reprinted in the

1872 volume *As A Strong Bird on Pinions Free,* in *Two Rivulets* in 1876, and ultimately in the cluster "From Noon to Starry Night" in the 1881 edition of *Leaves of Grass.*

For Whitman music is a great source of inspiration, as well as an invaluable resource for his poetry. "The Mystic Trumpeter" adopts as its theme music's inspiration—the vehicle for which is the trumpet. Whitman opens the poem by addressing this "strange musician" (section 1), calling it forward so "I may translate thee" (section 2). The trumpeter is ultimately called upon in each of the sections to provide music that will create, or re-create, various themes, allowing the poet an opportunity of expression.

W.L. Werner, in his "Whitman's 'The Mystic Trumpeter' as Autobiography," proposes that the last five sections of the poem are the poet's "attempt to divide his own life into five periods" (455). Section 4, he asserts, represents Whitman's early days, when he "revel'd in romance-reading" (456), referring primarily to his interest in the novels of Walter Scott. Section 5, it is proposed, "reproduces the ecstasy of the early *Leaves*" (457). Section 6 symbolizes the Civil War, while section 7 comments on the despair the poet has encountered, on the "wrongs of ages" (457). The final segment becomes one of "optimism and ecstasy" (457), a theme, it is suggested, with parallels to Whitman's poetry of the 1870s and beyond.

A similar reading on various divisions of this poem is presented by James E. Miller, Jr. He suggests that the trumpeter is the "spirit of poetry, the muse, grown 'wild' and 'strange'" (247). The intimation is that because the poet has reached old age, his poetic powers are declining. In section 4, Miller points to the various images that "conjure up" (247) the poetry of the past. Such "pageantry," he claims, is what "our poet has rejected as the theme of his poetry" (247). This view seems to play out Werner's notion that this "feudal element" was so important that Whitman "could never wholly free himself" from its influence (458). If we accept Werner's view that the poem portrays "moods parallel to Whitman's own life" (458), it also seems an appropriate position to stand with Miller's reading of the poem as *Leaves of Grass* "in miniature" (248).

"The Mystic Trumpeter" differs from many of Whitman's poems in that we see the poet looking outward, needing the "song," as it were, to expand his "numb'd imbonded spirit" (section 3). V.K. Chari, in his book *Whitman in the Light of Vedantic Mysticism,* suggests that this reaching out is more in accordance with Christianity than the poet's customary "conception of the cosmic self" (15) so prevalent in his early poetry. Yet throughout, the poet maintains that link between himself and the higher power. Even in moments "all lost," there is "endurance, resolution to the last" (section 7). And if, as Miller suggests, the muse plays a different tune to the older poet, Whitman never loses sight of those joyous moments when it is "enough to merely be" (section 8).

Frederick J. Butler

Bibliography

Chari, V.K. *Whitman in the Light of Vedantic Mysticism.* Lincoln: U of Nebraska P, 1964.

Miller, James E., Jr. *A Critical Guide to "Leaves of Grass."* Chicago: U of Chicago P, 1957.

Weis, Monica R., SSJ. "'Translating the Untranslatable': A Note on 'The Mystic Trumpeter.'" *Walt Whitman Quarterly Review* 1.4 (1984): 27–31.

Werner, W.L. "Whitman's 'The Mystic Trumpeter' as Autobiography." *American Literature* 7 (1936): 455–458.

Whitman, Walt. *Leaves of Grass: Comprehensive Reader's Edition.* Ed. Harold W. Blodgett and Sculley Bradley. New York: New York UP, 1965.

———. *Leaves of Grass: A Textual Variorum of the Printed Poems.* Ed. Sculley Bradley, Harold W. Blodgett, Arthur Golden, and William White. Vol. 3. New York: New York UP, 1980.

See also "FROM NOON TO STARRY NIGHT"; MUSIC, WHITMAN AND

Mysticism

The image of Whitman as a mystic and prophet has traditionally enjoyed a wide currency among scholars. This image was first promoted by Whitman's own friends and disciples—Richard Maurice Bucke, William Douglas O'Connor, William Sloane Kennedy, and Edward Carpenter—and corroborated by recent scholars, both Western and Eastern. There are evidently recognizable resemblances between some of Whitman's utterances and those of the classical mystics of the world. Recent Whitman studies have, however, tended to disfavor the mystical readings of his poetry and to focus on its sexuality or its political and cultural contexts.

Mysticism, however, comes in many brands, and there is no simple definition of that concept. But for our purposes it will suffice to distinguish between the I- or self-centered and the God-centered varieties. In either form, in essence, mystical experience may be said to consist in the intense and joyous realization of the oneness of all things and an ineffable sense of transport, enlargement, and emancipation. Mystical experience is more like an emotional state or immediate perception than like conceptual thinking. It is taken to be synonymous with religious experience. However, it should not be confused with the theological or metaphysical doctrine that it often presupposes or that might arise out of it.

Some of Whitman's justly celebrated poems of 1855 to 1860, like "Song of Myself," "The Sleepers," "Crossing Brooklyn Ferry," "Song of the Open Road," "Salut au Monde!," and "A Song of Joys," announce a new religion of man and a new conception of his selfhood that are in many respects radical and challenge conventional beliefs and modes of perception. The focal theme of these poems is the I or Myself which is also the self of all, a magnified ego which incorporates the whole cosmos—animate and inanimate—and becomes immersed in its activity. It breaks through subject-object barriers and spatial and temporal divisions, melting them down into a vast spiritual continuum. While merging in the life and motion of the world, the self is also aware of itself as a unique and separate identity, standing in its centripetal isolation, unattached and unperturbed, "watching and wondering" at the pageantry of life ("Song of Myself," section 4). There is also the distinct realization that all life is a miracle, that all things are holy and in their place, and that the soul is immortal and ever liberated and ever happy and beyond all contrarieties of good and evil, and sin and redemption.

Bucke calls this type of experience "cosmic consciousness" in his book of the same title and connects Whitman to a succession of mystics in the Western and Eastern traditions. William James in *The Varieties of Religious Experience* analyzes this phenomenon and cites Whitman as the supreme example of "healthy-mindedness" (83) or the inability to feel evil, as opposed to the "sick soul." It is a moot point as to whether the mystical illumination came to Whitman as a sudden revelation or epiphany or series of epiphanies, such as the one described in the fifth section of "Song of Myself," or whether it was a gradual realization. James calls the episode of this section a case of "sporadic" mysticism (387). But it is evident that, as James acknowledges, Whitman retained a permanent or "chronic" sense of this experience and the values communicated by it until the very end, through the many vicissitudes of his life.

There is, however, one chief difference between Whitman's mysticism in the early poems, described above, and the classical theistic types: here the emphasis is almost wholly on the self and its dominant "ego-centric" presence rather than on an external something called God or the Absolute. Whitman proceeds, not by positing a divine or transcendental reality to which, as in traditional mysticism, the individual ego is surrendered, but by the method of self-expansion. Hence Whitman's religion has been called a religion without God. God no doubt enters into his awareness of cosmic unity, as in section 5 of "Song of Myself." His optimistic faith and his sanctification of natural facts too may seem to imply the immanent presence of a divinity in nature. But still, God is not the focal object of his experience in the celebratory "Songs." However, in his old age, with the decline of his vitality and after he assumed the role of the Good Gray Poet, Whitman became increasingly theistic and introvertive, as opposed to the extrovertive or outgoing tendency of the early phase, and wrote "hymns to the universal God" ("The Mystic Trumpeter," section 8; also see "Passage to India" and "Prayer of Columbus"). This latter type of experience may be called "god-mysticism" or devotional mysticism, which is more akin to conventional notions of spirituality.

A good many scholars agree that Whitman is a mystic or a poet with an uncommon spiritual vision, but they differ in the explanatory models they bring to their interpretations. V.K. Chari argues that the dynamism of the early poems is best explained by the Vedantic concept of the Self, which is at once a unique identity and the world-all. Fred Carlisle agrees that identity or self is Whitman's central concern, but adopts the Buberian model of "I-Thou" and argues that Whitman discovers the essential self dialogically or relationally in the interaction between the "I" and the world. George Hutchinson sees Whitman's mysticism as a form of shamanism, in which the poet-shaman performs a public role, entering into trancelike states to make contact with the spirit world on behalf of his nation. David Kuebrich, on the other hand, reads Whitman in theistic terms as the founder of a new American religion, basically of traditional Christian inspiration, but adapted to the nineteenth-century evolutionary cosmology and millennialism.

Valid as these interpretations may be within their individual frameworks, they succeed only by emphasizing some poems or some aspects of those poems at the expense of others. It is doubtful whether any single model will work uniformly for all poems of *Leaves of Grass* and whether a holistic explanation of them as religious or mystical poetry is possible at all. Not all of Whitman's poems can be characterized as mystical in either of the forms presented above. For example, the poems of the "Calamus" group, the seashore lyrics, the elegiac and war poems, and many other sentimental lyrics of the later Whitman would hardly qualify as mystical expression. They are rather on the ordinary lyrical-emotional level.

Whitman's sexuality and his celebration of the body and the senses have been a major hurdle to interpretations of him as a mystic and religious prophet. Studies of his mysticism have tended either to deemphasize its sensuality or to spiritualize it altogether in the interests of the mystic theory, even as psychoanalytical criticism has tried to demysticize the spiritual element by reading into it pathological symptoms. However, two possible ways have been suggested in which the spiritual and the sensual in Whitman may be reconciled. It may be shown that, although the body or the physical self is the authentic center of Whitman's mysticism, it does not terminate in mere eroticism, but invariably opens out to him expanding universes; it also gives him a penetrating insight into the nature of his own identity. Sexuality thus becomes a solvent and a means of liberation and transcendence. Mystical states are often known to have been sparked by crises of sensual experience. Or alternatively, one can give a new name to Whitman's sensual ecstasies and call them physical or erotic mysticism—the kind in which erotic experience is itself exalted into something divine. But of course sex does not account for all manifestations of Whitman's cosmic consciousness (e.g., "Song of Myself," sections 4, 8, 15, 33; "Salut au Monde!"; "A Song of Joys"), for the rhapsodies of "Passage to India," or for the serene meditations of his old age ("Sands at Seventy"; "Good-Bye my Fancy"; "Old Age Echoes"; the nature notes at Timber Creek in *Specimen Days,* which have no ostensible connection with sex or body consciousness).

There is also a problem of a hermeneutical nature in dealing with Whitman's mysticism, namely, that of determining his precise meanings. There are obviously passages that are obscure and that admit of diverse constructions: e.g., the notorious first paragraph of section 5 of "Song of Myself." However, much of his mysticism is expressed in literal language and demands a straightforward reading. In fact, it is only when read literally that many of his affirmations and cosmic identifications will be recognized as mystical.

In any case, the canonized image of Whitman as prophet-mystic is no longer taken for granted today. Influential critical schools of our time have joined hands in questioning the very premises on which the mystical claims of the poet are based. The Self of Whitman's poems—which is the cornerstone of his mysticism—has been shown to be problematic and riddled with uncertainties and tensions, or, deconstructively viewed, uncentered and lacking in settled meaning. Studies from the New Historical and political standpoints, too, have given a new twist to his meanings. Whitman's poetic personality is no doubt seen to go through many vicissitudes when viewed in the total context of the *Leaves.* But it cannot be denied that at least some of his poems do present a coherent and consistent notion of the self. There is also no necessary conflict between Whitman's mysticism and the ideological, materialistic premises from which it was an outgrowth. Moreover, the vision of the self and of the cosmos that Whitman celebrated with such energy and originality is so far in excess of its cultural frame of reference that it can only be called mystical.

V.K. Chari

Bibliography

Allen, Gay Wilson. *The New Walt Whitman Handbook.* 1975. New York: New York UP, 1986.

Aspiz, Harold. "Sexuality and the Language of Transcendence." *Walt Whitman Quarterly Review* 5.2 (1987): 1–7.

Asselineau, Roger. *The Evolution of Walt Whitman: The Creation of a Book.* Trans. Asselineau and Burton L. Cooper. Cambridge, Mass.: Harvard, 1962.

Bucke, Richard Maurice. *Cosmic Conscious-*

ness: *A Study in the Evolution of the Human Mind*. New York: Dutton, 1901.

Carlisle, E. Fred. *The Uncertain Self: Whitman's Drama of Identity*. East Lansing: Michigan State UP, 1973.

Chari, V.K. *Whitman in the Light of Vedantic Mysticism*. Lincoln: U of Nebraska P, 1964.

Cowley, Malcolm. Introduction. *Walt Whitman's "Leaves of Grass": The First (1855) Edition*. Ed. Cowley. New York: Viking, 1959. vii–xxxvii.

Hutchinson, George B. *The Ecstatic Whitman: Literary Shamanism & the Crisis of the Union*. Columbus: Ohio State UP, 1986.

James, William. *The Varieties of Religious Experience*. 1902. New York: Modern Library, 1994.

Kuebrich, David. *Minor Prophecy: Walt Whitman's New American Religion*. Bloomington: Indiana UP, 1989.

Miller, James E., Jr. *A Critical Guide to "Leaves of Grass."* Chicago: U of Chicago P, 1957.

Miller, James E., Jr., Karl Shapiro, and Bernice Slote. *Start with the Sun: Studies in Cosmic Poetry*. Lincoln: U of Nebraska P, 1960.

See also COSMIC CONSCIOUSNESS; "CROSSING BROOKLYN FERRY"; HINDU LITERATURE; HUMAN BODY; JAMES, WILLIAM; RELIGION; "SALUT AU MONDE!"; SEX AND SEXUALITY; "SLEEPERS, THE"; "SONG OF JOYS, A"; "SONG OF MYSELF"; "SONG OF THE OPEN ROAD"; SOUL, THE; SWEDENBORG, EMANUEL

M

N

Native Americans (Indians)

Whitman's adult life was framed by two of the defining events in nineteenth-century Native American history—the infamous "Trail of Tears" in 1838 and 1839, when Whitman was twenty, and the Wounded Knee Massacre at the end of 1890, just over a year before his death. During Whitman's teenage years, the Choctaws, the Creeks, the Chickasaws, and finally the Cherokees were moved across the Mississippi and into the Oklahoma territory. During the formative years of *Leaves of Grass,* many of the most explosive western battles between natives and whites occurred, including the Pueblo uprising in 1847, the Grattan fight in 1854, and the Rains fight in 1855. As *Leaves of Grass* grew through its various editions, countless battles and skirmishes took place, and their names entered American memory: Birch Coulee, Canyon de Chelly, Rosebud, Warbonnet Creek, Sand Creek. By the time of Whitman's death, Wounded Knee had underscored the fact that active, armed Native American resistance to the United States was at an end.

Whitman was not unaffected by Native American life and events. While his own experience with Native Americans was limited, it was not insubstantial. He encountered American Indians as a boy on Long Island and as a young editor in New Orleans. He admired Indian troops who fought in the Civil War, and he was the only major American poet to work in the Indian Bureau of the Department of the Interior (1865), where he met several impressive Native delegations and had what he called "quite animated and significant" conversations with them (*Prose Works* 2:579). On his western trip in the 1870s, he commented on the Indians he met in Topeka, and he visited a Chippewa settlement during his trip to Canada in 1880.

Whitman's interest in Native Americans is evident from very early on in his writing. One of his earliest published poems is "The Inca's Daughter," about the noble suicide of a "captive Indian maiden" (*Early* 6), and his 1842 temperance novel, *Franklin Evans,* contains a long chapter ("The Death of Wind-Foot") that consists of a Native American revenge tale. A few years later, he wrote a novella, "The Half-Breed: A Tale of the Western Frontier," about a deformed and treacherous amalgam of the worst qualities of the white and red races. He wrote frequently about Native Americans and their history in various newspaper essays and articles. In the first edition of *Leaves of Grass,* Indians appear in five of the twelve poems, including the poem that would later be titled "The Sleepers," where Whitman records a haunting dream-memory of a "red squaw" (section 6) who visits his mother for an afternoon and then disappears forever, and the poem later titled "Song of Myself," where he offers an extended tableau of "the marriage of the trapper in the open air in the far west, the bride was a red girl" (section 10)—a scene that has been read as suggestive of the white domination of the Native, but also indicative of the possibility of a joining of the races and all they represented in nineteenth-century America.

In a notebook he kept in the late 1850s, Whitman sketched out plans for a *"poem of the aborigines"* that would incorporate "every principal aboriginal trait, and name" (*Notebooks* 1:275). He never wrote that poem, but *Leaves of Grass* contains more Native American elements than is generally noted. In "Starting from Paumanok," for example, Whitman pauses to "pronounce what the air holds of the red aborigines," and he goes on to catalogue their names—"Okonee, Koosa, Ottawa, Monongahela, Sauk, Natchez"—and to lament the Natives' disappearance while celebrating the way they have "charg[ed] the water and the land with names" (section 16). Whitman loved Native American words—"All aboriginal names sound good," he announced in his *American Primer* (18)—and he argued that Native names should replace the various classical and European names that had been imposed on the North American continent. His own efforts at reinstituting Native names included his insistence on calling Long Island "Paumanok" and New York City "Mannahatta." Native words had an authenticity for Whitman: they fit the American landscape, and, absorbed into English, they tinctured the language with native sounds. Whitman was therefore annoyed with the word "Indian" because it was an example of European misnaming, the imposition of a misidentification upon a whole group of cultures, "a great mistake perpetuated in a word . . . calling the American aborigines *Indians*," he wrote, is a lesson in how "names or terms get helplessly misapplied & wrench'd from their meanings" (*Notebooks* 5:1664). He preferred the term "aborigine," with its echo of "original," but mostly he loved to list and say the various tribal names—"Wabash, Miami, Saginaw, Chippewa" ("Starting from Paumanok," section 16).

While Whitman occasionally employed the language and assumptions of savagism— with its attendant belief in the inevitable demise of the natives in the face of the United States' claim to manifest destiny—he also was capable of questioning and complicating those assumptions, as he did in "Song of Myself," where he calls for a new "friendly and flowing savage" (section 39) whose mysterious appearance would help unsettle the already too repressed American civilization. Whitman's attitudes toward Native Americans remained ambivalent and wavering throughout his life. He could condemn Natives in reductive and stereotypical ways—"The real reds of our northern frontiers, of the present day, have propensities, monstrous and treacherous, that make them unfit to be left in white neighborhoods" (*Notebooks* 2:565)—but he could also celebrate them as some of the noblest examples of humanity: "There is something about these aboriginal Americans, in their highest characteristic representations, essential traits . . . arousing comparisons with our own civilized ideals" (*Prose Works* 2:578–579).

Finally, though, Whitman's evolutionary faith led him to accept the notion that Native Americans were doomed to extinction, the victims of a Darwinian struggle of races and cultures. He usually expressed sadness at this inevitable loss, as he did in his late poems "Red Jacket (from Aloft)," "Yonnondio," and "Osceola." These poems, written in the last decade of his life, were final acknowledgments of the importance he ascribed to the presence of Native Americans in the developing American poem; Whitman wanted to include them, even as they seemed to be disappearing as an active part of American history, and he wanted to afford them a kind of linguistic afterlife by employing their words, so that every time Americans spoke the names of the country's towns and states and rivers, their voices would echo with Native sounds.

Whitman, then, was ultimately more interested in the representation of Native Americans than in their actual cultures. He knew George Catlin, the artist who portrayed Indian cultures; he kept a print of Catlin's portrait of Osceola on the wall of his Camden home, and he supported the movement to have the United States government purchase Catlin's collection of Indian paintings so that the nation could have a collective visual memory of the tribes. One of Whitman's favorite paintings was John Mulvany's *Custer's Last Rally,* and he wrote a long meditation about the painting's conflicted portrayal of the Natives, a portrayal that resonated with Whitman's own handling of the Custer battle in his 1876 poem "From Far Dakota's Cañons."

Contemporary Native American writers have responded to Whitman's poetry in a variety of ways. Some, like Joseph Bruchac, find Whitman's poetry close in spirit and even style to Native American song and thus view him as a kind of spiritual brother. Others, like the Mohawk poet Maurice Kenny, attack Whitman's "indifference" to Natives and his complicit acceptance of manifest destiny. Still others, like the Acoma poet Simon Ortiz, record an ambivalent reaction to Whitman, curious about how the great poet of democracy reacted to the decimation of Native peoples, curious about why he did not say more than he did.

Ed Folsom

Bibliography

Bruchac, Joseph. "To Love the Earth: Some Thoughts on Walt Whitman." *Walt Whitman: The Measure of His Song.* Ed. Jim Perlman, Ed Folsom, and Dan Campion. Minneapolis: Holy Cow!, 1981. 274–278.

Folsom, Ed. *Walt Whitman's Native Representations.* Cambridge: Cambridge UP, 1994.

Kenny, Maurice. "Whitman's Indifference to Indians." *The Continuing Presence of Walt Whitman.* Ed. Robert K. Martin. Iowa City: U of Iowa P, 1992. 28–38.

Ortiz, Simon. *From Sand Creek.* Oak Park, N.Y.: Thunder's Mouth, 1981.

Whitman, Walt. *An American Primer.* 1904. Stevens Point, Wis.: Holy Cow!, 1987.

———. *The Early Poems and the Fiction.* Ed. Thomas L. Brasher. New York: New York UP, 1963.

———. *Notebooks and Unpublished Prose Manuscripts.* Ed. Edward F. Grier. 6 vols. New York: New York UP, 1984.

———. *Prose Works 1892.* Ed. Floyd Stovall. 2 vols. New York: New York UP, 1963–1964.

See also "Death of Wind-Foot, The"; *Franklin Evans;* "From Far Dakota's Cañons"; "Half-Breed, The"; Imperialism; Indian Affairs, Bureau of; "Osceola"; Place Names; Racial Attitudes; "Yonnondio"

"Native Moments" (1860)

"Native Moments" first appeared as number 8 in the cluster "Enfans d'Adam." In the final edition it assumes the twelfth position in the cluster. An interesting change in line 7 appears for the first time in 1881: the words "I take for my love some prostitute" have been dropped. In their context, 1860–1871, there is strong reason to believe the prostitute is male. M. Jimmie Killingsworth reads the original line as Whitman's attempt to shock his reading public. By 1876, however, Whitman had dropped personal references to prostitutes in several other poems, including "From Pent-up Aching Rivers."

Killingsworth classifies the poem as one of three "delirium" poems in "Children of Adam," the other two being "From Pent-up Aching Rivers" and "One Hour to Madness and Joy." But unlike the death metaphor for merge in the "Calamus" poems, the metaphor in "Native Moments" is madness. Thus, Killingsworth concludes, Whitman suggests that heterosexual fusion is incomplete and impossible. Harold Aspiz similarly reasons that the poem is masturbatory and thus represents Whitman's attempt to reach a transcendent mysticism through sexual release. For James Miller, the poem represents a dilemma for Whitman: torn between spontaneous Adamic joys and the harsh vulgarity of society, the narrator rejects convention and opts for natural law.

George Klawitter

Bibliography

Aspiz, Harold. "Sexuality and the Language of Transcendence." *Walt Whitman Quarterly Review* 5.2 (1987): 1–7.

Killingsworth, M. Jimmie. *Whitman's Poetry of the Body: Sexuality, Politics, and the Text.* Chapel Hill: U of North Carolina P, 1989.

Miller, James E., Jr. *A Critical Guide to "Leaves of Grass."* Chicago: U of Chicago P, 1957.

Whitman, Walt. *Leaves of Grass: A Textual Variorum of the Printed Poems.* Ed. Sculley Bradley, Harold W. Blodgett, Arthur Golden, and William White. 3 vols. New York: New York UP, 1980.

See also "Children of Adam"; "From Pent-up Aching Rivers"; "One Hour to Madness and Joy"; Sex and Sexuality

Nature

Nature is central to Whitman's thought and writing in two aspects: as the material world of objects and phenomena (*natura naturata*) or as the force—usually personified as feminine—that pervades and controls that material world (*natura naturans*). In Whitman's pre–Civil War poetry the *naturata* aspect of nature tends to predominate, as he focuses on specific natural objects. In such later works as *Democratic Vistas* (1871) or his last major poem, "Passage to India" (1871), the *naturans* aspect predominates and nature becomes largely an abstraction.

Like most of his contemporaries, including Emerson in his book *Nature* (1836), Whitman does not try to distinguish between the two aspects, simply declaring in the lines moved to the final version of "Song of Myself": "I permit to speak at every hazard / Nature without check with original energy" (section 1). For him as for William Cullen Bryant in the opening lines of "Thanatopsis," nature as *naturans* speaks through "her visible forms" (*naturata*). Thus John Burroughs, describing his first encounter with *Leaves of Grass* in 1861, when he read it in the woods as a naturalist, wrote that he found the book unique in producing the same impression on his moral consciousness as "actual Nature did in her material forms and shows" (10). Like Ralph Waldo Emerson, Whitman sees natural facts as inherently symbolic of spiritual facts, thus differing from Nathaniel Hawthorne, who depicts the symbolism of *naturata* as ambiguous, and from Herman Melville, who finds the symbolism of *naturata* not only ambiguous but often deceptive.

Whitman's poetic use of natural objects differs from that of his contemporaries such as William Wordsworth, Bryant, or Emerson chiefly by his inclusiveness. He rejects the prettified nature he finds in conventional poetry; in *Specimen Days* he describes that view of nature as artificial, repressing, and "constipating." Natural objects listed in his catalogues range from the "quintillions of spheres" that fill the universe to "brown ants," "mossy scabs," "pokeweed," and "beetles rolling balls of dung" ("Song of Myself," sections 33, 5, 24). Furthermore, like Emerson in the opening paragraphs of *Nature*, Whitman includes as natural objects products of human industry, such as the ships, foundries, and buildings of Manhattan in "Crossing Brooklyn Ferry." In the opening lines of "The Song of the Broad-Axe," that artifact is portrayed as though it were a natural object. And although like other romantic poets Whitman is strongly drawn to the unspoiled natural world, he is equally drawn to life in the city, which he is the first American poet to celebrate. Thus, after depicting the varied attractions of the countryside in the opening lines of "Give Me the Splendid Silent Sun," he rejects them for the excitement of the city, ending the poem with the line "Manhattan faces and eyes forever for me."

The natural object most frequently and conspicuously employed by Whitman is the sea. In "Out of the Cradle Endlessly Rocking," "When Lilacs Last in the Dooryard Bloom'd," and several of the shorter poems in the "Sea-Drift" section of *Leaves of Grass,* the sea is personified as an old mother or nurse and as-sociated with death. In "Reconciliation" Whitman has this personification of the sea in mind when he writes that "the hands of the sisters Death and Night incessantly softly wash again, and ever again, this soil'd world."

The air—used most frequently with the adjective "open"—generally symbolizes either freedom and happiness or the universality of Whitman's message. The sun figures prominently in *Leaves of Grass*—far more than the moon. Whitman makes frequent use of stars, listing them in "A Clear Midnight" as among his favorite themes, along with night, death, and sleep. The evening star, Venus, is a central and powerful symbol in "Lilacs."

Grass is a frequent symbol, most conspicuously in section 6 of "Song of Myself," as are leaves, which are often not merely parts of a plant but also parts of a book, as in "I Saw in Louisiana a Live-Oak Growing." The imagery of growing plants, with the use of words like "blossom" or "bloom," is used in such poems as "Song of Myself," "Song of the Universal," and "Passage to India" to symbolize the progress of the universe toward perfection.

Although Whitman occasionally mentions animals of the American wilderness such as alligators, bears, elk, moose, panthers, rattlesnakes, and wolves—most of which he had never encountered—his best-known reference to animals is the generalized one at the beginning of section 32 of "Song of Myself," where he seems to idealize the natural behavior of animals as contrasting sharply with the guilt feelings and frustrations found in artificial lives of human beings. Later, however, toward the end of "Passage to India," the behavior of animals, now referred to as "mere brutes," is something to be eschewed and transcended.

Whitman depicts birds conventionally in poems like "To the Man-of-War-Bird" or "The Dalliance of the Eagles," but his boldest and most distinctive use of them is as speaking characters in two of his greatest poems, "Out of the Cradle" and "Lilacs." The songs given to the mockingbird in the former and to the hermit thrush in the latter are used with great effectiveness to express naked, heartfelt emotional responses to death: loss, sorrow, and grief in one case; triumphant acceptance in the other.

Whitman's description of the hermit thrush depends heavily on information given to him by his friend Burroughs, since Whitman is admittedly no naturalist; he even asserts in *Specimen Days* that one enjoys the natural world more if one is not too precise or scientific about it. Rather, he sees the function of natural objects and phenomena as revealing the characteristics of *natura naturans*—that is, nature as a reified or personified abstraction. The closest he comes to defining this abstraction is in "Song of the Banner at Daybreak," where he can do little except to state that it is something separate from the natural objects and phenomena it pervades, much as Wordsworth refers in "Tintern Abbey" to a "presence," "something," "motion," and "spirit."

Historically, conceptions of nature as *naturans* have varied widely, and among Whitman's contemporaries nature as an abstraction is depicted in contradictory ways. For Wordsworth, nature is a benevolent goddess; for Alfred, Lord Tennyson in his "In Memoriam," nature is a cruel force, "red in tooth and claw." Emerson in *Nature* generally shares Wordsworth's view, but in his later essay, "Fate," he refers to nature as "the tyrannous circumstance" (Emerson 949).

For Whitman, nature as *naturans* has six predominant characteristics: process, purpose, sexuality, unity, divinity, and beneficence. He never sets forth this conception of nature explicitly or systematically, any more than did Emerson, Thoreau, and other transcendentalists, most of whom would generally agree with all of these characterizations of nature except sexuality. This last was for Whitman's contemporaries often the most conspicuous—and to many the most objectionable—aspect of his poetry.

Process simply means that the universe is not static, as it was often perceived in eighteenth-century thought, but is continually in flux, changing, growing, evolving. Furthermore, it is evolving in a purposive way toward a future perfection, a teleological view that Whitman sets forth succinctly in "Roaming in Thought (After reading Hegel)" and echoes in the section of *Specimen Days* headed "Carlyle from American Points of View." Whitman's outlook in this respect is consonant with the widely held nineteenth-century belief in progress, the belief reflected in the thinking of Georg Wilhelm Friedrich Hegel, Charles Darwin, and Karl Marx. But Whitman's depiction of progress is unique in identifying the force behind progress as sexual, an identification he made explicit in 1867 by adding the words "always sex" at the end of the Hegelian line 45 in "Song of Myself" (section 3).

For Whitman personally, sex was a force that often seemed to baffle him, overwhelm him, and leave him with guilty pleasure. But it may also have contributed to his empathy with the wounded young soldiers, and likewise his willingness to comfort them at times by kissing them, that made him such an assiduous and effective visitor to the Civil War army hospitals. This empathy is symbolized in the bold final gesture in "Reconciliation" and is stated most succinctly in "Song of Myself" (section 33): "I am the man, I suffer'd, I was there." In viewing sex as an essential component of nature, Whitman saw it as fulfilling two positive purposes: creating new life as the product of the attraction between men and women, and creating the organic unity of society as the product of a more inclusive attraction—for which he used the phrenological term "adhesiveness"—among all members of society, as set forth, for example, in "The Base of All Metaphysics," "I Hear It was Charged against Me," and *Democratic Vistas*.

The unity of nature is a central Emersonian belief that Whitman fully shares. Although he asserts this belief in such poems as "On the Beach at Night Alone," "Kosmos," or "Starting from Paumanok" (especially sections 6, 7, and 12), more often it is an unstated assumption. Whitman takes for granted an underlying unity, in which the individual components of his catalogues merge and blend, much like the diverse components of a successful photo montage, to create a single, unified impression.

Divinity as a fifth characteristic of nature as *naturans* is evidenced by Whitman's frequent use of the adjective "divine." Although he at times addresses God as a transcendent being, as in "Passage to India" (section 8) or "Prayer of Columbus," he also depicts God as immanent. In this latter sense the distinction between God and nature is not always clear, with the result that Whitman has sometimes been labeled a pantheist. Some support for this label may be found in Whitman's most theological poem, "Chanting the Square Deific," which depicts God as having four aspects—Jehovah, Christ, Satan, and Santa Spirita—the last of which includes not only the first three but everything else in the universe. Likewise, in "As They Draw to a Close," nature is described as "encompassing God."

Finally, Whitman sees nature as beneficent, a sharp contrast to the malevolent nature depicted by such contemporaries as Henry Adams in his *Education* and John Stuart Mill in his essay "Nature," or the morally indifferent nature of Herbert Spencer and the Social Darwinists. Whitman expresses this view of nature most explicitly in "A Song for Occupations" (section 3) and most succinctly in "Song of the Universal," where he speaks of "Nature's amelioration blessing all" (section 4).

This purposive, unified, divine, and beneficent nature plays a central role in "Passage to India," where Whitman sees the unification of the Eastern and Western halves of humanity as simultaneously bringing about the unity of humankind, nature, and God in a "trinitas divine" (section 5). In *Democratic Vistas,* written just a few years earlier, the *naturans* aspect of nature again plays a major role, this time as a model for democracy—referred to as nature's younger brother—and also for literature, which must always be tested against "the true idea of Nature, long absent" (Whitman 984).

Since Whitman was not a systematic thinker, his assertions about nature as *naturans* are inevitably characterized by a vagueness and inconsistency that frustrate those who want to reduce his thought to a static and logically coherent philosophy. Fittingly, in his final extended treatment of nature, in *Specimen Days,* Whitman returns to its *naturata* aspect and again reflects the joy, peace, and happiness he found in his solitary immersion at Timber Creek in the comforting maternity of the natural world.

Martin K. Doudna

Bibliography

Adams, Henry. *The Education of Henry Adams.* 1906. Boston: Houghton Mifflin, 1918.

Beach, Joseph Warren. *The Concept of Nature in Nineteenth-Century English Poetry.* 1936. New York: Pageant, 1956.

Burroughs, John. *Notes on Walt Whitman, as Poet and Person.* 1867. New York: Haskell House, 1971.

Doudna, Martin K. "'The Essential Ultimate Me': Whitman's Achievement in 'Passage to India.'" *Walt Whitman Quarterly Review* 2.3 (1984): 1–9.

Eby, Edwin Harold, ed. *A Concordance of Walt Whitman's "Leaves of Grass" and Selected Prose Writings.* 1955. New York: Greenwood, 1969.

Emerson, Ralph Waldo. *Essays & Lectures.* Ed. Joel Porte. New York: Library of America, 1983.

Foerster, Norman. "Whitman as a Poet of Nature." *PMLA* 31 (1916): 736–758.

Kaplan, Justin. *Walt Whitman: A Life.* New York: Simon and Schuster, 1980.

Mill, John Stuart. *Nature, the Utility of Religion, and Theism: Three Essays on Religion.* London: Longmans, Green, Reader, and Dyer, 1874.

Piasecki, Bruce. "Whitman's 'Estimate of Nature' in *Democratic Vistas.*" *Walt Whitman Review* 27 (1981): 101–112.

Whitman, Walt. *Complete Poetry and Collected Prose.* Ed. Justin Kaplan. New York: Library of America, 1982.

See also BRITISH ROMANTIC POETS; BRYANT, WILLIAM CULLEN; BURROUGHS, JOHN AND URSULA; CITY, WHITMAN AND THE; EMERSON, RALPH WALDO; PANTHEISM; ROMANTICISM; SEA, THE; SYMBOLISM; TIMBER CREEK; TRANSCENDENTALISM

Neruda, Pablo (1904–1973)

Pablo Neruda (Neftali Ricardo Reyes Basoalto), Chilean poet and winner of the 1971 Nobel Prize for Literature, attributed much of his achievement to an early exposure to Whitman. In his *Memoirs,* Neruda wrote of his own work, "If my poetry has any meaning at all, it is [its] tendency to stretch out in space, without restrictions, and not be happy to stay in one room. . . . I had to be myself, striving to branch out like the very land where I was born. Another poet of this same hemisphere helped me along this road, Walt Whitman, my comrade from Manhattan" (262). Neruda admired Whitman not only for his capacity for breaking through the boundaries of form but also for his depiction of what Neruda termed "the positive hero." Neruda lauded Whitman for bringing this hero, "not without suffering, into the intimacy of our physical life, making him share with us our bread and our dream" (*Memoirs* 294). Neruda, who wrote Spanish translations of many of Whitman's poems, claimed that Whitman had taught him how to be American.

Whereas Neruda's predecessors on the political left had tended to see Whitman as narrowly nationalistic and even jingoistic, Neruda regarded him as embodying a democratic ideal toward which rising nations and peoples might aspire. Neruda's 1956 *Nuevas Odas Elementales* includes "Ode to Walt Whitman," which acknowledges Whitman as an early formative influence. Neruda began his posthumously published *Incitación al nixonicidio y alabanza de la revolución chilena* (Incitation to Nixonicide and Praise for the Chilean Revolution) with the following invocation:

It is as an act of love for my land
That I call on you, necessary brother,
Old Walt Whitman of the gray hand.
("Comienzo" 17)

Although Whitman's influence can be observed virtually throughout Neruda's work, it is especially powerful in Neruda's great evocation of America, *Canto general* (1950), an epic reminiscent of "Song of Myself." Neruda's great esteem for Whitman can be observed in his 1972 article "We Live in a Whitmanesque Age," in which the poet called himself "the humble servant" of Whitman, "a poet who strode the earth with long, slow paces, pausing everywhere to love, to examine, to learn, to teach and to admire" (37).

John T. Matteson

Bibliography

Neruda, Pablo. *Canto general*. Buenos Aires: Losada, 1955.
———. "Comienzo por invocar a Walt Whitman." *Incitación al nixonicidio y alabanza de la revolución chilena*. Santiago: Editora Nacional Quimantu, 1973. 17–21.
———. *Memoirs*. Trans. Hardie St. Martin. New York: Farrar, Straus and Giroux, 1995.
———. "We Live in a Whitmanesque Age." New York *Times* 14 Apr. 1972: 37.
Nolan, James. *Poet-Chief: The Native American Poetics of Walt Whitman and Pablo Neruda*. Albuquerque: U of New Mexico P, 1994.
Sommer, Doris. "The Bard of Both Americas." *Approaches to Teaching Whitman's "Leaves of Grass."* Ed. Donald D. Kummings. New York: MLA, 1990. 159–167.

See also LEGACY, WHITMAN'S; SPAIN AND SPANISH AMERICA, WHITMAN IN

New Orleans *Crescent*

Established in 1848 by J.E. McClure and A.H. Hayes, the New Orleans *Crescent* joined the *Picayune* and the *Delta* as the third major newspaper in the Crescent City. It became an immediate success, gaining two thousand subscribers within a few weeks. The first issue was Sunday, 5 March 1848, but thereafter it appeared on weekdays only. Walt Whitman was associated with the fledgling newspaper from late February 1848 to late May 1848.

The exact nature of Whitman's position with the *Crescent* is uncertain. Though he may have been an editor, likely he was not the sole editor. The staff consisted of Whitman as "exchange editor," a full-time editorial writer named Larue, a city news reporter named Reeder, a translator of Mexican and foreign news items known as Da Poute, and Whitman's younger brother, Jeff, as office boy. Whitman's job was essentially twofold: to clip general news items in other newspapers received in the mail and thus make up the day's edition, and occasionally to contribute feature articles.

The first issue of the *Crescent* contained Whitman's poem "Sailing the Mississippi at Midnight" and a feature story entitled "Crossing the Alleghenies." The next day, 6 March 1848, his impressions of Cincinnati and Louisville appeared, along with a controversial editorial defending Dr. Collyer's "Model Artists," a show with scantily clad models. Four days later he published "The Habitants of Hotels" and other sketches of people types, such as Daggerdraw Bowie-Knife, Esq., a murderous scoundrel; John J. Jinglebrain, a New Orleans dandy; and a sentimental lover named Samuel Sensitive. His popular "Sketches of the Sidewalks and Levees," though inferior to his prior work on the Brooklyn *Daily Eagle*, reveal his fascination with New Orleans life and also his ability to mix pleasure with business. Some have judged these pieces to be flippant and sentimental, perhaps because Whitman was attempting humor, for which he was not well equipped. Better were the descriptive pieces about America's new frontier based on the notes he took on his twenty-four-hundred-mile trip from Brooklyn to New Orleans. Though not as impressive as later prose works, these articles were notably visual and show his developing ability to see as a painter.

On 25 May 1848, a mere three months after arriving in New Orleans, Whitman resigned his position at the *Crescent*, returned to New York, and started a weekly newspaper, the Brooklyn *Freeman*. The reason for his sudden departure after such a short tenure is a matter of conjecture. Whitman has written that for some reason unknown to him, the owners grew cold toward him and irritable toward Jeff, who had been ill most of the time while in the city. A squabble over a cash advance precipitated the final break that ended Whitman's association with the newspaper and sent the two brothers home. Even so, Whitman later characterized his situation with the *Crescent* as "a rather pleasant one" (*Prose Works* 2:607).

Maverick Marvin Harris

Bibliography
Allen, Gay Wilson. *The New Walt Whitman Handbook*. 1975. New York: New York UP, 1986.
———. *The Solitary Singer: A Critical Biography of Walt Whitman*. 1955. Rev. ed. 1967. Chicago: U of Chicago P, 1985.
Canby, Henry Seidel. *Walt Whitman: An American*. New York: Houghton Mifflin, 1943.
Kaplan, Justin. *Walt Whitman: A Life*. New York: Simon and Schuster, 1980.
Whitman, Walt. *Prose Works 1892*. Ed. Floyd Stovall. 2 vols. New York: New York UP, 1963–1964.
———. *The Uncollected Poetry and Prose of Walt Whitman*. Ed. Emory Holloway. 2 vols. Garden City, N.Y.: Doubleday, Page, 1921.
Zweig, Paul. *Walt Whitman: The Making of the Poet*. New York: Basic Books, 1984.

See also Journalism, Whitman's; New Orleans, Louisiana; New Orleans *Picayune*; Pre-*Leaves* Poems; Whitman, Thomas Jefferson

New Orleans, Louisiana

Since its founding in 1718 by Jean Baptiste Lemoine, Sieur de Boinville, New Orleans has been the largest, most important city in Louisiana. Located in the hollow of a three-sided bend of the Mississippi River as it reaches the Gulf of Mexico—hence its name "The Crescent City"—it has from earliest times been a commercial and cultural center. Walt Whitman's three-month stay there from 25 February to 25 May in 1848, while he worked for the newly founded New Orleans *Crescent*, significantly impacted his development as a poet and essayist.

The first occupants of this low-lying, swampy, palmetto-covered area were adventurers, gold hunters, thieves, pirates, and the riff-raff of society. As people of means and social standing were later drawn to the new land of opportunity, a Creole society evolved. New Orleans developed under the flags of Spain and France until 1803, at which time it passed to the young United States via the Louisiana Purchase.

The battle of New Orleans in 1815 and the Mexican War (1846–1848) highlighted the significance of the city as a port of entry to the interior regions of the growing nation.

Whitman, with his fourteen-year-old brother, Jeff, left New York in February 1848 at the invitation of J.E. McClure to help establish the New Orleans *Crescent*. Traveling by rail, coach, and boat for the twenty-four-hundred-mile trip, Whitman experienced the vastness of the American land and fixed in his mind the fullness and diversity of his beloved America.

Arriving on the *St. Cloud* on 25 February, Whitman and Jeff took temporary quarters but later moved into the Tremont House in the American district across from the St. Charles Hotel and the offices of the *Crescent*. The city was at the height of the festival season; General Taylor's men, back from the Mexican War, swarmed the streets. Over the next few weeks, as he roamed the streets in early morning, during break times, and late at night, Whitman observed bustling wharves lined with steamboats, active courtrooms, lively theaters, the opulent opera, the candlelit cathedral, gaming houses, fancy brothels, jaunty parades, and Saturday night balls. He absorbed the exotic French-Spanish flavor of the flowered courtyards. He enjoyed lounging in large barrooms and hotel saloons, drinking the select drinks they afforded. But most of all, he enjoyed strolling along the levees and marketplaces, where he listened to Indian and Negro hucksters proffer their wares and where he bought coffee and a biscuit for breakfast from a large Creole mulatto woman. These experiences and impressions formed the basis of feature articles in the *Crescent* and, later, "New Orleans in 1848" in *November Boughs* (1888).

Most scholars now reject the idea that Whitman was involved with a Creole woman of higher social rank than his own and that his sudden exit from New Orleans was due to complications deriving from this relationship. The theory of a New Orleans romance, started by Henry Bryan Binns in his *A Life of Walt Whitman* (1905), proposes to explain the mystery of Whitman's letter to John Addington Symonds in which he discussed his life down South and mentioned six illegitimate children (for which there is no documented evidence). It is also used to explain the dramatic change in Whitman after the New Orleans trip, his sexual awakening, and the inspiration for the first edition of

Leaves of Grass (1855). Some biographers think the lines "O Magnet-South! O glistening, perfumed South! My South! / O quick mettle, rich blood, impulse and love! good and evil! O all dear to me!" in "Longings for Home" (later "O Magnet-South") suggest a New Orleans romance. Some quote the first five lines of "I Saw in Louisiana a Live-Oak Growing" as support for the idea. Basil De Selincourt asserts in his 1914 critical study of Whitman that "Out of the Cradle Endlessly Rocking" bemoans the death of one who was all but wife to him—the genteel New Orleans lady. Still others see further evidence in "Once I Pass'd through a Populous City," in which Whitman penned, "Yet now of all that city I remember only a woman I casually met there who detain'd me for love of me . . . who passionately clung to me." However, Whitman's earlier manuscript, which read "the man" instead of "a woman," is telling. Current scholarship by and large rejects the theory.

A contentious relationship with the owners of the Crescent caused Whitman to resign on 25 May and return to New York.

Maverick Marvin Harris

Bibliography

Allen, Gay Wilson. *The New Walt Whitman Handbook*. 1975. New York: New York UP, 1986.

Binns, Henry Bryan. *A Life of Walt Whitman*. London: Methuen, 1905.

Bucke, Richard Maurice, Thomas B. Harned, and Horace L. Traubel. Introduction. *The Complete Writings of Walt Whitman*. By Whitman. Vol. 1. New York: Putnam, 1902. xiii–xcvi.

De Selincourt, Basil. *Walt Whitman: A Critical Study*. London: Martin Secker, 1914.

Holloway, Emory. *Whitman: An Interpretation in Narrative*. New York: Knopf, 1926.

Kaplan, Justin. *Walt Whitman: A Life*. New York: Simon and Schuster, 1980.

Miller, James E., Jr. *Walt Whitman*. 1962. Updated ed. Boston: Twayne, 1990.

Whitman, Walt. *Prose Works 1892*. Ed. Floyd Stovall. 2 vols. New York: New York UP, 1963–1964.

Zweig, Paul. *Walt Whitman: The Making of the Poet*. New York: Basic Books, 1984.

See also BINNS, HENRY BRYAN; JOURNALISM, WHITMAN'S; NEW ORLEANS CRESCENT; NEW ORLEANS PICAYUNE; TRAVELS, WHITMAN'S; WHITMAN, THOMAS JEFFERSON

New Orleans *Picayune*

Founded in 1836, the New Orleans *Picayune* was established during a period of the expansion of newspapers on the rapidly developing American frontier. After the war with Mexico was concluded in early 1848, New Orleans was an ideal locale for a newspaper, for the city flourished with trade going up and down the Mississippi River, bustled with soldiers returning from the war, quartered the best news and war correspondents, and had the ear of a young nation eager for news. Along with the New Orleans *Delta*, the *Picayune* faithfully provided that information.

In response to the *Picayune*'s invitation in 1887 to write about his possible work on its staff (he never did) during his brief tenure as editor of the New Orleans *Crescent* in 1848 or about journalism of that era, Walt Whitman responded with an article printed in the *Picayune* on 25 January 1887 and subsequently published as "New Orleans in 1848" in *November Boughs* (1888).

Maverick Marvin Harris

Bibliography

Allen, Gay Wilson. *The Solitary Singer: A Critical Biography of Walt Whitman*. 1955. Rev. ed. 1967. Chicago: U of Chicago P, 1985.

Whitman, Walt. "New Orleans in 1848." *Prose Works 1892*. Ed. Floyd Stovall. Vol. 2. New York: New York UP, 1964. 604–610.

See also NEW ORLEANS CRESCENT; NEW ORLEANS, LOUISIANA

New World, The (New York)

The New World (1839–1845) was a popular weekly paper that was founded by Park Benjamin and Rufus Griswold at a time when an increasingly aggressive entrepreneurial press was seeking to create and reach a mass public. Advertised as the "largest and cheapest" newspaper in the world, *The New World* was also known for publishing the works of famous British authors as "extras." While Whitman worked as a compositor at *The New World* in 1841, the paper published two of his poems, "Each Has His Grief" and "The Punishment of Pride," as well as "The Child's Champion," Whitman's erotically charged story of the love between an adolescent boy and a young man. In 1842 Benjamin offered Whitman a cash advance to write *Franklin Evans; or The Inebriate. A Tale of the Times.* Advertised as a temperance novel "By a Popular American Author," issued as an "extra" of *The New World* and aimed at "the widest circulation possible," *Franklin Evans* appears to have sold well (possibly twenty thousand copies). Like "The Child's Champion," *Franklin Evans* draws on the temperance genre to evoke the homoerotic subculture out of which the democratic comrade and lover of *Leaves of Grass* emerged. Although critics have tended to draw a sharp distinction between early journalist and later poet, Whitman's work for *The New World* as both printer and author suggests the multivarious sources of his later writing in the world of print journalism and the mass press, popular culture and temperance reform, working class radicalism and an increasingly visible same-sex subculture in the new urban space of the city.

Betsy Erkkila

Bibliography

Hoover, Merle M. *Park Benjamin, Poet & Editor.* New York: Columbia UP, 1948.

Hudson, Frederic. *Journalism in the United States from 1690 to 1872.* 1875. New York: Harper and Row, 1969.

Mott, Frank Luther. *A History of American Magazines, 1741–1850.* Cambridge, Mass: Harvard UP, 1957.

Warner, Michael. "Whitman Drunk." *Breaking Bounds: Whitman and American Cultural Studies.* Ed. Betsy Erkkila and Jay Grossman. New York: Oxford UP, 1996. 30–43.

See also "CHILD AND THE PROFLIGATE, THE"; GRISWOLD, RUFUS W.; *FRANKLIN EVANS*; PRE-*LEAVES* POEMS; SHORT FICTION, WHITMAN'S; TEMPERANCE MOVEMENT

New York *Aurora*

For two heady months in 1842 Walt Whitman edited the New York *Aurora*, a two-penny daily with a circulation of more than five thousand. At age twenty-two he was a peer of influential journalists like James Gordon Bennett and Horace Greeley, competing for readers in the city he considered the mecca of the New World. The *Aurora* targeted a more sophisticated demographic than Whitman would address for papers he later edited, and he adopted the appropriate accessories—a top hat, boutonniere, and walking cane. He soon claimed that circulation had grown another thousand under his editorship (Whitman 116).

The location of *Aurora* offices near Tammany Hall, New York's political hub, gave the young editor a taste for the rough and tumble of urban political life and reinforced his conviction that the written word can have political power. In the end, when his publisher wanted the paper to support a Whig presidential candidate, John Tyler, Whitman would not abandon his Jeffersonian loyalties and was fired.

As *Aurora* editor, Whitman joined public debates over presidential politics, public education, the desecration of revolutionary-era burial grounds, and "kidnappings" of prostitutes in a crackdown on Broadway. However, his editorials display less research and policy analysis than in his mature journalism, applying a simple interpretive frame of concern for republican principles of self-government. Even for the subject of his greatest attention on the *Aurora*, a controversy over schools for the influx of immigrant children, Whitman ignores the educational policy issues.

The New York governor—in touch with a leading educator, Horace Mann—had proposed granting funding authority to elected instead of appointed city school officials. More accountable to immigrant voters, elected authorities would probably have supported church and synagogue efforts to operate and improve schools. What Whitman wrote about, however, was not the need for schools nor who should be given authority for them, but the corruption he saw in the political process. He wrote editorials attacking "meddling" by "foreign" priests and decrying the disruptions of public meetings by immigrant political activists (Whitman 57–72).

Biographers since the mid-1980s have recognized more similarities between Whitman's *Aurora* writing and *Leaves of Grass* than were recognized previously. Catalogues of Americana, bombastic rhetoric, slang, French phrases, and a composite and democratic persona appear in the *Aurora* and later in Whitman's mature poetry. *Aurora* editorials also provide previews of the political agenda that would dominate Whitman's career—anxiety over the fragility of the Union as the foundation of New World hopes, suspicion of government as a threat to individual freedom, and fear that greed in the commercial world would undermine republican virtue.

Four years later, as editor of the Brooklyn *Daily Eagle,* Whitman expanded literary coverage, but in the *Aurora* he includes only a few small cultural items about J.F. Cooper, Charles Dickens, Italian opera, and Ralph Waldo Emerson. He does not display much interest in the content of Emerson's lecture "Poetry of the Times," other than Emerson's statement that "the first man who called another an ass was a poet." Instead he provides superficial details about the full house in attendance: only "a few beautiful maids" and too many "blue stocking" women were present, he reports. He mocks Horace Greeley's visible "ecstasies" when, every five minutes or so, Emerson said something "particularly good" (105).

Most *Aurora* articles by Whitman have been reprinted in *Walt Whitman of the New York Aurora.*

Dennis K. Renner

Bibliography

Erkkila, Betsy. *Whitman the Political Poet.* New York: Oxford, 1989.

Greenspan, Ezra. *Walt Whitman and the American Reader.* Cambridge: Cambridge UP, 1990.

Reynolds, David S. *Walt Whitman's America: A Cultural Biography.* New York: Knopf, 1995.

Rubin, Joseph Jay. *The Historic Whitman.* University Park: Pennsylvania State UP, 1973.

Whitman, Walt. *Walt Whitman of the New York Aurora.* Ed. Joseph Jay Rubin and Charles H. Brown. State College, Pa.: Bald Eagle, 1950.

See also EDUCATION, VIEWS ON; IMMIGRANTS; JOURNALISM, WHITMAN'S; POLITICAL VIEWS

New York City

"This is the city," wrote Whitman, "and I am one of the citizens" ("Song of Myself," section 42). For most of the first forty years of his life, New York was the great milieu that crucially affected every aspect of his existence. Yet he had not been born there, never really lived there, worked there only intermittently, and was devoted to the rival, "parasitical" town of Brooklyn. This may help explain his complex relationship to New York proper—his ability to relate to it simultaneously as spectator and participant, as knowing insider and dazed or chronically awed outsider; his easy accommodation of the contrasting claims of city and country (see "Give Me the Splendid Silent Sun"); his nonpossessive sense of the fluidity of New York's identity; and his antinativist appreciation of the hospitable openness of its "proud, friendly, turbulent" character ("First O Songs")—so different from that of its prim Yankee rival, Boston.

Moving from rooming house to dingy rooming house throughout 1835–1836 while working as a rookie printer, he grew into manhood amidst the feverish whirl of the city streets. Returning there in 1842 as rookie editor of the *Aurora,* he quickly joined in its ferocious political squabbles, and discovered the underlying violence, squalor, and degradation that served to heighten its social glitter. Even as the young autodidact set about acquiring his intellectual education from museums, sermons, speeches, and public lectures, he received an equally valuable streetwise education in the galvanic ways of a city caught in the throes of a socioeconomic revolution that turned it into the very image of the throbbingly modern.

As it exploded from 123,706 in 1820 into a metropolis of 813,669 (almost half of them immigrants) in 1860, New York disintegrated socially. Ethnic ghettos like *Kleindeutschland* appeared alongside such exclusive refuges of the rich as Astor Place. Plate-glass windows in that new wonder, the department store, displayed the goods and mirrored the fashion show on Broadway, while the immigrant poor were penned into the infamous Five Points district, where conditions, stinking of vice and crime, were appreciably worse than in the notorious East End of Dickens's London. No wonder that in his early poetry (1855–1860) Whitman worked to reintegrate society by means of such linking, collectivizing, or aggregating structures as choric rhythm, syntactical parallelism, and promiscuously inclusive cataloguing of activities and occupations.

He also produced a deliberately hybridized art, innovatively mixing high and low to create the verbal equivalent of that novel New York concoction, the cocktail. That ruffianly lower-class swell, the Bowery b'hoy—already a hero of the raucous popular theater frequented by Whitman—lent his outrageous swagger to "Song of Myself" (1855). Gaudy, vibrant New York glutted Whitman's passion for all the mixed entertainments of "art and heart"—from Italian opera to folksy harmonizing, from stylishly histrionic Shakespeare to the street theater of carnivalesque popular festivals and the cut-

Broadway stages, with St. Paul's Church in the background. By permission, Eno Collection, Miriam and Ira D. Wallach Division of Arts, Prints and Photographs, New York Public Library.

throat rivalry of the fire companies' chariot races. All these first became part of the young journalist who went forth every day during the 1840s, licensed to loafe at his ease around the streets, collecting "copy" that later, from *Leaves of Grass* (1855) onward, turned him into a Barnumesque self-promoter and a nineteenth-century Cecil B. De Mille who produced spectacular urban epics with casts of thousands, sometimes using the visual techniques he'd learned from the photographic studios he'd visited, or the grand dioramas and panoramas he'd seen.

Although beginning as a city dandy, and always a natural *flâneur,* he quickly became a hardened political infighter, social commentator and committed liberal reformer. As newspaper editor (on and off from 1842 through 1859), Whitman campaigned on issues ranging from ferry charges to clean water, raged against the appalling slum housing conditions, and argued for hygienic control of prostitution. Very much the product of the "new journalism" that had resulted from New York's invention, in the thirties, of that quintessentially urban phenomenon the mass

newspaper, Whitman was alive to both the responsibilities and the opportunities of his trade. He saw himself as an educator, helping to turn raw New Yorkers (many of them immigrants) into full democratic citizens. He was aware of the newspaper's capacity to act both as urban mirror and urban map—enabling readers to find their bearings in a chaotically changeful world and thereby helping them to create a new civic space.

But he was also mindful of the urban population's appetite for thrills and scandals. Although he came to despise the unprincipled opportunism of the sensationalizing penny press, he skillfully exploited the market for urban shockers in early fiction such as *Franklin Evans* (1842), a crude example of his fascination with the unbridled violence of New York's energies. And as Graham Clarke has shown, Whitman exhibits in a Poe-esque poem like "The Sleepers" (1855) a troubled psychic affinity with the twisted souls and poor misshapen bodies of New York's multitudinous social rejects, living in their own twin city of dreadful night. How far such an affinity implies a kind of covert identification remains an open question. There seems to be evidence aplenty in the poetry that a Whitman uneasy with fixed gender and social identity valued New York as an unprecedented solvent of traditional social ties and promoter of new (sometimes secret and proscribed) modes of relationship. Likewise, as one perhaps permanently in psychic transit, Whitman was fascinated with the stage drivers, horsecar conductors, and ferry pilots who participated in what a contemporary saw as an orgasm of locomotion. For this, as for many other reasons, it is appropriate that probably his single greatest urban poem is "Crossing Brooklyn Ferry" (1856).

However, the highly mediated manner in which the city is represented in that poem is typical of the difficulties the poetry puts in the way of critics who seek to assign it firmly to the actual, historical New York. Whitman himself signaled the separate, textual, and perhaps visionary, character of his poetry's city when, objecting to the hateful colonial provenance of the name "New York," he replaced it with the aboriginal "Mannahatta," supposedly the Indian word for *A rocky founded island— shores where ever gayly dash the coming, going, hurrying sea waves*" ("Mannahatta [My city's fit . . .]" [1888]). As the invocatory poem "Mannahatta [I was asking . . .]" (1860) shows, such redemptive renaming allowed Whitman to refashion a city that had been rigidly grid-blocked for the convenience of commerce, transfiguring it into a landscape as fluid with possibility as the surrounding waters that magically transformed New York for him into a city of ships. Such "metropolitan pantheism" (Conrad 12) allowed Whitman to assimilate New York to his evolutionary "kosmos," a strategy seen by some critics as a (suspect?) way of turning a real recalcitrant cityscape into a malleable personal mindscape. But others view it as Whitman's remarkable means of rendering the novel psychology of modern urban experience. Along with Baudelaire, he has therefore been credited with pioneering discourses for exploring anomie, estrangement, isolation, euphoric togetherness, and many of the other symptoms of urban consciousness that sociologists were later to identify and analyze.

Whitman's feelings about a New York he significantly preferred to apostrophize in maternal terms were deeply and fruitfully ambivalent, veering between ecstatic faith and deep misgivings. His doubts centered on the city's callous (and in his view antirepublican) "i-dollar-try," its increasingly selfish and cynical politics (the fifties saw Fernando Wood pave the way for Boss Tweed's Tammany machine), and its disregard for the egalitarianism that was for Whitman the very bedrock of democracy. His faith was placed in the indomitably radical spirit of New York's working class, in the irresistible energy for social progress he sensed in the dynamism of the streets, and in the newness that was inscribed in New York's very name and guaranteed by the regular influx of an immigrant population in flight from the old. But could such faith withstand the shock of discovering during the Civil War exactly how reactionary New York's politics could be, and the bewilderment of viewing, from a distance (for Whitman left Brooklyn in 1862 never really to return), the emergence of a booming postwar city more socially ravaged and riven than ever before? While most critics argue that these circumstances only intensified Whitman's longstanding arguments with himself, M. Wynn Thomas has suggested that from the early sixties there was a qualitative change in Whitman's relationship to the city, reflected in a decline in his poetry. His deepening bafflement made his affirmations increasingly hollow and his poetry correspondingly vapid, as he could no longer hold vision and contemporary urban reality in a single rapt focus. Thomas claims to find evidence for this in the way Whitman strains to address New York in *Democratic Vistas* (1871), and in those sections of *Specimen Days* (1882) where he records his nostalgia for the prewar years, exhaustively details what seems to be a compensatory postwar love of nature, and includes an unconvincingly portentous description of his recovered faith in a New York he briefly revisited in 1878. All this is seen by Thomas as touching evidence of the breakdown of the old authentic relationship that had been so memorably underwritten by creative engagement.

What is, however, certain beyond all such argument is that in his prime as a poet (about 1855–1865) Whitman was indeed "of Manhattan the son" ("Song of Myself," section 24) and that his yearningly boastful prediction about New York has proved true: "City whom that I have lived and sung in your midst will one day make you illustrious" ("City of Orgies").

M. Wynn Thomas

Bibliography

Brand, Dana. *The Spectator and the City in Nineteenth-Century American Literature.* Cambridge: Cambridge UP, 1991.

Clarke, Graham. *Walt Whitman: The Poem as Private History.* London: Vision, 1991.

Conrad, Peter. *The Art of the City.* Oxford: Oxford UP, 1984.

Jackson, Kenneth T., ed. *The Encyclopedia of New York City.* New Haven: Yale UP, 1995.

Johnson, John H. *The Poet and the City.* Athens: U of Georgia P, 1984.

Kaplan, Justin. *Walt Whitman: A Life.* New York: Simon and Schuster, 1980.

O'Connell, Shaun. *Remarkable, Unspeakable New York: A Literary History.* Boston: Beacon, 1995.

Reynolds, David S. *Walt Whitman's America: A Cultural Biography.* New York: Knopf, 1995.

Seaport: New York's History Magazine 26 (1992). Special Whitman number.

Sharpe, William Chapman. *Unreal Cities.* Baltimore: Johns Hopkins UP, 1990.

Spann, E.K. *The New Metropolis: New York City, 1840–1857.* New York: Columbia UP, 1981.

Thomas, M. Wynn. *The Lunar Light of Whitman's Poetry.* Cambridge, Mass.: Harvard UP, 1987.

———. "Whitman's Tale of Two Cities." *American Literary History* 6 (1994): 633–657.

Versluys, Kristiaan. *The Poet in the City.* Tübingen: Gunter Narr Verlag, 1987.

See also ACTORS AND ACTRESSES; ART AND DAGUERREOTYPE GALLERIES; BROADWAY HOSPITAL (NEW YORK); BROOKLYN, NEW YORK; CITY, WHITMAN AND THE; CRYSTAL PALACE EXHIBITION (NEW YORK); DEMOCRATIC PARTY; EGYPTIAN MUSEUM (NEW YORK); FERRIES AND OMNIBUSES; IMMIGRANTS; JOURNALISM, WHITMAN'S; LABOR AND LABORING CLASSES; LIBRARIES (NEW YORK); OPERA AND OPERA SINGERS; PFAFF'S RESTAURANT; POPULAR CULTURE, WHITMAN AND; ROUGHS; TAMMANY HALL; TEMPERANCE MOVEMENT; THEATERS AND OPERA HOUSES

New York *Evening Post*

The New York *Evening Post* was founded in 1801 at the behest of Alexander Hamilton. Its first editor was William Coleman, who served until 1829, when the reins were passed to William Cullen Bryant, who led the *Post* until his death in 1878. Bryant espoused almost everything Hamilton opposed: free trade, the rights of man, and the party of Andrew Jackson. But Bryant's literary abilities raised the *Post* above a partisan sheet, and it commanded respect throughout the nineteenth century for its editorial excellence. The paper promoted many reforms, and took a courageous early stand against the extension of slavery (unusual for a Democratic paper).

Whitman always esteemed the *Post,* led as it was by the pre-eminent poet of his day, and a Democrat to boot. On 29 July 1841, the paper favorably noted his remarks at a political event. On 29 March 1842, he returned the favor in the New York *Aurora,* assessing the *Post* as nearly the best paper in New York, but warning that "the reputation of a refined poet, and the course that must be pursued in order to make a readable paper, clash with each other" (112).

Despite this remark, Whitman contributed to the *Post* when convenient. Parke Godwin recalled later, "[U]pon our regular local staff we had at one time or another Walt Whitman, who did reporting for us, and, if I remember rightly, wrote a number of letters from Washington at the beginning of the war" (*One Hundredth Anniversary* 36). On 2 March 1850, he published his important early poem, "Song for Certain Congressmen" (later called "Dough-Face Song"). In 1851, Whitman wrote at least five articles for the *Post:* "Something About Art and Brooklyn Artists" (1 February), "A Letter from Brooklyn" (21 March), and three pieces headed "Letter from Paumanok" (27 June, 28 June, 14 August). In later life, too, after his fame spread, the *Post* published his poems on occasion.

Ted Widmer

Bibliography

Nevins, Allan. *The Evening Post: A Century of Journalism.* New York: Boni and Liveright, 1922.

The New York Evening Post One Hundredth Anniversary. New York: Evening Post Publishing, 1902.

Whitman, Walt. *Walt Whitman of the New York Aurora.* Ed. Joseph Jay Rubin and Charles H. Brown. State College, Pa.: Bald Eagle, 1950.

See also BRYANT, WILLIAM CULLEN

New York *Times*

First published by Henry J. Raymond and George Jones on 18 September 1851 as the New York *Daily Times,* it had no connection to the earlier *Sunday Times,* which Whitman edited between the summers of 1842 and 1843. While Myerson's Whitman bibliography lists over twenty-seven hundred items that Whitman published in newspapers and magazines before his death, fewer than twenty appeared in the New York *Times.* His first publication in the paper was a poem, "The Errand Bearers," 27 June 1860, honoring a Japanese delegation to America; a revised version, "A Broadway Pageant," appeared in *Drum-Taps* (1865) and in the 1881 edition of *Leaves of Grass.* Between 1863 and 1865, Whitman's work appeared in the paper eight times, mostly on his war-related activities and life in Washington. Most of these articles were reprinted in *Memoranda During the War* (1875–1876), *Specimen Days* (1882), and *The Wound Dresser* (1898), but often with slightly different titles, such as "Hospital Visits," the title used in *The Wound Dresser* for a piece that originally appeared in the paper on 11 December 1864 as "Our Wounded and Sick Soldiers— Visits Among Army Hospitals, at Washington, on the Field, and Here in New York." Whitman's association with John Swinton, managing editor of the paper, is cited as a factor that aided him in getting the government to arrange a prisoner exchange that reunited him with his brother George. His last entries in the New York *Times* were anonymous ones written in his old age: "The Good Gray Poet Still Cheerful" (7 October 1888) and "Walt Whitman Ill" (6 April 1890).

Walter Graffin

Bibliography

Allen, Gay Wilson. *The Solitary Singer: A Critical Biography of Walt Whitman.* 1955. Rev. ed. 1967. Chicago: U of Chicago P, 1985.

Myerson, Joel. *Walt Whitman: A Descriptive Bibliography.* Pittsburgh: U of Pittsburgh P, 1993.

Reynolds, David S. *Walt Whitman's America: A Cultural Biography.* New York: Knopf, 1995.

See also "BROADWAY PAGEANT, A"; SWINTON, JOHN

New York *Tribune*

Established by Horace Greeley on 10 April 1841, the New York *Tribune* was designed to be an inexpensive daily newspaper with a strong Whig orientation. Reform-oriented and mindful of his mission to publish a family newspaper, Greeley was determined to make the *Tribune* a successful venture. The paper had an initial circulation of fifty-five hundred and rose to forty-five thousand just before the Civil War. Aggressive in reporting the news of the day and in supporting causes such as abolition, the elimination of capital punishment, and temperance, Greeley was also interested in printing and promoting contemporary literature. He printed poems and short fiction, and he hired a number of talented New England intellectuals to write reviews and articles, including Charles A. Dana, Bayard Taylor, George Ripley, and Margaret Fuller, who after two years in New York (1844–1846) became the first woman foreign correspondent for an American newspaper and reported the revolutions of 1848 from the scene in Europe to the readers of the *Tribune.*

Greeley published three of Whitman's poems in the *Tribune* in 1850, all of which were politically inspired. The first, "Blood-Money" (22 March 1850), was undoubtedly written in response to Daniel Webster's speech in Congress on 7 March 1850 in which he voiced his support for the provisions of the Compromise of 1850, including the Fugitive Slave Law. Signed "Paumanok," as were other articles and poems written during this time, "Blood-Money" described the treachery of Judas, clearly analogous to the treachery of Webster. In "The House of Friends" (14 June 1850), later revised for *Specimen Days,* Whitman sharply criticized northern Democrats for their support of the Compromise of 1850. "Resurgemus" (21 June 1850), the only one of the poems of this period that would appear in *Leaves of Grass,* was inspired not by American events but by the European revolutions of 1848.

The *Tribune* also printed the first-known review of *Leaves of Grass* (by Charles A. Dana, 23 July 1855), but the most significant publication in the *Tribune* about Whitman was Ralph Waldo Emerson's famous private letter to Whitman of 21 July 1855, which Dana published as managing editor of the *Tribune* on 10 October 1855. Here Emerson greeted the poet "at the beginning of a great career," the ringing phrase that Whitman used throughout his life to promote the publication and positive reception of his most important work.

Susan Belasco Smith

N

Bibliography

Greenspan, Ezra. *Walt Whitman and the American Reader.* New York: Cambridge UP, 1990.

Kaplan, Justin. *Walt Whitman: A Life.* New York: Simon and Schuster, 1980.

Mott, Frank Luther. *American Journalism: A History of the Newspapers in the United States Through 250 Years: 1690–1940.* New York: Macmillan, 1941.

Myerson, Joel. *Walt Whitman: A Descriptive Bibliography.* Pittsburgh: U of Pittsburgh P, 1993.

Van Deusen, Glyndon G. *Horace Greeley: Nineteenth-Century Crusader.* Philadelphia: U of Pennsylvania P, 1953.

Whitman, Walt. *The Early Poems and the Fiction.* Ed. Thomas L. Brasher. New York: New York UP, 1963.

See also DANA, CHARLES A.; EMERSON, RALPH WALDO; "EUROPE, THE 72D AND 73D YEARS OF THESE STATES"; FULLER, MARGARET; PRE-*LEAVES* POEMS; REVOLUTIONS OF 1848; TAYLOR, BAYARD

Niagara Falls

Walt Whitman twice visited the famous falls on the Niagara River just north of Buffalo, New York, first in June 1848 on his return from New Orleans and again in June 1880. In "Seeing Niagara to Advantage" (from *Specimen Days*) he describes his second viewing as nothing less than a powerful moment of visual access which, as he writes, "gave me Niagara." Moving across a suspension bridge in a carriage he observed the falls "about a mile off, but very distinct, and no roar—hardly a murmur" (*Specimen Days* 236). He places this image in his private catalogue of important memories, which include a severe storm off Fire Island, Junius Brutus Booth in *Richard III* at the old Bowery theater, hearing Marietta Alboni sing, and the Civil War battlefields he had seen in Virginia.

Whitman's self-conscious memorialization of Niagara is wholly consistent with a central aspect of his overall poetic project, that of, as David Reynolds suggests, absorbing and being absorbed by America and thus fashioning a significant literary geography. In a very real sense, the poet's "perfect absorption of Niagara" (*Specimen Days* 237) in 1880 had been prefigured throughout *Leaves of Grass*. Niagara, perhaps the most easily recognized sublime artifact of the nineteenth-century American landscape, is typically a mark of Whitman's claims to geographical coverage or mapping America onto his own poetic vista. "Aware of mighty Niagara," he informs the reader in "Starting from Paumanok" (section 1); in "Song of Myself" he is situated "Under Niagara, the cataract falling like a veil over my countenance" (section 33). Frequently Niagara measures the intensity of the nation's mood, as in "long I watch'd Niagara pouring . . . Something for us is pouring now more than Niagara pouring," from "Rise O Days from Your Fathomless Deeps" (section 1), or as in the late poem "Election Day, November, 1884."

Stephen Rachman

Bibliography

Allen, Gay Wilson. *The Solitary Singer: A Critical Biography of Walt Whitman.* 1955. Rev. ed. 1967. Chicago: U of Chicago P, 1985.

Berton, Pierre. *Niagara: A History of the Falls.* Toronto: McClelland and Stewart, 1992.

Reynolds, David S. *Walt Whitman's America: A Cultural Biography.* New York: Knopf, 1995.

Whitman, Walt. *Complete Poetry and Collected Prose.* Ed. Justin Kaplan. New York: Library of America, 1982.

———. *Specimen Days.* Vol. 1 of *Prose Works 1892.* New York: New York UP, 1963.

See also ACTORS AND ACTRESSES; CIVIL WAR, THE; OPERA AND OPERA SINGERS; TRAVELS, WHITMAN'S

"Noiseless Patient Spider, A" (1868)

First published in *The Broadway Magazine* (London, October 1868), this poem was originally the third numbered section of what at first appeared to be a single larger poem, "Whispers of Heavenly Death," which itself later became a section (now clearly consisting of separate poems) of *Passage to India* (1871). "Spider" was finally incorporated into *Leaves of Grass* in 1881, still a part of "Whispers," which contained eighteen poems.

The poem's genesis may have been as early as the mid-1850s, when Whitman compared the human quest for knowledge of the spiritual world to a worm on the end of a twig reaching out into the immense vacant space beyond its own little world. The notebook passage stresses the limits of "our boasted knowledge" and the elusive nature of "spiritual spheres" as people attempt "to state them" with tongue or pen (*Notebooks* 6:2051). By 1862 or 1863, in another notebook entry (*Notebooks* 2:522–523; 700), the worm had become a spider, and the focus shifted from knowledge or expression of the infinite to homoerotic longing. The Soul, seeking love, is compared to a spider throwing filaments out of itself in attempts to make a connection beyond itself. The "oceans" in this early version of the poem are "latent souls of love . . . pent and unknown." To call the notebook entry a representation of gay cruising seems an exaggeration, but it certainly would have belonged in "Calamus" rather than the more metaphysical "Whispers" if Whitman had not transformed it.

In revision, "Spider" became one of Whitman's most powerful lyrics, a perfect illustration of Ralph Waldo Emerson's dictum that nature is a symbol of spirit. Whitman begins the poem with a description of a creature observed, then relates what he has seen to his own soul. The spider patiently launching forth filaments from itself in an attempt to connect across "the vacant vast surrounding" becomes an emblem for the soul reaching out, not only for love, but for any link with the "not-me." Apostrophizing his own soul ("And you O my soul"), the poet's analogical process is similar to Oliver Wendell Holmes's meditation on "The Chambered Nautilus" (1858), in which an empty mollusk shell inspires the poet to address his own soul, exhorting it to "Build . . . more stately mansions." But while Holmes is content to learn a pious lesson, hinting at the afterlife, Whitman suspends the soul in Pascal's terrifying empty spaces of the infinite—in "measureless oceans of space"—and suspends the reader as well in lines that form an incomplete sentence (the second stanza is a phrase followed by a subordinate clause, several participle phrases, then several subordinate clauses). "Spider" is an expression of hope that the soul will be able to connect (albeit with "ductile anchor" and "gossamer thread") to "the spheres" of the outside world, whether they be other souls or other worlds—or both, since to Whitman a soul is a "kosmos."

Whitman's final revisions of this poem included eliminating the repetition of the word "surrounded" in line 7, substituting the word "detached" to further describe the soul. Paul Diehl has shown how this and most of the punctuation changes from the 1871 to the 1881 version of the poem tend to emphasize the soul's existential isolation and therefore to intensify the soul's drive for connection. Moreover, contrasting the poem with Holmes's, one may vividly see the difference between a traditional and a modern lyric, in terms not merely of form but also of world view: whereas Holmes is strengthened in faith that his soul's final home will be heaven, Whitman is seeking—through the poem itself—to lessen the soul's existential loneliness.

Joseph Andriano

Bibliography
Diehl, Paul. "'A Noiseless Patient Spider': Whitman's Beauty—Blood and Brain." *Walt Whitman Quarterly Review* 6 (1989): 117–132.

Grier, Edward F., ed. *Walt Whitman: Notebooks and Unpublished Manuscripts.* 6 vols. New York: New York UP, 1984.

Krieg, Joann P. "Whitman's *Bel Canto* Spider." *Walt Whitman Quarterly Review* 4.4 (1987): 29–31.

White, Fred D. "Whitman's Cosmic Spider." *Walt Whitman Review* 23 (1977): 85–88.

Whitman, Walt. *Notebooks and Unpublished Prose Manuscripts.* Ed. Edward F. Grier. 6 vols. New York: New York UP, 1984.

See also METAPHYSICS; SOUL, THE; "WHISPERS OF HEAVENLY DEATH" (CLUSTER)

North American Review, The

A miscellany of politics, economics, religion, and literature, the *North American Review* was published in Boston (1821–1880) and New York (1881–1940).

Whitman's relationship with the periodical was contradictory before 1880, when it was an organ of the Boston-Harvard intelligentsia. In January 1856 Edward Everett Hale praised *Leaves of Grass* (1855) for its "freshness, simplicity, and reality" (275). And in January 1867 a mixed review of *Drum-Taps* by A.S. Hill still praised its "masculine directness of expression" (302). On the other hand, in October 1866 James Russell Lowell (editor, 1863–1872) described Whitman's poetry as "perfectly artificial" (rev. *Venetian*), and two years later he called *Leaves of Grass* "a cheap vision, for it cost no thought" (rev. *Poems*).

After the *North American Review* moved to New York under the editorship of Allan Thorndike Rice (1877–1889), it became less conservative and more receptive to Whitman, who became a frequent contributor. His publications in the *North American Review* include: "The Poetry of the Future" (February 1881); "A Memorandum at a Venture" (June 1882); "Slang in America" (November 1885); "Robert Burns as Poet and Person" (November 1886); "Some War Memoranda—Jotted Down at the Time" (January 1887); "Old Poets" (November 1890); and "Have We a National Literature" (March 1891).

William A. Pannapacker

Bibliography

Hale, Edward Everett. Rev. of *Leaves of Grass*, 1855 Edition. *North American Review* 83 (1856): 275–277.

Hill, A.S. Rev. of *Drum-Taps* and *Sequel*. *North American Review* 104 (1867): 301–303.

Lowell, James Russell. Rev. of *Poems*, by John James Piatt. *North American Review* 107 (Oct. 1868): 660–663.

———. Rev. of *Venetian Life*, by William Dean Howells. *North American Review* 103 (Oct. 1866): 611–612.

Mott, Frank Luther. "The North American Review." *A History of American Magazines*. Vol. 2. Cambridge, Mass.: Harvard UP, 1957. 219–261.

Whitman, Walt. *Prose Works 1892*. Ed. Floyd Stovall. 2 vols. New York: New York UP, 1963–1964.

See also HALE, EDWARD EVERETT; LOWELL, JAMES RUSSELL; "SLANG IN AMERICA"

Norton, Charles Eliot (1827–1908)

The prominence of Charles Eliot Norton among the New England cultural elite at mid-century gives special interest to his early review of *Leaves of Grass*. Still in his twenties in 1855, when he reviewed the book for *Putnam's Monthly Magazine*, Norton would have a lengthy, widely influential career at Harvard as a scholar, critic, and teacher. More reverent toward the literary past than Whitman, Norton shared with the new poet a humanist view of the power of art—and the moral example of the artist—to lift a nation out of mediocrity and materialism. Yet it is primarily the language of *Leaves*, its rough, slangy colloquialism, that most excited—and affronted—Norton. The poems seem to him "gross yet elevated," a "mixture of Yankee transcendentalism and New York rowdyism" ("Walt Whitman's" 15). These opposites perfectly combine, he writes, carrying with them "an original perception of nature, a manly brawn, and an epic directness . . . which belong to no other adept of the transcendental school" ("Walt Whitman's" 15).

Concurrently with his review, Norton expressed the same guarded enthusiasm about Whitman in a letter to his friend James Russell Lowell. He even composed a poem of his own in the manner of Whitman, titling it "A Leaf of Grass." Norton did not make known his authorship of the *Putnam's* review, nor did he publicly discuss Whitman again, though his attendance at a Whitman lecture and contribution to a fund for the poet (both in 1887) suggest that Norton remained at least distantly friendly. For his part, Whitman is silent on Norton, except for a comment to Horace Traubel in 1888 that Norton seems the sort of traditional moralist and scholar who "is bound to distrust a man like me" (Traubel 353).

Willis J. Buckingham

Bibliography

Hall, David D. "The Victorian Connection." *American Quarterly* 27 (1975): 561–574.

Norton, Charles Eliot. *A Leaf of Grass from Shady Hill*. Ed. Kenneth B. Murdock. Cambridge, Mass.: Harvard UP, 1928.

———. "Walt Whitman's *Leaves of Grass*." 1855. Rpt. in *Walt Whitman: The Contemporary Reviews*. Ed. Kenneth M. Price. Cambridge: Cambridge UP, 1996. 14–18.

Norton, Sara, and M.A. DeWolfe Howe, eds. *Letters of Charles Eliot Norton*. Vol. 1. Boston: Houghton Mifflin, 1913.

Rubin, Joan Shelley. *The Making of Middle/Brow Culture*. Chapel Hill: U of North Carolina P, 1992.

Traubel, Horace. *With Walt Whitman in Camden*. Vol. 1. Boston: Small, Maynard, 1906.

Vanderbilt, Kermit. *Charles Eliot Norton: Apostle of Culture in a Democracy*. Cambridge, Mass.: Harvard UP, 1959.

See also DANA, CHARLES A.; GRISWOLD, RUFUS W.; HALE, EDWARD EVERETT; LOWELL, JAMES RUSSELL; PARTON, SARA PAYSON WILLIS (FANNY FERN); *PUTNAM'S MONTHLY*

"Not Heat Flames Up and Consumes" (1860)

Appearing first as "Calamus" number 14 in the 1860 edition of *Leaves*, "Not Heat Flames Up and Consumes" took its present title in 1867. It was originally the first in a series of twelve poems entitled "Live Oak with Moss," which tells of Whitman's unhappy love affair with a man, possibly Fred Vaughan. Copied into a little notebook in the spring of 1859, the series was later called by Whitman "a Cluster of Poems, Sonnets expressing the thoughts, pictures, aspirations . . . fit to be perused during the days of the approach of Death" (qtd. in Helms 186). All twelve poems of the sequence were included among the forty-five poems of the 1860 "Calamus," but reordered so as to disguise the story, which Alan Helms regards as the only sustained treatment of homosexual love in all of Whitman's poetry.

"Not Heat Flames Up" remained in all subsequent editions of *Leaves,* escaping the fate of two other similarly revealing "Calamus" poems—["Long I Thought That Knowledge Alone Would Suffice"] and ["Hours Continuing Long"]—which were taken from the sequence and dropped after 1860. Whitman never published the sequence itself.

In "Not Heat Flames Up" the desire of the poet for "his love whom I love" is compared to various natural phenomena such as seawaves, the summer air, the tide, and the "high rain-emitting clouds." The most powerful of the images is the initial one ("Not heat flames up and consumes"), repeated in the fifth line—the flames likely connoting the danger involved in the relationship.

Richard Raleigh

Bibliography

Helms, Alan. "Whitman's 'Live Oak with Moss.'" *The Continuing Presence of Walt Whitman.* Ed. Robert K. Martin. Iowa City: U of Iowa P, 1992. 185–205.

Whitman, Walt. *Walt Whitman's Poems.* Ed. Gay Wilson Allen and Charles T. Davis. New York: New York UP, 1955.

See also "CALAMUS"; "LIVE OAK WITH MOSS"; VAUGHAN, FREDERICK B.

"Not Heaving from my Ribb'd Breast Only" (1860)

This poem—number 6 in the "Calamus" sequence—was part of the first appearance of the "Calamus" cluster in the 1860 edition of *Leaves of Grass.* Based on the first line, the title became official in the 1867 edition. "Not Heaving" was written after Whitman mailed the 1860 manuscript to the Rome brothers for typesetting in 1859, and some time before his arrival in Boston in March 1860 to oversee the printing by Thayer and Eldridge.

The poem's importance to Whitman may be judged by its placement in the group, and the fact that both the poem and its position remained unchanged in all succeeding editions. "Not Heaving" was not, however, one of the original twelve poems from the proposed "Live Oak with Moss" grouping, which was incorporated into "Calamus."

"Not Heaving" is related to "Calamus" numbers 13, 15, 26, and the last stanza of 3 (as numbered in the final edition) in the use of "not" or "nor" at the beginning of lines. In its frequency this rhetorical technique is unique to "Calamus" and reflects the emotional anguish which permeates the poems.

"Adhesiveness," which the poet addresses in "Not Heaving" as the "pulse of my life," is a term from phrenology, a popular pseudoscience in the mid-1800s. Defined as "male friendship," adhesiveness is believed to have been Whitman's code word for homosexual relationships.

Although not considered an important poem, "Not Heaving" is an integral part of "Calamus," a section of *Leaves* which attracts growing critical interest, especially among gay scholars.

Jack Field

Bibliography

Allen, Gay Wilson. *The Solitary Singer: A Critical Biography of Walt Whitman.* 1955. Rev. ed. 1967. Chicago: U of Chicago P, 1985.

Schwiebert, John E. *The Frailest Leaves: Whitman's Poetic Technique and Style in the Short Poem.* New York: Lang, 1992.

Whitman, Walt. *Leaves of Grass: Comprehensive Reader's Edition.* Ed. Harold W. Blodgett and Sculley Bradley. New York: New York UP, 1965.

———. *Whitman's Manuscripts: "Leaves of Grass" (1860).* Ed. Fredson Bowers. Chicago: U of Chicago P, 1955.

See also "CALAMUS"; COMRADESHIP; *LEAVES OF GRASS,* 1860 EDITION

Notebooks and Unpublished Prose Manuscripts (1984)

Part of New York University Press's *The Collected Writings of Walt Whitman* (Gay Wilson Allen and Sculley Bradley, general editors), this six-volume set edited by Edward F. Grier comprises all of Whitman's notebooks and unpublished prose manuscripts except those published in William White's *Daybooks and Notebooks* (1978). The material ranges from random aphoristic jottings to long trial runs for major works. Some of it is of limited interest and value (e.g., Whitman's factual notes on geography in volume 5); even William White questioned whether lists of melons and other meaningless or only partially legible fragments should be included in *The Collected Writings,* but as Betsy Erkkila points out, what appears useless now might some day turn out to be significant. In any case, the two thousand pages contain many treasures; indeed most of the material is indispensable to serious Whitman scholars and critics interested in the genesis of the poet's major works. And much of it is fascinating for readers who like to see a record of a genius exercising his mind. For these reasons—and the pervasive editorial excellence—this set is "an approved edition" of the MLA's Center for Scholarly Editions.

Of the thirteen hundred items included, about half were not previously published, but even the ones that can be found elsewhere (e.g., Emory Holloway, ed., *The Uncollected Poetry and Prose of Walt Whitman* [1921], or Clifton J. Furness, ed., *Walt Whitman's Workshop* [1928]) were never before edited so meticulously or presented so readably. Each manuscript is introduced with a lucid and concise headnote that lets the reader know where the manuscript is located (if extant), what it looks like, when it was probably written (dating the manuscripts was a daunting task for many reasons, including Whitman's occasional practice of going back to early jottings and reworking them), where it was first published, and how it relates to Whitman's published works. Each manuscript itself is printed plainly, with no attempt—save for a few choice illustrations—to typographically reproduce Whitman's random placement of passages (photocopies of many of the actual manuscripts are available elsewhere for scholars interested in the actual appearance of the page, and some of the notebooks have even been reproduced on the Internet). Copious footnotes for each manuscript give Whitman's

deletions and insertions, and often include valuable information linking the manuscript to Whitman's published works.

The set is organized in the most useful manner for scholars. The front matter of volume 1 contains a concise introduction, lists of abbreviations, illustrations, and titles (which comprise the first word or phrase of each manuscript and which are listed in the order in which they appear), and a chronology of Whitman's life and work. The first three volumes contain the manuscripts in roughly chronological order: Family Notes and Autobiography, Brooklyn and New York (volume 1); Washington (volume 2); Camden (volume 3). The last three volumes contain the notes, organized topically: Proposed Poems, Explanations/Introduction to *Leaves of Grass,* Attempts to Define the Poet's Role and Tradition, Needs of American Literature (volume 4); Study Projects, Words, notes on various writers, on history, geography, and natural history (volume 5); and notes on philosophy, religion, politics, slavery, education, oratory, and health (volume 6). The comprehensive index of titles and names is in volume 6 (in spite of the parenthetical note to the List of Titles on page xxix of volume 1 misinforming the reader that the index is at the end of volume 4—an erratum resulting from the last-minute expansion of the set to six volumes). The index is especially useful for scholars working on specific texts to discover quickly whether any mention of the texts is in the manuscripts and notebooks.

Ten of the notebooks Thomas B. Harned (one of Whitman's three literary executors) donated to the Library of Congress mysteriously disappeared in 1942, when they were being moved because of fear of aerial bombardment from Japan (it was not until the crates were opened in 1944 that the Library of Congress discovered they were missing). Since four of the missing notebooks (and the famous cardboard butterfly) turned up in early 1995, Grier's headnotes will have to be revised for them in the next printing. One of them is the earliest known notebook, and one of the most fascinating: "albot Wilson" (*Notebooks* 1:53–82). It contains prose (punctuated mainly with dashes) that eventually breaks into free verse, most of it obvious trial flights for the 1855 *Leaves.* Reading this and other notebooks will dispel any notion that Whitman's greatest lines—like "I believe a leaf of grass is no less than the journey-work of the stars" ("Song of Myself," section 31)—were born perfectly formed Athena-like from his head. Whitman wrote in his notebook: "And saw the journeywork of suns and systems of suns, / And that a leaf of grass is not less than they" (*Notebooks* 1:70–71). In imagining his soul enfolding "the countless stars" and asking whether it would then be satisfied, Whitman originally wrote: "No, when we fetch that height, we shall not be filled and satisfied but shall look as high beyond" (*Notebooks* 1:61). The line eventually became "No, we but level that lift to pass and continue beyond" ("Song of Myself," section 46). In another of the stolen manuscripts recently recovered, "You know how the One" (*Notebooks* 1:124–127), a striking prose passage about the power of operatic music is the embryonic form of section 26 of "Song of Myself."

While these notebooks and manuscripts give the reader a vivid picture of Whitman's creative processes, they do not give much insight into his personality. Indeed, some of the most personal passages were worked over, as he knew they would be read at least by Harned, Richard Maurice Bucke, and Horace Traubel, if not by posterity: for example, in "Epictetus," exhorting himself to "avoid seeing her, or meeting her" (*Notebooks* 2:889), he had originally written "him," referring to Peter Doyle, whom he felt he loved too much—to the point of "feverish disproportionate adhesiveness" (*Notebooks* 2:890). Here and in a few other notebooks, the reader gets a rare glimpse of the private, tormented soul of the man. But on the whole, these pieces are not for the literary voyeur; they are for the serious scholar and critic interested in the genesis and development of Whitman's great ideas, images, symbols, and themes.

Joseph Andriano

Bibliography

Birney, Alice L., ed. "The Thomas B. Harned Collection of the Papers of Walt Whitman." *Walt Whitman Home Page:* http://lcweb2.loc.gov/wwhome.html/

Erkkila, Betsy. Rev. of *Notebooks and Unpublished Prose Manuscripts,* ed. Edward F. Grier. *The Mickle Street Review* 10 (1988): 102–115.

Fineberg, Gail. "LC's Missing Whitman Notes Found in N.Y." *Library of Congress Gazette* 24 Feb. 1995. Rpt. http://lcweb2.loc.gov/wwhome.html/gazette1.html/

———. Rev. of *Notebooks and Unpublished Prose Manuscripts,* ed. Edward F. Grier. *Walt Whitman Quarterly Review* 3 (1985): 25–27.

Folsom, Ed. Rev. of *Notebooks and Unpublished Prose Manuscripts,* ed. Edward F. Grier. *Philological Quarterly* 65 (1986): 287–291.

Price, Kenneth M. Rev. of *Notebooks and Unpublished Prose Manuscripts,* ed. Edward F. Grier. *American Literary Realism, 1870–1910* 18 (1985): 271–277.

Whitman, Walt. *Daybooks and Notebooks.* Ed. William White. 3 vols. New York: New York UP, 1978.

———. *Notebooks and Unpublished Prose Manuscripts.* Ed. Edward F. Grier. 6 vols. New York: New York UP, 1984.

See also COLLECTED WRITINGS OF WALT WHITMAN, THE; DAYBOOKS AND NOTEBOOKS; FURNESS, CLIFTON JOSEPH; HARNED, THOMAS BIGGS; HOLLOWAY, EMORY; WHITE, WILLIAM

November Boughs (1888)

When Whitman suffered his physical collapse in 1888, from which he never fully recovered, he was working on a new collection of prose and poetry, intending to break a seven-year silence. With the help of Horace Traubel, who handled the details of publication, carrying copy to the printer, bringing proofs to Whitman, and acting as business manager, Whitman resumed work on the volume. David McKay published the volume, named *November Boughs,* later in 1888, purchasing from Whitman the rights to print further copies of the volume in 1888, 1889, and 1890 for a royalty fee of twelve cents per copy sold.

Like *Two Rivulets* (1876), the book is a mixture of prose and poetry. In the 140 pages are a long preface called "A Backward Glance O'er Travel'd Roads," approximately sixty very short poems which are collected under the title of "Sands at Seventy," and reprints of articles already published elsewhere. The preface, a combination of two articles that Whitman had published in 1884 and 1887, contains a retrospective on his literary theories and practices. He admits that he has not been accepted in his own time, but that he hopes for future recognition. He also recognizes that although *Leaves of Grass* was a

Walt Whitman, 1887, taken by George C. Cox and called by the poet "the Laughing Philosopher." Courtesy of the Library of Congress.

financial failure, it was always intended as an experiment. He explains his primary purpose in his poems: "to exploit that Personality [his own], identified with place and date, in a far more candid and comprehensive sense than any hitherto poem or book" (658). He also expresses reservations about his poetic form, no longer certain that his poems stand firmly on their unique employment of music and rhythm.

Whitman grouped the poems under the title "Sands at Seventy," perhaps reflecting not only his distress at aging and physical frailty, but also a recognition of his failing poetic powers. These poems he later annexed to *Leaves of Grass.* Clearly they lack the fire and lyricism of his early work, but they also contain a to-be-envied self-knowledge. And he is thankful that he was able to write them "in joy and hope" ("A Carol Closing Sixty-Nine"). Nevertheless he fears that his long poetic career may be drawing to a close, but he refuses to go gently, underscoring his unwillingness to depart and his expectation to be "[g]arrulous to the very last" ("After the Supper and Talk").

The collected prose pieces have received little critical attention, but read as a group they summarize many of Whitman's themes and concerns. They also serve as a kind of retrospective on the issues which both made Whitman the man and poet and which Whitman made the focus of his life and poetry. Central, of course, is Whitman's enthusiasm for democracy and the common man at the core of the American experiment. He urges eminent visitors to the United States not to be deluded by the effete Americans who entertain them in elevated segments of society: the real American genius is in the common people. Elias Hicks, the leader of the divisive movement which split the Quakers, Whitman praises for being the "most *democratic* of the religionists" (1221). And George Fox, the nearly illiterate founder of the Quaker movement and near contemporary of William Shakespeare, inspired Hicks, his open-air pulpit still remembered on Long Island.

In his comments on Shakespeare and his works, Whitman finds the democratic spirit the distinguishing essence. In the historical plays, Shakespeare undermines, perhaps unconsciously, the feudal system. He suggests that someday critics, "diving deeper . . . may discover . . . the inauguration of modern Democracy" (1150). In contrast, Shakespeare's sonnets are too medieval and feudal. Robert Burns, however, speaks to the American spirit, for he loved the plough and knew the workingman. Alfred, Lord Tennyson, although nondemocratic, is admired for his personal character and the moral dimensions of his work. Whitman points specifically to Tennyson's facility to charm with the English language and recommends the *Idylls of the King* by title.

Entranced by language, Whitman analyzes the place of slang in English, which he correctly sees as being an accretive language. English, he says, is a "universal absorber" (1165). In English, slang functions like the clowns in Shakespeare's plays. Slang is an attempt of common humanity to escape from bald literalism. Common people understand how slang operates, for they innately use circumlocution to enrich language which arises out of the work, needs, and joys of humanity.

In "The Bible as Poetry," Whitman finds the roots of American democracy in the Old and New Testaments. Rejecting aestheticism as one of the evils of his age, Whitman praises the scriptures for their depth. True, compared to Grecian epics, the scriptures may be "simple and meagre" (1140), but the daring metaphors, extravagant loves and friendships, accounts of religious ecstasy, and suggestions of mortality are unsurpassed. Thus, it is no surprise that Whitman finds the oratory of a preacher like Father Taylor extraordinary and similar to that of the Quaker Elias Hicks. In Taylor as in Hicks, one finds passion, tenderness, and firmness expressed in majestic, picturesque, and colloquial language borrowed from oriental and biblical forms.

Whitman also praises the multicultural sources of American society, noting the nobility of the Native American and the importance of the overlooked Spanish influence. The Indians stirred his artistic enthusiasm. Whitman quotes with approbation a correspondent who says, "They [the Indians] certainly have more of beauty, dignity and nobility mingled with their own wild individuality, than any of the other indigenous types of man" (1173). He doubts that any artistic representation, either visual or verbal, does the Native American justice. In a reprinted letter, he suggests that the Spanish influence has been marginalized in American culture, but he predicts it will see a resurgence.

Not to be omitted are Whitman's accounts of his days spent nursing the wounded and dying Civil War soldiers. In the midst of suffering, agony, death, and occasional survival, Whitman captures the nobility of the human spirit, of husbands and fathers yearning for word from home and desperate to send letters, but hampered by disease and poverty. In declining health and faced with incapacity, Whitman remembers what he had discovered years before: that sudden death, even death in battle, may not be the worst ending.

James E. Barcus, Jr.

Bibliography

Allen, Gay Wilson. *The Solitary Singer: A Critical Biography of Walt Whitman.* 1955. Rev. ed. 1967. Chicago: U of Chicago P, 1985.

———. *Walt Whitman Handbook.* Chicago: Packard, 1946.

Asselineau, Roger. *The Evolution of Walt Whitman: The Creation of a Book.* Trans. Roger Asselineau and Burton L. Cooper. Cambridge, Mass: Harvard UP, 1962.

———. *The Evolution of Walt Whitman: The Creation of a Personality.* Trans. Richard P. Adams and Roger Asselineau. Cambridge, Mass: Harvard UP, 1960.

N

Reynolds, David S. *Walt Whitman's America: A Cultural Biography.* New York: Knopf, 1995.

Whitman, Walt. *Complete Poetry and Collected Prose.* Ed. Justin Kaplan. New York: Library of America, 1982.

See also AGE AND AGING; "BACKWARD GLANCE O'ER TRAVEL'D ROADS, A"; BIBLE, THE; CIVIL WAR NURSING; HICKS, ELIAS; NATIVE AMERICANS (INDIANS); "SANDS AT SEVENTY" (FIRST ANNEX); SHAKESPEARE, WILLIAM; "SLANG IN AMERICA"; TAYLOR, FATHER (EDWARD THOMPSON); TENNYSON, ALFRED, LORD; TRAUBEL, HORACE L.

"O Captain! My Captain!" (1865)

Though stylistically atypical of his verse, "O Captain! My Captain!" is one of Walt Whitman's most popular poems. It first appeared in the *Saturday Press* (4 November 1865) and subsequently in *Sequel to Drum-Taps* (1865–1866). After modestly revising it, Whitman placed it in "President Lincoln's Burial Hymn" in *Passage to India* (1871) and finally in the "Memories of President Lincoln" cluster in *Leaves of Grass* (1881).

The rhyme, meter, stanza, and refrain in "O Captain" are conventional. The poem makes deliberate use of traditional metaphors, picturing the Union as a ship and the president as its captain. Although the ship has weathered the storm and re-entered the harbor safe and victorious, the captain (like the recently assassinated Abraham Lincoln) is dead. Capturing the triumph and grief of the war's end, "O Captain" is a public poem for a mass audience, an elegy remembering a beloved president.

Intended for a large, inclusive readership, "O Captain" became the most recited and popular of Whitman's works. It was usually a requisite selection at Whitman's readings and until recently his most widely anthologized poem. Because of its acclaim at the expense of his other poems, Whitman expressed some small regret about writing "O Captain," but insisted that it had an emotional, historically necessary purpose. No longer so celebrated, "O Captain" continues to be a revealing representation of the rhetorics of despair and celebration that followed the war, and it remains Whitman's most successful attempt to reach a national audience.

Gregory Eiselein

Bibliography
Erkkila, Betsy. *Whitman the Political Poet.* New York: Oxford UP, 1989.
Kaplan, Justin. *Walt Whitman: A Life.* New York: Simon and Schuster, 1980.
Whitman, Walt. *Leaves of Grass: Comprehensive Reader's Edition.* Ed. Harold W. Blodgett and Sculley Bradley. New York: New York UP, 1965.

See also Civil War, The; Lincoln, Abraham; "Memories of President Lincoln"; *Sequel to Drum-Taps;* "When Lilacs Last in the Dooryard Bloom'd"

"O Hymen! O Hymenee!" (1860)

First published in the 1860 edition of *Leaves of Grass* as an untitled member of the "Enfans d'Adam" cluster, the poem took its present title in the 1867 edition. Both the title and substance of the poem may have been suggested to Whitman by a passage in George Sand's *The Countess of Rudolstadt,* a novel he regarded as a masterpiece.

"O Hymen! O Hymenee!" is an apostrophic invocation to Hymen, the Greek goddess of marriage, in which the speaker chastises her for her inconstancy of affection toward him. The phrase itself is said to have accompanied marriages in preclassical Greece, and the word "hymen" itself later served as the root word of hymn, the holy songs of the Christian tradition—an etymological source Whitman may be playing on here to link his own song of physical love to the spirituality of the first couple, Adam and Eve.

Read in the larger context of the "Children of Adam" cluster, the poem offers a moment of meditation on the ability of the cluster's virile persona to sustain heterosexual passion in marriage. To the question of whether the Adamic lover can indeed sustain "mystic deliria" in such a union, the poem's speaker seems to reply in the negative. Permanent union would mean succumbing to the Transcendent, a spiritual apotheosis which results in bodily death.

Read in yet another way, the poem supports the claims of critics who have found the assertion of heterosexual sexuality in "Children of Adam" unconvincing and coldly rational. Whitman's use of the word "Hymenee" (apparently his own transformation of the Greek *hymenaie*) to refer to the bride's physical virginity, somewhat objectifies the woman and gives the holy hymn the air of a bawdy song in which the speaker explicates the travails of sexual intercourse from a somewhat clinical perspective.

Phillip H. Round

Bibliography

Killingsworth, M. Jimmie. *Whitman's Poetry of the Body: Sexuality, Politics, and the Text*. Chapel Hill: U of North Carolina P, 1989.

Larson, Kerry C. *Whitman's Drama of Consensus*. Chicago: U of Chicago P, 1988.

Miller, James E., Jr. *A Critical Guide to "Leaves of Grass."* Chicago: U of Chicago P, 1957.

Mullins, Maire. "'Act Poems of Eyes, Hands, Hips and Bosoms': Women's Sexuality in Walt Whitman's 'Children of Adam.'" *ATQ* 6 (1992): 213–231.

Shephard, Esther. *Walt Whitman's Pose*. New York: Harcourt, Brace, 1938.

See also "CHILDREN OF ADAM"; SAND, GEORGE; SEX AND SEXUALITY

"O Living Always, Always Dying" (1860)

Its publication history one of considerable shuffling, the poem first appeared as number 27 of "Calamus" in *Leaves of Grass* 1860, again in "Calamus" in *Leaves* 1867 as "O Living Always—Always Dying," then in the "Passage to India" supplement in *Leaves* 1871 and 1876, and finally in "Whispers of Heavenly Death" in *Leaves* 1881 as "O Living Always, Always Dying."

Writing to W.M. Rossetti, Whitman explained that "Whispers" would explore the "deep themes of Death & Immortality" (*Correspondence* 1:350). However, the poem is primarily concerned with the evolution of the self rather than with life and death. "Living" and "dying" become processes in the development of the self as it "cast[s]" off old selves, or "corpses," and takes on new identities, much like a snake shedding its skin. The self is portrayed in a state of Becoming, as opposed to Being (though Chari points out that Whitman, in general, adheres to a Vedantic belief in which Becoming and Being are coeval). Accordingly, change is to be celebrated rather than mourned; thus, the poet ignores funereal etiquette by choosing to "lament not" at the "burials" of his "corpses." More consonant with the purported theme of the cluster, the poem also accommodates a literal reading of "living" and "dying." Thus, the poem reiterates a familiar idea in "Whispers" by portraying life, or physical existence, as a type of death, and death as a type of life, or spiritual rebirth. Because "burials" and "corpses" are plural and since "always" indicates a continuous process, the poem echoes statements of belief in reincarnation which appear as early as "Song of Myself," where the poet states, "No doubt I have died myself ten thousand times before" (section 49).

Certainly the poem is a minor work in both the Whitman corpus and its resident cluster as well, often overshadowed by its companions "Whispers of Heavenly Death," "Chanting the Square Deific," and "A Noiseless Patient Spider," yet it displays a depth which its brevity and compactness belie.

Hadley J. Mozer

Bibliography

Chari, V.K. *Whitman in the Light of Vedantic Mysticism*. Lincoln: U of Nebraska P, 1964.

Miller, James E., Jr. *A Critical Guide to "Leaves of Grass."* Chicago: U of Chicago P, 1957.

Whitman, Walt. *The Correspondence*. Ed. Edwin Haviland Miller. 6 vols. New York: New York UP, 1961–1977.

———. *Leaves of Grass: Comprehensive Reader's Edition*. Ed. Harold W. Blodgett and Sculley Bradley. New York: New York UP, 1965.

See also DEATH; IMMORTALITY; REINCARNATION; "WHISPERS OF HEAVENLY DEATH" (CLUSTER)

"O Magnet-South" (1860)

This poem, the fifth in the "From Noon to Starry Night" cluster of the final edition of *Leaves of Grass,* was first printed in the 1860 edition under the title "Longings for Home." It was also published in the 15 July 1860 issue of *The Southern Literary Messenger* under the same title. In the 1860 edition, the poem was placed after "Crossing Brooklyn Ferry," between the "Calamus" cluster and the "Messenger Leaves" cluster. The poem itself, as well as its position, remained unchanged through the 1867, 1871, and 1876 editions. With the publishing of the 1881 edition, the poem received its present title and position and underwent two revisions: in line 19 the word "Tennessee" was replaced by the word "Kentucky," and the previous line 20, which read "An Arkansas prairie—a sleeping lake, or still bayou," was deleted.

The dominant theme of the poem is the irresistible, even mystical, allure the American South has for those who live there, as well as the infamous Southern love of place. The poem is passionate, but the wording is somewhat grandiose, and the emotions expressed almost factitious. Some Whitman biographers have used the poem to support the questionable claims of a New Orleans romance, referring to an alleged affair during Whitman's brief stay in that city, citing its sensual language and ambiguity as evidence. Even where such claims are not made, the consensus is that the poem was inspired by Whitman's journey to the South during the spring of 1848. Many of the images that appear in the poem would have been scenes that Whitman would have encountered during his brief travels south.

Perhaps the best commentary on the poem comes from Whitman himself in the form of his final placement of the poem. The "From Noon to Starry Night" cluster of *Leaves of Grass* contains twenty-two poems, collected from various sections spanning seven editions, which seem on the surface to have no unifying principle, either in terms of source or theme. And yet, all of the poems possess a certain lyricism and a reflective or retrospective quality.

Edward W. Huffstetler

Bibliography

Allen, Gay Wilson. *The Solitary Singer: A Critical Biography of Walt Whitman.* 1955. Rev. ed. 1967. Chicago: U of Chicago P, 1985.

———. *Walt Whitman Handbook.* 1946. New York: Hendricks House, 1962.

Kaplan, Justin. *Walt Whitman: A Life.* New York: Simon and Schuster, 1980.

Perlman, Jim, Ed Folsom, and Dan Campion, eds. *Walt Whitman: the Measure of His Song.* Minneapolis: Holy Cow!, 1981.

Schyberg, Frederick. *Walt Whitman.* Trans. Evie Allison Allen. New York: Columbia UP, 1951.

See also "From Noon to Starry Night"; New Orleans, Louisiana; South, The American

O'Connor (Calder), Ellen ("Nelly") M. Tarr (1830–1913)

Walt Whitman met Ellen O'Connor (later Calder) on 28 December 1862, in Washington, D.C. Calder's first husband, William Douglas O'Connor (married 22 October 1856), invited Whitman to live with them after his trip to the site of the battle of Fredericksburg, where Whitman had visited his brother George, who had been wounded. Whitman's stay at the O'Connor flat lasted over five months, and his stay in Washington lasted ten years, a time in which he regularly visited the O'Connors and the Union and Confederate soldiers hospitalized with war injuries and illnesses. After Whitman's first stroke in 1873, Calder visited the bedridden poet almost daily. Even after distance kept her away, she corresponded with the poet and with Anne and Horace Traubel, who sent her updated bulletins on Whitman's health. Whitman died four days after her second marriage on 22 March 1892 to a Providence businessman named Albert Calder.

As a teenager Calder worked in the Lowell, Massachusetts, mills and attended the Normal School in Newton. In her twenties, she first worked as a governess to the six children of abolitionists Dr. Gamaliel Bailey and Margaret Lucy Shands Bailey and then worked for two newspapers: William Lloyd Garrison's antislavery paper the *Liberator* and *Una,* a Providence paper dedicated to women's rights. Both prior to her first marriage and after raising her daughter Jean, Calder actively participated in the woman's rights and abolitionist movements. She was the secretary for the New England Woman's Rights Convention in 1855, and in 1879 she was vice president of the Woman's Rights Washington branch and attended the national convention in

Buffalo. After the Emancipation Proclamation, Calder devoted her abolitionist energy to educating the poor. She worked with Myrtilla Miner in her school for free Negro girls, about which she wrote in *Myrtilla Miner: A Memoir* (1885).

Calder was instrumental in encouraging her first husband's initial interest in and, perhaps, later displeasure with Whitman. Shortly after meeting O'Connor, she introduced him to the 1855 edition of *Leaves of Grass,* which William Henry Channing had loaned to Calder's sister Mary Jane ("Jeannie"). Years later, after Whitman walked out of one of his and O'Connor's many fervent debates concerning literature, politics, and social issues, Calder defended Whitman. Indignant with them both, O'Connor moved out of the house. He continued to visit his wife and their daughter, Jean, and sent them his paychecks, but kept a separate residence until shortly before his death.

Deshae E. Lott

Bibliography

Calder, Ellen M. Tarr O'Connor. Introduction. *The Good Gray Poet.* By William Douglas O'Connor. Toronto: Henry S. Saunders, 1927. i–ix.
———. *Myrtilla Miner: A Memoir.* Boston: Houghton Mifflin, 1885.
———. "Personal Recollections of Walt Whitman." *Atlantic Monthly* 99 (1907): 825–834.
———. "William O'Connor and Walt Whitman." *The Conservator* 17 (1906): 42.
Freedman, Florence Bernstein. *William Douglas O'Connor: Walt Whitman's Chosen Knight.* Athens: Ohio UP, 1985.

See also O'CONNOR, WILLIAM DOUGLAS; WASHINGTON, D.C.

O'Connor, William Douglas (1832–1889)

Walt Whitman met William Douglas O'Connor in 1860 at the short-lived firm of Thayer and Eldridge, which that year published Whitman's third edition of *Leaves of Grass* and O'Connor's only novel, *Harrington: A Story of True Love.* Two years later their paths crossed again when Whitman traveled to Washington, D.C., to search its military hospitals for his brother George, who had been wounded in the battle of Fredericksburg. O'Connor welcomed Whitman into his home and quickly became Whitman's friend and an ardent defender of Whitman's poetry. Since their first meeting, O'Connor had turned from his artistic pursuits as a daguerreotypist, poet, short-story writer, novelist, essayist, journalist, and editor (at the *Saturday Evening Post* in Philadelphia) to the more steady position of a clerk in the Treasury Department.

For five months Whitman lived with O'Connor and his family, sharing meals at their table. And for nearly another ten years he was a regular guest in the O'Connor home for nightly discussions on literature, politics, and social issues. During this time O'Connor helped procure Whitman a position as a clerk in the Indian Affairs Bureau of the Department of Interior (1865). A few months later, when Secretary of the Interior James Harlan fired Whitman due to the moral character of *Leaves of Grass,* O'Connor found his first significant opportunity to defend Whitman.

Risking his own career, O'Connor did two things: regain Whitman a governmental position and assail the forces of censorship in defense of *Leaves of Grass.* First, he went to his friend Assistant Attorney General J. Hubley Ashton, who spoke with both Harlan and Attorney General James Speed; the former agreed not to interfere, and the latter agreed to hire Whitman, who maintained that job until 1874, when the appointment was vacated because of Whitman's poor health. Second, O'Connor published *The Good Gray Poet: A Vindication* (1866), a forty-six-page pamphlet that criticized Harlan and other Whitman critics while lauding and joining those who admitted the merits of Whitman's poetry. The label "Good Gray Poet" was to stick, gaining Whitman many readers.

Further defenses of Whitman appeared as letters to the editor and fiction. For instance, letters by O'Connor defending Whitman appeared in *The Round Table* in 1866 and 1867 (for example, "Letter to the Editor," 3 February 1866, and "'C' on Walt Whitman," 16 February 1867); in the New York *Times* in 1866 and 1867 (for example, "Walt Whitman," 2 December 1866); and in the New York *Tribune* in 1876 and 1882 (for example, "Walt Whitman: Is He Persecuted?" 22 April 1876; "Suppressing Walt Whitman," 27 May 1882; and "Emerson and Whitman," 18 June 1882). In 1868 O'Connor published "The Carpenter," a short story with a Christlike portrayal of Whitman. O'Connor argued that he did not intend to depict Whitman as the reincarnated Christ; the character merely represented the spirit of Christ that he thought was present in any good man. Either way, O'Connor's edification of Whitman continued.

He also helped to place in *The Radical* "A Woman's Estimate of Walt Whitman" (1870), a favorable piece by the Briton Anne Gilchrist.

O'Connor had always favored liberal and noble causes. In the 1850s he worked for antislavery papers and wrote short stories dealing with the contemporary reform themes of prohibition, abolition, welfare, women's rights, divorce laws, and even spiritualism. His support of Whitman emanated from a similar spirit. However, he and Whitman often debated the efficacy of external, socially imposed reform as opposed to internal, personally motivated reform. One night near the close of 1872, Whitman walked out during their debate on Charles Sumner's war policies and Reconstruction legislation (the Fifteenth Amendment, giving black adult males the right to vote), which O'Connor supported and Whitman opposed.

After Whitman's departure, O'Connor's wife (Ellen M. Tarr O'Connor) defended Whitman's stance. O'Connor held a grudge against them both and promptly established a separate residence. Although he visited his daughter Jean and his wife and sent them each of his governmental paychecks, O'Connor would not again live with his wife until just before his death, when he needed her care.

The legend in family correspondence suggests that O'Connor saw Whitman in the street the day after their heated debate, that Whitman extended his hand, and that O'Connor bowed low but continued on his way. Although the two men would not directly converse for ten years, O'Connor faithfully supported Whitman's literary works. Following the reunion of their friendship in 1882, O'Connor allowed Whitman's friend, Dr. Richard Maurice Bucke, to reprint *The Good Gray Poet* in his biography of Whitman (1883). O'Connor also provided an introductory letter for the reprinted piece that carried an additional twenty-five pages in praise of Whitman and his poetry. In 1882 O'Connor created a fervor for the newspapers when he responded to Osgood and Company's withdrawal of its contract to publish *Leaves of Grass*. The Massachusetts State District Attorney Oliver Stevens, prompted by State Attorney General George Marston, had threatened prosecution unless extensive emendations were made. In fact, largely due to the publicity O'Connor created in the 1880s, for the first time Whitman received fairly steady royalties when his book subsequently was published in Philadelphia.

Deshae E. Lott

William Douglas O'Connor, Whitman's friend and supporter. Courtesy of the Library of Congress.

Bibliography

Freedman, Florence Bernstein. *William Douglas O'Connor: Walt Whitman's Chosen Knight.* Athens: Ohio UP, 1985.

Loving, Jerome. *Walt Whitman's Champion: William Douglas O'Connor.* College Station: Texas A&M UP, 1978.

O'Connor, William Douglas. "The Carpenter: A Christmas Story." *Putnam's Monthly Magazine* ns 1 (1868): 55–90.

———. *The Good Gray Poet: A Vindication.* New York: Bunce and Huntington, 1866.

See also ASHTON, J. HUBLEY; BOSTON, MASSACHUSETTS; BUCKE, RICHARD MAURICE; GILCHRIST, ANNE BURROWS; HARLAN, JAMES W.; INDIAN AFFAIRS, BUREAU OF; *LEAVES OF GRASS, 1860 EDITION*; *LEAVES OF GRASS, 1881–1882 EDITION*; O'CONNOR (CALDER), ELLEN ("NELLY") M. TARR; OSGOOD, JAMES R.; RECONSTRUCTION; SPEED, ATTORNEY GENERAL JAMES; STEVENS, OLIVER; THAYER AND ELDRIDGE; WASHINGTON, D.C.

"Of Him I Love Day and Night" (1860)

A celebration and condemnation of same-sex love, this poem charts Whitman's response to the homophobia of his day. The speaker reveals his pain and self-divided nature; he composes an elegy for his dream lover and for the democratic country that has lost its will to love freely. Whitman removed this poem from the "Calamus" section (1860 *Leaves*) and eventually fixed its place in "Whispers of Heavenly Death" (1871 *Leaves*).

The critical responses focus on politics and sexuality. Betsy Erkkila gives the most persuasive reading, indicating how the first half of the poem chronicles the poet's despair over his lover's death, the second his despair over the nation's death. She stresses the interweaving of personal and political motifs both in this poem and other "Calamus" poems. James Miller also stresses the function of death, arguing that the numerous references to burial sites suggest a commonality between the dead and the living. Robert Martin emphasizes the failure of men to love. Moreover, the affirmation of cremation reveals a shift in Whitman's values; as a memento mori, the poem concentrates on living intensely and denies any form of Christian rebirth. For Michael Moon, the poem's emphasis on spaces and spacing suggests a movement from contained (the tomb) to uncontained (America). Moon stresses Whitman's despair, as suggested by the speaker's vision of a necropolis. Read as "Calamus" number 17, the poem anticipates the Civil War and prophetically announces that the wide open spaces of America will become burial places.

Whitman's blending of politics and sexuality demonstrates that they are inseparable from his poetic vision. He intensifies his grief over losing someone he loves and dramatically conveys to readers that the contained grief in the poem's beginning becomes uncontained by the poem's end.

Jay Losey

Bibliography

Erkkila, Betsy. *Whitman the Political Poet.* New York: Oxford UP, 1989.

Martin, Robert K. *The Homosexual Tradition in American Poetry.* Austin: U of Texas P, 1979.

Miller, James E., Jr. *A Critical Guide to "Leaves of Grass."* Chicago: U of Chicago P, 1957.

Moon, Michael. *Disseminating Whitman: Revision and Corporeality in "Leaves of Grass."* Cambridge, Mass.: Harvard UP, 1991.

See also "CALAMUS"; DEATH; "WHISPERS OF HEAVENLY DEATH" (CLUSTER)

"Of the Terrible Doubt of Appearances" (1860)

"Of the Terrible Doubt of Appearances," one of the most significant of Whitman's philosophic poems, first appeared as "Calamus" number 7 in the 1860 edition of *Leaves of Grass.* The poem was given its present title in 1867. As is the case with nearly all of the "Calamus" poems, the year of composition of "Terrible Doubt" cannot be stated with confidence, but it is likely Whitman wrote it sometime between 1856 and 1860. While some "Calamus" poems were deleted from subsequent editions of *Leaves,* "Terrible Doubt" survived virtually unchanged through the 1892 Deathbed edition. Interestingly, in his revisions for the 1860 edition, Whitman deleted the poem's syntactically involved ninth line, then decided to let it stand.

In "Terrible Doubt" the same themes of attachment, crisis, and renunciation found in the other "Calamus" poems take on powerful form. As the "Calamus" poems show, Whitman's definitive optimism was not free from crises, and "Terrible Doubt" begins as a meditation on the uncertainties of existence. Reliance and hope are suspected of being merely "speculations," immortality "a beautiful fable only," and the phenomenal world "only apparitions." His questioning becomes terrifying as the speaker conceives of a dark and meaningless universe in which his very identity seems imperiled. Just when all seems lost, he is redeemed by the miracle of a touch: "He ahold of my hand has completely satisfied me." Only the experience of love can confirm reality. The speaker's newfound wisdom is an intuitive knowledge, beyond reason and verbal expression. In consequence, the world must be accepted, and therefore effectively renounced, as being of unreliable and perhaps unredeemable character. As in Matthew Arnold's "Dover Beach," one must seek in personal relationships the assurance the world cannot provide.

"Terrible Doubt" echoes the philosophy of other "Calamus" poems, perhaps most closely "Scented Herbage of My Breast," in which the "real reality" is contrasted with "these shifting forms of life." In "Herbage" as well, it is love that verifies reality.

Dena Mattausch

Bibliography

Crawley, Thomas Edward. *The Structure of "Leaves of Grass."* Austin: U of Texas P, 1970.

Knapp, Bettina L. *Walt Whitman.* New York: Continuum, 1993.

Miller, Edwin Haviland. *Walt Whitman's Poetry: A Psychological Journey.* New York: New York UP, 1968.

Whitman, Walt. *Leaves of Grass.* Ed. Sculley Bradley and Harold W. Blodgett. Norton Critical Edition. New York: Norton, 1973.

———. *Whitman's Manuscripts: "Leaves of Grass" (1860).* Ed. Fredson Bowers. Chicago: U of Chicago P, 1955.

See also "Calamus"; "Scented Herbage of My Breast"

"Old Age Echoes" (1897)

This group of thirteen poems was first added to *Leaves of Grass* in the edition issued in 1897, five years after Whitman's death. They are prefaced by Horace Traubel's "An Executor's Diary Note, 1891," recounting a conversation with Whitman shortly before his death in which he contemplated collecting "a lot of poetry and prose pieces—small or smallish mostly, but a few larger" to be published as a supplement, leaving the book complete as he left it for the Deathbed edition. When asked what he would do with them, Whitman said, "I have a title in reserve: Old Age Echoes—applying not so much to things as to echoes of things, reverberant, an aftermath" (Whitman 575).

The collection contains eleven previously unpublished poems, scraps, rough drafts, and reworked prose fragments; the other two pieces had appeared in the New York *Daily Graphic* in 1873–1874. One poem, "To Be at All," is a rough draft of stanza 27 of the 1855 "Song of Myself." Traubel rejected many of Whitman's trial titles and apparently supplied his own, drawn from a line in the poem.

Two poems are of especial interest. "Supplement Hours" confirms the notion that Whitman retained his poetic powers until the very end. This is a poem about extreme old age—about the bonus of tranquillity given to us after the striving and activity of a full life. Whitman apparently attached considerable importance to it, since many manuscript versions exist, as well as several different titles, such as "Notes as the wild Bee hums," "A September Supplement," and "Latter-time Hours of a half-paralytic."

"A Thought of Columbus" is said by Traubel to be Whitman's "last deliberate composition, dating December, 1891" (Whitman 575). Whitman apparently added some later touches and gave the manuscript to Traubel ten days before his death in March 1892. It was first printed in facsimile in *Once a Week* in July 1892, followed the next week by Traubel's account of its composition, in which he stated that it was "finished on his death-bed" ("Walt Whitman's Last"). This poem, written perhaps with the 1892 Columbian Exposition in mind, is a final tribute to the great discoverer with some ideas harking back to "Passage to India" and "Prayer of Columbus." In "Prayer," Columbus is viewed as the "batter'd wreck'd old man" suffering from defeat and despair. But in "A Thought of Columbus" he is a much more idealized figure. He is the agent of a divine plan bringing about the fulfillment of an ages-long process of completion, linking the growth of democracy in the Western Hemisphere with the unfolding of our cosmic destiny.

Like a number of Whitman's other late poems, "A Thought of Columbus" cannot be ignored or dismissed as the product of feebleness or senility. It demonstrates that he was still afoot with his vision, to which he remained faithful to the end. The characteristic exuberance, assurance, and strong rhythms may still be heard in this eloquent apostrophe to the discoverer of America and moving farewell from its solitary singer.

Donald Barlow Stauffer

Bibliography

Fillard, Claudette. "Le vannier de Camden: Vieillesse, Poésie, et les Annexes de *Leaves of Grass*." *Études Anglaises* 45 (1992): 311–323.

Stauffer, Donald Barlow. "Walt Whitman and Old Age." *Walt Whitman Review* 24 (1978): 142–148.

Traubel, Horace. "Walt Whitman's Last Poem." *Once a Week: An Illustrated Weekly Newspaper* 16 July 1892: 3.

Whitman, Walt. *Leaves of Grass: Comprehensive Reader's Edition.* Ed. Harold W. Blodgett and Sculley Bradley. New York: New York UP, 1965.

See also Age and Aging; Columbus, Christopher; "Prayer of Columbus"; "Supplement Hours"; "Thought of Columbus, A"; Traubel, Horace L.

"Old Age's Lambent Peaks" (1888)

This poem was first printed in *The Century* in September of 1888 and published in *Leaves of Grass* in 1888 as part of the "Sands at Seventy" annex. Whitman himself called it "an essential poem," by which he probably meant that it was essential to celebrate this period of life (Traubel 289).

At the beginning, the central image of the burst of the sun's flame just before sunset hints at an unacknowledged brightness possible in old age. The words "lambent [flickering] peaks" in the title and the final phrase of this eight-line lyric show the originality and accuracy of Whitman's word choice and his boldness in combining words for their suggestiveness.

The poem also illustrates his fondness for indirection. Old age is not mentioned till the end, the structure being periodic. The entire lyric is a metaphoric description not of old age, the topic avowed by the title, but of the gradually setting sun from the bright flames to the "calmer sight—the golden setting, clear and broad . . . so much (perhaps the best) unreck'd before."

Whitman used contractions frequently to control his beat. Here the contraction of "unreckoned," awkward as it is, reveals a need to follow a loose trochaic rhythmic pattern at all costs. The poem further illustrates Whitman's chronic habit of listing or naming items seriatim, not all of which need be of the same class, as with "passion" in line two: "O'er city, passion, sea—o'er prairie, mountain, wood—the earth itself." Yet if literally out of place in this line, the word "passion" does connect meaningfully to the central topic, which the reader is always aware of—the keen insight of old age.

David B. Baldwin

Bibliography

Stoddard, R.H. "Poetical Fads." *Independent* 40 (1888): 1131.

Traubel, Horace. *With Walt Whitman in Camden.* Vol. 2. New York: Appleton, 1908.

Whitman, Walt. *Leaves of Grass: Comprehensive Reader's Edition.* Ed. Harold W. Blodgett and Sculley Bradley. New York: New York UP, 1965.

———. *Leaves of Grass: A Textual Variorum of the Printed Poems.* Ed. Sculley Bradley, Harold W. Blodgett, Arthur Golden, and William White. Vol. 3. New York: New York UP, 1980.

See also AGE AND AGING; *LEAVES OF GRASS,* 1891–1892, DEATHBED EDITION; "SANDS AT SEVENTY" (FIRST ANNEX)

"On the Beach at Night" (1871)

"On the Beach at Night" was first published in the "Sea-Shore Memories" group in the 1871 *Passage to India.* The poem was transferred to the "Sea-Drift" cluster in the 1881 edition of *Leaves of Grass.* Significantly, this poem appears in the middle of the cluster (as the sixth of eleven poems) and is the longest poem after the opening poems, "Out of the Cradle Endlessly Rocking" and "As I Ebb'd with the Ocean of Life."

The poem opens with a narrative description of an event similar to that portrayed in Hopkins's "Spring and Fall," a father discussing a natural scene, here, the stars in the night sky, with his daughter. The father notices that the child begins to weep as she watches the "burial-clouds" cover over the stars. The poem then changes from a narrative description to a dramatic presentation of the father reassuring his daughter that the stars are immortal and will endure. The last stanza of the poem concludes the father's speech and includes two important parenthetical statements which explain that this reassurance is also a "first suggestion, the problem and indirection."

In the context of the "Sea-Drift" cluster as a whole, this central poem represents a shift from description of the growing awareness of the "outsetting bard" (initially depicted in "Out of the Cradle") of the meaning of life and death to description of the awareness of life after death. Significantly, the boy-poet of the earlier poems in the cluster has either disappeared and been replaced with a young girl or, more likely, has matured into a father figure who guides his child, offering hints and suggestions as Whitman does in his poems, to an understanding of the immortal nature of the human soul.

A. James Wohlpart

Bibliography

Fast, Robin Riley. "Structure and Meaning in Whitman's *Sea-Drift.*" *American Transcendental Quarterly* 53 (1982): 49–66.

Whitman, Walt. *Leaves of Grass.* Ed. Sculley Bradley and Harold W. Blodgett. Norton Critical Edition. New York: Norton, 1973.

Wohlpart, A. James. "From Outsetting Bard to Mature Poet: Whitman's 'Out of the Cradle' and the *Sea-Drift* Cluster." *Walt Whitman Quarterly Review* 9 (1991): 77–90.

See also DEATH; IMMORTALITY; "OUT OF THE CRADLE ENDLESSLY ROCKING"; "SEA-DRIFT"

"On the Beach at Night Alone" (1856)

Originally titled "Clef Poem" in the 1856 edition of *Leaves of Grass,* "On the Beach at Night Alone" is a truncated version of its precursor. Revising his poems for the 1867 edition of *Leaves of Grass,* Whitman, according to Thomas Crawley, made his poems more concise by reducing sexual references. Whitman cut nearly half of the lines from "Beach," removing passages treating death and sexuality. While the poet in the 1856 "Clef Poem" wonders if the "pink nipples" of his sleeping partners will "taste the same" in the afterlife, the poet in the 1867 "Beach" speaks in far more abstract terms.

Despite the title change, however, the motif of the "clef" remains in the latter version. Whitman retains the line "I think a thought of the clef of the universes," using the French word for key to indicate the clue or key with which to unlock the secrets of the cosmos. Whitman portrays himself as apprehending an insight into the universe that will grant the reader "key" insight. Recalling "Crossing Brooklyn Ferry" (1856), Whitman describes a "vast similitude" that unifies all time, all people, and all places.

"On the Beach at Night Alone" may be classed among Whitman's minor poems, but has been the focus of increasing critical attention due to the revisions between the 1856 and 1867 editions of *Leaves of Grass.* The poet in 1867 expresses himself with more confidence, no longer asking questions about the future, but offering answers. Although less startling than "Clef Poem," "Beach" emerges as a more unified poem, with Whitman focusing directly on the metaphysical issues that form the crux of his interest.

Joe Boyd Fulton

Bibliography

Crawley, Thomas Edward. *The Structure of "Leaves of Grass."* Austin: U of Texas P, 1970.

Killingsworth, M. Jimmie. *Whitman's Poetry of the Body: Sexuality, Politics, and the Text.* Chapel Hill: U of North Carolina P, 1989.

See also LEAVES OF GRASS, 1856 EDITION; SEA, THE

"Once I Pass'd through a Populous City" (1860)

Originally published in the third (1860) edition of *Leaves of Grass,* by Thayer and Eldridge, Boston, this poem was included in the "Enfans d'Adam" poem cluster and designated simply as number 9. The present title was affixed in 1867, when the title of this cluster was changed to "Children of Adam."

The poem records a visit to a crowded city and a woman "casually met there," the memory of whom takes precedence over all else that occurred or happened to the speaker. Lines 2, 3, and 4 describe the time that they spent together, absorbed in each other's presence. The last three lines of the poem shift to the present moment, when the memory of the "populous" city, with all its "shows, architecture, customs, traditions," is again displaced by the woman. These lines, etched from memory, recast how the two spent their time together: they "wander," "love," "separate," and hold hands. In the poem's last line the woman's face, "with silent lips sad and tremulous," appears "close beside" the speaker.

Early biographers read the poem as a record of Whitman's liaison with a woman in New Orleans. Whitman, accompanied by his younger brother Jeff, had spent three months there (February–May 1848) working as the chief editor of the *Crescent.*

The original manuscript of the poem, however, reveals a significant change in the text. Instead of "a woman I casually met there who detain'd me for love of me" in line 2, Whitman had originally written "the man who wandered with me, there, for love of me." In line 4, in place of "that woman who passionately clung to me" Whitman had written "one rude and ignorant man." Whitman may have made these changes because of the poem's inclusion in the "Children of Adam" poem cluster, or out of an attempt to disguise the homoerotic import of the lines.

The poem in its final form reflects the theme of the "Children of Adam" poem cluster: amativeness, a term Whitman borrowed from phrenology to signify the love of woman and man. Its length reflects the short, almost lyric form many of the poems in this cluster take. In its recreation of the mood of an intense, brief love affair, the poem looks forward to the themes of the "Calamus" cluster.

Maire Mullins

Bibliography

Allen, Gay Wilson. *The New Walt Whitman Handbook.* 1975. New York: New York UP, 1986.

———. *The Solitary Singer: A Critical Biography of Walt Whitman.* 1955. Rev. ed. 1967. Chicago: U of Chicago P, 1985.

Kaplan, Justin. *Walt Whitman: A Life.* New York: Simon and Schuster, 1980.

Killingsworth, M. Jimmie. *Whitman's Poetry of the Body: Sexuality, Politics, and the Text.* Chapel Hill: U of North Carolina P, 1989.

Waskow, Howard J. *Whitman: Explorations in Form.* Chicago: U of Chicago P, 1966.

See also BIOGRAPHIES; "CHILDREN OF ADAM"; *LEAVES OF GRASS,* 1860 EDITION; NEW ORLEANS, LOUISIANA

"One Hour to Madness and Joy" (1860)

"One Hour to Madness and Joy" was the sixth poem in "Enfans d'Adam," later called "Children of Adam," added to the greatly expanded 1860 *Leaves of Grass* along with the "Calamus" poems. It is the climactic poem of the group, a position it retained in successive editions. The words that became the title were added to the first line in 1867, three lines were dropped, and the poem altered very little after that. It is preceded by poems establishing the chastity and importance of the sexual impulse and followed by poems assimilating the ecstatic experience celebrated in "One Hour."

"One Hour" conveys the erotic charge impelling cosmic forces that combine in inevitable acts of creation in Whitman's universe: body and soul to create the self, earth and sun to create the natural world, reader and poet to regenerate culture. The transports of sexual ecstasy celebrated in the poem are a powerful metaphor for the moments of transcendent self-awareness achieved in the adventure of self-realization enacted in all of Whitman's poetry, particularly in "Song of Myself."

The union of mythic progenitors, Adam and Eve, recounted in "One Hour" by the line "O to return to Paradise!," recapitulates the union of the "earth by the sky staid with" in section 24 of "Song of Myself." In working notes, cited in *Leaves of Grass: Comprehensive Reader's Edition,* Whitman postulates a "fiery" Adam (90), and he begins "Children of Adam"

with the male lover "anew ascending" and ends the cluster with the hero "Facing west from California's shores." "One Hour" is the ecstatic apex of that progress which generates consciousness through the union of body and soul just as sunlight creates the visible world when it illuminates darkened matter. Similarly, the democratic poet is the "one complete lover" of the "known universe," Whitman says in the 1855 Preface (Whitman 715), and gives readers self-definition like "the sun falling around a helpless thing" (713).

Some critics have characterized the "Adam" poems, including "One Hour," as bombastic posturing, devoid of conviction. However, the sexual union celebrated in "One Hour" is mythic, not personal, and the perhaps unconvincing "mystic deliria" reflects the difficulty of achieving heroic language in modern times. The poem itself may lack dramatic tension, but in context it is part of a process of self-realization in which the anxiety of self-surrender—the need "to be yielded" "in defiance of the world"—must be overcome and the pain of leave-taking endured, as the poems following "One Hour" indicate.

Margaret H. Duggar

Bibliography

Aspiz, Harold. *Walt Whitman and the Body Beautiful.* Urbana: U of Illinois P, 1980.

Erkkila, Betsy. *Whitman the Political Poet.* New York: Oxford UP, 1989.

Killingsworth, M. Jimmie. *Whitman's Poetry of the Body: Sexuality, Politics, and the Text.* Chapel Hill: U of North Carolina P, 1989.

Miller, James E., Jr. *A Critical Guide to "Leaves of Grass."* Chicago: U of Chicago P, 1957.

Whitman, Walt. *Leaves of Grass: Comprehensive Reader's Edition.* Ed. Harold W. Blodgett and Sculley Bradley. New York: New York UP, 1965.

See also AMERICAN ADAM; "CHILDREN OF ADAM"; SEX AND SEXUALITY

"One Wicked Impulse!" (1845)

This short story was initially published in *United States Magazine and Democratic Review,* July–August 1845, as "Revenge and Requital: A Tale of a Murderer Escaped." It was given its current title in *Specimen Days & Collect* (1882). For publication particulars and Whitman's extensive revisions, see Brasher's edition of *The Early Poems and the Fiction.*

This Dickens-like story involves a corrupt lawyer, Adam Covert, guardian to brother and sister orphans. He dupes them out of their money, and he insults the young woman. Her brother, Philip, vows vengeance. While waiting out a storm, the two men fight and the young man kills Covert. Philip's psychology is noteworthy; the storm's wind, thunder, and rain kindle "a strange sympathetic fury" in Philip's mind (Whitman 312). The one witness, an African-American man, mercifully chooses not to testify against Philip, and Philip goes free.

In the original version, Philip finds peace after the murder from working with cholera victims in New York and in saving one of Covert's orphaned children. Philip eventually succumbs to cholera himself. In the final version, Philip finds peace in recognizing that his bloody hands will not wither roses, which smell as fragrant as ever: no cholera, no death for Philip.

Critics have preferred to comment on the first version. Thomas Brasher notes that the revisions weaken the story's original opposition to capital punishment. David Reynolds also sees the original version as sensationalism, mixing violence with criticism of the wealthy. Philip Callow reads the first version as a temperance tract, while Justin Kaplan sees elements that parallel Edgar Allan Poe's "Masque of the Red Death" (1842).

Patrick McGuire

Bibliography

Callow, Philip. *From Noon to Starry Night: A Life of Walt Whitman.* Chicago: Ivan R. Dee, 1992.

Kaplan, Justin. *Walt Whitman: A Life.* New York: Simon and Schuster, 1980.

Reynolds, David S. *Walt Whitman's America: A Cultural Biography.* New York: Knopf, 1995.

Whitman, Walt. *The Early Poems and the Fiction.* Ed. Thomas L. Brasher. New York: New York UP, 1963.

See also COLLECT; "DEATH IN THE SCHOOL-ROOM (A FACT)"; "HALF-BREED, THE"; SHORT FICTION, WHITMAN'S

"One's-Self I Sing" (1867)

O

A longer version of "One's-Self I Sing" first appeared as an "Inscription," heading the 1867 edition of *Leaves of Grass*. From the 1871 edition on, a shorter version, with the present title, became the first poem of *Leaves*, placed at the beginning of the opening poetic cluster, which was now called "Inscriptions." The longer version, with the new title "Small the Theme of My Chant," reappeared in the final, 1891–1892 edition, in "Sands at Seventy."

"One's-Self" is clearly a kind of framing poem, meant to point the reader's attention to certain paramount themes in what follows. "One's-Self I sing, a simple separate person," run the opening lines of *Leaves of Grass* from 1871 on, "Yet utter the word Democratic." A poetic universe of productive tension is hinted by that "Yet"; the tense equipoise between individualism and democracy, this poem suggests, is the foundational theme of Whitman's book.

The poem then goes on to introduce the site and symbol for this reconciliation of individual to mass: the body, "physiology from top to toe." We receive individual identity through our body, as Whitman had insisted in "Crossing Brooklyn Ferry" (1856), yet at the same time, physicality, and especially physical affection, are universal, binding us together in common humanity. Much of the boldly progressive politics of Whitman's poetry will follow from this emphasis on the body; thus his introduction of the theme of "physiology" is followed by his (then quite radical) insistence on the political equality of male and female.

After these dense indications of some major themes, "One's-Self" ends with a bland paean (absent from the 1867 version) to "Modern Man" in his "cheerful" freedom, and this soft ending, in turn, suggests the degree to which Whitman began to polish the rough edges of *Leaves* in the later editions. "One's-Self I Sing" is a relatively sanitized framing of Whitman's more extreme representations of physiology, of sexual relations, or of the violence involved in reconciling liberty to democracy, extremities which he had embraced, in earlier editions, as of the essence of *Leaves*. Most of these extreme representations are preserved in the later editions, but as this poem indicates, they are framed as particular instances of increasingly spiritualized and abstracted universal principles.

Terry Mulcaire

Bibliography

Cowley, Malcolm. Introduction. *The Works of Walt Whitman*. Vol. 1. New York: Funk and Wagnalls, 1968. 3–39.

Miller, James E., Jr. *Walt Whitman*. New York: Twayne, 1962.

Reynolds, David S. *Walt Whitman's America: A Cultural Biography*. New York: Knopf, 1995.

Whitman, Walt. *Leaves of Grass: Comprehensive Reader's Edition*. Ed. Harold W. Blodgett and Sculley Bradley. New York: New York UP, 1965.

See also DEMOCRACY; EQUALITY; HUMAN BODY; INDIVIDUALISM; "INSCRIPTIONS"; SEX AND SEXUALITY

Opera and Opera Singers

Italian opera and opera singers were an important influence on Whitman's creative development during those crucial years in the early 1850s when *Leaves of Grass* was germinating. Probably no other single influence is more important than this one. When we consider how many poems Whitman calls songs or chants, and how many references he makes to the voice and to singing, we come to realize that music and singing were central to the creation of his poetry. "But for the opera," he declared, "I could never have written *Leaves of Grass*" (qtd. in Trowbridge 166).

Even a quick glance at Whitman's poems will show the extent to which he thought of them in musical terms: from "Song of Myself" and the numerous other songs, to "Chants Democratic" and hundreds of references to the voice, singing, carols, hymns, choruses, musical instruments, and the like. Operatic singing in particular, with its emotions, its atmosphere of close rapport between singer and audience, and its varied styles—particularly recitative and aria—is the ground upon which Whitman built many of his poems. It is possible to conceive of many of the long passages in "Song of Myself" and other poems as recitative in the Italian opera style: not only the catalogues, which rhythmically enumerate his experiences and perceptions, but the narrative or dramatic passages as well. Interspersed throughout these recitative passages are lyrical sections, such as the apostrophe to "voluptuous cool-breath'd earth" in section 21, that approximate operatic arias. Such analogies with recitative and aria are made explicit in "Out of the Cradle Endlessly Rocking," where the mockingbird sings its aria of loss, and in "When Lilacs Last in the Dooryard Bloom'd," in which the hermit thrush sings its carol of death.

Whitman was particularly responsive to musical influences during the late 1840s and early 1850s, when *Leaves of Grass* was in its gestation stage and he was regularly attending the performances of Italian opera singers and companies in New York. The moods awakened in him by music played and sung in the streets, in the theater and in private shaped many of the poems he wrote. His own voice, "orotund sweeping and final," was a response to the almost mystical ecstasy he experienced when listening to grand opera and the singing of his favorite tenors and sopranos. In his manuscript notebooks he wrote of "the chanted Hymn whose tremendous sentiment shall uncage in my breast a thousand wide-winged strengths and unknown ardors and terrible ecstasies" (*Uncollected* 2:85)—a passage he reworked and included at the end of section 26 of "Song of Myself," beginning, "I hear the chorus, it is a grand opera, / Ah this indeed is music—this suits me."

Whitman was first exposed to opera in the 1840s, when the operas of Gaetano Donizetti and Giuseppe Verdi were performed in the Park Theater by companies featuring some of the great Italian singers of the day: Cesare Badiali, Marietta Alboni, Alessandro Bettini, and others. Although he had earlier denounced opera in 1845 as foreign and decadent, he quickly became a passionate convert, around the time when Don Francisco Marti's Italian opera company arrived from Havana in 1847 for a month-long season at the Castle Garden.

He began hearing opera regularly at the Astor Place Opera House from the time it opened in 1847; he also attended productions at the Park and Broadway theaters and others, and after 1854 at the beautiful new Academy of Music. It was during these years that he came to love the lyrical *bel canto* style of the operas of Gioacchino Rossini, Vincenzo Bellini, Donizetti, and the early Verdi and became a devoted opera lover. The *bel canto* style has its origins in the operas of Rossini, but was used by other Italian opera composers, including Donizetti, the early Verdi, and most notably Bellini, whose operas present a challenge to the singer's vocal technique. *Bel canto* consists of long passages of simple melody alternating with outbursts of elaborate vocal scrollwork, which turns the voice into a complex wind instrument. The desired effect was to heighten the dramatic meaning and significance of the words through attention to pitch, dynamics, melody, and rhythm. This highly emotional and intense use of the human voice was in Whitman's view the highest form of art.

In a piece in *Specimen Days* Whitman recalls his opera-going experiences in the early 1850s: "I heard, these years, well render'd, all the Italian and other operas in vogue, 'Sonnambula,' 'The Puritans' [both by Bellini], 'Der Freischutz' [Carl Maria von Weber], 'Huguenots' [Giacomo Meyerbeer], 'Fille d'Regiment' [Donizetti], 'Faust' [Charles Gounod], 'Etoile du Nord' [Meyerbeer], 'Poliuto' [Donizetti], and others. Verdi's 'Ernani,' 'Rigoletto,' and 'Trovatore,' with Donizetti's 'Lucia' or 'Favorita' or 'Lucrezia,' and Auber's 'Massaniello,' or Rossini's 'William Tell' and 'Gazza Ladra,' were among my special enjoyments" (*Prose Works* 1:20).

Whitman was an enthusiastic fan of the great Italian singers who came to New York. His favorite tenor was Alessandro Bettini, who had a deep and lasting effect on him. The voice of Bettini, who performed the title role of *Ernani* and sang in Donizetti's *La Favorita* in August 1851, moved Whitman to tears; "the singing of this man," he wrote, "has breathing blood within it; the living soul, of which the lower stage they call art, is but the shell and sham" (*Uncollected* 1:257). Bettini is almost certainly the tenor whom Whitman describes in section 26 of "Song of Myself." Another of his favorites was the great Cesare Badiali, in Whitman's opinion the "superbest of all superb baritones" in the world: "a big, coarse, broad-chested, feller, invested, however, with absolute ease of demeanor—a master of his art—confident, powerful, self-sufficient" (Traubel 173). Others include the soprano Angiolina Bosio, who later became the toast of Europe; Giulia Grisi and her husband Giuseppe Mario, who Whitman said was "inimitable" in *Lucrezia Borgia*. A poem written in Whitman's later years commemorates the death and funeral of another tenor, Pasquale Brignoli, whom he had heard years earlier in many roles in the 1840s and 1850s. The poem, "The Dead Tenor" (1884), acknowledges the strong influence of the singing voice on his own "chants."

But his favorite singer by far was the contralto Marietta Alboni, one of the greatest singers of the nineteenth century, who created a sensation in her only New York season in 1852–1853. In the fall she appeared at Niblo's Garden in twelve operas, and gave eleven more performances at other houses in the winter and spring. In addition she gave twelve operatic recitals and was a soloist in Rossini's *Stabat Mater*. One music critic wrote, "Alboni's performances are as purely and absolutely beautiful as it is possible for anything earthly to be" (qtd. in Faner 29). Whitman was obviously in agreement, since he recalled in *Specimen Days* that he "heard Alboni every time she sang in New York and vicinity" (*Prose Works* 1:20). His poem "To a Certain Cantatrice" (1860) is addressed to Madame Alboni, who he says is as deserving of his tribute as heroes, generals, and other "confronter[s] of despots." She is also prominently featured in the poem most richly commemorating his operatic enthusiasms, "Proud Music of the Storm" (1869): "The teeming lady comes, / The lustrous orb, Venus contralto, the blooming mother, / Sister of loftiest gods, Alboni's self I hear" (section 3). Alboni's most profound influence is on the aria of the mockingbird in "Out of the Cradle Endlessly Rocking" and the carol of the hermit thrush in "When Lilacs Last in the Dooryard Bloom'd," both of which are distillations of Whitman's experiences in listening to her singing.

These two poems, in fact, employ a recitative-aria structure quite consciously modeled on Italian operatic style. In "Out of the Cradle" the bird songs are printed in italics in order to emphasize the lyrical quality of the aria, while the recitative parts underline the dramatic content and structure of the poem, which, like Italian opera, tells a tragic story of love, separation, and death. "When Lilacs Last in the Dooryard Bloom'd" contains more recitative than aria, and does not so clearly distinguish between them. The arias are not italicized, but they have an effect similar to those in "Out of the Cradle." In construction, however, the poem is closer in form to the sonata or symphony than to opera.

The poem in which Whitman mentions opera most extensively is "Proud Music of the Storm" (1869), a kind of musical autobiography, in which he lists the variety of musical influences on his life and poetry. If he resisted the influence of European culture in many ways, he clearly did not when it came to music; he devotes over a third of the poem to the operas of Rossini, Meyerbeer, Donizetti, Verdi, Gounod and Mozart, singing out "Italia's peerless compositions" and the roles of Norma, Lucia, and Ernani. "Proud Music" also celebrates Rossini's *Stabat Mater* (in which he had heard Alboni perform), and the symphonies and oratorios of Ludwig von Beethoven, George Frederick Handel, and Franz Joseph Haydn, including *The Creation*.

His preference was clearly for the passionate Italian style of singing. He had little interest in what the critic Richard Grant White called "the thin, throaty, French way of singing" (qtd. in Faner 63), nor did he share the widespread popular enthusiasm for the dazzling recitals of the Swedish singer Jenny Lind, a creature of P.T. Barnum who became a great celebrity during her 1851–1852 New York season. After hearing her perform Whitman commented on the singing of this "strangely overpraised woman," writing that she "never touched my heart in the least," and that "there was a vacuum in the head of the performance . . . It was the beauty of Adam before God breathed into his nostrils" (*Uncollected* 1:257).

Another important influence upon Whitman's developing taste for operatic music was George Sand's novel *Consuelo* (1843), a story of the career of a great singer that he described to many of his friends as a masterpiece. In highly rhetorical and florid passages describing the almost unearthly quality of the heroine's voice, the novel's English translation gave Whitman a language for describing the effect on his readers he desired his poems to create. The reaction of Consuelo's lover to her singing, for example, is described in language that could be Whitman's own describing his poetry: "Music expresses all that the mind dreams and foresees of mystery and grandeur. It is the manifestation of a higher order of ideas and sentiments than any to which human speech can give expression. It is the revelation of the infinite; and when you sing, I only belong to humanity in so far as humanity has drunk in what is divine and eternal in the bosom of the Creator" (qtd. in Faner 47). The novel had much to do with forming his taste for great singing and the experience of listening to it, as well as inspiring in him a mystical response to the glories of the human voice.

In addition to his poems about opera and opera singers Whitman wrote a number of reviews and essays about them. In 1846–1847, when editor of the Brooklyn *Daily Eagle,* he published thirteen articles on musical subjects. His first critical opera review was of Rossini's

The Barber of Seville in March 1847. His most extended prose piece on opera and the pleasures of opera-going is "Letter from Paumanok," published on 14 August 1851, in the New York *Evening Post.* Another relatively long essay, "The Opera," appeared in *Life Illustrated* in November 1855, just four months after the publication of *Leaves of Grass.* In later years he included reminiscences of his opera-going days in *Specimen Days* and in an essay, "The Old Bowery," collected in the prose section of *Good-Bye My Fancy.*

Donald Barlow Stauffer

Bibliography

Cooke, Alice L. "Notes on Whitman's Musical Background." *New England Quarterly* 19 (1946): 224–235.

Faner, Robert D. *Walt Whitman & Opera.* 1951. London: Feffer and Simons, 1972.

Lawrence, Vera Brodsky. "'Unloos'd Cantabile': Walt Whitman and the Italian Opera." *Seaport* 26.1 (1992): 38–45.

Pound, Louise. "Walt Whitman and Italian Music." *American Mercury* 6 (1925): 58–63.

Spiegelman, Julia. "Walt Whitman and Music." *South Atlantic Quarterly* 41(1942): 167–176.

Traubel, Horace. *With Walt Whitman in Camden.* Vol. 2. New York: Appleton, 1908.

Trowbridge, John Townsend. "Reminiscences of Walt Whitman." *Atlantic Monthly* 89 (1902): 163–175.

Whitman, Walt. *Prose Works 1892.* Ed. Floyd Stovall. 2 vols. New York: New York UP, 1963–1964.

———. *The Uncollected Poetry and Prose of Walt Whitman.* Ed. Emory Holloway. 2 vols. Garden City, N.Y.: Doubleday, Page, 1921.

See also HUMAN VOICE; INFLUENCES ON WHITMAN, PRINCIPAL; MUSIC, WHITMAN AND; "OUT OF THE CRADLE ENDLESSLY ROCKING"; "PROUD MUSIC OF THE STORM"; SAND, GEORGE; "SONG OF MYSELF"; THEATERS AND OPERA HOUSES; "WHEN LILACS LAST IN THE DOORYARD BLOOM'D"

Optimism

The conclusion that optimism was Walt Whitman's dominant attitude is based on the bravado and affirmations of his early journalism and the first two editions of *Leaves of Grass,* when he was still buoyed by the legacy of the successful war for independence. The American Revolution seemed to prove that the universe was beneficent and historical conditions were malleable and could be changed for the better. By 1860 discouraging political developments had transformed such optimism into a hope that was sometimes desperate. As an attitude toward the future, hope differs from optimism in its larger measure of faith as opposed to expectations based on sensible evidence.

Whitman scholarship has followed the trend of American historians who are taking a darkening view of economic and political realities in antebellum America. Biographies by Gay Wilson Allen and Richard Chase demonstrated that in his family life and newspaper work, Whitman became all too familiar with disease, poverty, and political disorder, casting doubt on earlier views that his enthusiasms were grounded in firsthand experience of Jacksonian progress. Revisionist studies by Betsy Erkkila, M. Wynn Thomas, and David Reynolds have underscored Whitman's disillusionment over postcolonial economic and political developments in the United States. From this perspective, Whitman's bravado now seems less optimistic than strategic or a whistling in the dark, the poignant gesture Kenneth Burke once said he was certain Whitman knew he was making with his poems.

As a point of dispute in cultural criticism, Whitman's optimism has been critiqued from several perspectives. Literary critics look for evidence of Whitman's awareness of human limitation in tragic vision. Intellectual historians examine whether Whitman's ideas serve his own interests or the interests of the dominant classes in capitalistic society. Historians of religion question whether the language of millennialism in Whitman's poems is progressive or apocalyptic. From all three critical perspectives, optimism has seemed to be Whitman's characteristic attitude, but the evidence is often contradictory.

During the crisis decade leading to the American Civil War, for example, Whitman certainly lost confidence in the political process—parties, the press, even the electorate; pessimism became his dominant attitude. Then, late in his life—despite the harsh social criticism of *Democratic Vistas*—Whitman was again expressing optimism that the American electorate would eventually fulfill the promise of the American Revolution. Such shifting of attitudes, depending upon time and context, complicates generalizations about Whitman's optimism.

Just as Whitman's journalistic writing displays a full range of attitudes from extreme optimism to despair, so do his lyrics. Overall, however, *Leaves of Grass* displays a consistent tragic stance toward evil, indulging in neither absolute despair nor ill-founded optimism, concludes Henry Alonzo Myers, author of *Tragedy: a View of Life.* Myers ranks Whitman with Sophocles and Shakespeare as the preeminent tragic poets of world literature. In contrast, F.O. Matthiessen discerns in Whitman's work an optimism justifying W.B. Yeats's remark that Whitman lacks a vision of evil, and R.W.B. Lewis declares Whitman a prototypical American Adam, oblivious to history and preadolescent in his ignorance of human limitation. Discussions of Whitman's optimism have been influenced by Lewis's study, which shifted the focus of critical dispute from tragic vision and the problem of evil to ideology in Whitman's vision of nature.

Whitman's allusions to the Genesis creation story lead to the critical diagnosis that Whitman is mistakenly optimistic about political reform because his view of nature is Edenic and thus presocial, distracting him from a class analysis of oppositional forces in society. In short, like the republicanism of Thomas Jefferson, Whitman's political thought seems pastoral; as ideology, it serves the interests of dominant capitalistic classes by offering nature as an illusionary escape from struggling against exploitation by the social order. However, Whitman's notes on Jean Jacques Rousseau's "Social Contract" support M. Wynn Thomas's conclusion that Whitman uses nature not as an escape from society, but to argue for a specific kind of society—the democracy the American Revolution had supposedly begun. Whitman's Rousseau notes indicate he was attracted to the French philosopher's explanation that societies are formed to restrain self-interest by upholding moral principles that help to resolve conflicts between individuals peacefully. In nature, physical strength and prowess alone determine which creatures "wrest and acquire" what they want (*Notebooks* 5:1851), a situation that strikes Whitman as one of enslavement, not freedom. He views society as an escape from nature, not the reverse, his Rousseau notes suggest.

Whitman uses the Adam figure in his poems to model naturalness as an alternative to the artificiality he associates with aristocracy, but using the Adam figure to empower political resistance differs from believing in the Adamic innocence of human nature. In newspaper editorials Whitman expressed a contrary view, remarking that since God ordained evil, reformers could not eliminate it from human affairs and that anyone who has covered a police beat understands that the Calvinist notion of inherent evil rings truer than more positive doctrines.

Such evidence—even considering effusive Whitman pronouncements about human potential—suggests that Whitman's language of eugenic and millennial perfectionism in *Leaves of Grass* should not be interpreted literally. Like the Book of Revelation in the Bible, the millennialism of Whitman's poems may be allegorical. Instead of making literal predictions, the passages in Whitman's poems about perfectionist transformations in coming ages project the fulfillment of human aspirations into an imaginary future, a reading more consistent with metaphorical language for human history in *Leaves of Grass*. This language is organic and cyclical, not mechanistic, linear, and progressive. It encompasses not just birth and growth, but also death and decay.

At best Whitman seems to envision human progress as a laborious, eternal—oftentimes regressive—spiraling. This vision of human history is not the simple optimism often attributed to the poet. Whitman drew from the religions, sciences, and pseudosciences of his day for poetic language to portray the defeat of human aspirations as delays and thus project hope along quintillions of ages and into the cosmos.

Dennis K. Renner

Bibliography

Allen, Gay Wilson. *The Solitary Singer: A Critical Biography of Walt Whitman*. 1955. Rev. ed. 1967. Chicago: U of Chicago P, 1985.

Burke, Kenneth. "I, Eye, Ay—Emerson's Early Essay 'Nature': Thoughts on the Machinery of Transcendence." *Transcendentalism and Its Legacy*. Ed. Myron Simon and Thornton H. Parsons. Ann Arbor: U of Michigan P, 1966. 3–24.

Chase, Richard. *Walt Whitman Reconsidered*. New York: William Sloane Associates, 1955.

Erkkila, Betsy. *Whitman the Political Poet*. New York: Oxford UP, 1989.

Lewis, R.W.B. *The American Adam*. Chicago: U of Chicago P, 1955.

Matthiessen, F.O. *American Renaissance*. London: Oxford UP, 1941.

Meyers, Henry Alonzo. *Tragedy: A View of Life*. Ithaca, N.Y.: Cornell UP, 1956.

Reynolds, David S. *Walt Whitman's America: A Cultural Biography*. New York: Knopf, 1995.

Thomas, M. Wynn. *The Lunar Light of Whitman's Poetry*. Cambridge, Mass.: Harvard UP, 1987.

Whitman, Walt. *The Gathering of the Forces*. Ed. Cleveland Rodgers and John Black. Vol. 1. New York: Putnam, 1920.

———. "Human Nature Under an Unfavorable Aspect." Brooklyn *Daily Times* 7 October 1858.

———. *Notebooks and Unpublished Prose Manuscripts*. Ed. Edward F. Grier. 6 vols. New York: New York UP, 1984.

See also AMERICAN ADAM; AMERICAN REVOLUTION, THE; EVIL; EVOLUTION; HEGEL, GEORG WILHELM FRIEDRICH; POLITICAL VIEWS; RELIGION; STOICISM

"Orange Buds by Mail from Florida" (1888)

First published in the New York *Herald* on 19 March 1888, and later placed in "Sands at Seventy," this seven-line lyric echoes the staunch patriotism found in many of Whitman's other poems: that is, the Old World may be fine but the New gives promise of something finer. It also illustrates his penchant for turning the slightest incident into verse.

Whitman contrasts Voltaire's bragging about the heights of French civilization—shown by its grand opera and by a French warship (Whitman quotes Voltaire's view before his poem)—with his own delight in receiving an orange plant from Florida. America's greatness, "[p]roof of the present time," is shown to him by the nation's ability to ship the plant a great distance by mail, intact. The buds sprouting three days earlier unfold "their sweetness" into his room. As an old man cooped up and paralytic in his Camden, New Jersey, home, Whitman's isolation and winter loneliness play a part in understanding his joy in receiving this gift.

The lyric itself may seem somewhat forced because the occasion appears trivial when put beside Voltaire's brag. Also, the periodic device he uses, saving the phrase "bunch of orange buds" till the final line, appears anticlimactic.

Whitman may have been aware of the danger of this ending being thought absurd, but he would not have minded. Without being jingoistic, he was always secure in his preference for America.

David B. Baldwin

Bibliography

Thomas, M. Wynn. "A Study of Whitman's Late Poetry." *Walt Whitman Review* 27 (1981): 3–14.

Whitman, Walt. *Leaves of Grass: Comprehensive Readers Edition.* Ed. Harold W. Blodgett and Sculley Bradley. New York: New York UP, 1965.

See also "Sands at Seventy" (First Annex)

Oratory

Few institutions of nineteenth-century American culture influenced Whitman as much as oratory. Throughout his life, and especially during the time he was planning and drafting the first edition of *Leaves of Grass,* Whitman was fascinated by public speaking, an art form from which he would adapt devices for his poems.

Whitman's interest in oratory began early. At the age of sixteen he was a member of various debating societies, and he had begun by that age his lifelong habit of shouting declamatory speeches as he walked along the seashore. During his years as a journalist, Whitman reviewed collections of speeches and speech textbooks and reported on a number of sermons and lectures. At the same time, he was writing lectures on a variety of topics. Whitman's notebooks contain numerous references to oratory, and although contemporary scholars have discovered that most of the notes were copied by Whitman from publications dated after the first edition of *Leaves of Grass,* the entries nevertheless bear testimony to his interest in oratory.

In the late twentieth century it is difficult to appreciate the extent of the popularity of oratory during Whitman's lifetime. The closest analogy might be the cinema; successful public speakers were revered much as are today's movie stars. In the Golden Age of American Oratory, the three decades before the Civil War, a successful speaker could be both popular and rich. People crowded into lecture halls to hear orations on politics, travel, social customs, manners, and health. Whitman might

have seen a model in William Andrus Alcott, Bronson Alcott's cousin and the author of nearly a hundred volumes on physiology, hygiene, and practical education. For many writers of the day, like William Alcott and Ralph Waldo Emerson, writing led to a primary career in speaking. No wonder that Whitman imagined himself at the lectern and, in the 1840s, planned to undertake a series of lectures on diet, exercise, and health, probably to be addressed to audiences of young men. Why Whitman decided against a career in public speaking is not entirely clear, but it is possible that he lacked the right voice for it.

Barnet Baskerville, a historian of public speaking, and David Reynolds, a historian of popular culture, have shown that nineteenth-century public speaking fell into two main camps: the "grand" style with rolling lines, repetitions, and flourishes, and the "personal" style, with a conversational, more intimate approach. To the first group would belong speakers such as Edward Everett, Henry Ward Beecher, Daniel Webster, and Emerson. In the second group would be Edward T. Channing and the Quaker preacher Elias Hicks, whom Whitman heard as a child and continued to praise even in Whitman's advanced age. He valued most Hicks's ability to personalize his addresses, bringing the speech to bear upon the individual listener. This ability simultaneously to speak with authority and power and yet to relate intimately to the audience became a model for the poet-reader relationship in Whitman's poems.

From public speaking Whitman drew both a model for the poet-reader relationship and many rhetorical devices. C. Carroll Hollis's study of Whitman's rhetorical devices includes exclamations, rhetorical questions, parallelism, and direct addresses to the reader. In poems such as "A Song of Joys," Whitman praises oratory: "O the orator's joys! / To inflate the chest, to roll the thunder of the voice." At times, Whitman's poems seem almost to be speeches, with the poet-speaker addressing both a multitude and each individual hearer. Toward the end of "Song of Myself," the speaker asks, "Listener up there! what have you to confide to me?" (section 51). The identity of this "listener" is unclear, but it appears to be akin to the person sitting in the balcony of the lecture hall, captivated by a powerful, highly personalized address.

John B. Mason

Bibliography

Azarnoff, Roy S. "Walt Whitman's Concept of the Oratorical Ideal." *Quarterly Journal of Speech* 47 (1961): 169–172.

Baskerville, Barnet. "Principal Themes of Nineteenth-Century Critics of Oratory." *Speech Monographs* 19 (1952): 11–26.

Finkel, William L. "Walt Whitman's Manuscript Notes on Oratory." *American Literature* 22 (1950): 29–53.

Hollis, C. Carroll. *Language and Style in "Leaves of Grass."* Baton Rouge: Louisiana State UP, 1983.

Reynolds, David S. *Walt Whitman's America: A Cultural Biography.* New York: Knopf, 1995.

See also DOUGLASS, FREDERICK; EMERSON, RALPH WALDO; HICKS, ELIAS; HUMAN VOICE; INFLUENCES ON WHITMAN, PRINCIPAL; RHETORICAL THEORY AND PRACTICE; TAYLOR, FATHER (EDWARD THOMPSON)

Organicism

Walt Whitman's revolutionary style of poetry is largely based on what is commonly called the transcendental organic theory of literature. Following the pattern of growth and development characteristic of the natural world, Whitman constructed his poetry to reflect the primacy of the transcendental view of nature. He adhered to this practice in his choice and use of metaphor, verse form, language, and theme.

Whitman borrowed the notion of the organic principle from various prevailing ideas about literary form and nature that had crossed the Atlantic from Germany and England during the romantic period. In a lecture on William Shakespeare's work, the British romantic poet, Samuel Taylor Coleridge, rejected what he considered the traditional mechanic form of poetry and called for an organic poetic structure that shapes itself from within, and whose full development is seen in its outward form. The most direct influence on Whitman, however, came from Ralph Waldo Emerson, whose works Whitman greatly admired, especially Emerson's essay "The Poet" (1844). It is well known that Whitman envisioned himself to be the great American transcendental bard that Emerson wrote about and insisted the young developing nation required. Emerson defined the new original type of poetry that could best represent and capture the spirit of the vast, dynamic American land. Of course, in line with the principles of transcendental thinking, nature had to be the source and the model. Like the spirit and form of the plant or animal, the poem, Emerson explained, has its own architecture that displays the union of thought and form in equal measure.

Whitman explained his organic principle of literary creation in his 1855 Preface to *Leaves of Grass,* where he states that poems should develop their own metrical laws and "bud from them as unerringly and loosely as lilacs or roses on a bush" (714). The dark green cloth cover of the first edition of *Leaves of Grass* further attests to the emphasis Whitman wanted to place on the biological metaphors that are basic to his poetry. The decorative cover depicts flowers and plants, and the letters of the book's title send forth leaves, branches, and roots in different directions.

Understanding how Whitman relied on the example of nature for his poetic creations has guided scholars in their critical studies of his themes, forms, and techniques. The organic theory was central to Whitman's literary imagination. His lifetime work on the individual poems and their revisions and arrangements in the various editions of *Leaves of Grass* signified a growing body of poetry that matched the developing stages of his body and soul from youth and maturity to old age. Besides the central symbolic motif of the grass in "Song of Myself" and throughout the entire *Leaves of Grass,* many of the individual poems center on metaphors from the natural world, such as the sea with its endless waves hitting the beach and the mockingbird's solitary song in "Out of the Cradle Endlessly Rocking."

A good example of how Whitman applied the organic theory to his use of metaphors is seen in "When Lilacs Last in the Dooryard Bloom'd," where he works with the major symbols of lilac, star, cloud, and hermit thrush. Patterning the use of his symbols according to the natural processes of growth and development, Whitman first presents all his symbols in an undeveloped state at the beginning of his poem, and then he proceeds to invest them with additional meanings throughout the elegiac scenes relating to Abraham Lincoln's death. When at the end of the work Whitman again brings most of the major symbols together, the reader now sees them with all their full associative meanings and thematic relationships. The images in the final lines express the poet's peaceful mood of reconciliation now that he grasps the truth about death: "Lilac and star and bird twined with the chant of my soul, / There in the fragrant pines and the cedars dusk and dim" (section 16). Thus, the advanced understanding of the true and increased significance of the metaphors that Whitman uses from nature allows the reader to become fully aware of the emotional and thematic insights the poem can offer.

The organic idea of poetic creation enabled Whitman to invent a new style of form and technique that diverged dramatically from the conventional literary forms of his day. He viewed traditional patterns of verse, such as the sonnet, ballad, or epic, as artificial because the poet was forced to fit the thought to the preset metrical form. To eliminate this constraint, Whitman again turned to nature for his models. The free-verse form he devised has had profound effects on American poetic theory and practice and has achieved important influence on writers all over the world.

Besides patterning his poetic structures according to the developing forms of nature, Whitman attempted to imbue his creative work with a sense of the richness, diversity, and fecundity that characterizes the world of nature. All this can be felt in the dynamic spirit and vitality of his poems, with their prolific images, startling themes, and metrical rhythms that give the reader feelings of natural movements and actions, such as the sea waves washing up on the shore and the flight of mating eagles.

The first scholar to write at length about Whitman's organic principle was William Sloane Kennedy, who four years after Whitman's death in 1892 produced a study of the styles of *Leaves of Grass*. A groundbreaking work was published in 1939 by Sculley Bradley, who saw Whitman's organic rhythms and symmetrically formed lines as constituting the fundamental metrical principles in his poetry. Kennedy and Bradley have been joined by many other literary critics, such as Basil De Selincourt, Gay Wilson Allen, and James E. Miller, Jr., who have seriously studied Whitman's poetic technique of free-verse rhythms. They have tried to erase common misconceptions that Whitman's poetry is anarchic and shapeless. Although Whitman's invention of free verse follows no predetermined form, his new style presents a pattern constructed out of the thought processes and emotional levels of the creative work. Whitman's poems are characterized by his use of phrases and clauses and of such devices as repetitions, parentheses, free-flowing metric lines controlled by breath limitations, and catalogues or enumerations of persons, places, and objects that give weight and substance to images and themes. By analyzing these special poetic elements, scholars have demonstrated how most of the techniques Whitman used to produce his effects relate to the organic processes and structures present in nature.

All through his creative years, transcendentalism's essential link with nature gave Whitman the organic principle that he applied to his body of poems. This principle is pervasive in *Leaves of Grass* and is the foundation upon which the entire work is constructed. Whitman relied on the organic theory for his poetry's thematic concepts, metaphors, and verse techniques and forms. Thus, an understanding of Whitman's work must be grounded on a knowledge of his preoccupation with the organic realities of life.

Angelo Costanzo

Bibliography
Allen, Gay Wilson. *The New Walt Whitman Handbook*. 1975. New York: New York UP, 1986.
Bradley, Sculley. "The Fundamental Metrical Principle in Whitman's Poetry." *American Literature* 10 (1939): 437–459.
Christensen, Inger. "The Organic Theory of Art and Whitman's Poetry." *The Romantic Heritage: A Collection of Critical Essays*. Ed. Karsten Engelberg. Copenhagen: U of Copenhagen, 1983. 93–104.
Coleridge, Samuel Taylor. "Shakespeare, a Poet Generally." *Essays & Lectures on Shakespeare & Some Other Old Poets & Dramatists*. London: Dent, 1907. 38–42.
De Selincourt, Basil. *Walt Whitman: A Critical Study*. London: Martin Secker, 1914.
Kennedy, William Sloane. *Reminiscences of Walt Whitman*. London: Alexander Gardner, 1896.
Killingsworth, M. Jimmie. *The Growth of "Leaves of Grass": The Organic Tradition in Whitman Studies*. Columbia, S.C.: Camden House, 1993.
Miller, James E., Jr. *Walt Whitman*. Updated ed. Boston: Twayne, 1990.
Whitman, Walt. "Preface 1855—*Leaves of Grass*, First Edition." *Leaves of Grass: Comprehensive Reader's Edition*. Ed. Harold W. Blodgett and Sculley Bradley. New York: New York UP, 1965. 709–729.

O

See also EMERSON, RALPH WALDO; KENNEDY, WILLIAM SLOANE; LANGUAGE; NATURE; POETIC THEORY; PREFACE TO LEAVES OF GRASS, 1855 EDITION; PROSODY; ROMANTICISM; STYLE AND TECHNIQUE(S); SYMBOLISM; TRANSCENDENTALISM

"Osceola" (1890)

This ten-line poem preceded by a preface is one of the last thirty-one poems that Walt Whitman published in the two years before his death on 26 March 1892. It first appeared in *Munson's Illustrated World* in April 1890 and was included in Whitman's collection of prose and poetry *Good-Bye My Fancy* in 1891. Later that year Whitman added the poetry from that collection as an annex to the Deathbed edition of *Leaves of Grass* under the title "Good-Bye my Fancy."

In its preface Whitman states that the poem is a reminiscence of a report he heard in 1838 in Brooklyn, New York, when he was almost eighteen years old, from a U.S. marine returned from South Carolina who gave him his account of the death of the Seminole chief Osceola captured in the Florida war and imprisoned at Fort Moultrie, South Carolina. In his elegiac poem, Whitman vividly reconstructs half a century later Osceola's historic death as if he were a witness to the last hours of the young Seminole leader, evoking in the broken figure of this magnificent warrior all the courageous elements of lofty manhood that he admired, for, as he said in "By Blue Ontario's Shore, I am for those that have never been master'd' (section 17).

The origins and death of Osceola (whose name means rising sun) still remain obscure. Legend has it that he was the son of an English trader and an Indian Creek woman. Born around 1800, he opposed the forced relocation of his tribe and fought against Andrew Jackson in 1812 and 1818, then fled to Florida and joined the Seminoles. In 1834 he refused to sign a treaty to relocate west and, angry at the threats of General Thompson, stuck his knife through the document, defacing it. Soon, some white raiders kidnapped Osceola's wife. He went to Fort King to demand justice but, instead, was put in prison for twenty months. Set free, he returned on 28 December 1835 and killed the general and his secretary. When on 22 October 1837 he appeared under a flag of truce at Three Pines he was seized and taken prisoner to St. Augustine and later transferred to Fort Moultrie, where on 10 January 1838 he died.

Walt Whitman's early journalistic training and six months' work at the Indian Bureau in Washington, D.C., in 1865 helped him to understand the plight of the American Indians and, later, to see the need to add to *Leaves of Grass* his homage to Osceola, one of their bravest heroes.

Jesus Sierra-Oliva

Bibliography

Hartley, William B. *Osceola, the Unconquered Indian.* New York: Hawthorne Books, 1973.

Todd, Edgeley W. "Indian Pictures and Two Whitman Poems." *Huntington Library Quarterly* 19 (1955): 1–11.

Whitman, Walt. *Complete Poetry and Collected Prose.* Ed. Justin Kaplan. New York: Library of America, 1982.

See also INDIAN AFFAIRS, BUREAU OF; NATIVE AMERICANS (INDIANS); RACIAL ATTITUDES; "YONNONDIO""

Osgood, James R. (1836–1892)

Born in Fryeburg, Maine, James Ripley Osgood graduated from Bowdoin in 1854 and read law briefly in Portland before clerking for the Boston publishers Ticknor and Fields in September 1855. Rising to partner, with James T. Fields he established Fields, Osgood and Company in 1868. By 1871 the firm had become R. Osgood and Company, with Osgood and Benjamin Ticknor as partners. In 1878, the firm merged with H.O. Houghton, to form Houghton, Osgood and Company, which only lasted until 1880, when Osgood left to form James R. Osgood and Company.

In 1881 Osgood offered to publish *Leaves of Grass* and agreed to let Whitman "retain all the *beastliness* of the earlier editions" (qtd. in Ballou 282). On 1 October, Whitman finalized a ten-year contract with Osgood, and the seventh edition of *Leaves of Grass* (1881–1882), significantly revised by Whitman, was published in November at two dollars a copy. Although Whitman had removed some of the sexual content of *Leaves,* on 1 March 1882, the Boston district attorney, Oliver Stevens, acting under the influence of the New England Society for the Suppression of Vice, classified *Leaves* as obscene literature. Stevens ordered Osgood to remove several offending poems and passages or cease publication altogether. Although Whitman was willing to make some changes, he refused to completely expurgate *Leaves* and reached a settlement with Osgood on 17 May 1882: Osgood paid Whitman one hundred dollars in cash and gave him 225 copies of the book along with the stereotype plates.

After the Boston "suppression," Richard Maurice Bucke, John Burroughs, and William O'Connor rallied around Whitman and used the event to promote the poet as a victim of prudishness and comstockery. Using the plates from the Osgood edition, Rees Welsh and Company of Philadelphia sold about six thousand copies of *Leaves of Grass* (1882). Although not a direct result of the Whitman fiasco, James R. Osgood and Company went out of business in May 1885.

William A. Pannapacker

Bibliography

Allen, Gay Wilson. *The Solitary Singer: A Critical Biography of Walt Whitman.* 1955. Rev. ed. 1967. Chicago: U of Chicago P, 1985.

Ballou, Ellen B. *The Building of the House: Houghton Mifflin's Formative Years.* Boston: Houghton Mifflin, 1970.

Tryon, W.S. *Parnassus Corner: A Life of James T. Fields, Publisher to the Victorians.* Boston: Houghton Mifflin, 1963.

Weber, Carl J. *The Rise and Fall of James Ripley Osgood.* Colby College Monograph 22. Waterville, Me.: Colby College, 1959.

Winship, Michael. *American Literary Publishing in the Mid-Nineteenth Century: The Business of Ticknor and Fields.* Cambridge: Cambridge UP, 1995.

See also BOSTON, MASSACHUSETTS; COMSTOCK, ANTHONY; *LEAVES OF GRASS*, 1881–1882 EDITION; PHILADELPHIA, PENNSYLVANIA; SOCIETY FOR THE SUPPRESSION OF VICE; STEVENS, OLIVER

Osler, Dr. William (1849–1919)

Born in Bond Head, Ontario, Canada, Osler graduated from the McGill University medical school in 1872. In 1884, shortly after joining the University of Pennsylvania, he became Walt Whitman's physician at the request of Dr. Richard Maurice Bucke. For the next five years Osler treated without charge the ailing Whitman, seeing him through several crises but never joining the inner circle of worshipers such as Bucke, Thomas B. Harned, Thomas Donaldson, Horace Traubel, and others.

Though Whitman valued Osler's medical skills, he sometimes complained of the doctor's optimism, a characteristic for which generations of medical students idolized him as he transformed the coldly analytical method of making hospital rounds. Osler dispelled gloom and radiated cheer, listening attentively to each patient's complaints as an essential part of the clinical evaluation. In 1888, Whitman said Osler "is a great man—one of the rare men: I should be much surprised if he didn't soar way way up—get very famous at his trade—some day: he has the air of the thing about him—of achievement" (Traubel 391). Whitman's prediction proved accurate: Osler became the most beloved and famous medical doctor in the English-speaking world.

In late 1889 Osler left Philadelphia to help establish the Johns Hopkins medical school in Baltimore. There he completed his pathbreaking medical treatise *The Principles and Practice of Medicine,* published in 1892, the year of Whitman's death. By 1930 the book had gone into its eleventh edition and had been translated into four languages. Shortly after the publication of his book, Osler married a widow, Grace Revere Gross, a direct descendant of Paul Revere. In 1904 Osler accepted the chair of Regius Professor of Medicine at Oxford University, further ensuring his place as an icon of his profession. He was made a baronet by King George V in 1911.

Philip W. Leon

Bibliography

Cushing, Harvey. *The Life of Sir William Osler.* 2 vols. Oxford: Clarendon, 1925.

Leon, Philip W. *Walt Whitman and Sir William Osler: A Poet and His Physician.* Toronto: ECW, 1995.

Traubel, Horace. *With Walt Whitman in Camden.* Vol. 3. 1914. New York: Rowman and Littlefield, 1961.

See also BUCKE, RICHARD MAURICE; DRINKARD, DR. WILLIAM B.; HEALTH; LONGAKER, DR. DANIEL; MITCHELL, SILAS WEIR

"Our Old Feuillage" (1860)

"Our Old Feuillage" was apparently written at least in part in 1856, for a version of the poem in the Valentine-Barrett manuscript speaks of the "Eightieth year of These States" (1776 to 1856 would be eighty years), a phrase that Whitman changed to "eighty-third year of these States" in the 1860 and all subsequent editions of *Leaves of Grass.* Thus he was evidently revising the poem in 1859, when the secession crisis was rapidly coming to a head. The poem was first printed as number 4 of the "Chants Democratic," in the 1860 edition of *Leaves of Grass,* an edition that some critics see as an attempt on Whitman's part

O

to hold the Union together by sheer force of rhetoric. "Our Old Feuillage," with its celebration of the infinite heterogeneity of "These States," supports such a reading. In subsequent editions of *Leaves of Grass,* Whitman cut a few lines from this poem but made no major changes. The poem acquired its final title in the 1881 edition.

"Our Old Feuillage" is largely given over to one of the longest single catalogues in all of *Leaves of Grass.* The catalogue begins with a bird's eye perspective of the North American continent. From geography we move to demography, as Whitman lays out some census statistics designed to suggest the enormous scope and the "free range and diversity" of the "continent of Democracy." But then the camera eye swoops down to focus in on some specifics, and we find ourselves walking with the poet "[t]hrough Mannahatta's streets . . . these things gathering." Once we arrive at the level of the concrete particular, however, we (and the poet) soon leave Manhattan. Instead we leap from one region to another of "These States," in a series of strikingly concrete images of daily life in various regions of the nation—South, North, and West.

This series of images seeks to resolve itself in a declaration of the absolute unity of the nation. But implicitly Whitman seems to realize that merely announcing the unity of the states will not necessarily make them one, and midway through the poem he uneasily veers back from the political toward the personal. Again we find ourselves walking with the poet, but in the country this time, "rambling in lanes and country fields, Paumanok's fields." He returns to the political for a few lines describing an orator at work, but then he tries to resolve the tension between the universal and the particular in a metaphor, as the "I" of the poem becomes first a seagull and then a whole series of birds. And finally, Whitman concludes his poem with a passage—absent from the Valentine-Barrett manuscript and thus evidently added in late 1859 or early 1860—which includes a desperate declaration, shouted out in block capital letters, that the nation is indissolubly bound together into "ONE IDENTITY." This phrase hints at both his hopes and his fears, as he watched the Union break in two.

Burton Hatlen

Bibliography

Hatlen, Burton. "The Many and/or the One: Poetics versus Ideology in Whitman's 'Our Old Feuillage' and 'Song of the Banner at Daybreak.'" *American Transcendentalist Quarterly* ns 6 (1992): 189–211.
Thomas, M. Wynn. *The Lunar Light of Whitman's Poetry.* Cambridge, Mass.: Harvard UP, 1987.
Whitman, Walt. *Whitman's Manuscripts: "Leaves of Grass" (1860).* Ed. Fredson Bowers. Chicago: U of Chicago P, 1955.

See also CATALOGUES; CIVIL WAR, THE; *LEAVES OF GRASS,* 1860 EDITION

"Out from Behind This Mask" (1876)

First published in the New York *Tribune* (19 February 1876) and later included in the cluster "Autumn Rivulets," this two-stanza, twenty-four-line poem uses a self-portrait from a photograph (made by G.C. Potter of an engraving by W.J. Linton) as its reference. Whitman enjoyed being photographed; in fact here he fashioned a serious reflection on his own image, a dramatic reflection free from posturing.

Starting with the figure of a mask, the first section runs through a series of shifting equivalents for the poet's face and head: this "drama of the whole," this "common curtain," this "glaze" (God's) and this "film" (Satan's), this "map," this "small continent," this "soundless sea," "this globe," and finally the conceit, "[t]his condensation of the universe." At the very end of the stanza the poet shifts to a figure-free image, from the eyes in the portrait: "To you whoe'er you are—a look." The effect of the periodic syntax, holding off the main clause, is much like that from the long opening sentence in "Out of the Cradle Endlessly Rocking."

Whitman has established early that his portrait is more representative than unique ("This common curtain of the face contain'd in me for me, in you for you, in each for each"). In the second section he calls more attention to the reader. He now assumes the role of a traveler, much as he had done in the final sections of "Song of Myself," not an actual traveler but one who has traveled through "thoughts," through "youth," through "peace and war," through "middle age" and is now "[l]ingering a moment here and now" on his journey. Stopping the flow of time to seize the moment, he is lingering to greet the reader, the universal "you," not for a casual word or wave, but "[t]o draw and clinch your soul for once inseparably with mine." Then he will "travel travel on."

Both in skills, including the loose hexameter rhythm, the appropriate figures and images and word choices seemingly found without effort, as well as in idea and attitude, this poem shows Whitman at his most mature and attractive.

David B. Baldwin

Bibliography

Blodgett, Harold W. "Whitman and the Linton Portrait." *Walt Whitman Newsletter* 4.3 (1958): 90–92.

Folsom, Ed. *Walt Whitman's Native Representations.* Cambridge: Cambridge UP, 1994.

Whitman, Walt. *Leaves of Grass: Comprehensive Reader's Edition.* Ed. Harold W. Blodgett and Sculley Bradley. New York: New York UP, 1965.

See also "AUTUMN RIVULETS"; PHOTOGRAPHS AND PHOTOGRAPHERS

"Out of the Cradle Endlessly Rocking" (1859)

"Out of the Cradle Endlessly Rocking" is one of Whitman's most moving and difficult poems. The poem was first published under the title "A Child's Reminiscence" in the New York *Saturday Press* for 24 December 1859, with the opening verse paragraph bearing the heading "Pre-Verse." The issue contained also a notice on the editorial page probably written by Henry Clapp, the editor of the *Press* and a close friend of Whitman, which terms the poem "our Christmas or New Year's present to [our readers]." When the Cincinnati *Daily Commercial* published an attack upon the poem a few days later, the *Saturday Press* of 7 January 1860 reprinted the attack along with an anonymous response by Whitman entitled "All About a Mocking-Bird." There, in one of his first defenses against hostile criticism, Whitman justifies the poem and his craft and prophesies a new edition of *Leaves of Grass,* what would become the 1860 edition. "Out of the Cradle" appeared in that edition as "A Word Out of the Sea," with the heading "Reminiscence" placed between the first and second verse paragraphs. Whitman made several changes in the poem for the 1867 edition, used the title "Out of the Cradle Endlessly Rocking" for the first time in the 1871 edition, and gave the poem virtually its final form in the 1881 edition, where it stands prominently at the head of the "Sea-Drift" section.

"Out of the Cradle" dominates the "Sea-Drift" grouping because it condenses Whitman's themes of love, death, sexuality, loss, and their relation to language and poetry into a single setting and situation. On the beach at night, a curious boy wanders alone, witnessing two birds living and loving together. Then one vanishes, the other searches fruitlessly, the boy questions—only to hear the ocean's final assertion of death, and the man notes, "My own songs awaked from that hour." Here is Whitman narrating his awakening to death and his simultaneous projection into poesy. Out of this primal scene of eros and thanatos, of a "musical shuttle" made of "pains and joys," Whitman derives an intense and somber lesson in mortality and inspiration.

However, despite the ardor of the experience described, "Out of the Cradle" is remarkable in that here Whitman reveals a masterful formal control of his material. The opening of the poem is a tour de force of poetic suspense: a single sentence, twenty-two lines of sustained anaphora and parallelism, of gliding prepositional phrases and arousing half-allusions culminating in the simple bardic verb "sing." This haunting recitation introduces the four voices in the poem—bird, boy, man, sea—and arranges them into a sequence of "afflatus." That is, the bird calls "those beginning notes of yearning and love," the boy listens and "translat[es]" them as the italicized lines in the poem, the man records the translation and comments on the boy's condition, and the sea taciturnly provides the final word on the matter, the "word of the sweetest song and all songs"—death. And out of the boy's observance of love and loss and his hearkening to the sea's "hissing" iteration, "Death, death, death, death, death," comes a new destiny for the boy—to become a spirit dedicated to poetry. As the boy listens to the he-bird's progress from odes to timeless love to lament over the disappearance of the she-bird to peals of desperate hope that his love may return to piercing recognition of perpetual loss, the boy (as reflected upon by the man) turns to the sea for explanation, for some "clew" as to why such suffering comes about. The sea's patient answer solves nothing. Instead, it lifts the question out of its local context, provoking a universalization of the she-bird's departure, a conversion of individual pain into natural law.

This is the inspiration to sing, to write poetry. If death is not exactly the birth of language, it is the birth of song, the mother of beauty. As the essays by Stephen Whicher, Paul Fussell, Richard Chase, and Roy Harvey Pearce (all printed in an English Institute volume entitled *The Presence of Walt Whitman*) attest, "Out of the Cradle" raises the prospect of annihilation and concludes that there is nothing to do about it but sing it. In doing so, the poem places itself in a traditional genre of poems recounting the birth of poetry out of death. That is, "Out of the Cradle" dramatizes an archetypal experience of loss and reaches a familiar outcome: verse. In this genre, there is nothing else to do with irreversible loss but to describe its happening. How else can the bird recall his absent object of desire but by announcing its absence until his "carol" becomes in Whitman's rendition a worldwide annunciation? What else can Whitman make of his forsakenness but to dramatize it, to generalize bereavement into a human condition, the word of *all* songs? One love is lost, and all of life is changed.

This poetic psychodrama has led other scholars to interpret the love-loss-poetry pattern as it appears in "Out of the Cradle" in psychobiographical terms. Certainly the poem's language and narrative lend themselves to psychological description, with phrases such as "The unknown want, the destiny of me," or "A man, yet by these tears a little boy again," or "cries of unsatisfied love" virtually soliciting a reading that borrows from concepts of repression and the unconscious. Accordingly, critics such as Gustav Bychowski, Edwin Haviland Miller, Stephen Black, David Cavitch, and M. Jimmie Killingsworth have read the poem using a more or less psychoanalytical framework. Read within the purview of the unconscious, Whitman's poetic expressions come to be seen as the culmination of a psychic process, one characterized by sublimation and substitution and displacement. Psychoanalytical interpretation entails recovering clearly the psychic content which "Out of the Cradle" represents in a distorted fashion. That is, it begins with Whitman's Oedipal situation—a complex one, especially considering his excessively adoring portraits of his mother and his virtual silence about his father—and decodes the poem accordingly.

In this case, "Out of the Cradle" and its story of ideal love and traumatic separation and the abandoned he-bird's all-encompassing lament actually reenact Whitman's own trauma of separation. In the boy's humble testimony, Whitman vicariously expresses the pain of loss, the withdrawal of, perhaps, mother or recent lover (indeed, the latter would only be an aggravation of the former). The peremptory voice of the maternal sea marks Whitman expanding the source of that pain beyond his real mother, thereby expanding (or repressing) his desires away from the narcissistic needs of the infant. Whitman still desires to overcome separation, to reexperience the "oceanic feeling" character-

izing the mother-newborn relation, but that unity must now come at a cosmic level, not a personal one. (This may be because of his mother's threatening aspect, her tendency to absorb Walt's ego into her own, or because of his father's intemperate, distant attitude toward him.) Individual love means loss and dereliction, along with all the guilt and abjection that the ego takes upon itself to explain that catastrophe. But if that excruciating loneliness and self-recrimination—that emotional death—be linked to a universal lament, then Whitman may feel involved in a larger process of life and death, unified with all other things that experience the same pain. If this cosmic unification marks yet another sublimation, it is a creative one, more comprehensive and orderly than the he-bird's despairing cries or the boy's confused inquisitions.

Of course, this rough approximation of psychobiographical interpretations of "Out of the Cradle" smooths out differences in the readings offered by the critics mentioned above. It also does not take into account a methodological question: *How* does the poem represent Whitman's psycho-sexual tensions? This question is posed by another group of readings of "Out of the Cradle." These readings may be termed "theoretical" in that they not so much ask about the content of the representation as they explore the relation between representation and represented, psyche and word, intention and expression.

In theoretical readings of "Out of the Cradle" by critics such as Diane Wood Middlebrook, Kerry Larson, and Mark Bauerlein, the focus lies on the nature of the process of translation carried out in the poem. If the poem records Whitman's discovery of his "tongue's use," then the poem must proceed to show how the boy-man-poet learns to translate life and death into words that affect others, to transform formative experiences and dim memories into songs that transcend their circumstances. What is exceptional about "Out of the Cradle" in this respect is precisely the translation model Whitman sets his poetic inspiration within. For, as opposed to most conceptions of poetic origins, Whitman locates his inspiration in another's experience—the mockingbird's—and assumes the duty of translator, not originator of pathos. He becomes a singer of "warbling echoes" and "reverberations," imitating, "perpetuating" the bird, who is himself an imitator, a mockingbird. In other words, Whitman's birth as a poet happens when he joins a procession of singers and listeners—mockingbird, boy, man, poet, reader—attending to the cries of lonesome love.

This is what distinguishes his song from the bird's song. Upon losing his love, the bird remains frenzied, disbelieving, his cries addressing solely *his* loss, his pain allowing for no other realization but the return of his love. Even when he does begin to accept the loss, all he can do is repeat "Loved!" five times and say blankly, *"But my mate no more, no more with me!"* His lament remains self-centered, eventually trailing off into self-torture and despair. His song cannot succeed the way Whitman's does because he has no awareness of joining in a procession of communications, of communion. He fails to realize that poets work by "[t]aking all hints to use them, but swiftly leaping beyond them," beyond their contingent aspects and beyond the poet's own private concerns. Conceiving himself as an origin and end of song, the bird-poet can only insistently repeat his trauma. He needs a translator, one who can recast his notes as a beautiful permutation of elegiac narrative. Great poets require an apprehension of more than just their own individuality, and of course the absolute limit to individuality is death. This is why death is the "word of . . . all songs." It forces poets to see and sing beyond their own personal experience.

Such a conclusion reverses the romantic conception of the poet and belies the commonplace interpretation of Whitman as the most egotistical of writers. But in "Out of the Cradle," translation is not a fallen condition and self-absorption is a failure. The boy who sits in the bushes "translating" the "notes" seems free and natural, wholly devoid of irony or insincerity or narcissism. Perhaps the connection of innocence and interpretation contributes to the appeal of "Out of the Cradle." In any case, whether considered as a supreme instance of conventional elegy, a charged reflection of psychosexual tensions, or a complex meditation upon how to give words to trauma, "Out of the Cradle" remains a centerpiece of Whitman's poetry and poetics. In its poignant evocation of a lonely beach where a "curious boy" sits "peering, absorbing," hearing a mockingbird's natural cries of love and despair and feeling those notes turn to poems within him, "Out of the Cradle" embodies for many *the* Whitmanian poetic moment, the emotive origin and measure of his song.

Mark Bauerlein

Bibliography

Bauerlein, Mark. *Whitman and the American Idiom*. Baton Rouge: Louisiana State UP, 1991.

Black, Stephen. *Whitman's Journeys into Chaos*. Princeton: Princeton UP, 1975.

Bychowski, Gustav. "Walt Whitman: A Study in Sublimation." *Psychoanalysis and the Social Sciences*. Ed. Geza Roheim. New York: International Universities, 1950. 223–261.

Cavitch, David. *My Soul and I: The Inner Life of Walt Whitman*. Boston: Beacon, 1985.

Killingsworth, M. Jimmie. *Whitman's Poetry of the Body: Sexuality, Politics, and the Text*. Chapel Hill: U of North Carolina P, 1989.

Larson, Kerry. *Whitman's Drama of Consensus*. Chicago: U of Chicago P, 1988.

Lewis, R.W.B., ed. *The Presence of Walt Whitman*. New York: Columbia UP, 1962.

Middlebrook, Diane Wood. *Walt Whitman and Wallace Stevens*. Ithaca, N.Y.: Cornell UP, 1974.

Miller, Edwin Haviland. *Walt Whitman's Poetry: A Psychological Journey*. Boston: Houghton Mifflin, 1968.

Renner, Dennis K. "Reconciling Varied Approaches to 'Out of the Cradle Endlessly Rocking.'" *Approaches to Teaching Whitman's "Leaves of Grass."* Ed. Donald D. Kummings. New York: MLA, 1990. 67–73.

Whitman, Walt. *Leaves of Grass: Comprehensive Reader's Edition*. Ed. Harold W. Blodgett and Sculley Bradley. New York: New York UP, 1965.

See also CLAPP, HENRY; DEATH; *LEAVES OF GRASS*, 1860 EDITION; LONG ISLAND, NEW YORK; OPERA AND OPERA SINGERS; PSYCHOLOGICAL APPROACHES; *SATURDAY PRESS*; SEA, THE; "SEA-DRIFT"

"Out of the Rolling Ocean the Crowd" (1865)

"Out of the Rolling Ocean the Crowd," first published in *Drum-Taps* in 1865, was included in "Children of Adam" in 1871, where it follows the ecstatic celebration of sexual union, "One Hour to Madness and Joy." By tradition, according to notes in *Leaves of Grass: Comprehensive Reader's Edition,* the poem was originally addressed to a female admirer who championed Whitman's poetry against the resistance of her husband.

Though the occasion for the composition of the poem may have been personal, its function in "Adam" is thematic. It addresses the existential crisis of individuality occasioned by the fall into selfhood following the intense affirmation of the body and the sensory life celebrated in "One Hour" and other poems leading up to "Rolling Ocean." The "drop" cohered out of the "rolling ocean" expresses the fragility and vulnerability of the mortal flesh made self-aware. Though the drop is not specifically identified as female in the poem, the solicitous tone of the poetic persona and the humble demeanor of the drop suggest a self-effacing daring often represented as feminine in the nineteenth century.

The presumed femininity of the drop also fits Whitman's mythic structure. As he told Horace Traubel in 1888, "Leaves of Grass is essentially a woman's book" (Traubel 331). Of the forces that combine to produce the self, the body is "Physical matter . . . Female and Mother" but contains "corruption and decease"; "the Soul of the Universe is the Male and genital master," as Whitman wrote in notes published in *Walt Whitman's Workshop* (49). Thus the ecstatic celebration of the body designed to produce the fully realized identity in "Adam" also exposes the transience of the flesh expressed in the mutability of the individual drop.

The solution to this existential dilemma is the "great rondure," the pooled selfhood of self-aware souls. This spiritual community—"the common air that bathes the globe" in section 17 of "Song of Myself"—is best expressed in a democratic literature that, as in "Crossing Brooklyn Ferry," links kindred souls through space and time. "Every day at sundown" as the eternal light of the sun departs from physical matter, leaving it exposed to awareness of its own "corruption and decease," in "Rolling Ocean" the poet salutes "the air," the common spiritual bond; "the ocean," the mutable sensory life; and "the land," the fixed principles through which a reclaimed certainty ultimately may be achieved. In another poem, "In Cabin'd Ships at Sea," Whitman calls his book "not a reminiscence of the land alone" but a "lone bark" bearing "my love" through *"liquid-flowing syllables"* in *"ocean's poem."*

Margaret H. Duggar

Bibliography

Killingsworth, M. Jimmie. *Whitman's Poetry of the Body: Sexuality, Politics, and the Text*. Chapel Hill: U of North Carolina P, 1989.

Miller, James E., Jr. *A Critical Guide to "Leaves of Grass."* Chicago: U of Chicago P, 1957.

Traubel, Horace. *With Walt Whitman in Camden*. 1908. Vol. 2. New York: Rowman and Littlefield, 1961.

Whitman, Walt. *Leaves of Grass: Comprehensive Reader's Edition*. Ed. Harold W. Blodgett and Sculley Bradley. New York: New York UP, 1965.

———. *Walt Whitman's Workshop: A Collection of Unpublished Manuscripts*. Ed. Clifton Joseph Furness. Cambridge, Mass.: Harvard UP, 1928.

See also BEACH, JULIETTE H.; "CHILDREN OF ADAM"; SEA, THE

"Over the Carnage Rose Prophetic a Voice" (1865)

Although "Over the Carnage Rose Prophetic a Voice" appeared for the first time in the 1865 *Drum-Taps* collection, many of the poem's lines had been published in "Calamus" number 5 in the 1860 *Leaves of Grass*. Interested readers can get a glimpse of Whitman's revising process by consulting *Walt Whitman's Blue Book,* the facsimile edition of Whitman's personal copy of the 1860 text. Ultimately, "Over the Carnage" came to rest in the "Drum-Taps" cluster of *Leaves*.

"Calamus" number 5, or "States!," was an extremely optimistic, almost utopian celebration of the possibilities of American democracy. In it the bold poetic persona of the 1860 *Leaves* promises to inculcate "a new friendship" that will enable the states to be held together "as firmly as the earth itself is held together." "Affection," he declares, "shall solve every one of the problems of freedom"; "companionship thick as trees" will make legal agreements and armed struggle unnecessary.

In "Over the Carnage," Whitman's poetic persona looks out over a field full of dead young men, casualties of fratricidal war and irrefutable evidence of affection's failure. Out of this scene, over this carnage, he nonetheless attempts to conjure the optimism expressed in the earlier edition. Interestingly, though this poem again asserts the belief that affection could solve the problems of freedom, the speaker does not utter these words himself. Instead, he hears them pronounced by a "prophetic" voice. This externalized voice can at once comfort the poet's own despair, "Be not dishearten'd," and offer a mournful nation consolation by repeating what had been the now silent poet's own formulation, "affection shall solve the problems of freedom *yet*" (emphasis added).

The only wholly new lines to appear in "Over the Carnage" are "Sons of the Mother of All, you shall yet be victorious, / You shall yet laugh to scorn the attacks of all the remainder of the earth." Twice repeating the anticipatory "yet," the prophetic voice promises the mournful, divided nation a united future as a world power. Though not as striking in its descriptions or its imagery as the strongest of the "Drum-Taps" poems, "Over the Carnage" demonstrates the tenacity of Whitman's hope.

Rosemary Graham

Bibliography

Kaplan, Justin. *Walt Whitman: A Life.* New York: Simon and Schuster, 1980.

Reynolds, David S. *Walt Whitman's America: A Cultural Biography.* New York: Knopf, 1995.

Whitman, Walt. *Leaves of Grass: Comprehensive Reader's Edition.* Ed. Harold W. Blodgett and Sculley Bradley. New York: New York UP, 1965.

———. *Leaves of Grass: Facsimile of the 1860 Text.* Ed. Roy Harvey Pearce. Ithaca, N.Y.: Cornell UP, 1961.

———. *Walt Whitman's Blue Book.* Ed. Arthur Golden. 2 vols. New York: New York Public Library, 1968.

See also CIVIL WAR, THE; COMRADESHIP; "DRUM-TAPS"; *DRUM-TAPS*; LEAVES OF GRASS, 1860 EDITION; *WALT WHITMAN'S BLUE BOOK*

O

P

Paine, Thomas (1737–1809)

Walt Whitman's affection for Thomas Paine originated with his father, who both lovingly admired the patriot's writings and considered him an acquaintance. The poet's vision of an American spiritual democracy is historically rooted in Paine's example of political and religious radicalism.

Paine immigrated to Philadelphia in 1774, leaving in England his unsuccessful careers as a corset maker and excise officer. In January 1776, he published *Common Sense,* which sold as many as 150,000 copies and exerted an immeasurable influence on the cause for American independence. The same year Paine initiated a series of essays titled *The American Crisis* (1776–1783) which helped uphold colonial morale throughout the Revolutionary War. Paine's return to England in 1787 did not diminish his success as a political pamphleteer. *Rights of Man* (1791, 1792), a two-part response to Edmund Burke's attack on the French Revolution, was widely read for its brilliant defense of republican government. Paine's involvement with the French National Convention eventually led to his imprisonment in 1793–1794. While in France, he produced *The Age of Reason* (two volumes, 1794, 1795). The work's challenge to Christian superstition and biblical authority alienated many Americans, and upon his return to the United States in 1802, Paine was met with derision and scorn. The free-thinking Whitmans counted *The Age of Reason* among their favorite books.

Whitman told Horace Traubel that as a young man he had pledged to "do public justice" to Paine's much maligned reputation (Traubel 205–206). He received his finest opportunity when he spoke at the Thomas Paine Society Dinner in Philadelphia (28 January 1877). The speech was printed in *Specimen Days* (1882) under the title "In Memory of Thomas Paine." Relying on the testimony of Colonel John Fellows, an old friend of Paine's whom Whitman had met at Tammany Hall, the poet denied the many rumors about the old revolutionary's drunkenness and vulgarity. Whitman reminded his audience that Paine was largely responsible for the Union's independence, devotion to human rights, and freedom from religious tyranny. At the center of Whitman's comments was the issue of character, and the poet assuredly confirmed Paine's "noble personality," pointing to the philosophical calm with which he died (*Prose Works* 1:141).

Scholars have frequently noted Paine's legacy to *Leaves of Grass*. Both men were sympathetic to Quakerism, which provided them not only with a suspicion of priests, but also with a radically egalitarian vision of human divinity. Whitman retained much of Paine's deist belief in the self's capacity to comprehend moral truth through the study of the material world. As Betsy Erkkila has argued, however, when the language of natural law appears in *Leaves of Grass*, it tends to serve as a veil for the poet's partisan engagements. In this regard, what Whitman may have learned most from Thomas Paine was how democratic authors could convey their political opinions in the guise of candor and common sense.

David Haven Blake

Bibliography

Erkkila, Betsy. *Whitman the Political Poet.* New York: Oxford UP, 1989.

Foner, Eric. *Tom Paine and Revolutionary America.* New York: Oxford UP, 1976.

Keane, John. *Tom Paine: A Political Life.* New York: Little, Brown, 1995.

Paine, Thomas. *Collected Writings.* Ed. Eric Foner. New York: Library of America, 1995.

Traubel, Horace. *With Walt Whitman in Camden.* Vol. 2. New York: Appleton, 1908.

Vanderhaar, Margaret M. "Whitman, Paine, and the Religion of Democracy." *Walt Whitman Review* 16 (1970): 14–22.

Whitman, Walt. *Prose Works 1892.* Ed. Floyd Stovall. 2 vols. New York: New York UP, 1963–1964.

See also AMERICAN REVOLUTION, THE; HARRIS, FRANK; INFLUENCES ON WHITMAN, PRINCIPAL; POLITICAL VIEWS; WHITMAN, WALTER, SR.

Painters and Painting

Whitman's engagement with the visual arts grew out of his experiences as a journalist in Brooklyn in the 1840s and 1850s. He once admitted spending "[l]ong, long half hours" in front of a single painting (qtd. in Rubin 339) and in his journalistic rambles through Manhattan and Brooklyn focused nearly as much attention on painting as on photography. Whitman valued the creative process and individual achievement over the art product and considered painting's spiritual essence more important than its technical proficiency. Landscape painting, portraiture, and religious subjects elicited his strongest responses, and although he often expressed as much sympathy for a beautifully illustrated book or an inexpensive reproduction as for an original painting, he never wavered in his commitment to the essentiality of the arts in a democracy.

In his reviews, Whitman reserved special praise for the efforts of two of his friends, genre painter Walter Libbey and landscapist Jesse Talbot. He particularly admired the simplicity and democratic egalitarianism implicit in Libbey's rural genre scenes. Tonal gradations resulting from the close observation of nature, muted outlines and a "richness of coloring" adjusted to the scene's temporal requirements were among the formal qualities Whitman admired most (*Uncollected* 1:238).

Whitman regularly reviewed New York's principal art exhibitions and in 1850 and 1851 championed the activities of the struggling Brooklyn Art Union. Like the larger and more established American Art Union, whose president in the mid-1840s was Whitman's friend William Cullen Bryant, the Brooklyn Art Union sponsored exhibitions administered by the artists themselves. Whitman valued both the visual stimulation and the communal spirit manifest in such endeavors and called for the creation of "a close phalanx [of artists], ardent, radical and progressive" to strengthen this country's artistic base (*Uncollected* 1:237). On 31 March 1851 Whitman delivered the keynote address at the organization's first annual distribution of prizes. In this, his only lecture on art, Whitman echoed Emerson in his emphasis on art's moral value and his equation between the "perfect man" and the "perfect artist" (*Uncollected* 1:243). Whitman also stressed art's mediating presence, especially with regard to death, a theme he would develop further in his poetry. Had the federal government not forced the closure of all art unions before the Brooklyn Art Union elected its president, Whitman might well have been chosen, as his friends had placed his name in nomination for the post.

Whitman's fascination with the power inscribed in visual images contributed significantly toward the visual emphasis of his poetry. Scholars have discussed a variety of thematic and structural affinities between Whitman's verse and the contemporaneous artistic modes of genre painting, the diorama, luminism, realism, and impressionism. James Dougherty notes a shift toward a more extended and conventional pictorialist image in Whitman's later poems. At least two of Whitman's last poems, "The Dismantled Ship" and "Death's Valley," were written in response to specific paintings, the last a work by American landscape painter George Inness.

After the Civil War, with both his health and poetic skills in decline, Whitman demonstrated renewed interest in the visual arts. In *Specimen Days* he described spending "two rapt hours" in 1881 viewing a large private collection of the paintings and pastels of the French Barbizon painter Jean-François Millet (*Prose Works* 1:267). Millet's visually subdued yet tonally rich landscapes of French peasants toiling in the fields were phenomenally popular with the American public, who, like Whitman, were attracted by the works' moral and ethical suasion. Years later Whitman confided to Horace Traubel that the thing that most impressed him in Millet's work "was the untold something behind all that was depicted—an essence, a suggestion, an indirection, leading off into the immortal mysteries" (*With Walt Whitman* 2:407). This, coupled with the sympathetic portrayal of ordinary laborers, prompted Whitman to proclaim *Leaves of Grass* "only Millet in another form" (*With Walt Whitman* 1:7).

In painting as in photography, Whitman repeatedly sought visual analogues for his verse, particularly in the painted portraits which he eagerly encouraged and for which he willingly sat. Walter Libbey was the first artist to paint Whitman's portrait from life, and in 1859 Whitman sat for his friend the New York artist Charles Hine. An engraved version of Hine's portrait was chosen as the frontispiece for the 1860 *Leaves of Grass,* the only time Whitman selected a painting as a frontispiece.

During the 1870s and 1880s Whitman enjoyed increasing contact with painters, among them Colonel John R. Johnston, a Camden neighbor with whom he often shared Sunday dinner, and Herbert Gilchrist, son of Whitman's British admirer, Anne Gilchrist. Gilchrist produced at least three oil paintings of the poet, in addition to several sketches of Whitman at Timber Creek and an intaglio which Richard Maurice Bucke chose as the frontispiece for his 1883 Whitman biography. Gilchrist's most successful effort was the seated Whitman portrait (University of Pennsylvania), painted on his return visit in 1887. Painted with the loose brushwork and lighter palette adapted from the impressionists, the painting was widely criticized by Whitman and his circle, who dubbed it the "parlor" Whitman (*With Walt Whitman* 1:39) and mocked the intrusion of the Italian curls into the poet's hair and beard. Whitman was particularly dissatisfied with the portrait's acquiescence to the orthodoxy of the academy, claiming "the Walt Whitman of that picture lacks guts" (*With Walt Whitman* 1:154).

Whitman was no more complimentary about the portrait completed under commission from *Scribner's Monthly* by the rising young American portraitist John White Alexander. Alexander sketched Whitman at his home in February 1886, but in the finished portrait (Metropolitan Museum of Art) abandoned the intimacy and informality of the sketch, which showed Whitman in his reading glasses, for a more distant and patriarchal representation. Alexander's portrait, although generally admired by critics since its completion in 1889, masks Whitman's roughness behind a facade of impeccable dignity and restraint. Whitman harshly criticized the work's idealized presence as representative of what he perceived as the all-too-common tendency among artists to disregard the "real" in favor of the "ideal."

Whitman's favorite among the portrait painters was the Philadelphia-born Thomas Eakins, with whom he shared a dedication to the materiality of the human form and a fascination with the physiognomy of the human countenance. A black and white print of Eakins's gripping *Gross Clinic*, given him by the painter, graced Whitman's parlor, testimony both to their love of science and their history of rejection by their peers. Eakins's half-length portrait of the poet (Pennsylvania Academy of the Fine Arts), which the two men owned jointly, inaugurated the artist's late portrait manner. The painting resonates with the poignancy of old age, a theme with which Whitman himself was grappling in several of the poems in *November Boughs*, published the same year. Whitman especially appreciated the work's simplicity and what he held to be its unmediated presence. As he confided to Traubel, "the subject is not titivated, not artified, not 'improved'—but given simply as in nature" (*With Walt Whitman* 6:416).

Eakins visited Whitman regularly following the completion of the portrait and painted portraits of several Whitman associates, including Talcott Williams, who had introduced them. Two of Eakins's associates, sculptors William R. O'Donovan and Samuel Murray (with whom Eakins fashioned Whitman's death mask) sculpted busts of Whitman in Eakins's studio, and it was there, following Whitman's funeral, that Bucke and others gathered to hear Whitman's friend Weda Cook, a young Camden singer, sing "O Captain! My Captain!"

In the twentieth century Whitman's verse has stimulated considerable response among painters of widely varying stylistic, thematic, and philosophical persuasions. Especially in the early decades of the century, such American painters as Robert Henri, Marsden Hartley, and Joseph Stella discovered in Whitman's poetry an inspiring native voice for their excursions into the unmapped terrain of visual modernism.

Ruth L. Bohan

Bibliography

Alcaro, Marion Walker. *Walt Whitman's Mrs. G: A Biography of Anne Gilchrist*. Madison, N.J.: Fairleigh Dickinson UP, 1991.

Dougherty, James. *Walt Whitman and the Citizen's Eye.* Baton Rouge: Louisiana State UP, 1993.

Miller, Edwin Haviland, ed. *The Artistic Legacy of Walt Whitman.* New York: New York UP, 1969.

Reynolds, David S. *Walt Whitman's America.* New York: Knopf, 1995.

Rubin, Joseph Jay. *The Historic Whitman.* University Park: Pennsylvania State UP, 1973.

Sill, Geoffrey M., and Roberta K. Tarbell, eds. *Walt Whitman and the Visual Arts.* New Brunswick, N.J.: Rutgers UP, 1992.

Traubel, Horace. *With Walt Whitman in Camden.* Vol. 1. 1906. New York: Rowman and Littlefield, 1961; Vol. 2. 1908. New York: Rowman and Littlefield, 1961; Vol. 6. Ed. Gertrude Traubel and William White. Carbondale: Southern Illinois UP, 1982.

Whitman, Walt. *The Gathering of the Forces.* Ed. Cleveland Rodgers and John Black. 2 vols. New York: Putnam, 1920.

———. *Prose Works 1892.* Ed. Floyd Stovall. 2 vols. New York: New York UP, 1963–1964.

———. *The Uncollected Poetry and Prose of Walt Whitman.* Ed. Emory Holloway. 2 vols. Garden City, N.Y.: Doubleday, Page, 1921.

See also "DEATH'S VALLEY"; EAKINS, THOMAS; GILCHRIST, HERBERT HARLAKENDEN; MILLET, JEAN-FRANÇOIS; PHOTOGRAPHS AND PHOTOGRAPHERS; SCULPTORS AND SCULPTURE

Pantheism

Pantheism involves a belief in the complete identity of God and the world, the idea that everything is God and God is everything, and the conviction that everything in the universe is sacred. A poetic description of pantheism is found in Alexander Pope's *Essay on Man* (1733): "All are but parts of one stupendous whole / Whose body Nature is, and God the soul."

Pantheistic strains are found throughout *Leaves of Grass* and Whitman's prose works. In an 1847 journal entry Whitman suggests that the "soul or spirit transmits itself into all matter" (Whitman 57) such as rocks and trees and even earth, sun, and stars. "The unseen is proven by the seen," the poet adds in "Song of Myself" (section 3). He beholds God in "every object"

and even finds "letters from God dropt in the street" (section 48). Here the pantheistic element in Whitman's thought becomes clear. Whitman is attempting to erase the usual dichotomy found between spirit and matter, as in this passage from "Song of Myself": "I have said that the soul is not more than the body, / And I have said that the body is not more than the soul, / And nothing, not God, is greater to one than one's self is" (section 48).

Karl Shapiro says in *Start with the Sun* that Whitman was trying "to obliterate the fatal dualism of body and soul" (Miller, Shapiro, and Slote 67). In *Studies in Classic American Literature* D.H. Lawrence adds that Whitman "was the first to smash the old moral conception that the soul of man is something 'superior' and 'above' the flesh" (184). Whitman was "as nearly pure pantheist as anything else" (6), Floyd Stovall notes in "Main Drifts in Whitman's Poetry," but "drifted" over his lifetime from a "materialism pantheism" in the direction of a highly "spiritualized idealism" (21). Gay Wilson Allen, in *A Reader's Guide to Walt Whitman*, notes that Whitman wanted to establish a new religion in which "man would worship the divinity incarnated in himself" (21).

Many observers, including Henry David Thoreau, noted similarities between *Leaves of Grass* and the philosophy of Hinduism, which centers on "non dualism" and which sees God and the world as one. In *Whitman in the Light of Vedantic Mysticism* (1964), originally written as a dissertation for Benares Hindu University in India, V.K. Chari details some of those similarities.

It would seem to be impossible to categorize Whitman's work in one single category. Certainly elements of materialism and naturalism are also found there. Pantheism has to be one of the categories to be considered, however, in any adequate understanding of Whitman's thought.

Ronald W. Knapp

Bibliography

Allen, Gay Wilson. *A Reader's Guide to Walt Whitman.* 1970. New York: Octagon, 1986.

Brennan, Joseph Gerard. *The Meaning of Philosophy.* New York: Harper and Row, 1953.

Chari, V.K. *Whitman in the Light of Vedantic Mysticism.* Lincoln: U of Nebraska P, 1965.

Lawrence, D.H. *Studies in Classic American Literature*. New York: Boni and Liveright, 1923.

Miller, James E., Jr., Karl Shapiro, and Bernice Slote. *Start With the Sun: Studies in Cosmic Poetry*. Lincoln: U of Nebraska P, 1960.

Stovall, Floyd. "Main Drifts in Whitman's Poetry." *American Literature* 4 (1932): 3–21.

Whitman, Walt. *Notebooks and Unpublished Prose Manuscripts*. Ed. Edward F. Grier. Vol. 1. New York: New York UP, 1984.

See also HINDU LITERATURE; MYSTICISM; RELIGION

Parodies

Although Whitman himself was not a parodist, he has been much parodied. In 1888, Walter Hamilton included him in the fifth and last volume of his vast collection of parodies of English and American authors. Hamilton pointed out that most of the parodies of Whitman were unfair because so few people had actually read him; it was therefore impossible for readers ignorant of the original to appreciate the parody. In an attempt to remedy this situation, Hamilton provided an excerpt from "Song of Myself," as well as a few minor poems from *Leaves of Grass*. Most of these early parodies collected by Hamilton ridicule Whitman's notorious (alleged) egotism: the earliest (1868) shows no understanding of Whitman's Self expanded beyond mere ego: "I am Walt Whitman. / You are an idiot" (Hamilton 257). A similar sentiment is expressed in a parody that appeared in *Judy* (a publication that favored rhyming over free verse) in 1884.

Occasionally, Whitman's celebratory and incantatory tone was parodied not so much to poke fun at him but to ridicule someone else: e.g., Walter Parke's "St. Smith of Utah" finds Whitman's idiom particularly appropriate for a mock-heroic mistreatment of the patron saint of the Mormons, who "profited" from his role as a "prophet" and is summed up as a "boss saint" (Hamilton 261–262). As one might expect, most parodies of Whitman's style lack his genius for converting mere "inventories" into song (despite Emerson's famous complaint). Readers whose ears were used to traditional verse could not recognize the musical qualities of Whitman's free verse; their parodies often make this pain-

fully clear: e.g., H.C. Bunner's frequently anthologized "Home Sweet Home with Variations (As Walt Whitman might have written all around it.)" (1881). Far more tedious than any of Whitman's catalogues, Bunner's evokes the quotidian with more banality than Whitman was ever capable of. More successful is the anonymous "A Whitman Waif," hilariously incoherent as it enumerates a Whitmanesque catalogue of cities and states, then intrudes editorially: "The poet's MS is here lost in space. [See] Colton's Intermediate Geography" (Falk 138).

Some parodies were downright mean-spirited, like Richard Grant White's "After Walt Whitman" (1884), which does occasionally succeed at exaggerating Whitman's exuberance into gush: "Put all of you and all of me together, and agitate our particles by rubbing us up into eternal smash . . ." (Falk 135). But mainly White views Whitman as a drunken, disreputable boaster reveling in physical corruption—"Of the purity of compost heaps . . . and the ineffable sweetness of general corruption" (Falk 135)—while remaining naive about political corruption—"Of the honesty and general incorruptibility of political bosses" (Falk 136). White especially takes umbrage at Whitman's vision "Of the beauty of flat-nosed, pock-marked" Africans (Falk 135), whom Whitman supposedly extols over genteel respectable white men, who are of no more account "than a possum or a woodchuck" (Falk 137).

Most Whitman parodies are more reverent, however; some even aspire to emulate rather than ridicule Whitman (e.g., Bayard Taylor's "Camerados" [1876]). Swinburne's "The Poet and the Woodlouse," though included in Carolyn Wells's *A Parody Anthology* (1922), is not a parody at all—it is a reverent rhyming variation on a theme in "Out of the Cradle Endlessly Rocking."

By far the funniest and most famous of parodies of Whitman is E.B. White's "A Classic Waits for Me" (1944), obviously spoofing "A Woman Waits for Me," with amusing allusions to other poems ("Into an armchair endlessly rocking") (Macdonald 145). Unlike most of the early parodies by Whitman's contemporaries, "A Classic" does not satirize Whitman (to whom he apologizes). Instead, White imitates his celebratory voice to gently mock the pseudo-elitist exclusivity of the Classics Club: "And I will not read a book nor the least part of a book but has the approval of the Committee . . ." (Macdonald 146).

G.K. Chesterton also wrote a Whitman parody, as part of a parodic cluster of "Variations . . . on Old King Cole" (1932). Again, Whitman himself is not the butt of satire; rather, his style is appropriated by the parodist for mock-heroic effect. Perhaps the cleverest parody of Whitman, besides E.B. White's, is Helen Gray Cone's verse dialogue, "Narcissus in Camden: A Classical Dialogue of the Year 1882" (Zaranka 211–214). Whitman's name in the poem is Paumanokides, and his interlocutor (it becomes clear when one recalls that the two writers met and chatted that year in Camden) is Oscar Wilde, called here "Narcissus." The poem records, in stanzas alternating between Whitman-like free verse and Wilde-like Swinburnesque doggerel, an actual conversation they had about aestheticism. That Whitman may have confided to Wilde that he too was gay is also implied in the poem, which satirizes Wilde's narcissism and seems to side with Whitman.

Parodies of Whitman, then, seem to fall into three categories: those that ridicule him, those that revere or emulate him, and those that imitate his style to satirize someone or something else.

Joseph Andriano

Bibliography

Falk, Robert P., ed. *American Literature in Parody*. New York: Twayne, 1955.

Hamilton, Walter, ed. *Parodies of the Works of English and American Authors*. 1888. Vol. 5. New York: Johnson Reprint, 1967.

Macdonald, Dwight, ed. *Parodies: An Anthology from Chaucer to Beerbohm—and After*. New York: Random House, 1960.

Saunders, Henry S., comp. *Parodies on Walt Whitman*. New York: American Library Service, 1923.

Wells, Carolyn, ed. *A Parody Anthology*. New York: Scribner's, 1922.

Zaranka, William, ed. *The Brand-X Anthology of Poetry. A Parody Anthology*. Cambridge, Mass.: Apple-Wood Books, 1981.

See also HUMOR

Parton, James (1822–1891)

Before establishing himself as a popular biographer in the 1850s, James Parton worked as a writer and editor for N.P. Willis's popular magazine *The New York Home Journal*. Parton chose to leave journalism in 1854 when he signed a contract to write *The Life of Horace Greeley*. The research and narrative methods that Parton subsequently developed earned him the epithet "father of modern biography." Parton's biography of Andrew Jackson (1860) is considered a classic of nineteenth-century historical writing. In reviewing Jackson's many biographers Robert V. Remini concludes that Parton "cut deeply into his subject . . . striking the hard bone of Jackson's personality" (xxx).

Parton and Whitman knew each other as members of New York's journalistic and literary community. Shortly after Parton's 1854 marriage to the newspaper columnist Fanny Fern (Sara Willis), Whitman became a frequent visitor in the Parton-Fern household. This friendship turned sour over a two-hundred-dollar loan which Parton made to Whitman in 1857. Whitman's failure to repay the loan led to a lawsuit in which some of his personal property was seized. This scandal embarrassed Whitman and, apparently, he blamed Parton's wife for the lawsuit and its outcome. When queried about the incident late in life, Whitman held that Fanny Fern "kept alive what . . . James Parton would have let die" (Traubel 236). Following Fern's death in 1872 Parton continued to write productively, focusing especially on historically important women, but never rekindled his friendship with Whitman.

T. Gregory Garvey

Bibliography

Flower, Milton E. *James Parton, The Father of Modern Biography*. Durham: Duke UP, 1951.

Remini, Robert V. Introduction. *The Presidency of Andrew Jackson*. By James Parton. New York: Harper and Row, 1967. vii–xxx.

Reynolds, David S. *Walt Whitman's America*. New York: Knopf, 1995.

Traubel, Horace. *With Walt Whitman in Camden*. Vol. 3. New York: Mitchell Kennerley, 1914.

See also PARTON, SARA PAYSON WILLIS (FANNY FERN)

Parton, Sara Payson Willis (Fanny Fern) (1811–1872)

Sara Payson Willis Parton took the pseudonym "Fanny Fern" in 1851 while she was writing several articles a week for two Boston newspapers, the *Olive Branch* and the *True Flag*. By 1856, the year her husband, James Parton, introduced her to his friend Walt Whitman, Fanny Fern had become a famous woman. The author of four books, including a best-selling novel, *Ruth Hall,* Fern was also the celebrated author of weekly articles for the New York *Ledger* and the first woman in America to be a professional newspaper columnist. Although Fern wrote about many social issues, especially the status of women and women's rights, she was also interested in the place of literature and the arts in American life.

Impressed by Whitman's originality, Fern published first a brief comment on Whitman's fine speaking voice in an article on New York celebrities for the *Ledger* on 19 April 1856 and then a laudatory review of *Leaves of Grass* on 10 May 1856. She was the first woman to praise Whitman's generally unnoticed book. Calling attention to the contrast between Whitman's "fresh, hardy" poems and "forced, stiff, Parnassian exotics," Fern applauded the "unmingled delight" of *Leaves of Grass* and defended Whitman against charges of coarseness and sensuality ("Fresh Fern" 4). The emerging friendship between Fern and Whitman was short-lived, for reasons that have been a subject of some highly charged speculation among Whitman biographers. But recent studies of Fern's life suggest a fairly straightforward story. Accepting a loan of two hundred dollars from James Parton as an advance against payment he was to receive for a "literary project" (Warren, "Subversion" 60), Whitman was unable to pay his debt when it was due in February 1857. The unpaid loan, as well as the Partons' feeling that they had been ill used by a friend, ended the relationship.

Susan Belasco Smith

Bibliography

Coad, Oral S. "Whitman *vs.* Parton." *The Journal of the Rutgers University Library* 4 (1940): 1–8.

Fern, Fanny. "Fresh Fern Leaves: *Leaves of Grass.*" New York *Ledger* 10 May 1856: 4.

———. *Ruth Hall and Other Writings.* Ed. Joyce W. Warren. New Brunswick, N.J.: Rutgers UP, 1986.

Kaplan, Justin. *Walt Whitman: A Life.* New York: Simon and Schuster, 1980.

Warren, Joyce W. *Fanny Fern: An Independent Woman.* New Brunswick, N.J.: Rutgers UP, 1992.

———. "Subversion versus Celebration: The Aborted Friendship of Fanny Fern and Walt Whitman." *Patrons and Protegees: Gender, Friendship, and Writing in Nineteenth-Century America.* Ed. Shirley Marchalonis. New Brunswick, N.J.: Rutgers UP, 1988. 59–93.

See also PARTON, JAMES; WOMEN AS A THEME IN WHITMAN'S WRITING

"Passage to India" (1871)

First appearing in 1871 in a separate publication containing the title poem, a few other new poems, and a number of poems previously published in *Leaves of Grass,* "Passage to India" was subsequently included in a 120-page supplement to the fifth edition of *Leaves of Grass* in 1871. Some printings of the 1871 edition contained the supplement, but, hoping for additional revenue, Whitman also had the supplement issued separately. The chronology of the poem's composition is not entirely clear, but portions were written as early as 1868, a year before the appearance of two of the three modern achievements that the poem extols. In 1869, the Suez Canal was completed, as was the Union and Central Pacific transcontinental railroad. The third achievement, the completion of the Atlantic cable, had taken place four years earlier in 1866.

The last major poem of Whitman's career, "Passage to India" celebrates the achievement of material science and industry, but the poem merely used these physical forms to accomplish what he termed the "unfolding of cosmic purposes" (Traubel 167). In his mature years, Whitman returned to the dominant theme of the early poems: the transcendental journey to the Soul. With the world linked by the modern wonders of transportation and communication, Whitman envisioned a world ready for its final accomplishment: the creation of spiritual unity.

The poet in section 5 presents himself as the "true son of God, the poet" who will settle the doubts of man (Adam and Eve) and justify their innate desire for exploration. The poet will assuage such doubts by showing that the world is not disjoined and diffuse, but integrated and whole. Part of that integration must entail an account of the past, a time in which previous explorers, like Columbus, failed. To transform previous failure into success, the poet celebrates America, the continent that Columbus discovered accidentally but which ultimately gave reality to his dream of connecting East and West.

In section 7 the poet begins to express his impatience with waiting for the Soul to make its journey to "primal thought," to "realms of budding bibles." At the beginning of section 8, the poet urges the Soul to action, and in that section and the last, the poet celebrates the exuberant flight of the Soul. Through reconciling the thoughts and deeds of the past, the Soul, merged with the poet, unleashes itself in flight toward a merger with God, "the Comrade perfect."

"Passage to India" can be approached on at least three levels: the philosophical, the political, and the aesthetic. Philosophically, the poem is thoroughly transcendental. The title suggests Whitman's longtime interest in the East and in mysticism. India represents the historical cradle of civilization and religion and also the ultimate goal of the spiritual journey, yet, as Whitman says at the beginning of the poem's last section, the goal is "Passage to more than India!" (section 9). Whitman's brand of mysticism was Western at its core, embracing the physical world as a vehicle to the spiritual. Hegelian in his conception of progress, Whitman sees an ongoing confrontation of opposites (physical and spiritual, ancient and modern, life and death), a mediation between them, and the creation of a new entity that enters into an endless cycle of creation. The physical is just as vital as is the spiritual to provide a pathway to the Soul.

In "Crossing Brooklyn Ferry," Whitman referred to physical phenomena as the "dumb, beautiful ministers" (section 9) that provide the pathway to the Soul. A decade and a half later, he returned to his transcendental argument—that spirituality will be achieved through an embracing of the physical world, not through its denial. Yet the poem does not convey the gritty physical realities of the early poems. In "Passage to India," the achievements of modern science are linked to the monumental wonders of the ancient world. However, Whitman presents them as far less robust entities than even the everyday Brooklyn ferry and its passengers. In the first section of "Passage to India," the poet praises the "light works" of engineers and the "gentle wires" of modern communication. Later, in section 3, the steel rails that cross the American continent are envisioned as "duplicate slender lines." For Whitman, modern science and technology, no less than religion and art, unify the world, dissolve the limits of time and space, and connect the individual to God.

But in his last great poetic effort—what Gay Wilson Allen likened to Milton's epic justification of God's ways to man—Whitman's vision, as had his language, had softened. Even the Soul itself, which he terms "thou actual Me," operates gently (section 8). The Soul "gently masterest the orbs" (section 8). For many years, Whitman had repeated his transcendental praise of unity and had insisted upon it even as he graphically constructed an earthy, multitudinous panorama. In "Passage to India" he is too impatient to construct the panorama, and he yearns for the journey to be accomplished. "Have we not stood here like trees in the ground long enough?" he asks (section 9).

Politically, "Passage to India" can be seen as a questioning of the materialistic values of the Gilded Age. On one hand, Whitman embraces American capitalism and its products. David Reynolds sees a marked difference in Whitman's depiction of capitalism and labor in the early poems and in the later poems. In the early poems, he says, Whitman praises individual laborers; in his later poems he extols the virtues of industry and the workforce, not workers. The armies of the past would be replaced by "armies" of workers. However, as Reynolds notes, Whitman was not entirely comfortable with America's growing materialism. In *Democratic Vistas*, completed the same year as "Passage to India," Whitman envisioned America evolving beyond its preoccupation with commerce. Betsy Erkkila sees in the poem the same repudiation of materialistic values as it "leaps" toward spiritual transcendence, but she sees also a reconciliation of materialism and spiritualism in the figure of Columbus. In Columbus, Erkkila argues, Whitman found his ideal merger of the explorer of the physical world and the religious prophet whose dream of reaching India had been achieved through the creation of an industrialized nation. The poet then becomes the spiritual heir of Columbus. As the poet-explorer, he could praise both individualism and national unity.

The poem's aesthetic qualities have earned it mixed reviews. For some readers, Whitman's turning to traditional poetic diction ("thee," "thou," "seest") is disappointing. For others, like Stanley Coffman, the poem's imagery more than compensates. For Coffman, the dominant motif of the poem is metamorphosis, and Whitman uses images of "passage" of forms into higher forms, spiraling to the Soul. He connects the past with the present, the present with the future, with images of projection; the natural growth of the past into the present projects or propels the present into the future. A duality of images reconciles a duality of concepts.

If "Passage to India" is less pleasing than Whitman's earlier verse, the reason is not because the poem deals with a more abstract or "universal" theme. The striving for a transcendent state is the theme of both "Passage to India" and the major early poems. Aside from its archaic language, what marks the poem is its self-constraint and self-containment. Lacking are the grand catalogues of the early poems and the personal, oratorical appeals to the reader. Whitman was master of both the long and the short lyric. "A Noiseless Patient Spider," one of the poems included in the *Passage to India* supplement, illustrates well Whitman's mastery of the short form. Both poems echo each other. Adam and Eve in "Passage to India" are said to be "wandering, yearning, curious, with restless explorations" (section 5). The speaker on his journey to the Soul passes the "Promontory" (section 3). In both poems he was dealing with the figure of the poet striving to reach the Soul through making connections among physical phenomena. Without the catalogues, the interspersed narratives, and the expansive rhetorical features of the early long poems, Whitman's talent, at least for some readers, found its best expression in the short poem such as "A Noiseless Patient Spider."

John B. Mason

Bibliography

Coffman, Stanley K., Jr. "Form and Meaning in Whitman's 'Passage to India.'" *PMLA* 70 (1955): 337–349.

Erkkila, Betsy. *Whitman the Political Poet.* New York: Oxford UP, 1989.

Lovell, John, Jr. "Appreciating Whitman: 'Passage to India.'" *MLQ* 21 (1960): 131–141.

Reynolds, David S. *Walt Whitman's America: A Cultural Biography.* New York: Knopf, 1995.

Traubel, Horace. *With Walt Whitman in Camden.* Vol. 1. Boston: Small, Maynard, 1906.

See also COLUMBUS, CHRISTOPHER; *LEAVES OF GRASS, 1871–1872 EDITION*; SOUL, THE; TECHNOLOGY

"Patroling Barnegat" (1880)

In the 1881 edition of *Leaves of Grass,* Whitman placed "Patroling Barnegat" as the second to last poem in the "Sea-Drift" cluster, a rather important position because, with this poem, the cluster moves toward its closure. "Patroling Barnegat" was originally published in June 1880 in *The American* and then reprinted in April of 1881 in *Harper's Monthly* and remained in its penultimate position in the "Sea-Drift" cluster in the Deathbed edition of *Leaves of Grass.*

"Patroling Barnegat" is broken into two linked sections, the first of which describes the wild and stormy sea as it crashes on the beach during a windy night and the second of which describes a coast patrol as it watches for wrecked vessels and confronts the sea and the wind. The poem has often been noted for its evocative power as it represents, through its use of the present participle, of assonance and consonance, and of specific metrical patterns, the terror and force of the sea and the pathos of humans struggling against their environment.

However, read in the context of the "Sea-Drift" cluster as a whole and the cluster's movement toward recognition of the immortality of the human soul, the poem appears less dark. While "Patroling Barnegat" seems to describe a confrontation with death and mortality, such a confrontation, when read with the other poems in the cluster, and especially the final poem, "After the Sea-Ship," only heralds the ultimate immortality of humanity.

A. James Wohlpart

Bibliography

Chari, V.K. "Whitman Criticism in the Light of Indian Poetics." *Walt Whitman: The Centennial Essays.* Ed. Ed Folsom. Iowa City: U of Iowa P, 1994. 240–250.

Fast, Robin Riley. "Structure and Meaning in Whitman's *Sea-Drift.*" *American Transcendental Quarterly* 53 (1982): 49–66.

French, R.W. "Whitman's Dark Sea: A Note on 'Patroling Barnegat.'" *Walt Whitman Quarterly Review* 1.3 (1983): 50–52.

Haynes, Gregory M. "Running Aground in Barnegat Bay: Whitman's Symbols and Their Rhetorical Intentionalities." *Walt Whitman: Here and Now.* Ed. Joann P. Krieg. Westport, Conn.: Greenwood, 1985. 115–124.

Malbone, Raymond G. "Organic Language in 'Patroling Barnegat.'" *Walt Whitman Review* 13 (1967): 125–127.

Whitman, Walt. *Leaves of Grass*. Ed. Sculley
 Bradley and Harold W. Blodgett. Norton
 Critical Edition. New York: Norton,
 1973.
Wohlpart, A. James. "From Outsetting Bard
 to Mature Poet: Whitman's 'Out of the
 Cradle' and the *Sea-Drift* Cluster." *Walt
 Whitman Quarterly Review* 9 (1991):
 77–90.

See also LEAVES OF GRASS, 1881–1882
EDITION; SEA, THE; "SEA-DRIFT"

Pennell, Joseph (1857–1926), and Elizabeth Robins (1855–1936)

Joseph Pennell and Elizabeth Robins were
friends of Whitman in Camden, New Jersey.
Pennell was an etcher who illustrated and/or
wrote more than one hundred books. Robins
was a writer and collaborator with Pennell
who had met Whitman in her youth in Camden.

Pennell was born in Philadelphia, and he
attended Quaker schools. By 1880 he opened
his own art studio. Pennell did illustrations for
many well-known writers, including George
Washington Cable, William Dean Howells,
Washington Irving, and Henry James. Pennell
and Robins were married in 1884, and the following year they produced *A Canterbury Pilgrimage* (1885), a collection of his sketches and
her annotations. Pennell started an art criticism
column for the London *Star*. Robins, however,
soon began writing for the column and for the
London *Daily Chronicle* as well.

Pennell's style was clearly influenced by
Whistler, while his technique was influenced by
Charles S. Reinhart. Together, Pennell and Robins published *The Life of James McNeill Whistler* (1908). Pennell later published *The Whistler Journal* (1921). After Pennell and Robins
died, the Library of Congress acquired their
estate and founded the Chalcographic Museum,
which contained both the Whistler and Pennell
collections.

Pennell and Robins were contemporaries
of Whitman, and their work was published
extensively in his lifetime. Pennell's illustrations
were in many works Whitman would have read,
and Whitman knew them both from contacts in
the bohemian artist area of Camden in which
Robins had lived and which all three artists
often visited.

Paula K. Garrett

Bibliography

Allen, Gay Wilson. *The Solitary Singer: A
 Critical Biography of Walt Whitman*.
 1955. Rev. ed. 1967. Chicago: U of Chicago P, 1985.
Baigell, Matthew. *Dictionary of American
 Art*. New York: Harper and Row, 1979.
Traubel, Horace. *With Walt Whitman in
 Camden*. Vol. 1. Boston: Small,
 Maynard, 1906.

See also CAMDEN, NEW JERSEY; PAINTERS
AND PAINTING

Periodicals Devoted to Whitman

Periodicals devoted to the study of Whitman's
poetry, ideas, and influence began to appear
around the time of the poet's death and have in
recent years proliferated. The earliest such periodical was Horace Traubel's monthly paper,
The Conservator, which he published in Philadelphia from March 1890 until his death in
1919. Devoted to Felix Adler's Ethical Movement, the paper endorsed a wide range of social
and philosophical reform movements, from
socialism to antivivisectionism, but above all it
carried articles about Whitman, usually offering socialist reform readings of his work (a typical title of an essay was "Walt Whitman's Significance to a Revolutionist"). Traubel also
regularly printed his own Whitman-inspired
poetry and prose, along with poems about Whitman by other writers. Whitman's words from
Democratic Vistas—"Moral conscientiousness,
crystalline, without flaw, not godlike only, entirely human, awes and enchants forever"—
appeared on the masthead, and ads for and reviews of Whitman's books and books about
Whitman appeared in every issue.

Traubel was also instrumental in setting up
the Walt Whitman Fellowship, an organization
formally begun in 1894 and devoted to the
study of Whitman. This group met regularly in
New York, Boston, and Philadelphia and issued
a set of *Walt Whitman Fellowship Papers*—124
of them over twenty-four years (the number of
issues per year varied from two to fifteen). Most
of the issues were devoted to the business and
programs of the fellowship, but thirty of the
issues contained brief but valuable articles about
Whitman by writers like Richard Maurice
Bucke, Charlotte Porter, Oscar Lovell Triggs,
and Thomas Harned. In 1895, Kelly Miller of
Howard University gave a speech to the fellow-

ship on "What Walt Whitman Means to the Negro"; it was published as Paper 10 that year, the first extended written comment by an African American about Whitman's significance. Like *The Conservator*, the *Fellowship Papers* ceased with Traubel's death in 1919.

The Whitman Fellowship had by this time spawned chapters in other cities, and one of the most active was in Toronto, Canada. The Canadian branch of the fellowship was centered on what came to be known as the Whitman Club of Bon Echo, and this group published a little magazine called *The Sunset of Bon Echo;* six issues appeared from 1916 through 1920. Flora MacDonald Denison edited the journal and wrote many of its articles; other notable contributors included Traubel and Charlotte Perkins Gilman. Denison died in 1921, and the journal died with her.

With the death of the first generation of Whitmanites, no journals devoted to Whitman's work appeared for the next couple of decades. But when the state of New Jersey in 1947 took title to Whitman's Mickle Street house in Camden, the Walt Whitman Foundation (which had in 1946 reorganized and renamed itself, while tracing its lineage back to the original Walt Whitman Fellowship) began to issue *The Walt Whitman Foundation Bulletin*. The first number appeared in 1948; it was an annual publication with regular contributions by such distinguished scholars as Gay Wilson Allen, Sculley Bradley, and Robert E. Spiller. The journal lasted, however, only through 1955, with its final issue celebrating the centennial of the first edition of *Leaves of Grass*.

Another Camden-based annual Whitman journal began publication in 1979, this one sponsored by the successor to the foundation, the Walt Whitman Association. Edited by Geoffrey M. Sill, *The Mickle Street Review* initially focused on poems, stories, and essays celebrating Whitman or showing his influence, but during the final few years (1988–1990), the journal presented the collected papers from important annual Whitman conferences sponsored by the Whitman Studies Program at the Rutgers University Camden campus. These issues—"Whitman and the World," "Whitman and the Foundations of America," "Whitman, Sex, and Gender," and "Whitman and the Visual Arts"—contained work by many eminent Whitman scholars and commentators, and most of these essays were later published in two books (*Walt Whitman and the Visual Arts* and *Walt Whitman of Mickle Street*).

The Walt Whitman Birthplace Association in Huntington, Long Island, organized in 1949, began issuing its own journal, the *Walt Whitman Birthplace Bulletin,* in the fall of 1957. A mixture of association news and short articles about Whitman's life and work, the journal, edited by Verne Dyson, lasted only four years. However, in 1979 the Birthplace Association began another journal, *West Hills Review: A Walt Whitman Journal*. Dedicated to publishing both original poetry and Whitman scholarship, this annual publication lasted until 1988. Over the years, it emphasized poetry far more than scholarship, although significant essays by critics like Gay Wilson Allen, Joann Krieg, Aaron Kramer, and Harold Blodgett appeared there. In 1995, the Birthplace Association restarted *West Hills Review* in a much reduced format.

The first academic journal devoted to Whitman studies had a modest beginning as a four-page newsletter, the *Walt Whitman Newsletter,* initially developed by Gay Wilson Allen to publicize events and publications during the 1955 centennial celebration of the first edition of *Leaves of Grass*. Published for free by New York University Press (which had just announced plans for the *Collected Writings of Walt Whitman* project), the newsletter was slated to cease at the end of 1955; the press and Allen had no interest in carrying it on. Scholars, however, found Allen's newsletter so valuable that they wanted it continued, and a Detroit Whitman collector, Charles Feinberg, along with William White, a professor at Wayne State University, decided to take on the task, with backing from the Wayne State University Press. Beginning in 1956, the *Walt Whitman Newsletter* quickly became the central outlet for Whitman scholarship. By 1959 the publication had grown beyond newsletter size and was renamed the *Walt Whitman Review*. Under White's editorship, and with an advisory board of Allen, Blodgett, and Sculley Bradley, the *Review* became the place where a whole generation of Whitman scholars first saw their work in print (Harold Aspiz, Mutlu Blasing, Florence Freedman, Scott Giantvalley, George B. Hutchinson, Karl Keller, M. Jimmie Killingsworth, Donald D. Kummings, Jerome Loving, and M. Wynn Thomas are just a few prominent Whitman scholars whose early work appeared there). White also oversaw the production of several special issues and publications, including *Walt Whitman in Europe Today* and *Walt Whitman's Journalism,* White's valuable bibliography of Whitman's newspaper pieces.

In 1982 Wayne State University Press abruptly withdrew its support of the *Review,* and White and Feinberg joined with Ed Folsom to move the journal to the University of Iowa, where, sponsored by Iowa's Graduate College and English Department, it was recast as the *Walt Whitman Quarterly Review.* With White and Folsom as coeditors and an editorial board made up of some of the most renowned Whitman scholars (Allen, Harold Aspiz, Roger Asselineau, Betsy Erkkila, Arthur Golden, Loving, James E. Miller, Jr., and Thomas), the journal grew in size, began to referee submissions rigorously, and published more substantial essays. *WWQR* continued the tradition of special book-length issues, including a complete collection of Whitman photographs, edited by Folsom, and a supplementary volume of Whitman's correspondence, edited by Edwin Haviland Miller. Folsom took over sole editorship of the journal in 1990. In addition to critical and biographical essays, *WWQR* now publishes shorter notes, reviews of Whitman-related books, news of interest to Whitman scholars, and an ongoing annotated bibliography of work about Whitman; each volume of the journal contains over two hundred pages.

There have been a variety of other, smaller Whitman-related serials. In 1959, the *Long Islander,* the newspaper Whitman founded and edited, began publishing a "Walt Whitman Page" (later a "Supplement") each year, containing short articles by leading Whitman experts, usually around a single theme. The Whitman Supplement was reprinted and widely distributed. Guest-edited by various Whitman scholars until 1974, the supplement from that point on was compiled by William White until it was discontinued after the 1985 issue. In Japan, William L. Moore of Toho Gakuen University of Music edited *Calamus: Walt Whitman Quarterly, International* from 1969 through 1986. Twenty-eight issues appeared during its seventeen-year run, each with a handsome calligraphy cover printed on fine Japanese paper. Advised by an international group of Whitman scholars, Moore included in his journal a variety of reprinted essays, essays with an international perspective, and his own essays endorsing evolution as the key to understanding Whitman's work.

Various Whitman organizations and interest groups have in recent years issued newsletters, which often contain short essays on Whitman. The Walt Whitman Association in Camden publishes *Conversations* (1990–); the Walt Whitman Birthplace Association on Long Island publishes *Starting from Paumanok* (1984–); the Leisure World Walt Whitman Circle in California sponsors a quarterly newsletter edited by Robert Strassburg, *The Walt Whitman Circle* (1991–); Fredrick Berndt of San Francisco edited *The Bulletin of the Walt Whitman Music Library* (1993–1994); and Bruce Noll publishes an occasional newsletter about Whitman performance, *Afoot and Lighthearted* (1992–).

Ed Folsom

Bibliography

Greenland, Cyril, and John Robert Colombo, eds. *Walt Whitman's Canada.* Willowdale, Ontario: Houslow, 1992.

Hutchinson, George B. "Whitman and the Black Poet: Kelly Miller's Speech to the Walt Whitman Fellowship." *American Literature* 61 (1989): 46–58.

Sill, Geoffrey M., ed. *Walt Whitman of Mickle Street.* Knoxville: U of Tennessee P, 1994.

Sill, Geoffrey M., and Roberta K. Tarbell, eds. *Walt Whitman and the Visual Arts.* New Brunswick, N.J.: Rutgers UP, 1992.

White, William. "The Walt Whitman Fellowship: An Account of Its Organization and a Checklist of Its Papers." *Papers of the Bibliographical Society of America* 51 (1957): 67–84, 167–169.

See also ALLEN, GAY WILSON; ASSOCIATIONS, CLUBS, FELLOWSHIPS, FOUNDATIONS, AND SOCIETIES; BON ECHO; CAMDEN, NEW JERSEY; CANADA, WHITMAN'S RECEPTION IN; DENISON, FLORA MACDONALD; JAPAN, WHITMAN IN; *LONG ISLANDER;* MICKLE STREET HOUSE; TRAUBEL, HORACE L.

Perry, Bliss (1860–1954)

Bliss Perry was born in Williamstown, Massachusetts, and graduated from Williams College in 1881. Two years later he took his M.A. and then studied abroad for two years. In 1893 he became a professor at Princeton University, but he resigned in 1899 to become editor of the *Atlantic Monthly,* a position he held until 1909. In 1907 he joined the faculty at Harvard as a professor of literature, taking the chair vacated by James Russell Lowell.

Perry wrote fiction, literary biography, and criticism. He was an authority on Ralph Waldo Emerson's life and work. In 1906 he published *Walt Whitman,* considered a model of literary biography. A second edition appeared in 1908. Though he gathered material from S. Weir Mitchell, E.C. Stedman, John Burroughs, Talcott Williams, J.T. Trowbridge, Horace Traubel, and others who knew Whitman personally, Perry's book was one of the first to approach Whitman with objectivity, eschewing the hero worship found in previous biographies.

Perry was also one of the first critics to note the parallels of certain passages from Whitman's poetry with the speeches of Krishna in the *Bhagavad-Gita.*

Philip W. Leon

Bibliography

"Perry, Bliss." *The National Cyclopedia of American Biography.* Vol. 46. 1893. Ann Arbor, Mich.: University Microfilms, 1967. 50.

Perry, Bliss. *Walt Whitman: His Life and Work.* Boston: Houghton Mifflin, 1906.

See also ATLANTIC MONTHLY, THE; BIOGRAPHIES

Personae

While consistently natural and unaffected in his personal relationships with family and friends, Whitman nevertheless projected, with deliberate artifice, several distinct public personae during the years he was, as newspaperman or as poet, subject to public scrutiny. In his awareness of the power of photography and journalism to create desired identities, Whitman was significantly ahead of his time. His efforts at self-promotion, however, had little effect in achieving their purpose of gaining a large audience for himself and his poems.

Whitman's projection of public "image," however, was not entirely artifice, for always it had much to do with his conception of a self appropriate to his desires. To a certain extent, particularly in his later years, he *became* what he imagined himself to be, and the evidence is in the poetry as well as in his public pronouncements. Whitman seems to have had a remarkable ability to will himself into being.

As a young reporter and editor in the 1840s, Whitman appeared as a stylish and worldly man about town, a sophisticated denizen of the great cities of Brooklyn and Manhattan; then,

as the poetry began to take form in the early 1850s, he adopted in certain poems and other writings the identity of a common man, a carpenter, Christlike and mystical, one whose intuitive awareness embraced the entire universe and its mysterious ways. While not completely abandoning this pose, with the publication of the radically aggressive and challenging first edition of *Leaves of Grass* in 1855, Whitman became the figure of the frontispiece: a man of the people still, dressed in worker's clothing, but insolently and arrogantly poised with one hand on his hip, the other in a pocket, eyes staring directly at the reader, unflinching, unapologetic, and strongly assertive, as if *daring* his audience to respond. Emphasizing his physical nature—as in his later years he would emphasize his spirituality—Whitman proclaimed himself to be, as he insists in section 24 of "Song of Myself," "one of the roughs, a kosmos, / Disorderly fleshy and sensual . . . eating drinking and breeding" (1855 *Leaves*). From this unlikely source, however, there emerged the prophetic speaker of much of the poem, the bardic poet who, knowing all time and all space, chanted his vision in tones of absolute certainty.

In 1860, with the publication of the third edition of *Leaves of Grass,* an altogether different figure appears in the frontispiece: a well-groomed character, moody and melancholy, with a short, neatly trimmed beard, wearing a large loosely knotted scarf and, under his jacket, a shirt with flowing Byronic collar. This identity, which does not reappear after 1860, seems to reflect the romantic and personal nature of some of the poems added for this edition, the "Calamus" group in particular. It also underlines the warning of the 1860 poem "Whoever You are Holding Me Now in Hand": "I am not what you supposed, but far different."

The 1860s brought about profound changes for Whitman as for the nation. He moved to Washington and performed extensive labors in the hospitals there, as companion and confidant to many injured and dying soldiers, Southern as well as Northern. Aging prematurely, he now became the Good Gray Poet of William O'Connor's polemical pamphlet published in January of 1866. This figure, congenial to Whitman's self-conception of the time, was almost the exact antithesis of the radically offensive, subversive figure of the 1850s. "The good gray poet" appeared to be a man misunderstood, and therefore unfairly abused by those who found his poetry offensive; but in truth, the portrayal contends, he was a great and good citizen, a noble servant both compassionate and selfless, and a poet who has kept the faith and is worthy of respect, even of veneration. Such, for example, is the figure portrayed in the 1865 poem "The Wound-Dresser" or the 1874 "Prayer of Columbus."

In his later years, particularly after the paralytic stroke of 1873 which left him a semi-invalid, Whitman moved naturally into the role of the sociable Sage of Camden, a wise elder revered by a growing circle of friends and admirers, visited by travelers from afar, and honored by the select few, including Alfred, Lord Tennyson, the poet laureate of England, with whom he maintained a correspondence. Withdrawn from the struggles of earlier years, Whitman could now rest content, at ease with himself and confident of the ultimate rightness of his ways.

R.W. French

Bibliography

Allen, Gay Wilson. *The Solitary Singer: A Critical Biography of Walt Whitman.* 1955. Rev. ed. 1967. Chicago: U of Chicago P, 1985.

Chase, Richard. *Walt Whitman Reconsidered.* New York: William Sloane Associates, 1955.

Kaplan, Justin. *Walt Whitman: A Life.* New York: Simon and Schuster, 1980.

Miller, James E., Jr. *Walt Whitman.* Updated ed. Boston: Twayne, 1990.

O'Connor, William. *The Good Gray Poet: A Vindication.* New York: Bunce and Huntington, 1866.

Price, Kenneth M. *Whitman and Tradition: The Poet in His Century.* New Haven: Yale UP, 1990.

Whitman, Walt. *Leaves of Grass: Comprehensive Reader's Edition.* Ed. Harold W. Blodgett and Sculley Bradley. New York: New York UP, 1965.

Zweig, Paul. *Walt Whitman: The Making of the Poet.* New York: Basic Books, 1984.

See also Biographies; Leaves of Grass, 1855 Edition; Leaves of Grass, 1860 Edition; O'Connor, William Douglas; Photographs and Photographers; "Prayer of Columbus"; "Wound-Dresser, The"

Pessoa, Fernando (1888–1935)

A poet's poet and a modernist of the first rank, Fernando Pessoa grew up in Durban, South Africa, but lived subsequently in his native city of Lisbon, Portugal. He eked out a marginal livelihood there as a commercial translator. The magnitude and quality of his literary output came largely as a surprise to posterity and are still being assessed. He devised a series of alter egos (heteronyms), each one with a distinctive poetic style, to whom he attributed much of his writing.

Pessoa mastered English at an early age and was annotating a copy of *Leaves of Grass* at a crucial moment in his literary development. It was at this time that his celebrated poem "Salutation to Walt Whitman" (1914) was written. The "Salutation" makes deft use of Whitman's stylistic tics and recreates a Whitmanesque mood of transcendental enthusiasm. However, it does so in a way that makes *Leaves of Grass* seem faintly preposterous. In fact, the work is a puckish send-up.

Yet Pessoa made use of Whitman's technical advances to great effect elsewhere in his more reflective verse. It also appears that his pastoral lyrics were, at bottom, an elaborate philosophical commentary on *Leaves of Grass.* Such links between the two poets were of a serious and substantial character.

N.J. Mason-Browne

Bibliography

Brown, Susan Margaret. "Pessoa and Whitman: Brothers in the Universe." *The Continuing Presence of Walt Whitman.* Ed. Robert K. Martin. Iowa City: U of Iowa P, 1992. 167–181.

Pessoa, Fernando. *Poems of Fernando Pessoa.* Ed. and trans. Edwin Honig and Susan M. Brown. New York: Ecco, 1986.

Sena, Jorge de. "Fernando Pessoa: The Man Who Never Was." *The Man Who Never Was: Essays on Fernando Pessoa.* Ed. George Monteiro. Providence, R.I.: Gávea-Brown, 1982. 19–31.

See also Portugal and Brazil, Whitman in; Leaves of Grass; Legacy, Whitman's

Pfaff's Restaurant

In the age before air conditioning many an oyster bar, beer hall, or restaurant was in a basement or cellar. And so was Pfaff's, the Bohemian gathering place Whitman visited frequently in

New York between 1859 and 1862, when he departed for Washington. The restaurant, its regulars, and the depth and importance of their influence on him remain uncertain, principally because of scanty and contradictory evidence. An undisputed fact is that Whitman's reputation was enhanced by his relations with Henry Clapp, king of the Pfaffian Bohemians; the first version of "Out of the Cradle" appeared in Clapp's weekly *Saturday Press* and Whitman was one of the journal's main subjects. While some of the Pfaff's crowd lionized Whitman, some challenged him in print. The point is that they gave him recognition and publicity.

Located at 647 Broadway, two buildings north of Bleecker Street and on the west side of the thoroughfare, Charles Ignatius Pfaff's restaurant was in New York's popular "Left Bank" entertainment district, which included theaters, restaurants, music halls, and saloons stretching to Spring Street in lower Manhattan. The Bohemians were nonconforming, frequently intellectual, engaged in the arts, and in opposition to bourgeois conventions. Among the most visible were King Clapp and the queen, Ada Clare, Fitz-James O'Brien, George Arnold, William Winter, Elihu Vedder, and, among the more "genteel," E.C. Stedman. They gathered in the smoke-filled, badly ventilated, and reeking cellar, the insiders often seated at a long table almost, it seems, to attract the visitors and tourists such as Howells who did not like the scene. (The often reproduced picture in his *Literary Friends and Acquaintance,* by the way, was made thirty years after the fact, and in it Whitman appears more a version of an 1890s gentleman than the free and imposing figure he had cut in the 1860s.) Whitman appears to have sat most often at one of the smaller tables, as he does in the picture, whether because he preferred to listen and observe—remain somewhat detached—or because of his reluctance or inability to compete in the snappy and witty conversations. He offers a vivid impression of the gathering place in "The Two Vaults," an unfinished poem. But one of the best signals of his involvement was his bringing the staid Ralph Waldo Emerson for a visit to the vault, this despite his minimizing his connection with the place and the gang.

The greatest benefit Whitman enjoyed from the Pfaff's connection, aside from the good fellowship and fun, was the constant focus offered by the *Saturday Press,* especially in 1860, which gave him visibility. Pfaff's and its habitués offered an unconventional life style—for instance, they were among the many period groups that promoted free love—and validated and encouraged many of Whitman's predilections.

Donald Yannella

Bibliography

Howells, William Dean. *Literary Friends and Acquaintance.* New York: Harper, 1900.

Hyman, Martin D. "'Where the Drinkers and Laughers Meet': Pfaff's: Whitman's Literary Lair." *Seaport* 26 (1992): 56–61.

Lalor, Gene. "Whitman among the New York Literary Bohemians: 1859–1862." *Walt Whitman Review* 25 (1979): 131–145.

Parry, Albert. *Garrets and Pretenders: A History of Bohemianism in America.* 1933. New York: Dover, 1960.

Stansell, Christine. "Whitman at Pfaff's: Commercial Culture, Literary Life and New York Bohemia at Mid-Century." *Walt Whitman Quarterly Review* 10 (1993): 107–126.

See also CLAPP, HENRY; CLARE, ADA (JANE MCELHENEY); GRAY, FRED; MENKEN, ADAH ISAACS; *SATURDAY PRESS;* STEDMAN, EDMUND CLARENCE; SWINTON, JOHN

Philadelphia, Pennsylvania

Known as the Quaker City and the City of Brotherly Love, Philadelphia should have sounded promising to Walt Whitman, an admirer of Elias Hicks and a poet of comradely affection. With over a million inhabitants in 1890, Philadelphia was the third most populous city in the United States when Whitman resided across the Delaware River in Camden, New Jersey, from 1873 until his death in 1892. During these years Philadelphia was an expanding industrial city that rivaled Boston as a center of culture, education, and high society. In addition to numerous libraries, lecture halls, newspapers, and publishers, Philadelphia possessed the Pennsylvania Academy of Fine Arts, the American Philosophical Society, and the University of Pennsylvania. For nearly twenty years Whitman and his supporters used the resources of the Philadelphia-Camden area as a forum in which to promote the poet and his poetry.

Whitman's poetry had been sold through various outlets in Philadelphia since 1856, but his personal association with the city began after suffering a paralytic stroke in 1873. Nearly an invalid, Whitman moved from Washington, D.C., to Camden in June to live with his brother George and sister-in-law Louisa. Whitman knew hardly anyone in Camden or Philadelphia when he arrived, but, as he slowly recovered, he began to make acquaintances at the nearby factories and rail yards and on the ferries which regularly plied the Delaware between Camden and Philadelphia. The relationship between the two cities was reminiscent of what he had known in Brooklyn and Manhattan, and before long Whitman was visiting Philadelphia's Mercantile Library on Tenth Street, frequenting the downtown printing offices, drinking at the waterfront saloons, and befriending the streetcar conductors along Market Street. Over the next two decades Whitman continued to make friends in Philadelphia, some of them wealthy and capable of influencing public opinion, but he also continued to be regarded by many Philadelphians as the immoral author of an indecent book.

Although Whitman's self-promotional activities were international in scope, he exerted considerable effort at establishing a reputation in Philadelphia, particularly in 1876, when national attention was focused on the city. While enormous preparations were being made for Philadelphia's Centennial Exposition, Whitman prepared his Centennial edition of *Leaves of Grass* in two volumes. Possibly hoping for an invitation to read the opening poem of the exposition, Whitman changed the title of *After All, Not to Create Only,* which he read at the opening of New York's National Industrial Exhibition in 1871, to "Song of the Exposition." In January 1876 he also published an anonymous article in the *West Jersey Press* exposing how he had been abused by American publishers and now lived in poverty. A pastiche of exaggerations, the article was reprinted in London and caused a press war between England and the United States which included the Philadelphia *Times* (24 February). Although these efforts failed to gain Whitman the opening poem of the exposition, they did gain him several influential supporters in Philadelphia. George W. Childs, publisher of the Philadelphia *Public Ledger,* became a devoted patron. He offered to publish an edited version of *Leaves of Grass* in 1878 and loaned Whitman five hundred dollars to buy a house in 1884. An English admirer, Anne Gilchrist, moved to Philadelphia with her children in September 1876 and settled at 1929 North 22nd Street,

where Whitman became a frequent overnight guest during the next three years. And John Wien Forney, owner of the Philadelphia *Press,* helped sponsor Whitman's trip to the American West in 1879.

In 1881 the suppression of James Osgood's edition of *Leaves of Grass* in Boston confirmed the belief among some Philadelphians that Whitman was indeed the victim of prudishness and comstockery. Using the plates of the Osgood edition, Rees Welsh and Company of Philadelphia risked prosecution by publishing *Leaves of Grass* and a companion volume, *Specimen Days,* in 1882. As a result of the publicity of the Boston banning, Rees Welsh sold about six thousand copies of *Leaves.* From 1882 until his death, most of Whitman's American publications were handled in Philadelphia by David McKay, the successor of Rees Welsh, including *November Boughs* and a new printing of *Leaves* in 1888, *Good-Bye My Fancy* in 1891, and the Deathbed edition of *Leaves* in 1891–1892. McKay also published Richard M. Bucke's adulatory biography, *Walt Whitman,* in 1883, and *Camden's Compliment to Walt Whitman* in 1889.

After the Boston suppression of *Leaves,* new admirers from Philadelphia began to rally around Whitman. Talcott Williams, a journalist for the Philadelphia *Press* (1881–1912), managed to get the Boston prohibition of *Leaves* revoked. Robert Pearsall Smith, a glass manufacturer and Quaker evangelist, visited Whitman in Camden at the encouragement of his daughter, Mary Whitall Smith, and the poet soon became a guest at their house in Germantown. About this time Whitman also was a frequent guest of Thomas Donaldson, a Philadelphia lawyer who provided Whitman with free ferry passes and organized a collection to buy him a horse and buggy in 1885. During the 1880s Whitman acquired other notable allies in Philadelphia, including two on the faculty of the University of Pennsylvania, Horace Howard Furness, a Shakespearean scholar, and Daniel Garrison Brinton, an anthropologist. Others were George Henry Boker, a dramatist, poet, and diplomat; Charles Godfrey Leland, a writer and translator of Heine; Elizabeth Robins, a journalist; Joseph Pennell, a magazine illustrator; and Thomas Eakins, former director of the Academy of Fine Arts.

Whitman's growing network of friends enabled him to augment his reputation in Philadelphia through publications in local newspapers and charitable benefits in the form of lectures. From 1879 to 1887, Whitman published numerous articles in the Philadelphia *Press* and occasionally contributed to the Philadelphia *Public Ledger* and Philadelphia *Times*. Whitman's lecture on the death of Abraham Lincoln was profitably delivered in Philadelphia at least twice: at the Chestnut Street Opera House in 1886, and at the Contemporary Club in 1890. From the late 1880s, Whitman's birthday celebrations, arranged by friends in Camden and Philadelphia, were covered in the local press, particularly in 1890, when Robert G. Ingersoll, a professional speaker and agnostic, lectured on Whitman's behalf at C.H. Reisser's Restaurant in Philadelphia. After being refused by two other auditoriums, Ingersoll gave another lecture on 21 October at Philadelphia's Horticultural Hall attended by at least fifteen hundred people. After Whitman's death, his supporters continued to observe the poet's birthday and spread his fame, forming the Walt Whitman Fellowship, which lasted until 1919.

A century after the first publication of *Leaves of Grass* in 1855, the Delaware River Port Authority decided to name a new bridge after the poet so closely associated with both banks of the river. Many Philadelphians still remembered Whitman's reputation for indecency, and during the next two years the decision was disputed in the local papers, but on 15 May 1957 the Walt Whitman Bridge was officially dedicated.

William A. Pannapacker

Bibliography

Allen, Gay Wilson. *The Solitary Singer: A Critical Biography of Walt Whitman.* 1955. Rev. ed. 1967. Chicago: U of Chicago P, 1985.

Baedeker, Karl, ed. *The United States with an Excursion into Mexico: A Handbook for Travellers.* 1893. New York: Da Capo, 1971.

Giantvalley, Scott. *Walt Whitman, 1838–1939: A Reference Guide.* Boston: Hall, 1981.

Kummings, Donald D. *Walt Whitman, 1940–1975: A Reference Guide.* Boston: Hall, 1982.

McCullough, John M. "Walt Whitman Bridge—Philadelphia, 1957." *Walt Whitman Newsletter* 3 (1957): 42–44.

Reynolds, David S. *Walt Whitman's America: A Cultural Biography.* New York: Knopf, 1995.

See also ASSOCIATIONS, CLUBS, FELLOWSHIPS, FOUNDATIONS, AND SOCIETIES; BOKER, GEORGE HENRY; CAMDEN, NEW JERSEY; CENTENNIAL EXPOSITION (PHILADELPHIA); COSTELLOE, MARY WHITALL SMITH; DONALDSON, THOMAS; EAKINS, THOMAS; GILCHRIST, ANNE BURROWS; INGERSOLL, ROBERT GREEN; *LEAVES OF GRASS, 1876, AUTHOR'S EDITION*; *LEAVES OF GRASS, 1881–1882 EDITION*; LELAND, CHARLES GODFREY; MCKAY, DAVID; OSGOOD, JAMES R.; PENNELL, JOSEPH, AND ELIZABETH ROBINS; SMITH, ROBERT PEARSALL; "SONG OF THE EXPOSITION"; *WEST JERSEY PRESS*; WILLIAMS, TALCOTT

Phillips, George Searle ("January Searle") (1815–1889)

A journalist and writer of books, pamphlets, and journal articles, under the pseudonym January Searle, Phillips was an early supporter of Whitman. He was educated at Trinity College, Cambridge, where he received an A.B., although his name does not appear on the list of graduates. After immigrating to America, he was associated with the New York *World,* the *Herald,* and the Chicago *Tribune,* before becoming literary editor of the New York *Sun.*

Phillips wrote a favorable review of *Leaves of Grass* for the New York *Illustrated News* (26 May 1860), reprinted in the *Saturday Press* (30 June 1860). His laudatory poem, "Letter Impromptu" (1857), written in hexameters, appeared in *Leaves of Grass Imprints* (1860).

Patricia J. Tyrer

Bibliography

"Phillips, George Searle." *The Dictionary of National Biography.* 1897. Ed. Leslie Stephen and Sidney Lee. Vol. 15. London: Oxford UP, 1937–1938. 1087.

Glicksberg, Charles I. "Walt Whitman and 'January Searle.'" *American Notes and Queries* 6 (1946): 51–53.

Whitman, Walt. *Notebooks and Unpublished Prose Manuscripts.* Ed. Edward F. Grier. Vol. 1. New York: New York UP, 1984.

See also LEAVES OF GRASS IMPRINTS

Photographs and Photographers

"No man has been photographed more than I have," Whitman said late in his life (*With Walt Whitman* 2:45), and he was in fact the most photographed writer of the nineteenth century. There are over 130 extant photographic portraits, far more than of any other author who died before 1900 (by which time portable cameras and roll film had moved photography out of the hands of artisan-photographers and into the hands of everyone who could afford inexpensive cameras). The earliest photos of Whitman were taken in the 1840s (soon after the first daguerreotypes were made in the United States), and his last photos were taken the year of his death. While Whitman often had his portrait painted, he always preferred his photographic portraits, and, toward the end of his life, he wanted to publish a portfolio of the most representative pictures. While this project was never completed, his various editions of *Leaves of Grass* serve as a kind of cumulative gallery, beginning with his use of the famous 1854 daguerreotype (with Whitman in an open shirt, one arm akimbo, a hand in his pocket, his hat cocked on his head, his eyes fixing the viewer), an engraving of which he used as the frontispiece for his first edition of *Leaves*. As *Leaves* went through its various editions, Whitman experimented with the portraits he used in his book; in the 1889 issue of *Leaves,* he included five photographic portraits (or engravings of photographs) and created a kind of visual progression of his life, as well as a kind of exhibit of the evolution of nineteenth-century techniques of photographic reproduction, from wood-engraving to half-tone reproduction.

For Whitman, photography was one of the great examples of how nineteenth-century technological advancement provided a concomitant spiritual advancement. Just as the railroad and telegraph had shortened time and shrunk space, making the world a smaller place, so had the photograph frozen time and space by holding a moment and a place permanently in view: it transformed the fleeting into the permanent. Whitman was of the first generation of humans who, by the end of their lives, could look back on a sequence of accurate visual traces of their entire life, could track their aging, and could view accurate images of their dead friends and relatives. These "miraculous mirrors," as photographs were often called in the nineteenth century, provided the tools for a whole new conception of identity and a new relationship with one's own past. Stumbling on photos of himself that he had forgotten about, Whitman once spoke humorously of the kind of identity crisis photography had initiated: "I meet new Walt Whitmans every day," he said; "I don't know which Walt Whitman I am" (*With Walt Whitman* 1:108). Whitman's tone turned serious, though, as he considered the implications of a lifetime of photographs, each portraying a different phase of his life: "It is hard to extract a man's real self . . . from such historic débris" (*With Walt Whitman* 1:108). Unlike painted portraits, which attempted to render a full identity in a single image, photographic portraits were records of precise moments, each one "useful in totaling a man but not a total in itself" (*With Walt Whitman* 3:72), as Whitman formulated it. He wondered whether all the photos of himself finally suggested that life was "evolutional or episodical" (*With Walt Whitman* 4:425), a unified sweep of a single identity or a fragmented series of disjointed and even contradictory identities. Photographs, then, helped Whitman struggle with one of the most essential questions that his poetry dealt with: how a self is defined as it journeys through time and space.

His photographs of himself suggested a kind of cluttered identity, and that seemed to be in the very nature of the photographic enterprise. When photographs first became widely available in the 1840s and 1850s, observers were often struck by the cluttered representation of the world they rendered. In the early days of photography, one thing that distinguished photographic representations of reality from painted representations was that photography did not edit its subject; it did not remove unnecessary or unaesthetic details; it in fact ignored nothing that appeared in the photographic field of vision. The clutter that bothered many viewers of photographs excited Whitman. He noted that the "advantage" of photography is that "it lets nature have its way" (*With Walt Whitman* 4:124–125). Whitman would try in his own poetry to do the same thing. Through the development of techniques like the poetic catalogue, Whitman attempted to create a poetic field just as cluttered as a photograph; he would try to maintain an open attentiveness to the things of the world so that he could absorb in his poem anything that the sun illuminated, just as photos did.

"I find I often like the photographs better than the oils," Whitman said; "they are perhaps mechanical, but they are honest" (*With Walt Whitman* 1:131). That same honesty was the quality he sought in his poetry, where he attempted to open his lines to the marginalized subjects and people who had been excluded from the poetry of the past. The poet who in "As I Ebb'd with the Ocean of Life" defined himself as "but a trail of drift and debris" learned from photography how the cluttered and neglected objects of the world were part of its unity. He learned that union, wholeness, was achieved only by including all the extraneous detail that composed that wholeness; unity could not be represented by leaving things out, by ignoring the unpleasant or evil or apparently insignificant. Photography was literally "light writing," and for Whitman the sun was the great democrat, shining on things great and small, illuminating everything that composed the world. So when Whitman wrote "Not till the sun excludes you do I exclude you" ("To a Common Prostitute"), he presented himself as the poet who was every bit as impressionable and absorptive as a photographic plate. "In these *Leaves*," Whitman wrote, "everything is literally photographed. Nothing is poetized, no divergence, not a step, not an inch, nothing for beauty's sake, no euphemism, no rhyme" (*Complete Writings* 6:21).

Photography also extended the human field of vision, allowing people actually to see places they had never been, observe persons they had never encountered, and witness events they had not experienced. While Whitman earned his knowledge of Civil War strife through his service in hospitals, he had no actual battlefield experience, and he gathered his visual impressions of those battlefields largely through the widely distributed photographs of Mathew Brady, Alexander Gardner, and the other photographers who followed the troops. Photographic technology at the time lent itself more to capturing the preparations and aftereffects of battles (corpses on a battlefield) than the actual fighting itself, and Whitman's poetry similarly focused on battlefields before and after the battles; he also bathed his war poems in moonlight, reminiscent of the dark black and white surfaces of Civil War photos. In the same way, much of his imagery of the far West derives from the photos that Gardner took for the Union Pacific as the railroad built its way across the prairies. Part of the easy absorptive quality of Whitman's poetry—his claims of having been everywhere and his catalogues of faraway places presented with the authority of someone who had tramped the ground—are the result of a life lived during the heady early days of photography, when it seemed that everyone's eyes were being extended around the world, when it

became possible to travel by opening a photograph album.

Whitman knew and admired many of the best of the first generation of photographers. These early photographers were a colorful group of skilled artisans, the kind of independent businessmen—part scientist, part artist, and part salesman—that Whitman admired. As a young reporter in New York, he frequented the daguerreotype galleries and published articles about his enchantment at seeing on the walls the "great legion of human faces" (*Gathering* 2:116) whose eyes followed him as he wandered among the portraits. One of his favorite galleries was John Plumbe's, whose Broadway studio was unsurpassed in its collection of daguerreotypes of the famous; Whitman met Plumbe in 1846, and one of the first daguerreotypes of Whitman may well have been taken at that time. Gabriel Harrison, who took the well-known daguerreotype that Whitman used for his 1855 *Leaves* frontispiece, was a writer, actor, painter, and stage manager, as well as an award-winning photographer, and he remained for Whitman one of the true artisanheroes of the era. Whitman admired Mathew Brady and claimed to have had many conversations with him, but the photographer he most admired was Gardner, who began as Brady's assistant, but who during the Civil War set up his own studio. Whitman thought Gardner's portraits of him were the best, and Gardner in return was a great admirer of *Leaves*. Whitman called Gardner a "real artist," a photographer who "saw farther than his camera—saw more" (*With Walt Whitman* 3:346).

After the Civil War, Whitman was photographed by some of the most successful commercial photographers in America—Jeremiah Gurney, George G. Rockwood, Napoleon Sarony, and Frederick Gutekunst. By successfully marketing photographs of actors, writers, adventurers, and politicians, these men were in large part responsible for the creation of the modern idea of "celebrity." The widespread distribution of photographic images of people with well-known names made them instantly recognizable across the country, and Whitman was one of the people whose image was in demand. During the last decade of his life, he collected royalties on sales of his photographs and had a taste of celebrity: "my head gets about: is easily recognized" (*With Walt Whitman* 3:532). At the end of his life, he was photographed and painted by the then controversial artist Thomas

P

Eakins; the photographs made by Eakins and his assistants are some of the most effective portraits we have of the poet, portraying him as a wise old prophet.

Almost all of Whitman's photographic portraits are of him alone; he was seldom photographed with others, and never with any members of his family or any of his adult friends. On three occasions, he allowed himself to be photographed with the children of friends; the resultant images seem symbolic representations of the American bard preparing the generation of poets to come. On four occasions, he was photographed with young male friends—Peter Doyle in the 1860s, Harry Stafford in the 1870s, Bill Duckett in the 1880s, and Warren Fritzinger in the 1890s. These images are some of the most intimate portraits of the poet; unpublished during his lifetime, they record his personal Calamus relationships. But the majority of his photographs record the carefully controlled evolution of his poetic identity, from the young New York reporter/*flâneur* to the working class rough to the careworn Civil War nurse to the Good Gray Poet and finally to the ancient sage of democracy.

Ed Folsom

Bibliography

Clarke, Graham. *Walt Whitman: The Poem as Private History.* New York: St. Martin's, 1991.

Dougherty, James. *Walt Whitman and the Citizen's Eye.* Baton Rouge: Louisiana State UP, 1993.

Folsom, Ed. *Walt Whitman's Native Representations.* Cambridge: Cambridge UP, 1994.

Orvell, Miles. *The Real Thing: Imagination and Authenticity in American Culture, 1880–1940.* Chapel Hill: U of North Carolina P, 1989.

Trachtenberg, Alan. *Reading American Photographs: Images as History, Mathew Brady to Walker Evans.* New York: Hill and Wang, 1989.

Traubel, Horace. *With Walt Whitman in Camden.* Vol. 1. Boston: Small, Maynard, 1906; Vol. 2. New York: Appleton, 1908; Vol. 3. New York: Kennerley, 1914; Vol. 4. Ed. Sculley Bradley. Philadelphia: U of Pennsylvania P, 1953.

Whitman, Walt. *The Complete Writings of Walt Whitman.* Ed. Richard Maurice Bucke, Thomas B. Harned, and Horace L. Traubel. 10 vols. New York: Putnam, 1902.

———. *The Gathering of the Forces.* Ed. Cleveland Rodgers and John Black. 2 vols. New York: Putnam, 1920.

See also ART AND DAGUERREOTYPE GALLERIES; CIVIL WAR, THE; DOYLE, PETER; EAKINS, THOMAS; FRITZINGER, FREDERICK WARREN; POETIC THEORY; STAFFORD, HARRY L.; TECHNOLOGY

Phrenology

Walt Whitman's growing interest from the late 1840s to the mid-1850s in the newly emerging science of phrenology, and the details of his business association with the phrenological cabinet of Fowler and Wells during this period, have been thoroughly documented. Early in 1846 he had clipped and heavily underlined an article from the *American Review* entitled "Phrenology: A Socratic Dialogue." Later in that same year Whitman reviewed J.G. Spurzheim's *Phrenology, or the Doctrine of Mental Phenomena* (1834), the first of the several favorable reviews on books devoted to phrenology that he was to write for the Brooklyn *Daily Eagle.* His growing interest in phrenology and his confidence that this was a legitimate field of study are evident in the brief notices he wrote of newly published phrenological works for the *Eagle.* Their subject matter ranged widely—from an exposition of the general principles of phrenology (J.G. Spurzheim's *Phrenology, or the Doctrine of the Mental Phenomena*) to a study of the relation of the body to the mind (George Moore, *The Use of the Body in Relation to the Mind*), to marriage (Lorenzo Niles Fowler, *Marriage: Its History and Ceremonies*); others that he noticed treated health and education from a similar phrenological perspective. In the meantime, notebooks from these formative years show Whitman familiarizing himself with the technical jargon of phrenology, copying out excerpts from phrenological works (most notably, George Combe's *Lectures on Phrenology*), and clipping articles to save, including three from the *American Phrenological Journal.* He also took a more direct step to acquaint himself with phrenology when on 16 July 1849 he presented himself at the phrenological cabinet of Fowler and Wells at 131 Nassau Street for a head reading. The impetus that brought him there can only be guessed at: acting on his interest in heredity and genealogy, he may have wanted to meet Orson Fowler who, in *Hereditary Descent,* mentioned a long-lived ancestor, John Whitman; or he may have been drawn to these men whose interests, judging from the notes and clippings Whitman was steadily accumulating on matters related to physique, health, water cure, and temperance, so nearly accorded with his own. Or, as an aspiring poet, he may simply have come to believe, as scientific fact, that the ideal poet needed an ideal phrenology and he wanted confirmation of his own ambitions. Lorenzo Niles Fowler's reading of Whitman was so astonishing that Whitman could only conclude that nature emphatically chose him for the profession of poet, more so than Oliver Wendell Holmes, William Cullen Bryant, Nathaniel Parker Willis, or Fitz-Greene Halleck, all of whose phrenological endowments were conspicuously less developed. That it would have impressed nineteenth-century devotees of phrenology may account for the fact that he published its results five times during his lifetime.

During the ensuing years leading up to the first edition of *Leaves of Grass,* Whitman's ties with the firm of Fowler and Wells grew close, seemingly inspired by personal friendship and maintained by mutual admiration and intellectual sympathies. Around 1850 and 1851, in addition to other activities, Whitman became a bookseller whose stock included some Fowler and Wells imprints; and four years later, in November 1855, Whitman was listed as a "voluntary correspondent" when he published an article in a Fowler and Wells newspaper, *Life Illustrated;* this position changed to staff writer in April 1856 and he contributed a series titled "New York Dissected."

Most importantly, Fowler and Wells published, advertised, and sold the 1855 edition of *Leaves of Grass* and published the second edition. Whitman's close association with the firm paid dividends: it extended to Whitman an enviable opportunity, beginning with the 28 July 1855 issue, to promote his poetry by publishing self-reviews and puffs of *Leaves of Grass* in *Life Illustrated.* As its publisher and distributor, Fowler and Wells actively promoted Whitman's volume: it listed Whitman's volume for sale at the Phrenological Depot in an ad that ran in the New York *Tribune* from 6 July 1855 and sporadically thereafter through February 1856; published Whitman's joint review of Tennyson's *Maud* and *Leaves of Grass,* titled "An English

and American Poet," in the October 1855 issue of the *American Phrenological Journal;* and sent out review copies, among them, presumably, the one that led Emerson to write the famous congratulatory letter Whitman was to use unabashedly in furthering his career, and others to the firm's representatives in England, a move that brought him to the attention of the British public.

The Depot's involvement in the 1856 edition was more muted, however; though Fowler and Wells published this edition, it withheld its imprint from the inside cover, perhaps because it had enough controversy in its championing of a host of unpopular reforms—among them, sex—without being too prominently associated with an edition that included the likes of "A Woman Waits for Me" and "Spontaneous Me." Nevertheless, the 16 August 1856 issue of *Life Illustrated* carried an announcement of its anticipated publication of the second edition, followed this with an advertisement on 11 September and included a leaf at the end of the published volume that listed agents in several cities in this country and abroad where the volume could be purchased. The volume sold poorly and relations between the poet and the phrenologists rapidly cooled. By July 1857 Whitman declared that "Fowler & Wells are bad persons for me.— They retard my book . . ." (*Correspondence* 1:44), a turn of events probably encouraged by Samuel R. Wells, the firm's chief publishing officer. Ironically, their like-minded views about liberalizing sexual attitudes had driven the two parties apart.

Though his physical ties with the phrenologists were severed, Whitman's intellectual and spiritual ties to them were to remain intact through his lifetime. As late as 1888 he said of phrenology to Horace Traubel: "I guess most of my friends distrust it—but then you see I am very old fashioned—I probably have not got by the phrenology stage yet" (Traubel 385). He could say so with good reason, because he built a career by fulfilling the promise of his phrenological analysis and by drawing inspiration and subject matter from this pseudoscience's doctrines.

From the details of Lorenzo Fowler's "Phrenological Notes on W. Whitman," Whitman constructed the concept of the cosmically chosen poet-prophet in his poetry, self-reviews, and prose essays from which he never varied in his lifetime. The features attributed to the ideal poet in the 1855 Preface (and found by Fowler to be highly developed in Whitman) can be readily converted into phrenological jargon— "fondness for women and children" (amativeness and philoprogenitiveness), "a perfect sense of the oneness of nature" (sublimity)—while "large hope . . . alimentiveness and destructiveness" are themselves phrenological propensities. Told that he was "undoubtedly descended from the soundest and hardiest stock" (Hungerford 363), Whitman created both for himself and the poet-prophet an impeccable family lineage. In "Song of Myself" the poet asserts: "Before I was born out of my mother generations guided me, / My embryo has never been torpid, nothing could overlay it" (section 44). Described by Fowler as having a "grand physical constitution" himself (qtd. in Hungerford 363), Whitman in the Preface assigned "the soundest organic health" to the poet-prophet. In short, the greatest poet "is complete in himself," much the same conclusion Fowler drew from his examination of Whitman.

The allure of phrenology was as compelling to Whitman as it was to a host of prominent and respectable nineteenth-century figures. From its theory that the mind is a composite of thirty-seven independent faculties and powers, each one governed by a corresponding organ located in an identifiable region of the brain, phrenology offered an orderly exposition of the organization of mankind's mind and body and the laws of nature; it also asserted the innate goodness of man and the indefinite improvability of human institutions. As a consequence, it figured prominently in the major social issues of this period: education, health reform, human sexuality, eugenics, religion, political speculation, and philosophy. Contemporaneous, even daringly liberal, yet intelligible, practical, and seemingly scientifically based, phrenology's appeal was considerable, particularly so for an aspiring poet with a limited formal education.

Some of Whitman's individual poems reflect the presence of explicitly phrenological doctrine. For instance, the structure and content of "There was a Child Went Forth" depict the systematic and progressive exercising by the poem's young persona of different groups of phrenological faculties as he grows to triumphant maturity. His growth is enhanced by the poem's superior mother from whom he inherits his first-rate physical and mental organization. "Faces" is also structured according to and informed by phrenological (and physiognomical) doctrine; the final section, with its image of the deific grandmother who looks upon her gifted progeny, conveys Whitman's own optimistic vision about the creation's goodness and the latent perfection inherent in all people. This eugenic material emerges as the keynote in "Unfolded Out of the Folds." Using "unfold" as a synonym for evolution or upward spiraling, Whitman fuses the emergence of the physically and spiritually superior child, whose emotional, physical, and intellectual attributes are inherited from superior parents, with the emergence of the Great Republic and, beyond that, with successive unfoldings of the soul to eternity.

The issues implicitly and explicitly raised in the above poems—the role of women, education, eugenics, sexuality, health, social reform, progress, millennialism—are less systematically presented throughout Whitman's canon, but are nevertheless there. It should be added, however, that the phrenologists were eclectic, much as were the other pseudoscientists, and were prone to draw on and adapt to their own purposes a rich potpourri of nineteenth-century ideas, hopes, philosophical theories, and assumptions related to the ancient dream of renovating mankind and its institutions. Thus the attempt to assign phrenological influence to specific passages is often problematical. However, the presence of phrenological content goes far in accounting for Whitman's poetic origins and may well have been at least as important in bringing him to "a boil" as was Emerson.

Arthur Wrobel

Bibliography

Allen, Gay Wilson. *The Solitary Singer: A Critical Biography of Walt Whitman.* 1955. Rev. ed. 1967. Chicago: U of Chicago P, 1985.

Aspiz, Harold. "Educating the Kosmos: 'There Was a Child Went Forth.'" *American Quarterly* 18 (1966): 655–666.

———. "A Reading of Whitman's 'Faces.'" *Walt Whitman Review* 19 (1973): 37–48.

———. "Unfolding the Folds." *Walt Whitman Review* 12 (1966): 81–87.

Davies, John D. *Phrenology: Fad and Science: A 19th-Century Crusade.* New Haven: Yale UP, 1955.

Hungerford, Edward. "Walt Whitman and His Chart of Bumps." *American Literature* 2 (1931): 350–384.

Kaplan, Justin. *Walt Whitman: A Life.* New York: Simon and Schuster, 1980.

Stern, Madeleine B. *Heads & Headlines: The Phrenological Fowlers.* Norman: U of Oklahoma P, 1971.

Traubel, Horace. *With Walt Whitman in Camden.* Vol. 1. New York: Appleton, 1906.

Wallace, James K. "Whitman and *Life Illustrated:* A Forgotten 1855 Review of *Leaves.*" *Walt Whitman Review* 17 (1971): 135–138.

Whitman, Walt. *The Correspondence.* Ed. Edwin Haviland Miller. 6 vols. New York: New York UP, 1961–1977.

Wrobel, Arthur. "A Poet's Self-Esteem: Whitman Alters His 'Bumps.'" *Walt Whitman Review* 17 (1971): 129–135.

———. "Whitman and the Phrenologists: The Divine Body and the Sensuous Soul." *PMLA* 89 (1974): 17–23.

See also American Phrenological Journal; "Faces"; Fowler, Lorenzo Niles and Orson Squire; Health; Influences on Whitman, Principal; *Life Illustrated*; New York Tribune; Prophecy; Pseudoscience; Sex and Sexuality; "Spontaneous Me"; "There was a Child Went Forth"; "Unfolded Out of the Folds"; Wells, Samuel Roberts

"Pioneers! O Pioneers!" (1865)

"Pioneers! O Pioneers!" first appeared in *Drum-Taps* (1865) and was then moved to the "Marches now the War is Over" cluster (1871), and finally appeared as the second poem in "Birds of Passage" (1881). In its position in *Drum-Taps* following "The Centenarian's Story" and preceding "Quicksand Years," "Pioneers" announced the more universal theme of the continuity of life in the midst of the suffering of the Civil War poems. In its placement in the section "Marches now the War is Over," "Pioneers" followed "As I sat Alone by Blue Ontario's Shore" and preceded "Respondez!," probably the most savage poem Whitman ever wrote. Between this early version of "By Blue Ontario's Shore," which concerns itself with the nation's destiny following the Civil War, and the deeply ironical "Respondez!," "Pioneers" seems a pallid assertion of amelioration.

In its final position in the "Birds of Passage" cluster (1881), "Pioneers" finds a happier place, following "Song of the Universal" and preceding "To You [Whoever you are . . .]." These three poems form a sequence on the general theme of the evolution of the human race. In all three poems we have the call to the soul: in "Song of the Universal" the idea of soul seeks the ideal; in "Pioneers" the idea of America seeks its destiny; and in "To You [Whoever you are . . .]" the idea of the individual seeks its true identity. The task of dramatizing the idea of America seeking its true identity is undertaken in the larger context of the soul of creation seeking the ideal. This is not another American "westering" poem; it describes a spiritual migration.

The main line of critical attention has been on this poem's themes, but the four-line trochaic stanza form has also received notice. Trochaic meter is suited not only to light, tripping tones, but also to a serious incantatory quality which Whitman attempts in this poem. The criticism recognizes that *Drum-Taps* is itself more conventional in form and style than earlier poems in *Leaves* and that the marching rhythms of "Pioneers" are among the most regular of all Whitman's poems.

Charles W. Mignon

Bibliography

Allen, Gay Wilson. *Walt Whitman Handbook.* 1946. New York: Hendricks House, 1962.

Miller, James E., Jr. *A Critical Guide to "Leaves of Grass."* Chicago: U of Chicago P, 1957.

Shapiro, Karl, and Robert Beum. *A Prosody Handbook.* New York: Harper and Row, 1965.

Stovall, Floyd. Introduction. *Walt Whitman: Representative Selections.* Ed. Stovall. New York: Hill and Wang, 1961. xi–lii.

Whitman, Walt. *Leaves of Grass: A Textual Variorum of the Printed Poems.* Ed. Sculley Bradley, Harold W. Blodgett, Arthur Golden, and William White. 3 vols. New York: New York UP, 1980.

See also "Birds of Passage"; Drum-Taps; West, The American

Place Names

Fascinated by onomastics and very interested in place names, Whitman had strong opinions on which names were appropriate—"appropriateness" being extremely important to him. Best were all indigenous, aboriginal names, followed by names accurately expressing the place being named; borrowed classical and European names were not acceptable. He often used names in his poetry. Names were powerful. As Whitman indicates in *An American Primer* (1904), "*Names* are magic.—One word can pour such a flood through the soul" (18).

P

According to Whitman, a nation leads all other nations if it produces its own names and prefers them to all other names. In fact, a nation that "begs" names from other nations "has no identity, marches not in front but behind" (*Primer* 34). Americans must reclaim control of the land by renaming all of the places hastily named by Europeans. Some of the mountains in the West, for example, were inappropriately named for European explorers. Restoring the land to the people and to democracy, new names would replace the names born of the aristocracy and tyranny.

Place names must not be given arbitrarily, but must be considered deliberately with concern for aesthetics, the American experience, and the character of the place. Names, above all, should be appropriate. The names of American cities should reflect their physical features and life of their citizens—expressing the essence of the cities.

Some of the best names, he believed, were the ones given by Native Americans, as shown by his praise of their "sonorous beauty" (*Gathering* 2:137) in the Brooklyn *Daily Eagle* as early as 1846. In "Slang in America" (1885), he indicates his fascination with the sounds of many Northwestern Indian place names. America would reclaim its true history by absorbing into its language and landscape the powerful original names given by Native American tribes. Whitman particularly objected to replacing Indian place names with borrowed European names; in fact, not using the aboriginal names amounted to lost opportunities.

Whitman preferred the Native American name "Mannahatta" instead of "New York City" (honoring the Duke of York, an English tyrant), "Paumanok" instead of "Long Island," "Tacoma" rather than "Washington," and "Kanawtha" rather than "West Virginia." He frequently used "Mannahatta" (seventeen times) and "Paumanok" (eighteen), and centered some of his poems on names, such as "Mannahatta" (1860, a second poem 1888), "Yonnondio" (1887), and "Starting from Paumanok" (1860).

Native names were particularly suited for poetry that would be truly American. American Indian names and his poetry were "original," "not to be imitated—not to be manufactured . . . nothing . . . so significant—so individual—so of a class—as these names" (Traubel 488). Incorporating Indian place names into his poetry was essential, because his role as a poet involved his revealing, his expressing, the authentic American experience.

Even though Whitman wanted words to be magic, or at least to have an inherent relation with what they named, he came to realize that such a relationship did not exist. Simply listing or evoking the place names for physical entities would not create the same images for each reader and not even necessarily the same images as the ones he himself visualized. Whitman's poetry, however, was distinctly American, not merely transplanted English poetry, partially a result of his inclusion of American place names.

Sherry Southard

Bibliography

Dressman, Michael R. "Goodrich's *Geography* and Whitman's Place Names." *Walt Whitman Review* 26 (1980): 64–67.

———. "'Names Are Magic': Walt Whitman's Laws of Geographic Nomenclature." *Names* 26 (1978): 68–79.

Folsom, Ed. *Walt Whitman's Native Representations.* Cambridge: Cambridge UP, 1994.

Hollis, C. Carroll. "Names in *Leaves of Grass.*" *Names* 5 (1957): 129–156.

Read, Allen Walker. "Walt Whitman's Attraction to Indian Place Names." *Literary Onomastics Studies* 7 (1980): 189–204.

Southard, Sherry. "Whitman and Language: His 'Democratic' Words." Diss. Purdue U, 1972.

Traubel, Horace. *With Walt Whitman in Camden.* Ed. Gertrude Traubel. Vol. 5. Carbondale: Southern Illinois UP, 1964.

Warren, James Perrin. *Walt Whitman's Language Experiment.* University Park: Pennsylvania State UP, 1990.

Whitman, Walt. *An American Primer.* Ed. Horace Traubel. 1904. Stevens Point, Wis.: Holy Cow!, 1987.

———. *The Gathering of the Forces.* Ed. Cleveland Rodgers and John Black. 2 vols. New York: Putnam, 1920.

See also AMERICAN PRIMER, AN; LANGUAGE; NATIVE AMERICANS (INDIANS); SLANG; "SLANG IN AMERICA"

Poe, Edgar Allan (1809–1849)

Whitman's appreciation of Edgar Allan Poe's work as author and editor is barely a footnote in the larger studies of Walt Whitman. Though scholars have argued that Whitman's early work was thematically and lyrically influenced by Poe and that Whitman was well aware of Poe and his work, in his final discussion of Poe in *Specimen Days* (1882) he remains undecided and ambiguous about its quality.

An essay by Whitman entitled "Heart-Music and Art-Music" was reprinted as "Art-Singing and Heart-Singing" in the *Broadway Journal,* which was edited by Poe at the time, on 29 November 1845. The essay responded to the American music Whitman had heard in New York. Poe's editorial footnote acknowledged Whitman's lack of "scientific knowledge of music" yet noted that he agreed "with our correspondent throughout." Shortly after the article was published, Poe and Whitman met for the first and only time, during which meeting Whitman collected his fee for the article. In *Specimen Days* Whitman notes that he had "a distinct and pleasing remembrance" of Poe as a kind but jaded man (Whitman 17).

Several references to Poe and his work were included by Whitman in the *Daily Eagle.* Not only did he reprint Poe's "A Tale of the Ragged Mountains" in the paper, but satires of Poe's work as well, including the unsigned "A Jig in Prose," a parody of "The Raven." Whitman also included notices on Poe's death, his wife's sickness, and her subsequent death.

Whitman attended Poe's reburial and monument dedication, the ceremony of which was held in Baltimore in 1875. Though Whitman sat on the platform during the ceremony, he refused to speak publicly on Poe's work or life. Later commenting in *Specimen Days,* Whitman expressed his divided sentiments on Poe, citing "an indescribable magnetism" about Poe, but concluding that while the excessive rhyming and "demoniac undertone" of his work dazzled, they provided "no heat" (Whitman 231). However, in a 16 November 1875 Washington *Star* article, Whitman recognizes Poe's status in literary history.

Amy E. Earhart

Bibliography

Allen, Gay Wilson. *The Solitary Singer: A Critical Biography of Walt Whitman.* 1955. Rev. ed. 1967. Chicago: U of Chicago P, 1985.

Fussell, Paul. "The Persistent Itchings of Poe and Whitman." *Southern Review* ns 3 (1967): 235–247.

Price, Kenneth M. *Whitman and Tradition: The Poet in His Century.* New Haven: Yale UP, 1990.

Thomas, Dwight. *The Poe Log: A Documentary Life of Edgar Allan Poe, 1809–1849.* Boston: Hall, 1987.

Whitman, Walt. *Prose Works 1892.* Ed. Floyd Stovall. Vol. 1. New York: New York UP, 1963.

See also BROADWAY JOURNAL; INFLUENCES ON WHITMAN, PRINCIPAL; POETIC THEORY; SPECIMEN DAYS

Poetic Theory

To the question "What is Whitman's theory of poetry?" the best response probably would be the Buddha-like gesture of silently holding up a copy of *Leaves of Grass.* Next best is to be cautious when abstracting general principles from Whitman's many prose and verse pronouncements on what poetry should be and should do. Whitman is uncomfortable with system, and shares with his fellow cultural nationalists the reflex American suspicion of the word "theory," even as he uses it. "Who is satisfied with the theory, or a parade of the theory?" he blusters in "The Eighteenth Presidency!"; "I say, delay not, come quickly to its most courageous facts and illustrations" (Whitman 1307). General statements of principle and program play their part, but the part is strictly limited to introducing and framing the concrete particularities that matter.

This reversal of the relationship of the particular and the general marks Whitman's ineradicable point of departure from Emerson, to whom he was greatly indebted for language describing the poet's character and mission. Whitman's stridently "new" aesthetic, like others before and after, relies heavily on such reversals of precedent, gaining the specificity of what it is not. If the forms of the old poetry are preset and regular, those of the new will be spontaneous and organic, regular or irregular as the occasion demands. Poems will be divided into sections, though nothing so constrictive, repetitive, and numbingly familiar as the rhyming quatrain stanza. Size will vary with content, mood, and intent. To the rigid metrics of traditional verse, Whitman opposes a looser and more changeable rhythm. (William Carlos Williams credits Whitman with foreshadowing the "variable foot," though it is difficult to state precisely what the term means in the prosody of either poet, beyond a studied avoidance of tick-tock mechanics [Perlman, Folsom, and Campion 119].) The most appropriate organic analogue for Whitman's sense of rhythm may be the human heartbeat. Its rhythm changes with the body's need, calm and quiet in repose, rushed and pounding when excited, always circulating energy in appropriate measure. Musicality is incidental: if the poem is true to life, and it should be, it will naturally sound life's music.

The idea that poetry above all else must be true to life is Whitman's first principle. His is a deeply mimetic, realist commitment. Rhythms and forms, content, language, all must be drawn from life. Poetry should seek immersion in the real, never escape from the mundane into the romance of fairyland or the transcendent spirit. To be sure, Whitman's sense of what life comprises is very broad. Life includes the homely realities of everyday existence in city and country, but also the facts of commerce, politics, war, the sciences and arts, religion, the intricate geographies and demographies of American life. Whitman wants much more than to titillate readers with the "blab of the pave"; he wants to awe them with the magnitude, diversity, and connectedness of a real world they inhabit but only minimally comprehend. Jorge Luis Borges remarks that Whitman's verse scans "Life and its splendor" (Perlman, Folsom, and Campion 142). Typically, the remark sounds banal when it is exact. The extraordinary length of Whitman's line, his most visible signature on the page, signals his uniquely expansive reception of the complex and continuous rhythms and contents of the inward and outward realities he experiences. Moreover, for all his immediacy and presentism, Whitman is not obsessively original. He acknowledges the value of continuity with the living past, and borrows technical devices from Homer, the Bible, and Shakespeare without embarrassment, simply because they still serve.

Whitman sings the near, the low, the common that Emerson affirms in his prose but avoids in his poetry. And mimesis demands that the everyday world be presented in its own language. He is the first great poet of the American vernacular, as Twain is its first great prose fiction writer. Before Whitman, vernacular poetry is mostly a vehicle of satire and class consciousness, the lettered poking fun at uncouth lower beings. More than any other nineteenth-century author (more even than Twain, who wobbles throughout his adult life on the relative value of the vernacular and the genteel), Whitman insists on the dignity, creativity, and propriety of the vernacular. It is a vernacularism largely of vocabulary and idiom. The rolling, chanting verse is more a literary adaptation than a direct echo of contemporary speech. Nevertheless, as Donald D. Kummings argues, the vernacularism is thorough enough to be prescriptive: the American poet must be a vernacular hero, at once a common and uncommon culture hero who represents and inspires. Whitman, though, is not a linguistic nationalist. He thinks English a wonderful vernacular medium; it "befriends the grand American expression," he declares in 1855 (Whitman 25). Like the poet-hero, English is a "universal absorber, combiner, and conqueror"; it "stands for Language in the largest sense" (1165). Whitman's catalogues of American place names, his use of Native American and Spanish words, of street slang, his coinages, gorge an imperial English in its American moment. That is only as it should be, for in Whitman's thought the American moment culminates and fulfills the *translatio studii,* absorbing, fusing all past centers of civilization.

Whitman's mimesis acts and shapes. The verse forms, subject matters, and vernacular language contribute to the multifaceted reality they reflect, affirm its immense variety and render it intelligible and inviting. All of his poetic utterance "smacks of the living physical identity, date, environment, individuality" (Whitman 1345), the better to perceive, express, and add to the great poems of the Soul and America. The trademark anaphoric parallelism of many of Whitman's lines, for example, is more than an extension of one of Shakespeare's tricks. It is a way of displaying the Many and the One without collapsing the former into the latter, conveying an ensemble conceived as a "full armory of concrete actualities, observations, humanity, past poems, ballads, facts, technique, war and peace, politics, North and South, East and West, nothing too large or too small, the sciences as far as possible" (Whitman 1345). Purely as sound pattern, rhyming parallelism dissolves difference in a succession of lines that begin uniquely but end in echo, building a sense of punctuated similarity. Anaphoric parallelism begins with formal similarity and ends with the differences of distinct concrete example. The form is useful for elaborating variations on a theme, differences within a unity, and, important to Whitman, for implying the equality of the many manifestations that constitute the One as Ensemble.

In the longer poems, the method in the madness of Whitman's irregular stanzas and his nonlinear or "spatial" thematic development also is rooted in his desire for form indicative of the dynamic relationship between sharp, irreducible individualities and the whole within which they commune. One of the curiosities in Whitman's statements on poetic theory is his remark in "A Backward Glance O'er Travel'd Roads" that he agrees with Poe's argument that "there can be no such thing as a long poem." Whitman says the thought had haunted him before, but Poe's essays "work'd the sum out and proved it to me" (665). But Whitman grasps the corollary: there may be no such thing as a long poem, but there is such a thing as a sequence of short poems. The sections of his long poems may more profitably be read not as ill-assorted stanzas but as distinct poems, each with its own organic integrity and its assigned communicant's place within the whole. The agreement with Poe also suggests that there may be less compulsive meddling and more deliberation in Whitman's habit of carving out short poems from long to stand on their own (e.g., the excision of "Transpositions" and "Reversals" from "Respondez!") or to be shuffled into other long poems. Collage and bricolage are tempting modern terms for this process, but the working spirit is closer to the anthological.

Similarly, Whitman's lists within poems resist conflation with varied sizes, rhythms, and contents. He invests in the surprise of disjunctive juxtaposition to protect against the danger inherent in successive roll calls—the numbing of the reader to inattention. The list, as list, defies replacement by summary generalization. "The following chants each for its kind I sing," he decrees in "Starting from Paumanok" (section 10); each item is identified and secured in the catalogue, granted the recognition due each member of the poetic community that is always, in Whitman's verse, evocative of the democratic community of the nation. The One, poem or nation, is the ever mutable outcome of the interactions of its constituents. In *Democratic Vistas* he describes the health of the open society (but could be describing the organic health of the open poem) as dependent on "an infinite number of currents and forces, and contributions, and temperatures, and cross purposes, whose ceaseless play of counterpart brings constant restoration and vitality" (929). The moral intent of this national, social, personal, and literary poesis is best expressed by a devout and subtle reader of Whitman, the philosopher William James, who calls, in like phrasing, for "the greatest possible enrichment of our ethical consciousness, through the intensest play of contrasts and the widest diversity of characters" (169).

Vernacular language has its active contribution also. Only the vernacular, "its bases broad and low, close to the ground" (Whitman 1166), is living, evolving language. A poem in the vernacular is inescapably entwined in that growth. The multiple, evanescent, contradictory agent of growth is slang. Slang is language "fermentation"; it is the catalytic ingredient in the process in which "froth and specks are thrown up" (1166), some to vanish, some to live. Furthermore, slang, which he also calls "indirection" (1165), one of his favorite words for his creative method, is radically literary. Slang goes beyond "bald literalism" (1165) into the metaphoric coupling of diverse concretes and "produces poets and poems" and in primal ages "the whole immense tangle of the old mythologies" (1166). For Whitman, as for other poets of sacred affection, from the author(s) of "The Song of Songs" to Dante to Blake, metaphor formation, poesis, eros, are cognates. The poet's most important obligation is to seize difference and particularity, static in their unperceived potential, and induce through poetry the ferment and dynamism of attraction, binding, friendship, love, union. Metaphor couples, rhythm drums the joining; assonance, consonance, rhyme, anaphora incarnate the mystery dance patterns of echo and contact.

What sets Whitman apart is the totality of the sphere of eros. In Whitman, affection binds much more than body, soul, and God. It connects race to race, state to state, land to land. Eros is the foundation principle of national political union of the great poem of the United States. Dissolution, unthinkably, would mean the fall of America out of poetry into severed, isolated, inert, and dying units. Affection, as the title of one poem states, is "The Base of All Metaphysics." Certainly Whitman's homoerotic imagery (here leaving aside the question of its relation to his sexual identity) is crucial to his project of universal, democratic metaphorization. The language of manly affection and bonding provides Whitman with an alternative to the implications of opposition, hierarchy, and restrictive family inevitably associated with traditional models of heterosexual eros. What he calls in "I Hear It was Charged against Me" the "dear love of comrades" is unrestrictive, egalitarian, more easily transportable to the nonhuman, for example to the "inseparable cities with their arms about each other's necks" ("For You O Democracy"). Whitman's "procreant urge of the world" ("Song of Myself," section 3) is ungendered or infinitely gendered. Each individuum is uniquely composed, desirous, and capable of unpredictable and multiple connection.

The poet, supremely, is the magus of attachment and generativity; "only the poet begets," he claims in "Song of the Answerer." Poetry absorbs the urge and urge, and casts spells that strengthen it, conjuring and multiplying "the act-poems of eyes, hands, hips and bosoms" ("Pent-up Aching Rivers") performed by all beings and things. To the reader, the poet bequeaths an enlarged capacity for the delights and possibilities of the world, an opening forced by constant astonishment at improbable feats of union and metaphoric transformation. The mortal sins in Whitman's aesthetic are reduction, simplification, summary conclusion, and closure. However convenient, however necessary, they murder aspects of the real. "I resist anything better than my own diversity," says Whitman in "Song of Myself" (section 16). It is a wry and knowing maxim, and a reminder to readers of Whitman scholarship and criticism to be suspicious of any abstract or outline of his poetic theory.

Robert Johnstone

Bibliography

Allen, Gay Wilson. *The New Walt Whitman Handbook.* 1975. New York: New York UP, 1986.

Emerson, Ralph Waldo. *Essays & Lectures.* Ed. Joel Porte. New York: Library of America, 1983.

James, William. *The Will to Believe and Other Essays in Popular Philosophy, and Human Immortality.* New York: Dover, 1956.

Kummings, Donald D. "Walt Whitman's Vernacular Poetics." *Canadian Review of American Studies* 7 (1976): 119–131.

Matthiessen, F.O. *American Renaissance.* London: Oxford UP, 1941.

Perlman, Jim, Ed Folsom, and Dan Campion, eds. *Walt Whitman: The Measure of His Song.* Minneapolis: Holy Cow!, 1981.

Preminger, Alex, ed. *Princeton Encyclopedia of Poetry and Poetics.* Princeton: Princeton UP, 1974.

Reynolds, David S. *Walt Whitman's America: A Cultural Biography.* New York: Knopf, 1995.

Whitman, Walt. *Complete Poetry and Collected Prose.* Ed. Justin Kaplan. New York: Library of America, 1982.

Zweig, Paul. *Walt Whitman: The Making of the Poet.* New York: Basic Books, 1984.

See also "Backward Glance O'er Travel'd Roads, A"; Catalogues; Democracy; Emerson, Ralph Waldo; Language; Organicism; Preface to *Leaves of Grass*, 1855 Edition; Prosody; Rhetorical Theory and Practice; Sex and Sexuality; Slang; Style and Technique(s); Symbolism

"Poetry To-day in America—Shakspere—The Future" (1881)

This essay, Walt Whitman's most succinct commentary on the evolution of poetry in America, was written in 1881 and published in the February issue of the *North American Review.* It first appeared under the name "The Poetry of the Future" and was later included in Whitman's collected works. Historically, it has remained in the shadows of his other, more prominent prose pieces.

In the essay, Whitman argues that America must produce a class of poets that reflects not only the democratic principles of our country, but one that moves beyond the feudalism of Europe, illustrated most obviously by Shakespeare—and by his followers Sir Walter Scott and Alfred, Lord Tennyson. His understanding of feudalism in the British Islands led him to see beyond its "tyrannies, superstitions, [and] evils" and to believe that from the great poetry it produced, America could learn valuable lessons in the development of its own democratic society and representative bards. It was Whitman's firm belief that the United States should, from the "mass of foreign nutriment" found in the feudalism of Europe, expand, nationalize, and—through its growth process—present its own great literatures (476).

Whitman's praise for William Shakespeare's profound influence on American literature and its poets did not, however, preclude him from waging "hornet-stinging criticism" (477) on Shakespeare's representation of the feudalistic society in his writing. Such representation, in Whitman's mind, served to undermine the development of great poetry in America because of Shakespeare's (and other great writers') portrayal of the caste system, which the United States had come to destroy. Whitman's reference in the article to Thomas Jefferson's verdict on Scott's Waverley novels suggests that they shed "entirely false lights and glamours over the lords, ladies, and aristocratic institutes of Europe" (477), and then ignored the suffering of the lower class citizens. Whitman rejected this model as unfit for America because he believed that the emerging identity of a young and radical republic should be rooted in the identity and convictions of its great poets—past, present, and future.

The future of poetry in America becomes central to this essay. Whitman reiterated what he had earlier professed in 1855, when he wrote the Preface to the first edition of *Leaves of Grass* that the poetry of the future would embody the individual, the free expression of emotion, the powerful uneducated masses, and the central identity of the country. He believed that liberty and freedom, cornerstones of a democratic nation, would become paramount in producing the true poets and the true poems of the world. Only then would the universal appeal of American literature rise above the great works of John Milton, Shakespeare, and others, and serve as a model for the rest of the world.

Whitman also believed that if a great literature of the United States was to emerge, the poets of the future would have to rely on nature as much as they would rely on history. His comparison of the future of poetry to "outside life and landscapes" (481) is a theme present not only in this essay, but one woven intricately into *Leaves of Grass*. For Whitman, nature represented a clear reflection of the individual, a reflection he believed must be fully absorbed by the poets of the future.

Robert W. Barnett

Bibliography

Clarke, Graham. *Walt Whitman: The Poem as Private History*. New York: St. Martin's, 1991.
Dvorak, Angeline Godwin. "A Response to Nature: Prelude to Walt Whitman." *CEA Critic* 54.1 (1991): 58–61.
Mulqueen, James E. "Walt Whitman: Poet of the American Culture-Soul." *Walt Whitman Review* 22.4 (1976): 156–162.
Whitman, Walt. "Poetry To-day in America—Shakspere—The Future." *Prose Works 1892*. Ed. Floyd Stovall. Vol. 2. New York: New York UP, 1964. 474–490.

See also DEMOCRACY; FEUDALISM; *LEAVES OF GRASS*; POETIC THEORY; "POETS TO COME"; PREFACE TO *LEAVES OF GRASS*, 1855 EDITION; SCOTT, SIR WALTER; SHAKESPEARE, WILLIAM; TENNYSON, ALFRED, LORD

"Poets to Come" (1860)

"Poets to Come" was first published as number 14 of "Chants Democratic" in the 1860 edition of *Leaves of Grass*. It was shortened and improved in 1867, transferred to "The Answerer" group in 1871 and 1876, and finally moved to the opening "Inscriptions" section of *Leaves of Grass* in 1881.

In this poem Whitman addresses future American poets, "a new brood, native, athletic, continental," and encourages them to "justify" him. The poem exhorts his successors to take up the work Whitman hints he has only begun in *Leaves of Grass*. That work includes his development of the poetic line, the incorporation of colloquial speech into American poetry, and a willingness to treat in a direct way both physical and spiritual matters. In the last two lines of the poem he challenges his poetic descendants to complete what he has initiated: "Leaving it to you to prove and define it / Expecting the main things from you."

The ongoing poetic response is accounted for in *Walt Whitman: The Measure of His Song* (1981), in which the editors organize chronologically the vast number of poems, letters, essays, and tributes that have been written to and about Walt Whitman. "Poets to Come" serves as an apt epigraph for that collection. As Ed Folsom indicates in his introductory essay "Talking Back to Walt Whitman," "most American poets after Whitman have directly taken him on—to argue with him, agree with him, revise, question, reject and accept him—in an essay or a poem" (xxi).

Thus, "Poets to Come" is an historic invitation, responded to in one way or another by poets who have followed in Whitman's footsteps. Fully cognizant of his own mortality in this poem—"I but advance a moment only to wheel and hurry back in the darkness"—Whitman anticipates an immortal link between himself and future generations of poets.

Steven P. Schneider

Bibliography

Folsom, Ed. "Talking Back to Walt Whitman: An Introduction." *Walt Whitman: The Measure of His Song*. Ed. Jim Perlman, Ed Folsom, and Dan Campion. Minneapolis: Holy Cow!, 1981. xxi–liii.
Martin, Robert K. *The Continuing Presence of Walt Whitman*. Iowa City: U of Iowa P, 1992.
Whitman, Walt. *Leaves of Grass*. Ed. Sculley Bradley and Harold W. Blodgett. Norton Critical Edition. New York: Norton, 1973.

See also "INSCRIPTIONS"; *LEAVES OF GRASS*; LEGACY, WHITMAN'S

Political Views

Walt Whitman's editorial writing on politics began at an early age, influenced by his father, who was attracted to the radical political and religious thought of the Enlightenment and felt empathy for working class people. Other influences on Walt Whitman's politics were the panics of 1819, 1837, 1857, and 1873, which triggered economic depressions, and his exposure to the political and economic life in Brooklyn and Manhattan (in the 1820s–1840s). In 1831, at age twelve, Whitman worked as a journalist's apprentice on the *Long Island Patriot,* a partisan newspaper for the Democratic party in Kings County (Brooklyn), switching, however, to the *Long Island Star* (the Whig weekly paper, also in Brooklyn) by the summer of 1832. An ardent Jacksonian Democrat, he revered William Leggett, the party's foremost spokesman in the 1830s. In that decade Whitman worked on the *Long Island Democrat* (in Jamaica, Queens County, from 1838 to 1839), and from 1846 to 1848 he edited the *Brooklyn Daily Eagle and King's County Democrat* (the paper's full title). He considered the Democratic party the protector of the ideals of the American Revolution, venerating the freethinking of Thomas Paine, the heroic qualities of George Washington, and the wisdom of the Founding Fathers.

Whitman believed in the two-party system and praised national (and presidential) elections. He thought that differing principles dividing the nation into opposing parties—Democrats and Whigs—would not cause the Union to erode. He welcomed partisan conflict as being beneficial to the body politic, placing his confidence in the Democratic party leadership and, indeed, commending the office of the president as "the most sublime on earth" (qtd. in Reynolds 116). The Democratic party was that of Thomas Jefferson and Andrew Jackson, Whitman affirmed, and the American republic was rooted in Jefferson's revolutionary principles of political equality and the inalienable rights of the individual. Whitman's belief that "the best government is that which governs the least" (*Gathering* 1:60) borrowed Jefferson's language, echoing his attack in the Declaration of Independence on George III and the monarchy.

Influenced by the Locofoco party (a radical New York democratic group opposed to bank monopolies and paper money), Whitman considered Jackson the heir to Jeffersonian republicanism, for his 1832 veto of the bank re-charter bill had ended the operation of the privately owned second Bank of the United States, charged with monopoly and special privilege. Whitman supported a "tight money" policy and the subtreasury system (depository for the government's funds) established in 1840 by Jackson's successor, President Martin Van Buren. In the age of Jacksonian democracy and the so-called rise of the common man (actually class conflict and economic inequality expanded in antebellum America), Whitman addressed many other public issues. He advocated freedom of speech and of the press, abolition of the slave trade and of capital punishment, reform of schools and prisons, temperance, the widest suffrage, women's rights (including the right to retain property after marriage), sexual liberty for men and women, promotion from the ranks in the army and navy, the sale of public lands at cheap prices to settlers, tenement housing reform, and most vociferously, free trade (a cardinal principle in the democratic creed). Although he feared that aggressive social action portended social disorder, he deplored the existence of slavery, anti-immigration movements (nativism), oppression of the poor, low wages for women, rapidly widening class differences, political corruption in all levels of government, and greed for wealth.

With the coming of the Democratic machine, organized by 1836–1837, Whitman served as a party activist, forming ties with the New York City Democratic party and in 1845 becoming secretary of its Kings County General Committee. In Brooklyn's 1846 and 1847 elections, he worked to get out the Democratic vote, although the Whigs—the anti-Jackson party—won them both. In 1840 Whitman campaigned for Democratic presidential candidate Martin Van Buren, who lost his reelection bid to Whig candidate William Henry Harrison. Whitman was saddened by Van Buren's defeat, and on 29 July 1841, at a huge rally of Democrats from New York, Kings, and Richmond counties at City Hall Park in Manhattan, he implored the faithful to carry on the fight for the party's principles; presciently, he also announced that the Democratic candidate in 1844 would be "carried into power on the wings of a mighty reaction" (*Uncollected* 1:51).

Whitman enthusiastically supported the expansionist policies of James K. Polk, the 1844 Democratic victor, who achieved a huge electoral margin, followed by the annexation of Texas (1845) as well as Oregon (with the 49th parallel as the boundary) and the Mexican War (both in 1846). Whitman felt that annexation of a large amount of territory from Mexico was inevitable and justifiable. It was not greed or the lure of power that motivated his calculations for the creation of new states ("continentalism"), but the desire for American democracy to spread, as it already had in the West.

No public issue engaged Whitman more passionately than slavery and disunion. He had accepted the Missouri Compromise of 1820, which prohibited slavery in the Louisiana Purchase territory north of the line of 36°30' (except in the state of Missouri, admitted as a slave state). A quarter of a century later David Wilmot, the radical Democratic congressman from Pennsylvania, conditionally stipulated in 1846 that slavery be excluded forever from any territories acquired from Mexico, but the so-called Wilmot Proviso was rejected. Influenced in his thinking by Silas Wright, a rigorous opponent of slavery expansion, Whitman adopted a similar view. He had endorsed Wright in his successful campaign for the governorship of New York in 1844 and campaigned for him in Kings County in 1846, though the governor was defeated for a second term.

At their state convention at Syracuse in 1847, the conservative New York State Democrats (Hunkers) defeated the resolutions against the extension of slavery. The radical wing of the party (Barnburners) bolted and at their own convention at Herkimer hailed the principle of "free soil," bringing down the Syracuse ticket in the local election. Whitman's uncompromising Barnburner opposition to the extension of slavery caused his dismissal from the Brooklyn *Daily Eagle*. Isaac Van Anden, the paper's owner, sided with the proslavery extensionist Democrats. Whitman blamed the party's defeat on its indifference to the Wilmot Proviso. Nevertheless, he was not extremist and in fact was highly critical of the extremist Northern abolitionists and Southern fire-eaters, both of whom he considered serious threats to national unity. As for President Polk, Whitman was disturbed by his opposition to the Wilmot Proviso, but he remained loyal.

Whitman defended the rights and dignity of free male labor—white workingmen, i.e., mechanics and farmers, as opposed to the system of slave labor. He criticized the Southern planter class—a minority of 350,000 seeking to create more slave territory and slave states; a larger majority of both parties in the non-slaveholding states, on the other hand, favored opening the territories to free laborers of the North and South.

In the 1848 presidential election, Whitman spurned both nominees: Governor Lewis Cass of Michigan, the Democratic candidate who opposed the Wilmot Proviso, advocating instead "popular sovereignty" (only the people living in the territories, not Congress, had the power to decide the slavery issue there), and Zachary Taylor, the Virginia-born Whig candidate who became a Louisiana sugar planter and slave owner. When the New York State Democrats nominated Cass at their convention in 1848, Democrats committed to free-soilism walked out of the party. Whitman was one of them: he and fourteen other delegates from Brooklyn attended the Free Soil party national convention at Buffalo in August 1848, when ex-President Van Buren was nominated president. A month later, Whitman founded and edited a free-soil newspaper, the Brooklyn *Freeman* (1848–1849), dedicated to the election of Van Buren and opposing the addition to the Union "of a single inch of slave land, whether in the form of state or territory" (qtd. in Kaplan 145). (Van Buren won 10 percent of the vote.)

The Compromise Law in 1850 (signed by New York's Millard Fillmore, for Taylor had died) infuriated Whitman. It opened up the Mexican Cession (except California) to "popular sovereignty" and included also a more stringent Fugitive Slave Act, which smacked of federal interference. Whitman castigated Northern Democrats like Senator Daniel Webster of Massachusetts—"dough faces"—for supporting Clay's Compromise of 1850 to subject the Union to the influence of the slave owners. This could cause the destruction of the party system and the Union itself, he warned.

Although the Free Soil party had been badly beaten in 1848, Whitman persuaded John Parker Hale of New Hampshire to accept the nomination in 1852. His advocacy of the free-soil policy had long been applauded by Whitman, who hoped the nomination would lead to a "renewed and vital [Free Soil] party" (*Correspondence* 1:39–40). Reorganizing his supporters as the Free Democratic party, Hale won 5 percent of the vote. More disastrous was the election of Franklin Pierce of New Hampshire, the Democratic candidate who, as the Free-Soilers feared, yielded to the proslavery forces.

The issues dividing the North and South were intensified in 1854 when Congress passed and President Pierce signed the Kansas-Nebraska Act. Sponsored by Senator Stephen A. Douglas of Illinois, it created two territories—Kansas and Nebraska—opened to "popular sovereignty" and thus specifically repealing the Missouri Compromise. "Civil war" came to Kansas when a proslavery territorial legislature was elected, made possible by proslavery Missourians who in March 1855 crossed the border to vote. Whitman remained adamant on the issue of slavery extension—arguing for no sectional compromise and asserting that Kansas would continue to "bleed" until it was redeemed. The failure of the Pierce administration to challenge political corruption in Kansas contributed to his disillusionment with America's elected rulers and to his apprehension about the future of the republic.

Whitman was also angered by the presidential nominations in 1856: James Buchanan, the "dough face" Pennsylvania Democrat who had been closely connected to the Compromise of 1850, and Millard Fillmore, the American or Know-Nothing party candidate; he viewed both as disunionists. He was particularly frustrated with the Democratic party because he believed that the proslavery policies of Fillmore, Pierce, and Buchanan contributed to a backlash and consequent growth of the Republican party (he thought it perilous to approve of Republicans for agitating against slavery). These Democratic presidents, "our topmost warning and shame" (*Prose Works* 2:429), proved unable to hold the Union together, he concluded. In the presidential election of 1856, Whitman left the Democratic party and voted for John C. Frémont, the nominee of the Republican party, founded two years earlier to "save Kansas"; it shifted the nation's course away from compromise by espousing the cause of "free labor and free soil."

Whitman described the events that transpired in the several years before Lincoln's presidency as "more lurid and terrible than any war" ("Death" 3). He feared sectionalism because the jurisdiction of the federal government over matters involving the states was tenuous; this made it unlikely that the South, eager to nationalize slavery, would yield to the national interest. The solution to the issue of states' rights and centralized authority, he believed, lay in a Union conceived as a league in which the national government functioned as a consolidation to achieve certain objectives. Each state operated in its own sphere, but while Whitman, a Jeffersonian democrat, continually referred to the nation as "these states," he had no doubt that the national sovereignty, possessing superior power, nourished them.

When the Civil War started, Whitman turned the issue of states' rights vs. national power into the issue of secession vs. union. He observed that Northern sympathy for secession—disunion—was significant and that the North and South were equally culpable for the conflict. But in his view the war was not a "struggle of two distinct and separate peoples" (*Prose Works* 2:426). South Carolina's declaration (on 20 December 1860) that the Union was dissolved and the 1861 collapse of the Democratic party culminated in the disruption of American democracy. Whitman called it the "Secession War" or preferably the "Union War"—rarely the "Civil War"—confident at least in his public writing that the Union would ultimately survive.

Whitman cherished Lincoln for his full commitment to nationalism and to the Union and claimed to have voted for him in 1860. (Whitman was not a zealous Republican.) He fervently supported the first national military conscription law passed by the 37th Congress in early 1863, even though he was disappointed that it was not a universal draft (men won exemption either by paying substitutes or by paying three hundred dollars outright). Whitman championed the war, denouncing Northern Democrats who impeded the war effort and who wanted to recognize the Southern confederacy: the so-called Copperhead Democrats. The war strengthened his faith in the average human, and it restored his respect for political leaders and government institutions. The absolute defeat of the attempted secession demonstrated the steadiness of the democratic republic and, with the abolition of slavery, settled more than the issue of free soil: but like Lincoln and the majority of the people of the Union, Whitman was not prepared to accept the political and social equality of white and black races.

He backed the reconciliation policies of Presidents Andrew Johnson and Ulysses S. Grant, which he believed would ease the return of the secessionists and reestablish a sense of nationality. The Thirteenth, Fourteenth, and Fifteenth Amendments, moreover, afforded federal guarantees of civil and political rights for the black race. The disputed election of 1876, however, led to another deal—the Compromise of 1877, which awarded the presidency to Rutherford B. Hayes, the Republican candidate, in return for the withdrawal of the last federal troops from the South—and this end of radical Reconstruction led to the Republican abandonment of the freedmen. Still, Whitman thought that Hayes helped strengthen ties between the North and South.

Whitman berated the crass materialism of the Gilded Age and, disturbed by corruption among avaricious and wealthy businessmen as well as the growing "trust" problem and bitter labor-capital strife, he feared for American democracy. But he also recognized that material progress improved American life, and he welcomed the accelerated pace of industrialization and technological invention. He hoped that all people would share in the nation's wealth and come to have a stake in society, not penetrating the dark side of economic individualism.

Whitman was fundamentally optimistic about the average individual, believing that democratic government, with all of its possibilities, would work itself out in future generations and promote human happiness. Constantly dwelling on this theme, he asserted that there must be continual additions to our "great experiment of how much liberty society will bear" (*Gathering* 1:11). The nation would then become truly unified. But Whitman contradicted himself (as he suggested) by continuing to hark back to America's past, the republican traditions of the Revolution of 1776.

Bernard Hirschhorn

Bibliography

Allen, Gay Wilson. *The Solitary Singer: A Critical Biography of Walt Whitman.* 1955. Rev. ed. 1967. Chicago: U of Chicago P, 1985.

Brower, Brock. "Patriot Days." *Civilization* May–June 1995: 38–45.

Erkkila, Betsy. "The Political Whitman." *Democracy's Poet: A Walt Whitman Celebration.* New York: Museum of the City of New York, 1992. 4–5.

———. *Whitman the Political Poet.* New York: Oxford UP, 1989.

Kaplan, Justin. *Walt Whitman: A Life.* New York: Simon and Schuster, 1980.

Parrington, Vernon Louis. "The Afterglow of the Enlightenment—Walt Whitman." *Main Currents in American Thought: The Beginnings of Critical Realism in America.* Vol. 3. New York: Harcourt, Brace, 1930. 69–86.

Pessen, Edward. *Jacksonian America: Society, Personality, and Politics.* Homewood, Ill.: Dorsey, 1969.

Reynolds, David S. *Walt Whitman's America: A Cultural Biography.* New York: Knopf, 1995.

Schlesinger, Arthur M., Jr. *The Age of Jackson.* 1945. Boston: Little, Brown, 1950.

Sixbey, George L. "Conscription and Walt Whitman." *Long Island Forum* (Feb. 1942): 25–26, 35–36.

Thomas, M. Wynn. *The Lunar Light of Whitman's Poetry.* Cambridge, Mass.: Harvard UP, 1987.

Trachtenberg, Alan. "Whitman's Visionary Politics." *The Mickle Street Review* 10 (1988): 15–31.

Whitman, Walt. *The Correspondence.* Ed. Edwin Haviland Miller. 6 vols. New York: New York UP, 1961–1977.

———. "Death of Abraham Lincoln." *Memoranda During the War & Death of Abraham Lincoln.* Ed. Roy P. Basler. Bloomington: Indiana UP, 1962. 1–14.

———. *"The Eighteenth Presidency!" A Critical Text.* Ed. Edward F. Grier. Lawrence: U of Kansas P, 1956.

———. *The Gathering of the Forces.* Ed. Cleveland Rodgers and John Black. 2 vols. New York: Putnam, 1920.

———. *Prose Works 1892.* Ed. Floyd Stovall. 2 vols. New York: New York UP, 1963–1964.

———. *The Uncollected Poetry and Prose of Walt Whitman.* Ed. Emory Holloway. 2 vols. Garden City, N.Y.: Doubleday, Page, 1921.

Zweig, Paul. *Walt Whitman: The Making of the Poet.* New York: Basic Books, 1984.

See also BARNBURNERS AND LOCOFOCOS; BUFFALO FREE SOIL CONVENTION; CIVIL WAR, THE; COMPROMISE OF 1850; DEMOCRACY; DEMOCRATIC PARTY; DOUGLAS, STEPHEN ARNOLD; FREE SOIL PARTY; HUNKERS; JACKSON, ANDREW; JEFFERSON, THOMAS; JOURNALISM, WHITMAN'S; LABOR AND LABORING CLASSES; LEGGETT, WILLIAM L.; LINCOLN, ABRAHAM; MEXICAN WAR, THE; PAINE, THOMAS; PRESIDENTS, UNITED STATES; RADICALISM; RECONSTRUCTION; REPUBLICAN PARTY; SLAVERY AND ABOLITIONISM; WHIGS; WILMOT PROVISO; WOMAN'S RIGHTS MOVEMENT AND WHITMAN, THE

P

Popular Culture, Whitman and

Whitman had deep roots in popular culture. He wrote in "A Song for Occupations" (1856), "The popular tastes and employments tak[e] precedence in poems or anywhere" (section 6). In his period of literary apprenticeship, from 1838 to 1850, he was primarily a writer for the mass audience. During this time he wrote twenty poems, twenty-four short stories, a novel, and countless pieces of journalism. His interest in the themes of sensationalism, death, religion, and reform surfaced early in his periodical writings and reappeared, in revised forms, in his major poetry.

Whitman was weaned in the cut-and-thrust world of penny-press urban journalism, and he noted the extreme popularity of what he called "blood and thunder romances with alliterative titles and plots of startling interest" (*Uncollected* 2:20). As chief editor of the Brooklyn *Daily Eagle* and later the Brooklyn *Daily Times* he accommodated to popular taste by printing horrid stories of crime and violence. Before that, he had reported murders for the New York *Tattler* and wrote police and coroner's stories for the New York *Sun*.

Several of his early poems and stories were sensational in a straightforward way, like the plot- and action-driven yellow-covered novels of the day. In his magazine tale "Richard Parker's Widow" (1845), for instance, a maddened woman disinters her husband's coffin, opens it, and embraces and kisses the rotting corpse.

A certain amount of sensationalism runs through *Leaves of Grass*, suggesting that on some level Whitman was trying to appeal to the predominantly working class readers who consumed such literature. One thinks particularly of the bloody adventure narratives at the heart of "Song of Myself," describing the massacre of the 412 young men and then the bloody sea battle, or of the graphic images scattered throughout his poems, such as the amputated leg that falls horribly into the pail or the mashed fireman or the suicide sprawled on the bloody bedroom floor. Still, Whitman makes every effort in his major poetry to juxtapose sensational images with life-affirming ones, as though tragic occurrences are a natural part of an ongoing cycle of life and death.

His revised treatment of sensationalism was linked to a revised treatment of death. Whitman started out largely as a writer of gloom and skepticism, in the vein of popular poets like William Cullen Bryant and Lydia H. Sigourney. In one early poem, "The Love That Is Hereafter" (1840), he writes that since on earth there is "[n]ought but wo," the heart must "look above, / Or die in dull despair" (*Early* 9). In "Each Has His Grief" (1840) he points out that "All, all know care" and that since death ends human agony, none should fear "the coffin, the pall's dark gloom" (*Early* 16–17). This kind of lachrymose writing filled popular periodicals.

Over time Whitman's almost nihilistic fear of death was largely alleviated by his exposure to two popular developments of the late 1840s: chemical science and spiritualism. Chemical scientists such as Justus Liebig introduced an explanation for the recombination of atoms in an eternal cycle of decay and regeneration. Whereas in his early poetry Whitman had expressed terror that everything physical must decay, in *Leaves of Grass* decay creates new life through a ceaseless exchange of atoms. A part of his poetic mission was the coinage of fresh metaphors to communicate this democratic exchange of physical substances, such as the grass as dark hair growing from the roofs of pink mouths or the image of the corpse as good manure.

Whitman also felt the direct influence of spiritualism, which surfaced in 1848 and spread with amazing rapidity, gaining millions of adherents. Spiritualism was nineteenth-century America's most influential movement challenging the idea of the finality of death. By 1857 Whitman could note in the *Daily Times* that there were some three to five million spiritualists in America and that the movement was "blending itself in many ways with society, in theology, in the art of healing, in literature, and in the moral and mental character of the people of the United States" (Brooklyn *Daily Times,* 26 June 1857). One of the things it blended with was his poetry. His constant affirmations of immortality through his poetry were linked to spiritualism, as when he wrote, "I know I am deathless . . . I laugh at what you call dissolution" ("Song of Myself," section 20). Although Whitman was never a card-carrying spiritualist, he did befriend spiritualists, attended séances at least twice, and actually wrote a poem about immortality he said was inspired by a talk with a spiritualist. On some level, he wished to be identified with this popular movement. In a self-review of the 1855 edition he wrote of himself as poet: "He is the true spiritualist. He recognizes no annihilation, or death or loss of identity" ("Walt" 19).

Just as science and spiritualism helped him overcome his earlier fears of death, so certain religious developments of the 1850s expanded and intensified his philosophical vision. The expressions of religion and morality in Whitman's early magazine writings were largely conventional. Visionary tales like "The Angel of Tears" (1842) and "The Love of Eris: A Spirit Record" (1844) and moral stories like "A Legend of Life and Love" (1842) and "The Shadow and the Light of a Young Man's Soul" (1848) were staidly pious works that accorded with the benign liberal Protestantism permeating much popular fiction and poetry of the time. The rise of Harmonialism and Swedenborgianism between 1848 and 1854 brought to the fore new kinds of mysticism and spiritual eroticism that Whitman would experiment with in *Leaves of Grass*. His outlook in some ways corresponded with that of the era's leading Harmonialist, Andrew Jackson Davis. Several things Davis popularized—mesmeric healing, trance writing, and mental time-space travel through what Davis called "traveling clairvoyance"—were manifested in Whitman's poetry. Small wonder that the 1855 edition of *Leaves of Grass* received a long, positive review in the Harmonial magazine *The Christian Spiritualist*.

Closely allied to Harmonialism was Swedenborgianism, another popular movement that affected Whitman as he made the transition from periodical writer to poet. Swedenborgianism, which became widely diffused through American culture after 1848, was a religious movement that showed how the erotic and the mystical could be combined. In the 1850s Whitman became close to several people active in Swedenborgian circles, discussing some of them, such as Thomas Lake Harris and James John Garth Wilkinson, in his notebooks. In a Brooklyn *Daily Times* article of 1858 he reviewed the Swedenborgian movement in America and said Swedenborg would have "the deepest and broadest mark upon the religions of future ages here, of any man that ever walked the earth" (*Uncollected* 2:18).

There was an eroticism, even a kind of homoeroticism, intrinsic to Swedenborgian worship. Swedenborg had called God the Divine Man, or *Homo Maximus,* with the so-called highest heaven extending from the Divine Man's head down to the neck, the middle heaven from the breast to the loins, the lowest from the feet to the soles and the shoulders to the fingers. Whitman echoed this body-specific view when he addressed God in a poem as follows: "thou, the Ideal Man . . . Complete in body and dilate in spirit, / Be thou my God" ("Gods") or when in the 1855 version of "Song of Myself" he called God "a loving bedfellow [who] sleeps at my side all night and close on the peep of the day" (section 3). Whitman used the Swedenborgian words "influx" and "efflux" in *Leaves of Grass* several times. More important, he fused intense religiosity with body-specific mysticism, as in the famous section 5 of "Song of Myself," where his persona is pictured lying with his soul on the transparent summer morning.

In his apprentice writings Whitman endorsed many popular reforms. Early on, his reform was very much *anti:* anti-drinking, anti–capital punishment, anti-tobacco, and so forth. His temperance novel *Franklin Evans* (1842), which he emphasized was "written *for the mass,*" sold some twenty thousand copies with its diverting episodes illustrating the nefarious operations of the so-called Liquor Fiend (*Early* 127). To some degree, this "anti" voice is heard even in his mature poetry, as when he denounced in his poems the "putridity of gluttons or rum-drinkers" or the "privacy of the onanist" ("Song of Prudence"), or when he wrote, "No diseas'd person, no rum drinker, or venereal taint is permitted here" ("Song of the Open Road," section 10).

More characteristically, though, his poetry made affirmative statements that reveal the influence of positive health reforms of the day, particularly those popularized by the publishing firm of Fowler and Wells, distributor of the first edition of *Leaves of Grass* and publisher of the second. In particular, the Fowlers' popular versions of phrenology and physiology contributed to his outlook. The Fowlers called for frank, open treatment of the body and sexuality. They also advised keeping the brain and other bodily functions in equilibrium. Theirs was a holistic outlook that emphasized maintaining balance in every aspect of physical and mental being. Anything that threatened this balance could cause insanity or disease. The healer-persona of Whitman's poetry was directly linked to the Fowlers' notion of health. Whitman wrote that the poet was the one in perfect equilibrium, the one to whom the diseased or troubled could look for help.

Indeed, Whitman wrote *Leaves of Grass* largely because he thought the nation itself lacked equilibrium and needed immediate help. The political crisis of the 1850s, in which the Whig party collapsed and the Democratic party gave itself over to proslavery forces, made him now view social rulers as corrupt beyond hope. His anti-authoritarian position was expressed in four political protest poems of 1850: "Resurgemus," "Blood-Money," "Dough-Face Song," and "The House of Friends." Establishing a whole new tone that anticipated the bracingly rebellious moments in *Leaves of Grass,* these poems adopted the kind of gothicized, subversive rhetoric that had been popularized by best-selling working class writers like George Lippard.

Whitman now thought redemption could be found only in average people. Among his models for the brashly independent but fundamentally sound American, he turned to the Bowery b'hoy, a figure of urban street culture who had been mythologized in popular plays and novels. Whitman's poetic persona as "one of the roughs" reflected the defiance and hearty good nature of this popular figure.

The imminent unraveling of the United States after the passage in May 1854 of the Kansas-Nebraska Act drove him to create a unifying poetic document that brought together the diverse, sometimes contradictory cultural images under one literary roof. He offered his poetry as a gesture of healing and togetherness to a nation on the brink of war.

David S. Reynolds

Bibliography

Reynolds, David S. *Beneath the American Renaissance: The Subversive Imagination in the Age of Emerson and Melville.* New York: Knopf, 1988.

———. "From Periodical Writer to Poet: Whitman's Journey Through Popular Culture." *Periodical Literature in Nineteenth-Century America.* Ed. Kenneth M. Price and Susan Belasco Smith. Charlottesville: UP of Virginia, 1995. 35–50.

———. *Walt Whitman's America: A Cultural Biography.* New York: Knopf, 1995.

Whitman, Walt. *The Early Poems and the Fiction.* Ed. Thomas L. Brasher. New York: New York UP, 1963.

———. *Leaves of Grass: Comprehensive Reader's Edition.* Ed. Harold W. Blodgett and Sculley Bradley. New York: New York UP, 1965.

———. *Leaves of Grass: A Textual Variorum of the Printed Poems.* Ed. Sculley Bradley, Harold W. Blodgett, Arthur Golden, and William White. 3 vols. New York: New York UP, 1980.

———. *The Uncollected Poetry and Prose of Walt Whitman.* 1921. Ed. Emory Holloway. 2 vols. Gloucester, Mass.: Peter Smith, 1972.

———. "Walt Whitman and His Poems." *In Re Walt Whitman.* Ed. Horace L. Traubel, Richard Maurice Bucke, and Thomas B. Harned. Philadelphia: McKay, 1893. 13–21.

Zweig, Paul. *Walt Whitman: The Making of the Poet.* New York: Basic Books, 1984.

See also BROOKLYN *DAILY EAGLE;* BROOKLYN *DAILY TIMES;* FOWLER, LORENZO NILES AND ORSON SQUIRE; *FRANKLIN EVANS;* HARRIS, THOMAS LAKE; JOURNALISM, WHITMAN'S; LIEBIG, JUSTUS; PRE-*LEAVES* POEMS; "RICHARD PARKER'S WIDOW"; ROUGHS; SENTIMENTALITY; SHORT FICTION, WHITMAN'S; SWEDENBORG, EMANUEL

Portugal and Brazil, Whitman in

The multiple and contradictory Whitman "kosmos" made a major impression on Fernando Pessoa (1888–1935), Portugal's most important modern poet. Pessoa wrote poems not only under his name but also as distinctive fictional poets whom he called his heteronyms. According to critic Eduardo Lourenço in *Pessoa Revisitado: Leitura Estruturante do Drama em Gente,* it was *Leaves of Grass* that sparked the creation of two interrelated heteronyms who sound like transfigurations of Whitman: Álvaro de Campos and Alberto Caeiro. Campos, the most obvious Whitmanian heteronym and the author of the ode "Saudação a Walt Whitman," presents the American poet's comprehensive vision of the world, but as he lacks his "camaraderie" he is unable to merge with the crowd. Although Pessoa tried to diminish Whitman's imprint in Caeiro's work (*Obra* 2:1063), Susan M. Brown has convincingly demonstrated in the essays "The Whitman/Pessoa Connection" and "Pessoa and Whitman: Brothers in the Universe" Whitman's essential presence in Campos's poetic sequence entitled "O Guardador de Rebanhos" (The Keeper of Sheep).

In the nineteenth century, Joaquim de Sousa Andrade (1831–1902)—or Sousândrade as he preferred to sign his name—was the only Brazilian writer who felt the impact of Whitman's work. Nevertheless, in the beginning of the twentieth century, Whitman's voice, which was brought to Brazil by the symbolist and the avant-garde movements, reached a significant number of writers and their respective publics. In the 1920s, Whitman was praised as a forerunner of a new aesthetics by members of the literary movement known as Modernismo. As the "traditionalists" also regarded him as one of them, both groups requested Whitman to close ranks with them. Among the modernists who gave critical and creative response to Whitman's work, Mário de Andrade (1893–1945) is the most important figure. Andrade, a careful and attentive reader of *Leaves of Grass*, used this book as inspiration for some of his own poems, and there are passages in his work that are better understood in the light of Whitman's achievements, because they have become integral elements in Andrade's DNA poetic structure. The name of Ronald de Carvalho (1893–1935) became unequivocally associated with Whitman's after the publication of *Toda a América* (1926), an attempt to enlarge Whitman's Americanism to include all the Americas. Whitman's prophetic gospel was also very important for Tasso da Silveira (1895–1968). Silveira's free rhythm resembles the model given by Èmile Verhaeren (1855–1916), but Whitman's diction—in Christian array—is clearly present in many of the poems of *Alegorias do Homem Novo* (1926) and of *Cantos do Campo de Batalha* (1945), which includes a poem called "Palavras a Whitman."

The dates of publication of these books reveal two privileged moments of Whitman's literary reception in Brazil. Whereas in the 1920s Whitman was regarded as a symbol of artistic freedom, in the 1940s he became a symbol of social freedom, being highly regarded by those who were on the political right and left. Essays were written and collections of poems were translated and published to support both views. The most popular translation of that period was *Cantos de Walt Whitman* (1946) by the socialist Oswaldino Marques (1916–1964) and the best book was the internationally acclaimed *O Camarada Whitman* (1948) by the sociologist Gilberto Freyre (1900–1987), who was regarded as being on the right.

In 1964, Geir Campos (1924–) translated and published the most popular collection of Whitman's poems in Brazil, entitled *Fôlhas de Relva* (1964), reedited five times from 1983 to 1993 with the title *Folhas das Folhas de Relva*. Although Whitman continues attracting each new generation of Brazilian readers, a complete Portuguese translation of *Leaves of Grass* has not been forthcoming.

Maria Clara B. Paro

Bibliography

Allen, Gay Wilson, and Ed Folsom, eds. *Walt Whitman & the World*. Iowa City: U of Iowa P, 1995.

Andrade, Mário de. *Poesias Completas*. Ed. D.Z. Manfio. Belo Horizonte: Itatiaia, São Paulo: Editora da U de São Paulo, 1987.

Brown, Susan Margaret. "Pessoa and Whitman: Brothers in the Universe." *The Continuing Presence of Walt Whitman*. Ed. Robert K. Martin. Iowa City: U of Iowa P, 1992. 167–181.

———. "The Whitman/Pessoa Connection." *Walt Whitman Quarterly Review* 9 (1991): 1–14.

Campos, Geir, trans. *Folhas das Folhas de Relva*. São Paulo: Brasiliense, 1983.

———, trans. *Fôlhas de Relva*. Rio de Janeiro: Civilização Brasileira, 1964.

Carvalho, Ronald de. *Toda a América*. São Paulo: Hispano-Brasileña, 1935.

Freyre, Gilberto. *O Camarada Whitman*. Rio de Janeiro: José Olympio, 1948.

Lourenço, Eduardo. *Fernando Pessoa Revisitado: Leitura Estruturante do Drama em Gente*. Porto: Editorial Inova, 1973.

Marques, Oswaldino, ed. and trans. *Cantos de Walt Whitman*. Rio de Janeiro: José Olympio, 1946.

Paro, Maria Clara B. "As Leituras Brasileiras da Obra de Walt Whitman." Diss. U de São Paulo, 1995.

———. "Walt Whitman in Brazil." *Walt Whitman Quarterly Review* 11 (1993): 57–66.

Pessoa, Fernando. *Obra Poética e em Prosa*. 3 vols. Porto: Lello and Irmãos, 1986.

See also INTERCULTURALITY; PESSOA, FERNANDO; SPAIN AND SPANISH AMERICA, WHITMAN IN

Pound, Ezra (1885–1972)

Over the course of his artistic life Ezra Pound's attitude toward Walt Whitman was ambivalent. At heart an American chauvinist much in the Whitman mold, Pound "equated his own hope for an American Risorgimento with Whitman's faith in man's [especially the American's] ability to realize his divine potential" (Willard, "'Message'" 95). Moreover, *Leaves of Grass* taught Pound important lessons that helped to shape Pound's *Cantos*—that one could sing one's self as a national and even universal paradigm, and "that a modern American long poem including history could be a cumulative, open-ended, personal record built up over the author's lifetime as a work in progress" (Witemeyer 83).

On the minus side, however, Pound long felt that Whitman, although he was "to my fatherland . . . what Dante is to Italy" (Pound, *Selected* 116), was too instinctual, insufficiently attuned to European culture, and insufficiently careful as a craftsman. In the 1934 *The ABC of Reading*, for example, Pound claimed that "If you insist . . . on dissecting [Whitman's] language you will probably find that it is wrong" (192).

There are traces of Whitman in Pound's earlier *Cantos* (e.g., Canto 47), but with the *Pisan Cantos* in 1948 (e.g., Cantos 80 and 82), Pound, like many sons who come to terms with filial misgivings, was ready to accept Whitman practically without hesitation. By then his affinity for Whitman was so great that "There is no more callow talk about Whitman's not being 'master of the forces which beat upon him'"—Pound's complaint decades before in *The Spirit of Romance* (Witemeyer 99). Oddly, however, Pound could never seem to see that in Whitman's open form and direct treatment of the *thing* in such poems as "The Runner," he was a direct precursor of the imagist movement over which Pound was to preside.

Alan Shucard

Bibliography

Pound, Ezra. *ABC of Reading.* London: Faber and Faber, 1963.

———. *Selected Prose, 1909–1965.* Ed. William Cookson. London: Faber and Faber, 1973.

Willard, Charles B. "Ezra Pound and the Whitman 'Message.'" *Revue de littérature comparée* 31 (1957): 94–98.

———. "Ezra Pound's Appraisal of Walt Whitman." *Modern Language Notes* 72 (1957): 19–26.

Witemeyer, Hugh. "Clothing the American Adam: Pound's Tailoring of Walt Whitman." *Ezra Pound Among the Poets.* Ed. George Bornstein. Chicago: U of Chicago P, 1985. 81–105.

See also LEAVES OF GRASS; LEGACY, WHITMAN'S

"Prairie States, The" (1881)

Whitman's short poem "The Prairie States" first appeared in the 1881–1882 edition of *Leaves of Grass* in the "Autumn Rivulets" cluster. One of twenty new poems he added for this edition, "The Prairie States" was inspired by the poet's 1879 trip west, during which he journeyed as far as Colorado. Although the poem is considered one of Whitman's minor works, it nevertheless reveals the celebratory wonder with which he regarded the western landscape and the men and women who erected homes, towns, and cities upon that landscape.

Whitman's tone of celebration is recognizable early in the poem when he lauds the region for its potential as a "newer garden of creation." The allusion to the biblical Garden of Eden is clear, but what follows is not so much a hymn to beauty, innocence, or creative fertility as it is a hymn in praise of population growth. Whitman's western garden will not be a remote and isolated paradise. Instead, it will be a place of human density and diversity, a place capable of drawing millions of people from all corners of the world. These millions will form an interconnected society in which qualities like freedom, law, and thrift shine so brightly they become the crowning virtues of the population.

Whitman's boast about the future of the prairie states is characteristic of his enthusiasm for his steadily expanding nation, but it should not be forgotten that the boast—indeed, the entire poem—turns memorably upon the final four words: "to justify the past." Through this phrase Whitman offers a sober reminder that nothing, not even a "newer garden of creation," springs into existence without an antecedent. The task of future generations will be to "justify," in the many ways the word can be interpreted, that which came before.

C.D. Albin

Bibliography

Allen, Gay Wilson. *The New Walt Whitman Handbook.* 1975. New York: New York UP, 1986.

Asselineau, Roger. *The Evolution of Walt Whitman: The Creation of a Personality.* Trans. Richard P. Adams and Roger Asselineau. Cambridge, Mass.: Harvard UP, 1960.

Erkkila, Betsy. *Whitman the Political Poet.* New York: Oxford UP, 1989.

Whitman, Walt. *Leaves of Grass: Comprehensive Reader's Edition.* Ed. Harold W. Blodgett and Sculley Bradley. New York: New York UP 1965.

See also "Autumn Rivulets"; Great Plains and Prairies, The; "Prairie-Grass Dividing, The"; Travels, Whitman's; West, The American

"Prairie-Grass Dividing, The" (1860)

"The Prairie-Grass Dividing" was originally number 25 in the "Calamus" cluster. After some minor changes, it took its final form in 1867.

The poem celebrates the inhabitants of the prairies, "Those of the open atmosphere, coarse, sunlit, fresh, nutritious." Throughout his poetic career, Whitman envisioned the prairies as the home of a mythical race. Long before the poet ever visited the plains states, he incorporated into his poetry the geography of the plains and the men who inhabited them.

Whitman's romanticized description of those who lived in the prairies reflects his faith in inland America: "Those of earth-born passion, simple, never constrain'd, never obedient." Characteristically, Whitman fails to consider that those whom he extols with such sweeping praise may have had a hand in the slaughter of the buffalo or the killing of Native Americans and the seizure of their lands.

That Whitman places this poem in the "Calamus" section distinguishes it from several other prairie poems. Whitman's use of the verb "demand" near or at the beginning of lines 2, 3, and 4 of the poem suggests the sense of urgency the speaker feels: "Demand the most copious and close companionship of men." Just as the short and tall prairie grasses grow close together, so too did Whitman envision the "close companionship of men." Thus, the prairie grass itself is both an image and a metaphor, the landscape out of which an audacious and lusty race has emerged and the sweet-smelling perfume of copious manly love. The poem is an integral part of Whitman's poetic program in "Calamus," what he describes in *Democratic Vistas*

as "the counterbalance and offset of our materialistic and vulgar American democracy" (*Prose Works* 2:414).

"The Prairie-Grass Dividing" is a key poem in Whitman's canon. It echoes the sentiment that the westward plains states, with their vast expanses of prairie, are the seat of a vigorous and healthy manhood. The poem also seeks and manifests a "correspondence" between geography and the human body, and between Whitman's love of the land and of his fellow Americans.

Steven P. Schneider

Bibliography

Olson, Steven. *The Prairie in Nineteenth-Century American Poetry.* Norman: U of Oklahoma P, 1994.

Whitman, Walt. *Prose Works 1892.* Ed. Floyd Stovall. 2 vols. New York: New York UP, 1963–1964.

———. *Leaves of Grass.* Ed. Sculley Bradley and Harold W. Blodgett. Norton Critical Edition. New York: Norton, 1973.

See also "Calamus"; Comradeship; Great Plains and Prairies, The; "Prairie States, The"; West, The American

"Prayer of Columbus" (1874)

Whitman wrote "Prayer of Columbus" in late 1873 and published it with a prefatory note in *Harper's Monthly* in March 1874. The poem was collected in the Centennial edition of *Two Rivulets* (1876) and entered *Leaves of Grass* with the 1881 edition.

Whitman wrote "Prayer" during one of the darkest periods of his life. He was already demoralized by the scandals of the Grant administration, the failures of Reconstruction and the country's descent into the Gilded Age, when in 1872 his opposition to black suffrage cost him his important friendship with William Douglas O'Connor. In January 1873 Whitman suffered a paralytic stroke; in February, his sister-in-law, Mattie, died; in May, his mother died; and finally, in October, Tom Olser, a Camden friend, was killed in an accident. While recuperating in Camden, he saw his most recent books ignored or panned.

As his despair deepened, Whitman turned to the figure of Columbus for inspiration. In "Prayer," Whitman expresses his own despair through the voice of the defeated Columbus of the fourth and final voyage, who, his ships badly damaged by worms, was forced to run ashore in Jamaica where his crew threatened mutiny and the natives staged guerrilla attacks. The poem presents a dramatic dialogue by Columbus in which he addresses God and himself and struggles with doubt. In a letter to Ellen O'Connor, Whitman wrote of the poem, "As I see it now, I shouldn't wonder if I have unconsciously put a sort of autobiographical dash in it" (*Correspondence* 2: 272).

The Columbus of the opening stanza is a "batter'd, wreck'd old man . . . [v]enting a heavy heart." In the second stanza, he sinks deeper into despair until he finally says, "Haply I may not live another day." But, then, as he turns to God in prayer, Columbus becomes angry and gains resolve. His voice becomes Job-like and defiant, and the prayer becomes a long list of his accomplishments, meant to remind God that he has been faithful. Though he tries to remain pious, he cannot accept his fate or put aside his pride. He claims his "[i]ntentions, purports, [and] aspirations" as his own and only grudgingly accepts that the "results" belong to God.

Throughout the poem Columbus wavers between self-doubt and pride. His uncertainty reflects the loss of faith Whitman felt at the time, for like Columbus, he was "[o]ld, poor, and paralyzed." In the final stanzas, the crisis comes to a head when Columbus addresses not God but himself and asks, "Is it the prophet's thought I speak, or am I raving?" At this point, Whitman borrows a conceit from Joel Barlow's *The Columbiad* and Washington Irving's *The Life and Voyages of Christopher Columbus,* each of whom had portrayed Columbus as a prophet. At the close of "Prayer," Whitman's Columbus is consoled by a vision of "countless ships" sailing to the new world he has discovered.

Critics have generally admired "Prayer," seeing it as a striking and sustained example of dramatic monologue. Its controlled intensity is often compared favorably to the more ambitious and mystical, but also more histrionic "Passage to India," which features Columbus as well and immediately precedes "Prayer" in *Leaves of Grass.*

Ned C. Stuckey-French

Bibliography

Allen, Gay Wilson. *The Solitary Singer: A Critical Biography of Walt Whitman.* 1955. Rev. ed. 1967. Chicago: U of Chicago P, 1985.

Barlow, Joel. *The Columbiad.* Philadelphia: C. and A. Conrad, 1807.

Irving, Washington. *The Life and Voyages of Christopher Columbus.* 1828. Ed. John Harmon McElroy. Boston: Twayne, 1981.

Whitman, Walt. *The Correspondence.* Ed. Edwin Haviland Miller. 6 vols. New York: New York UP, 1961–1977.

———. *Leaves of Grass: A Textual Variorum of the Printed Poems.* Ed. Sculley Bradley, Harold W. Blodgett, Arthur Golden, and William White. 3 vols. New York: New York UP, 1980.

See also COLUMBUS, CHRISTOPHER; "PASSAGE TO INDIA"; "THOUGHT OF COLUMBUS, A"; *TWO RIVULETS,* AUTHOR'S EDITION

Preface to *As a Strong Bird on Pinions Free* (1872)

In 1872 Whitman issued a pamphlet publication from Washington, D.C., called *As a Strong Bird on Pinions Free and Other Poems.* It introduced seven new poems and the significant prose Preface announcing his desire to produce a book of "democratic nationality" to serve as a companion volume to *Leaves of Grass.* This 1872 Preface, though published as a prefix to *As a Strong Bird on Pinions Free* (later "Thou Mother with Thy Equal Brood"), belonged to the textual archaeology of the growth of *Leaves,* insofar as the poet set out an apology for the relevancy of *Leaves* in lucid terms while pressing ahead with his plans for the companion volume. Whitman's project had already begun to fragment after the war, beginning with *Drum-Taps* (1865), *Sequel to Drum-Taps* (1866), *Songs Before Parting* (1867), and *Passage to India* (1871). All these supplementary texts still bore the imprint "Leaves of Grass" on their title pages, but their rhetorical energies were leading Whitman to believe that he had already commenced in the production of a second volume of work to accompany his major work, *Leaves of Grass.*

Undiminished in his desire to represent the events of "our Nineteenth Century" (Whitman 740), Whitman's 1872 Preface argues that his historical desire to be embedded in his time would represent America not simply in materialistic terms, but also as the "composite nation" (741) which welcomed with tolerance all immigrants to be assimilated as Americans. As in the

1871 *Democratic Vistas,* the Preface articulates a desire for native literary organizations which would bind together the material advantages of the nation, in pursuit of "the great Ideal Nationality" (741) of succeeding generations. Such a democratic nationality would result from the separation of religion from its conventional institutional structures, and the realignment of religion to the masses and to literature. The Civil War had already begun to be erased from the popular imagination, and Whitman applauds the postwar amnesia as a salve for the earlier sectional and racial hatreds that had led to a fracturing of the Union in 1861. While there is more than a little compensation in Whitman's pronouncements that the "strange, sad war" (743) was quickly losing its hold on the nation's memory, the poet's rhetoric suggests an even more important representational function: the desire for the departure from the divisive social balkanization between section and section, between races, or between federal authorities and unruly state and municipal authorities. In other words, Whitman was bidding a nostalgic farewell to the unbridled heterogeneity of America as a confederacy of states. The poet was thus enabled to welcome the renovated compact of United States which Americans could increasingly turn to in their self-understanding.

Having distanced the Reconstruction nation from the divided past, Whitman's dominant accent in his political agenda in the 1872 Preface continues to be the future of democracy. The aspiration for a more socially cohesive solidarity among citizens underscores the popular displeasure with the contemporary squabbles between races, in the white resistance to black equality, and between the federal government and recalcitrant Southern states over black civil rights. In effect, Whitman had made the move from the plural "United States" to the pluralized citizens within a singular nation. Likewise, in his discussion of his work, this federalizing ambition had crystallized into a willingness to look on *Leaves of Grass* ("the song of a great composite *Democratic Individual*" [743]) as the first installment in a project which would include a companion volume focused on "electric *Democratic Nationality*" (744). Though critics have uniformly assumed that such a supplement was not completed, due to the onset of ill health and a decline of creative powers, Whitman did deliver the companion volume *Two Rivulets* (1876) to supplement the Centennial edition of *Leaves of Grass* in the same year. In the 1872 Preface Whitman registers uncertainty over whether such a book of democratic nationality would be completed, and his publication of *Two Rivulets* four years later has met with almost complete critical indifference from then until now. Whatever its merits, *Two Rivulets* becomes a summa of the majority of Whitman's major Reconstruction texts: *Democratic Vistas* (1871), *As a Strong Bird on Pinions Free* (1872), *Memoranda During the War* (1875–1876), and *Passage to India* (1871). Arguably, Whitman's prospectus in the 1872 Preface came closest to fulfillment in *Two Rivulets,* with its rhetorical insistence on centralizing the energies of the nation.

Always placing social affection above mere political machinations, in the 1872 Preface Whitman returned to his earlier texts with an undiminished confidence that his creative energies had not been misplaced, though he seems to have sensed his own physical deterioration. The notion of American nationality, as the culmination of Western history, reverberates throughout the Preface, though Whitman's evolutionary model of progress will not concede that America has incarnated its destiny in 1872. Thus, the 1872 Preface elaborates many of the preoccupations of Whitman's earlier work (democracy, individualism, literary religion, the Civil War, social solidarity), while the rhetoric also points to Whitman's desire for a fuller embodiment of democratic nationality down the open road of the future.

Luke Mancuso

Bibliography

Allen, Gay Wilson. *The New Walt Whitman Handbook.* 1975. New York: New York UP, 1986.

Erkkila, Betsy. *Whitman the Political Poet.* New York: Oxford UP, 1989.

Mancuso, Luke. "'The Strange Sad War Revolving': Reconstituting Walt Whitman's Reconstruction Texts in the Legislative Workshop, 1865–1876." Diss. U of Iowa, 1994.

Whitman, Walt. *Leaves of Grass: Comprehensive Reader's Edition.* Ed. Harold W. Blodgett and Sculley Bradley. New York: New York UP, 1965.

See also COMRADESHIP; DEMOCRACY; DEMO-CRATIC VISTAS; INDIVIDUALISM; LEAVES OF GRASS, 1871–1872 EDITION; LEAVES OF GRASS, 1876, AUTHOR'S EDITION; RECONSTRUCTION; TWO RIVULETS, AUTHOR'S EDITION

Preface to *Leaves of Grass,* 1855 Edition

It was the unfortunate fate of Whitman's Preface to the 1855 edition of *Leaves of Grass* to vanish almost immediately after publication into a shadowy existence that effectively obscured its place as a pioneering manifesto of American literary and cultural history. Whitman never allowed the complete text of 1855 to be reprinted in America during his lifetime, nor did he permit the Preface to be reissued in any form in an American edition of his poems.

After 1855, the next reprinting came in London thirteen years later, in the 1868 selected *Poems of Walt Whitman* edited by W.M. Rossetti. In this text of the Preface, punctuation was normalized, and with Whitman's consent deletions were made in a few passages in order to eliminate potentially objectionable language. After another thirteen-year interval, the Preface was again published in London, in an 1881 pamphlet issued by Trübner and Company under the title "*Leaves of Grass* By Walt Whitman. Preface to the Original Edition, 1855." The Trübner text restored deleted words and phrases, and in various other ways it was closer to Whitman's original.

The 1855 Preface was not reissued in America until 1882, in *Specimen Days & Collect.* For this printing Whitman made extensive revisions; besides changes in punctuation and style, and some slight additions, there were deletions that reduced the length of the Preface by about one-third, with a consequent diminution of force. This abbreviated version was reprinted in the *Complete Poems & Prose* of 1888 and in the *Complete Prose Works* of 1892.

At the same time that the 1855 Preface was disappearing as a prose document, it was taking on a new life, of sorts, in Whitman's poetry. Many of its lines and phrases were transcribed, revised, or paraphrased to become parts of poems, particularly in the 1856 and 1860 editions of *Leaves of Grass.* Most indebted were (to give the poems their final titles) "By Blue Ontario's Shore" and "Song of Prudence"; other poems dependent in varying degrees on the Preface were "Song of the Answerer," "To You [Whoever you are . . .]," "Tests," "Perfections," "Suggestions," "Assurances," "A Child's Amaze," and "To a Foil'd European Revolutionaire." The ultimate transformation of the Preface into poetry was not, however, Whitman's; it came in 1982 when William Everson arranged the entire Preface into verse under the title *American Bard.*

That the Preface should be finally recast as poetry is entirely appropriate, since it shares many of the qualities of Whitman's early poems. Its voice is energetic and impassioned; its language is full of concrete imagery and specific details, including extended catalogues that would not be out of place in "Song of Myself." In structure the Preface is Emersonian, as in Ralph Waldo Emerson's essay "The Poet," which Whitman heard Emerson deliver in 1842 and to which the Preface may be profitably compared. The coherence of the Preface is not that of ordered development, but rather that of active thought, as it ranges freely over concepts of the American nation and of the poet; in addition, statements about the *soul* recur throughout, so that the word gathers the structural force of a leitmotif.

Whitman's primary focus is on the identity and aesthetics of the poet. He leads indirectly, although purposefully, into this subject by describing America as a nation still in the process of creating itself; the implication, as the rest of the Preface makes clear, is that the United States has yet to find the poet it deserves and requires. Calling America "a teeming nation of nations," distinguished from others by its "ampler largeness and stir," Whitman approaches his major theme by asserting that the nation is itself no less than poetry. "The Americans," he states grandly, "of all nations at any time upon the earth have probably the fullest poetical nature. The United States themselves are essentially the greatest poem" (*Comprehensive* 709).

Most important in the composition of this "poem" are the characteristics of the common people: "these too," Whitman declares, "are unrhymed poetry" (*Comprehensive* 710). Now the time has come for the American bard to come forth and write the poetry of his nation and its people, giving his subject "the gigantic and generous treatment worthy of it" (710). This treatment demands that the poet take into himself all the dynamic variety of America. First of all, the poet is to be "commensurate with a people," and second, he is to incorporate the landscape into his being: "His spirit responds to his country's spirit . . . he incarnates its geography and natural life and rivers and lakes" (711). The poet must then write poetry both "transcendant and new," poetry suitable for the "psalm" of the American republic (712).

Restating a central assertion, Whitman declares that "Of all nations the United States with veins full of poetical stuff most need poets and will doubtless have the greatest and use them the greatest" (712). The Preface then turns from consideration of the American identity to focus in detail on characteristics of the poet, or, more particularly, of "the greatest poet," to use Whitman's dominant epithet. Although this poet will write the songs of America, he transcends nationality, as he is also a mythic poet "of the kosmos," godlike in knowledge and judgment, a true creator who brings the perceived world into being: "He bestows on every object or quality its fit proportions neither more nor less" (712).

The poet is also a "seer" who guides his people into visionary knowledge (713). Depictions of "dumb real objects" are good in themselves, but, Whitman goes on to say, people expect the poet to do more: "they expect him to indicate the path between reality and their souls" (714). That purpose is central, as the soul itself is central: "Only the soul is of itself . . . all else has reference to what ensues" (724). Like Emerson, Whitman begins with an exalted concept of *soul*.

In order to accomplish his essential purposes, the poet must have aesthetic as well as political freedom. The *form* of poetry is crucial. "The rhyme and uniformity of perfect poems," Whitman states, "show the free growth of metrical laws and bud from them as unerringly and loosely as lilacs or roses on a bush, and take shapes as compact as the shapes of chestnuts and oranges and melons and pears, and shed the perfume impalpable to form" (714). Poetic form must be *organic*, as free to follow its own development as any object in nature; otherwise the poem can never be wholly true.

Similarly, if the soul is to find its way into truth, it must follow its own laws above all. The poet is to be an Emersonian nonconformist, that "heroic person [who] walks at his ease through and out of that custom or precedent or authority that suits him not" (717). The truth cannot be imposed, for it comes from within: "Whatever satisfies the soul is truth" (725). This truth of the soul must be expressed simply and directly, unobscured by ornaments of style. "What I tell," Whitman declares, "I tell for precisely what it is" (717).

It follows from this aesthetic of truth that the findings of science are of central importance to poetry. "Exact science," Whitman insists, "and its practical movements are no checks on the greatest poet but always his encouragement and support" (718). The object, always, is to know *reality*, even at the cost of displacing traditional belief; confronted with scientific truth, Whitman writes, "The whole theory of the special and the supernatural and all that was twined with it or educed out of it departs as a dream" (719). In a revolutionary statement that leads directly into "Song of Myself," Whitman declares that it is "not consistent with the reality of the soul to admit that there is anything in the known universe more divine than men and women" (719).

The divinity of men and women demands their freedom; thus the poet must be liberator as well as creator. "In the make of the great masters," Whitman writes, "the idea of political liberty is indispensible"; and, he adds, "the attitude of great poets is to cheer up slaves and horrify despots" (720). As the Preface nears its conclusion, Whitman presents a climactic apocalyptic vision in which figures of authority—he mentions priests in particular—will disappear, to be replaced by a new order of freedom in which "every man shall be his own priest" (727). Like the poet of "Song of Myself," the poet of the Preface points the way to freedom.

Although overshadowed by the poetry that followed, the 1855 Preface remains a major critical document and a compelling manifesto. In language of unusual excitement and vitality, it offers a compilation of romantic values and attitudes, including such central themes as these: exaltation of the common people; sympathy for the oppressed and unfortunate; rejection of traditional authority; affirmation of individual autonomy; insistence on human rights and universal freedom; commitment to progress; trust in the soul as the ultimate source of power and knowledge; love of nature; belief in the possibilities of apocalyptic renewal; assertion of the poetic imagination as an index of truth; and faith in the poet, and in poetry, as means to enlightenment. As this summary may suggest, Whitman's 1855 Preface deserves comparison with the works of Robert Burns, William Blake, William Wordsworth, Percy Bysshe Shelley, John Keats, and, of course, Emerson.

In 1855, the Preface closed with the sentence, "The proof of a poet is that his country absorbs him as affectionately as he has absorbed it" (729). Whitman deleted that sentence from all future printings published in America during his lifetime, perhaps as a result of his awareness that the country had *not* absorbed him, affectionately or otherwise, and that the truth of the matter was what he expressed in that essay of his mellow old age (as the 1855 Preface is the essay of his iconoclastic youth), "A Backward Glance O'er Travel'd Roads," published in 1888. In that work Whitman stated with disarming frankness, "I have not gain'd the acceptance of my own time, but have fallen back on fond dreams of the future" (*Prose Works* 2:712). In its revised and abbreviated text, the Preface concludes with the sentence, "The soul of the largest and wealthiest and proudest nation may well go half-way to meet that of its poets" (*Prose Works* 2:458). The burden of response is left with the nation.

R. W. French

Bibliography

Duerksen, Roland A. "Shelley's 'Defence' and Whitman's 1855 'Preface': A Comparison." *Walt Whitman Review* 10 (1964): 51–60.

Everson, William. *American Bard*. The Original Preface to *Leaves of Grass* Arranged in Verse. New York: Viking, 1982.

Whitman, Walt. *Leaves of Grass: Comprehensive Reader's Edition*. Ed. Harold W. Blodgett and Sculley Bradley. New York: New York UP, 1965.

———. *Prose Works 1892*. Ed. Floyd Stovall. 2 vols. New York: New York UP, 1963–1964.

See also "BACKWARD GLANCE O'ER TRAVEL'D ROADS, A"; "BY BLUE ONTARIO'S SHORE"; EMERSON, RALPH WALDO; EVERSON, WILLIAM (BROTHER ANTONINUS); LEAVES OF GRASS, 1855 EDITION; POETIC THEORY; PROPHECY; "SONG OF THE ANSWERER"; SOUL, THE

Preface to *Two Rivulets* (1876)

Little has been written about the 1876 Preface. It opens the Author's edition of *Two Rivulets*. Critics up to now have ignored it or given it cursory attention. Generally speaking, the Preface has been understood as Whitman's reflections on the democratic nationality in the main body or upper text and on the purpose of *Leaves of Grass* in the discursive footnote sequence or lower text. But it is more. It is Whitman's final moral apologia (see lower text) as well as his literary ars poetica (see upper text). But—it is even more. Even beyond this, as a fused text it is an imaginative piece of lyric criticism. Whitman's own characterization, "this rambling Prefatory gossip" (*Comprehensive* 744), points to the essential nature of this important text.

If the reader considers Whitman's lower text equal—democratically speaking—to the upper text and visualizes the two texts as "two rivulets" themselves, then the 1876 Preface shifts into a new dimension. A new rhetorical strategy exists. It is the rhetorical strategy of "double texts" simultaneously chatting while traveling—as "[c]ompanions, travelers, gossiping as they journey" (Whitman's verse words in the opening poem of the first section of *Two Rivulets*). After all, for seven of nine and a half pages of the Preface, Whitman has double texts overlapping—much like the first of *Two Rivulets* that strings poetry above prose on the same page for eighteen pages. By reading the bottom and top parts dialectically rather than thematically, the 1876 Preface becomes a lyrical piece of imaginative literary criticism and not just a prose treatise summarizing Whitman's literary and cultural theories for a New World democracy.

Whitman enacts this rhetorical "gossip" method—a method of "easy, unrestrained talk or writing" (as the *OED* defines it) with two graphically visual techniques. First, he uses different type sizes and linking printer's "reference marks" to create a dynamic encounter between the upper and lower texts. Second, he allows each text to take turns assuming or demanding more space on the page depending upon the needs or importance of the text-topic. For example, the lower text occupies seventy-five percent of page seven when it requires room to process its moral and psychic traumas. Likewise, when the upper text feels compelled to carve out an ideal American plan for moral democracy, it uses ninety percent of page eight to stake out its claim.

After the double texts negotiate spacing for seven pages, both finally merge into one unit for the last two and a half pages. They bond indistinguishably and form an "interpenetrating, composite, inseparable Unity" (*Comprehensive* 749). When the lower text meets and joins the upper, when the defiantly confessional meets the prescriptively oratorical, then the moment brings joy and vatic faith. The 1876 Preface is an imaginative piece of moral criticism on Whitman's poetry and politics of living holistically. In union, Whitman's poetic, cultural, and spiritual theories have talked each other into personal and national moral health. Amid nature's antiseptic powers, celebrating both his fifty-sixth birthday and the nation's centennial birthday, he can testify and poetically sing:

> I therefore now bequeath Poems and Essays as nutriment . . . to furnish . . . what The States most need of all, and which seems to me yet quite unsupplied in literature, namely, to show them . . . Themselves distinctively, and what They are for. I count with such absolute certainty on the Great Future of The United States . . . America, too, is a prophecy. What, even of the best and most successful, would be justified by itself alone? . . . All ages, all Nations and States, have been such prophecies. But where any former ones with prophecy so broad, so clear, as our times, our lands—as those of the West?
>
> (*Comprehensive* 752)

The 1876 Preface is thus the disquisitional meditation of a troubled yet coyly defiant and brave singer (see lower text). In the guise of the metaphysician-poet, he inspires with righteous indignation and guides with kind instruction (see upper text). Then as ideal prophet-bard and moral "sponsor" (curiously, another *OED* definition for *gossip*), Whitman interprets the "Eternal Soul of Man" for "future Poetry" (*Comprehensive* 753).

He bequeaths all of his poetic "escapades," his private and public voices, to his readers and baptizes them (his poems, his essays, his readers, his two volumes *Leaves of Grass* and *Two Rivulets*) into the poet's real mission—the pure spirit or ideal form—the poetics of "Eidólons" (his own verse excerpt placed into the fused text):

> The Prophet and the Bard,
> Shall yet maintain themselves—
>   in higher circles yet,
> Shall mediate to the Modern,
>   to Democracy—interpret yet
>   to them, God and Eidólons.
>   (*Comprehensive* 753)
>   *Frances E. Keuling-Stout*

Bibliography

Allen, Gay Wilson. Introduction. *Two Rivulets*. By Walt Whitman. Norwood, Pa.: Norwood, 1979. iii–vi.
———. *The New Walt Whitman Handbook*. 1975. New York: New York UP, 1986.

Erkkila, Betsy. *Whitman the Political Poet*. New York: Oxford UP, 1989.
Whitman, Walt. *Leaves of Grass: Comprehensive Reader's Edition*. Ed. Harold W. Blodgett and Sculley Bradley. New York: New York UP, 1965.
———. *Prose Works 1892*. Ed. Floyd Stovall. Vol. 2. New York: New York UP, 1964.
———. *Two Rivulets*. Camden, N.J.: Author's Edition, 1876.

See also LEAVES OF GRASS, 1876, AUTHOR'S EDITION; *TWO RIVULETS*, AUTHOR'S EDITION

Pre-*Leaves* Poems

Whitman published roughly twenty poems in various newspapers and magazines before he published his first volume of *Leaves of Grass* in 1855.

Probably the first poem Whitman published was "Our Future Lot." A conventional poem in rhyme, meter, and content, "Our Future Lot" was first published in the *Long Islander*, a paper which Whitman founded in the spring of 1838. Although no copies of the paper are known to exist, the poem was reprinted on 31 October 1838 in the *Long Island Democrat* and labeled "from the *Long Islander.*" The poem was revised and retitled "Time to Come" and was printed in the New York *Aurora* on 9 April 1842.

Whitman had several poems published in the *Long Island Democrat* from 1838–1840, including "Young Grimes," "The Inca's Daughter," "The Love That Is Hereafter," "The Spanish Lady," "The Columbian's Song," "The End of All," "The Winding-Up" (a revision of "The End of All"), "We Shall All Rest at Last," "Fame's Vanity," and "My Departure." Many of these early works are reflections on the end of life or the afterlife.

The remainder of Whitman's pre-*Leaves* poems were all published in or before 1850. Most of the poems were published in various New York area newspapers and magazines. These include "Each Has His Grief" (a revision of "We Shall All Rest at Last"), "The Punishment of Pride," "Ambition" (revision of "Fame's Vanity"), "The Death and Burial of McDonald Clarke. A Parody," "Death of the Nature-Lover" (revision of "My Departure"), "The Play-Ground," "Ode," "The House of Friends" (appears as "Wounded in the House of Friends" in *Specimen Days & Collect*), "Resurgemus," "Song for Certain Congressmen" (appears as "Dough-Face

Song" in *Collect*), "Blood-Money," "Tale of a Shirt," and "A Sketch." It is easy to see that even at this early stage Whitman was not content to let poems rest but constantly was tinkering with them and revising them and their titles.

The only poem not published in the New York area was "The Mississippi at Midnight," which was printed in the New Orleans *Crescent* during Whitman's brief stint there. The poem later appeared as "Sailing the Mississippi at Midnight" in *Collect*.

Other poems deserving special attention are "Resurgemus," "Tale of a Shirt," and "A Sketch." "Resurgemus" was the only poem published prior to 1855 which was incorporated into *Leaves of Grass*. It appeared untitled as the eighth of twelve poems in the 1855 *Leaves of Grass*. In the 1860 edition of *Leaves* it was revised and retitled "Europe, The 72d and 73d Years of These States." "Tale of a Shirt" and "A Sketch" are the only two pre-*Leaves* poems which do not appear in the definitive edition of the early works, *Walt Whitman: The Early Poems and the Fiction,* edited by Thomas Brasher. "Tale of a Shirt" was discovered in 1982 by Herbert Bergman in the 31 March 1844 issue of the New York *Sunday Times & Noah's Weekly Messenger.* "A Sketch" was discovered by Jerome Loving in 1993 in the December 1842 issue of *The New World.*

Whitman's earliest poetry was sentimental in nature and imitative of William Cullen Bryant and other popular nineteenth-century American poets. Whitman did experiment with parody and comic verse but the majority of his earliest poems are indistinguishable from the flood of poetry being produced in the 1840s. Many of them contain four- or five-line stanzas, regular meter, and rhymed verse. The themes are also conventional and revolve around the folly of pride, the brevity of life, and the hope of a life to come.

By 1850, however, Whitman had turned to political themes and his poetry had taken on more of the characteristics of *Leaves of Grass.* His poetry around this time was often occasional and was angrier and more satirical in tone. He began to experiment with less conventional metrics and abandoned rhyme altogether.

For the most part critics have ignored or given only a cursory glance at the pre-*Leaves* poems and rightly so. These poems are important primarily for insight into Whitman's origin and growth as a poet. The forms and subject matter of the poetry are conventional and bland at best.

Brent L. Gibson

Bibliography

Bergman, Herbert. "A Hitherto Unknown Whitman Story and a Possible Early Poem." *Walt Whitman Review* 28 (1982): 3–15.

Loving, Jerome. "A Newly Discovered Whitman Poem." *Walt Whitman Quarterly Review* 11 (1994): 117–122.

Reynolds, David S. *Walt Whitman's America: A Cultural Biography.* New York: Knopf, 1995.

Whitman, Walt. *The Early Poems and the Fiction.* Ed. Thomas Brasher. New York: New York UP, 1963.

———. *Specimen Days.* Vol. 1 of *Prose Works 1892.* Ed. Floyd Stovall. New York: New York UP, 1963.

———. *The Uncollected Poetry and Prose of Walt Whitman.* Ed. Emory Holloway. 2 vols. Garden City, N.Y.: Doubleday, Page, 1921.

See also BRYANT, WILLIAM CULLEN; COLLECT; "EUROPE, THE 72D AND 73D YEARS OF THESE STATES"; LEAVES OF GRASS, 1855 EDITION; LONG ISLAND DEMOCRAT; LONG ISLANDER; POLITICAL VIEWS; POPULAR CULTURE, WHITMAN AND; SENTIMENTALITY; SHORT FICTION, WHITMAN'S; "SKETCH, A"; STYLE AND TECHNIQUE(S)

Presidents, United States

Throughout his life Whitman was a close observer of public affairs, and his ideas and opinions about them often appear in his writings. As with most Americans, Whitman looked to the president more than any other leader, both to deal with the great questions of the day and to embody the ideals and aspirations of Americans past, present, and future. In his political tract "The Eighteenth Presidency!" (written in 1856), Whitman had much to say about the sort of man he most wanted to see at the head of the government: "heroic, shrewd, fully-informed, healthy-bodied, middle-aged, beard-faced American blacksmith or boatman come down from the West . . . dressed in a clean suit of working attire, and with the tan all over his face, breast, and arms" (21). This description suggests Abraham Lincoln, but it was written before Lincoln became a national figure, probably before Whitman had ever heard of him.

The early presidents, especially Washington, Jefferson, and Jackson, were the principal yardsticks against whom he measured later leaders. In his poem "The Sleepers" he called forth the image of Washington weeping as he watched his soldiers defeated in the battle of Brooklyn, and it is unmistakable that Whitman is looking ahead to the Civil War, calling Washington's men "Southern braves" (section 5). At the end of his life Whitman's admiration for Washington remained as strong as ever, as in "Washington's Monument, February, 1885": "Courage, alertness, patience, faith, the same— e'en in defeat defeated not, the same."

Whitman's parents, in common with many Americans of their time, named three of their sons after George Washington, Thomas Jefferson, and Andrew Jackson, showing their uncritical acceptance of these past heroes. Walt Whitman was further influenced by the writing of William Leggett of the New York *Evening Post,* who showed the Jeffersonian basis for the policies of Jackson. Whitman owned a nine-volume edition of the *Writings of Thomas Jefferson* (1854) and listed "the official lives of Washington, Jefferson, Madison" as examples for his countrymen to follow (*Workshop* 105). He referred to the Democratic party as "the party of the sainted Jefferson and Jackson" (*Gathering* 1:219). Whitman had been in the crowd which greeted President Jackson's visit to Brooklyn (1833) and later referred to Jackson as "true gold . . . unmined, unforged . . . the genuine ore in the rough" (qtd. in Winwar 58). Justin Kaplan points out in his *Walt Whitman: A Life* that Whitman was of the generation which saw the departure of the last of the legendary heroes of the founding of the republic. In his early years Whitman could and did talk with those who had seen and corresponded with these heroes.

Whitman enthusiastically supported Jackson's hand-picked successor, Martin Van Buren, in his first campaign (1836) and took an active part in Van Buren's unsuccessful reelection effort (1840), attending rallies and debating Whig partisans. Four years later the Democrats made a comeback, and Whitman, still loyal to his party, enthusiastically supported the new president, James K. Polk. He attended Polk's speech in Brooklyn (1847) and compared him to two of his greatest heroes, Jefferson and Jackson. When Polk led the nation into war with Mexico, Whitman supported the war, favoring the expansion of the nation to include Texas, Or-

egon, California, even Cuba and Canada. He disagreed with Polk over the slavery question, however, calling for Democrats to support the Wilmot Proviso, which would have outlawed slavery in the new territories. Whitman's feelings against slavery eventually became strong enough to drive him out of the Democratic party. Although he had cheered Zachary Taylor's victories in the war, Whitman didn't think that was enough to recommend the general to be president. Seeing Taylor in a New Orleans theater, Whitman described him as a "jovial, old, rather stout, plain man, with a wrinkled and dark-yellow face," and lacking "conventional ceremony or etiquette" (*Prose Works* 2:606). Rather than support either the Whig Taylor or the Democrat Lewis Cass, Whitman turned to the new Free Soil party, becoming a delegate to their convention (1848) and supporting their nomination of former President Van Buren.

The 1850s was a discouraging period for Whitman politically. The campaign of 1852 offered little for him, for neither the politically inept General Winfield Scott nor the largely unknown Franklin Pierce was willing to meet the slavery issue head on. By the next election Whitman was ready to express his bitter contempt for the three presidents whose terms spanned the decade. Referring to Millard Fillmore, who succeeded upon Taylor's death (1850), and Franklin Pierce, and later amending his text to include James Buchanan, the victor of 1856, Whitman said, "Never were publicly displayed more deformed, mediocre, snivelling, unreliable, false-hearted men!" Writing of Pierce's pro-Southern policies, Whitman said, "The President eats dirt and excrement for his daily meals, likes it, and tries to force it on The States" (*Eighteenth Presidency* 24). He used similar language to describe Pierce, "the weakest—the very worst of the lot," and Buchanan, "perhaps the weakest of the President tribe—the very unablest" (*With Walt Whitman* 3:30). A paragraph of "The Eighteenth Presidency!" suggests he had some hope for John Frémont, the candidate of the new Republican party, but at the same time he did not consider Frémont to be the ideal leader he longed for, the "Redeemer President" (39).

Whitman's feelings about Abraham Lincoln are well known and are dealt with at greater length elsewhere in this volume, but it may be useful to point out that for all his passionate statements of principle, Whitman's support, even adoration, of Lincoln may have had little to do with the president's policies. Lincoln was not the passionate abolitionist that the antislavery people wanted. He moved slowly and cautiously toward a policy of limited emancipation. When Lincoln said that the purpose of the Civil War was to preserve the Union and not to abolish slavery, Whitman agreed. Had Pierce or Buchanan said such a thing only a few years before, Whitman would undoubtedly have heaped scorn on them. His observations on Taylor (1848), indicating that his main objection was that the general was too plain looking, gives a clue that with Whitman, what counted the most was something intangible and hard to define. Taylor was a plain man of the people— so far so good—but that was all he was. Lincoln was that and more, and it was the more that Whitman saw, before most others, that made all the difference. This may also help to explain why it was that, although Whitman saw Lincoln many times, he passed up every chance to meet his hero. Was it that he was shy, in spite of the brashness of his poems? Or perhaps he dared not look beyond the archetype lest he discover merely human flaws and weaknesses. Like most others, Whitman had occasional doubts about Lincoln and his policies, but by late 1863 he conceded, "I still think him a pretty big President" (*Correspondence* 1:174) and defended Lincoln before his doubting brother Jeff. Lincoln's assassination moved Whitman to compose his masterpiece, "When Lilacs Last in the Dooryard Bloom'd," in which he suggested the idea that Lincoln's death, like his life, stood as a symbol whose significance went far beyond the man himself. Although he labeled four of his poems "Memories of President Lincoln," nowhere in any of these poems does Lincoln's name appear, further suggesting that the poet used the president as a symbol, an embodiment of ideas and feelings not to be limited to one man.

Attending the Grand Review of the victorious armies in 1865, Whitman "saw the President [Andrew Johnson] several times," thought him "very plain and substantial," and marveled that such an "ordinary man . . . should be the master of all these myriads of soldiers." On the same occasion he saw General Ulysses S. Grant, who would be Johnson's successor in the White House, and thought him "the noblest Roman of them all" (*Correspondence* 1:261). His initial impression of Johnson, "I think he is a good man" (*Correspondence* 1:267), remained, and he did not favor the impeachment and trial (1868). His defense of the unpopular Johnson

mystified his friends, but again, it probably arose from his idea of celebrating what the man stood for, at least in Whitman's mind, rather than from what he was. This same attitude of uncritical acceptance applied to Grant, who was the center of storm and scandal as president. Whitman was certainly aware of the scandals and disappointments of the Grant years, as his poem "Respondez!" shows, but the president himself retained Whitman's respect for his wartime service and again because he was "good, worthy, non-demonstrative, average-representing" (*Correspondence* 2:15). "What a man [Grant] is! . . . A mere plain man—no art—no poetry— only practical sense, ability to do, or try his best to do, what devolv'd upon him" (*Prose Works* 1:226–227). This same tendency to see good when he wanted to see it led him to speak well of Grant's successor, Rutherford B. Hayes. Judging the man only from his speeches, Whitman pronounced Hayes "genial, good-natured, sensible, helping things along" (*With Walt Whitman* 2:556).

James A. Garfield, narrowly elected president in 1880, was an admirer of Whitman, the two having met in Washington during the war, when Garfield was a congressman. Garfield's shooting (1881) "has depressed me much," Whitman wrote (*Correspondence* 3:232), and the president's death two months later moved Whitman to memorialize him in "The Sobbing of the Bells." Whitman met Grover Cleveland when the latter was governor of New York and another admirer of the poet. Whitman liked Cleveland, in spite of his being a Democrat, much more than he liked Benjamin Harrison, who first defeated Cleveland (1888) and then was defeated by him (1892). "I lean rather to the Cleveland side," he wrote (*Correspondence* 4:221), calling Harrison "insignificant," "an unprecedentedly humdrum President" (*Correspondence* 4:328, 5:21), and "the smallest egg ever laid in Uncle Sam's basket" (qtd. in Thayer 303). In spite of Harrison's election (1888), however, he expressed his ultimate faith in America; this election was but "one tack . . . the ship will go on her voyage many a sea and many a year yet" (*Correspondence* 4:232).

Frederick Hatch

Bibliography

Allen, Gay Wilson. *The Solitary Singer: A Critical Biography of Walt Whitman.* 1955. Rev. ed. 1967. Chicago: U of Chicago P, 1985.

Erkkila, Betsy. *Whitman the Political Poet.* New York: Oxford UP, 1989.

Kaplan, Justin. *Walt Whitman: A Life.* New York: Simon and Schuster, 1980.

Reynolds, David S. *Walt Whitman's America: A Cultural Biography.* New York: Knopf, 1995.

Thayer, William Roscoe. "Personal Recollections of Walt Whitman." *Whitman in His Own Time.* Ed. Joel Myerson. Detroit: Omnigraphics, 1991. 283–308.

Traubel, Horace. *With Walt Whitman in Camden.* Vol. 2. New York: Appleton, 1908; Vol. 3. New York: Mitchell Kennerley, 1914.

Whitman, Walt. *The Correspondence.* Ed. Edwin Haviland Miller. 6 vols. New York: New York UP, 1961–1977.

———. *The Eighteenth Presidency!* Ed. Edward F. Grier. 2nd ed. Lawrence: U of Kansas P, 1956.

———. *The Gathering of the Forces.* Ed. Cleveland Rodgers and John Black. 2 vols. New York: Putnam, 1920.

———. *Prose Works, 1892.* Ed. Floyd Stovall. 2 vols. New York: New York UP, 1963–1964.

———. *Walt Whitman's Workshop: A Collection of Unpublished Manuscripts.* Ed. Clifton J. Furness. Cambridge, Mass.: Harvard UP, 1928.

Winwar, Frances. *American Giant: Walt Whitman and His Times.* New York: Harper, 1941.

See also DEMOCRATIC PARTY; "EIGHTEENTH PRESIDENCY!, THE"; FREE SOIL PARTY; JACKSON, ANDREW; JEFFERSON, THOMAS; LINCOLN, ABRAHAM; POLITICAL VIEWS; REPUBLICAN PARTY; WASHINGTON, GEORGE; WHIGS

Price, Abby Hills (1814–1878)

Abby Hills, born in Windham, Connecticut, married Edmund Price in 1838; in 1842 the Prices moved to Hopedale, Massachusetts, to become part of the founding of Adin Ballou's Hopedale Community, a Practical Christian commune subscribing not only to pacifism but also to a form of pre-Marxian socialism, temperance, and abolitionism. The community was also unusual in its practice of women's rights. Abby Price lived in Hopedale until 1853, when she was publicly reprimanded for counseling a married couple and single woman in what turned out to be an adulterous relationship. The Price family left Hopedale in 1853 to live at the Raritan Bay Union, outside Perth Amboy, New Jersey, where they stayed until 1855, when they moved to Brooklyn. Price and Whitman became close friends in 1856 and remained so until her death in 1878.

Of utmost importance to Whitman studies is the fact that Abby Price, a person who would now qualify as a "radical feminist," befriended Whitman and his family, offering present-day scholars a view which runs counter to that of Charles Eldridge, likewise Whitman's friend, who said in 1902 that Whitman "delighted in the company of old fashioned women; mothers of large families preferred, who did not talk about literature or reforms" (381). Abby Price, anything but an old-fashioned woman, did talk about literature and reform. Numerous articles written by her appear in the Hopedale newspaper, *The Practical Christian* (1842–1853). Articles by her appear, as well, in *The Una* and the *Liberator,* and her speeches given at the 1850, 1851, and 1852 National Woman's Rights conventions appear in the New York *Tribune* and in *History of Woman Suffrage,* as well as the proceedings of the conferences.

By reading the speeches given at the national, state, and local women's rights conferences in the decade of the 1850s, a person soon begins to hear points of view similar to those expressed in *Leaves of Grass.* Whitman was not antipathetic to the issues forwarded by women's rights activists, though, admittedly, he did not create images of women working outside the home nearly so much as activists like Price and her activist friend Paulina Wright Davis promoted. But a critical evaluation of Whitman and/ or *Leaves* must take into account women like Abby Price, who was one of Whitman's closest friends in his most creative years, 1850–1860. In evaluating Whitman's stance toward women in his poetry and prose, Abby Price is a key figure in regard to any feminist critique of Whitman.

Sherry Ceniza

Bibliography

Ceniza, Sherry. "Walt Whitman and Abby Price." *Walt Whitman Quarterly Review* 7 (1989): 49–67.

———. "Whitman and Democratic Women." *Approaches to Teaching Whitman's "Leaves of Grass."* Ed. Donald D. Kummings. New York: MLA, 1990. 153–158.

Eldridge, Charles. "Walt Whitman as a Conservative." *Saturday Review of Books and Art* supp. to New York *Times* 7 June 1902: 381.

Stanton, Elizabeth Cady, Susan B. Anthony, and Matilda Joslyn Gage, eds. *History of Woman Suffrage.* 1881. 3 vols. Rochester: Susan B. Anthony, Charles Mann, 1992.

Whitman, Walt. *The Correspondence.* Ed. Edwin Haviland Miller. Vols. 1–2. New York: New York UP, 1961.

See also FARNHAM, ELIZA W.; PRICE, HELEN E.; WOMAN'S RIGHTS MOVEMENT AND WHITMAN, THE; WOMEN AS A THEME IN WHITMAN'S WRITING

Price, Helen E. (b. 1841)

Helen Price, daughter of Abby and Edmund Price, did not take the active public role in women's rights that her mother did, but that is not to say that she was a passive observer of her culture. She comes alive, historically, through her two articles on Whitman and her mother and through the detailed letters she wrote to Whitman's mother. We also know her through the letters she wrote to Horace Traubel, and to Richard Maurice Bucke in answer to his requests for information on Whitman and for copies of her and Louisa's letters.

Price was an infant when her parents moved to Hopedale, Massachusetts, the community Adin Ballou founded in 1841. She went with her parents to the Raritan Bay Union in 1853, outside of Perth Amboy, New Jersey, and then to Brooklyn, where she lived with them until they moved to Red Bank, where her mother Abby died in 1878. Helen lived in Woodside, New Jersey, following her mother's death.

Fortunately for Whitman scholarship, she wrote a chapter in Bucke's biography of Whitman, as well as a 1919 newspaper article. Both contain background information on Whitman in the 1850s and early 1860s, as well as on the Price family. In her personal letters, Helen Price mentions numerous names of people who came to the Price home to visit and she also mentions events she and her mother attended, thus providing readers with a sense of the Price home and the Prices' mindset. The close friendship Whitman shared with the Price family and the culturally significant nature of the Price household provide valuable insights into the life and interests of Whitman.

Sherry Ceniza

Bibliography

Bucke, Richard Maurice. *Walt Whitman.* Philadelphia: McKay, 1883.

Price, Helen. "Reminiscences of Walt Whitman." New York *Evening Post Book Review* 31 May 1919.

See also BIOGRAPHIES; BUCKE, RICHARD MAURICE; PRICE, ABBY HILLS; TRAUBEL, HORACE L.; WHITMAN, LOUISA VAN VELSOR

Pride

In his open letter to Emerson, which was attached to the 1856 edition of *Leaves of Grass,* Whitman confidently anticipated that in a "few years . . . the average annual call for my Poems [will be] ten or twenty thousand copies—more, quite likely" (*Comprehensive* 731). While such demand was never to be approached during the poet's lifetime, periodic moments such as this of Whitman's ambitious self-projection nevertheless garnered him a popular reputation as an egotist of sorts. His own projects of self-promotion throughout his career—publishing reviews of his own work, writing or controlling the content of his early "biographies"—contributed to this image of Whitman as a proud and self-aggrandizing figure. Yet Whitman's pride, although undeniable, is an unavoidable product and an integral component of his enormous and expansive poetic vision.

In early poems such as "Punishment of Pride" (1841) and "Ambition" (published as "Fame's Vanity" in 1842), Whitman's view of pride is generally as conventional as that of those who would later criticize him for the sensual and arrogant aspects of his verse. By 1855, however, Whitman's vision of both passion and pride had undergone substantial development, a fact he proudly admits in section 21 of "Song of Myself": "I chant the chant of dilation or pride, / We have had ducking and deprecating about enough, / I show that size is only development." This development in Whitman's vision emerged, it seems, out of an epiphany of the psychical immensity of himself and of the physical immensity of his cosmos: "Encircling all, vast-darting up and wide, the American Soul, with equal hemispheres, one Love, one Dilation or Pride" ("Our Old Feuillage").

For Whitman, this "American Soul" necessitated a level of pride equal to the enormous task of an American poetry: "I know perfectly well my own egotism," he admits, "[k]now my omnivorous lines and must not write any less." Here in section 42 of "Song of Myself," Whitman makes clear that he is cognizant of his boastful and bragging nature. More important, however, is that Whitman sees his braggadocio as necessary to the creation of a truly American poetry, democratic in voice yet infused with personal identity and pride.

Whitman's idea for his poetry signals a break from literary ties to Europe, where, for Whitman, the common individual's value had been neglected and his or her pride obfuscated by themes and characters inappropriate to an American vision of self and world. In "A Backward Glance O'er Travel'd Roads," Whitman writes, "Defiant of ostensible literary and other conventions, I avowedly chant 'the great pride of man in himself,' and permit it to be more or less a *motif* of nearly all my verse. I think this pride indispensable to an American. I think it not inconsistent with obedience, humility, deference, and self-questioning" (*Comprehensive* 571). Viewed in this positive light, pride—conceived as an exuberant confidence in the grandeur and goodness of both the individual and the cosmos—is inextricable from, and in fact necessary to, Whitman's poetry.

Although in his poetry Whitman often praises himself as the one true bard of both the individual and the nation, he points out that whatever pride he claims for himself, he claims for all humanity; as such, Whitman's pride is inherent in all, and he urges all to discover it in themselves. "These are really the thoughts of all men in all ages and lands," he writes; "they are not original with me, / If they are not yours as much as mine they are nothing, or next to nothing" ("Song of Myself," section 17). Such was Whitman's hope in an age generally ambivalent or hostile toward his work.

Despite a turgid morality, the latter half of the nineteenth century revealed an America exploding with energy and invention, yet haunted by the specter of war. *Leaves of Grass* was a song of prideful expansiveness—of the world generally and of America specifically. Whitman's nationalistic pride manifested itself most prominently in the early editions of *Leaves of Grass*. With the advent of the Civil War and the publication of *Drum-Taps* and *Sequel to Drum-Taps,* Whitman retained and built upon his national, as well as personal, pride, although the sobering effects of the conflict can be seen in the postbellum poems.

Despite a lowering of key during and after the war, Whitman continued to sing the pride of animate beings as well as inanimate objects. Pride is seen as a creative force, absolutely necessary for accessing the highest beauty and holiness inherent in the individual as well as in the commonest materials of the universe. An evangelist of sorts, Whitman after the Civil War saw himself clearly as a poetic historian of the conflict as well as a hopeful herald of a new world, calling women and men forth to exalt in themselves, their surroundings, and their united freedom.

During the war, Whitman saw young men facing death daily on the most gruesome of terms. Nevertheless, his unflinching gaze into the mystery of death did not falter as he himself approached death. In the final poem before the various annexes of the 1891–1892 *Leaves of Grass,* Whitman's voice is clear: "I announce uncompromising liberty and equality, / I announce the justification of candor and the justification of pride. . . . I announce an end that shall lightly and joyfully meet its translation" ("So Long!"). Whitman's joyful egotism rings forth as brightly from his deathbed as it did before the war.

Christopher O. Griffin

Bibliography

Allen, Gay Wilson. *The Solitary Singer: A Critical Biography of Walt Whitman.* 1955. Rev. ed. 1967. Chicago: U of Chicago P, 1985.

Whitman, Walt. *Leaves of Grass: Comprehensive Reader's Edition.* Ed. Harold W. Blodgett and Sculley Bradley. New York: New York UP, 1965.

———. *The Uncollected Poetry and Prose of Walt Whitman.* 1921. Ed. Emory Holloway. 2 vols. Gloucester, Mass.: Peter Smith, 1972.

See also "Backward Glance O'er Travel'd Roads, A"; Individualism; Preface to *Leaves of Grass,* 1855 Edition; Self-Reviews of the 1855 *Leaves,* Whitman's Anonymous; "Song of Myself"

Printing Business

During Whitman's lifetime, innovations in printing technology revolutionized the printing business in America. Improvements in printing presses and typesetting machines in the early decades of the nineteenth century indicated the beginning of an era, the industrial age in the printing craft. The steam-powered cylinder press, introduced in 1814, would replace the slower flatbed press. A method for casting stereotype plates, introduced around 1820, would facilitate the production of multiple editions of a work. The "Hoe Type Revolving Machine," which Whitman would celebrate in his "Song of the Exposition" (1871), would appear in 1847, employing an automatic "fly" for paper removal. Typesetting would improve with the patenting, in 1822, of a keyboard-operated composition machine.

As a result of these innovations the book trade in America soared from 2.5 million dollars in 1820 to sixteen million in 1856, while newspapers increased from two hundred in 1800 to over twenty-five hundred by 1850. As publishing became increasingly geared toward mass production, traditional work arrangements changed. In the early 1800s the head of a newspaper often served simultaneously as proprietor, editor, compositor, press operator, and even distributor. As operations expanded, however, work became increasingly specialized, and in some respects, more impersonal.

In 1831, however, when at the age of twelve Whitman went to work for a small political sheet called the *Long Island Patriot*, printing was still an artisan craft. There Whitman was initiated into the mysteries of the trade, including the painstaking work of setting type by hand. In 1832 he worked briefly for a Brooklyn printer, then for the Brooklyn *Star* under successful editor and publisher Alden Spooner. By age sixteen Whitman was a full-fledged "journeyman printer," working as a compositor in New York. From these early experiences Whitman gained an appreciation for craftsmanship and the single-person production technique.

This appreciation would translate into a lifelong desire to control every aspect of the publication of his poetry. Each edition of *Leaves of Grass* was personally supervised by Whitman in virtually every detail of production. The first edition was produced at the Brooklyn establishment of the Rome brothers, printer friends of Whitman, where he spent much of the spring of 1855 setting type for the volume and revising and correcting proof. Subsequent editions of *Leaves* received the same careful attention. Whitman designed the covers, selected the type, and supervised the printing. In his final years, too frail to worry his book through the press, he persuaded his friend Horace Traubel to do it for him.

Whitman called printing "the craft preservative of all crafts" (Whitman 45) and said that Traubel's four years working in a print shop were "better than so many years at the university" (Traubel 166). Whitman's controlling hand made each edition of *Leaves* a unique extension of its author in form as well as content.

Dena Mattausch

Bibliography

Lehmann-Haupt, Hellmut. *The Book in America: A History of the Making, the Selling, and the Collecting of Books in the United States.* New York: Bowker, 1939.

Reynolds, David S. *Walt Whitman's America: A Cultural Biography.* New York: Knopf, 1995.

Traubel, Horace. *With Walt Whitman in Camden.* Vol. 1. Boston: Small, Maynard, 1906.

Whitman, Walt. *Walt Whitman's New York: From Manhattan to Montauk.* 1963. Ed. Henry M. Christman. New York: New Amsterdam, 1989.

See also HARTSHORNE, WILLIAM; *LONG ISLAND PATRIOT*; ROME BROTHERS, THE

"Promise to California, A" (1860)

Whitman's "A Promise to California" originally appeared as number 30 in the "Calamus" cluster of the 1860 edition of *Leaves of Grass* and did not assume its current title until the 1867 edition. In fact, as Blodgett and Bradley point out, in the Barrett manuscript Whitman makes no reference to California in the opening line. Instead, the promise is issued to the states of Indiana, Nebraska, Kansas, Iowa, and Minnesota.

The "Calamus" section of *Leaves of Grass* has generated a great deal of discussion because of the nature of its sexual imagery, but "A Promise To California" is less sexually charged than many of the "Calamus" poems. In fact, it has even been described as didactic, primarily because of the tone in which the speaker promises to travel west and teach his fellow citizens about the vigorous camaraderie necessary for American democracy. Despite this tone, the poem contains subtle images of exploration and discovery that refer as much to the speaker's inner self as they do to the nation. For instance, the speaker declares himself willing to remain a bit longer in the familiar East, but he is also drawn inexorably "inland" and to the "Western sea." Such journeys would invite at least a symbolic charting of new territory, and in this way he links his own inner exploration with the continued westward expansion of the nation.

Although "A Promise to California" is a relatively minor poem in the Whitman canon, it does reveal Whitman's belief in an intimate connection between the deep, often unspoken impulses of the individual and the more public and collective impulses of the democracy. As a result, the poem also stands as a reminder of the vital and public role of poetry in the shaping of any nation dedicated to freedom.

C.D. Albin

Bibliography

Allen, Gay Wilson. *The New Walt Whitman Handbook*. 1975. New York: New York UP, 1986.

Waskow, Howard J. *Whitman: Explorations in Form*. Chicago: U of Chicago P, 1966.

Whitman, Walt. *Leaves of Grass: Comprehensive Reader's Edition*. Ed. Harold W. Blodgett and Sculley Bradley. New York: New York UP, 1965.

See also "CALAMUS"; "PRAIRIE-GRASS DIVIDING, THE"; WEST, THE AMERICAN

Prophecy

In 1921 Will Hayes published an extended comparison between Whitman and Christ in which the object was obviously to make Whitman out as a religious prophet. Hayes was not writing in a vacuum; many early Whitman boosters viewed *Leaves of Grass* as Scripture and Whitman as sacred spokesman for a new religion. By the end of the twenties, however, the Cult of Whitman had pretty well died out.

That Whitman presented himself as a prophet is beyond doubt. In the Preface to *As a Strong Bird on Pinions Free* (1872) he makes clear that from early on his purpose was religious. Further, in a discussion of Brooklyn as a "City of Churches," David Reynolds contends that Brooklyn was the best possible place in America for new religious developments in the nineteenth century (35). Eighteenth-century deists had posited a God who ruled the world by laws—natural laws. Based on reason, natural religion was opposed to revealed religion, and science seemed to support the former. By the time Charles Darwin published his *Origin of Species* in 1859, that old ideas about religion would not suffice was obvious, and in the Preface to his 1855 *Leaves,* Whitman envisioned a new order in which "the new breed of poets [shall] be interpreters of men and women and of all events and things" (Whitman 25).

As early as "Starting from Paumanok" (1860) Whitman writes, "I too . . . inaugurate a religion, I descend into the arena." He viewed religion as the essential glue bringing all things into union: "I say that the real and permanent grandeur of these States must be their religion, / Otherwise there is no real and permanent grandeur" (section 7). Being a visionary is not necessarily the same as being a prophet, and Whitman was a visionary: "I am afoot with my vision" ("Song of Myself," section 33). He finds "letters from God" dropped in the street ("Song of Myself," section 48), and in "To Think of Time" he writes, "[E]very thing has an eternal soul! . . . I swear I think there is nothing but immortality!" (section 9).

As for the nature of this new religion that Whitman thought would mold America into a great moral force—a feat not accomplished by priests, creeds, and churches—he first recognized the role of conscience: "Conscience [is] the primary moral element" (Whitman 964). Whitman's idea is that personality (Personalism), caught up in the eternal flow of things, is directed by conscience. Thus his evolutionary view of things embraces both the material and the spiritual. That is why Whitman responded as he did to Robert G. Ingersoll's expression of religious doubts: "What is this world without a further Divine Purpose in it all?" (Whitman 1282).

How could Whitman as poet-prophet bring people into a religious union, a union with God, through love and democracy? In *Democratic Vistas* he says that poets should be "possess'd of the religious fire and abandon of Isaiah" (Whitman 988). The reference to Isaiah is not misplaced, for in it one finds both Whitman's purpose and his method. In "The Bible as Poetry" he cites Frederic de Sola Mendes's observation that religion was the basis of Judaism and that ancient Jewish poetry was by its very nature religious, "[i]ts subjects, God and Providence" (Whitman 1140). In "Five Thousand Poems," he asserts, "In a very profound sense *religion is the poetry of humanity*" (Whitman 1185). That Whitman saw himself in the role of the prophet in the Jewish sense is made clear in his discussion of Thomas Carlyle as prophet in "Carlyle from American Points of View" (Whitman 893), and in "Slang in America" he makes clear that the role of the prophet is to reveal God (Whitman 1166).

In spite of the fact that Whitman viewed himself as poet-prophet in the ancient Hebraic sense, since World War II critics have been reluctant to accept his estimate of himself. Arthur E. Briggs, for example, sees the thrust of Whitman's prophecy as encouraging faith in the future, and Roy Harvey Pearce contends that Whitman lacked the disciplined imagination of such poet-prophets as Blake and Yeats. Although the early Whitman prophesied, says Pearce, he failed to bring about his own transformation from poet to prophet. Pearce considers the later Whitman no more than a "visionary poet" (68). C. Carroll Hollis also limits Whitman's role to that of poet. Says Hollis, Whitman's posturing allowed him to speak convincingly in the early years, but he was never more than a poet. Finally, the two critics who have written most, and probably most perceptively, about Whitman and prophecy are George B. Hutchinson and David Kuebrich. Hutchinson sees Whitman as both shaman and revitalization prophet, because Whitman possessed characteristics of both. Hutchinson, therefore, is interested in connections and distinctions pertaining to revitalizing the culture and at the same time maintaining a personal or individual religious experience. As for Kuebrich, while admitting that "Song of Myself," for example, presents the reader with a coherent world view, Whitman fails, he contends, because "Song of Myself" does not contain enough information about that world view to make it accessible. For Kuebrich this seems to be a good summary of Whitman's effort to found a new religion. That Jeremiah and Isaiah both worked within a religion already established seems beside the point. On the other hand, Whitman rejected established religions in favor of inaugurating his own, and he failed. In that fact, perhaps, lies the entire argument over whether or not Whitman was a prophet, especially for modern readers.

J.R. LeMaster

Bibliography

Briggs, Arthur E. *Walt Whitman: Thinker and Artist.* New York: Philosophical Library, 1952.

Hayes, Will. *Walt Whitman: The Prophet of a New Era.* 1905. London: Daniel, 1921.

Hollis, C. Carroll. *Language and Style in "Leaves of Grass."* Baton Rouge: Louisiana State UP, 1983.

Hutchinson, George B. *The Ecstatic Whitman: Literary Shamanism & the Crisis of the Union.* Columbus: Ohio State UP, 1986.

Kuebrich, David. *Minor Prophecy: Walt Whitman's New American Religion.* Bloomington: Indiana UP, 1989.

Pearce, Roy Harvey. "Whitman Justified: The Poet in 1860." *Walt Whitman.* Ed. Harold Bloom. New York: Chelsea House, 1985. 65–86.

Reynolds, David S. *Walt Whitman's America: A Cultural Biography.* New York: Knopf, 1995.

Whitman, Walt. *Complete Poetry and Collected Prose.* Ed. Justin Kaplan. New York: Library of America, 1982.

See also DEMOCRATIC VISTAS; RELIGION; "SONG OF MYSELF"; "STARTING FROM PAUMANOK"

Prosody

Prosody is the study of sound patterning in verse, traditionally line and verse organization (quantitative) and assonance (qualitative). Whitman was the first to write modern free verse, and his contemporaries, along with poets and critics for several decades, tended to class his verse as heightened prose. (For reception and context, see Finch.) He himself thought of his poems as growing freely and loosely from the seeds of metrical laws, fulfilling themselves in natural shapes according to the same laws that governed music and oratory (1855 Preface). C. Carroll Hollis has traced the series of dots in the 1855 *Leaves of Grass* to rhetoric handbooks, which prescribed the marks to indicate long pauses for delivery.

The merging of spoken language, text, music, and poetry in the verse practice has made distinguishing an organizing principle for the prosody difficult and varied. Some scholars have located his prosody in the tradition of alliterative accentual verse or that of accentual syllabic verse. Others see it as composed of phrasal units, or as being wholly unsystematic. Lines and parts of lines that fit the parameters of traditional metrical or strong-stress poetry abound. Annie Finch examines mixtures of iambic and dactylic patterns, studying the verse in relation to nineteenth-century metrical codes.

Attempts to determine the basic principle of rhythmic organization examine syntax. Syntactic units are units of meaning whose boundaries are marked by some slight or long break in the stream of speech, often, though not necessarily, indicated by punctuation. The intonation unit is coextensive with the information unit; the unit of sound and meaning occur together and are not separable. Thus the "thought unit" is the unit of rhythmic organization, not the foot. Rhythmic cohesion depends on syntactic repetition, and repetition and variation of intonation (accentual) patterns. Whitman's lines are end-stopped; groupings of clauses or phrases (not feet) constitute lines; lines were originally divided into units for oral reading by series of dots; and syntactic repetition often serves as a cohesive and rhythmic device (e.g., "I" plus verb series, or prepositional phrase series). Further cohesion is made through patterns of accentual contours that are stylized, repeated, and varied, achieving force, fluidity, musicality, and delicacy. Familiar metrical patterns occur frequently but never so much as to invoke a consistent regularity which would identify a poem as metrical since metricality is determined by rule and context. For instance, consider the opening lines of "Song of Myself":

> I celebrate myself, and sing myself,
> And what I assume you shall assume,
> For every atom belonging to me as good
>   belongs to you.

While the first line can be scanned as iambic pentameter (iambic trimeter in the 1855 edition, before "and sing myself" was added) and the second and third lines as a mix of iambic, anapestic, and dactylic, we could scan most prose in the same way if read in the heightened manner reserved for poetry. Rather, rhythmic cohesion depends on the numbers and placement of accents within each phrasal group and the repetition and variation of accentual patterns. In line 1, there are two phrasal groups, each containing two accents, falling in the same positions—primary accents on *cel-* and *sing*, both verbs, and secondary accents on *-self* and *-self*, reflexive pronouns. The two groups have the same accentual contour—falling 1–2, primary to secondary prominence. Line 2 does not pick up the iambic rhythm of line 1 but rather this 1–2 falling contour. Again there are two

groups, with 1–2 contours, with the first accent on pronouns—*I* and *you* and *-sume* and *-sume*. The falling of the accents on the same syntactic items reinforces the rhythmic cohesion. Line 3 has seven accents, four on one side of a mid-line break, three on the other. The rhythmic contour is again supported by syntactic and same word repetition—*belonging, belongs, me, you*. Many lines have too many unaccented syllables to be scanned, but they repeat the accentual contour types established at the poem's outset:

> The distillation would intoxicate me
>   also, but I shall not let it.
> The atmosphere is not a perfume,
>   it has no taste of the distillation,
>   it is odorless. . . .
>   ("Song of Myself," section 2)

Many poems ask to be read at a rapid, exuberant pace, with no time for the heightened accents of meters. Whitman's musical working of regularized accentual contours drawn from speech is able to contain the play of traditional meters in a rich fabric.

Rosemary Gates Winslow

Bibliography

Allen, Gay Wilson. *American Prosody.* New York: American, 1935.

Bradley, Sculley. "The Fundamental Metrical Principle in Whitman's Poetry." *American Literature* 10 (1939): 437–459.

Finch, Annie. *The Ghost of Meter: Culture and Prosody in American Free Verse.* Ann Arbor: U of Michigan P, 1993.

Gates, Rosemary L. "The Identity of American Free Verse: The Prosodic Study of Whitman's 'Lilacs.'" *Language and Style* 18 (1985): 248–276.

Hollis, C. Carroll. *Language and Style in "Leaves of Grass."* Baton Rouge: Louisiana State UP, 1983.

Mitchell, Roger. "A Prosody for Whitman?" *PMLA* 84 (1969): 1606–1612.

See also LEAVES OF GRASS; STYLE AND TECHNIQUE(S)

"Proud Music of the Storm" (1869)

This poem was first published as "Proud Music of the Sea-Storm" in the *Atlantic Monthly,* February 1869, to which it was submitted by

Ralph Waldo Emerson as a personal favor to Whitman. It was first included in *Leaves of Grass,* with the new title, in 1871 and was presented in its final version in 1881.

Sidney Krause divides the poem's six numbered sections into three parts: I, section 1; II, sections 2 through 5; III, section 6. The organization can also be seen as an envelope, the first and last sections enclosing the intervening ones, which provide overlapping forays into the experience of different music. This music is revealed to be or emanate from a spiritual substance and will become the force behind a new poetic vision. In the envelope, sleep or dream is the locus of music, at first multifold and mysterious and at last multifold but beginning to be understood. Otherwise, sleep is mentioned only once, toward the beginning of section 2. In the final section, the poet emerges from his sleep with his new realization. The two major and intertwined themes are specified respectively in line 51, "And man and art with nature fused at last" (section 1) and in line 163, where the poet discovers that music will form the basis of "Poems bridging the way from Life to Death" (section 6), which will provide for a new departure in his poetry.

In section 1 varied sounds, from nature and from human activity, enter the poet's sleep and mysteriously seize him. In section 2 music from human activities, human music-making, and nature blend into one orchestra which under God's direction creates unity of man, art, and nature. Section 3 divides into two parts. In the first, the poet reminds himself that since he was a child all sounds have become music for him. This enables him to move to his family's voices and then to sounds of nature, popular songs, and tragic operas. The operatic motifs suggest that music gives heartbreaking experiences a deep significance.

Section 4 continues to enumerate the parts of the one great orchestra, moving from other operas to dance music and then to music expressing worldwide religions, mostly Asian, each suggesting ecstatic union of the human and divine. Although the operas mentioned in section 5 reintroduce European material, the poet says that he moves from Asia to Europe because most of his material is now based on European, not Asian, religions. He then asserts that this music expresses the godhead and he experiences it as it fuses with nature, and by filling him gives him a sense of universal unity. He awakes "softly" in section 6 because the tumultuous sounds have brought him to a calming realization. As in "Out of the Cradle" he has found a "clew" but from all sounds rather than just the sea. He can walk amidst the real world "[n]ourish'd henceforth by the celestial dream" (section 6) that he has described in sections 1 through 5 because music transforms reality into the celestial dream of unity, with everything ideal that lies within and beyond it. Thus what he has heard is given a dimension greater than its surface substance. All that he has heard comprises the rhythmic impulsion that will lie behind new poems "bridging the way from Life to Death" (section 6). They have been "vaguely wafted" because the human and natural music have only suggested what he must embody in words that he hopes to write.

The poem echoes the arrival of a new bard announced in "Starting from Paumanok"; the bridging of matter and spirit central to "Passage to India"; the passage from life to death symbolized in "Crossing Brooklyn Ferry" and "Out of the Cradle"; and the stimulation of inexpressible feelings by music described in "Song of Myself," section 26. It also hints of deep unformed feelings mentioned in "Scented Herbage of My Breast," whose "O I do not know what you mean there" is echoed by "I think O tongues ye tell this heart, that cannot tell itself, / This brooding yearning heart, that cannot tell itself" (section 2). Gay Wilson Allen found a symphonic structure in the poem, as in Sidney Lanier's poems. Sidney Krause denied the possibility of this by maintaining that music is the inspiration of Whitman's feeling and insight rather than its substance. James C. McCullagh proposed that Whitman reconciles diverse human states represented by sounds by reconciling natural and man-made sounds and sounds of worldwide religions and cultures. Several critics propose that the poem's real subject is Whitman's announcement of a new poetic program which will stress the connection of life to death and be more explicitly religious than his earlier work.

Mordecai Marcus

Bibliography

Allen, Gay Wilson. *The Solitary Singer: A Critical Biography of Walt Whitman.* 1955. Rev. ed. 1967. Chicago: U of Chicago P, 1985.

———. *Walt Whitman Handbook.* Chicago: Packard, 1946.

Kramer, Lawrence. "Conclusion: On Time and Form." *Music and Poetry: The Nineteenth Century and After.* Berkeley: U of California P, 1984. 223–241.

Krause, Sidney. "Whitman, Music and 'Proud Music of the Storm.'" *PMLA* 72 (1957): 705–721.

McCullagh, James C. "'Proud Music of the Storm': A Study in Dynamics." *Walt Whitman Review* 21 (1975): 66–73.

Schyberg, Frederik. *Walt Whitman.* Trans. Evie Allison Allen. New York: Columbia UP, 1951.

See also MUSIC, WHITMAN AND; "MYSTIC TRUMPETER, THE"

Bibliography

McLoughlin, William G. *Rhode Island: A History.* New York: Norton, 1986.

Rosenfeld, Alvin H. "Whitman and the Providence Literati." *Books at Brown* 24 (1971): 82–106.

Whitman, Walt. *The Correspondence.* Ed. Edwin Haviland Miller. Vol. 2. New York: New York, 1961.

Woodward, William, and Edward F. Sanderson. *Providence: A Citywide Survey of Historic Resources.* Providence: Rhode Island Historical Preservation Commission, 1986.

See also DOYLE, PETER; O'CONNOR, WILLIAM DOUGLAS

Providence, Rhode Island

A city at the head of Narragansett Bay, Providence is the seat of Brown University and the metropolis of Rhode Island. Now the state capital, it shared capital status with Newport in the nineteenth century. Founded in 1636 by Roger Williams, who wished to acknowledge divine assistance in his forced relocation from Massachusetts, the city early gained a reputation for attracting dissenters and freethinkers.

Providence emerged as an important mercantile port in the eighteenth century, and grew even more quickly with the Industrial Revolution. The first successful cotton mill in America (1790) was financed with Providence capital, and throughout the nineteenth century it was a major industrial center (Whitman addressed it as such in "The Eighteenth Presidency!"). The Dorr Rebellion, a contest over suffrage extension, took place there in 1842. And the giant steam engine that powered the Centennial Exposition in 1876 (admired by Whitman) was built by the Corliss firm in Providence. During Whitman's lifetime, the city's population rose from 11,767 (1820) to 132,146 (1890).

Whitman had many admirers in Providence (including the young Charlotte Perkins Gilman) and spent a pleasant vacation there in October 1868. He boasted to Pete Doyle of his "capacity of flirtation & carrying on with the girls" (Whitman 62), adding he was "having a devil of a jolly time" (63). But he also found its intellectual society "good & smart, but too constrained & bookish for a free old hawk like me" (61).

Ted Widmer

Pseudoscience

A notebook entry from the late 1850s suggests the appeal that an array of contemporary, interrelated radical movements—phrenology, mesmerism, spiritualism, and natural therapies—had for Whitman: "the real science is omnient, is nothing less than all sciences, comprehending all the known names, and many unknown" (*Notebooks* 5:1998). Amidst a world of fragmenting disciplines, each of these pseudosciences laid claim to the compelling nineteenth-century dream that all knowledge was interrelated and unitary and that its doctrines represented a grand synthesis. Purporting to study objective models of natural law, each nevertheless made room for subjective consciousness; each also attempted to forge links between natural law and social theory, between the material and spiritual. Optimistic, visionary, and dynamic, the more radical doctrines of these pseudosciences challenged religious, scientific, medical, sexual, and gender orthodoxies in order to hasten the coming of the City of Regenerated Man.

Many of their publications could be found for sale at the phrenological cabinet of Fowler and Wells in lower Manhattan which Whitman frequented during the 1840s and where in July 1849 L.N. Fowler gave Whitman his now famous cranioscopical examination. Considering that its proprietors, Orson Squire Fowler and his brother Lorenzo Niles, made the cabinet into an unofficial clearinghouse for the writings of radical reformers, it is no wonder that they were prepared to risk publishing and distributing the 1855 edition of *Leaves of Grass* and publishing the 1856 edition. They would have recognized therein, now transformed into poetry, "faint clews" and broader concepts explicitly derived from their own discipline and from the writings of the authors whose books they stocked: Orson Fowler on hereditary descent, parentage, and sexuality; Sylvester Graham on dietary and sexual reform; John Bovee Dods on mesmerism and electrical psychology; Andrew Jackson Davis on spiritualism; Amelia Bloomer on dress reform; Russell Trall and Joel Shew on water cure; and Margaret Fuller on women's rights.

Whitman's exposure to phrenological theory was more systematic and probably more extensive than to the other pseudosciences, and the conclusions he drew from his immersion in phrenology influenced the way he deployed the doctrines of the other pseudosciences in his poetry and prose: that a poet should be richly endowed with the gifts or faculties peculiar to each of the pseudosciences, and that the ensuing poetry should demonstrate these gifts and be grounded in the doctrines of each of the pseudosciences.

In the case of phrenology, Whitman constructed a mythical persona, based in large part on the results of his own phrenological examination, whose splendid physique, superb genealogy, virility, and sound physiology indicated formidable spiritual, moral, and intellectual powers. Poems, in the early editions particularly, reflect Whitman's incorporation of materials central to phrenological thought: the relation of sexuality and hereditary descent to perfection ("Unfolded Out of the Folds"); the generative act to physical and racial amelioration ("A Woman Waits for Me"); and the benevolent and progressive character both of cosmic teleology and human experience and institutions ("Crossing Brooklyn Ferry" and "A Song of the Rolling Earth").

Mesmerism, or animal magnetism, another area of interest to the phrenological Fowlers, premised the existence of a magnetic, electrical ether or fluid called the odic force that linked all phenomena. As a healing therapy, physicians attempted to effect a cure by manipulating the fluid in a patient's afflicted area using either magnets or, if they possessed vast odic powers, by passing their hands over the body. As a form of stage entertainment, however, mesmerism developed occult overtones: mesmeric operators using their odic powers appeared to control the mind of and even elicit clairvoyant visions from

a trance subject. Initially skeptical, Whitman announced his conversion to animal magnetism as early as August 1842 when he asserted that "it reveals at once the existence of a whole new world of truth, grand, fearful, profound, relating to that great mystery, in the shadow of which we live and move" (qtd. in Reynolds 260). Animal magnetism's vocabulary and lore surfaces in much of *Leaves of Grass,* while magnetic power comprises the constitutive element of the persona.

The persona's electrical "conductors," we learn, "seize every object and lead it harmlessly through me" ("Song of Myself," section 27); charged with an enormous store of vitalizing life force, the persona disseminates curative electricity to his weakened countrymen, as in sections 39, 40, and 41. A resemblance between mesmeric healers and the Christ/healer is evident in such poems as "To You [Whoever you are . . .]" and "To Him That was Crucified." In the latter, the persona's electrical vitality, in the form of his boundless healing powers of sympathy and friendship as conveyed through his breath and touch, accounts for his purported ability to cheer up and even restore wounded soldiers. And, in "The Sleepers," the healer makes electrical healing pass over diseased sleepers (section 1). The persona's shape-shifting and even sex-changing, in this poem and elsewhere, recall similar changes that operators effected during mesmeric performances on tranced subjects.

The language of the magnetists informs as well Whitman's depiction of sex. The persona's powerful electro-sexuality vivifies all; as the nation's poet and Columbia's lover, he plunges "his seminal muscle" into her, to charge her with vivifying force ("By Blue Ontario's Shore," section 6). In section 21 of "Song of Myself," Whitman takes the magnetic-sexual imagery to another level; here the cosmic persona embraces the "voluptuous" and "prodigal" earth to beget new celestial bodies and animate life. This spermatic trope, so called by Harold Aspiz, has its most sustained development in some of the "Children of Adam" poems and, elsewhere, in "Song of the Answerer," "By Blue Ontario's Shore," and sections 24 and 25 of "Song of Myself." In the latter, nature's sexual "[t]rickling sap" and "soft-tickling genitals" so heighten the persona's awareness of his phallic self that when his own "[s]eas of bright juice suffuse heaven" (section 24), he reaches the climax both of his physiological and poetic/imaginative processes. Such electro-biological lore, including the notion that sperm was the distillation of mind and body, came to Whitman from a potpourri of contemporary sources, including animal magnetism, phreno-magnetism, and phrenology.

Though the various roles played by the Whitman persona—as hypnotist, clairvoyant, visionary seer, and healer—were largely defined by practitioners of animal magnetism, these were also variously present in the newly emerging phenomenon of spiritualism. Surely, spiritualistic séances, where mediums assisted by a "spirit guide" communicated with the spirits of the deceased, did not go unnoticed by a poet whose aim was to demonstrate the interpenetration of the spiritual and material. Whitman reported in the Brooklyn *Daily Times* in 1857 that the "spiritual movement is blending itself in many ways with society, in theology, in the art of healing, in literature and in the moral and mental character of the people of the United States" (qtd. in Reynolds 263). In the 1855 Preface he included the spiritualist as a lawgiver of the poet. As with mesmerism, Whitman's adaptation of specific spiritualistic systems to his poetry is absent; David Reynolds suggests that Whitman garnered spiritualist ideas from an assortment of sources—the 1844 lectures of Professor George Bush on Emanuel Swedenborg, the idiosyncratic brand propagated by Thomas Lake Harris whose Brooklyn church Whitman most likely attended, and the writings of a leading British Swedenborgian, James John Garth Wilkinson.

Spiritualism lent its authority to Whitman's many optimistic declarations in *Leaves of Grass* about immortality. As a divine medium, the persona senses in "These I Singing in Spring" that "the spirits of dear friends dead or alive, thicker they come, a great crowd, and I in the middle." In "Mediums" Whitman associates bards with mediums who will "illustrate Democracy and the kosmos"; these same "divine conveyers" will communicate "[c]haracters, events, retrospections, . . . [d]eath, the future," and even what he called "the invisible faith," namely spiritualism. "Apostroph" contains an explicit call to "mediums" to "journey through all The States" and "convey the invisible faith"; and in "These Carols" the persona dedicates his poetic output to "the Invisible World." In "The Mystic Trumpeter," the "ecstatic ghost" of the "dead composer," who hovers unseen in the air and fills the night with "capricious tunes" that recall the past and predict a joyous future, resembles the invisible musicians of séances (sections 1 and 2).

The notion peculiar to Swedenborgianism, which Whitman associated with spiritualism, namely the doctrine of correspondences, constitutes a major component of Whitman's cosmic optimism. In "Starting from Paumanok," Whitman writes, "[H]aving look'd at the objects of the universe, I find there is no one nor any particle of one but has reference to the soul" (section 12), and in "Crossing Brooklyn Ferry" he asserts that "none else is perhaps more spiritual" than the "dumb, beautiful ministers" (section 9). The persona makes similar declarations in "A Song of Joys." Swedenborgian terms are also present in Whitman's poetry: the title of his 1876 poem "Eidólons" is a Swedenborgian term referring to the ultimate spiritual reality that lies behind all material appearances, as are two other companion words: "influx" or "afflatus" (inspiration that comes from the spiritual atmosphere through inhalation) and "efflux" (the wisdom issuing from an inspired subject's exhalation). In "Song of the Open Road" Whitman's persona asserts that the "efflux of the soul is happiness" and curiously links this efflux with the electrical "charge" of the animal magnetists: "Now it [the efflux] flows unto us, we are rightly charged" (section 8).

Whitman's canon also suggests his familiarity with more idiosyncratic outgrowths of Swedenborgianism. The erotic mysticism so powerfully exemplified in section 5 of "Song of Myself," where the contemplation of the personified soul by the poem's "I" leads to the revelation of God, resembles the physical-mystical spirit found in the writings of James John Garth Wilkinson. Elsewhere, Whitman's notebooks tell of his entering into an exultant, visionary trance that closely resembles Andrew Jackson Davis's brand of "traveling clairvoyance," namely Davis's mental travels removed in time and space. In "Song of Myself" the persona's freeing himself of "ties and ballasts" and "skirt[ing] the sierras, my palms cover[ing] continents" (section 33) allows him to communicate with future generations; he does so also in "Crossing Brooklyn Ferry" ("I am with you, you men and women of a generation, or ever so many generations hence" [section 3]). Another area of Whitman's thought also bears Davis's Harmonial stamp, namely the restorative, sexually magnetic powers of nature, appearing in "Song of Myself": "Press close bare-bosom'd night— press close magnetic nourishing night!" (section 21).

Unlike the aforementioned pseudosciences, the lore of pseudomedical practices and various health therapies rarely inspired in Whitman startling imagery and exciting flights of poetic imagination. Rather, they were put to the service of a frankly prescriptive end: he fashioned from his readings in several vitalistic medical theories—Thompsonism, homeopathy, and hydropathy—and from a scattering of other books devoted to health matters, both a persona and images of men and women who, as models of superior physical and moral training, were intended to counteract contemporary fears about the deterioration of America's citizenry. Fowler and Wells carried an extensive stock of books that preached temperance, advocated vegetarianism and hydropathy, and provided instructions about the regulation of diet, swimming, and even ventilation—all measures to ensure mental and physical health. Believing with many of his contemporaries that national regeneration lay in physical culture, Whitman even projected a series of lectures on various aspects of physical culture for young men, lectures that lifted his own lifelong commitment to temperance, bathing, and mild healing therapies to a moral imperative. References to water therapy, being in contact with nature, diet, habits, healthy-mindedness, and positive thinking as health-imparting restoratives are scattered throughout "Song of Myself"; here the persona exudes confidence that his health and cheer can overcome disease, the limitations of death, and impart his own health to his fellows and the nation. In his guise as Adam-hero, Whitman endows the physically and morally superior persona with the potential to found a heroic race; in "Spontaneous Me," "One Hour to Madness and Joy," and "A Woman Waits for Me," the persona acts not only out of humanistic and patriotic fervor, but in response to the Lamarckian urge toward racial improvement. Scenes in *Leaves of Grass* depicting idealized married life and ecstatic coupling, driven by such eugenic and racial considerations, have their origins in literature of these alternative therapies.

In the final analysis, Whitman's adaptation of these natural therapies is not very different from his adaptation of the other pseudosciences; they all contribute to the prescriptive intent he had for *Leaves of Grass*—that it could, like all great poetry, transform nations, evolve great societies, inspire the creation of gifted individuals, and point the way to a splendid future.

Arthur Wrobel

Bibliography

Aspiz, Harold. "'The Body Electric': Science, Sex, and Metaphor." *Walt Whitman Review* 24 (1978): 137–142.

———. "Educating the Kosmos: 'There Was a Child Went Forth.'" *American Quarterly* 18 (1966): 655–666.

———. "A Reading of Whitman's 'Faces.'" *Walt Whitman Review* 19 (1973): 37–48.

———. "Unfolding the Folds." *Walt Whitman Review* 12 (1966): 81–87.

———. "Walt Whitman: The Spermatic Imagination." *American Literature* 56 (1984): 379–395.

———. *Walt Whitman and the Body Beautiful.* Urbana: U of Illinois P, 1980.

Davies, John D. *Phrenology, Fad and Science: A 19th-Century Crusade.* New Haven: Yale UP, 1955.

Finkel, William L. "Sources of Walt Whitman's Manuscript Notes on Physique." *American Literature* 22 (1950): 308–331.

Hungerford, Edward. "Walt Whitman and His Chart of Bumps." *American Literature* 2 (1931): 350–384.

Reiss, Edmund. "Whitman's Debt to Animal Magnetism." *PMLA* 78 (1963): 80–88.

Reynolds, David S. *Walt Whitman's America: A Cultural Biography.* New York: Knopf, 1995.

Stern, Madeleine B. *Heads & Headlines: The Phrenological Fowlers.* Norman: U of Oklahoma P, 1971.

Whitman, Walt. *Leaves of Grass: Comprehensive Reader's Edition.* Ed. Harold W. Blodgett and Sculley Bradley. New York: New York UP, 1965.

———. *Notebooks and Unpublished Prose Manuscripts.* Ed. Edward F. Grier. 6 vols. New York: New York UP, 1984.

See also "CHILDREN OF ADAM"; "EIDÓLONS"; "FACES"; FOWLER, LORENZO NILES AND ORSON SQUIRE; HEALTH; HUMAN BODY; "I SING THE BODY ELECTRIC"; PHRENOLOGY; POPULAR CULTURE, WHITMAN AND; SCIENCE; "SLEEPERS, THE"; "SONG OF JOYS, A"; "SONG OF MYSELF"; "SONG OF THE OPEN ROAD"; SWEDENBORG, EMANUEL; "THERE WAS A CHILD WENT FORTH"; TRALL, DR. RUSSELL THACHER; "UNFOLDED OUT OF THE FOLDS"; "WOMAN WAITS FOR ME, A"

Psychological Approaches

Given that Whitman made the self his principal poetic topic, it was inevitable that he attracted psychological attention from the first *Leaves of Grass* on. He insisted that the poems were inseparable from himself, he confided that he created himself by writing poems, and he even dictated the identities of his readers. Nearly all studies of the poetry have been biographical, nearly all biographies have studied the poems to learn of their author, and most questions asked by interpreters and biographers have been psychological questions. Even among the early disciples, speculations about the poet's magnetism and prophetic quality had psychological overtones.

Of books by disciples, the most psychologically interesting is Edward Carpenter's *Days with Walt Whitman,* the first book to try to understand a mind extremely subtle, complex, and secretive. Carpenter was the first to say that beneath the affirmations of health and self-satisfaction lay something he thought tragic, something unfulfilled in the poet's sexual life. The first scholarly biographer, Emory Holloway, was fascinated by the variety of sexual poems in *Leaves of Grass* and catalogued their types. By the questions he suggested, and by making documentary material widely available, Holloway opened the door to the full-scale psychological research that followed.

The first critic to make an explicitly psychoanalytic exploration, Jean Catel wrote in 1929 of the poet's growth in a book that shows the influence of the analytic pioneer Wilhelm Stekel. Attentive to problems in the Whitman family, Catel erroneously posited an adolescent Whitman estranged from his family and judged that the young Whitman revealed himself in journalistic writing as a maladjusted failure. Catel believed that during the 1848 New Orleans trip, Whitman discovered a sexual peculiarity, namely that he was by nature autoerotic, and Catel reasoned that this quality lay behind Whitman's maladjustment. Writing poetry became Whitman's chief mode of sexual expression; the sexual force of the poems accounts for the transformation of the failing journalist into the great poet. Catel's general point about the poet's autoerotic sexuality was modified by Stephen Black (1975) and followed by Justin Kaplan (1980) and Paul Zweig (1984). Catel believed that writing poetry had therapeutic value for Whitman.

In 1933 the Danish theater critic Frederik Schyberg wrote a somewhat broader Freudian study which argued with Catel's claim that Whitman was autoerotic, positing instead an extremely delayed psychosexual development. Schyberg concluded that Whitman remained identified with his mother throughout his life, and often played a maternal role in poems and in life. Schyberg, like Holloway, studied all the editions of *Leaves of Grass,* and went much further than Holloway in using changes in the poems to construe the poet's personal development. It is Schyberg who first suggested a psychological crisis occurring before new poems of the third (1860) *Leaves of Grass* were written. The crisis is reflected in "Out of the Cradle," and "As I Ebb'd with the Ocean of Life," and in the sexual poems of "Calamus," which Schyberg considered unmistakably homoerotic. Schyberg asserted that if Whitman were fully aware of the homoeroticism in the poems he would not have published them. (Whitman seemed surprised and taken aback when an admirer, J.A. Symonds, inquired whether the "Calamus" poems referred to "the love of man for man" and rejected the inference as "damnable" [Traubel 75–76].) Schyberg regarded the successive revisions and editions as attempts to suppress such unwitting revelations from early editions and to create a picture of a life more unified and idealized than the life actually led.

Psychological thinking among literati fell under academic ban during the reign of the New Criticism, and, perhaps by no coincidence, Whitman also went into eclipse. In the 1960s psychological criticism resumed, and a new sense of Whitman began to emerge. Edwin Miller showed why the New Critics had been rendered mute by *Leaves of Grass.* The poems have meanings that are elusive because they are emotional rather than intellectual. Also, he asserted, the poems have unity undiscovered by the New Critics because it is a psychic unity. Without ignoring conflicts in Whitman's life and psyche, Miller emphasizes the poet's joy, a joy that, like Nietzsche's, takes poet and reader beyond good and evil, beyond tragedy. Opposing a trend that still prevails, Miller asserts the primacy of earliest printed texts of the poems because they stand closest to the originating psychic impulses.

Like Miller, Stephen Black finds the earliest printed texts most interesting psychologically and (usually) most satisfactory aesthetically. Black studies Whitman's creative processes from the standpoint of psychoanalytic ego psychology. Emphasizing that nearly all Whitman's major poems were composed between early 1855 and the end of 1859, he argues that after 1860 Whit-

P

man seems unable or unwilling to return to the psychic sources of his poetry. The sources can only be reached by regressions in which Whitman escapes various inhibitions, including conventions of thought and language; therefore, the regressions simultaneously give the poetry its power and originality. Where Miller assumes that Whitman's homoeroticism was conscious and overt from an early age, Black argues that Whitman repressed knowledge of physical homosexual wishes until some crisis occurred in 1857–1859. Possibly the crisis was the very act of writing the "Calamus" poems. Afterwards, the poet was increasingly furtive, never becoming comfortable with the love of either men or women and remaining primarily autoerotic.

Biographies and interpretations of the poems, psychological or otherwise, leave unanswered two questions that have intrigued readers from the beginning: how can someone who seems as ordinary as Whitman become a great poet? And, how can one account for the magnetism that captivated numerous people, many of them far from credulous? David Cavitch, building on Miller and Black, offers a single striking answer to both riddles: Whitman surprises himself with the discovery that an ordinary man may represent everyone else. Cavitch convincingly establishes his thesis that Whitman re-created in his poetic voice and structures the relationships that existed between him and his parents, brothers and sisters, and found his true poetic power in "struggling against his poetry," a struggle that reproduced his "loving conflict with his family" (xii).

The approaches of psychological critics have shown their most direct influence in recent biographies of Whitman by Justin Kaplan and Paul Zweig.

Stephen A. Black

Bibliography

Black, Stephen A. *Walt Whitman's Journeys into Chaos*. Princeton: Princeton UP, 1975.

Carpenter, Edward. *Days with Walt Whitman*. London: Allen, 1906.

Catel, Jean. *Walt Whitman: la naissance du poète*. Paris: Les Editions Rieder, 1929.

Cavitch, David. *My Soul and I: The Inner Life of Walt Whitman*. Boston: Beacon, 1985.

Holloway, Emory. *Whitman: An Interpretation in Narrative*. New York: Knopf, 1926.

Kaplan, Justin. *Walt Whitman: A Life*. New York: Simon and Schuster, 1980.

Miller, Edwin Haviland. *Walt Whitman's Poetry: A Psychological Journey*. Boston: Houghton Mifflin, 1968.

Schyberg, Frederik. *Walt Whitman*. Trans. Evie Allison Allen. New York: Columbia UP, 1951.

Traubel, Horace. *With Walt Whitman in Camden*. Vol. 1. Boston: Small, Maynard, 1906.

Zweig, Paul. *Walt Whitman: The Making of the Poet*. New York: Basic Books, 1984.

See also BIOGRAPHIES; CARPENTER, EDWARD; CATEL, JEAN; HOLLOWAY, EMORY; MILLER, EDWIN HAVILAND; SCHYBERG, FREDERIK; SEX AND SEXUALITY

Putnam's Monthly

Founded in New York by George Palmer Putnam and Company in January 1853, *Putnam's Monthly Magazine* was one of the most prestigious nineteenth-century literary periodicals. It continued under the editorship of Charles Briggs until September 1857, when it merged with *Emerson's United States Magazine* to form *Emerson's Magazine and Putnam's Monthly*. With Briggs as editor, it reemerged in January 1868, as *Putnam's Magazine: Original Papers on Literature, Science, Art, and National Literature* and continued until November 1870.

Putnam's Monthly published one of the first reviews of *Leaves of Grass* (1855); in September 1855 Charles Eliot Norton called *Leaves* "a mixture of Yankee transcendentalism and New York rowdyism," and found it "preposterous yet somehow fascinating" (25). In January 1868 *Putnam's* new series contained an effort by William D. O'Connor, author of *The Good Gray Poet* (1866), to mythologize Whitman. O'Connor's story, "The Carpenter," presents Whitman as a modern Christ, able to perform miracles and heal people with his personal magnetism.

William A. Pannapacker

Bibliography

Loving, Jerome. *Walt Whitman's Champion: William Douglas O'Connor*. College Station: Texas A&M UP, 1978.

Norton, Charles Eliot. "Charles Eliot Norton's Review 1855." *Walt Whitman: The Critical Heritage*. Ed. Milton Hindus. London: Routledge and Kegan Paul, 1971. 24–28.

Mott, Frank Luther. "Putnam's Monthly Magazine." *A History of American Magazines, 1850–1865*. Cambridge, Mass.: Harvard UP, 1938. 419–431.

See also NORTON, CHARLES ELIOT; O'CONNOR, WILLIAM DOUGLAS

Quakers and Quakerism

Whitman's Quaker antecedents can be summarized briefly. In his early years on Long Island and in Brooklyn (1819–1841) he grew up near Quaker relatives and neighbors. During his final years of illness in Camden, New Jersey (1873–1892), he enjoyed free-ranging conversations with local Quaker acquaintances.

His maternal grandmother, Naomi Williams (Van Velsor), brought Quaker culture from the Williams home when she married Cornelius Van Velsor. Her daughter, Louisa Van Velsor (Whitman), absorbed Quaker lore and language from her, and passed it on to her own children when she married Walter Whitman. Walt seems to have absorbed her affectionate regard for the culture.

Neither of Whitman's parents was a member of the Society of Friends (the formal name for Quakers), but they were both admirers of the radical Quaker Elias Hicks, their Long Island neighbor (1748–1839). Hicks was at the center of a controversy that developed in the Society in the 1820s, between the radical Hicksite Quakers, who wanted to keep to the "pure" (radical, un-orthodox) spirit of the movement's seventeenth-century founder, George Fox (1624–1691), and the orthodox Quakers, who wanted to move Quakerism closer to other evangelical Protestant churches. In 1827 the dispute climaxed in a formal separation which split the Society of Friends in the United States for over a century. The aging Hicks, endorsed by his local meeting, continued to make his living by farming and to travel as a visiting minister to distant meetings of the Society of Friends. In 1829 Whitman's parents attended the last public sermon that Hicks delivered before his death; Walt, ten years old, was indelibly impressed by his earnest eloquence.

Years later, in a letter to his mother from Washington, Whitman invoked Hicks. He was explaining why his own volunteer ministry with wounded soldiers was of a different order from the professional efforts of government agents and chaplains. Elias Hicks would call them *hirelings*, he told her, expecting her to understand that he, like Hicks, would minister to the world's needs out of love rather than for money.

The biographical record shows these impressions made by Quakers. Critics disagree as to their critical significance. The Quakers were an influence on Whitman's world view, undoubtedly; but what kind of influence, and where? The references to Quakers in Whitman's verse seem self-contained and of minor importance: the "mother of men" in "Faces," who may have been modeled on his grandmother Naomi, and an allusion to George Fox in "An Old Man's Thought of School." More informative are the references to Quakerism in the prose coming out of Whitman's Camden years: memories of Long Island Quakers in *Specimen Days;* positive remarks made to Traubel about a felt affinity toward Quakers and Quakerism; and in 1888 a pair of biographical essays on Elias Hicks and George Fox.

In both essays what Whitman most admires is the respect that each Quaker accords to individual subjectivity. The traditional core belief of Quakers is usually worded as "there is that of God in every person." Whitman notes the version of this belief as preached by Hicks, that "the fountain of all naked theology, all religion, . . . all the truth to which you are possibly eligible" lies "in *yourself* and your inherent relations" (*Prose Works* 2:627). Whitman shows that the same idea was preached by Fox, who came to "direct people to the spirit that gave forth the Scriptures" (*Prose Works* 2:650)—the Holy Spirit implanted at creation in each human being. The imaginative consequences of this idea ("there is that of God within every person") are profoundly democratic. Quakers imagined "that" as neither male nor female but as an elemental form of generative energy: a seed, an inner light, a spirit-within corresponding mysteriously to the Universal Spirit that created it. Thus, each human soul is as uniquely precious to the universe, and as divinely equal, as any other; and thus it is wrong for any human being to defer to, or to do violence to, any other. There is a clear affinity between the democratic meanings in the radical Quaker world view and the democratic meanings Whitman expresses in a poem like "Song of Myself": "Stop this day and night with me and you shall possess the origin of all poems" (section 2).

Both Fox and Hicks were willing to endure massive disapproval from the external world because of their loyalty to their own internal intuition of truth. With his truth George Fox founded a minority sect; with his, Elias Hicks split it in two. Whitman notes at one point in the Hicks essay that there are no longer "any such living fountains of belief" (*Prose Works* 2:647) being offered by the sects and churches of the late nineteenth century—a generalization which includes the Society of Friends. Thus in 1888 Whitman was drawn to the radical vision of a Fox and a Hicks, but not to the outlook of the orthodox to whom they were the exceptions. This outlook, which tended to judge the world in moralizing categories of "bad" and "good," he associated with the Quaker-poet John Greenleaf Whittier. If orthodox Quakers were dull to the radical force of their group's most inspiring idea ("that of God"), then Quakerism had become a dormant culture whose chief contribution to democracy lay in the past.

In 1889 one of Whitman's supporters, William Sloane Kennedy, undertook to write about Whitman's Quaker traits. He produced a brief list of common resemblances, concluding that Quakerism conferred only a somewhat perceptible "tinge" to Whitman's writings. Since Kennedy's account was edited and approved by Whitman, it is understandable that subsequent critics also would treat it as a "tinge."

But Quaker influence is being reevaluated. Since the 1960s Americanists are increasingly realizing the power of minority cultures to preserve and release energies for social change, and are looking more closely at the cultural background of nonconformist writers like Whitman. Once Whitman critics begin to trace unconventional forms and features in *Leaves of Grass* back to the exchanges that Whitman may have had with minority cultures such as Quakerism, they discover that such exchanges typically occur gradually, through diffusion beneath the level of consciousness, rather than in moments of conscious decision.

Critics of intercultural exchange look at Quakerism not only as a belief system but also as an active culture. They ask not only what its ideas could have meant to Whitman but also how the example of its activism might have influenced him. Both aspects of Quakerism, its historical beliefs and its activist history, were there to support Whitman in his lifelong effort (implicit in the verse, explicit in his prose) to move readers to accept and trust and treasure their sexual natures. For the radical Quaker belief in "that of God" leads to the further belief that nature and human nature are infused with God's Spirit. It is this belief that Whitman appeals to in one of his most extended treatments of sexual frankness and censorship, "A Memorandum at a Venture" (1882), which to support its arguments for tolerance invokes the biblical story of creation, in which God looks upon all that he has made and finds it good.

Quakerism's history of cultural activism is directly relevant to Whitman. In the seventeenth century English Quakers insisted on the right to dress, speak, and behave in symbolic accord with their religious beliefs. Their group testimony included not only public demonstrations but also the punishments that they drew down upon themselves, their nonresistance to those punishments, and the reasoned protests, defenses, and explanations that they wrote and published to the world. After four decades of this irrepressible testimony, the public toleration and freedoms they sought were secured for them and others in a far-reaching Act of Toleration (1689). An exemplary precedent was established: a "Friendly" minority brought about a major change in the attitudes and laws of the majority by nonviolent persuasion.

This example, which Whitman knew because he praised it in his Fox essay, was a silent presence giving psychological as well as legal protection to his life-experiment of writing truthful, liberating, self-liberating poetry. A dual appreciation of Quakerism, as an activist culture with an activating faith, shows how much Whitman resembled the Friends. It illuminates not only his unorthodox ideas but also the unorthodox confidence with which he persisted in bringing those ideas to public attention and keeping public orthodoxy from ignoring them—like an irrepressible Friend.

Susan Day Dean

Bibliography

Brinton, Howard H. *Friends for 300 Years: The History and Beliefs of The Society of Friends since George Fox Started the Quaker Movement.* 1952. Wallingford, Pa.: Pendle Hill Publications, 1965.

Dean, Susan. "Whitman's Democratic Vision in Multicultural Perspective." Unpublished manuscript, 1995.

Kennedy, William Sloane. "Quaker Traits of Walt Whitman." *In Re Walt Whitman.* Ed. Horace Traubel, Richard Maurice Bucke, and Thomas B. Harned. Philadelphia: McKay, 1893. 213–214.

Traubel, Horace. *With Walt Whitman in Camden.* 1908. Vol. 2. New York: Rowman and Littlefield, 1961.

Whitman, Walt. *The Correspondence.* Ed. Edwin Haviland Miller. Vol. 1. New York: New York UP, 1961.

———. *Prose Works 1892.* Ed. Floyd Stovall. 2 vols. New York: New York UP, 1963–1964.

See also DEMOCRACY; EQUALITY; GENEALOGY; HICKS, ELIAS; KENNEDY, WILLIAM SLOANE; RELIGION; VAN VELSOR, NAOMI ("AMY") WILLIAMS; WHITMAN, LOUISA VAN VELSOR; WHITTIER, JOHN GREENLEAF

"Quicksand Years" (1865)

"Quicksand Years" first appeared as "Quicksand years that whirl me I know not whither" in *Drum-Taps* (1865), which was subsequently annexed to the 1867 edition of *Leaves of Grass.*

In 1871 the poem was moved (under its final title) to the "Whispers of Heavenly Death" cluster within *Passage to India,* which was annexed to the 1871 *Leaves.* In the 1881 edition, the cluster, including "Quicksand Years," was integrated into *Leaves.*

This six-line poem depicts "politics, triumphs, battles, life" as undependable substances, mere "shows" which whirl the speaker aimlessly and then give way and elude him. The one dependable, lasting substance is "One's-Self," the "soul."

The change in placement of "Quicksand Years" suggests a shift in meaning. In *Drum-Taps,* Whitman was attempting to capture the spirit and actions of a particular time and place, Civil War America. In this context, the "politics, triumphs, battles" appear to refer particularly to that historical cataclysm, against which only one's own inner self is proof. The poem's repositioning in the "Whispers" cluster changes the referent, for as both Blodgett and Miller point out, this grouping is more deliberately spiritual in emphasis. Miller argues that in this cluster the spiritual is shown to be true reality and the apparently real, mere illusion. Within this context, "Quicksand Years" takes on a more universal significance—the concept that when external supports fail, one's only surety is the soul.

Gay Barton

Bibliography

Blodgett, Harold W. "Whitman's *Whisperings.*" *Walt Whitman Review* 8 (1962): 12–16.

Megna, B. Christian. "Sociality and Seclusion in the Poetry of Walt Whitman." *Walt Whitman Review* 17 (1971): 55–57.

Miller, James E., Jr. *A Critical Guide to "Leaves of Grass."* Chicago: U of Chicago P, 1957.

See also DRUM-TAPS; SOUL, THE; "WHISPERS OF HEAVENLY DEATH" (CLUSTER)

R

Racial Attitudes

Whitman has commonly been perceived as one of the few white American writers who transcended the racial attitudes of his time, a great prophet celebrating ethnic and racial diversity and embodying egalitarian ideals. He has been adopted as a poetic father by poets of Native American, Asian, African, European, and Chicano descent. Nonetheless, the truth is that Whitman in person largely, though confusedly and idiosyncratically, internalized typical white racial attitudes of his time, place, and class.

The poet not only grew up in a racist environment, a descendant of slave owners, but also followed (without always embracing) forms of "ethnological science" that throughout the nineteenth century presented racist arguments contradicting the poet's egalitarian principles. As a result, Whitman's racial attitudes were unstable and inconsistent. The inconsistencies particularly appear in differences between his journalism and unpublished notes, on the one hand, and his poetry and visionary essays on the other—as if Whitman did not trust himself on racial issues and therefore largely avoided them, or veiled his attitudes in the work by which he wanted to revitalize American culture and finally to be remembered as democracy's bard.

Concerning people of African descent, what little is known about the early development of Whitman's racial awareness suggests he imbibed the prevailing white prejudices of his place and time, thinking of black people as servile, shiftless, ignorant, and given to stealing, although he would remember individual blacks of his youth in positive terms. His later experiences in the South apparently did nothing to mitigate early impressions, although readers of the twentieth century, including black ones, imagined him as a fervent antiracist.

Whitman's attitudes to people of African descent must be distinguished from his attitudes toward slavery. In an 1857 editorial for the Brooklyn *Daily Times,* for example, he articulated his antislavery position in white nationalist terms, opposing "the great cause of American White Work and Working people" to "the Black cause" (*I Sit* 88). The misnomer "the Black cause," by which Whitman means the *slave owners'* cause, betrays the psychological slippage between his attitude toward the institution of slavery and his attitude toward its contemporary victims. Indeed, its victims awaken in him a feeling of dread. Elsewhere he refers to slave labor as a "black tide" threatening white workingmen. At one point Whitman suggested regarding the whole debate over slavery in terms of racial nationalism, as a contest between "the totality of White Labor" and the interference of "Black Labor, or of bringing in colored persons on any terms" (*I Sit* 90). And yet in his unpublished manuscript "The Eighteenth Presidency!" (written in 1856) he expresses a definite sense of black working people as "American" working people with no less importance to the democratic cause than white workers. Moreover, only a few years prior to his expressions of a racial nationalist stance, Whitman editorialized in the New York *Aurora* against all immigration restriction, insisting that America must embrace immigrants of all backgrounds, including Africans. He still held these views in the last years of his life.

When Whitman defended exclusion of blacks from the new western territories, he rationalized his position (which he recognized as morally suspect) by suggesting that separation would best serve both blacks and whites—an argument also made by some black nationalists of the time. He argued, for example, that blacks would only become an "independent and heroic race" if they were out from under the heel of white racism, which he saw as endemic in the United States (*I Sit* 90).

In fact, if there is one consistent strain in Whitman's confused and contradictory prose meditations on race and slavery, it is an emphasis on the importance of self-determination to human dignity. Late in life, Whitman said that his ambivalence about "ultra-abolitionism," and even his suspicions about black inferiority, derived from his perception that the masses of black people lacked a defiant love of liberty and the drive for self-reliance. (These views, it must be said, matched contemporary racial theories that identified different "temperamental" and "cultural" attributes with different "races.") Particularly in old age, his private argument against African Americans was that he saw little tendency to self-determination in their "group" character. Nor was he disposed to recognize such self-determination where it revealed itself. When reminded of Wendell Phillips's famous oration on Toussaint L'Ouverture, he replied that he thought it exaggerated; and when mentioning Frederick Douglass, he could not help bringing up that eloquent freedom fighter's "white blood." Moreover, in the wake of the Civil War he feared the idea of blacks gaining political power.

After the war, Whitman began wondering whether blacks were innately inferior to whites and bound to disappear. He even considered that fate "most likely" though far off. Contact with the "stronger" and more arrogant white race, Whitman generally suspected, would finally prove fatal. His reading of post–Civil War "ethnological science" deeply influenced Whitman on this issue. To Horace Traubel he said, "The nigger, like the Injun, will be eliminated: it is the law of races, history, what-not" (*With Walt Whitman* 2:283). His statements along these lines are sometimes hesitant and ambiguous, sometimes quite certain.

One does not find suggestions of the disappearance of the Negro before the Civil War. The early poetry occasionally reveals a view of blacks as being at an early stage of evolutionary development but with the assumption that they will in time reach the poet's side. They have a great future before them, not a tragic or merely pathetic end. In the late 1850s Whitman rejected racist ethnologists' arguments that Negroes were incapable of developing great "civilizations," considering early Egypt a refutation of this view.

Whitman was surely aware of how his racist tendencies belied the fundamental convictions that suffused *Leaves of Grass,* particularly since some of his most devoted early supporters were antiracists. He admitted to Horace Traubel that he had probably been "tainted" by the "New York" attitude toward antislavery, and he came to blame his split with William Douglas O'Connor upon his own shortcomings in this respect (*With Walt Whitman* 3:75–76). His solution to the contradiction was to avoid racial issues, much as he would avoid issues concerning the genocide being perpetrated against Native Americans. Clearly, Whitman could not consistently reconcile the ingrained, even foundational, racist character of the United States with its egalitarian ideals. He could not even reconcile such contradictions in his own psyche.

African-American readers of the late nineteenth and early twentieth centuries greatly admired Whitman's poetic treatment of their people; they did not find in *Leaves of Grass* the condescension and exoticism they found in virtually all other white literature with black characters. They considered Whitman uniquely immune to the racism of his countrymen and a model to black authors themselves, treasuring lines that glorified the "divine-soul'd African, large, fine-headed, nobly-form'd, superbly destin'd, on equal terms with me!" ("Salut au Monde!," section 11). Even "Ethiopia Saluting the Colors," today generally considered stereotypical if not racist in its portrait of an old slave woman, was widely admired by black intellectuals before World War II, and was set to music as a "war song" for World War I by Harry T. Burleigh, a prominent black composer. Black writers lamented that Whitman's influence had been limited by the unpopularity of his poetic form. Only in the mid-twentieth century would Whitman's actual racial attitudes begin to be more broadly recognized by both white and black readers, mainly specialists in American literature.

Just as Whitman suspected late in life that blacks would not survive in the long run, he accepted the dominant view that Native Americans (whom he often called "aborigines" in preference to "Indians") would "die out" in the competition for survival—an idea shared by his friend and admirer Daniel Brinton, at the time America's premier ethnological "authority" on Native American languages. Poems such as "Pioneers! O Pioneers!" and "Song of the Redwood-Tree" suggest that Whitman viewed the displacement of Native Americans by whites inevitable and even fitting. He could admire individual "specimens" of aboriginal humanity—particularly elders who had not been corrupted by white civilization and therefore maintained their rugged "natural" beauty and eloquence; but he appears to have seen no place for them in the future nation of nations. His views are suggested in "Song of the Redwood-Tree," where "a mighty dying" redwood, having *"fill'd [its] time,"* yields willingly to the axes of *"a superber race."* He told Horace Traubel point-blank, "the Injun, will be eliminated" (*With Walt Whitman* 2:283).

Once again, Whitman's postwar social Darwinism clashes with the egalitarian spirit of his poetry. In *Leaves of Grass* we find a poet who celebrates racial difference and embraces diversity: "Of every hue and caste am I, of every rank and religion" ("Song of Myself," section 16). In "Song of Myself" he tenderly depicts the marriage between a white trapper and a young Native American girl—a portrayal that conflicts with his negative portrayal of "half-breeds" in other contexts. Whitman's "friendly and flowing savage" in "Song of Myself" (section 39), a sort of model American, is a cultural hybrid of "red" and "white" attributes; yet Whitman found many of the Indians he met or saw in "white" towns and cities "degraded" and "shiftless." Even Whitman's idealization of what he often regarded as Native "nobility" and its "relics" could waver during fits of indignation over, for example, reports of an Indian massacre of whites in Minnesota. Whitman never felt driven to take up the cause of the multitudes of Native Americans massacred by white soldiers and settlers throughout his poetic career. Instead, he eulogized the idea of the "vanishing" Indian whose positive traits he hoped would be absorbed by white Americans to help distinguish them from Europeans.

In contrast to his belief in the inferiority of African Americans and Native Americans, Whitman viewed the peoples of Asia in what could be considered an egalitarian light. The poet's great appreciation for the ancient Asian spiritual texts probably accounts for his admiration for those cultures. In fact Whitman's privileging of Asian cultures over African and Native American ones might be based in part on a respect for cultures with a written tradition and a devaluing of those that he believed had not independently developed methods of writing—a crucial distinction to Enlightenment thinkers. In private conversations, Whitman adamantly attacked popular anti-immigration attitudes directed against Asian newcomers. This does not mean he was beyond the influence of long-established stereotypes. Whitman accused Sadakichi Hartmann, a Whitman admirer of Japanese and German heritage, of having a "Tartaric makeup" and embodying an "Asiatic craftiness, too—all of it!" (*With Walt Whitman* 5:38). Nonetheless, as Xilao Li has observed, Whitman viewed Asia as the origin of the human race and of all religions. In "Passage to India" the final connection made between Old Asia and New America suggests the ultimate fruition of human civilization. Whitman seems to have no trouble fitting people of Asian descent into his personal world vision, or his vision of American identity.

Because of the radically democratic and egalitarian aspects of his poetry, readers generally expect, and desire for, Whitman to be among the literary heroes that transcended the racist pressures that abounded in all spheres of public discourse during the nineteenth century. He did not, at least not consistently; nonetheless his poetry has been a model for democratic poets of all nations and races, right up to our own day. How Whitman could have been so prejudiced, and yet so effective in conveying an egalitarian and antiracist sensibility in his poetry, is a puzzle yet to be adequately addressed.

George Hutchinson and David Drews

Bibliography

Aspiz, Harold. *Walt Whitman and the Body Beautiful.* Urbana: U of Illinois P, 1980.

Folsom, Ed. *Walt Whitman's Native Representations.* Cambridge: Cambridge UP, 1994.

Klammer, Martin. *Whitman, Slavery, and the Emergence of "Leaves of Grass."* University Park: Pennsylvania State UP, 1995.

Li, Xilao. "Walt Whitman and Asian American Writers." *Walt Whitman Quarterly Review* 10 (1993): 179–194.

Loving, Jerome. *Walt Whitman's Champion: William Douglas O'Connor.* College Station: Texas A&M UP, 1978.

Peeples, Ken, Jr. "The Paradox of the 'Good Gray Poet' (Walt Whitman on Slavery and the Black Man)." *Phylon* 35 (1974): 22–32.

R

Price, Kenneth. "Whitman's Solutions to 'The Problem of the Blacks.'" *Resources for American Literary Study* 15 (1985): 205–208.

Sill, Geoffrey. "Whitman on 'The Black Question': A New Manuscript." *Walt Whitman Quarterly Review* 8 (1990): 69–75.

Traubel, Horace. *With Walt Whitman in Camden.* Vol. 2. New York: Appleton, 1908; Vol. 3. New York: Mitchell Kennerley, 1914; Vol. 5. Ed. Gertrude Traubel. Carbondale: Southern Illinois UP, 1964.

Whitman, Walt. *I Sit and Look Out: Editorials from the Brooklyn Daily Times.* Ed. Emory Holloway and Vernolian Schwarz. New York: Columbia UP, 1932.

———. *Notebooks and Unpublished Prose Manuscripts.* Ed. Edward F. Grier. Vol. 6. New York: New York UP, 1984.

———. *Walt Whitman of the New York Aurora.* Ed. Joseph J. Rubin and Charles H. Brown. State College, Pa.: Bald Eagle, 1950.

See also DOUGLASS, FREDERICK; "ETHIOPIA SALUTING THE COLORS"; INDIAN AFFAIRS, BUREAU OF; LABOR AND LABORING CLASSES; MEXICAN WAR, THE; NATIVE AMERICANS (INDIANS); RECONSTRUCTION; SLAVERY AND ABOLITIONISM; "SONG OF MYSELF"; "SONG OF THE REDWOOD-TREE"

Radicalism

Whitman's adulthood coincided with an extremely tumultuous time in American politics and society. From 1840 onward, politically active Americans like Whitman were energized and agitated not only by the burgeoning, robust debate over slavery but by such vital and divisive political and social issues as dirty tricks and corruption, the prohibition of alcohol, and women's rights. Disagreements over these and other issues contributed to the increasing fractiousness among Americans along class and ideological lines. While Whitman's ideas on many of these issues put him among those people who were categorized at the time as "radical," his identity as a political and social radical is actually complex, as Whitman himself indicated when he told Horace Traubel, "Be radical—be radical—be not too damned radi-cal!" (Traubel 223). As one might expect from a figure whose persona is "large" and "contain[s] multitudes" ("Song of Myself," section 51), Whitman's connection to radicalism in his life and work is flexible and, frequently, contradictory: at times he uncompromisingly stakes out positions on the margins, at other times he holds positions that seek a delicate balance between the extremes.

The evolution of Whitman's participation in the national conflict over slavery provides the clearest example of his complicated connection to nineteenth-century political radicalism. From early in his journalistic career (as editor of the Brooklyn *Daily Eagle*), Whitman wrote articles expressing his strong opposition to the spread of slavery. Faithful Democrat that he was at this time, Whitman initially espoused views on slavery that were close to the party's mainstream. However, as Democratic leaders began to make compromises that Whitman believed were morally wrong—such as President James Polk's opposition to the Wilmot Proviso—he aligned himself with the radical wing of the Democratic party, referred to as the "Barnburners." In 1848 Whitman left the Democratic party altogether to join the Free Soil party (he even attended their national convention), whose members were unflinchingly opposed to the spread of slavery into any newly acquired territories. A few years later, after Whitman realized that there were no political leaders with the will or integrity to confront the slavery issue without compromising on essential moral questions, he fled party politics entirely.

This brief chronology of events in Whitman's political evolution indicates the principled position he took regarding the issue of slavery: believing that this institution was not morally tenable, Whitman rejected any compromise on its extension beyond the South. Whitman's radicalism on slavery, however, was limited to this single dimension. For a variety of reasons, Whitman took less radical positions on such issues as the abolition of slavery, the return of fugitive slaves, and the necessity of disuniting North from South. To a great extent, Whitman's views on these other critical issues were greatly influenced by his belief in American democracy and his fear of disunion. Thinking that extreme positions on these key issues threatened to rip the country and its institutions apart, Whitman was unwilling to sacrifice the nation's present and future existence to uncompromising stands on these issues.

However, Whitman's willingness to resolutely oppose slavery's extension but not to support immediate emancipation, the unconditional return of fugitive slaves, or principled disunion also reflects his inability to fully transcend the racism that was widespread in the nineteenth century. Although Whitman's later poetry in *Leaves of Grass* reflects his humanitarian belief in the value of all human beings, his deepest sympathy was with white workingmen and thus he took positions on slavery that put their interests first. Extension of slavery was the single most important issue for Whitman because of its potentially devastating effect on the status and livelihood of white workingmen.

Whitman's position in the debate over slavery was truly only marginally radical. Although he held his strong position on the extension of slavery, he did not at any time join with the abolitionists. After the Civil War, moreover, Whitman's political writings suggest that he has become more conservative. *Democratic Vistas,* Whitman's 1871 reply to Thomas Carlyle's writings attacking radical democracy, for example, reveals that Whitman has become more disenchanted with contemporary American society and less sure that the promise of American democracy will be fulfilled in the future. Whitman's rhetoric in *Democratic Vistas* borders on the apocalyptic in his warnings about the possibility that the American experiment will fail. Moreover, this essay includes Whitman's endorsement of American "business energy" (*Democratic Vistas* 487) and its essential contribution to the establishment of an ideal democracy.

Whitman's radicalism is not, however, simply a matter of politics. At least three other elements of Whitman's life and work must be examined in connection with the topic of radicalism: his literary style, sexuality, and humanitarianism. When *Leaves of Grass* is compared to the work of Whitman's poetic contemporaries—John Greenleaf Whittier, William Cullen Bryant, Ralph Waldo Emerson, James Russell Lowell, and Henry Wadsworth Longfellow—there is no underestimating the revolutionary nature of his literary achievement. While these poets composed verse on topics and in forms that owed at least as much to British tradition as to American experience, Whitman depicted everyday American life in language that was informal and rough, thereby staking out literary territory on the margins of the nineteenth-century literary establishment. Although Whit-

man's poetry was widely published and positively reviewed during his lifetime, his unquestioned inclusion into the pantheon of American poets would have to wait until the twentieth century.

Similarly, Whitman's frank poetic examination of his own sexuality, although containing elements (such as friendship among male comrades) that were familiar to readers of his time, marks a radically open stance to topics that continue to cause great controversy in American society. Whitman's determination to claim a homosexual identity in the "Calamus" poems (and elsewhere in *Leaves of Grass*) is more evidence of his courageous, radical spirit. Further evidence of the revolutionary nature of Whitman's asserted sexual identity in his poetry is provided by the generations of readers who have refused to read his work as proclaiming anything other than a platonic love for men.

Constant through all of Whitman's work is a humanitarianism that is radical in its unyielding commitment to the common man and woman. Whitman's belief in the ultimate triumph of American democracy is fundamentally a profound faith in the ability of the American people to construct institutions that will allow and encourage the formation of a moral and spiritual society. This radical humanitarian spirit even comes shining through the cynicism and doubts Whitman expresses in *Democratic Vistas*: in this extraordinary document Whitman calls for men and women to rise above tradition and convention to fulfill the promise of democracy.

A final measure of Whitman's radical spirit is provided by the overwhelmingly positive responses of later self-styled radical writers and thinkers. From Ezra Pound and D.H. Lawrence to Allen Ginsberg and June Jordan, Whitman's admirers have claimed and celebrated the most controversial aspects of his life and work. Perhaps Whitman's greatest impact and most profound legacy can be found in his appeal to those Americans who heed his "barbaric yawp" as a call to arms.

Jon Panish

Bibliography

Erkkila, Betsy. *Whitman the Political Poet.* New York: Oxford UP, 1989.

Kaplan, Justin. *Walt Whitman: A Life.* New York: Simon and Schuster, 1980.

Martin, Robert K. "Whitman and the Politics of Identity." *Walt Whitman: The Centennial Essays.* Ed. Ed Folsom. Iowa City: U of Iowa P, 1994. 172–181.

R

Reynolds, David S. *Walt Whitman's America: A Cultural Biography.* New York: Knopf, 1995.

Rubin, Joseph Jay. *The Historic Whitman.* University Park: Pennsylvania State UP, 1973.

Traubel, Horace. *With Walt Whitman in Camden.* 1905. Vol. 1. New York: Rowman and Littlefield, 1961.

Whitman, Walt. *Democratic Vistas. Leaves of Grass and Selected Prose.* Ed. Lawrence Buell. New York: Modern Library, 1981. 468–524.

———. *Leaves of Grass.* Ed. Sculley Bradley and Harold W. Blodgett. Norton Critical Edition. New York: Norton, 1973.

See also BARNBURNERS AND LOCOFOCOS; DEMOCRATIC VISTAS; FREE SOIL PARTY; LABOR AND LABORING CLASSES; POLITICAL VIEWS; RACIAL ATTITUDES; SEX AND SEXUALITY; SLAVERY AND ABOLITIONISM; STYLE AND TECHNIQUE(S); WILMOT PROVISO; WOMAN'S RIGHTS MOVEMENT AND WHITMAN, THE

Reading, Whitman's

"My reading," Whitman remarked to Horace Traubel in 1888, "is wholly without plan: the first thing at hand, that is the thing I take up" (*With Walt Whitman* 2:492). Such seems to have been the case throughout his life; and while Whitman always declined the role of man of letters, the fact is that from an early age he read widely in many areas: not only in English and American literature, but also in history, science, philosophy, biography (a particular favorite), and translations of various works in foreign languages. Ralph Waldo Emerson was quick to perceive the distance between image and reality when at one of his early meetings with Whitman he is said to have expressed his surprise at finding the poet "a copious book man" (*With Walt Whitman* 3:401–402).

Emerson's surprise is evidence of Whitman's success in concealing the breadth of his reading. The concealment was a deliberate strategy, as indicated by a notebook entry dating between 1847 and early 1855: "Make no quotations, and no reference to any other writers" (*Notebooks* 1:159). Whitman, wishing to appear as a new poet in a new land, a bard of nature, maintained this resolve with remarkable consistency throughout his life.

Few writers have been so free of literary debt. Whatever his response to individual authors, Whitman rejected foreign literatures, both past and present, as irrelevant, if not actually hostile, to American democracy. Still, he had his enthusiasms, and first among them was Sir Walter Scott, whom he discovered early in life, perhaps as early as 1829 or 1830 according to an entry in *Specimen Days,* and who remained with him right to the end, as may be seen in the volumes of Traubel's *With Walt Whitman in Camden.* In 1888 Whitman commented to Traubel that "If you could reduce the Leaves to their elements you would see Scott unmistakably active at the roots" (1:96), and in the following year he listed Scott among those select few authors constituting what he called his "daily food" (4:67).

Of other British writers, three were particularly important: William Shakespeare, Thomas Carlyle, and Alfred, Lord Tennyson. As a representative of the feudal past, Shakespeare was unsuitable for the American ideal; still, there was no denying the imaginative force of the poetry or the power of the drama, of which Whitman was a devotee, frequently attending performances on the New York stage.

Carlyle was valued as a writer who knew and recorded the violent complexities of his times with passion, energy, and moral commitment: a Hebrew prophet in nineteenth-century England. Still, Whitman notes in *Specimen Days,* while Carlyle was the most indignant protester against the growing evils and injustices of the age, he was also "a mark'd illustration" of the maladies he condemned (*Prose Works* 1:261); furthermore, Whitman objected to Carlyle's disdain for common people.

Tennyson, with whom Whitman conducted a sporadic and respectful correspondence for some twenty years, was admired for his artistry: "Tennyson is an artist even when he writes a letter," Whitman commented in 1888 (*With Walt Whitman* 1:36). The admiration, however, was always qualified by Tennyson's Old World sympathies—"the bard of ennui and of the aristocracy," Whitman called him in an 1855 essay ("An English and an American Poet" 39)—and by Whitman's awareness that Tennyson's poetry challenged his own in the most basic, apparently irreconcilable ways. Stylistically and thematically, the two poets would forever be opposed, yet Whitman could not deny Tennyson's mastery.

Among the Americans, Emerson is surely of the greatest significance, as Whitman's testimony, however qualified, makes clear, from the "dear Friend and Master" letter prefacing the 1856 *Leaves of Grass* to statements made near the end of his life. Whitman began reading Emerson in the 1840s, although he may not have felt the full power of Emerson's voice until he began to find his own in the early 1850s. The story of Whitman's relationship with Emerson is long and complex; but whatever may be said, Emerson's centrality remains, for it was Emerson, above all, who showed the way and, in his person as in his writings, did much to sustain Whitman throughout his long poetic career.

Other American writers for whom Whitman had high regard, despite his differences from them in style and substance, were William Cullen Bryant, John Greenleaf Whittier, and Henry Wadsworth Longfellow; these three, together with Emerson, were for Whitman the four best American poets. Whitman also had high praise for James Fenimore Cooper, whose novels he had read extensively and was rereading during the last years of his life.

Beyond literature in English, Whitman paid particular tribute to Epictetus, whom he claimed to have discovered at the age of sixteen, and to whom he was still expressing indebtedness more than half a century later. "He sets me free," Whitman proclaimed in 1888, "in a flood of light—of life, of vista" (*With Walt Whitman* 2:71). The following year Whitman included Epictetus among those writers whom he read repeatedly on a daily basis. Also on that list were Homer and Aeschylus, as well as the Bible. While Whitman complained in *Democratic Vistas* about the "shreds of Hebrews, Romans, Greeks" that dominated attention (*Prose Works* 2:411), he possessed at least a broad, general knowledge of classical and biblical literature. His familiarity with both Old and New Testaments is evident throughout his life.

Mention should be made of Frederic H. Hedge's anthology, *Prose Writers of Germany*, published in 1847, from which Whitman derived much of his knowledge of German literature. "I can hardly tell how many years," he commented in 1890; "it has been inspiration, aid, sunlight" (*With Walt Whitman* 7:111). Whitman also read variously in translations of French literature, including works by Voltaire and Rousseau; and from 1859, when he first read the *Inferno* (in the Carlyle translation), Whitman maintained an interest in Dante.

A rarity among major poets in not being a particularly avid reader of poetry, Whitman read indiscriminately in fiction; in *Specimen Days* he described himself as a "most omnivorous novel-reader" in his youth and afterwards (*Prose Works* 1:15). His most valued reading included Frances Wright's philosophical novel, *A Few Days in Athens*, which presented concepts, largely Epicurean, that were later to find their way into *Leaves of Grass*, and two novels by George Sand, *Consuelo* and *The Countess of Rudolstadt*, which Whitman admired for the truth and economy of their styles and representations. Charles Dickens was an early favorite, and Whitman read widely in the novels; his 1842 essay "Boz and Democracy" defended Dickens as "a democratic writer" in that his works promoted love of humanity despite the differences of social distinctions (*Uncollected* 1:69). Not least important, Whitman knew the popular fiction of his time; among his own contributions to the genre were his early short stories and his temperance novel, *Franklin Evans*.

A full account of Whitman's reading would have to include not only the reading he did in following his own interests, but also the many books he reviewed as a journalist. Despite his acquaintance with hundreds of writers, however, only a few came to be of enduring significance. Whitman remained to the end of his life stubbornly true to his own perceptions and resistant to literary influence.

R.W. French

Bibliography

Loving, Jerome. *Emerson, Whitman, and the American Muse*. Chapel Hill: U of North Carolina P, 1982.

Price, Kenneth M. *Whitman and Tradition: The Poet in His Century*. New Haven: Yale UP, 1990.

Reynolds, David S. *Beneath the American Renaissance: The Subversive Imagination in the Age of Emerson and Melville*. New York: Knopf, 1988.

Stovall, Floyd. *The Foreground of "Leaves of Grass."* Charlottesville: UP of Virginia, 1974.

———. "Notes on Whitman's Reading." *American Literature* 26 (1954): 337–362.

Traubel, Horace. *With Walt Whitman in Camden*. 9 vols. Vols. 1–3. 1906–1914. New York: Rowman and Littlefield, 1961; Vol. 4. Ed. Sculley Bradley.

R

Carbondale: Southern Illinois UP, 1959; Vol. 5. Ed. Gertrude Traubel. Carbondale: Southern Illinois UP, 1964; Vol. 6. Ed. Gertrude Traubel and William White. Carbondale: Southern Illinois UP, 1982; Vol. 7. Ed. Jeanne Chapman and Robert MacIsaac. Carbondale: Southern Illinois UP, 1992; Vols. 8–9. Ed. Jeanne Chapman and Robert MacIsaac. Oregon House, Calif.: W.L. Bentley, 1996.

Whitman, Walt. "An English and an American Poet." *Walt Whitman: A Critical Anthology.* Ed. Francis Murphy. Baltimore: Penguin, 1970. 37–42.

———. *Notebooks and Unpublished Prose Manuscripts.* Ed. Edward F. Grier. 6 vols. New York: New York UP, 1984.

———. *Prose Works 1892.* Ed. Floyd Stovall. 2 vols. New York: New York UP, 1963–1964.

———. *The Uncollected Poetry and Prose of Walt Whitman.* 1921. Ed. Emory Holloway. 2 vols. Gloucester, Mass.: Peter Smith, 1972.

See also BIBLE, THE; BRYANT, WILLIAM CULLEN; CARLYLE, THOMAS; COOPER, JAMES FENIMORE; DICKENS, CHARLES; EMERSON, RALPH WALDO; EPICTETUS; EPICURUS; HOMER; INFLUENCES ON WHITMAN, PRINCIPAL; LONGFELLOW, HENRY WADSWORTH; SAND, GEORGE; SCOTT, SIR WALTER; SHAKESPEARE, WILLIAM; TENNYSON, ALFRED, LORD; WHITTIER, JOHN GREENLEAF; WRIGHT, FRANCES (FANNY)

Realism

Although entrenched in the "American Renaissance," Whitman wrote through the period of American realism. Although his poetic project is squarely romantic, and although realism is associated more with fiction than poetry, facets of Whitman's artistic, social, and political philosophies bear striking affinities with realism. Warner Berthoff even suggests that Whitman inspired the realists' theories of realistic representation, their ideals of a democratic literature, and their enthusiasm for the language of the common person.

Whitman's technique of cataloguing particulars is similar to the realists' attempts to capture the empirical detail of "real" existence. Interest in dense surface detail is not surprising

in latter nineteenth-century America with the rise of technology, especially photography, which provided an unprecedented ability to reproduce the world with mechanical accuracy. Whitman was fascinated with photography, but both he and the realists were interested in subjective beauty and significance, not just linguistic photographs. Among the realists, Henry James's theory of organicism in *The Art of Fiction* (1888) best expresses the ways in which depths of truth emerge out of surface detail.

Creating democracy is arguably the core of both Whitman's and the realists' work and the end of their technique. As Paul Zweig notes, for both Whitman and later realists like Frank Norris and Theodore Dreiser (and William Dean Howells, too), the United States contained democratic possibilities unfilled. A decline in kindliness toward one's fellows led to moral failures of the likes of Howells's Silas Lapham; Whitman would call this necessary fellow-feeling "adhesiveness," especially in the "Calamus" poems (1860). As the century progressed, when beliefs in determinism grew, the realists and later the naturalists became more pessimistic about a benevolent America, yet all held to belief in a kind universe, as exemplified in the power of the wheat in Norris's *The Octopus* (1901).

Perhaps the most important literary technique contributing to an American democratic art is the common person's plain language. Whitman is well noted for celebrating the "divine average," even through later works like *Democratic Vistas* (1871), written at the height of realism. An American indigenous voice, originating in the speech of the democratic individual, devoid of excessive ornamentation and eschewing a romanticized past, assisted readers in confronting reality according to the likes of Whitman and the realists. This theory of the representation of the common person in literature, expressed in works like Howells's *Criticism and Fiction* (1891) and Hamlin Garland's *Crumbling Idols* (1894), was put into practice in the use of vernacular. Whitman and Twain especially share the immediacy of a first-person native voice, as well as the political point of view underlying the vernacular style advocating egalitarianism.

It is surprising, though, how little Whitman and the realists encountered and commented upon each other (with the exception of Garland). Howells encountered Whitman only three brief times, not even mentioning these meetings in writing until 1895 in an article on literary New

York, which mostly puzzled over the paradox of Whitman's gentle nature and his "uncouth" work. Henry James's review of *Drum-Taps* (1865) is notorious for its revulsion toward Whitman's poetry, dubbing it obvious, shallow, and self-aggrandizing. Yet in 1898, James finds Whitman's posthumously published letters to Peter Doyle in *Calamus* "positively delightful" (260). Most critics have puzzled over this conversion, but Eric Savoy has recently read it as a conflict between affiliation and detachment: James's flight from and self-affirmation of his own homosexuality, manifested in rejection of homosexual writers early in his career and acceptance at the turn of the century. Perhaps Whitman's most direct influence on a major writer of the realistic period is in issues of sexuality rather than literary technique or political philosophy.

Thomas K. Dean

Bibliography

Berthoff, Warner. *The Ferment of Realism: American Literature, 1884–1919.* New York: Free Press, 1965.

Folsom, Ed. *Walt Whitman's Native Representations.* Cambridge: Cambridge UP, 1994.

Hindus, Milton, ed. *Walt Whitman: The Critical Heritage.* London: Routledge and Kegan Paul, 1971.

Howells, William Dean. "First Impressions of Literary New York." *Walt Whitman: The Critical Heritage.* Ed. Milton Hindus. London: Routledge and Kegan Paul, 1971. 246–247.

James, Henry. "Henry James on Walt Whitman. 1865." *Walt Whitman: The Critical Heritage.* Ed. Milton Hindus. New York: Barnes and Noble, 1971. 110–114.

———. "Henry James on Walt Whitman. 1898." *Walt Whitman: The Critical Heritage.* Ed. Milton Hindus. New York: Barnes and Noble, 1971. 259–260.

Marx, Leo. *The Pilot and the Passenger.* New York: Oxford UP, 1988.

Savoy, Eric. "Reading Gay America: Walt Whitman, Henry James, and the Politics of Reception." *The Continuing Presence of Walt Whitman.* Ed. Robert K. Martin. Iowa City: U of Iowa P, 1992. 3–15.

Zweig, Paul. *Walt Whitman: The Making of the Poet.* New York: Basic Books, 1984.

See also CHOPIN, KATE; CLEMENS, SAMUEL LANGHORNE (MARK TWAIN); GARLAND, HAMLIN; HOWELLS, WILLIAM DEAN; JAMES, HENRY; LANGUAGE; ROMANTICISM; SEX AND SEXUALITY

"Reconciliation" (1865)

"Reconciliation" is one of Whitman's short lyrics about the Civil War. It first appeared in *Sequel to Drum-Taps* (1865–1866), but was later incorporated into *Leaves of Grass.* Whitman's first poems on the subject exhibited an attitude of factionalism and martial excitement, but this stance gave way to a more sober appreciation of what large-scale, fearsomely sanguinary battles such as Fredericksburg (1862) and Chancellorsville (1863) actually entailed. The muted and pensive realism of the work reflects this evolution of the poet's feelings, and it speaks to us in a way that most Victorian war poetry does not. "Reconciliation" deserves to be recognized as one of the first modern war poems.

The text evokes a small, wartime scene of the sort which Whitman, in his capacity as a nurse's aide, might well have observed. A Confederate soldier has died while in enemy hands. He is laid out in his coffin. Moved to pity, an onlooker bends down to kiss him. The moment, depicted with a few matter-of-fact strokes, is passionately felt, and its conciliatory spirit is like that of Abraham Lincoln's Second Inaugural (which Whitman heard). But the poet himself had comforted the Confederate sick and wounded in the hospitals where he worked. He expressed great fondness and respect for them in his journals. In the end, their humanity mattered more to him than their politics, and it was this scale of priorities which was installed in the poem.

Concise in the extreme, "Reconciliation" comprises, in its revised form, a single, elaborate sentence. The poem begins with a lovely rhetorical gesture which invokes the concept of reconciliation by comparing it to the sky. In a series of rapid and imperceptible shifts, the poem descends thereafter from a realm of abstraction to the particularities of death and the physical immediacy of a kiss.

N.J. Mason-Browne

Bibliography

Asselineau, Roger. *The Evolution of Walt Whitman: The Creation of a Book.* Trans. Roger Asselineau and Burton L. Cooper. Cambridge, Mass.: Harvard UP, 1962.

Hesford, Walter. "The Efficacy of the Word, the Futility of Words: Whitman's 'Reconciliation' and Melville's 'Magnanimity Baffled.'" *Walt Whitman Review* 27 (1981): 150–155.

R

Lowenfels, Walter, ed. *Walt Whitman's Civil War*. New York: Knopf, 1960.

Whitman, Walt. *Complete Poetry and Collected Prose*. Ed. Justin Kaplan. New York: Library of America, 1982.

See also CIVIL WAR, THE; "DRUM-TAPS"

Reconstruction

In many ways, the Reconstruction years (1865–1877) were a time of disruption for Walt Whitman. As the United States came apart in civil war, and then sought to recompose its Union ideology, so Whitman experienced the war and its aftermath with disquieting intensity. Reconstruction America became activated for Whitman in December 1862, when the poet journeyed to Fredericksburg, Virginia, in order to find his wounded brother, George, after notice that he had been injured in battle. Rather than return home to Brooklyn, Whitman relocated to the nation's hub, Washington, D.C., and thus inaugurated his first geographical displacement from New York, which would last until he suffered a debilitating stroke in January 1873. Whitman supported himself (and to some extent his mother) first as a part-time clerk in the Army Paymaster's Office (1863–1865), then as a clerk in the Department of the Interior (1865), and finally as a clerk in the Attorney General's Office (1865–1873). Aside from his desultory schedule as a government employee, Whitman's consuming passion remained his visits to Civil War hospitals, where he visited and consoled up to one hundred thousand veterans from all corners of the United States.

Whitman widened his circle of friends, meeting Peter Doyle, his closest personal friend who was a streetcar conductor and former Confederate soldier, as well as William Douglas O'Connor, his literary companion who published the first Whitman biography, *The Good Gray Poet* (1866). A year later, American naturalist John Burroughs published the second Whitman biography, *Notes on Walt Whitman as Poet and Person* (1867), and William Michael Rossetti attracted British readers to Whitman's work by a laudatory notice in July 1867 in the London *Chronicle*. When Rossetti published an expurgated English edition of Whitman in 1868, called simply *Poems,* Mrs. Anne Gilchrist fell in love with the poet, began a series of love letters in 1871, and actually moved to Philadelphia in 1876 in order to be near the poet. Whitman also encountered resistance to his poetic reputation, most notably in his firing from the Secretary of the Interior's Office by Senator James Harlan in 1865, on the grounds that he was the author of the notoriously frank *Leaves of Grass*. Shortly after Whitman's first major stroke in 1873, his mother passed away, and the poet was forced to leave Washington, D.C., for the confines of his brother George's home in Camden, New Jersey. Thus, after initiating Reconstruction in search of his brother George, Whitman ends the Reconstruction decade as a convalescent with his brother George.

Aside from geographical displacement, the Reconstruction years were constituted by a prolific outpouring of editorial and creative work. Critics have largely ignored this pivotal period in Whitman's long career, outside of biographical and bibliographical notices, but the direction of Whitman's work splinters across eight major publications: *Drum-Taps* (1865), *Sequel to Drum-Taps* (1865–1866), *Leaves of Grass* (1867 edition), *Democratic Vistas* (1871), *Leaves of Grass* (1871–1872 edition), *Memoranda During the War* (1875–1876), and the Centennial edition of *Leaves of Grass* and *Two Rivulets* (1876). There are two significant points about such a dispersion of his creative output. First, the previous organic unity of *Leaves* gives way to a fracturing of his major work into multiple annexes appended to *Leaves* along the way: *Drum-Taps, Sequel, Songs Before Parting* in 1867; *Passage to India* and *After All, Not to Create Only,* or later "Song of the Exposition," in 1871–1872; and the gathering of all his major Reconstruction statements into *Two Rivulets* in 1876. Second, Whitman makes a bid as a serious prose writer in such essays as *Democratic Vistas* and *Memoranda During the War,* in which the poet both looks forward to the evolution of American democracy and backward to the Civil War as the impetus for the growth of American promise. This intriguing middle period of Whitman's poetic career has been hastily passed over by critics, who have reinforced the notion that after the Civil War, Whitman's output indicates a period of decline following his spectacular debut as an antebellum genius. Whitman himself assisted such a dismissal, when he decreed that the final arrangement of *Leaves* (1881) should guide the readers of the future. Though recently critics have recovered the 1855 *Leaves,* the 1860 *Leaves, Drum-*

Taps, Democratic Vistas, and even *Memoranda During the War,* the gap has yet to be bridged across his other Reconstruction publications as artifacts worthy of attention in their own right.

The improvisational nature of many of these arrangements of texts can be analyzed across the discourses afloat in the Reconstruction years, as the Union sought to replace the secession years with the consolidation of national interests over against regional and sectional differences. Even in their physical manifestations, Whitman's editions were broken into "sectional" pieces, seeking coherence in their shuffling of older and newer compositions with each appearance. In the 1872 Preface to *As a Strong Bird on Pinions Free,* Whitman makes a proposal to accompany *Leaves,* which he called the book of the *"Democratic Individual,"* with a companion volume which would fulfill nationalist aspirations (the book of *"Democratic Nationality"*). While Whitman's assertion is hesitant, the poet persists in his prospectus for such a centralizing volume. In fact, Whitman delivered the volume *Two Rivulets* to accompany the 1876 *Leaves,* and the former comes closest to representing any book of "democratic nationality" as Whitman ever produced. In *Two Rivulets,* Whitman gathered together most of his major Reconstruction documents (including *Passage to India, Democratic Vistas,* and *Memoranda During the War*) in a strategy that can be read as either a haphazard or deliberate alignment of centralizing statements to be used for national purposes.

The disruption of America's governmental structure by the Civil War created a divide between the localized understandings of regional identity before the war and the hegemony of federal authority asserting a national identity after the war. The reconstructive energies of postwar culture lurched forward during the Reconstruction years, not least in the coercive domination of the Republican North over against the resistance of the unreconstructed South. In the legislative workshop of Washington, civil and political rights for ex-slaves were grudgingly affirmed from 1865 to 1870 through such landmark statutes as the Civil War amendments to the Constitution: the Thirteenth Amendment (1865), which abolished slavery; the Fourteenth Amendment (1868), which recognized African-American citizenship; and the Fifteenth Amendment (1870), which granted suffrage to African-American males. Such Constitutional reform provoked widespread resistance, and required federal surveillance of state jurisdictions on a scale that was not equaled until the 1950s and 1960s. Whitman's Reconstruction texts continually collapse federal-state frictions in favor of cooperative alliances between the two jurisdictional forums, but they also place a greater rhetorical weight on centralization through their deployment of nationalist images. As the representative poet, Whitman legislates unlimited promise for the national identity knitting together in the turbulent postwar years, while recognizing the continual dangers inherent in representative democracy. By 1876, just as Radical Reconstruction was breaking apart under the forces of racist violence and segregation, Whitman nonetheless issued *Two Rivulets* as a summa of his Reconstruction projects. This underrated volume is dominated by images of a radical democracy that seeks to dismantle discrimination in all its forms, through the implementation of a nationality that promotes localized social barriers giving way to the federated identity of cooperative citizens. The Reconstruction Whitman remains the Whitman who has yet to be fully scrutinized by Whitman scholars and readers alike.

Luke Mancuso

Bibliography

Allen, Gay Wilson. *The New Walt Whitman Handbook.* 1975. New York: New York UP, 1986.

———. *The Solitary Singer: A Critical Biography of Walt Whitman.* 1955. Rev. ed. 1967. Chicago: U of Chicago P, 1985.

Erkkila, Betsy. *Whitman the Political Poet.* New York: Oxford UP, 1989.

Mancuso, Luke. "'The Strange Sad War Revolving': Reconstituting Walt Whitman's Reconstruction Texts in the Legislative Workshop, 1865–1876." Diss. U of Iowa, 1994.

See also ATTORNEY GENERAL'S OFFICE, UNITED STATES; CIVIL WAR, THE; CIVIL WAR NURSING; *DEMOCRATIC VISTAS;* DOYLE, PETER; *DRUM-TAPS;* HARLAN, JAMES W.; HEALTH; *LEAVES OF GRASS,* 1867 EDITION; *LEAVES OF GRASS,* 1871–1872 EDITION; *LEAVES OF GRASS,* 1876, AUTHOR'S EDITION; *MEMORANDA DURING THE WAR;* O'CONNOR, WILLIAM DOUGLAS; PREFACE TO *AS A STRONG BIRD ON PINIONS FREE;* PREFACE TO *TWO RIVULETS; SEQUEL TO DRUM-TAPS; TWO RIVULETS;* WASHINGTON, D.C.; WHITMAN, GEORGE WASHINGTON

R

"Recorders Ages Hence" (1860)

"Recorders Ages Hence" was first published in the 1860 edition of *Leaves of Grass*. It was the tenth poem of forty-five in the "Calamus" section. In the late 1850s, Whitman began writing poems for this section, and grouped twelve poems under the heading "Live Oak with Moss." "Recorders" was the seventh poem in this original cluster. In 1867 the first two lines were dropped, and the poem remained unchanged in later editions.

In this poem, Whitman addresses his future audience, asking readers to remember him not as a poet, but as a loving and emotional person. He then tells them of his love for another man. The poet, however, could not use the language of his era to express this love because there were no positive terms for homosexual desire. Homosexuality in the nineteenth century was referred to as a sin or disease, if it was even mentioned at all.

Whitman labored to create positive terms for "the measureless ocean of love within him." He called himself "the tenderest lover" to counter the negative terms that a homophobic society would use to label him. In "Recorders," he writes of the sadness when he is separated from his lover, "the sick, sick dread" of unreturned love, and the joy of holding the hand of "his friend his lover." Such emotional expressions could be shared and understood by readers of any sexual orientation. In "Recorders," and in many other "Calamus" poems, Whitman uses sentimentality to cover his homosexuality.

Robert K. Martin notes that in this poem Whitman challenges the gender roles of his day by performing "feminine" activities; he loves tenderly, he waits for his lover's return, and he saunters with his lover.

In the last two lines of the poem we see the dual aspects of this love. Whitman is with his lover, but the two are alone, "apart from other men," in "fields, in woods, on hills." The natural environment reflects the naturalness of their desire. Their private display is soon public, as they "saunter'd the streets" with their arms around each other's shoulders.

Conrad M. Sienkiewicz

Bibliography

Cady, Joseph. "Not Happy in the Capitol: Homosexuality and the 'Calamus' Poems." *American Studies* 19.2 (1978): 5–22.

Killingsworth, M. Jimmie. "Sentimentality and Homosexuality in Whitman's 'Calamus.'" *ESQ* 29 (1983): 144–153.

Martin, Robert K. *The Homosexual Tradition in American Poetry.* Austin: U of Texas P, 1979.

Whitman, Walt. *Leaves of Grass: Comprehensive Reader's Edition.* Ed. Harold W. Blodgett and Sculley Bradley. New York: New York UP, 1965.

———. *Whitman's Manuscripts: "Leaves of Grass" (1860).* Ed. Fredson Bowers. Chicago: U of Chicago P, 1955.

See also "CALAMUS"; "LIVE OAK WITH MOSS"; LOVE; SEX AND SEXUALITY

Redpath, James (1833–1891)

In a time when lyceums were failing, James Redpath began the Boston Lyceum Bureau in 1869. In order to provide his audience variety he booked such speakers as Ralph Waldo Emerson and Mark Twain. Abolitionist author of *The Public Life of Captain John Brown* and editor of the *North American Review,* Redpath published some of Whitman's articles. Redpath was a writer for the firm of Thayer and Eldridge, who were closely identified with abolition. Although he remained a moderate, Whitman befriended such radical writers as Redpath and William Douglas O'Connor.

In a long letter written from Washington to Redpath dated 8 August 1863 Whitman asked for his friend's help in soliciting funds to carry on his work in the hospitals there. A short time later, 21 October 1863, Whitman wrote Redpath about publishing a book entitled *Memoranda of a Year,* but nothing came of it. It was published by the author in 1876 as *Memoranda During the War* and was included in *Two Rivulets* in the same year. For details see especially volumes 1, 2, and 4 of *The Correspondence,* edited by Edwin Haviland Miller, and volume 2 of Horace Traubel's *With Walt Whitman in Camden.*

J.R. LeMaster

Bibliography

Allen, Gay Wilson. *The Solitary Singer: A Critical Biography of Walt Whitman.* 1955. Rev. ed. 1967. Chicago: U of Chicago P, 1985.

Kaplan, Justin. *Walt Whitman: A Life.* New York: Simon and Schuster, 1980.

Myerson, Joel. *Walt Whitman: A Descriptive Bibliography.* Pittsburgh: U of Pittsburgh P, 1993.

Reynolds, David S. *Walt Whitman's America: A Cultural Biography.* New York: Knopf, 1995

Whitman, Walt. *Selected Letters of Walt Whitman.* Ed. Edwin Haviland Miller. Iowa City: U of Iowa P, 1990.

See also MEMORANDA DURING THE WAR; O'CONNOR, WILLIAM DOUGLAS; THAYER AND ELDRIDGE

Reincarnation

That Whitman believed in reincarnation or rebirth of the soul in some form may be gathered from his poems, especially "Song of Prudence," "To Think of Time," "Song of Myself" (sections 44 and 49), and "Unnamed Lands." This idea proceeds from his belief that the soul is deathless because it is distinct from the perishable body and that it has not only an endless existence but endless possibilities for enrichment. Whitman's triumphant optimism rests upon this faith, but it is also fused with the notion of evolutionary progress and meliorism. However, the idea of progressive improvement and a future perfection is inconsistent with his other statements affirming the fullness and felicity of the present moment—an inconsistency that needs to be explained.

The belief in reincarnation was shared by many primitive cultures, but it was in the Indian religious systems that it was formulated more elaborately and erected into a major theological doctrine. Briefly stated, this doctrine postulates a soul that does not perish with the material form with which it is invested, but passes through a cycle of births and rebirths until it realizes its true identity or it is finally reunited with the supreme being. Pain and imperfection, which are a necessary part of its incarnated state, appertain to its material nature and hence are illusory or impermanent.

Associated with the idea of reincarnation is the doctrine of karma (action), which states that the soul is driven by desire to engage in action as long as it is attached to its material body and that since every action, good or bad, must produce its consequences, man's happiness or sorrow is the result of the deeds willed by him over many lives. Karma, like Ralph Waldo Emerson's "compensation," is an inexorable law whose fruits must be enjoyed till all traces of it, even from previous lives, are completely extinguished and the soul is liberated. Karma and rebirth are not immutable, however: they may be obviated through the discriminative knowledge of the soul's true nature (in Vedanta and Samkhya) or through surrender to the will of God (in theistic Hinduism).

Whitman expresses similar ideas regarding soul, body, and existence beyond death. The interior soul or "real body," he says, is immaterial and transcends the senses and flesh, and it is impregnable to the laws of nature ("A Song of Joys"). "Prudence" or spiritual knowledge he defines (echoing Emerson in his essay of the same title and in "Compensation") as the understanding that whatever a man says, does, or thinks has consequences beyond death and affects his past, present, and future, and that no consummation exists that does not follow from long previous consummations. This leads him to the conviction that the entire cosmic process, the known life, is duly tending toward, and is a preparation for, the unknown, permanent life ("To Think of Time"). Life is a seamless continuity and should not be viewed partitively. In many places, he expresses the belief that there are many births (he does not, however, speak of transmigration of souls) and that life is the "leavings" of many previous deaths. He says that he himself has died many times before ("Song of Myself," section 49). But, like Emerson again, he asserts that while all else is caught up in the law of action and consequence, the soul is "of itself" ("Song of Prudence")—that is, autonomous and untouched by the law of karma, as the Hindu would say. Also suggested is the idea that the spirit's attachment to its material form is not an ineluctable modality, but is simply what is contributed by the soul itself—an idea presupposed in the Hindu conception of karma and one that ensures the possibility of the soul's eventual liberation (although the implication of Whitman's statement bearing on this point that "The spirit receives from the body just as much as it gives to the body" ["Song of Prudence"] is not exactly clear).

In the Hindu systems, including Buddhism, the doctrine of reincarnation, and its corollary, the doctrine of karma, are resorted to as a solution to the problem of evil, sin, and suffering. The Hindu conception, however, is more austere and regards the chain of births and deaths as the outcome of man's false attachment to his material nature and hence as a bondage, liberation from which is the highest goal of life; Whitman, on the other hand, sees rebirths and continued existence as a guarantee of the soul's immortality and as an opportunity for the soul's endless self-enrichment. He is alive to the presence of evil, disease, and death, but minimizes them as being inessential. He views them as parts of an harmonious becoming and hence as being in their rightful place. And this belief is the source of his euphoria, his "unrestricted faith" ("Starting from Paumanok," section 7). (In his later period he came to believe, under the influence of Hegel, that evil is dialectically necessary for the progressive unfoldment of universal good; see "Song of the Universal.") Yet, almost in the same breath, he declares that he is beyond good and evil, that there is in fact no evil. There was never any more perfection than there is now, he declares ("Song of Myself," section 3); he has "the best of time and space" (section 46). Thus Whitman's faith in progressive evolution and meliorism, on the one hand, and in eternal perfection—the mystic's eternal now—on the other, continue side by side.

One way of explaining this discrepancy may be to view the two statements as referring to two different planes of existence—one representing his own enlightened state, in which he feels that he is at the acme of the evolutionary ladder, and the other representing the state of being of other people, of unrealized potentialities, in whose development Whitman had a passionate concern. To such people, other births can bring opportunities to evolve spiritually. But with reference to his own accomplished self, which he celebrates, more births can only bring more richness and variety ("Song of Myself," section 44), so as to satisfy the "glut" of his soul ("Song of Prudence").

In the final analysis, it appears that Whitman seizes upon the idea of reincarnation, not as a serious religious belief with its implication of sin and personal salvation, but rather as an additional support to his own intuited faith in the goodness of the universal order, or alternatively as a dynamic symbol, the amplitude of time—the extensive future and the extensive past—providing an infinite scope for the spirit's self-expansion. In his last writings, however, he does not think of rebirth, but more and more of union with God and of death as deliverance.

V.K. Chari

Bibliography

Asselineau, Roger. *The Evolution of Walt Whitman: The Creation of a Book.* Trans. Roger Asselineau and Burton L. Cooper. Cambridge, Mass.: Harvard UP, 1962.

Chari, V.K. *Whitman in the Light of Vedantic Mysticism.* Lincoln: U of Nebraska P, 1964.

Mercer, Dorothy F. "Walt Whitman on Reincarnation." *Vedanta and the West* 9 (1946): 180–185.

Sharma, Om Prakash. "Walt Whitman and the Doctrine of Karma." *Philosophy East and West* 20 (1970): 169–174.

See also DEATH; HINDU LITERATURE; IMMORTALITY; MYSTICISM; RELIGION; "SONG OF MYSELF"; "SONG OF PRUDENCE"; "TO THINK OF TIME"

Religion

Whitman once complained to Horace Traubel, companion and note-taker of his final years, that people "speak of the *Leaves* as wanting in religion." But this was not, Whitman emphasized, his "view of the book—and I ought to know." *Leaves of Grass* was "the most religious book among books: crammed full of faith" (Traubel 372). This retrospective assessment was not a whimsical recollection, for Whitman made such assertions throughout his career. Some early readers and critics were in ardent agreement, considering Whitman the prophet of a new religion that would inform the future culture of the United States and eventually the world. Subsequent academic criticism, while rightfully freeing itself from such intemperate claims, has, nevertheless, frequently lost sight of the prophetic and mystical dimensions of Whitman's intention and achievement. This essay will indicate important religious influences that fed into Whitman's conception of his poetic project, outline the structure and principal beliefs of his world view, and suggest some guidelines for interpreting *Leaves* as a religious text.

A version of evangelical Protestantism permeated the social life and intellectual discourse of the culture in which Whitman matured. In contrast to Catholicism, or even Episcopal and Lutheran forms of Protestantism, which emphasize ritual and the authority of the church hierarchy, the dominant Christian culture of this period was Bible-centered. Sermons and religious tracts, while less influential than in the colonial period, were still important forms of popular literature; and school books, imaginative writings, political orations, and journalism routinely espoused Christian beliefs and values. Not surprisingly, such a culture nurtured writers who instinctively resorted to the use of biblical materials. Even though Whitman wanted to use his poetry to lay the foundation for a post-Christian cultural order, he nevertheless sometimes found it useful to draw upon biblical symbols, and as Gay Wilson Allen has demonstrated, Whitman's style was greatly influenced by the syntactic forms and sonorous rhythms of the King James Bible. More important, from his understanding of the Bible's central role in Christian culture, Whitman aspired to formulate a new order of poetry that would serve the same functions the Bible had in an earlier age.

Antebellum American society was also notable in that it had no state-sponsored church and was officially committed to religious freedom, thus providing fertile ground for a large number of denominations and sects. This lack of governmental support and competitive context, in combination with a rapidly increasing and westward-migrating population constantly in need of new churches, meant that the various religious bodies were not only dependent upon their own resources but also had a clear need for a committed and active laity. At the same time, Christianity in the United States had theological resources that could be drawn upon to meet these needs. For example, many of the nation's religious groups, including the large Congregational and Presbyterian denominations, held to a Reformed theology that called for spiritually active Christians who would make a personal commitment to Christ. These same denominations had also cultivated a tradition of viewing the United States as a new Israel with the special mission of creating a truly Christian society. This confluence of the institutional needs, opportunities, and theological traditions of the churches led to the formation of a dynamic Christianity which sought to develop organizations and practices (for example, Bible and tract societies, revivals, and temperance and abolitionist movements) for disseminating the biblical message, recruiting new members, and creating a Christian nation. It was, in short, a Christianity that attempted to inculcate its members with a high degree of moral earnestness and social engagement. This cultural milieu helped to nurture a literature, ranging from the prophetic writings of Emerson and Whitman to the domestic fiction of Harriet Beecher Stowe, that sought to effect the spiritual renovation of both individual readers and the larger society.

The material and religious context of the times also nurtured several distinctive forms of religious enthusiasm. One of these was a combination of progressive millennialism and religious nationalism which defined the United States as the primary agent for effecting God's will in history. Endowed with a unique combination of blessings—Protestant Christianity, political democracy, vast geographical expanse, burgeoning population, and material abundance—God's new Israel was ordained to advance toward a millennial state in which the spirit of Christ would rule the hearts of the people and govern their social institutions. A second type of enthusiasm, known as "perfectionism," maintained that individual Christians could attain to a state of complete sanctification, and radical perfectionists even asserted themselves to be free from Christian precepts and civil law. A third, "illuminism," held that it was possible to attain to more profound understandings of previous revelation or to arrive at fresh revelation. Given the existence of these theological emphases, it is appropriate to view Whitman's call for a future religious democracy, a citizenry of spiritual athletes who would "think lightly of the laws" ("Song of the Broad-Axe," section 5), and a new order of religious poetry as post-Christian versions of themes that pervaded the prevailing Protestantism.

In addition to a general exposure to the surrounding Christian culture, Whitman also had direct contact with the churches of his day. The Whitman family were not church members, but Whitman went to Sunday school for periods of his childhood, and he also attended and reported on the services of various churches while working as a newspaperman in the 1840s. Yet Whitman never joined a church, and there is no evidence that he ever subscribed to a Christian world view. This indifference can be attributed to other influences upon Whitman's religious development, for in his youth and early adulthood he was also exposed to various marginal religious discourses which were critical of Christianity and exalted the religious imagination as the source of fresh revelation.

From his father Whitman inherited an interest in the deism of Count Volney, Thomas Paine, and Frances Wright, and throughout his adulthood his writings consistently give expression to several deistic themes: a denial of Christ's divinity, a distrust of clergy and organized religion, a concern to reconcile science and faith, and an openness to non-Christian religions. The deistic concern to extract a common-denominator faith from the various religions of the world also encouraged some nineteenth-century United States religious figures (chiefly first- and second-generation transcendentalists such as Ralph Waldo Emerson, Theodore Parker, James Freeman Clarke, and Samuel Johnson) to entertain the possibility that the comparative study of religion might contribute to the creation of a new syncretic or universal religion. This approach to world religions is evident in Whitman's notes on religion, which frequently present earlier and existing religions as rudimentary expressions of a more perfect future faith. It is also clearly reflected in passages in the *Leaves,* such as sections 41 and 43 of "Song of Myself," in which he speaks of drawing upon the "rough deific sketches" of previous religions and asserts that his vision encloses "worship ancient and modern and all between ancient and modern."

Whitman's childhood also furnished him with an understanding of the human soul as a faculty of religious prophecy. Whitman's paternal grandfather and his parents were admirers of the Long Island Quaker prophet, Elias Hicks, who in 1829 became the leader of a faction of dissenting ("Hicksite") Quakers. Hicks extended the Quaker doctrine of the soul's inner light beyond the bounds of Christian orthodoxy by proclaiming, much as Emerson would in "The Divinity School Address," that the religious imagination of the individual believer was the source of religious revelation and thus of higher authority than the Bible. Hicks's abiding significance for Whitman is indicated by the fact that in his old age Whitman composed a brief biographical sketch that praises him for pointing to "the fountain of all naked theology, all religion, all worship . . . namely in *yourself*" (*Prose Works* 2:627).

However, in the years prior to the 1855 edition of the *Leaves,* when Whitman was conceiving of his epic project, it was the image of the poet as prophet projected by the writings of Thomas Carlyle and Emerson that gave crucial shape to his poetic identity. Whitman was familiar with Carlyle's impassioned call for an inspired poet-prophet, and he read various of Emerson's essays such as "Nature," "The Divinity School Address," and "The Poet," which

Americanized Carlyle, transforming the nation's post-revolutionary demand for a national literature into a call for fresh revelation and defining the poet as a religious prophet. As Whitman aspired to forge a new myth for the modern world, Emerson's poetics provided him with helpful guidance and, more important, needed psychological support for his ambitious sense of vocation.

Taken out of its historical setting, Whitman's effort to found a new religion can easily seem naive if not pathological, and criticism has often found it convenient to ignore the poetry's prophetic claims. However, properly situated within the theological traditions, intense enthusiasm, and critical ferment of antebellum religious culture, Whitman's grand aspirations appear to be an astonishing but nevertheless understandable response to the intellectual and spiritual imperatives of his age. Whitman strove to muster the requisite intellectual integrity and imaginative power to forge a new religious vision, and his poetry is best understood as an attempt to outline the beginnings of a post-Christian myth that would give religious depth and ideological coherence to the democratic and scientific culture developing in the United States.

Although Whitman himself never achieved a fully elaborated religious vision (nor perhaps ever thought of this as a possible or desirable objective) or a completely realized formal design for his ever growing book of poems, yet prior to 1855 he did formulate a basic world view, sufficiently general to accommodate new historical events (for example, the Civil War) and additional themes and changes in emphasis, which provided a coherent intellectual structure for the first and all subsequent editions of his poetry. *Leaves* is informed by a theistic cosmology that is, in gross outline, a fusion of transcendentalism, mid-nineteenth-century evolutionary science and the millennial religious nationalism of the period. Like the transcendentalists, Whitman believed that the external world was immanent with spirit and that this immanent spirituality provided the basis for a system of correspondences between natural and historical facts and the human soul. In addition, drawing upon contemporary ideas of progress and the emerging evolutionary sciences, he imagined the evolution of nature and the course of history to be the manifestation of divine immanence ascending toward reunion with its transcendent source.

Consistent with his process theism, Whitman conceived of history as the human race's ongoing struggle for freedom and development (for example, see "To Thee Old Cause" and "To a Certain Cantatrice"), and he envisioned the United States as playing the lead role in the climactic scene of this long historical drama. Whitman felt that America's political institutions and general prosperity had created a situation in which, for the first time in history, the masses were freed from political and material oppression. Now what was needed was a new order of poetry which would deliver them from all forms of psychological repression. If this were achieved, the U.S. citizenry would become fully developed women and men living in what Whitman termed a "religious democracy." Then the United States would have realized its divinely ordained mission and history would have attained to its grand culmination.

Accordingly, many of the most important themes in *Leaves* are designed to emancipate the human subject and promote his or her development. After announcing himself as a saving prophet in "Song of Myself," Whitman immediately leads the reader through two sequences: "Children of Adam," designed to sanctify the body and liberate heterosexual passion; and "Calamus," designed to liberate men from emotional repression, call forth new levels of male intimacy, and unite the soul with God. In addition, to free the working class masses from a sense of shame and social inferiority, Whitman stresses the absolute value of the human soul as the basis for affirming a democratic equality and the inherent dignity and unlimited potential of all human beings. Most important of all, to deliver his readers from the fear that life has no ultimate meaning, he presents a vision of a loving God who not only provides for evolutionary and historical progress but also personal immortality and the soul's ongoing development in the afterlife.

To understand Whitman's religious vision, it is necessary to keep certain interpretive norms in mind. One is that *Leaves* should be read, as Whitman always insisted, not as an anthology of individual poems but as a unity. To do so reveals not only a coherent world view but also a special religious vocabulary. In articulating his post-Christian vision, Whitman uses some traditionally religious (but not specifically Christian) terms such as "God" or "soul." But in addition he develops his own religious lexicon by subtly investing many terms, for example,

"real," "secret," "love," "aroma," "pride," "pine," "electric," and "want," with a level of religious meaning. Whitman also consistently exploits the symbolic potential of certain natural facts that have been privileged in numerous religious systems, such as the stars, the waters, and the earth; and he creates some new religious symbols, for instance, the grass, the calamus plant, and the lilacs. In reading *Leaves,* it is crucial to grasp the religious significance of these terms and symbols, and this requires attending to their recurring usage throughout the entire text.

The reader must also properly conceptualize the religious dimension of Whitman's poetry. Religion is not one theme in *Leaves* to be considered alongside others such as democracy, sexuality, or nature, but rather the matrix and marrow of other aspects of Whitman's thought. The central and inclusive role of religion is clearly indicated in the long prefatory poem, "Starting from Paumanok" (1860): "For you [the reader] to share with me two greatnesses, and a third one rising inclusive and more resplendent, / The greatness of Love and Democracy, and the greatness of Religion" (section 10). For Whitman, love, democracy, and other important themes such as sexuality, nature, science, etc.—all are infused with religious meaning.

Whitman's readers must also exercise a certain sympathy for religious language and experience. Whitman asks a great deal of his readers not only because his mystical meanings are ultimately ineffable but also because he intentionally uses a suggestive method which leaves much unsaid. Whitman called for athletic readers, that is, spiritual athletes, who would subordinate worldly concerns to spiritual development and read *Leaves* as a spiritual guide, preferably alone in the midst of nature. Such readers will, Whitman suggests, arrive at an existential realization of the spiritual secrets of his poetry.

Academic scholarship has largely overlooked the unity of Whitman's world view and text. When it does consider Whitman's spirituality, it usually betrays a misconception of religion as a theme that can be detached from the larger vision; and sometimes, especially in recent decades, dismisses the religion of *Leaves* as an addendum "inflicted" (to quote one critic) upon the later editions by a chastened older poet wishing to dilute the radical sexuality of the earlier poetry. Although the explication of hidden ideology is a hallmark of current literary studies, Whitman criticism is not without its unexamined secular assumptions. Accordingly, it sometimes shows little interest in attending to the spiritual meanings of this "most religious book among books" (Traubel 372).

David Kuebrich

Bibliography

Ahlstrom, Sydney. *A Religious History of the American People*. New Haven: Yale UP, 1972.

Allen, Gay Wilson. *The New Walt Whitman Handbook*. 1975. New York: New York UP, 1986.

———. *The Solitary Singer: A Critical Biography of Walt Whitman*. 1955. Rev. ed. 1967. Chicago: U of Chicago P, 1985.

Finke, Roger, and Rodney Stark. *The Churching of America, 1776–1790*. New Brunswick, N.J.: Rutgers UP, 1992.

Handy, Robert T. *A Christian America: Protestant Hopes and Historical Realities*. Rev. ed. New York: Oxford UP, 1984.

Hutchinson, George B. *The Ecstatic Whitman: Literary Shamanism & the Crisis of the Union*. Columbus: Ohio State UP, 1986.

Jackson, Carl T. *The Oriental Religions and American Thought: Nineteenth-Century Explorations*. Westport, Conn.: Greenwood, 1981.

Kuebrich, David. *Minor Prophecy: Walt Whitman's New American Religion*. Bloomington: Indiana UP, 1989.

Rubin, Joseph Jay. *The Historic Whitman*. University Park: Pennsylvania State UP, 1973.

Traubel, Horace. *With Walt Whitman in Camden*. Vol. 1. Boston: Small, Maynard, 1906.

Whitman, Walt. *Notebooks and Unpublished Prose Manuscripts*. Ed. Edward F. Grier. Vol. 6. New York: New York UP, 1984.

———. *Prose Works 1892*. Ed. Floyd Stovall. 2 vols. New York: New York UP, 1963–1964.

See also BIBLE, THE; CARLYLE, THOMAS; COMRADESHIP; DEATH; EMERSON, RALPH WALDO; HICKS, ELIAS; IMMORTALITY; MYSTICISM; PAINE, THOMAS; QUAKERS AND QUAKERISM; SCHOLARSHIP, TRENDS IN WHITMAN; "SONG OF MYSELF"; SOUL, THE; TRANSCENDENTALISM; VOLNEY, CONSTANTIN; WRIGHT, FRANCES (FANNY)

Republican Party

The Republican party originally drew its support from free laborers, farmers, and working people in general, the same sort of people whom Whitman had celebrated in his writings. The modern Republican party was formed through a coalition of interests, foremost among them being opposition to slavery. Even those who were willing to tolerate slavery's existence often opposed its spread into new territories. Whitman, the former Democrat, shared this point of view with Abraham Lincoln, the former Whig. When the Kansas-Nebraska Act (1854) allowed the spread of slavery into new territories, opponents of the administration joined forces with abolitionists and other interests in protest meetings. Out of these meetings was born the new party.

The success of the Republican party was surprising. By 1860 the Republicans had majorities in both houses of Congress and had elected a president. The Republicans won six successive presidential elections (1860–1880), the longest unbroken winning streak in the history of American presidential elections. The Civil War had a lot to do with the Republican success at the polls. Republican strategy was to link their opponents with the Southern cause, accusing them of disloyalty. Even though none of the Democrats nominated for president after 1860 was a Southerner until well into the twentieth century, the Republicans used the issue of "waving the bloody shirt" to remind voters of which party was associated with secession. Rebellion was not the only issue, however. From the beginning, Republicans championed ideas associated with America's growing industrialization and expansion, promoting the building of roads, railroads, and canal and river navigation, and encouraging westward settlement. Republican strength in the western states, which persists down to the present, is partly due to the popularity of these expansionist ideas. Likewise, Republican anti-Southern strategy prevented the Republicans from building any major strength in the South until recently. Republican support of sound money and business expansion would eventually carry the party away from its origins as a defender of the workingman, but that tendency was much less obvious during Whitman's lifetime.

Disagreements over the slavery issue and over how to go about reconstruction of the defeated South brought about the rise of the Radical Republicans. This faction sought to make a harsh peace, with the South occupied and deprived of statehood. The Radicals considered President Andrew Johnson a traitor and eventually sought his removal from office through impeachment. Whitman did not favor the Radicals' ideas and generally supported President Johnson, though by this time (1868) he was employed in the Attorney General's Office and feared changes at the top, which might well have cost him his livelihood.

Whitman's interest in national affairs lasted throughout his life, but in later years he was content to be a spectator. By 1888 he wrote of "our election trial" (*Correspondence* 4:221) and admitted he felt no great enthusiasm for the election. By the term of President Benjamin Harrison (1889–1893) he was clearly disappointed with the direction the leadership of the Republican party had taken. In a letter to Dr. Richard Maurice Bucke (1890) he wrote of Harrison's "damnable diseased" trade policies and cried out for "the once glorious live Lincoln party" (*Correspondence* 5:84).

Frederick Hatch

Bibliography

Greene, Jack P., ed. *Encyclopedia of American Political History.* New York: Scribner's, 1984.

Holt, Michael F. *Political Parties and American Political Development from the Age of Jackson to the Age of Lincoln.* Baton Rouge: Louisiana State UP, 1992.

Mayer, George H. *The Republican Party 1854–1966.* New York: Oxford UP, 1967.

Reynolds, David S. *Walt Whitman's America: A Cultural Biography.* New York: Knopf, 1995.

Smith, Page. *The Nation Comes of Age.* New York: Penguin, 1990.

Whitman, Walt. *The Correspondence.* Ed. Edwin Haviland Miller. 6 vols. New York: New York UP, 1961–1977.

See also DEMOCRATIC PARTY; LINCOLN, ABRAHAM; POLITICAL VIEWS; PRESIDENTS, UNITED STATES

"Respondez!" (1856)

This poem was first published in the 1856 edition of *Leaves of Grass* under the title "Poem of the Propositions of Nakedness," the word "nakedness" used as a figure for stripping or unmasking corruptions, pretensions, delusions, and hidden motives such as greed or arrogance. The title "Respondez!" suggests a more heated, personal attitude. Whitman excluded the poem from *Leaves of Grass* after 1876, probably because its negative tone was too insistent for the general thrust of the work.

The poem consists of sixty-eight lines, only eight of which do not begin with "Let," as in "Let murderers, bigots, fools, unclean persons, offer new propositions," a typical rhetorical line recommending the opposite of what he actually wants. Angry as he is, Whitman is not asking for a revolution of roles or a turning over of the status quo. Rather, his irony is used to affirm the true, natural order of the world and to warn against the chaos that would result from disrupting this order: "Let the worst men beget children out of the worst women!" and "Let marriage slip down among fools, and be for none but fools!"

The effect of the anaphoric and ironic rhetorical mode is powerful. Rarely in *Leaves of Grass* is Whitman so relentlessly worked up over such a long list of evils or potential evils. It is not possible to locate the particular stimulus for his outburst, if there was one. But there is a thematic pattern through the poem: that firsthand reality is preferable to second ("O seeming! seeming! seeming!"); that competence and order are to be preferred over their opposites; that faith in the scheme of things and in God is absolutely vital; and that happiness is to be found within oneself.

Occasionally he mars the rhetorical consistency, as if amused by his own angry stance. Near the beginning he announces, "Let me bring this to a close," and later he mocks, "Let him who is without my poems be assassinated!"

The final lines, addressing the reader directly, widen out to embrace the issue of how anyone should approach life, and reinforce the implication all through that Whitman is not attacking the political or cultural condition of America but is simply shaking up unexamined assumptions of any reader: "(What real happiness have you had one single hour through your whole life?) / Let the limited years of life do nothing for the limitless years of death! (What do you suppose death will do, then?)."

Other poems in a similar tone of sustained anger or dismay, though entirely different in treatment, are "I Sit and Look Out" and "Are You the New Person Drawn toward Me?"

David B. Baldwin

R

Bibliography

Berger, James A. "Whitman's Rejection of 'Respondez!'" *Essays in Literature* 19 (1992): 221–230.

Golden, Arthur. "Whitman's 'Respondez!,' 'A Rounded Catalogue Divine Complete,' and Emerson." *Études Anglaises* 48 (1995): 319–327.

Whitman, Walt. *Leaves of Grass: Comprehensive Reader's Edition.* Ed. Harold W. Blodgett and Sculley Bradley. New York: New York UP, 1965.

See also LEAVES OF GRASS, 1856 EDITION

"Return of the Heroes, The" (1867)

As part of the cluster entitled "Autumn Rivulets," this poem celebrates an important theme in Whitman's post–Civil War works, that of venerating the soldiers who gave their lives in that conflict.

These soldiers are seen as the one essential ingredient in America's defining moment. A terrible sacrifice has been offered. Now America must affirm this supreme sacrifice if these deaths are to have meaning. Viewing the nation with newly focused eyes, Whitman discovers a way to give eternal meaning to that slaughter of young men, many of whom he had nursed in their final hours. He provides perpetual significance as he suggests that the return of these "heroes" can be realized in a "fecund," or newly productive, America that will thrive and flourish as never before in the great democratic experiment (section 3).

Echoing the cyclical nature of the "parturient" earth that he had earlier described in his 1856 poem "This Compost," Whitman pays tribute to the miracle of nature found in God's "calm annual drama" as life eternally springs from death (section 2). He refers to America as a miracle and calls it the "envy of the globe" (section 3) as he carries this nostalgic reminiscence forward with a consideration of how he can discover a meaning in these "sad, unnatural shows of war" (section 4). He must find a means of synthesizing these memories of dead heroes with the awareness that America has survived and will now flourish in "these days of brightness" (section 5).

Whitman places the war heroes on a precarious pedestal. Only a prosperous and flourishing nation will provide affirmation of these heroic deaths that Whitman has insistently eulogized in countless poems and prose passages since the end of the war. Their triumphant return will be realized by a nation that will be able to rejoice in a larger victory—the saving of a prosperous and democratic Union. That victory will now culminate in a series of "saner," "sweet," and "life-giving" wars (section 6) when soldiers trade in their guns for their tools and work the fields of one nation with "boundless fertility" (section 7) that will become the envy of the world.

Whitman sees these productive fields as "the true arenas of my race" where heroes wield "better weapons" both North and South to harvest the products of a great nation (section 7). No longer will his cameradoes wield weapons of destruction. Now they will wield the "human-divine inventions" (section 8), powerful machines imbued with life-giving qualities that will dominate the earth under the eyes of an ever-observant world.

In states all over the nation, both North and South, farmers will harvest those crops unique to each state. This harvest will be a tribute and a vindication of the bloody sacrifice made by former soldiers to preserve the nation. The crops will grow and ripen "under the beaming sun and under thee" (section 8), Whitman concludes. The heroes have returned.

Julian B. Freund

Bibliography

Bowers, Fredson. "The Manuscript of Walt Whitman's 'A Carol of Harvest, for 1867.'" *Modern Philology* 52 (1954): 29–51.

Whitman, Walt. *Complete Poetry and Collected Prose.* Ed. Justin Kaplan. New York: Library of America, 1982.

See also "AUTUMN RIVULETS"; CIVIL WAR, THE; DRUM-TAPS; SPECIMEN DAYS

"Reuben's Last Wish" (1841)

This short story was published on 21 May 1842, in the *Washingtonian.* For publication information, see Brasher's edition of *The Early Poems and the Fiction.*

This temperance story is openly didactic. Whitman announces in the first paragraph that the story "may haply teach a moral and plant a seed of wholesome instruction" (110). The story is told by a narrator who heard it directly from Frank Slade at a temperance meeting. This narrative ploy is a compromise between Whitman's usual omniscience and the technique used in "Bervance: or, Father and Son" (1841).

Frank Slade is a good man, but he drinks too much, and his drinking has caused some economic hardship and humiliation for him and his family. Slade's sickly son, Reuben, arranges for his mother to embroider a blue border around an unsigned temperance pledge. As death approaches the boy, he holds out to his father the unsigned pledge and dies pointing to the line his father should sign.

Though the story is sentimental, Whitman's prose has a carefulness perhaps unparalleled in all his fiction. A rhythmic string in one paragraph, for example, may echo a rhythmic string in other paragraphs. In line with the sentimentality, the effect of the prose is almost precious at times.

While not as cruel as the many unhappy fathers in Whitman's stories—"Bervance," for example—Frank Slade regains happiness. Also, this tale is thematically related to "The Child's Champion" (1841) in that a man's love for a boy leads to the man's reformation.

Reynolds reads "Reuben" as a typical example of the sensationalism of temperance writings of the time. Kaplan asserts that Whitman borrowed the child's name from "Roger Malvin's Burial" (1832), by Nathaniel Hawthorne.

Patrick McGuire

Bibliography

Kaplan, Justin. *Walt Whitman: A Life.* New York: Simon and Schuster, 1980.

Reynolds, David S. *Walt Whitman's America: A Cultural Biography.* New York: Knopf, 1995.

Whitman, Walt. *The Early Poems and the Fiction.* Ed. Thomas L. Brasher. New York: New York UP, 1963.

See also "BERVANCE: OR, FATHER AND SON"; "CHILD AND THE PROFLIGATE, THE"; SHORT FICTION, WHITMAN'S

Revolutions of 1848

Walt Whitman's tendency for liberal political thought was fostered at an early age by his father's interest in radical thinkers such as Frances Wright and Thomas Paine. Nevertheless, years would pass before Whitman became profoundly liberal in his views and truly committed to man's struggle for freedom. Decisive in the development of his politics was the outbreak of the European revolutions of 1848.

In 1846 and 1847, Whitman edited the Brooklyn *Daily Eagle.* This position intensified his interest in the politics of the underclass as it challenged authority, and he watched the European situations, predicting uprisings. In 1848, Whitman accepted a position at the New Orleans *Crescent,* moving to the city at a time of intense interest in Europe. There, working as an editor, he read articles from newspapers abroad and added his comments to "create" foreign news. He was caught up in New Orleans's interest in French politics, and he eagerly followed the imminent French revolt led by poet-statesman Alphonse de Lamartine. On 22–24 February 1848 King Louis Philippe was overthrown, and Lamartine quickly organized a provisional government. News of the French revolt consumed New Orleans, and Lamartine became Whitman's hero, about whom he wrote several articles that spring. Meanwhile, the revolution in France had sparked a succession of uprisings throughout Europe. The general goal of the conflicts was the overthrow of despotic leadership. Austria, Italy, Prussia, and smaller German states overthrew their leaders, and over fifty smaller revolutions broke out.

Although the revolutions were fairly quickly squelched, Whitman had gained a taste of the revolutionary spirit. His development from newspaper journalist to democracy-proclaiming poet occurred most dramatically in the years between the mid-1840s and mid-1850s, and although some point to Whitman's work against slavery as his motivation for becoming freedom's poetic leader, others point to the revolutions of Europe as his inspiration.

In direct response to the revolutions, Whitman wrote "Resurgemus," a poem printed in the New York *Daily Tribune* on 21 June 1850. Intended to encourage, support, and glorify the revolutionaries, "Resurgemus" reflected Whitman's optimistic idea that the uprisings, which by 1850 had already failed, would someday regain their strength and be successful. He even included biblical allusions in "Resurgemus" to highlight his belief that the revolutions were a holy event. The nature imagery used throughout "Resurgemus" is an important artistic step for Whitman, since he clearly uses it to link the replenishing power of nature to the rejuvenation of revolution and liberation. This poem was among those chosen for inclusion in the first (1855) *Leaves of Grass,* and it continued

R

to resurface in various forms throughout his later editions. Although printed without a title in the 1855 *Leaves,* it was renamed "Poem of The Dead Young Men of Europe, The 72d and 73d Years of These States" in 1856, and in 1860, it was shortened to "Europe, The 72d and 73d Years of These States." With this title, Whitman strengthened a correlation between Europe's freedom and that of the United States, illustrating his belief that the European liberation was an echo of American freedom.

Jennifer J. Stein

Bibliography

Allen, Gay Wilson. *The Solitary Singer: A Critical Biography of Walt Whitman.* 1955. Rev. ed. 1967. Chicago: U of Chicago P, 1985.

Erkkila, Betsy. *Whitman the Political Poet.* New York: Oxford UP, 1989.

Reynolds, David S. *Walt Whitman's America: A Cultural Biography.* New York: Knopf, 1995.

Reynolds, Larry J. *European Revolutions and the American Literary Renaissance.* New Haven: Yale UP, 1988.

Whitman, Walt. *Leaves of Grass: Comprehensive Reader's Edition.* Ed. Harold W. Blodgett and Sculley Bradley. New York: New York UP, 1965.

See also DEMOCRACY; "EUROPE, THE 72D AND 73D YEARS OF THESE STATES"; FREEDOM

Rhetorical Theory and Practice

Rhetoric, according to Aristotle, is "the faculty of observing in any given case the available means of persuasion" (24). As such, rhetoric's goals are practical. It is not concerned with uncovering absolute, permanent truths, but rather with the ways in which people arrive at practical truths, such as for whom to vote or which school to attend.

Classical rhetoricians, such as Plato, Aristotle, and Cicero, were concerned with articulating systems and defining the different modes of persuasion. Aristotle divides rhetoric into three main areas: *forensic* rhetoric, which is concerned with establishing the justice of a particular event or course of action; *epideictic* rhetoric, which is concerned with establishing the honor of a person; and *deliberative* rhetoric, which is concerned with determining the expedience of a course of action. Cicero divides

rhetoric into five areas: invention, arrangement, style, memory, and delivery.

For centuries rhetoric was considered the queen of knowledge. But during the Renaissance people began to turn away from rhetoric, with its emphasis on contingent truths, in favor of science and logic, with their claims on absolute truth. Rhetoric became more and more circumscribed until it came to mean only style. This is the origin of the popular idea of rhetoric as a pejorative term, as in "that's just rhetoric."

However, in the last half of the twentieth century, with the postmodern emphasis on the multiple nature of truth, rhetoric has undergone a resurgence. Unlike classical rhetoric, with its emphasis on creating systems, contemporary rhetoric is concerned with describing the ways in which persuasion and argumentation create knowledge. Rhetoricians such as Kenneth Burke, Chaim Perelman and Lucie Olbrechts-Tyteca, and Michel Foucault have looked at how different political, social, and ideological assumptions underlie supposedly objective areas of discourse, including the natural sciences.

One of the key terms of contemporary rhetorical theory is "identification." This term, developed by Kenneth Burke in his book *A Rhetoric of Motives,* stems from the idea that in order for a group of people to act toward the same goal, they must first have a common sense of identity. Identity is not a monolithic concept; in fact, individuals have many intertwined identities. So a person may simultaneously identify herself as an American, a rugby player, an economist, a woman, and a pickup truck owner. The rhetorician is interested in the ways that writers play on these different identities, highlighting some and discounting others in an attempt to move the reader to identify with the writer or a particular group based on certain shared identities.

As an approach to literature, rhetoric differs from other forms of criticism in that it treats language as an act rather than an artifact. Because of its concern with action, rhetoric asks certain questions about the dynamic qualities of the text: Who did it? What scene or context was it done in? Why was it done? What, exactly, is it that was done? And how was it done? These five questions reflect the five terms of Kenneth Burke's pentad: act, scene, agent, agency, and purpose. The pentad provides the critic with a systematic means for examining all the various aspects and contexts of an act. This approach helps the rhetorician to come to terms with the flexible nature of meaning and to avoid what I.A. Richards calls the "proper meaning superstition," the belief that a word or text has a single, static meaning. Instead, rhetorical criticism locates meaning in negotiations between author, text, and reader. Most contemporary rhetoricians see these negotiations as occurring in group contexts. Thus different discourse communities, groups which share certain assumptions, may derive different meanings from a single text.

There are many rich areas of inquiry for the rhetorical critic who is interested in Whitman. To date, most rhetorical studies of Whitman, such as that of C. Carroll Hollis, have been concerned with style, how the arrangement of the words on the page works to create literary and rhetorical effects. But other important areas of rhetorical analysis are beginning to be explored, including questions of audience, invention, and epistemology.

Foremost in recent rhetorical studies of Whitman is a concern with the poet's relationship to his audience. Unlike poststructuralist criticism, which views Whitman's addresses to his audience as ultimately a futile attempt to bridge the physical gap between himself and his audience, rhetorical criticism stresses the way these addresses work to create a bond of identification between the reader and the poet. This identification is not illusory, but very real because it can lead to a change in the reader's actions or attitudes. Unlike historicist approaches, which are primarily concerned with readers who were contemporaries with Whitman, the rhetorical critic is interested in the different audiences that have read Whitman since 1855, especially present-day readers, and how the different expectations and reading conventions those audiences bring to the text affect the meaning produced.

Other areas of interest to the rhetorical critic include Whitman's concept of what language does and how it functions; the epistemologies of *Leaves of Grass,* how Whitman creates knowledge in the poetry; and the stylistic strategies Whitman employs to make his arguments in the poems.

Andrew C. Higgins

Bibliography

Aristotle. *The Rhetoric and the Poetics of Aristotle.* Trans. W. Rhys Roberts. New York: Modern Library, 1984.

Booth, Wayne. *The Rhetoric of Fiction.* 2nd ed. Chicago: U of Chicago P, 1983.
Burke, Kenneth. *A Rhetoric of Motives.* 2nd ed. Berkeley: U of California P, 1969.
Foucault, Michel. *The Archaeology of Knowledge and the Discourse on Language.* Trans. A.M. Sheridan Smith. New York: Pantheon, 1972.
Hollis, C. Carroll. *Language and Style in "Leaves of Grass."* Baton Rouge: Louisiana State UP, 1983.
LeFevre, Karen Burke. *Invention as a Social Act.* Carbondale: Southern Illinois UP, 1987.
Richards, I.A. *The Philosophy of Rhetoric.* 1936. New York: Oxford UP, 1965.

See also ORATORY; POETIC THEORY

Rhys, Ernest Percival (1859–1946)

Ernest Percival Rhys, an author and editor, is best known for beginning the Everyman's Library series of inexpensive reprintings of popular works, 983 volumes of which appeared between 1906 and Rhys's death. He went to a private school in Newcastle and later became a mining engineer. In 1886 he moved to London to be a writer. Rhys was a member of the Rhymers' Club, which included Arthur Symons and William Butler Yeats among its members, and contributed poetry and reviews to the magazines. He married in 1891 and had three children.

Rhys was instrumental in securing from Whitman his permission and assistance in publishing three of his volumes in Britain by the firm of Walter Scott. He wrote Whitman in 1885 about a one-shilling edition of *Leaves of Grass* in Scott's Canterbury Poets series, and when it appeared the following year, it sold eight thousand copies within two months. This edition of *Leaves* presented many of the poems from the 1881 edition—although about one hundred were omitted—in approximately the same order. Whitman received ten guineas for the book, whose sale was restricted to England. *Leaves of Grass* remained in print from Scott through at least 1911. In 1886, at Whitman's suggestion, Rhys helped publish *Specimen Days in America* in Scott's Camelot Series; the following year, he helped with *Democratic Vistas* in the same series. This was a clever way for Whitman to make two books out of *Specimen Days & Collect.* Whitman received another ten guineas for each book, and they were both in print through at least 1902. In 1887 Rhys met Whitman during a trip to America, and the two got along famously.

Joel Myerson

Bibliography

Rhys, Ernest. *Everyman Remembers*. New York: Cosmopolitan Book Corporation, 1931.

Thomas, M. Wynn. "Walt Whitman's Welsh Connection: Ernest Rhys." *Anglo-Welsh Review* 82 (1986): 77–85.

See also BRITISH ISLES, WHITMAN IN THE

"Richard Parker's Widow" (1845)

This short story first appeared in *The Aristidean* in April 1845. For publication details, see Brasher's edition of *The Early Poems and the Fiction*.

The story begins with the narrator and his friend on a tour of a London police station. There they see a pitiable woman. The friend supplies the narrator with details of her misfortune. Richard Parker was executed for mutiny. The woman is his widow, and she had tried desperately to get a stay of execution. When that failed, she tried in vain to see her husband before he died. In his last words, he denied his guilt, but accepted his death sentence so that order might be restored among British seamen. After the wife was then denied his remains, she climbed the wall of the cemetery and disinterred her husband's corpse. She kissed and embraced it in her grief; she intended to remove it from London. But the lord mayor learned of her plight and arranged a safe burial in Whitechapel churchyard. Later, she was duped out of a small fortune. Forty years later, when the narrator and his friend see her, she is in the habit of seeking charity.

Critics have noted that Whitman borrowed heavily for this story from the same source regarding the 1797 Nore mutiny that Herman Melville used for *Billy Budd, Sailor* (1924): Camden Pelham's *Chronicles of Crime; or, The New Newgate Calendar* (1841). David Reynolds sees the widow's kisses as sensationalism bordering on necrophilia. Justin Kaplan notes that the mutiny, with Parker as leader, parallels Whitman's theme of son versus father: the hangman's noose here paralleling the rope around the rebellious son's wrist in "Wild Frank's Return" (1841). Gay Wilson Allen, however, sees in the story Whitman's ability to share the emotions of women.

Patrick McGuire

Bibliography

Allen, Gay Wilson. *The Solitary Singer: A Critical Biography of Walt Whitman*. 1955. Rev. ed. 1967. Chicago: U of Chicago P, 1985.

Kaplan, Justin. *Walt Whitman: A Life*. New York: Simon and Schuster, 1980.

Reynolds, David S. *Walt Whitman's America: A Cultural Biography*. New York: Knopf, 1995.

Whitman, Walt. *The Early Poems and the Fiction*. Ed. Thomas L. Brasher. New York: New York UP, 1963.

See also SHORT FICTION, WHITMAN'S; "WILD FRANK'S RETURN"

Riverby

John Burroughs (1837–1921), the well-known naturalist, writer, and friend of Walt Whitman, built a house with a spectacular view of the Hudson River on nine acres in the Catskill Mountains, about a hundred miles north of Manhattan. He purchased the land in September 1873 and called the home "Riverby" (meaning "by the river" and pronounced "river bee"). Walt Whitman made three trips to Riverby, the last of which, in 1879, he recounted in *Specimen Days*.

Riverby turned out to be something of a disappointment for Burroughs. He ignored all advice on the house, even disregarding Whitman's recommendation of a carpenter. Burroughs himself was the architect of the stone house, built according to aesthetic principles of environmental harmony.

The house was entirely impractical. Built into a hillside and partly underground, the lower floors remained perpetually dark and damp, and bone-numbingly cold in winter. The absence of water pumps required Burroughs's wife, Ursula, to climb narrow stairways carrying heavy buckets of water for bathing and for house cleaning.

Whitman first visited Riverby for a week in June 1878 to see Burroughs's two-month-old son, Julian, who was the offspring of a liaison with an Irish maid employed by a nearby household, although the fact was a closely guarded secret even after John Burroughs's death. Almost two miles from Riverby was a particularly beautiful spot so loved by Whitman that Burroughs referred to it as "The Whitman Land." Burroughs began *Whitman: A Study* with a reference to a "primitive and secluded" (2) spot which is itself like Whitman in that the poet does not suggest the wild and unkempt as he seems to do to many mistaken readers, but, rightly perceived, Whitman suggests the "cosmic and the elemental" (2). In *Specimen Days* Whitman described the same spot in an entry entitled "An Ulster County Waterfall," which contains the combination of precise detail along with aesthetic appreciation that characterizes the nature writing of John Burroughs himself.

Indeed, Burroughs and Riverby influenced Whitman in a number of ways. In general, Burroughs heightened Whitman's appreciation for paying close attention to the natural world, for observing and recording exact detail. Specifically, Burroughs's description of the midair mating of eagles, which Burroughs observed while hiking near Riverby and recorded in a journal which Whitman read, inspired Whitman to watch the eagles when he was at Riverby, and culminated in Whitman's "The Dalliance of the Eagles" (1880). Also, even before building Riverby, Burroughs compellingly described the hermit thrush to Whitman, providing Whitman with just the unifying image he needed while writing his long elegy, in 1865, on the death of Abraham Lincoln, "When Lilacs Last in the Dooryard Bloom'd."

Burroughs's dissatisfaction with Riverby and his love of "The Whitman Land" led to his building a cabin called "Slabsides" on the spot in 1895. The first chapter of *Whitman: A Study* and the final revision of the work were completed at Slabsides in 1895–1896.

Carmine Sarracino

Bibliography

Barrus, Clara. *Whitman and Burroughs, Comrades.* New York: Houghton Mifflin, 1931.
Burroughs, John. *Riverby.* New York: Houghton Mifflin, 1894.
———. *Whitman: A Study.* New York: Houghton Mifflin, 1896.
Renehan, Edward J., Jr. *John Burroughs, An American Naturalist.* Post Mills, Vt.: Chelsea Green, 1992.
Whitman, Walt. *Specimen Days.* Vol. 1 of *Prose Works 1892.* Ed. Floyd Stovall. New York: New York UP, 1963.

See also BURROUGHS, JOHN AND URSULA; "DALLIANCE OF THE EAGLES, THE"; HUDSON RIVER; *SPECIMEN DAYS;* "WHEN LILACS LAST IN THE DOORYARD BLOOM'D"

Rocky Mountains

The Rocky Mountains, also known as the Rockies, are a range of mountains spanning thirty-two hundred miles from present-day Alaska to New Mexico. First brought to the attention of Europe by the sixteenth-century conquistador Coronado, these mountains became part of the American imagination through the tales of early nineteenth-century explorers. Several mountain peaks in the Rockies are over fourteen thousand feet high, and the entire region is noted for its varied and majestic landscapes.

Trappers and fur traders produced the first nonindigenous settlements in the Rockies during the first half of the nineteenth century, but the discovery of gold in Pike's Peak prompted a dramatic increase in the population. Once the gold deposits neared depletion, miners discovered silver. This discovery inaugurated a second, larger wave of population growth in the Rockies. Drawn by the stories of instant wealth to be found in the mountains, tourists traveled by the thousands to see the Rockies. Walt Whitman joined the ranks of these tourists when he, along with J.M.W. Geist, E.K. Martin, and William W. Reitzel, traveled to the Colorado Rockies in September of 1879. Despite his later claim that he had visited Leadville, a booming mining town, Whitman's visit to the Rockies was limited to the sights accessible by railroad; in 1879 the Denver, South Park, and Pacific Railroad ended at Guiraud—thirty-five miles short of Leadville. Whitman's visit to the Rocky Mountains came after he had written most of his poetry, but Whitman was impressed by both the beautiful terrain and the hardy population, and he saw in this region the "great naturalness and rugged power" he ascribed to his poems (qtd. in Eitner 83).

Timothy Stifel

Bibliography

Eitner, Walter H. *Walt Whitman's Western Jaunt.* Lawrence: Regents Press of Kansas, 1981.
Ubbelohde, Carl, Maxine Benson, and Duane A. Smith. *A Colorado History.* 3rd ed. Boulder: Pruett, 1972.

See also DENVER, COLORADO; "SPIRIT THAT FORM'D THIS SCENE"; TRAVELS, WHITMAN'S; WEST, THE AMERICAN

Roe, Charles A. (b. 1829)

Born during February of 1829 in Little Bay Side, in the town of Flushing, Long Island, Charles A. Roe attended the classes taught by Walt Whitman in the Little Bay Side School during the late 1830s. Horace Traubel interviewed Roe in 1894, and the information from this interview provides a unique view of Whitman as teacher.

Roe describes Whitman as a man who "strangely attracted our respect and affection" (qtd. in Traubel 116). Whitman conducted class orally, rather than from books, and his lessons in reading, writing, arithmetic, and grammar were punctuated with stories. Although Roe characterizes his former teacher as "a boy among boys, always free, always easy, never stiff" (qtd. in Traubel 110), he also mentions that Whitman kept his classroom well disciplined—he never used corporal punishment, but he occasionally used the dunce cap. Roe also offers details of Whitman's life outside the classroom. Whitman boarded with a widow who was concerned with what she considered his atheism, but Whitman was liked and respected by the parents of his students. Roe remembers him as a healthy young man who always ate heartily, never drank alcohol, and apparently shunned the company of women. Whitman taught in the school at Little Bay Side only one year, so the precise memories Roe recalled over fifty years later attest to Whitman's effectiveness in the classroom.

Timothy Stifel

Bibliography

Allen, Gay Wilson. *The Solitary Singer: A Critical Biography of Walt Whitman*. 1955. Rev. ed. 1967. Chicago: U of Chicago P, 1985.

Traubel, Horace L. "Walt Whitman, Schoolmaster: Notes of a Conversation with Charles A. Roe, 1894." *Whitman in His Own Time*. Ed. Joel Myerson. Detroit: Omnigraphics, 1991. 109–116.

See also EDUCATION, VIEWS ON; PRE-*LEAVES* POEMS; TRAUBEL, HORACE L.

Rolleston, Thomas William Hazen (1857–1920)

Thomas William Hazen Rolleston's interest in a German translation of Whitman can be attributed to his interest in German literature (which he studied in Germany from 1879–1883) and his Irish nationalism. Educated at Dublin's Trinity College, he came from an intellectual environment which fostered (under the leadership of Edward Dowden) an enthusiasm for Whitman. Germany, as an economic competitor and potential military adversary of England, was considered a natural ally for Irish nationalists and, therefore, what strengthened Germany seemed good for Ireland. German passiveness and dry positivism could be overcome by a hefty dosage of Whitman's poetry.

Together with Karl Knortz, Rolleston was the coauthor of the first book-length translation of Whitman's poetry. He contributed the major portion of the translated poetry, attempting to make the German translation as shocking to German readers as the original had been to Americans. In a letter to Richard Maurice Bucke, he wrote: "A German translation of W. which should never startle the 'ordinary reader' or seem ridiculous or coarse to him, would not be Whitman at all" (qtd. in Grünzweig 27). Whereas Knortz provided an interpretation of Whitman as a political poet, Rolleston stressed Whitman's aesthetic revolution. Both conceptions were important for Whitman's German success in the twentieth century.

Rolleston's close affiliation with Whitman is documented in an extensive correspondence relating to Germany, the Irish question, and Whitman's reception in Europe.

Walter Grünzweig

Bibliography

Cotterill, H.B., and T.W. Rolleston. *Ueber Wordsworth und Walt Whitman: Zwei Vorträge gehalten vor dem Literarischen Verein zu Dresden*. Dresden: C. Tittmann, 1883.

Frenz, Horst, ed. *Whitman and Rolleston: A Correspondence*. Bloomington: Indiana UP, 1951.

Grünzweig, Walter. *Constructing the German Walt Whitman*. Iowa City: U of Iowa P, 1995.

Rolleston, Charles Henry. *Portrait of an Irishman: A Biographical Sketch of T.W. Rolleston*. London: Methuen, 1939.

Whitman, Walt. *Grashalme: Gedichte*. Trans. Karl Knortz and T.W. Rolleston. Zurich: Schabelitz, 1889.

See also BRITISH ISLES, WHITMAN IN THE; GERMAN-SPEAKING COUNTRIES, WHITMAN IN THE; KNORTZ, KARL

Romanticism

When Walt Whitman boasted in 1884 that he was "the greatest *poetical* representative of German philosophy" (*Workshop* 236, n138), he explicitly situated his "language experiment" within the phase of Western culture known as romanticism. A reaction to Enlightenment rationalism and classicism, romanticism was an egalitarian and utopian movement in philosophy, literature, politics, and the arts which valued subjective expression, formal experimentation, and unmediated connection with nature and the divine. While European romanticism extended from the French revolutionary period in the 1780s to the beginning of the British Victorian period in the 1840s, American romanticism began in the 1820s and ended with the Civil War in 1865. At the height of the American romantic period, during a phase of literary emergence known as the American Renaissance, Whitman published the first edition of *Leaves of Grass* (1855), twelve poems whose "barbaric yawp" revitalized and revolutionized romanticism.

The principal catalysts for European romanticism were the rise of the middle class and capitalism, the democratic and revolutionary movements, and the Protestant Reformation. Romanticism was also profoundly influenced by two Enlightenment figures: Jean Jacques Rousseau, who championed the innate goodness of human nature before its corruption by civilization, and Immanuel Kant, who held that objective reality may be known only as it is mediated by the structures of human consciousness. Kant's transcendental idealism inspired the German idealists Johann Fichte, Friedrich Schelling, and Georg Wilhelm Friedrich Hegel, who conceived the objective world as a phenomenal expression of absolute spirit. Writers such as Johann Wolfgang von Goethe and Friedrich Schlegel in Germany, and Victor Hugo and George Sand in France, worked out the literary implications of romantic philosophy. In Britain, Thomas Carlyle and Samuel Taylor Coleridge were the chief analysts of the creative imagination, while Coleridge, William Blake, William Wordsworth, Lord Byron, Percy Bysshe Shelley, and John Keats were its poetic exemplars.

In the United States, romanticism developed somewhat later in response to this larger European movement, particularly British romanticism. After the American Revolution, romantic tendencies were nurtured by a realized political democracy, Protestant culture, frontier expansion and agrarian life, individualism and optimism as dominant values, and the unavoidable fact of the North American wilderness. Early romantic literature included the gothic romances of Charles Brockden Brown, the frontier romances of James Fenimore Cooper, and the elegiac nature poetry of William Cullen Bryant. Edgar Allan Poe would later fully realize the gothic strain of romanticism, while Nathaniel Hawthorne would perfect the American romance.

The chief architects of romantic ideology in the United States, however, were the transcendentalists. Beginning as a reform movement within the Unitarian Church, American transcendentalism expressed itself primarily through the literary writings of such authors as Ralph Waldo Emerson, Margaret Fuller, Amos Bronson Alcott, and Henry David Thoreau. Emerson's "Divinity School Address" (1838) repudiates his church's emphasis on religious forms in favor of direct inspiration in and contact with God. In this respect, transcendentalism epitomizes the religious expression of romanticism. Emerson's *Nature* (1836), a manifesto of American romanticism, conceives nature as the embodiment and "symbol" of spirit.

Of all the influences on the early editions of Whitman's *Leaves of Grass*, Emerson's was undoubtedly the most important. As editor (1846–1848) at the Brooklyn *Daily Eagle*, Whitman attended Emerson's lectures in New York and reviewed other key romantics, such as Carlyle, another major influence, Coleridge, Goethe, Fuller, Herman Melville, Schlegel, and Sand. In his editorial columns, Whitman quoted from European and American romantics alike, including Bryant, Byron, Hawthorne, Hugo, and Poe. After the first two editions of *Leaves*, Whitman began exploring the German metaphysicians, especially Gottfried Leibniz, Kant, Fichte, Schelling, and Hegel. Whitman was also influenced by organic language theory, particularly as developed by Wilhelm von Humboldt. Whitman's synthesis of the historical and spiritual theories of language prevalent in the nineteenth century is evident in *An American Primer* (1904), "America's Mightiest Inheritance" (1856), "Slang in America" (1885), and his ghostwriting for William Swinton's *Rambles Among Words* (1859).

With the publication of F.O. Matthiessen's landmark study *American Renaissance: Art and Expression in the Age of Emerson and Whitman* (1941), critics began to identify Whitman as a central figure in the mid-nineteenth-century

R

efflorescence of literature which Matthiessen described as the "American Renaissance." For Matthiessen, the defining "classics" that emerged during this time constituted the core of a new national literature devoted to the "possibilities of democracy" (ix): Emerson's *Representative Men* (1850), Hawthorne's *The Scarlet Letter* (1850), Melville's *Moby-Dick* (1851), Thoreau's *Walden* (1854), and *Leaves of Grass* (1855). In *The Romantic Foundations of the American Renaissance* (1987), however, Leon Chai argues that the period represents instead the final, decadent phase of European romanticism. Chai omits Whitman, asserting that he was influenced by romanticism only indirectly through Emerson. Yet the poet who proclaimed "I am the poet of the body, / And I am the poet of the soul" ("Song of Myself," section 21, 1855 *Leaves*) undermines Chai's argument that the shift from European to American romanticism involved increasing subjectivization and deepening opposition between materialism and spiritualism. Jerome Loving argues that Whitman advanced transcendentalism by contradicting the assumption that the body and senses were merely emblems of the soul. Unlike other nineteenth-century poets, Whitman insisted on the equality of body and spirit.

Whitman's *Leaves of Grass* was a revolutionary departure in American as well as European romanticism. Like Emerson's "The American Scholar" (1847), Whitman's Preface to the 1855 edition was a declaration of America's literary independence from Europe, yet it may also be read in the tradition of Wordsworth's Preface to the *Lyrical Ballads* (1800). Whitman wanted to become the national poet for a new country, a romantic commonplace. He astonished his contemporaries with his equations of democracy and divinity, sexuality and spirituality, but these were also versions of the romantic desire to fuse opposites. Nevertheless, Whitman revised his romantic inheritance. He synthesized romantic universalism and nationalism when he declared in the 1855 Preface, "America is the race of races" (*Complete* 6–7). His poet was a seer, prophet, and priestly giver of imperatives, yet assumed a democratic equality with the reader: "every man shall be his own priest" (25). And Whitman ardently articulated the union of subject and object in calling his poet the "lover" of the universe—"burning" for "contact and amorous joy" (12).

In "Song of Myself," the central poem of *Leaves of Grass,* Whitman's poetic innovations range from the variable length and rhythms of his lines, to his reconstruction of the romantic lyric "I" and his explosion of the meditative lyric. As Paul Zweig suggests, Whitman's poems dissolved the conventional narrative form of the romantic poem and ventured into pure feeling and sensation. Whitman's poetry was autobiographical, but it also unlocked the lyric of self-reflection and welcomed the multiple selves of American democracy: "Through me many long dumb voices" (section 24). In his catalogues Whitman creates a formal equivalent for the democratic ideals of romanticism. He revolutionizes the union of subject and object by reconstructing the relationship between poet and reader: "what I assume you shall assume" (section 1). To accomplish this transformation, Whitman radically alters the romantic "I." Donald Pease argues that Whitman's "I" is intimately bound up with his "you," a poetic "intersubject" reducible to neither self nor other (158). But Whitman also dramatizes the epiphanic union of self and soul, most memorably as two lovers in the grass.

Although Whitman's poems were motivated by the desire to regenerate the people with democratic ideals, in the 1860s he became more doubtful about America's future and his desired role as its bard. The Civil War brought more realism to Whitman's poetry, yet his tragic treatment of a new nation at war with itself falls within the ethos of romanticism. Although his earlier poetry is characterized by celebration, his later poems are no less romantic for being elegiac. *Drum-Taps* (1865) may lack the innovative risk of Whitman's earlier work, but it stands among celebrated literary responses to the Civil War, and "When Lilacs Last in the Dooryard Bloom'd" (1865), Whitman's last great poem, may be read in the company of the eminent romantic elegies.

Whitman was steeped in the romanticism of his age, both European and American, but his poetry does not represent a mannered response to romantic aesthetics and philosophy. Rather, Whitman reinvented the romantic quest for selfhood by embracing collective as well as personal consciousness; he freed the creative imagination to voice experiences untouched by previous poets; he opened poetic form to the rhythms of the mundane and the sublime; he rewrote the romantic lyric with the urgent vernacular of America's working class; and he recovered prelapsarian innocence in the flux of modern life. In *Leaves of Grass,* Whitman revolutionized and thus revitalized the essential modes of romanticism.

Harbour Fraser Hodder

Bibliography

Abrams, M.H. *Natural Supernaturalism: Tradition and Revolution in Romantic Literature.* New York: Norton, 1971.

Allen, Gay Wilson. *The New Walt Whitman Handbook.* 1975. New York: New York UP, 1986.

Chai, Leon. *The Romantic Foundations of the American Renaissance.* Ithaca, N.Y.: Cornell UP, 1987.

Loving, Jerome. "Walt Whitman." *Columbia Literary History of the United States.* Ed. Emory Elliott et al. New York: Columbia UP, 1988. 448–462.

Matthiessen, F.O. *American Renaissance.* London: Oxford UP, 1941.

Pease, Donald. "Walt Whitman's Revisionary Democracy." *The Columbia History of American Poetry.* Ed. Jay Parini and Brett C. Millier. New York: Columbia UP, 1993. 148–171.

Warren, James Perrin. "Organic Language Theory in the American Renaissance." *Papers in the History of Linguistics, Princeton, August 1984.* Ed. Hans Aarsleff, Louis Kelly, and Hans Niedereche. Amsterdam Studies in the Theory and History of Linguistic Science. Vol. 38. Amsterdam: Benjamins, 1987. 531–522.

Whitman, Walt. "America's Mightiest Inheritance." *Life Illustrated* (1856). Rpt. *New York Dissected.* Ed. Emory Holloway and Ralph Adimari. New York: Rufus Rockwell Wilson, 1936. 55–65.

———. *Complete Poetry and Collected Prose.* Ed. Justin Kaplan. New York: Library of America, 1982.

———. *Notebooks and Unpublished Prose Manuscripts.* Ed. Edward Grier. 6 vols. New York: New York UP, 1984.

———. *The Uncollected Poetry and Prose of Walt Whitman.* 1921. Ed. Emory Holloway. 2 vols. Gloucester, Mass.: Peter Smith, 1972.

———. *Walt Whitman's Workshop: A Collection of Unpublished Manuscripts.* Ed. Clifton J. Furness. Cambridge, Mass.: Harvard UP, 1928.

Zweig, Paul. *Walt Whitman: The Making of the Poet.* New York: Basic Books, 1984.

See also BRITISH ROMANTIC POETS; CARLYLE, THOMAS; EMERSON, RALPH WALDO; GERMAN-SPEAKING COUNTRIES, WHITMAN IN THE; GOETHE, JOHANN WOLFGANG VON; HEGEL, GEORG WILHEM FRIEDRICH; HUGO, VICTOR; MATTHIESSEN, F.O.; ORGANICISM; POETIC THEORY; PREFACE TO *LEAVES OF GRASS,* 1855 EDITION; READING, WHITMAN'S; REALISM; SAND, GEORGE; TRANSCENDENTALISM

R

Rome Brothers, The

Because he was a printer and editor, Walt Whitman placed high demands on those who worked in publishing, and the production of the 1855 edition of *Leaves of Grass* was no exception. Just three years before, Whitman had competed for business with various printers in Brooklyn and had assessed their competence. For his prized manuscript, Whitman selected the Rome brothers. Immigrants from Scotland, brothers Andrew, James, and Thomas Rome ran a print shop known primarily for its legal publications. Andrew Rome had known Whitman since 1849, and the Rome family saw Whitman as someone who soon would make his mark on the world.

When Whitman approached them in the spring of 1855, they happily agreed to print the first edition of *Leaves of Grass.* Letting Whitman supervise (and even set approximately ten pages of type), the brothers consulted with Whitman on all facets of the publication, including typefaces, ink, type of paper and layout. Whitman selected a typeface from Scotland. The twelve pages of the Preface were set in ten-point type; the eighty-three pages of poetry, in twelve-point type. The printers provided him with eight hundred copies in quarto format, and then the sheets were sent to an engraver and binder.

In addition, the Rome brothers provided access to a comfortable, small print shop, similar to the one where Whitman had done his apprenticeship years before. Most mornings that spring Whitman appeared at the shop, read the New York *Tribune,* and settled in to work on page proofs. While there he also wrote a prose piece about the role of the poet and poetry in American life and included the essay at the beginning of the volume.

In 1858–1859 the Rome brothers set Whitman's new poems in type and gave him copies for prospective publishers of a new and enlarged edition of *Leaves of Grass.*

Jan Whitt

Bibliography

Allen, Gay Wilson. *The Solitary Singer: A Critical Biography of Walt Whitman.* 1955. Rev. ed. 1967. Chicago: U of Chicago P, 1985.

Greenspan, Ezra. *Walt Whitman and the American Reader.* Cambridge: Cambridge UP, 1990.

Rubin, Joseph Jay. *The Historic Whitman.* University Park: Pennsylvania State UP, 1973.

Stovall, Floyd. *The Foreground of "Leaves of Grass."* Charlottesville: UP of Virginia, 1974.

See also LEAVES OF GRASS, 1855 EDITION; PRINTING BUSINESS

Rossetti, William Michael (1829–1915)

One of Whitman's most important European editors, critics, and supporters, William Michael Rossetti, brother of Dante Gabriel and Christina Rossetti, was the editor of *The Germ* (1850), journal and manifesto of the Pre-Raphaelite Brotherhood. Rossetti received a copy of *Leaves of Grass* (1855) soon after its publication, as a gift from William Bell Scott, who had been introduced to it by Thomas Dixon of Sunderland. Rossetti responded enthusiastically and discussed it with many other British writers, among them A.C. Swinburne. An article by Rossetti in the London *Chronicle* (6 July 1867) created great interest in Whitman in Britain and America and was much appreciated by John Burroughs, William D. O'Connor, and Whitman himself. It was reprinted in several publications in the United States. At the suggestion of Moncure D. Conway, who gained Whitman's permission for the publication of a selection of his poems, with a few changes in text, and at the invitation of London publisher John Camden Hotten, Rossetti agreed to edit a selection of *Leaves of Grass* from the 1867 edition, omitting any poem he thought likely to offend English readers (and censors). His editing of Whitman's *Poems* (1868), including the 1855 Preface (which Whitman doubted was worth republishing), was a major event in the growth of Whitman's reputation and readership in America and Europe. Rossetti's prefatory notice admitted that Whitman had what Rossetti considered many faults of diction and subject matter, but asserted that Whitman was among the greatest poets of the English language. Rossetti's edition contained about one half of the 1867 text; the poems included were printed without omissions or emendations, though a few changes were made in the text of the Preface. Rossetti insisted that his edition was unexpurgated and only preliminary to an English publication of the complete *Leaves of Grass,* but O'Connor and Whitman had strong reservations about it, and Whitman later referred to it as "the horrible dismemberment of my book" (*Correspondence* 2:133).

Throughout the rest of his life Rossetti championed Whitman, praising him even in his 1870 edition of Henry Wadsworth Longfellow as by far the greatest American poet. In 1872 Rossetti published *American Poems,* "dedicated with homage and love to Walt Whitman," including thirty-two poems by Whitman. He included one poem ("A Boston Ballad (1854)") by Whitman in his anthology *Humorous Poems* (1872). He brought out a new edition of Whitman's *Poems* in 1886. Rossetti's letters and diaries contain many references to Whitman and show his deep affection for Whitman as poet and correspondent, as well as his sympathy with Whitman's social and political ideals.

Rossetti was important in the editing and publishing of Anne Gilchrist's "An Englishwoman's Estimate of Walt Whitman" (Boston *Radical,* 1870), and suggested the beginning of the correspondence between Whitman and Mrs. Gilchrist which led to her visit to Philadelphia in 1876.

In 1876, after an article appeared in the *West Jersey Press* (Camden) about Whitman's poverty and neglect in the United States, and subsequent heated discussions of this in English and American journals, Rossetti offered Whitman the assistance of his English admirers, and Whitman agreed to accept it. Rossetti's efforts led to many generous subscriptions to the 1876 Centennial edition of *Leaves of Grass,* which Whitman said "pluck'd me like a brand from the burning, and gave me life again" (*Prose Works* 2:699–700). Famous personages among the subscribers were John Ruskin, Edmund Gosse, George Saintsbury, Alfred, Lord Tennyson, and Edward Dowden. In 1886, Rossetti directed the collection and distribution of the equivalent of almost two thousand dollars in cash gifts from British friends. Tireless in his efforts, he even wrote a letter to President Grover Cleveland proposing that the United States grant Whitman a government pension.

Sherwood Smith

Bibliography

Blodgett, Harold. *Walt Whitman in England.* Ithaca, N.Y.: Cornell UP, 1934.

Rossetti, William Michael. *The Diary of W.M. Rossetti, 1870–1873.* Ed. Odette Bornand. Oxford: Clarendon, 1977.

———. *Letters . . . Concerning Whitman, Blake, and Shelley.* Ed. Clarence Gohdes and Paull Franklin Baum. Durham, N.C.: Duke UP, 1934.

———. *Selected Letters of William Michael Rossetti.* Ed. Roger W. Peattie. University Park: Pennsylvania State UP, 1990.

———, comp. *Rossetti Papers, 1862 to 1870.* 1903. New York: AMS, 1970.

———, ed. *American Poems.* London: E. Moxon, 1872.

———, ed. *Humorous Poems.* London: E. Moxon, 1872.

Whitman, Walt. *The Correspondence.* Ed. Edwin Haviland Miller. 6 vols. New York: New York UP, 1961–1977.

———. *Poems.* Ed. William Michael Rossetti. London: John Camden Hotten, 1868.

———. *Prose Works 1892.* Ed. Floyd Stovall. 2 vols. New York: New York UP, 1963–1964.

See also BRITISH ISLES, WHITMAN IN THE; GILCHRIST, ANNE BURROWS; HOTTEN, JOHN CAMDEN; *LEAVES OF GRASS*, 1867 EDITION; *WEST JERSEY PRESS*

Roughs

Aspiring to produce the first distinctly American poetry, Whitman modeled *Leaves of Grass* on explicitly democratic principles and in doing so made the common man thematically central, seeking to give to the majority the prominence allotted them by the provisions of egalitarianism. David Reynolds and Justin Kaplan treat Whitman's conception of the common man as an outgrowth of his journalistic career through which he achieved intimate familiarity with urban-dwelling, working class figures—common men who made up the masses in industrializing centers such as New York. In his notebooks, Whitman identified this assortment of figures as the "divine aggregate" from which there should be "none excluded—not the ignorant, not the roughs or laboring persons" (*Notebooks* 6: 2092). "The Roughs," a class of gang members in Manhattan's poorer districts also known as "rowdies," "loafers," and "toughs," are mentioned five times in his poetry and have attracted attention from Whitman scholars due to the poet's bold announcement of himself in the first three editions of *Leaves of Grass* as "Walt Whitman, an American, one of the roughs, a kosmos" ("Song of Myself"). Whitman substantiated his characterization of himself as a rough with the frontispiece to the 1855 edition. Here Whitman—with bearded face and a muscular physique, casual workman's trousers, open collar, cocked hat, and arm akimbo in a strikingly nonchalant, even arrogant pose—deliberately mirrors the coarse appearance of the working class rough, who in every way was a product of industrial environment. Whitman saw great potential in "the rough of the streets who may underneath his coarse skin possess the saving graces" (Traubel 177) and embraced this character as his first poetic persona so that the common man, whom he envisioned as his audience, might find a reflection of himself in *Leaves of Grass*.

Reactions to Whitman's self-identification have varied. While some of Whitman's contemporaries appreciated his proletarian pose, they tended to resist his choice of the rough as his focus. One can understand why Whitman's contemporaries, who would have been familiar with accounts of a low-class, often violent gang of loafers notorious for instigating political riots, might have attempted to defend his reputation against the poet's own self-identification. Ed Folsom relies on John Kasson's account of nineteenth-century social standards to demonstrate how Whitman's unconventional persona would have posed a direct affront to the sensibilities of a contemporary reviewer such as William Sloane Kennedy, who opposed Whitman's use of the frontispiece. Kasson cites unpolished features and casual, unrestrained demeanor as external evidence, according to the methods of popular physiognomy, of the rough's supposedly unrefined internal character. Whitman's audience, which consisted largely of the educated elite, would likely have felt alienated and offended by his image, which suggested to them a rude and ignorant character. Likewise, Reynolds discusses Charles Eliot Norton, another contemporary of Whitman, who hoped that by emphasizing the poet's transcendental qualities he might compensate for Whitman's use of slang terms such as "rough," a practice that Norton condemns as unsophisticated but one which Whitman valued for its immediacy.

Scott Giantvalley discusses the reaction of Thomas Wentworth Higginson, who hoped that Whitman might replace "rough" with a less charged term, such as "boweriness," to depict the masculinity of his persona.

Twentieth-century scholars have continued to speculate about how much a rough the author of *Leaves of Grass* actually was. While Frederik Schyberg depicts a rowdy, loaferish young Whitman, Reynolds, Whitman's most recent biographer, believes Whitman's true personality revealed few of these traits and suggests other figures, such as Mike Walsh, a working class editor and defender of the common man, who may have influenced the persona. As the historical accurateness of Whitman's persona has come into question, scholars have come to view his poetic character not as a literal rough but primarily as a character type which serves a specific poetic purpose in *Leaves of Grass*. For Griffith Dudding and Ernest Lee Tuveson, the coupling of the terms "rough" and "kosmos" creates a dual-sided persona for Whitman. Dudding asserts that Whitman's characterization of himself as a rough, which grounds him in his reality, counterbalances his description of himself as a "kosmos," which allows him to encompass the larger, metaphysical truths of existence. Tuveson views the rough as the destructive elements of Whitman's cosmic nature. Similarly, James Dougherty describes Whitman's persona as part rough and part Shakespeare and Dante.

Other critics have looked toward Whitman's self-identification in terms of its potential effect on the common man. Reynolds's interpretation, based on his argument that the poet was somewhat disturbed by the violent tendencies of the roughs, claims that Whitman places the term between "American" and "kosmos" in order to elevate the rough to the level of ideas such as patriotism and mysticism. Larzer Ziff, on the other hand, argues that Whitman's purpose is not to elevate the rough, but rather to show the rough his potential, providing for him a sense of identity that would allow the common man to appreciate the strengths of his daily existence. Van Wyck Brooks, who drew a connection between Whitman's rough and Ralph Waldo Emerson's Berserkers, emphasized the potential for social reform Whitman saw in the common man. Similarly, Folsom's most recent interpretation sees Whitman's persona as one that bridges the gap between worker and poet, thereby promoting the nineteenth-century rise of the common man.

In 1867 *Leaves of Grass* appeared with Whitman's self-identification as a rough and the accompanying photograph removed. Reynolds discusses Whitman's actions around the same time, when he sent a letter to William D. O'Connor in which he offers some suggestions for a review, which Whitman requested that O'Connor write, stating that "personally the author of *Leaves of Grass* is in no sense or sort whatever the 'rough,' the 'eccentric,' 'vagabond' or queer person, that the commentators . . . persist in making him" (*Correspondence* 1:348). In time, Whitman's persona was recast, largely through O'Connor's effort, into its second incarnation, the Good Gray Poet. Schyberg suggests that specifically the removal of the frontispiece and, in general, the rejection of the persona was a reaction to criticism from his reviewers, who were among the educated elite and representative of Whitman's audience. Reynolds and Ziff believe that Whitman was alarmed by political corruption in the Democratic party with which the rough, frequently performing in the service of political bosses, certainly would have been involved. In general, scholars recognize this as a period of disillusionment for Whitman, whose poetry failed to find his audience in the common man. Perhaps, it is finally in these terms that we can best make sense of the poet's eventual rejection of his first poetic persona, that of the "rough."

Danielle L. Baker and Donald C. Irving

Bibliography

Brooks, Van Wyck. *The Times of Melville and Whitman*. New York: Dutton, 1947.

Dougherty, James. *Walt Whitman and the Citizen's Eye*. Baton Rouge: Louisiana State UP, 1993.

Dudding, Griffith. "The Function of Whitman's Imagery in 'Song of Myself,' 1855." *Walt Whitman Review* 13 (1967): 3–11.

Folsom, Ed. *Walt Whitman's Native Representations*. Cambridge: Cambridge UP, 1994.

Giantvalley, Scott. "'Strict, Straight Notions of Literary Propriety': Thomas Wentworth Higginson's Gradual Unbending to Walt Whitman." *Walt Whitman Quarterly Review* 4.4 (1987): 17–27.

Kaplan, Justin. *Walt Whitman: A Life*. New York: Simon and Schuster, 1980.

Kasson, John F. *Rudeness & Civility, Manners in Nineteenth-Century Urban America*. New York: Hill and Wang, 1990.

Miller, Edwin Haviland. *Walt Whitman's "Song of Myself": A Mosaic of Interpretations.* Iowa City: U of Iowa P, 1989.

Reynolds, David. *Walt Whitman's America: A Cultural Biography.* New York: Knopf, 1995.

Schyberg, Frederik. *Walt Whitman.* Trans. Evie Allison Allen. New York: Columbia UP, 1951.

Traubel, Horace. *With Walt Whitman in Camden.* Vol. 2. New York: Appleton, 1908.

Tuveson, Ernest Lee. *The Avatars of Thrice Great Hermes: An Approach to Romanticism.* Lewisburg: Bucknell UP, 1982.

Whitman, Walt. *The Correspondence.* Ed. Edwin Haviland Miller. 6 vols. New York: New York UP, 1961–1977.

———. *Notebooks and Unpublished Prose Manuscripts.* Ed. Edward F. Grier. 6 vols. New York: New York UP, 1984.

Ziff, Larzer. *Literary Democracy.* New York: Viking, 1981.

See also DEMOCRACY; *LEAVES OF GRASS,* 1855 EDITION; PERSONAE; PHOTOGRAPHS AND PHOTOGRAPHERS

"'Rounded Catalogue Divine Complete, The'" (1891)

A seven-line free-verse poem, "'The Rounded Catalogue Divine Complete'" (1891) first appeared in the annex "Good-Bye my Fancy." An earlier draft and the printer's copy are in the Charles E. Feinberg Collection at the Library of Congress. Comparing the draft with the published version reveals a number of Whitman's revisions, which include the deletion of several lines before the poem was published.

In a bracketed prefatory note, Whitman explains that he is responding to a sermon he had heard in which a professor-pastor purported to list "the rounded catalogue divine complete." Whitman complains, however, that this catalogue only included *"the esthetic things."* Whitman's poem appropriates the preacher's phrase and lists what was neglected, the "low and evil, crude and savage."

The theme of "'Rounded Catalogue'" is highly characteristic of Whitman's oeuvre. Whitman's democratic insistence on all-inclusiveness pervades the majority of his poems: he praises both heterosexual and homosexual love in the "Children of Adam" (1860) and the "Calamus" (1860) poems, and the narrator of "Song of Myself" (1855) empathizes with blacks and whites, women and men, young and old, virtue and vice. In "'Rounded Catalogue'" Whitman continues to unite apparent opposites. Whitman's verse complements the preacher's sermon, so that they together comprise an ontological democracy in which heaven is united with earth and sermon is reconciled with poetry. In "'Rounded Catalogue'" Whitman reasserts his belief that a balanced harmony between apparent opposites is necessary in order to complete the divine.

Matthew C. Altman

Bibliography
Golden, Arthur. "Whitman's 'Respondez!,' 'A Rounded Catalogue Divine Complete,' and Emerson." *Études Anglaises* 48 (1995): 319–327.

Whitman, Walt. *Leaves of Grass.* Ed. Sculley Bradley and Harold W. Blodgett. Norton Critical Edition. New York: Norton, 1973.

See also "CHANTING THE SQUARE DEIFIC"; "GOOD-BYE MY FANCY" (SECOND ANNEX)

Rukeyser, Muriel (1913–1980)

Muriel Rukeyser was an important figure in American feminist and radical poetry, whose work, beginning with her *Theory of Flight* (1935), celebrated the diversity of women's accomplishments, the physical and metaphorical power of technology, and the importance of political and social activism. She was attracted to Whitman as a predecessor who shared these concerns. During her forty-five-year writing career, she covered a vast range of historical, political, social, and personal topics, and she was one of the first female poets in the United States to write outside of the narrow realms of romantic and domestic concerns that the literary public had come to expect from women writers.

She also shared with Whitman a fascination with urban experience, a frankness about sexuality and the body, and a desire to break out of traditional poetic forms and discover a new poetic language that would capture areas of experience not previously articulated in poetry. It is not surprising, then, that Whitman occasionally appears by name in her poetry, as he does as early as 1935 in "The Lynchings of Jesus." What is surprising is that Rukeyser's most extended commentary on Whitman centers on her claim that he is androgynous. Her essay, "Whitman and the Problem of Good," in *The Life of Poetry* (1949), discusses Whitman as "the poet of possibility"—that is, the poet whose "imagination of *possibility*" allowed him to explore areas of experience, particularly of sexuality, beyond his culture's operable definitions of "good" and "evil" ("Whitman" 109). And one of his great achievements in his "struggle for identity," according to Rukeyser, was his forging of "a resolution of components that are conventionally considered to be male and female—a resolution that expresses very much indeed" ("Whitman" 104). Rukeyser goes so far as to suggest that Whitman's autopsy revealed certain glandular changes that indicated a physical manifestation of his new dual-gendered "inclusive personality" ("Whitman" 104). Whitman-as-androgyne was an important concept for her, because her own desire was to write her way beyond traditional sex roles and to experience a unified human personality.

Ed Folsom

Bibliography

Rukeyser, Muriel. *The Collected Poems*. New York: McGraw-Hill, 1978.

———. *The Life of Poetry*. New York: Current Books, 1949.

———. *Theory of Flight*. New Haven: Yale UP, 1936.

———. "Whitman and the Problem of Good." *Walt Whitman: The Measure of His Song*. Ed. Jim Perlman, Ed Folsom, and Dan Campion. Minneapolis: Holy Cow!, 1981. 102–110.

See also LEGACY, WHITMAN'S; SEX AND SEXUALITY

Russia and Other Slavic Countries, Whitman in

Whitman's importance in twentieth-century Russia is immense, and in other Slavic countries substantial: the populist vigor of his verse, its nondogmatic spirituality, and the bold energy of its innovative techniques have helped make him beloved. Many editions of Kornei Chukovsky's often revised Russian translation of *Leaves of Grass* (from 1907 to the posthumous version of 1970) have sold in huge numbers, especially in wartime, while Whitman's poetic influence has been felt most notably by the futurists Velimir Khlebnikov and Vladimir Mayakovsky.

The third (1860) edition of Whitman's book was the first to be noticed in Russia when an anonymous reviewer in *Annals of the Fatherland* mistook the work for a novel, but *Leaves of Grass* was not noticed again until 1882, in a translation of John Swinton's lecture on Whitman which appeared in *Foreign Herald*. When N. Popov reviewed Whitman's book in the following year, he not only compared the poet to Johann Wolfgang von Goethe's Faust and John Milton's Satan but further alarmed the censors with praise for "This Compost." Whitman's ability to attain "rapture through the lessons of putrid corpses" seemed dangerously decadent: the reviewer was jailed, the magazine suspended. When part of this review was translated and published in the American journal *Critic* (16 June 1883), Whitman, who read it, was convinced that Popov must be a pseudonym of Swinton.

Ivan Turgenev, author of *Fathers and Sons* (1859), tried to translate Whitman's "Beat! Beat! Drums!" but left his failed attempt unfinished (the manuscript was discovered in Paris in 1966). In 1890 Count Leo Tolstoy wrote to his friend L. Nikiforov suggesting that the latter translate some Whitman, but nothing came of this. In an *Encyclopedic Dictionary* article of 1892, Z.A. Vengerova saw Whitman as wholly outside all European literary tradition, but I.V. Shklovsky (pseudonym Dioneo) opposed this view in his "Oscar Wilde and Walt Whitman" (*Russian Riches* 1898). In 1899 V.G. Bogoraz (pseudonym Tan) published a poem, generally known as "Song of Labor and Struggle," with the subheading "From Walt Whitman." A member of the radical "People's Will" group who had suffered imprisonment and exile, Bogoraz sought to evade the censors by attributing his own poetical offspring (written in strictly regular meter and rhyme) to the American bard.

Though Whitman's death in 1892 was extensively reported in Russian newspapers, it was still dangerous even to translate him. Konstantin Balmont's 1905 selections were confiscated and most copies destroyed; Kornei Chukovsky was taken to court in 1905 and again in 1911, when his book of translations was destroyed by court order. In 1913 at least four Russian cities banned public lectures on Whitman's life and poetry.

Balmont (called by Osip Mandelstam the Father of Russian Symbolism) and Chukovsky were Whitman's most eager and influential Russian proponents. Chukovsky also inaugurated the rigorous scholarly investigation of Whitman criticism in his 1906 article "Russian Whitmaniana" (in *The Scales*). Here he insists on accuracy in biography, thoroughness in bibliography, and faithfulness in translation. Chukovsky correctly criticizes Balmont for regularizing Whitman's meter and generalizing his diction, and he points to outright errors in the Balmontian renditions. Chukovsky's critique, extended in succeeding years into a fierce attack on Balmont's temperament and opinions, is marred by excessive zeal from the start, as when he insists that "human form" must be translated as "human body" because Whitman is using the word "form" to refer to the body. But Chukovsky's accurate Whitman translations are rightly honored and deservedly endure.

Chukovsky and Balmont are both fine essayists on Whitman, and often their insights are either identical or mutually complementary. In *My Whitman* (1966) Chukovsky defines Whitman's unique visionary attribute as a continual awareness of the infinity of time and space. This somehow allows Whitman to reconcile materialism and idealism. Whitman is as scientific-minded as Bazarov, the "nihilist" of Turgenev's *Fathers and Sons* whose perspective is shaped by such books as Ludwig Büchner's *Force and Matter*. Yet Whitman expresses with equal fervor idealistic sentiments like those of Georg Wilhelm Friedrich Hegel or Ralph Waldo Emerson. Chukovsky sees in the poet's all-in-oneness a perilous obliteration of individuality: in the Whitman world of "identity" we could hardly distinguish Nikolai Gogol's comical Korobochka from Tolstoy's tragic Karenina. But Chukovsky still admires what he calls "cosmic enthusiasm," a phrase Balmont had borrowed from J.A. Symonds to describe the Whitman world view.

Balmont, building on metaphors he found in Symonds, sees Whitman as Leviathan, Yggdrasil, earth-titan, eagle. In "Polarity" (1908, later used as preface to his 1911 *Shoots of Grass*) Balmont contrasts Edgar Allan Poe's self-preoccupation to the Whitman emphasis on self-transcendence; for Balmont Whitman is an oceanic poet, a sea-beast immersed in the larger element. (In *Marine Phosphorescence* [1910] Balmont movingly re-creates "As I Ebb'd with the Ocean of Life" in a meditation on the Russo-Japanese War, with mounds of the dead in Manchuria tossed up by the Ocean of Night.) As all-inclusive poet of the plenitude of Being,

Whitman is like Yggdrasil, the mythic Norse World Tree, but he is also like the creative-destructive Broad-Axe. In *White Summer Lightnings* (1908) Balmont sees the earth-titan Whitman as "building" utopian future cities of friendship. Balmont not only acknowledges the homosexual element in this friendship but praises Whitman for expressing it with naturalness and conviction. Finally, Balmont sees Whitman as a soaring eagle, rising above his era with prophetic insight, so that his American poems of 1860 illuminate the Russian revolution of 1905.

Russian futurists enjoyed Whitman. Chukovsky says Velimir Khlebnikov liked listening to Whitman's poems declaimed in English, though he knew but little of the language; influence may be seen in "O Garden of Animals!" (1910). Chukovsky read his own translations of Whitman to Vladimir Mayakovsky, whose poems "The Cloud in Trousers" (1915) and "To His Beloved Self, the Author Dedicates These Lines" (1916) show a clear kinship with "Song of Myself." Other poets of the period who learned from Whitman were Mikhail Larionov and Ivan Oredezh.

D.S. Mirsky, whose "Poet of American Democracy" introduces the ninth (1935) edition of Chukovsky's Whitman, finds the essence of the American poet's spirit in "The Dalliance of the Eagles"; he also thinks Whitman's respect for the equality of women and men is unprecedented in poetry (though influenced by the prose of Saint-Simon). Zhanna Ivina, citing the "Calamus" poems, compares Whitman with Marina Tsvetaeva in her "Sapphic purity." Most recently, in "Epos of One's Personal Fate" (1987) O. Aliakrinsky finds in Whitman's compression of time and space a precedent for a modern poetic genre extending from Guillaume Apollinaire and Blaise Cendrars to Yevgeny Yevtushenko's "Mama and the Neutron Bomb."

Though Polish discussion of Whitman began in 1887, a taste conditioned by "realism" delayed Whitman's influence in Poland until the rise of the free-rhythm Skamander poets, whose views are summed up in Julian Tuwim's 1917 "Manifesto of General Love (Walt Whitman)." Stanisław de Vincenz translated *Three Poems* in 1921; S. Napieralski did *75 Poems* in 1934. Juliusz Zuławski edited translations in 1965, Hieronym Michalski in 1973. Zuławski also published a 1971 Whitman biography, emphasizing Polish contributions to American history.

The great Czech poet Jaroslav Vrchlický began translating Whitman in 1895. The year

R

1906 saw more renditions, by Vrchlický and also by Emanuel z Lěshradu. The former's translations were attacked by Pavel Eisner, whose own *Democracy, Ma Femme* came out in 1945. Two more Czech translators, Jiři Kolář and Zdeněk Urbánek, offered in 1955 a selection of Whitman's poetry and prose. *Democratic Vistas* has twice been rendered into Czech, and Zdeněk Vančura has written a popular biography of Whitman. A Slovak translation, whose title translates as *Salut au Monde!* (1956), contains fifty poems (translated by Ján Boor) as well as *Democratic Vistas* (done by Magda Seppová).

Serbian Book Herald has twice featured Whitman translations (1912, 1920) and also Bogdan Popovich's "Walt Whitman and Swinburne" (1925), reportedly an attack on Whitman's coarseness from A.C. Swinburne's perspective (but that is a puzzle: in *William Blake* Swinburne praises Whitman highly). Though Whitman extracts in Croatian were published in 1900, 1909–1912, and 1919 by such writers as Borivoj Jevtić, Ljubo Wiesner, and Ivo Andrić, not until 1951 did more extensive Croatian selections (translated by the masterly poet Augustin Ujević) appear in Zagreb. For the Nobel Prize winner Ivo Andrić, Whitman "helps us to forget our own selves and our dark, Slavic sadness" (qtd. in Basic 25). Bulgaria first showed interest in Whitman when Rusi Rusev's "The Literary Judgments of Walt Whitman" appeared in the 1946 *Annual of the Faculty of History and Philology at the University of Sofia.* Slovenian and Macedonian translations of Whitman also exist. No other nineteenth-century American poet has equaled Whitman's impact in Eastern Europe.

Martin Bidney

Bibliography

Abieva, N.A. "Nachalo znakomstva s Uoltom Uitmenom v Rossii." *Russkaia Literatura* 4 (1986): 185–195.
Aliakrinskii, O. "Èpos chastnoi sud'by." *Voprosy Literatury* 12 (1987): 130–159.
Allen, Gay Wilson. *The New Walt Whitman Handbook.* 1975. New York: New York UP, 1986.
———, ed. *Walt Whitman Abroad.* Syracuse: Syracuse UP, 1955.
Allen, Gay Wilson, and Ed Folsom, eds. *Walt Whitman & the World.* Iowa City: U of Iowa P, 1995.
Basic, Sonja. "Walt Whitman in Yugoslavia." *Walt Whitman in Europe Today.* Ed. Roger Asselineau and William White. Detroit: Wayne State UP, 1972. 24–26.
Bidney, Martin. "Leviathan, Yggdrasil, Earth-Titan, Eagle: Balmont's Reimagining of Walt Whitman." *Slavic and East European Journal* 34 (1990): 176–191.
Chukovskii, Kornei. *Moi Uitmen.* Moscow: Progress, 1966.
———. "Russkaia Whitmaniana." *Vesy* 10 (1906): 43–45.
Ivina, Zhanna. "With the grandeur of Homer and the purity of Sappho. . . ." *Women and Russia: Feminist Writings from the Soviet Union.* Ed. Tatyana Mamonova with Sarah Matilsky. Trans. Rebecca Park and Catherine A. Fitzpatrick. Boston: Beacon, 1984. 155–163.
Khlebnikov, Velimir. *The King of Time: Selected Writings of the Russian Futurian.* Ed. Charlotte Douglas. Trans. Paul Schmidt. Cambridge, Mass.: Harvard UP, 1975.
Leighton, Lauren G. "Whitman in Russia: Chukovsky and Balmont." *Calamus: Walt Whitman Quarterly International* 22 (1972): 1–17.
Mayakovsky, Vladimir. *The Bedbug and Selected Poetry.* 1960. Ed. Patricia Blake. Trans. Max Hayward and George Reavey. Bloomington: Indiana UP, 1975.

See also CHINA, WHITMAN IN; INTERCULTURALITY

S

St. Louis, Missouri

Pierre Laclede founded St. Louis in 1764 to be a focal point for French trade on the Mississippi River. On 10 March 1810 the United States military took command of the post under the terms of the Louisiana Purchase, but the city did not become prominent until the 1850s, when it developed into an important railway center. By late 1879—when Walt Whitman made his only extended visit—St. Louis's population was more than three hundred thousand, making it the fourth largest city in the United States.

Whitman first toured St. Louis on 3 June 1848 when his brother Jeff Whitman and he stopped for a few hours as they returned east after working for the New Orleans *Crescent.* Jeff Whitman, who studied to become a civil engineer specializing in waterworks, later moved to St. Louis in 1867 to supervise its water department.

On 12 September 1879 Walt Whitman returned to St. Louis for another one-day visit as part of a group traveling to Kansas to celebrate the Old Settlers' Quarter Centennial celebration. On his return trip later in the month, Whitman again stopped in St. Louis. He subsequently decided to extend his visit and lived with his brother's family from 27 September to 5 January 1880. Although he complained that illness delayed his departure from St. Louis, Whitman thoroughly enjoyed his stay. He spent his afternoons either at Eads Bridge, which he greatly admired for its size, or in the Mercantile Library. Occasionally, he visited neighborhood kindergartens to entertain the children with his stories.

Jim McWilliams

Bibliography

Allen, Gay Wilson. *The Solitary Singer: A Critical Biography of Walt Whitman.* 1955. Rev. ed. 1967. Chicago: U of Chicago P, 1985.

Eitner, Walter H. *Walt Whitman's Western Jaunt.* Lawrence: Regents Press of Kansas, 1981.

McWilliams, Jim. "An Unknown 1879 Profile of Whitman." *Walt Whitman Quarterly Review* 11 (1994): 141–143.

Whitman, Thomas Jefferson. *Dear Brother Walt: The Letters of Thomas Jefferson Whitman.* Ed. Dennis Berthold and Kenneth M. Price. Kent, Ohio: Kent State UP, 1984.

See also TRAVELS, WHITMAN'S; WHITMAN, THOMAS JEFFERSON

"Salut au Monde!" (1856)

"Salut au Monde!," first published as the third poem of the 1856 edition of *Leaves of Grass,* was originally entitled "Poem of Salutation." Receiving its present title in 1860, the piece underwent minor revisions throughout the different editions of *Leaves of Grass.* In the interest of aesthetic and thematic unity, Whitman dropped the American "genre painting" scene of section 8 from the thirteen sections in 1881 and reprinted it as a separate poem, "A Paumanok Picture." Though Whitman may have begun work on the poem before 1855, there are preliminary fragments of some of its lines in an 1855–1856 notebook, along with a jotting which would appear to make plans for the piece: "Poem—comprehending the / sentiment of /

saluting Helo!" (*Notebook* 17). This poem of democratic salutation is influenced by the vision of international harmony of Constantin Volney's *Ruins* (1802).

"Salut au Monde!" is Whitman's calling card to the world, as well as one of his most successful compositions. With its close-ups and panoramic visions of the earth, the poem extends and internationalizes the outward progression of the first person seer in "Song of Myself." It begins the journey motif in what James E. Miller has classified as the "Song Section" ("Song of the Open Road," "Song of the Rolling Earth," etc.) of *Leaves of Grass*. As one of the twenty new poems of the second edition of *Leaves of Grass*, "Salut au Monde!" typifies Whitman's early optimism and exuberant engagement in the world. While the poem initially included American scenes, the poet deleted these by 1881, unifying "Salut au Monde!" as an international vision reaching beyond America to a universal ensemble.

From American brotherhood to a universal unity, Whitman's ongoing poetic aspiration is toward an "internationality of poems and poets, binding the lands of the earth closer than all treaties and diplomacy" (*Prose Works* 2:512). This "solidarity of the world," as Whitman called it in 1884 (*Correspondence* 3:369), is a manifestation of the poet's emphasis on "sympathy," the outward movement of self and nation, counterbalancing the "pride" of individualism and nationalism.

Argentine writer Jorge Luis Borges notes Whitman's dialogue technique in "Salut au Monde!," as seen in the line "What do you see, Walt Whitman?" (section 4), suggesting that the poet incorporates the reader (or perhaps the world) as questioner in his poem. The questions are answered in sounds and visions encompassing what Allen and Folsom list as Whitman's central concerns in his own nation: religion, politics, art, and sexuality. In typical Whitmanic fashion, the poet addresses these categories in wide-panning vistas and short strokes of detail. Along with historical summaries and sky-view grids of railroads and rivers, he records the Cossack's cry, Spanish dancing, and Hebrew prayer.

It is important to note that the poet who embraces the world in his song of foreign songs is also the critic who states that, as for national expression, "I know not a land except ours that has not, to some extent . . . made its title clear" (*Prose Works* 2:413). "Salut au Monde!" exhibits not only international good will but also

the national pride of an American bard attempting a "New World" art in which "the other continents arrive as contributions" ("Preface 1855" 711). Ironically, such a declaration may illustrate a recent problematic in Whitman studies, one in which a cordial nationalism would be found to accompany an imperialist chauvinism (see González de la Garza and Martin). The bard reaching out to the world in America's name would also support the expansionism of Manifest Destiny. This contradiction is examined by Roger Asselineau, who finds in Whitman an ingenuous belief in America as prime vehicle of democracy. And while an insistence on American identity has also left the bard of brotherhood open to accusations of xenophobia, it is important to note that "Salut au Monde!" reflects an earnest bid for international solidarity, just as it asserts an autonomous American identity—an identity Whitman found stunted not only by a national dependence on foreign cultural models but by the deep divisions caused by slavery, materialism, and surging immigration (see Erkkila and Reynolds).

In the free verse of "Salut au Monde!," Whitman's characteristic use of anaphora ("I hear . . . I hear . . ."), parallelism, and enthusiastic enumeration, create not only a sense of conviction and plenitude, diversity and unity, but insistently stake a claim: in his international inventory of visions and songs, Whitman as New World poet does not imitate; he appropriates. His relentless "I" with its roll call to the world (e.g., "You Spaniard, You Norwegian") takes the seer's journey while remaining on an American soil that underlines the raised "perpendicular hand" (added in 1860). It is this extended hand of lineal relation that intersects with and assumes the world. This intersection is emphasized in the choice of the French for a title. As Betsy Erkkila has observed, throughout *Leaves of Grass* French is the language of bonding and unity ("ensemble," "en masse," "rapport," "mélange") (86).

The ardent Whitmanic intersection that celebrates and penetrates difference in "Salut au Monde!" represents, with international accent, the "pride" and "sympathy" of *Leaves of Grass*, a work received around the world mainly in the spirit in which it was sent. Folsom and Allen note the prophetic nature of "Salut au Monde!," with its climactic declaration: "I have look'd for equals and lovers and found them ready for me in all lands" (section 13). In effect, no American writer has found "equals and lovers" in more lands than Whitman, who has, most noticeably through "Salut au Monde!," provoked a response in the tongues of all the continents he salutes. In their response to Whitman, these other lands, in turn, help America to understand its own identity. Whitman, in his own all-assuming identity, with dilating internal atlas ("Within me latitude widens, longitude lengthens" [section 2]), transcending self and nation to shape the world, is the international American poet who celebrates not only cultural difference, but the essential and universal songs of the soul.

Carol M. Zapata-Whelan

Bibliography

Allen, Gay Wilson. *The New Walt Whitman Handbook*. 1975. New York: New York UP, 1986.

Asselineau, Roger. *The Evolution of Walt Whitman*. 2 vols. Cambridge, Mass.: Harvard UP, 1960, 1962.

Erkkila, Betsy. *Whitman the Political Poet*. Oxford: Oxford UP, 1989.

Folsom, Ed, and Gay Wilson Allen. "Introduction: 'Salut au Monde!'" *Walt Whitman & the World*. Ed. Allen and Folsom. Iowa City: U of Iowa P, 1995. 1–10.

González de la Garza, Mauricio. *Walt Whitman: Racista, Imperialista, Antimexicano*. México: Colección Málaga, 1971.

Martin, Robert K., ed. *The Continuing Presence of Walt Whitman*. Iowa City: U of Iowa P, 1992.

Miller, James E., Jr. *A Critical Guide to "Leaves of Grass."* Chicago: U of Chicago P, 1957.

Perlman, Jim, Ed Folsom, and Dan Campion, eds. *Walt Whitman: The Measure of His Song*. Minneapolis: Holy Cow!, 1981.

Reynolds, David S. *Walt Whitman's America: A Cultural Biography*. New York: Knopf, 1995.

Whitman, Walt. *The Correspondence*. Ed. Edwin Haviland Miller. 6 vols. New York UP: New York, 1961–1977.

———. "Preface 1855—*Leaves of Grass*, First Edition." *Leaves of Grass: Comprehensive Reader's Edition*. Ed. Harold W. Blodgett and Sculley Bradley. New York: New York UP, 1965. 709–729.

———. *Prose Works 1892*. Ed. Floyd Stovall. 2 vols. New York: New York UP, 1963–1964.

———. *Walt Whitman: An 1855–56 Notebook Toward the Second Edition of "Leaves of Grass."* Ed. Harold Blodgett. Carbondale: Southern Illinois UP, 1959.

See also FOREIGN LANGUAGE BORROWINGS; INTERCULTURALITY; VOLNEY, CONSTANTIN

S

Sanborn, Franklin Benjamin (Frank) (1831–1917)

An 1855 Harvard graduate, Frank Sanborn—unreliable biographer of Henry David Thoreau, John Brown, and Bronson Alcott—boarded with the Thoreaus for several years while he taught school in Concord, Massachusetts. An active supporter of John Brown, Sanborn was the person who introduced Brown to Thoreau and one of the Secret Six who conspired to help Brown by acquiring money and arms for Brown's violent antislavery activities in Kansas and at Harper's Ferry.

Sanborn first encountered Walt Whitman on 4 April 1860 in a courtroom in Boston, where Sanborn had been brought (after a foiled arrest attempt in Concord, Massachusetts) to testify as to his involvement with John Brown's 16 October 1859 raid on Harper's Ferry; Sanborn looked out over the packed courtroom and saw, sitting at the rear of the courtroom, Walt Whitman, who had come to Boston to supervise the printing of the third edition of *Leaves of Grass*. Whitman would later say that he came to make sure that, if Sanborn were convicted, he—Whitman—might take part in an attempt to free him. Sanborn was not convicted. (See Jeffrey Rossbach's excellent documentation of this complex sequence of events in *Ambivalent Conspirators*.)

In his poem "Year of Meteors (1859–60)," Whitman devoted a few lines to John Brown, who had been executed in 1859. Years later, Sanborn corresponded with Whitman, gave a favorable review of Whitman's *Drum-Taps*, became editor of the *Springfield Republican*, and in 1881 took Whitman to his own home in Concord where he hosted the poet. Whitman once told Horace Traubel, "I always hold Sanborn, Frank Sanborn, to be a true friend—to stand with those who wish me well" (Traubel 285).

Linda K. Walker

Bibliography

Reynolds, David S. *Walt Whitman's America: A Cultural Biography.* New York: Knopf, 1995.

Rossbach, Jeffrey. *Ambivalent Conspirators: John Brown, The Secret Six, and a Theory of Slave Violence.* Philadelphia: U of Pennsylvania P, 1982.

Traubel, Horace. *With Walt Whitman in Camden.* Vol. 1. 1906. New York: Rowman and Littlefield, 1961.

See also BOSTON, MASSACHUSETTS; DRUM-TAPS; LEAVES OF GRASS, 1860 EDITION; SLAVERY AND ABOLITIONISM; THOREAU, HENRY DAVID; "YEAR OF METEORS (1859–60)"

Sand, George (1804–1876)

Author of more than fifty novels, George Sand (Amandine Lucile Aurore Dudevant) was perhaps the most famous woman writer in nineteenth-century France, certainly the most prolific. Her first novel, *Indiana* (1832), prepared the stage for much of her later work in its unconventional portrait of an unhappy wife who tries to free herself from the prison of marriage and a society that emphasized male dominance. Her subsequent novels shocked her nineteenth-century readers with frank studies of women's sexual feelings and the promotion of women's rights. Her iconoclastic themes in her novels were only enhanced by her unconventional behavior: leaving her husband and living with other men, occasionally dressing in men's clothing, smoking cigars. Her literary reputation was worldwide in the 1840s, and this seems to have been the time when Whitman first read her *Consuelo* (1842). Whitman had a profound interest in French romantic novelists, and as editor of the Brooklyn *Daily Eagle,* he especially reviewed the current French writers such as Sand.

In 1842, at age twenty-three, Whitman came across *Consuelo* in his mother's library, and he read and reread this novel in various translations. He thought it "truly a masterpiece . . . the noblest in many respects, on its own field, in all literature" (Traubel 423). According to the critics, this work was seminal for Whitman, perhaps the work that inspired his democratic view of men and women, and his vision of the poet as spokesman for all mankind. Whitman thought Consuelo superior to all of Shakespeare's women. In this Sand novel and its sequel, *La Comtesse de Rudolstadt* (1844), Whitman was to find soul nourishment for much of the political, religious, and artistic vision that he would employ in *Leaves of Grass* just a decade later. Whitman might have been led to employ specific seminal images such as the carpenter poet and the pure contralto from Sand. It was particularly in Sand that Whitman's liberated perspective toward sex, the body, spirituality, and equality for women took shape. Whitman possibly took from her novels not only some ideas that inspired *Leaves of Grass* but also his dress, his role, and his pose as the poet of democracy.

Sand's international influence upon other novelists, musicians, and poets is staggering: Honoré de Balzac, Fyodor Dostoevsky, Ivan Turgenev, William Makepeace Thackeray, George Eliot, Gustave Flaubert, Henry James, Frédéric Chopin, Thomas Carlyle, Karl Marx, Margaret Fuller, Elizabeth Barrett Browning, Robert Browning, Matthew Arnold, and preeminently, Walt Whitman. Whitman was a fervent reader of George Sand all of his adult life, and she remained a vibrant force in his democratic inspiration and outlook.

Andy J. Moore

Bibliography

Asselineau, Roger. *The Evolution of Walt Whitman: The Creation of a Personality.* Trans. Richard P. Adams and Roger Asselineau. Cambridge, Mass.: Harvard UP, 1960.

Erkkila, Betsy. *Walt Whitman Among the French: Poet and Myth.* Princeton: Princeton UP, 1980.

Roy, G.R. "Walt Whitman, George Sand and Certain French Socialists." *Revue de Littérature Comparée* 29 (1955): 550–561.

Shephard, Esther. *Walt Whitman's Pose.* New York: Harcourt Brace, 1938.

Traubel, Horace. *With Walt Whitman in Camden.* Vol. 3. 1914. New York: Rowan and Littlefield, 1961.

Zweig, Paul. *Walt Whitman: The Making of the Poet.* New York: Basic Books, 1984.

See also DEMOCRACY; INFLUENCES ON WHITMAN, PRINCIPAL; WOMEN AS A THEME IN WHITMAN'S WRITING

Sandburg, Carl (1878–1967)

As a critic Carl Sandburg once inventoried the "particulars" that make *Leaves of Grass* "the most peculiar and noteworthy monument amid the work of American literature." First, Sandburg notes, "as to style, . . . it is regarded as the most original book" and "the most sublimely personal creation in American literary art." Second, "It is the most highly praised and the most deeply damned book that ever came from . . . an American writer." Sandburg's third point is that *Leaves* is "the most intensely personal book in American literature" and, fourth, that the book "packs within its covers . . . the life and thought and feeling of one man." Fifth, Sandburg asserts that no other American poet except Poe has achieved the worldwide stature that Whitman has, nor—Sandburg's sixth point—has any other American book as ardent a following in America. Finally, Sandburg proclaims *Leaves of Grass* "the most wildly keyed solemn oath that America means something and is going somewhere that has ever been written" (Sandburg iii–iv).

While Sandburg's enumeration is essentially accurate and his introduction to *Leaves* thoughtfully places Whitman's call to individual and artistic freedom in historical context, his failure to discuss the soul in Whitman's work reflects the tendency of Sandburg the poet to follow Whitman's technique without Whitman's empathetic spirituality. Pearce points out that in Sandburg's Whitman-*sounding* poems, such as "Chicago" and "The People, Yes," he "lacked Whitman's extraordinarily mobile sensibility" and became a speech maker. While Sandburg became, for a time, a poet of the people, unlike Whitman he merely "registered the people's sentiments and did little to change them" or even to understand them (Pearce 270–271).

Alan Shucard

Bibliography

Niven, Penelope. *Carl Sandburg: A Biography*. New York: Scribner's, 1991.
Pearce, Roy Harvey. *The Continuity of American Poetry*. Princeton: Princeton UP, 1961.
Sandburg, Carl. Introduction. *Leaves of Grass*. By Walt Whitman. New York: Modern Library, 1921. iii–xi.

See also Leaves of Grass; Legacy, Whitman's

"Sands at Seventy" (First Annex) (1888)

This collection of sixty-five poems, along with selected prose pieces, including "A Backward Glance O'er Travel'd Roads," first appeared in the book entitled *November Boughs*. The poems were bound into the 1888 reprint of *Leaves of Grass* as an annex, and appeared again in the 1889 reprint. In the 1891–1892 edition the collection is introduced by a separate title page which reads: "ANNEX / TO PRECEDING PAGES. / SANDS AT SEVENTY. / Copyright, 1888, by Walt Whitman. / (*See* 'NOVEMBER BOUGHS')."

This "First Annex" (the Second Annex contains poems from a previously published miscellany entitled *Good-Bye My Fancy* [1891]) includes poems written after 1881 and published in newspapers or periodicals, many of them in the New York *Herald*. In the years from 1860 to 1881 Whitman had revised, added, excluded, and rearranged the poems of *Leaves of Grass* to make up what he came to think of as a single poem reflecting the chronological experience of the "average" man whose life spanned the nineteenth century. Because he felt that poems published after 1881 would detract from his carefully worked-out thematic unity he chose to distinguish these two groups of poems in bound editions of *Leaves of Grass* as "annexes" (the 1881 edition concludes with the section called "Songs of Parting," the last poem of which is "So Long!").

The dominant themes of the collection are old age and death, but there are a number of occasional poems on such subjects as Election Day 1884, the death of General Ulysses S. Grant, the burial of the famous Iroquois chief Red Jacket, the Washington Monument, the death of an operatic tenor, and John Greenleaf Whittier's eightieth birthday. Many poems reflect his conflicting feelings about maintaining a positive outlook in the face of his increasing infirmities. Talking to Traubel about the subject matter of these poems, Whitman said, "Of my personal ailments, of sickness as an element, I never spoke a word until the first of the poems I call Sands at Seventy were written, and then some expression of invalidism seemed to be called for" (Traubel 234). He realized that if he were to be true to his own stated goal of reflecting the life of an old man in his poems he had to include references to his sickness and invalidism, since they had become so much a part of his life. In writing about his own aging he remained faithful to his purpose to record as accurately as he could what he himself experienced. "Queries to

My Seventieth Year" reveals some of the ambiguous feelings he has about the year to come. In "A Carol Closing Sixty-Nine" he is happy to be still alive, "the jocund heart yet beating in my breast." "The Dismantled Ship" describes an "old, dismasted, gray and batter'd ship" that "[l]ies rusting, mouldering" in a poem whose tone recalls that of the "batter'd, wreck'd old man" of "Prayer of Columbus," written in 1874, about a year after Whitman had suffered his first paralytic stroke. In "As I Sit Writing Here" he writes, "Not my least burden is that dulness of the years, querilities, / Ungracious glooms, aches, lethargy, constipation, whimpering *ennui,* / May filter in my daily songs."

Poems about the negative aspects of his illness and aging are countered by poems like "Halcyon Days," "Thanks in Old Age," and "Old Age's Lambent Peaks," which celebrate their positive aspects: his memories, his heightened appreciation and understanding of life, and his spiritual serenity.

A notable feature of the "Sands at Seventy" annex is the group of eight poems entitled "Fancies at Navesink." Like the "Sea-Drift" cluster, compiled for the 1881 edition, their unifying theme is Whitman's love of the sea. From the vantage point of the Atlantic highlands on the New Jersey coast Whitman contemplates and addresses the sea: the rhythms of the waves and the tides, and their relationship to his own poetic rhythms, his mystical vision and the cycle of life.

The collection concludes with "After the Supper and Talk," containing a typical upbeat self-characterization in the context of a "last supper," at the end of which he turns in the exit door to say farewell to his friends, "garrulous to the very last."

Donald Barlow Stauffer

Bibliography

Fillard, Claudette. "Le vannier de Camden: Vieillesse, Poésie, et les Annexes de *Leaves of Grass.*" *Études Anglaises* 45 (1992): 311–323.

Stauffer, Donald Barlow. "Walt Whitman and Old Age." *Walt Whitman Review* 24 (1978): 144–148.

Traubel, Horace. *With Walt Whitman in Camden.* Vol. 2. New York: Appleton, 1908.

Whitman, Walt. *Leaves of Grass: A Textual Variorum of the Printed Poems.* Ed. Sculley Bradley, Harold W. Blodgett, Arthur Golden, and William White.

Vol. 3. New York: New York UP, 1980.

See also AGE AND AGING; "BACKWARD GLANCE O'ER TRAVEL'D ROADS, A"; DEATH; "GOOD-BYE MY FANCY" (SECOND ANNEX); *NOVEMBER BOUGHS;* "OLD AGE ECHOES"; SEA, THE; "SEA-DRIFT"

Santayana, George (1863–1952)

Philosopher, poet, and critic, George Santayana was a man divided intellectually as well as personally. Born in Europe of Spanish parents, he was brought to America as a young man. His ambivalence about the relationship of America to European culture and tradition was repeatedly expressed in his troubled evaluations of Walt Whitman.

Santayana's divided mind is vividly present in the form as well as the content of "Walt Whitman: A Dialogue" (1890). The two speakers debate Whitman's worth, McStout arguing that what Whitman creates is not poetry at all but barbarism. Van Tender accepts the critique of Whitman's style but maintains that he offers inspiration. Santayana returns to the subject in "The Poetry of Barbarism" (1900). The poetry of barbarism, including Whitman's, offers "passion" not constrained by "clear thought" (89). This is not meant as a totally negative judgment. Whitman's "genius" is "this wealth of perception without intelligence and of imagination without taste" (93) which frees him from the cold decline of the genteel tradition. Santayana grants Whitman a grandeur of diction and inspiration. Whitman's poetic barbarism is not inferior, but corresponds to part of our natures, offering "frankness and beauty" (97). These opposing sides of his personality, as of his national identity, Santayana could only hold in precarious balance.

Robert K. Martin

Bibliography

Aaron, Daniel. "George Santayana and the Genteel Tradition." *Critical Essays on George Santayana.* Ed. Kenneth M. Price and Robert C. Leitz III. Boston: Hall, 1991. 223–231.

Dawidoff, Robert. *The Genteel Tradition and the Sacred Rage: High Culture vs. Democracy in Adams, James, & Santayana.* Chapel Hill: U of North Carolina P, 1992.

Santayana, George. "The Poetry of Barbarism." *Interpretations of Poetry and Religion.* 1900. Rpt. in *Selected Critical*

Writings of George Santayana. Ed. Norman Henfrey. Vol. 1. Cambridge: Cambridge UP, 1968. 84–116.

———. "Walt Whitman: A Dialogue." 1890. *George Santayana's America: Essays on Literature and Culture.* Ed. James Ballowe. Urbana: U of Illinois P, 1967. 97–107.

See also CRITICS, WHITMAN'S; LEGACY, WHITMAN'S; SCHOLARSHIP, TRENDS IN WHITMAN

Sarrazin, Gabriel (1853–1935)

Born in Laval, France, Gabriel Sarrazin first encountered Whitman's work while in England researching a book on the English romantic poets, *La Renaissance de la Poésie Anglaise, 1778–1889.* Sarrazin, deeply impressed, inserted a chapter called "Walt Whitman," which was published separately in *La Nouvelle Revue* on 1 May 1888. In January 1889, Sarrazin sent Whitman a copy of the well-received article.

Horace Traubel reports that Whitman asked two friends, William Sloane Kennedy and Dr. Richard Maurice Bucke, each to translate the Sarrazin article. Whitman then had two versions to compare, and he was well pleased with Sarrazin's work, pronouncing it to be among the "strongest pieces of work which Leaves of Grass has drawn out" (Traubel 109). Whitman wrote to Sarrazin, and the two continued to correspond until almost the very end of Whitman's life.

After a brief introduction, the essay is divided into four parts: Pantheism, The New World, *Leaves of Grass,* and Walt Whitman. The first section is the most striking, for Sarrazin connects Whitman with the Oriental mystics and, further, compares him with the ancient prophets.

Carmine Sarracino

Bibliography

Asselineau, Roger. "Walt Whitman to Gabriel Sarrazin: Four Unpublished Pieces." *Walt Whitman Review* 1 (1959): 8–11.

Sarrazin, Gabriel. "Walt Whitman." *In Re Walt Whitman.* Ed. Horace Traubel, Richard Maurice Bucke, and Thomas Harned. Philadelphia: McKay, 1893. 159–194.

Traubel, Horace. *With Walt Whitman in Camden.* Ed. Sculley Bradley. Vol. 4. Philadelphia: U of Pennsylvania P, 1953.

See also BUCKE, RICHARD MAURICE; FRANCE, WHITMAN IN; KENNEDY, WILLIAM SLOANE

Saturday Press

Founded in October 1858, by Henry Clapp, the *Saturday Press* was perhaps best known for its publication of works by American Bohemians. On 24 December 1859, on its front page, the periodical published Whitman's "A Child's Reminiscence," later retitled "A Word Out of the Sea" and then, finally, "Out of the Cradle Endlessly Rocking." Occupying two columns, the poem was described by Clapp (in words possibly supplied by the poet himself) as a "curious warble" and a "wild and plaintive song, well-enveloped, and eluding definition . . . like the effect of music" (qtd. in Allen 231). In the 7 January 1860 issue of the *Press,* Whitman himself responded to an attack on the poem that had appeared in the Cincinnati *Daily Commercial.* At the same time he announced a forthcoming edition of *Leaves of Grass* (that is, the third, or 1860, edition), maintaining that its popularity would surely spread from literary circles to the general public and claiming that thousands of copies would be needed, especially in the "great West." Clapp, too, promoted the 1860 *Leaves,* stating in the *Press* on 28 April that large orders had been placed already. In the 9 June 1860 issue of the journal, Mary A. Chilton and a woman identifying herself as C.C.P. defended Whitman's purity in their description of their own innocent readings of his poems. According to David Reynolds, between 24 December 1859 and 15 December 1860, the *Saturday Press* printed twenty-five pieces about or by Whitman. This abundant publication kept his name in the public eye.

Amy M. Bawcom

Bibliography

Allen, Gay Wilson. *The Solitary Singer: A Critical Biography of Walt Whitman.* 1955. Rev. ed. 1967. Chicago: U of Chicago P, 1985.

Mott, Frank Luther. *A History of American Magazines 1850–1865.* Vol. 2. Cambridge, Mass.: Harvard UP, 1938.

Reynolds, David S. *Walt Whitman's America: A Cultural Biography.* New York: Knopf, 1995.

See also CLAPP, HENRY; LEAVES OF GRASS, 1860 EDITION; "OUT OF THE CRADLE ENDLESSLY ROCKING"; PFAFF'S RESTAURANT

Sawyer, Thomas P. (b. ca. 1843)

Although Walt Whitman was attracted to many of the young men he met in the Civil War hospital wards, his feelings for Sergeant Thomas P. Sawyer might best be described as an infatuation. The two men met early in 1863 while Whitman was nursing Sawyer's friend Lewy Brown, and soon Whitman was in full pursuit.

Whitman's letters to Sawyer were full of ardor, declaring that no other comrade but Sawyer suited him "to a dot" (Whitman 92). He proposed that after the war he and Sawyer and Brown might all live together, declaring that Sawyer had his love "in life and death forever" and assuring the young soldier that "my soul could never be entirely happy, even in the world to come, without you, dear comrade" (93). He made a point of mentioning that Brown had given him long kisses, implying that Sawyer might wish to do the same, but cautiously declaring: "I do not expect you to return for me the same degree of love I have for you" (107).

Sawyer was a soapmaker from Cambridge, Massachusetts, whose reserved Yankee manner and near illiteracy would not have permitted him to respond in kind, even had he been so disposed. More likely, he was bemused by the passionate attentions of this older man, whose interests he did not share.

Before Sawyer left for his military post, Whitman prepared a package with a shirt and a pair of drawers, hoping that Sawyer would "be wearing around his body something from me" (Whitman 93) which would contribute to his comfort, but Sawyer never came by to pick up the package. In a letter to Brown, who had evidently written to him of Whitman's disappointment, Sawyer apologized for not having had the time to get the clothes, and he sent along his thanks to Whitman for a book (possibly Leaves of Grass). Eventually, in January 1864, Sawyer wrote directly to Whitman, stiltedly addressing him as "Brother," and assuring him of his friendship in less than passionate terms (Whitman 90, n86). Their correspondence faded after that, doubtless to Whitman's sad dismay.

Arnie Kantrowitz

Bibliography

Allen, Gay Wilson. *The Solitary Singer: A Critical Biography of Walt Whitman.* 1955. Rev. ed. 1967. Chicago: U of Chicago P, 1985.

Shively, Charley. *Calamus Lovers: Walt Whitman's Working Class Camerados.* San Francisco: Gay Sunshine, 1987.

Whitman, Walt. *The Correspondence.* Ed. Edwin Haviland Miller. Vol. 1. New York: New York UP, 1961.

See also BROWN, LEWIS KIRK; CIVIL WAR NURSING; COMRADESHIP; SEX AND SEXUALITY

Scandinavia, Whitman in

The interest taken in Whitman and his poetry in Denmark, Norway, and Sweden in the closing decades of the nineteenth century reflected dominant social as well as literary concerns in each country. Norway, independent since 1814 but with close ties still to Denmark, was increasingly intent on establishing an unequivocal national identity; at the same time Norwegians were emigrating to America in numbers exceeded only by the Irish. Swedes and Danes were also emigrating but in smaller proportions. Concurrently, industry and commerce were transforming the Scandinavian countries. Unprecedented economic prosperity brought increasingly insistent popular demands for a democratic distribution of its benefits. Curiosity about life and literature in the American democracy was understandably intense in all three countries. When Whitman offered a Danish editor his recently completed *Democratic Vistas* for translation, it was quickly accepted and became a focal text for commentary on American democracy as well as Whitman's poetry.

Rudolf Schmidt, the translator of *Democratic Vistas*, was the enterprising editor of a new journal, *For Idé og Virkelighed* (Idea and Reality), in which he published in 1872 a long enthusiastic essay on Whitman. Alerted to Whitman's existence by an article in *The Fortnightly Review*, Schmidt had ventured to write to the poet in Washington; Whitman's grateful reply enclosed a copy of *Leaves of Grass* and of the newly published *Democratic Vistas*. Within months Schmidt's essay appeared presenting *Leaves of Grass* as "a new departure in humanity" (qtd. in Allen 357) better understood in Europe than in America, where it was more likely to be ridiculed than praised. *Demokratiske Fremblik*, Schmidt's translation of *Democratic Vistas,* followed in 1874.

No less a personage sat on Schmidt's editorial board than Norway's national poet, Bjørnstjerne Bjørnson, famous in Scandinavia as an unyielding exponent of free thought. He concurred in Schmidt's appraisal of Whitman, which he confirmed, with reservations, after a lengthy American tour in 1881. In that same year Kristofer Janson, a young Lutheran pastor who as a Bjørnsonian freethinker had been obliged to leave his post in Norway for a Unitarian church in Minneapolis, published *Amerikanske Forholde, Fem Foredrag* (American Life, Five Lectures) on the merits and risks inherent in American democracy as he had observed them at first hand and as they had been powerfully revealed in Whitman's poetry and *Demokratiske Fremblik*.

Janson had briefly in his employ in Minneapolis a talented but footloose Norwegian immigrant, Knut Hamsun, who soon left America after two failed attempts to establish himself as a novelist and poet among the Norwegian settlers. In 1889 he published in Copenhagen *Fra det moderne Amerikas Aandsliv* (The Cultural Life of Modern America), based on lectures given before the Student Union. He disparaged the positive views of America promulgated by Schmidt, Bjørnson, and Janson, and ridiculed Whitman's unorthodox poetics and lofty aspirations for American democracy. Hamsun privately discounted his book as being no more than a way of gaining notoriety (and a publication fee) for its indigent author—thirty years old, in debt, and virtually unknown except for the recent publication of a fragment of *Hunger,* the first novel in a career that would bring him the Nobel Prize thirty years later. The strategy succeeded all too well; in later years Hamsun repeatedly denied permission to reissue the book, dismissing it as worthless.

A decisive moment early in Johannes V. Jensen's Chicago novel *Hjulet* (The Wheel, 1905) directed Danish readers to his translations of several poems by Whitman read *con amore* by a young male character. Jensen had visited America in 1902–1903 and had sensed, he later reported in *Den ny Verden* (The New World, 1907), both the powerful regenerative force as well as the risks of self-deception present in Whitman's poems and in America itself. Nevertheless, the translations in *Hjulet* apparently served to introduce Whitman to many Scandinavian readers. Jensen later provided the introduction to translations by Otto Gelsted in a centenary volume (Copenhagen, 1919) that was adopted by a whole generation of Scandinavian readers as a basic text in literary modernism. In 1933 the Danish drama critic Frederik Schyberg published *Walt Whitman* (enlarged English translation, 1951), a remarkable, wide-ranging study of Whitman as an American poet whose achievement had made of him quite simply *"a trend in world literature"* (Schyberg 3). Schyberg skillfully analyzed textual revisions and rearrangements Whitman had made in successive editions of *Leaves of Grass* over the course of four decades. In a concluding chapter his findings allowed him to place Whitman in the company of major poets of worldwide renown. Translations continue to appear in Denmark: for example, Paul Borum's *Fremtidens historie* (The History of the Future, 1976) and Annette Mester's *Demokratiske Visioner* (1991).

The first display of Swedish interest in Whitman, apart from passing references, appeared in 1905 in a long essay by Andrea Butenschön, a Norwegian by birth who had traveled in India. She placed Whitman's poetry in the context of ancient Wisdom literature like that of India and translated "Proud Music of the Storm" in an inflated epic style. Whitman's real impact in Sweden came later, when a number of Swedish-language poets in Finland discovered in his poetry a primal source of their modernist ambitions. Edith Södergran's first volume of strikingly unconventional poetry appeared in 1916 and was soon followed by poetry and criticism by Elmer Diktonius. Both were quickly denominated the New Generation of poets by the critic Hagar Olsson. She attributed their power largely to the visionary force exemplified in *Leaves of Grass*. Whitman, she wrote, had shown these new poets how to restore poetry to its true function and rescue it from stale romantic lyricism. Revolution became a byword of the New Generation, not surprisingly in Finland, which had succeeded in asserting its independence in 1918 after a century of Russian rule. In mainland Sweden the New Generation of Finland-Swedish poets seemed dangerously radical to some critics, but the young poet Artur Lundkvist, describing himself as "a proletarian of the soil" (qtd. in Anderson 344), was completely won over. He later testified to a quickening of his own revolutionary spirit (carefully distinguished from communism) after having read in 1925 Gelsted's Danish translations of

Whitman. Lundkvist became a leading spokesman in the following decades in Sweden for what he termed "dynamic modernism." In that role he paid tribute in both prose and poetry to Whitman as a "pioneer and path breaker" who "identifies himself with nature, the cosmos" (qtd. in Anderson 345). Lundkvist's enthusiasm drew together Harry Martinson and other writers in the important group known as *fem unga* (Five Youths), but late in life it soured as he perceived Whitman to have been a false prophet, given the failure of America to fulfill its lofty promise of freedom and democracy.

Translations of Whitman in Scandinavia, where English has increasingly become the second language of choice, have been limited to selections, never the whole of his corpus, as in Russia and France. Translators have gradually improved their skills in dealing with intransigent problems of syntax, diction, and prosody and in learning how to annul the lingering influence of their own great poets. Especially noteworthy translations of "Song of Myself" have been published, by Per Arneberg (1973, in Neo-Norwegian), and of the 1855 edition of *Leaves of Grass*, by Rolf Aggestam (1983, in Swedish).

Carl L. Anderson

Bibliography

Allen, Gay Wilson. "Whitman in Denmark and Norway." *Walt Whitman & the World*. Ed. Gay Wilson Allen and Ed Folsom. Iowa City: U of Iowa P, 1995. 357–362.

Anderson, Carl L. "Whitman in Sweden." *Walt Whitman & the World*. Ed. Gay Wilson Allen and Ed Folsom. Iowa City: U of Iowa P, 1995. 339–351.

Naess, Harald. *Knut Hamsun og Amerika*. Oslo: Gyldendal Norsk Forlag, 1969.

Peltola, Niilo. "Whitman in Finland." *Walt Whitman & the World*. Ed. Gay Wilson Allen and Ed Folsom. Iowa City: U of Iowa P, 1995. 381–385.

Schyberg, Frederik. *Walt Whitman*. Trans. Evie Allison Allen. New York: Columbia UP, 1951.

See also ALLEN, GAY WILSON; INTERCULTURALITY; SCHYBERG, FREDERIK

"Scented Herbage of My Breast" (1860)
The second of the "Calamus" poems continues many of the themes introduced in the opening poem. Once again there is a sense of awakening and release, represented here in the figure of the "herbage" (or "blossoms," in the manuscript) that is brought out of its concealment. Whitman shifts subtly from chest hair to pubic hair, and from the body to the earth, from leaves of grass to the leaves of his book. He struggles against an allegorical, transcendental tradition that would read the herbage as "emblematic," seeking instead a way of speaking directly. This new speech amounts to a coming to awareness, a rejection of false identity ("the sham that was proposed to me" in 1860, originally "the costume, the play," later dropped altogether), and a new mission to speak for comrades.

The context for this discovery is a contemplation of death and rebirth, stimulated perhaps by the model of Osiris, represented as sprouting leaves of grain. Whitman links death and repression, the newly freed self being like someone reborn. In his manuscript revisions Whitman apparently sought to make less precise his original conception of the power of sexual denial. The "burning and throbbing" of line 8, with its incomplete phallic desire, was originally joined to "O these hungering desires!," which made the nature of the refusal as well as of what "will one day be accomplished" clear. This cutting is consistent with a general attempt to reduce the specific references to sexuality, resulting in a certain coy indefiniteness. Thus "I will sound myself and love" became "I will sound myself and comrades," while the concluding apostrophe to Death lost its correlative "and manly Love."

The joining of love and death in "Herbage" is an early expression of a theme that would dominate later poems such as "When Lilacs Last in the Dooryard Bloom'd." The ending of the poem reflects Whitman's Platonism, in its evocation of a "real reality" that lies "behind the mask of materials." Whitman returned repeatedly to his attempt to understand death, finding consolation in cycles of rebirth and reincarnation, and in an ascension "to the atmosphere of lovers," a Platonic paradise. His view of writing sees the poet's words as leaves or blossoms that may only flower after his death, but that can offer a testament to his life and desires.

James E. Miller emphasizes the poem's treatment of spiritual love, while Edwin Miller calls attention to a simultaneous exhibition and sublimation of desire. Killingsworth sees a rich psychological drama with the poet-lover fearing rejection, but ultimately going beyond the individual self. Almost all readers remark the complexity of thought and imagery in the poem, unusual in the context of "Calamus."

Robert K. Martin

Bibliography

Killingsworth, M. Jimmie. *Whitman's Poetry of the Body: Sexuality, Politics, and the Text.* Chapel Hill: U of North Carolina P, 1989.

Miller, Edwin Haviland. *Walt Whitman's Poetry: A Psychological Journey.* Boston: Houghton Mifflin, 1968.

Miller, James E., Jr. *A Critical Guide to "Leaves of Grass."* Chicago: U of Chicago P, 1957.

See also "CALAMUS"; COMRADESHIP; DEATH; LOVE; SEX AND SEXUALITY

Scholarship, Trends in Whitman

Because Whitman was a poet who claimed a strong identity between his life and his work, as well as his life and his times, it is not easy to separate the scholarship he has inspired into neat categories and types—biographical, bibliographical, historical, formal, and linguistic. All these approaches appear as trends that rise to prominence at various moments of history, but always interpenetrate and overlap one another. The richness of this scholarly tradition has been matched by the astounding proliferation of studies. By the time of the poet's death in 1892, Whitman scholarship was already in full swing, with friends like John Burroughs and literary executors like Richard Maurice Bucke and Horace Traubel leading the way. By the time of the centennial of the first edition of *Leaves of Grass* in 1955, the bibliography of works about Whitman was growing at the average rate of one hundred items per year, in the estimate of Donald Kummings.

Though from the time of Bucke and Burroughs a mingling of scholarly approaches has been the norm, the great tradition of Whitman scholarship has been biographical; scholars appear to have accepted the word of the poet who named his most famous poem "Song of Myself." The first biographical works appeared in the years just after the Civil War. Whitman's circle of literary admirers rushed to his defense when he was dismissed from a government clerkship allegedly for writing an immoral book. The first defender was William Douglas O'Connor, whose famous 1866 pamphlet *The Good Gray Poet* argued that Whitman was not only blameless in the face of the attacks upon himself and his book, but in fact superior both in character and artistic accomplishment to most poets of the day. The picture of Whitman as a man of extraordinary moral and artistic development, the genius of the American people—in the sense of both his personal ability and his representative power—is yet more fully developed in Burroughs's *Notes on Walt Whitman as Poet and Person* (1867). *Notes* stresses the republican theme, the view of Whitman as a kind of medium for the spirit of American life. Whitman preferred this interpretation to the view of himself as a special case of poetic genius and fostered it by actually contributing prose accounts of his life as a representative American character to the biographies of both Bucke and Burroughs. In the later work, *Whitman: A Study,* published in 1896 after the death of the master, Burroughs all but abandoned the republican theme and emphasized the poet's uniqueness and exalted status among men of genius. In the view of his other contemporaneous biographer, Richard Maurice Bucke, the poet's greatness was the result of an experience of special insight, a dawning of "cosmic consciousness" literally recorded in "Song of Myself," section 5, and elsewhere in the poems. In his 1883 *Walt Whitman,* Bucke suggested that this mystical experience explains Whitman's transcendence of his character as a minor writer of fiction, poems, and journalism before *Leaves of Grass* and his ascendance to the role of poet-prophet of democracy suddenly in 1855. In the chapter on Whitman in his 1903 *Cosmic Consciousness,* now a classic work of popular mysticism, Bucke universalizes Whitman's significance and puts his experience on a par with that of Jesus and Buddha. Though this view was discredited by the scholarship of high modernism in the first half of the twentieth century, when scientific skepticism, philosophical materialism, and existentialism ruled the day, the prophetic cast and mystical character of *Leaves of Grass* has again been treated seriously in more recent anthropologically oriented studies such as Lewis Hyde's *The Gift: Imagination and the Erotic Life of Property* (1979) and George Hutchinson's *The Ecstatic Whitman: Literary Shamanism & the Crisis of the Union* (1986), both of which relate Whitman's mysticism to his vision of democratic politics, as well as in the thematic study *Minor Prophecy: Walt Whitman's New American Religion* (1989) by David Kuebrich.

Biographical work after the turn of the century reflected the professionalization of literary scholarship by striving for objectivity and impartiality, treating Whitman as a literary subject rather than as an extraordinary man. Even Horace Traubel's multivolume and worshipful *With Walt Whitman in Camden* advanced this trend by carefully, indeed minutely, documenting the sayings and activities of Whitman in his last years. Henry Bryan Binns's *A Life of Walt Whitman* (1905), which has the distinction of being the first modern literary biography, is remembered mainly for perpetrating the questionable story that Whitman fell in love with a mysterious woman during his brief stay in New Orleans and even fathered children by her. The next year saw the publication of Bliss Perry's *Walt Whitman,* a book distinguished by greater scholarly caution and a deeper interest in the poems and the circumstances of their composition. Perry rejects the idea of sudden inspiration as a way of accounting for the emergence of *Leaves of Grass* in 1855, arguing for a slower, steadier development of the poet's artistic ability. This claim formed the basis of an important trend in Whitman scholarship. The study of Whitman's reading and early works of prose and poetry as antecedents of his greatest poems became the key concern of books such as Floyd Stovall's *The Foreground of "Leaves of Grass"* (1974) and a number of collections and critical evaluations of the poet's journalistic writings by such scholars as Thomas Brasher, Joseph Jay Rubin, and Emory Holloway. Holloway's own detailed study of Whitman's published and unpublished writings outside of *Leaves of Grass* undergirded his 1926 biography *Whitman: An Interpretation in Narrative.* While giving a full and influential account of Whitman's literary apprenticeship and the changes observable in the different editions of *Leaves of Grass*, notably the decline of the radical power of the early *Leaves* in the later editions, Holloway stubbornly refused to consider the strong evidence of homoeroticism that he himself uncovered in Whitman's personal experience and works and stayed with the heterosexual myths inherited from Binns.

After Holloway, Whitman biography developed in two directions—toward an increasing concern with Whitman's relation to his social and historical context, on the one hand, and toward an intensifying interest in the texts of his most important writings, on the other. These two biographical types—"life and times" studies and "critical biography"—prepared the way for the further development of historical criticism and textually oriented criticism, including formalist, structuralist, and poststructuralist studies.

In the historical vein, the way was prepared by Vernon Parrington's *Main Currents in American Thought* (1927) and Newton Arvin's *Whitman* (1938), both of which analyze Whitman's poems in light of contemporaneous politics and social movements, and by Henry Seidel Canby's 1943 biography *Walt Whitman: An American.* Unlike the historical materialists Parrington and Arvin, Canby accepted the importance earlier biographies assigned to the development of the inner life of the poet but insisted on placing this inner development in a dialectical relationship with Whitman's sensitivity to changes in his social and political milieu. With this double emphasis, he anticipated the feminist contention that the personal is political (and vice versa). Unfortunately, Canby's influence was diminished because his work was separated from scholarship pursuing the same social and historical spirit by the intervention of the era of New Criticism, when formalist approaches prevailed and historical context was reduced to "background." When historical criticism did reemerge in the 1970s, however, it was destined to become the dominant trend of Whitman scholarship. Thematic studies have followed Parrington, Arvin, and Canby in emphasizing, for example, the significance of physical life and sexuality in the texts and contexts of Whitman's poems. Such is the case with Robert K. Martin's *The Homosexual Tradition in American Poetry* (1979), Harold Aspiz's *Walt Whitman and the Body Beautiful* (1980), Charley Shively's *Calamus Lovers: Whitman's Working Class Camerados* (1987), M. Jimmie Killingsworth's *Whitman's Poetry of the Body: Sexuality, Politics, and the Text* (1989), Michael Moon's *Disseminating Whitman: Revision and Corporeality in "Leaves of Grass"* (1991), and Byrne Fone's *Masculine Landscapes: Walt Whitman and the Homoerotic Text* (1992). New studies of Whitman's political vision have also appeared, including M. Wynn Thomas's *The Lunar Light of Whitman's Poetry* (1987), Betsy Erkkila's *Whitman the Political Poet* (1989), and Martin Klammer's study of Whitman's attitudes toward slavery, *Whitman, Slavery, and the Emergence of "Leaves of Grass"* (1995). Other cultural studies include James Dougherty's book on the image of the city in *Leaves of Grass, Walt Whitman and the Citizen's Eye* (1993) and Ed Folsom's consideration of four surprisingly intertwined themes—baseball, American Indians, photography, and lexicography—in *Walt Whitman's Native Representations* (1994). The life and times tradition inaugurated by Canby came full circle with the 1995 publication of David S. Reynolds's *Walt Whitman's America: A Cultural Biography.*

Though Whitman was certainly no darling of the New Critics in the years of their dominance, textually oriented criticism of his work did not lag during the 1950s, 1960s, and 1970s, and work in this area continues vigorously today. Somewhat ironically, biographies also led the way in this work, beginning with Roger Asselineau's *The Evolution of Walt Whitman*, the French version of which appeared in 1954, followed by an English translation in 1960. Asselineau devoted a volume to the development of Whitman the man and another volume to the evolution of *Leaves of Grass* as a book, thus defining the twin focus that would concern a number of critical biographers from Gay Wilson Allen (*The Solitary Singer*, 1955) to Justin Kaplan (*Walt Whitman: A Life*, 1980), Jerome Loving (*Emerson, Whitman, and the American Muse*, 1982), and Paul Zweig (*Walt Whitman: The Making of a Poet*, 1984) and including the psychoanalytical work of Edwin Haviland Miller (*Walt Whitman's Poetry: A Psychological Journey*, 1968) and Stephen A. Black (*Whitman's Journeys into Chaos: A Psychoanalytical Study of the Poetic Process*, 1975). These scholars differ from earlier biographers in their critical spirit. They are critical in two senses: they leave off the hero worship of the earlier writers and treat the poet with attitudes ranging from respectful distance (as in Allen, Kaplan, Loving, and Zweig) to clinical skepticism (as in Miller and Black), and they are more likely than the earlier writers to give critical readings and extended interpretations of the poems. Of them all, Allen's *Solitary Singer*, a biography written in the heyday of New Criticism, has had the most sustained influence on Whitman studies. Allen set the standard for later biography, but he also initiated a tradition of close reading of Whitman's texts, a distinction he shared with Richard Chase, whose ground-breaking work of rhetorical criticism, *Walt Whitman Reconsidered* (1955), was published in the same year as Allen's biography. An interest in close reading also informed the work of James E. Miller, Jr. (*A Critical Guide to "Leaves of Grass,"* 1957) and Howard J. Waskow (*Whitman: Explorations in Form*, 1966). This tradition has evolved in recent years to accommodate new theories of language and textuality. Works in this vein include C. Carroll Hollis's *Language and Style in "Leaves of Grass"* (1983), James Perrin Warren's *Walt Whitman's Language Experiment* (1990), Mark Bauerlein's *Whitman and the American Idiom* (1991), Tenney Nathanson's *Whitman's Presence: Body, Voice, and Writing in "Leaves of Grass"* (1992), and a book that mingles semiotics with political and historical study, Kerry Larson's *Whitman's Drama of Consensus* (1988).

In addition to these strong threads and concentrated periods of Whitman scholarship, there have been scattered studies of reception and influence—notably the work of Esther Shephard, Harold Blodgett, Gay Wilson Allen, V.K. Chari, Harold Bloom, Betsy Erkkila, Kenneth Price, and Ed Folsom—that over the years have accumulated into an impressive account of Whitman's position as a major author in world literature. In textual and bibliographical scholarship, the same cumulative effect has been achieved, thanks to such scholars as William White, Arthur Golden, Scott Giantvalley, Donald Kummings, Joel Myerson, and the various editors of the New York edition of Whitman's works. Much remains to be done, however, before bibliographical work and reception study can be said to match the strongest tradition of Whitman scholarship in biography and historical criticism.

M. Jimmie Killingsworth

Bibliography

Allen, Gay Wilson. *The New Walt Whitman Handbook*. 1975. New York: New York UP, 1986.
———. *Walt Whitman Handbook*. 1946. New York: Hendricks House, 1962.
Giantvalley, Scott. *Walt Whitman, 1838–1939: A Reference Guide*. Boston: Hall, 1981.
Hindus, Milton, ed. *Walt Whitman: The Critical Heritage*. New York: Barnes and Noble, 1971.
Killingsworth, M. Jimmie. *The Growth of "Leaves of Grass": The Organic Tradition in Whitman Studies*. Columbia, S.C.: Camden House, 1993.
Kummings, Donald D. *Walt Whitman, 1940–1975: A Reference Guide*. Boston: Hall, 1982.

See also ALLEN, GAY WILSON; ARVIN, NEWTON; ASSELINEAU, ROGER; BIBLIOGRAPHIES; BINNS,

HENRY BRYAN; BIOGRAPHIES; BUCKE, RICHARD MAURICE; BURROUGHS, JOHN AND URSULA; CANBY, HENRY SEIDEL; CHASE, RICHARD VOLNEY; CRITICS, WHITMAN'S; HOLLOWAY, EMORY; MILLER, EDWIN HAVILAND; MILLER, JAMES EDWIN, JR.; O'CONNOR, WILLIAM DOUGLAS; PERRY, BLISS; TRAUBEL, HORACE L.

Schyberg, Frederik (1905–1950)

Frederik Schyberg edited a selection of Walt Whitman's poetry in Copenhagen in 1933. In the same year he wrote a companion biography to the collection entitled simply *Walt Whitman*. While it built on Jean Catel's *Walt Whitman: La naissance du poète,* published in Paris in 1929, Schyberg's biography is notable because it not only places Whitman in a world context, but more importantly because it blends biography and textual issues. Schyberg traces the changes and alterations between the various editions of *Leaves of Grass,* suggesting Whitman's psychological development at each stage of the composing process. Schyberg sees biography affecting text just as text reveals biography. It was Schyberg, for example, who first suggested in a formal biography that the doomed love affair which apparently gave rise to "Live Oak with Moss" was homosexual in nature when other biographers pointed to the actress Ellen Grey as the love interest.

Schyberg also emphasizes, for the first time in Whitman biography, that Whitman was not out of touch with his age, but rather was caught up in the social and moral currents of his time, reacting to people and events around him on an intimate level. Whitman operates, then, for Schyberg as a prophetic mystic not only seeing his own surroundings clearly, but able to see them in a larger spiritual context as well. This provides the basis for Whitman's worldwide appeal, according to Schyberg.

Walt Whitman was translated into English by Evie Allison Allen and first published in the United States of America in 1951.

David G. Miller

Bibliography

Allen, Gay Wilson. *The New Walt Whitman Handbook.* 1975. New York: New York UP, 1986.

Killingsworth, M. Jimmie. *The Growth of "Leaves of Grass": The Organic Tradition in Whitman Studies.* Columbia, S.C.: Camden House, 1993.

See also ALLEN, GAY WILSON; BIOGRAPHIES; CATEL, JEAN; GREY, ELLEN; SCANDINAVIA, WHITMAN IN

Science

In the 1855 Preface to *Leaves of Grass* Whitman asserts that scientists are "the lawgivers of poets and their construction underlies the structure of every perfect poem," and credits the scientist with generating the "fatherstuff" that creates "sinewy races of bards." As we might expect in a relationship depicted in familial terms, however, Whitman claims the dominant position for the poet-son: "In the beauty of poems are the tuft and final applause of science" (*Comprehensive* 718–719). Still, Whitman's assertion that scientific and poetic laws are interconvertible sets the terms of a lifelong engagement with science. In 1876, with his major works behind him, he wrote in the Centennial edition Preface that "Without being a scientist, I have thoroughly adopted the conclusions of the great Savans and Experimentalists of our time, and of the last one hundred years, and they have interiorly tinged the chyle of all my verse for purposes beyond" (*Comprehensive* 752). One of his last poems, "L. of G.'s Purport" (1891), uses the most important scientific idea of the century, evolution, to summarize the animating idea of his poetry: "To span vast realms of space and time, / Evolution—the cumulative—growths and generations" (*Comprehensive* 555).

Whitman did not have to wait until Charles Darwin's *Origin of Species* in 1859 to be introduced to a theory of evolution. The publication in London in 1844 of Robert Chambers's *Vestiges of the Natural History of Creation,* a lucid exposition of the "development hypothesis," sparked a wide-ranging debate in the press both in Great Britain and America. Chambers combined the nebular hypothesis of Pierre Simon Laplace with evidence for transmutation of the species drawn from such sciences as geology, chemistry, embryology, paleontology and plant biology to offer a revolutionary theory of the origins, development, and destiny of the human species. An attack on fixed hierarchies, *Vestiges* became associated with all manner of radical causes. Despite some egregious errors, *Vestiges* withstood the attempts of the scientific and clerical establishments to crush it, and likely became Whitman's most important source for science. Section 44 of "Song of Myself," a creation story told from the perspective of the latest science, reframes *Vestiges* in thirty-six lines.

During Whitman's pre-1855 career as a journalist, New York became the nation's center for the popular exploration of science. Astronomers, geologists, and naturalists lectured to capacity lyceum audiences and their talks were routinely reproduced verbatim in the daily press. Whitman covered some of these lectures himself, praising the eloquent Cincinnati astronomer O.M. Mitchel in an editorial for the Brooklyn *Daily Eagle* on 20 March 1847 which urged the construction of an observatory in Brooklyn (*Gathering* 2:146–149).

On 1 January 1851 the journalist Parke Godwin wrote in "The Last Half-Century," published in the New York *Evening Post,* that "it is within the memory of men still young that the most important doctrines of Astronomy, of Geology, of Optics, of Mineralogy, of Chemistry, of Zoology, of Comparative and Fossil Anatomy, of Paleontology, of Magnetism, of Electricity, of Galvanism, of Actinism, etc. have been first published" (Godwin 158). Godwin argued in the essay, which he included in *Out of the Past,* published by Putnam in 1870, that discoveries in those fields—each important to Whitman—revealed connections between the human and natural worlds: "modern science, lately threatened to be engulfed in the deluge of its own materials, finds its chief glory in exploring the wonderful analogies of creation" (169). Godwin's reference to "wonderful analogies" reflects a fundamental assumption of the tradition of *Naturphilosophie* as expounded variously by Friedrich Schelling, Samuel Taylor Coleridge, and Ralph Waldo Emerson, that there exist fundamental connections between mind and matter, self and external world. In "Carlyle from American Points of View" from *Specimen Days,* Whitman explained that Schelling's "answer" to the question of the relationship of self to the external world is that "the same general and particular intelligence, passion, even the standards of right and wrong, which exist in a conscious and formulated state in man, exist in an unconscious state, or in perceptible analogies, throughout the entire universe of external Nature . . . thus making the impalpable human mind, and concrete Nature . . . convertible, and in . . . essence one" (*Complete* 895). Artist and scientist share the work of exploring the cosmos and articulating the connections between the self and the external world.

At the heart of this tradition is the scientific concept of polarity, which applies to an ongoing, dynamic process of reconciling opposing forces within nature. The German nature philosophers thought of all nature in terms of a dynamic, ongoing moving system which was propelled by the interaction of opposed but related forces, including the real and ideal, male and female, repulsion and attraction, centrifugal and centripetal, and self and external world. (Reconciling such opposites is both a subject and a structural principle in "Song of Myself.") The "development hypothesis" or evolution is a logical consequence of the idea of polarity, for the progressive development of the universe takes place through the resolution of the fundamental opposites and antitheses in the world. A far-reaching egalitarianism is also implicit in this view of the world, because it does away with the notion of fixed hierarchies and substitutes a world in which change is an ongoing process. Since each side in the polar relationship contributes to the higher synthesis, it is impossible to rank one above the other. Hence this scientific tradition could be interpreted as supporting democracy. In the 1876 Preface, Whitman linked science and democracy by remarking that *Leaves of Grass* is "an utterance adjusted to, perhaps born of, Democracy and Modern Science" (*Comprehensive* 751). During the 1840s and 1850s, as Godwin's "The Last Half-Century" implies, romantic ideas such as polarity, equality, evolution, and the principle of the conservation of energy (the first law of thermodynamics) were finding empirical verification, confirming the assumptions of this tradition.

Whitman was also attracted to phrenology, mesmerism, and other pseudosciences, which were the subject of great interest by a large and broad cross section of the population. Parke Godwin referred to these fields as "not yet science" and spoke of the "wonderful manifestations of Animal Magnetism, which are too well authenticated as facts to be denied, though not yet referred to any satisfactory laws" (168). Harold Aspiz has shown that in such works as "I Sing the Body Electric," "Song of Myself," and "There was a Child Went Forth," Whitman incorporates ideas and images drawn from various pseudosciences. But he wrote as a poet, not as a scientist, and so avoided a literalism in the use of terms that would ultimately prove limiting. In a notebook entry included by Richard Maurice Bucke in *Notes and Fragments,* he reminded himself, "Remember in scientific and similar allusions that the theories of Geology,

History, Language, &c., &c., are continually changing. Be careful to put in only what *must* be appropriate centuries hence" (55). This balance between a willingness to explore all manner of new thinking and a fundamental conservatism in the area that mattered most, language, served Whitman well. He approached poetry and science as ways of knowing that were complementary but different. As important as science was to him, he carefully reframed its concepts within his poetry.

Whitman's ability to make use of scientific laws to articulate the interconnected lives of human beings with the external world is nowhere more evident than in "Song of Myself." The affectionate, sexual, haughty, electrical speaker articulates analogous qualities in the external world; informed by the principle of polarity, he depicts in section 3 the unfolding of self and the cosmos: "Out of the dimness opposite equals advance, always substance and increase, always sex, / Always a knit of identity, always distinction, always a breed of life." The poem's most dramatic instance of the reconciliation of polar opposites occurs in section 5, where the speaker unites body and soul in an ecstatic union. What begins as a statement of equality between two opposites, "I believe in you my soul, the other I am must not abase itself to you, / And you must not be abased to the other, " ends in rapturous bliss: "Swiftly arose and spread around me the peace and knowledge that pass all the argument of the earth." That reconciliation leads to new insights and launches speaker and reader on a voyage of discovery. In bringing together supposed opposites, the speaker articulates the principle of cosmic evolution: "All goes onward and outward, nothing collapses, / And to die is different from what any one supposed, and luckier" (section 6).

The theme of immortality is based on the scientific principles of Correlation of Forces and Conservation of Energy, which were just then being expounded. Chemists and physicists alike—including Justus Liebig and Michael Faraday—were demonstrating that not even the smallest known element ever disappears but that elements are constantly being transformed. These ideas are developed throughout "Song of Myself," as in section 49, where the speaker offers an apostrophe: "O suns—O grass of graves—O perpetual transfers and promotions." This idea supports the fluid identity of a speaker who in section 16 "resist[s] any thing better than my own diversity." These principles

lie at the heart as well of the 1856 masterpiece "This Compost."

The process of articulating such fundamental principles gives the speaker imaginative control over them. In section 44 of "Song of Myself" he reverses the process of evolution and imaginatively returns to the beginning of time, "the huge first Nothing, I know I was even there." His ability to recall all of evolutionary history is bolstered by another idea of romantic nature philosophy, that ontogeny recapitulates phylogeny: "Before I was born out of my mother generations guided me, / My embryo has never been torpid, nothing could overlay it." Even as he can reverse time, so the speaker, "the acme of things accomplish'd, and I am encloser of things to be," projects himself into the future, combining biology and astronomy, space and time, in a cosmic dance: "My feet strike an apex of the apices of the stairs, / On every step bunches of ages, and larger bunches between the steps, / All below duly travel'd—and still I mount and mount." In celebrating the evolutionary process—"Births have brought us richness and variety, / And other births will bring us richness and variety"—Whitman affirms the egalitarian principle everywhere present in the cosmos: "I do not call one greater and one smaller, / That which fills its period and place is equal to any."

Given the centrality of science within the poem, the speaker feels the need to define boundaries, and in section 23 directly addresses the scientists: "Gentlemen, to you the first honors always! / Your facts are useful, and yet they are not my dwelling, / I but enter by them to an area of my dwelling." During the antebellum period the growing prominence of science and its increasing specialization threatened to displace writers. The word "scientist" had been coined to refer to professional investigators, who were claiming for themselves the primary authority to know the external world. Whitman met the issue head-on, appropriating for his own purposes the astounding insights of the scientists. But, as John Burroughs wrote in an essay on Whitman included in *Birds and Poets with Other Papers,* in his "thorough assimilation of the modern sciences," he "transmut[ed] them for strong poetic nutriment" (241).

In "Great are the Myths," an 1855 poem which he dropped from *Leaves of Grass* in 1881, he claimed that language itself "is the mightiest of the sciences, / It is the fulness, color, form, diversity of the earth, and of men and women, and of all qualities and processes, / It is greater than wealth—it is greater than buildings, ships, religions, paintings, music" (1860 *Leaves*). The poet's challenge, then, is to go beyond the secondhand reports, including those of scientists, to use words that can be presented as the authentic speech of nature itself. Whitman's "A Song of the Rolling Earth" calls attention to the artificiality of conventional language by asking, "Were you thinking that those were the words, those upright lines? those curves, angles, dots? / No, those are not the words, the substantial words are in the ground and sea, / They are in the air, they are in you" (section 1). Whitman's goal was to write a poetry that encompasses the "substantial" words of nature itself: "There can be no theory of any account unless it corroborate the theory of the earth, / No politics, song, religion, behavior, or what not, is of account, unless it compare with the amplitude of the earth, / Unless it face the exactness, vitality, impartiality, rectitude, of the earth" (section 3).

Similarly, the poem "Kosmos," an implicit reference to Alexander von Humboldt's great five-volume scientific compendium which had appeared in German under the title *Kosmos* and was during the 1850s appearing in a translation published by the Harpers, sets as a goal for human conduct the ability to incorporate into our identities those qualities that scientists and poets alike discover in the material world. The "kosmos" is that individual "Who includes diversity and is Nature, / Who is the amplitude of the earth, and the coarseness and sexuality of the earth, and the great charity of the earth, and the equilibrium also." Implicit in this view is the idea that it is not the poet alone or the scientist alone who is capable of articulating the meaning of the natural world. Each of us, in becoming a "kosmos," takes on that function and "out of the theory of the earth and of his or her body understands by subtle analogies all other theories, / The theory of a city, a poem, and of the large politics of these States."

Leaves of Grass itself fulfills the requirement that Whitman set for the "kosmos," who is to be an individual who creates a self in the context of the fullest possible understanding of the external world. The kosmos is one who "believes not only in our globe with its sun and moon, but in other globes with their suns and moons, / Who, constructing the house of himself or herself, not for a day but for all time, sees races, eras, dates, generations, / The past, the future, dwelling there, like space, inseparable together" ("Kosmos"). The laws of science were essential building blocks for Whitman in that magnificent and haughty construction.

Robert J. Scholnick

Bibliography

Aspiz, Harold. *Walt Whitman and the Body Beautiful*. Urbana: U of Illinois P, 1980.

Beaver, Joseph. *Walt Whitman: Poet of Science*. Morningside Heights, N.Y.: Kings Crown, 1951.

Burroughs, John. *Birds and Poets*. 1877. Boston: Houghton Mifflin, 1904.

Godwin, Parke. *Out of the Past*. New York: Putnam, 1870.

Reynolds, David S. *Walt Whitman's America: A Cultural Biography*. New York: Knopf, 1995.

Scholnick, Robert J. "'The Password Primeval': Whitman's Use of Science in 'Song of Myself.'" *Studies in the American Renaissance 1986*. Ed. Joel Myerson. Charlottesville: UP of Virginia, 1986. 385–425.

Whitman, Walt. *Complete Poetry and Collected Prose*. Ed. Justin Kaplan. New York: Library of America, 1982.

———. *The Gathering of the Forces*. Ed. Cleveland Rodgers and John Black. 2 vols. New York: Putnam, 1920.

———. *Leaves of Grass: Comprehensive Reader's Edition*. Ed. Harold W. Blodgett and Sculley Bradley. New York: New York UP, 1965.

———. *Notes and Fragments*. 1899. Ed. Richard Maurice Bucke. Folcroft, Pa.: Folcroft Library Editions, 1972.

See also BROOKLYN, NEW YORK; DARWIN, CHARLES; EVOLUTION; HUMBOLDT, ALEXANDER VON; "I SING THE BODY ELECTRIC"; "L. OF G.'S PURPORT"; LAMARCK, JEAN BAPTISTE; LIEBIG, JUSTUS; MITCHEL, O.M. (ORMSBY MACKNIGHT); PHRENOLOGY; PSEUDOSCIENCE; "SONG OF MYSELF"; TECHNOLOGY; "THERE WAS A CHILD WENT FORTH"; "THIS COMPOST"

Scott, Sir Walter (1771–1832)

Sir Walter Scott was one of the most influential and prolific literary figures of the early nineteenth century. Scott achieved fame primarily as a writer of narrative poems, which include *The Lay of the Last Minstrel* (1805), *Marmion* (1808), and *The Lady of the Lake* (1810). After George Gordon, Lord Byron displaced Scott as Britain's most popular poet, Scott turned to novel writing. As a novelist, Scott is best remembered for his Waverley Novels, which include *Waverley* (1814) and *The Heart of Midlothian* (1818). Also a talented scholar and editor, Scott compiled traditional Scottish ballads into a three-volume text entitled *Minstrelsy of the Scottish Border* (1802–1803), and he edited the works of John Dryden and Jonathan Swift.

First introduced to Scott's writing as a child, Whitman describes himself to Horace Traubel in the 1880s as a passionate reader of Scott's work, insisting, for instance, that Scott "does not stale for me" (*With Walt Whitman* 2:243) and even that Scott's novels are his "chief pleasure nowadays" (2:251). Whitman also tells Traubel that Scott had greatly influenced his own writing, particularly *Leaves of Grass,* though Whitman's description of the nature of this influence is vague—Scott, he says, as well as James Fenimore Cooper, taught him to "look for the things that take life forward" (1:97).

Though Whitman admired Scott's artistic talents, he censured his Tory political beliefs. In two articles he wrote which appeared in the Brooklyn *Daily Eagle* in 1846 and 1847, Whitman includes Scott among British Tory authors who glorified the aristocracy in their writings and whose works posed a potential threat to the extension of democracy in America. Whitman repeats his assertion that Scott's antidemocratic sentiment made the political message of his writing unfit for an American audience in his essay "Poetry To-Day—Shakspere—the Future": "Walter Scott and Tennyson, like Shakspere, exhale that principle of caste which we have come on earth to destroy" (*Prose Works* 2:476). Whitman, however, does not state that Scott's works should be dismissed because of their elitist overtones. In the same essay, Whitman insists that he, as well as every American, owes a "debt of thanks" to Scott for being the "noblest, healthiest, cheeriest romancer that ever lived" (2:477).

Vickie L. Taft

Bibliography
Traubel, Horace. *With Walt Whitman in Camden.* Vol. 1. Boston: Small, Maynard, 1906; Vol. 2. New York: Mitchell Kennerley, 1915.
Whitman, Walt. *The Gathering of the Forces.* Ed. Cleveland Rodgers and John Black. 2 vols. New York: Putnam, 1920.
———. *Prose Works 1892.* Ed. Floyd Stovall. 2 vols. New York: New York UP, 1963–1964.

See also FEUDALISM; INFLUENCES ON WHITMAN, PRINCIPAL; "POETRY TO-DAY IN AMERICA—SHAKSPERE—THE FUTURE"

Sculptors and Sculpture

Although Whitman demonstrated less concern with sculpture than with either painting or photography, he thought highly enough of it to classify himself as "one among the wellbeloved stonecutters" in the 1855 Preface to *Leaves of Grass* (*Leaves* 714). Whitman's scattered comments on sculpture are found principally in his early journalistic writings and in his later conversations with Horace Traubel.

In both published reviews and private commentaries, Whitman endorsed the idealist stance of the transcendentalists, which placed a premium on the moral and spiritual value of a work of art, while generally disregarding its technical requirements. As with painting, Whitman made little distinction between original works of sculpture and cheap reproductions intended primarily for the home. Above all Whitman admired sculpture's emphasis on the human figure and took strong exception to the complete absence of a human presence in works like the Washington Monument in the nation's capital and Boston's "chimney-shaped" Bunker Hill Monument (*Uncollected* 1:242). Despite his fondness for the cemetery, Whitman found tombstone inscriptions more compelling than the sculpted monuments.

During his Brooklyn years Whitman reserved his most explicit praise for the work of Henry Kirke Brown, an American sculptor whose 1846 solo exhibition at the National Academy of Design followed four years of study in Florence and Rome. In the Brooklyn *Daily Eagle,* Whitman cited Brown as an artist of "genius and industry" (*Uncollected* 1:142). Whitman later became a regular visitor at Brown's Brooklyn studio, where he enjoyed the company of a lively group of painters, writers, and sculptors, many of whom, like John Quincy Adams Ward, would establish distinguished careers over the next quarter century. Brown was a leader in the transformation of American sculpture from its emphasis on neoclassical forms and mythological subjects toward a more robust naturalism and a concern with nativist themes. Whitman appreciated both the workshop atmosphere and the free exchange of ideas that distinguished Brown's studio from the more hidebound literary circles of writers like Henry Wadsworth Longfellow. The experience helped to stimulate both Whitman's visualist poetics and his maturing national consciousness.

In his later years in Camden Whitman enjoyed the friendship of writer, editor, and sculptor Sidney H. Morse. The founding editor of *The Radical* and a self-taught artist of only modest talent, Morse constituted a striking contrast to either Brown or Ward. Although Morse's initial effort at modeling Whitman's likeness, undertaken in Philadelphia in 1876, proved a miserable failure, a later attempt, one of several executed on a return visit in 1887, garnered some of Whitman's highest praise. Whitman much preferred Morse's bust to the painted portraits of either John White Alexander or Herbert Gilchrist; at times he even preferred it to Thomas Eakins's portrait. Whitman regarded the bust's rough-hewn quality and focused treatment of the eyes as tropes for the rugged individualism and visionary presence of his verse, judging it "exceedingly fine—a revelation of what art can do at its best, when it becomes nature!" (Traubel 63). In 1889, at Whitman's urging, the bust appeared as the frontispiece in *Camden's Compliment*.

In the last year of Whitman's life Samuel Murray and William R. O'Donovan, both associates of Thomas Eakins, commenced bust-length sculptures of the poet in Eakins's Philadelphia studio. Housebound and in declining health, Whitman seems never to have seen either work. He did, however, greatly admire a profile photograph which Murray took in preparation for his bust, inscribing one print "Walt Whitman (Sculptor's profile May 1891)." Following Whitman's death, Murray, accompanied by Eakins, made plaster casts of Whitman's head, hand, and shoulder.

Ruth L. Bohan

Bibliography
Allen, Gay Wilson. "The Iconography of Walt Whitman." *The Artistic Legacy of Walt Whitman*. Ed. Edwin Haviland Miller. New York: New York UP, 1970. 127–152.
Morse, Sidney H. "My Summer With Walt Whitman, 1887." *In Re Walt Whitman*. Ed. Horace L. Traubel, Richard Maurice Bucke, and Thomas B. Harned. Philadelphia: McKay, 1893. 367–391.
Sill, Geoffrey M., and Roberta K. Tarbell, eds. *Walt Whitman and the Visual Arts*. New Brunswick, N.J.: Rutgers UP, 1992.
Traubel, Horace. *With Walt Whitman in Camden*. Ed. Gertrude Traubel and William White. Vol. 6. Carbondale: Southern Illinois UP, 1982.
Whitman, Walt. *Leaves of Grass*. Ed. Sculley Bradley and Harold W. Blodgett. Norton Critical Edition. New York: Norton, 1973.
———. *The Uncollected Poetry and Prose of Walt Whitman*. Ed. Emory Holloway. 2 vols. Garden City, N.Y.: Doubleday, Page, 1921.

See also ART AND DAGUERREOTYPE GALLERIES; EAKINS, THOMAS; PAINTERS AND PAINTING; PHOTOGRAPHS AND PHOTOGRAPHERS

Sea, The

Along with such natural phenomena as the stars, the earth, and the grass, the sea is one of the natural facts that serves as a major religious symbol in *Leaves of Grass*. It has a pervasive presence: making its initial appearance in the third poem, "In Cabin'd Ships at Sea," it frequently reappears throughout the succeeding pages, sometimes rising up prominently to give its name to poems and sequences, for example, "Song for All Seas, All Ships" and "Sea-Drift," but more often serving as a leitmotif that subtly infuses a range of spiritual values. It forms the thematic center of a larger pattern of aquatic symbolism in *Leaves* which includes the rain, sea breezes, rivers, the pond in "Calamus," and other bodies of water such as the swamp of "When Lilacs Last in the Dooryard Bloom'd." Taken as a whole, these waters constitute the most important symbolism in Whitman's poetry.

An adequate approach to Whitman's use of the sea and other waters must consider his symbolic practice within the context of two related aspects of his poetic. The first, which pertains to the existential dynamics of religious symbolism, is grounded in the fact that although the conceptual meaning of a religious symbol can be grasped intellectually, its existential power derives from the natural fact being encountered as a religious experience that speaks to the depths of the human personality, which Whitman terms the "soul." Accordingly, Whitman enjoins his readers to encounter the sea and other symbols not only in *Leaves* but also in the book of nature, inscribed by God, where they can be experienced in their numinous power. In addition, he calls for a spiritually active or "athletic" reader who will bring a prepared soul both to the divine text and the poet's commentary on it.

The second relevant aspect of the poetic pertains to the interpretation of the symbol. Whitman requires that the reader join in the creation of meaning in a process in which the poet provides accompanying "hints" and "suggestions" which the reader is to fuse with the emotions induced by her or his soul's encounter with natural fact. In this way, the reader will be able to realize the text's implied but ineffable spiritual meanings. To grasp Whitman's full range of accompanying commentary, the reader must recognize, as Whitman himself always insisted, that *Leaves* has a considerable amount of textual coherence, and so it must be read not as an anthology of individual poems but as a unified work. Accordingly, it is necessary to attend to the meanings that Whitman's symbols assume as they recur throughout the text, and to bring to any particular instance of a symbol possible related meanings that are attached to its other occurrences in the larger text.

Whitman adapts the structure of his aquatic symbolism to fit diverse thematic contexts and he invests it with a number of related meanings. However, despite this surface multiplicity, an analysis of the essential form and import of this symbolism reveals it to be consistent with the usage of aquatic symbolism in various religious systems: the waters are associated with purification and renewal and with a spiritual matrix or divinity that precedes the creation and takes it back to itself. An awareness of the transhistorical structure and meaning of aquatic symbolism can serve a heuristic purpose in interpreting Whitman's usage; however, it is always necessary to supplement an archetypal reading with the specific nuances of Whitman's text.

In both Whitman's poetry and prose, the sea functions as a symbol of the divine source of humanity and the rest of creation. (This level of meaning is often implicit and must be inferred, as noted above, from its recurring usage.) In "As I Ebb'd with the Ocean of Life," Whitman imagines the entities of the natural world as having emerged from a divine sea, and he establishes his spiritual unity with the soil of Long Island by pointing to their common emergence out of these mysterious waters: "I too have bubbled up, floated the measureless float, and been wash'd on your shores" (section 3). Similarly, in "Crossing Brooklyn Ferry" he draws upon the symbolic power of the waters of the harbor to establish a sense of a timeless spiritual realm, and then he uses this to create a spiritual kinship with his future readers by reminding them that at an earlier time he also proceeded from the same eternal waters as they have: "I too had been struck from the float forever held in solution" (section 5). Conversely, after their finite existence, humans are conceived of as flowing back into these mystical waters. In "To Old Age" human death and the soul's return to God are analogized to an "estuary that enlarges and spreads itself grandly as it pours in the great sea." Whitman uses the same comparison in *Democratic Vistas*: "[M]ortal life is most important with reference to the immortal, the unknown, the spiritual, the only permanently real, which as the ocean waits for and receives the rivers, waits for us each and all" (*Prose Works* 2:403).

In a related use of this symbolism, Whitman frequently compares death and the soul's journey into the afterlife to a ship's voyage into the open sea. The soul's human existence is analogous to a ship at anchor, and the lifting of the anchor symbolizes the soul's emancipation and eligibility for a higher stage of existence characterized by a more comprehensive participation in the divine nature. For instance, in "Joy, Shipmate, Joy!," Whitman depicts himself jubilantly calling to his soul at the moment of death: "The long, long anchorage we leave, / The ship is clear at last, she leaps!"

To a certain extent this symbolism also reflects Whitman's concern to adapt traditional symbols to modern thought, in this case contemporary evolutionary science. For instance, in "Eidólons" (a Greek term Whitman uses for "symbols"), he asserts that the modern poet is "impell'd" to "newer, higher pinnacles / From science and the modern." One important way Whitman altered his thought in response to science was to develop a new understanding of the afterlife as an ongoing process. Because then contemporary theory in geology, astronomy, and pre-Darwinian evolutionary biology indicated a process of ongoing, progressive development, Whitman formulated a new understanding of the afterlife as a process in which the soul continues to advance toward progressively higher stages of participation in divinity. Thus Whitman never describes the soul's embarkation after human death as a final voyage but rather as the soul's entrance into a higher spiritual state: "I will not call it our concluding voyage, / But outset and sure entrance to the truest, best, maturest" ("Sail Out for Good, Eidólon Yacht!"). As Whitman projects the soul's posthuman existence in "Passage to India," it will travel through many future seas, but it can do so without fear ("O daring joy, but safe!"), for "are they not," he asks, "all the seas of God?" (section 9).

With the sea representing the divine or the spiritual in Whitman's poetry, the land represents the natural world, and the shoreline becomes a meeting point between the two worlds and thus an appropriate location for spiritual perception and poetic inspiration. In various poems, for instance, "Out of the Cradle Endlessly Rocking," "By Blue Ontario's Shore," "When I Heard at the Close of the Day," and "As I Ebb'd with the Ocean of Life," Whitman receives an important revelation at the seashore. Also the margins of lesser bodies of water sometimes function in a similar way. For example, in "Calamus" Whitman indicates that the calamus grass is the symbol of a manly love which has a spiritual source and significance by plucking it from the margins of a pond that, like Thoreau's Walden, has an otherworldly depth. After announcing that he has collected symbols from across the world, Whitman passes beyond "the gates" so he can "now draw from the water" the calamus root, "the token of comrades" ("These I Singing in Spring").

Whitman's immersions in the sea are another permutation of the above elements of sea symbolism. They entail a crossing of the mystical juncture and also a form of death and rebirth in which the poet returns to the spiritual source of his being and reemerges in a more pure or noetic state. Thus in section 22 of "Song of Myself," it is appropriate that Whitman immerses himself in the sea just prior to his explicit celebration of the sanctity of his body and sexuality. Similarly, in the most intimate of the "Calamus" poems, "When I Heard at the Close of the Day," Whitman indicates the spiritual dimensions of this love by bathing himself in the sea prior to meeting his comrade. In a related use of this imagery, Whitman describes his effort to sanctify U.S. democracy ("Thou Mother with Thy Equal Brood") and to bless Lincoln's death ("When Lilacs Last in the Dooryard Bloom'd") as a sending of sea sounds and sea breezes across the seashore and onto the land.

Because the sea and associated waters are so pervasive and can assume so many forms, the symbolism is an apt vehicle for conveying a rich multiplicity of meanings. Throughout *Leaves,* in one guise or another, it whispers to the soul messages of divine love, of immortality, of personal renewal, and of the sanctity of the body, manly love, the democratic nation, and the entire creation.

David Kuebrich

Bibliography

Eliade, Mircea. *Patterns in Comparative Religion.* 1958. Trans. Rosemary Sheed. Cleveland: World, 1970.

Kuebrich, David. *Minor Prophecy: Walt Whitman's New American Religion.* Bloomington: Indiana UP, 1989.

Miller, James E., Jr. *Walt Whitman.* Updated ed. Boston: Hall, 1990.

Whitman, Walt. *Prose Works 1892.* Ed. Floyd Stovall. 2 vols. New York: New York UP, 1963–1964.

See also IMMORTALITY; RELIGION; "SEA-DRIFT"; SOUL, THE; SYMBOLISM

"Sea-Drift" (1881)

The "Sea-Drift" cluster, a group of eleven poems including "Out of the Cradle Endlessly Rocking" and "As I Ebb'd with the Ocean of Life," was first incorporated into *Leaves of Grass* in 1881. The cluster consisted of two new poems, two poems from the 1876 *Two Rivulets,* and seven poems from the "Sea-Shore Memories" cluster in the 1871 *Passage to India.* With the exception of "Out of the Cradle" and "As I Ebb'd," both of which were composed in 1859 and went through a series of major revisions, most of the poems in this cluster are short lyrics which underwent little change in their inclusion in "Sea-Drift" in 1881.

Critics and scholars often discuss the relative importance of the "Sea-Drift" cluster to an analysis of the structure of the whole of the 1881 *Leaves of Grass.* Thomas Edward Crawley notes that this arrangement of poems suggests a significant shift from land and pioneering imagery to sea imagery, representing a shift in emphasis from exploration, materialism, and individuality to introspection, spiritualism, and all-inclusive spirituality. Similar readings suggest that the cluster achieves its unity and importance through its description of the poet's encountering, reading, and assimilating the voice and rhythm of the sea, which represents

S

the transfiguration of despair and darkness into faith and hope.

While "Sea-Drift" is often pointed to as a pivotal cluster in *Leaves of Grass,* very few readings closely analyze the entire series of poems. Central to such a reading, and to the debate about the relationship of the cluster to the whole of *Leaves of Grass,* is the question of the poetic voice (or voices) described in the cluster, and especially in "Out of the Cradle" (the first poem in the cluster). Because in "Out of the Cradle" Whitman offers a variety of voices that often conflate into one another, critics generally suggest that the boy-poet at the end of his dramatic encounter with the sea is the same as the mature poet who speaks the opening lines and understands the immortal nature of the human soul. Indeed, Robin Riley Fast argues that "Out of the Cradle" is a microcosm of the "Sea-Drift" cluster as a whole in that both offer a vision of the poet's incipient testing and then eventual confirmation of his poetic vision and vocation; the poems in the cluster after "Out of the Cradle" become for Fast a detailed recounting of the maturation process in which the poet comes to understand mortality and then immortality.

Yet a close inspection of the voices in "Out of the Cradle" suggests a clear demarcation between the voice of the "outsetting bard" who at the end of the poem has learned about loss of love and loss of life and the mature poet who in the opening lines of the poem reveals his knowledge of birth and death as intertwined and recurring processes that point to the immortality of the human soul. Thus the knowledge of the boy-poet in the first poem in the cluster is incomplete; indeed, it is in the remainder of the cluster that Whitman describes the maturation process of the poet and thus closes the gap existing in "Out of the Cradle" between the boy-poet's knowledge of death and the mature poet's understanding of immortality.

Whitman develops this growth through a shift in the primary imagery in the cluster from that of the bird to that of the ship, a shift that occurs in "To the Man-of-War-Bird." The bird imagery in the first part of the cluster, arising out of and closely connected to the land (suggesting the physical aspect of humans), is used to symbolize the boy's growing awareness of mortality; the ship imagery in the second part of the cluster, on the other hand, offers the possibility of crossing the sea of time to immortality (suggesting the spiritual aspect of humans). Significantly, the ship imagery becomes a recurring motif in the remainder of *Leaves of Grass* as Whitman turns

from describing the individual and material to describing the inclusive nature of the spiritual.

A. James Wohlpart

Bibliography

Crawley, Thomas Edward. *The Structure of "Leaves of Grass."* Austin: U of Texas P, 1970.

Fast, Robin Riley. "Structure and Meaning in Whitman's *Sea-Drift.*" *American Transcendental Quarterly* 53 (1982): 49–66.

LaRue, Robert. "Whitman's Sea: Large Enough for Moby Dick." *Walt Whitman Review* 12 (1966): 51–59.

Miller, James E., Jr. *A Critical Guide to "Leaves of Grass."* Chicago: U of Chicago P, 1957.

———. *Walt Whitman.* Updated ed. Boston: Twayne, 1990.

Wohlpart, A. James. "From Outsetting Bard to Mature Poet: Whitman's 'Out of the Cradle' and the *Sea-Drift* Cluster." *Walt Whitman Quarterly Review* 9 (1991): 77–90.

See also "As I Ebb'd with the Ocean of Life"; Immortality; "Out of the Cradle Endlessly Rocking"; Sea, The

Self-Reviews of the 1855 *Leaves,* Whitman's Anonymous

Throughout his career, Whitman used his connections in journalism to defend and promote his literary work. As early as 1842, Whitman anonymously "puffed" his novel *Franklin Evans* and quoted from his own short story "Death in the Schoolroom (a Fact)." In later years, the poet provided friendly reviewers with the equivalent of news releases, prose passages that could be easily incorporated into articles signed by others. His behind-the-scenes self-promotion peaked in 1855, when he placed anonymous self-reviews of the first edition of *Leaves of Grass* in no fewer than three periodicals—the *United States Review,* the *American Phrenological Journal,* and the Brooklyn *Daily Eagle.*

Whitman used these reviews not only to advertise but also to enhance the effects of his poems and Preface. The one in the *United States Review*—which begins with the now famous exclamation "An American bard at last!" (Price 8)—accomplishes directly what the 1855 Preface could do only by indirection: it tells the reader that the poems of the book are intended to embody the poetic ideals set forth in the Preface. "With light and rapid touch," the self-reviewer says of the poet, "he first indicates in prose the principles of the foundation of a race of poets . . . to spring from the American people. . . . He [then] proceeds himself to exemplify this new school, and set models for their expression and range of subjects" (Price 9). All the self-reviews sketch out a course of historical criticism by which to account for the poetic experimentation of *Leaves of Grass*. This agenda is especially clear in the piece written for the *American Phrenological Journal*. Entitled "An English and an American Poet," the article reveals the confidence and aplomb of the 1855 Whitman. Quite willing to grant Alfred, Lord Tennyson the respect due to the English poet laureate, the eager self-reviewer praises Whitman the poet for breaking free of the European tradition. "In the verse of all those undoubtedly great writers, Shakespeare just as much as the rest," he writes, "there is the air which to America is the air of death. The mass of the people, the laborers and all who serve, are slag, refuse" (Price 23). But now, the review continues, "a strange voice" (Price 25) calls forth in the name of common people. Conceding that "critics and lovers and readers of poetry as hitherto written, may well be excused their shudders which will assuredly run through them, to their very blood and bones, when they first read Whitman's poems" (Price 25), the self-reviewer explains that what makes the poet seem strange is the psychological depth and physiological reality he reveals in the life of the ordinary citizen: "every sentence," he says, "and every passage tells of an interior not always seen, and exudes an impalpable something which sticks to him that reads" (Price 25). Likewise, in the *Daily Eagle* review, Whitman prepares the audience to receive this new breed of poet and his poetry. *Leaves of Grass,* he writes, "conforms to none of the rules by which poetry has ever been judged" (Price 18). Thus, the theoretical project of the first edition is defended and advanced in these reviews, and the poet's relationship with his readers is varied.

Early on, Whitman's most attentive readers discovered his game. In a review of the 1856 *Leaves,* William Swinton of the New York *Times* identified Whitman's hand in the three anonymous reviews. Unabashed, Whitman reprinted Swinton's exposé along with the original self-reviews in *Leaves of Grass Imprints,* the publicity packet distributed with the 1860 edition. The elderly Whitman discussed his self-promotional campaign openly with Horace Traubel, who as literary executor published the 1855 self-reviews

and attributed them directly to Whitman. Nearly every biography since Emory Holloway's 1929 article "Whitman as His Own Press-Agent" has taken up the topic, at least in passing.

Whitman's practice of self-reviewing alternately offended and fascinated students of his biography. It represents a rare case of a poet acting as his own critic and biographer not, as is usual, in the voice of the autobiographer or memoirist, but in the guise of a created persona presuming to represent, and redirect, the tastes and cultural trends of his times.

M. Jimmie Killingsworth

Bibliography

Hindus, Milton, ed. *Walt Whitman: The Critical Heritage.* New York: Barnes and Noble, 1971.

Hollis, C. Carroll. "Whitman and William Swinton." *American Literature* 30 (1959): 425–449.

Holloway, Emory. "Whitman as His Own Press-Agent." *American Mercury* 18 (1929): 482–488.

Kaplan, Justin. *Walt Whitman: A Life.* New York: Simon and Schuster, 1980.

Price, Kenneth M., ed. *Walt Whitman: The Contemporary Reviews.* Cambridge: Cambridge UP, 1996.

Shephard, Esther. "Walt Whitman's Whereabouts in the Winter of 1842–1843." *American Literature* 29 (1957): 289–296.

See also AMERICAN PHRENOLOGICAL JOURNAL; BROOKLYN *DAILY EAGLE*; *DEMOCRATIC REVIEW*; *LEAVES OF GRASS*, 1855 EDITION; *LEAVES OF GRASS IMPRINTS*; SWINTON, WILLIAM

Sentimentality

The relationship between Walt Whitman and sentimentality seems, at first glance, to be quite clear. In the famous section 24 of "Song of Myself," where the speaker is finally identified as "Walt Whitman, a kosmos," he goes on to define himself in negatives. He is "No sentimentalist, no stander above men and women or apart from them." The term "sentimentalist," as used here, serves as a foil to the previous stream of positive adjectives defining this son of Manhattan: "Turbulent, fleshy, sensual, eating, drinking and breeding." If this section makes clear what relationship Whitman claims to sentimentality, it does not explain what is at stake in this claim. Two issues that are of increasing critical interest concern the role played by sentimentality in shaping Whitman's career as a poet and the degree to which sentimentality inflects Whitman's poetic project.

Like Mark Twain, who is celebrated as an opponent of sham sentiment and false genteel virtues, Whitman began his literary career as an author of sentimental verse and prose. In several places in *Specimen Days* the practice of sentimentality figures importantly in Whitman's mythic stories of his own beginnings. His start in the newspaper business, for example, is due to his facility with sentimental genres: "I commenced when I was but a boy of eleven or twelve writing sentimental bits for the old 'Long Island Patriot'" (*Complete* 919). He continued through his early thirties writing in the popular and sentimental modes of the day for magazines and newspapers. Although few examples of this work are commonly anthologized, Thomas Brasher's *Walt Whitman: The Early Poems and the Fiction* (1963) and the Library of America edition of the *Complete Poetry and Collected Prose* make these readily available to scholars.

This early sentimental work, both verse and fiction, is for the most part conventional in subject matter, diction, and form. It is highly didactic, featuring narrators who, in contrast to the speaker of "Song of Myself," stand apart from and above the characters they judge. And yet, these pieces also show Whitman exhausting given literary forms, and they provide the opportunity to deduce what remains of these conventional forms and subjects in Whitman's later work. Some of the factors that remain important in Whitman's later work include the sentimental topoi of death, broken families, childhood innocence, and transcendent love. Other, more formal factors include his didacticism, his use of apostrophe, and his celebration of socially and politically marginal people.

Again like Mark Twain, Whitman's anxiety about sentimentality marks his continued reliance on it. Although the expression of emotion is often poorly executed in his juvenile and pre–*Leaves of Grass* works, emotion remains the key element that Whitman, like standard sentimentalists such as Lydia H. Sigourney and Henry Wadsworth Longfellow, uses to bridge the distance between himself and his reader. He echoes the feelings of these writers and many of his readers in what has been called a "culture of sentiment" when he asks, "what is humanity in its faith, love, heroism, poetry, even morals, but *emotion?*" (*Complete* 921). In his mature work, Whitman eschewed "verbal melody," which he

considered the "idiosyncrasy, almost a sickness" of nineteenth-century poetry, best exemplified by Longfellow's work. Nevertheless, he embraced and even amplified many of the sentimental tropes and topoi of popular sentimental culture. One superficial example of Whitman's amplification of sentimental values is the presentation of the first edition of *Leaves of Grass*. With its green embossed slip case and its private printing, the physical book itself is indistinguishable from the numerous floral titles of poetry collections by the many women writers of the day. Unlike Sara Willis Parton's ironic use of this kind of title for her humorous editions of *Fern Leaves from Fanny's Portfolio,* Whitman seems to be earnest in describing his work and its succeeding exfoliations (for example, *November Boughs*) with the floral titles common to sentimental authors.

Never denying the importance of sentimentality to his own professional life, Whitman nevertheless represented it as something left well behind when he found his "true" voice as a poet. For the most part this view has been accepted uncritically by twentieth-century critics. However, the recent critical reappraisal of nineteenth-century popular literature, and in particular sentimentality, has begun a reexamination of the relationship between sentimentality and Whitman's revolutionary poetics. This can be seen particularly in work devoted to examining the gendered dimension of Whitman's work. As early as 1966 Michael Lasser published an article on "Sex and Sentimentality in Whitman's Poetry" which begins to trace the connection between one of Whitman's most recognized subjects and one of the most reviled of literary modes. Brasher indirectly points out that early sentimental temperance tales such as "The Child and the Profligate" suggest that sentimentality provided both a rationale and a literary form for the celebration of homoerotic relationships. These ideas are taken up and expanded by critics such as M.J. Killingsworth, who argued in 1983 that sentimentality is crucial to Whitman's homoerotic poetics as laid out in the "Calamus" poems. The role of sentimentality in Whitman's ability to produce an American epic is also beginning to be explored. To what degree, it might be asked, is the "grand American expression" which melds with the "English language" to produce the "language of resistance" and the "dialect of common sense" (*Complete* 25) synonymous with what can also be called sentimentality?

Mary Louise Kete

Bibliography

Killingsworth, M. Jimmie "Sentimentality and Homosexuality in Whitman's 'Calamus' Poems." *ESQ* 29 (1983): 144–153.

Lasser, Michael. "Sex and Sentimentality in Whitman's Poetry." *Emerson Society Quarterly* 43 (1966): 94–97.

Whitman, Walt. *Complete Poetry and Collected Prose.* Ed. Justin Kaplan. New York: Library of America, 1982.

———. *The Early Poems and the Fiction.* Ed. Thomas L. Brasher. New York: New York UP, 1963.

See also "Child and the Profligate, The"; Parton, Sara Payson Willis (Fanny Fern); Popular Culture, Whitman and; Pre-*Leaves* Poems; Short Fiction, Whitman's

Sequel to Drum-Taps (1865)

By the time *Drum-Taps* was published in New York in May 1865, the Union had won the Civil War the previous month, Abraham Lincoln had been assassinated, and the Thirteenth Amendment to the Constitution (abolishing slavery) had been floating in Congressional debates for over a year. Whitman began work on a "little book" to accompany *Drum-Taps*. This "little book" was completed later in 1865 and appended to *Drum-Taps* with the title page *Sequel to Drum-Taps (Since the Preceding Came from the Press.) When Lilacs Last in the Door-Yard Bloom'd. And Other Pieces. Washington. 1865–6.* The *Sequel* gathered together eighteen poems in a twenty-four-page booklet, which was bound into some of the copies of *Drum-Taps* and included some of Whitman's most recognizable poetry: "When Lilacs Last in the Dooryard Bloom'd," "O Captain! My Captain!," and "Chanting the Square Deific." Little critical analysis has engaged the *Sequel* as a discrete cluster of poems, for, characteristically, Whitman later displaced several of the poems and dispersed them in the final edition (1881) of *Leaves of Grass*. Along the way, the *Sequel* was bound into the 1867 edition of *Leaves,* but such was its final appearance as a separate publication.

Given the evanescent moment of the publication of the *Sequel* in the unstable evolution of *Leaves,* it is not surprising that critics have largely ignored the *Sequel* as a unique artifact for critical scrutiny. Recently, this critical indifference has begun to be reversed. Betsy Erkkila has offered a historical reading of "Lilacs" and "O Captain! My Captain!" in the context of the national grief over Lincoln's assassination. Gregory Eiselein has persuasively argued that the *Sequel* offers an alternative, less coercive model of mourning practices than those practices in nineteenth-century popular culture, which exacted dutiful responses from the mourners. Luke Mancuso has argued that the *Sequel,* and "Lilacs" in particular, inaugurates the Reconstruction project of breaking the bonds of the inherited model of slave economics in favor of a model of federalized social solidarity, which includes civil liberties for African Americans.

As the centerpiece of the *Sequel,* "Lilacs" remains one of the most prolific sites of critical discourse in Whitman studies. Conventionally, "Lilacs" has been read biographically as the elegy written primarily for Lincoln which moves from the "black, black, black" aftermath of the assassination to the consolation present in its closing lines. Whitman never actually names Lincoln in this, or any, of his poems later clustered under the rubric "Memories of President Lincoln," though the unnamed subject of the historical Lincoln is never far from the poetic content. However, the natural images in the poem remain ambiguous enough to allow for embedding "Lilacs" in the cultural landscape as well. Which image of "Lincoln" is Whitman addressing in "Lilacs"? Arguably, because of the text's appearance in 1866, Whitman is writing from a Reconstruction (postwar) position, and therefore the unnamed Lincoln suggests the Reconstruction Lincoln, who had since 1863 inaugurated a dual purpose for reconstructing the Union: reunification and emancipation of slaves. While never an abolitionist himself, Whitman was adamantly opposed to the institution of slavery, and he never recorded any displeasure over Lincoln's reluctant but growing support for the abolition of slavery as a war aim. Later in his address, "Death of Abraham Lincoln" (1879), Whitman attributed the knitting together of "a Nationality" with emancipation as the dual qualities of Lincoln's lasting significance. This condensation of democratic nationality would evolve into Whitman's main preoccupation in his Reconstruction project, from 1865–1876, and "Lilacs" can be read as its preface. In such a case, the occasional poem of Lincoln's passing expands its ideological scope to include the image of the "coffin" of the nation's continuity with the sanctioning of slavery.

Another recognizable poem, "Chanting the Square Deific," makes its appearance in the 1865–1866 *Sequel*. Although the text finally settled in the "Whispers of Heavenly Death" cluster in *Leaves* (1881), George Fredrickson has persuasively argued that "Chanting" is Whitman's final word on the Civil War. Composed of four symmetrical sections, the poem represents a political allegory, though disguised in the form of theological conundrum. Each of these four sections enacts a verbal testimony by four persons in a fictional "divine quaternity": Jehovah, Christ, Satan, and Santa Spirita. Reading it as an allegory, Kerry C. Larson has interpreted "Chanting" as a narrative which reproduces in large gestures the unfolding of the history of American democracy—from the Founding Fathers (Jehovah) to the Founders' descendants (Christ) to the dissenters (Satan) to the larger ideology which holds these forces together (Santa Spirita). Such a historical reading embeds an identifiably theological text in the material social forces that produced the anxieties over the Civil War in its aftermath. Indeed, if the "Satan" persona represents the defiant Confederacy, then Whitman recognizes that such a threat of destabilization is always already present in American democratic politics.

Other poems in Whitman's *Sequel* deploy images that are suffused with a collage of consolatory, pessimistic, and defiant images. These dissonant images collide against each other, in much the same way that the survivors of the Civil War everywhere attempted to pick up the pieces and push ahead in reconstructing their lives, cities, states, and nation. In "Reconciliation," Whitman calls for a kind of amnesia through which to forget the carnage of the war, but in "Spirit whose Work is Done," the poet requires the convulsions of conflict to identify his songs to future readers. Likewise, in "As I Lay with My Head in Your Lap Camerado," Whitman employs a defiant persona who unsettles any social inertia embodied by "majorities" in favor of resistance to a quick forgetfulness of the revolutionary energies unleashed by the Civil War. In fact, "As I Lay" concludes on the uncertain note that the fruits of victory for the Union had hardly begun to ripen into a secure future for American democracy. The final poem, "To the Leaven'd Soil They Trod" appeals to the natural landscape as a mute witness to the reconciliation of the North and South, but the muteness also suggests that the vertigo of the Civil War's violence will never be fully recoverable.

Luke Mancuso

Bibliography

Allen, Gay Wilson. *The New Walt Whitman Handbook.* 1975. New York: New York UP, 1986.

Blasing, Mutlu Konuk. "Whitman's 'Lilacs' and the Grammars of Time." *PMLA* 97 (1982): 31–39.

Eiselein, Gregory. "Whitman and the Humanitarian Possibilities of Lilacs." *Prospects.* Ed. Jack Salzman. Vol. 18. New York: Cambridge UP, 1993. 51–79.

Erkkila, Betsy. *Whitman the Political Poet.* New York: Oxford UP, 1989.

Fredrickson, George M. *The Inner Civil War: Northern Intellectuals and the Crisis of the Union.* New York: Harper and Row, 1965.

Larson, Kerry C. *Whitman's Drama of Consensus.* Chicago: U of Chicago P, 1988.

Mancuso, Luke. "'The Strange Sad War Revolving': Reconstituting Walt Whitman's Reconstruction Texts in the Legislative Workshop, 1865–1876." Diss. U of Iowa, 1994.

Whitman, Walt. *Walt Whitman's "Drum-Taps" (1865) and "Sequel to Drum-Taps" (1865–6): A Facsimile Reproduction.* Ed. F. DeWolfe Miller. Gainesville, Fla.: Scholars' Facsimiles and Reprints, 1959.

See also "Chanting the Square Deific"; "Death of Abraham Lincoln"; Drum-Taps; *Leaves of Grass, 1867 Edition*; "Memories of President Lincoln"; "O Captain! My Captain!"; Reconstruction; "When Lilacs Last in the Dooryard Bloom'd"

Sex and Sexuality

Themes of sex and sexuality have dominated *Leaves of Grass* from the very beginning and have shaped the course of the book's reception. The first edition in 1855 contained what were to be called "Song of Myself," "The Sleepers," and "I Sing the Body Electric," which are "about" sexuality (though of course not exclusively) throughout. From the very beginning, Whitman wove together themes of "manly love" and "sexual love," with great emphasis on intensely passionate attraction and interaction, as well as bodily contact (touch, embrace) in both. Simultaneously in sounding these themes, he equated the body with the soul, and defined sexual experience as essentially spiritual experience. He very early adopted two phrenological terms to discriminate between the two relationships: "amativeness" for man-woman love and "adhesiveness" for "manly love." Although Whitman did not in the 1855 Preface call direct attention to this element in his work, in one of his anonymous reviews of his book ("Walt Whitman and His Poems," 1855) he wrote of himself and the 1855 *Leaves:* "The body, he teaches, is beautiful. Sex is also beautiful. . . . Sex will not be put aside; it is a great ordination of the universe. He works the muscle of the male and the teeming fibre of the female throughout his writings, as wholesome realities, impure only by deliberate intention and effort" (*Poetry and Prose* 535).

Whitman added other sex poems to his book in 1856, including "Poem of Procreation" (now "A Woman Waits for Me") and "Bunch Poem" ("Spontaneous Me"). At the end of the volume he included, without permission, Emerson's letter praising the 1855 *Leaves* (its "great power," and "free and brave thought"), and alongside it he published his own letter in reply. He may have been misled by the nature of Ralph Waldo Emerson's praise to emphasize the centrality of his themes of adhesiveness and amativeness: "As to manly friendship, everywhere observed in The States, there is not the first breath of it to be observed in print. I say the body of a man or woman, the main matter, is so far quite unexpressed in poems; but the body is to be expressed, and sex is" (*Poetry and Prose* 529).

It was not until the 1860 edition of *Leaves* that Whitman gathered the poems celebrating sexuality into the cluster "Enfans d'Adam" ("Children of Adam") and the poems celebrating "manly love" into "Calamus." When Whitman came to Boston to see his book through the press there, Emerson tried to persuade him to withdraw the sex poems, but Whitman refused. He probably understood that if he really de-sexed *Leaves* it would be like self-castration. Although Emerson never publicly withdrew his endorsement of Whitman, he passed up opportunities to repeat it. Emerson's silence together with Whitman's loss of his job at the Interior Department in 1865, charged with writing "indecent poems," were early warning signs that

he and his *Leaves* were embarked on a difficult road ahead.

In subsequent editions of *Leaves,* Whitman revised and shifted his poems of amativeness and adhesiveness, but by and large his dominant themes became not the body but the soul, not youth but old age—and death. His experience in the Civil War hospitals seems to have provided a turning point for Whitman's focus. He even claimed, in "A Backward Glance O'er Travel'd Roads" (1888), that the war revealed to him, "as by flashes of lightning," the "final reasons-for-being" of his "passionate song" (*Poetry and Prose* 516). In his Civil War poems, *Drum-Taps* (1865, later included in the 1867 *Leaves*), the "Calamus" theme runs throughout—"cropping out" as Whitman himself said of it in his 1876 Preface to *Two Rivulets* (*Prose Works* 2:471). Whitman critics have not failed to notice in "Drum-Taps" the poet's theme of adhesiveness—the joy in the physical transmuted by the war into pain and anguish—in such poems as "The Wound-Dresser," "Vigil Strange I Kept on the Field One Night," and "A March in the Ranks Hard-Prest, and the Road Unknown."

In 1868 W.M. Rossetti published a British edition of Whitman's poetry, *Poems by Walt Whitman.* In effect, this was an expurgated *Leaves,* with "Song of Myself," "Children of Adam," and "Calamus" omitted, except for a few poems of the "Calamus" cluster placed in a section entitled "Walt Whitman." In spite of Rossetti's gutting of the book, it established Whitman's reputation in England and attracted many ardent admirers. Some, when they became familiar with the poems purged by Rossetti, became even more ardent, while others turned hostile. The former included Anne Gilchrist, who fell in love with Whitman and wrote an article "An Englishwoman's Estimate of Walt Whitman" (Boston 1870), especially praising Whitman's sex poems. Algernon Swinburne wrote a poem in praise of Whitman in *Song Before Sunrise* (1871), but loudly reversed himself in his 1887 essay "Whitmania," after encountering all of *Leaves.* John Addington Symonds read Whitman's poems as a young man, and, bowled over, found his way to the whole of "Calamus." He would later strike up a correspondence with Whitman in Camden, pressing him on the real meaning of his "Calamus" poems, leading Whitman ultimately to reply in a notorious letter in 1890 claiming to have had six illegitimate children during his "jolly" "times south" (*Poetry and Prose* 958).

Although in the fifth edition (1871–1872) of *Leaves,* Whitman seemed temporarily to lose his way in shaping *Leaves* to contain his new work ("Passage to India" and related poems), some ten years later, in the sixth edition (1881–1882), he adopted his earlier practice of integrating the poems of a lifetime into a single structure. Before the book could be distributed by its publisher in Boston, however, it was found to be immoral by the Society for the Suppression of Vice; because Whitman refused to remove the offensive parts, the book was withdrawn and published in Philadelphia. The Boston censors found offensive not only the whole of "A Woman Waits for Me," "The Dalliance of the Eagles," and "To a Common Prostitute," but also passages vital to the life of a number of Whitman's greatest works, including "Song of Myself." But the "Calamus" cluster with its songs of "manly love" was left intact!

In "A Backward Glance," Whitman made his final assessment of the sex poems that had given him so many problems. Writing a bit after the most recent attempt to censor his book, Whitman affirms boldly that "'Leaves of Grass' is avowedly the song of Sex and Amativeness, and even Animality. . . . Of this feature . . . I shall only say the espousing principle of those lines so gives breath of life to my whole scheme that the bulk of the pieces might as well have been left unwritten were those lines omitted" (*Poetry and Prose* 518). A similar claim might have been made for the "Calamus" poems of adhesiveness; that no such claim was made was attributable, surely, to the fact that they had never inspired public controversy as had the sex poems.

Whitman said in "A Backward Glance," "I have not gain'd acceptance of my own time, but have fallen back on fond dreams of the future" (507). It is clear that near the end of the twentieth century, Whitman's book has won a worldwide reputation that would astonish him. The story of that acceptance, beginning after his death in 1892, has been told only in part—and is still unfolding. At the center of the story is a shift from concern about his poems of "Sex and Amativeness" to concern about his poems of "manly attachment" and adhesiveness. Providing a frame of reference for understanding this shift are changes in perspective brought about in the first half of the century by Freudian and psychoanalytic thought, and in the latter half by

the rights movements of gays, lesbians, and feminists (allied to the black civil rights movement).

Emory Holloway, in his *Whitman: An Interpretation in Narrative* (1926), provided the first scholarly biography of the poet, and his experience may stand as an example of the continuing controversy over Whitman. In his research, Holloway happened to run across the manuscript of a "Children of Adam" poem, "Once I Pass'd through a Populous City," and discovered that it had originally been addressed to a man—and therefore "belonged" in the "Calamus" cluster. He was the first biographer to agonize over how to write about Whitman's sexuality. A revealing footnote to Holloway's biography is that he later became obsessed with demonstrating that Whitman was telling the truth in his claims to fatherhood in his letter to Symonds; his obsession led to his publication, after long years of research, of *Free and Lonesome Heart: The Secret of Walt Whitman* (1960), claiming discovery of "Whitman's son."

Holloway's dilemma has been inherited, in one form or another, by subsequent biographers and critics of Whitman. What can be assumed factually about sexuality in Whitman's life? What may be said validly about sexuality in his poetry?

As to the life: Gay Wilson Allen's biography, *The Solitary Singer,* published first in 1955, revised in 1967, and reprinted in 1985, remains indispensable. In his preface to the latest edition, Allen pointed out that attitudes toward Whitman's sexuality had changed since he first wrote his book. He had decided, he explained, to use the word "homoerotic" to indicate that his "sexual emotions were stronger for men than for women"; he had avoided the use of "homosexual," he said, because "at the time that term implied a practitioner of pederasty," for which there was no evidence (Allen xi). Justin Kaplan, whose biography, *Walt Whitman: A Life,* appeared in 1980, followed Allen in using the word "homoerotic." And in his essay "The Biographer's Problem" (1989), Kaplan pointed out that the biographer's requisite "intimate evidence" on Whitman's sexuality remained elusive (25). Kaplan's point is borne out by a brief and informative biography of Peter Doyle, Martin G. Murray's "'Pete the Great': A Biography of Peter Doyle" (1994), which sketches Whitman's relationship with the horsecar conductor he met in Washington at the end of the Civil War—a relationship well known since

1897, after the appearance of a collection of Whitman's letters to Doyle under the deliberately chosen title *Calamus*. Though the warmth and intensity of the bonding are clear, the "intimate evidence" is still missing. About Doyle, Kaplan concluded: "Maybe it doesn't matter"; the "evidence" for Whitman's homosexuality exists, he asserted, in his poetry and letters (26).

As to the poetry: Robert K. Martin's *The Homosexual Tradition in American Poetry* (1979) has brought the controversy about how to interpret the sexuality of Whitman's *Leaves* into clear focus. His opening chapter on Whitman begins: "Although Whitman intended his work to communicate his homosexuality to his readers, and although homosexual readers have from the very beginning understood his homosexual meanings, most critics have not been willing to take Whitman at his word" (3). Martin's edited volume, *The Continuing Presence of Walt Whitman: The Life After the Life* (1992), brings together an international array of critics and poets who start from Martin's basic assumption. By their very nature these works set new directions for the continuing discussion of Whitman. Two other critics have taken Whitman "at his word" and assume his homosexuality a given: Michael Moon, *Disseminating Whitman: Revision and Corporeality in "Leaves of Grass"* (1991), and Byrne R.S. Fone, *Masculine Landscapes: Walt Whitman and the Homoerotic Text* (1992). In their approaches, all these critics have brought new and valuable insights into the many meanings of *Leaves*.

But have they, in clearing away some distortions, contributed others of their own? There are many critics who agree on the pervasive homoeroticism in Whitman's life, letters, and poetry, and even on his latent if not overt homosexuality; they are not, however, ready to adopt such a singular and reductive assumption about what Whitman "intended" in his *Leaves*—"to communicate his homosexuality to his readers." Throughout his prefaces and "A Backward Glance"—and in his poetry—Whitman wrote at length about his purposes, including his themes of amative and adhesive love, but also (among others) his themes of selfhood and freedom, being and becoming, democracy and equality, war and tragedy, spirituality and death. Nor are all critics ready to accept the assumption that such seismic chasms divide readers as implied by such ponderous sexual labeling. There remains the fact that innumerable "heterosexual" readers, both men and women, have felt the power, sexual and other, of Whitman's *Leaves*. His appeal is universal, not exclusive. Sexual labels are simplistic, distorting as they do the complexity of any "real" individual's sexuality. In short, all readers can share, consciously and/or unconsciously, Whitman's omnisexual vision—omnisexual in the all-encompassing sense of embracing auto-, homo-, and heteroerotic impulses. Individuals possess these impulses within them by the fact of being human and sexual, assimilated in passing through the stages of growing up. There is much more in their sexuality that brings human beings together than divides them, whatever the nature of their "sexual preference," whatever the nature of their sexual experience—experience central to *human* experience, and allied closely always, as Whitman reiterated, to the spiritual: "Lacks one lacks both" ("Song of Myself," section 3).

James E. Miller, Jr.

Bibliography

Allen, Gay Wilson. *The Solitary Singer: A Critical Biography of Walt Whitman*. 1955. Rev. ed. 1967. Chicago: U of Chicago P, 1985.

Aspiz, Harold. *Walt Whitman and the Body Beautiful*. Urbana: U of Illinois P, 1980.

Folsom, Ed, ed. *Walt Whitman: The Centennial Essays*. Iowa City: U of Iowa P, 1994.

Fone, Byrne R.S. *Masculine Landscapes: Walt Whitman and the Homoerotic Text*. Carbondale: Southern Illinois UP, 1992.

Kaplan, Justin. "The Biographer's Problem." *Walt Whitman of Mickle Street: A Centennial Collection*. Ed. Geoffrey M. Sill. Knoxville: U of Tennessee P, 1994. 18–27.

Killingsworth, M. Jimmie. *Whitman's Poetry of the Body: Sexuality, Politics, and the Text*. Chapel Hill: U of North Carolina P, 1989.

Martin, Robert K. *The Homosexual Tradition in American Poetry*. Austin: U of Texas P, 1979.

———, ed. *The Continuing Presence of Walt Whitman: The Life After the Life*. Iowa City: U of Iowa P, 1992.

Miller, James E., Jr. *A Critical Guide to "Leaves of Grass."* Chicago: U of Chicago P, 1957.

———. *"Leaves of Grass": America's Lyric-Epic of Self and Democracy*. Twayne's Masterwork Studies 92.

New York: Twayne, 1992.

Moon, Michael. *Disseminating Whitman: Revision and Corporeality in "Leaves of Grass."* Cambridge, Mass.: Harvard UP, 1991.

Murray, Martin G. "'Pete the Great': A Biography of Peter Doyle." *Walt Whitman Quarterly Review* 12 (1994): 1–51.

Shively, Charley, ed. *Drum Beats: Walt Whitman's Civil War Boy Lovers.* San Francisco: Gay Sunshine, 1989.

Whitman, Walt. *The Poetry and Prose of Walt Whitman.* Ed. Louis Untermeyer. New York: Simon and Schuster, 1949.

———. *Prose Works 1892.* Ed. Floyd Stovall. 2 vols. New York: New York UP, 1963–1964.

See also "CALAMUS"; "CHILDREN OF ADAM"; COMRADESHIP; "DALLIANCE OF THE EAGLES, THE"; "DRUM-TAPS"; HUMAN BODY; "I SING THE BODY ELECTRIC"; *LEAVES OF GRASS,* 1860 EDITION; LOVE; "ONCE I PASS'D THROUGH A POPULOUS CITY"; "SLEEPERS, THE"; SOCIETY FOR THE SUPPRESSION OF VICE; "SONG OF MYSELF"; "SPONTANEOUS ME"; "TO A COMMON PROSTITUTE"; "WOMAN WAITS FOR ME, A"

"Shadow and the Light of a Young Man's Soul, The" (1848)

This autobiographical piece, more exemplum than short story, first appeared in the *Union Magazine of Literature and Art,* June 1848.

The story is told broadly. The Dean family suffered severe financial loss from the New York fire of 1835. The widow Dean overcomes such hardships and cheerfully raises her two boys, David, who is sickly, and Archibald, who is temperamentally uneven. Like the poet in "Lingave's Temptation," Archie knows his talents, but bristles under the injustice of his poverty. He takes an unwanted position as a teacher in a country school and writes letters of despair to his loving mother. Country living, however, sweetens Archie's disposition; he comes to admire the simplicity of the country folk around him.

Archie hears of an old spinster whose family had long ago lost its wealth. Resolved to regain the family farm, she had worked endlessly and eventually bought back the farm in time for her father to enjoy it in his last years. Archie sees the spinster's story as a rebuke of his own conduct and resolves to be more hard-working and less bitter. When his brother dies, Archie moves back with the widow. The last paragraph extols Archie's change and warns against "morose habits" that spread bitterness over one's existence (Whitman 330).

"The Shadow and the Light" is considered autobiographical for several reasons, chief of which is that Whitman, like Archie, was forced by poverty to take a country-school teaching position. Callow, however, has a different view: Archie's resolve at the making of his manhood parallels Whitman's own task of inventing himself in the years following this story.

Patrick McGuire

Bibliography

Allen, Gay Wilson. *The Solitary Singer: A Critical Biography of Walt Whitman.* 1955. Rev. ed. 1967. Chicago: U of Chicago P, 1985.

Callow, Philip. *From Noon to Starry Night: A Life of Walt Whitman.* Chicago: Ivan R. Dee, 1992.

Whitman, Walt. *The Early Poems and the Fiction.* Ed. Thomas L. Brasher. New York: New York UP, 1963.

See also "LINGAVE'S TEMPTATION"; SHORT FICTION, WHITMAN'S

Shakespeare, William (1564–1616)

The author of two lyric poems, *Venus and Adonis* (1593) and *The Rape of Lucrece* (1594), and 154 sonnets, this Renaissance poet and playwright remains best known for his plays, which include histories, comedies, tragicomedies (the so-called problem plays), tragedies (most notably *Hamlet* [1600–1601], *Othello* [1604], *King Lear* [1605], and *Macbeth* [1606]), and romances. Over the years, Shakespeare has evolved into one of the representative icons of the Western literary tradition.

Whitman's view of Shakespeare can best be characterized as ambivalent. While he recognized and acknowledged Shakespeare's poems and plays as masterpieces, he at the same time felt compelled to criticize them for espousing what he considered "feudal" principles.

In his youth, Whitman became intimately familiar with Shakespeare's works, reading and rereading them and even carrying a copy of the *Sonnets* or one of the plays torn out from "some broken or cheap edition" in his pocket so that he could read it "when the mood demanded" (*Prose Works* 1:294). Indeed, Whitman memorized long passages from Shakespeare's plays (especially from *Richard II*), then "spouted" them "on the Broadway stage-coaches, in the awful din of the street" and on the Brooklyn ferries (Traubel 246). Yet Whitman did not content himself with simply memorizing excerpts; he somewhat methodically compared the written texts with stage productions. Whitman would read the plays "carefully the day beforehand," then attend performances of them, frequenting "the old Park, the Bowery, Broadway and Chatham-square theatres" (*Prose Works* 1:21, 19). These performances, given during the heyday of Shakespeare on the American stage, clearly made a lasting impression on Whitman, for he was able to recall details of the players and performances years later. Perhaps it was such close familiarity with Shakespeare that led Whitman to refer to Shakespeare more than to any other poet.

Despite his obvious admiration for Shakespeare, Whitman nevertheless considered the poet-playwright the key representative and proponent of what he terms the "feudal" literary tradition, which he believed to be "poisonous to the idea of the pride and dignity of the common people, the lifeblood of democracy" (*Prose Works* 2:388). Consequently, Whitman repeatedly and adamantly criticized Shakespeare and "his legitimate followers, Sir Walter Scott and Alfred, Lord Tennyson," at one point even going so far as to claim that they "exhale that principle of caste which we Americans have come on earth to destroy" (*Prose Works* 2:475–476).

Ultimately, however, Whitman tempered his criticism of Shakespeare and feudal poetry, acknowledging his—and, by extension, American literature's—debt: "If I had not stood before those poems with uncover'd head, fully aware of their colossal grandeur and beauty of form and spirit, I could not have written 'Leaves of Grass'" (*Prose Works* 2:721).

Phyllis McBride

Bibliography

Furness, Clifton Joseph. *Walt Whitman's Estimate of Shakespeare.* Cambridge, Mass.: Harvard UP, 1932.

Harrison, Richard Clarence. "Walt Whitman and Shakespeare." *PMLA* 44 (1929): 1201–1238.

Traubel, Horace. *With Walt Whitman in Camden.* 1908. Vol. 2. New York: Rowman and Littlefield, 1961.

Whitman, Walt. *Prose Works 1892.* Ed. Floyd Stovall. 2 vols. New York: New York UP, 1963–1964.

See also ACTORS AND ACTRESSES; FEUDALISM; "POETRY TO-DAY IN AMERICA—SHAKSPERE—THE FUTURE"; SCOTT, SIR WALTER; "SHAKSPERE-BACON'S CIPHER"; THEATERS AND OPERA HOUSES

"Shakspere-Bacon's Cipher" (1891)

This six-line poem, first published in the second annex to the 1891 edition of *Leaves of Grass,* "Good-Bye my Fancy," probably reflects Whitman's familiarity with Ignatius Donnelly's theory that a hidden system of ciphers in Shakespeare's works conveys the identification of Francis Bacon as the author. With elaborate documentation, Donnelly set forth his proposition in the two-volume *The Great Cryptogram: Francis Bacon's Cipher in the So-Called Shakespeare Plays* (1888). A flurry of articles, primarily as rebuttals, appeared in American and British journals. The Bacon-authorship proposal had been launched first in book form—*Was Lord Bacon the Author of Shakespeare's Plays?* (1856) by William Henry Smith. The theory gained prominence through Delia Bacon's *The Philosophy of the Plays of Shakespeare Unfolded* (1857), in which she cites the existence of a cipher to reveal the true author.

Without adhering to the Baconian camp, Whitman sidesteps the controversy to find another type of "mystic cipher . . . infolded." It lies within "every object, mountain, tree, and star." Nowhere in the poem itself is either Shakspere (Whitman's usual spelling of the name throughout all of his prose and poetry) or Bacon mentioned. Whitman echoes words from the books and articles about the Shakespeare-Bacon controversy, but he finds "meaning, behind the ostent"—the universal spirit that breathes throughout nature and persons.

Robert G. Collmer

Bibliography

Friedman, William F., and Elizebeth S. Friedman. *The Shakespeare Ciphers Examined.* Cambridge: Cambridge UP, 1957.

Stovall, Floyd. "Whitman's Knowledge of Shakespeare." *Studies in Philology* 49 (1952): 643–669.

See also SHAKESPEARE, WILLIAM

Shephard, Esther (1891–1975)

Esther Shephard, scholar, poet, and folklorist (she compiled a popular edition of Paul Bunyan stories) was the author of *Walt Whitman's Pose* (1938), an early source study which doggedly demonstrates the influence of some of Whitman's reading on *Leaves of Grass*. In particular, while she places undue emphasis on it, Shephard convincingly shows that George Sand's *Countess of Rudolstadt* and *Journeyman Joiner* influenced Whitman's literary persona of the "vagabond poet, dressed in laborer's garb" (141). However, Shephard's sense of Whitman as poseur and dissembler is so extreme that it colors her judgment of *Leaves of Grass* to the point that she has virtually no sympathy or ear for Whitman and his work. By the end, Shephard throws up her hands, suggesting that "a consideration of Walt Whitman in his career as the self-styled metaphysician and philosoph [*sic*] of the nineteenth century is a saddening experience" (396). Despite these drawbacks, as Gay Wilson Allen suggests, Shephard's work was important in redirecting Whitman biography toward a more thorough investigation of his literary sources. Shephard taught for most of her career at San Jose State (presently California State University at San Jose) and contributed scholarly articles on Whitman through the 1940s and 1950s.

Stephen Rachman

Bibliography

Allen, Gay Wilson. *The New Walt Whitman Handbook.* 1975. New York: New York UP, 1986.

———. *The Solitary Singer: A Critical Biography of Walt Whitman.* 1955. Rev. ed. 1967. Chicago: U of Chicago P, 1985.

"Shephard, Esther." *Contemporary Authors, Permanent Series.* Ed. Christine Nasso. Vol. 2. Detroit: Gale Research, 1978.

Shephard, Esther. *Walt Whitman's Pose.* New York: Harcourt, Brace, 1938.

See also INFLUENCES ON WHITMAN, PRINCIPAL; PERSONAE; READING, WHITMAN'S; SAND, GEORGE

"Shirval: A Tale of Jerusalem" (1845)

This short story appeared in *The Aristidean*, March 1845. Whitman revised the story for *Specimen Days & Collect* (1882), though he did not use it. For publication details and revisions see Brasher's edition of *The Early Poems and the Fiction.*

In "Shirval" Whitman retells a story from the New Testament, Luke 7: 11–18. The characters, except for Jesus, are unnamed in Luke, but Whitman gives them names and adds the maiden Zar. Shirval is the young man who is raised from the dead. Unni is the widow and mother of Shirval, and Zar is Shirval's beloved.

Whitman avoids the name Jesus in his telling by using words like Being, Presence, Man of Wo, and Nazarine—the first three printed completely in capitals. Whitman's portrayal of Jesus emphasizes physical manifestations of the spiritual. The hearts of the crowd throb at "the nearness of an UNDEFINABLE PRESENCE, more than mortal" (294).

According to David Reynolds, Whitman's humanizing a tale from the Bible sets Whitman in line with progressive literary practices of his day. Whitman addresses that very issue in the story when he defines a function of literature: "It is the pen's prerogative to roll back the curtains of centuries . . . and make them live in fiction" (292).

Reynolds also notes that "Shirval" is a lighter, happier tale than Whitman's other fiction. However, it involves much of the same thematic interest in death and grief, only here Whitman begins in gloom—"O Earth! huge tomb-yard of humanity" (292)—and ends in awe: widow, son, and maiden "knelt upon the ground and bent their faces on the earth-worn sandals of the MAN OF WO" (295).

Noteworthy also is Whitman's use of parallelism in an emotional apostrophe addressed to the Nazarene. The cadences are biblical and not unlike those of the poetry.

Patrick McGuire

Bibliography

Reynolds, David S. *Walt Whitman's America: A Cultural Biography.* New York: Knopf, 1995.

Whitman, Walt. *The Early Poems and the Fiction.* Ed. Thomas L. Brasher. New York: New York UP, 1963.

See also BIBLE, THE; SHORT FICTION, WHITMAN'S

Short Fiction, Whitman's (1841–1848)

Whitman's roughly two dozen short stories and vignettes were initially published between 1841 and 1848 in news and literary papers. Whitman collected and edited nine of them for *Specimen Days & Collect* (1882). Many of the stories were republished, with slight alterations, during the years Whitman spent working on newspapers in New York City and Brooklyn. In style and theme the stories reflect the mass-market reading taste in the America of Whitman's youth; their relation to his later work has recently become a question of critical interest.

In many cases the stories were published under a pseudonym or anonymously, making exact identification of Whitman's authorship uncertain; there may still remain unidentified short works by Whitman. Nine of the short stories appeared first in the *United States Magazine and Democratic Review,* beginning with "Death in the School Room (a Fact)" in August 1841. *Columbian Magazine* and *The Aristidean* also published many of Whitman's fictional efforts. The last known short-story debut was "The Shadow and the Light of a Young Man's Soul," published in June 1848 in the *Union Magazine of Literature and Art.* An excellent review of the complex publication history of Whitman's fiction is found in Thomas Brasher's edition of *The Early Poems and the Fiction.*

To some extent one can ascertain the stylistic and thematic content of Whitman's short fiction from the story titles. The sensationalism of "Death in the School-Room (a Fact)" and the pathos of "Dumb Kate.—An Early Death" (1844) reflect the popular taste in magazine fiction Whitman exploited in these early tales. Many of the stories, in tune with their contemporaries, concern death and dying, apparitions, and the conversion of guilty consciences. The short fiction also treats many of the often debated reform issues of the day, including temperance and the disciplining of children. Some of the stories, such as "The Little Sleighers. A Sketch of a Winter Morning on the Battery" (1844) are mere vignettes, reminiscent of the

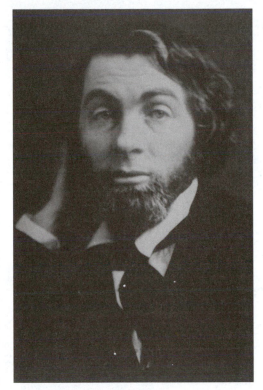

Walt Whitman, early 1840s. By permission, Walt Whitman Association.

snatches of city life listed in Whitman's later poetry. Others, like "The Child-Ghost; a Story of the Last Loyalist" (1842), show Whitman's early patriotism and enthusiasm for American democracy.

Some of the stories contain autobiographical elements. "My Boys and Girls" (1844), critics agree, is a reminiscence about Whitman's many brothers and sisters. "The Shadow and the Light of a Young Man's Soul" concerns a man who is forced by poverty out of the city into a rural teaching position—an experience Whitman had after the great fire of 1835 in New York City hindered his career as a printer there.

Whitman's short fiction is relatively little studied. These stories show a journalist's sense of popular taste and reveal the early Whitman grappling with popular issues of the day. Early biographers such as Gay Wilson Allen use the stories to illustrate the progress of Whitman's adaptation to the literary marketplace of New York City, but criticize the lack of originality shown in the fiction. Paul Zweig's psychoanalytic approach sees in these stories a Whitman obsessed with his father and anxious about leaving his familial responsibilities behind. Critics continue to find the artistic gap between the early fiction and *Leaves of Grass* tantalizing, but recent scholarly work forgoes aesthetic judgments and attempts to show the connections between Whitman and his political and artistic contemporaries. Despite Whitman's pervasively symptomatic fictional style and subject matter, for example, he was being published in the *Democratic Review* along with the greatest American literary luminaries of his time. Several scholars have pointed out, for example, that Whitman borrowed from Edgar Allan Poe and Nathaniel Hawthorne in his stories; all three published in the *Democratic Review*. David Reynolds has made the most systematic exploration of the connections between the early stories and the concerns of the later poetry. Reynolds and other recent Whitman students emphasize the tension shown in the early fiction (and poetry) between Whitman's economic need to publish and his desire to produce literature that would be considered artistic by the standards of his day.

Ultimately, the stories speak not only to Whitman's early life and artistic development, but to the literary atmosphere in which he worked and lived. The short fiction has only been touched on by critics so far, and despite Whitman's dismissal of his early publications, they are an important piece of the aesthetic puzzle Whitman represents.

Matt Cohen

Bibliography

Allen, Gay Wilson. *The Solitary Singer: A Critical Biography of Walt Whitman*. 1955. Rev. ed. 1967. Chicago: U of Chicago P, 1985.

Kaplan, Justin. *Walt Whitman: A Life*. New York: Simon and Schuster, 1980.

Reynolds, David S. *Walt Whitman's America: A Cultural Biography*. New York: Knopf, 1995.

Whitman, Walt. *The Early Poems and the Fiction*. Ed. Thomas L. Brasher. New York: New York UP, 1963.

Zweig, Paul. *Walt Whitman: The Making of the Poet*. New York: Basic Books, 1984.

See also "ANGEL OF TEARS, THE"; "BERVANCE: OR, FATHER AND SON";

"BOY LOVER, THE"; "CHILD AND THE PROFLIGATE, THE"; "DEATH IN THE SCHOOL-ROOM (A FACT)"; "DEATH OF WIND-FOOT, THE"; "DUMB KATE"; "FIREMAN'S DREAM, THE"; *FRANKLIN EVANS*; "HALF-BREED, THE"; JOURNALISM, WHITMAN'S; "LAST LOYALIST, THE"; "LAST OF THE SACRED ARMY, THE"; "LEGEND OF LIFE AND LOVE, A"; "LINGAVE'S TEMPTATION"; "LITTLE JANE"; "LITTLE SLEIGHERS, THE"; "LOVE OF ERIS: A SPIRIT RECORD, THE"; "MADMAN, THE"; "MY BOYS AND GIRLS"; "ONE WICKED IMPULSE!"; POPULAR CULTURE, WHITMAN AND; PRE-*LEAVES* POEMS; "REUBEN'S LAST WISH"; "RICHARD PARKER'S WIDOW"; SENTIMENTALITY; "SHADOW AND THE LIGHT OF A YOUNG MAN'S SOUL, THE"; "SHIRVAL: A TALE OF JERUSALEM"; "SOME FACT-ROMANCES"; "TOMB BLOSSOMS, THE"; "WILD FRANK'S RETURN"

"Sight in Camp in the Daybreak Gray and Dim, A" (1865)

In a December 1862 notebook entry written at Falmouth, Virginia, Whitman recorded the prose description of a scene that closely parallels the one described in this poem. "A Sight in Camp in the Daybreak Gray and Dim" was first published in *Drum-Taps* (1865) and incorporated into the body of *Leaves* in 1871 as part of the "Drum-Taps" cluster, where it remained in subsequent editions of *Leaves*.

The poem's three-stanza symmetrical shape prompts Allen to associate it, structurally and metrically, with sonnet form. Emerging from his tent at daybreak, the speaker encounters the bodies of three dead soldiers. In the third he discerns "the face of the Christ himself, / Dead and divine and brother of all."

The poem is interesting, on a literal level, for its reportorial accuracy of description. In addition, the literal images evoke Whitman's larger symbolic sense of the war, its everyday heroes, and its place in history. For instance, the three soldiers, collectively, may represent all dead soldiers; the image of the dead "Christ," with its connotations of redemptive sacrifice, matches what Whitman saw as the similarly redemptive sacrifice of the Civil War dead; and the emphatic reference to "all" in the last line suggests Whitman's sense of the war as a unifying cause in furtherance of community and comaraderie, which can temper selfish individualism and materialism.

John E. Schwiebert

Bibliography

Allen, Gay Wilson. *A Reader's Guide to Walt Whitman.* New York: Farrar, Strauss and Giroux, 1970.

Glicksberg, Charles I., ed. *Walt Whitman and the Civil War.* Philadelphia: U of Pennsylvania P, 1933.

Schwiebert, John E. *The Frailest Leaves: Whitman's Poetic Technique and Style in the Short Poem.* New York: Lang, 1992.

Whitman, Walt. *The Uncollected Poetry and Prose of Walt Whitman.* Ed. Emory Holloway. 2 vols. Garden City, N.Y.: Doubleday, Page, 1921.

See also CIVIL WAR, THE; "DRUM-TAPS"; FALMOUTH, VIRGINIA; NOTEBOOKS AND UNPUBLISHED PROSE MANUSCRIPTS

Simpson, Louis (1923–)

Louis Simpson won the Pulitzer Prize for his collection of poetry *At the End of the Open Road* in 1964. He has written ten books of poetry, several critical studies, a novel, and an autobiography, and he edited the anthology *New Poets of England and America* (1957). Born in the West Indies, the son of a lawyer of Scottish descent and a Russian mother, Simpson immigrated to the United States at the age of seventeen. Since 1967 he has taught at the State University of New York at Stony Brook.

One of Simpson's best-known poems is "Walt Whitman at Bear Mountain," which first appeared in his collection *At the End of the Open Road.* In this poem Simpson addresses a bronze statue of Whitman and inquires: "Where are you, Walt? / The Open Road goes to the used car lot" (*Open Road* 64). Simpson expresses his disappointment here and elsewhere in his work that the American dream and myth, so often expressed in grandiose terms by Whitman, has been tragically corrupted by materialism. In his poetry and prose, Simpson has played an influential role in the ongoing "dialogue" between post–World War II American poets and Walt Whitman.

Steven P. Schneider

Bibliography

Lazer, Hank. "Louis Simpson and Walt Whitman: Destroying the Teacher." *Walt Whitman Quarterly Review* 1.3 (1983): 1–21.

Perlman, Jim, Ed Folsom, and Dan Campion, eds. *Walt Whitman: The Measure of His Song.* Minneapolis: Holy Cow!, 1981.

Simpson, Louis. *At the End of the Open Road.* Middletown: Wesleyan UP, 1963.

———. *The Character of the Poet.* Ann Arbor: U of Michigan P, 1986.

———. *People Live Here: Selected Poems 1949–1983.* Brockport, N.Y.: BOA Editions Ltd., 1983.

See also LEGACY, WHITMAN'S

"Sketch, A" (1842)

"A Sketch" was first published in the December issue of *The New World,* edited by Park Benjamin, but it has never been included in any editions of Whitman's poetry. In fact, the poem had not been known to exist until Jerome Loving discovered it in the Rare Book and Manuscript Library, Columbia University, and republished it in the Winter 1994 issue of the *Walt Whitman Quarterly Review.*

Loving offers compelling evidence that authenticates the authorship of "A Sketch" as Whitman's: it was signed "W.," and it resembles, in theme and metrics, Whitman's "Each Has His Grief" and "The Punishment of Pride"; its theme also echoes "Our Future Lot," published in Whitman's own *The Long Islander* in 1838. Loving further points out that it was perhaps Whitman's first "seashore poem," anticipating later great pieces such as "Out of the Cradle Endlessly Rocking," "As I Ebb'd with the Ocean of Life," and "Out of the Rolling Ocean the Crowd." The narrator of the poem is "ultimately concerned with the significance of love in the context of the unknown" (Loving 119), expressing the loneliness found in parts of "Song of Myself" and other major pieces.

Guiyou Huang

Bibliography

Loving, Jerome. "A Newly Discovered Whitman Poem." *Walt Whitman Quarterly Review* 11 (1994): 117–122.

See also PRE-*LEAVES* POEMS; SEA, THE

Slang

Slang, containing powerful words, was to be one of the main sources of words in Whitman's poetry. American poetic expression, he advocated, should use all slang terms, including bad as well as good. This slang should encompass all areas of the life of the common American man and woman; it should come from the daily speech of the workingman. In "Slang in America" (1885) and *An American Primer* (1904), Whitman called for the use of slang; however, he used slang somewhat infrequently.

Sporadically before 1855, regularly between 1856 and 1860, and intermittently thereafter, Whitman searched for slang phrases and idiomatic expressions wherever he could find them. He took notes on slang sayings and provincialisms, and interviewed workmen, recording his findings in private journals so that he could later incorporate them into his poetry. For some of the terms in his collection of slangy idiomatic expressions, he attempted to indicate the meanings along with the pronunciation and intonation for each.

In "Slang in America," Whitman claimed that slang was an important factor in the development of the language. Referring to slang as a "lawless germinal element" (*Prose Works* 2:572), he believed that slang terms would outlive and surmount their disapprobation to become accepted expressions, exerting a powerful force in the evolution of the language. This national American language would come from the daily speech of the common man or woman. The masses would be most influential in determining the nature of the American language. Because many frequently used words, he contended, were originally slang, slang could be considered to have breathed life into the language. Slang was the beginning of a national language for America, more than most realized.

This new language would be necessary for him as a poet to be able to relate the unique experiences of the new, developing nation. Pushing language to its fullest capacity, he would incorporate any word he found necessary without regard to social conventions. Slang would be part of the raw materials he would use as the poet of the working class. While he relished the slang he heard in ordinary talk and viewed slang as expressing the poetry of human utterances, he realized that many slang terms were short-lived. Some slang had a "naturalness" and "fittingness"; not all of it, though,

was equally good because for some slang words and phrases, he could discover no meaning or no appropriate meaning. Slang, nonetheless, was earthy, basic, and real—therefore the true vehicle for poetic expression.

As Whitman proclaimed America and Americans in his poetry, he used slang and colloquialisms; however, he also indiscriminately mixed words from all stages of language, all languages, all levels of language, and all areas (all professions and fields). When discussing Whitman's diction, scholars invariably comment on his use of slang and dialect terms as well as his frequent juxtaposition of slang and learned, formal diction. Some critics argue that his use of slang declined after 1860 and 1865. Most agree that his poetical language became more conventional in later years.

The oral, conversational nature of his poetry as well as his use of Americanisms, place names and other names, and technical terms related to the occupations of the workingman may create the illusion that Whitman liberally used slang, especially in the earlier editions of *Leaves of Grass*. Persons studying the types of words used in Whitman's poetry should first define the labels they are using, such as slang, colloquialisms, Americanisms, dialect, and idioms.

Whitman as a poet wanted to express the experiences of the common man and woman, borrowing from the language of those in all walks of ordinary life, incorporating slang from the streets and from various professions. Yet his poetry was not accepted by the uneducated and semi-educated, the audience he wrote for. By using terms probably not understood by the general public (obsolete, archaic, and poetic terms; learned words; neologisms; and foreign terms), Whitman made it difficult for them to embrace his poetry as he wished.

Sherry Southard

Bibliography

Allen, Irving Lewis. *The City in Slang: New York Life and Popular Speech*. New York: Oxford UP, 1993.

Bauerlein, Mark. *Whitman and the American Idiom*. Baton Rouge: Louisiana State UP, 1991.

Folsom, Ed. *Walt Whitman's Native Representations*. Cambridge: Cambridge UP, 1994.

Southard, Sherry G. "Whitman and Language: Great Beginnings for Great

American Poetry." *Mt. Olive Review* 4 (1990): 45–54.

———. "Whitman and Language: His 'Democratic' Words." Diss. Purdue U, 1972.

Warren, James Perrin. *Walt Whitman's Language Experiment.* University Park: Pennsylvania State UP, 1990.

Whitman, Walt. *Prose Works 1892.* Ed. Floyd Stovall. 2 vols. New York: New York UP, 1963–1964.

See also AMERICAN PRIMER, AN; DICTIONARIES; LANGUAGE; PLACE NAMES; "SLANG IN AMERICA"

"Slang in America" (1885)

This essay by Walt Whitman is his last prose statement published during his lifetime on the topic of language. It represents the final fruits of a career of collecting, annotating, and synthesizing materials on language in general and the English language in particular. "Slang in America" is approximately eighteen hundred words long and first appeared as an article in the *North American Review* in November 1885. It was later reprinted, with some editorial revisions, in *November Boughs* (1888).

The working title among Whitman's manuscript notes for much of the linguistic material he collected was "Names and Slang in America." Whitman told Horace Traubel in 1888 that the editors of the *North American Review* had approached him and asked for "a piece—anything." He claimed that all he had at hand were some collected observations on slang, so he submitted "Slang in America," with some assurance, remarking that slang was "one of my specialties" (Traubel 462).

In this piece, Whitman calls "slang" the "lawless germinal element, below all words and sentences, and behind all poetry," and he connects the language-refreshing, omnivorous nature of slang to what he sees as the essential genius of the United States's "most precious possession"—the English language (572).

One of his major points is that the creative element in language, its ability to adapt and develop, is as alive today with just as much fervor and intensity as it was at any point in the past. Whitman cites his characteristic favorites—working people at their labors, using their special jargon—as his chief examples: on city horsecars, the conductor is called a "snatcher"

because it is his job "to constantly pull or snatch the bell-strap, to stop or go on" (575).

Under the heading of slang, Whitman includes semantic change and other dynamic aspects of language, and most especially metaphor itself as a source for common words: "many of the oldest and solidest words we use, were originally generated from the daring and license of slang" (573).

Whitman celebrates neologisms, both English-based terms and those from Native American languages. He likes the Tennessee term "barefoot whiskey" for an undiluted drink, and he quotes several pieces of New York restaurant lingo: "stars and stripes" (ham and beans), "sleeve-buttons" (codfish balls), and "mystery" (hash) (575). He favors native names, such as "Oklahoma," for new territories.

Reflecting the original working title, the essay has as much about names as about slang. There are extensive lists and several quotations exhibiting American western place names (such as "Squaw Flat," "Shirttail Bend," and "Toenail Lake") and names of newspapers (such as *The Solid Muldoon,* of Ouray" and "*The Jimplecute,* of Texas"). There is also a list of striking or unusual American Indian names, including "Two-feathers-of-honor" and "Spiritual woman" (576).

Whitman praises and cites examples of aptness in nicknames (e.g., "Uncle Billy" Sherman [574]) and lists the nicknames of citizens of the various states. Some of these are common and still current, such as Indiana "Hoosiers" or Vermont "Green Mountain Boys." Others are less immediately identifiable, such as Rhode Island "Gun Flints" and South Carolina "Weasels" (575).

Whitman calls language "the grandest triumph of the human intellect" (574). He demonstrates his awareness of British and German studies in comparative philology, and he identifies the scientific examination of language with other sciences, such as geology (because of the strata in languages) or biology (because of the organic nature of language).

In his presentation of etymologies, Whitman actually quotes without acknowledgment from Ralph Waldo Emerson's *Nature.* For example, Whitman has "the term *right* means literally only straight. *Wrong* primarily meant twisted" (573). Emerson has "*Right* originally meant *straight; wrong* means twisted" (18). Such borrowing was, however, far from casual or random. Whitman's notions of the place and importance of language appear to be drawn from or are, at least, parallel to Emerson's seminal essay, especially the fourth chapter.

In "Slang in America" Whitman gives his readers and admirers additional encouragement to see his poetry and his attitude toward language as exemplifying a cause. America is the inheritor of all that has come before. English, America's language, is the heir and absorber of all human languages before it. Walt Whitman, America's poet and master of a dynamic slang-filled American English, speaks for America and all of humankind.

Michael R. Dressman

Bibliography

Dressman, Michael R. "Another Whitman Debt to Emerson." *Notes and Queries* ns 26 (1979): 305–306.

Emerson, Ralph Waldo. "Nature." *The Collected Works of Ralph Waldo Emerson.* Ed. Alfred R. Ferguson. Vol. 1. Cambridge, Mass.: Harvard UP, 1971. 3–45.

Nathanson, Tenney. *Whitman's Presence: Body, Voice, and Writing in "Leaves of Grass."* New York: New York UP, 1992.

Traubel, Horace. *With Walt Whitman in Camden.* Vol. 1. Boston: Small, Maynard, 1906.

Warren, James Perrin. *Walt Whitman's Language Experiment.* University Park: Pennsylvania State UP, 1990.

Whitman, Walt. "Slang in America." *Prose Works 1892.* Ed. Floyd Stovall. Vol. 2. New York: New York UP, 1964. 572–577.

See also AMERICAN PRIMER, AN; "AMERICA'S MIGHTIEST INHERITANCE"; DICTIONARIES; FOREIGN LANGUAGE BORROWINGS; LANGUAGE; NATIVE AMERICANS (INDIANS); PLACE NAMES; SLANG; SWINTON, WILLIAM

Slavery and Abolitionism

Walt Whitman's seemingly inconsistent and self-contradictory attitudes toward slavery have long been a source of critical debate. On one hand, Whitman's opposition to slavery is demonstrated in *Leaves of Grass* by the way in which he consistently includes African Americans in his vision of an ideal, multiracial republic and portrays them as beautiful, dignified, and intelligent. On the other hand, various Whitman texts show that he had little tolerance for abolitionism, that he thought blacks were inferior to whites, and that his opposition to the extension of slavery had little, if anything, to do with sympathy for slaves.

Whitman's attitudes toward slavery and abolitionism can best be understood by tracing the development of his thinking in the context of the national debate over slavery from the mid-1840s until the Civil War. Whitman began his journalistic career as an ardent free-soiler, but within several years his poetry experiments articulated a much different and more sympathetic attitude toward slaves. Whitman held these two attitudes in unresolved tension until 1854, when national events related to slavery radicalized Northern opinion and so encouraged Whitman to publish his poetry. In the 1855 *Leaves of Grass* Whitman's passages on slaves and slavery proclaim a radically egalitarian vision of persons of African descent while at the same time argue for popular political positions, such as opposition to the Fugitive Slave Law. A brief review of how Whitman's attitudes evolved makes clear the significant role slavery plays in his development as a poet.

Whitman's involvement with slavery began with his newspaper editorials on the 1846 Wilmot Proviso. The proviso, which stated that slavery was to be excluded from territory acquired in the war with Mexico, was eventually blocked by the Senate in March 1847 after rancorous sectional debate. But despite the proviso's defeat, the bill gave rise to the "free-soil" sentiment that would lead in 1848 to the formation of the Free Soil party.

Whitman consistently supported the Wilmot Proviso and the free-soil movement, beginning with his first editorials at the Brooklyn *Daily Eagle* until the 1850 Compromise. In his *Eagle* editorials in 1846–1847 Whitman argues, as did free-soil Northerners in Congress, that the introduction of slavery into new territories would discourage, if not prohibit, whites from migrating to those areas because white labor could not economically compete with slave labor and would be "degraded" by it. In this way, Whitman's opposition to slavery was directly connected to his dreams for the settlement and expansion of democracy into the West. "The voice of the North proclaims that *labor must not be degraded,*" Whitman writes in a 27 April 1847 editorial. "The young men of the free States must not be shut out from the new domain (where slavery does not now exist) by the *introduction* of an institution which will render their honorable industry no longer respectable" (*Gathering* 1:205–206).

From 1846 until the Civil War Whitman consistently opposed the extension of slavery on these grounds. He did not directly criticize the institution of slavery in the South and in fact opposed abolitionism, which he considered the work of radical extremists to destroy the compact of the Union. Such attitudes were already apparent in his 1842 temperance novel, *Franklin Evans; or The Inebriate*. In one episode of the novel, Whitman's protagonist journeys south to a Virginia plantation where he comes to understand from a wise slave owner that, contrary to abolitionist arguments, slavery is not sinful but beneficial, a source of sustenance and happiness for slaves. Moreover, Whitman's depiction of a Creole slave woman in this episode as sexually alluring yet also violent and vengeful suggests that his attitudes about blacks were drawn largely from contemporary racist stereotypes. Whitman's seeming indifference to the plight of blacks in his journalism and early fiction reflects a standard attitude of many white Northerners, including the New York Democratic party's Barnburner faction, of which Whitman was a member.

In 1848 Whitman became more active in the free-soil movement, serving as a local delegate to a national convention in Buffalo that August, when the Free Soil party was born, and editing a short-lived free-soil newspaper, the Brooklyn *Freeman*. While the Free Soil party elected only a few members to Congress that November, it succeeded in forcing the Whigs and Democrats to consider slavery as the primary issue on the national agenda.

By 1850, however, compromises between North and South so weakened the free-soil movement that Whitman abandoned his free-soil journalism. When regional divisions cast the future of the Union in doubt, Congress passed a series of resolutions that cumulatively came to be known as the 1850 Compromise. Whitman and Free-Soilers were outraged by several of these resolutions, including the organization of some western territories without restrictions on slavery and a stringent Fugitive Slave Law. Yet Unionist sentiment prevailed, and Whitman, who had focused much of his journalistic writing on slavery, wrote three letters to the free-soil journal *National Era* that fall, but was not to be heard from again for several years.

In these same years, however, Whitman was experimenting with an altogether different voice and attitude toward slavery in his notebook poetry experiments. Begun in 1847, this poetry makes clear the vital link between Whitman's emerging sense of a poetic self and attitudes toward slaves and slavery which are startlingly unlike those of his free-soil journalism. When Whitman breaks into poetry in these notebooks, his first fragment proclaims: "I am the poet of slaves and of the masters of slaves / I am the poet of the body / I am" (*Notebooks* 1:67). Whitman defines his very vocation as poet in terms of slavery, leveling the differences created by slavery and claiming to represent both slaves and their masters. Further on Whitman adds: "I go with the slaves of the earth equally with the masters . . . Entering into both so that both will understand me alike" (*Notebooks* 1:67). Neither Whitman's radical egalitarianism nor his identification with slaves could have been anticipated by his free-soil journalism, with its focus on white labor.

How Whitman achieved such a vision is difficult if not impossible to trace. One possibility is that Whitman's reading of Ralph Waldo Emerson, which occurred at about the same time, may have prompted Whitman toward a sense of his own divinity which he recognized as connected to the divinity of all others, including slaves. He may later have been sensitized to the plight of slaves during a four-month stint as editor of the New Orleans *Crescent* in 1848, when he wrote about persons of color he encountered and likely witnessed slave auctions. At any rate, by the late 1840s Whitman had established a pattern of opposing the extension of slavery as a free-soil journalist while imagining persons of African descent in radically sympathetic and inclusive terms in his poetry.

Whitman was not heard from as a journalist or a poet in the early 1850s. Yet when two national events in 1854 radically altered Northern attitudes about slavery, Whitman discovered an audience that would now be receptive both to his free-soil concerns and his new poetry about slaves. The passage of the Kansas-Nebraska Act in May infuriated many Northerners because the bill repealed the 1820 Missouri Compromise ban on slavery north of 36°30'. Such a repeal seemed to reserve Nebraska for freedom and Kansas for slavery, violating the fragile trust between North and South that had emerged with the 1850 Compromise.

Northern reaction was further galvanized a short time later when Anthony Burns, an escaped slave from Virginia, was arrested in Boston and placed under federal guard. When anger fomented by the Kansas-Nebraska bill inspired an attempt to rescue Burns in an attack on the courthouse, federal troops were called in to ensure Burns's return to his master. By June 1854 these two events ignited an explosion of antislavery sentiment in the North. Several Northern state legislatures called for the immediate repeal of both the Kansas-Nebraska Act and the Fugitive Slave Law.

With the public mood shifting, Whitman felt liberated, perhaps even compelled, to publish his poems in 1855. In the wake of recent events, *Leaves of Grass* portrays both the suffering and the dignity of African Americans, seen in the present as victims of slave-catchers but envisioned in the future as partners with whites in an egalitarian democracy. In the "hounded slave" episode from "Song of Myself" (section 33), the speaker not only sympathizes with, but in fact identifies with, the fugitive slave: "I am the hounded slave, I wince at the bite of the dogs." Whitman's change of the pronoun from "He" to "I" some time earlier in his notebooks now signals a central moment in the poem as the speaker merges his identity with others in the world: "I do not ask the wounded person how he feels, I myself become the wounded person." Yet this passage also reveals how Whitman's portrayal of slaves could serve his political purposes, especially his opposition to the Fugitive Slave Law, which was based, in fact, not on sympathy for slaves but on what he felt was the unwarranted intrusion of federal authority in a local matter.

Elsewhere in *Leaves of Grass* Whitman portrays African Americans with great depth and sensitivity. In the portraits of the "negro" drayman in "Song of Myself" or of the slaves at auction in "I Sing the Body Electric," Whitman celebrates African-American beauty, dignity, and strength in contrast to popular stereotypes, and he demonstrates the centrality of black persons to the democratic future of America. "Examine these limbs, red, black or white" ("I Sing," section 7), Whitman says of the auctioned slave, figuring him as emblem of a multiracial body politic. In the 1855 poem that later became "The Sleepers," Whitman gives voice to the slave's desire for vengeance which most Americans wished not to acknowledge: "I have been wronged . . . . I am oppressed . . . . I hate him

that oppresses me, / I will either destroy him, or he shall release me" (1855 *Leaves*).

After 1855 Whitman would diminish the power of these images and claims by the diffusion of focus on blacks through the addition of new poems. None of the new poems in 1856 or 1860 contain passages longer than two lines on slavery. Moreover, Whitman's prose writings in these years appear to apologize for slavery and disavow any humane commitment to slaves. In an 1857 editorial he avers that "the institution of slavery is not at all without its redeeming points" (*I Sit* 88), and in 1858 he editorializes: "Who believes that the Whites and Blacks can ever amalgamate in America? Or who wishes it to happen?" (*I Sit* 90).

Whitman's seeming change of heart must be understood in light of the effect of historical circumstance on his fundamental understanding of slavery. Whitman consistently believed that slavery was to be judged according to its threats to democracy. In the late 1840s Whitman's free-soil writings respond to the threat to democracy posed by the extension of slavery into the West. By the late 1850s Whitman's antislavery rhetoric turns conciliatory in response to the threat to the very existence of the Union.

Yet these political positions do not explain the eloquent empathy in his passages about blacks in the 1855 *Leaves of Grass*. One way to make sense of Whitman's seeming inconsistencies on slavery is to recognize that his journalism addressed the realities of the present, while his poetry pointed toward his hopes for America's democratic future. Whitman writes in the 1855 Preface concerning the great poet: "As he sees the farthest he has the most faith" (*Complete* 9). In this way Whitman's poetry about slaves captured what his politics could not, a faith in the humanity and dignity of African Americans and in their rightful place as free and equal citizens in the United States.

Martin Klammer

Bibliography

Allen, Gay Wilson. *The Solitary Singer: A Critical Biography of Walt Whitman.* 1955. Rev. ed. 1967. Chicago: U of Chicago P, 1985.

Foner, Eric. *Politics and Ideology in the Age of the Civil War.* New York: Oxford UP, 1980.

Klammer, Martin. *Whitman, Slavery, and the Emergence of "Leaves of Grass."* University Park: Pennsylvania State UP, 1995.

McPherson, James M. *Battle Cry of Freedom:*

The Civil War Era. New York: Oxford UP, 1988.

Rubin, Joseph Jay. *The Historic Whitman*. University Park: Pennsylvania State UP, 1973.

Thomas, M. Wynn. *The Lunar Light of Whitman's Poetry*. Cambridge, Mass.: Harvard UP, 1987.

———. "Walt Whitman and the Dreams of Labor." *Walt Whitman: The Centennial Essays*. Ed. Ed Folsom. Iowa City: U of Iowa P, 1994. 133–152.

Whitman, Walt. *Complete Poetry and Collected Prose*. Ed. Justin Kaplan. New York: Library of America, 1982.

———. *The Early Poems and the Fiction*. Ed. Thomas L. Brasher. New York: New York UP, 1963.

———. *The Gathering of the Forces*. Ed. Cleveland Rodgers and John Black. 2 vols. New York: Putnam, 1920.

———. *I Sit and Look Out: Editorials from the Brooklyn Daily Times*. Ed. Emory Holloway and Vernolian Schwarz. New York: Columbia UP, 1932.

———. *Notebooks and Unpublished Prose Manuscripts*. Ed. Edward F. Grier. 6 vols. New York: New York UP, 1984.

See also BARNBURNERS AND LOCOFOCOS; "BOSTON BALLAD (1854), A"; BROOKLYN *DAILY EAGLE*; BROOKLYN *FREEMAN*; BUFFALO FREE SOIL CONVENTION; BURNS, ANTHONY; COMPROMISE OF 1850; FREE SOIL PARTY; LABOR AND LABORING CLASSES; NEW ORLEANS *CRESCENT*; RACIAL ATTITUDES; "SONG OF MYSELF"; SOUTH, THE AMERICAN; WILMOT PROVISO

"Sleepers, The" (1855)

The poem that has become known as "The Sleepers" was first published as the fourth of the twelve untitled poems in the 1855 edition of *Leaves of Grass*. In the 1856 edition it became "Night Poem," and in the 1860 and 1867 editions it is titled "Sleep-Chasings." It acquired its final title in the 1871 edition. The poem was much revised as it passed through these various editions. Most significantly, after the 1871 edition Whitman excised from the end of section 1 a strikingly explicit description of sexual arousal and orgasm, and at the end of section 7 he eliminated a passage in which the persona identifies first with Lucifer, then with a slave whose "woman" has been

sold downriver, and finally with a whale. Some scholars have felt that these deletions were motivated more by Whitman's desire to accommodate his critics than for aesthetic concerns, and for this reason almost all serious students of the poem have returned to the 1855–1871 version. There is a widespread consensus that "The Sleepers" is, among the poems in the 1855 volume, second in significance only to what eventually became "Song of Myself," and one of the five or six most important poems in Whitman's entire poetic corpus. Paul Zweig calls "The Sleepers" the "dark twin of 'Song of Myself'" (245), and other critics have echoed this judgment. "The Sleepers" probes deep into the unconscious dream-world, the "night" side of human consciousness. Many critics have attempted to define what Whitman discovers on this voyage into the darkness, and in the process they have demonstrated that "The Sleepers" is one of Whitman's most complex and rewarding poems.

"The Sleepers" begins with the speaker's uneasy entry into the night-world; proceeds through various episodes, some persuasively dreamlike and others less so; and arrives finally at a luminous vision of the entire human race drawn together in sleep, under the shade of a maternal night. The movement of the poem is partly cyclic: the poem begins as the speaker's portion of the earth's surface passes into darkness, and it ends as that portion begins to re-emerge into the light. But the movement is also linear, insofar as the poem moves from troubled doubt concerning the speaker's relationship to the darkness and to his fellows, to a confident affirmation of the unity of humankind and a soaring celebration of the maternal darkness as the ultimate ground of human existence. Among the major critical questions that the poem poses are, first, does the poem hang together? In our passage from the beginning of the poem to the end, we encounter a series of episodes—an extended image of a drowning swimmer, the story of a shipwreck in which Whitman helped pull bodies from the sea, two vignettes of George Washington, and the story of a Native American woman who visited the poet's mother—that succeed one another more or less arbitrarily. Do these episodes help to develop some unified theme? If not, can we justify Whitman's decision to include these episodes in the poem? And critics have also focused on a second and more important question: how does the poem get from point A to point B, from doubt to certainty? And is the faith that Whitman affirms at the end truly earned and thus rhetorically convincing, or is he simply attempting to hypnotize himself and us with the incantatory power of his language?

One plausible and widely accepted reading of "The Sleepers" sees it as an account of a mystical experience. Thus James E. Miller, Jr., in one of the first (1957) full studies of "The Sleepers," argues that for Whitman "night symbolizes the world of spirituality, and sleep represents death's release of the soul" (130). Miller explains the middle episodes of the poem in accordance with this overall schema, arguing that the story of the "gigantic swimmer" and the story of the shipwreck serve to dramatize the speaker's encounter with death, while the Washington episodes and the story of the Native American woman offer examples of "deep spiritual love" (137). Armed with the knowledge he has gained in these episodes, the speaker emerges into a full spiritual enlightenment in the last two sections of the poem. "The effect of night and sleep—or submergence in the mystical state of the spiritual world—is twofold," Miller asserts; "there is a leveling and there is a healing" (139). More recently, George Hutchinson has taken this interpretation a step further, suggesting that the poem describes the soul-journey of a shaman who acquires through his visions the power to heal both himself and his nation. Readers who come to "The Sleepers" convinced that Whitman was a mystic and that the word "mystic" has a clear significance may find these readings satisfactory. Others, however, may feel that the probing, exploratory movement of the poem argues against any assumption that Whitman has here developed a consciously worked-out system of symbols concerning human spiritual life.

Starting from the genuinely dreamlike, even surrealistic feel of this poem, a second group of critics has applied psychoanalytic methods of analysis to "The Sleepers." As early as 1955, Richard Chase described the poem as dramatizing "the descent of the as yet unformed and unstable ego into the id, its confrontation there of the dark, human tragedy, its emergence in a new, more stable form" (54). The psychoanalytic approach has been further explored by Edwin Haviland Miller, who suggested in 1968 that "The Sleepers" is "not only a confession, one of Whitman's most personal revelations, but, more important, a reenactment of ancient puberty rites" (72). In his dream, Miller sug-

gests, the "I" engages in a confused and fumbling exploration of his own sexuality. In the wet dream or masturbatory climax of section 1, the dreamer's penis, in the symbol of a pier, reaches out into the water (a feminine symbol), but the dreamer sees the vagina as "toothed" and threatening and therefore recoils. In parts 3 and 4, the sea, still feminine, is still destructive. Section 5 attempts to invoke Washington as a reassuring father figure, but he is ineffectual, and the Native American woman who appears only to vanish "is another destructive maternal figure" (E.H. Miller 81). Sections 7 and 8 attempt to move beyond such negative images of the woman, and Miller believes that Whitman has by the end of the poem emerged into a full adult sexuality. But other psychoanalytic critics, notably Stephen Black, have questioned this reading of the final sections, seeing in them instead an unconvincing attempt to conceal beneath an affirmative rhetoric Whitman's deeply regressive desire to recover a state of undifferentiated unity with the mother.

Orthodox Freudians like E.H. Miller and Black assume that normal adult sexuality is heterosexual, and they judge Whitman as either approaching this norm or deviating from it. But some other critics, although also touched by the influence of psychoanalysis, reject the hypothesis that there is a single model of normal sexuality. Two such critics, Robert K. Martin and Byrne R.S. Fone, have interpreted the sexual feelings expressed in "The Sleepers" as explicitly and unabashedly homosexual. These critics have persuasively interpreted the tangled imagery accompanying the wet dream of section 1 as a fantasy of homosexual fellatio. Fone contends that in the poem, "as the speaker confronts the most primal and irrational facets of his sexuality . . . he will literally eat the phallic flesh and drink the seminal blood of his now fully confirmed homosexual identity" (117). This reading, while offering a persuasive explanation of sections 1 and 2, has more difficulty justifying the presence in the poem of the middle episodes. Martin suggests, not too plausibly, that the story of the Native American woman and the poet's mother offers an example of homoerotic desire between women, but Fone dismisses these episodes in a sentence, describing them as merely "confused nightmare visions of public and conscious loss" (127). But the homosexual reading of the poem does offer a simple explanation of the final sections, where the sense of "love, completion, and well-being"

(Fone 127) can be read as a postorgasmic glow. From this perspective, then, the poem follows a natural pattern of rising tension leading to climax and a sense of fulfillment and unity with the cosmos.

Other recent critics, while by no means rejecting the homoerotic reading, have seen important political dimensions in "The Sleepers." For example, Betsy Erkkila has argued that the persona of the poem enters not only into his own unconscious mind but also into "a kind of political unconscious of the nation" (120). Not surprisingly, Erkkila focuses primarily on the middle sections of the poem, where the image of Washington as the tender and loving but also tragic father of the nation suggests some of Whitman's own anxieties about the future of the Union. She sees the story of the Native American woman and Whitman's mother as an idyllic image of a lost ideal: a nation united by bonds of love that transcend racial and regional differences (122). Similarly, in a brilliant recent interpretation, Kerry Larson sees "The Sleepers" as an attempt to mediate between the "I" and the "Union." The "I" of the poem, Larson notes, is shifting and unstable, as it seeks to establish its own existence by identifying in turn with one individual after another. This "I" is "both overspecified and secondary, both at the center of the story and inconsequential to it" (62). This perspective can both account for the sexual confusions of section 1 and the later, more public episodes. In section 3, for example, the gigantic swimmer is the "I" itself, which struggles heroically but vainly to survive in these treacherous seas, and the Washington, Native American woman, and Lucifer episodes all suggest the fragility of the social order. From a political perspective, the upbeat conclusion of the poem suggests that Whitman is whistling in the dark; both Erkkila and Larson find this conclusion unpersuasive, but Larson also senses a deep pathos in the poem's search for a way to "restore a splintered community" (72).

But perhaps the most fruitful line of inquiry in critical discussions of "The Sleepers" has focused on the poem itself as an empowering, liberating and even potentially healing verbal act. In 1966 Howard Waskow suggested that "The Sleepers" is a new and distinctive kind of poem, a "monodrama"—that is, a poem in which the speaker, rather than "describing an action and giving us guides to it," is actually "*going through* the action" as the poem occurs (139). "The Sleepers" thus becomes a kind of "action poem," a poem that is primarily "about" the action it is itself performing. What sort of action is "The Sleepers" performing? In a subtle and provocative essay, Mutlu Blasing has argued that the poem issues out of an impulse of transcendence, a desire to merge the self in a larger whole. Whitman, she suggests, recognizes that self-transcendence means the death of the self, but nevertheless he risks this gambit, confident that he can recover his annihilated self in the act of poetic enunciation. Similarly, James Perrin Warren has shown how the language of Whitman's poem creates a "transcendental or poetic self . . . [which] mediates between the poet and the numberless others, between the one and the many" (18). The catalogue in particular, Warren shows, makes possible such mediation, by mingling stative and dynamic causal structures. The muscular movement of Whitman's language can do things that logic knows not of; and it is by trusting the movement of language itself, not by appealing to some mystical and/or erotic power lying beyond language, that Whitman wins his way through to the sense of harmony and unity we hear in the final sections of "The Sleepers."

Burton Hatlen

Bibliography

Abrams, Robert E. "The Function of Dreams and Dream-Logic in Whitman's Poetry." *Texas Studies in Literature and Language* 17 (1975): 599–616.

Black, Stephen A. *Whitman's Journeys into Chaos.* Princeton: Princeton UP, 1975.

Blasing, Mutlu. "'The Sleepers': The Problem of the Self in Whitman." *Walt Whitman Review* 21 (1975): 111–119.

Chase, Richard. *Walt Whitman Reconsidered.* New York: William Sloane Associates, 1955.

Durand, Régis. "'A New Rhythmus Fitted for Thee': On Some Discursive Strategies in Whitman's Poetry." *North Dakota Quarterly* 51.1 (1983): 48–56.

Erkkila, Betsy. *Whitman the Political Poet.* New York: Oxford UP, 1989.

Fone, Byrne R.S. *Masculine Landscapes: Walt Whitman and the Homoerotic Text.* Carbondale: Southern Illinois UP, 1992.

French, R.W. "Whitman's Dream Vision:

A Reading of 'The Sleepers.'" *Walt Whitman Quarterly Review* 8 (1990): 1–15.

Hutchinson, George. *The Ecstatic Whitman: Literary Shamanism & the Crisis of the Union.* Columbus: Ohio State UP, 1986.

Larson, Kerry C. *Whitman's Drama of Consensus.* Chicago: U of Chicago P, 1988.

Martin, Robert K. *The Homosexual Tradition in American Poetry.* Austin: U of Texas P, 1979.

Miller, Edwin Haviland. *Walt Whitman's Poetry: A Psychological Journey.* Boston: Houghton Mifflin, 1968.

Miller, James E., Jr. *A Critical Guide to "Leaves of Grass."* Chicago: U of Chicago P, 1957.

Warren, James Perrin. "'Catching the Sign': Catalogue Rhetoric in 'The Sleepers.'" *Walt Whitman Quarterly Review* 5.2 (1987): 16–34.

Waskow, Howard J. *Whitman: Explorations in Form.* Chicago: U of Chicago P, 1966.

Zweig, Paul. *Walt Whitman: The Making of the Poet.* New York: Basic Books, 1984.

See also LEAVES OF GRASS, 1855 EDITION; MYSTICISM; PSYCHOLOGICAL APPROACHES; SEX AND SEXUALITY

Smith, Alexander (ca. 1830–1867)

A minor Scottish poet, essayist, and lace-pattern designer (a profession learned from his father), Alexander Smith received little formal education. Born in Kilmarnock, Smith mainly educated himself by reading Sir Walter Scott, James Fenimore Cooper, William Wordsworth, Lord Byron, Percy Bysshe Shelley, John Keats, and Alfred, Lord Tennyson.

In 1850 Smith published in the "Poet's Corner" of the Glasgow *Evening Citizen*. These short poems received little notice, but his *A Life Drama and Other Poems* (1853) attracted enough attention by 1855 to have run through several editions. Whitman took notice of *A Life Drama* in 1854, and while he was largely unmoved by the work, he nevertheless was excited by a passage announcing the advent of "a mighty poet whom this age shall choose / To be its spokesman to all coming times" (qtd. in Zweig 149). For the most part, Whitman learned from Smith and other nineteenth-century poets how not to write.

Critics dubbed Smith a "spasmodic" poet and attacked him throughout his career for pro-

ducing ineffectively organized long poems and essays plagued by overwrought images, feverish emotions, and obscure meanings—labels Smith never overcame. Whitman learned from Smith's dubious example—he wished to write clearly and simply.

Stephen A. Cooper

Bibliography
Kaplan, Justin. *Walt Whitman: A Life.* 1980. New York: Bantam Books, 1982.

Scott, Mary Jane W. "Alexander Smith: Poet of Victorian Scotland." *Studies in Scottish Literature* 14 (1979): 98–111.

Smith, Alexander. *The Poetical Works of Alexander Smith.* Ed. William Sinclair. Edinburgh: Nimmo, 1909.

Zweig, Paul. *Walt Whitman: The Making of the Poet.* New York: Basic Books, 1984.

See also INFLUENCES ON WHITMAN, PRINCIPAL

Smith, Logan Pearsall (1865–1946)

Logan Pearsall Smith was an essayist, literary critic, and writer of aphorisms. In 1913 he helped Robert Bridges establish the Society for Pure English. His works include *The Life and Letters of Sir Henry Wotton* (1907), *The English Language* (1912), and *Milton and His Modern Critics* (1940). Smith is probably best known for *All Trivia* (1933) and *Unforgotten Years* (1938).

Smith was born in Millville, New Jersey, son of Quakers Hannah Whitall and Robert Pearsall Smith. He was educated at Haverford, Harvard, and Oxford. In 1888 he made England his permanent residence, and in 1913 he became a British citizen. Smith and his sister Mary Whitall Smith, who had read *Leaves of Grass* as a student at Smith College, admired Whitman's writing. Invited by their father, Whitman first visited the Smith home in Germantown, Pennsylvania, at Christmas time in 1882. During Whitman's many visits with the Smiths, he participated in family activities—after-dinner conversations, singing, and recitations. Logan Pearsall Smith was strongly influenced by Whitman's "familiar presence" in their home (Smith, "Walt Whitman" 100). The poet provided him with "ideas in solution tho' not yet crystallized," thereby affecting Smith's ways of seeing and thinking (Smith, *Chime of Words* 41). Smith devoted a chapter of *Unforgotten Years* to his remembrances of Whitman; however, William White has noted errors in Smith's account of the poet's first visit with the Smiths. Moreover, Barbara Strachey's version of the Smiths' arrangements for this visit differs from accounts found in sources cited by White.

Whitman and Smith's relationship revealed a mutual fondness and caring. They remained friendly until the poet's death.

Christina Davey

Bibliography

Smith, Logan Pearsall. *A Chime of Words: The Letters of Logan Pearsall Smith.* Ed. Edwin Tribble. New York: Ticknor and Fields, 1984.

———. "Walt Whitman." *Unforgotten Years.* By Smith. Boston: Little, Brown, 1939. 79–108.

Strachey, Barbara. *Remarkable Relations: The Story of the Pearsall Smith Family.* London: Victor Gollancz, 1980. Rpt. as *Remarkable Relations: The Story of the Pearsall Smith Women.* New York: Universe Books, 1982.

White, William. "Logan Pearsall Smith on Walt Whitman: A Correction and Some Unpublished Letters." *Walt Whitman Newsletter* 4 (1958): 87–90.

Whitman, Walt. *The Correspondence.* Ed. Edwin Haviland Miller. 6 vols. New York: New York UP, 1961–1977.

See also COSTELLOE, MARY WHITALL SMITH; PHILADELPHIA, PENNSYLVANIA; QUAKERS AND QUAKERISM; SMITH, ROBERT PEARSALL

Smith, Robert Pearsall (1827–1898)

Philadelphia Quaker Robert Pearsall Smith was a map publisher, glass manufacturer, and evangelist popular in the United States and England, and on the European Continent. He fostered the evolution of the map publishing industry in the United States by being one of the first to reproduce maps using the anastatic process of lithography, an easier and less expensive method of reproducing maps (1846). His religious works include *Holiness through Faith* (1870).

Smith, son of John Jay and Rachel Pearsall Smith, was educated at Haverford College. In 1851, he married Hannah Whitall. Smith and his family befriended Whitman at Christmas time, 1882. The eldest child, Mary Whitall Smith, had wanted to meet Whitman after reading his work, so her father invited the poet to their Germantown home. Robert Pearsall Smith joined Whitman's American supporters. In 1883 he gave Whitman two hundred shares in the Sierra Grande Mines, Lake Valley, New Mexico;

however, the mines failed. Moreover, he took Whitman to New York to deliver the Lincoln lecture at the Madison Square Theater on April 14, 1887, and planned Whitman's reception held at the Westminster Hotel. There, the poet enjoyed the attention of two hundred to three hundred admirers.

Both Smith and Whitman valued their relationship. Although Hannah Whitall and Robert Pearsall Smith moved permanently to England in 1888, Whitman's friendship with Smith and his family continued until the poet's death.

Christina Davey

Bibliography

Ristow, Walter W. "The Map Publishing Career of Robert Pearsall Smith." *Quarterly Journal of the Library of Congress* 26 (1969): 170–196.

Strachey, Barbara. *Remarkable Relations: The Story of the Pearsall Smith Family.* London: Victor Gollancz, 1980. Rpt. as *Remarkable Relations: The Story of the Pearsall Smith Women.* New York: Universe Books, 1982.

Whitman, Walt. *The Correspondence.* Ed. Edwin Haviland Miller. 6 vols. New York: New York UP, 1961–1977.

———. *Daybooks and Notebooks.* Ed. William White. Vol. 2. New York: New York UP, 1978.

See also COSTELLOE, MARY WHITALL SMITH; LINCOLN'S DEATH; PHILADELPHIA, PENNSYLVANIA; QUAKERS AND QUAKERISM; SMITH, LOGAN PEARSALL

Smuts, Jan Christian (1870–1950)

Jan Christian Smuts was an influential South African leader and prime minister who played a key role in world politics for over five decades. As a student at Cambridge in England, Smuts was greatly influenced by Whitman, on whom he wrote an unpublished book and developed a philosophy called Holism.

As a distinguished law student and former theology major, Smuts was on scholarship and known for voracious reading and daunting study habits. Whitman's poetry encouraged Smuts to move "beyond" theology into a transformative realm that married philosophy, science, and spiritualism. Coming from a fundamentalist religious background, Smuts compared his release from his family-induced religious upbringing to that of St. Paul's liberation from the dominion of law by the revelation of the power of grace. Whitman's writing helped Smuts create an understanding of natural man and in turn aided his study of the development of individual personality that was to remain an interest his entire life.

While at Cambridge, Smuts completed a large scholarly work on Whitman; his treatise was to remain unpublished as he was unable to retain a publisher while in England or upon his return to South Africa. Influenced by Whitman's universality, Smuts developed Holism, a minor if overlooked philosophy that sought to explain an invisible link between seemingly unrelated principles in nature. Holism involves an expanded vision and a new paradigm of organization that involves "seeing" the whole to understand the small. Inherent in this philosophy is the idea that the mind evolves just as living matter does. Holism bears a strong resemblance to Hindu philosophy, particularly as seen through Whitman's eyes and eclectic knowledge.

D. Neil Richardson

Bibliography

Crafford, F.S. *Smuts: A Bibliography.* Garden City, N.Y.: Doubleday, 1943.

Friedman, Bernard. *Smuts: A Reappraisal.* New York: St. Martin's, 1976.

Ingham, Kenneth. *Jan Christian Smuts: The Conscience of a South African.* New York: St. Martin's, 1986.

Smuts, Jan Christian. *Walt Whitman: A Study in the Evolution of Personality.* Ed. Alan L. McLeod. Detroit: Wayne State UP, 1973.

See also AFRICA, WHITMAN IN; EVOLUTION; HINDU LITERATURE; RELIGION

"So Long!" (1860)

Whitman first added "So Long!" to *Leaves of Grass* in 1860, and in this and all later editions it is the final poem in the volume, even though the two annexes added in the 1888 and 1891 editions partly obscure the climactic position of the poem. Whitman revised the poem extensively: the 1860 text runs eighty-nine lines, but in the 1867 edition Whitman cut twenty-one lines, and in the 1871 and subsequent editions he added three lines. "So Long!," as Kenneth M. Price and Cynthia G. Bernstein note, stands within the tradition of the poetic envoi, in which the poet bids farewell to his book and sends it on its way to the reader. This envoi is distinctively Whitmanesque not only in its substitution of the colloquial American "so long!" for the elegant French label but also, as George B. Hutchinson has argued, in its evocation of an ecstatic, even orgasmic union between the poet, his book, and the reader. But "So Long!," as other critics have noted, is also shadowed by a sense of dark foreboding, perhaps triggered by the impending war, and the poem is as interesting for the conflicts that it tries to overcome as for the moment of orgasmic union that it proclaims.

In the climactic lines of "So Long!," Whitman says farewell to his poetic project ("My songs cease, I abandon them") and announces that he will now step forward in the flesh ("From behind the screen where I hid I advance personally solely to you"). There follow the most famous lines in the poem:

> Camerado, this is no book,
> Who touches this touches a man,
> (Is it night? are we here together alone?)
> It is I you hold and who holds you,
> I spring from the pages into your arms—
>   decease calls me forth.

The declaration that the man and the book are one and the same is clearly a pivotal moment in *Leaves of Grass,* at once offering a kind of immortality (as long as the book is read, the man lives) and claiming a radical authenticity for the words on the page, which are no longer mere signifiers, traces pointing toward an absent plenitude, but rather become an incarnation (more "real," perhaps, than the material flesh) of Walt Whitman himself, so that "decease" thereby opens the way to a new life.

But "So Long!" is a poem of enduring interest not simply because it makes the claim that man and book are one, but because of the rhetorical strategies it employs to arrive at this moment. As the poem begins, Whitman assumes a prophetic stance: he will "conclude" by announcing "what comes after me." What follows is a vision of an emerging superrace (as Harold Aspiz notes, the eugenics movement has left its imprint on this poem) united by a steadily increasing "adhesiveness." But then, more or less midway in the poem, the poet finds himself overwhelmed by his vision of the future: "I foresee too much, it means more than I thought, / It appears to me I am dying." There follows an extended and syntactically tangled series of participles, developing an almost hallucinatory image of the poet passing through the world, "Screaming electric," scattering about him "[s]parkles hot, seed ethereal down in the dirt dropping." Clearly, Whitman wants to spread his seed—but also he fears that his seed may simply fall, onanistically, in the dirt. (Or perhaps this seed will bring the dirt itself to life?) If this passage carries us toward a moment of orgasmic climax, then, the poet seems to feel some anxiety that this moment might be merely masturbatory.

The ambiguities that hover about the "seed ethereal"—both spermatic and spiritual, "seminal" in both senses—also pervade the final stanzas of "So Long!" Having met his reader in the night and in a privacy that invites intimacy, the poet foresees a moment of erotic bliss, as he springs from the pages into the reader's arms:

O how your fingers drowse me,
Your breath falls around me like dew,
   your pulse lulls the tympans of my ears,
I feel immerged from head to foot,
Delicious, enough.

The erotic experience here evoked seems oddly infantile, as the poet assumes a wholly passive role, stroked, cradled, and finally swallowed up—"immerged" suggests both immersion and merger. Ironically, too, even though the poet earlier announced that he has stepped out from behind his book, every line in this passage could as easily be spoken by the book itself—stroked by the reader's fingers, etc.—as by the man. The poet has sought to cast aside the book to achieve a total, unmediated union with his reader. But his own language reveals that this union can come only through and in language, so that the fusion of person and book ends by generating a new and endless indeterminacy.

Burton Hatlen

Bibliography

Aspiz, Harold. *Walt Whitman and the Body Beautiful.* Urbana: U of Illinois P, 1980.

Erkkila, Betsy. *Whitman the Political Poet.* New York: Oxford UP, 1989.

Hutchinson, George B. *The Ecstatic Whitman: Literary Shamanism & the Crisis of the Union.* Columbus: Ohio State UP, 1986.

Nathanson, Tenney. *Whitman's Presence: Body, Voice, and Writing in "Leaves of Grass."* New York: New York UP, 1992.

Price, Kenneth M., and Cynthia G. Bernstein. "Whitman's Sign of Parting: 'So long!' as l'envoi." *Walt Whitman Quarterly Review* 9 (1991): 65–76.

Snyder, John. *The Dear Love of Man: Tragic and Lyric Communion in Walt Whitman.* The Hague: Mouton, 1975.

See also DEATH; "GOOD-BYE MY FANCY!"; IMMORTALITY; *LEAVES OF GRASS, 1860 EDITION*; "SONGS OF PARTING"

Society for the Suppression of Vice

Vice societies flourished in the late nineteenth century in many American cities. Funded by the wealthy, these watchdog groups were powerful lobbies for anti-obscenity and anticontraception laws, which they also helped to enforce. Although they eventually earned the ridicule and contempt of a majority of thinking people, they were initially philanthropic in intent and practice, until an overly zealous vice hunter, Anthony Comstock (1844–1915), gave them a bad name by both deviously entrapping suspects and pruriently enjoying the very vices he was supposed to be suppressing.

In 1882 James Osgood was pressured by Boston district attorney Oliver Stevens, himself under the influence of the New England Society for the Suppression of Vice (later known as the Watch and Ward Society), to withdraw *Leaves of Grass* from publication because it violated "the Public Statutes concerning obscene literature." Osgood, not up for a fight, sent Whitman a list of passages and whole poems that would have to be amended or deleted for publication to continue. Included among the allegedly obscene material were "A Woman Waits for Me," "To a Common Prostitute," "I Sing the Body Electric," and "Spontaneous Me." At first, Whitman was willing to make some revisions, but when they were not sufficient for Osgood, Whitman wrote back that expurgation "will not be thought of under any circumstances." Thus began a controversy that would eventually boost the sales of *Leaves of Grass,* now "banned in Boston."

In 1872 Anthony Comstock, under the auspices of the YMCA, founded the New York Society for the Suppression of Vice. By 1882 his influence and power were so pervasive that several of Whitman's friends (e.g., William Douglas O'Connor) were convinced that the Boston district attorney had merely been his tool. In any event, when liberal reformists and anarchist free-love advocates began to champion Whitman, Comstock became a more direct threat. George Chainey provocatively published "To a Common Prostitute" in Boston, and when he boldly attempted to mail it, ran up against the Comstock Act, which prohibited the distribution of obscene material in the mail. (After three weeks delay in the post office, the postmaster general declared the poem inoffensive.) And Benjamin Tucker, also in Boston, publicly challenged the vice society to prosecute him for publishing *Leaves* from Osgood's plates. (Tucker had made an offer directly to Whitman, who ignored it, not wanting to be associated with free love and anarchy.) But it was Ezra Heywood, president of the New England Free-Love League, who piqued Comstock enough to make him threaten to suppress Whitman's book if anyone attempted to publish it in New York. Heywood was arrested for publishing (along with antimarriage literature) "Prostitute" and "A Woman Waits for Me." When these poems were excluded from the indictment by the judge, Whitman was glad to know that Comstock finally "retire[d] with his tail intensely curved inwards" (*Correspondence* 3:338–339).

William Douglas O'Connor's vituperative diatribes against Comstock—most notably, "Mr. Comstock as Cato the Censor" (*New York Tribune*, August 1882)—reminded the "mousing owl" of the vice society that the protection afforded literary classics like *The Decameron* should also be given to the Good Gray Poet's great book. Fortunately, after Heywood's trial, the scandal surrounding *Leaves* faded. And though Whitman did not like being associated with the free-love league (or being lumped with the likes of *The Lustful Turk*), the Comstockery of the vice societies in Boston and New York made his book a little more famous, and—apparently more delectable as a piece of forbidden fruit—for a brief while it sold well and made the poet some respectable royalties.

Joseph Andriano

Bibliography

Boyer, Paul S. *Purity in Print: The Vice-Society Movement and Book Censorship in America*. New York: Scribner, 1968.

D'Emilio, John, and Estelle B. Freedman. *Intimate Matters: A History of Sexuality in America*. New York: Harper and Row, 1988.

Loving, Jerome. *Walt Whitman's Champion: William Douglas O'Connor*. College Station: Texas A&M UP, 1978.

Reynolds, David S. *Walt Whitman's America: A Cultural Biography*. New York: Knopf, 1995.

Whitman, Walt. *The Correspondence*. Ed. Edwin Haviland Miller. 6 vols. New York: New York UP, 1961–1977.

See also BOSTON, MASSACHUSETTS; "CHILDREN OF ADAM"; COMSTOCK, ANTHONY; HEYWOOD, EZRA H.; "I SING THE BODY ELECTRIC"; O'CONNOR, WILLIAM DOUGLAS; OSGOOD, JAMES R.; SEX AND SEXUALITY; "SPONTANEOUS ME"; STEVENS, OLIVER; "TO A COMMON PROSTITUTE"; "WOMAN WAITS FOR ME, A"

"Some Fact-Romances" (1845)

This work, a collection of five numbered short tales and an introduction, first appeared in *The Aristidean,* December 1845. Several of the tales were later published separately: the first as "A Fact-Romance of Long Island," the second as "The Old Black Widow," and the fifth as "An Incident on Long Island Forty Years Ago." For publication history and revisions, see Brasher's edition of *The Early Poems and the Fiction.*

Whitman's purpose in gathering the tales under one title is obscure. In the introduction, he pledges that the stories are true and, therefore, more charming than fiction. The fifth Fact-Romance involves Whitman's mother and grandparents.

The first Fact-Romance has been singled out by Brasher as, perhaps, Whitman's best effort at fiction writing. After a boat capsizes, a young man, helping his sister to shore, hears his fiancée's call for help. He abandons his sister, who then drowns. Within a year, the couple marries, but the man becomes weaker and weaker and finally sinks into a death caused by grief.

In the second Fact-Romance, a pious old African-American widow saves an innocent deaf-and-dumb girl from the indecency of their Broadway neighborhood. The third tells of an émigré French couple. When the wife becomes ill, they consult several New York physicians. The wife dies on the return trip, and the husband becomes a madman. In the fourth, a villain is captured because he tries to retrieve from a pawnbroker his mother's keepsake instead of trying to escape. In the final Fact-Romance, during a storm, two frightened women mistake the sound of falling peaches for footsteps of a ghost.

Reynolds sees each tale as a variety of sensationalism, though the second seems more sentimental than sensational and the fifth includes humor.

Patrick McGuire

Bibliography

Reynolds, David S. *Walt Whitman's America: A Cultural Biography*. New York: Knopf, 1995.

Whitman, Walt. *The Early Poems and the Fiction*. Ed. Thomas L. Brasher. New York: New York UP, 1963.

See also "BOY LOVER, THE"; "DUMB KATE"; POPULAR CULTURE, WHITMAN AND; SHORT FICTION, WHITMAN'S

"Sometimes with One I Love" (1860)

Originally number 39 in the "Calamus" cluster, "Sometimes with One I Love," a four-line poem, first appeared in *Leaves of Grass* in 1860. It advances Whitman's view that for all the ups and downs of friendship or love, there can be no "unreturn'd love." The reward is certain "one way or another" because even the rage of unrequited love produces "these songs." The poem reworks a universal poetic theme: art is born of anguish; the sorer the lover feels, the better for his/her art.

Few readers of this poem seem to have missed the revision its third line has undergone. The 1860 text had for its third line, "Doubtless I could not have perceived the universe, or written one of my poems, if I had not freely given myself to comrades, to love." Whitman deletes this line in 1867 and replaces it with "(I loved a certain person ardently and my love was not return'd, / Yet out of that I have written these songs.)" Often enough, this has invited some biographical speculations. Edwin Haviland Miller, for one, finds the revision rather pointless because he feels that for all the poet's supposed intimacy with Peter Doyle in 1867, love is more brotherly and universal in "Calamus" as a whole.

K. Narayana Chandran

Bibliography

Helms, Alan. "'Hints . . . Faint Clews and Indirections': Whitman's Homosexual Disguises." *Walt Whitman: Here and Now*. Ed. Joann P. Krieg. Westport, Conn.: Greenwood, 1985. 61–67.

Miller, Edwin Haviland. *Walt Whitman's Poetry: A Psychological Journey*. New York: New York UP, 1969.

Miller, James E., Jr. "'Calamus': The Leaf and the Root." *A Century of Whitman Criticism*. Ed. Edwin Haviland Miller. Bloomington: Indiana UP, 1969. 303–320.

Whitman, Walt. *Leaves of Grass: Comprehensive Reader's Edition*. Ed. Harold W. Blodgett and Sculley Bradley. New York: New York UP, 1965.

See also COMRADESHIP

"Song at Sunset" (1860)

This poem was first published in the 1860 edition of *Leaves of Grass* as number 8 under the heading "Chants Democratic." It was annexed to *Leaves of Grass* as one of the *Songs Before Parting* in 1867 and later under the cluster "Songs of Parting" in 1871. In the Barrett manuscript the title reads "A Sunset Carol."

We find Whitman once again celebrating the joys of life, the simple miracles of daily living: "To breathe the air . . . To speak—to walk—to seize something by the hand!" Throughout his poetry, Whitman attempts to communicate the richness life affords him. This is a simple, yet rich and elegant song extolling the sheer and profound nature of life as witnessed by the poet. This celebration, as proclaimed in "Song at Sunset," is a consistent theme that finds itself again and again in so much of Whitman's work.

In his evaluation of this poem, James E. Miller, Jr., points to the poet's "resolution to inflate his throat and sing" (251). Whitman himself exclaims in "Song of Myself" that the sunrise would kill him if he could not "now and always send sun-rise out of me" (section 25). Words become the necessary vehicle for the expression of this "sun-rise." To Whitman, words are not only necessary, but are, of themselves, transcendental in nature. He writes in his *American Primer* that nothing is "more spiritual than words" (1).

The poet's relationship with language is as spiritual as his relationship with nature; the former is a celebration of the latter. For Whitman, the "real words" transcend what is written on the page. In "A Song of the Rolling Earth" he tells us that these "curves, angles, dots" are not the words. The "substantial words" are all around us—in the "ground and sea . . . in the air . . . in you" (section 1). Carmine Sarracino calls this the poet's "language of nature, a language of perfection and silence" (8).

It is out of this silence, what Whitman in *Democratic Vistas* has termed "the devout ecstasy, the soaring flight" (*Prose Works* 2:398), that "Song at Sunset" springs. "Illustrious every one! . . . Good in all . . . Wonderful to be here!" Each phrase echoes an ever familiar strain of what Whitman calls the "noiseless operation of one's isolated Self" (*Prose Works* 2:399). The poem accords the reader yet another glimpse into the "endless finalés of things," a theme of which the poet never tires—a theme which aims at undressing the mysteries and revealing life's affirmation of itself.

Frederick J. Butler

Bibliography

Miller, James E., Jr. *A Critical Guide to "Leaves of Grass."* Chicago: U of Chicago P, 1957.

Sarracino, Carmine. "Figures of Transcendence in Whitman's Poetry." *Walt Whitman Quarterly Review* 5.1 (1987): 1–11.

Whitman, Walt. *An American Primer.* 1904. Ed. Horace Traubel. Stevens Point, Wis.: Holy Cow!, 1987.

———. *Leaves of Grass: Comprehensive Reader's Edition.* Ed. Harold W. Blodgett and Sculley Bradley. New York: New York UP, 1965.

———. *Leaves of Grass: A Textual Variorum of the Printed Poems.* Ed. Harold W. Blodgett, Sculley Bradley, Arthur Golden, and William White. Vol. 2. New York: New York UP, 1980.

———. *Prose Works 1892.* Ed. Floyd Stovall. 2 vols. New York: New York UP, 1963–1964.

———. *Whitman's Manuscripts: "Leaves of Grass" (1860).* Ed. Fredson Bowers. Chicago: U of Chicago P, 1955.

See also AGE AND AGING; "SONGS OF PARTING"

"Song for Occupations, A" (1855)

The poem that became "A Song for Occupations" in the 1881 and subsequent editions of *Leaves of Grass* originated as the second of the untitled poems in the 1855 edition, where it immediately follows what eventually became "Song of Myself." In later editions it became "Poem of The Daily Work of The Workmen and Workwomen of These States" (1856), chant number 3 of the "Chants Democratic" (1860), "To Workingmen" (1867), and "Carol of Occupations" (1871 and 1876). The poem also passed through extensive internal revisions. To the 178 lines of the original, Whitman had added 27 lines by 1860, when the poem reached its maximum length of 205 lines; but then he began to cut, and by 1881 he had pruned away 59 lines of the 1860 version while adding five new lines, for a total of 151 lines. Throughout these changes the poem is concerned, as its various titles suggest, with work and working people. But the changes are so radical that the 1855–1860 text is in some important ways a different kind of poem from the post-1881 text.

M. Wynn Thomas has argued that "A Song for Occupations" is principally concerned with "the loss of the conception of the complete human being . . . Whitman commits himself to pitting his ineffectual strength against the whole weight of the American predilection for respecting the power of money to decide personal worth and to dictate the terms of personal relations" (13). Whitman has great difficulty, as Mark Bauerlein notes, in saying precisely what has been lost: "I do not know what it is except that it is grand, and that it is happiness" (section 3). But the primary symptom of the loss seems to be the tendency of the citizens of the republic to think ill of themselves:

> Why what have you thought of yourself?
> Is it you then that thought yourself less?
> Is it you that thought the President greater
>   than you?
> Or the rich better off than you? or the
>   educated wiser than you?
>
> (section 1)

More broadly, the image has taken precedence over substance, the abstract simulacra has replaced the thing itself: "Have you reckon'd that the landscape took substance and form that it might be painted in a picture? / Or men and women that they might be written of, and songs sung?" (section 3).

What has been lost is a sense of "wholeness," both in things and in the self. "Will the whole come back then?" the poet asks a little wistfully, at the turning point of the poem (the beginning of section 5 in the post-1881 version). "A Song for Occupations" seeks to recover wholeness by affirming the dignity of human labor, as the process that generates both the material and the social world. The poem works back from the commodities produced by labor, through the labor process itself, to the person behind it all. Commodities thereby become units of energy, and energy in turn becomes human power at work. Whitman shows little awareness of how mechanization, capitalist consolidation, and racism were affecting the lives of nineteenth-century working people. But as Alan Trachtenberg argues in a brilliant essay, although the "social logic of the wage system escaped him," Whitman "grasped the difference, if not its cause, between use-value (the value itself) and exchange-value, and he joined in powerful tropes and a music of amalgamation, use with being, work with art," to create in "A Song for Occupations" an "heroic celebration of labor as life, work as art" (131).

Whitman's revisions may not change the theme of this poem, but they decisively affect its tone. The post-1881 text begins with an appeal to abstract principles and an explicit declaration of a unifying theme:

> A song for occupations!
> In the labor of engines and trades and the
>   labor of fields I find the developments,
> And find the eternal meanings.
>   (section 1)

But the earlier version begins on an intimate, even erotic note:

> Come closer to me,
> Push closer, my lovers, and take the best
>   I possess,
> Yield closer and closer, and give me the best
>   you possess.
> This is unfinished business with me—
>   How is it with you?
> I was chilled with the cold types, cylinder,
>   wet paper between us.
>   (1860 Leaves)

In both early and late versions, this poem is concerned with the relationship between the feeling/touching/knowing self and the active, laboring self. But the earlier version moves from the former to the latter, while the later versions reverse this path, starting with and always returning to the external, public self. We can see this shift especially in the most heavily revised section of the poem, the long catalogue of occupations in section 5 of the 1881 version. Whitman's cuts in this section make it less fluid and personal, transforming it finally into a mere list of occupations.

Burton Hatlen

Bibliography

Bauerlein, Mark. *Whitman and the American Idiom*. Baton Rouge: Louisiana State UP, 1991.

Knapp, Bettina L. *Walt Whitman*. New York: Continuum, 1993.

Thomas, M. Wynn. *The Lunar Light of Whitman's Poetry*. Cambridge, Mass.: Harvard UP, 1987.

Trachtenberg, Alan. "The Politics of Labor and the Poet's Work: A Reading of 'A Song for Occupations.'" *Walt Whitman: The Centennial Essays*. Ed. Ed Folsom. Iowa City: U of Iowa P, 1994. 120–132.

Whitman, Walt. *Leaves of Grass: Facsimile Edition of the 1860 Text*. Ed. Roy Harvey Pearce. Ithaca, N.Y.: Cornell UP, 1961.

See also CATALOGUES; LABOR AND LABORING CLASSES; *LEAVES OF GRASS*; "SONG OF JOYS, A"; "TRAMP AND STRIKE QUESTIONS, THE"

"Song of Joys, A" (1860)

Entitled "Poem of Joys" when it first appeared in 1860, and "Poems of Joy" in 1867, the poem resumed its first title in 1871 and 1876. It took its present title, "A Song of Joys," in 1881. Based on memories of Whitman's early life, but designed, like "Song of Myself" and "Song of the Open Road," to celebrate the vitality and variety of the American experience, the poem has been much revised by excision and addition. An important change was the addition of lines 121 through 133 and 166 through 170 in 1871. This addition may indicate the poet's feelings of optimism after the Civil War. Whitman's entry in a pre-1855 notebook indicates his early interest in the poem's theme: "Poem incarnating the mind of an old man, whose life has been magnificently developed—the wildest and most exuberant joy—the utterance of hope and floods of anticipation—faith in whatever happens—but all enfolded on Joy Joy Joy, which underlies and overtops the whole effusion" (Whitman 102).

"Poem of Joys" proclaims the poet's discovery of his poetical powers and his ability to use words to give vivification to his world and himself in it. The poetic self journeys forth, singing of the beauty of the tasks of various occupations along the way. The catalogues of average people at work enact textually the poet's blending with the many identities he encounters. He celebrates the dignity of all workers and he ennobles all jobs. As David Reynolds suggests in *Walt Whitman's America,* Whitman's passage on the orator's joys emphasizes his desire to incorporate participatory oratorical style into his poetics.

In the poem Whitman embraces all equally: female and male, infancy and old age. Everything gives him joy. The "vast elemental sympathy" generated and emitted by the poetic self's soul is not independent of the material objects which give the soul its identity. This cosmic emotion enables his merging into new identities and gives substance and beauty to his spiritual body.

At the poem's conclusion, the physical body returns to the "eternal uses of the earth," and the "real body," the spiritual, leaves for other spheres. For Whitman, death is beautiful because it allows the soul to pass beyond, ever changing. Death is part of the "perpetual journey" ("Song of Myself," section 46) and a step

toward an "unknown sphere more real than I dream'd" ("So Long!"). Therefore, like everything else, it should be celebrated. In contrast to works like "Song of Myself" and "Children of Adam," "A Song of Joys" proclaims that the life of the spirit transcends the flesh.

Deborah Dietrich

Bibliography

Reynolds, David S. *Walt Whitman's America: A Cultural Biography.* New York: Knopf, 1995.

Whitman, Walt. *Notebooks and Unpublished Prose Manuscripts.* Ed. Edward F. Grier. Vol. 1. New York: New York UP, 1984.

See also CATALOGUES; JOURNEYING; OPTIMISM; ORATORY; "SONG FOR OCCUPATIONS, A"

Walt Whitman, ca. 1854, called by Richard Maurice Bucke "the Christ likeness." By permission, Beeghly Library, Ohio Wesleyan University.

"Song of Myself" (1855)

In the 1855 edition of *Leaves of Grass,* "Song of Myself" came first in the series of twelve untitled poems, dominating the volume not only by its sheer bulk, but also by its brilliant display of Whitman's innovative techniques and original themes. Whitman left the poem in the lead position in the 1856 edition and gave it its first title, "Poem of Walt Whitman, an American," shortened to "Walt Whitman" in the third edition of 1860. By the time Whitman had shaped *Leaves of Grass* into its final structure in 1881, he left the poem (its lines now grouped into fifty-two sections) in a lead position, preceded only by the epigraph-like cluster "Inscriptions" and the programmatic "Starting from Paumanok."

"Song of Myself" portrays (and mythologizes) Whitman's poetic birth and the journey into knowing launched by that "awakening." But the "I" who speaks is not alone. His camerado, the "you" addressed in the poem's second line, is the reader, placed on shared ground with the poet, a presence throughout much of the journey. As the poem opens, the reader encounters the poet "observing a spear of summer grass" and extending an invitation to his soul. He vows to "permit to speak at every hazard, / Nature without check with original energy" (section 1). Leaving "[c]reeds and schools" behind, he goes "to the bank by the wood to become undisguised and naked" (sections 1 and 2), clearly preparing himself for the soul's visit of section 5, which dramatizes the transfiguring event that launches the poet on his lifelong quest.

This event may best be described as the organic union of the poet's body and soul, the latter appearing first in the disembodied "hum" of a "valvèd voice." In highly charged erotic imagery, the soul settles his head "athwart" the poet's hips, "gently" turns over upon him, parting his shirt from his "bosom-bone" and plunging his "tongue" to the poet's "bare-stript heart"—while reaching simultaneously to *feel* his "beard" and to *hold* his "feet." In short, the soul with his phallic tongue (instrument of his "valvèd voice") penetrates directly to the poet's heart, bestowing there, without aid of mind or "reason," the teeming sperm of life-affirming intuitive knowledge, in effect the foundation for transcendent self-assurance that will sustain the poet on his search. Held in the trancelike grip of the soul from beard to feet, the poet suddenly awakens to the "peace and knowledge that pass all the argument of the earth," a fragmentary but certain knowledge: "that the spirit of God is the brother of my own," "that all the men ever born are also my brothers, and the women my sisters and lovers," "that a kelson of the creation is love." These sweeping affirmations trail off into what seems a heap of incoherent images—"limitless" "leaves," "brown ants," "elder, mullein and poke-weed." In effect, the incomprehensible multiplicity of nature, in its smallest manifestations, is also embraced in the all-inclusive affirmations of God and brotherhood.

As the awakening portrayed in section 5 has prepared the poet for a new kind of knowledge, section 6 launches him on his journey into knowing, beginning with exploration of a child's question, *"What is the grass?"* This phase of the journey extends through section 32, providing ample occasion for the poet to establish many of the subjects and themes that are addressed elsewhere in *Leaves of Grass.* From the focus on the grass imagery in section 6, the poet moves on to the theme of "en-masse," in sections 7–16. He becomes Walt Whitman, American, roaming the continent, celebrating everyday scenes of ordinary life. He presents himself (in section 13) as the "caresser of life wherever moving . . . Absorbing all to myself and for this song." This movement rises in a crescendo to the extended catalogue of section 15, with its rapid-fire snapshots of American types and scenes.

Moving away from American diversity in section 17, the poet turns to human common-ality—to "the grass that grows wherever the land is and the water is." In sections 18–24, the poet proceeds to collapse traditional discriminations, celebrating "conquer'd and slain persons" (section 18) along with victors, the "righteous" along with the "wicked"—extending his embrace to include outcasts and outlaws. But increasingly his focus fixes on the equality of body and soul and ways of rescuing the body from its inferior status. He turns to himself and his own body, presenting in section 24 a nude portrait of "Walt Whitman, a kosmos," providing a catalogue, meticulously metaphoric, for every item of his anatomy ("Firm masculine colter," "duplicate eggs").

Throughout sections 18–32 of "Song of Myself," the poet celebrates the erotic dimension of all the senses, but he turns to the miraculous touch in section 28: "Is this then a touch? quivering me to a new identity?" In some of the most surrealistic lines in all of *Leaves,* the poet proceeds to portray himself in a scene of self-induced sexual arousal to the climactic point of orgasm. Section 29 presents the poet's tender farewell to complicit touch, while sections 30–32 explore the knowledge bestowed by the experience: "What is less or more than a touch?" Having experienced and affirmed the most intense of physical ecstasies, the poet contemplates becoming one with the animals: he mounts and races a "gigantic beauty of a stallion." But he ends by "resign[ing]" the stallion, realizing that deeper knowledge lies in wait.

Adjusted to his new identity bestowed by touch, he is now ready for the second major phase of his journey. Section 33 begins with new and higher affirmations: "Space and Time! now I see it is true, what I guess'd at, / What I guess'd when I loaf'd on the grass." In this longest section of "Song of Myself," the poet feels the exhilaration of being no longer bound by the ties of space and time: he is "afoot with" his "vision." He feels able, indeed, to range back and forth over all time, and to soar like a meteor out into space. But in one of the strangest reversals in "Song of Myself," this peak of exaltation in section 33 glides into its opposite as the poet begins to identify more and more closely with the outcasts and rejected: "I am the man, I suffer'd, I was there." He becomes the "old-faced infants and the lifted sick," the mother "condemned for a witch," "the hounded slave." A note of despair sounds louder and louder through sections 34–37, until at the end the poet becomes a homeless beggar. Such despair, unfelt during similar identifications with outcasts in sections 17–20, suggests that the poet has moved obscurely beyond the knowledge of his previous phase.

Section 38, opening with strong rejection of the role of beggar he has assumed ("Enough! enough! enough!") suddenly resets the direction for the poet on his journey: "I discover myself on the verge of a usual mistake." Although he is never quite explicit about the basis for what he knows, he says that he "remember[s] now" and resumes "the overstaid fraction." He suggests metaphorically that the nature of this "overstaid fraction" is contained in the resurrection that followed (or follows) crucifixion, in lines implying humankind's identification with the universalized experience of Christ: "The grave of rock multiplies what has been confided to it, or to any graves, / Corpses rise, gashes heal, fastenings roll from me." Thus out of his despair, the poet emerges "replenish'd with supreme power," a power that reaches beyond identification with the downtrodden and rejected, a power indeed to bring "help for the sick as they pant on their backs" as well as "yet more needed help" for "strong upright men" (section 41).

This stage, in which the poet is confident in his transcendent power, extends through the closing sections, 38–49. In section 43 the poet affirms all religious faiths ("worship ancient and modern and all between ancient and modern"), and in section 44 he celebrates his place in evolutionary theory: both religion and science contain the seeds that provide the source for his supreme power.

The reader learns in section 46 that the poet's is a "perpetual journey," that he has "no chair, no church, no philosophy," that he cannot travel the road for "you," but "you must travel it for yourself." In sections 48–49, he again affirms the body equal with the soul, as he affirms the identity of selfhood and Godhead. And similarly, he proclaims death and life so inseparably bonded as to render one unimaginable without the other. Near the end of section 49, the poet appears to give up further effort to convey in words what he knows and turns to the natural world for help: "O suns— O grass of graves—O perpetual transfers and promotions, / If you do not say any thing how can I say any thing?"

In section 50 the poet seems to be emerging from a trancelike state similar to the one he entered in section 5: "Wrench'd and sweaty—calm and cool then my body becomes, / I sleep—I sleep long." Coming out of his deep sleep, the poet stammers almost incoherently: "I do not know it . . . it is a word unsaid, / It is not in any dictionary, utterance, symbol" (emphasis added). Readers may guess that "it" refers to the ineffable transcendent meaning of the poet's experience on his dreamlike journey. That meaning can be conveyed only by oblique analogy: "Something it swings on more than the earth I swing on, / To it the creation is the friend whose embracing awakes me" (emphasis added). In the end the poet addresses those "brothers and sisters" first evoked in section 5, trying to hit upon a word that might convey some notion, however inadequately, of the transcendent meaning discovered on his journey: "It is not chaos or death—it is form, union, plan—it is eternal life—it is Happiness."

As the poet's camerado from the beginning, "you" the reader come to the fore in the two concluding sections (51–52) of the poem. The poet does not deny but dismisses his "contradictions," asserting, "I am large, I contain multitudes." On beginning his journey (section 1) he promised he would "permit to speak at every hazard, / Nature without check with original energy"; similarly, at the end, he describes himself as "not a bit tamed," as "untranslatable," as one who sounds his "barbaric yawp over the roofs of the world." His journey over and done, he prepares for departure, bequeathing himself "to the dirt to grow from the grass" he loves, and tells the reader: "If you want me again look for me under your boot-soles." To the end, the poet insists that his transcendental knowledge gained on his spiritual journey cannot be embodied in words, but that nevertheless it can be conveyed indirectly. Readers will come to "know," not because he has conveyed his meaning abstractly, but rather because he has come to "filter and fibre" their blood. At the end, the poet admonishes his readers to "keep encouraged" and continue their search for him, promising: "I stop somewhere waiting for you."

Like most poetic works of genius, "Song of Myself" has defied attempts to provide a definitive interpretation. In a very real sense, no reading of the poem has clarified the sum of its many mysteries. Critics have provided useful readings, concentrating on one or another dimension of the poem: Carl F. Strauch on the solidity of a fundamental structure, Randall Jarrell on the brilliance of individual lines, James E. Miller, Jr., on the portrayal of an "inverted mystical experience," Richard Chase on the often overlooked comic aspects, Malcolm Cowley on the affinities with the inspired prophecies of antiquity, Robert K. Martin on the resemblance to a "dream vision based on sexual [essentially homosexual] experience." In addition, Edwin Haviland Miller has provided a guide through the various readings in *Walt Whitman's "Song of Myself": A Mosaic of Interpretations* (1989). In the final analysis, readers must find their own way through "Song of Myself." They will know that they are on the right path when they begin to feel something of the "great power" that Ralph Waldo Emerson felt in 1855 (Whitman 1326).

James E. Miller, Jr.

Bibliography
Chari, V.K. *Whitman in the Light of Vedantic Mysticism*. Lincoln: U of Nebraska P, 1964.
Cohen, B. Bernard. *Whitman in Our Season: A Symposium*. Hartford: Transcendental Books, 1971.
Kummings, Donald D., ed. *Approaches to Teaching Whitman's "Leaves of Grass."* New York: MLA, 1990.
Martin, Robert K. *The Homosexual Tradition in American Poetry*. Austin: U of Texas P, 1979.
Miller, Edwin Haviland. *Walt Whitman's "Song of Myself": A Mosaic of Interpretations*. Iowa City: U of Iowa P, 1989.
Miller, James E., Jr. *"Leaves of Grass": America's Lyric-Epic of Self and Democracy*. New York: Twayne, 1992.
———, ed. *Whitman's "Song of Myself": Origin, Growth, Meaning*. New York: Dodd, Mead, 1964.
Whitman, Walt. *Complete Poetry and Collected Prose*. Ed. Justin Kaplan. New York: Library of America, 1982.

See also CATALOGUES; DEATH; DEMOCRACY; EQUALITY; EVOLUTION; HUMAN BODY; HUMOR; INDIVIDUALISM; JOURNEYING; LANGUAGE; MYSTICISM; PERSONAE; PSEUDOSCIENCE; SCIENCE; SEX AND SEXUALITY; SOUL, THE; STYLE AND TECHNIQUE(S)

"Song of Prudence" (1856)

"Song of Prudence" first appeared in the 1856 edition of *Leaves of Grass* as "Poem of The Last Explanation of Prudence." It is a sometimes verbatim poetic transcription of paragraph 22 of the 1855 Preface. In the 1860 edition of *Leaves* the poem appeared as number 5 in the "Leaves of Grass" cluster and in 1867 and 1871 as "Manhattan's Streets I Saunter'd, Pondering." It took its final title in the 1881 edition, where it was incorporated into the newly created cluster, "Autumn Rivulets."

The key idea in "Song of Prudence" is that everything a person does, says, or thinks "is of consequence." The consequences of actions are significant both temporally and metaphysically; what is done today reverberates forever, and what the body does affects the soul. Therefore the prudence the poet espouses is "the prudence that suits immortality." Whitman plays with the conventional meaning of the word "prudence" by employing the vocabulary of finance—good actions are the only worthwhile "investments," whoever is wise "receives interest," and the grand deeds of the past are what we "inherit."

Yet Whitman's concept of prudence is not conventional. The Preface spends several sentences elaborating the contrast between the poet's "higher notions of prudence" and ordinary "caution." The kind of prudence which would entice beings capable of divinity into wasting their lives on mere moneymaking is a "fraud" (Whitman 20–21). Although the poem omits most of the discussion of this contrast, it does make clear that genuine prudence is quite different from what is usually thought: the "young man who composedly peril'd his life and lost it" has been more truly prudent than the careful man who lives "to old age in riches and ease" without noble deeds.

The middle section of the poem consists of a catalogue of good actions—those involving love, honesty, nobility of mind—which constitute worthy investments for the soul. Yet it is not good actions only which accrue immortal "interest." Each "venereal sore, discoloration, privacy of the onanist, / Putridity of gluttons or rum-drinkers, peculation, cunning, betrayal, murder, seduction, prostitution" will have its eternal consequence. This list of vices raises the issue of one of Whitman's often discussed contradictions; in a number of passages he accepts every kind of person, but in others rejects the corrupt, a contradiction especially apparent in sections 2 and 10 of "Song of the Open Road." David Reynolds suggests that the moralizing passages in "Open Road" and "Prudence" are simply carryovers from the language of moral reform which had characterized Whitman's early journalism. Compared with its source, the poem deemphasizes the negative. The Preface includes a much longer catalogue of evils whose "interest will come round" (22).

Prudence was one of the qualities attributed to Whitman by the phrenologist Fowler, but the poet redefines the word (which Fowler equated with "cautiousness" and "provision") in terms reminiscent of Ralph Waldo Emerson's more metaphysical definition. The poem's concept of moral retribution may also be influenced by Emerson's "Compensation" or by the law of karma. Another possible influence on the poem may be the teachings of Stoicism.

A number of critics feel that the "Autumn Rivulets" cluster represents a transition between the past (especially the Civil War crisis depicted in the preceding "Drum-Taps" poems) and the future. Paul Lizotte notes that while other poems in the cluster address the relationship of past to future for the individual or for historical humanity, "Song of Prudence" examines such a relationship in terms of the soul.

Gay Barton

Bibliography

Asselineau, Roger. *The Evolution of Walt Whitman: The Creation of a Book*. Trans. Roger Asselineau and Burton L. Cooper. Cambridge, Mass.: Harvard UP, 1962.

Giantvalley, Scott. *Walt Whitman, 1838–1939: A Reference Guide*. Boston: Hall, 1981.

Kummings, Donald D. *Walt Whitman, 1940–1975: A Reference Guide*. Boston: Hall, 1982.

Lizotte, Paul A. "'Time's Accumulations to Justify the Past': Whitman's Evolving Structure in 'Autumn Rivulets.'" *ESQ* 26 (1980): 137–148.

Reynolds, David S. *Walt Whitman's America: A Cultural Biography*. New York: Knopf, 1995.

Weathers, Willie T. "Whitman's Poetic Translations of His 1855 Preface." *American Literature* 19 (1947): 21–40.

Whitman, Walt. *Complete Poetry and Collected Prose*. Ed. Justin Kaplan. New York: Library of America, 1982.

See also "Autumn Rivulets"; Epicurus; Evil; Fowler, Lorenzo Niles and Orson Squire; Hindu Literature; Metaphysics; Preface to *Leaves of Grass*, 1855 Edition; Stoicism

"Song of the Answerer" (1881)

In preparing the 1881 edition of *Leaves of Grass*, Whitman formed "Song of the Answerer" by joining together two poems with long prehistories. What became in 1881 the first part of "Song of the Answerer" originated as an untitled section of the 1855 edition, became "Poem of the Poet" in the 1856 edition, "Leaves of Grass" number 3 in 1860, and "Now List to My Morning Romanza" (from the new opening line of the poem) in the 1867 and subsequent editions until the 1881 edition. The eventual second part of "Song of the Answerer" originated in some phrases in the Preface to the 1855 edition, took form as "Poem of The Singers and of The Words of Poems" in the 1856 edition, became "Leaves of Grass" number 6 in the 1860 edition, and appeared as "The Indications" in the 1867 and later editions, until it became part of "Song of the Answerer" in the 1881 edition. Both poems were from the beginning concerned with the role of the poet in the human community, and this thematic affinity perhaps explains why Whitman linked them together.

"Song of the Answerer" celebrates the poet as "the glory and extract thus far of things and of the human race" (section 2). In section 1, he takes on the mysterious name of the Answerer (always capitalized in the later editions) and becomes a kind of redeemer: "Him all wait for, him all yield up to, his word is decisive and final." The poet passes freely among all varieties of people, all of whom see themselves in him: "the mechanics take him for a mechanic, / And the soldiers suppose him to be a soldier." Everything the poet sees he "strangely transmutes," so that in him "[t]he insulter, the prostitute, the angry person, the beggar . . . are not vile any more, they hardly know themselves they are so grown." In section 2 the tone shifts somewhat, as Whitman develops an elaborate distinction between the poet and the mere "singer": "The singers do not beget, only the Poet begets." What the singer does is thus secondary to and derivative from the work of the poet. In the last two stanzas of section 2, however, Whitman returns to the larger themes of the first section, declaring that "[t]he words of true poems give you more than poems," inviting the reader "[t]o launch off with absolute faith, to sweep through the ceaseless rings, and never be quiet again."

There are, however, some ambiguities in "Song of the Answerer." In the 1855 Preface Whitman sees the poet as at once a unique, world-transforming figure as well as a common, ordinary man, not essentially different from any of the other citizens of a democracy. Traces of this same paradox also play through "Song of the Answerer." As the Answerer addresses his fellow citizens, they mutually immerse one another. There seems to be here, as Tenney Nathanson notes, a two-way process. Especially in section 1, the vision of the poet as an all-permeating divine force, something like Ralph Waldo Emerson's Brahma, serves to undercut the potentially egoist pretensions of the individual poet, Walt Whitman. Instead, the Answerer is anonymous, with no determinate identity. Early versions of what becomes section 1 also include a passage, excised when Whitman created "Song of the Answerer," that redefines poetry in broadly democratic terms: "But what are verses beyond the flowing character you could have? or beyond beautiful manners and behavior? / Or beyond one manly and affectionate deed of an apprentice-boy? or old woman? or man that has been in prison, or is likely to be in prison?" (1860 *Leaves*). If, as these lines suggest, poetry encompasses all human gesture and action, then Whitman's own poems become, not world-mastering imperialist acts, but rather simply his contribution to the universal choir.

Burton Hatlen

Bibliography

Nathanson, Tenney. *Whitman's Presence: Body, Voice, and Writing in "Leaves of Grass."* New York: New York UP, 1992.
Whitman, Walt. *Leaves of Grass: Facsimile Edition of the 1860 Text.* Ed. Roy Harvey Pearce. Ithaca, N.Y.: Cornell UP, 1961.

See also EMERSON, RALPH WALDO; LEAVES OF GRASS; POETIC THEORY; PREFACE TO LEAVES OF GRASS, 1855 EDITION

"Song of the Banner at Daybreak" (1865)

"Song of the Banner at Daybreak" constitutes Whitman's longest poem on the Civil War, unless we count "When Lilacs Last in the Dooryard Bloom'd" as a war poem. "Song of the Banner" was probably written early in the war, for in 1861 Whitman's publishers, Thayer and Eldridge, advertised 'Banner at Day-Break' as the title poem of a book Whitman was preparing. However, the poem did not see print until 1865, when it was published in *Drum-Taps*. As *Leaves of Grass* evolved, Whitman redesigned several of the subsections so that they pivot on a long poem: "I Sing the Body Electric" in "Children of Adam," or "Out of the Cradle Endlessly Rocking" in "Sea-Drift." "Song of

the Banner" plays a similar role in what eventually became the "Drum-Taps" cluster. (In the original *Drum-Taps* volume, it has a rival in "Pioneers! O Pioneers!," but Whitman later moved "Pioneers!" to the "Birds of Passage" section.) Any attempt to understand Whitman's response to the war must therefore pay close attention to "Song of the Banner."

"Song of the Banner" is structured as a masque or choric text, with five speakers: the Poet, the Child, the Father, the Pennant, and the Banner. At the beginning of the poem, the Pennant summons the Child to battle, while the Father, alarmed, tries to persuade his Child to stay home. Despite this apparently dialogic structure, however, there is no true debate within the poem. For the Poet gets both the first word and the last, and from the beginning the Poet greets the war with enthusiasm: "I'll pour the verse with streams of blood, full of volition, full of joy, / Then loosen, launch forth, to go and compete, / With the banner and pennant a-flapping." As for the Father, he is defined for us as simply a greedy materialist. Rather than inviting a dialogue between pro- and antiwar parties, Whitman suggests that all idealists are joyously committed to the war, while those opposed to it are motivated solely by selfishness. Not surprisingly, then, the Child adopts the Banner as his new soul-father; and although the poem breaks off before we know what the Child will do, it seems clear that he will plunge into the battle, to the applause of the Poet.

Tonally, "Song of the Banner" contrasts sharply with many of the other poems gathered in "Drum-Taps." The anguished tenderness toward the dead that we find in "Vigil Strange I Kept on the Field One Night" or "A Sight in the Camp in the Daybreak Gray and Dim," the almost surrealist sense of the horror of war so striking in "A March in the Ranks Hard-Prest, and the Road Unknown"—these tonalities are entirely absent from "Song of the Banner." The strong probability that Whitman wrote this poem early in the war, before he had seen for himself the effects of combat, may in part explain its tone. Although as the struggle went on Whitman could not ignore the human costs of the war, at the start he greeted the idea of the war with a rush of euphoria, and "Song of the Banner" gives expression to this euphoria, which at times seems to shade into blood-lust. Despite the central position it occupies in the "Drum-Taps" cluster of *Leaves of Grass*, therefore, "Song of the Banner" has seemed to many readers less the thematic center of the group than an awkward, even embarrassing anomaly.

Burton Hatlen

Bibliography

Hatlen, Burton. "The Many and/or the One: Poetics Versus Ideology in Whitman's 'Our Old Feuillage' and 'Song of the Banner at Daybreak.'" *American Transcendental Quarterly* ns 6 (1992): 189–211.

Larson, Kerry C. *Whitman's Drama of Consensus.* Chicago: U of Chicago P, 1988.

Moon, Michael. *Disseminating Whitman: Revision and Corporeality in "Leaves of Grass."* Cambridge, Mass.: Harvard UP, 1991.

Sweet, Timothy. *Traces of War: Poetry, Photography, and the Crisis of the Union.* Baltimore: Johns Hopkins UP, 1990.

Thomas, M. Wynn. *The Lunar Light of Whitman's Poetry.* Cambridge, Mass.: Harvard UP, 1987.

Whitman, Walt. *Leaves of Grass: Comprehensive Reader's Edition.* Ed. Harold W. Blodgett and Sculley Bradley. New York: New York UP, 1965.

See also CIVIL WAR, THE; "DRUM-TAPS"; THAYER AND ELDRIDGE

"Song of the Broad-Axe" (1856)

"Song of the Broad-Axe" was first published in the 1856 edition of *Leaves of Grass*, as "Broad-Axe Poem." In the 1860 edition it became number 2 of the "Chants Democratic," and it acquired its final title in the 1867 edition. Whitman also cut the 290 lines of the earlier editions to 254 lines in later editions. Almost all the cuts come at the end of the poem, where Whitman excised two substantial passages, one describing the "full-sized men, / Men taciturn yet loving" (1860 *Leaves*) who will emerge in the future, and another describing Whitman himself—"Arrogant, masculine, näive, rowdyish" (1860 *Leaves*)—as the ideal embodiment of American manhood. The poem moves from an opening meditation on the various uses of the axe to a progressively broader vision of the various "shapes" that will eventually "arise" from the work of the axe. The structure of the poem thus invites a symbolic reading, and most critical commentary on the poem has been devoted to elucidating the symbolic meanings—whether private or public, psychosexual or sociopolitical—that come to cluster around the image of the axe.

"Song of the Broad-Axe" begins with an atypical (for Whitman) passage of rhyming, metrical verse (we can read it either as iambic tetrameter with some elided initial syllables, or as trochaic tetrameter with some elided end syllables), although Whitman has partly disguised this pattern by twice placing two tetrameter units on the same line:

> Weapon shapely, naked, wan,
> Head from the mother's bowels drawn,
> Wooded flesh and metal bone,
>   limb only one and lip only one,
> Gray-blue leaf by red-heat grown,
>   helve produced from a little seed sown,
> Resting the grass amid and upon,
> To be lean'd and to lean on.
>
> (section 1)

The emphatic rhythm of these lines suggests a riddle (see Peavy), or perhaps, as M. Wynn Thomas has argued, a ritual incantation, "the modern, democratic equivalent of the baptismal spell chanted by primitives to confer sacred power upon a newly fashioned weapon" (141). In either case, the percussive rhythms and condensed, allusive language of these opening lines invite us to see the axe as something more than merely a tool—as, in sum, a symbol, but of what?

Whitman, according to Richard Maurice Bucke, wanted to make the broad-axe "the American emblem preferent to the eagle" (*Notes* 35). In Europe, Whitman reveals as the poem proceeds, the axe served primarily as an instrument of war and oppression, culminating in the figure of the bloody headsman described in section 8. But in America the axe is transformed into the means by which a free people clears the forest and transforms the landscape to build the ideal city, as described in section 5. Thus we can, with Thomas, read the poem's opening lines as a ritual purification of the axe so that it can play this new social role. To this end the poem systematically downplays the violence of the European invasion of America and the settlers' assault on the forest. Instead Whitman portrays this process as the expression of a "natural" vitality, "Muscle and pluck forever" (section 4). We can thus read the axe as a symbol of America seen as "a nonprofit association of purely heroic adventurers and spirited workingmen, in anticipation of the brave New Jerusalem, the heavenly city, to be built eventually on American soil" (Thomas 145).

However, we can also read the opening lines of this poem in more personal terms, for a flood of sexual imagery washes through these lines. The image of the axe-head "drawn . . . from the mother's bowels" has seemed to many critics as inescapably sexual. "The axe, drawn out of the mother's bowels, is not only the emerging infant but also the phallus of the father" (Gregory 2). As phallus, the axe becomes the focus of an Oedipal drama, compounded of admiration for the potency of the father (thus the emphasis on the power of the axe to generate new life) and fear of castration (thus the recurrent images of the axe as an instrument of destruction, climaxing in the sinister image of the masked headsman, "clothed in red, with huge legs and strong naked arms" [section 8]). Whitman attempts to resolve this ambivalence through identification with the father (thus the celebration of the "power of personality just or unjust" [section 3] in the middle sections of the poem), but in the end Whitman identifies not with the father but with the mother (thus the invocation of the ideal woman whose "shape arises" in section 11, at the end of the poem).

Burton Hatlen

Bibliography

Black, Stephen A. *Whitman's Journeys into Chaos*. Princeton: Princeton UP, 1975.

Cavitch, David. "The Lament in 'Song of the Broad-Axe.'" *Walt Whitman: Here and Now*. Ed. Joann P. Krieg. Westport, Conn.: Greenwood, 1985. 125–135.

———. *My Soul and I: The Inner Life of Walt Whitman*. Boston: Beacon, 1985.

Gregory, Dorothy M-T. "The Celebration of Nativity: 'Broad-Axe Poem.'" *Walt Whitman Quarterly Review* 2.1 (1984): 1–11.

Knapp, Bettina L. *Walt Whitman*. New York: Continuum, 1993.

Miller, James E., Jr. *A Critical Guide to "Leaves of Grass."* Chicago: U of Chicago P, 1957.

Moon, Michael. *Disseminating Whitman: Revision and Corporeality in "Leaves of Grass."* Cambridge, Mass.: Harvard UP, 1991.

Peavy, Linda. "'Wooded Flesh and Metal Bone': A Look at the Riddle of the Broad-Axe." *Walt Whitman Review* 20 (1974): 152–154.

Rosenfeld, Alvin H. "The Eagle and the Axe: A Study of Whitman's 'Song of the Broad-Axe.'" *American Imago* 25 (1968): 354–370.

Thomas, M. Wynn. *The Lunar Light of Whitman's Poetry*. Cambridge, Mass.: Harvard UP, 1987.

Whitman, Walt. *Leaves of Grass: Facsimile Edition of the 1860 Text*. Ed. Roy Harvey Pearce. Ithaca, N.Y.: Cornell UP, 1961.

———. *Notes and Fragments*. Ed. Richard Maurice Bucke. London, Ontario: A. Talbot, 1899.

See also AMERICAN CHARACTER; *LEAVES OF GRASS*, 1856 EDITION; PROSODY; PSYCHOLOGICAL APPROACHES; SYMBOLISM

"Song of the Exposition" (1871)

This poem was written for the fortieth National Industrial Exposition of the American Institute and recited in New York by Whitman on 7 September 1871. The poem was first printed alone in a pamphlet by Roberts Brothers with the title *After All, Not to Create Only* in 1871 and appeared under the same title at the end of the 1872 *Leaves of Grass*. In 1876 it appeared in *Two Rivulets* under the current title and was prefaced for the Centennial Exposition at Philadelphia although Whitman was not asked to read there. It was retained in the 1881 *Leaves of Grass*, with the addition of the opening parenthetical expression and the deletion of nineteen satirical lines and numerous dashes, capitalizations, and other alterations.

Whitman was solicited by the American Institute Board of Managers a month prior to the event. The Institute offered him payment of one hundred dollars and traveling expenses and guaranteed publication in the "metropolitan press" (*With Walt Whitman* 1:326–329). Whitman accepted the invitation four days later. The poem was reprinted in twelve newspapers, and several editorials appeared on the day of or soon after the reading. As was his tendency, Whitman probably authored several of them. The New York *Tribune* published excerpts, and soon after, a parody by Bayard Taylor.

Critical attention has given this poem a secondary place. It is true that it does not bear multiple readings. The fault does not lie in construction or in vocabulary, but perhaps in its

S

origin. The poem was written in a month's time, and was intended to be spoken and deserves to be treated so. As an oration it carries cadences in the transition of language that are missed in the silent reading. From the opening section's grand style to the third section's arrogant sales pitch, to the seventh section's passionate sincerity, Whitman takes full advantage of his subject, industrial civilization, and his object of elevating the common man based on this societal advance.

In *The Solitary Singer,* Gay Wilson Allen calls it a "pathetic episode" which was "unfortunate in every respect" (435). In the *Comprehensive Reader's Edition,* Harold Blodgett and Sculley Bradley note, "it remains one of WW's comparative failures because it does not surmount its own rhetoric" (196n). Whitman himself, in 1889, dubs the occasion "memorandum" and of the Board of Managers' tender of thanks says, "'magnificent original poem' is putting it on pretty thick" (*With Walt Whitman* 4:484).

The poem's purpose is much like that of *Democratic Vistas* or "A Song for Occupations," though in *Democratic Vistas* Whitman acknowledges the people's "crude defective streaks" (*Prose Works* 2:379). In comparison, the laborer in "Song of the Exposition" is likened unto God and as a worker becomes the theme the Muse should inspire. A few years later Whitman would write "Song of the Universal," which expresses much the same idea, compacted, and speaks directly to the Muse.

The Muse in "Song of the Exposition" approaches the scene at the beck of Whitman. His treatment of her, as it is with most of the "sacred" things of the Old World, is irreverent, though not derogatory. He conveys her image of arrival to the audience with the famous "She's here, install'd amid the kitchen ware!" (section 3). Contrast this to the reverence he displays when describing the people and works of America, "the People themselves . . . elate, secure in peace" (section 6).

Whitman employs his catalogues in this poem to demonstrate the diversity of the present, in honor of and exampled by the exhibition, and also to demarcate the Old World from the New. In the switching from old to new is also the shift in tone, so that the sacred mountains of Greece are to be leased and the Muse may take up residence in the "great cathedral sacred industry" (section 5). After this shift, in the fifth section, the poem becomes more and more intent and loses much of its potential in overstatement.

Section 7 is one of the better sections, in which Whitman's years spent nursing wounded Civil War soldiers infuse his remarks with a true passion—"Away with themes of war! away with war itself!" This directive is accompanied by one to be rid of old romance, so that the Muse will inspire songs of society and progress and the laboring life.

The concluding stanza, like the opening, is a poetic contrast to the dogma of the body of the poem, and alone is purpose enough to justify the final inclusion of the poem in the canon: material production and profit are but the manifestation of the spiritual growth of the nation.

Karen Wolfe

Bibliography

Allen, Gay Wilson. *The Solitary Singer: A Critical Biography of Walt Whitman.* 1955. Rev. ed. 1967. Chicago: U of Chicago P, 1985.

Blodgett, Harold W., and Sculley Bradley, eds. *Leaves of Grass: Comprehensive Reader's Edition.* By Walt Whitman. New York: New York UP, 1965.

Kennedy, William Sloane. *The Fight of a Book for the World.* West Yarmouth, Mass.: Stonecroft, 1926.

Reynolds, David S. *Walt Whitman's America: A Cultural Biography.* New York: Knopf, 1995.

Traubel, Horace. *With Walt Whitman in Camden.* Vol. 1. Boston: Small, Maynard, 1906; Vol. 4. Ed. Sculley Bradley. Philadelphia: U of Pennsylvania P, 1953.

Whitman, Walt. *The Correspondence.* Ed. Edwin Haviland Miller. Vol. 2. New York: New York UP, 1961.

———. *Leaves of Grass: A Textual Variorum of the Printed Poems.* Ed. Sculley Bradley, Harold W. Blodgett, Arthur Golden, and William White. Vol. 3. New York: New York UP, 1980.

———. *Prose Works 1892.* Ed. Floyd Stovall. 2 vols. New York: New York UP, 1963–1964.

See also CENTENNIAL EXPOSITION (PHILADELPHIA); *DEMOCRATIC VISTAS;* LABOR AND LABORING CLASSES; "SONG FOR OCCUPATIONS, A"; TECHNOLOGY

"Song of the Open Road" (1856)

Originally published as "Poem of The Road," the poem received its present imaginative title in 1867; in 1881 its 224 lines were divided into fifteen sections. Whitman's own interpretation of the work is most nearly expressed in a book on which he collaborated. There it is called "a mystic and indirect chant of aspiration toward a noble life, a vehement demand to reach the very highest point that the human soul is capable of attaining . . . a religious poem in the truest and best sense of the term" (*Autograph Revision* 88–89). It has remained popular because its insights into human frailty are offset by its rousing call to freedom and fraternity, by its dynamic persona who is at once the poem's subject and the spokesman for Whitman's exuberant gospel of hope, and by its stirring musicality.

During the 1850s the open road was a distinctively American symbol of progress—an imagined escape route toward the quasi-mythical open spaces where one was free to prosper, to commune with nature, to discover one's selfhood, and to undergo spiritual regeneration. Whitman translates the nineteenth-century doctrine of progress into a vision of a hard-fought but inevitable individual advancement—"the procession of souls along the grand roads of the universe" (section 13). In *Democratic Vistas* he contends that the attainment of personal and societal betterment must be preceded by a powerful poetic vision of the future. "Song of the Open Road"—one attempt to create such a vision—affirms his faith that the (somewhat vague) "goal that was named cannot be countermanded" (section 14). Regarding humanity's progress along the mythic road, the poem's persona declares: "I know not where they go, / But I know that they go toward the best—toward something great" (section 13).

Essentially a dramatic monologue, the poem is divisible into three "movements": the persona's absorption of the road's sights and sounds and his translation of them into a visionary consciousness (sections 1–5), his transfigurative voice conjuring up visions of limitless possibilities (sections 6–8), and his quasi-oratorical call to companions to undertake the mystic trek. In the first "movement"—with its exuberant apostrophe to the mystic road—his perception and his inner sight merge: the road and everything on it become a nexus of symbols. He reads these symbols inscribed on the road's ostensibly "impassive" (section 3) surfaces and interprets them for everyone's benefit. The experience fills him with a sense of transcendence. Envisioning a race of perfect men and women, he exclaims: "I think I could stop here myself and do miracles. . . . I ordain myself loos'd of limits and imaginary lines . . . my own master total and absolute" (sections 4–5). Although the poem is esteemed for its evocation of nature and wanderlust, it contains little description of nature. Rather, nature becomes an extension of the persona's capacious imagination, for, as Whitman elsewhere explains, nature is always filtered through the mind of the observer ("Poetry To-Day" 485).

The poem's second "movement" (sections 6–8) brings the persona to the height of his absorptive powers and forms a bridge to his call to action. His capacity for personal attraction is called by the innovative ("not previously fashion'd") word "adhesiveness" (adapted from the phrenological term for the supposed instinct of male bonding) and is said to be consistent ("apropos") with nature's laws (section 6). The persona distills "the charm that mocks beauty and attainments," "charm" being the mesmerists' code word for one's hypnotic and clairvoyant powers. Becoming "rightly charged" and exuding the soul's "efflux" of happiness (section 8), he is eligible to become the dynamic leader of the poem's second half. Nevertheless, his confidence is tempered in section 7, where, in sexually charged imagery, he questions the meanings of his own "thoughts in the darkness," his ability to attract others, and his "yearnings" for companions.

Scattered throughout the poem's second half (sections 9–15) are ten stirring lines beginning with the command "Allons!"—"the poem's framing 'Marseillaise' cry" (Hollis 118). The persona challenges his reader-companions to abandon their conventional beliefs and relationships, to perfect themselves, and to embrace life and death joyously. In a rare pun, he urges them to develop limitless powers of imagination (to become poets?): "To see no possession, but you may possess it, enjoying all without labor or purchase, abstracting the feast yet not abstracting one particle of it" (section 13). (The "feast" encompasses love, beauty, and even godhood.) By pausing to question whether diseased and depraved persons or secretly self-loathing conformists are eligible to undertake the proposed limitless journey, the persona reflects Whitman's known doubts about transforming the flawed American masses into ideal personalities. Nevertheless, he remains confident, rallying all persons to the martial rhythms of the poem's penultimate stanza. In the closing stanza of the earlier versions of the poem, the fatherly persona (in his only direct address to an individual) had invited "Mon enfant" (a "Calamus" lad? the reader?) to accompany him down the uncharted road. In 1881 Whitman changed "Mon enfant" to "Camerado," thus elevating the "enfant" to parity with the persona.

Although he does not classify "Song of the Open Road" among Whitman's first-rank achievements, Gay Wilson Allen calls it "a carefree, lighthearted . . . universal vision of joy and brotherhood" (86). The poem is a virtuoso experiment in innovative prosody and in poet-reader relations. Its lines are varied in rhythm, diction, and melody. Its language, although sometimes lapsing into the sermonic or even the banal, is generally innovative and—with its out-flashings of emotion—exhilarating. And taking advantage of the fact that the pronoun "you" is both singular and plural, Whitman achieves a brilliant interplay between formal (at times oratorical) address and intimate conversation.

Harold Aspiz

Bibliography

Allen, Gay Wilson. *The New Walt Whitman Handbook*. 1975. New York: New York UP, 1986.

Bloom, Harold, ed. *Walt Whitman*. Modern Critical Views. New York: Chelsea House, 1985.

Collins, Christopher. "Whitman's Open Road and Where It Led." *The Nassau Review* 1 (1965). 101–110.

Hollis, C. Carroll. *Language and Style in "Leaves of Grass."* Baton Rouge: Louisiana State UP, 1983.

Miller, James E., Jr. *Walt Whitman*. New York: Twayne, 1962.

Rosenfeld, Alvin. "Whitman's Open Road Philosophy." *Walt Whitman Review* 14 (1968): 3–16.

Whitman, Walt. *Leaves of Grass: A Textual Variorum of the Printed Poems*. Ed. Sculley Bradley, Harold W. Blodgett, Arthur Golden, and William White. 3 vols. New York: New York UP, 1980.

———. "Poetry To-Day in America—Shakspere—The Future." *Prose Works 1892*. Ed. Floyd Stovall. Vol. 2. New York: New York UP, 1964. 474–490.

———. *Walt Whitman's Autograph Revision of the Analysis of Leaves of Grass (For Dr. R.M. Bucke's Walt Whitman)*. Ed. Stephen Railton. New York: New York UP, 1974.

Zweig, Paul. *Walt Whitman: The Making of a Poet*. New York: Basic Books, 1984.

See also COMRADESHIP; DEMOCRACY; FREEDOM; JOURNEYING; KEROUAC, JACK; NATURE; PERSONAE; RELIGION; SIMPSON, LOUIS; SYMBOLISM

"Song of the Redwood-Tree" (1874)

Written in the fall, 1873, "Song of the Redwood-Tree" was first published *in Harper's New Monthly Magazine* with "Prayer of Columbus" in February 1874. Whitman was paid one hundred dollars for the poem. He included it in "Centennial Songs—1876," which was annexed to *Two Rivulets* (1876), and then in *Leaves of Grass* (1881) in its present position among an unnamed group of twelve "songs" between the clusters "Calamus" and "Birds of Passage." "Redwood-Tree" appeared in volume 2 of *Half-Hours with the Best American Authors* (4 vols., 1886–1887). The poem's title remained consistent from its original appearance, and Whitman made no significant revisions.

A poem of the westering experience and Manifest Destiny, "Redwood-Tree" celebrates the popular nineteenth-century ideology of human progress and its culmination in the New World. It shares these themes with several other poems with which it is grouped, especially "Song of the Broad-Axe" (1856) and "Song of the Exposition" (1871).

In "Redwood-Tree" a tree speaks for all his brother trees. The poet, like the speaker in "Out of the Cradle Endlessly Rocking" (1859), hears the tree's voice in his "soul" (section 1) and thus internalizes the emotions and essence of nature. The tree recognizes that its time has come, that it will now pass from the earth and provide for the human race, which is "Promis'd to be fulfilled" (section 3). This implied divine promise will be the culmination of humankind in an *"empire new"* (section 1), which will become a thriving world seaport. Such imagery reflects that of "Facing West from California's Shores" (1860) and "Passage to India" (1871), both of which also suggest America's prominence in the encircled and fulfilled world. The New World also claims distinction in history because it incorporates the past and will "build a grander future" ("Redwood-Tree," section 3).

In "Redwood-Tree" Whitman's politics are very much those of the public poet extolling the popular ideology, or myth, that America is the spiritual union of humankind and nature. Whereas Cecelia Tichi suggests that Whitman's poem is understandable in light of two hundred years of the myth, Betsy Erkkila claims that Whitman is simply content not to explore the irony of cutting down trees to unite humans with nature. According to M. Wynn Thomas, a number of writers and painters were concerned about the mass destruction of trees in the virgin territory.

While aware of this concern, Whitman wrote "Redwood-Tree," which rationalizes, even credits, such destruction. Thomas further posits that, while the poem is in a sense disgraceful, it demonstrates Whitman's attempt to use poetry to transcend less respectable human actions and to raise the ideology to a higher level.

In letters to Rudolf Schmidt (4 March and 28 July 1874) Whitman himself explained that the poem was meant to idealize the Pacific West and that it pleased him more than any of his other later poems. Perhaps the poem pleased him not so much because of its political import, however, but because of its personal significance. Gay Wilson Allen suggests that "Redwood-Tree" grew out of Whitman's loneliness and despair during the fall and winter of 1873–1874 and that his identification with the tree is his attempt at reconciliation with a deteriorating life.

These various readings of "Redwood-Tree" perhaps demonstrate that this poem, which sounds typical Whitmanian themes, does not reach its potential. That is, it leaves the political ramifications unexplored, the spiritual intentions unfulfilled, and the poet's life not clearly related.

Steven Olson

Bibliography

Allen, Gay Wilson. *The Solitary Singer: A Critical Biography of Walt Whitman.* 1955. Rev. ed. 1967. Chicago: U of Chicago P, 1985.

Erkkila, Betsy. *Whitman the Political Poet.* New York: Oxford UP, 1989.

Thomas, M. Wynn. *The Lunar Light of Whitman's Poetry.* Cambridge, Mass.: Harvard UP, 1987.

Tichi, Cecelia. *New World, New Earth: Environmental Reform in American Literature from the Puritans through Whitman.* New Haven: Yale UP, 1979.

Whitman, Walt. *The Correspondence.* Ed. Edwin Haviland Miller. 6 vols. New York: New York UP, 1961–1969.

———. *Leaves of Grass: Comprehensive Reader's Edition.* Ed. Harold W. Blodgett and Sculley Bradley. New York: New York UP, 1965.

See also "Facing West from California's Shores"; Imperialism; Nature; "Passage to India"; "Prayer of Columbus"; "Song of the Broad-Axe"; "Song of the Exposition"; *Two Rivulets*; West, The American

"Song of the Rolling Earth, A" (1856)

The poem that eventually became "A Song of the Rolling Earth" was first included in the 1856 edition of *Leaves of Grass,* under the title "Poem of The Sayers of The Words of The Earth." It later became "To the Sayers of Words" (in the 1860 and 1867 editions) and "Carol of Words" (in the 1871 and 1876 editions), before acquiring its final title in the 1881 edition. Internal revisions in the poem are fairly minor, except for the excision of the original opening lines:

> Earth, round, rolling, compact—
>   suns, moons, animals—
>   all these are words to be said,
> Watery, vegetable, sauroid advances—
>   beings, premonitions,
>   lispings of the future,
> Behold, these are vast words to be said.
>   (1860 *Leaves*)

These lines, dropped by Whitman in the 1881 edition, emphasize that the central concern of this poem is the relationship between the earth and words. Among all of Whitman's poems, Tenney Nathanson argues, "'A Song of the Rolling Earth' gives most sustained attention to linguistic issues" (175). But Whitman's decision to drop these lines, as well as the changes in the title of the poem, suggest some ambivalence on Whitman's part concerning the relationship between the earth and words.

The first part of this poem emphasizes primarily the superiority of "substantial words"—things themselves, "air, soil, water, fire"—to mere artificial words—"those upright lines . . . those curves, angles, dots." The "inaudible words of the earth" speak truth, in contrast to ordinary human discourse: "The earth does not argue . . . Does not scream, haste, persuade, threaten, promise. . . ." The "masters"—i.e., the true poets—"know the earth's words and use them more than audible words" (section 1). In his desire to find an authentic speech, Whitman thus collapses the distinction between signifier and signified, declaring that the true word is the thing itself. But if so, then the thing itself also becomes a word: the equation of the two opens up the possibility of an authentic speech, but it also defines reality itself as essentially linguistic. The result is a fundamental instability, which this poem elaborates without resolving. This instability may in part explain the extraordinary proliferation of negative grammatical constructions in the poem. And a fundamental problem emerges immediately: if

S

the true words are "inaudible"—and, as Whitman later adds, "untransmissible by print" (section 1)—then what happens when the poet actually speaks or writes? Do the words become, at that moment, false?

Impelled forward by these unanswerable questions, Whitman shifts his attention from language toward the earth itself, which he envisions dancing through space in a grand cotillion, accompanied by the twenty-four hours of the day and the 365 days of the year. This image of the "divine ship sail[ing] the divine sea" (section 2) may seem unequivocally positive. But the passage pivots on a description of the earth as a woman, "her ample back towards every beholder" (section 1) staring into a mirror—this mirror is, James Griffin suggests, the moon. Thus translated into visual terms, the "eloquent dumb great mother" (section 1) begins to seem oddly narcissistic and self-involved. And in the second section of the poem, when Whitman urges us to emulate the grand self-sufficiency of the earth, the end result seems to be a fundamental breakdown in communicative interchange:

> The song is to the singer,
>   and comes back most to him,
> The teaching is to the teacher,
>   and comes back most to him,
> The murder is to the murderer,
>   and comes back most to him. . . .
> (section 2)

Although Whitman here seems to be addressing us in Orphic tonalities, a world in which all speech turns back on the speaker without reaching any sort of audience is deeply antithetical to Whitman's own ideal of the democratic community.

In section 3, Whitman returns to the issue of language, but now the emphasis shifts from the superior authenticity of "substantial words" to the inadequacy of human speech, including the words of the poet. It is better to "leave the best untold," he realizes, because when he attempts to "tell the best," he finds that he cannot:

> My tongue is ineffectual on its pivots,
> My breath will not be obedient to its organs,
> I become a dumb man.

We may, with Griffin, read these lines as implying a union of the poet with the "eloquent dumb great mother": "if Whitman can emulate the earth's dumb-greatness, then in fact, he may inherit as well its fecundity and expressiveness"

(7). But as Mark Bauerlein argues, when a poet goes dumb, something has gone wrong: "The Orphic mastery he had affirmed in 'Song of Myself' . . . has lapsed into a stifling impotence" (116). Depending upon which of these two readings we accept, the final section ("Say on, sayers! sing on, singers! / Delve! mould! pile the words of the earth" [section 4]) may seem a triumphant resolution or a last, desperate attempt to conceal the irresolvable paradoxes of this poem.

Burton Hatlen

Bibliography

Bauerlein, Mark. *Whitman and the American Idiom.* Baton Rouge: Louisiana State UP, 1991.

Griffin, James D. "The Pregnant Muse: Language and Birth in 'A Song of the Rolling Earth.'" *Walt Whitman Quarterly Review* 1.1 (1983): 1–8.

Hollis, C. Carroll. *Language and Style in "Leaves of Grass."* Baton Rouge: Louisiana State UP, 1983.

Larson, Kerry C. *Whitman's Drama of Consensus.* Chicago: U of Chicago P, 1988.

Nathanson, Tenney. *Whitman's Presence: Body, Voice, and Writing in "Leaves of Grass."* New York: New York UP, 1992.

Whitman, Walt. *Leaves of Grass: Facsimile Edition of the 1860 Text.* Ed. by Roy Harvey Pearce. Ithaca, N.Y.: Cornell UP, 1961.

See also LANGUAGE; *LEAVES OF GRASS,* 1856 EDITION; POETIC THEORY

"Song of the Universal" (1876)

This poem was written to be read at the Tufts College commencement 17 June 1874. Since Whitman was unable to attend, the poem had to be read for him. Whitman considered this poem to be one of his "Centennial Songs," that is, poems written to celebrate one hundred years of American Independence. "Song of the Universal" celebrates the dream of what America could be, in spite of perceived faults in the country. Beneath the "measureless grossness" which the poet witnessed in America following the Civil War "[n]estles the seed perfection" (section 1).

There appears to be a general consensus that by the time this poem was written Whitman's creative energy had all but evaporated. Richard Chase, in *Walt Whitman Reconsidered,* writes that in this poem "Whitman has given up poetry and become a speechmaker" (147).

"Song of the Universal" is found in the "Birds of Passage" cluster of *Leaves of Grass,* a cluster that Gay Wilson Allen sees as being "bound by a fragile thread-theme of the search of the human race for perfections" (*Reader's Guide* 106–107). Henry Seidel Canby notes that Whitman is suggesting that to lack faith in the American dream is to "dream of failure" (287). Harold Aspiz asserts that Whitman is praying that the "therapeutic electric spirituality" contained in *Leaves of Grass* may "purge America's future of corruption" (152). James E. Miller believes that "Song of the Universal" suggests that "evil exists only in time" (211) and that evil disappears and good triumphs in eternity.

Apparently, the poem was written after Whitman first became acquainted with the writings of the German philosopher Georg Wilhelm Friedrich Hegel (1770–1831). Hegel taught that there is inherent in the universe a continuous process of change and progress which reveals itself in what is now known as the Hegelian dialectic. According to the Hegelian dialectic, any concept (thesis) inevitably generates its opposite (antithesis), and the struggle and interaction between the two results in a new concept (synthesis) which in turn becomes a new thesis in an ever continuing dialectic. In *The New Walt Whitman Handbook,* Gay Wilson Allen says that this poem is "another Hegelian expression" of Whitman's faith in "the ultimate triumph of the poet's ideals" (146).

In "Song of the Universal," Whitman suggests that the universe moves towards a remote ideal "[i]n spiral routs by long detours" but always the "real to the ideal tends" (section 2). In the pursuit of this ideal, the world must embrace science and must reject the "measured faiths of other lands" in order to embrace "grandeurs" of its own (section 4). For Whitman, this is one of the aspects of a new song which the modern world needs to hear and which modern poets need to celebrate.

Ronald W. Knapp

Bibliography
Allen, Gay Wilson. *The New Walt Whitman Handbook.* 1975. New York: New York UP, 1986.

———. *A Reader's Guide to Walt Whitman.* 1970. New York: Octagon, 1986.

Aspiz, Harold. *Walt Whitman and the Body Beautiful.* Urbana: U of Illinois P, 1980.

Canby, Henry Seidel. *Walt Whitman: An American.* Boston: Houghton Mifflin, 1943.

Chase, Richard. *Walt Whitman Reconsidered.* New York: William Sloane Associates, 1955.

Miller, James E., Jr. *A Critical Guide to "Leaves of Grass."* Chicago: U of Chicago P, 1957.

See also "Birds of Passage"; Hegel, Georg Wilhelm Friedrich; *Two Rivulets,* Author's Edition

"Songs of Parting" (1871)

"Songs of Parting" stands prominently as the final cluster in Walt Whitman's *Leaves of Grass,* but the sense of conclusion appears in the 1860 edition (before this cluster was formed) with its final poem "So Long!," a poem that comes into "Songs of Parting" in 1871 and remains through the 1881 edition. The 1867 edition uses the title *Songs Before Parting* for a separate book of poems bound with *Leaves* and *Drum-Taps,* and in 1871 "Songs of Parting" appears as a cluster in *Leaves.* As the cluster takes shape through the editions, the imminence of departure, farewell, and death becomes apparent in 1871, especially with the addition of the Civil War poems. Little critical material exists concerning this cluster although one often finds discussions of "Song at Sunset" and "So Long!"

In the seventeen poems of the 1881 edition, there is a cohesive, psychological development beginning with the somber, oppressive tone in "As the Time Draws Nigh" to soaring exhilaration in "Song at Sunset" with its ecstatic "Wonderful to depart! / Wonderful to be here!" After that climactic, contradictory utterance, the cluster moves calmly toward the farewell in "So Long!" In this arbitrarily chosen pattern, it is after the pitch of "Song at Sunset" that Whitman inserts two poems (the only two written for this cluster) that deal with specific deaths: "As at Thy Portals Also Death," an elegy for his mother, and "The Sobbing of the Bells," a poem for the recently assassinated President James Garfield.

These two poems and the Civil War poems make death a dominant subject of the cluster. Whitman's approach is ambivalent and contradictory: death is a conclusion, a delivery from life, and a fulfillment; it is at once terrible and terrifying, beautiful and enticing. Death entices in that its fulfillment leads to a consideration of

Walt Whitman, early 1880s, with cardboard butterfly—the poet's favorite photo of himself. Courtesy of the Library of Congress.

an afterlife, and it is associated with the sea. In "Joy, Shipmate, Joy!," the speaker says, "Our life is closed, our life begins"; and as the ship loses its anchorage, it "leaps" away from the shore. Excitement is evident in this poem but is absent from another, "Now Finalè to the Shore," as the speaker peacefully takes leave of those he loves and departs upon an "endless cruise."

Faced with the horror of death in this cluster, Whitman works to undermine death's power and his pessimistic emotions. He sees in the earth's beauty that "not an atom be lost" in "Pensive on Her Dead Gazing"; he envisions America's democracy and its future in "Years of the Modern" and "Thoughts"; and, finally, he leaves his poetry to his readers in "So Long!" Whitman constructs three futures or ways to subvert death: in the earth's beauty of which his body will be a part, in the ideals of democracy which are prominent in earlier poems, and in his eternal wooing of readers in and with his poetry.

In "Songs of Parting," Whitman reveals his conflicting attitudes toward death, a reality he had been conscious of since 1860 in that "delicious word death" in "Out of the Cradle Endlessly Rocking." In its final form, this cluster exhibits familiar echoes of other parts of *Leaves of Grass* in the Civil War poems, Whitman's belief and disbelief in democracy, his love of his readers, and his belief in the power of poetry.

Susan Rieke

Bibliography

Allen, Gay Wilson. *The Solitary Singer: A Critical Biography of Walt Whitman.* 1955. Rev. ed. 1967. Chicago: U of Chicago P, 1985.

Carlisle, E. Fred. *The Uncertain Self: Whitman's Drama of Identity.* East Lansing: Michigan State UP, 1973.

Crawley, Thomas Edward. *The Structure of "Leaves of Grass."* Austin: U of Texas P, 1970.

Erkkila, Betsy. *Whitman the Political Poet.* New York: Oxford UP, 1989.

Kaplan, Justin. *Walt Whitman: A Life.* New York: Simon and Schuster, 1980.

Miller, James E., Jr. *Walt Whitman.* New York: Twayne, 1962.

See also "As at Thy Portals Also Death"; Death; Immortality; "So Long!"; "Song at Sunset"

Soul, The

Whitman's understanding of the soul is extremely complex, and it plays an integral role in various aspects of his larger vision. Two of his most important ideas about the soul, that it is an immortal spiritual principle and an agency of religious knowledge, are shared by Christianity and many other religious systems. It seems likely that Whitman derived these views from the Christian culture in which he matured and from the writings of such religious romanticists as Samuel Taylor Coleridge, Thomas Carlyle, and Ralph Waldo Emerson. But the influence of other sources cannot be discounted, and critics have pointed to parallel conceptions in Indian religions, phrenology, and shamanism. However, Whitman ultimately developed a rather original theory of the soul because of the manner and extent to which he integrated his understanding of the soul with a process world view. In the final analysis, no aspect of Whitman's thought is more important to his vision than his notion of "soul," for it is an essential element of his understanding of God, the processes of evolution and history, human existence, and the purpose of the material world.

Whitman conceived of "soul" as part of the divinity, and so his theory of the soul must be related to his understanding of God. In its basic structure, Whitman's theology is theistic. That is, in contrast to both deism, which places God above the natural world, and pantheism, which locates God totally within nature, Whitman posited the existence of a God who both transcends the material universe and is also immanently present within the creation. However, he altered traditional theism by adapting it to his process world view. Consistent with conventional formulations of theism, Whitman conceived of a transcendent God who creates the universe, but he transformed the traditional notion of divine immanence by defining it not only as a spiritual substance that informs the material universe but also as the dynamic spiritual force which impels the evolution of nature, the advancement of history, and the development of human beings.

From this conception of divinity and its relationship to the world and human beings, Whitman derived two important corollaries. One was the idea that every part of nature "without exception has an eternal soul! / The trees have, rooted in the ground! the weeds of the sea have! the animals!" ("To Think of Time," section 9). The other was the belief that the souls which infused the creation were incessantly striving for fuller development and higher stages of existence. Accordingly, in order to describe this world, Whitman developed a poetic vocabulary which included what might be termed a "diction of the divine urge." For instance, in "Song of Myself" he speaks of the "Urge and urge and urge, / Always the procreant urge of the world" (section 3). And his lexicon is laced with such terms as "longing," "yearning," "pining," "burning," "struggling," "pang," "need," "dissatisfaction," and "want." Placed within the context of Whitman's theology, all of these words are used to describe the souls (of inanimate nature, plant, animal, and human life) that collectively make up the continuous progression of divine immanence toward reunion with its transcendent source.

Accordingly, human life, as Whitman conceived of it, is not the beginning of the soul's existence, as it is in Christian theology, but rather marks a particular phase in the ascent of divine immanence in which the soul becomes a depth dimension of the human personality. Also, in contrast to much of Western religious and philosophical thought, Whitman did not think of the body and its desires as an antagonist or hindrance to the soul, but instead depicted the body and soul as capable of harmonious integration. In his poetry, such fundamental human needs as sex, love, freedom, and immortality are presented as manifestations of the instinctive desires of the soul yearning to realize its full potential. History is the record of humanity's ongoing struggle, consciously or unconsciously, to fulfill the cravings of the soul: "Ever the soul dissatisfied, curious, unconvinced at last; / Struggling to-day the same—battling the same" ("Life"). Thus Whitman could conceive of the historical process as a warfare waged to liberate the human race from all forms of oppression (for example, in "To Thee Old Cause" and "To a Certain Cantatrice"). The significance of the United States in this grand historical drama was that it was the first country to establish constitutional rights and material conditions that freed the masses from political and material oppression. To complete the liberation of the human race, Whitman now called for a new religious vision (for which he tried to provide the beginnings) which would free the U.S. citizenry from psychological repression. The result would be, for the first time in history, the creation of complete men and women with fully developed souls who lived in accordance with their inner divinity. Thus Whitman's ideal future democracy was a form of spiritual anarchism in which the kingdom of God is realized on earth: "Land in the realms of God to be a realm unto thyself, / Under the rule of God to be a rule unto thyself" ("Thou Mother with Thy Equal Brood," section 6).

But even if history were to arrive at such a millennial culmination, the soul's journey would still be far from complete, for Whitman believed that the soul would continue to develop in the afterlife. Human death was just one more transition that the soul traversed in its long evolutionary ascent. Whitman depicted his own impending death as but one of his soul's many incarnations and promotions: "I receive now again of my many translations, from my avataras ascending, while others doubtless await me" ("So Long!"). The soul was engaged in an "endless march" ("Going Somewhere"), a "perpetual journey" ("Song of Myself," section 46), or a "journey ever continued" ("Thoughts" [Of ownership—as . . .]), because after its human existence it would continue to develop in what Whitman refers to as other "spheres."

In addition to being part of the divine immanence and the essence and motive force of the human personality, the soul was also conceived of by Whitman as a faculty of religious knowledge which enabled humans to encounter the external world as spirit. Mircea Eliade, the distinguished phenomenologist of religion, has described the experience of encountering an object or aspect of the natural world as sacred as having two distinctive qualities. First, the experience establishes itself in the mind of the religious subject as an especially intimate form of knowledge in which the subject feels a sense of psychological union with the inner spirit of that which is known. Second, because the soul is a depth dimension of the personality, religious experience impresses the subject as an especially meaningful or powerful form of knowledge. Consistent with this description of religious knowing, Whitman speaks of his religious experience of the natural world as an especially profound or "real" form of experience which develops or "identifies" his soul: "O the joy of my soul . . . receiving identity through materials . . . My soul vibrated back to me from them . . . The real life of my senses and flesh transcending my senses and flesh" ("Song of Joys").

This sense of the soul's higher knowledge gives rise to a crucial paradox in Whitman's thought. Although Whitman lovingly celebrated the natural world and the human body, he also held that these material realities were ultimately important only because they were indispensable to the soul's development. Seen from the higher spiritual perspective of an "envision'd soul," the objects of the natural world were "illusions! apparitions! figments all!" (Whitman 418). Unlike the youthful Emerson of "Nature," Whitman's sense of the greater reality of religious experience did not lead him to adopt a strict philosophical idealism which denied the matter-of-fact reality of the natural world. Yet he did always insist that this world, which he celebrated so lovingly, existed not for its own sake but to promote the development of immortal souls during their human incarnation.

David Kuebrich

Bibliography

Chari, V.K. *Whitman in the Light of Vedantic Mysticism*. Lincoln: U of Nebraska P, 1964.

Cowley, Malcolm. Introduction. *Walt Whitman's "Leaves of Grass": The First (1855) Edition*. Ed. Cowley. New York: Viking, 1959. vii–xxxvii.

Eliade, Mircea. *Patterns in Comparative*

Religion. Trans. Rosemary Sheed. New York: Sheed and Ward, 1958.

———. *The Sacred and the Profane*. Trans. Willard R. Trask. New York: Harcourt, Brace, 1959.

Hutchinson, George B. *The Ecstatic Whitman: Literary Shamanism & the Crisis of the Union*. Columbus: Ohio State UP, 1986.

Kuebrich, David. *Minor Prophecy: Walt Whitman's New American Religion*. Bloomington: Indiana UP, 1989.

———. "Whitman's New Theism." *ESQ* 24 (1978): 229–241.

Whitman, Walt. *Prose Works 1892*. Ed. Floyd Stovall. Vol. 2. New York: New York UP, 1964.

Wrobel, Arthur. "Whitman and the Phrenologists: The Divine Body and the Sensuous Soul." *PMLA* 89 (1974): 17–23.

See also CARLYLE, THOMAS; COMRADESHIP; EMERSON, RALPH WALDO; EVOLUTION; HINDU LITERATURE; HUMAN BODY; IMMORTALITY; NATURE; PANTHEISM; PHRENOLOGY; RELIGION

South, The American

Consisting of fifteen states, eleven of which would eventually form the Southern Confederacy, along with four border states, the American South held a place in Whitman's imagination and poetry before the Civil War, but his depictions became less romanticized and more emotionally charged after the war, even taking somewhat of a bitter tone after Abraham Lincoln's death. Whitman spent time in the South twice during his life, once in 1848 for a three-month stint as editor of the New Orleans *Crescent* and later to check on his brother George at the army field hospital in Falmouth, Virginia, during the Civil War, a trip which resulted in his remaining in Washington—which Whitman considered a Southern city, for eleven years, working as a clerk for various governmental agencies from 1862 until he suffered a stroke in 1873.

After Whitman was fired from the Brooklyn *Daily Eagle* because of his free-soil politics, he ran into J.E. McClure in the lobby of a Broadway theater. McClure was starting a new daily in New Orleans called the New Orleans *Crescent* and made Whitman an offer on the spot. Forty-eight hours later, on 11 February 1848,

Whitman and his fourteen-year-old brother Jeff, an apprenticed printer, were on their way south, arriving in New Orleans on 25 February 1848. While Whitman and his brother enjoyed the atmosphere of the famed Southern city, the position at the *Crescent* was not ideal. Whitman's political views were controversial, and somewhat of an embarrassment to McClure, who became cold toward the brothers, finally terminating their employment in May after a squabble over a cash advance. The brothers left on 27 May, arriving in New York sometime in mid-June.

Whitman wrote extensively in letters and in his journal about the South, often presenting a rather stylized, romanticized view of its exotic qualities and its genteel, aristocratic appeal. The poems concerning the South, or set in the South, written prior to the Civil War—of which there were essentially three: "I Saw in Louisiana a Live-Oak Growing," "Once I Pass'd through a Populous City," and "O Magnet-South"—depict a rather stereotypical South with lush, sensual images, indicating to some biographers the possibility of a New Orleans romance. This inference began with the English biographer Henry Bryan Binns, who speculated that these poems, along with a written statement that Whitman had made to John Addington Symonds (in response to Symonds's suggestion that Whitman was homosexual) in which he claimed to have Southern offspring and at least one Southern grandchild, revealed that Whitman had had an affair with an upper class Creole lady of Spanish descent. More recent biographers discount the "New Orleans romance" altogether, but the poems remain, nevertheless, emblematic of Whitman's somewhat romanticized, passionate view of the South he had seen during this period.

Whitman's second excursion to the South occurred in 1862, when, upon receiving word that his brother George had been wounded in battle, Whitman traveled south, reaching the army field hospital at Falmouth, Virginia, just after the battle of Fredericksburg in September. Upon finding his brother relatively well, he stayed with him for a week, then moved to Washington, D.C., where he took a job as clerk at the army paymaster's office. Later, he would work for the Department of Interior's Bureau of Indian Affairs, and later still, the Attorney General's Office, remaining in Washington until he suffered from a stroke in 1873. But living in the South, and the experience of the Civil War itself, would change Whitman's opinion of the South in general. No longer would he speak in his poetry of the mystical, Spanish moss–laden place of his earlier imaginative poetry. The realities of the war, and the South's role in it, would alter his stereotypes, and would perhaps give him a more realistic, more critical view of the region. However, in the poems included in "Drum-Taps," Whitman makes a great effort to include the South in his lamentations so as to heal the wounds left by the war. For instance, in "To the Leaven'd Soil They Trod," the terminal poem to "Drum-Taps," Whitman ends the poem with the statement that while the North would always nourish him, it is the hot sun of the South that is to "fully ripen" his songs. In many of the "Drum-Taps" poems, the South is evoked as having been just as brave, just as honorable, and just as devastated by the war as the North. And yet, the South Whitman describes is far more realistic, far more accurately drawn than his earlier descriptions. The enormity of the landscape and the problems facing the South are depicted especially in the poem "The Return of the Heroes," printed in the "Autumn Rivulets" section of Leaves of Grass. Here Whitman celebrates the returning armies and their ability to dissolve and once again turn their energies to planting crops, running farms and industries, producing the fruits of democracy.

But while it is true that Whitman's "Drum-Taps" sought to heal the wounds of the Civil War, and while it is true that Whitman depicted the South in these poems immediately following the Civil War in a particularly magnanimous fashion, the poems written several years later, in the early 1870s, were not as generous or forgiving. In his poem "Virginia—the West," first printed in the March 1872 issue of The Kansas Magazine and later added to "Drum-Taps" in the 1881 edition of Leaves of Grass, Whitman refers to Virginia, and by extension the South in general, as "the noble sire fallen on evil days." The irony for Whitman was that Virginia had been so instrumental in forming the very democracy it was now seeking to dissolve. His tone in the poem could be described as bitter, even satiric, especially when he describes Washington—for Whitman the very image of the Union—as having been provided by Virginia and reminds us that the Confederate soldiers who attacked the Union were also partly provided by Virginia.

But nowhere do Whitman's feelings for the South take on a more bitter tone than in the poem "This Dust was Once the Man," first printed in the 1871 Passage to India, later added to the "Memories of President Lincoln" section of the 1881 edition of Leaves of Grass. In this poem, Whitman laments the death of Lincoln, whom he describes as the man who saved the Union "[a]gainst the foulest crime in history known in any land or age," referring, of course, to the secession. Despite his earlier romanticized view of the South, and despite his magnanimity just after the Civil War, Whitman's view of the South was more emotional and bitter after the war and after the death of Lincoln.

Edward W. Huffstetler

Bibliography

Allen, Gay Wilson. The Solitary Singer: A Critical Biography of Walt Whitman. 1955. Rev. ed. 1967. Chicago: U of Chicago P, 1985.

Asselineau, Roger. The Evolution of Walt Whitman. 2 vols. Cambridge, Mass.: Harvard UP, 1960–1962.

Binns, Henry Bryan. A Life of Walt Whitman. London: Methuen, 1905.

Hudgins, Andrew. "Walt Whitman and the South." Southern Literary Journal 15 (1982): 91–100.

Kolb, Deborah S. "Walt Whitman and the South." Walt Whitman Review 22 (1976): 3–14.

Schyberg, Frederik. 1993. Walt Whitman. Trans. Evie Allison Allen. New York: Columbia UP, 1951.

See also BINNS, HENRY BRYAN; CIVIL WAR, THE; "I SAW IN LOUISIANA A LIVE-OAK GROWING"; LINCOLN'S DEATH; NEW ORLEANS CRESCENT; NEW ORLEANS, LOUISIANA; "O MAGNET-SOUTH"; "ONCE I PASS'D THROUGH A POPULOUS CITY"; "RETURN OF THE HEROES, THE"; "TO THE LEAVEN'D SOIL THEY TROD"; WASHINGTON, D.C.; WHITMAN, GEORGE WASHINGTON; WHITMAN, THOMAS JEFFERSON

Space

Space is a large trope for Walt Whitman. He conceives of it as geographical, extraterrestrial, inner or psychological, and as three-dimensional physical space. These different spaces often carry symbolic significance, ranging from the social and political union of the United States, to global unity, to spiritual fulfillment, to transcendence of death, and to divinity. While he treats space similarly in his poetry and prose, his poetry serves as the clearest example.

In addition to grounding Whitman's poetry primarily in the New World, geographical space ("space," place names, immensity, etc.) commonly represents humankind's culminating social potential, especially in terms of democracy and the Union. Geographical space also extends his vision to the entire world, claiming global unity and placing the United States in a key role in the evolution of human consciousness. "Facing West from California's Shores" is perhaps his clearest poetic example of this grounding.

Whitman's references to geographical space commonly suggest a figurative movement upward and outward, a notion extended in his references to extraterrestrial space. Images of the firmament obviously connote the larger, that is, more encompassing and complete notion of universe or "Kosmos," as in section 24 of "Song of Myself." "When I Heard the Learn'd Astronomer" is a clear assertion of Whitman's strongly figurative use of space. The astronomer and by implication his audience see only physical outer space, what is measurable. In the "stars" Whitman, however, sees the metaphysical and the mystical. Thus the trope expands its significance from extraterrestrial to inner or psychological space.

Whitman also conceives of space as that concept which acknowledges physical existence. In this sense, space is an essential of perception, of understanding, and of knowing. Using this sense of space symbolically, he can extend beyond the physical, as in "Crossing Brooklyn Ferry," where he proclaims that space is a physical limit only: "distance avails not" (section 3). This basic denial of space is a transcendence of physical boundaries, and as such is Whitman's essential statement of the limitlessness of humankind.

"Passage to India" is arguably Whitman's most important poem about space because of how it extends from the geographical, to the extraterrestrial, to the psychological, and to the metaphysical. At the beginning of this poem the movement is on the earth and westerly to the continental United States, where the "rondure" of the world is completed and fulfilled (section 4). Then the poem's frame of reference shifts to outer space as the speaker pictures the earth in the larger cosmological and universal "Rondure"

(section 5). With the completion of the world's "rondure" in the United States and the attendant implied completion of the evolution of human consciousness, extraterrestrial space becomes an appropriate symbol of humankind's spiritual potential, the vast capacity of the human soul's movement toward divinity. The poem finally invokes such meaning by associating the universe, "Time and Space," the human soul, and God (section 8).

These uses of space are displayed throughout Whitman's works. The Preface to the 1855 edition of *Leaves of Grass* introduces the poet's attitude toward space by first relating nature's and a nation's largeness to "the spirit of the citizen" (*Comprehensive* 710). The Preface further states that the American poet spans the continent, that the poet is the "one complete lover" of the universe (715) and that "American bards . . . shall be Kosmos" (718). A later prose work, *Democratic Vistas* (1871), appeals to the space of the United States in its very title. A number of sections in *Specimen Days* (1882) also describe various kinds of space. Some, like "Begin a Long Jaunt West," promulgate the geographic openness of the land. Others, like "Scenes on Ferry and River," celebrate the heavens. Still others, like "The Prairies and Great Plains in Poetry," directly associate the spaciousness of the new country with its literature.

Citing references to space in the order of their appearance in the 1891–1892 edition of *Leaves of Grass* indicates Whitman's expansive use of the trope in his poetry. "Song of Myself" catalogues geographic areas of the United States and the world, portending unity on earth. It associates the poet's poems and the earth with the stars, punning that a "leaf of grass is no less than the journey-work of the stars" (section 31). It relates "Space and Time" to the poet's vision as his "palms cover continents" (section 33). Finally, it projects humankind outward and upward to "a million universes" (section 48).

Several other poems catalogue geographic areas of the United States and the world. The whole of "Starting from Paumanok" asserts the essential characteristic of the New World—immensity. "Salut au Monde!" establishes a world geography, identifies America's place in it, and proclaims the limitlessness of the human spirit. "Song of the Open Road" also relates a world geography to cosmic space.

In "From Paumanok Starting I Fly like a Bird," early in the "Drum-Taps" cluster, Whitman promulgates a geographic and political "all," associating it with the "inseparable" Union. At the end of "Drum-Taps" and at the end of the war, the soldiers return to the "endless vistas" of the nation, which is whole again ("To the Leaven'd Soil They Trod").

The Union is clearly associated with the heavens in "When Lilacs Last in the Dooryard Bloom'd." President Lincoln is the "western fallen star" (section 2)—signifier of the Union he helped to retain, of the geographic spaces of the nation through which his coffin is carried, and finally of the mystical conquering of death.

The cluster "Whispers of Heavenly Death" also relates space to the metaphysical. Echoing "Passage to India," the first poem in the cluster, "Darest Thou Now O Soul," claims that at this point in the journey through life, the soul is equal with time and space and equipped to fulfill them, to fulfill existence. "A Noiseless Patient Spider" characterizes the soul by comparing the spider's casting out its filaments to the soul's constant search in "measureless oceans of space." In "Night on the Prairies" the speaker is walking alone and gazing into space, which allows him to attain immortality and understand that death will reveal to him what life has not, for death is not limited by time and space.

The final cluster of *Leaves*, "Songs of Parting," reasserts the relationship between geographical space and the United States in "Thoughts." Finally, the first and second annexes underscore and bring to a close the essential meanings of space with three poems that recall "Passage to India": "To the Sun-Set Breeze," "You Tides with Ceaseless Swell," "Sail Out for Good, Eidólon Yacht!"

With all its connotations—geographical, political, psychological, spiritual—space is a major concept for Whitman. He strews images and symbolic meanings of space throughout the final edition of *Leaves of Grass*. While he does not develop these meanings linearly throughout *Leaves* nor throughout his writing career, he uses them continuously. They ebb and flow, ebb and flow. They bud and wither and flourish again.

Steven Olson

Bibliography

Allen, Gay Wilson. "The Influence of Space on the American Imagination." *Essays on American Literature in Honor of Jay B. Hubbell*. Ed. Clarence Gohdes. Durham, N.C.: Duke UP, 1967. 329–342.

————. "Walt Whitman's Inner Space." *Papers on Language and Literature* 5 (1969): 7–17.

Olson, Steven. *The Prairie in Nineteenth-Century American Poetry*. Norman: U of Oklahoma P, 1994.

Roche, John. "Democratic Space: The Ecstatic Geography of Walt Whitman and Frank Lloyd Wright." *Walt Whitman Quarterly Review* 6 (1988): 16–32.

Whitman, Walt. *Leaves of Grass: Comprehensive Reader's Edition*. Ed. Harold W. Blodgett and Sculley Bradley. New York: New York UP, 1965.

————. *Prose Works 1892*. Ed Floyd Stovall. 2 vols. New York: New York UP, 1963–1964.

Zanger, Jules. "The Twelfth Newberry Library Conference on American Studies." *Newberry Library Bulletin* 5 (1961): 299–314.

See also "Crossing Brooklyn Ferry"; "Darest Thou Now O Soul"; *Democratic Vistas;* "Facing West From California's Shores"; "Noiseless Patient Spider, A"; "Passage to India"; Preface to *Leaves of Grass*, 1855 Edition; "Salut au Monde!"; "Song of Myself"; "Song of the Open Road"; "Starting from Paumanok"; Time

Spain and Spanish America, Whitman in

Walt Whitman's presence in Spain and Spanish America began when the exiled poet José Martí (Cuba, 1853–1895) witnessed Whitman's 1887 Lincoln address and wrote "El poeta Walt Whitman." Published in Argentina's *La Nación* and disseminated throughout the Spanish-speaking world, this letter of introduction set the tone for the "Whitman cult" in Hispanic letters. While Martí begins his essay citing a portrait of Whitman as aged prophet-bard, the composite he draws is of the New World "natural man" of relation who is transcendental brother and lover, spawn of "man on a new continent" with a "robust philosophy." Martí hears Whitman's charging verse as "sounds [that] ring like the earth's mighty shell when it is trodden by triumphant armies, barefoot and glorious" (Martí 211). It is Whitman the bearded bard, the all-embracing liberator, who arrives in Spain and Spanish America in Martí's essay.

Like Chilean poet-critic Fernando Alegría in his cornerstone study, *Walt Whitman en His-*

panoamérica, critics Doris Sommer and Enrico Mario Santi address a history of myth and misreading that has idealized Whitman and used his name and rhetoric at cross purposes. Santi points to the secondhand biographies and twice-removed translations of Whitman that have informed his "cult." In unwitting illustration of this difficult culture transfer, a would-be Whitman of Spanish America, José Santos Chocano (Peru, 1875–1934), announces that "Walt Wihtman [*sic*]" has the North, but he has the South (Chocano 13).

Critics note the irony of poets like Rubén Darío and Pablo Neruda invoking Whitman to combat a U.S. imperialism the poet himself represented. Yet Roger Asselineau defends Whitman's naive expansionism as an idealistic desire to disseminate democracy. In such a spirit the poet is received; as recently as 1981 the Nicaraguan Ministry of Culture published *Poesía libre,* an anthology of freedom poems featuring Whitman as voice of the people and model for Nicaraguan poets. As Ed Folsom and Gay Wilson Allen note, Whitman has helped writers around the world "to formulate and to challenge democratic assumptions" (3).

In Spain and Spanish America, Whitman in all his contradiction is invoked as voice, model, emblem, theme; he is translated, imitated, adapted, appropriated, and answered. In the cultures of profound spiritual tradition, of damning division and impassioned relation, of popular exuberance in a verse that expresses nature as often as ideology, Whitman, "the poet of the Body and . . . of the Soul" ("Song of Myself," section 21), sounds, as Gilberto Freyre has said, like a Latin translated into English.

Whitman's initial appearance in Hispanic poetry is in the Spanish American verse of *modernismo* (an Hispanic ambivalence to modernity informed by cosmopolitan currents). Alegría notes that Whitman's philosophical, religious, and political ideas were not fully understood until the era of post-*modernismo* (post-1916). Nevertheless, Martí's sophisticated, if idealized, portrait of the poet, which solidly outlines Whitman, harbors the intuitive comprehension Whitman himself sought. This embrace of recognition will characterize the reception of writers, from the *modernistas* to the post-*modernistas* to the avant-garde and social poets of Spain and Spanish America.

Relying directly or indirectly on Whitman's autobiographical writings as well as on Léon Bazalgette's *Walt Whitman: L'Homme et son oeuvre* (1908), early Hispanic biographers extend Whitman's own public relations image, one which approaches the titanic Walt Whitman persona of *Leaves of Grass.* Jorge Luis Borges would demythify this Whitman, distinguishing the "modest journalist" from "the semi-divine hero of *Leaves of Grass*" (qtd. in Santi 172). Octavio Paz on the other hand would argue simply: the "mask . . . is his true face" (qtd. in Santi 157).

Alegría calls the Catalan Cebriá Montoliú's *Walt Whitman, L'homme i sa tasca* (1913) the first systematic biography of the Hispanic world. Other significant critic-biographers are, as Alegría lists, A. Torres Ríoseco (*Walt Whitman,* 1922), who renewed Hispanic interest in Whitman after World War I; José Gabriel (*Walt Whitman, la voz democrática de América,* 1944); Luis Franco (*Walt Whitman,* 1945); and Miguel de Mendoza (*Walt Whitman,* 1944). Briefer readings include those of Enrique Gómez del Carrillo, who speaks like a benign Santayana, Luis Sánchez, Alberto Zum Felde, José Lezama Lima, and Armando Donoso, who like others after him yokes Whitman to Friedrich Nietzsche. Representing a demythified Whitman, Mauricio Gonzáles de la Garza culls the poet's prose for his *Walt Whitman: Racista, imperialista, anti-mexicano* (1971). To these writings the Spanish poet León Felipe would respond, "Walt has no biography. . . . His truth and his life are not in his prose. They are in his song" (Felipe 23).

Alvaro Armando Vasseur's 1912 *Walt Whitman, poemas,* published in several editions as the first Hispanic translation of Whitman, becomes, as Alegría observes, the breviary in which Hispanic writers first read from *Leaves of Grass.* Santi suggests that Vasseur's work, loosely translated from Italian and not English, both informs and reflects the second- and third-hand Whitman myth in Hispanic letters.

Other significant translations include Torres Ríoseco's *Walt Whitman* (1922); León Felipe's *Walt Whitman: Canto a mí mismo* (1941); Concha Zardoya's popular *Okras escogidas* (1946); Francisco Alexander's *Hojas de hierba* (1953), which includes Whitman's prefaces and informs Borges's *Hojas de hierba* (1969); Enrique Lopez Castellón's *Canto a mí mismo* and *El Cálamo, Hijos de Adán* (1981); Mauro Armiño's *Canto de mí mismo* (1984); and Alberto Manzano's *Hojas de hierba* (1984).

Rubén Darío (Nicaragua, 1867–1916), master of *modernismo* and "liberator" of Hispanic verse, merits a place comparable to Whitman's in his America's literary history. Conscious of this comparison, Rubén Darío both revered and petulantly dismissed Whitman, defending a New World art of the old and the noble with his famous lines, "the rest is yours, Democrat Walt Whitman." It is possible that Darío, unlike most of his contemporaries, read Whitman in English and soon honored this reading in his undervalued *Azul* sonnet, "Walt Whitman" (1890). Darío, the poet who wrote the anti-imperialist "A Roosevelt" (1905) in free "versos de Walt Whitman" and who in seeming about-face honored the United States in "Salutación al águila" (1906), revered not the nation of Roosevelt, but the ideal "América de Whitman." Darío subtly employed the "Yankee," his style, his name, to make this critical point. In his prose Darío refers repeatedly to the older poet and quotes from memory from "Salut au Monde!" It is in response to "Salut au Monde!" that Darío "talks back" to Whitman in his Americanist "Desde la Pampa," with the repeated "os saludo" ["I salute you"] returning Whitman's wave to the Argentine Pampas. And it is this Argentina that Darío celebrates with Whitmanic exuberance and enumeration in "Canto a la Argentina" (1916).

Pablo Neruda (Chile, 1904–1973), telluric and epic poet of America and of the people, declares, "I hold [Whitman] to be my greatest creditor" ("We Live" 41). In Neruda's "Oda a Walt Whitman," Whitman's hand, in a "mission of circulatory peace," leads the Chilean to an American identity ("Oda" 122). In Whitmanesque tribute to this identity, Neruda writes "Que despierte el leñador" ("Let the Railsplitter Awaken"). In a less tender poem, "Comienzo por invocar a Walt Whitman," Neruda invokes his mentor against Richard Nixon and U.S. violation. Though Neruda might be seen as the Whitmanesque poet par excellence, Alegría calls the similarities between Whitman and Neruda "illusory," and Santi maintains that Neruda resisted his predecessor's influence until the New World tribute *Canto General* (1950), the epic song of America with Whitmanic lists, repetition, and aphorism. However, *Canto General* parts ways with *Leaves of Grass* as an ideological tract in which "comrade" denotes communism: Neruda shares Whitman's sensual materialism, but rejects the transcendental beliefs fundamental to the American poet's world view. Still, Neruda's own world view, humbly composed in *Odas elementales*

(1954–1957), met with the popular success Whitman craved.

Jorge Luis Borges (Argentina, 1899–1986), the great metaphysical prankster and would-be gaucho, struggled with Whitman's influence, pronouncing him early on not only a great poet but "the only poet." Though amending this view, Borges's fascination with Whitman the poet of multiple masks continued in his prose and took shape in his poem "Camden, 1892," where he places the Good Gray Poet before a mirror. This characteristic Borgean preoccupation with identity informs essays like "Nota sobre Whitman" (*Otras inquisiciones*, 1960), "El otro Whitman" (*Discusión*, 1932) and "La nadaría de la personalidad" (*Inquisiciones*, 1925). In his philosophical inclusiveness, which invites the reader to share identity with the author, Borges parallels Whitman's own projection of the reader who will form a "general partnership" with the writer.

Octavio Paz (Mexico, 1914–) has denied any direct Whitman influence. Yet his focus on the tensions between individual, national, and American identity as well as his transcendentalism and sensual investment in the earth suggest an innate kinship. As Santi notes, Whitman becomes a standard bearer for Paz's pan-Americanist ideology. In Paz's essay, "Walt Whitman, poeta de América" (*El arco y la lira*, 1967), Whitman, like Paz himself, becomes an inventor of America.

Some additional poets Alegría lists as important readers of Whitman are Leopoldo Lugones (Argentina); Whitman translator Alvaro Armando Vasseur and Carlos Sabat Ercasty (Uruguay); Ezequiel Martínez Estrada (Argentina); Ernesto Cardenal and José Coronel Urtecho (Nicaragua); César Vallejo (Peru); Gabriela Mistral, Vicente Huidobro, and Pablo de Rokha (Chile); Jacinto Fombona Pachano (Venezuela); Luis Llorens Torres (Puerto Rico); Melvin René Barahona (Guatemala); and Pedro Mir (Dominican Republic).

According to critic Concha Zardoya, Miguel de Unamuno (Spain, 1864–1936), who translated fragments of "Salut au Monde!," is the first Spanish writer to exhibit Whitman's direct influence. Unamuno translates Whitman's ideas in prose in "Sobre la consecuencia; la sinceridad" (1906). In "El canto adánico" (*El espejo de la muerte*, 1913) Unamuno honors Whitman's re-creative enumeration—which he adapts in his poem "Canción de la puesta del sol." Whitman's stylistic presence is strong in the innovative poems "El cristo de Velásquez" and "Credo poético" (1920). Unamuno shares with Whitman a passionate stake in immortality, fearless innovation, and mistrust of reason and classification.

Federico García Lorca (Spain, 1898–1936) bears no discernible traces of Whitman. Yet, the Andalusian giving voice to the guitar, the earth, the gypsies articulates his Spain as Whitman himself uttered his America. Lorca wrote "Oda a Walt Whitman" as part of his lyrical collection of angst in America, *El poeta en Nueva York* (1930). The Spanish poet pays tribute to Whitman's redeeming presence. Surreal with the logic of the body, the poem is a note of gratitude; it intimately addresses a Whitman with beard of butterflies as a fellow sublimated homosexual.

Alegría calls attention to Lorca's fellow poets of the Spanish Civil War who saw in Whitman a brother in arms. Rafael Alberti, neopopulist, declares Whitmanesquely, "I send you a greeting / and I call you comrades" (qtd. in Zardoya 12). Other antifascist poets, Antonio Machado and Gabriel Celaya, find example in Whitmanic tone and enumeration, and Jorge Guillén finds confirmation, if not influence, in Whitman as the poet who relates breathing with poetry.

León Felipe (Camino) (1884–1968), poet of "earth" (*barro*), owes to Whitman, according to Zardoya, poetic parallels in which biography, poetry, and destiny are equal terms. Felipe "becomes" Whitman in his 1941 translation of "Song of Myself," declaring in his long verse prologue, "And so what if I call myself Walt Whitman? I have justified this . . . old American poet of Democracy, I have extended him and I have contradicted him" (qtd. in Zardoya 10).

Carol M. Zapata-Whelan

Bibliography

Alegría, Fernando. *Walt Whitman en Hispanoamérica*. Mexico City: Ediciones Studium, 1954.

Allen, Gay Wilson, and Ed Folsom, eds. *Walt Whitman & the World*. Iowa City: U of Iowa P, 1995.

Chocano, José Santos. *Oro de Indias*. Vol. 1. Santiago, Chile: Editorial Nascimiento, 1939.

Erkkila, Betsy. *Whitman the Political Poet*. New York: Oxford UP, 1989.

Felipe, León. *Canto a mí mismo de Walt Whitman*. Madrid: Visor, 1981.

Jaén, Didier Tisdel. *Homage to Walt Whitman*. Tuscaloosa: U of Alabama P, 1969.

Martí, Jose. "The Poet Walt Whitman." Trans. Arnold Chapman. *Walt Whitman Abroad*. Ed. Gay Wilson Allen. Syracuse: Syracuse UP, 1955. 201–213.

Neruda, Pablo. "Oda a Walt Whitman." *Walt Whitman & the World*. Ed. Gay Wilson Allen and Ed Folsom. Iowa City: U of Iowa P, 1995. 118–126.

———. "We Live in a Whitmanesque Age." *Walt Whitman in Europe Today*. Ed. Roger Asselineau and William White. Detroit: Wayne State UP, 1972. 41–42.

Nolan, James. *Poet-Chief: The Native American Poetics of Walt Whitman and Pablo Neruda*. Albuquerque: U of New Mexico P, 1994.

Perlman, Jim, Ed Folsom, and Dan Campion, eds. *Walt Whitman: The Measure of His Song*. Minneapolis: Holy Cow!, 1981.

Saldívar, José David. *The Dialectic of America*. Durham, N.C.: Duke UP, 1990.

Santi, Enrico Mario. "The Accidental Tourist: Walt Whitman in Latin America." *Do the Americas Have a Common Literature?* Ed. Gustavo Perez Firmat. Durham, N.C.: Duke UP, 1991. 156–176.

Sommer, Doris. "The Bard of Both Americas." *Approaches to Teaching Whitman's "Leaves of Grass."* Ed. Donald D. Kummings. New York: MLA, 1990. 159–167.

———. "Supplying Demand: Walt Whitman as the Liberal Self." *Reinventing the Americas: Comparative Studies of Literature of the United States and Spanish America*. Ed. Bell Gale Chevigny and Gary Laguardia. Cambridge: Cambridge UP, 1986. 68–91.

Zardoya, Concha. "Walt Whitman in Spain." *Walt Whitman in Europe Today*. Ed. Roger Asselineau and William White. Detroit: Wayne State UP, 1972. 9–12.

See also BORGES, JORGE LUIS; GARCÍA LORCA, FEDERICO; INTERCULTURALITY; NERUDA, PABLO; PORTUGAL AND BRAZIL, WHITMAN IN

"Sparkles from the Wheel" (1871)

"Sparkles from the Wheel" has been singled out by several critics as one of Whitman's best short lyrics. It is first of all a "picture poem"—one of the sharp descriptive sketches that Whitman frequently wrote and in which he anticipates the work of the imagists in the early twentieth century. The subject here is a mundane city sight: a knife-grinder practicing his trade on a sidewalk, unremarked except by the group of children (and the poet) who have gathered around him to watch.

"Sparkles" would be an admirable poem for its descriptive glimpse alone, but beyond this it also has a rich suggestiveness. It resonates with both clarity and possibilities. Among those possibilities, critics have seen, for example, a correspondence between the knife-grinder and the creative artist—another craftsman whose skill produces sparks of beauty, and who is often overlooked by the world around him. The scene also contains a commentary on modern life, the small group drawn aside and the archaic, soon-to-be-obsolete craftsman, human fragments nearly lost among the vastness and rush of the city. Or the sparkles can be seen as an image of the cosmos itself—an image which in turn might transform the knife-grinder into a Jehovah-like presence, a creator whirling out stars and worlds with a dignified, detached power and ease.

The themes of transience and flux hover throughout the poem. The central image of the sparkles whispers them. In "Sparkles" Whitman's dual awareness of the exquisite, sharp physical reality of things, and of their evanescence, is expressed perhaps as well as anywhere in Whitman's poetry. The scene the poem catches, a closely observed bit of nineteenth-century American life, is itself a sparkle from the great wheel of life. The poem is, therefore, a subtle poising of small and large, solid and fluid, momentary and timeless, caught by the senses, imagination, and language. The poet is careful to include himself in this: "Myself effusing and fluid, a phantom curiously floating, now here absorb'd and arrested."

In terms of structure, "Sparkles" is one of Whitman's finest unions of the formal and the free. The poem has sixteen lines, and while the first two are a separate sentence and set off, they introduce the next six, giving the poem in effect two eight-line stanzas or movements. In both, the images and syntax gracefully build, until Whitman brings us back again to the turning wheel, the next-to-last line describing the sparks, the last coming to rest with the simple title phrase and central image, now also musical refrain: "Sparkles from the wheel."

Howard Nelson

Bibliography

Beaver, Joseph. *Walt Whitman: Poet of Science.* Morningside Heights, N.Y.: King's Crown, 1951.

Miller, James E., Jr. *A Critical Guide to "Leaves of Grass."* Chicago: U. of Chicago P, 1957.

Pascal, Richard. "Whitman's 'Sparkles from the Wheel.'" *Walt Whitman Review* 28 (1982): 20–24.

Snyder, John. *The Dear Love of Man: Tragic and Lyric Communion in Walt Whitman.* The Hague: Mouton, 1975.

Thomas, M. Wynn. *The Lunar Light of Whitman's Poetry.* Cambridge, Mass.: Harvard UP, 1987.

See also "Autumn Rivulets"; Style and Technique(s)

Specimen Days (1882)

Specimen Days first appeared in 1882 within a volume entitled *Specimen Days & Collect,* published by Rees Welsh and Company in Philadelphia. Composed in 1881 largely out of notes, sketches, and essays written at various stages of the poet's life from the Civil War on, it is the closest thing to a conventional autobiography Whitman ever published.

The largest and arguably the most important work of Whitman's old age (except for the reordering of *Leaves of Grass* during the same period), the book deserves attention as more than a source of information or for its moving descriptions of the poet's experiences in the Civil War, which have in the past been the chief sources of its interest to scholars. The book attempts to link Whitman's life history to national and natural history while presenting itself as the casual reminiscence of a man approaching death. It therefore resembles what students of aging term "life review."

The volume was provoked in part by a trip to Whitman's childhood haunts and the family graveyards on Long Island that the poet took with Richard Maurice Bucke in 1881, in connection with Bucke's aim to write his biography. The text is presented as a series of brief, titled fragments, almost like a scrapbook, and is divisible into five sections or "acts" framed by introductory and concluding remarks. The sections cover the author's genealogy and early life, the Civil War, Whitman's recuperation from a stroke during a few months spent on a farm near Philadelphia, a brief trip to Canada and then another trip west in 1879–1880, and finally the author's thoughts about a variety of earlier authors such as Ralph Waldo Emerson, Thomas Carlyle, and Edgar Allan Poe.

Many of the fragments that compose the book had been published previously in periodicals, and most of the Civil War section had formed a book entitled *Memoranda During the War* (1875–1876). By piecing the fragments together and bathing them in an informal tone of reminiscence, Whitman creates a casual mood that conveys authenticity yet veils the seriousness of his structure and the carefully constructed nature of his pose. The rhetorical effect is thus to make Whitman's prophetic interpretation of his life all the more convincing, because apparently unstudied and "natural."

Throughout, Whitman emphasizes that his personal history has been shaped by geography and history, which in turn are the results of cosmic, natural processes. At the same time, he implies that he was in just the right places at the right moments to experience the epic transformations of the nineteenth century. The result is a kind of justification of his life course as the author accommodates himself to his physical debility and the approach of death—and strives to ensure his place in the continuum of American democratic development.

Specimen Days presents the formation of a self through participation in communal and even ecological process; unlike most confessional autobiographies in the Western tradition, Whitman's emphasizes the dependence of individual identity upon community identity, and thus upon historical placement. Even in the early genealogical portion of the book (the conventional starting point for biographies of the day) the poet links his family experience to the public experience of the nation as a whole. Meditating on the succession of generations buried in the Whitman and Van Velsor cemeteries on Long Island, representing a lineage going back to the first European settlement of the area, he also describes the setting in nationalistic terms, drawing attention to a grove of old black walnuts, "the sons or grandsons, no doubt, of black-walnuts during or before 1776" (*Specimen Days* 6).

Similarly, when narrating the key experiences of his early life, Whitman emphasizes such events as learning to set type under a man who remembered the American Revolution, being lifted up as a child and kissed by the marquis de Lafayette a half century after the signing of the

Declaration of Independence, and experiencing the growth of New York City—which for Whitman epitomizes the emergence of modern America. Throughout the book one finds such links between geography and historical epochs. Thus the Civil War memoranda dramatize how Whitman participated in the nation's terrifying rite of passage. At the same time, he refers to the conflict in metaphors of natural catastrophe. The will of "the people" for Union, for example, he describes as a stratum of bedrock "capable at any time of bursting all surface bonds, and breaking out like an earthquake" (25). The fatefulness of the war implies the fatefulness of his own life course at the defining moment for both the poet and the nation. Moreover, much of the Civil War section is composed of diary notes, thus forcing the reader's participation in the construction of the narrative. We are invited to discover the design supposedly immanent in Whitman's life history—a brilliant strategy not only for making readers experience the war as part of a common world continuous with the present but also for making us believe the poet's career has been written in the book of fate, that he was destined to be the bard of the nation at the turning point of its history. Whitman's assertions that *Leaves of Grass* "revolves around the Four Years' War" (*Comprehensive* 750) are connected with this self-justifying function. But they also reveal how the very process of composing *Specimen Days* was part of his own process of accommodating himself to a new "self"—that of the half-paralytic, made so, he liked to assert, by the blows the war experience delivered to his own body.

Following the Civil War section, Whitman presents a series of meditative descriptions of the natural world written when he lived at the Stafford Farm on Timber Creek, in part attempting to recover from a paralytic stroke. Here we follow the change in the bodily rhythms of the poet as he puts himself in "rapport" with trees, water, and clear skies. He describes the elements of the natural world around him, but also his own physical immersion in that world, whether bathing in the stream or "wrestling" with trees in exercises he invented for physical therapy. Inasmuch as this section of the narrative begins in May 1876, as Linck Johnson has suggested, Whitman symbolically connects his own rejuvenation with that of the nation in the centennial celebrations. This explains a ten-year gap in the narrative between the end of the war and the centennial year. The

S

decade 1865–1875 was very lonely and depressing for the poet, not easy to integrate into the story he is trying to construct of his life course and the nation's.

Finally Whitman emerges into the public world again, experiencing city life, sailing up the Hudson to John Burroughs's home, and then taking a trip to Denver. The notes on the trip west, when Whitman first crossed the Great Plains and saw the Rocky Mountains, balance the earlier notes concerning his youth in New York and suggest the poet's projected relationship to the next generation of American bards. The poet envisions the new American poets emerging from the geography of the trans-Mississippi West to produce a literature "altogether our own, without a trace or taste of Europe's soil, reminiscence, technical letter or spirit" (*Specimen Days* 219). The western poets to come will realize the prophetic implications of Whitman's own life's work.

This section also seeks to ground the chronological development of the nation in geographical features. The immensity of the mountains and rivers themselves match, for Whitman, the immensity of the democratic experiment; and what the Mediterranean was to early Europe the poet believes the Mississippi is to the new democratic epoch of the United States. This relationship between geography, geological scales of time, and human history further suggests the fit Whitman strives to make between interlocking personal, national, and cosmic cycles in his life story.

Ultimately the narrative of *Specimen Days* returns us to Camden and meditations on intellectual or literary predecessors and contemporaries—Carlyle, Emerson, Poe, Elias Hicks, Henry Wadsworth Longfellow, John Greenleaf Whittier, and William Cullen Bryant. Whitman stresses particularly the old age and death of these men, in addition to their contributions to the tradition with which he identifies. In this way he incorporates himself into a cultural continuum and at the same time models his own pose for his declining years. Moreover, he once again places individual identity amid the process of nature. He asks, for example, whether Carlyle (one of Whitman's early models) does not remain "an identity still," though chemically dissolved, "perhaps now wafted in space among those stellar systems, which, suggestive and limitless as they are, merely edge more limitless, far more suggestive systems?" (253). Such meditations are, in part, a means of bolstering the faith of the Good Gray Poet in the integrity of his own identity and in its immortality.

Specimen Days is, then, a new form of autobiography shaped in part by new challenges to the aging self brought on by rapid modernization and swift transformations of society that have characterized the industrializing and postindustrial period. For all its emphasis on memory and continuity, it is a peculiarly "modern" book.

The key to this deceptively informal and colloquial text may lie in what recent students of aging have to say about the uses of reminiscence in modern societies. Reminiscences, unlike histories, convey a rich sense of individual lives as components of larger social and historical processes; they create a complex identification with the world held in common with others both alive and dead, a deep sense of interconnectedness with other forms of being. Reflecting on *Specimen Days,* one comes to see how such interconnectedness is less a natural given than a creative achievement of self-making and of human desire.

George Hutchinson

Bibliography

Aarnes, William. "Withdrawal and Resumption: Whitman and Society in the Last Two Parts of *Specimen Days*." *Studies in the American Renaissance.* Ed. Joel Myerson. Boston: Twayne, 1982. 401–432.

Allen, Gay Wilson. *The Solitary Singer: A Critical Biography of Walt Whitman.* 1955. Rev. ed. 1967. Chicago: U of Chicago P, 1985.

Erkkila, Betsy. *Whitman the Political Poet.* New York: Oxford UP, 1989.

Hutchinson, George B. "Life Review and the Common World in Whitman's *Specimen Days*." *South Atlantic Review* 52 (1987): 3–23.

Johnson, Linck C. "The Design of Walt Whitman's *Specimen Days*." *Walt Whitman Review* 21 (1975): 3–14.

Kazin, Alfred. Introduction. *Specimen Days.* By Walt Whitman. Ed. Lance Hidy. Boston: Godine, 1971. xix–xxiv.

Price, Kenneth M. "Whitman on Other Writers: Controlled 'Graciousness' in *Specimen Days*." *Emerson Society Quarterly* 26 (1980): 79–87.

Whitman, Walt. *Leaves of Grass: Comprehensive Reader's Edition.* Ed. Harold W. Blodgett and Sculley Bradley. New

York: New York UP, 1965.

———. *Specimen Days.* Vol. 1 of *Prose Works 1892.* Ed. Floyd Stovall. New York: New York UP, 1963.

See also BRYANT, WILLIAM CULLEN; BUCKE, RICHARD MAURICE; CARLYLE, THOMAS; CIVIL WAR, THE; EMERSON, RALPH WALDO; GREAT PLAINS AND PRAIRIES, THE; HARTSHORNE, WILLIAM; HICKS, ELIAS; LAFAYETTE, MARQUIS DE; LONDON, ONTARIO, CANADA; LONG ISLAND, NEW YORK; LONGFELLOW, HENRY WADSWORTH; *MEMORANDA DURING THE WAR;* MISSISSIPPI RIVER; POE, EDGAR ALLAN; RIVERBY; ROCKY MOUNTAINS; TIMBER CREEK; TRAVELS, WHITMAN'S; WHITTIER, JOHN GREENLEAF

Speed, Attorney General James (1812–1887)
Born in Kentucky, James Speed received his education there, began his law practice in Louisville (1833), and served in the Kentucky legislature (1847), although his opposition to slavery hampered his political career. Speed taught law at the University of Louisville (1856–1858), then served in the Kentucky State Senate (1861–1863). He was appointed U.S. Attorney General by President Lincoln (1864). When Whitman was fired from the Interior Department (1865), friends recommended him to Speed, who was not offended by Whitman's poetry, as Secretary James Harlan had been. Referring to Speed and his successors, Whitman said, "I couldn't wish to have better bosses" (Whitman 26).

When Lincoln was assassinated, Speed soon found himself in disagreement with President Johnson's reconstruction policies and resigned (1866). Returning to Kentucky, Speed ran unsuccessfully for the U.S. Senate (1867) and for the House of Representatives (1870), and again taught law (1872–1879).

Whitman remained friendly with Speed, writing to keep him up to date on affairs at the office, and, in applying for pardon clerk (1871), gave Speed's name as a reference. In 1868 he recalled Speed's having treated him with "distinguished consideration" (Whitman 26). When Speed was asked to speak at the unveiling of a bust of Lincoln in Louisville, he asked Whitman to polish the speech for him, saying, "[H]e can do it better than any man I know" (qtd. in Allen 377).

Frederick Hatch

Bibliography
Allen, Gay Wilson. *The Solitary Singer: A Critical Biography of Walt Whitman.* 1955. Rev. ed. 1967. Chicago: U of Chicago P, 1985.
Collins, Margaret B. "Walt Whitman: Ghost Writer for James Speed? or 'None Goes His Way Alone.'" *Filson Club History Quarterly* 37 (1963): 305–324.
Reynolds, David S. *Walt Whitman's America: A Cultural Biography.* New York: Knopf, 1995.
Speed, James. *James Speed: A Personality.* Louisville: J.P. Morton, 1914.
Speed, Thomas. *Records and Memorials of the Speed Family.* Louisville: Courier-Journal Job Printing, 1892.
Whitman, Walt. *The Correspondence.* Ed. Edwin Haviland Miller. Vol. 2. New York: New York UP, 1961.

See also ATTORNEY GENERAL'S OFFICE, UNITED STATES; HARLAN, JAMES W.; WASHINGTON, D.C.

"Spirit That Form'd This Scene" (1881)
This short poem (subtitled "Written in Platte Cañon, Colorado") invokes Earth's Creator in the title and first line, then briefly marvels at western scenery—rocks, peaks, and gorges—before turning to the subject of Whitman and *his* creations. The poet claims inspiration by the same creative spirit. The issue of poetic form emerges: critics have "charged" that his poems lack disciplined art or formal skill. They are not "measur'd" or "wrought" or "polish'd." The conclusion apostrophizes that his poems—his "wild arrays"—honor instead the playful, unconstrained, and mysterious spirit that revels in nature.

Whitman traveled to the West for the first and only time in September 1879, and from the experience he produced for the 1881 edition this poem and two others, "The Prairie States" and "Italian Music in Dakota." The latter is especially relevant, since it too connects the spirit of nature with human artifice. The open spaces and large scale of the West powerfully confirmed Whitman's sweeping concept of nature, to which his ideals of democracy and poetry were intimately related. In *Specimen Days* Whitman summed up the impact of the West: "I have found the law of my own poems" (*Specimen Days* 210).

That law, governing both nature and poetry, was an open-ended creative force, not to be confined to neat meters or clipped gardens. "Spirit" is a carefully constructed apologia which embodies Emersonian organic form: it creates its own shape from inner necessity, like the "lilacs or roses" of Whitman's 1855 Preface (*Comprehensive* 714). Whitman's technique impressed contemporary English poet Gerard Manley Hopkins, who found troubling yet compelling the poem's "savage" artistry.

A close technical reading reveals that artistry. "Spirit" exemplifies Whitman's favored form, growing from short lines to long and then coming to rest again in short. The first and last lines are identical in rhythm and alliteration; those between develop artful changes on the basic three-beat line.

David Oates

Bibliography

Aarnes, William. "'Free Margins': Identity and Silence in Whitman's *Specimen Days*." *ESQ* 28 (1982): 243–260.

Aspiz, Harold. "Whitman's 'Spirit That Form'd This Scene.'" *Explicator* 28 (1969): Item 25.

Hopkins, Gerard Manley. "A Letter to Robert Bridges." *Walt Whitman: The Measure of His Song*. Ed. Jim Perlman, Ed Folsom, and Dan Campion. Minneapolis: Holy Cow!, 1981. 13–14.

Lehmberg, P.S. "'That Vast Something': A Note on Whitman and the American West." *Studies in the Humanities* 6 (1978): 50–53.

Mitchell, Roger. "A Prosody for Whitman?" *PMLA* 84 (1969): 1606–1612.

Piasecki, Bruce. "Conquest of the Globe: Walt Whitman's Concept of Nature." *Calamus* 23 (1983): 29–44.

Whitman, Walt. *Leaves of Grass: Comprehensive Reader's Edition*. Ed. Harold W. Blodgett and Sculley Bradley. New York: New York UP, 1965.

———. *Specimen Days*. Vol. 1 of *Prose Works 1892*. Ed. Floyd Stovall. New York: New York UP, 1963.

See also "FROM NOON TO STARRY NIGHT"; "ITALIAN MUSIC IN DAKOTA"; ORGANICISM; "PRAIRIE STATES, THE"; ROCKY MOUNTAINS; STYLE AND TECHNIQUE(S); WEST, THE AMERICAN

"Spirit whose Work is Done" (1865–1866)

"Spirit whose Work is Done" is from *Sequel to Drum-Taps* (1865–1866), printed in Washington. *Drum-Taps* and *Sequel to Drum-Taps* were first bound with *Leaves of Grass* in 1867. With only minor revisions, "Spirit" has remained in the "Drum-Taps" cluster through all editions. The title note, (*Washington City, 1865.*), was added in 1871.

"Spirit," which appears near the end of "Drum-Taps," was written after Whitman had witnessed the Grand Review in May 1865. In this poem the speaker addresses the Spirit of War, remembering the "dreadful hours" of battle, now ended. As he watches the review, he sees the Spirit lingering on the bristling, slanted bayonets. The drum-taps are now "hollow and harsh," quite disparate from the "stretch'd tympanum" in the opening poem of "Drum-Taps" ("First O Songs for a Prelude"). The anticipatory excitement is gone; in its place stands the Spirit of "solemn day" and "savage scene." He entreats the Spirit to allow him to remember and record its "pulses of rage" and "currents convulsive." His words will identify the Spirit of War to future generations as a record and a warning of this precious American experience.

In the last four lines of "Spirit," the imperative has been read as an invocation for literary inspiration and a desire for the poet to become a disciple of strife, retaining and understanding the rage and convulsions of war. The poet wants to absorb the Spirit of War back into himself, leaving the world at peace, once again Wound-Dresser to the nation. Those lines are also visionary, the "chants" and "songs" serving as a warning to the future of the terrible powers of the Spirit of War. Through their re-creation and captivity within the text the speaker hopes to hold them there, allowing the nation to avoid their consequences and live in peace.

"Spirit" reveals a mature and sober speaker, well acquainted with the horrors of war. It is a poem of wisdom, revealing the painful reality behind the "beat and beat [of] the drum"; it is a poem of prophecy, identifying the scorch and blister of war as a warning for future generations. With the harsh and hollow drum beats all across the land, the nation is now immune to the glamour and spectacle of war. Even in its proudest moment, thoughts turn away from victory to reflect on the terrible price that has been paid. "Spirit whose

Work is Done" is both a recollection of the conflict and a prayer that it is well and truly finished.

Sheree L. Gilbert

Bibliography
Allen, Gay Wilson. *The New Walt Whitman Handbook.* 1975. New York: New York UP, 1986.
Askin, Denise T. "Retrievements Out of the Night: Prophetic and Private Voices in Whitman's *Drum Taps.*" *American Transcendental Quarterly* 51 (1981): 211–223.
Cannon, Agnes Dicken. "Fervid Atmosphere and Typical Event: Autobiography in *Drum-Taps.*" *Walt Whitman Review* 20 (1974): 79–96.
McWilliams, John P., Jr. "'Drum Taps' and *Battle-Pieces:* The Blossom of War." *American Quarterly* 23 (1971): 181–201.
Whitman, Walt. *Walt Whitman's "Drum-Taps" (1865) and "Sequel to Drum-Taps" (1865–6): A Facsimile Reproduction.* Ed. F. DeWolfe Miller. Gainesville, Fla.: Scholars' Facsimiles and Reprints, 1959.

See also Civil War, The; "Drum-Taps"; Sequel to Drum-Taps; Washington, D.C.

Spontaneity

"Spontaneity" is a word with particular meaning to Walt Whitman, associated not only with his vision of the sort of poetry he was attempting to write, but also with the larger vision he had of the relationship of the soul to the world, representing a philosophy that influenced several twentieth-century poets and writers. The word itself, or some form of it, only occurs in three poems, and furnishes the title in only one, but the concept infuses most of Whitman's work.

Whitman, with the publication of the 1855 *Leaves of Grass,* was attempting to create poetry that appeared spontaneous, completely new, utterly cut off from its European or foreign antecedents. With its open verse form, its lack of rhyme and regular meter, its longer-line format, and its lack of literary or biblical allusions, Whitman sought to give the impression of poetry created spontaneously, arising from the mind of the quintessentially democratic man interacting with the landscape of America. The concept of spontaneity was crucial to his understanding of the poet's role in *Leaves of Grass,* whereby the poet's persona, his language, his actions, etc., were supposed to arise spontaneously from the atmosphere of democracy.

Further, the concept of spontaneity was at the heart of Whitman's philosophy as well, in that his understanding of the soul and its relationship to nature—much of which he had taken from Ralph Waldo Emerson—was rooted in the spontaneous interaction of the soul in its environment. As described in "There was a Child Went Forth," the soul interacts with the environment, accumulates experience, which then furnishes and creates the soul as it develops. The entire process is based on the spontaneity of the soul's interaction with the world. It is from this source, many would argue, that Whitman's poetry emerges, in his desire to demonstrate and enact this process.

Many later poets and writers were influenced by this aspect of Whitman's philosophy, most especially the British writer D.H. Lawrence, who wrote in an essay in the *Nation and Athenaeum* (1921) that Whitman's poetry "springs sheer from the spontaneous sources of his being . . . the highest loveliness of human spontaneity" (618). For Lawrence, Whitman's concept of spontaneity represents his true achievement as a poet, for the spontaneity reflects Whitman's ability to let his soul speak out, not in the controlled, mechanical way of a classical poet, but in the spontaneous, instinctive way of the natural world.

The word "spontaneity," or "spontaneous," appears in only three poems, however. In "A Thought of Columbus," the earth, that "mystery of mysteries," which is said to be thoughtless, is described as spontaneous. In "Give Me the Splendid Silent Sun," Whitman describes the desire to "warble spontaneous songs recluse by myself" (section 1), indicating the soul's natural tendency to speak out and give voice to itself, something Lawrence says is the basis of Whitman's poetry. And finally, in the poem "Spontaneous Me," in the "Children of Adam" cluster, Whitman fully illustrates his philosophy concerning the concept of spontaneity, a concept many critics associate with Whitman's autoerotic poetry, that is, the poetry that expresses the poet's consciousness of his own body and the healthy love of self seen in most of the "Children of Adam" poems. In this poem, Whitman depicts the poet behaving naturally, spontaneously, enjoying nature, his own body, the bodies of others, with a complete lack of self-consciousness, a complete lack of pretension. In the poem, nature itself is spontaneous, dropping its fruit wherever it falls, spreading its

S

branches wherever it will, the wind blowing in whatever direction, etc. The poet seeks to achieve the spontaneity of nature in order to realize his own spontaneous nature, which in large measure can be indicated by his honest, casual acceptance of sex. Sex, in the "Children of Adam" section and elsewhere, like all natural functions, should be a spontaneous occurrence when souls interact because sex itself is a spontaneous function of nature, just as all of the natural occurrences the poet lists are spontaneous. Like the dancing of the honey bee, or the descending of dew on the grass, sex is the natural, instinctive result of the spontaneity of souls interacting, and the poem seeks to celebrate that concept.

Edward W. Huffstetler

Bibliography

Kaplan, Justin. *Walt Whitman: A Life*. New York: Simon and Schuster, 1980.

Lawrence, D.H. "Whitman." *Nation and Athenaeum* 29 (1921): 616–618.

Perlman, Jim, Ed Folsom, and Dan Campion, eds. *Walt Whitman: The Measure of His Song*. Minneapolis: Holy Cow!, 1981.

Schyberg, Frederik. 1933. *Walt Whitman*. Trans. Evie Allison Allen. New York: Columbia UP, 1951.

See also "CHILDREN OF ADAM"; "GIVE ME THE SPLENDID SILENT SUN"; LAWRENCE, D.H.; SEX AND SEXUALITY; SOUL, THE; "SPONTANEOUS ME"; "THERE WAS A CHILD WENT FORTH"; "THOUGHT OF COLUMBUS, A"

"Spontaneous Me" (1856)

First published as the twenty-eighth poem in the second edition (1856) of *Leaves of Grass*, and originally titled "Bunch Poem," "Spontaneous Me" was included as number 5 in the "Enfans d'Adam" (later "Children of Adam") cluster. The first line of this poem was added in 1860, and became the title in 1867.

Without the opening line, the emphasis of the beginning of the poem would shift dramatically to the relationship between the speaker of the poem and the "friend" who accompanies him. The poem describes not a particular relationship but a way of relating to nature and to sexuality, and posits an attitude of acceptance and openness to the human body and to the physicality of the natural world. Lines 4 and 5 collapse time, from the "blossoms of the mountain ash" in spring to the "same late in au-

tumn," providing a sense of cyclical change as a backdrop for the change which is recorded later in the poem, from nighttime fantasies of adolescence to the maternity and paternity of adulthood.

Whitman had marked line 10 for deletion in his Blue Book (Whitman's personal copy of the 1860 *Leaves*). The line, however, remained. This section of the poem names directly the connection between the human male body and poetry; out of this connection comes the catalogue of "Love-thoughts," which culminate in the description of the bee "that gripes" the flower as an analogy for human sexual intercourse.

The second half of the poem begins with an image of two lovers sleeping peacefully together (perhaps the "friend" of line 2, now after having made love). This image of restful repose is followed by a new character in the poem, a boy who "confides" to the speaker his dreams of unsatisfied longing, and these dreams offer a direct contrast to the "Love-thoughts" section. Instead of "love-juice" and "love-odor," the "no-form'd stings" and the "hubb'd sting of myself" take precedence. As in "The Sleepers," the speaker merges with other sleepers (both young men and young women) like the boy, who also suffer from unquenched desire for physical contact. Their desire culminates only in frustrated acts of "torment."

The final section of the poem (divided by a semicolon, as the second section is at the end of line 17) begins with a striking image of reciprocity in contrast to the frustration of the preceding section: the speaker accepting the "souse upon me of my lover the sea, as I lie willing and naked." The catalogue which follows contains images of fruition and ripeness in nature and in humanity. The poem ends with a salutation to procreation, and a parting gesture in which this "bunch" (of semen, of words, of poems) is tossed "carelessly to fall where it may" because forethought and calculation would go against the spontaneous impulse which the poem advocates.

Maire Mullins

Bibliography

Chosy, Shirley Ann. "Whitman's 'Spontaneous Me': Sex as Symbol." *Walt Whitman Review* 25 (1979): 113–117.

Gordon, Travis. "Whitman's 'Spontaneous Me.'" *Explicator* 52 (1994): 219–222.

Killingsworth, M. Jimmie. *Whitman's Poetry of the Body: Sexuality, Politics, and the Text*. Chapel Hill: U of North Carolina P, 1989.

Larson, Kerry C. *Whitman's Drama of Consensus*. Chicago: U of Chicago P, 1988.

Miller, Edwin Haviland. *Walt Whitman's Poetry: A Psychological Journey*. 1968. New York: New York UP, 1969.

Waskow, Howard J. *Whitman: Explorations in Form*. Chicago: U of Chicago P, 1966.

See also "CHILDREN OF ADAM"; *LEAVES OF GRASS, 1856 EDITION*; SEX AND SEXUALITY; SPONTANEITY; *WALT WHITMAN'S BLUE BOOK*

Stafford, George and Susan M.

George and Susan Stafford were the parents of Harry Stafford, a young man Whitman met and befriended in the mid-1870s. Harry's parents were tenant farmers in Laurel Springs, outside of Glendale, near Camden, New Jersey. Harry invited Whitman to his family home, and Whitman immediately fell in love with the homestead and the intimate atmosphere. It reminded him of the Whitman family farm on Long Island that his parents had inherited from Whitman's paternal grandparents, Jesse and Hannah Whitman. After the initial visit to the Stafford farm, Whitman was to return several times over the following years, often staying for weeks at a time and paying for his lodging in order to help with family finances.

While he was with the Staffords, Whitman found the time to work on *Specimen Days*, an autobiographical piece in which he, among other things, wanted to record his reactions to the war. In that memoir he turns from the horrors of war's destruction to the comforts and joys of his adopted home. The Stafford family serves as a counterpoint to the disruption of the Civil War. At the farm he also planned much of the 1881 edition of *Leaves of Grass*. Whitman only stopped going to the farm when his friendship with Harry Stafford became strained, which made the visits uncomfortable. He later wrote that among the Staffords he felt both loved and able to love, and that they had in a real way saved his life after the horrors of the Civil War.

David G. Miller

Bibliography

Kaplan, Justin. *Walt Whitman: A Life*. 1980. New York: Bantam Books, 1982.

Reynolds, David S. *Walt Whitman's America: A Cultural Biography*. New York: Knopf, 1995.

Walt Whitman, ca. 1879, with Harry Stafford. By permission, Edward Carpenter Collection, Sheffield [England] Archives.

Whitman, Walt. *The Correspondence*. Ed. Edwin Haviland Miller. 6 vols. New York: New York UP, 1961–1977.

See also CIVIL WAR, THE; *LEAVES OF GRASS, 1881–1882 EDITION*; *SPECIMEN DAYS*; STAFFORD, HARRY L.; TIMBER CREEK

Stafford, Harry L. (b. 1858)

Harry Stafford was only eighteen years old in 1876 when he took a job as an errand boy at the Camden *New Republic*. He was a moody adolescent, given to fits of brooding and impulsive behavior. Walt Whitman, then fifty-seven and still recovering from his stroke of 1873, came to the office to work on the Centennial edition of *Leaves of Grass*, and the two began one of the most intense relationships of the poet's life.

Stafford took Whitman to visit his parents at White Horse Farm, near Kirkwood, New Jersey. The farm adjoined Timber Creek (now called Laurel Springs), and Whitman made his way down to the creek to regenerate his health by wrestling with birch saplings and taking "Adamic" mud baths. He also found time to meet there with a Stafford farmhand named Ed Cattell, but he kept those encounters secret from Stafford.

Stafford and Whitman slept together in the same top floor bedroom, and when they traveled together Whitman referred to him as "my nephew" and insisted that they be accommodated in the same bed (Whitman 68). Whitman's friend John Burroughs complained that they "cut up like two boys" (qtd. in Whitman 79, n19), and he found their frolicsome behavior annoying. The Stafford family, however, were pleased to see the well-known man act as mentor to their son and gladly forgave any bad manners, chalking them up to artistic temperament. They hung a picture of the poet on their sitting room wall.

Despite the frolicking, the relationship was a stormy one. They quarreled frequently, and several times Stafford returned a friendship ring given to him by Whitman. Stafford wrote that there was "something wanting to compleete [sic] our friendship" (qtd. in Shively 143), perhaps meaning sexual relations. At another time, he wrote of wanting to buy a suit of clothes like Whitman's so he could earn the admiration of his friends. He also wrote, "I am thinking of what I am shielding, I want to try and make a man of myself" (qtd. in Miller 6), perhaps referring to guilt about homosexuality or simply to immaturity.

The nature of their bond remains mysterious, and critics have interpreted it as everything from asexual and paternal to erotic and promiscuous. Whitman seems to have been less ambivalent. He wrote in his notebooks of their peaceful times together and of his dismay at Stafford's mercurial anxiety. At one point, he wrote of his gratitude for Stafford's help in his medical recovery, declaring that *"you, my darling boy, are the central figure of them all"* (Whitman 215).

Stafford went from one job to another until he returned to the family farm. He and Whitman remained close until Stafford married Eva Westcott in 1884, after which the poet visited occasionally. When he died, Whitman left Stafford his silver watch, originally intended for Peter Doyle.

Arnie Kantrowitz

Bibliography

Allen, Gay Wilson. *The Solitary Singer: A Critical Biography of Walt Whitman.* 1955. Rev. ed. 1967. Chicago: U of Chicago P, 1985.

Callow, Philip. *From Noon to Starry Night: A Life of Walt Whitman.* Chicago: Ivan R. Dee, 1992.

Kaplan, Justin. *Walt Whitman: A Life.* New York: Simon and Schuster, 1980.

Miller, Edwin Haviland. Introduction. *The Correspondence.* By Walt Whitman. Ed. Miller. Vol. 3. New York: New York UP, 1964. 1–9.

Shively, Charley. *Calamus Lovers: Walt Whitman's Working Class Camerados.* San Francisco: Gay Sunshine, 1987.

Whitman, Walt. *The Correspondence.* Ed. Edwin Haviland Miller. Vol. 3. New York: New York UP, 1964.

See also Burroughs, John and Ursula; Doyle, Peter; Stafford, George and Susan M.; Timber Creek

"Starting from Paumanok" (1860)

Although it is a complex and fascinating poem on its own, the primary importance of "Starting from Paumanok" is that it introduces *Leaves of Grass.* As Fredson Bowers has shown, Whitman began to work on it soon after the publication of the first (1855) edition. Entitled "Premonition" in manuscript (Barrett Collection, University of Virginia), the poem was first printed in the third (1860) edition, in which, under the title "Proto-Leaf," it led off the volume. It received its present title in the fourth (1867) edition and its present position, immediately after "Inscriptions," the opening cluster of brief poems, in the fifth (1871). The 271 lines of the final version are divided into nineteen sections of various lengths.

After identifying himself and announcing that he "will strike up for a New World" (section 1), the speaker of the poem spends the rest of his time explaining what he will sing about and to whom. He is a typical, "generic" American, who declares that he will sing in "endless announcements" to "[w]hoever you are" (section 14) about three "greatnesses": Love, Democracy, and, "a third one rising inclusive and more resplendent," Religion (section 10).

The emotion at the poem's core is the speaker's elated discovery that life is affirmation and joy. Having understood that "starting from Paumanok" he has also come from everywhere else—California, the Dakotas, anywhere—and that in his "[s]olitary" identity all other identities are fused, he will "strike up" for "a New World" (section 1) disclosed by his vision in which life is "[v]ictory, union, faith, identity, time, / The indissoluble compacts, riches, mystery, / Eternal progress, the kosmos, and the modern reports" (section 2). Glancing through "vast trackless spaces" and "projected through time" (section 2), this generic Self who is the speaker places himself at the heart of space and time, and his chants go "forth from the centre . . . Shooting in pulses of fire ceaseless to vivify all" (section 3).

His exuberance and excitement do not allow the speaker to advance a carefully reasoned argument; the poem plays variations, instead, on the two themes of "Love" and "Democracy": the powerful though diffuse erotic and affective energies present throughout *Leaves of Grass* and the community implied by the conviction "that all the things of the universe are perfect miracles, each as profound as any" (section 12). Woven through these variations is the third theme, "Religion." Although this sounds at times like Whitman's version of Emersonian idealism, of the conviction that "Nature is the symbol of spirit" (Emerson 20), at other times it works the other way around: "the body includes and is the meaning, the main concern, and includes and is the soul" (section 13). This tension is not resolved in the poem. The keynote throughout is "the soul," the inner eye that enables him to see and believe in the coherence and purposeful goodness of it all.

In the long coda which concludes the poem (sections 14 to 19), the speaker appoints his audience. As if falling in step with the "[e]ternal progress" (section 2) of the "marches humanitarian" (section 3), he hurries on with ever increasing speed, inviting "you" to "haste on" with "me firm holding" (section 15), to see and experience a "world primal again" (section 17). At first, this "you" is anybody ("[w]hoever you are" [section 13]), but the person whom he embraces at last with the "music wild" of his shouts of ecstatic release is a "camerado close" (section 19). This camerado strongly resembles the "pensive and silent" young man to whom he earlier explained that "[i]t is a painful thing to love a man or woman to excess, and yet it satisfies, it is great" (section 9). With this gradual identification of the audience as well as with the impression it creates of a spontaneous, improvisational structure, "Starting from Paumanok" recalls the 1855 Preface, which it was clearly

designed to replace. It is, to borrow Emerson's phrase, yet another of Whitman's "incomparable things said incomparably well" (qtd. in Whitman, *Comprehensive* 730); the identification does not restrict the audience but infinitely enlarges it. The "camerado close" has become all humanity responding to the song just as the speaker, though he may have started from Paumanok, is all humanity singing.

Readers who do not simply browse in *Leaves of Grass* but make their way through it, as Whitman seems to have expected them to, from the first page to the last will find that, subordinated to Love, Democracy, and Religion, many, if not most, of the other major themes and motifs that dominate *Leaves of Grass* are also introduced in this poem. Thus, his chant of the "greatness" of Love will also be "the song of companionship" and of "manly love" (section 6) or, as Whitman often refers to it, "adhesiveness," celebrated in "Calamus" and, indeed, throughout the volume. The "century marches" (section 3) of Democracy sweep down the Open Road onto which all *Leaves of Grass* invites its readers, and the soul is the speaker's "mistress" (section 5) not just in this poem but in virtually all of Whitman's poems, from "Song of Myself" to "Passage to India" and "So Long!" The catalogues, so characteristic of the entire book, first appear in this poem ("Interlink'd, food-yielding lands!" etc. [section 14] and "See, steamers steaming through my poems," etc. [section 18]), and a number of other poems will remind the reader of the declaration that "I am myself just as much evil as good, and my nation is" (section 7). An indication that the poem was meant to be a sampler of the rest of the volume is that the 1867 version has added a reference not just to the pair of mockingbirds from Alabama (section 11) prominent in "Out of the Cradle Endlessly Rocking," which was composed in 1858–1859, but to "the hermit thrush from the swamp-cedars" (section 1) that sings the serenade to death in "When Lilacs Last in the Dooryard Bloom'd," which was composed in 1865.

One of the many revisions that Whitman made between 1860 and 1881, this addition has enriched and improved the text; most of the others have not. Betsy Erkkila has found that in its final form the poem is weaker than in the first largely because the revisions, reflecting the turbulence in Whitman's and the nation's life between 1860 and 1867, tend to dull the 1860 version's intensity of personal feeling and clarity of political conviction. M. Jimmie Killingsworth's careful review of the poem in its several versions leads to a similar conclusion.

"Starting from Paumanok" has received critical attention in all major studies of Whitman. No readers will deny its importance as the introduction to *Leaves of Grass,* but few are likely to claim that it is one of Whitman's truly great poems, like "Song of Myself" or "When Lilacs Last in the Dooryard Bloom'd." Passages in which shrillness and platitudes take the place of inspiration are not difficult to find. For all its flaws, however, it also has its moments of genuine power and subtle beauty. Although it refers to itself as "a programme of chants" (section 3), "Starting from Paumanok" is not an account of what is to follow but an illustration of it. Like an overture to one of the poet's beloved Italian operas, it is not a description but a tonal entry into Whitman's world, not the program of the concert but part of the performance itself.

Ivan Marki

Bibliography

Cameron, Ann M. "Whitman's 'Starting from Paumanok.'" *Explicator* 49.2 (1991): 86–89.

Emerson, Ralph Waldo. *Essays & Lectures.* Ed. Joel Porte. New York: Library of America, 1983.

Erkkila, Betsy. *Whitman the Political Poet.* New York: Oxford UP, 1989.

Killingsworth, M. Jimmie. *Whitman's Poetry of the Body: Sexuality, Politics, and the Text.* Chapel Hill: U of North Carolina P, 1989.

Whitman, Walt. *Leaves of Grass: Comprehensive Reader's Edition.* Ed. Harold W. Blodgett and Sculley Bradley. New York: New York UP, 1965.

———. *Whitman's Manuscripts: "Leaves of Grass" (1860).* Ed. Fredson Bowers. Chicago: U of Chicago P, 1955.

See also DEMOCRACY; HUMAN BODY; *LEAVES OF GRASS,* 1860 EDITION; LOVE; RELIGION; SOUL, THE; STYLE AND TECHNIQUE(S)

Stedman, Edmund Clarence (1833–1908)

The November 1880 Whitman essay Edmund Clarence Stedman wrote dramatically enhanced the poet's stature among intellectuals as well as the more general audience *Scribner's* appealed to. Whitman later expressed his appreciation, and they remained friendly over the years. The piece was later included in *Poets of America* (1885), probably Stedman's finest work. The series of critical essays sought canon reform, and the less recognized Edgar Allan Poe as well as Whitman received extraordinary care. The Whitman piece remains the best in the volume, and he also received more space than any other poet in the ten-volume Library of American Literature.

Stedman began as one of the more genteel Pfaffian Bohemians, helped them materially, and admired and promoted the 1876 Centennial edition of *Leaves.* He was an esteemed and powerful literary and cultural critic, as well as a poet, but earned his living as a stockbroker in a volatile, unregulated market. A serious intellectual, he struggled as did others in his period with the challenges rapidly maturing scientific thought created for traditional views and institutions. Noting in the essay that Whitman had been rejected or "canonized, not criticized," Stedman wrote "judicially" about the work rather than the man—a cardinal principle embraced by the critical group he was part of—in order to provide a fair introduction and assessment which was in keeping with his nondeterministic Tainean views. The weakest part of his treatment is the judgment that Whitman was insufficiently modest when treating sex, but this is far outweighed by his understanding of the prosody; he pointedly demonstrated that the seemingly innovative poetics was conventional, with roots in English Bible translations and William Blake's experiments, among others. Whitman, a poet of nature, was employing an Emersonian romantic organicism in which function dictated form. Stedman was a committed nationalist in the Emersonian tradition, though not as radical as the midcentury's Young America group, and strongly opposed to Anglophilism. There is irony in the essay's being published first in *Scribner's,* since the editor, J.G. Holland, was vehemently opposed to Whitman and his work—as well as to that of Poe and Henry David Thoreau; but Stedman gave him the choice of publishing all or none of the essays which eventually composed *Poets of America.*

Stedman took exception to the fact that the common people Whitman celebrated, at the expense of the conventional, intelligent, and educated middle class, did not and probably would not read him in the future. He was not far off the mark, however, when suggesting that Whitman stood the best chance among his contemporaries of being read by future generations.

Donald Yannella

Bibliography
Scholnick, Robert J. *Edmund Clarence Stedman.* Boston: Twayne, 1977.
Stedman, Edmund Clarence. *Poets of America.* Boston: Houghton Mifflin, 1895.
———, ed. *An American Anthology, 1787–1900.* 2 vols. Cambridge, Mass.: Riverside, 1900.
———, ed. *A Library of American Literature: From the Earliest Settlement to the Present Time.* 10 vols. New York: Webster, 1889.

See also Critics, Whitman's; Pfaff's Restaurant; Scholarship, Trends in Whitman

Stevens, Oliver (b. 1825)

In a letter dated 1 March 1882 Boston District Attorney Oliver Stevens advised James R. Osgood and Company to cease publication of *Leaves of Grass* on the grounds that it violated anti-obscenity laws. When Stevens, under pressure from State Attorney General George Marston and Anthony Comstock, threatened legal action if specific passages were not deleted, he ignited a public controversy that launched Whitman's poetry into the center of a national debate over First Amendment rights.

Initially, Whitman received Stevens's threat lightly and agreed to self-censure, thinking the objections applied to only "half a dozen words and phrases." When he learned that three whole poems, "A Woman Waits for Me," "To a Common Prostitute," and "The Dalliance of the Eagles," required deletion, Whitman became obdurate, refusing to make even the slightest revision. Osgood subsequently declined to challenge Stevens's legal authority in the matter, forcing Whitman to secure publication elsewhere.

Whitman, recognizing that Marston and Comstock were the prime movers in the affair, expressed no significant degree of animosity toward Stevens. Little is known about Stevens, a native of Massachusetts who briefly studied law at Harvard, but his apparent silence in the face of abusive attacks in the press by Whitman's defender, William Doug-

las O'Connor, indicates that he was at least in partial agreement with the morally conservative views of Marston and Comstock.

Joseph P. Hammond

Bibliography
Freedman, Florence Bernstein. *William Douglas O'Connor: Walt Whitman's Chosen Knight.* Athens: Ohio UP, 1985.
Loving, Jerome. *Walt Whitman's Champion: William Douglas O'Connor.* College Station: Texas A&M UP, 1978.
Whitman, Walt. *The Correspondence.* Ed. Edwin Haviland Miller. Vol. 3. New York: New York UP, 1964.

See also Boston, Massachusetts; Comstock, Anthony; Heywood, Ezra H.; O'Connor, William Douglas; Osgood, James R.; Society for the Suppression of Vice

Stevens, Wallace (1879–1955)

Wallace Stevens, a major twentieth-century American poet, is best known for his ingenious explorations of the relationship between reality and the imagination. His most representative poems come from *Harmonium* (1923), *Ideas of Order* (1936), *The Man with the Blue Guitar* (1937), and *Notes Toward a Supreme Fiction* (1942). His *Collected Poems* (1954) won him the National Book Award and the Pulitzer Prize. He had one significant book of literary criticism, *The Necessary Angel* (1951).

At a first reading, Stevens's poems seem to be distant from the Whitman tradition of American poetry or even from things American. His early kinship appeared to be with the French symbolist poets, but it is obvious that Stevens was familiar with the poetry of Whitman. In the opening lyric of "Like Decorations in a Nigger Cemetery," Stevens has great praise for Whitman's poetic sensibility. Critics explore Stevens's "The Owl in the Sarcophagus" and see its elegiac roots in Whitman's "The Sleepers" and "When Lilacs Last in the Dooryard Bloom'd." They also compare its rock, leaf, and lilac images to those in "Song of Myself."

Stevens's ties to Whitman seem to rest in his delight and vitality in the power of language, his images of light, color, seascape, and death, as well as his spaciousness. In a 1955 letter to Joseph Bennett, Stevens said that a reading of Whitman's poetry "remains highly vital for many people . . . a gatherings-together of precious Americana . . . The superbly beautiful and moving things are those that he wrote naturally, with an extemporaneous and irrepressible vehemence of emotion" (Stevens 870). Both poets focus on the configuration of the role of the poet as an arbiter of reality.

Andy J. Moore

Bibliography
Bloom, Harold. *Wallace Stevens: The Poems of Our Climate*. Ithaca, N.Y.: Cornell UP, 1976.
Middlebrook, Diane Wood. *Walt Whitman and Wallace Stevens*. Ithaca, N.Y.: Cornell UP, 1974.
Riddel, Joseph N. "Walt Whitman and Wallace Stevens: Functions of a 'Literatus.'" *South Atlantic Quarterly* 61 (1962): 506–520.
Stevens, Wallace. *Letters*. Ed. Holly Stevens. New York: Knopf, 1966.
Yukman, Claudia. "An American Poet's Idea of Language." *Critical Essays on Wallace Stevens*. Ed. Steven Gould Axelrod and Helen Deese. Boston: Hall, 1988. 230–245.

See also LEGACY, WHITMAN'S; POETIC THEORY

Stevenson, Robert Louis (1850–1894)

Scottish novelist, essayist, poet, Stevenson became acquainted with *Leaves of Grass* while a student in his native Edinburgh. He was soon reading, reciting, and preaching Whitman to his friends, and in 1871 began an essay which appeared as "The Gospel According to Walt Whitman" in the *New Quarterly Magazine*, London, October 1878, and as "Walt Whitman" in *Familiar Studies of Men and Books*, 1882. Stevenson presented a curious mixture of praise and censure, toning down much of his rapturous early drafts. In his preface to *Familiar Studies*, he half apologized for his essay as an effort to explain Whitman "credibly to Mrs. Grundy" (xvii). Though the essay received favorable critical comment, Whitman did not care for it or for Stevenson's public image or his writings. Stevenson, however, remained an ardent admirer of Whitman, praising him in an article, "Books Which Have Influenced Me," as of critical importance in his life and work (*The British Weekly*, 13 May 1887). He took *Leaves of Grass* with him to Samoa, where he often read aloud "Song of the Open Road." Stevenson was among the contributors to the fund raised for Whitman by W.M. Rossetti in 1885.

Sherwood Smith

Bibliography
Caldwell, Elsie Nobel. *Last Witness for Robert Louis Stevenson*. Norman: U of Oklahoma P, 1960.
Maxiner, Paul, ed. *Robert Louis Stevenson: The Critical Heritage*. London: Routledge and Kegan Paul, 1981.
Stevenson, Robert Louis. *Familiar Studies of Men and Books*. 1882. London: Chatto and Windus, 1924.
Swearingen, Roger G. *The Prose Writings of Robert Louis Stevenson: A Guide*. Hamden, Conn.: Archon Books, 1980.

See also BRITISH ISLES, WHITMAN IN THE

Stoddard, Charles Warren (1843–1909)

A minor literary figure in his own day, and until recently all but forgotten, Stoddard was a journalist, poetaster, and essayist who exchanged a few letters with Walt Whitman (from 1867 to 1870). Stoddard is also known for his brief stint as Mark Twain's secretary and companion in London in 1873. Whitman read Stoddard's charming sketches about Hawaiian natives in *The Overland Monthly* (1869–1870) that would be collected as *South Sea Idylls* (1873), his most popular book. It may be compared favorably with Herman Melville's *Typee* (1846) and the early chapters of *Moby-Dick* (1851) in its provocative—and humorous—tribute to the sensuous lifestyle of "barbarism." Like Melville, Stoddard focused on homoerotic affection between the Christian and the barbarian.

It is not surprising, then, that he would react so enthusiastically to Whitman's "Calamus" poems. His letter of 2 April 1870 opens, "In the name of CALAMUS listen to me!" (Traubel 444) and proceeds to sing the joys of barbarism as opposed to the hypocrisy and "frigid manners of the Christians" (445). Whitman's response was guardedly sympathetic: he "warmly approve[d]" of Stoddard's "adhesive nature," but felt compelled to remind him of the virtues of "American practical life" (Whitman 97).

Although Stoddard was vastly inferior to Whitman as a poet, they were kindred spirits in their need for discreet homoerotic attachments, though Whitman preferred his in civilized society. And though Whitman in the two surviving letters to Stoddard sincerely hoped they would some day meet, they apparently never did.

Joseph Andriano

Bibliography

Austen, Roger. *Genteel Pagan: The Double Life of Charles Warren Stoddard.* Amherst: U of Massachusetts P, 1991.

Katz, Jonathan, ed. *Gay American History: Lesbians and Gay Men in the U.S.A.* New York: Crowell, 1976.

Traubel, Horace. *With Walt Whitman in Camden.* Vol. 3. 1914. New York: Rowman and Littlefield, 1961.

Whitman, Walt. *The Correspondence.* Ed. Edwin Haviland Miller. Vol. 2. New York: New York UP, 1961.

See also "Calamus"; Sex and Sexuality

Stoddard, Richard Henry (1825–1903)

Whitman endured a tempestuous relationship with this New York poet, critic, and editor. Throughout his lengthy career, and especially after 1870 when he had established a reputation, Stoddard formed a link between older, well-established writers and the younger New York crowd.

Born in Hingham, Massachusetts, Stoddard was raised in poverty after his sea-captain father was lost at sea. Stoddard went to work at eleven at various odd jobs before being apprenticed to an iron foundry. After marrying Elizabeth Drew Barstow, writer of fiction and poetry, Stoddard received Nathaniel Hawthorne's help in obtaining a New York Custom House post, a position he held for seventeen years.

Reports vary concerning Stoddard's connection to Whitman via the crowd of literary Bohemians that frequented Pfaff's Broadway restaurant. Gay Wilson Allen and Edwin Haviland Miller include Stoddard, along with his friends Edmund Clarence Stedman and Thomas Bailey Aldrich, with Whitman in the group that occupied a reserved table at the pub. But Stoddard was critical of the Bohemian crowd, and claimed in his *Recollections* that he had never entered Pfaff's but only once looked in the window.

Stoddard, whose poetry is compared with that of John Keats and Percy Bysshe Shelley, may not have understood Whitman's style. In *Poets' Homes,* Stoddard refers to "Song of My-

self" as the piece that Whitman "oddly enough named for himself" (2:41), and most strongly praises one of Whitman's most conventional lyrics, "O Captain! My Captain!"

Stoddard's published criticism of Whitman widened the gap between the two. In his satirical review of William Douglas O'Connor's *The Good Gray Poet* in the *Round Table,* Stoddard criticized both the poet and O'Connor. Whitman speculated that Stoddard and New York *Tribune* drama critic William Winter had collaborated on negative reviews of *Leaves of Grass* in 1882. Most importantly, Whitman believed that a scathing letter on obscenity in *Leaves of Grass,* published under the pseudonym "Sigma" in the New York *Tribune* in 1882, was Stoddard's.

Jennifer A. Hynes

Bibliography

Allen, Gay Wilson. *The Solitary Singer: A Critical Biography of Walt Whitman.* 1955. Rev. ed. 1967. Chicago: U of Chicago P, 1985.

Macdonough, A.R. "Richard Henry Stoddard." *Scribner's Monthly* 20 (Sept. 1880): 686–694.

O'Connor, William. *The Good Gray Poet: A Vindication.* New York: Bunce and Huntington, 1866.

Stedman, Edmund Clarence. *Genius and Other Essays.* New York: Moffat, Yard, 1911.

Stoddard, Richard Henry, et al. *Poets' Homes: Pen and Pencil Sketches of American Poets and Their Homes.* 2 vols. in one. Boston: D. Lothrop, 1879.

———. *Recollections, Personal and Literary.* Ed. Ripley Hitchcock. New York: A.S. Barnes, 1903.

———. Rev. of *The Good Gray Poet,* by William Douglas O'Connor. *Round Table* 3 (1866): 37.

Whitman, Walt. *The Correspondence.* Ed. Edwin Haviland Miller. 6 vols. New York: New York UP, 1961–1977.

See also "O Captain! My Captain!"; O'Connor, William Douglas; Pfaff's Restaurant

Stoicism

An important philosophical influence on Whitman's entire career, Stoicism began as a Greek school of philosophy under Zeno in the third century B.C. It has since been a "perennial philosophy" in Western culture, revived particularly in periods of storm and stress. It was to become particularly important to Marcus Aurelius in the period of Rome's decline, to William Shakespeare and other Renaissance authors, and even to the transcendentalists such as Ralph Waldo Emerson in Whitman's own day.

Chief features of the stoic philosophy (which in Whitman's case should perhaps be regarded more as an attitude or stance) include the precept of keeping one's moral purposes in harmony with nature, maintaining imperturbability, acknowledging the kinship of all people, and practicing indifference to one's own experiences of pain, suffering, and death. Moreover, Stoics tend to see one's personal existence as a role in a play directed by nature, thus conceiving the self in dualistic terms. One aspect of the person is involved in the everyday perturbations of life, the other looks on calmly from its position within the larger cosmic scheme. Four of Whitman's pre–Civil War poems have been singled out as particularly stoical in theme and effect: "Song of Prudence" (1856, largely taken from the 1855 Preface), "I Sit and Look Out" (1860), "Me Imperturbe" (1860), and "A Song of Joys" (1860). "Me Imperturbe" can serve virtually as a definition of the stoic stance:

> Me imperturbe,
>   standing at ease in Nature,
> Master of all or mistress of all,
>   aplomb in the midst
>   of irrational things,
> Imbued as they, passive, receptive,
>   silent as they,
> Finding my occupation, poverty,
>   notoriety, foibles, crimes,
>   less important than I thought,
>
> . . . .
>
> Me wherever my life is lived,
>   O to be self-balanced
>   for contingencies,
> To confront night, storms, hunger,
>   ridicule, accidents, rebuffs,
>   as the trees and animals do.

That several of the most stoical poems of Whitman's antebellum career were written in 1860 suggests the intensity of Whitman's personal and political disappointments at this time.

The most important Stoic text for Whitman was the *Encheiridion* of Epictetus, which he first discovered at about the age of sixteen. "It was like being born again," he would later tell Horace Traubel (*With Walt Whitman* 2:71–72). He returned to this text recurrently during his life, particularly in old age, when it became for him a kind of manual for daily living. In a manuscript notebook of 1868–1870, Whitman paraphrases Epictetus's description of a wise man, one who neither reproves nor praises others, nor attends to praise or insult of himself; one who maintains moderate appetites and allows desire only for those things that are within his own power to obtain. During the period that he wrote this note, Whitman was struggling to control the "perturbation" of what he seems to have considered a vain sexual pursuit.

Later in life, Stoicism aided Whitman's accommodation to paralysis and the approach of death. In fact it formed a key element of his "Good Gray" persona. In the concluding paragraph of *Specimen Days* (1882), he quotes the Roman Stoic Marcus Aurelius's definition of virtue as "only a living and enthusiastic sympathy with Nature" (295). This "sympathy with Nature" allows Whitman in old age to think of his life as part of the world's great flux. It also helps him stem anxieties about both his reputation and the direction of American democracy. Marcus Aurelius had written that "fluxes and flows" continually renewed the world (qtd. in Allen 56). In Whitman's later work, images of tides and slow-wheeling stars, always important to him, become far more prevalent features than "leaves" as he abandons the ecstatic modes of his greatest earlier poems, yet attempts in a different manner to link the rhythms of his life with those of the cosmos.

He returned to the *Encheiridion* frequently for support in his daily affliction, attesting to Horace Traubel that "the source of [his] great peace" was Epictetus's prescription that what is good for nature is good for oneself (*With Walt Whitman* 1:423). A pocket-sized 1881 translation of Epictetus's book by T.W.H. Rolleston became his constant companion; he called the book "sacred, precious, to me: I have had it about me so long—lived with it in terms of such familiarity" (*With Walt Whitman* 3:253). Indeed, he paraphrased it constantly. The book was a kind of manual for coping with infirmity and pain, calumny, vilification, and death.

If the importance of Stoicism in Whitman's life has perhaps not received its due, this is understandable. Aspects of his work—particularly his antebellum work—reveal that Stoicism was only one resource in his ethical universe, always waxing and waning depending on his circumstances and often alternating with quite different tendencies. His ecstatic intensity, the burning loves and disappointments of some of his most famous poems, conflict with the stoic ethos—although even in "Song of Myself," the speaker repeatedly falls back from intense emotion and participation to stoic detachment. After the Civil War, ecstaticism largely disappears and the stoic attitude becomes dominant, inflected by a comic sensibility and a rather unstoical, prophetic hope for the future.

The symbolism of tides remains constant, however, suggesting that Stoicism, connected emotionally in Whitman's sensibility with the massive imperturbability of nature and the ultimately indestructible nature of the self, remains a constant resource for the poet through the immense highs and lows, great hopes and disappointments of his life.

George Hutchinson

Bibliography

Allen, Gay Wilson. "Walt Whitman and Stoicism." *The Stoic Strain in American Literature.* Ed. Duane J. MacMillan. Toronto: U of Toronto P, 1979. 43–60.

Epictetus. *The Encheiridion of Epictetus.* Trans. T.W.H. Rolleston. London: Kegan Paul, Trench, 1881.

Hutchinson, George B. "'The Laughing Philosopher': Whitman's Comic Repose." *Walt Whitman Quarterly Review* 6 (1989): 172–188.

Kahn, Sholom J. "Whitman's Stoicism." *Scripta Hierosolymitana* 9 (1962): 146–175.

Pulos, C.E. "Whitman and Epictetus: The Stoical Element in *Leaves of Grass.*" *Journal of English and Germanic Philology* 55 (1956): 75–84.

Traubel, Horace. *With Walt Whitman in Camden.* Vol. 1. Boston: Small, Maynard, 1906; Vol. 2. New York: Appleton, 1908; Vol. 3. New York: Mitchell Kennerley, 1914.

Wenley, R.M. *Stoicism and Its Influence.* 1924. New York: Cooper Square, 1963.

Whitman, Walt. *Specimen Days.* Vol. 1 of *Prose Works 1892.* Ed. Floyd Stovall. New York: New York UP, 1963.

See also EPICTETUS; "I SIT AND LOOK OUT"; "ME IMPERTURBE"; PERSONAE; "SONG OF JOYS, A"; "SONG OF PRUDENCE"; *SPECIMEN DAYS*

Style and Technique(s)

From the publication of the first *Leaves of Grass* in 1855, Walt Whitman has been justly honored as the first great innovator in American poetry. Indeed, persistent innovation marks Whitman's style in every phase of his long career, though many readers find Whitman's most characteristic style in the poems of 1855–1865, from "Song of Myself" to "When Lilacs Last in the Dooryard Bloom'd." Whitman himself stated, "I sometimes think the Leaves is only a language experiment" (qtd. in Traubel viii), and the experimental spirit imbues both his poetry and his prose.

One area of particularly successful experimentation, in the 1855 and 1856 editions of *Leaves of Grass,* is poetic diction. Whitman creates a rich mixture of words borrowed or adapted from foreign languages, colloquialisms, Americanisms, geographical place names, and slang expressions. Some of Whitman's characteristic foreign borrowings in the 1855 "Song of Myself" include *omnibus, promenaders, experient, savans, embouchures, vivas, venerealee, amies, foofoos, en-masse, kosmos, eleves, promulges, accoucheur,* and *debouch.* Even this brief list suggests a range of stylistic choices, from the commonly accepted borrowing to the surprising adaptation or coining. The stylistic texture created by other dictional elements can be fairly suggested by four lines from "Song of Myself" in which the speaker attempts to answer the child's question, *"What is the grass?":*

> Or I guess it is a uniform hieroglyphic,
> And it means, Sprouting alike in broad
>   zones and narrow zones,
> Growing among black folks as among white,
> Kanuck, Tuckahoe, Congressman, Cuff,
>   I give them the same, I receive them
>   the same.

(section 6)

Whitman combines the more formal language of "uniform hieroglyphic" with colloquialisms,

Americanisms, and slang to create the figure of a democratic speaker who answers the child inclusively and familiarly.

Whitman's exotic and familiar words exist alongside a host of standard English words used in grammatically surprising ways. Thus the processes of word formation in the English language become a resource for Whitman's experiments. In particular, he employs the processes of suffixation, conversion, and compounding in remarkable ways. He creates new words by grafting the *-ee* and *-er* suffixes to lexically established words, by converting verbs into nouns, and by synthesizing compounds from temporary, ad hoc relations. The result of these grammatical experiments is a dynamic, verbal style in which agents and activities coalesce.

Perhaps the most obvious stylistic trait of Whitman's poetry is the long line, written in free verse. Whitman abandons, almost completely, the metrical tradition of accentual syllabic verse and embraces instead the prosody of the English Bible. The most important techniques in Whitman's prosody are syntactic parallelism, repetition, and cataloguing. These stylistic innovations combine to create an expansive, oracular, and often incantatory effect.

Syntactic parallelism has rightly been seen as the basic technique of Hebrew poetry, and Whitman's innovative free verse owes a fundamental debt to the rhythms of the Bible. That being said, the nature of the poet's debt remains far from clear. Bishop Robert Lowth's early attempts to classify the types of biblical parallelism have, according to modern scholars, proven limited in usefulness. Similarly, Gay Wilson Allen's accounts of biblical analogies for Whitman's unconventional prosody, based on Lowth's taxonomy, do not describe the variety and complexity of Whitman's poetic practice. More important than the types of parallelism, in any case, is the basic structure of syntactic parallelism itself. Whitman tends to establish a sequence of coordinate clauses, from two to four lines long, based on the parallelism between syntactic units within lines. So, for example, this stanza from "Song of Myself" features coordinate syntax both within and between lines, employing a *subject-verb* parallelism: "I loafe and invite my soul, / I lean and loafe at my ease observing a spear of summer grass" (section 1).

The second, related technique is repetition. The three techniques of repetition usually carry their Greek names from Demetrius and Longi-

nus. *Anaphora* (or *epanaphora*) refers to the repetition of the same word or words at the beginning of lines. *Epistrophe* (or *epiphora*) refers to the repetition of the same word or words at the end of lines. *Symploce* (or *complexio*) refers to the combination of anaphora and epistrophe. In the lines quoted above, anaphora names the initial repetition of the word "I." A lengthier stanza from "Song of Myself" shows the complexity and variety of Whitman's repetitions:

> Swiftly arose and spread around me the
>   peace and knowledge that pass all
>   the argument of the earth,
> And I know that the hand of God is the
>   promise of my own,
> And I know that the spirit of God is the
>   brother of my own,
> And that all the men ever born are also
>   my brothers, and the women my
>   sisters and lovers,
> And that a kelson of the creation is love,
> And limitless are leaves stiff or drooping
>   in the fields,
> And brown ants in the little wells be-
>   neath them,
> And mossy scabs of the worm fence,
>   heap'd stones, elder, mullein and
>   poke-weed.
>
> (section 5)

The repetition of "And" at the beginning of lines sets a firm rhythmical frame based on anaphora, but Whitman employs symploce, elision, variation of line length, and variation of syntactic structure to create a complex weave of assertion.

The third technique, cataloguing, can be seen as the expansive synthesis of syntactic parallelism and rhetorical repetition. The catalogue typically expands beyond the rhythmical frame of two to four coordinate clauses, it features parallelism of clause, phrase, or some mixture of the two, and it employs the full repertoire of rhetorical devices of repetition. The catalogue is particularly important in the first three editions of *Leaves of Grass,* and it functions significantly in long poems such as "Song of Myself," "The Sleepers," "Crossing Brooklyn Ferry," "Song of the Open Road," "Salut au Monde!," "By Blue Ontario's Shore," "Song of the Broad-Axe," and "Starting from Paumanok." A representative example of the clausal catalogue appears as section 15 of "Song of Myself," while an example of the phrasal catalogue appears as section 41. Whitman's most extensive catalogue, section 33 of "Song of Myself," is a complexly ordered composition of phrasal and clausal lines.

A final element of Whitman's free verse relates to the effective irregularity of stanza form. In contrast to a regular repetition of a given stanza, usually marked by a definite pattern of meter and rhyme, Whitman's style features the persistent irregularity of stanza length. In this respect, Whitman's practice with stanzas parallels his treatment of the poetic line. The stanzas tend to form units of expression, elaborating on a figure or theme that is announced in the first line of the stanza. The length of the stanza is thus a function of the poet's expressive thought, not a formal requirement. The stanzas vary from one line to dozens of lines, and at these two extremes the word "stanza" hardly seems descriptive. Between the two ends of the spectrum, however, Whitman displays great artistry in the play of stanza form. Section 11 of "Song of Myself," for instance, owes much of its dreamlike tone to the delicate play of tercet and couplet.

In the 1860 edition of *Leaves of Grass*, Whitman begins to show his concern for larger units of poetic form. Always conscious of the printed format of the poems, Whitman numbers stanzas in the 1860 edition, and in the 1867 edition he first uses section numbers (as well as stanza numbers) in the long poems. By 1881, in the sixth edition, he deletes stanza numbers but preserves the section numbers. The fifty-two sections of "Song of Myself" are thus a postwar revision of the poem.

A second and perhaps more important concern also appears in 1860: Whitman begins to organize poems into special groups he calls "clusters," and this technique of arranging poems persists through the remaining editions of *Leaves*. Although many poems occupy a rather stable position in a given cluster, Whitman goes through a long, complicated process of arranging and rearranging the poems into thematic, figural, or topical clusters. The titles and contents of a particular cluster go through a constant process of experimentation, and in many cases the cluster disappears altogether, its contents dispersed to form some other arrangement. Although Whitman claimed that the cluster arrangements of the 1881 edition are definitive, the annexes that appear after 1881—"Sands at Seventy" and "Good-Bye my

Fancy"—suggest the same method of organization and the same restless spirit of experimentation. Indeed, in the preface to the second annex (written in 1891) Whitman calls it "this little cluster, and conclusion of my preceding clusters" (Whitman 537), as if he recognizes a formal similarity between the patterns of the definitive edition and those of the two later additions.

The idea that there is stylistic and thematic continuity between the poems of 1855–1865 and those of Whitman's last twenty-seven years has remained a minority view throughout the twentieth century. The general tendency of criticism has been to tell a tragic story of decline and failure, seeing the three postwar editions of *Leaves of Grass*, the Deathbed edition of 1891–1892, and the voluminous prose of *Democratic Vistas, Specimen Days,* and *Prose Works 1892* as somehow inescapably tinged by Whitman's life of illness, depression, and artistic isolation. The problem with the tragic narrative is its implied value judgment concerning Whitman's postwar style, for there is certainly a palpable change in the style. For instance, Whitman employs archaic forms of direct address much more frequently in the postwar poems than in the first three editions of *Leaves:* "thou" and "thee" abound in such poems as "Proud Music of the Storm" (1869), "Passage to India" (1871), "Thou Mother with Thy Equal Brood" (1872), "The Mystic Trumpeter" (1872), and "To a Locomotive in Winter" (1876). Perhaps the only poem to escape censure in this regard is "When Lilacs Last in the Dooryard Bloom'd" (1865), and its date troubles both the neatness of the stylistic paradigm and the negative evaluation of archaisms themselves. The new style of address parallels, in most cases, Whitman's focus on the soul's "[p]assage to more than India" ("Passage to India," section 9). He often addresses abstract, spiritualized entities, such as democratic America or an idealized past, as if his poems were an attempt to call them into being.

A stylistic corollary to this form of address is the withdrawal of the poet from the physical, material world he describes so luxuriantly in the 1855–1865 poems. In "Proud Music of the Storm," for instance, the speaker is less an active participant or dynamic observer, more a passive receiver of sonorous, otherworldly intimations. A fine dramatic monologue like "Prayer of Columbus" (1874) dwells more on the abstract, general memories and meditations of the speaker than on the physical, concrete situation itself.

The final stylistic change in the postwar poetry is the increased number of short lyrics. It should be noted, however, that from the very beginning of his career Whitman writes both long and short poems, and it could be argued that a masterpiece like "Song of Myself" is, in some ways, more aptly described as a sequence of short poems than as one single poem. The cluster arrangements of the 1860 edition feature many short lyrics, and the texture of *Leaves of Grass* from 1860 to 1892 owes a great deal to the mixture of long poems with clusters of short lyrics. The poems of Whitman's last decade tend to run to fewer than twenty lines, and they often run to fewer than ten lines. Because of this reduction in length, Whitman engages in significantly less artistic manipulation of stanza forms. Finally, the subjects in the last decade tend to create an effect of occasional verse, whether the occasion be public or private. Although these facts suggest a waning of poetic power, it is well to note that the long line remains a prominent feature in the late poems, as do the characteristic techniques of Whitman's unconventional prosody.

Whitman's innovative experiments with language extend beyond the rather permeable boundary separating poetry from prose. In this regard, Whitman's prose style is at its best, for many readers, when it most nearly approximates his poetic style. Thus the 1855 Preface to *Leaves of Grass* employs the very same techniques that mark Whitman's free verse, and the poet cannibalized the Preface for poems in the 1856 edition, especially "By Blue Ontario's Shore." The 1856 "Letter to Ralph Waldo Emerson" and the unpublished pamphlet "The Eighteenth Presidency!" resemble the 1855 Preface in style and technique, and in all three texts the effect is that of language threatening to expand beyond the borders of sentence and paragraph. Some readers have described this effect as the presence or voice of the speaker resisting the confines of written language.

Effects of presence or voice persist in the postwar prose, particularly in *Democratic Vistas* (1871). Whitman employs syntactic parallelism, catalogue techniques, and compounds to create a complex figure of eloquence, a speaker-writer who is both an active, individualized observer of postwar urban America and a more withdrawn, retrospective, general diagnostician of postwar America's materialistic disease. Though marked by more complex and demanding syntactic struc-

tures, Whitman's style in *Democratic Vistas* recalls the oratorical style of the 1850s. In *Specimen Days* (1882), as well as in the short essays of the 1880s, Whitman's style parallels the reductions in scale and scope that characterize the poems of the final decade. But like the short poems of the annexes, the wartime memoranda and nature descriptions in *Specimen Days* maintain a certain stylistic expansiveness on the level of the sentence. The postwar prose awaits an extensive critical analysis and appraisal.

James Perrin Warren

Bibliography

Allen, Gay Wilson. *The New Walt Whitman Handbook.* 1975. New York: New York UP, 1986.

Folsom, Ed, ed. *Walt Whitman: The Centennial Essays.* Iowa City: U of Iowa P, 1994.

Hollis, C. Carroll. *Language and Style in "Leaves of Grass."* Baton Rouge: Louisiana State UP, 1983.

Nathanson, Tenney. *Whitman's Presence: Body, Voice, and Writing in "Leaves of Grass."* New York: New York UP, 1992.

Southard, Sherry G. "Whitman and Language: An Annotated Bibliography." *Walt Whitman Quarterly Review* 2.2 (1984): 31–49.

Traubel, Horace. Foreword. *An American Primer.* By Walt Whitman. Boston: Small, Maynard, 1904. v–ix.

Warren, James Perrin. *Walt Whitman's Language Experiment.* University Park: Pennsylvania State UP, 1990.

Whitman, Walt. *Leaves of Grass: Comprehensive Reader's Edition.* Ed. Harold W. Blodgett and Sculley Bradley. New York: New York UP, 1965.

See also BIBLE, THE; CATALOGUES; DICTIONARIES; EPIC STRUCTURE; FOREIGN LANGUAGE BORROWINGS; LANGUAGE; ORGANICISM; PERSONAE; PLACE NAMES; POETIC THEORY; PROSODY; SLANG; SYMBOLISM

"Supplement Hours" (1891)

Found among Whitman's papers after his death, "Supplement Hours" became a part of the posthumous "Old Age Echoes" annex to *Leaves of Grass.* Manuscript evidence suggests that Whitman reworked this poem several times, trying out a number of different titles, such as "Notes as the wild Bee hums," "A September Supplement," and "Latter-time Hours of a half-paralytic."

In this poem of reconciliation with old age and the passage of time, Whitman displaces the exuberant self of his earlier poetry for the tranquil present of individual contemplative moments. The poem's focus, as Whitman's final title selection suggests, is upon the natural "hours" that mark the passing observations of a consciousness which yet rests in the "[s]ane" experience of things in "themselves." The tone Whitman develops here as he observes the yearly round of insects, fields, and seasons is reminiscent of the mood he developed in the nature pieces of *Specimen Days* and reflects a continuation of one of his favorite themes—the movement away from books and into nature. The fourth line of this poem in fact echoes a similar line in Whitman's "A Clear Midnight."

The poem's sense of homecoming, of the returning of natural objects to their right places, is complicated by the autobiographical irony Whitman develops in the disjunction between his own "half-paralytic" body and his "sane" poetic consciousness. In a sense, the poem points to the cerebral ecstasy he has learned to appreciate as his earlier and more celebrated bodily ecstasy wanes. The poem's final images expand this celebration of contemplative tranquility outward to encompass the entire universe. An almost Ptolemaic cosmos emerges in which the stars "roll round" the speaker. The concluding line's assertion of silence represents a gentle reconciliation of the "barbaric yawp" of the poet's youth ("Song of Myself," section 52) to the poetic cadences of old age, here enunciated in the sibilance of "silent sun and stars." It may have been this sort of residual sound that Whitman thought of when he gave his literary executors the title, "Old Age Echoes," for this annex. As Whitman wished the whole annex would, the sonorous final line of "Supplement Hours" exhibits "echoes of things, reverberant, an aftermath" (Whitman 575).

Phillip H. Round

Bibliography

Traubel, Horace. "An Executor's Diary Note, 1891." *Complete Poetry and Selected Prose.* By Walt Whitman. Ed. James E. Miller, Jr. Boston: Houghton Mifflin, 1959. 385.

Stauffer, Donald Barlow. "Teaching Whitman's Old-Age Poems." *Approaches to Teaching Whitman's "Leaves of Grass."* Ed. Donald D. Kummings. New York: MLA, 1990. 105–111.

Whitman, Walt. *Leaves of Grass: Comprehensive Reader's Edition.* Ed. Harold W. Blodgett and Sculley Bradley. New York: New York UP, 1965.

See also AGE AND AGING; "CLEAR MIDNIGHT, A"; "OLD AGE ECHOES"

Swedenborg, Emanuel (1688–1772)

It is not clear whether Whitman read Swedenborg or simply was acquainted with him through other sources, most notably William Fishbough and Andrew Jackson Davis. Whatever the case, however, the Swedish scientist, philosopher, and mystic intrigued Whitman, who considered Swedenborg one of the great prophets. "He is a precursor," wrote Whitman, "in some sort of great differences between past thousands of years, and future thousands" (*Notebooks* 6:2034). Whitman also mentions Swedenborg in a footnote in *Democratic Vistas* in a list of thinkers whose thoughts are, for Whitman, rightfully fueled by the religious impulse (*Prose Works* 2:417). Such an opinion accords with the growing popularity of Swedenborgian thought in Whitman's own day. In theories such as the doctrine of correspondence, Swedenborg demonstrated a genius for connecting science and religion, for seeing the material and spiritual worlds as an intricately connected system, a vision which appealed to many transcendentalists and mystics of the nineteenth century, particularly Emerson who, in *Representative Men,* made Swedenborg the prime example of "The Mystic."

Andrew Ladd

Bibliography

Emerson, Ralph Waldo. *The Collected Works of Ralph Waldo Emerson.* Ed. Joseph Slater. Vol. 4. Cambridge, Mass.: Harvard UP, 1987.

Reynolds, David S. *Walt Whitman's America: A Cultural Biography.* New York: Knopf, 1995.

Whitman, Walt. *Notebooks and Unpublished Prose Manuscripts.* Ed. Edward F. Grier. 6 vols. New York: New York UP, 1984.

———. *Prose Works 1892.* Ed. Floyd Stovall.

2 vols. New York: New York UP, 1963–1964.

See also ARNOLD, GEORGE B.; EMERSON, RALPH WALDO; POPULAR CULTURE, WHITMAN AND

Swinburne, Algernon Charles (1837–1909)

Swinburne, British Victorian poet and critic, may own the second most notorious repudiation of Whitman, behind Ralph Waldo Emerson; however, Swinburne's retraction is more vehement. Yet Swinburne does not entirely deserve his disgrace in Whitman studies, for, despite enthusiasm, his early writings on Whitman are tempered with careful criticism and his late "attack" on Whitman was as much an attack on the excesses of Whitman's devotees as it was criticism of Whitman's poetry.

Swinburne borrowed Whitman's 1855 *Leaves of Grass* and in 1862 bought a copy of the 1860 edition, finding himself especially taken with "A Word Out of the Sea," later titled "Out of the Cradle Endlessly Rocking." His *William Blake* (1868) includes a favorable comparison of Blake and Whitman, noting their identical "passionate" advocacy of "sexual [and] political freedom," the similarity of their poetry to "the Pantheistic poetry of the East," and their prophetic stature. Noting that they both have flaws, Swinburne calls William Blake's work more profound but finds Whitman's "fresh and frank," praising "Out of the Cradle" and "When Lilacs Last in the Dooryard Bloom'd" (*William Blake* 300–304). Swinburne, inspired by political reform in Italy and France, dedicated his collection of poetry *Songs Before Sunrise* (1871) to Mazzini and included "To Walt Whitman in America," addressing Whitman and the United States as symbols of freedom. Less flattering is *Under the Microscope* (1872), in which Swinburne complains that the poet and the formalist clash in Whitman, who would better advance the cause of democracy by abandoning his catalogues for his more lyrical expressions. Published in 1887, "Whitmania" is a far cry from the admiration expressed in *William Blake*. Denying that Whitman is much of a poet, Swinburne criticizes the latest wave of his admirers who would attempt to rank him in the literary "pantheon." Swinburne accords Whitman some praise, granting him enthusiasm, love of nature, faith in freedom, and a dignified attitude toward death, but holds Whitman's work to be underdeveloped rhetoric rather than poetry. Whitman never publicly responded to Swinburne's attack, though the controversy from this famous disavowal kept Whitman in the public eye, ensuring his fame.

Alan E. Kozlowski

Bibliography

Blodgett, Harold. *Walt Whitman in England.* Ithaca, N.Y.: Cornell UP, 1934.

Gosse, Edmund. *The Life of Algernon Charles Swinburne.* New York: Macmillan, 1917.

Swinburne, Algernon Charles. *The Letters of Algernon Charles Swinburne.* London: Heinemann, 1918.

———. *Songs Before Sunrise.* London: Ellis, 1871.

———. *Under the Microscope.* London: White, 1872.

———. "Whitmania." *Fortnightly Review* ns 42 (1887): 170–176. Rpt. in *Walt Whitman: The Critical Heritage.* Ed. Milton Hindus. New York: Barnes and Noble, 1971. 199–209.

———. *William Blake: A Critical Essay.* London: Hotten, 1868. Rpt. in *Walt Whitman: The Critical Heritage.* Ed. Milton Hindus. New York: Barnes and Noble, 1971. 134–136.

See also BLAKE, WILLIAM; BRITISH ISLES, WHITMAN IN THE

Swinton, John (1829–1901)

A respected journalist, reformer, and labor activist, John Swinton knew Whitman and admired the man and his work from their first meeting, probably between 1855 and 1857. He was one of the regular Bohemian crowd that gathered at Pfaff's, an enthusiast about *Leaves of Grass*—he apparently read the first edition right after publication—and was instrumental in arranging the prisoner exchange which freed Whitman's brother George by contacting General Grant. Swinton was usually well connected.

Born in Scotland, as was his brother William, he resided there until the family's migration to Canada in 1843; like Whitman, he learned the journalism trade from the ground up, beginning as an apprentice printer in Montreal, then working as a journeyman in New York. He took courses in the classics, studied medicine, worked in South Carolina as a compositor, and went to Kansas when matters were heating up, though he arrived too late to witness John Brown's engagement with the Border Ruffians. He became a major figure on the editorial staff of Henry J. Raymond's New York *Times* through most of the 1860s, having started there around 1858. Not a socialist, but an acquaintance and admirer of Karl Marx, Swinton espoused radical social views, and the devout Scottish Calvinist worked for numerous papers including the more conservative *Sun*, edited by Charles A. Dana, which is probably a testament to an integrity uncompromised by radical views. He ran a controversial labor weekly, *John Swinton's Paper*, from 1883 to 1887, and wrote a few short books. He remained loyal and close to Whitman until the end.

Donald Yannella

Bibliography

Hollis, C. Carroll. "Whitman and William Swinton." *American Literature* 30 (1959): 425–449.

Hyman, Martin D. "'Where the Drinkers and Laughers Meet': Pfaff's: Whitman's Literary Lair." *Seaport* 26 (1992): 56–61.

Lalor, Gene. "Whitman among the New York Literary Bohemians: 1859–1862." *Walt Whitman Review* 25 (1979): 131–145.

Parry, Albert. *Garretts and Pretenders: A History of Bohemianism in America*. 1933. New York: Dover, 1960.

Waters, Robert. *Career and Conversation of John Swinton*. Chicago: Stokes, 1902.

White, William. "Whitman and John Swinton: Some Unpublished Correspondence." *American Literature* 39 (1968): 547–553.

See also NEW YORK TIMES; PFAFF'S RESTAURANT; SWINTON, WILLIAM

Swinton, William (1833–1892)

Although William Swinton held many titles during the course of his life (war correspondent, author, philological expert, professor, and translator), he is best remembered as one of Walt Whitman's friends. William and his older brother, John, became intimates of Whitman in the mid-1850s. The intense, yet short-lived friendship which formed between Whitman and Swinton was based on a common interest in philology. Fluent in several languages, Swinton indulged Whitman's fascination with the French language by becoming his tutor and translator, and stimulated his interest in language studies by introducing him to philological texts.

In 1855, Swinton accepted a job with the New York *Times* as a book reviewer, a position which enabled him to affect Whitman's literary career. He is believed to be the author of the unsigned review of *Leaves of Grass* (1856), which appeared in the *Times* on 13 November 1856. The review was strangely ambivalent; Swinton praised Whitman's skill as a poet, but viciously attacked his character, labeling him arrogant and indecent. Swinton also accused Whitman of manufacturing and publishing favorable reviews of the collection and exposed the fact that he published a private letter of praise from Emerson without the author's permission. Some believe that Whitman himself informed Swinton of these improprieties because he welcomed the attention a scandal would generate, an idea which would be consistent with the fact that the review seemed not to have affected the friendship in any negative way.

Of particular interest to Whitman scholars is Swinton's *Rambles Among Words* (1859), a collection of loosely connected etymological essays. Although the book is signed only by Swinton, some believe that the eleventh and twelfth chapters, as well as other sections of the book, were actually written by Whitman. These passages provide important insights into Whitman's theories of language, particularly concerning its evolution (nonstatic nature) and power.

Sherry Southard and Sharron Sims

Bibliography

Hollis, C. Carroll. "Whitman and William Swinton: A Cooperative Friendship." *American Literature* 30 (1959): 425–449.

"Swinton, William." *Dictionary of American Biography*. Vol. 18. New York: Scribner's, 1936. 252–253.

Warren, James Perrin. "Whitman as Ghostwriter: The Case of *Rambles Among Words*." *Walt Whitman Quarterly Review* 2.2 (1984): 22–30.

See also EMERSON, RALPH WALDO; LANGUAGE; *LEAVES OF GRASS*, 1856 EDITION; SWINTON, JOHN

Symbolism

Although symbolism is an inherent part of the poet's art, the idea of a symbolist movement did not enter the vocabulary of literary critics until the last decade of the nineteenth century, at about the time of Walt Whitman's death. Since that time, the extent to which Whitman can be called a symbolist in theory or practice has been the subject of debate. Most of the basic critical studies have suggested a strong symbolist impulse in Whitman's work, including F.O. Matthiessen's exploration of Whitman's place in the "American Renaissance" (1941), Henry Seidel Canby's biography/critical analysis (1943), and, most directly, Charles Feidelson's book on symbolism in American literature (1953). Recent studies have also demonstrated Whitman's direct influence upon the French symbolists and through them the major symbolist writers of the twentieth century.

There are, however, some factors which complicate the designation of Whitman as symbolist. These include the self-contradictory statements in the various prefaces to *Leaves of Grass,* the comparisons that suggest Whitman uses symbolism in a very different way than do the poets of the symbolist school, and the question raised in recent studies as to whether even Whitman's more obvious symbols are indeed symbols in the contemporary sense of that term.

Those who view Whitman as a symbolist point out the repeated references throughout the prefaces to *Leaves of Grass* to the technique he calls "indirection." In the 1855 Preface, Whitman states emphatically that his poems are "indirect and not direct" (714), adding that his readers "expect of the poet to indicate *more* than the beauty and dignity which always attach to dumb real objects" (716, emphasis added). Such statements of his poetic theory concur completely with the definition of symbolism as the transcendentalists had been using the term. In one of Whitman's favorite books, *Sartor Resartus,* Thomas Carlyle defines the symbol in virtually identical terms, as that which "reveals and conceals" (Symons 2), noting that through the symbol the unseen is indirectly represented by the visible. Ralph Waldo Emerson, also, in two essays which Whitman knew well, "The Poet" and "Nature," writes of the symbol as that which links an object with an "unconscious truth" (Bickman 9). Emerson's transcendental definition, like Carlyle's, accords with Whitman's view of his art as that which indicates "the path between reality and their souls" (Whitman 716).

In addition to the statements in the prefaces, there are numerous explicit statements within the poems themselves of Whitman's method, which again emphasize his link with

Carlyle and transcendental symbolism. He continually refers to something that inheres in reality and radiates a meaning beyond it. In "Song of Myself" the poet emphasizes that "the unseen is proved by the seen" (section 3). In "Calamus" he suggests that crucial meaning hides in "shifting forms of life." He further refers to life as a "mask of materials" for the "real reality" that lurks behind a "show of appearance" ("Scented Herbage of My Breast"). In virtually every poem there is some statement that suggests a symbolic meaning transcending the objects which embody it. In "Song of the Open Road," Whitman apostrophizes the "objects that call from diffusion" his meanings and "give them shape" (section 3).

The problem, however, is in relating Whitman's idea of symbolism with contradictory comments that appear elsewhere in the prefaces. While insisting on indirection, Whitman also writes that "nothing can make up for . . . the lack of definiteness" (719). His readers expect more than "dumb real objects" (716), yet he will have nothing stand between the poet and the reader "like curtains" (719). In the same vein, he compares his technique with that of the representational artist who simply invites his audience to participate in immediate experience and "look in the mirror" with him (719). Many of these statements would suggest an imagist rather than symbolist aesthetic. The only resolution for these conflicting statements of his intent is to explore the extent to which Whitman actually employs symbols in the poems, while bearing in mind his warning that he does not fear to contradict himself ("Song of Myself," section 51).

It is evident that Whitman employs symbols both as a structural principle for *Leaves of Grass* as a whole and as points of emphasis within the individual poems. At the beginning of "Song of Myself," when a child asks the poet *"What is the grass?"* (section 6), he begins to "guess" about some of its symbolic meanings. The entire book continues these explorations of grass as his basic symbol for the particular in its links with the cosmic. Most of the individual "leaves" likewise employ a central symbol as a unifying principle, such as the calamus root as an erotic symbol, the various roads and travels as symbols of life's journeys, the drum taps which symbolize both the excitement of parade and the death music of war, and the rivulets from the ocean of life that symbolize the end of the poet's journey at old age. Within these larger units, each section of *Leaves of Grass* contains individual patterns of symbols such as, for example, the lilac, the star, and the hermit thrush in "When Lilacs Last in the Dooryard Bloom'd" and the ferry, the sea journey, and the people in transit in "Crossing Brooklyn Ferry."

Many of the poems are further unified by Whitman's use of the poet himself as a symbol of everyman's questing soul that finds the cosmos within himself. For example, in "Salut au Monde!" the poet becomes a symbol of the geography of the earth: "Within me latitude widens, longitude lengthens . . . Within me zones, seas, cataracts, forests, volcanoes, groups" (section 2). In recent years, critics have also found patterns of psychological symbolism in Whitman's exploration of the cosmic man. In these terms, *Leaves of Grass* as a whole can be interpreted as a symbolic representation of the pattern of psychic development in the soul from the exuberant selfhood of youth in "Song of Myself" to the cosmic consciousness of the individuated Jungian "wise old man" in "Sands at Seventy."

In spite of all these symbols and symbolic structures in his work, a comparison with the later symbolists reveals that Whitman's concept may differ in certain fundamental ways from their practice. Starting with Matthiessen, critics have been troubled by the way that Whitman "could shuttle back and forth from materialism to idealism without troubling himself about any inconsistency" (521). Moreover, Whitman's reality remains infused with a mystical correspondence that differs from the symbolist concept of objects as "objective correlatives" for an emotion or a mood (Chari 174). Whitman's objects remain particular and concrete, swallowed whole by the poet's mystical imagination. In his mystical flights, Whitman unites opposites through paradoxical utterance as often as he employs symbols as a method to mediate between reality and the unseen.

This topic is far from a final resolution. That Whitman employed symbols is a matter of evidence; the extent to which Whitman can, however, be called a "symbolist," with all the critical assumptions attached to that word, remains a matter of controversy.

Lorelei Cederstrom

Bibliography

Bickman, Martin. *The Unsounded Centre: Jungian Studies in American Romanticism.* Chapel Hill: U of North Carolina P, 1980.

Canby, Henry Seidel. *Walt Whitman: An American.* Boston: Houghton Mifflin, 1943.

Cederstrom, Lorelei. "A Jungian Approach to the Self in Major Whitman Poems." *Approaches to Teaching Whitman's "Leaves of Grass."* Ed. Donald D. Kummings. New York: MLA, 1990. 81–89.

———. "Walt Whitman and the Imagists." *Walt Whitman of Mickle Street.* Ed. Geoffrey M. Sill. Knoxville: U of Tennessee P, 1994. 205–223.

Chari, V.K. "The Limits of Whitman's Symbolism." *Journal of American Studies 5* (1971): 173–184.

Erkkila, Betsy. *Walt Whitman Among the French: Poet and Myth.* Princeton: Princeton UP, 1980.

Feidelson, Charles, Jr. *Symbolism and American Literature.* Chicago: U of Chicago P, 1953.

Jones, P. Mansell. *The Background of Modern French Poetry.* Cambridge: Cambridge UP, 1951.

Matthiessen, F.O. *American Renaissance.* New York: Oxford UP, 1941.

Symons, Arthur. *The Symbolist Movement in Literature.* New York: Dutton, 1958.

Whitman, Walt. "Preface 1855—*Leaves of Grass*, First Edition." *Leaves of Grass.* Ed. Sculley Bradley and Harold W. Blodgett. Norton Critical Edition. New York: Norton, 1973. 711–731.

See also LANGUAGE; POETIC THEORY; SEA, THE; TRANSCENDENTALISM

Symonds, John Addington (1840–1893)

John Addington Symonds, a prominent biographer, literary critic, and poet in Victorian England, was in his time most famous as the author of the seven-volume history *The Renaissance in Italy.* But in the smaller circles of the emerging upper class English homosexual community, he was also well known as a writer of homoerotic poetry and a pioneer in the study of homosexuality, or sexual inversion as it was then known.

After receiving his A.B. degree from Oxford, Symonds became a fellow of Magdalen College in 1862. However, within a short time charges of homosexuality were leveled against him. Symonds, though cleared of the charges, was forced to leave. Soon after this he began his career as an independent scholar and reviewer, and over the next thirty years produced studies of Dante, Shelley, Shakespeare, Michelangelo, various other Renaissance figures, and Walt Whitman.

In 1891 Symonds published *A Problem in Modern Ethics,* which explored the notion of sexual inversion. This work gave him his first widespread exposure as a homosexual. He was subsequently sought out by the young psychologist Havelock Ellis to write a scientific exploration of homosexuality. The work, titled *Sexual Inversion,* was first published in Germany in 1896, and a year later in England. Symonds, however, had died in Rome on 19 April 1893, the same day on which his biography of Walt Whitman was published in London.

Symonds first read Whitman in 1865, and began corresponding with him six years later. His most famous letter was written in August 1890 wherein, after years of indirect questioning, Symonds directly asked Whitman about the homosexual content of the "Calamus" poems. This prompted Whitman's famous reply in which he denied the "morbid inferences" (Whitman 282) and, as way of proof, claimed to have fathered six children, apparently unaware that Symonds himself had fathered four. Whitman's fantastic paternal claim has since been the source of many a wild goose chase on the part of Whitman biographers intent on proving the poet's heterosexuality. Critics who acknowledge Whitman's homosexual leanings have also given this letter much thought, offering a range of reasons for its tone and exaggeration, from Whitman's concern about his public image and literary reputation to his hostility to Symonds's rigid conception of sexuality.

Andrew C. Higgins

Bibliography

Grosskurth, Phyllis. *John Addington Symonds.* New York: Holt, Rinehart and Winston, 1964.

Symonds, John Addington, Jr. *The Letters of John Addington Symonds.* Ed. Herbert M. Schueller and Robert L. Peters. 3 vols. Detroit: Wayne State UP, 1967–1969.

———. *Memoirs of John Addington Symonds.* Ed. Phyllis Grosskurth. New York: Random House, 1984.

———. *Walt Whitman: A Study.* 1893. New York: Dutton, 1906.

Whitman, Walt. *Selected Letters of Walt Whitman.* Ed. Edwin Haviland Miller. Iowa City: U of Iowa P, 1990.

See also BIOGRAPHIES; BRITISH ISLES, WHITMAN IN THE; SEX AND SEXUALITY

T

Tammany Hall

The Society of St. Tammany (its name derived from Tammanend, the legendary chief of the Delaware Indians known for his wisdom and love of liberty) was founded in 1788 as a fraternal order dedicated to opposing the development of a hereditary aristocracy in the United States. Increasingly a partisan organization from the 1790s onward, Tammany became identified with the Democratic party and by the mid-1800s had become infamous for exercising political control in New York City through a boss-centered combination of charity and patronage.

Walt Whitman's relationship with Tammany Hall began in 1841 when the *New Era,* the official Tammany newspaper, quoted a speech he had given at a Democratic rally. A short time later, as editor of the New York *Aurora,* Whitman became entangled in a political controversy over state-supported parochial education that brought him into collision with the Tammany political machine, but this did not prevent him, he claimed, from writing *Franklin Evans,* his first novel, in the Tammany reading room. It was, in all probability, at Tammany Hall that Whitman met the Democratic editors, journalists, and politicians that led to his being offered the editor's chair first at the Democratic *Statesman* and then at the New York *Democrat.*

While at the *Democrat,* Whitman again challenged the Tammany party bosses by advocating the nomination of a liberal candidate for governor and for his efforts was summarily removed as editor. This defeat at the hands of political bosses would not be Whitman's last, as the Tammany machine continued to flourish, ruling over an era of gang fights and political abuses. The most infamous of Tammany's bosses, Boss Tweed, virtually controlled the state in the late 1860s and presided over a predatory band of looters responsible for the theft of tens of millions of dollars. This corruption continued into the twentieth century until an investigation finally discredited Tammany and forced the resignation of Mayor James Walker in 1932.

Charles B. Green

Bibliography

Allen, Gay Wilson. *The Solitary Singer: A Critical Biography of Walt Whitman.* 1955. Rev. ed. 1967. Chicago: U of Chicago P, 1985.

Jackson, Kenneth T., ed. *The Encyclopedia of New York City.* New Haven: Yale UP, 1995.

See also DEMOCRATIC PARTY; *FRANKLIN EVANS;* JOURNALISM, WHITMAN'S; NEW YORK *AURORA;* NEW YORK CITY; POLITICAL VIEWS

Taylor, Bayard (1825–1878)

Whitman once suggested to Traubel that several of the least effectual allies in his campaign for free speech were eventually turned into adversaries by professional jealousy and an "awful belief in respectability" (*With Walt Whitman* 6:62). A.C. Swinburne and Bayard Taylor were at the top of this list. Taylor was a prolific Philadelphia travel writer, novelist, and poet. His poetic style, rooted in the classics and Victorian sentiment, brought him so little acclaim that he began to resent the mass appeal of his travel writing. Only his *Faust* translation is well known today.

In *John Godfrey's Fortunes* (1864), Taylor portrays Whitman as the Bohemian poet Mr.

Smithers, who prefers "the fireman, in his red flannel shirt, with the sleeves rolled up to his shoulders" over fools with "the morbid sensitiveness which follows culture" (278). Taylor's "Echo Club" parodies, published in the *Atlantic Monthly* in 1872, called *Leaves of Grass* a "modern, half-Bowery-boy, half-Emersonian apprehension of the old Greek idea of physical life . . . A truer sense of art would have prevented . . . offensive frankness" (*Echo Club* 179–180).

Whitman noted that Taylor's *Poems of the Orient* (1854) "indirectly has a meaning" (*Notebooks* 5:1771), which, according to Byrne Fone, was Whitman's way of indicating a homosexual discourse. Thus Whitman was hardly surprised when Taylor confided that he found in his own nature both Whitman's "physical attraction" and "tender and noble love of man for man" (qtd. in *Correspondence* 1:295). Taylor offered his suspicious Quaker neighbors *The Story of Kennett* (1866) as an alternative to the fad of "exceptional or morbid" kinds of "psychological problems" (*Kennett,* Prologue ix), and his two male characters avoided a tender embrace because that "was the custom of the neighborhood" (*Kennett* 237). However, his odd novel *Joseph and His Friend* (1870) showed heroes holding hands and kissing, as dictated by "a loftier faith, a juster law," and "instincts, needs, knowledge, and rights—ay, rights! of their own" (214).

In 1856, George Boker, who was married, wrote Taylor, who was widowed, that he had "never loved anything human as I love you. It is a joy and a pride to my heart to know that this feeling is truly returned" (qtd. in Evans 115). In the years after 1874, Whitman may have intruded upon their Philadelphia turf, when the "florid, almost effusive" Boker (*With Walt Whitman* 6:226) invited him to dine "two or three times" (*With Walt Whitman* 6:234). By 1876, Taylor was blasting Whitman in the New York *Tribune,* and after that, the two never reconciled.

Mitch Gould

Bibliography

Beatty, Richmond. *Bayard Taylor, Laureate of the Gilded Age.* Norman: U of Oklahoma P, 1936.

Evans, Oliver H. *George Henry Boker.* Boston: Twayne, 1984.

Fone, Byrne. *Masculine Landscapes: Walt Whitman and the Homoerotic Text.* Carbondale: Southern Illinois UP, 1992.

Taylor, Bayard. *The Echo Club and Other Literary Diversions.* Boston: Osgood, 1876.

———. *John Godfrey's Fortunes.* New York: Putnam, 1864.

———. *Joseph and His Friend.* New York: Putnam, 1870.

———. *Poems of the Orient.* Boston: Ticknor and Fields, 1854.

———. *The Story of Kennett.* New York: Putnam, 1866.

Traubel, Horace. *With Walt Whitman in Camden.* Vol. 2. New York: Appleton, 1908; Vol. 6. Ed. Gertrude Traubel and William White. Carbondale: Southern Illinois UP, 1982.

Whitman, Walt. *The Correspondence.* Ed. Edwin Haviland Miller. 6 vols. New York: New York UP, 1961–1977.

———. *Notebooks and Unpublished Prose Manuscripts.* Ed. Edward F. Grier. 6 vols. New York: New York UP, 1984.

See also BOKER, GEORGE HENRY; CENTENNIAL EXPOSITION (PHILADELPHIA)

Taylor, Father (Edward Thompson) (1793–1871)

Born in Richmond, Virginia, on 25 December 1793, Edward Thompson Taylor was orphaned as an infant and went to sea as a cabin boy at the age of seven. Upon conversion to Methodism in 1811, he aspired to preach. He began as lay chaplain to fellow prisoners while held by the British during the War of 1812, was licensed in 1814, and ordained in 1819. He traveled extensively as a missionary, including duty in 1827 as chaplain aboard the *Macedonian,* but after 1830 he primarily served the Methodist Seamen's Bethel in Boston. There, in a chapel noted for its resemblance to a timbered ship, he paced his quarterdeck pulpit, exhorting in a sincere, joyous, spontaneous, colorful, idiomatic manner that enthralled all who heard him. For literati no trip to Boston was complete without taking in the hallelujah drama of Father Taylor and his congregation of rough-and-ready sea dogs grappling to rescue impenitent sinners from storm-tossed brine and rock-bound coasts. Ralph Waldo Emerson exalted Taylor as the near perfect master of oratory. William Ellery Channing, Charles Dickens, Jenny Lind, Harriet Martineau, and countless others chorused similar paeans, while Herman Melville immortalized Father Taylor by transforming him into Father Mapple of *Moby-Dick*. During his visit to Boston in 1860, Walt Whitman, too, pilgrimaged to experience Taylor's struggle for sailors' souls. Father Taylor died on 6 April 1871, but Whitman's memory of him remained vivid. In 1884, a brief "reminiscence" of Father Taylor fetched Whitman fifty dollars from *Century* magazine. Echoing Emerson, Whitman characterized Taylor as the "one essentially perfect" practitioner of oratory, "the rarest and most profound of humanity's arts" (Whitman 549). The article was published in *Century* in 1887 and was included, with minor editorial changes, as "Father Taylor (and Oratory.)" in *November Boughs* (1888).

John Lee Jellicorse

Bibliography

Oliver, Egbert S. "Emerson's Almost Perfect Orator: Edward Taylor." *Today's Speech* 8 (1960): 20–22.

"Taylor, Edward Thompson." *The Columbia Encyclopedia*. 5th ed. New York: Columbia UP, 1993. 2700.

"Taylor, Edward Thompson." *The National Cyclopaedia of American Biography*. Vol. 8. New York: J.T. White, 1906. 464.

Whitman, Walt. *Prose Works 1892*. Ed. Floyd Stovall. Vol. 2. New York: New York UP, 1964.

See also BOSTON, MASSACHUSETTS; *NOVEMBER BOUGHS*; ORATORY

Teaching of Whitman's Works

The teaching of Walt Whitman begins with a good and appropriate edition of his writings. On the college level, the Norton Critical Edition (1973), edited by Sculley Bradley and Harold W. Blodgett, has been among the most popular, and among the most influential, having introduced *Leaves of Grass* to several generations of students. The Norton is notable for its authoritative texts, extensive footnotes, and wide-ranging selection of criticism. Because the Norton is now sorely in need of updating, its critical essays and bibliographies in particular, a revised edition is being prepared (by Michael Moon). Another highly regarded college-level edition is Justin Kaplan's *Complete Poetry and Collected Prose* (1982)—a volume in the distinguished Library of America series. Featuring both the 1855 and 1891–1892 *Leaves,* as well as ample selections of prose writings, the Library of America edition is the most comprehensive one-volume collection of Whitman ever published.

Other good "teaching editions," each of which is suitable for students at all levels, include *Walt Whitman's "Leaves of Grass": The First (1855) Edition* (1959), edited by Malcolm Cowley; *Walt Whitman: Complete Poetry and Selected Prose* (1959), edited by James E. Miller, Jr.; *"Leaves of Grass" and Selected Prose* (1981), edited by Lawrence Buell; *Walt Whitman: The Complete Poems* (1975), edited by Francis Murphy; *Walt Whitman: "Leaves of Grass"* (1990), edited by Jerome Loving; *Walt Whitman: "Leaves of Grass"* (1955), edited by Gay Wilson Allen; and *The Portable Walt Whitman* (1973), edited by Mark Van Doren and revised by Malcolm Cowley. Each of these contains reliable texts, an illuminating introduction, and helpful notes, each is available in paperback, and each is more modestly priced than either the Norton or Library of America edition.

Few instructors, if any, assign *Leaves of Grass* in its entirety, at least as far as the 1891–1892 or Deathbed edition is concerned. The question becomes, then, which Whitman works to teach, and of course the answer depends on the level on which one is teaching and the nature of the course for which one is responsible. Nevertheless, for most experienced teachers any list of Whitman's greatest poems would include "Song of Myself," "Crossing Brooklyn Ferry," "Out of the Cradle Endlessly Rocking," "When Lilacs Last in the Dooryard Bloom'd," and "The Sleepers." Other poems frequently assigned include selections from (or, in advanced courses, all of) the "Children of Adam," "Calamus," and "Drum-Taps" clusters. Still others are "Passage to India," "There was a Child Went Forth," "As I Ebb'd with the Ocean of Life," "A Noiseless Patient Spider," "When I Heard the Learn'd Astronomer," "The Dalliance of the Eagles," "To a Locomotive in Winter," "This Compost," "Starting from Paumanok," "Song of the Open Road," "A Song of the Rolling Earth," "Prayer of Columbus," "Chanting the Square Deific," and "So Long!" Seasoned instructors tend to agree that Whitman's best prose is to be found in the Preface to the 1855 *Leaves,* "A Backward Glance O'er Travel'd Roads," *Democratic Vistas, Specimen Days,* and *An American Primer*. Though meritorious in its own right, Whitman's prose is often useful in contextualizing his poems.

To what secondary sources should an instructor turn for guidance in preparing a class or course on Whitman? This is a difficult question, for the poet's writings have inspired a massive amount of scholarship. Any short-list of "essential books" is necessarily partial and bound to exclude something that no doubt deserves to be included. With the hope that this caveat will be kept firmly in mind, here are some suggestions: (1) biographies: Gay Wilson Allen's *Solitary Singer*, David S. Reynolds's *Walt Whitman's America*, Justin Kaplan's *Walt Whitman: A Life*, and Paul Zweig's *Walt Whitman: The Making of the Poet*; (2) general introductions: Allen's *New Walt Whitman Handbook*, James E. Miller's *Critical Guide to "Leaves of Grass,"* and Roger Asselineau's *Evolution of Walt Whitman: The Creation of a Book*; (3) critical studies: Betsy Erkkila's *Whitman the Political Poet*, Harold Aspiz's *Walt Whitman and the Body Beautiful*, Edwin Haviland Miller's *Walt Whitman's Poetry: A Psychological Journey*, Jerome Loving's *Emerson, Whitman, and the American Muse*, Kenneth M. Price's *Whitman and Tradition*, C. Carroll Hollis's *Language and Style in "Leaves of Grass,"* M. Wynn Thomas's *Lunar Light of Whitman's Poetry*, Ed Folsom's *Walt Whitman's Native Representations*, M. Jimmie Killingsworth's *Whitman's Poetry of the Body*, David Kuebrich's *Minor Prophecy: Walt Whitman's New American Religion*, V.K. Chari's *Whitman in the Light of Vedantic Mysticism*, and Kerry C. Larson's *Whitman's Drama of Consensus*; (4) anthologies of criticism: *Walt Whitman: The Measure of His Song*, edited by Jim Perlman, Ed Folsom, and Dan Campion; *Walt Whitman: A Critical Anthology*, edited by Francis Murphy; and *Walt Whitman and the World*, edited by Gay Wilson Allen and Ed Folsom; (5) background studies: F.O. Matthiessen's *American Renaissance*, Lawrence Buell's *Literary Transcendentalism*, David S. Reynolds's *Beneath the American Renaissance*, Robert K. Martin's *Homosexual Tradition in American Poetry*, and Roy Harvey Pearce's *Continuity of American Poetry*; (6) bibliographies: Joel Myerson's *Walt Whitman: A Descriptive Bibliography*, Scott Giantvalley's *Walt Whitman, 1838–1939: A Reference Guide*, and Donald D. Kummings's *Walt Whitman, 1940–1975: A Reference Guide*.

Many instructors enhance their teaching of Whitman's writings through use of audiovisual materials, aids such as facsimile editions; photographs; slide programs; illustrations; reproductions of paintings; compact discs, audiocassettes, and records; films, filmstrips, and videocassettes; and original or reprinted nineteenth-century materials (for example, newspapers, works of popular literature, political pamphlets, reform tracts, and physiology and sex manuals). Space limitations here preclude the possibility of providing a thorough survey of resources, but a few recent items can be noted. One of these is a superb facsimile—indeed, the most accurate facsimile to date—of the 1855 *Leaves of Grass*. It was published in 1992, the centennial of Whitman's death, by the Library of American Poets, 92 Barrow Street, New York, New York 10014, and can be purchased for one hundred dollars. The most complete collection of photographs of Whitman—accompanied by detailed notes—can be found in a special double issue of the *Walt Whitman Quarterly Review* (Vol. 4, Nos. 2–3, 1986–1987). Now available on audiotape (for ten dollars from the *WWQR*) is what appears to be an 1889 or 1890 Edison-cylinder recording of Whitman himself reading four lines of his 1888 poem "America." One of the best film treatments of the poet is *Walt Whitman* (1987), a one-hour video program that is part of a biographical and critical series entitled *Voices and Visions: Modern American Poetry*. Also excellent is the Canadian film *Beautiful Dreamers* (1992), directed by John Kent Harrison. Starring Rip Torn as Whitman, the film portrays a dramatic episode in the relationship between the poet and Richard Maurice Bucke.

Pedagogical resources on Whitman have recently increased substantially with the publication of *The Teachers & Writers Guide to Walt Whitman* (1991), edited by Ron Padgett, and *Approaches to Teaching Whitman's "Leaves of Grass"* (1990), edited by Donald D. Kummings. The Padgett volume contains nineteen essays, all by poets, about teaching Whitman's work and about using that work to inspire students to write their own poetry and prose. The essays are mainly directed toward elementary and secondary school teachers, and many provide practical exercises and suggestions that can be adapted for classrooms from kindergarten through college. Particularly noteworthy among the essays are Kenneth Koch's "Whitman's Words," Gary Lenhart's "Whitman's Informal History of His Times: *Democratic Vistas* and *Specimen Days*," and Bill Zavatsky's "Teaching Whitman in High School." Padgett concludes the book with a nine-page annotated bibliography of "Whitman Resources."

The Kummings volume contains essays written by nineteen college teachers and Whitman scholars. Aimed primarily at those who instruct undergraduates, the essays are grouped under four headings: "Teaching 'Song of Myself,'" "Teaching Other Major Works," "Whitman in the Lower-Division Course," and "Whitman on the Upper Level." Essayists explore a broad range of subjects and issues central to Whitman studies—narrative techniques, elements of language and style, prosodic innovations, biographical concerns, literary relations, cultural backgrounds, philosophical perspectives, and strategies for interpreting individual poems and prose works. The collection as a whole reflects a variety of pedagogical philosophies and methodologies and addresses a variety of teaching situations, from introductory writing classes and required surveys to specialized upper-division courses. The *Approaches* volume begins with a lengthy chapter, written by the editor, on "Materials"—that is, on preferred editions of *Leaves of Grass,* required and recommended student readings, essential secondary studies, and valuable teaching aids. "Materials" discusses in some detail most of the books mentioned earlier in this essay.

Donald D. Kummings

Bibliography

Armistead, J.M. "Ending with Whitman." *Journal of English Teaching Techniques* 7 (1974): 14–21.

Blodgett, Harold W. "Teaching 'Song of Myself.'" *Emerson Society Quarterly* 22 (1961): 2–3.

Bradley, Sculley. "The Teaching of Whitman." *College English* 23 (1962): 618–622.

Freed, Richard. "Teaching Whitman to College Freshmen." *English Record* 29.1 (1978): 9–12.

Gerber, John C. "Varied Approaches to 'When Lilacs Last in the Dooryard Bloom'd.'" *Reflections on High School English.* NDEA Institute Lectures 1965. Ed. Gary Tate. Tulsa: U of Tulsa, 1966. 214–230.

Katz, Sandra L. "A Reconsideration of Walt Whitman: A Teaching Approach." *Walt Whitman Review* 27 (1981): 70–74.

Kummings, Donald D., ed. *Approaches to Teaching Whitman's "Leaves of Grass."* New York: MLA, 1990.

Marx, Leo. "*Democratic Vistas:* Notes for a Discussion." *Emerson Society Quarterly* 22 (1961): 12–15.

Miller, James E., Jr. "The Mysticism of Whitman: Suggestions for a Seminar Discussion." *Emerson Society Quarterly* 22 (1961): 15–18.

Padgett, Ron, ed. *The Teachers & Writers Guide to Walt Whitman.* New York: Teachers & Writers Collaborative, 1991. 197–206.

Romano, Tom. "Of Whitman and Friend." *English Journal* 73 (1984): 26–27.

Sealts, Merton M., Jr. "Melville and Whitman." *Melville Society Extracts* 50 (1982): 10–12.

See also BIBLIOGRAPHIES; BIOGRAPHIES; CHRONOLOGY; MEDIA INTERPRETATIONS OF WHITMAN'S LIFE AND WORKS; SCHOLARSHIP, TRENDS IN WHITMAN; STYLE AND TECHNIQUE(S)

Technology

The analogy of poetry to leaves of grass immediately suggests a certain romantic preference for nature over artifice. For all its natural organicism, however, the very title of Whitman's book punningly invokes its own artifice, the fact that it comes in printed "leaves" or pages, and indeed, Whitman returns to this pun over and over in his poetry, worrying over, or, perhaps, insisting on the technological echo in *Leaves of Grass,* rather than attempting to deny it.

This traditionally romantic sense of an opposition between natural immediacy and technological artifice continues to inform important, recent works of cultural criticism on Whitman, in which technology figures as the symbol and agent of the alienating and dehumanizing social transformations brought about by the rise of industrial capitalism in the nineteenth century. For M. Wynn Thomas, in *The Lunar Light of Whitman's Poetry* (1987), *Leaves* expresses Whitman's ambivalent attempts to come to terms with inescapable technological changes which were eroding the possibilities for individual autonomy, and social community, in the United States. In some ways the romantic continuity is even clearer in *Disseminating Whitman* (1991), Michael Moon's important study of Whitman's homosexual poetics, even though Moon does not address issues of technology directly. For Moon, the sexual body takes the place of nature as a kind of poetic touchstone prior to all artificial mediation, but Whitman's drive to free this body from the repressive toils of a bourgeois capitalist society is finally frustrated, he contends, by the mediating form of the poetic text. For both Moon and Thomas, then, the book—what might be called the literary technology of *Leaves of Grass*—is a kind of ineradicable residue of technology, and thus an ultimate barrier to Whitman's radical drive to make intimate contact with his readers.

In contrast to this new work on Whitman, with its radical anti-technological and anticapitalist bias, an older tradition of cultural studies, exemplified by Leo Marx's *The Machine in the Garden* and Henry Nash Smith's *Virgin Land,* has described a Whitman whose career displays something more like a romanticism of technology itself. In the 1840s, the New York journalist known as Walter Whitman embraced a westward-looking ideology of American manifest destiny, an ideology which expressed itself, as Marx argued, in symbolic fusions of frontier pastoralism with technological futurism. Walter Whitman found this technological romanticism in the democratic politics of the Free Soil party, which was committed above all to preserving open western lands for an egalitarian economy of entrepreneurial capitalism. The raw nature of the frontier, for theorists of free soil such as Horace Greeley or Henry C. Carey, was literally a kind of proto-industrial entity, a natural factory, or capital fund, waiting for human agents to develop it.

This ideology appears, largely intact, in poems from *Leaves* such as "Song of the Broad-Axe"(1856), "The Return of the Heroes" (1867), and "Passage to India"(1871). What is startlingly original in *Leaves* is its transformation of the individualist boosterism of free soil into a complex poetics of the self. Two broad insights, one psychological and one bodily, may be said to underlie this transformation. First, Walt Whitman located in the psychological depths of the self the endlessly progressive, open-ended historical drive of manifest destiny, so that selfhood, for him, came to mean a sense of perpetual incompletion, of always unsatisfied desire. As a consequence of this personal identification with the technological romance of manifest destiny, Walt Whitman's poetic persona can appear alternately as a romantic rebel, bursting through social conventions on his journey to the heart of nature, or as the poetic embodiment of a technologically driven American imperialism, who "colonizes the Pacific, the archipelagoes," as he writes in "Years of the Modern"(1865), "[w]ith the steamship, the electric telegraph, the newspaper, the wholesale engines of war."

Second, Whitman imagined the human body as a microcosmic field for this fusion of natural and technological drives: the body, like the locomotives or steamships which he described (in his 1856 letter to Emerson) as "resistless splendid poems" (Whitman 737), was a kind of engine for the generation, and vehicle for the transmission, of an inexhaustible, progressive desire. His masterpiece, in this regard, is "Crossing Brooklyn Ferry" (1856), where a ride on the ferry across the East River provokes his epiphany that to be a self, located in a body, is to be an essentially mobile entity, in endless, progressive movement toward the future; the ferry is both a symbol and literally a component of selfhood thus conceived. Thus at poem's end he "plants" within himself the machinery of industrial civilization, assimilating its momentum and power to his own. Factories, ships, ferries, the "dumb, beautiful ministers" (section 9) of human desire, are grafted onto *Leaves of Grass*.

As Moon and Thomas contend, however, the vector of Whitman's desire aims most characteristically at physical intimacy with other human beings. Here the pun of *Leaves* takes on a positive meaning which cannot adequately be explained in terms of hostility to artifice or technological mediation: the book—the physical artifact, print, pages, and binding—becomes not an obstacle to intimacy, but the literary vehicle of an intimacy which enables him symbolically to extend his physical presence beyond the limits set by time or space; this accounts for his expressed desires literally and figuratively to touch even those readers who will come to his book years or generations after his death. One may grant that Whitman's drive for intimacy has radical implications, then, as these recent critics have compellingly argued, but one is left with the paradox that this poetic intimacy is grounded, as it were, in the apparatuses and technologies of industrial civilization. "I was chilled with the cold types and cylinder and wet paper between us," he writes in "A Song for Occupations" (1855); "I must pass with the contact of bodies and souls." Here the technologies of a modern publishing industry, for all their "chilling," alienating power, become the visible vehicle for Whitman's poetic incarnation as a kind of bodily poem in the presence of his readers.

Terry Mulcaire

Bibliography

Foner, Eric. *Free Soil, Free Labor, Free Men.* New York: Oxford UP, 1970.

Greeley, Horace. *An Overland Journey.* London: Knopf, 1963.

Kasson, John. *Civilizing the Machine: Technology and Republican Values in America, 1776–1900.* New York: Grossman, 1976.

Marx, Leo. *The Machine in the Garden.* New York: Oxford, 1964.

Matthiessen, F.O. *American Renaissance.* New York: Oxford UP, 1941.

Moon, Michael. *Disseminating Whitman: Revision and Corporeality in "Leaves of Grass."* Cambridge, Mass.: Harvard UP, 1991.

Morrison, Rodney J. *Henry C. Carey and American Economic Development.* Philadelphia: Transactions of the American Philosophical Society, 1986.

Mulcaire, Terry. "Publishing Intimacy in *Leaves of Grass.*" *ELH* 60 (1993): 471–501.

Smith, Henry Nash. *Virgin Land: The American West as Symbol and Myth.* Cambridge, Mass.: Harvard UP, 1950.

Thomas, M. Wynn. *The Lunar Light of Whitman's Poetry.* Cambridge, Mass.: Harvard UP, 1987.

Whitman, Walt. *Leaves of Grass: Comprehensive Reader's Edition.* Ed. Harold W. Blodgett and Sculley Bradley. New York: New York UP, 1965.

See also Centennial Exhibition (Philadelphia); "Crossing Brooklyn Ferry"; Crystal Palace Exhibition (New York); Imperialism; "Passage to India"; Political Views; "Return of the Heroes, The"; Science; "Song for Occupations, A"; "Song of the Broad-Axe"; "Song of the Exposition"; "To a Locomotive in Winter"; "Years of the Modern"

Temperance Movement

Whitman's journalism and early fiction exhibit his changing stand on this social-reform movement, which rivaled the abolition of slavery in its intensity and political force in antebellum America.

Temperance reform responded to a history of heavy alcohol consumption in America beginning in colonial times. As late as the 1820s alcohol was served at nearly all social functions and drunkenness was common in all classes. In 1830 per capita consumption of absolute alcohol in the United States was 3.9 gallons; by 1845, at the height of the temperance crusade, this figure had dropped to one gallon. The temperance movement apparently was successful. By midcentury, drinking had ceased to be respectable and alcohol was outlawed in many states.

The first phase of temperance reform, beginning in about 1825, relied on moral suasion and spread with the rise of the Whig party. Evangelical preachers like Lyman Beecher warned against the evils of drink and urged signing a pledge of partial abstinence (swearing off hard liquor only). Temperance reformers urged their cause both as a religious imperative and as a way of combating social problems arising in a rapidly industrializing society: crime, immorality, poverty, and insanity. And during this early period the backers of temperance included many of those who would gain from a sober, industrious work force: the owners of industry. By 1830 temperance crusaders claimed that about ten percent of the population abstained from alcohol; this figure was higher in the Northeastern states and much lower in the South.

By the 1830s the standard pledge of partial abstinence, which allowed signers to partake of moderate amounts of beer and wine, was largely replaced by a pledge of total abstinence. With the rise of the Washingtonians, a group with working class origins, which began in April of 1840 in Baltimore and which focused on reforming drunkards, temperance became a way of life. Washingtonian societies, named for the nation's first president, saw their membership grow to about a hundred thousand by 1841 and nearly a half million by 1843. Temperance saloons, hotels, theaters, festivals, steamboats, and boarding houses offered an alternative lifestyle that would provide support to the reformed. Junior temperance groups were organized for children, warning them to "beware of the first glass." Another group, the Sons of Temperance, urged respectable dress, language, and behavior as the means to avoid backsliding.

Whitman's attitude toward alcohol and temperance apparently relaxed over time. Gay Wilson Allen claims that Whitman took a pledge of total abstinence while an apprentice in Brooklyn in the 1820s and that he was a prohibitionist while a schoolmaster on Long Island.

Whitman had seen the evils of alcohol; his father, brother-in-law Ansel Van Nostrand, and brother Andrew suffered bouts with drink. But Whitman was a moderate drinker. He took part in both the libations and the conversation when he joined his friends of the Bohemian crowd at Pfaff's Broadway restaurant before the Civil War. In Whitman's old age, Thomas Harned frequently sent the poet a bottle of champagne, although he recalled that the bottle would last a long while. Indeed, Whitman was apt to condemn extremism of any kind—whether overindulgence or puritanism.

But Allen argues that Whitman most likely was "an ardent prohibitionist" (58) when he wrote the temperance novel *Franklin Evans; or The Inebriate* (1842), although later in life he was embarrassed by the book. In Whitman's various accounts of its writing he claims that he did so only for money, and wrote under the influence of alcohol (variously reported as port, gin, or whiskey). But Whitman appears sincere in the novel's introduction, in which he warns readers of the dangers of overindulgence in drink and praises sober, virtuous habits.

Whitman's journalism shows a distinct leaning toward the Washingtonian brand of temperance. This style of reform, which targeted the working class and appealed to the masses by acting out the miseries of drunkenness as warnings, appealed to Whitman's democratic sensibilities. (Indeed, *Franklin Evans* relies on drama and moralistic sensationalism to make its appeal.) David Reynolds argues that Whitman enjoyed the dramatic speeches of the day's greatest temperance orator, John Bartholomew Gough. After this former actor and reformed drunk was found in an alcohol-induced stupor in a whorehouse, Whitman defended the temperance cause—apart from its fallen leader—in a series of articles for the Brooklyn *Star*. In an article that appeared in the New York *Aurora* in 1842, "Temperance Among the Firemen!," Whitman describes a day of temperance rallies, processions, and orations. Although the article focuses in part on the physical and moral attributes of the young men who take part in the procession, he also praises this kind of popular activity as an effective weapon against "the enemy."

In the 1840s and 1850s the temperance fight had evolved into a political battle for prohibition. By 1855 Maine Laws (so named because the first prohibition law was passed in that state) were enacted in thirteen states and territories. Reynolds argues that Whitman was opposed to prohibition, and insisted that reform could only be achieved by persuasion and appeals to common sense, not by legal action. Indeed, in articles published for the Brooklyn *Daily Times* during the late 1850s Whitman seems to counsel individual restraint rather than any kind of group effort at reform. In his article "Liquor Legislation," he admonishes the "impracticable . . . ultraists" who push for Maine Laws, urging instead a kind of community action to punish those who sell liquor to known problem drinkers (48). And in his article "The Temperance Movement" Whitman sharply criticizes the impracticality of "over-zealous" reformers who disdain "half-way measures" and have thus actually brought on a rise in alcohol consumption (49). As was characteristic of Whitman's opinion on many subjects, he called for moderation both in liquor consumption and in reform.

Jennifer A. Hynes

Bibliography

Allen, Gay Wilson. *The Solitary Singer: A Critical Biography of Walt Whitman.* 1955. Rev. ed. 1967. Chicago: U of Chicago P, 1985.

Blocker, Jack S., Jr., ed. *Alcohol, Reform and Society: The Liquor Issue in Social Context.* Contributions in American History 83. Westport, Conn.: Greenwood, 1979.

Holloway, Emory. "Editor's Introduction." *Franklin Evans; or The Inebriate.* By Walt Whitman. New York: Random House, 1929. v–xxiv.

Reynolds, David S. *Walt Whitman's America: A Cultural Biography.* New York: Knopf, 1995.

Rorabaugh, W.J. *The Alcoholic Republic: An American Tradition.* New York: Oxford UP, 1979.

Tyrrell, Ian R. *Sobering Up: From Temperance to Prohibition in Antebellum America, 1800–1860.* Contributions in American History 82. Westport, Conn.: Greenwood, 1979.

Whitman, Walt. "Liquor Legislation." Brooklyn *Daily Times* 23 Jan. 1858. Rpt. in *I Sit and Look Out: Editorials from the Brooklyn Daily Times.* 1932. Ed. Emory Holloway and Vernolian Schwarz. New York: AMS, 1966. 47–49.

———. "Temperance Among the Firemen!" New York *Aurora* 30 Mar. 1842. Rpt. in *Walt Whitman of the New York Aurora.* State College, Pa.: Bald Eagle, 1950. 35–36.

———. "The Temperance Movement."
Brooklyn *Daily Times* 10 March 1858.
Rpt. in *I Sit and Look Out: Editorials
from the Brooklyn Daily Times*. 1932.
Ed. Emory Holloway and Vernolian
Schwarz. New York: AMS, 1966. 49.

See also BROOKLYN *DAILY TIMES;* BROOKLYN,
NEW YORK; "CHILD AND THE PROFLIGATE,
THE"; *FRANKLIN EVANS;* "LITTLE JANE";
"MADMAN, THE"; NEW YORK *AURORA;*
POPULAR CULTURE, WHITMAN AND;
"REUBEN'S LAST WISH"

Tennyson, Alfred, Lord (1809–1892)

Walt Whitman's relationship to Tennyson divides into two phases: first, rejection of his
work as affected and overstylized, and later,
acceptance in old age with much the same reservation. Whitman highly respected Tennyson
as a man, defending his character as warm and
"worthy of any man's regard and respect" (qtd.
in Ditsky 76), and valuing his letters so much
that he carried them in the inside pocket of his
gray coat. Nevertheless, in spite of Tennyson's
admiration, the poets' friendly, twenty-year
correspondence, their habit of exchanging gifts
via intermediaries throughout the latter half of
Whitman's life, and an invitation by Tennyson
for Whitman to visit him, their views on poetry
differed dramatically.

Whitman's criticism of Tennyson began
almost immediately after publication of the first
edition of *Leaves of Grass* in 1855 with a combined review of Tennyson's *Maud and Other
Poems* and *Leaves of Grass,* published by the
American Phrenological Journal in October of
that year and penned anonymously by Whitman. In the review, he casts himself as the spokesman of a newer, more dynamic civilization that
questions the validity of following the old models of poetic form represented by Tennyson. He
linked Tennyson with Shakespeare as a poet of
the old school, describing him as a "bard of
ennui and of the aristocracy" ("An English"
39), a writer strictly for the English upper class
and not America's democratized common man.

Arthur Briggs sees Whitman's easing of
criticism of Tennyson in his later years as a
possible result of his susceptibility to Tennyson's
expressed admiration for his work and acknowledgment of him as an equal more than
any change in his opinion of his work. In 1888,
near the end of his life, Whitman expressed his
final public assessment of Tennyson in an essay
entitled "A Word about Tennyson." He considered his character vital and genuine, but still
immersed in the sensibilities of the upper class,
"a little queer and affected," admiring what he
called his "verbalism" and "cunning colloca-
tions" ("A Word" 570–571). In his later years,
Whitman believed that, although Tennyson had
accepted him as an equal, he may not have really understood his character or the intentions
of *Leaves of Grass*—that Tennyson still considered his work decadent, but only as a result of
the literary tastes and inclinations of his time.

Thomas Sanfilip

Bibliography

Allen, Gay Wilson. *The Solitary Singer: A
Critical Biography of Walt Whitman.*
1955. Rev. ed. 1967. Chicago: U of Chicago P, 1985.
Briggs, Arthur E. *Walt Whitman: Thinker
and Artist.* 1952. New York: Green-
wood, 1968.
Ditsky, John M. "Whitman-Tennyson Corre-
spondence: A Summary and Commen-
tary." *Walt Whitman Review* 18 (1972):
75–82.
Traubel, Horace. *With Walt Whitman in
Camden.* Ed. Gertrude Traubel and
Willam White. Vol. 6. Carbondale:
Southern Illinois UP, 1982.
Whitman, Walt. "An English and American
Poet." *Walt Whitman: A Critical Anthol-
ogy.* Ed. Francis Murphy. Baltimore: Pen-
guin, 1969. 37–42.
———. "A Word about Tennyson." *Prose
Works 1892.* Ed. Floyd Stovall. Vol. 2.
New York: New York UP, 1964. 568–572.

See also AMERICAN PHRENOLOGICAL JOURNAL;
POETIC THEORY; SELF-REVIEWS OF THE 1855
LEAVES, WHITMAN'S ANONYMOUS;
SHAKESPEARE, WILLIAM

"That Music Always Round Me" (1860)

This ten-line poem originally was number 21 of
the "Calamus" cluster in the 1860 *Leaves of
Grass.* Whitman made no changes to the poem
after its first publication (except to give it a title
in 1867) but in 1871 he transferred it to the new
section of *Leaves of Grass* called "Whispers of
Heavenly Death."

Whitman may have thought the transfer
appropriate because "That Music Always

Round Me," like many of the poems in the new "Whispers," and unlike much of Whitman's earlier work, puts emphasis upon sounds, rather than upon picture images.

The transfer from "Calamus" may have seemed to Whitman to be fitting for another reason also; "That Music" does not deal directly with manly love. However, in the context of the 1860 "Calamus," it certainly may include this subject, with Whitman announcing in his first line, "That music always round me, unceasing, unbeginning, yet long untaught I did not hear."

Whitman proceeds in the next line to describe a chorus of four elements to the music, represented by human voices, two male and one female, together with "the triumphant tutti, the funeral wailings with sweet flutes and violins." (*Tutti* is an Italian word which Whitman here uses correctly; it is the musical notation for full tonality of all instruments in an orchestra played simultaneously.)

"That Music" is Whitman's direct recognition of the power of music in his inspiration. It often has been compared with the later "Proud Music of the Storm" (1869). In "Proud Music," however, Whitman will present himself even yet as the seeker, finding poems "vaguely wafted in night air, uncaught, unwritten" (section 6). In "That Music" Whitman claims he is able to hear all of the music, "not the volumes of sound merely, I am moved by the exquisite meanings." This poem may represent the peak of Whitman's sure self-confidence, and that may be why he chose never to change a word of its text.

Jerry F. King

Bibliography

Allen, Gay Wilson. *The Solitary Singer: A Critical Biography of Walt Whitman.* 1955. Rev. ed. 1967. Chicago: U of Chicago P, 1985.

Miller, James E., Jr. *A Critical Guide to "Leaves of Grass."* Chicago: U of Chicago P, 1957.

Whitman, Walt. *Leaves of Grass.* Ed. Sculley Bradley and Harold W. Blodgett. Norton Critical Edition. New York: Norton, 1973.

See also "CALAMUS"; HUMAN VOICE; LEAVES OF GRASS, 1860 EDITION; MUSIC, WHITMAN AND; "MYSTIC TRUMPETER, THE"; "PROUD MUSIC OF THE STORM"; "WHISPERS OF HEAVENLY DEATH" (CLUSTER)

Thayer (William Wilde, 1829–1896) and Eldridge (Charles W., 1837–1903)

Thayer and Eldridge was a Boston publishing firm responsible for the third edition of Walt Whitman's *Leaves of Grass* (1860). The firm also published *Echoes of Harper's Ferry* (1860), by James Redpath, and William Douglas O'Connor's *Harrington* (1860), as well as other abolitionist books and pamphlets.

When the publishers, who saw Whitman's poetry as consistent with their politics, learned the New York firm Fowler and Wells (printers of the 1855 and 1856 volumes of *Leaves of Grass*) had severed its relationship with Whitman, they composed a letter imploring the poet to allow them to publish his work. According to William Wilde Thayer's unpublished autobiography (1892), the letter was drafted by Thayer and approved by his partner, Charles W. Eldridge. Whitman readily agreed.

Whitman oversaw all the details of the printing himself with little interference from Thayer and Eldridge. His letters show that his plans for the book met with skepticism from the printers at first because of its idiosyncratic design, with multiple typefaces and illustrations. But like the poet's two previous editions, the Thayer and Eldridge publication showed that Whitman's ability as a designer was nearly as great as his poetic genius, and even the taciturn Boston printers were won over in the end.

According to Thayer's account, Whitman's stereotype plates cost eight hundred dollars, apparently the highest figure Thayer and Eldridge ever paid for plates. The poet was to receive a ten percent royalty on the sales of the book. The book was first issued in May, and by July the publishers announced that they expected a second printing to sell out in a month's time, proposing that the third printing be split between a cheaper paperback and a deluxe hardbound edition.

Buoyed by his publisher's enthusiasm, Whitman planned a new volume of poems, *Banner at Day-Break,* which Thayer and Eldridge advertised in November. But by December the expectation of prolonged hostilities between the North and South dried up the capital for investments, and Thayer and Eldridge, overextended and victimized by poor business dealings, declared bankruptcy. Neither Whitman's new volume nor the planned third issue of the 1860 *Leaves of Grass* ever came to fruition.

After the collapse of the publishing firm, Thayer drifted out of publishing and became a newspaper editor in the Midwest and West, remaining a committed activist and republican. Eldridge maintained a friendship with Whitman for many years, and in fact helped the poet secure his position in the Army Paymaster's Office in Washington, D.C., during the war.

David Breckenridge Donlon

Bibliography

Allen, Gay Wilson. *The Solitary Singer: A Critical Biography of Walt Whitman.* 1955. Rev. ed. 1967. Chicago: U of Chicago P, 1985.

Callow, Phillip. *From Noon to Starry Night: A Life of Walt Whitman.* Chicago: Ivan R. Dee, 1992.

Thayer, William Wilde. "Autobiography of William Wilde Thayer." Unpublished manuscript, 1892. Library of Congress, Manuscript Division.

See also BOSTON, MASSACHUSETTS; *LEAVES OF GRASS*, 1860 EDITION

Theaters and Opera Houses

Throughout his career, the theater and the opera were important influences on the work of Walt Whitman. In *Specimen Days* (1882), *November Boughs* (1888), and *Good-Bye My Fancy* (1891), as well as his early newspaper articles and poems such as "Song of Myself" and "Proud Music of the Storm," Whitman demonstrates his interest in both the theater and the opera and takes note of having visited some of the most important theaters and opera houses of his day. These establishments, located in New York City, included the Astor Place Opera House, the Bowery Theater, the Broadway Theater, Castle Garden, Niblo's Garden and Theater, the Olympic Theater, Palmo's Opera House, and the Park Theater.

The Astor Place Opera House was originally built for Italian opera and opened on 22 November 1847. In 1849 the rivalry between British actor William Charles Macready and the American star Edwin Forrest erupted in the infamous Astor Place Riot, in which thirty-one people lost their lives. One of Whitman's favorite opera singers, the tenor Alessandro Bettini, appeared at the Astor Place Opera House. Bettini inspired Whitman to write in "Song of Myself" of him, "A tenor large and fresh as creation fills me" (section 26). The Astor Place Opera House was eventually closed in 1850 and converted into a library and lecture room.

The Bowery Theater originally opened in 1826 but was destroyed by fire in 1828, 1836, 1838, and 1845 and was rebuilt each time. A succession of famous and talented actors appeared on its boards, among them Junius Brutus Booth, Edwin Forrest, Thomas Abthorpe Cooper, Charlotte Cushman, and Edward Eddy. The Bowery Theater came to be the gathering place of the lower class New York groundlings as opposed to the more elite audiences of the Park Theater. Whitman fondly remembered the Bowery as a democratic theater, and he enjoyed attending its productions alongside the leading authors, poets, and editors of the time as well as the cartmen, butchers, firemen, and mechanics who also attended the theater.

The Broadway Theater opened in 1847 and, when the Park Theater burned down, became the home for foreign stars. Forrest was appearing at the Broadway Theater during the Astor Place Riot, and Cushman appeared there as well. The contralto Marietta Alboni, whom Whitman claimed to have heard sing twenty times, appeared at the Broadway as well as at Niblo's Garden.

The Castle Garden featured Jenny Lind in her debut in 1850, and it was there that Whitman saw her perform. The Castle Garden also presented such opera singers as Balbina Steffanone, soprano, Ignazio Marini, basso, Angiolina Bosio, soprano, and Cesare Badiali, baritone, all of whom are mentioned by Whitman in his prose works in the 1880s and 1890s.

Niblo's Garden and Theater, built in 1827, became popular when the Bowery was destroyed by fire in 1828. The Olympic Theater opened in 1837 and then came under the management of William Mitchell in 1839 through 1850. For many years the Olympic operated outside the star system and provided lower class audiences popular entertainment. Whitman heard the popular singer Mary Taylor sing at the Olympic in 1847.

Palmo's Opera House was built by Ferdinand Palmo to introduce the Italian opera to New York. After two bad seasons, Palmo lost control of the Opera House, and the theater languished until taken over by William E. Burton in 1848. Palmo's was renamed Burton's Chambers Street Theater and became one of the most important theaters of the day.

Finally, the Park Theater, originally built in 1798, became the first important theater in New York and was known as the "Old Drury" of America. More aristocratic and elite than its rival, the Bowery, the theater specialized in performances by British actors such as Thomas Abthorpe Cooper, Edmund Kean, and Macready. By 1847 Whitman had become disillusioned with the bad taste and vulgarity prevalent at so many theaters, but he exempted the Park from his complaints, commending it on its intelligent audiences and its "dash of superiority thrown over the Performances" (Whitman 311).

Susan M. Meyer

Bibliography

Bogard, Travis, Richard Moody, and Walter J. Meserve. *American Drama.* Vol. 8 of *The Revels History of Drama in English.* London: Methuen, 1977.

Faner, Robert D. *Walt Whitman & Opera.* Carbondale: Southern Illinois UP, 1951.

Hartnoll, Phyllis. *The Oxford Companion to the Theatre.* 4th ed. Oxford: Oxford UP, 1983.

Levine, Lawrence W. *Highbrow/Lowbrow: The Emergence of Cultural Hierarchy in America.* Cambridge, Mass.: Harvard UP, 1988.

Odell, George C.D. *Annals of the New York Stage.* 15 vols. New York: Columbia UP, 1927–1938.

Reynolds, David S. *Walt Whitman's America: A Cultural Biography.* New York: Knopf, 1995.

Stovall, Floyd. *The Foreground of "Leaves of Grass."* Charlottesville: UP of Virginia, 1974.

Whitman, Walt. *The Gathering of the Forces.* Ed. Cleveland Rodgers and John Black. Vol. 2. New York: Putnam, 1920.

See also ACTORS AND ACTRESSES; HUMAN VOICE; OPERA AND OPERA SINGERS

"There was a Child Went Forth" (1855)

Untitled in the first edition, called "Poem of The Child That Went Forth, and Always Goes Forth, Forever and Forever" in 1856, and grouped in the "Leaves of Grass" cluster in 1860 and 1867, the poem received its present title in 1871. Successive revisions improved its style but probably lessened its emotional impact.

Called by Whitman "the most innocent thing I ever did" (Traubel 157) and by Edwin Haviland Miller "one of the most sensitive lyrics in the language and one of the most astute diagnoses of the emergent self" (27–28), this thirty-nine-line poem is a retrospective view describing the absorption of everything the poem's child beholds. Each sensation becomes "part of" the child (a phrase repeated six times) and by implication foreshadows his maturation into the Whitman poet-persona.

Sandwiched between the poem's opening assertion that each experience "became part of" the child and the closing line's recapitulation of the same idea, a compact catalogue records an astounding four dozen metaphorically charged images or sounds that the child absorbs (in a phrase deleted in later editions) "with wonder or pity or love or dread" (1855 *Leaves*). His development is shown objectively by interlinked patterns of space, colors, passing time, and social phenomena; subjectively by his developing cognitive powers.

Coincidentally or not, the poem illustrates the phrenological formula for educating the superior child by cultivating its powers of observing all surrounding phenomena. "The inductive method of studying nature, namely, by *observing facts* and ascending through *analogous* facts up to the laws that govern them is the only way to arrive at correct conclusions" (Spurzheim 16–17). The young child progressively observes a colorful array of plant and animal life, including the grass, "early lilacs," the ovoid "white and red morning-glories" (corresponding to the glorious morning of his world), young farmyard animals, and—in language suggesting the intersection of his objective and subjective worlds—fish "curiously" suspended in "the beautiful curious liquid." In an intimation of good and evil, he views the passing spectacle of children and adults. The statement that "all the changes of city and country" became "part of him" signals his growing powers of cognition.

The poem's second half tests the child's cognitive powers. Whitman was aware of the phrenological principles that a child's character is basically formed by the blending of the physical and mental characteristics of its parents and by its familial nurture. These principles also state that great poets are descended from gifted mothers—hence the poem's eugenically significant statement that the child's parents "became part of him." Lines 22–25 are sometimes read as literal portraits of Whitman's parents, but the mild, sweet-smelling matriarch resembles the idealized mother figures in Whitman's poems and the "strong, self-sufficient, manly" father is not demonstrably Walter Whitman, Sr. In phrenological terms, the father's aggressive traits endow the child with the self-confidence needed to balance the gentler traits inherited from the mother.

The growing child's innocence—his perceptions and his "yearning and swelling heart"—is threatened by "The doubts of day-time and the doubts of night-time." His questionings are not resolved, but his departure from home, through the bustling city, affords him auguries of divinity: views of sunset "[s]hadows, aureola, and mist" and the "strata of color'd clouds, the long bar of maroon-tint away solitary by itself, the spread of purity it lies motionless in." (These luminous tints complement the pastels of the child's earlier sightings.) The final image of the "horizon's edge . . . salt marsh and shore mud" mingles metaphors of land and sea, suggesting the man-child's initiation into the mysteries of life and death.

The poem's ending repeats the idea that this child who "will always go forth every day" has been molded by his absorptions. The first published version ends with the (deleted) line: "And these become [part] of him or her that peruses them now" (1855 Leaves), implying that the poem can recapture the child's wonder world for every reader. Although the poem's child-persona is apparently an isolated observer, Whitman's musical and sensuous rendering of its observations has kept the poem perennially fresh.

Harold Aspiz

Bibliography
Aspiz, Harold. "Educating the Kosmos: 'There Was a Child Went Forth.'" *American Quarterly* 18 (1966): 655–666.
———. *Walt Whitman and the Body Beautiful*. Urbana: U of Illinois P, 1980. 108–141.
Doherty, Joseph P. "Whitman's 'Poem of the Mind.'" *Semiotica* 14 (1975): 345–363.
Miller, Edwin Haviland. *Walt Whitman's Poetry: A Psychological Journey*. Boston: Houghton Mifflin, 1968.
Spurzheim, J.G. *Education: Its Elementary Principles Founded on the Nature of Man*. 1821. New York: Fowler and Wells, 1847.
Traubel, Horace. *With Walt Whitman in Camden*. Ed. Gertrude Traubel and William White. Vol. 6. Carbondale: Southern Illinois UP, 1982.
Waskow, Howard J. *Whitman's Explorations in Form*. Chicago: U of Chicago P, 1966.
Whitman, Walt. *Leaves of Grass: A Textual Variorum of the Printed Poems*. Ed. Sculley Bradley, Harold W. Blodgett, Arthur Golden, and William White. Vol. 1. New York: New York UP, 1980.

See also "AUTUMN RIVULETS"; LEAVES OF GRASS, 1855 EDITION; PHRENOLOGY; WHITMAN, LOUISA VAN VELSOR; WHITMAN, WALTER, SR.

T

"These I Singing in Spring" (1860)

"These I Singing in Spring" was first published in the 1860 edition of *Leaves of Grass*. It was the fourth poem of forty-five in the "Calamus" section. In 1867 it was given a title, and the poem remained unchanged in later editions.

Whitman begins this poem alone, walking through "the garden the world." "Alone I had thought," he writes, "yet soon a troop gathers around me." "Some walk by my side" as equals, "some behind" as followers, "and some embrace my arms or neck" as lovers. The poet has withdrawn from society only to discover a community of others who think and love as he does.

He soon begins picking and exchanging flowers with this new community, and these flowers become "tokens" of friendship. The moss from a live-oak represents the poet's need for friendship and love, as expressed in another "Calamus" poem, "I Saw in Louisiana a Live-Oak Growing." The lilac is a symbol of the perennial aspect of love, and Whitman uses this flower in other poems such as "When Lilacs Last in the Dooryard Bloom'd" and "Warble for Lilac-Time."

The most important symbol, however, is the calamus root. This "token of comrades," with its phallic bloom, is the unifying symbol for the "Calamus" section of *Leaves of Grass*. It represents homosexual desire, or what Whitman calls "adhesiveness," one man's love for another man. Whitman had to be careful when expressing this love, for his was a homophobic society. In the closing lines of this poem, Whitman states that he gives away this token cautiously, "only to them that love as I myself am capable of loving."

By using natural imagery, Whitman shows that the love of him who "tenderly loves me" is a natural desire, contrary to the common beliefs of nineteenth-century American society. In this poem, fences are man-made dividers that represent the defining aspects of a society that is trying to limit and contain him. "Old stones" are symbols of the established yet outdated ideas of his society. A new and radical growth is beginning, however, as Whitman writes, "Wildflowers and vines and weeds come up through the stones and partly cover them." As Robert K. Martin notes, Whitman moves from the artificiality of the cultivated garden to the natural realm of the forest.

In "Singing," we see several themes that are common to other poems in the "Calamus" section. Whitman withdraws from society to be "the poet of comrades." Once alone, he defines and expresses his gay desire in natural and positive terms. Like the spring, it is new, lush, and characterized by growth. Like the plants, it is beautiful, stimulating to the senses, and natural. Lastly, he discovers that there are others who love as he does.

Conrad M. Sienkiewicz

Bibliography

Cady, Joseph. "Not Happy in the Capitol: Homosexuality and the 'Calamus' Poems." *American Studies* 19.2 (1978): 5–22.

Killingsworth, M. Jimmie. "Sentimentality and Homosexuality in Whitman's 'Calamus.'" *ESQ* 29 (1983): 144–153.

Martin, Robert K. *The Homosexual Tradition in American Poetry.* Austin: U of Texas P, 1979.

Whitman, Walt. *Leaves of Grass: Comprehensive Reader's Edition.* Ed. Harold W. Blodgett and Sculley Bradley. New York: New York UP, 1965.

See also "CALAMUS"; COMRADESHIP; "I SAW IN LOUISIANA A LIVE-OAK GROWING"; *LEAVES OF GRASS,* 1860 EDITION; SEX AND SEXUALITY

"This Compost" (1856)

Originally titled "Poem of Wonder at The Resurrection of The Wheat," this exquisite lyric meditation on death was number 4 in the "Leaves of Grass" cluster in the 1860 edition, received its present intriguing title in 1867, and (having undergone several textual changes over the years) attained its present form in 1881, when it was placed in the "Autumn Rivulets" cluster of *Leaves of Grass* together with many other poems about death.

Although compost generally refers to decomposing vegetable and animal matter used as fertilizer, the poem's title more specifically designates putrefying human carrion; the present line 17 originally read, "Behold! / This is the compost of billions of premature corpses" (1856 *Leaves*). The speaker appears terrified at the thought of such an ignominious destiny for all humanity and at the earth's apparent indifference toward mankind. (The poem makes brilliant use of the pathetic fallacy.) But since compost is a universal nutrient, he also beholds this compost as an element in nature's renewing and transformative powers and, paradoxically, as a promise of universal immortality.

The poem, whose subtext is the poet's struggle between his faith in spiritual regeneration and his fears of annihilation, expresses terror ("Something startles me where I thought I was safest" [section 1]) at the thought of coming in contact with the infectious earth. (Here Whitman echoes the widely accepted theory of miasma—the concept that living matter decomposes into infectious effluvia and poisonous vapors.) In a series of rhetorical questions, the speaker demands to know how the earth, "every mite" (section 2) of which is packed with "all the foul liquid and meat" of "distemper'd corpses" (section 1), can perpetually create wholesome life out of such corruption. Then he opens his eyes to the landscape. Out of the decay he beholds an awful beauty. Observing the leafing and flowering of plants and savoring the earth's bounty, he concludes that "The summer growth is innocent and disdainful above all those strata of sour dead" (section 2). Echoing the poem's 1856 title, a key line—"The resurrection of the wheat appears with pale visage out of its graves" (section 2)—alludes to the earth's vegetational cycle but also, by analogy, to spiritual immortality. Saint Paul's sermon on the conquest of death and the rebirth of the soul (1 Corinthians 15) speaks of the sown wheat resurrected in a divine body and of "the resurrection of the dead . . . sown in corruption" but "raised in incorruption" as a "spiritual body."

In the penultimate paragraph the speaker tries to allay his fears of death and decay with the thought that, despite the corruption and fevers deposited in the earth, he can enjoy the sea, the winds, and the vegetation without catching "any disease." "What chemistry!" he exclaims (section 2). Although "chemistry" is clearly a metaphor for nature's power to compost living and dead elements together to create new life, this exclamation also recalls Whitman's enthusiasm over Justus Liebig's 1846 textbook on chemistry, which defined "fermentation, or putrefaction" as "metamorphosis"—the simultaneous breakdown and re-creation of matter (Aspiz 63–64). Such a chemical "metamorphosis" suggests a dynamic metaphor for the transformative powers of nature, for what Whitman called American democracy's "kosmical, antiseptic power" to digest and transform its corrupt persons into worthy citizens (*Prose Works* 2:382), for the transformation of death into life, and for the poet's power to transform morbid experience into inspirational poetry.

This forty-seven-line masterpiece melds Whitman's anguished confessional mode and his strivings to accept and glorify life and death. Its series of parallel, anaphoric lines (generally forming short catalogues) have an almost breathless quality. Rich in detailed visual images, "This Compost" is also one of Whitman's finest nature poems.

Harold Aspiz

Bibliography

Aspiz, Harold. *Walt Whitman and the Body Beautiful*. Urbana: U of Illinois P, 1980.

Marriage, Anthony X. "Whitman's 'This Compost,' Baudelaire's 'Out of Decay Comes an Awful Beauty.'" *Walt Whitman Review* 27 (1981): 143–149.

Whitman, Walt. *Leaves of Grass: A Textual Variorum of the Printed Poems*. Ed. Sculley Bradley, Harold W. Blodgett, Arthur Golden, and William White. Vol. 1. New York: New York UP, 1980.

———. *Prose Works 1892*. Ed. Floyd Stovall. 2 vols. New York: New York UP, 1963–1964.

See also "Autumn Rivulets"; Death; Immortality; *Leaves of Grass*, 1856 Edition; Liebig, Justus; Nature; Science

Thoreau, Henry David (1817–1862)

Henry David Thoreau, best remembered for his stay at Walden Pond, was one of the Concord school of writers, a transcendentalist, and a naturalist. In addition to *Walden* (1854), Thoreau's major works include *A Week on the Concord and Merrimack Rivers* (1849), "Resistance to Civil Government" (later known as "Civil Disobedience") (1849), and his prodigious *Journal* (1906). The standard edition of Thoreau's works is the 1906 Walden edition, but it is being superseded by the new, controversial Princeton edition, to run to twenty-five volumes (1971–).

Earning a living at odd jobs, teaching, lecturing, pencil making, and surveying, Thoreau never realized the success of his writing, dying of tuberculosis at age forty-four. He was, however, well regarded by his friends, who included Ralph Waldo Emerson, Ellery Channing, Bronson Alcott, and the children of Concord. An ardent admirer of nature, Thoreau devoted much of his time to sauntering through its domain and closely observing its inhabitants. Composed initially to explain his two-year stay at Walden Pond while composing the memorial to his brother John (*A Week*), *Walden* is regarded as America's best example of nature writing. A critic of American life and politics, Thoreau infused *Walden* with biting commentary on the mundane life, and in "Civil Disobedience" he argued for the individual's right to resist government when it runs counter to higher laws. Though "Civil Disobedience" has been one of his most influential pieces, making an impact on the politics of Gandhi and Martin Luther King, Jr., the lectures on his excursions to the Maine Woods, Cape Cod, and Canada were popular with his contemporaries.

Thoreau met Whitman on an excursion he took with Alcott to New York in November 1856. Thoreau was already familiar with Whitman's poetry, having a copy of the 1855 edition of *Leaves of Grass* in his library and having sent a copy to Thomas Cholmondeley. The visit made an impression on him, as his letter to Harrison Blake attests (19 November 1856). He describes Whitman as "the greatest democrat the world has seen" but feels himself "somewhat in a quandary about him." Thoreau's mixed reaction to Whitman continued even after his reading of the second edition of *Leaves of Grass*. Again sharing with Harrison Blake his reaction (7 December 1856), Thoreau commented that he found "two or three pieces . . . which are disagreeable, to say the least, simply sensual." Even so, he found it "exhilarating encouraging" and Whitman to be "a great fellow" (qtd. in Harding 374–375). Whitman's reaction to Thoreau was similarly mixed, for though he liked Thoreau he found him to be morbid. They seemed to appreciate each other, despite their differences.

Though never a great champion of Whitman's poetry, Thoreau recognized its truthfulness and urgency, themes in his own writing.

Susan L. Roberson

Bibliography

Buell, Lawrence. "Whitman and Thoreau." *Calamus* 8 (1973): 18–28.

Cavell, Stanley. *The Senses of "Walden."* New York: Viking, 1972.

Harding, Walter. *The Days of Henry Thoreau.* New York: Knopf, 1965.

Metzger, Charles R. *Thoreau and Whitman: A Study of Their Esthetics.* Seattle: U of Washington P, 1961.

Scharnhorst, Gary. *Henry David Thoreau: A Case Study in Canonization.* Columbia, S.C.: Camden House, 1993.

Thoreau, Henry David. *The Writings of Henry David Thoreau* (Walden Edition). Ed. Bradford Torrey. 20 vols. Boston: Houghton Mifflin, 1906.

See also ALCOTT, AMOS BRONSON; EMERSON, RALPH WALDO; NATURE; TRANSCENDENTALISM

"Thou Mother with Thy Equal Brood" (1872)

Appearing as the title poem in *As a Strong Bird on Pinions Free* (1872), "Thou Mother" subsequently appeared as a supplement to the 1876 *Leaves of Grass;* the poem was finally placed in *Leaves of Grass* in 1881. Generally reviled as one of Whitman's worst poems, "Thou Mother" has elicited a wide range of critical responses. Most treat the poem's prophetic nature, but some isolate unusual features, indicating that the poem, despite its hyperbole and structural flaws, has vibrancy. As Gay Wilson Allen notes, the poem is derivative, repeating ideas and moods presented in *Democratic Vistas.* Still, this poem reveals a facet of Whitman that has been gaining much recent currency: his internationalism.

Most critics acknowledge Whitman's artificial scripting of nature while praising his unblinking gaze at America's potential for "moral consumption" (section 6). Cast as an epic, "Thou Mother" contains a bard singing, which, according to Thomas Crawley, intensifies the poem's internationalism. Like Crawley, James E. Miller, Jr., views the poem as Whitman's final statement on nationalism, on national destiny. America's destiny, in Whitman's rendering, affects international destiny. This international scope gives vibrancy to the poem.

Yet the inevitability of corruption and rhetorical excess make the poem less a visionary utterance than a prosaic assertion. Hurriedly composed for the Dartmouth College commencement in 1872, the poem, according to M. Wynn Thomas, reveals Whitman's postwar tendency to use rhetorical excess to overcome doubts. Thomas gives the most persuasive of all critical readings, arguing that America has no permanency except for the permanency Whitman authorizes in his poem. Thomas presents a tragic Whitman, whose crises cause him to rely on "leaves" (paper) and "chants" (poetic utterances).

The most intriguing responses to the poem deal with its political and religious meaning. Betsy Erkkila stresses Whitman's political aims, arguing that he scripts both a democratic self and a national self. She stresses the conflation of male and female in the poet's assertion "I merely thee ejaculate" (section 5). By extension, the nation is a construct because it has been scripted by a poet like Whitman. (See also Longfellow's "Building of the Ship," which, for Kenneth Price, reveals Whitman's borrowing without acknowledgment.) For V.K. Chari, "Thou Mother" reveals a religious-spiritual dimension in Whitman. He argues that while the self is real for Whitman, substances are unreal. The self, grounded in nature, must interpret phenomena, a view that W.B. Yeats affirms in poems like "A Dialogue of Self and Soul." However, the unseen soul, the "real real," corresponds to the Upanishadic view that Brahma is the "real of the real." The poem may be a failed visionary utterance, but Whitman strove to make it visionary.

Clearly, Whitman composed too rapidly, striving to meet the commencement deadline. As C. Carroll Hollis persuasively notes, the poem's vagueness may have resulted from Whitman's desire to be an oracular poet; but Whitman was a poet, not a prophet. Whitman may have despaired over ending his *Leaves of Grass* project. A poem like "Passage to India" indicates he wanted to widen his national vision, but "Thou Mother" remains one of a handful of poems that treat in sustained measure the international theme Whitman hoped to stress in his next volume.

Jay Losey

Bibliography

Allen, Gay Wilson. *Walt Whitman Handbook.* 1946. New York: Hendricks House, 1962.

Chari, V.K. *Whitman in the Light of Vedantic Mysticism.* 1964. Lincoln: U of Nebraska P, 1969.

Crawley, Thomas Edward. *The Structure of "Leaves of Grass."* Austin: U of Texas P, 1970.

Erkkila, Betsy. *Whitman the Political Poet.* New York: Oxford UP, 1989.

Hollis, C. Carroll. *Language and Style in "Leaves of Grass."* Baton Rouge: Louisiana State UP, 1983.

Miller, James E., Jr. *A Critical Guide to "Leaves of Grass."* Chicago: U of Chicago P, 1957.

Price, Kenneth M. *Whitman and Tradition: The Poet in his Century.* New Haven: Yale UP, 1990.

Thomas, M. Wynn. *The Lunar Light of Whitman's Poetry.* Cambridge, Mass.: Harvard UP, 1987.

Whitman, Walt. *Leaves of Grass: A Textual Variorum of the Printed Poems.* Ed. Sculley Bradley, Harold W. Blodgett, Arthur Golden, and William White. Vol. 3. New York: New York UP, 1980.

See also DARTMOUTH COLLEGE; *DEMOCRATIC VISTAS*; PREFACE TO *AS A STRONG BIRD ON PINIONS FREE*; RECONSTRUCTION

"Thou Orb Aloft Full-Dazzling" (1881)

Published with the title "A Summer Invocation" in *The American* on 4 June 1881, this is the first poem of the miscellaneous cluster "From Noon to Starry Night" in the 1881 edition of *Leaves of Grass*. The manuscript contains two alternative titles, "Sun-up" and "A Seashore Invocation." Whitman reported that the editor of *Harper's* magazine returned it to him because he judged the magazine readers would not understand it.

Nevertheless, the poem is easily accessible to any attentive reader. Whitman is clearly calling on the sun, addressing it by an ancient rhetorical device—the apostrophe, which he often used—as if it were human. Here it is a call for help, an invocation, a word Whitman actually uses ("as now to thee I launch my invocation"). Although the poem is positive and confident, its form as a prayer or entreaty does not allow for a sustained affirmative tone.

For Whitman, the apostrophe as a device yields both a formal and an intimate effect, aided often by the use of inverted word order: "Thou canst not with thy dumbness me deceive." Exactly what he wants from the sun is withheld until the final lines of this twenty-five-line lyric. Earlier he has described dramatically the vast role of the sun in providing the earth vitality, as well as its role in his own life, in which he addresses the sun as "lover." He assures himself that a "fitting man" would understand the silent but pervasive operation of the sun. He seems to link the "perturbations" of the sun, its sudden shafts of flame, with his own anxieties, without revealing what these might be. Finally, he asks for help: "Shed, shed thyself on mine and me, with but a fleeting ray out of thy million millions, / Strike through these chants." Not for his songs only does he ask aid, but in the last line he also asks for himself as he prepares for old age and death, as his images may hint: "Prepare the later afternoon of me myself—prepare my lengthening shadows / Prepare my starry nights."

Although the sun figures in other poems, most notably in the title and opening line of a major one, "Give Me the Splendid Silent Sun," Whitman was no sun worshiper, except as the sun focused attention on nature's bounty. When recovering from his stroke at the Stafford farm in New Jersey (1876–1878), he gained much in health from yielding to the restorative power of the natural scene. But always more important were the resources of men and women, and of himself, as objects to treasure and to address in his poems, as he argues even in "Give Me the Splendid Silent Sun." The conventional invocation or prayer is therefore rare, with exceptions being "Gods," "The Last Invocation," "Look Down Fair Moon," and "Prayer of Columbus." Whitman's calling on the sun in "Thou Orb Aloft" is a case of the poet's using a conceit, not exercising a belief, and this is Whitman at his imaginative best.

David B. Baldwin

Bibliography

Allen, Gay Wilson. *The Solitary Singer: A Critical Biography of Walt Whitman.* 1955. Rev. ed. 1967. Chicago: U of Chicago P, 1985.

Whitman, Walt. *Leaves of Grass: Comprehensive Reader's Edition.* Ed. Harold W. Blodgett and Sculley Bradley. New York: New York UP, 1965.

———. *Leaves of Grass: A Textual Variorum of the Printed Poems.* Ed. Sculley Bradley, Harold W. Blodgett, Arthur Golden, and William White. Vol. 3. New York: New York UP, 1980.

———. *Specimen Days.* Vol. 1 of *Prose Works 1892.* Ed. Floyd Stovall. New York: New York UP, 1963.

See also "FROM NOON TO STARRY NIGHT"; "GIVE ME THE SPLENDID SILENT SUN"; *LEAVES OF GRASS*, 1881–1882 EDITION; "PRAYER OF COLUMBUS"

"Thought of Columbus, A" (1892)

Horace Traubel claimed that "A Thought of Columbus" (1892) was the last poem Walt Whitman wrote. He said Whitman gave him the pieced-together manuscript on 16 March 1892, just ten days before the poet's death. The poem was first published in *Once a Week*, 9 July 1892, and Traubel's description of its composition appeared in the same magazine a week later. "Thought" was then added to the tenth edition of *Leaves of Grass* (1897) as part of "Old Age Echoes."

In 1891 the United States was preparing to celebrate the four hundredth anniversary of the "discovery." Whitman undoubtedly followed the news of the Quatercentennial, for during his final winter he worked on "Thought," his third poem about Columbus. In "Passage to India" (1871) he celebrated Columbus as one of history's great heroes. In "Prayer of Columbus" (1874), Whitman, having recently suffered a paralytic stroke, expressed his own despair through the voice of the old and broken Columbus of the final voyage. "Thought" resembles "Prayer" in that it also uses a dramatic monologue to establish unity between Whitman and Columbus. If "Thought" and "Prayer" are similar in form, they are very different in theme and tone. "Prayer" focuses on the defeated Columbus of the final voyage, but "Thought" presents a young Columbus, looking out at the Atlantic from Europe and pondering the possibility of sailing west to the Indies. "Thought," then, is about two men about to embark upon the unknown—a young explorer setting out for the New World and an old poet about to die.

Ned Stuckey-French

Bibliography

Traubel, Horace. "Walt Whitman's Last Poem." *Once a Week: An Illustrated Weekly Newspaper* 16 July 1892: 3.

Whitman, Walt. *Leaves of Grass: A Textual Variorum of the Printed Poems*. Ed. Sculley Bradley, Harold W. Blodgett, Arthur Golden, and William White. 3 vols. New York: New York UP, 1980.

See also COLUMBUS, CHRISTOPHER; "OLD AGE ECHOES"; "PASSAGE TO INDIA"; "PRAYER OF COLUMBUS"

Timber Creek

Timber Creek, a tributary of the Delaware River, runs through southern New Jersey. A spot on the creek about twelve miles from Camden, where Whitman had moved in 1873, became a favorite retreat for the poet for several years in the late 1870s and into the 1880s, playing an important role in both his life and his work.

The site of Whitman's Timber Creek retreat lies in the town of Laurel Springs, then only a rural crossroads. Whitman first visited there in 1876. His residence was with the Stafford family—George, Susan, and their children. It was through one of the Stafford sons, Harry, whom he met in a print shop where his pamphlet *Two Rivulets* was being set, that Whitman came to know the Staffords. Whitman's status in the Stafford home was that of a paying guest but also a friend, and his visits sometimes extended through most of the summer.

In the years just before Whitman began to visit Timber Creek, he had experienced some of the hardest blows of his life: he was semi-paralytic from a stroke, and his mother had died. Whitman was at a low ebb, physically and emotionally. Timber Creek was a place of recuperation for him. Some, Whitman among them, have suggested that the place and the relationships associated with it saved his life.

The Stafford farmhouse was on a rise above the creek, and Whitman made his way down to it along a lane, lined with an old rail fence that became a footpath as it approached the water. At first he went slowly and with assistance, with a companion carrying a chair for him to stop and rest at short intervals. As time went on he became more mobile and independent, and he would spend many hours down along the creek, resting, observing, musing, jotting, and practicing a program of physical therapy that partially rehabilitated his body, as the entire Timber Creek experience rejuvenated his spirit.

Whitman's days at Timber Creek are memorably recorded in *Specimen Days*, in some of his best nature writing and freshest prose. Whitman referred to the unspoiled creek, which afforded both privacy and natural beauty, as "the secluded-beautiful" (121). He observed and absorbed the water and trees, the plants, birds, and insects, the sun and wind and changes in the weather, and he experienced states of great pleasure, relaxation, and receptiveness that blended the therapeutic and the mystical: "How they and all grow into me, day after day—everything in keeping—the wild, just-palpable perfume, and the dapple of leaf-shadows, and all the natural-medicinal, elemental-moral influences of the spot" (121).

The physical therapy he practiced here included sun-bathing, mud-bathing, bathing at a flowing spring, scrubbing his skin with a hard brush, sauntering along the bank wearing only shoes and a straw hat, singing bits of opera and folksongs and reciting poetry, and wrestling with the saplings that grew along the bank. Whitman and most biographers have emphasized the solitude of Timber Creek, but human relationships were also important. Mrs. Stafford had a special fondness for Whitman, and his relationship with her son Harry became one of the most intense attachments of his life. The company of Harry and other young men from the neighborhood was a key part of the powerful attraction, both idyllic and emotional, that Timber Creek had for Whitman.

Some of Whitman's admirers raised a fund for the purpose of building the poet a cottage along the creek, but the plan never materialized. Today the spring where Whitman bathed (its flow now much diminished) and a section of creek bank are a public park in the town of Laurel Springs. From the 1930s through the 1950s the site lay beneath the town dump, but through the efforts of local citizens it was cleaned up and restored. The Stafford house, now called the Whitman Stafford House, has also been restored and is open to the public.

Howard Nelson

Bibliography

Aspiz, Harold. "*Specimen Days:* The Therapeutics of Sun-Bathing." *Walt Whitman Quarterly Review* 1.3 (1983): 48–50.

Binns, Henry Bryan. *A Life of Walt Whitman.* London: Methuen, 1905.

Bradley, Sculley. "Walt Whitman on Timber Creek." *American Literature* 5 (1933): 235–246.

Kaplan, Justin. *Walt Whitman: A Life.* New York: Simon and Schuster, 1980.

Shively, Charley. *Calamus Lovers: Walt Whitman's Working Class Camerados.* San Francisco: Gay Sunshine, 1987.

Whitman, Walt. *Specimen Days.* Vol. 1 of *Prose Works 1892.* Ed. Floyd Stovall. New York: New York UP, 1963.

See also CAMDEN, NEW JERSEY; HEALTH; NATURE; SPECIMEN DAYS; STAFFORD, GEORGE AND SUSAN M.; STAFFORD, HARRY L.

Time

The concept of time held mystical significance for Walt Whitman, and his poetry represents time not merely as an adversary with which the poet must contend but also a vast force with which the soul may merge itself to achieve peace and transcendence. In the Preface to the 1855 *Leaves of Grass,* Whitman observes that the poet who seeks to bring the spirit of events home to the reader is compelled "to compete with the laws that pursue and follow time" (13). Through the work of the great poet, Whitman continues, "Past and present and future are not disjoined but joined. The greatest poet forms the consistence of what is to be from what has been and is . . . [H]e places himself where the future becomes present" (13). In "Starting from Paumanok," Whitman promises to "thread a thread through my poems that time and events are compact" (section 12). For Whitman, the problem is at least twofold: How does a person confront time as an emblem of mortality, and how does a poet conquer time by making his poetry pertinent to unborn generations? In response to these challenges, Whitman's poetry strives in general to show time not as a succession of moments trisected into past, present, and future, but as a single sublime unity that comprehends all experience in an eternal "now." Whitman achieves this appearance of unity through a number of devices. He describes states of mystical awareness in which the restraints of time are transcended; he propounds a theory of cyclical biological renewal in which individual bits of matter may change but the cosmos remains unchanged, and he uses rhetorical structures to imply that the experiences and feelings of the poet are one with those of future readers.

In the 1855 and 1856 editions of *Leaves of Grass,* Whitman's meditations on time emphasize natural cycles as an emblem of the eternal now and propose the text of the poem itself as a place where writer and reader may interact outside the constraints of time. The former idea is prominent in the untitled 1855 poem that later became "To Think of Time." Whitman begins by supposing that the reader is troubled by the passage of time and the prospect of death:

> Have you guessed you yourself would
> not continue? Have you dreaded
> those earth-beetles?
> Have you feared the future would be
> nothing to you?
>
> (1855 *Leaves*)

Whitman answers this disquieting thought by observing that nature will be felt in the same way by future generations and that, therefore, there is a constancy to human experience that transcends time:

> To think that the rivers will come to
>   flow, and the snow fall, and fruits
>   ripen . . and act upon others as
>   upon us now . . . . yet not act upon
>   us;
> To think of all these wonders of city and
>   country . . . and others taking great
>   interest in them . . and we taking
>   small interest in them.
>
> (1855 *Leaves*)

The poet proceeds to suggest that whereas individual lives may pass away, the matter and processes that build, destroy, and rebuild life will endure forever, and that this cyclicality in some sense makes illusions of time and death:

> The vegetables and minerals are all
>   perfect . . and the imponderable
>   fluids are perfect;
> Slowly and surely they have passed
>   on to this, and slowly and surely
>   they will yet pass on.
>
> . . . .
>
> I swear I see now that every thing has
>   an eternal soul!
> The trees have, rooted in the ground . . . .
>   weeds of the sea have . . . . the
>   animals.
> I swear I think there is nothing but
>   immortality!
>
> (1855 *Leaves*)

Whitman voices a similar but more carefully elaborated vision of eternity in the 1856 poem later entitled "Crossing Brooklyn Ferry." The voyage of the ferry is itself a metaphor both for the apparent passage of time and for its circular repetitions. Continually crossing and recrossing, the boat and its passengers are both static and in motion, just as for Whitman time both moves forward and repeats itself. Accentuating the circularity of time, the poet observes that the sun that is now "half an hour high" (section 1) will appear in the same position "[f]ifty years hence" (section 2). As in "To Think of Time," Whitman elides the passage of years

by stating that his perceptions will be repeated by those who will follow him: "Just as you stand and lean on the rail, yet hurry with the swift current, I stood yet was hurried" (section 3). Whitman further accentuates the unity of past, present, and future by his subtle use of verb tenses. In the second section of the poem, Whitman's perceptions are related in the present tense, and those of generations to come are set in the future tense. In the third section, however, the poet's experiences are in the past tense and those of his future readers are in the present tense. Moreover, when, in this section, Whitman shifts his own moment to the past, his descriptions of what he sees are spangled with a series of present participles, preserving a sense of ongoing progression within seemingly past recollection. Within this carefully constructed frame of shared experiences and meticulously modulated verb forms, Whitman asserts his view that "It avails not, time nor place—distance avails not" (section 3).

In later poems, Whitman continues to suggest that the passage of time is somehow an illusion. In these works, however, the triumph over time and mortality is less likely to arise out of biological theories of regeneration or litanies of experiences shared between generations. As Whitman's career moves forward, he comes to view the mastering of time as the result of a mystical expansion of the soul. In "Chanting the Square Deific" (1865–1866), a poem about participation in divine being, Whitman implies that the great soul does not resist time but becomes one with it. He writes, "Not Time affects me—I am Time, old, modern as any" (section 1). In "Passage to India," Whitman again affirms the power of the soul both to transcend and to ally itself with time:

> Swiftly I shrivel at the thought of God,
> At Nature and its wonders,
>   Time and Space and Death,
> But that I, turning, call to thee O soul,
>   thou actual Me,
> And lo, thou gently masterest the orbs,
> Thou matest Time, smilest content at
>   Death,
> And fillest, swellest full the vastnesses
>   of Space.
>
> (section 8)

Although Whitman never attempted a precise elaboration of his concept of time, his poetry plainly suggests that time should not be considered as a line, but perhaps as a circle, or, better still, as a single, ubiquitous point. Whitman observes that people of all times share the same biological origins and the same feelings and experiences and that the individual soul has the mystical power to absorb, "mate," and merge itself into time. Whitman thus suggests that, to both sense and spirit, the present is eternal.

John T. Matteson

Bibliography
Kagle, Steven. "Time as a Dimension in Whitman." *American Transcendental Quarterly* 12 (1971): 55–60.
McGhee, Richard D. "Concepts of Time in Whitman's Poetry." *Walt Whitman Review* 15 (1969): 76–85.
Orlov, Paul A. "On Time and Form in Whitman's 'Crossing Brooklyn Ferry.'" *Walt Whitman Quarterly Review* 2.1 (1984): 12–21.
Poulet, George. "Whitman." *Studies in Human Time*. Trans. Elliott Coleman. Baltimore: Johns Hopkins UP, 1956. 342–345.
Whitman, Walt. 1855 Preface. *Complete Poetry and Collected Prose*. Ed. Justin Kaplan. New York: Library of America, 1982. 4–26.

See also "Chanting the Square Deific"; "Crossing Brooklyn Ferry"; Immortality; Mysticism; "Passage to India"; Soul, The; Space; "To Think of Time"

"To a Certain Civilian" (1865)

One of the later poems in "Drum-Taps," this poem was written in 1865, revised in 1871 and included in the 1891–1892 edition of *Leaves of Grass*.

Perhaps harsher in tone than other Whitman poems addressed to the reader, this work presents a stern, unsympathetic Whitman whose admonition to the reader is to leave his work and go elsewhere if the subjects of his poems are not "dulcet," "languishing," and "peaceful" enough.

This intimacy in the relationship between Whitman and reader is best understood by a close reading of "Crossing Brooklyn Ferry" (1856), wherein Whitman transcends the barriers of time to "approach" his reader and establish an intimate relationship by inquiring "What is it then between us?" and thereby sug-

gesting a relationship that is compassionate, sympathetic, and understanding. But as the reader approaches the end of the "Drum-Taps" cluster, Whitman is wearying of his theme much as he did the Civil War in its final years.

The interplay between Whitman and his reader in the poems preceding "To a Certain Civilian" shows a tired and forlorn Whitman, one reduced to a few short lines written at brief intervals as he continues his labors nursing in the various field hospitals, lamenting the carnage and suffering of the young men he cares for. Whitman sees himself urging onward his "cameradoes" to an unknown destiny much as the Union urged its young men forward to an uncertain future.

And now in "To a Certain Civilian," the poet explodes in quiet anger toward that reader who may be tiring of his message and his portraits of misery and tragedy. Whitman proclaims that he is not "singing" in order to comfort his reader with understanding or "dulcet" and "languishing" rhymes. His work is a dirge, an elegy to those who have paid the ultimate price, for it is they who have demonstrated understanding all along. In one line Whitman declares "I have been born of the same as the war was born," suggesting that from the agony of war the poet's maturity was assured.

Whitman explains in *Specimen Days* that in his youth the poet is charged with sunshine and optimism, but as dusk approaches he realizes there is greater truth in the "half-lights" of evening (Whitman 923). He then explains the soul's joy in capturing what cannot be defined by the intellect. To grasp these truths one must enter or contribute of one's own volition.

So it is with the reader who cannot identify with Whitman's "cameradoes" on the battlefields of the Civil War. He suggests these readers "lull" themselves with those piano tunes that they can comprehend. He then concludes "Drum-Taps" by returning to his tributes for the fallen soldiers and the sacred soil their blood saturates.

Julian B. Freund

Bibliography
Miller, James E., Jr. *A Critical Guide to "Leaves of Grass."* Chicago: U of Chicago P, 1957.
Whitman, Walt. *Complete Poetry and Collected Prose*. Ed. Justin Kaplan. New York: Library of America, 1982.

See also Civil War, The; "Crossing Brooklyn Ferry"; "Drum-Taps"

"To a Common Prostitute" (1860)

Whitman added more than a hundred new poems to the 1860 edition of *Leaves of Grass,* including "To a Common Prostitute." Attempting for the first time to group poems thematically, Whitman placed "To a Common Prostitute" in a loosely organized section called "Messenger Leaves." Allen sees this section as thematically unified only by the prominence of the "Messiah-role" in several poems, including "Prostitute."

The sexuality of the 1860 edition (which, in addition to "Prostitute," included for the first time fifteen untitled erotic poems in a section called "Enfans d'Adam") troubled Thayer and Eldridge, the Boston publishers who went bankrupt just after they brought out the third (1860) edition of *Leaves.* Whitman resisted their pressures to expurgate the edition, and resisted as well the similar "vehement arguments" of Ralph Waldo Emerson, America's preeminent man of letters, who urged that "Prostitute" be dropped.

"Prostitute" was again the focus of controversy in 1881, when James R. Osgood and Company, publishers, planned to bring out the sixth edition of *Leaves.* When the District Attorney put Osgood under notice that the book violated obscenity laws, Osgood proposed deleting three whole poems ("Prostitute," "A Woman Waits for Me," and "The Dalliance of the Eagles"). Whitman took the book away from Osgood.

Although the subject of prostitution was considered inappropriate for poetry, a prostitute also appears in "Song of Myself," "draggl[ing] her shawl" drunkenly down the street while surrounded by men who wink and jeer (section 15). Whitman condemns not the prostitute, but rather the mob's ridicule, and, as in "Prostitute," extends compassion to the woman.

As editor of the Brooklyn *Daily Eagle* (1846–1848) and, later, of the Brooklyn *Daily Times* (1857–1859), Whitman had editorialized about prostitution. Interestingly, in his role as a newspaper editor commenting on social problems, Whitman condemned the vice of prostitution as a destroyer of families, spreader of venereal disease, and polluter of bloodlines. A careful reading of "Prostitute" clarifies this apparent inconsistency. As Allen notes, the voice in this poem is that of Whitman as a Messiah; it is not the voice of a time/space-bound observer such as a newspaper editor.

In the very first line of the poem Whitman identifies himself with "Nature," and speaks thereafter from an all-encompassing, cosmic perspective. Just as elemental nature itself does not reject this virtual child, neither does the cosmic Whitman.

If we bring to this poem Whitman's expansive vision of reincarnation, we understand that this young woman is an evolving soul who at this moment finds herself in the debased role of the prostitute. Through the long journey of every soul's growth ("make preparation to be worthy to meet me"), we ourselves, by subtle implication, may have passed through debasement similar to that of the prostitute, and all, including her, will rise ultimately to join the Messiah in a meeting of equals ("be patient and perfect till I come").

We find in this poem, then, one of the main functions of Whitman's Messiah-role: an expansion of perspective that inspires in readers a sense of compassion and acceptance, as well as an awareness of the finally triumphant patterns of human evolution.

Carmine Sarracino

Bibliography

Allen, Gay Wilson. *The New Walt Whitman Handbook.* 1975. New York: New York UP, 1986.

———. *The Solitary Singer: A Critical Biography of Walt Whitman.* 1955. Rev ed. 1967. Chicago: U of Chicago P, 1985.

Aspiz, Harold. *Walt Whitman and the Body Beautiful.* Urbana: U of Illinois P, 1980.

Crawley, Thomas Edward. *The Structure of "Leaves of Grass."* Austin: U of Texas P, 1970.

Whitman, Walt. *Prose Works 1892.* Ed. Floyd Stovall. Vol. 2. New York: New York UP, 1964.

See also BOSTON, MASSACHUSETTS; "CHILDREN OF ADAM"; EMERSON, RALPH WALDO; *LEAVES OF GRASS,* 1860 EDITION; *LEAVES OF GRASS,* 1881–1882 EDITION; OSGOOD, JAMES R.; THAYER AND ELDRIDGE

"To a Foil'd European Revolutionaire" (1856)

"To a Foil'd European Revolutionaire" appeared in the second edition of *Leaves of Grass* (1856) as "Liberty Poem for Asia, Africa, Europe, America, Australia, Cuba, and The Archipelagoes of the Sea." It contains a number of lines from the 1855 Preface. Succeeding editions presented many changes of title, cluster position, and wording. It became "To a Foiled Revolter or Revoltress" in 1860 and 1867, and took its familiar title thereafter.

In 1860, "Foil'd" was included in the "Messenger Leaves" cluster; it was in no cluster in 1867; then in 1871 and 1876 it appeared as one of six poems in "Songs of Insurrection." Finally Whitman placed it in "Autumn Rivulets."

"Foil'd" is a speech of encouragement in the midst of political failure. Its apparent addressee is the European "revolter" or "revoltress," who is exhorted not to give up hope—for the personified "Liberty" is an inexpungable element in the very nature of life. The poem concludes by turning defeat on its head, claiming that not only victory but also "death and dismay are great."

That final word hints at pregnancy ("great with child"), particularly when read in context of the "latent" figure of Liberty, "patiently waiting." It expresses the theme of natural cycle and regeneration implicit in Whitman's master metaphor of the grass. Here the cycle is both political and spiritual, but its earthy roots are suggested in the poem's positioning after "The City Dead-House" and "This Compost" and before "Unnamed Lands." All proclaim Whitman's faith in a moral and natural economy in which nothing is ever lost. The 1850 poem "Resurgemus"—included in *Leaves of Grass* as "Europe"—also voices it: "Not a grave of the murder'd for freedom but grows seed for freedom, in its turn to bear seed."

Like "Resurgemus," "Foil'd" is a product of the politically turbulent decade preceding 1855, during which the activist Whitman speechified for his Democratic party and edited partisan newspapers. It embodies both the heady hopes of 1848, the "year of revolutions," and the dismal aftermath of the 1850s, when the cause of democracy abroad and antislavery at home became mired in setback and compromise. The original poem's several references to slavery, later removed—like the excoriating political letter Whitman appended to the 1856 edition—indicate a domestic dimension.

David Oates

Bibliography

Allen, Gay Wilson. *The New Walt Whitman Handbook.* 1975. New York: New York UP, 1986.

Erkkila, Betsy. *Whitman the Political Poet.* New York: Oxford UP, 1989.

Reynolds, Larry J. "1848 and the Origins of *Leaves of Grass.*" *ATQ* 1 (1987): 291–299.

See also "Autumn Rivulets"; "Europe, The 72d and 73d Years of These States"; Political Views; Radicalism; Revolutions of 1848

"To a Historian" (1860)

When this poem first appeared in the third (1860) edition of *Leaves of Grass,* it was number 10 of sixteen new poems that were combined with six old ones to form a cluster titled "Chants Democratic." These poems, intended to sing of nationalistic purposes first mentioned in the Preface to the 1855 edition, actually trace Whitman's attempt to describe the fundamental basis of an ethical democracy. In the third edition, "To a Historian" consisted of fifteen lines, but it was trimmed to the present seven lines when the fourth (1867) edition broke up the "Chants Democratic" cluster and placed the poem in a new cluster called "Inscriptions," where it has remained ever since.

The poem prophesies the ideal man that the American of the future will be. Whitman holds his vision to be superior to that of the historian, for whereas the historian "celebrates bygones," he "project[s] the history of the future." The historian has limited vision, seeing only the "outward," the exhibited surface of the world's peoples, the life that has been rather than the life that can be. His approach is to consider humanity only in terms of politics in which the individual is ignored as he considers people as "aggregates." In contrast, Whitman treats of the inner individual, seeking the "pulse of life" which defines him but which he seldom overtly displays. Hence, as the "Chanter of Personality," he clearly grasps the essence of America's people, allowing him to project what the historian cannot envision: "the history of the future."

By calling himself the "habitan of the Alleghanies" (his spelling), the oldest mountains in the United States, Whitman associates himself with the ancient foundation and fundamentals of his beloved America. His use of such foreign words as *habitan,* however, has been criticized by some critics, who consider them a blemish and an ugly trick.

Appearing during the period of bitter conflict and eventual war between the states, North and South, the poem reminds readers that the true destiny of a nation lies not in the observable facts of its history but in the hidden character of its people.

Maverick Marvin Harris

Bibliography

Miller, Edwin Haviland. *A Century of Whitman Criticism.* Bloomington: Indiana UP, 1969.

Whitman, Walt. *Leaves of Grass: Comprehensive Reader's Edition.* Ed. Harold W. Blodgett and Sculley Bradley. New York: New York UP, 1965.

See also "Inscriptions"

"To a Locomotive in Winter" (1876)

Having first appeared 19 February 1876, in the New York *Daily Tribune,* as part of a preview of the volume *Two Rivulets* (1876), "To a Locomotive in Winter" was added to *Leaves of Grass* in 1881, in the cluster "From Noon to Starry Night." Whitman probably wrote the poem in the winter of 1875, when he felt old and "shattered" by his recent stroke (1873). Feeling his own life in "winter-day declining," the poet attempts to tap into the potent power of the locomotive, invoking it to "serve the Muse."

In a note on the manuscript, Whitman conceived the train as an emblem of modern "Power & Motion." But "Locomotive" is not simply a poem celebrating a technological triumph. Nor is it merely a postromantic attempt to glean something poetic out of industry and technology. The poet transforms the train into a poem, then listens to its "lawless music." Whitman hears dissonant music—*modern* music—in the "shrieks" and "rumbling" of the train: "No sweetness debonair of tearful harp or glib piano thine." What makes the locomotive a "[t]ype of the modern," then, is not merely its synecdochal representation of technology but also its assertion that any subject may be poetical—and cacophony may be beautiful ("Fierce-throated beauty!").

The poem is divided into two unnumbered sections. The first (lines 1–17) is a chanting apostrophe, cast as a "recitative." In opera, the recitatives are the passages in which characters appear to be talking; the half-sung, half-spoken vocal style is rhythmically free so that the singer may imitate the natural inflections of speech. Thus Whitman is not only making his free verse more operatic, he is attempting to enter into a dialogue with the locomotive. In the first section he appears to do all the talking, but actually he embeds the locomotive's song in his sound effects. Most of the explicit imagery of the first seventeen lines is visual (as French has shown), but the implicit imagery is auditory: if the poem is read aloud (as it really must be), the locomotive comes alive—assonance ("serve . . . merge," "buffeting gusts") and alliteration ("pale . . . vapor-pennants . . . purple") especially compensate for the lack of auditory imagery that French noticed, and the iambic thrust of many of the lines ("Thy black cylindric body, golden brass and silvery steel") more subtly suggests the pulsing power of the locomotive.

In the pulsing rhythm of the locomotive's poetry, Whitman finds the systolic and diastolic rhythm of heartbeat and spirit. But he knows that it is a living thing only when he instills it with life through his poem. It is not a poem until he makes it one; no one hears its song until he, the poet, writes the notes. So in the second section (lines 18–25), he implies that the only way the train can join the dialogue of the recitative is through him ("Roll through my chant"). An exchange has occurred: the machine has been animated and vitalized by the poet; and the man crippled by stroke has absorbed the energy of the locomotive.

Though Whitman's body was now feeble, his spirit could still find strength, and his language still had the power to move. "Locomotive" is often anthologized, not only because it begs comparison with a famous poem by Emily Dickinson ("I like to see it lap the miles—," also about a train that speaks dissonant poetry in "horrid hooting stanza"), but perhaps especially because it evokes—and invokes—the Ghost in the Machine.

Joseph Andriano

Bibliography

Christ, Ronald. "Walt Whitman: Image and Credo." *American Quarterly* 17 (1965): 92–103.

Faner, Robert. *Walt Whitman & Opera.* Carbondale: Southern Illinois UP, 1951.

French, Roberts W. "Music for a Mad Scene: A Reading of 'To a Locomotive in Winter.'" *Walt Whitman Review* 27 (1981): 32–39.

Jerome, Judson. "Type of the Modern." *University of Dayton Review* 19.1 (1987–1988): 69–78.

See also "FROM NOON TO STARRY NIGHT"; TECHNOLOGY; *TWO RIVULETS,* AUTHOR'S EDITION

"To a President" (1860)

The president addressed and disparaged by Walt Whitman in this poem is James Buchanan, in the eighteenth term of the U.S. presidency (from 1857 to 1861). The poet called Buchanan and his two predecessors "deform'd, mediocre, snivelling, unreliable, false-hearted men" (*Complete* 996) and considered Buchanan to be "perhaps the weakest of the President tribe—the very unablest" (Traubel 30). Solely on the issue of corruption in government, the Buchanan administration was the worst ever, in his view. Whitman was disenchanted with the people's choice when they let such "scum floating atop of the waters" into the presidency ("To the States, To Identify the 16th, 17th, or 18th Presidentiad"), but he also was contemptuous of the 1856 Democratic convention for its machinations. A minority president who won 45 percent of the popular vote nationally, Buchanan scored a narrow victory (with 59 percent of the electoral vote. He was indebted to the South, carrying every slave state except Maryland (112 electoral votes of the 174 he had won).

Northern Democrats chose Buchanan thinking that he (a Northerner) would rein in Southern power and hold the Union together. During the campaign Buchanan endorsed the "popular sovereignty" plank of the Democratic platform, assuming that it would pacify the South. Yet, as Whitman noted, Buchanan was unaware of growing antislavery expansion sentiment.

Indeed, the irresolute and pliable Buchanan remained a "dough-face." Whitman charged that his proslavery compromises went beyond those of Millard Fillmore and Franklin Pierce; they antagonized the Northern wing of the party, causing it to split. Buchanan had influenced a Northern United States Supreme Court justice to join the Southern majority on the court in the Dred Scott case (decided 6 March 1857), holding that the Congress had no power to prohibit slavery in the territories. In his inaugural address, Buchanan had assured all Kansas settlers the right to express freely and independently their views on the slavery question. Yet when a small minority of proslavery settlers drafted a constitution at Lecompton in September 1857, voters had to vote either for a constitution "with slavery" or "without the further introduction of slavery." (With the Free-Soilers refusing to participate in the referendum, the constitution was overwhelmingly adopted.) Buchanan accepted the Lecompton Constitution and recommended that the Congress admit Kansas as the sixteenth slave state.

Whitman rebuked Buchanan for failing to embrace the North and the South; instead, he said, the president "labored with might and main in the interests of slavery" (*I Sit* 94). In "To a President" Whitman, who associated democracy with nature, reprimands Buchanan for not having learned of the "politics of Nature." In his pre-Darwinian outlook, Whitman ascribes to nature such traits as fullness, righteousness, fairness, equality, and dignity. He accuses the president of not understanding that these qualities are necessary for the nation and that anything less than these attributes will be sloughed off.

Bernard Hirschhorn

Bibliography

Nicols, Roy Franklin. *The Disruption of American Democracy.* New York: Macmillan, 1948.

Pressly, Thomas J. *Americans Interpret Their Civil War.* New York: Free Press, 1962.

Reynolds, David S. *Walt Whitman's America: A Cultural Biography.* New York: Knopf, 1995.

Traubel, Horace. *With Walt Whitman in Camden.* Vol. 3. 1914. New York: Rowman and Littlefield, 1961.

Whitman, Walt. *Complete Poetry and Collected Prose.* Ed. Justin Kaplan. New York: Library of America, 1982.

———. *I Sit and Look Out: Editorials from the Brooklyn Daily Times.* Ed. Emory Holloway and Vernolian Schwarz. New York: Columbia UP, 1932.

See also DEMOCRATIC PARTY; "EIGHTEENTH PRESIDENCY!, THE"; PRESIDENTS, UNITED STATES; "TO THE STATES, TO IDENTIFY THE 16TH, 17TH, OR 18TH PRESIDENTIAD"

"To a Stranger" (1860)

The twenty-second of the "Calamus" poems underwent almost no changes from the manuscript for the 1860 to later editions. It is a very tightly joined narrative of encounter and desire. Of the ten lines, half begin with "I," four with "You," and the first- and second-person pronouns structure every line, moving toward a union of self and other. The passing stranger becomes an object of desire who can evoke all earlier objects, recall the past, and promise a future.

Although the poem somewhat self-consciously tries to universalize its erotic desire by adding a feminine alternative in two lines ("You must be he I was seeking, or she I was seeking"), it is clearly written in celebration of urban male desire. Whitman manages to make out of a chance encounter a moment of deep significance and permanence. Such encounters are seen as marking the self indelibly. The poem records the loneliness of unfulfilled desire and the pleasure of visual contact, the longing for connection.

Although Edwin Miller has seen in the poem a need for secrecy, in fact the erotic attraction is the product of a public encounter that recalls a past dreamlike state of comradeship. Whitman makes of such a simple poem a touching record of desire and its expression, once again celebrating a transitory moment over a claimed permanence.

Robert K. Martin

Bibliography

Miller, Edwin Haviland. *Walt Whitman's Poetry: A Psychological Journey.* Boston: Houghton Mifflin, 1968.

See also "CALAMUS"

"To a Western Boy" (1860)

Originally written in 1860 as number 12 in the "Calamus" series of the third edition of *Leaves of Grass,* this four-line poem was extensively revised by Whitman before he considered it finished in 1881. At one point, probably in 1867, he added a different opening line ("O Boy of the West!") and its present title, although he later dropped the opening line in order to make the poem a single interrogative sentence.

In the question it poses to his "eleve," or pupil, this love poem sums up Whitman's belief in the necessity of spiritual communion between men and boys. Using his familiar persona of an aged and wise benefactor, Whitman tells his "eleve" that if he neglects communion with Whitman—"if blood like mine circle not in your veins"—then there is no point in his trying to learn from his teacher. In other words, Whitman's message is that if the boy consciously or unconsciously excludes himself from the circle of men, then Whitman and his student have nothing in common and should sever their relationship. By stating the importance of love between males so strongly, Whitman reinforces a theme he develops in other poems such as "Song of the Open Road" and "Among the Multitude."

Jim McWilliams

Bibliography

Allen, Gay Wilson. *The Solitary Singer: A Critical Biography of Walt Whitman.* 1955. Rev. ed. 1967. Chicago: U of Chicago P, 1985.

Miller, Edwin Haviland. *Walt Whitman's Poetry: A Psychological Journey.* Boston: Houghton Mifflin, 1968.

Whitman, Walt. *Leaves of Grass: Comprehensive Reader's Edition.* Ed. Harold W. Blodgett and Sculley Bradley. New York: New York UP, 1965.

———. *Whitman's Manuscripts: "Leaves of Grass" (1860).* Ed. Fredson Bowers. Chicago: U of Chicago P, 1955.

See also "CALAMUS"; *LEAVES OF GRASS,* 1860 EDITION

"To One Shortly to Die" (1860)

Included in a cluster of poems ("Whispers of Heavenly Death") contemplating the mysteries of life and death, this poem contains a number of themes and elements Whitman explored earlier in a variety of works. Philosophical in its outlook, "To One Shortly to Die" echoes in part his earlier poem "Crossing Brooklyn Ferry" (1856), and also suggests the theme of physical decay he explored in "This Compost" (1856).

As he speaks directly to his reader, Whitman assumes the persona of one who has successfully transcended the barrier of time, a theme he explored in greater detail in "Crossing Brooklyn Ferry." Claiming that he is "more than nurse," "more than parent or neighbor," Whitman approaches the reader, absolves the reader of all but the spiritual body, and gently prepares him for the inevitability of physical death, while reminding his subject that spiritual existence is eternal.

Whitman speaks from the standpoint of a god, one who claims to be "exact" and "merciless," yet one who professes deep love for his subject. Whitman becomes a comforter. "Softly I lay my right hand upon you," he proclaims as he prepares the appointed one for a celestial journey. The physical self will remain behind, becoming "excrementitious," a term reminiscent of the "foul meat" and "sour dead" he alluded to in "This Compost." Physical life is rank in stark contrast to eternal life where "the sun bursts through," and Whitman assures his reader that medicines and friends become irrelevant as "strong thoughts fill you, and confidence."

Both poems reflect Whitman's conviction of the fetid, putrid nature of physical existence, a theme he was about to experience in all of its loathsome reality as he nursed the victims of physical brutality during the Civil War. Death is inevitable, yet tolerable. Whitman does not experience sorrow at the thought of death; he "congratulates" his reader as he comforts him with the assurance that "I am with you."

Julian B. Freund

Bibliography

Miller, James E., Jr. *A Critical Guide to "Leaves of Grass."* Chicago: U of Chicago P, 1957.

Whitman, Walt. *Complete Poetry and Collected Prose.* Ed. Justin Kaplan. New York: Library of America, 1982.

See also "CROSSING BROOKLYN FERRY"; "THIS COMPOST"; "WHISPERS OF HEAVENLY DEATH" (CLUSTER)

"To Rich Givers" (1860)

Included in the "Messenger Leaves" cluster of the third (1860) edition of *Leaves of Grass*, this poem was published in Boston by Thayer and Eldridge. The "Messenger Leaves" cluster was dropped in 1867, and its fifteen poems dispersed throughout *Leaves of Grass*. In 1871 "To Rich Givers" was placed in the cluster "Songs of Parting," and was moved to its present placement in "By the Roadside" in 1881. The same title was used throughout all editions.

The poem describes the relationship between the poet and "rich givers," who could literally be patrons or readers of the poem. Gay Wilson Allen, in his biography of Whitman, notes that in this poem Whitman expresses a wish for wealthy patrons, but the poem does not have to be read in a strictly biographical way. Unashamed to accept "sustenance" from "rich givers," the "I" of the poem accepts "cheerfully" a "hut and garden" and "a little money"—images evocative of Henry David Thoreau's *Walden* (1854).

Giving becomes a form of enrichment for the giver, as the title of the poem indicates. The givers are rich because what the poet bestows upon them enriches them even more. Thus, the wealth of the givers comes from what the poetry gives to them—"the entrance to all the gifts of the universe"—an open-ended world. By the end of the poem, the meanings and implications of "rich givers" widen to include the poet, this poem, and the "poems" of line 2. The "you" and "I" of line 1 thus become interchangeable, with "you" as reader/patron or poet.

Maire Mullins

Bibliography

Allen, Gay Wilson. *The Solitary Singer: A Critical Biography of Walt Whitman.* 1955. Rev. ed. 1967. Chicago: U of Chicago P, 1985.
Larson, Kerry C. *Whitman's Drama of Consensus.* Chicago: U of Chicago P, 1988.
Zweig, Paul. *Walt Whitman: The Making of the Poet.* New York: Basic Books, 1984.

See also "BY THE ROADSIDE"; *LEAVES OF GRASS, 1860 EDITION*

"To Soar in Freedom and in Fullness of Power" (1897)

Written in 1890 or 1891, "To Soar in Freedom and in Fullness of Power" was first published in *Leaves of Grass* in the posthumous tenth edition of 1897–1898. "To Soar" is the first in a group of thirteen poems added to *Leaves* as a third annex. Horace Traubel, one of Whitman's three literary executors, prefaces the 1897 addendum with a conversation in which Whitman apparently authorizes and names this third annex "Old Age Echoes." However, the conversation is ambiguous, and many editors exclude the entire annex from their editions of *Leaves*, considering the 1891–1892 edition to be the final, authorized version.

The two sentences of "To Soar" were transcribed directly from a two-page, unpublished prose fragment entitled "My Poetry is more the Poetry of Sight than Sound." This title gives some hints at a theme for the poem. In "To Soar" Whitman challenges the tradition of poetry as bard-song or bird-song and chooses rather a visual ("more sight than sound") or experiential (flights, broad circles, soaring) metaphor for a poet's work. Whitman seeks a new metaphor for a new poetry for a New World.

Many critics hold that Whitman's best poetry had already been written several decades before his death, so these final poems are largely, and perhaps unjustly, ignored. These five lines obviously belong in any study of birds in Whitman, and the poem houses those ubiquitous Whitman boarders, the neat Psalmic parallelism and contrast. The fact that "To Soar" was part of a possible prose preface to "Echoes" suggests the poem as a guide to reading the entire third annex. It may also be helpful to consider the poem a retrospective work, a piece to be read in conjunction with Whitman's essay entitled "A Backward Glance O'er Travel'd Roads" (1888).

Nathan C. Faries

Bibliography

Whitman, Walt. *Leaves of Grass: Comprehensive Reader's Edition.* Ed. Harold W. Blodgett and Sculley Bradley. New York: New York UP, 1965.

See also "BACKWARD GLANCE O'ER TRAVEL'D ROADS, A"; "OLD AGE ECHOES"

"To the Garden the World" (1860)

First published in *Leaves* (1860) as number 1 in "Enfans d'Adam," this poem was retitled "To the Garden the World" in the 1867 edition of *Leaves* and placed as the lead poem in the "Children of Adam" cluster, where it remained through subsequent editions. Whitman heralds the "Adam" cluster (1860) as "A string of Poems . . . embodying the amative love of woman" and treating Adam "as a central figure and type" of the new man (*Notebooks* 1:412–413).

With annunciatory confidence, "To the Garden" validates the religious sacredness of the natural and sensual world. Juxtaposing "the garden" (with its religious-mythic associations) and "the world" (conventionally viewed as the antithesis of Edenic joy), the opening line posits a new holy garden that is the physical/sensual/sexual world itself. The poem suggests a sense, simultaneously, of cyclical and linear time: the new Adam is resurrected out of the "revolving cycles" of the past; yet he also advances into an altogether new age of human history that honors material things (the body, the senses, sex) that were formerly disparaged.

"To the Garden" evokes, explicitly and implicitly, many of the "Adam" cluster's inspiriting themes and preoccupations: sex, the physical urge toward re-creation and regeneration (both sexual and spiritual), unashamed celebration of the self and identity, and a subversive attitude toward traditional and conventionally repressive notions about both the human body and the world's body.

John E. Schwiebert

Bibliography

Allen, Gay Wilson. *Walt Whitman as Man, Poet and Legend.* Carbondale: Southern Illinois UP, 1961.

Aspiz, Harold. *Walt Whitman and the Body Beautiful.* Urbana: U of Illinois P, 1980.

Killingsworth, M. Jimmie. *Walt Whitman's Poetry of the Body: Sexuality, Politics, and the Text.* Chapel Hill: U of North Carolina P, 1989.

Schwiebert, John E. *The Frailest Leaves: Whitman's Poetic Technique and Style in the Short Poem.* New York: Lang, 1992.

Whitman, Walt. *Notebooks and Unpublished Prose Manuscripts.* Ed. Edward F. Grier. 6 vols. New York: New York UP, 1984.

See also AMERICAN ADAM; "CHILDREN OF ADAM"; HUMAN BODY; SEX AND SEXUALITY

"To the Leaven'd Soil They Trod" (1865–1866)

First published as the last poem in *Sequel to Drum-Taps* (1865–1866), "To the Leaven'd Soil They Trod" was later added, also as the last poem, to the "Drum-Taps" cluster of *Leaves of Grass* in 1871. While its title remained consistent, in the 1881 edition of *Leaves of Grass* two significant changes were made. What had been the second line was dropped: "Not cities, nor man alone, nor war, nor the dead" (1871 *Leaves*). The present line 11 was moved from its original position as line 7 and revised from the following: "To the average earth, the wordless earth, witness of war and peace" (1871 *Leaves*).

As the last poem of the "Drum-Taps" cluster, "Leaven'd Soil" provides a definite conclusion to these poems about the Civil War. The war over, America's soil is "leaven'd": it is rising and growing, not desiccated by the death and destruction of the war. Furthermore, the pun on "leaven'd"—given leaves or once again adorned with leaves—suggests that the land is enlivened. This newly fertile land becomes the "average earth"—average because from a human standpoint it has absorbed the blood of common men from both sides in the war and because from a political standpoint it has proven the strength of democracy and the Union. It is average, too, because the equality implied in the surviving and strengthened Union distributes the worth of the nation equitably (implied by the balanced references to North and South and the key references to the Allegheny Mountains and the Mississippi River, which geographically link the North and South).

The pun on "leaven'd" also associates the war, the resulting "leaven'd soil," and Whitman's poems. The nation's land answers the poet, "but not in words." It answers by its demonstration of unity, by its persistence to exist on its terms rather than on those imposed by human beings. The poem's last two lines provide the most effective reconciling and unifying imagery: the opposites of Northern ice and Southern sun join to nourish the poet's songs, to sustain the leaves of grass. Finally, the reciprocity between the poet's songs and the land indicates that Whitman is "commensurate with [the] people" and that "he incarnates [his country's] geography," essential criteria which he established for the American poet in the 1855 Preface to *Leaves of Grass* (*Comprehensive* 711).

Steven Olson

Bibliography

Whitman, Walt. *Leaves of Grass: Comprehensive Reader's Edition.* Ed. Harold W. Blodgett and Sculley Bradley. New York: New York UP, 1965.

———. *Leaves of Grass: A Textual Variorum of the Printed Poems.* Ed. Sculley Bradley, Harold W. Blodgett, Arthur Golden, and William White. 3 vols. New York: New York UP, 1980.

See also CIVIL WAR, THE; "DRUM-TAPS"; SEQUEL TO DRUM-TAPS

"To the States" (1860)

Titled "Walt Whitman's Caution" in 1860, on its first appearance in *Leaves of Grass* as one of the "Messenger Leaves," and also in 1871 and 1876 as one of the "Songs of Insurrection," "To the States" acquired its final title in 1881 when it appeared in "Inscriptions."

This three-line poem is important beyond its size, less for any reasons of poetic form than for its illumination of political conditions around the time of the Civil War in the United States, when challenges to federal authority—perceived as the enemy within—prefigured the post–Cold War 1990s.

Repetitions connect the three lines—obey/obedience, enslaved/enslaved—and this connectedness reflects the logical structure of the cautionary miniature. The opening line's injunction is explained and justified by lines 2 and 3, which have a syllogistic force: unquestioning obedience leads to enslavement, and enslavement leads to permanent loss of liberty. The causal progression in lines 2 and 3 is echoed by the gradual limiting of the opening line's address from plural states to one state and then finally to one city within that state.

"States" in line 1 is not a shorthand for a radically unified and single-willed United States of America but represents the plurality of states with their own independent rights. Presumably "any city" is being enjoined to resist its own state. By calling on all smaller units to resist the larger units in which they find themselves, Whitman is implicitly extending his call to the individual, who must likewise resist conformity to the group. In fact, in an 1856 political tract not published until after his death—"The Eighteenth Presidency!"—Whitman asserts that "the rights of individuals" are "signified by the impregnable rights of The States, the substratum of this Union" (Whitman 1321).

In its historical context, the poem's ultimate complication is revealed; the poet who took as his hero Abraham Lincoln, the savior of the Union, here takes a stand seemingly seditious. It is important to remember, however, that the forces of the North, meant to quell rebellion by secessionists, were organized throughout the Civil War into units designated by each soldier's state of origin.

The popularity of the imperative *"Resist much, obey little"* is clear from its being co-opted for commercial use by a footwear firm in the November 1992 issue of *Glamour* (with credit to Whitman).

Philip Dacey

Bibliography

Erkkila, Betsy. *Whitman the Political Poet.* New York: Oxford UP, 1989.

Whitman, Walt. *Complete Poetry and Collected Prose.* Ed. Justin Kaplan. New York: Library of America, 1982.

See also "EIGHTEENTH PRESIDENCY!, THE"; "INSCRIPTIONS"

"To the States, To Identify the 16th, 17th, or 18th Presidentiad" (1860)

This eight-line poem was originally published under its present title as the eighth poem in the "Messenger Leaves" cluster in the 1860 *Leaves of Grass.* In its earliest manuscript, however, it bore the title "A Past Presidentiad, and one to come also." Its text remained unchanged in all succeeding editions, except for minor alterations in punctuation and capitalization. Whitman placed it in the "By the Roadside" cluster in 1881.

Betsy Erkkila calls "Messenger Leaves" "a kind of political jeremiad," with "To the States" being one of the main examples of Whitman's excoriation of contemporary national politicians (183). The 16th, 17th and 18th presidentiads of the poem's subtitle identify the presidencies of Millard Fillmore (1850–1853), Franklin Pierce (1853–1857), and James Buchanan (1857–1861), respectively. Whitman takes all three to task, along with the Congressmen and the "great Judges," for their political opportunism and corruption. The poem objects as well to the political atmosphere stemming from the Compromise of 1850, which accommodated slavery in the territories at the expense of free soil.

"To the States" envisions the solution to national corruption as a natural process—the political awakening of the democratic masses figured as a gathering storm. Whitman draws a similar opposition between organic popular politics and official corruption in another of the "Messenger Leaves," "To a President" (1860). The storm imagery in "To the States" foreshadows the Civil War as well as Whitman's attempts to rationalize it as part of an inevitable, natural cycle. The poem's role as a harbinger of war was reinforced by its final placement as the last poem in the "By the Roadside" cluster, immediately preceding "Drum-Taps."

Though the poem's tones of anger and sarcasm are unusual in Whitman's writing of the later 1850s, they are not unprecedented. Besides the other "Messenger Leaves," this poem's political invective recalls one of the earliest *Leaves of Grass* poems, "A Boston Ballad (1854)" (1855), which satirizes the trial of Anthony Burns, a fugitive slave, as the return of British tyranny. The characterization of politicians in "To the States" as "scum floating atop of the waters," "bats and night-dogs," also echoes the language of Whitman's 1856 lecture-essay "The Eighteenth Presidency!" The poem's parenthetical concluding lines offer a milder version of the essay's call for young, white workingmen to rise up and cleanse the Republic of its political corruption.

Carl Smeller

Bibliography
Erkkila, Betsy. *Whitman the Political Poet.* New York: Oxford UP, 1989.
Whitman, Walt. *Complete Poetry and Collected Prose.* Ed. Justin Kaplan. New York: Library of America, 1982.
———. *Whitman's Manuscripts: "Leaves of Grass" (1860).* Ed. Fredson Bowers. Chicago: U of Chicago P, 1955.

See also "BOSTON BALLAD (1854), A"; "BY THE ROADSIDE"; COMPROMISE OF 1850; "EIGHTEENTH PRESIDENCY!, THE"; POLITICAL VIEWS; PRESIDENTS, UNITED STATES; "TO A PRESIDENT"

"To the Sun-Set Breeze" (1890)

"To the Sun-Set Breeze" was first published in *Lippincott's Magazine* in December of 1890 and included in the second annex, "Good-Bye my Fancy," in the 1891–1892 edition of *Leaves of Grass*.

While many readers have dismissed the poems of Whitman's later years, a major poet, Ezra Pound, singled out this very late one as representing Whitman's best artistry: "And yet if a man has written lines like Whitman's 'To the Sunset Breeze' one has to love him. I think we have not yet paid enough attention to the deliberate artistry of the man, not in details but in the large" (qtd. in Bergman 60).

The poet describes himself: "Me, old, alone, sick, weak-down, melted-worn with sweat" and the relief he gains one hot day from a late breeze, which he speaks to as if alive. In fact he addresses the breeze (as "thou" or its variants) twelve times during the sixteen lines, an archaic device that would appear ludicrous here in a lesser poet. Later he attributes divinity to the breeze, broadening its origins and influence, without, characteristically, letting go of its material attributes: "For thou art spiritual, Godly, most of all known to my sense." The earlier images are highly sensual, appropriately stressing the tactile, for which Whitman's verse is well known, as in line 7: "So sweet thy primitive taste to breathe within—thy soothing fingers on my face and hands."

But the kinesthetic sense is seldom celebrated for its own sake in Whitman. Throughout this poem the cooling breeze is given mystical and symbolic stature. At the end, in a cross between doubt and faith, he asks: "Hast thou no soul? Can I not know, identify thee?" Yet he has already established the breeze as curative, spiritual, and emanating from the world of his dead companions, the other vast world, God's world, inscrutable but benign. His final questions, then, are probably rhetorical; yes, the breeze does have a soul, and, yes, he can identify it.

For a more extensive analysis of this important poem, see "Whitman and the Correspondent Breeze," by Dwight Kalita, who connects it to the poems of other romantic poets, notably William Wordsworth.

David B. Baldwin

Bibliography
Bergman, Herbert. "Ezra Pound and Walt Whitman." *American Literature* 27 (1955): 56–61.
Kalita, Dwight. "Whitman and the Correspondent Breeze." *Walt Whitman Review* 21 (1975): 125–130.
Whitman, Walt. *Leaves of Grass: Comprehensive Reader's Edition.* Ed. Harold W. Blodgett and Sculley Bradley. New York: New York UP, 1965.

—. *Leaves of Grass: A Textual Variorum of the Printed Poems.* Ed. Sculley Bradley, Harold W. Blodgett, Arthur Golden, and William White. Vol. 3. New York: New York UP, 1980.

See also AGE AND AGING; "GOOD-BYE MY FANCY" (SECOND ANNEX); LEAVES OF GRASS, 1891–1892 EDITION

"To Thee Old Cause" (1871)

"To Thee Old Cause" invokes a term, "good old cause," with political currency from the time of the British Puritan Commonwealth, when it referred to efforts to secure civil and religious liberty through expanded powers of Parliament. In jottings in *Notes and Fragments* Whitman defined the term "good old cause," which also resonated strongly in American political struggles as that "which promulges liberty, justice, the cause of the people as against infidels and tyrants" (55).

The association of the term with Puritan struggles for self-determination against monarchical and ecclesiastical hierarchies fits Whitman's preoccupation with enlightened self-determination for individual democratic citizens as explored in "Song of Myself" and other poems, as well as various prose works, including his prefaces to his poems. In fact, the Puritan practice of self-examination, separated from doctrinal religious concerns, may be said to lead directly to "Song of Myself" through Emerson and other such apostles of the self.

However, "Old Cause," first published in 1871, claims for Whitman's work at least two historical dimensions. In his poetry, he addresses not only the political independence of citizens growing out of the Revolutionary War but the necessity for union affirmed by the recently concluded American Civil War; "my book and the war are one," he says in the poem. How Whitman reconciled the apparently contradictory claims of independence and union he revealed in "Origins of Attempted Secession," where he defined the Civil War as an internal struggle, not of "two distinct and separate peoples, but a conflict (often happening, and very fierce) between the passions and paradoxes of one and the same identity" (*Prose Works* 2:426–427). In his 1872 Preface to *As a Strong Bird on Pinions Free,* he called *Leaves of Grass* "the song of a great composite *democratic individual,* male or female" which is the basis of

"an aggregated, inseparable, unprecedented, vast, composite, electric *democratic nationality*" (*Prose Works* 2:463).

Whitman's assertion in the poem that "all war through time was really fought" for the "old cause" reflects his belief that recent scientific theories of evolution suggest that all human struggles are essentially strivings for self-determination. In the 1872 Preface, he rejoices that "the old theology of the East," hierarchical authoritarianism, will "disappear" while "science . . . prepares the way" for "the new theology." It will be the basis for a "sane and complete personality" and ultimately a "grand and electric nationality" which will unite the nation in a spiritual—that is, secular-religious—bond (*Prose Works* 2:462). This he says in "Old Cause" is the "axis" on which *Leaves* turns.

Margaret H. Duggar

Bibliography
Erkkila, Betsy. *Whitman the Political Poet.* New York: Oxford UP, 1989.
Gohdes, Clarence. "Whitman and the 'Good Old Cause.'" *American Literature* 34 (1962): 400–403.
Whitman, Walt. *Leaves of Grass: Comprehensive Reader's Edition.* Ed. Harold W. Blodgett and Sculley Bradley. New York: New York UP, 1965.
—. *Notes and Fragments.* Ed. Richard Maurice Bucke. 1899. Folcroft, Pa.: Folcroft Library Editions, 1972.
—. *Prose Works 1892.* Ed. Floyd Stovall. 2 vols. New York: New York UP, 1963–1964.

See also AMERICAN REVOLUTION; FREEDOM; INDIVIDUALISM; "INSCRIPTIONS"

"To Think of Time" (1855)

In the first edition of *Leaves of Grass,* this important poem (now neglected) appeared between "A Song for Occupations" and "The Sleepers." The pioneer biographers (especially Asselineau), concerned with Whitman's early explorations of "problems" of evil and death (1855–1860), gave it prominence. Allen writes: "If Walt Whitman has a major theme, this is it, in 1855 and later" (*Walt Whitman* 79). Originally untitled, it was named "Burial Poem" in 1856, became "Burial" in 1860 and 1867, and "To Think of Time" in 1872.

In the final edition of *Leaves,* this poem concludes the "Autumn Rivulets" cluster. In his *Critical Guide* Miller shows how—"without central symbol or metaphor"—it contributes, together with other major poems, to the transition to "Whispers of Heavenly Death," "bridg[ing] the way 'from Life to Death'" (237). However, Miller's unfavorable evaluation of the poem is unfair. "To Think of Time" is broadly representative of the early Whitman and has many realistic and symbolic links to other early poems: the "old stagedriver" to "Occupations," river and sea passages to "Crossing Brooklyn Ferry," and so forth. Its strong central metaphor-idea is the flow of time toward death and immortality.

Allen and Davis (1955) describe it well: its thoughts and "factual details" make a structure that "logically builds up" to Whitman's conclusion; its effects range from implicit ironies that yield to "flow" and heavenly transcendence; its pattern is systematic (150). Furthermore, in content and language "To Think of Time" exhibits qualities that place it among Whitman's best. Two parts are especially vivid: the deathbed scene (section 2) and the funeral scenes (section 4). As a whole, this is a metaphysical poem, with subtle ironies conveyed by quiet wit and even humor: "The living look upon the corpse with their eyesight, / But without eyesight lingers a different living [spirit] and looks curiously on the corpse" (section 2). Section 8 contains a powerful list of people who are "not nothing" (an attractive double negative), and in "Do you think I could walk pleasantly and well-suited toward annihilation?" there may be a pun in "well-suited."

This poem earns its emphatic conclusion: "I swear I think there is nothing but immortality!" (section 9). Beginning with penetrating questions (somewhat as in "This Compost")— "Have you dreaded those earth-beetles?" (section 1)—it develops persuasive answers. Though the "black lines" of burial (section 3) do indeed "stand out starkly," as Miller points out, the rest is far from the "paleness" he feels characterizes the poem as a whole (238), and the reader comes to believe with the poet that "We must have the indestructible breed of the best, regardless of time" (section 8, 1855 *Leaves*)—that is, immortality.

Finally, as an effective American treatment of an ancient theme, this poem helps establish Whitman as a precursor of modernism. Wyndham Lewis made the connection (1927), em- phasizing not "thought," however, but immersion in nature, history, and life (his example is *Specimen Days*): "Whitman was . . . its earliest professor" (368). Whitman's broodings on time and humanity produced rich results, of which "To Think of Time" is a metaphysical epitome.

Sholom J. Kahn

Bibliography

Allen, Gay Wilson. *Walt Whitman.* 1961. Rev. ed. Detroit: Wayne State UP, 1969.

Allen, Gay Wilson, and Charles T. Davis, eds. *Walt Whitman's Poems.* New York: New York UP, 1955.

Asselineau, Roger. *The Evolution of Walt Whitman.* 2 vols. Cambridge, Mass.: Harvard UP, 1960–1962.

Kahn, Sholom J. "Whitman's Wit and Wisdom." *Essays in Honour of A.A. Mendilow.* Hebrew University Studies in Literature. Jerusalem: Magnes, 1982. 268–286.

Lewis, Wyndham. *Time and Western Man.* 1927. Boston: Beacon, 1957.

Miller, James E., Jr. *A Critical Guide to "Leaves of Grass."* Chicago: U of Chicago P, 1957.

See also "AUTUMN RIVULETS"; DEATH; IMMORTALITY; *LEAVES OF GRASS, 1855* EDITION; TIME

"To You [Whoever you are . . .]" (1856)

This poem first appeared in the 1856 edition of *Leaves of Grass* as "Poem of You, Whoever You Are," and took the title "To You" in 1871. It is one of three poems Whitman published with the same title in various editions of *Leaves.* One of these, a two-line fragment, appears in the "Inscriptions" section of the final edition; the second appeared in the 1860 and 1867 editions, but was dropped by Whitman from later editions. The 1856 version, of around fifty lines, may reasonably be taken, then, as his fullest direct expression on an important theme in *Leaves:* the theme of his dependence on each of his individual readers to bring to completion, or, as he puts it in "Full of Life now" (1860), to "realize" his poems.

"To You" shares with numerous other poems in *Leaves* an insistence that Whitman is intimately, physically present to his readers. "I place my hand upon you," he writes; "I whisper with my lips close to your ear." But "To

You" is distinct in its aggressive foregrounding of the paradoxical logic of such a sensuous intimacy. In order to get this close to every possible reader or "you," in other words, Whitman has to strip away all particularities, good and bad, all that might limit his offer of a democratic embrace to less than all of humanity. What's left, paradoxically, is a universalized and curiously anonymous individualism, a cosmic and spiritual essence which constitutes what is most perfect and beautiful in each individual, but only in the abstract.

What Whitman asks his readers to complete, in "To You," is a relation of erotic spiritualism, which miraculously elevates the absolute particularity of sensuous, physical experience to the level of a cosmic universal. He can only proffer the abstract universal; it remains up to each reader to animate it, so to speak, with his or her own particular, embodied experiences and desires. "Whoever you are," he pleads, then, "you be my poem." The reward for the reader's returned desire, his or her self-transformation into his "poem," is a kind of apotheosis; thus he pictures a halo, a "nimbus of gold-color'd light," around the head of each "you" that he addresses.

In *Pragmatism* (1907) William James praised "To You" for its philosophical pluralism, in its exhortations that each individual reader, each "you," should strive to realize his or her potential greatness, in whatever particular form it might take. Justin Kaplan notes that James also hailed Whitman as an apostle of the "religion of healthy-mindedness" (qtd. in Kaplan 56). David Reynolds has expanded on the optimistic religiosity of "To You," suggesting that the nimbus image in this poem marks Whitman's debt to the Luminist school of American painting, in which effulgent light was the sign of God's immanent presence. Indeed, in 1857 Whitman described his ongoing work on *Leaves* as "the Great Construction of the New Bible" (*Notebooks* 1:353), and "To You" might be described as an expression of Whitman's religion of progressive democracy, where the circulation of mutual desire transforms individualism into a poetic principle of universal, spiritual identity.

Terry Mulcaire

Bibliography

Breitweiser, Mitchell. "Who Speaks in Whitman's Poems?" *Bucknell Review* 28.1 (1983): 121–143.

James, William. *Pragmatism: A New Name for Some Old Ways of Thinking.* New York: Longmans, Green, 1907.
Kaplan, Justin. *Walt Whitman: A Life.* New York: Simon and Schuster, 1980.
Moon, Michael. *Disseminating Whitman: Revision and Corporeality in "Leaves of Grass."* Cambridge, Mass.: Harvard UP, 1991.
Reynolds, David S. *Walt Whitman's America: A Cultural Biography.* New York: Knopf, 1995.
Whitman, Walt. *Leaves of Grass: Comprehensive Reader's Edition.* Ed. Harold W. Blodgett and Sculley Bradley. New York: New York UP, 1965.
———. *Notebooks and Unpublished Prose Manuscripts.* Ed. Edward F. Grier. 6 vols. New York: New York UP, 1984.

See also "Birds of Passage"; Leaves of Grass, 1856 Edition; Poetic Theory

"Tomb Blossoms, The" (1842)

This short story appeared first in *United States Magazine and Democratic Review,* January 1842. For further publication history, see Brasher's edition of *The Early Poems and the Fiction.*

In this well-balanced story, the frets of city life are opposed to the peacefulness of country living and death itself. The reminiscent narrator recalls something that happened when he lived in a country village. Tired and sullen, he returned home from a short visit to New York City. Next morning, refreshed, he sauntered off for a walk and came upon an old woman tending two graves, old Mrs. Delaree, a widow and inmate of the almshouse. She and her husband were miserably poor and, as foreigners from the West Indies, unwelcome. He died of poverty while she was ill. She tended two graves because no one knew in which one her husband lay. The narrator recognized the grave as a kind of friend. He admits that lately he does not dread dying.

The title is syntactically ambiguous. The blossoms, of course, are the flowers that the woman sets upon the graves; the tomb, as a symbol of death, blossoms into a friend. Kaplan sees the title as one of the central tropes of Whitman's *Leaves of Grass,* while Callow sees in the story Whitman's compulsive interest in doubles and in death.

Critics consign this tale to Whitman's early "dark" works.

Patrick McGuire

Bibliography

Allen, Gay Wilson. *The Solitary Singer: A Critical Biography of Walt Whitman.* 1955. Rev. ed. 1967. Chicago: U of Chicago P, 1985.

Callow, Philip. *From Noon to Starry Night: A Life of Walt Whitman.* Chicago: Ivan R. Dee, 1992.

Kaplan, Justin. *Walt Whitman: A Life.* New York: Simon and Schuster, 1980.

Reynolds, David S. *Walt Whitman's America: A Cultural Biography.* New York: Knopf, 1995.

Whitman, Walt. *The Early Poems and the Fiction.* Ed. Thomas L. Brasher. New York: New York UP, 1963.

See also POPULAR CULTURE, WHITMAN AND; SHORT FICTION, WHITMAN'S

Trall, Dr. Russell Thacher (1812–1877)

Dr. Trall, a hydropathic physician, established the first water-cure establishment in New York City (1844) and in the 1850s—when the water-cure fad crested—became "the high priest" of the water-cure system (qtd. in Aspiz 44). He wrote some thirty books on a broad range of health reform topics, integrating the principles of hydropathy with those of other hygienic and reformist cults; edited Fowler and Wells's *Water-Cure Journal* and other periodicals; and headed the coed drug- and alcohol-free New York Hygieo-Therapeutic College—a gathering place for reformist intellectuals. His career was involved with Fowler and Wells, who published his books and sponsored many of his lectures.

Although unsympathetic to the extremism of the "cold-water worshippers" (qtd. in Aspiz 46), Whitman shared many of Trall's interests: the need for clean water, pure food, fresh air, and personal hygiene; opposition to alcohol and drugs; and advanced views on women and sexuality. Whitman was familiar with Trall's work. He reviewed Trall's *Family Gymnasium* (1857) and his manuscript notes on physique are derived, in part, from Trall's writings. Trall was assistant editor for Fowler and Wells's *Life Illustrated* in 1855–1856, when Whitman wrote several man-about-town essays for that journal.

Harold Aspiz

Bibliography

Aspiz, Harold. *Walt Whitman and the Body Beautiful.* Urbana: U of Illinois P, 1980.

Logan, Marshall Scott. "Hydropathy, or Water Cure." *Pseudo-Science and Society in Nineteenth-Century America.* Ed. Arthur Wrobel. Lexington: UP of Kentucky, 1987. 74–99.

Stern, Madeleine B. *Heads & Headlines: The Phrenological Fowlers.* Norman: U of Oklahoma P, 1971.

Whorton, J.C. "Russell Thacher Trall." *Dictionary of American Medical Biography.* Ed. Martin Kaufman et al. Westport, Conn.: Greenwood, 1984. 751.

See also FOWLER, LORENZO NILES AND ORSON SQUIRE; *LIFE ILLUSTRATED*; PSEUDOSCIENCE; WELLS, SAMUEL ROBERTS

"Tramp and Strike Questions, The" (1882)

Written in 1879 and published in *Specimen Days* (1882), "The Tramp and Strike Questions" marks a low point in Walt Whitman's hopes for the evolution of a successful New World democracy. Part of a proposed but undelivered public lecture, it expresses Whitman's profound disenchantment with the social upheavals and economic travails that swept across Reconstruction-era America after the crash of 1873, and it stands as the inconclusive end of Whitman's remarks on the growing divide between rich and poor in Gilded Age America. What he described in passing in *Democratic Vistas* (1871) as "that problem, the labor question, beginning to open like a yawning gulf, rapidly widening every year" (*Complete* 990), has become the "grim and spectral dangers" (1063) of tramps and strikes. After a span of years which had endured the failed Long Strike in the anthracite mines of Pennsylvania and the terrorist activities of the Molly Maguires, the great railroad strike of 1877, the use of federal troops against civilian Americans, the riots of the unemployed in Tompkins Square, New York, and, in Whitman's home city of Camden, the many sufferings of working people, Whitman had come to fear that the intractable problems of the Old World were infecting the United States. No longer was the "abstract question of democracy" most pressing but rather those "of social and economic organization, the treatment of working-people by employers, and all that goes along with it—not only the wage-payment part, but a certain spirit and principle, to vivify anew these relations" (1064).

Casting the American and French Revolutions as "great strikes," Whitman hints of the impending "homœopathic" cure (1064) that the "vast crops of poor, desperate, dissatisfied, nomadic, miserably-waged populations" might inflict upon the diseased nation, and if the status quo continues, he laments that the republican experiment must be considered "at heart an unhealthy failure" (1065). As Newton Arvin has observed, it was in this same humor that Whitman created for his sixth edition of *Leaves of Grass* the eventually discarded cluster "Songs of Insurrection," calling for healthy revolt in the "more and more insidious grip of capital" (*Workshop* 229). In "Tramp and Strike," Whitman, who had long celebrated and sympathized with workers and laborers and captured the vigorous spirit of the artisan "roughs" of 1850s New York, recorded his puzzlement at this new class of working poor. The piece concludes with a diary entry from February 1879 in which Whitman is astonished by the sight of three "quite good-looking American men, of respectable personal appearance, two of them young" (*Complete* 1065) tramping along, scrounging for scraps. Dismay and bewilderment predominate. Because he cannot reconcile the healthy workingmen's bodies with their broken spirits, Whitman, who would have placed these setbacks within the context of a country evolving toward a visionary democracy in *Democratic Vistas,* can neither defer these "questions" nor offer poetic or practical solutions to them.

Stephen Rachman

Bibliography

Allen, Gay Wilson. *The Solitary Singer: A Critical Biography of Walt Whitman.* 1955. Rev. ed. 1967. Chicago: U of Chicago P, 1985.

Arvin, Newton. *Whitman.* New York: Macmillan, 1938.

Erkkila, Betsy. *Whitman the Political Poet.* New York: Oxford UP, 1989.

Reynolds, David S. *Walt Whitman's America: A Cultural Biography.* New York: Knopf, 1995.

Whitman, Walt. *Complete Poetry and Collected Prose.* Ed. Justin Kaplan. New York: Library of America, 1982.

———. *Walt Whitman's Workshop: A Collection of Unpublished Manuscripts.* Ed. Clifton Joseph Furness. Cambridge, Mass.: Harvard UP, 1928.

Wilentz, Sean. *Chants Democratic: New York City & the Rise of the American Working Class, 1788–1850.* New York: Oxford UP, 1984.

See also Arvin, Newton; Democracy; *Democratic Vistas;* Labor and Laboring Classes; Reconstruction

Transcendentalism

Properly speaking, for geographical and social reasons, Walt Whitman was not a transcendentalist, since transcendentalism was a New England phenomenon affecting American scholars and clergymen's relatives. Yet he can be considered the poet of transcendentalism whose coming Emerson had prophesied, but which he failed to be himself, because his poetry was more intellectual than inspired and was, besides, hampered by the straitjacket of traditional prosody. Emerson remained on the threshold of the Promised Land, but his works were the fountain-spring of Whitman's poetry, if we are to believe what Whitman himself said on several occasions, notably to J.T. Trowbridge in 1860: "I was simmering, simmering, simmering; Emerson brought me to a boil" (qtd. in Trowbridge 166). Trowbridge adds: "He freely admitted he could never have written his poems if he had not first 'come to himself,' and that Emerson helped him to 'find himself'" (166). No wonder Whitman addressed Emerson as "Master" in the open letter he appended to the 1856 edition of *Leaves of Grass.* Later, however, he tried to minimize and even deny Emerson's influence, particularly through the medium of John Burroughs's *Notes on Walt Whitman as Poet and Person:* "[U]p to the time he published the quarto edition [of 1855] . . . [he] had never read the Essays or Poems of Mr. Emerson at all. This is positively true" (16–17). He was even more categorical in 1887 in a letter to W.S. Kennedy: "It is of no importance whether I had read Emerson before starting L of G or not. The fact happens to be positively that I had *not*" (*Correspondence* 4:69).

Actually, whether Emerson was the direct source of Whitman's ideas or not, the fact remains that there are striking similarities between the main themes of *Leaves of Grass* and the basic tenets of New England transcendentalism. First of all, both Emerson and Whitman had the revelation of the existence of God in the course of a mystical experience. "Standing on the bare ground," Emerson felt "the currents of the Universal Being circulate through me" and "became part or parcel of God" (Emerson 10). Similarly, Whitman on "a transparent summer morning" discovered "the peace and knowledge that pass all the argument of the earth" and knew that the "spirit of God is the brother of my own" ("Song of Myself," section 5). He never used the word "oversoul," as did Emerson, but his "general soul" ("Chanting the Square Deific," section 4) also circulates through everything that exists and consequently makes all creatures equally divine, men in particular. For Whitman as for Emerson, the true miracles were not those which are reported in the Bible, but the humblest existences around us, the "limitless . . . leaves stiff or drooping in the fields, / And brown ants . . . And mossy scabs of the worm fence, heap'd stones, elder, mullein and poke-weed" ("Song of Myself," section 5). Whitman knew "of nothing else but miracles . . . To me every hour of the light and dark is a miracle, / Every cubic inch of space is a miracle" ("Miracles"). The catalogues he so frequently inserted in his poems were catalogues of miracles. In his eyes, all things were both physical and spiritual presences. The "general soul" was the sum total of innumerable individual souls. According to him, material things have a secret meaning which transcends them. They are symbols; they carry messages. "I hear and behold God in every object . . . I find letters from God dropt in the street, and every one is sign'd by God's name" ("Song of Myself," section 48). Grass is "the handkerchief of the Lord . . . Bearing the owner's name someway in the corners, that we may see and remark, and say *Whose?*" ("Song of Myself," section 6). "Surely there is something more in each of the trees, some living soul. . . . O spirituality of things!" ("Song at Sunset"). In the same way, for Emerson, "the world is a temple whose walls are covered with emblems, pictures and commandments of the Deity" (454).

Transcendentalism, as Emerson pointed out, was a form of idealism: "[T]he Idealism of the present day acquired the name of Transcendental from the use of that term by Immanuel Kant, of Königsberg . . ." (198). There were times when Whitman, too, tended toward idealism: "May-be the things I perceive, the animals, plants, men, hills, shining and flowing waters, . . . may-be these are (as doubtless they are) only apparitions, and the real something has yet to be known" ("Of the Terrible Doubt of Appearances"). Transcendentalism is a form of monism, but Whitman's implicit metaphysics is based on the dualism matter-spirit.

For the transcendentalists as for Whitman, the poet is a seer; he sees the "vast similitude" which "interlocks all" ("On the Beach at Night Alone"). In the dislocated physical world made up of apparently separate objects in which we live, he knows how to reattach them to the great Whole. He has a sense of the infinity and unity of space and time. He is constantly aware of the existence of the soul, "the permanent identity, the thought, the something . . . that fully satisfies . . . That something is the All, and the idea of All, with the accompanying idea of eternity" (*Prose Works* 2:420). Poets are thus constantly in touch with the divine something which speaks through them. "The poets," Whitman wrote in the margin of an article on poetry, "are the divine mediums—through them come spirits and materials to all the people, men and women" (qtd. in Asselineau 95). They are inspired and their songs spring from "irresistible impulses" (["So Far, and So Far, and on toward the End"]). True poems are the result of an inner urge and their growth is organic. For Emerson a poem, "like the spirit of a plant or an animal . . . has an architecture of its own and adorns nature with a new thing" (450); for Thoreau similarly, "As naturally as the oak bears an acorn, and the vine a gourd, man bears a poem" (74); and for Whitman, "The rhyme and uniformity of perfect poems show the free growth of metrical laws, and bud from them as unerringly and loosely as lilacs and roses on a bush" (*Prose Works* 2:440).

There is thus a constant parallelism between *Leaves of Grass* and Emerson's thought, but actually, for all his admiration and possible indebtedness to Emerson, Whitman did not in all respects follow the example of his so-called Master. He parted company with him and boldly struck out for himself, preferring the open road leading to the future rather than the beaten tracks of the genteel tradition.

The greatest originality of *Leaves of Grass* and Whitman's most important departure from transcendentalism was the place he gave to the body. In his poems the word "body" is surrounded by the same halo of mystery and infinity as the word "soul" in the works of other poets. He never uses the word "soul" without immediately reminding us of the existence of the body: "I am the poet of the Body and I am the poet of the Soul" ("Song of Myself," section

21). "I believe materialism is true and spiritualism is true, I reject no part" ("With Antecedents," section 2). He went even further; he exalted sex, which was not even mentioned or alluded to by the New England transcendentalists, heirs of the Pilgrim Fathers' puritanism. "I believe in the flesh and the appetites," Whitman proudly proclaims, and he describes himself as "[t]urbulent, fleshy, sensual, eating, drinking and breeding" ("Song of Myself," section 24). He was no "transparent eyeball" like Emerson (Emerson 10). He had a solid body covered with feelers all over; he was "the caresser of life" ("Song of Myself," section 13). Emerson and Thoreau would not willingly have subscribed to such a statement as "[c]opulation is no more rank to me than death is" ("Song of Myself," section 24). Such sensuality was alien to the transcendentalists.

Another difference was that Whitman, although he sometimes referred to himself as "solitary," believed in man "en-masse" and had faith in democracy: "mine a word of the modern, the word En-Masse," he declares in "Song of Myself" (section 23), and adds, "I speak the pass-word primeval, I give the sign of democracy" (section 24). Emerson, on the other hand, affirms, "Society is good when it does not violate me, but best when it is likest to solitude" (195). He felt that the "solitary and fastidious manners" of the transcendentalists "not only withdraw them from the conversation, but from the labors of the world . . . They do not even like to vote" (202–203). There was a considerable difference between living in rural Concord or Cambridge and living in cosmopolitan and turbulent New York. It was difficult for a New Yorker to ignore politics.

Despite a number of differences, Whitman was fundamentally in communion with the transcendentalists. He was like them the priest of a new religion without priests, although he was in a way excommunicated by Emerson, who did not include him in his *Parnassus*. A further resemblance between Emerson and Whitman is that neither the pure transcendentalists nor Whitman were set in their attitudes. They were equally open-minded and contemptuous of rational consistency. "Do I contradict myself? / Very well then I contradict myself," said Whitman" ("Song of Myself," section 51), echoing Emerson's "Suppose you should contradict yourself, what then?" (265).

Roger Asselineau

Bibliography

Allen, Gay Wilson. *The New Walt Whitman Handbook*. 1975. New York: New York UP, 1986.

Asselineau, Roger. *The Evolution of Walt Whitman: The Creation of a Book*. Cambridge, Mass.: Harvard UP, 1962.

Burroughs, John. *Notes on Walt Whitman as Poet and Person*. 1867. New York: Haskell House, 1971.

Carpenter, Frederick Ives. *Emerson Handbook*. New York: Hendricks House, 1953.

Emerson, Ralph Waldo. *Essays and Lectures*. Ed. Joel Porte. New York: Library of America, 1983.

Fredman, Stephen. *The Grounding of American Poetry: Charles Olson and the Emersonian Tradition*. Cambridge: Cambridge UP, 1993.

Gura, Philip F., and Joel Myerson, eds. *Critical Essays on American Transcendentalism*. Boston: Hall, 1982.

Loving, Jerome. "Walt Whitman." *The Transcendentalists: A Review of Research and Criticism*. Ed. Joel Myerson. New York: MLA, 1984. 375–383.

Matthiessen, F.O. *American Renaissance*. London: Oxford UP, 1941.

Thoreau, Henry David. *A Week on the Concord and Merrimack Rivers; Walden, or, Life in the Woods; The Maine Woods; Cape Cod*. Ed. Robert F. Sayre. New York: Library of America, 1985.

Trowbridge, John Townsend. "Reminiscences of Walt Whitman." *Atlantic Monthly* 89 (1902): 163–175.

Whitman, Walt. *The Correspondence*. Ed. Edwin Haviland Miller. 6 vols. New York: New York UP, 1961–1977.

———. *Prose Works 1892*. Ed. Floyd Stovall. 2 vols. New York: New York UP, 1963–1964.

See also CONTRADICTION; DEMOCRACY; EMERSON, RALPH WALDO; HUMAN BODY; MYSTICISM; ORGANICISM; RELIGION; ROMANTICISM; SOUL, THE; THOREAU, HENRY DAVID; TROWBRIDGE, JOHN TOWNSEND

T

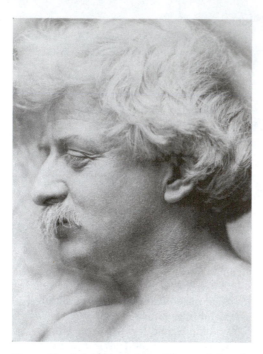

Horace Traubel, Whitman's confidant and disciple. By permission, Harry Ransom Humanities Research Center, University of Texas at Austin.

Traubel, Horace L. (1858–1919)

Horace Traubel is best known as the author of a nine-volume biography of Whitman's final four years, *With Walt Whitman in Camden*. He visited the poet virtually daily from the mid-1880s until Whitman's death in 1892, and he began taking copious notes of their conversations in March of 1888. Every night he transcribed his notes and published three large volumes of them (1906, 1908, 1914) before his death, leaving behind manuscripts for six more. His original goal had been to bring out one volume a year until all were in print, but the final two volumes did not appear until 1996, over a century after they were written.

Traubel described himself as Whitman's "spirit child," and for the twenty-seven years he lived on after Whitman's death, he served the poet as a dutiful son: he became the most active of Whitman's three literary executors (the other two were Richard Maurice Bucke and Thomas Harned); he founded, edited, and published *The Conservator,* a journal dedicated to keeping Whitman's works alive; he published his own Whitman-inspired poetry and prose in three large volumes; and he carried on a tireless correspondence with Whitman enthusiasts around the country and around the world, weaving together an international fellowship of disciples who worked to assure Whitman's immortality.

Only thirty-three years old at the time of Whitman's death, Traubel had already known the poet for nearly twenty years. Born and reared in Camden, New Jersey, Traubel first met Whitman soon after the half-paralyzed poet decided to live in his brother George's Camden home in 1873. Traubel was then not yet fifteen years old, but he soon became Whitman's companion; they took walks and discussed books endlessly. At first, the young man's relationship with Whitman caused something of a scandal; Traubel recalled that neighbors went to his mother and "protested against my association with the 'lecherous old man'" (Traubel, Introduction ix).

Following in his master's footsteps, Traubel stopped his formal education by the age of twelve and spent his teenage years learning the printing trade and newspaper business; after leaving school, he became a typesetter, a skill he would employ throughout his life as he often set the type for his monthly journal and for his various pamphlets. By the time he was sixteen, he had become foreman of the Camden *Evening Visitor* printing office. After that, he worked in his father's Philadelphia lithographic shop, was a paymaster in a factory, and became the Philadelphia correspondent for the Boston *Commonwealth*. None of these jobs paid well, but they gave him a wealth of experience, a confidence in his writing skills, and an understanding of how words could be made public and powerful through the labor of printing. Traubel's middle name was Logo, a sign of the faith in words his father Maurice—a German immigrant artist—instilled in him.

As a young adult, Traubel became increasingly involved with radical reformist thought and persistently urged a reluctant Whitman to admit that *Leaves of Grass* endorsed a socialist agenda. Traubel was indefatigable in his support of Whitman's work, and he made sure that the major radical leaders of his day read and discussed it. He founded the Walt Whitman Fellowship International and served as its secretary-treasurer from 1894 until a year before his death.

His own books can be read as socialist refigurings of Whitman's work, each of his titles subtly adjusting Whitman's terminology: *Chants Communal* (1904) took the individualistic edge off Whitman's "Chants Democratic"; *Optimos*

(1910) redefined Whitman's "kosmos" as an optimized "cheerful whole" (qtd. in Bain 39); and his ecstatically revolutionary essays, *Collects* (1914), collectivistically pluralized Whitman's *Collect*. His journal, *The Conservator,* which he began two years before Whitman's death and continued until his own death in 1919, was an influential organ of radical ideas about everything from women's rights to animal rights. Every issue began with one of Traubel's idiosyncratic "Collect" essays, always written in his repetitive, staccato style.

Traubel traced his liberalism and egalitarianism not only to Whitman but to his hybrid heritage, especially to his father's Jewish background; he said he loved "being a Jew in the face of your prejudices and your insults" (qtd. in Wiksell 119). He always retained his democratic identification with the persecuted and remained a dedicated political and intellectual radical. He kept up a tireless correspondence with leftist and reformist political and artistic figures—including Eugene Debs, Emma Goldman, and Upton Sinclair—and he was involved with the arts and crafts movement and helped publish *The Artsman* from 1903 to 1907, espousing the belief that radical reforms in art, design, and production were essential to social reform.

Traubel's radicalism did not come without cost. His one stable, salaried position was as a clerk in a Philadelphia bank, a job he began during the last years of Whitman's life and held until 1902, when he published an attack on one of Philadelphia's most powerful businessmen. Under pressure from the bank, Horace resigned and began a life of self-imposed poverty, living on the meager proceeds from his writings and gifts from his supporters.

His principled decision affected more than just himself, for by then he had a family to support. Traubel had married Anne Montgomerie in Whitman's home 28 May 1891; their daughter Gertrude was born the following year, and their son Wallace the year after that. In 1898, young Wallace died of scarlet fever. Three months later, Horace's beloved father committed suicide. Horace, however, was always on the rebound and refused to allow personal tragedy to drain his optimism and energy. He enlisted his wife and remaining child in his causes: Anne became associate editor of *The Conservator* in 1899, and Gertrude, whom Horace and Anne educated at home, joined the staff of the journal when she was fourteen.

During the decade after he quit his bank job, Traubel lived an energetic life. He read most nights until four or five in the morning, then took the morning ferry to Philadelphia so he could work in his garret office on Chestnut Street. While riding the Camden ferry in 1909, he was trampled by a horse and suffered severe rib injuries. By 1914, his health had become a major concern, as rheumatic fever left him with a faulty heart valve. The outbreak of the Great War was particularly traumatic for this pacifist and believer in universal brotherhood, and over the next few years he steadily declined, suffering his first heart attack in June 1917, the night before Gertrude's wedding in New York. He suffered additional heart attacks during the next year, and in the summer of 1918 he had a cerebral hemorrhage. He and Anne moved to New York in the spring of 1919 to be close to Gertrude and their new grandson. Traubel was determined to live through the centenary anniversary of Whitman's birth, and on 31 May he attended the New York celebration, where he was given a standing ovation by the two hundred Whitmanites (including Helen Keller) in attendance.

Traubel attended one last centenary event—the August dedication of a huge granite cliff at the Bon Echo estate in Canada, to be named "Old Walt" and inscribed with Whitman's words in giant letters. On 28 August Traubel, while sitting in a tower room where he could look out on Old Walt, shouted that Whitman had just appeared above the granite cliff "in a golden glory": "He reassured me, beckoned to me, and spoke to me. I heard his voice but did not understand all he said, only 'Come on'" (qtd. in Denison 196). Traubel died at Bon Echo on 3 September and was buried in Harleigh Cemetery in Camden, close to Whitman's tomb.

Ed Folsom

Bibliography

Bain, Mildred. *Horace Traubel.* New York: Albert and Charles Boni, 1913.

Denison, Flora MacDonald. "A Dedication and a Death." *Walt Whitman's Canada.* Ed. Cyril Greenland and John Robert Colombo. Willowdale, Ontario: Hounslow, 1992. 196–200.

Karsner, David. *Horace Traubel: His Life and Work.* New York: Egmont Arens, 1919.

Traubel, Horace. *Chants Communal.* Boston: Small, Maynard, 1904.

———. *Collects.* New York: Albert and Charles Boni, 1914.

———. Introduction. *Leaves of Grass (I) & Democratic Vistas.* By Walt Whitman. London: Dent, 1912. vii–xiii.

———. *Optimos.* New York: B.W. Huebsch, 1919.

———. *With Walt Whitman in Camden.* 9 vols. Vols. 1–3. 1906–1914. New York: Rowman and Littlefield, 1961; Vol. 4. Ed. Sculley Bradley. Philadelphia: U of Pennsylvania P, 1953; Vol. 5. Ed. Gertrude Traubel. Carbondale: U of Southern Illinois P, 1964; Vol. 6. Ed. Gertrude Traubel and William White. Carbondale: U of Southern Illinois P, 1982; Vol. 7. Ed. Jeanne Chapman and Robert MacIsaac. Carbondale: U of Southern Illinois P, 1992; Vols. 8–9. Ed. Jeanne Chapman and Robert MacIsaac. Oregon House, Calif.: W.L. Bentley, 1996.

Walling, William English. *Whitman and Traubel.* 1916. New York: Haskell House, 1969.

Wiksell, Percival. "Horace Traubel." *The FRA* 7 (1911): 117–121.

See also ARTS AND CRAFTS MOVEMENT; ASSOCIATIONS, CLUBS, FELLOWSHIPS, FOUNDATIONS, AND SOCIETIES; BIOGRAPHIES; BON ECHO; BUCKE, RICHARD MAURICE; CAMDEN, NEW JERSEY; HARLEIGH CEMETERY

Travels, Whitman's

Other than periodic travel in New England and his war-related stay in Washington, D.C., Whitman made only three journeys of length during his lifetime: to New Orleans in 1848, to Denver in 1879, and to Canada in 1880. For a poet who catalogued hundreds of places both in the United States and around the world in *Leaves of Grass,* his excursions away from home were surprisingly few.

Several factors may have limited his opportunity to travel. The New Orleans trip, his first outside the confines of New York, was made possible by newspaper employment. Upon his return, after a one-year stint at the Brooklyn *Freeman,* he entered a seven-year phase of odd employment and real estate ventures while supporting his family. During this time he became the poet of *Leaves.*

In 1857 he accepted the editorship of the Brooklyn *Daily Times.* The following year he planned a series of lectures which would take him "through all these states, especially West and South and through Kanada" (qtd. in Allen 219). But Whitman was fired from his position in the summer of 1859, and spent the next three years living a bohemian lifestyle without the funds necessary for his proposed trip. He did stay in Boston from 15 March until 13 May 1860 to oversee the printing of the 1860 edition.

Having read in the New York *Herald* that his brother George had been wounded in the battle of Fredericksburg, Walt immediately rushed to Falmouth, Virginia, in December of 1862 and found him relatively unhurt. Shortly afterwards he established residency in Washington, D.C., where for the next ten years (punctuated by trips back to Brooklyn) he lived and worked as volunteer nurse and paid government clerk.

In January 1873 he suffered a paralytic stroke and was forced to move in with his brother George in Camden, New Jersey. After time and therapeutic visits to the nearby Stafford family farm at Timber Creek, Whitman was well enough to embark on the long awaited journeys out West and to Canada, which were primarily funded by friends and admirers. These two trips, along with the earlier sojourn to New Orleans, served to fortify the poet's belief in the greatness of America.

New Orleans

On 9 February 1848 Whitman accepted an offer (from a businessman he happened to meet at the theater) to help start a newspaper in New Orleans. Two days later, accompanied by his younger brother Jeff, Walt boarded a train in Brooklyn and traveled to Cumberland, Maryland. There they joined a stagecoach, with seven other passengers, for a trip over the Allegheny Mountains to Wheeling, West Virginia. Upon arriving on 13 February, they boarded the steamboat *St. Cloud* and traveled down the Ohio River. Whitman was impressed with Cincinnati and Louisville, and in Cairo, Illinois, they arrived at the junction of the Mississippi, which Walt called "the great father of waters" (*Uncollected* 1:189).

The remaining trip south was "monotonous and dull" (*Prose Works* 2:607) except for the bluffs at Memphis and Natchez, Mississippi. The Whitmans arrived in New Orleans on

25 February, and notes he made during the voyage became "Excerpts From a Traveller's Notebook," which appeared in the *Crescent* in three weekly installments.

After a pleasant beginning, with Walt working as assistant editor and Jeff as office boy, the brothers (especially Jeff, who was plagued with bouts of dysentery) became homesick and found their employers to be increasingly hostile. Toward the end of May, Walt resigned, and they began the return trip on 27 May.

Taking a different route than in February, the steamer *Pride of the West* took them to St. Louis on 3 June, where they boarded the *Prairie Bird* and proceeded to La Salle, Illinois, arriving on 5 June. They transferred to a canal boat headed for Chicago, which they reached the next day. There they explored the city for a day, boarding at the American Temperance hotel.

The next day they took the steamboat *Griffith* across Lake Michigan. Whitman was impressed with Wisconsin, noting that if he were to move from Long Island, "Wisconsin would be the proper place to come to" (*Prose Works* 2:608). They arrived in Buffalo on 12 June and boarded a train to Niagara, where they saw the falls. Another train took them to Albany, and from there they traveled by boat down the Hudson River to New York City, arriving on 15 June.

The importance of this journey on Whitman's development as a poet cannot be overemphasized. According to his friend Dr. Bucke, Whitman believed that the New Orleans trip helped him gather "the main part" of the "physiology" of *Leaves of Grass*.

Denver

In September 1879 Whitman was invited to participate in the Old Settlers' Quarter Centennial celebration in Lawrence, Kansas. His railroad pass and most expenses were included. Traveling with four companions who were newspaper men and well-known Free-Soilers (as was the poet), Whitman planned after the event to continue west as far as his health and finances would allow.

On 10 September they traveled by train from Philadelphia to St. Louis. Near Urbana, Ohio, the train had a bad collision, but only one person was hurt, and they continued after a delay of several hours, arriving on the twelfth. While his companions stayed in a hotel, Walt spent the night at his brother Jeff's house. Ironi-

cally, the brothers had explored St. Louis together on their return trip from New Orleans, and must have noted the many changes as Jeff showed Walt the sights. The poet said, in an interview published in the 13 September 1879 St. Louis *Daily Globe-Democrat*, that he was "in sympathy and preference Western—better fitted for the Mississippi valley." The next day the five travelers boarded a train for Kansas City. They were met at the station by a committee from the Quarter Centennial, and were escorted to Lawrence on another train.

During the first day of the event, the fifteenth, Whitman sat on the outdoor stage and endured the heat. He failed to appear the next day, when he was expected to read a poem, complaining of ill health. That evening the party traveled to Topeka by train, and the next day toured the city. Legend has it that Walt was taken to view some Indian prisoners, who responded only to him.

On the eighteenth, minus one companion, they headed to Colorado on the Kansas Pacific railroad. The group arrived in Denver on the evening of the nineteenth in time to see the Rocky Mountains at sunset. Denver was a growing city in 1879, with a streetcar system, telephone company, and construction for electric lights in progress. Whitman spent time touring the city rather than join his friends on a rugged excursion to the mining town of Leadville, although in later newspaper "interviews" he claims to have gone there.

He did visit Platte Canyon by train, which was the inspiration for his poem "Spirit That Form'd This Scene" (1881). The next morning, the twenty-third, the four men departed and headed east, although Whitman had wished to travel further west. In Pueblo they boarded the Atchison, Topeka and Santa Fe Railroad, arriving in Kansas City on the twenty-fifth. They stopped on the way in Sterling, Kansas, where Whitman visited with a former soldier he had befriended during the Civil War.

From Kansas City they took a train and reached St. Louis on the twenty-seventh. There Whitman parted with his friends, who returned East, and began an extended visit with Jeff which became necessary when Walt suffered a relapse around 11 October.

When he felt better, Whitman spent his time visiting the Mississippi River, the Mercantile Library, and a kindergarten near Jeff's house where he entertained the children with stories. He sent several of his correspondents at this time a map of his travels.

T

He finally departed St. Louis on 4 January, receiving the necessary funds for the trip from an unknown donor via Dr. Bucke. His train arrived in Philadelphia the next day, and he returned to his brother's house in Camden. The trip West had been the great journey of his life.

Canada

In the summer of 1880, Whitman began his only trip outside of the United States. Dr. Richard Maurice Bucke, his friend and eventual literary executor, had been encouraging the poet to visit him in London, Ontario, where he was superintendent of the Asylum for the Insane. Bucke came to Camden and on 3 June accompanied Whitman on the rail trip to Canada. They stopped en route so that Walt could view Niagara Falls for the second time in his life (the first was on the return trip from New Orleans).

Whitman spent his first two weeks in London observing conditions at the asylum and exploring the spacious ornamental grounds and farmland there. On 19 June they took a sixty-mile trip west to Sarnia, a city on the banks of the St. Clair River and on the Canada–Michigan border fifty-five miles northeast of Detroit. On the twenty-first they enjoyed a moonlight excursion on Lake Huron, and the next day visited a school and Indian settlement in the area on their way back to London.

For the next month Whitman remained at the sanitarium, enjoying the natural surroundings and activities. On 26 July he and Dr. Bucke took a train to Toronto, and the next day boarded a steamboat on Lake Ontario and proceeded to Kingston on the Canada–New York border, two hundred miles northwest of Syracuse. They stayed there a week, sightseeing and touring the Lakes of the Thousand Islands twenty-five miles east of Kingston. On 3 August they took a steamer to Montreal, arriving that evening. On the fifth they proceeded to Quebec, and the next day continued 134 miles to Tadoussac, at the mouth of the Saguenay River. A steamboat took them up that river to Chicoutimi and Ha Ha Bay, then back again to Quebec on the eighth. The next day they continued on to Montreal, Toronto, and Hamilton, arriving back in London on 14 August.

Whitman spent his remaining forty-five days in Canada resting and observing nature at the asylum. On the twenty-eighth he traveled by rail with Bucke as far as Niagara, then returned home by himself on the twenty-ninth.

Other than a short trip the following year to Boston to oversee the printing of the 1881 *Leaves* and to visit Emerson in Concord, this Canadian "jaunt" was the final travel experience of his life.

Jack Field

Bibliography

Allen, Gay Wilson. *The Solitary Singer: A Critical Biography of Walt Whitman.* 1955. Rev. ed. 1967. Chicago: U of Chicago P, 1985.

———. *Walt Whitman.* 1961. Rev. ed. Detroit: Wayne State UP, 1969.

Barrus, Clara. *Whitman and Burroughs, Comrades.* 1931. New York: Kennikat, 1968.

Eitner, Walter H. *Walt Whitman's Western Jaunt.* Lawrence: Regent's Press of Kansas, 1981.

Greenland, Cyril, and John Robert Colombo, eds. *Walt Whitman's Canada.* Willowdale, Ontario: Hounslow, 1992.

Nicholl, James R. "Walt Whitman's 1879 Visit to Missouri, Kansas, and Colorado." *Heritage of the Great Plains* 14.1 (1981): 33–42.

Whitman, Walt. *The Correspondence of Walt Whitman.* Ed. Edwin Haviland Miller. 6 vols. New York: New York UP, 1961–1977.

———. *Daybooks and Notebooks.* Ed. William White. 3 vols. New York: New York UP, 1978.

———. *Prose Works 1892.* Ed. Floyd Stovall. 2 vols. New York: New York UP, 1963–1964.

———. *The Uncollected Poetry and Prose of Walt Whitman.* 1921. Ed. Emory Holloway. 2 vols. Gloucester, Mass.: Peter Smith, 1972.

See also BOSTON, MASSACHUSETTS; BUCKE, RICHARD MAURICE; CAMDEN, NEW JERSEY; CANADA, WHITMAN'S VISIT TO; DENVER, COLORADO; FALMOUTH, VIRGINIA; HUDSON RIVER; JOURNEYING; LAWRENCE, KANSAS; LONDON, ONTARIO, CANADA; MISSISSIPPI RIVER; NEW ORLEANS *CRESCENT*; NEW ORLEANS, LOUISIANA; NIAGARA FALLS; PHILADELPHIA, PENNSYLVANIA; ROCKY MOUNTAINS; ST. LOUIS, MISSOURI; "SPIRIT THAT FORM'D THIS SCENE"; WASHINGTON, D.C.; WHITMAN, GEORGE WASHINGTON; WHITMAN, THOMAS JEFFERSON

Treasurer's Office, Solicitor of the

Walt Whitman's brief tenure as a clerk at the Solicitor of the Treasurer's Office, a division of the United States Justice Department, in Washington, D.C., was his last regular employment. It is not clear when he started to work there, but by late January 1872 he had been transferred from the Attorney General's Office, and was occupying an office with several other clerks. At the Solicitor of the Treasurer's Office Whitman performed the same types of bureaucratic and secretarial duties that he had at the Attorney General's Office, which was also located in the Treasury Building. Unlike his departure from the Department of the Interior a decade earlier, Whitman left the Treasurer's Office because of illness rather than scandal.

Whitman failed to mention the Treasurer's Office when he described the period in "An Interregnum Paragraph" in *Specimen Days,* and also misremembered the date of the onset of the illness that led to his departure, claiming it took place in February rather than in January. From Whitman's description, it appears that he worked no harder for the Solicitor of the Treasury than he had for the Attorney General. In addition to using his office as a home-away-from-home during his leisure time—Whitman particularly enjoyed the office window's southern view of the Potomac and the mountains of Virginia—in 1872 he took several leaves of absence to work on a new edition of *Leaves of Grass.*

According to his later description to Richard Maurice Bucke, Whitman had decided to remain in his office on the frigid evening of 22 January 1873, rather than return to his unheated apartment nearby. He was reading a popular novel while reclining by the fire when he was struck with a dizziness that would develop into paralysis later that night while he slept at home. After several months of convalescence, Whitman returned to work part time in March, but in June he moved to Camden, New Jersey. In July he asked the chief clerk of the office for a continued leave of absence, which was granted, and the next month successfully petitioned for a friend to substitute in his place. Despite an appeal to President Grant in 1874, Whitman was eventually discharged.

Jonathan Gill

Bibliography

Allen, Gay Wilson. *The Solitary Singer: A Critical Biography of Walt Whitman.* 1955. Rev. ed. 1967. Chicago: U of Chicago P, 1985.

Bucke, Richard Maurice. *Walt Whitman.* Philadelphia: McKay, 1883.

Reynolds, David S. *Walt Whitman's America: A Cultural Biography.* New York: Knopf, 1995.

See also ATTORNEY GENERAL'S OFFICE, UNITED STATES; HEALTH; *LEAVES OF GRASS,* 1871–1872 EDITION; WASHINGTON, D.C.

"Trickle Drops" (1860)

This poem was originally published, without its present opening line, as number 15 in the "Calamus" cluster of the 1860 *Leaves of Grass.* In 1867 and 1871 the initial line—"Trickle, drops!"—was added; this was emended to the present line in 1881. Otherwise, its text remained the same in all succeeding editions, except for minor alterations in punctuation and capitalization. It took "Trickle Drops" as its title from 1867 onward; in manuscript the poem was called "Confession Drops."

"Trickle Drops" presents the curious image of the poet wounding himself in the face and chest so that his blood may drip out onto the pages of his book, staining his poems. Unlike most of the "Calamus" poems, "Trickle Drops" does not deal directly with male same-sex love. The poem's only intimation of a connection to homosexuality is its sixth line, which speaks of concealment and confession, motifs often signifying repressed homoerotic desire in *Leaves of Grass.*

Both M. Jimmie Killingsworth and Kerry Larson correlate the freeing of the drops of blood with masturbation, an act commonly associated with homosexual behavior in Whitman's day. Indeed, the drops are said to be "ashamed," reflecting the social stigma against masturbation. Killingsworth reads the drops of blood as poems that Whitman "extracts" from himself, much as "bunches" of semen are figured as poems, and ejaculation as poetic expression, in "Spontaneous Me!" (1856). By contrast, Larson interprets the "bloody drops" as the failure of poetry to provide aesthetic restitution for sublimated (homo)sexual desire: the violent discharge of pent-up sexual urges precludes the possibility of liberating literary representation of those urges.

The violence of the poet's self-wounding recalls other instances of sadomasochistic fantasy in *Leaves of Grass,* such as the plunging of the tongue to the "bare-stript heart" in section 5 of "Song of Myself" (1855) and the erotic strangulation induced in the poet by grand opera in "Song of Myself," section 26. Michael Moon sees "Trickle Drops" as the literalization of the fantasy of self-wounding implicit in the lexical conversion of "leaves" of grass into knife-like "blades" in "Scented Herbage of My Breast" (1860). Killingsworth likewise traces the poet's transformation of himself from Osiris in "Scented Herbage" to crucified Christ figure in "Trickle Drops," whose death permits the transcendence of self which is the essence of love.

Carl Smeller

Bibliography

Killingsworth, M. Jimmie. *Whitman's Poetry of the Body: Sexuality, Politics, and the Text.* Chapel Hill: U of North Carolina P, 1989.

Larson, Kerry C. *Whitman's Drama of Consensus.* Chicago: U of Chicago P, 1988.

Moon, Michael. *Disseminating Whitman: Revision and Corporeality in "Leaves of Grass."* Cambridge, Mass.: Harvard UP, 1991.

Whitman, Walt. *Complete Poetry and Collected Prose.* Ed. Justin Kaplan. New York: Library of America, 1982.

———. *Walt Whitman's Manuscripts: "Leaves of Grass" (1860).* Ed. Fredson Bowers. Chicago: U of Chicago P, 1955.

See also "CALAMUS"; SEX AND SEXUALITY

Triggs, Oscar Lovell (1865–1930)

An educator and author, Triggs in his book *Browning and Whitman* (1892) examined parallels in the verse of the two authors, revealing Triggs as an early supporter of Whitman, whom he called the embodiment of the democratic ideal. Triggs also edited *Selections from the Prose and Poetry of Walt Whitman* (1898) and the third volume of *The Complete Writings of Walt Whitman* (1902), in which he is credited with sanctioning the "cathedral analogy" of the organic theory of *Leaves of Grass* first expounded by Richard Maurice Bucke.

Triggs was educated at the University of Minnesota and the University of Chicago, where he received his A.M. and Ph.D. degrees. Triggs was an outspoken exponent of modern movements, and according to friend and fellow Whitmanite,

Arthur E. Briggs, was dismissed from the University of Chicago for proclaiming Whitman "a poet of high rank" (300). Along with Briggs, Triggs organized the first Whitman dinner at the Men's City Club in Los Angeles, which later evolved into the Annual Whitman Fellowship Celebration.

Patricia J. Tyrer

Bibliography

Allen, Gay Wilson. *The New Walt Whitman Handbook.* 1975. New York: New York UP, 1986.

Briggs, Arthur E. *Walt Whitman: Thinker and Artist.* New York: Philosophical Library, 1952.

See also COMPLETE WRITINGS OF WALT WHITMAN, THE; LEAVES OF GRASS, VARIORUM EDITION

Trowbridge, John Townsend (1827–1916)

One of the earliest and most even-handed of Walt Whitman's admirers, John Townsend Trowbridge left a deft and important portrait of their relationship in his autobiography, *My Own Story.* New York born but Boston based, Trowbridge was editor, novelist, poet, antislavery reformer and writer of many juvenile stories and serials. He enjoyed acclaim and popularity for his novels, especially *Neighbor Jackwood* (1857), *Cudjo's Cave* (1864), *Coupon Bonds* (1866), the widely read "Jack Hazard Series" (1871–1874), and his best-known light verse about a hubristic boy, "Darius Green and His Flying-Machine." He was an important voice in literature for children, editing *Our Young Folks* and contributing to *St. Nicholas* and *The Youth's Companion,* and he was also a frequent contributor of verse to the *Atlantic.*

In *My Own Story* Trowbridge relates how he first came across excerpts of *Leaves of Grass* while staying in Paris during 1855; he read the book upon his return to the United States and liked it very much while objecting to its explicit sexuality. In a letter dated November 1856, he called it "a marvel & a monstrosity." "The author is a sort of Emerson run wild—glorious, graphic, sublime, ridiculous, spiritual, sensual, great, powerful, savage, tender, sweet, and filthy" (qtd in. Coleman, "Trowbridge" 262–263). Trowbridge met Whitman for the first time in Boston in 1860 when the poet was preparing the third edition of *Leaves of Grass,* and he was surprised to find a "simple, well-mannered man" (Trowbridge, "Reminiscences"

164). When Whitman called on Trowbridge at his home in Somerville, their friendship blossomed, and the latter inquired into the poet's familiarity with Emerson's writings. Whitman explained that, when he was building houses with his father in 1854, he had read Emerson's essays on his lunch breaks and Emerson had "helped him to 'find himself.'" "I was simmering, simmering, simmering," Whitman was reported to have said; "Emerson brought me to a boil" (qtd. in Trowbridge, "Reminiscences" 166). Given Whitman's subsequent denials of having read Emerson before writing *Leaves of Grass,* Trowbridge's testimony remains an important contravention.

Over a period of weeks in 1863, Trowbridge spent a good deal of time with Whitman along with John Burroughs and William D. O'Connor in the poet's "terrible" garret in Washington, D.C., and made unsuccessful attempts to secure for Whitman a government clerkship from Salmon P. Chase, Lincoln's Secretary of Treasury. While keeping his distance from the more sycophantic circles of Whitman's admirers, Trowbridge remained a steadfast friend through the 1880s and beyond. "The way Trowbridge stuck to me through thick and thin was beautiful to behold," Whitman told Horace Traubel. "He had objections to me always; has objections today; but he accepted me on general principles and has never so far as I know revised his original declaration in my favor" (Traubel 506).

Trowbridge is a significant contemporary reader of Whitman precisely for the way he could take from *Leaves of Grass* what he enjoyed and still be offended. Very little scholarship exists which examines Whitman's influence on Trowbridge but surely poems such as "My Comrade and I" from *The Vagabonds and Other Poems* (1869) evoke the sentiments of "Calamus" cast in conventional meter and mores. Undoubtedly, Trowbridge always found the sexual parts of *Leaves of Grass* unpleasant and unnecessary and yet often felt that Whitman's later verse was too conventional in its phraseology, preferring the 1855 edition. While his appreciation does not fit the radical mold of the typical nineteenth-century champion of the Good Gray Poet, it does offer evidence of a frequently overlooked part of nineteenth-century Whitmanian readership—a conventional Victorian sensibility that could perceive, as he writes, "the great original force" (Trowbridge, "Reminiscences" 175) of Whitman's verse.

Stephen Rachman

Bibliography

Allen, Gay Wilson. *The Solitary Singer: A Critical Biography of Walt Whitman.* 1955. Rev. ed. 1967. Chicago: U of Chicago P, 1985.

Coleman, Rufus A. "Further Reminiscences of Walt Whitman." *Modern Language Notes* 63 (1948): 266–268.

———. "Trowbridge and Whitman." *PMLA* 63 (1948): 262–273.

Reynolds, David S. *Walt Whitman's America: A Cultural Biography.* New York: Knopf, 1995.

Traubel, Horace. *With Walt Whitman in Camden.* Vol. 3. New York: Mitchell Kennerley, 1914.

Trowbridge, John Townsend. *My Own Story.* Boston: Houghton Mifflin, 1903.

———. *The Poetical Works of John Townsend Trowbridge.* Boston: Houghton Mifflin, 1903.

———. "Reminiscences of Walt Whitman." *Atlantic Monthly* 89 (1902): 163–175.

See also BURROUGHS, JOHN; CHASE, SALMON P.; EMERSON, RALPH WALDO; O'CONNOR, WILLIAM DOUGLAS; TRAUBEL, HORACE L.

Tupper, Martin Farquhar (1810–1889)

Martin Farquhar Tupper was an enormously popular poet in Victorian England. Although literary critics disparaged his work, his middle class audience loved him. His most famous and popular work was *Proverbial Philosophy* (1838), which he published fairly early in his career and which sold over a quarter of a million copies in England alone. American sales were estimated at over one million.

Although he continued to publish profusely, his popularity waned dramatically during his lifetime so that by the end of his life, "Tupperish" was a term of literary derision.

Tupper was born the son of a successful physician in London in 1810. He received an extensive education, attending Oxford and later studying law. His career was stymied, however, by an acute stuttering problem. He turned to writing as a career and became the most popular poet of his day, outselling even Tennyson. Tupper is remembered for popularizing a form of prose-poetry that used no regular rhyme or meter.

When Whitman published *Leaves of Grass* in 1855, he was widely compared to Tupper by literary critics, including Henry James and Algernon Swinburne. Whitman did read Tupper's poetry, and Whitman's personal copy of *Proverbial Philosophy* contains one passage, heavily marked and annotated in Whitman's handwriting, that bears a striking resemblance to the style of prose-poetry found in Whitman's catalogues.

Brent L. Gibson

Bibliography

Hudson, Derek. *Martin Tupper: His Rise and Fall*. London: Constable, 1949.

Reynolds, David S. *Walt Whitman's America: A Cultural Biography*. New York: Knopf, 1995.

Rubin, Joseph J. "Tupper's Possible Influence on Whitman's Style." *American Notes & Queries: A Journal for the Curious* 1 (1941): 101–102.

See also CATALOGUES; LEAVES OF GRASS, 1855 EDITION; READING, WHITMAN'S; STYLE AND TECHNIQUE(S)

Two Rivulets, Author's Edition (1876)

The Author's edition of *Two Rivulets* is the companion volume to the 1876 Author's edition of *Leaves of Grass*. In the past, this two-volume centennial set was ignored in large measure by critics for a number of reasons. Whitman ran off only 750–800 copies of *Rivulets* at the New Republic Print shop in Camden (see Myerson 194–205 for detailed facts of publication). In addition to the scarce number of originals, the first known reprint or facsimile did not become available for over a hundred years, in 1979. Also, up until recently, the volume was considered either a hodgepodge of printing methods and poetic techniques or simply the miscellaneous overflow from an already too bulky *Leaves*. Today, though, *Rivulets*'s reputation is being rescued from obscurity and disrepute. Ed Folsom in 1994 offered the dramatic possibility that it—as well as the 1876 *Leaves*—might represent Whitman's culminating poetic moment.

Indeed, rather than an illustration of the poet's decline, *Rivulets* presents an impressive number of graphic "firsts" to help make it a startling venture into breaking down "the barriers of form between Prose and Poetry" (*Rivulets* 28). Whitman clearly announces this poetic mission in "NEW POETRY"—a small prose unit of the first section in *Rivulets*. Further, by using the visible mediums of print and photo to "talk" to its verbal composition (Whitman's dialectical strategy) *Rivulets* sets up novel typographic and visual experiments on the page.

For the first time, Whitman creates a two-volume matched set in which he imprints "Author's Edition" on the title pages of *Rivulets* and *Leaves*. And in an odd printing move, he transfers *Passage to India* out of *Leaves* and into *Rivulets*. He also has a photo (see Linton engraving) and a poem ("The Wound-Dresser") in *Leaves* talk to the poem "Out from Behind This Mask" in *Rivulets*. In *Rivulets*, Whitman interweaves prose sections with poetry sections: *Two Rivulets* (poetry with prose), *Democratic Vistas* (prose), *Centennial Songs—1876* (poetry), *As a Strong Bird on Pinions Free* (poetry), *Memoranda During the War* (prose), and *Passage to India* (poetry). In the first section of *Rivulets,* he has prose and a bold wavy line (a printer's ornament) run simultaneously under poetry for eighteen pages. Strangely, too, in the same printing issue of *Rivulets,* Whitman labels his book spine differently. He stamps "Verse" on some copies and "Prose and Verse" on others (Myerson 201). He also inserts not one but two prefaces in *Rivulets* (1876 and 1872). And finally, in the introductory Preface (1876), Whitman tries to define as well as market his 1876 set (*Leaves* and *Rivulets*) as one of his "wilful" and poetic "escapades" (11).

In *Rivulets,* the poet seeks an original way to celebrate America's second century in this 1876 centennial year. He does so by envisioning an "ideal" America of limitless possibilities without relinquishing the "real" America of national, political, and economic embroilments.

To give a sense of how radical an experiment this volume was, there follows a short lyric unit excerpted from the first section of *Rivulets* (28). The poem is entitled "Wandering at Morn" and its prose "rivulet" is entitled "NEW POETRY":

> Yearning for thee, harmonious Union!
>   thee, Singing Bird divine!
> Thee, seated coil'd in evil times, my
>   Country, with craft and black dis-
>   may—with every meanness, treason
>   thrust upon thee;

I see of course that the really maturing America is at least just as much to loom up, expand, and take definite shape; . . . from the States drain'd by the Mississippi and from those flanking the Pacific, or bordering the Gulf of Mexico.

Whitman places his prose (set in smaller type) under a wavy line beneath the wings of his characteristically long lines of verse (set in larger type). The prose offers expansive assertions of hope in a typographically reciprocal reply to the poem's yearning apostrophe. Whitman thus attempts to bond poetry and prose together by a new form that can be seen as the visual interacting of texts. It is the poet's graphically symbolic model for overcoming traditional barriers between forms.

At this juncture, an important question to ask is, why did Whitman call his new volume *Two Rivulets?* The *OED* defines *rivulet* as both a small stream and as a specific type of moth/ (butterfly?) called "GRASS RIVULET." So Whitman—from the very title itself—subtly fuses *Leaves of "GRASS"* to *Two "RIVULETS"* as he warns the reader in the 1876 Preface:

> The arrangement in print of *TWO RIVULETS*—the indirectness of the name itself . . . —are but parts of the Venture which my Poems entirely are. (11)

It is this type of indirection that creates, drives, and sustains his 1876 two-volume, one-unit "Venture" for *Leaves* and *Rivulets.*

To grant the possibility that Whitman, at age fifty-seven, still possessed his full poetic powers is to accept the 1876 *Rivulets* as the work of a mature master. And it permits us to see *Rivulets* as an effective literary composition rather than a mere bibliographic curiosity.

Frances E. Keuling-Stout

Bibliography

Allen, Gay Wilson. *The New Walt Whitman Handbook.* 1975. New York: New York UP, 1986.

———. Introduction. *Two Rivulets.* By Walt Whitman. Norwood, Pa.: Norwood, 1979. iii–vi.

Folsom, Ed. "Prospects for the Study of Walt Whitman." *Resources for American Literary Study* 20 (1994): 1–15.

Myerson, Joel. *Walt Whitman: A Descriptive Bibliography.* Pittsburgh: U of Pittsburgh P, 1993.

Scovel, J.M. "Walt Whitman. His Life, His Poetry, Himself. 'The Good Gray Poet' Self-Estimated." *Springfield Daily Republican* 23 July 1875, sec. 3: 1–3.

Whitman, Walt. *The Correspondence.* Ed. Edwin Haviland Miller. Vol. 3. New York: New York UP, 1964.

———. *Two Rivulets.* Camden, N.J.: Author's Edition, 1876.

See also LEAVES OF GRASS, 1876, AUTHOR'S EDITION; PREFACE TO *TWO RIVULETS*

Tyndale, Hector (1821–1880)

Hector Tyndale was a prominent glass and china merchant in Philadelphia and served as a brigadier general in the Union Army. In 1868, he was narrowly defeated as the Republican candidate for mayor of Philadelphia.

Tyndale was the son of Robinson and Sarah Thorn Tyndale, who introduced him to Walt Whitman. He turned down an appointment to the United States Military Academy at the request of his mother, but during the Civil War he served in many battles, including Antietam. In 1859 Tyndale escorted John Brown's wife to visit her husband in Harper's Ferry before Brown's execution even though Tyndale did not support Brown's raid. Tyndale, a polished man who traveled widely in Europe, became a good friend of Whitman and his family. On 25 February 1857 he dined with Whitman, who asked him for advice on how to improve *Leaves of Grass* for the third edition. Tyndale encouraged him to use York Cathedral as a model—to focus on the massiveness of his poetry without paying too much attention to the individual parts.

Tyndale's advice and architectural metaphor seem to have influenced Whitman, who later compared writing *Leaves of Grass* to building a cathedral.

Denise Kohn

Bibliography

Allen, Gay Wilson. *The Solitary Singer: A Critical Biography of Walt Whitman.* 1955. Rev. ed. 1967. Chicago: U of Chicago P, 1985.

Kaplan, Justin. *Walt Whitman: A Life.* New York: Simon and Schuster, 1980.

McLaughlin, John. *A Memoir of Hector Tyndale.* Philadelphia: Collins, 1882.

Reynolds, David S. *Walt Whitman's America: A Cultural Biography.* New York: Knopf, 1995.

See also TYNDALE, SARAH THORN

Tyndale, Sarah Thorn (1792–1859)

Sarah Thorn Tyndale was an abolitionist and Fourierist from Philadelphia. She was married to Robinson Tyndale, a glass and china merchant, and was the mother of Hector Tyndale, a brigadier general in the Union Army.

Sarah Tyndale first met Whitman when she visited him in Brooklyn with Bronson Alcott and Henry David Thoreau on 10 November 1856. Whitman received them in his attic bedroom—

the bed he shared with his brother Edward was unmade and the chamber pot was in view. He told his visitors that he bathed daily in midwinter and enjoyed riding atop the city omnibus all day. Alcott's efforts to foster conversation between Thoreau and Whitman failed, but Tyndale stayed to talk more with Whitman after her companions had left. She and Whitman became friends and began a correspondence. She later introduced her son Hector to the poet. On 20 July 1857 Whitman wrote to her that he had a hundred poems for a third edition of *Leaves of Grass* and wanted to buy the plates of the second edition from the publishers Fowler and Wells, who he believed were not helping his career. Tyndale concurred with his assessment of his publishers in her reply on 27 July 1857 and offered to lend him fifty dollars to buy the plates.

Tyndale was important to Whitman as a friend and confidante. Although she was concerned that some of his poetry might be misunderstood and thus dangerous to the weak-minded, the two seemed to share many of the same beliefs and interests.

Denise Kohn

Bibliography

Allen, Gay Wilson. *The Solitary Singer: A Critical Biography of Walt Whitman.* 1955. Rev. ed. 1967. Chicago: U of Chicago P, 1985.

Johnson, Allen, and Dumas Malone, eds. *Dictionary of American Bibliography.* New York: Scribner's, 1964.

Kaplan, Justin. *Walt Whitman: A Life.* New York: Simon and Schuster, 1980.

Reynolds, David S. *Walt Whitman's America: A Cultural Biography.* New York: Knopf, 1995.

Zweig, Paul. *Walt Whitman: The Making of the Poet.* Basic Books: New York, 1984.

See also ALCOTT, AMOS BRONSON; FOWLER, LORENZO NILES AND ORSON SQUIRE; THOREAU, HENRY DAVID; TYNDALE, HECTOR; WELLS, SAMUEL ROBERTS; WOMAN'S RIGHTS MOVEMENT AND WHITMAN, THE

U

"Unfolded Out of the Folds" (1856)

First published as "Poem of Women," its original placement immediately following "Poem of Walt Whitman, An American" ("Song of Myself") suggests its importance in the eugenic program that pervaded the second edition. In the poem, pseudoscientific principles governing conception and gestation are applied to the birth of the perfect child. In 1860 and 1867, the poem was included, untitled, in the "Leaves of Grass" cluster; it acquired its present title in 1871, and in 1881 it was placed in the "Autumn Rivulets" cluster, thus diminishing its sexual implications.

The twelve-line poem begins, "Unfolded out of the folds of the woman man comes unfolded, and is always to come unfolded." Each of the following nine anaphoric lines is also an independent clause beginning with "Unfolded" and affirming that all elements of male greatness derive from the mother. The idea is recapitulated in the poem's last two lines. The repeated terms "unfolded" and "folds" highlight the poem's overlapping themes. These include Whitman's plea for a race of physiologically and spiritually sound women, freed from the restrictions of Victorian mores; a vision that predicates human evolution on a race of perfect mothers; the concept that the gift of poetry is inherited from an ideal mother; and, by implication, the celebration of the birthing of the wonder child who is destined to become his nation's poet.

The poem's imagery involves the "unfolding" of the foetus, the mother's vulval "folds," and the brain "folds" of mother and child. Phrenologists maintained that the attributes of the unborn child are encoded and "folded up or concentrated" (Fowler, *Love and Parentage* 26) in the parents' brains, which are constituted of faculties that govern each human trait and (to the degree that they are developed in the parents) transmitted to the child to form its character. Thus the poem declares that "[u]nfolded out of the folds of the woman's brain come all the folds of the man's brain, duly obedient" and that from "the folds of the superbest woman" will "come the superbest man." The mother's and child's attributes of "friendliness" are associated with the phrenological faculty of adhesiveness; their "justice" and "sympathy" with the group of faculties called the moral sentiments. Accepting the phrenological linkage of creativity with maternal sexuality, the poem celebrates the mother's "perfect body" and sexual stamina: "Unfolded by brawny embraces from the well-muscled woman I love, only thence come the brawny embraces of the man." (Paradoxically, the persona assumes the roles of both wonder child and Adamic begetter.) The declaration that "[u]nfolded only out of the inimitable poems of woman can come the poems of man, (only thence have my poems come)" illustrates Orson Fowler's dictum that "[a]ll poetry is inherited" (*Hereditary Descent* 203–204). The phrenological faculty of ideality was originally called the faculty of poetry. As in Whitman's self-portraits, Goethe, Schiller, and Burns were said to be descended from perfect mothers.

Harold Aspiz

Bibliography

Aspiz, Harold. "Unfolding the Folds." *Walt Whitman Review* 12 (1966): 81–87.

Fowler, Orson Squire. *Hereditary Descent: Its Laws and Facts Applied to Human Improvement.* New York: Fowler and Wells, 1847.

———. *Love and Parentage, Applied to the Improvement of Offspring*. New York: Fowler and Wells, 1844.

Killingsworth, M. Jimmie. *Whitman's Poetry of the Body: Sexuality, Politics, and the Text*. Chapel Hill: U of North Carolina P, 1989.

Whitman, Walt. *Leaves of Grass*. Ed. Sculley Bradley and Harold W. Blodgett. Norton Critical Edition. New York: Norton, 1973.

See also "Autumn Rivulets"; Evolution; Fowler, Lorenzo Niles and Orson Squire; Human Body; *Leaves of Grass*, 1856 Edition; Motherhood; Phrenology; Pseudoscience; Women as a Theme in Whitman's Writing

"Unseen Buds" (1891)

"Unseen Buds" first appeared in 1891 in the second annex of *Leaves of Grass*, "Good-Bye my Fancy." Gay Wilson Allen points out that this poem is an elaboration of the concept of "evolving plenitude" expressed earlier in the 1860 poem eventually entitled "Germs." Both of these poems constitute simply one more expression of an idea ubiquitous in Whitman's poetry, his belief in an "inner force or principle which propels the universe through its cosmic development" (Allen 288). Roger Asselineau reads the poem as an expression of the evolu-

tion of the poet's work—a certain theme would exist as a germ in an earlier edition and would then develop organically through later editions.

However, when read along with "The Unexpress'd," "Grand is the Seen," and "Good-Bye my Fancy!," all published in 1891, the poem seems to express the poet's regret that, in his seventies, he has the urge but lacks the energy to produce more poetry; a good part of the poet, "infinite, hidden well," has not yet been revealed. In "Grand is the Seen" Whitman declares, "Grand is the seen . . . But grander far the unseen soul of me." Perhaps the unseen buds represent this same unseen soul of the poet.

Guiyou Huang

Bibliography

Allen, Gay Wilson. *Walt Whitman Handbook*. 1946. New York: Hendricks House, 1962.

Asselineau, Roger. *The Evolution of Walt Whitman: The Creation of a Personality*. Trans. Richard P. Adams and Roger Asselineau. Cambridge, Mass.: Harvard UP, 1960.

Whitman, Walt. *Leaves of Grass*. Ed. Sculley Bradley and Harold W. Blodgett. Norton Critical Edition. New York: Norton, 1973.

See also "Good-Bye my Fancy" (Second Annex)

V

Van Velsor, Cornelius (1768–1837)

Known as "the Major," Cornelius Van Velsor was Whitman's jocular, hearty, loud-voiced maternal grandfather. He was born to Garrett Van Velsor and Mary Kossabone. The Major married Naomi (Amy) Williams and, after her death, remarried. Residing on the Van Velsor homestead near Cold Spring, Long Island, he bred and raised horses, which Whitman sometimes rode. As a boy, Whitman would sit next to his grandfather on their large farm wagon and travel some forty miles to deliver produce to Brooklyn. The "old race of the Netherlands," says Whitman in *Specimen Days,* "so deeply grafted on Manhattan Island and in Kings and Queens counties, never yielded a more mark'd and full Americanized specimen than Major Cornelius Van Velsor" (8).

Amy M. Bawcom

Bibliography

Allen, Gay Wilson. *The Solitary Singer: A Critical Biography of Walt Whitman.* 1955. Rev. ed. 1967. Chicago: U of Chicago P, 1985.

Whitman, Walt. *Specimen Days.* Vol. 1 of *Prose Works 1892.* Ed. Floyd Stovall. New York: New York UP, 1963.

See also LONG ISLAND, NEW YORK; VAN VELSOR, NAOMI ("AMY") WILLIAMS

Van Velsor, Naomi ("Amy") Williams (d. 1826)

Affectionately known as "Amy," Naomi Williams was Whitman's maternal grandmother. She married Cornelius Van Velsor and in 1795 gave birth to the daughter, Louisa, who would become Whitman's mother. According to John Burroughs, Amy "was a Friend, or Quakeress, of sweet sensible character, housewifely proclivities, and deeply intuitive and spiritual" (qtd. in Whitman 9). Her death in February 1826 profoundly saddened the six-year-old Walt. However, he would inherit from Amy Van Velsor a sympathy with Quaker customs as well as a number of family stories, some of which would find their way into *Leaves of Grass.* For instance, in section 35 of "Song of Myself," Whitman recounts a tale involving Amy's father, Captain John Williams, who served under John Paul Jones in an "old-time sea-fight" on 23 September 1779, a battle between Jones's ship, the *Bon Homme Richard,* and the British *Serapis.*

Amy M. Bawcom

Bibliography

Allen, Gay Wilson. *The Solitary Singer: A Critical Biography of Walt Whitman.* 1955. Rev. ed. 1967. Chicago: U of Chicago P, 1985.

Whitman, Walt. *Specimen Days.* Vol. 1 of *Prose Works 1892.* Ed. Floyd Stovall. New York: New York UP, 1963.

See also QUAKERS AND QUAKERISM; VAN VELSOR, CORNELIUS; WHITMAN, LOUISA VAN VELSOR

Vaughan, Frederick B. (b. 1837)

Canadian born in 1837 of Irish parents, Frederick B. Vaughan lived with Walt Whitman while the poet finished his "Calamus" poems which their love helped shape. After hearing Emerson lecture, Vaughan wanted New York to erect a

Fred-Walt statue "with an immense placard on our breasts, reading *Sincere Freinds* [sic]!!!" (qtd. in Shively 39). In 1860 Whitman sent Vaughan galleys from Boston when the 1860 *Leaves of Grass* went to press.

Bemoaning lover problems, Whitman in 1870 compared Vaughan with Peter Doyle, admonishing himself: "Remember Fred Vaughan" (Whitman 890). Vaughan confessed to Whitman: "Father used to tell me I was lazy. Mother denied it. . . . I used to tell your mother you was lazy and she denied it" (qtd. in Shively 49). Vaughan's drinking (frequently in Pfaff's) ended in what he called their "estrangement" (qtd. in Shively 49).

In 1862 Vaughan married, and he eventually became the father of four children. Whitman left New York and seldom returned. After Vaughan visited Camden in 1890, Whitman told Traubel, "Yes: I have seen him off and on—but now, poor fellow, he is all wrecked from drink" (Traubel 399). The date of Vaughan's death is unknown. Despite his estrangement from Whitman, Vaughan continued to write to Whitman, often destroying the letters without mailing them. Enclosed with one letter that he did mail was a description of a summer day in Williamsburgh which reads in part: "From among all out of all. Connected with all and yet distinct from all arrises [sic] thee Dear Walt" (qtd. in Shively 49).

Charley Shively

Bibliography

Shively, Charley. *Calamus Lovers: Walt Whitman's Working-Class Camerados.* San Francisco: Gay Sunshine, 1987.

Traubel, Horace. *With Walt Whitman in Camden.* Ed. Gertrude Traubel and William White. Vol. 6. Carbondale: Southern Illinois UP, 1982.

Whitman, Walt. *Notebooks and Unpublished Prose Manuscripts.* Ed. Edward F. Grier. Vol. 2. New York: New York UP, 1984.

See also DOYLE, PETER; "LIVE OAK WITH MOSS"; SEX AND SEXUALITY

"Vigil Strange I Kept on the Field One Night" (1865)

"Vigil Strange I Kept on the Field One Night" (1865) was first published in Walt Whitman's *Drum-Taps* (1865). The poems in the *Drum-Taps* volume, along with those in *Sequel to Drum-Taps* (1865–1866), were eventually incorporated into *Leaves of Grass*, where most of them, including "Vigil Strange," ended up in the "Drum-Taps" cluster.

The poem relates a Civil War incident that the poet may either have witnessed or experienced when he visited the front; however, critics do not agree as to the source of the incident that served as the impetus for the poem. Emory Holloway believes that Whitman is the first-person narrator in the poem. Holloway suggests that Whitman may have lived the incident in the poem when he went to Culpepper, Virginia, in the company of General Lyman Hapgood. Holloway alleges that during the visit to the front Whitman "kept vigil all night with the body of a fallen comrade" (219). On the other hand, M. Wynn Thomas ascribes the narration to a persona invented by Whitman. He reads the poem literally and states that both the father and the son are soldiers. When the son is killed the father advances in battle and then, at the end of the day, returns to the scene of the son's death and buries him "where he fell." Whitman may have meant for the soldier to be a composite American. Whatever his intent, the poem's power lies in its dramatic narrative.

The poem is a dramatic monologue in which the narrator feels all the emotional impact of his comrade's death, yet he seems to transcend to a spiritual level. He carries out his "vigil" in the starlight, feeling the "cool . . . moderate night-wind." The repetition of the word "vigil" from the title throughout the poem becomes the "central 'meaning'" (Miller, *Critical* 159). The narrator must surely feel anguish as he returns to his fallen companion, yet no anguish is overtly expressed. Only the lonely "vigil of night and battlefield dim" fills the thoughts of the narrator. The speaker, the dead comrade, and the universe are linked by the experience. As the soldier waits under the stars for the dawn, he is aware of his comrade's death and that he is powerless to save a person whom he cared for and loved. "I think," the narrator states, "we shall surely meet again." That line in the poem marks a change in the narrator's voice. Until then he speaks directly to the dead "son-soldier," but after that line to the end of the poem, the narrator speaks not to the dead comrade, but in a detached voice refers to the comrade in third person as he goes about burying the body. Miller regards this poem as "one of the really great poems in the language" (*Critical* 158).

William G. Lulloff

Bibliography

Holloway, Emory. *Whitman: An Interpretation in Narrative*. 1926. New York: Biblo and Tannen, 1969.

Miller, James E., Jr. *A Critical Guide to "Leaves of Grass."* Chicago: U of Chicago P, 1957.

———. *Walt Whitman*. New York: Twayne, 1962.

Thomas, M. Wynn. *The Lunar Light of Whitman's Poetry*. Cambridge, Mass.: Harvard UP, 1987.

Whitman, Walt. *Leaves of Grass*. Ed. Sculley Bradley and Harold W. Blodgett. Norton Critical Edition. New York: Norton, 1973.

———. *Walt Whitman's "Drum-Taps" (1865) and "Sequel to Drum-Taps" (1865–6): A Facsimile Reproduction*. Ed. F. DeWolfe Miller. Gainesville, Fla.: Scholars' Facsimiles and Reprints, 1959.

See also CIVIL WAR, THE; "DRUM-TAPS"

Volney, Constantin (1757–1820)

French linguist, historian, politician, philosopher, Constantin François Chasseboeuf, Comte de Volney was the author of *Les Ruines; ou, Méditations sur les révolutions des empires* (Paris, 1791; translated in the United States by Joel Barlow and Thomas Jefferson, about 1802). Greatly admired by Whitman's father, *The Ruins* was one of the books on which Whitman told Traubel he had been "raised" (Traubel 445). It was the principal channel to Whitman of the ideas and values of the French Enlightenment. A meditation begun at the ruins of Palmyra on the natural causes of the rise and fall of great cities and nations, *The Ruins* influenced many of Whitman's early writings, and echoes of it may be heard throughout *Leaves of Grass,* from the 1855 Preface to "Passage to India."

Volney believed that the source of all human woes was the ignorance of the weak and the greed of the strong, abetted by organized religions and tyrannical governments. This belief was tempered by his hope that by open-eyed study of nature and enlightened self-love mankind might devise a truly natural religion and thereby reach moral "perfection."

His book had far-reaching influence not only on Whitman's social and political ideas, but on his literary imagery and techniques as well. It was also one of the sources of Whitman's prodigious knowledge of comparative religion. Though Whitman greatly admired Volney, he was far from complete acceptance of Volney's mechanistic cosmology and was closer to Jean Jacques Rousseau in his assumption of innate human goodness.

Sherwood Smith

Bibliography

Allen, Gay Wilson. *The New Walt Whitman Handbook*. 1975. New York: New York UP, 1986.

Erkkila, Betsy. *Walt Whitman Among the French: Poet and Myth*. Princeton: Princeton UP, 1980.

———. *Whitman the Political Poet*. New York: Oxford UP, 1989.

Goodale, David. "Some of Walt Whitman's Borrowings." *American Literature* 10 (1938): 202–213.

Traubel, Horace. *With Walt Whitman in Camden*. Vol. 2. New York: Appleton, 1908.

Volney, C.F. *The Ruins, or, Meditations on the Revolutions of Empires; and the Laws of Nature*. 1791. Baltimore, Md.: Black Classics, 1991.

See also PAINE, THOMAS; RELIGION; WRIGHT, FRANCES (FANNY)

Wallace, James William (1853–1926)

James William Wallace, an English architect, was a Whitman enthusiast, a founding member of Bolton "College," a Whitman correspondent, a visitor to Walt Whitman in Camden in 1891, and coauthor of a book with Dr. John Johnston (d. 1918), fellow Bolton "College" Member, about their separate visits to Whitman.

In 1885 Wallace, thirty-one and unmarried, organized Monday night meetings at his father's house on Eagle Street in Bolton, England. Known locally as "the Eagle Street 'College'" and abroad as Bolton "College," this group included mostly working class men with limited educational backgrounds. The appellation "College" shows the humor of the group, which met without formal organization or purpose for discussion of local interest topics, politics, humor, and spiritual matters.

After the death of his mother in January of 1885, Wallace had a mystical experience about which he wrote and which Dr. Richard Maurice Bucke (1837–1902) included in his *Cosmic Consciousness*.

Wallace and Johnston began a correspondence with Walt Whitman in 1887. By the time of his death, Whitman had written the two men more than 120 letters and postcards. Whitman also presented his stuffed canary to Wallace. Today, the Metropolitan Library in Bolton holds the canary and other Whitman gifts to the group.

In 1891 Wallace visited Whitman in Camden and Bucke in London, Ontario. Wallace also visited Andrew H. Rome in New York and the Cranberry Street room where the Romes printed *Leaves of Grass* (1855). He visited the Whitman Birthplace, Jayne's Hill, both Whitman maternal and paternal homesteads and

burial grounds, and various Whitman relatives on Long Island.

Larry D. Griffin

Bibliography

Bucke, Richard Maurice. *Cosmic Consciousness: A Study in the Evolution of the Human Mind.* Philadelphia: Innes, 1901.

Hamer, Harold. *A Catalogue of Works by and Relating to Walt Whitman in the Reference Library, Bolton.* Bolton, England: Libraries Committee, 1955.

Johnston, John, and J.W. Wallace. *Visits to Walt Whitman in 1890–1891.* London: Allen and Unwin, 1917.

Salveson, Paul. *Loving Comrades: Lancashire's Links to Walt Whitman.* Bolton, England: Worker's Educational Association, 1984.

Wallace, J.W. *Walt Whitman and the World Crisis.* Manchester: The National Labour Press, 1920.

See also BOLTON (ENGLAND) "EAGLE STREET COLLEGE"; BRITISH ISLES, WHITMAN IN THE; BUCKE, RICHARD MAURICE; JOHNSTON, DR. JOHN

Walt Whitman's Blue Book (1968)

The Blue Book (bound in blue paper wrappers) was Whitman's personal, annotated copy of the 1860 (third) edition of *Leaves of Grass*. Over the span of the Civil War (1861–1865), Whitman carefully revised the bulk of the poems in the third edition, bringing them more closely in line with his on-the-spot responses to the war. The Blue Book was to serve as the revised text of the next (1867) edition of *Leaves*, but Whitman, for the most part, rejected many of these revisions in favor of the 1860 text. For this reason, the Blue Book enables one to recover Whitman's overall poetic strategies for *Leaves of Grass* under the urgent pressures of war during this crucial period of his career.

Whitman had termed the third edition of *Leaves of Grass* his "New Bible" (*Blue Book* 2:xxxi). To the thirty-two poems of the 1855 and 1856 editions Whitman added 146 new poems to *Leaves*. These included most of the poems that formed the programmatic-nationalistic "cluster," or grouping of poems, "Chants Democratic and Native American"; the "Children of Adam" cluster, celebrating heterosexual love; the "Calamus" cluster, in which Whitman often interwove an intense homosexual emotion with the general theme of the "Brotherhood of Man"; and various miscellaneous clusters. Very little had escaped Whitman's attention in the Blue Book. All but 34 of its 456 pages often show heavy revisions, excisions, paste-on slips containing fresh lines, marginal notations, and erasures, all variously in ink and pencils of different colors.

Throughout *Leaves of Grass*, Whitman's integral nationalist bonding metaphor was that of the celebration of the "divine average," of the American people "en-masse." The war stifled this idea of the organic oneness of the states. In the Blue Book, Whitman's aim was to bring the divided nation to a prewar visionary nationalistic homogeneity. In effect, his revisory strategy was to hold in suspension two separate attitudes toward the South. For example, in his heavy revisions for the "Chants Democratic" poem "By Blue Ontario's Shore," it was as though the South, not mentioned by name, was some *foreign* aggressor attacking the United States. In a paste-on addition, we get these lines, retained in 1867:

The menacing, arrogant one, that strode
    and advanced with his senseless
      scorn, bearing the murderous knife!
Lo! the wide swelling one, the braggart
    that would yesterday do so much!
Already a carrion dead, and despised of
    all the earth—an offal rank,
This day to the dunghill maggots spurn'd.
                (*Blue Book* 2:114)

But for the "other" South, the South of the "people," in the 1860 poem "Longings for Home" ("O Magnet-South"), Whitman in light revision retained almost intact his antebellum romantic view of the South.

In this connection, faced at the early stages of the war with the possible dissolution of the Union, and with such foreign powers as England and France antagonistic to the Union cause, Whitman's intense nationalism at times shifted during this period to the xenophobic. In the poem "Our Old Feuillage," Whitman wished to "demain [or cut America off from the rest of] the continent!" (*Blue Book* 2:160). With a Northern victory, he rejected this revision in 1867. Following the end of the war, with an occasional exception (e.g., "By Blue Ontario's Shore") Whitman rejected in 1867 most of his harshest nationalistic revisions.

In the Blue Book Whitman was also preoccupied with subjecting the forty-five-poem "Calamus" cluster to heavy revision. The calamus image derives from the calamus plant, a phallic-shaped, aromatic plant found in remote marshy areas. It served Whitman as the combined metaphor for the themes of the "Brotherhood of Men" and the often intense homosexual emotion. Elsewhere in the Blue Book, Whitman in revision regularly interwove the "Calamus" theme with the nationalistic theme, as, for example, in "Starting from Paumanok," thus giving its initial democratic motif a more intense bonding of "manly love."

In this connection, in the revised "Calamus" grouping, Whitman often considerably strengthened the homosexual motif. In an apparent effort to tighten matters and avoid repeating the same theme and emotion he had explored variously in 1860, Whitman initially had rejected no fewer than thirteen poems, later restoring four. Had he followed through on his Blue Book revisions in 1867, one-fifth of the "Calamus" cluster would have disappeared. Had Whitman intended to suppress passages or entire poems that delineated his homosexual sensibility, he certainly would have done so in the extensively revised "Calamus" group. That is, any logical assumption of suppression would presuppose the outright elimination, or the watering down, of the "Calamus" metaphor in poems, stanzas, lines. On the contrary, in poem after poem Whitman retained through extensive revision passages as revealing in the intensity of the "Calamus" emotion as anything he had rejected. And, for example, in "Whoever You are Holding Me Now in Hand," the revised version was, if anything, even more intensely evocative and personal than in 1860. On the other hand, the quietly suggestive "A Glimpse" remained more or less as in 1860. Whitman saw fit to reject most of the "Calamus" revisions in 1867. The three 1860 "Calamus" poems he dropped from the 1867 edition were certainly highly personal, but no more so contextually than the revised Blue Book "Calamus" poems, or the sexually explicit "Calamus" poems he retained in 1867. In all, forty poems were variously rejected, with six restored. It appears to have been Whitman's aim not merely to revise the poems, but also to achieve overall a broader economy of statement. Only six new poems appeared in the 1867 edition. During this period, Whitman had also completed the *Drum-Taps* (1865) poems.

The Blue Book had gained notoriety over the years as the volume that led to Whitman's dismissal in 1865 from his clerkship in the Indian Office of the Department of the Interior. Whitman had kept the book in his desk. Secretary of the Interior James Harlan somehow got hold of the copy, was scandalized by its openness, and fired Whitman. Through the influence of friends, Whitman was hired the next day in the Attorney General's Office, where he remained free from official smut-hounds until 1873, when he suffered a stroke and left government service.

One of Whitman's literary executors, Horace Traubel, tried unsuccessfully over the years to issue a facsimile edition of the Blue Book. In 1968 the noted Whitman collector Oscar Lion, who gave to the New York Public Library his important Whitman collection, generously made possible the publication of an exact facsimile edition of the Blue Book and an accompanying introduction and analysis of all the revisions. One can now follow Whitman's advice to Traubel and take "a glimpse into the workshop" without being put off by the myths that had obscured its importance over the years.

Arthur Golden

Bibliography

Golden, Arthur. "New Light on *Leaves of Grass:* Whitman's Annotated Copy of the 1860 (Third) Edition." *Bulletin of the New York Public Library* 69 (1965): 283–306.

Killingsworth, M. Jimmie. *Whitman's Poetry of the Body: Sexuality, Politics, and the Text.* Chapel Hill: U of North Carolina P, 1989.

Miller, James E., Jr. *A Critical Guide to "Leaves of Grass."* Chicago: U of Chicago P, 1957.

Whitman, Walt. *Prose Works 1892.* Ed. Floyd Stovall. 2 vols. New York: New York UP, 1963–1964.

———. *Walt Whitman's Blue Book.* Ed. Arthur Golden. 2 vols. New York: New York Public Library, 1968.

———. *Walt Whitman's Civil War.* Ed. Walter Lowenfels. New York: Knopf, 1960.

———. *Whitman's Manuscripts: "Leaves of Grass" (1860).* Ed. Fredson Bowers. Chicago: U of Chicago P, 1955.

See also CIVIL WAR, THE; HARLAN, JAMES W.; LEAVES OF GRASS, 1860 EDITION

Warren, Samuel (1807–1877)

Samuel Warren, poet and author of *Ten Thousand a Year* (1840–1841), was born 23 May 1807, at the Rackery, near Wrexham. His father, a Wesleyan minister, formed the Wesleyan Methodist Association, or "Warrenites," which later became the United Methodist Free Churches. The younger Warren, eldest son of Dr. Samuel Warren, studied medicine at Edinburgh (1826–1827), where he won a prize for poetry in 1827. Thus began Warren's career in creative literature, intermittent at times with a career in law, which finally culminated in *The Lily and the Bee: An Apologue of the Crystal Palace* (1851).

This prose-poetry work bears some rather curious similarities to Whitman's *Leaves of Grass.* Whitman's contemporaries commonly believed Warren to be an influence, and speculation among scholars continues even at present. Allen, Reynolds, Zweig, and Carpenter all notice similarities such as parallelism, apostrophe, declamation, and sweep between the authors. Carpenter, however, posits that a closer examination of these will dispel any notions of similarities, stating in addition that Whitman had found his "new style" by March 1851 (42).

Stephen A. Cooper

Bibliography

Allen, Gay Wilson. *Walt Whitman Handbook.* 1946. New York: Hendricks House, 1962.

Carpenter, George Rice. *Walt Whitman.* New York: Macmillan, 1909.

Reynolds, David S. *Walt Whitman's America: A Cultural Biography.* New York: Knopf, 1995.

Zweig, Paul. *Walt Whitman: The Making of the Poet.* New York: Basic Books, 1984.

See also INFLUENCES ON WHITMAN, PRINCIPAL; TUPPER, MARTIN FARQUHAR

Bird's Eye View of Washington, D.C., and Environs, 1865. By permission, Kiplinger Washington Collection.

Washington, D.C. (1863–1873)

The decade that Walt Whitman lived in the nation's capital proved remarkably rich for him both professionally and personally. Whitman's Civil War experiences gave rise to *Drum-Taps* and *Memoranda During the War,* his grief for the slain president was expressed in the Lincoln elegies, and his disgust with the corruption and materialism of postwar society erupted in *Democratic Vistas.* The man who had proclaimed himself the "poet of comrades" ("These I Singing in Spring") formed loving friendships with Charles Eldridge, Lewy Brown, William and Ellen O'Connor, John and Ursula Burroughs, and Peter Doyle. But for a stroke that caused him to retire to Camden, New Jersey, Whitman might have spent the remainder of his days in the federal district.

Drawn initially to D.C. to nurse his brother George, a Union soldier who had been wounded at the battle of Fredericksburg (13 December 1862), Whitman remained in the capital to comfort the casualties of the Civil War. Psychically wounded by the prospect that the Union would falter, Whitman found healing in the willingness of his countrymen to defend the republic against the evil twins, Secession and Slavery. A self-styled "dweller in camps" ("Hush'd be the Camps Today"), Whitman could easily walk to barracks set up in government office buildings, as well as in larger campgrounds such as Carver Barracks on the grounds of Columbian College or in the numerous defensive forts that ringed the city. Daily visiting one of the dozens of Washington hospitals—Armory Square, Finley, and Harewood being a small sample—Whitman befriended scores of soldiers. The camaraderie that Whitman witnessed and often shared with such convalescents as Lewy Brown, Tom Sawyer, and Reuben Farwell affirmed the belief expressed in "Over the Carnage Rose Prophetic a Voice" that "affection shall solve the problems of freedom yet."

Whitman's poetical response to the war, *Drum-Taps,* was ready for the printer when Robert E. Lee's army surrendered to Ulysses S. Grant at Appomattox Court House, Virginia, on 9 April 1865. This zenith for the Union was succeeded five days later by its nadir, the assassination of President Abraham Lincoln at Ford's Theater in Washington, D.C. The poet's quaternary on the death of Lincoln includes Whitman's most popular poem, "O Captain! My Captain!," and one of his most critically acclaimed, "When Lilacs Last in the Dooryard Bloom'd."

During his Washington years, Whitman published nearly a hundred new poems. He shepherded *Leaves of Grass* through two new editions (1867 and 1871) and separately published a major poem, *Passage to India* (1871).

He also cooperated with William Michael Rossetti's publication of a selection of Whitman's poems in England (1868), an edition which gained Whitman an appreciative and influential British audience that included Anne Gilchrist, Edward Carpenter, Edward Dowden, Bram Stoker, and John Addington Symonds.

Between 1863 and 1873 Whitman supported himself in the same manner as most Washingtonians, by working for the federal government. Through Charles Eldridge, the publisher of the third edition of *Leaves of Grass* (1860) who was serving as Assistant Army Paymaster during the war, Whitman obtained part-time employment in the paymaster's office. A full-time berth came in January 1865, when Whitman was appointed to a first class (lowest grade) clerkship in the Interior Department's Bureau of Indian Affairs, located in the Patent Office Building. There the "poet-chief" (*Notebooks* 2:881) welcomed visiting delegations of Indian tribes, when not performing the more prosaic duties of his job, such as writing reports for Congressional oversight committees. Dismissed on 30 June 1865 by Interior Secretary James Harlan for authoring "that book" (*Notebooks* 2:799), Whitman started work the next day through the influence of his friends in the Attorney General's Office in the Treasury Building, adjacent to the White House. Investigating government malfeasance during the Johnson and Grant administrations provided steady employment for Whitman, who rose to a third class clerkship.

Whitman lived modestly on his clerk's salary, settling for inexpensive rooms in boardinghouses. He relied on his married friends, William and Ellen O'Connor, and John and Ursula Burroughs, to provide social stimulation. At the O'Connors' evening salons, Whitman met many of Washington's political and literary elite, including John and Sarah Piatt (poets), John Hay (Lincoln's personal secretary), Count Adam Gurowski (Polish ex-patriot and radical abolitionist), and Frank Baker (later head of the National Zoo).

O'Connor and Burroughs were strong Whitman loyalists. After Whitman was fired from Interior, O'Connor took on the poet's persecutors in a stirring polemic he titled *The Good Gray Poet* (1866). In the process, Whitman obtained additional celebrity status and a lasting sobriquet. Burroughs provided a more balanced assessment in the poet's first critical biography, *Notes on Walt Whitman as Poet and Person* (1867).

Whitman found friendship with Peter Doyle. The twenty-one-year-old horsecar conductor and former Confederate soldier became acquainted with the forty-five-year-old Whitman in the early months of 1865. Thereafter, the comrades were inseparable, spending long hours riding on Doyle's streetcar, or taking moonlight walks along the Potomac, or feasting on melons at Center Market on Pennsylvania Avenue.

With its unpaved roads and swampy terrain, wartime Washington was notorious as a city of mud. After the war, Washington experienced a building boom under the leadership of Alexander "Boss" Shepherd, whose administration laid sewers, paved roads, and built schools. Municipal corruption mirrored national scandals such as the Crédit Mobilier and formed the backdrop to *Democratic Vistas* (1871), Whitman's lamentation on the unfulfilled promise of the "American Experiment."

During and after the war, the city's population was swelled by Southern refugees, especially African Americans escaping oppression and poverty. The large influx of poor blacks exacerbated racial tensions in the nation's capital, whose residents had long regarded themselves as more Southern than Northern in their beliefs and practices. While Eldridge and the O'Connors worked tirelessly to improve the life of the district's freedmen, Whitman refrained from personal involvement in their plight. David Reynolds attributes Whitman's conservative political perspective, in part, to his warm personal regard for Attorneys General Henry Stanbery and William Evart, under whom Whitman served. Both Stanbery and Evart were closely tied to President Andrew Johnson's Reconstruction policies favoring Southern whites at the expense of blacks. William O'Connor's advocacy of Negro suffrage and Whitman's indifference bordering on hostility was the fault line running through their friendship, which finally ruptured in 1872.

While reading in his office in the Treasury Building on the evening of 23 January 1873, Whitman suffered a stroke. Exactly four months later, on 23 May, he was dealt an equally painful blow when his mother died. Moving that summer to his brother George's home in Camden, New Jersey, Whitman never regained the health that would have enabled him to return to Washington.

Martin G. Murray

Bibliography

Allen, Gay Wilson. *The Solitary Singer: A Critical Biography of Walt Whitman*. 1955. Rev. ed. 1967. Chicago: U of Chicago P, 1985.

Freedman, Florence Bernstein. *William Douglas O'Connor: Walt Whitman's Chosen Knight*. Athens: Ohio UP, 1985.

Green, Constance McLaughlin. *Washington, A History of the Capital, 1800–1950*. 1962. Princeton: Princeton UP, 1976.

Leech, Margaret. *Reveille in Washington, 1860–1865*. New York: Harper, 1941.

Reynolds, David S. *Walt Whitman's America: A Cultural Biography*. New York: Knopf, 1995.

Wecter, Dixon. "Walt Whitman as Civil Servant." *PMLA* 58 (1943): 1094–1109.

Whitman, Walt. *Notebooks and Unpublished Manuscripts*. Ed. Edward F. Grier. 6 vols. New York: New York UP, 1984.

See also BROWN, LEWIS KIRK; BURROUGHS, JOHN AND URSULA; CIVIL WAR, THE; CIVIL WAR NURSING; *DEMOCRATIC VISTAS;* DOYLE, PETER; *DRUM-TAPS;* GUROWSKI, COUNT ADAM DE; *LEAVES OF GRASS, 1867 EDITION; LEAVES OF GRASS, 1871–1872 EDITION;* LINCOLN'S DEATH; *MEMORANDA DURING THE WAR;* O'CONNOR (CALDER), ELLEN ("NELLY") M. TARR; O'CONNOR, WILLIAM DOUGLAS; RECONSTRUCTION

Washington, George (1732–1799)

A Virginia planter, surveyor, and an officer in the French and Indian War (1753–1759), Washington's first major political office was in the Virginia House of Burgesses (1758–1774). Washington also served as a delegate to the first and second Continental Congresses (1774, 1775). He is best known as commander of the Continental Army in the American Revolution (1775–1783) and first president of the United States (1789–1797).

By the time of Walt Whitman's birth, Washington was the mythical Father of his Country, nearly deified in popular iconography and in Mason Weems's best-selling *Life of Washington* (1809). Washington was part of Whitman's family history; the poet's early youth was spent in the West Hills, where his granduncle had served under Washington at the battle of Brooklyn (1776), an event retold by Whitman in "The Centenarian's Story" and "The Sleepers." One

of Whitman's brothers was named "George Washington," and Whitman treasured a memory of Washington's beloved general, the Marquis de Lafayette, kissing him as a child on 4 July 1825. In Whitman's short story, "The Last of the Sacred Army," published in the *Democratic Review* (March 1842), an adoring crowd beseeches an aged soldier of Washington's army, "Speak to us of him, and of his time'" (*Early* 98–99). In an *Eagle* column of 4 December 1846 Whitman recounts Washington's farewell to his officers, a scene which also reappears in "The Sleepers": "The chief encircles their necks with his arm and kisses them on the cheek" (section 5). In later years, Whitman is said to have compared himself to Washington: as Washington freed America from English political domination, so Whitman would free America from European ideals.

William A. Pannapacker

Bibliography

Binns, Henry Bryan. *A Life of Walt Whitman*. London: Methuen, 1905.

Freeman, Douglass Southall. *George Washington: A Biography*. Completed by J.A. Carroll and M.W. Ashworth. 7 vols. New York: Scribner's, 1948–1957.

Reynolds, David S. *Walt Whitman's America: A Cultural Biography*. New York: Knopf, 1995.

Weems, Mason L. *The Life of Washington*. 1809. Ed. Marcus Cunliffe. Cambridge, Mass.: Harvard UP, 1962.

Whitman, Walt. *The Early Poems and the Fiction*. Ed. Thomas L. Brasher. New York: New York UP, 1963.

———. *The Gathering of the Forces*. Ed. Cleveland Rodgers and John Black. 2 vols. New York: Putnam, 1920.

See also AMERICAN REVOLUTION, THE; BROOKLYN, NEW YORK; "CENTENARIAN'S STORY, THE"; GENEALOGY; LAFAYETTE, MARQUIS DE; "LAST OF THE SACRED ARMY, THE"; "SLEEPERS, THE"; WHITMAN, GEORGE WASHINGTON

"We Two Boys together Clinging" (1860)

This nine-line poem was originally published as number 26 in the "Calamus" cluster of the 1860 *Leaves of Grass*. Its original eighth line was dropped in 1867; otherwise, its text remained the same in all succeeding editions, except for minor alterations in punctuation. The poem's first line was used as its title from 1867 onward. However, in the poem's earliest manuscript version, entitled "Razzia," the first two lines are not present and the pronouns are all first person singular. Thus between manuscript and publication Whitman converted a poem of singular self-assertion into a representation of exclusive love between two young men.

Unlike the mere joy in the lover's presence extolled in other "Calamus" poems such as "A Glimpse" (1860) or "When I Heard at the Close of the Day" (1860), the affection between the two boys is enacted through shared physical activities. Harold Aspiz notes that the boys, like other idealized male figures in Whitman's poems, drink only water, reflecting Whitman's interest in hydrotherapy and bodily health. Some of the boys' activities—"thieving, threatening, . . . priests alarming, . . . statutes mocking"—are moderately antisocial, suggesting the lawless Bowery toughs with whom Whitman liked to associate and whose pose he adopted in the frontispiece to the 1855 *Leaves of Grass*. The boys' youth and activeness also recalls the wrestling apprentices in "I Sing the Body Electric" (1855), the kind of young white workingmen who serve as the primary objects of erotic attraction for the poet throughout *Leaves of Grass* and whom he addresses as the republic's best political hope in his lecture/essay "The Eighteenth Presidency!" (1856).

Michael Moon notes that, despite the idealized glow cast on the two boys, such dyadic pairing in this and some other "Calamus" poems is exceptional in *Leaves of Grass*. Most same-sex interactions in Whitman's poetry involve the poet with an indeterminable number of male others, such as the journeying companions in "Song of the Open Road" (1856) or the "gay gang of blackguards" in section 1 of "The Sleepers" (1855).

Carl Smeller

Bibliography

Aspiz, Harold. *Walt Whitman and the Body Beautiful*. Urbana: U of Illinois P, 1980.
Fone, Byrne R.S. *Masculine Landscapes: Walt Whitman and the Homoerotic Text*. Carbondale: Southern Illinois UP, 1992.
Moon, Michael. *Disseminating Whitman: Revision and Corporeality in "Leaves of Grass."* Cambridge, Mass.: Harvard UP, 1991.
Whitman, Walt. *Complete Poetry and Collected Prose*. Ed. Justin Kaplan. New York: Library of America, 1982.
———. *Leaves of Grass: Facsimile Edition of the 1860 Text*. Ed. Roy Harvey Pearce. Ithaca, N.Y.: Cornell UP, 1961.
———. *Walt Whitman's Manuscripts: "Leaves of Grass" (1860)*. Ed. Fredson Bowers. Chicago: U of Chicago P, 1955.

See also "CALAMUS"; COMRADESHIP; ROUGHS; SEX AND SEXUALITY

"We Two, How Long We were Fool'd" (1860)

"We Two, How Long We were Fool'd" first appeared as poem number 7 in the cluster "Enfans d'Adam." It assumed its present title in the 1867 edition. After the 1860 edition, two lines were dropped from the poem. Before the present line 1 there appeared, "You and I—what the earth is, we are," and the following after line 10: "We are what the flowing wet of the Tennessee is—we are two peaks of the Blue Mountains, rising up in Virginia." Whitman apparently changed his mind several times as he worked on revisions of the 1860 edition of this poem. From an analysis of Whitman's copy, Golden concludes that the poet first transposed lines 1 and 2, by writing "We two—how long we were fool'd" but then rejected the printed line "You and I—what the earth is, we are" altogether. Whitman may have considered using printed line 3 as an opener but then decided to stay with the opening line (and title) as we have them today. For the new line 2, Whitman struck the word "delicious" and switched the position of "swiftly" and "we." Although it is clear from Whitman's Blue Book that he moved the words "we are as two comets" one line higher (to follow "we soar above and look down"), the change does not appear in editions subsequent to the Blue Book, nor do Whitman's manipulations with line breaks in the Blue Book for lines 14 and 15.

Killingsworth sees in this poem a significant shift in Whitman's attitude on sexual acceptance. Whereas in 1855 Whitman wanted men and women to accept their own bodies so that they might be vehicles for contact with others, in a "Children of Adam" poem like "We Two, How Long We were Fool'd," Whitman turns inward and stresses the need for his unwilling female readers to accept his male body and his poem as given, even though they are separate from his readers' desires. Although E.H. Miller understands the two to be a modern Adam and Eve in search of a new spirit, he finds the poem actually celebrates male-male attraction, and Allen notes that the theme of the poem stresses that the pair were gulled by abstinence. In a sequence of poems that stresses elemental imagery with water and earth predominating over air and fire, the poem "We Two" mixes images of nature.

George Klawitter

Bibliography

Allen, Gay Wilson. *Walt Whitman Handbook*. 1946. New York: Hendricks House, 1962.

Killingsworth, M. Jimmie. *Whitman's Poetry of the Body: Sexuality, Politics, and the Text*. Chapel Hill: U of North Carolina P, 1989.

Miller, Edwin Haviland. *Walt Whitman's Poetry: A Psychological Journey*. New York: New York UP, 1969.

Stephens, Rosemary. "Elemental Imagery in 'Children of Adam.'" *Walt Whitman Review* 14 (1968): 26–28.

Whitman, Walt. *Leaves of Grass: A Textual Variorum of the Printed Poems*. Ed. Sculley Bradley, Harold W. Blodgett, Arthur Golden, and William White. 3 vols. New York: New York UP, 1980.

———. *Walt Whitman's Blue Book*. Ed. Arthur Golden. 2 vols. New York: New York Public Library, 1968.

See also "CHILDREN OF ADAM"; HUMAN BODY

Wells, Samuel Roberts (1820–1875)

The publication of the second edition of *Leaves of Grass* without an imprimatur by the phrenologist-publishers Fowler and Wells in 1856 is attributable in large measure to S.R. Wells. In 1843 Wells joined the business founded by O.S. and L.N. Fowler, married their sister Charlotte in 1844, and became a member of the firm, renamed Fowlers and Wells. Wells headed the publishing department, his list including phrenological handbooks and manuals on related reforms: vegetarianism, temperance, and water cure.

By June 1856, when Whitman was contributing to *Life Illustrated*, one of the firm's periodicals, the possibility of a new edition of *Leaves of Grass* had been broached. That Wells was reluctant is reflected in his letter of 7 June 1856 to "Friend Whitman," insisting upon the omission of "objectionable passages" and sug-

gesting that the work would be better published elsewhere. Wells's ambivalence and timidity certainly contributed to the firm's compromise decision to publish the expanded second edition of *Leaves of Grass* without a firm imprimatur. Fowler and Wells (the firm had been renamed with Orson S. Fowler's withdrawal in September 1855) agreed to print and sell one thousand copies of the new *Leaves of Grass*—the edition that reprinted Whitman's phrenological analysis made by Lorenzo N. Fowler in 1849 and carried on the spine of each volume Emerson's endorsement without Emerson's authorization. The firm's support was still anonymous and halfhearted, however, and after the book's unfavorable reception, the relationship of Walt Whitman to Fowler and Wells ceased.

Madeleine B. Stern

Bibliography

Myerson, Joel. *Walt Whitman: A Descriptive Bibliography*. Pittsburgh: U of Pittsburgh P, 1993.

Stern, Madeleine B. *Heads & Headlines: The Phrenological Fowlers*. Norman: U of Oklahoma P, 1971.

Wells, Samuel Roberts. Letter to Walt Whitman. 7 June 1856. Charles E. Feinberg Collection. Library of Congress.

See also FOWLER, LORENZO NILES AND ORSON SQUIRE; *LEAVES OF GRASS*, 1856 EDITION; *LIFE ILLUSTRATED*; PHRENOLOGY

West Jersey Press

The *West Jersey Press* was a weekly newspaper published in Camden. On 26 January 1876 the *Press* published the anonymous article "Walt Whitman's Actual American Position," written by the poet himself. In the piece, Whitman complained with hyperbolic self-pity that he had been almost completely ignored by the American people. He lamented, "[W]ith the exception of a very few readers . . . Whitman's poems in their public reception have fallen still-born in their country. They have been met . . . with the determined denial, disgust and scorn of orthodox American authors . . . and, in a pecuniary and worldly sense, have certainly wrecked the life of their author" (qtd. in Reynolds 516).

The day the article appeared, Whitman sent a copy to William Rossetti, calling his real situation "even worse than described in the article" and asking that the piece be printed in

London (Whitman 20). Excerpts printed in the 11 March 1876 *Athenaeum* touched off a flurry of accusations and denials. Periodicals ranging from the London *Daily News* to *Harper's*, *Scribner's*, and the New York *Tribune* took up the issue of Whitman's status, both aesthetic and pecuniary. On 24 May 1876 Whitman added to the controversy by publishing a second anonymous article in the *West Jersey Press*, confirming his destitution and describing himself as "a continuous target for slang, slur, insults, gas-promises, disappointments, caricature—without a publisher, without a public" (qtd. in Reynolds 520). The two *West Jersey Press* articles brought Whitman a good deal of public notice and boosted both his reputation and his morale. Although the articles greatly exaggerated Whitman's actual poverty and neglect, they accurately reflected the poet's personal frustrations at having achieved neither the level of cultural influence nor the popular adulation of which he deemed himself worthy.

John T. Matteson

Bibliography

Allen, Gay Wilson. *The Solitary Singer: A Critical Biography of Walt Whitman.* 1955. Rev. ed. 1967. Chicago: U of Chicago P, 1985.

Reynolds, David S. *Walt Whitman's America: A Cultural Biography.* New York: Knopf, 1995.

Whitman, Walt. *The Correspondence.* Ed. Edwin Haviland Miller. Vol. 3. New York: New York UP, 1964.

See also BRITISH ISLES, WHITMAN IN THE; CAMDEN, NEW JERSEY; ROSSETTI, WILLIAM MICHAEL; SELF-REVIEWS OF THE 1855 *LEAVES*, WHITMAN'S ANONYMOUS

West, The American

For Walt Whitman, the American West represented a point of intersection between the concrete reality of the present and his own idealized dream of the nation's future. Although he never lived for an extensive period of time in the West and rarely traveled there, he did reserve the latter months of 1879 for what he referred to as "quite a western journey" (*Specimen Days* 850). He traveled from Philadelphia as far west as Colorado, finding himself impressed on an almost daily basis by the region's visual beauty and by the physical and spiritual endurance of its inhabitants. Not surprisingly, this trip helped to confirm one of his deepest intuitive beliefs: that the West was the place where his vision of the ideal American democracy would find its ultimate and definitive fruition.

Although Whitman was born in the East and lived most of his life in cities such as New York or Washington, D.C., he was still willing to say, in an interview published on 13 September 1879 by the St. Louis *Daily Globe-Democrat*, that he was "in sympathy and preference Western—better fitted for the Mississippi Valley." His sympathies lay with the West because, as he had previously written, it seemed probable that the very "spine-character of the States" would be located there (*Democratic Vistas* 952). He believed the region to be populated by sturdy, determined, unpretentious people, the kind of people who would become the collective progenitors of his golden American future. He wished to name himself among such people.

Significantly, the two men Whitman considered most representative of this western ideal were Abraham Lincoln and Ulysses S. Grant. These were "vast-spread, average men," but they possessed "foregrounds of character altogether practical and real," accompanied by the "finest backgrounds of the ideal" (*Specimen Days* 854). Whitman knew historians would forever link these men with that great conflagration of the American past, the Civil War, yet he believed their efforts to preserve the Union sprang not merely from a commitment to a unified nation, but also from a commitment to an as yet unrealized American future. He believed their status as native westerners, as men accustomed to a constantly changing and retreating frontier, had helped to fortify them in their struggle to achieve an intangible and elusive ideal. Thus, his faith in a grand national future was bolstered by his assumption that the fellow citizens of Lincoln and Grant—citizens of the plains, prairies, and swelling western cities—would possess the same instinctive dedication to the future as did his two representative men.

Whitman's own faith in the West as the great stage of the American future may be seen in *Democratic Vistas*, where many of his remarks about the region are pointedly placed in the context of the future. "In a few years," he declares, "the dominion-heart of America will be far inland, toward the West" (951). The same paragraph contains his speculation that the nation's capital may one day be moved far west and restructured according to newer and superior principles, the implication being that the physical movement westward will signify a moral and spiritual movement forward for the nation. Such a speculation contrasts sharply with those caustic passages in *Democratic Vistas* where Whitman rails against the materialism of the East and argues that, even though this materialism has created great cities, it has also created a superficial society that is spiritually dry, empty, and desolate. Exasperated by what he perceived as the shallow spirit of the American present, and equally troubled by an American past permanently seared by the horrors of the Civil War, he invested his hopes in the American future: "To-day, ahead, though dimly yet, we see, in vistas, a copious, sane, gigantic offspring" (*Democratic Vistas* 929).

Whitman's 1879 trip across the Great Plains to the Rockies helped confirm his belief that such an offspring would come from the gigantic American West. For him the region meant far more than mighty rivers, fertile soil, and apparently limitless natural resources. As he crossed the prairies he saw a length and breadth of land to which his Eastern eye was unaccustomed, and he came to feel the presence of a "vast Something, stretching out on its own unbounded scale, . . . combining the real and the ideal, and beautiful as dreams" (*Specimen Days* 853). He was sure that here, on this vast canvas, the great American epic of flesh and spirit would unfold, revealing the country's "distinctive ideas and distinctive realities" (854).

Much of this distinctiveness had to do with the particular kind of beauty Whitman encountered in the West, a beauty to which he believed he had been intuitively alluding in his own poetry. Looking out upon the jagged, looming majesty of a mountain peak, or the raw, river-forged scoop of a gorge, or even the opaque flow of a stream gone brown with clay and sediment, he could say to himself, "I have found the law of my own poems" (*Specimen Days* 855). This was a law—whether it be applied to nature, beauty, or art—that placed no predetermined restrictions upon form. As a result, when Whitman looked at the raw, elemental landscape of the West, he saw a landscape that seemed to confirm his own poetic instincts. Moreover, this landscape seemed somehow prophetic to him, as if its enormous scale and remarkable variety of forms held out a sure promise that the people who dwelt here would also achieve great scale and diversity. He knew the distinctive face of the West had been forged by tangible elements like sun, wind, rain, fire, and ice,

but he believed a less tangible force, something akin to national destiny, was at work as well. This force would ensure that westerners of the future embodied both the real and ideal qualities of their land. In doing so, they would shape democracy into new, grand, and unanticipated forms.

At the end of 1879 Walt Whitman ended his western journey and returned to the East, having traveled, according to his own estimation, more than ten thousand miles. His mind was still bathed in memories of the immense landscape he had traversed, but the journey seemed to have wearied him as well. He wished to retire for a while to the small woods and creek where he felt most at home. Yet there was no question in his mind as to the worth of his journey. In one of his final entries on the West in *Specimen Days*, he asserts that no one can "know the real geographic, democratic, indissoluble American Union in the present, or suspect it in the future" without viewing the prairies, the states of the Midwest, or the Mississippi River (871). The fact that he had journeyed even farther west than these destinations may hint at his desire to think of himself as a truly Western man, as someone whose eyes instinctively turned toward the far horizon in search of an eternal and ideal tomorrow.

C.D. Albin

Bibliography

Eitner, Walter H. *Walt Whitman's Western Jaunt.* Lawrence: Regents Press of Kansas, 1981.

Fussell, Edwin. "Walt Whitman's *Leaves of Grass.*" *Frontier: American Literature and the American West.* By Fussell. Princeton: Princeton UP, 1965. 397–441.

Hubach, Robert R. "Walt Whitman and the West." Diss. Indiana U, 1943.

Smith, Henry Nash. "Walt Whitman and Manifest Destiny." *Virgin Land: The American West as Symbol and Myth.* By Smith. Cambridge, Mass.: Harvard UP, 1950. 47–51.

Whitman, Walt. *Democratic Vistas. Complete Poetry and Collected Prose.* Ed. Justin Kaplan. New York: Library of America, 1982. 929–994.

———. *Specimen Days. Complete Poetry and Collected Prose.* Ed. Justin Kaplan. New York: Library of America, 1982. 689–926.

See also DEMOCRATIC VISTAS; DENVER, COLORADO; GREAT PLAINS AND PRAIRIES, THE; IMPERIALISM; LAWRENCE, KANSAS; LINCOLN, ABRAHAM; MISSISSIPPI RIVER; ROCKY MOUNTAINS; SPECIMEN DAYS; TRAVELS, WHITMAN'S

Westminster Review, The

Among the powerful arbiters of taste in nineteenth-century England were periodicals like the *Edinburgh Review,* Blackwood's *Edinburgh Magazine,* and the *Westminster Review,* a liberal Benthamite journal that the critics and editors of the *Democratic Review* often praised. These popular British magazines were often pirated in American editions. Whitman apparently received these editions for reviews while he was still in newspaper work, especially in 1848 and 1849 and again in 1857–1859, when he was editing the Brooklyn *Daily Times.* A survey of his critical summaries of these periodicals in his editorial pages reveals that ideas which some have thought he picked up from American sources could have come from these British reviews.

Considering Whitman's enthusiasm for the *Westminster Review* during the 1850s, the attack on his poems in the October 1860 issue must have hurt the poet deeply and may have sparked his decision again to write anonymous reviews of his work. A defense of *Leaves of Grass* in the Brooklyn *City News* on 10 October was almost certainly written by Whitman.

However, by 1871 the *Westminster Review* redeemed itself when it published in the July number an article entitled "The Poetry of Democracy: Walt Whitman," written by Edward Dowden, Professor of English at Trinity College in Dublin. After receiving rejections from *Macmillan's* and a last-minute decision not to publish from the *Contemporary Review,* Dowden's essay finally appeared, pronouncing Whitman to be "the first & only representative in art of American Democracy" (qtd. in Whitman 914, n49). This delayed approbation provided Whitman with some compensation for the attack a decade earlier.

James E. Barcus, Jr.

Bibliography

Allen, Gay Wilson. *The Solitary Singer: A Critical Biography of Walt Whitman.* 1955. Rev. ed. 1967. Chicago: U of Chicago P, 1985.

Whitman, Walt. *Notebooks and Unpublished Prose Manuscripts.* Ed. Edward F. Grier. Vol. 2. New York: New York UP, 1984.

See also BRITISH ISLES, WHITMAN IN THE; DOWDEN, EDWARD; IRELAND, WHITMAN IN

Wharton, Edith (1862–1937)

Edith Wharton, the author of twenty-five novels, including the Pulitzer Prize–winning *The Age of Innocence* (1920), greatly admired Whitman and his poetry. She alludes to him in fiction and verse and honors him in notes she made for a critical essay. Wharton also shared a reverential love of Whitman's poetry with friends Henry James and George Cabot "Bay" Lodge, who thought him the best American poet, and with other female writers, who responded to his unabashed depictions of female sensuality.

In notes for an unwritten essay, Wharton applauds Whitman's conscious artistry, rhythms, adjectives, ability to express "the inherences of things," and "sense of the absolute behind the relative" ("Sketch"). As Kenneth Price notes, she valued him as a philosopher as well as a poet, finding his models of love and friendship both exhilarating and troubling. Whitman influenced Wharton personally and artistically. During a passionate love affair, she composed "Terminus," a Whitman-like celebration of sexuality. Biographer R.W.B. Lewis reprinted the poem and noted its erotic candor and expansive lines and rhythms. Biographers Cynthia Wolff and Shari Benstock also describe its Whitman-like expression of the profound ordinariness of human passion. Susan Goodman writes that Wharton was most affected by a "Cosmic Whitman" who offered her alternatives to conventional religion and thought; Carol Singley argues that Whitman's romanticism inspired her depictions of nature, particularly in the novel *Summer* (1917). Wharton pays homage to Whitman in novels of artistic development such as *The Custom of the Country* (1912), *Hudson River Bracketed* (1929), *The Gods Arrive* (1932), and "Literature" (unpublished); in war-related novellas *The Son at the Front* (1922) and *The Spark* (1924); and in her autobiography, *A Backward Glance* (1933), titled after Whitman's "A Backward Glance O'er Travel'd Roads."

Wharton's love of Whitman defied the staid conventionality of her upper-class Victorian society. His life and poetry provided her with important new models of comradeship, artistry, and emotional and sexual freedom.

Carol J. Singley

Bibliography

Benstock, Shari. *No Gifts from Chance: A Biography of Edith Wharton.* New York: Scribner, 1994.

Goodman, Susan. "Edith Wharton's 'Sketch of an Essay on Walt Whitman.'" *Walt Whitman Quarterly Review* 10 (1992): 3–9.

Lewis, R.W.B. *Edith Wharton: A Biography.* New York: Harper and Row, 1975.

Price, Kenneth M. "The Mediating 'Whitman': Edith Wharton, Morton Fullerton, and the Problem of Comradeship." *Texas Studies in Literature and Language* 36 (1994): 380–402.

Singley, Carol J. *Edith Wharton: Matters of Mind and Spirit.* New York: Cambridge UP, 1995.

Wharton, Edith. "Sketch of an Essay on Walt Whitman." Edith Wharton Collection. Beinecke Rare Book and Manuscript Library, Yale University, New Haven, Conn.

Wolff, Cynthia Griffin. *A Feast of Words: The Triumph of Edith Wharton.* 1977. 2nd ed. Radcliffe Biography series. Reading, Mass.: Addison-Wesley, 1995.

See also JAMES, HENRY; LEGACY, WHITMAN'S; SEX AND SEXUALITY

"What Think You I Take My Pen in Hand?" (1860)

Originally number 32 of the "Calamus" cluster, this poem is one of a number devoted to a contrast between two sets of values, such as the opposition of worldly success and personal love in "No Labor-Saving Machine." In this case, the poem opposes two possible subjects of art, to be recorded by the poet. At one level this is an aesthetic distinction, between the epic and the lyric, or between the sublime and the picturesque, but it is also an evocation of the meaning of personal love against more social or political themes.

After the introductory question, the poem is divided in half, with three lines listing possible "great" subjects of art, concluding with a forceful "No," and a series of three more lines, beginning "But" and recounting a glimpse of two men kissing good-bye on the pier. Whitman's outdoor scene, a moment of time, contrasts with the pretensions of the more dramatic scenes of the majestic battleship or the glory of the great city.

Whitman identified that spontaneous moment with male love, which represents in the poem a life of simplicity, passion, and affection. The poem troubles its readers not by its assertion of the natural over the historical and social but by identifying that natural with the men's

kiss, a moment of affection that takes place "in the midst of the crowd," that asserts its right to public space for affection. Martin has called attention to this poem as the search for a "feminine" poetics and linked Whitman's strategies to those of women writers.

Robert K. Martin

Bibliography
Martin, Robert K. *The Homosexual Tradition in American Poetry.* Austin: U of Texas P, 1979.

See also "CALAMUS"; LOVE

"When I Heard at the Close of the Day" (1860)

Published initially as "Calamus" poem number 11 in the 1860 edition of *Leaves,* "When I Heard at the Close of the Day" was given its present title in 1867. "When I Heard" was originally the third in a series of twelve poems entitled "Live Oak with Moss" which Whitman copied into a notebook in the spring of 1859.

In his notes Whitman referred to the "Calamus" poems as being in the style of sonnets, and "When I Heard" is perhaps the best example of this. Though not in iambic pentameter, and without rhyme and stanzaic pattern, the poem has a structure similar to that of the sonnet, with thirteen lines of similar length, and a transition from sadness to joy. Indeed, the poem might be regarded as an inverted Italian sonnet, with the transition announced by the "But" at the beginning of the third line and coming to full closure in the final line of the opening sestet. The shortened "octave" then narrates the activities of the three days that separate the speaker from the meeting with his "lover."

Gay Wilson Allen and Charles T. Davis suggest that the "plaudits in the capitol" of the first line of the poem might be a reference to a review of *Leaves* published in the Washington, D.C., *National Intelligencer* of 18 February 1856. The happiness enters when the setting moves from the capitol, with all of its regulations, to the beach, where the speaker bathes in the sea and watches the sun rise and thinks how "my dear friend my lover was on his way coming." The rippling rhythmical lines that follow build to a climax, with the speaker sleeping with his lover on the beach "under the same cover in the cool night," as nature, in the form of the rolling waters, congratulates him. One of the finest love poems in all of American literature, "When I Heard" is skillful, candid, and tender—with Whitman at his happiest.

Richard Raleigh

Bibliography

Greenspan, Ezra. *Walt Whitman and the American Reader.* New York: Cambridge UP, 1990.

Helms, Alan. "Whitman's 'Live Oak with Moss.'" *The Continuing Presence of Walt Whitman.* Ed. Robert K. Martin. Iowa City: U of Iowa P, 1992. 185–205.

Killingsworth, M. Jimmie. *Whitman's Poetry of the Body: Sexuality, Politics, and the Text.* Chapel Hill: U of North Carolina P, 1989.

Whitman, Walt. *Walt Whitman's Poems.* Ed. Gay Wilson Allen and Charles T. Davis. New York: New York UP, 1955.

See also "CALAMUS"; "LIVE OAK WITH MOSS"

"When I Heard the Learn'd Astronomer" (1865)

"When I Heard the Learn'd Astronomer" originally appeared in *Drum-Taps* (1865). This brief eight-line poem entered *Leaves of Grass* in 1867 when *Drum-Taps* was appended to the main body of *Leaves;* in 1871, Whitman moved the poem to his "Songs of Parting" cluster, where it remained until the 1881 edition, when he moved it finally to the "By the Roadside" cluster. While the poem's subject is obviously not the Civil War, the tenor of the war times is nonetheless reflected in the speaker's desire to escape a place of fragmentation (where the unified cosmos is broken down and divided into "columns") and to regain a sense of wholeness. Union and oneness, pulling together that which has been separated—these are the subjects of many of Whitman's Civil War poems, and they are also the focus of this poem.

The first half of "Astronomer" consists of four anaphoric lines of steadily increasing length; the insistent repetition of the opening "When" joins with the accumulating verbiage to build to a peak point of exacerbation, after which the speaker expresses in a final group of four brief lines his relief at getting out of the "lecture-room" and into "the mystical moist night-air." The two halves of the poem, then, imitate the contrasting sounds of the scene: the first four lines (evoking the astronomer's lecture) contain sixty-four noisy syllables, while the last four (moving toward the speaker's "perfect silence") contain only fifty syllables and diminish into the relative quiet of the final ten-syllable line with its hushed concluding fourfold assonance ("silence at the stars").

As the speaker moves from the lecture room—with its demonstration of book learning—out into the night, he repeats a familiar pattern in Whitman's poetry, as when the speaker of "Song of Myself" puts "Creeds and schools in abeyance" (section 1) and leaves the "Houses and rooms" to "go to the bank by the wood" (section 2). The erudite astronomer presents the cosmos as an intellectual abstraction—a series of proofs and figures and diagrams—and receives applause for, in effect, having broken the cosmos down into charts and moved it into a lecture room, where the only brilliance the audience can see belongs to the astronomer, not to the stars. One has to go outside to see the actual stars, which speak their proofs in "perfect silence." The speaker of the poem becomes "unaccountable . . . tired and sick" of the lecture, and the term "unaccountable" resonates with the speaker's desire to experience the cosmos again as "uncountable," as beyond the clever adding, dividing, and theorizing of the scientist.

And yet, as the speaker looks up at the sky, he does not forget the lessons he learned in the lecture room. He describes how he looked "from time to time" into the heavens, and the phrase signals one of the newly formulated concepts that the astronomer would have explained in his lecture: that when we look at the stars, we are not only looking across vast distances of space, but vast distances of time as well. When we look at the night sky, we are looking from our time to the light from distant pasts, "from time to time." As so often happens in Whitman, the scientist's lessons are not rejected but are absorbed by the poet, who employs them in surprising ways to create poetic truth. "Hurrah for positive science!," Whitman writes in "Song of Myself"; "Your facts are useful, and yet they are not my dwelling, / I but enter by them to an area of my dwelling" (section 23).

Ed Folsom

Bibliography

Lindfors, Bernth. "Whitman's 'When I Heard the Learn'd Astronomer.'" *Walt Whitman Review* 10 (1964): 19–21.

Schwiebert, John E. *The Frailest Leaves: Whitman's Poetic Technique and Style in the Short Poem.* New York: Lang, 1992.

See also "BY THE ROADSIDE"; SCIENCE

"When I Read the Book" (1867)

This poem exists in two versions. The earlier version was published in 1867 and contains five lines; in 1871, Whitman moved it from the "Leaves of Grass" cluster to the new cluster "Inscriptions," replacing the fifth line with three additional lines.

Acknowledging the later version as a better inscription, Harold Blodgett and Sculley Bradley nevertheless assert that the earlier version expresses "genuine power and insight" in the last line (613). Gay Wilson Allen and Roger Asselineau, on the other hand, both suggest that the new poems in the 1867 edition, including "When I Read the Book," are rather trivial and of minor significance.

Other critics have found more significance in the poem. V.K. Chari observes that the real life of a person is transcendental and eludes the grasp of the empirical mind; as Whitman himself admitted in "As I Ebb'd with the Ocean of Life," he had not the least idea of who or what he was. Thus, the poem may be viewed as an expression of his constant quest for the self. David Cavitch finds that to Whitman a person's life is not a biography, which offers old-fashioned or even deceptive information; the poet is instead objecting to "the distortions of conventional biographies" (Cavitch 4). James E. Miller, Jr., views it as Whitman's warning to scholars who would probe deep into his personal life that obviously defies recording.

The speaker is talking to his soul, which, Whitman asserts in "Song of Myself," is as great as "the other I am," the body (section 5). When a biography is written, only a small portion of the person's life is revealed; the truer and larger character is unseen, unexpressed, and defiant of investigation and probing. Whitman seems to suggest that no biography is accurate or truthful to the person whose life is little known even to the self.

Guiyou Huang

Bibliography

Allen, Gay Wilson. *Walt Whitman Handbook.* 1946. New York: Hendricks House, 1962.
Asselineau, Roger. *The Evolution of Walt Whitman: The Creation of a Personality.* Trans. Richard P. Adams and Roger Asselineau. Cambridge, Mass.: Harvard UP, 1960.
Blodgett, Harold W., and Sculley Bradley, eds. *Leaves of Grass: Comprehensive Reader's Edition.* New York: New York UP, 1965.
Cavitch, David. *My Soul and I: The Inner Life of Walt Whitman.* Boston: Beacon, 1985.
Chari, V.K. *Whitman in the Light of Vedantic Mysticism.* Lincoln: U of Nebraska P, 1964.
Miller, James E., Jr. *Walt Whitman.* New York: Twayne, 1962.

See also "Inscriptions"

"When Lilacs Last in the Dooryard Bloom'd" (1865)

As an elegy on the death of Abraham Lincoln, "When Lilacs Last in the Dooryard Bloom'd" may be placed in contexts both historical and literary. The historical facts need only brief mention. While attending a performance at Ford's Theater in Washington, D.C., on the evening of 14 April 1865, President Lincoln was shot by the actor John Wilkes Booth; mortally wounded, he died the following morning. On 20 April his body lay in state at the Capitol, and the next day it began a 1,600-mile journey by rail across the landscape and through major cities on its way to Springfield, Illinois, for interment on 4 May.

At the time of the assassination Whitman was with his mother in Brooklyn. As he recalls in *Specimen Days,* "The day of the murder we heard the news very early in the morning. Mother prepared breakfast—and other meals afterward—as usual; but not a mouthful was eaten all day by either of us. We each drank half a cup of coffee; that was all. Little was said. We got every newspaper morning and evening, and the frequent extras of that period, and pass'd them silently to each other" (*Prose Works* 1:31). Composition of "Lilacs" began almost immediately after the assassination and was completed within weeks. Initial publication was in *Sequel to Drum-Taps,* issued by Gibson Brothers in the fall of 1865 and bound with *Drum-Taps;* the poem made its first appearance in the text of *Leaves of Grass* in 1881, although *Sequel,* along with *Drum-Taps* and *Songs Before Parting,* had been bound with the fourth (1867) edition.

Whitman had for years admired and defended the president. "I believe fully in Lincoln," he commented in an 1863 letter; "few know the rocks & quicksands he has to steer through" (*Correspondence* 1:163–164). Whitman had been present at Lincoln's second inauguration just weeks before the assassination. The president, he noted in a *Specimen Days* entry, "look'd very much worn and tired; the lines, indeed, of vast responsibilities, intricate questions, and demands of life and death, cut deeper than ever upon his dark brown face; yet all the old goodness, tenderness, sadness, and canny shrewdness, underneath the furrows. (I never see that man without feeling that he is one to become personally attach'd to, for his combination of purest, heartiest tenderness, and native western form of manliness.)" (*Prose Works* 1:92).

While the assassination of President Lincoln is the *occasion* of "When Lilacs Last in the Dooryard Bloom'd," the *subject*, in the manner of elegy, is both other and broader than its occasion. "Lilacs" turns out to be not just about the death of Abraham Lincoln, but about death itself; in section 7, just after the poet has placed a sprig of lilac on the coffin, the poem makes a pointed transition: "Nor for you, for one alone," the poet chants, "Blossoms and branches green to coffins all I bring." Significantly, Lincoln is never mentioned by name in "Lilacs," nor does the poem relate the circumstances of his death; indeed, the *absence* of the historical Lincoln in the poem is one of its more striking features. Historical considerations give way to universal significance. The fact of assassination, for example, is not mentioned, for, while all people die, assassination is the fate of only a few.

Discussion of the poem has focused largely on its style, on its structure, on the significance of its three major symbols of lilac, star, and thrush, and on the nature of the final resolution, with its distinction between "the thought of death" and "the knowledge of death," with whom the poet walks as companions (section 14). Stylistically, as opposed to the earlier Whitman of "Song of Myself," the poet of "Lilacs" works in a more Tennysonian mode, creating a poetry refined, mellifluous, and carefully controlled. Making no pretense of spontaneity, the poem proclaims on every line its artifice and its artistry.

The general structure of "Lilacs" follows the traditional pattern of elegy in its movement from grief to consolation, and it includes such traditional elegiac elements as the funeral procession, the mourning of nature, the placing of flowers upon the coffin, the contrast between nature's cyclical renewal and humanity's mortality, the eulogy, and the final resolution of sorrow; the development, however, is notably indirect. "Lilacs" circles and turns back on itself, seeking direction until it finds rest in the concluding reconciliation; the pattern suggests the fluctuations of emotion rather than the strict progressions of logical development. The structure of "Lilacs" has also been likened to music, with its use of themes and motifs recurring in isolation and set off against each other, but moving always toward a concluding harmony.

The three major symbols of the elegy—lilac, star, and hermit thrush—had particular significance for Whitman. In his lecture on Lincoln, delivered on a number of occasions from 1879 to 1890, Whitman recalled the day of the assassination. "I remember," he said, "where I was stopping at the time, the season being advanced, there were many lilacs in full bloom. By one of those caprices that enter and give tinge to events without being at all a part of them, I find myself always reminded of the great tragedy of that day by the sight and odor of these blossoms. It never fails" (*Prose Works* 2:503).

The star—actually, the planet Venus—was indeed low in the sky at the time of the assassination, as Whitman describes in the poem. In a *Specimen Days* entry dating from around the time of Lincoln's second inauguration, Whitman wrote, "Nor earth nor sky ever knew spectacles of superber beauty than some of the nights lately here. The western star, Venus, in the earlier hours of evening, has never been so large, so clear; it seems as if it told something, as if it held rapport indulgent with humanity, with us Americans" (*Prose Works* 1:94).

A notebook entry of 1865 suggests the significance of the hermit thrush in the elegy: "Solitary Thrush . . . sings oftener after sundown sometimes quite in the night / is very secluded / likes shaded, dark, places in swamps . . . his song is a hymn . . . he never sings near the farm houses—never in the settlement / is the bird of the solemn primal woods & of Nature pure & holy" (*Notebooks* 2:766).

In "Lilacs," the three major symbols accumulate meaning as the poem develops. While there are differing interpretations of each, the three being resonant and profound, in the nature of complex symbols, still, it is generally agreed that the star introduced in section 2 ("O great star disappear'd") is to be associated with the man who has died, although by no means is it to be considered simply as "Lincoln," and the lilac that enters the poem in section 3 ("tall-growing with heart-shaped leaves of rich green") suggests an exuberant, vital, sensuous nature, a nature of fecundity and eternal renewal. The thrush is of course also of nature, but in the poem it becomes more than merely natural. A creature "of Nature pure & holy," it expresses itself in song, and thus has been considered a figure of the bardic poet or the seer, a visionary singer of ultimate insight.

While attention has been focused on the three major symbols, other images in the poem also take on symbolic value, most notably the cloud and the swamp. The cloud appears early, in section 2, as an image of oppression ("O harsh surrounding cloud that will not free my soul"), and it returns late, in section 14; significantly, it is seen in that section immediately prior to the moment when the poet attains enlightened knowledge ("And I knew death, its thought, and the sacred knowledge of death"), an illumination it is unable to prevent, for by then it has become powerless, and the poet is free to make his journey to the swamp.

Home of the secluded thrush, the swamp is a place of revelation, where words are given to intuitive knowledge. Like the beach, another setting important to Whitman as a site of revelation, the swamp is an in-between state, a meeting place of earth and water; the poet specifically describes himself in section 14 as going "Down to the shores."

As the major symbols suggest, "Lilacs" is firmly based in the natural world, and it is there that the poem must find its consolations. Whitman refused to seek comfort in the supernatural; the Christian vision of eternal life in heaven that Milton found in "Lycidas" was not available to him, and he deliberately avoided any suggestion of it. The lilacs will return; Lincoln will not, and he will have no life other than the one he has lost, not even in nature, for Whitman significantly refrained from invoking the view taken in section 6 of "Song of Myself," that death is no more than part of the continuum of life ("The smallest sprout shows there is really no death . . .") and thus may be dismissed as inconsequential. Whitman's experience of the Civil War, including of course his service in the hospitals, had evidently tempered his outlook; he had seen too much of death to dismiss it so readily.

"Lilacs" offers the explicit consolation that death is a release from the sufferings of life. But if that rationale were all, there would be no need of the thrush, whose song is a joyous carol in praise of death, not a lament about the sorrows of human life. When the poet is ready to hear that song, he has already reconciled "the thought of death" with "the sacred knowledge of death" (section 14). While interpretations differ, it is significant that the word "sacred" is applied only to the latter. A *thought* may be fleeting and changeable, concerned with a particular death, while *sacred knowledge* suggests ultimate insight: complete comprehension of death itself and its place in the universal order.

Whitman has the tact not to try to explain this insight, for it is necessarily intuitive and inexpressible. It comes suddenly, without prelude, at the unlikely moment when the cloud returns: "And I knew death, its thought, and the sacred knowledge of death" (section 14). One simply *knows,* as in the visionary passage of "Song of Myself," section 5, when the poet attains enlightenment: "Swiftly arose and spread around me the peace and knowledge that pass all the argument of the earth . . ."

"Passing the visions, passing the night," the poet of "Lilacs" moves on toward conclusion (section 16), ready to reclaim the life he has left, putting the experience of the night behind him, but by no means abandoning it. "Yet each to keep and all, retrievements out of the night," he chants, knowing that the experience has been transforming, for the vision granted him has brought ultimate knowledge of life and death. At the end of "Lilacs," all disparate elements have been reconciled: "Lilac and star and bird twined with the chant of my soul, / There in the fragrant pines and the cedars dusk and dim."

R. W. French

Bibliography

Adams, Richard P. "Whitman's 'Lilacs' and the Tradition of Pastoral Elegy." *PMLA* 72 (1957): 479–487.

Betts, William W., Jr., ed. *Lincoln and the Poets.* Pittsburgh: U of Pittsburgh P, 1965.

Erkkila, Betsy. *Whitman the Political Poet.* New York: Oxford UP, 1989.

Whitman, Walt. *The Correspondence.* Ed. Edwin Haviland Miller. 6 vols. New York: New York UP, 1961–1977.

———. *Leaves of Grass: Comprehensive Reader's Edition.* Ed. Harold W. Blodgett and Sculley Bradley. New York: New York UP, 1965.

———. *Notebooks and Unpublished Prose Manuscripts.* Ed. Edward F. Grier. 6 vols. New York: New York UP, 1984.

———. *Prose Works 1892.* Ed. Floyd Stovall. 2 vols. New York: New York UP, 1963–1964.

———. *Walt Whitman's Civil War.* Ed. Walter Lowenfels. New York: Knopf, 1960.

See also CIVIL WAR, THE; DEATH; LINCOLN, ABRAHAM; LINCOLN'S DEATH; "MEMORIES OF PRESIDENT LINCOLN"; "O CAPTAIN! MY CAPTAIN!"; *SEQUEL TO DRUM-TAPS*; SYMBOLISM

Whigs

An American political party of the early 1830s to the mid-1850s, the Whigs tended to represent the moneyed business and professional people, along with the larger-holding agricultural interests. Andrew Jackson's opposition to a national bank was a major issue for the Whigs. "Whigs—what a ridiculous name for an American party," Whitman scoffed (*Daybooks* 3:683). Opponents of the king of England, both in the seventeenth century and at the time of the American Revolution, had called themselves Whigs. The term began to appear in American politics at the local level as early as 1832. Certainly by the summer of 1834 the anti-Jacksonians were calling themselves Whigs and organizing a national party.

Throughout their history the Whigs were plagued by divisions arising from the many differences among their supporters. Generally, Whigs sought support in the North by emphasizing Union, while in the South they opposed high tariffs and in the West they sought the support of conservative Democrats by claiming that Jackson was concentrating too much power in one man's hands. Following the battle over the bank, which caused many Democrats to switch parties, the Panic of 1837 gave the Whigs a potent new issue, leading to their greatest success (1840).

Whitman was a Democrat and campaigned for fellow New Yorker Martin Van Buren (1840). In his newspaper editorials he pointed to the Whigs' nativist tendencies, an especially potent issue in Brooklyn in the 1840s, with its growing immigrant population.

The Whigs declined in the 1850s as their best leaders left public life to take advantage of the reviving economy. The Whigs had advocated government intervention to improve the economy, but the California gold rush (1849) helped to accomplish that without new government programs. Although individuals would retain the name for a few more years, the Whig party was finished after the campaign of 1856.

Frederick Hatch

Bibliography

Brasher, Thomas L. *Whitman as Editor of the Brooklyn Daily Eagle*. Detroit: Wayne State UP, 1970.

Burnham, W. Dean. *Presidential Ballots, 1836–1892*. Baltimore: Johns Hopkins UP, 1955.

Carroll, E. Malcolm. *Origins of the Whig Party*. Durham: Duke UP, 1925.

Erkkila, Betsy. *Whitman the Political Poet*. New York: Oxford UP, 1989.

Holt, Michael F. *Political Parties and American Political Development from the Age of Jackson to the Age of Lincoln*. Baton Rouge: Louisiana State UP, 1992.

Porter, Kirk H., comp. *National Party Platforms*. New York: Macmillan, 1924.

Sellers, Charles Grier, Jr. "Who Were the Southern Whigs?" *American Historical Review* 59 (1954): 335–346.

Smith, Page. *The Nation Comes of Age*. New York: Penguin, 1990.

Whitman, Walt. *The Correspondence*. Ed. Edwin Haviland Miller. 6 vols. New York: New York UP, 1961–1977.

———. *Daybooks and Notebooks*. Ed. William White. 3 vols. New York: New York UP, 1978.

See also AMERICAN WHIG REVIEW; DEMOCRATIC PARTY; POLITICAL VIEWS; REPUBLICAN PARTY

"Whispers of Heavenly Death" (1868)

First published in the English *Broadway Magazine* (October 1868), the poem "Whispers of Heavenly Death" was later included in the cluster of the same name in the supplement *Passage to India* (1871). Essentially unchanged since its first printing, it was included as the second poem of the cluster "Whispers of Heavenly Death" in *Leaves of Grass* (1881), where it remained. Whitman sent it to the *Broadway* in response to that magazine's request of December 1867 for some prose or poetry by him. He was paid ten pounds in gold (fifty dollars) for the poem.

As the title poem of the cluster, "Whispers" sounds the section's main themes, and its quiet tone echoes its gentle acknowledgment of approaching death. Though death is not fully understood, because not completely heard, by the speaker, its approach is auspicious rather than ominous: this characterization is connoted by the images in the opening four lines, which suggest pleasant choruses, a walking journey upward, soft breezes, and flowing tides. Line 5 adds a note of sorrow in its reference to human tears.

The second stanza continues on this somber note, acknowledging the mournfulness and sadness of death. But the third (and final) stanza introduces the idea that approaching death is in fact a rebirth, a new "frontier."

While the essential statement of the poem is a cliché, the poem's beauty is in its quiet and controlled treatment of the subject. An immediate implication of order and control is suggested in the three stanzas because of their visible length—the first one is five lines long, the second is four lines, and the third is three. Furthermore, the sounds and rhythms do not simply produce an actual whisper when the poem is read aloud; they produce a soothing and flowing quality, perfectly matching the attitude of the speaker and the connotations of the images. Consonants are primarily continuants, and vowels tend to be medium to low register. In the first line, for example, of twenty consonant sounds, only three are stops; of twelve vowel sounds, only three are in the upper register. Though these proportions do not continue throughout the poem, the first line sets the tone and emphasizes the aural quality. Additionally, the fluidity of the present participles and the implied movement in the images of breezes, water, and clouds add to the artistry of this poem. Like "A Noiseless Patient Spider," "Cavalry Crossing a Ford," and "The Dalliance of the Eagles," "Whispers" shows Whitman's ability to compose highly crafted poems, and his ability to work in a compact poetic medium something like that of his contemporary Emily Dickinson.

Steven Olson

Bibliography

Allen, Gay Wilson. *The Solitary Singer: A Critical Biography of Walt Whitman.* 1955. Rev. ed. 1967. Chicago: U of Chicago P, 1985.

Whitman, Walt. *The Correspondence.* Ed. Edwin Haviland Miller. 6 vols. New York: New York UP, 1961–1977.

———. *Leaves of Grass: Comprehensive Reader's Edition.* Ed. Harold W. Blodgett and Sculley Bradley. New York: New York UP, 1965.

See also DEATH; "WHISPERS OF HEAVENLY DEATH" (CLUSTER)

"Whispers of Heavenly Death" (cluster) (1871)

Originally a cluster of thirteen poems, "Whispers of Heavenly Death" was first incorporated under its present title in the supplement *Passage to India* (1871). It was added to *Leaves of Grass* in 1881 with five more poems written between 1856 and 1871 for a total of eighteen poems. The cluster is a statement about the transcendence of death, death as a beginning rather than an end—a typical theme for Whitman since 1855, when he wrote in "Song of Myself," "Has any one supposed it lucky to be born? / I hasten to inform him or her it is just as lucky to die . . ." (section 7).

The cluster's main theme explains its position in *Leaves of Grass.* Following the cluster "Autumn Rivulets," "Whispers" addresses the winter of life, when death is imminent. As Betsy Erkkila sees these final sections of *Leaves of Grass,* they progress not only through the stages of life; they move from material to spiritual concerns of existence. They also incorporate poems written at various times in Whitman's career to offer a sense of unity, closure, and grand design.

The design of "Whispers" itself reflects the psychological and spiritual reconciliations to death and demonstrates the artfulness of the cluster. While the cluster moves constantly toward the moment of death, the poet's emotional mood ebbs and flows as he adjusts to the inevitability of death.

The first four poems establish the essential themes and lyrical quality of the cluster in a quiet, but celebratory, tone. "Darest Thou Now O Soul" introduces the journey of the soul into the "unknown region" of death, where without body the soul is unbounded and free in time and space. The second and title poem of the cluster lyrically clarifies just how near the subject is to death, so near that death's whisper is audible. "Chanting the Square Deific" then characterizes the pervasive spirituality of the cosmos. "Of Him I Love Day and Night" laments the death of a loved one, but emphasizes the sense of satisfaction, even in the presence of death.

An emotional ebb, "Yet, Yet, Ye Downcast Hours" and "As if a Phantom Caress'd Me," displays the desire to escape death and that desire's resulting isolation and paranoia. These poems, however, are followed by the flood tide of "Assurances" and "Quicksand Years," which assert faith in the power of the soul, the greatness of death, and the certainty that at the end of life "One's-Self" will remain.

A series of short, lyrical poems then creates congenial imagery. "That Music Always Round Me" associates death with beauty, emotional pleasantness, and the fulfillment of a cosmically pervasive harmony. Reflecting the transcendent imagery of "Passage to India," "What Ship Puzzled at Sea" offers the "most perfect pilot" to give sure direction on the spiritual journey. "A Noiseless Patient Spider" presents the hope of the soul's casting into the "vacant" vastness until it connects to something, as it certainly will. "O Living Always, Always Dying" again implies nautical imagery as the soul casts off bodily existence in order to pass to the afterlife.

The last six poems speak directly about the transition from life to death. In "To One Shortly to Die" death speaks to a person he is claiming, and while death's inevitability is clear, he approaches softly and invitingly. In "Night on the Prairies" the poet, looking to the heavens, is assured that in passing to death new knowledge unavailable in life will be exhibited. Death thus becomes a continuation and fulfillment. A last brief ebb in the psychological adjustment to death, "Thought" questions whether souls are "drown'd and destroy'd." It also begins to unite images from other poems in the cluster: the first line recalls the supper of "Night on the Prairies" and the music of "That Music Always Round Me"; the rest of the poem reasserts the metaphor of the journey and the imagery of sailing. "The Last Invocation" quickly returns to an optimistic tone and echoes the "noiseless[ness]" of the spider as the speaker asks for release from his body and for continuance of his soul. "As I Watch'd the Ploughman Ploughing" presents the concluding, if stock, analogy of life and death to tilling and harvesting, respectively. Thus, it implies both the fulfilling and cyclical quality of death. Finally, "Pensive and Faltering" asserts that the dead might be the real living souls and the living body the "apparition."

The cluster is a highly crafted poetic design of interwoven themes, tones, and images. This design nicely complements its subject—the quiet, beautiful, assuring, and infinite nature of death.

Steven Olson

Bibliography

Blodgett, Harold W. "Whitman's *Whisperings*." *Walt Whitman Review* 8 (1962): 12–16.
Erkkila, Betsy. *Whitman the Political Poet.* New York: Oxford UP, 1989.
Ledbetter, J.T. "Whitman's Power in the Short Poem: A Discussion of 'Whispers of Heavenly Death.'" *Walt Whitman Review* 21 (1975): 155–158.
Megna, B. Christian. "Sociality and Seclusion in the Poetry of Walt Whitman." *Walt Whitman Review* 17 (1971): 55–57.
Whitman, Walt. *Leaves of Grass: Comprehensive Reader's Edition.* Ed. Harold W. Blodgett and Sculley Bradley. New York: New York UP, 1965.

See also "CHANTING THE SQUARE DEIFIC"; "DAREST THOU NOW O SOUL"; DEATH; "NOISELESS PATIENT SPIDER, A"; "O LIVING ALWAYS, ALWAYS DYING"; "OF HIM I LOVE DAY AND NIGHT"; "QUICKSAND YEARS"; SOUL, THE; "THAT MUSIC ALWAYS ROUND ME"; "TO ONE SHORTLY TO DIE"; "WHISPERS OF HEAVENLY DEATH"

White, William (1910–1995)

From the 1950s to the 1990s, William White was a strong presence in literary studies in general and in Whitman studies in particular. By the end of his career he had contributed roughly twenty-five hundred articles and reviews to professional journals and had authored, edited, or compiled nearly forty books. Some of his books were on figures as widely divergent as John Donne, A.E. Housman, Sir William Osler, Ernest Hemingway, and Nathanael West. Only a handful of White's important contributions to Whitman scholarship can be noted here: he authored *Walt Whitman's Journalism: A Bibliography* (1968); edited Whitman's *Daybooks and Notebooks* (3 volumes, 1978); coedited *Leaves of Grass: A Textual Variorum of the Printed Poems* (3 volumes, 1980); and coedited volume 6 of Horace Traubel's *With Walt Whitman in Camden* (1982). His crowning achievement, however, may well be his work on periodicals devoted to Whitman. From 1956 to 1982 he edited the *Walt Whitman Review,* and from 1983 to 1989 he coedited the *Walt Whitman Quarterly Review.* In these editorial positions, "he had," says Ed Folsom, "a Whitmanlike commitment to a diversity of ideas and to a democratic access to print . . ." (207).

Born in Paterson, New Jersey, and educated at the University of Tennessee at Chattanooga (B.A., 1933), the University of Southern California (M.A., 1937), and the University of London (Ph.D., 1953), White taught courses in journalism and American studies at numerous colleges and universities but spent most of his academic career at Wayne State University (1947–1980). Along with his various teaching positions, White also held jobs as reporter, columnist, and editor of more than a dozen daily and weekly newspapers.

Donald D. Kummings

Bibliography

Folsom, Ed. "William White, 1910–1995." *Walt Whitman Quarterly Review* 12 (1995): 205–208.

See also COLLECTED WRITINGS OF WALT WHITMAN, THE; PERIODICALS DEVOTED TO WHITMAN

Whitman, Andrew Jackson (1827–1863)

The sixth of Walter and Louisa Whitman's nine children, Andrew Jackson Whitman was born in Brooklyn, New York, on 9 April 1827. Andrew was one of three Whitman sons named after an American hero, a reflection of the patriotic ardor imbued in the Whitman children by their parents.

Andrew appears in an early Whitman prose work, "My Boys and Girls," published in *The Rover* (20 April 1844). The piece celebrates the high spirits and wrestling skills of Walt's younger brother.

As an adult, Andrew took up his father's trade of carpenter, and worked at the Brooklyn Navy Yard. He took Nancy McClure as his wife. They had three children: James Cornwell (also spelled Cornell), named after the Brooklyn police justice who was featured in an early Whitman newspaper sketch; George; and Andrew, Jr.

References to Andrew in family correspondence indicate that he was often sickly, and that he may have been an alcoholic. Perhaps the family's nickname for Andrew—"Bunkum"—was an ironic tribute to one who must have often complained, "I don't feel so bunkum." Despite his chronic health problems, Andrew joined the Union Army, enlisting as a "three-months' man" during the summer of 1862. He served as a private in Company H of the Thirteenth Regiment, New York State Militia—the same regiment that his brother, George, had served with in the spring of 1861.

Upon returning to Brooklyn, Andrew began a decline that ended in his death on 3 December 1863, at the age of thirty-six. His doctor listed the cause of death as laryngitis, an indication that Andrew had tuberculosis. Carriages provided by Andrew's friend Cornwell took the family to Evergreens' Cemetery, where Andrew was buried. Whitman had said his good-byes in a visit he made to Brooklyn shortly before his brother's death, but he was back in Washington nursing the war wounded when his brother died, and did not attend the funeral.

Andrew's estate was limited to the contents of his carpenter's tool box, which were auctioned off by his navy yard comrades. The proceeds were given to his widow, pregnant with their third son, Andrew, Jr. This youngest child was killed by an errant brewer's wagon in 1868, but at least one of Andrew's boys, James, lived to adulthood and was named in Walt Whitman's last will.

Martin G. Murray

Bibliography

Loving, Jerome M., ed. *Civil War Letters of George Washington Whitman.* Durham, N.C.: Duke UP, 1975.
Molinoff, Katherine. *Some Notes on Whitman's Family.* Brooklyn: Comet, 1941.
Murray, Martin G. "Bunkum *Did* Go Sogering." *Walt Whitman Quarterly Review* 10 (1993): 142–148.

See also "MY BOYS AND GIRLS"; WHITMAN, EDWARD; WHITMAN, GEORGE WASHINGTON; WHITMAN (HEYDE), HANNAH LOUISA; WHITMAN, JESSE (BROTHER); WHITMAN, NANCY; WHITMAN, THOMAS JEFFERSON; WHITMAN (VAN NOSTRAND), MARY ELIZABETH

Whitman, Edward (1835–1892)

Though there is some uncertainty about details, virtually all the evidence indicates that this youngest of Walt Whitman's siblings was from early childhood, if not indeed from birth, significantly retarded mentally, epileptic, and physically handicapped. Consequently, Whitman's relationship with "Eddy" was a special one. These two matters—the fact of Edward's disabilities, complicated by questions about their nature and extent; and the poet's responding attachment to the afflicted brother—are of continuing interest to Whitman studies.

Clara Barrus reports that Walt Whitman, attributing his brother's condition to their father's alcoholism, declared that Edward had been stunted almost from the first and had virtually no mental life. Persons who knew Edward in middle age described him as severely retarded, crippled in one hand and leg, and racked by frequent violent seizures. However, references in various Whitman family letters make clear that during much of his life he was capable of being out in the city streets unattended, of doing simple errands, and of attending church with interest. In 1939, Whitman's niece, Jessie Louisa Whitman—vehemently denying any insanity in the family—insisted that Edward had been normal until his mind was affected by scarlet fever at age three and his limbs by infantile paralysis a few years later. She also maintained that he had been trusted to take her and her sister out for pushcart excursions in Brooklyn when they were little girls in the 1860s. Such long-distance memories, however, from a woman determined to put the family in the best light, must be viewed with caution.

While the specifics of Edward's incapacities are thus somewhat blurred, there is little question regarding the closeness of the relationship between him and his brother Walt. In the mid-1850s the two shared a bed in the attic of their mother's house in Brooklyn. Referring to entries in the poet's notebooks of that time, Paul Zweig suggests that Whitman's feelings for Edward may have been complicated by guilt-producing eroticism. Such is not unlikely but remains unverifiable; what appears certain is the bond of affection that lasted throughout their lives. In 1888, days after Walt Whitman had suffered a series of debilitating strokes, Eddy, on the way to enter the asylum at Blackwood, New Jersey, where he would spend his last four years, was brought to see the aging poet. According to Horace Traubel, the two exchanged a few words, then sat for a long time in silence, Walt holding Eddy's hand. In the intervening decades Whitman had not only contributed generously to Eddy's support and seen to it that he was well cared for, but had treated him with a humane respect and brotherly affection not forthcoming from the other Whitman brothers. He made Edward the principal beneficiary of his will, though the largesse was unnecessary, for Eddy lived only eight months longer than Walt.

Along with the oldest Whitman brother, Jesse (who also died in an asylum), Edward raises questions about the issue of mental aberration in the troubled family that produced perhaps America's greatest poet. Further, he illuminates in a unique way those qualities of tender affection, compassion, and comradely brotherhood—perhaps never quite separable from homoeroticism—that are so central to Walt Whitman's character and work.

Randall Waldron

Bibliography

Allen, Gay Wilson. *The Solitary Singer: A Critical Biography of Walt Whitman.* 1955. Rev. ed. 1967. Chicago: U of Chicago P, 1985.

Barrus, Clara. *Whitman and Burroughs, Comrades.* Boston: Houghton Mifflin, 1931.

Molinoff, Katherine. *Some Notes on Whitman's Family.* Brooklyn: Comet, 1941.

Traubel, Horace. *With Walt Whitman in Camden.* Vol. 2. New York: Appleton, 1908.

Waldron, Randall. "Jessie Louisa Whitman: Memories of Uncle Walt, et al., 1939–1943." *Walt Whitman Quarterly Review* 7 (1989): 15–27.

Whitman, Walt. *The Correspondence.* Ed. Edwin Haviland Miller. 6 Vols. New York: New York UP, 1961–1977 (with a *Second Supplement* published by the *Walt Whitman Quarterly Review,* 1991).

Zweig, Paul. *Walt Whitman: The Making of the Poet.* New York: Basic Books, 1984.

See also WHITMAN, ANDREW JACKSON; WHITMAN, GEORGE WASHINGTON; WHITMAN (HEYDE), HANNAH LOUISA; WHITMAN, JESSE (BROTHER); WHITMAN, THOMAS JEFFERSON; WHITMAN (VAN NOSTRAND), MARY ELIZABETH

Whitman, George Washington (1829–1901)

As a soldier in war and a workman in peace, George Washington Whitman manifested the common American manliness that his brother Walt Whitman lauded in poetry and prose. George's lack of interest in Whitman's art was also typical of the average American, much to the poet's eternal frustration and disappointment.

Ten years Walt's junior, George Whitman was born in Brooklyn, New York, on 29 November 1829. His boyhood was spent in the Long Island countryside to which Walter and Louisa Whitman had moved the family in 1834. In "My Boys and Girls" Whitman fondly recalls carrying on his shoulders young George, "his legs dangling down upon my breast, while I trotted for sport down a lane or over the fields" (248). George learned his "3 Rs" from Walt during Whitman's brief career as a village schoolmaster.

George Whitman (the poet's brother) in his Civil War uniform. By permission, Special Collections Library, Duke University.

then enlisted that fall with the Fifty-first New York Volunteers to serve for the remainder of the Civil War. Walt Whitman's war ministry in the capital's hospitals followed upon his nursing of brother George on the camp grounds of Falmouth, Virginia, after the battle of Fredericksburg. In *Specimen Days* Whitman has left a permanent record of familial pride in this brother whose battleground heroism at New Bern, Antietam, Fredericksburg, Second Bull Run, the Wilderness, and Petersburg was reflected in the stripes (sergeant, captain, major, breveted lieutenant colonel) he successively earned.

After the war was won, George Whitman returned to Brooklyn. Unsuccessful in his initial house-building ventures, he obtained work inspecting iron pipes in Brooklyn and Camden, New Jersey. He married Louisa Orr Haslam on 14 April 1871 and settled in Camden. A year later, he moved his ailing mother and retarded brother Edward in with them. Mother Whitman died on 23 May 1873. Walt Whitman, who had suffered a debilitating stroke in January, came to George's home to convalesce in the summer of 1873, and never left Camden.

The brothers lived amicably together. George and Louisa named their first son, who died in infancy, after Walt. (A second boy, named for his father, was stillborn.) Walt relieved George of much of the emotional and financial burden caused by Eddie's care.

George Whitman held responsible positions as a pipe inspector for the city of Camden and the New York Metropolitan Water Board, giving rise to Whitman's quip that George was interested "in pipes, not poems" (Traubel, *With Walt Whitman* 1:227). In 1884 George and Louisa moved into a new house they had built on a small farm outside Camden. When Walt decided to remain in the city, buying a house of his own on Mickle Street, a rift between the brothers occurred. Although Whitman remained close to his sister-in-law, he never again had warm relations with George.

Walt Whitman died on 26 March 1892. Later that year, Louisa died, followed by Edward. George Whitman lived alone on his farm in Burlington, New Jersey, until his death on 20 December 1901. He left a sizable estate, which supported his sister Hannah and niece Jessie (Jeff's daughter). George and Louisa Whitman are buried in Harleigh Cemetery in Walt Whitman's tomb.

Martin G. Murray

George Whitman was trained in carpentry by his father and worked alongside his brothers Andrew and Walt in the family's house-building ventures in Brooklyn. The publication of the first edition of *Leaves of Grass* (1855) did not impress George, who recalled: "I saw the book—didn't read it all—didn't think it worth reading—fingered it a little" (Traubel, "Notes" 35).

George Washington Whitman proved he was fittingly named after America's first patriot when he responded with full measure to his country's call following the Rebel attack on Fort Sumter. George joined the local militia (Thirteenth New York) in the spring of 1861 and

Bibliography

Loving, Jerome M., ed. *Civil War Letters of George Washington Whitman.* Durham, N.C.: Duke UP, 1975.

Traubel, Horace. "Notes from Conversations with George W. Whitman, 1893: Mostly in His Own Words." *In Re Walt Whitman.* Ed. Traubel, Richard Maurice Bucke, and Thomas B. Harned. Philadelphia: McKay, 1893. 33–40.

———. *With Walt Whitman in Camden.* Vol. 1. Boston: Small, Maynard, 1906.

Whitman, Walt. *The Early Poems and the Fiction.* Ed. Thomas L. Brasher. New York: New York UP, 1963.

See also CAMDEN, NEW JERSEY; CIVIL WAR, THE; FALMOUTH, VIRGINIA; HARLEIGH CEMETERY; "MY BOYS AND GIRLS"; WHITMAN, ANDREW JACKSON; WHITMAN, EDWARD; WHITMAN (HEYDE), HANNAH LOUISA; WHITMAN, JESSE (BROTHER); WHITMAN, LOUISA ORR HASLAM (MRS. GEORGE); WHITMAN, THOMAS JEFFERSON; WHITMAN (VAN NOSTRAND), MARY ELIZABETH

Whitman, Hannah Brush (1753–1834)

Hannah Brush Whitman, married to Jesse Whitman, was Walt Whitman's paternal grandmother. She worked as a schoolteacher and was skilled in needlework.

She impressed the young Walt with her stories of the family's patriotism during the Revolutionary War and their prosperous past as landholders on Long Island. She told Walt about his unconventional great-grandmother, Sarah White Whitman, who chewed tobacco and rode like a man out into the fields to oversee the slaves. Hannah and Jesse Whitman were the last in the family to own a substantial tract of land.

Walt Whitman warmly admired his grandmother. Jesse Whitman died before he was born, so Hannah Whitman was an important source of information to him about his family's past.

Denise Kohn

Bibliography

Allen, Gay Wilson. *The Solitary Singer: A Critical Biography of Walt Whitman.* 1955. Rev. ed. 1967. Chicago: U of Chicago P, 1985.

Kaplan, Justin. *Walt Whitman: A Life.* New York: Simon and Schuster, 1980.

Reynolds, David S. *Walt Whitman's America: A Cultural Biography.* New York: Knopf, 1995.

See also AMERICAN REVOLUTION, THE; GENEALOGY; WHITMAN, JESSE W. (GRANDFATHER)

Whitman (Heyde), Hannah Louisa (d. 1908)

Hannah Louisa Whitman was the younger sister of Walt Whitman, and she was the single family member who seemed to understand Whitman's writing. She attended the Hempstead Female Seminary and taught school prior to her marriage in March 1852 to Charles L. Heyde, a landscape artist to whom Whitman had introduced her. She moved with Heyde to Rutland, Vermont, where they lived a tumultuous, impoverished life together.

Named for her paternal grandmother, Hannah Brush Whitman, and her mother, Louisa Van Velsor Whitman, Hannah Whitman appears to have been Whitman's favorite sister, and they shared a love of literature. Hannah Whitman appears in Whitman's story "My Boys and Girls" (1844) as a fair and delicate youth.

Throughout her married life, Hannah and Walt exchanged many letters; in fact, in the last two years of his life Whitman wrote almost forty letters to her. She speaks favorably of his writing in her early letters, particularly admiring *Leaves of Grass* (1855). Her husband, Charles Heyde, grew uncomfortable around Whitman, even leaving when Whitman would visit, and he had a particular dislike of *Leaves*.

Having visited his sister in Vermont, and having seen the conditions in which she was living, with his letters Whitman often sent the Heydes money for clothes and furnishings. Hannah and Charles also received money from neighbors in spite of the fact that many of them witnessed violent fights between the two.

Later in life, Hannah became reclusive and hypochondriacal, and her letters reveal a neurotic tendency to overstate the family's wealth and social position. In his first will Whitman left Hannah one gold ring; in his final will, however, he left her one thousand dollars.

Charles Heyde died in an insane asylum in 1892, and Hannah Whitman Heyde died sixteen years later in 1908. She is buried in the Whitman mausoleum in Harleigh Cemetery (Camden, New Jersey), as the poet had planned.

Walt Whitman's sister Hannah appears to have been an important figure in his life. Not only did he care for her financially, but he was close to her. She seems to have been the one favorable connection between his family and his writing, since she read and enjoyed her brother's work.

Paula K. Garrett

Bibliography

Allen, Gay Wilson. *The Solitary Singer: A Critical Biography of Walt Whitman.* 1955. Rev. ed. 1967. Chicago: U of Chicago P, 1985.

Kaplan, Justin. *Walt Whitman: A Life.* New York: Simon and Schuster, 1980.

Molinoff, Katherine. *Some Notes on Whitman's Family.* Brooklyn: Comet, 1941.

Reynolds, David S. *Walt Whitman's America: A Cultural Biography.* New York: Knopf, 1995.

See also HARLEIGH CEMETERY; HEYDE, CHARLES L.; "MY BOYS AND GIRLS"; WHITMAN, ANDREW JACKSON; WHITMAN, EDWARD; WHITMAN, GEORGE WASHINGTON; WHITMAN, JESSE (BROTHER); WHITMAN, THOMAS JEFFERSON; WHITMAN (VAN NOSTRAND), MARY ELIZABETH

Whitman, Jesse (brother) (1818–1870)

The oldest of Whitman's eight siblings, Jesse Whitman was born on 2 April 1818 and died, unmarried and childless, on 21 March 1870. Named for his paternal grandfather, Jesse seems to have inherited elements of his father's moody, unstable temperament, as well. Less is known about Jesse than any of the other Whitman children who lived to adulthood—virtually nothing, in fact, aside from a few uncertain details about his troubled personality and its effects on the family.

As a young man Jesse went to sea on a merchant vessel, and by 1861 he was working in the Brooklyn Navy Yard preparing provisions for Union ships while living in his mother's house (along with his brothers Walt and Jeff and Jeff's family). About this time, his fragile disposition began to deteriorate; he became given to violent outbursts, particularly upon waking in the night, and he often vomited his meals. These problems were so severe that he was no longer able to hold a job, and the family began to fear for their safety, particularly that of Jeff's wife and children, at whom Jesse frequently raged. Jeff and Walt (who for part of the time was living in Washington and keeping abreast of the situation through the mail) favored hospitalizing him, but their mother resisted. When Jesse threatened to strike her with a chair, however, Walt committed him to the Kings County Lunatic Asylum on 5 December 1864; he died there of a burst aneurysm in 1870 and was buried, without family present, on the hospital grounds.

The cause of Jesse's problem is obscure. His mother claimed that he had always been "passionate almost to frenzy" (qtd. in Allen 308); the record of his admission to the asylum notes that he had injured his head in a fall about sixteen years earlier; and his niece reported that he had been "attacked by thugs and hit on the head with brass knuckles . . . he was considered to have the best mind of any of the children, until this happened" (Molinoff 19). All of that may be true, but Jeff's explanation seems best to fit Jesse's symptoms and course of deterioration: he had contracted syphilis from an "Irish whore" with whom he had lived (Whitman, Thomas Jefferson 85).

Horace Traubel notes that Whitman never discussed Jesse and even deflected a natural opportunity to do so. To varying degrees, he seems to have suppressed (or even repressed) the stories of the family's darker, more troubled members—Jesse, Andrew, Edward, their father—perhaps fearing that part of his own psychic inheritance. Certainly Jesse's story is the darkest and most thoroughly suppressed, and it helped to form the fearful background of mental and physical decay from which Whitman asserted the perfect health and equanimity of his poetic persona.

John Rietz

Bibliography

Allen, Gay Wilson. *The Solitary Singer: A Critical Biography of Walt Whitman.* 1955. Rev. ed. 1967. Chicago: U of Chicago P, 1985.

Gohdes, Clarence, and Rollo Silver, eds. *Faint Clews & Indirections: Manuscripts of Whitman and His Family.* Durham, N.C.: Duke UP, 1949.

Molinoff, Katherine. *Some Notes on Whitman's Family.* Brooklyn: Comet, 1941.

Traubel, Horace. *With Walt Whitman in Camden.* Vol. 1. Boston: Small, Maynard, 1906.

Whitman, Martha Mitchell. *Mattie: The Letters of Martha Mitchell Whitman.* Ed. Randall H. Waldron. New York: New York UP, 1977.

Whitman, Thomas Jefferson. *Dear Brother Walt: The Letters of Thomas Jefferson Whitman.* Ed. Dennis Berthold and Kenneth M. Price. Kent, Ohio: Kent State UP, 1984.

Whitman, Jesse W. (grandfather) (1749–1803)

Walt Whitman never knew his paternal grandfather Jesse W. Whitman directly, but he certainly heard of him through family stories, particularly the stories of his paternal grandmother, Hannah Brush Whitman. Jesse Whitman was the son of Nehemiah and Phoebe (Sarah White) Whitman; he inherited the family farm on Long Island from his parents. There he raised three sons, Jesse, Walter, and Treadwell, and one daughter, Sarah. The farm and homestead in West Hills amounted to nearly five hundred acres of land and became an important part of Walt Whitman's sense of home. The character of his mother undoubtedly contributed to Jesse Whitman's character. Phoebe Whitman was portrayed in family legend as a hardworking, tobacco-chewing, cursing woman who was able to oversee the farm single-handedly.

David G. Miller

Bibliography

Reynolds, David S. *Walt Whitman's America: A Cultural Biography.* New York: Knopf, 1995.

See also GENEALOGY; WHITMAN, HANNAH BRUSH; WHITMAN, WALTER, SR.

Whitman, Louisa Orr Haslam (Mrs. George) (1842–1892)

Walt Whitman's sister-in-law, Louisa, married George Washington Whitman in 1871, and moved with him to Camden in 1872. Whitman moved to Camden to live with the couple in 1873, and remained until 1884, when they bought a farm in Burlington County. Louisa also cared for Mrs. Whitman and Edward Whitman in Camden. Louisa was named executrix to Whitman's will. She also approved the autopsy performed on Whitman, despite the objections of Mrs. Mary Oakes Davis, Whitman's housekeeper.

Whitman appears to have been somewhat ambivalent about Lou, as he addressed her. She is usually mentioned in letters to friends and family as being "well" or "well as usual." As the wife of George, who "believes in pipes, not poems" (*With Walt Whitman* 1:227), Louisa was probably also somewhat business-minded, or if not, at least not poetically inclined. There are seven extant letters from Louisa to Whitman (see index in *Correspondence*). Louisa appears to be rather plain, though genuine and loving, and above all capable of being entrusted with Whitman's estate.

Whitman wrote to Louisa, mostly in the late 1870s and early 1880s, describing his travels and occasionally containing instructions for her to follow concerning his mail. The tone is one of familiarity, which might be contrasted with his remarks to others of how it was to live with Louisa and George: "[I] have for three years, during my paralysis, been boarding here, with a relative, comfortable . . . but steadily paying just the same as at an inn—and the whole affair in precisely the same business spirit" (*Correspondence* 3:47), and "My sister-in-law is very kind in all housekeeping things, cooks what I want, has first rate coffee for me & something nice in the morning, & keeps me a good bed and room—all of which is very acceptable—(then, for a fellow of my size, the *friendly presence & magnetism needed,* somehow, is not here)" (*Correspondence* 2:245).

Louisa gave birth to "Walter" in 1875, but the child died within the year (*Correspondence* 3:54). Whitman was evidently very pleased with the child and was distressed at its death: "I am miserable—he knew me so well—we had already had such good times—and I was counting so much" (*Correspondence* 3:54). She became pregnant again in 1877, this time with "George," but the baby was stillborn. Louisa is buried in Whitman's mausoleum.

Karen Wolfe

Bibliography

Allen, Gay Wilson. *The Solitary Singer: A Critical Biography of Walt Whitman.* 1955. Rev. ed. 1967. Chicago: U of Chicago P, 1985.

Traubel, Horace. *With Walt Whitman in Camden.* Vol. 1. Small, Maynard, 1906; Vol. 4. Ed. Sculley Bradley. Philadelphia: U of Pennsylvania P, 1953.

Whitman, Walt. *The Correspondence.* Ed. Edwin Haviland Miller. Vols. 2–3. New York: New York UP, 1961–1964.

See also CAMDEN, NEW JERSEY; DAVIS, MARY OAKES; MICKLE STREET HOUSE (CAMDEN, NEW JERSEY); WHITMAN, GEORGE WASHINGTON

Louisa Van Velsor Whitman, the poet's mother. Courtesy of the Library of Congress.

Whitman, Louisa Van Velsor (1795–1873)

Louisa Van Velsor Whitman, mother of nine children, eight of whom lived to adulthood, is best known, of course, for her second child, Walt, born when Louisa was twenty-four years old. It has turned out that this second son not only is known for his innovative poetry, but is also the child whom Louisa came to cherish and depend on more than any of her other children. Walt returned the love and the emotional connection, saying to his friend Horace Traubel, "How much I owe her! It could not be put in a scale—weighed: it could not be measured—be even put in the best words: it can only be apprehended through the intuitions. Leaves of Grass is the flower of her temperament active in me. . . . I wonder what Leaves of Grass would have been if I had been born of some other mother" (Traubel 113–114).

Louisa's letters to Walt are filled with news about the family, which Walt desired, but also with her observations on the political events of the day. The letters contain, as well, Louisa's repeated words of thanks and appreciation for Walt's generosity; not only did he consistently send her money, but he also sent her books, newspapers, almanacs, and articles. She, in turn, spoke frequently to him about critical reviews of his work which she had read, astutely assessing, at the time of its appearance, the value of Anne Gilchrist's 1870 "A Woman's Estimate of Walt Whitman," appearing in the Boston *Radical*.

Louisa's own style of writing merits attention. Louisa, often described as being "illiterate," did not use standard punctuation. She rarely capitalized letters; she frequently misspelled words, and sometimes did not observe what is to contemporary readers correct grammar. She was not "literate" in the written sense, but she read; she was intelligent and aware of her world, the public as well as her own private world. Reading Louisa's letters, a person soon becomes aware of learning to read in a new way—of following the rhythm of Louisa's prose, of actively creating the sentence breaks. Louisa's prose encourages active reading and also rewards the reader with a recognition of Louisa's unique sense of storytelling. A careful reader of her letters soon senses the import of Whitman's recognition of her own writing-thinking skills. "I favor her," Whitman said to Traubel, "'favor' they call it up on Long Island—a curious word so used, yet a word of great suggestiveness. Often people would say—men, women, children, would say—'You are a Whitman: I know you.' When I asked how they knew they would up with a finger at me: 'By your features, your gait, your voice: they are your mother's.' I think all that was, is, true: I could see it in myself" (280).

In addition to contributing to the formation of her son's style, Louisa's effect on her son can be seen in Whitman's representation of gender. Louisa's own strength contributed to Walt's sense of gender fluidity. Accordingly, in one of his notebooks, Whitman wrote: "Could we imagine such a thing—let us suggest that before a manchild or womanchild was born it should be suggested that a human being could be born" (*Uncollected* 2:76). Though Whitman certainly was at times caught in his culture's ideology, and in this regard at times essentializes women and men, there is a more pervasive move in his thinking, a move toward what is now called social construction. That is, Whitman could see the role society played in formulating a person's view of self and of others. Thus, he wished to inscribe in his poetry and prose a view of democracy much more idealized than the actuality in which he lived, outside his home.

Louisa also contributed to Walt's evolving understanding of the concept of "comradeship." This concept came to take on a progressively more inclusive meaning for Whitman, especially as a result of the Civil War. The war caused Whitman to fear the possible failure of democracy in the United States. He frequently revised in order to inscribe into his poetry more and more the ethic of care. "Comradeship" became an inclusive term for Whitman, not narrowed by gender, age, sexual orientation, or relationship. Though the strong individual was ever a concern for Whitman, he came to fear the excess of unthinking individualism, resulting in the fracturing of his country. Thus, the image of the Mother of All, representing comradeship, became intensified, post Civil War. Certainly, Louisa Van Velsor Whitman served as a model for Whitman for this Mother of All image.

Sherry Ceniza

Bibliography

Erkkila, Betsy. *Whitman the Political Poet.* New York: Oxford UP, 1989.

Traubel, Horace. *With Walt Whitman in Camden.* Vol. 2. 1908. New York: Rowman and Littlefield, 1961.

Whitman, Louisa Van Velsor. The largest collection of Louisa's letters to Walt is held in the Trent Collection at the Duke University Library. Also see her letters in the Hanley Collection, held in the Harry Ransom Humanities Research Center in Austin, Texas, and her letters to Helen Price held in the Pierpont Morgan Library in New York City. Helen Price's letters to Louisa are held in the Trent Collection. Letters to Louisa from various friends and relatives are found in the Whitman-Feinberg Collection, Library of Congress.

Whitman, Walt. *The Correspondence.* Ed. Edwin Haviland Miller. Vols. 1–2. New York: New York UP, 1961.

———. *The Uncollected Poetry and Prose of Walt Whitman.* Ed. Emory Holloway. 2 vols. Garden City, N.Y.: Doubleday, Page, 1921.

See also MOTHERHOOD; WHITMAN, WALTER, SR.; WOMEN AS A THEME IN WHITMAN'S WRITING

Whitman, Martha ("Mattie") Mitchell (1836–1873)

Next to his mother, whom Walt Whitman loved above all other persons, the woman for whom he appears to have had the deepest affection was his "Sister Matty," wife of his favorite brother, Thomas Jefferson. The poet had more in common with Mattie (as her familiar name was spelled by all but himself) than with his two natural sisters, and apparently felt more deeply about her as well. She and his mother, he wrote, were "the two best and sweetest women I have ever seen or known" (*Correspondence* 2:240).

Very little is known of Martha Mitchell's life before she married into the Whitman family. Her death certificate indicates she was born in New York (no city or town is given), and her daughter Jessie reported that she was an orphan whose stepmother had vanished with Martha's money upon learning of her intention to marry Jeff Whitman. When the newly married couple moved into the Whitman household, Mattie became an integral part of the family. She was industrious (making shirt-fronts at home for a local manufacturer) and energetic, and got along well with everyone except the emotionally unstable and sometimes violent oldest brother, Jesse. Mattie and her mother-in-law, Louisa Van Velsor Whitman, formed an unusually close bond, though occasional tensions did arise between the two strong-willed women. George Whitman believed, no doubt rightly, that Walt was drawn to Mattie because she was so good to his mother, but there were other reasons as well. Like him, she was gregarious, affectionate, sociable, and they shared interests in common, most notably music. Addressing her in a letter to his mother from Washington, Walt fondly remembered their going together to hear Guerrabella and having an oyster supper afterwards.

Only one of Walt Whitman's letters to Mattie survives, but hers to him and to his mother indicate that he wrote her a number of others, mostly after 1868, when she and her two daughters joined Jeff in St. Louis, where he had recently become superintendent of water works. By that time Mattie had begun to suffer acutely from the throat and respiratory disease (probably cancer) that would cause her death five years later. As her letters show, she endured her long and finally agonizing illness with a courage and cheerfulness that undoubtedly further endeared her to Walt. She was evidently much on his mind in her final months, for her last letter to him, in October 1872, acknowledges "a good many letters and books" he had sent her (Whitman, Martha 83).

The early months of 1873 were devastating ones for Walt Whitman. In late January he suffered a stroke that left him permanently weakened and disabled. The paralyzing early effects of that stroke prevented him from traveling to see his dear Sister Matty before she died in mid-February. Three months later, his beloved mother was also dead. In swift succession he had lost the bodily health and vitality he so much prized, and "the two best and sweetest women" he had ever known.

Randall Waldron

Bibliography

Allen, Gay Wilson. *The Solitary Singer: A Critical Biography of Walt Whitman.* 1955. Rev. ed. 1967. Chicago: U of Chicago P, 1985.

Whitman, Martha Mitchell. *Mattie: The Letters of Martha Mitchell Whitman.* Ed. Randall H. Waldron. New York: New York UP, 1977.

Whitman, Thomas Jefferson. *Dear Brother Walt: The Letters of Thomas Jefferson Whitman.* Ed. Dennis Berthold and Kenneth M. Price. Kent, Ohio: Kent State UP, 1984.

Whitman, Walt. *The Correspondence.* Ed. Edwin Haviland Miller. 6 vols. New York: New York UP, 1961–1977 (with *A Second Supplement* published by *Walt Whitman Quarterly Review,* 1991).

See also WHITMAN, LOUISA VAN VELSOR; WHITMAN, THOMAS JEFFERSON

Whitman, Nancy

Criticized both for her financial irresponsibility and her neglect of her children, Nancy Whitman was married to the poet's brother, Andrew Jackson Whitman. The couple had two children. On 3 December 1863 Andrew Whitman died of alcoholism and tuberculosis of the throat. According to the Whitman family, his wife was drunk at the time of his death. Furthermore, hours before Andrew died, his siblings had tried to take him to his mother's home (at his request), but his wife had prevented it.

Nancy is called a "streetwalker" and "prostitute" by Walt Whitman's biographers, and little is known about her life. An alcoholic, she is alleged to have been a poor mother, sending her children out onto city streets to beg. In 1868 her five-year-old son was run over by a brewery wagon and killed.

Martha Mitchell Whitman, wife of the poet's brother Thomas Jefferson ("Jeff") Whitman, told Walt on 21 December 1863 that when she saw Nancy earlier that month, Nancy had only a crust of bread. Martha gave her a dollar, explaining that it was all she had at the time. Jeff then wrote on 28 December that Andrew's death had left Nancy destitute. He said that, as usual, she "seems to have no idea of getting along" (91).

While married to Nancy, Andrew visited his mother often, taking food home for his wife and children. Although Walt's mother, Louisa Van Velsor Whitman, wrote Walt regularly complaining about his sister-in-law's lack of personal hygiene and parenting skills, the poet remained generous, often sending her kind greetings. Louisa, however, blamed Nancy for the couple's quarrels and for her son's drinking and early death.

The dates of Nancy Whitman's birth and death are not known, although she was still alive in 1888 when Whitman apportioned her fifty dollars in his will.

Jan Whitt

Bibliography

Allen, Gay Wilson. *The Solitary Singer: A Critical Biography of Walt Whitman.* 1955. Rev. ed. 1967. Chicago: U of Chicago P, 1985.

Whitman, Martha Mitchell. *Mattie: The Letters of Martha Mitchell Whitman.* Ed. Randall H. Waldron. New York: New York UP, 1977.

Whitman, Thomas Jefferson. *Dear Brother Walt: The Letters of Thomas Jefferson Whitman.* Ed. Dennis Berthold and Kenneth M. Price. Kent, Ohio: Kent State UP, 1984.

See also WHITMAN, ANDREW JACKSON; WHITMAN, LOUISA VAN VELSOR; WHITMAN, MARTHA ("MATTIE") MITCHELL; WHITMAN, THOMAS JEFFERSON

Whitman, Thomas Jefferson (1833–1890)

Walt Whitman's favorite brother, "Jeff," was the only one with whom he had much in common by way of interests and sensibility and the only one to achieve distinction in life beyond being kin to the famous poet. In Jeff's youth, Walt helped him learn to read, played games with him, and stimulated his love of music. In 1848, when Walt left Brooklyn to edit the New Orleans *Crescent,* Jeff went along, working as office boy at the paper and writing newsy letters to the family back home. Later, Walt helped make the connections that would lead Jeff into the civil engineering career in which he became, as superintendent of water works in St. Louis, a nationally recognized figure in his field.

Without suggesting any actual sexual intimacy, Dennis Berthold and Kenneth Price (editors of Jeff's letters) argue convincingly that Walt Whitman's love for Jeff may have been the earliest manifestation of the brother–son–beloved-comrade relationships he formed throughout his life and celebrated in his work. Perhaps an indicator of the nature and intensity of the poet's feeling for Jeff is that it was profoundly shaken and altered by the latter's marriage in 1859—though Jeff's wife Martha ("Mattie") was herself to become an object of Walt's deep affection. It would be a mistake, however, to suggest that the two brothers were drawn together only by the pull of strong emotion, for they had interests and traits of personality in common as well. Their many letters to one another testify to shared enthusiasms for music (especially opera), politics, and other subjects. Jeff worked assiduously to raise money for Walt's hospital work and—alone among the Whitmans—took fervent interest in his literary career. For his part, undoubtedly with pride in Jeff's accomplishments in mind, Walt praised the great achievements of modern engineering in his poems, most notably in "Passage to India" (1871), where such marvels of the day as the Suez Canal and the Atlantic cable figure as transcendent symbols for the coming together of all people, nations, and cultures in universal oneness. Ironically, while the poet's imagination was thus stirred by the great feats of his brother's profession, Jeff's own advancement in the field may have had some chilling effect on their relationship. As Berthold and Price point out, communication between Jeff and Walt dropped off radically in 1869, possibly because the younger man's suc-

Thomas Jefferson Whitman (the poet's favorite brother), ca. 1872. By permission, Missouri Historical Society, St. Louis.

cess and self-sufficiency had put him outside the sphere of dependency which nourished Walt's affections. Though perhaps driven somewhat apart in this way, they were drawn together powerfully in feeling when Mattie died in 1873, and in the winter of 1879–1880 Walt spent several months in St. Louis with Jeff and his daughters, Manahatta and Jessie Louisa. During the next ten years the brothers saw one another only occasionally, when Jeff was in the East on business, but the warmth between them was again rekindled, sadly enough, by the sudden death of Manahatta in 1886 and by Walt's illness and progressive weakening.

When Jeff Whitman died in 1890, numerous obituaries, including several in major engineering journals, testified to his stature as a professional and public figure. One of these, written by Walt for the *Engineering Record,* added to that testimony while also recalling the intimate and exuberant affection in which the poet held the most beloved of his brother-comrades: "how we loved each other—how many jovial good times we had!" (*Prose Works* 2:693).

Randall Waldron

Bibliography

Allen, Gay Wilson. *The Solitary Singer: A Critical Biography of Walt Whitman.* 1955. Rev. ed. 1967. Chicago: U of Chicago P, 1985.

Kaplan, Justin. *Walt Whitman: A Life.* New York: Simon and Schuster, 1980.

Whitman, Martha Mitchell. *Mattie: The Letters of Martha Mitchell Whitman.* Ed. Randall H. Waldron. New York: New York UP, 1977.

Whitman, Thomas Jefferson. *Dear Brother Walt: The Letters of Thomas Jefferson Whitman.* Ed. Dennis Berthold and Kenneth M. Price. Kent, Ohio: Kent State UP, 1984.

Whitman, Walt. *The Correspondence.* Ed. Edwin Haviland Miller. 6 Vols. New York: New York UP, 1961–1977 (with a *Second Supplement* published by *Walt Whitman Quarterly Review,* 1991).

——. *Prose Works 1892.* Ed. Floyd Stovall. 2 Vols. New York: New York UP, 1963–1964.

See also NEW ORLEANS, LOUISIANA; ST. LOUIS, MISSOURI; TECHNOLOGY; WHITMAN, ANDREW JACKSON; WHITMAN, EDWARD; WHITMAN, GEORGE WASHINGTON; WHITMAN (HEYDE), HANNAH LOUISA; WHITMAN, JESSE (BROTHER); WHITMAN, MARTHA ("MATTIE") MITCHELL; WHITMAN (VAN NOSTRAND), MARY ELIZABETH

Whitman (Van Nostrand), Mary Elizabeth (b. 1821)

Mary Elizabeth Whitman, the younger sister of Walt Whitman, separated herself from much of the Whitman family decline. In 1840, at the age of nineteen, she married a shipbuilder, Ansel Van Nostrand, and moved to Greenport on the north fork of Long Island. There Mary led a conventional life; her husband was hardworking and successful at shipbuilding, and the Van Nostrands raised five children.

Mary Elizabeth appears in several of Walt Whitman's stories, and she often seems to be the subject of Whitman's inquiries about loss of innocence. She is an unnamed fourteen-year-old in his story "My Boys and Girls" (1844) and is presented as the sweet Sister Mary in his children's story "The Half-Breed: A Tale of the Western Frontier" (1845).

Whitman often visited Mary and Ansel in Greenport, and he delighted in the comfortable life that Mary lived despite her husband's heavy drinking. Their home, a small white house in a small town, represented for Whitman idyllic hearth-and-home living. Mary, unlike many of her siblings, enjoyed an average, normal existence, and she separated herself from the eccentricities of the Whitman family. For Whitman, time spent with Mary in Greenport was peaceful and contented. In his first will, Whitman had arranged to leave a gold ring for Mary, but in his final will he left her two hundred dollars.

Mary Elizabeth was an important influence on Walt Whitman because she represented for him ideals he wanted to believe in. She read about him in newspapers, but she did not follow his literary career carefully. Instead, she seems to have provided a haven for him where he could visit for rest and where he could rediscover his dream for the Whitman family.

Paula K. Garrett

Bibliography

Allen, Gay Wilson. *The Solitary Singer: A Critical Biography of Walt Whitman.* 1955. Rev. ed. 1967. Chicago: U of Chicago P, 1985.

Kaplan, Justin. *Walt Whitman: A Life.* New York: Simon and Schuster, 1980.

Molinoff, Katherine. *Some Notes on Whitman's Family.* Brooklyn: Comet, 1941.

Reynolds, David S. *Walt Whitman's America: A Cultural Biography.* New York: Knopf, 1995.

See also "HALF-BREED, THE"; LONG ISLAND, NEW YORK; "MY BOYS AND GIRLS"; WHITMAN, ANDREW JACKSON; WHITMAN, EDWARD; WHITMAN, GEORGE WASHINGTON; WHITMAN (HEYDE), HANNAH LOUISA; WHITMAN, JESSE (BROTHER); WHITMAN, THOMAS JEFFERSON

Whitman, Walter, Sr. (1789–1855)

Appropriate to his politics, Walter Whitman, Sr., the poet's father, was born the day the Bastille was stormed, 14 July 1789, to Jesse W. and Hannah (Brush) Whitman. A freethinking rationalist who rejected organized religion and regularly read left-leaning books and journals, he was proud to have known Thomas Paine personally, and he took his son Walt to hear Elias Hicks, the Quaker iconoclast, and Frances Wright, the feminist-socialist reformer, when they spoke in New York. All three became family heroes about whom the poet spoke admiringly all his life. But if Whitman readily embraced his father's radical politics, he was reluctant to recognize the more general influence of his father's troubled personality.

On 8 June 1816 Walter Whitman married Louisa Van Velsor, with whom he had nine children, the second being the poet, his namesake. The Whitmans had lived in Huntington and West Hills, Long Island, since their Puritan forebears settled there in the seventeenth century, but in 1823 Walter Whitman moved his family to Brooklyn, where they changed addresses frequently. He was a skilled, hardworking carpenter who, once in Brooklyn, tried to better the family's fortunes through real estate speculation: buying a lot, building on it, moving his family there for a few months, and then selling and moving again once he had built the next house. His business ventures failed perennially.

Even before his worldly failures made him bitter, however, Whitman's father was, by all accounts, moody, dour, and inflexible, and the one surviving photographic portrait seems to reflect such a temperament. In "There was a Child Went Forth" (1855), the father is described as "strong, self-sufficient, manly, mean, anger'd, unjust," a man associated with "[t]he blow, the quick loud word, the tight bargain, the crafty lure," a fair description of the poet's own father. That slight, indirect, and unflattering reference is typical of Whitman, who rarely spoke of his father—far less often, certainly, than he spoke of his mother, whose gentle, affectionate disposition he openly admired and emulated. Clearly, the poet wanted to see himself as being more like his mother and struggled against the latent tendency toward brooding rigidity he inherited from his father. That interior struggle was not only outwardly manifest in conflicts between the poet and his father in the 1840s but was also reflected in Whitman's fiction from that period; stories like "Bervance: or, Father and Son" (1841) and "Wild Frank's Return" (1841) express Whitman's sense of suffocation and resentment in melodrama: a protagonist son is rejected by a cruel father who is later filled with remorse when that rejection results in the son's utter destruction (e.g., insanity or hideous death).

Walter Whitman, Sr., the poet's father. Courtesy of the Library of Congress.

Their antagonism (and Whitman's apparent desire for self-destructive revenge) seems to have eased when, in the late 1840s, Whitman began to take control of the family as his father's health failed. That reversal, made complete by his father's death on 11 July 1855, seems to have been liberating, perhaps even freeing him to launch his poetic career. When, in the opening lines of the Preface to *Leaves of Grass* (published just a week earlier), Whitman spoke of the son who calmly observes the father's corpse being borne from the house, essentially dismissing it as irrelevant, he was announcing the triumph of the sunny, healthy poetic persona over the brooding and unstable shadow he had repressed. Images of the father became as scarce in the subsequent poetry as they had been pervasive in the earlier fiction, and it was at this time, too, that he first cast off his father's name and signed his work "Walt" rather than "Walter." Only late in life could Whitman acknowledge, "As I get older, and latent traits come out, I see my father's [influence] also" (*Daybooks* 3:658).

John Rietz

Bibliography

Allen, Gay Wilson. *The Solitary Singer: A Critical Biography of Walt Whitman.* 1955. Rev. ed. 1967. Chicago: U of Chicago P, 1985.

Kaplan, Justin. *Walt Whitman: A Life.* New York: Simon and Schuster, 1980.

Molinoff, Katherine. *Some Notes on Whitman's Family.* Brooklyn: Comet, 1941.

Whitman, Walt. *Daybooks and Notebooks.* Ed. William White. 3 vols. New York: New York UP, 1978.

———. *Leaves of Grass: Comprehensive Reader's Edition.* Ed. Harold W. Blodgett and Sculley Bradley. New York: New York UP, 1965.

———. *The Uncollected Poetry and Prose of Walt Whitman.* Ed. Emory Holloway. Vol. 1. Garden City, N.Y.: Doubleday, Page, 1921.

Zweig, Paul. *Walt Whitman: The Making of the Poet.* New York: Basic Books, 1984.

See also "BERVANCE: OR, FATHER AND SON"; HICKS, ELIAS; LONG ISLAND, NEW YORK; PAINE, THOMAS; WHITMAN, HANNAH BRUSH; WHITMAN, JESSE W. (GRANDFATHER); WHITMAN, LOUISA VAN VELSOR; "WILD FRANK'S RETURN"; WRIGHT, FRANCES (FANNY)

Whittier, John Greenleaf (1807–1892)

John Greenleaf Whittier—poet, essayist, hymn writer, journalist, and editor—was, like Whitman, born of Quaker parentage and was best-loved for "Barbara Frietchie" (1863) and "Snow-Bound: A Winter Idyl" (1866). Whittier was initially averse to Whitman, throwing his complimentary copy of *Leaves of Grass* into the fire; in later years, however, he became more cordial to Whitman.

It was Whittier who first celebrated the common man in six "Songs of Labor"—"The Shoemakers," "The Fishermen," "The Lumbermen," "The Ship-Builders," "The Drovers," and "The Huskers"—which he contributed to the *Democratic Review* and the *National Era* in 1845–1847. Whittier engaged the attention of Whitman with his stern editorial pronouncements in the *Haverhill Gazette* rejecting war, imprisonment for debt, capital punishment, and the denial of voting rights for women. Despite Whitman's moving descriptions of the wounded in Washington hospitals in *Leaves,* Whittier, having published a collection of war songs, *National Lyrics* (1865), still refused to acknowledge the merit of Whitman's work.

However, in August of 1885, along with a ten-dollar contribution toward a horse and buggy for the lame gray poet, Whittier included a warm note to Thomas Donaldson about Whitman, stating, "I am sorry to hear of the physical disabilities of the man who tenderly nursed the wounded Union soldiers and as tenderly sung the dirge of their great captain" (qtd. in Allen 523).

Julie A. Rechel-White

Bibliography

Allen, Gay Wilson. *The Solitary Singer: A Critical Biography of Walt Whitman.* 1955. Rev. ed. 1967. Chicago: U of Chicago P, 1985.

Pollard, John A. *John Greenleaf Whittier, Friend of Man.* Boston: Houghton Mifflin, 1949.

See also CIVIL WAR NURSING

"Who Learns My Lesson Complete?" (1855)

First published without a title in *Leaves of Grass* (1855), "Who Learns My Lesson Complete?" was called "Lesson Poem" in the second (1856) edition of *Leaves.* Whitman gave it the present title in *Passage to India* (1871). The latest and the most commonly available text of this poem is in the 1891–1892 edition of *Leaves of Grass.*

In the opening stanza Whitman asks himself whom he should consider the best of his clientele. Among his "students" he counts manual and intellectual labor; the high and the low; the more and the less gifted; the young and the old—in fact the whole gamut of humanity, so long as they "draw nigh and commence" learning. And learning, for the poet, means breaking self's barriers, being able to converse and exchange views freely.

The three stanzas that follow describe the poet himself: one who is withdrawn and passive, and yet not overawed by the phenomenal world. What he comprehends but cannot articulate is the sheer *wonder* of this world. This forms the subject of stanzas 4, 5, and 6. The wonders include the rotation and revolution of our planet, the vastness of time and our consciousness of it, the immortality of one's soul, the levels and orders of ocular perception, and one's very birth and growth.

The last two stanzas state the "lesson" of the poem rather obliquely. In a way the "lesson" here is the wonder of its rhetoric—"that I can think such thoughts . . . And that I can remind you, and you think them and know them to be true." The wonder of it all, in other words, is the realization one's self commands and communicates.

K. Narayana Chandran

Bibliography

Bogen, Don. "'I' and 'You' in 'Who Learns My Lesson Complete?': Some Aspects of Whitman's Poetic Evolution." *Walt Whitman Review* 25 (1979): 87–98.

Hollis, C. Carroll. *Language and Style in "Leaves of Grass."* Baton Rouge: Louisiana State UP, 1983.

Whitman, Walt. *Leaves of Grass: Comprehensive Reader's Edition.* Ed. Harold W. Blodgett and Sculley Bradley. New York: New York UP, 1965.

See also "Autumn Rivulets"; *Leaves of Grass, 1855 Edition*

"Whoever You are Holding Me Now in Hand" (1860)

The third of the "Calamus" poems is a warning to readers and would-be disciples. The "me" of the title is both the poet's body and his book, and a commitment to either requires a loss of a former self. Whitman demands of his acolytes submission to him as to God, for he is "your God, sole and exclusive" (1860 *Leaves*). Like Jesus he calls on those who would follow to give up "all conformity."

After such a warning about the consequences of disciplehood, Whitman offers a very different view of himself, one not available in the house or the library, but only in the open air. If he can find a safe place, away from the gaze of others, then he can accept the disciple and offer him the "comrade's long-dwelling kiss." Unlike the enthusiasm of many of the "Calamus" poems in the celebration of achieved love, this poem situates love between men in a context of social danger and ostracism, and makes clear the price one will have to pay for "coming out."

Whitman also makes himself available as his book, not to be read, but rather to be thrust "beneath your clothing." By insisting on the bodily, Whitman refuses his idealist heritage. He

recognizes that much of what he says about the body will be misunderstood. Those who cannot grasp his meanings, cannot see him as the new evangel of male love, must simply release him. At the same time, Whitman makes understanding difficult, always refusing to identify clearly the "one thing" that should make the rest clear, which can only be called "that which you may guess at."

Underlying Whitman's play is a sense of the opacity and elusiveness of language. He will not be pinned down, any more than meaning can be prevented from dissemination. Whitman himself is fleeting, evanescent, his language in constant deferral. He places in question the idea of a true meaning, like a true self. The reader is left with what Edwin Miller has called "the chill of the type face" (153), the book as object, with the self that produced it having vanished. At the same time the reader has been offered a glimpse of another response, if only he (women are absent in the poem) can make the necessary sacrifice.

Robert K. Martin

Bibliography

Grossman, Allen. "Whitman's 'Whoever You Are Holding Me Now in Hand': Remarks on the Endlessly Repeated Rediscovery of the Incommensurability of the Person." *Breaking Bounds: Whitman and American Cultural Studies.* Ed. Betsy Erkkila and Jay Grossman. New York: Oxford UP, 1996. 112–122.

Miller, Edwin Haviland. *Walt Whitman's Poetry: A Psychological Journey.* Boston: Houghton Mifflin, 1968.

See also "Calamus"

"Wild Frank's Return" (1841)

This short story appeared in November 1841 in *United States Magazine and Democratic Review.* For publication history and revisions, see Brasher's edition of *The Early Poems and the Fiction.*

This story is Whitman's first use of the theme of two brothers going separate ways. In a dispute between Richard and Wild Frank, the father sides with the older. The second son, Wild Frank, leaves home. After two years of a dissolute life at sea, he reconciles with his brother and begins his journey home on a favored horse, Black Nell. The journey is tiring, so

Frank stops to give himself and the horse a little rest. He ties the horse to his wrist and falls asleep. So deep is his sleep that an ensuing storm cannot wake him, but the horse bolts and drags him the several miles home, where his family awaits his return. His mother, whose favorite he was, faints in a deadly swoon.

Reynolds, seeing in the story psychological parallels to its author, asks if Whitman, as prodigal son, projected this story to shock his mother. Kaplan sees it as Whitman's revenge against his own family, but he notes some hidden sexual symbols, such as Black Nell, and a correspondence between an umbilical cord and the cord around Frank's wrist, which correspondence Callow also sees. Allen sees this story, along with "Bervance: or, Father and Son" (1841), as evidence of Whitman's obsession with cruel fathers.

Patrick McGuire

Bibliography

Allen, Gay Wilson. *The Solitary Singer: A Critical Biography of Walt Whitman.* 1955. Rev. ed. 1967. Chicago: U of Chicago P, 1985.

Callow, Philip. *From Noon to Starry Night: A Life of Walt Whitman.* Chicago: Ivan R. Dee, 1992.

Kaplan, Justin. *Walt Whitman: A Life.* New York: Simon and Schuster, 1980.

Reynolds, David S. *Walt Whitman's America: A Cultural Biography.* New York: Knopf, 1995.

Whitman, Walt. *The Early Poems and the Fiction.* Ed. Thomas L. Brasher. New York: New York UP, 1963.

See also "BERVANCE: OR, FATHER AND SON"; SHORT FICTION, WHITMAN'S; WHITMAN, WALTER, SR.

Wilde, Oscar (1854–1900)

Born Oscar Fingal O'Flahertie Wills Wilde in Dublin, Wilde is most famous for his only novel, *The Picture of Dorian Gray* (1891), his dramatic comedy *The Importance of Being Earnest* (1895), and the poem "The Ballad of Reading Gaol" (1898), written after his release from jail where he served two years after being found guilty of homosexual offenses under the Criminal Law Amendment.

On 18 January 1882 Wilde visited Walt Whitman in Camden, where the poet was then living with his brother and sister-in-law. Wilde told Whitman that his mother had purchased a copy of *Leaves of Grass* when it was first published, that Lady Wilde had read the poems to her son, and that later, at Oxford, he and his friends carried *Leaves* to read on their walks. Flattered, Whitman offered Wilde, whom he later described as "a fine large handsome youngster" (Whitman 264), some of his sister-in-law's homemade elderberry wine, and they conversed for two hours. Asked later by a friend how he managed to get the elderberry wine down, Wilde replied: "If it had been vinegar I would have drunk it all the same, for I have an admiration for that man which I can hardly express" (qtd. in Allen 502). In a letter to Whitman postmarked 1 March, Wilde writes: "Before I leave America I must see you again. There is no one in this wide great world of America whom I love and honour so much" (100). Wilde was true to his word, making a second visit to Whitman the following May.

The chief proponent of the aesthetic movement, Wilde was notorious for his eccentricity in appearance and manner, and his court trial in London in 1895, when he was at the peak of his career, became a public sensation.

Bankrupt and in ill health, he lived the last three years of his life in France under the pseudonym Sebastian Melmoth, dying in Paris after converting to Roman Catholicism.

Richard Raleigh

Bibliography

Allen, Gay Wilson. *The Solitary Singer: A Critical Biography of Walt Whitman.* 1955. Rev. ed. 1967. Chicago: U of Chicago P, 1985.

Ellman, Richard. "Oscar Meets Walt." *New York Review of Books* 3 December 1987: 43–44.

———. *Oscar Wilde.* New York: Knopf, 1988.

Whitman, Walt. *The Correspondence.* Ed. Edwin Haviland Miller. Vol. 3. New York: New York UP, 1964.

Wilde, Oscar. *The Letters of Oscar Wilde.* Ed. Rupert Hart-Davis. London: Rupert Hart-Davis, 1962.

See also IRELAND, WHITMAN IN

Williams, Captain John

Captain John Williams, great-grandfather of Walt Whitman, was a Welsh master and part owner of a West Indies trading ship. As a young man Williams served under John Paul Jones on the *Bon Homme Richard;* notably, he fought in the famous naval battle on 23 September 1779, against the English *Serapis*. Williams's daughter, Naomi ("Amy") Williams Van Velsor, told Whitman of his great-grandfather's sea adventures, and Whitman wrote of the famous Independence sea fight in "Song of Myself": "Would you hear of an old-time sea-fight? / Would you learn who won by the light of the moon and stars? / List to the yarn, as my grandmother's father the sailor told it to me" (section 35).

Stephen A. Cooper

Bibliography

Allen, Gay Wilson. *The Solitary Singer: A Critical Biography of Walt Whitman.* 1955. Rev. ed. 1967. Chicago: U of Chicago P, 1985.

Whitman, Walt. *Complete Poetry and Collected Prose.* Ed. Justin Kaplan. New York: Library of America, 1982.

See also AMERICAN REVOLUTION, THE; VAN VELSOR, NAOMI ("AMY") WILLIAMS

Williams, Talcott (1849–1928)

Talcott Williams was born in Beirut en route to Turkey where his parents were missionaries. He graduated from Phillips Academy and went on to Amherst, graduating in 1873. He learned journalism in New York City at the *World* and at the *Sun.* He joined the Philadelphia *Press* in 1881, remaining there for thirty-one years until he became the first head of the Columbia University School of Journalism. In Philadelphia, Williams was a regular at the literary gatherings on Saturday nights at the home of his neighbor and Whitman patron, Dr. S. Weir Mitchell. Among Williams's friends were the Shakespeare scholar Horace Howard Furness, the artist Thomas Eakins, and Whitman, whose poems he sometimes published. Whitman respected Williams, saying, "The only thing that saves the [Philadelphia] Press from entire damnation is the presence of Talcott Williams" (Traubel 341). He was one of the thirty-six subscribers who gave ten dollars each to buy a horse and buggy for Whitman. In 1887 Williams introduced Eakins to Whitman so that he could paint his portrait. A founder of Philadelphia's Contemporary Club, he arranged for Whitman to speak at one of its first meetings. Williams's biographer credits him with obtaining the revocation of the court order barring *Leaves of Grass* from the federal mail as pornographic material. As one of the honorary pallbearers at Whitman's funeral he read selections from the Bible, the Greek philosophers, Confucius, and the Koran.

Philip W. Leon

Bibliography

Dunbar, Elizabeth. *Talcott Williams: Gentleman of the Fourth Estate.* Brooklyn: Robert E. Simpson, 1936.

Paneth, Donald, ed. *The Encyclopedia of American Journalism.* New York: Facts on File, 1983.

Traubel, Horace. *With Walt Whitman in Camden.* Vol. 1. 1906. New York: Rowman and Littlefield, 1961.

Williams, Talcott. *The Newspaperman.* New York: Scribner, 1922.

See also EAKINS, THOMAS; PHILADELPHIA, PENNSYLVANIA

Williams, William Carlos (1883–1963)

The influence of Walt Whitman's poetic practice on William Carlos Williams was both seminal and immensely rich. After Whitman, Williams is the great revolutionary in American prosody. Although he ultimately rejected Whitman's long and, to him, chaotic line, Whitman's willingness to break away from conventional metric practice, and to base a poetic rhythm in the rhythms of American language, was the founding impetus for American poetry. Likewise with modernism: Williams wrote (1955) that Whitman's dual discoveries that "the common ground is of itself a poetic source" and that the American language demanded a new and "free" verse were the true origin of modernism (22).

Williams, who worked in relative isolation and obscurity for most of his life, found sustenance as well as substance in Whitman's rebelliousness toward received forms, his determination to celebrate the democratic American culture around him, and his energetic celebration of the physical world. Despite Williams's move beyond Whitman's prosody into what he called measure or the variable foot, other concrete aspects of Whitman's practice had a continuing influence on Williams. Williams's *Paterson* (1963), for instance, is structured by Whitman's discovery, evidenced in the catalogues of "Song of Myself" and in "Crossing Brooklyn Ferry," that poetry must explore the deep morphology between the modern American city and modern consciousness.

James Breslin argues that Whitman's empathy for objects is the motivating force behind Williams's poetics, which the poet summarized as "no ideas but in things." Stephen Tapscott emphasizes that Williams, especially in his epic *Paterson,* is the leading modern exponent of Whitman's expansionist and democratic poetic voice, and that Whitman's persona presides over and in that poem.

Williams, a New Jersey poet, felt an emotional bond with Whitman, who spent his later years in Camden. In turn, both Williams and Whitman were spiritual mentors to yet another New Jersey poet, Allen Ginsberg.

Huck Gutman

Bibliography
Breslin, James E. *William Carlos Williams: An American Artist.* New York: Oxford UP, 1970.
Tapscott, Stephen. *American Beauty: William Carlos Williams and the Modernist Whitman.* New York: Columbia UP, 1984.
Williams, William Carlos. "An Essay on Leaves of Grass." *"Leaves of Grass" One Hundred Years After.* Ed. Milton Hindus. Stanford: Stanford UP, 1955. 22–31.

See also GINSBERG, ALLEN; LEGACY, WHITMAN'S

Willis, Nathaniel Parker (1806–1867)

During the 1850s N.P. Willis embodied the magazine editor as man-about-town. Whitman worked under him at the New York *Mirror* in 1844. Willis gained a reputation as an editor of popular magazines and as a prolific writer of poetry, sketches, and travelogues. Between 1827 and 1860 he published six volumes of poetry, nine books of sketches, and six volumes of travel writing. His prominence was such that Melville included Willis's name in a list of eight leading American authors (which he subsequently deleted) in his essay "Hawthorne and His Mosses." Willis's travel writing had international appeal and won him a following in Great Britain.

But it is as an editor that Willis remains noteworthy. He was a significant advocate of American literary nationalism. In response to Britain's refusal to offer American authors copyright protection, Willis founded the short-lived journal *The Corsair* (1839–1840), which sub-sisted by publishing pirated texts of British authors. He achieved his greatest stature between 1846 and 1864 as editor of the *New York Home Journal,* which still exists as the upscale magazine *Town and Country.*

Willis's reputation was marred, however, by accusations that he lacked substance. His reputation received a serious blow when Fanny Fern, his sister and author of the novel *Ruth Hall,* used Willis as the model for the character Hyacinth Ellet, a cold-hearted social climber who abandons his widowed sister.

T. Gregory Garvey

Bibliography
Auser, Cortland P. *Nathaniel Parker Willis.* New York: Twayne, 1969.
Rathbun, John W. *American Literary Criticism, 1800–1860.* Boston: Hall, 1979.
Stovall, Floyd. *The Foreground of "Leaves of Grass."* Charlottesville: UP of Virginia, 1974.

See also PARTON, JAMES; PARTON, SARA PAYSON WILLIS (FANNY FERN)

Wilmot Proviso (1846)

Introduced by Representative David Wilmot of Pennsylvania in the United States Congress in August 1846, the proviso stated that, as a condition to the United States acquiring territory from Mexico, "neither slavery nor involuntary servitude" could exist in any part of that territory. The proviso served as a lightning rod to the Congressional debates over slavery which dominated the national agenda from 1846 until the 1850 Compromise, intensifying divisions between North and South and giving rise to the free-soil movement which would find institutional form in 1848 in the Free Soil party and, in 1854, in the Republican party. Walt Whitman's editorial support of the Wilmot Proviso throughout the late 1840s positioned him solidly within the Free Soil camp and showed his thinking on slavery to be motivated more by concern for white labor than by sympathy for slaves, a position he consistently held in his journalism up through the Civil War.

Disputes over slavery had supposedly been settled by compromises in the United States Constitution and agreements such as the 1820 Missouri Compromise, and the abolitionists of the 1830s and 1840s had proved ineffective in moving Congress to reconsider the issue. But with a vast new territory including California,

New Mexico, and Texas opened up by United States victory in its war with Mexico, the debate over slavery exploded. Northerners who came to be known as Free-Soilers promoted the Wilmot Proviso as a means by which free (i.e., white) labor could enter the new territories without having to compete with—and, thus, be "degraded" by—slave labor. Southerners vigorously opposed the Wilmot Proviso, fearing that additional free states would decisively tip the balance of power to the North. The House passed the Wilmot Proviso along sectional lines in both 1846 and 1847, but the Senate, in which the South had greater power, blocked the proviso in March of 1847.

Despite the proviso's defeat, debate over the bill gave rise to the free-soil movement which Whitman would promote in Brooklyn *Eagle* editorials from December 1846 until his departure in January 1848. Whitman's editorials largely echo the Free-Soilers' position that the introduction of slavery would discourage, if not prohibit, white laborers from migrating to the new territories. Whitman's distinction between abolitionist "interference" with slavery in the South and the question of the extension of slavery into the West invokes the memory of Thomas Jefferson as the prototypical Free-Soiler and characterizes the debate as an issue not of race but of class between white labor and the aristocracy of the South. While Whitman's position follows the Free-Soilers' emphasis on white labor and not on moral opposition to slavery, Whitman, unlike many Free-Soilers, does not evoke white anxiety about associating with blacks as a reason to support the proviso.

Debate over the Wilmot Proviso divided both the Whig and Democratic parties, whose dissenters merged to form the Free Soil party in 1848. While the proviso became largely irrelevant with passage of the 1850 Compromise, it ignited and intensified the divisions between North and South that led to Civil War.

Martin Klammer

Bibliography

Allen, Gay Wilson. *The Solitary Singer: A Critical Biography of Walt Whitman.* 1955. Rev. ed. 1967. Chicago: U of Chicago P, 1985.

Klammer, Martin. *Whitman, Slavery, and the Emergence of "Leaves of Grass."* University Park: Pennsylvania State UP, 1995.

McPherson, James M. *Battle Cry of Freedom: The Civil War Era.* New York: Oxford UP, 1988.

Rubin, Joseph Jay. *The Historic Whitman.* University Park: Pennsylvania State UP, 1973.

Whitman, Walt. *The Gathering of the Forces.* Ed. Cleveland Rodgers and John Black. 2 vols. New York: Putnam, 1920.

See also BROOKLYN *DAILY EAGLE;* COMPROMISE OF 1850; DEMOCRATIC PARTY; FREE SOIL PARTY; REPUBLICAN PARTY; SLAVERY AND ABOLITIONISM

"With Husky-Haughty Lips, O Sea!" (1884)
First published in *Harper's Monthly* (March 1884), this twenty-three-line poem describes Whitman's response to the sea during a week's visit to Ocean Grove, New Jersey, with John Burroughs in September and October, 1883. Found in the *Leaves of Grass* cluster "Sands at Seventy," it joins numerous other poems involving the sea, most especially the eight-poem group "Fancies at Navesink," composed around the same time, and the earlier cluster, "Sea-Drift."

The poem's structure follows a familiar Whitman pattern, fashioned to provide the most dramatic impact. The central image is first presented with the poet's involvement immediately established as he addresses the sea, which responds with its "varied strange suggestions." Extending this personification in a series of descriptive lines, he portrays the sea's complex, shifting moods until there takes place a kind of apotheosis: the sea sounds have seemed to the listener "the first and last confession of the globe." That confession, for Whitman, is "the tale of cosmic elemental passion." The connection with the poet, prepared for in the parenthetical "sounding, appealing to the sky's deaf ear—but now, rapport for once," is made through a key word in the last line, "kindred": "Thou tellest to a kindred soul." The arrangement has been less linear than circular, less descriptive than reflective. The poet retains the opening role as listener but has added a major idea: that his role is also that of a companion.

This poem is dominated by the use of personification, a device much favored by nineteenth-century writers and one that often led to mawkish sentimentality or absurd exaggeration. Whitman's poetry is seldom guilty of the first, but sometimes falls into the second, as can be felt here. An ocean seen with an "ample, smiling face" or a "brooding scowl and murk," with "many tears" and in a "lonely state," having a "vast heart, like a planet's" might not be the ocean another onlooker would see. Whitman does perhaps admit to himself that an ocean and a human are not comparable, as he suggests that the ocean can never attain true greatness: there is "a lack from all eternity in thy content / (Naught but the greatest struggles, wrongs, defeats, could make thee greatest—no less could make thee,)"—but this is a stretching of the comparison into the absurd.

By now Whitman is letting his fancy run free with a conceit in which the sea, "by lengthen'd swell, and spasm, and panting breath," is viewed sympathetically because held back, chained, thwarted, letting off a "serpent hiss, and savage peals of laughter / And undertones of distant lion roar." When this sea, constricted like Prometheus, becomes the voice of the earth's cosmic passion, the conceit has become more obscure than apt, remaining admirable only as an instance of Whitman's imaginative reach.

The qualities of the sea selected by the poet are its mixture of moods, its "unsubduedness, caprices, wilfulness," its loneliness, its being forcibly controlled by some greater power, and its passion. With these, to some unspecified degree, Whitman feels allied. The bond is wisely left vague and cryptic. This is not one of his confessional poems; the role of Whitman himself remains generalized. The poem's effectiveness depends on the taste of the reader, who may or may not enter into the poet's imaginative response to the sea on this occasion.

David B. Baldwin

Bibliography

Allen, Gay Wilson, and Charles T. Davis, eds. *Walt Whitman's Poems: Selections with Critical Aids.* New York: New York UP, 1955.

Whitman, Walt. *Leaves of Grass: Comprehensive Reader's Edition.* Ed. Harold W. Blodgett and Sculley Bradley. New York: New York UP, 1965.

See also "Sands at Seventy" (First Annex); Sea, The; "Sea-Drift"

"Woman Waits for Me, A" (1856)
This poem was first published by Fowler and Wells in Brooklyn as the thirteenth poem in the second (1856) edition of *Leaves of Grass* and originally entitled "Poem of Procreation." In 1860 this title was dropped and the poem was moved to the "Enfans d'Adam" poem cluster as poem number 4. In 1867 the poem was given its present title.

Comprised of eight loose stanzas, the poem catalogues the speaker's desire for a woman who will meet his sexual agenda in the same bold and brash spirit as it is proclaimed here. The first stanza emphasizes fullness versus emptiness, since the woman who waits, "sex," and "the right man" must be present in order for procreation to take place.

The second stanza develops the idea of "sex" as an integral part of all aspects of creation. Here Whitman unpacks all that sex "contains," echoing the first line, but applies it to sex rather than to the woman. In the third stanza, both the man and the woman know and testify to the "deliciousness" of sex. By repeating the line and substituting "woman" for "man," Whitman calls attention to the natural attitude each brings to sex, an attitude contradicted by the "impassive" women of line 11. The third and fourth stanzas emphasize the mutual understanding and capacity that exist between the woman who "knows and avows" her sexuality and her physical prowess and that of the speaker, who appreciates and admires the "divine suppleness and strength" of their flesh. Apart from the ability to bear children, these women possess markedly masculine traits and abilities.

The last half of the poem describes the procreative act, as the "right man" and the woman who "contains all" come together. The tone of these lines changes, however; instead of the reciprocity and mutual understanding figured in the inclusive "knows and avows" of lines 9 and 10 and the following stanza, the lines attest to a man, "stern, acrid, large, undissuadable," who "make[s] [his] way." Despite the speaker's claim that these women are not "one jot less than I am," in these lines their desire does not match his, and, as such, they are found lacking. Now the single "woman" of the title becomes plural, as "you women" are drawn close to the speaker and forced to receive his "slow rude muscle." The procreative urge takes precedence over the women's "entreaties" and the speaker does not "withdraw" until he has "deposit[ed] what has so long accumulated."

In a rare moment of specificity for the pronoun "you" in Whitman's work, the final lines of the poem are addressed to the women who will make possible the speaker's procreative vision. Strong, healthy, unabashed, these women receive his "gushing showers" and in turn "grow fierce and athletic girls." The latter part of the poem collapses Whitman's poetic and political agendas in its use of hyperbolic rhetoric. As such, the poem should probably be read figuratively rather than literally; that is, insemination in this instance is directed toward those capable of bringing Whitman's poetic vision into being. Although it attempts to transform the constrictions placed upon women by nineteenth-century American society, the poem ultimately fails to extricate itself from contemporary discourse.

Maire Mullins

Bibliography

Aspiz, Harold. *Walt Whitman and the Body Beautiful.* Urbana: U of Illinois P, 1980.

Baym, Nina. "The Portrayal of Women in American Literature, 1790–1870." *What Manner of Woman: Essays on English and American Life and Literature.* Ed. Marlene Springer. New York: New York UP, 1977. 211–234.

Erkkila, Betsy. *Whitman the Political Poet.* New York: Oxford UP, 1989.

Killingsworth, M. Jimmie. *Whitman's Poetry of the Body: Sexuality, Politics, and the Text.* Chapel Hill: U of North Carolina P, 1989.

Lawrence, D.H. *Studies in Classic American Literature.* New York: Seltzer, 1923.

Mullins, Maire. "'Act Poems of Eyes, Hands, Hips and Bosoms': Women's Sexuality in Walt Whitman's 'Children of Adam.'" *ATQ* 6 (1992): 213–231.

See also "CHILDREN OF ADAM"; SEX AND SEXUALITY; SOCIETY FOR THE SUPPRESSION OF VICE

Woman's Rights Movement and Whitman, The

The terms "woman's rights" refers to the first wave of an organized and ongoing movement for women's rights, "woman" the word used by the activists in the decade of the 1850s. Though the 1848 Seneca Falls meeting inaugurated the movement, it was in 1850 in Worcester, Massachusetts, at the first National Woman's Rights Convention, which Paulina Wright Davis organized and at which she presided as president, that a precedent was established. For the next ten years, until the Civil War began, national meetings were held yearly, as well as numerous state and local assemblies. These conventions received widespread coverage by the press. The New York *Tribune,* for example, printed the speeches and step-by-step coverage in its over-sized pages. These conventions were going on in the exact period of Whitman's most creative breakthroughs. They focused on the issue of consuming importance to Whitman—the analysis of just what American democracy meant in actuality and what the Declaration of Independence said it meant, or could mean. For this reason, given Whitman's like concerns, it is doubtful that he ignored the extensive press coverage given the movement.

There is also the matter of Fowler and Wells. Not only was this publishing firm a part of Whitman's life in terms of the first two editions of *Leaves of Grass* and in terms of its focus on phrenology and numerous other reform-related issues, Whitman also wrote for one of its journals, *Life Illustrated.* This firm frequently published the proceedings of the woman's rights conventions and Lydia Fowler frequently served as secretary, meaning that Whitman had firsthand opportunities to hear (as well as read) about the issues discussed by these early woman's rights activists. In addition, one of the movement's early speakers moved to Brooklyn in 1855 and in time became one of Whitman's closest friends—Abby Hills Price. In turn, he became acquainted with two more of the most active female activists in the 1850s—Paulina Wright Davis and Ernestine L. Rose.

What were the issues? Suffrage, of course, stands out as a burning concern, but the speeches reveal that this first concerted effort by activists for women's rights stands out for its boldness and comprehensive grasp both of history and of women's existential situation. A major concern was the institution of marriage. Marriage laws penalized women in every respect. Women lost not only their last names, but also their property, their wages, their homes, and often their children, if the husband died or the couple managed to obtain a divorce. Equally important to these activists were the issues of work, education, and dress. These activists wanted not to be closed out of the workplace, wanted the opportunities to develop their minds and skills and to use them to become financially independent. The more radical activists did not want the separation of home and the public sphere.

Abby Hills Price spoke at the first three National Woman's Rights conventions in 1850, 1851, and 1852. She also read a poem she wrote at the twenty-year celebration of the National Woman's Rights movement, held in New York City, 1870, organized by her close friend and frequent visitor at her home, Paulina Wright

Davis. Davis was a force in the woman's rights movement until her death in 1876 and the publisher/editor of the woman's journal *The Una*. Whitman also knew and visited Ernestine L. Rose, considered in her time one of the movement's most eloquent public speakers. Rose frequently served on National Woman's Rights committees alongside Price and Davis, and she influenced Whitman sufficiently that he used her words in one of his poems, "France." Rose's speeches stand out for their tight use of logical argument, as well as for their fearlessness, and their repudiation of the status quo which enforced female subservience.

There can be no convincing critical work on Whitman and women if the ties he had with the woman's rights movement are not taken into account. Because of the woman's movement and the women in his life, Whitman became more sensitized to the issue of women and American democracy. Beginning with the 1856 edition of *Leaves,* Whitman's poetry and prose become much more radicalized in terms of his stance toward equality. "The Primer of Words" (an 1850s manuscript published in 1904 as *An American Primer*) and *Democratic Vistas* (published by Whitman in 1871, after two of the segments had already appeared in the *Galaxy*) provide eloquent insights into the woman's rights cause. Also of importance is the extensive oratory carried on by activists for woman's rights in the decade of the 1850s. When one notes the importance that oratory played in Whitman's mind and writing, the presence of such orators-activists-friends as Price, Davis, Rose cannot be ignored.

Sherry Ceniza

Bibliography

Ceniza, Sherry. "Walt Whitman and 'Woman Under the New Dispensation.'" Diss. University of Iowa, 1990.

———. *Walt Whitman and 19th-Century Women Reformers.* Tuscaloosa: U of Alabama P, 1998.

———. "Whitman and Democratic Women." *Approaches to Teaching Whitman's "Leaves of Grass."* Ed. Donald D. Kummings. New York: MLA, 1990. 153–158.

Davis, Paulina Wright. *A History of the National Woman's Rights Movement.* New York: Journeymen Printers' Co-Operative Association, 1871.

DuBois, Ellen Carol. *Feminism and Suffrage: The Emergence of an Independent Women's Movement in America, 1848–1869.* Ithaca, N.Y.: Cornell UP, 1978.

Stanton, Elizabeth Cady, Susan B. Anthony, and Matilda Joslyn Gage, eds. *History of Woman Suffrage.* 6 vols. Rochester, N.Y.: Susan B. Anthony, Charles Mann, 1881–1922.

Stern, Madeleine B. *Heads & Headlines: The Phrenological Fowlers.* Norman: U of Oklahoma P, 1971.

Suhl, Yuri. *Ernestine L. Rose and the Battle for Human Rights.* New York: Reynal, 1959.

Whitman, Walt. *The Correspondence.* Ed. Edwin Haviland Miller. 6 vols. New York: New York UP, 1961–1977.

See also EQUALITY; FARNHAM, ELIZA W.; FOWLER, LORENZO NILES AND ORSON SQUIRE; *LIFE ILLUSTRATED;* ORATORY; PRICE, ABBY HILLS; WELLS, SAMUEL ROBERTS; WOMEN AS A THEME IN WHITMAN'S WRITING

Women as a Theme in Whitman's Writing
Women have admired Whitman's *Leaves of Grass* from the first, though, of course, there have been dissenters. In 1856 Fanny Fern (Sara Payson Willis Parton) wrote in praise of Whitman and of *Leaves* in the New York *Ledger,* inaugurating a pattern which exists to this day. Fern represents the pattern in that hers was a celebratory reception of Whitman's work, yet the subsequent falling out which occurred in the Whitman-Parton friendship—Whitman's borrowing money from the Partons and then failing to meet the repayment date—illustrates the negative side of this relationship. To this day it is cited as an example of Whitman's unfairness, especially to women, as Joyce Warren does in her biography *Fanny Fern.* To simplify the issue and to bring it up to date: is Whitman's writing enabling for women readers? How does Whitman portray women in his work?

The first question—is Whitman's writing enabling for women readers?—is phrased in a way which assumes a universal type of woman reader, which is, of course, a gross oversimplification. Presently, critics such as Betsy Erkkila find Whitman was and is enabling for women readers; critics such as Joyce Warren find the opposite. It is tempting to say that the proof lies in the details, but these, too, can be manipulated, often unconsciously, by one's general political stance.

What *are* the details? The details are so abundant and intricate that to do justice to the topic one would have to write a complete book. However, a look at the topic will be presented here, considering the following: a brief noting of major figures who wrote about Whitman's representation of women, many of whom were female writers-critics; a brief noting of actual women important in Whitman's life and thinking; and ways Whitman went about inscribing "the new woman, the democratic woman" into his writing.

Four years after Fanny Fern wrote in praise of Whitman and *Leaves,* three women wrote, in Henry Clapp's *Saturday Press,* defending Whitman's third (1860) edition. Mary Chilton, Juliette Beach, and C.C.P. praised Whitman's representation of women and defended him against charges of immorality. Adah Menken also lauded Whitman's thinking and writing in 1860, and Eliza Farnham quoted Whitman in her 1864 *Woman and Her Era.* The decade of the 1870s is important for the publication of Anne Gilchrist's "A Woman's Estimate of Walt Whitman" and Nora Perry's "A Few Words about Walt Whitman." In the decade of the 1880s many women wrote positive reviews of Whitman's work, and one woman, Elizabeth Porter Gould, published an edition of selected poems from *Leaves,* calling it *Gems from Walt Whitman.*

The range of personalities and viewpoints more or less covers the spectrum, from Porter's discreet Bostonian point of view to activist Elmina D. Slenker's anything but cautious outspokenness. The responses to Whitman continue. Interestingly, many of the women's responses have dropped out of the critical dialogue, but one response has remained present: D.H. Lawrence's article on Whitman written in 1921 and then appearing in revised form in 1923 in his *Studies in Classic American Literature.* Lawrence's negative view of Whitman's representation of women is still repeated as authority in present-day scholarship, even though scholars such as Harold Aspiz, Jerome Loving, M. Jimmie Killingsworth, Sherry Ceniza, and Betsy Erkkila offer readings which, in large measure, contradict Lawrence's.

Though Whitman's representation of women in his writing is not consistently in touch with contemporary feminism, it must be put into its historical perspective. If one views any writer as both caught in the language and ideology of his or her times while at the same time, for writers like Whitman, attempting to break out of those ideologies, then it is difficult to view Whitman's literary representation of women as anything but positive. One way to account for this positiveness is to note the presence of actual women in his life who influenced

or at least educated him. The strongest influence in his life was his mother, Louisa Van Velsor Whitman. She was a woman who took matters into her own hands, although her lack of formal education and the circumstances of her times seemed to work against her. She prepared the way for Whitman to listen to and admire women such as Frances Wright, whom he placed alongside Elias Hicks and Thomas Paine as three people in American history who had been overlooked, even maligned. When Whitman heard and read women's words in the 1840s and more pervasively in the 1850s, Louisa's essence enabled him, as well, to listen intently to what *they* were saying. His friendship with Abby Hills Price, Paulina Wright Davis, and Ernestine L. Rose, all activists in the woman's rights cause, as well as antislavery supporters, associationists, and advocates of other reforms, attests to his ability and readiness to listen to (and to learn from) reform-minded women.

Whitman's 1856 letter of reply to Emerson, ostensibly a preface to the 1856 edition, needs to be taken into consideration when assessing his representation of women in *Leaves.* Whitman said, "This filthy law [that one cannot mention sexuality in writing] has to be repealed—it stands in the way of great reforms. Of women just as much as men, it is the interest that there should not be infidelism about sex, but perfect faith." He then makes the following statement: "Women in These States approach the day of that organic equality with men, without which, I see, men cannot have organic equality among themselves" (*Comprehensive* 737). A bedrock tenet in Whitman's concept of American democracy was his belief in each person's having the opportunity to develop to the extent she or he desired. Call it freedom, or equality of opportunity. Regardless, the poetry and prose overall make the distinction between "feudalism" and democracy, between an individual controlled by outside forces and an individual taking responsibility for her or his own actions. Whitman states it this way in *Democratic Vistas:*

> The purpose of democracy . . . is . . . to illustrate, at all hazards, this doctrine or theory that man, properly train'd in sanest, highest freedom, may and must become a law, and series of laws, unto himself, surrounding and providing for, not only his own personal control, but all his relations to other individuals, and to the State.
>
> (*Prose Works* 2:374–375)

Assuming Whitman meant what he said, how did he go about accomplishing his aims, to portray "democratic" women as well as men; black, brown, and red as well as white; same-sexed unions as well as male-female unions? The first issue—gender representation—is the one of concern here. One accomplishment, judging by the research made of women's written reactions to *Leaves*, was Whitman's appeal to many different readers, female as well as male. When he says, as he does in "Song of the Open Road," "Whoever you are, come forth! or man or woman come forth! / You must not stay sleeping and dallying there in the house, though you built it, or though it has been built for you" (section 13), the reader, male or female, is addressed. Whitman's lines seek to create an expansive space for women, something very much against the grain of his times, at least for white, middle-class women, who were exhorted to observe "the separation of the spheres." Along with his address to readers aiming at expansiveness, Whitman's frequent use of both gendered pronouns (as well as his frequent use of "man and woman" and "woman and man") was revolutionary. In fact, today the generic "man" is still used regularly, seemingly unquestioningly, in the popular media, and still at times in academia, as well.

Concerning images of women, the cluster of poems most attacked in his times was "Children of Adam," and the specifics in individual poems most problematic to his readers were the passages in which women's bodies were spoken of in ways other than those pertaining to the docile, dutiful mother or the chaste, single woman. Whitman's women often "swim, row, ride, wrestle, shoot, run, strike, retreat, advance, resist, defend themselves," as they do in his poem "A Woman Waits for Me." But in an earlier poem, "I Sing the Body Electric," they also dutifully wait: "Girls, mothers, house-keepers, in all their performances, / The group of laborers seated at noon-time with their open dinner-kettles, and their wives waiting" (section 2).

Interestingly, a refrain runs through women's responses to Whitman, at least from the late 1850s to the 1920s. That refrain is the valorization of Whitman's inscription of the strong "I." In an 1860 personal letter to Henry Clapp, the publisher and editor of the New York *Saturday Press*, Juliette Beach says it well: "Its egotism delights me—that defiant ever recurring 'I,' is so irresistibly strong and good" (7 June 1860, Library of Congress). Once a person has read countless nineteenth-century women's words and words written to women or about women, it comes as no surprise that women, at least some women, responded to the call made in *Leaves* for the independent "I."

Whitman made the point early on, in his 1855 Preface, that "the soul has that measureless pride which consists in never acknowledging any lessons but its own. But it has sympathy as measureless as its pride and the one balances the other and neither can stretch too far while it stretches in company with the other" (*Comprehensive* 716). In *Democratic Vistas* pride and sympathy are discussed in more public terms. Whitman speaks of the individual citizen in a democratic society, emphasizing the unified amalgamation of individuals into a country. In his poetry after the Civil War, Whitman focused more than before on creating images of unity, and certainly one of the primary images was that of the Mother of All. Birthing always held top value for Whitman, who, in many ways, saw literal birthing and the creation of *Leaves* as analogous. He wanted strong mothers, but he also wanted women to participate in the public life in his country. In the 1856 and 1860 editions of *Leaves*, the public images become more pronounced. For example, the 1856 "Song of the Broad-Axe," section 11, inscribes a public role for the woman, as does the 1856 "Primer of Words."

The disturbing element in *Leaves* for many contemporary women is the lack of representation of women working outside the home. Most of the images of women working are those of a domestic nature. There are strong images of women using language, such as in the poems "Vocalism" and "Mediums." However, just as the women defending the 1860 *Leaves* said, one has to take the whole of *Leaves*, not the fragments. The words of poet Adrienne Rich provide the kind of anticlosure that the present topic requires because of its dense ties to the culture and Whitman's own sensibility. In her essay "Beginners" in her 1993 book *What Is Found There*, Rich says of Whitman: "Yet that woman [Dickinson] and that man [Whitman] were beginners; . . . the man overriding Puritan strictures against desire and insisting that democracy is of the body, by the body, and for the body, that the body is multiple, diverse, untypic" (95).

Finally, Whitman's words on his "intentionality" merit notation. He said to Horace Traubel in 1888:

Leaves of Grass is essentially a woman's book: the women do not know it, but every now and then a woman shows that she knows it: it speaks out the necessities, its cry is the cry of the right and wrong of the woman sex—of the woman first of all, of the facts of creation first of all—of the feminine: speaks out loud: warns, encourages, persuades, points the way.

(Traubel 331)

Sherry Ceniza

Bibliography

Erkkila, Betsy. *Whitman the Political Poet.* New York: Oxford UP, 1989.

Fern, Fanny. "Fresh Fern Leaves. 'Leaves of Grass.'" New York *Ledger* 10 May 1856.

Rich, Adrienne. "Beginners." *What Is Found There: Notebooks on Poetry and Politics.* By Rich. New York: Norton, 1993. 90–101.

Stansell, Christine. *City of Women: Sex and Class in New York, 1789–1860.* Urbana: U of Illinois P, 1987.

Traubel, Horace. *With Walt Whitman in Camden.* Vol. 2. 1908. New York: Rowman and Littlefield, 1961.

Warren, Joyce W. *Fanny Fern: An Independent Woman.* New Brunswick, N.J.: Rutgers UP, 1992.

Whitman, Walt. *Leaves of Grass: Comprehensive Reader's Edition.* Ed. Harold W. Blodgett and Sculley Bradley. New York: New York UP, 1965.

———. *Leaves of Grass: A Textual Variorum of the Printed Poems.* Ed. Sculley Bradley, Harold W. Blodgett, Arthur Golden, and William White. 3 vols. New York: New York UP, 1980.

———. *Prose Works 1892.* Ed. Floyd Stovall. 2 vols. New York: New York UP, 1963–1964.

See also BEACH, JULIETTE H.; "CHILDREN OF ADAM"; DEMOCRACY; *DEMOCRATIC VISTAS*; EQUALITY; FARNHAM, ELIZA W.; GILCHRIST, ANNE BURROWS; "I SING THE BODY ELECTRIC"; LAWRENCE, D.H.; "LETTER TO RALPH WALDO EMERSON"; MENKEN, ADAH ISAACS; MOTHERHOOD; PARTON, SARA PAYSON WILLIS (FANNY FERN); PRICE, ABBY HILLS; *SATURDAY PRESS*; SEX AND SEXUALITY; WHITMAN, LOUISA VAN VELSOR; "WOMAN WAITS FOR ME, A"; WOMAN'S RIGHTS MOVEMENT AND WHITMAN, THE; WRIGHT, FRANCES (FANNY)

"World Below the Brine, The" (1860)

Receiving its present title in 1871, when it was placed in the grouping entitled "Sea-Shore Memories" in *Passage to India,* "The World Below the Brine" was originally published in the "Leaves of Grass" cluster as number 16 in the 1860 edition and number 4 in the 1867 edition. The poem was transferred to the "Sea-Drift" cluster in the 1881 edition of *Leaves of Grass.*

"The World Below the Brine" describes, in progressive detail, first, plant life existing at the bottom of the ocean's floor, then animal life swimming dumbly and sluggishly in the ocean, and then, finally, those swimmers who occasionally rise to the surface and perhaps walk on land. The poem concludes with a terse contrast between this ocean life and humans who walk the earth, a contrast that points onward to "beings who walk other spheres." Such a clear progression has suggested, variously, Whitman's adherence to the neo-Platonic concept of the Great Chain of Being, possibly through Locke, or his acceptance of nineteenth-century geological and biological descriptions of the evolution of humans.

In addition to implications of a metaphysical or a scientific nature, "The World Below the Brine," with its placement in the "Sea-Drift" cluster, is important for its implications about poetic theory and the role of the poet. In relation to transcendental theories, the poem suggests, through the consciousness of the poet, the possibility of transcendence of the physical and material world. More specifically, in relation to the progress of the poems in the cluster as a whole, "The World Below the Brine" offers a partial vision, a hint, of the immortality of the human soul, a vision which has been described in increasing detail as the cluster has progressed and which is then fully delineated in "On the Beach at Night Alone," the next poem in the series.

A. James Wohlpart

Bibliography

Fasel, Ida. "Whitman's 'The World Below the Brine.'" *Explicator* 25 (1966): Item 7.

Fast, Robin Riley. "Structure and Meaning in Whitman's *Sea-Drift.*" *American Transcendental Quarterly* 53 (1982): 49–66.

Freedman, William A. "Whitman's 'The World Below the Brine.'" *Explicator* 23 (1965): Item 39.

Stillgoe, John R. "Possible Lockean Influence in 'The World Below the Brine.'" *Walt Whitman Review* 21 (1975): 150–155.

Wohlpart, A. James. "From Outsetting Bard to Mature Poet: Whitman's 'Out of the Cradle' and the *Sea-Drift* Cluster." *Walt Whitman Quarterly Review* 9 (1991): 77–90.

See also EVOLUTION; "ON THE BEACH AT NIGHT ALONE"; SEA, THE; "SEA-DRIFT"

Worthington, Richard (1834–1894)

Richard Worthington was a printer in New York who published unauthorized editions of *Leaves of Grass* in the 1860s. For two hundred dollars, Worthington purchased the publishers' plates for the 1860 edition of the book at the bankruptcy auction of Thayer and Eldridge. He then proceeded to print and sell copies without Whitman's permission.

Whitman was outraged by the piracy and railed against "Holy Dick," as he ironically nicknamed Worthington. Although as many as ten thousand spurious copies may have been sold, Whitman never took Worthington to court because he felt it was too much trouble. Biographers, however, also point out that Whitman was willing to receive royalties from the pirated editions, which may have kept him from pursuing legal action.

David G. Miller

Bibliography

Allen, Gay Wilson. *The New Walt Whitman Handbook*. 1975. New York: New York UP, 1986.

Reynolds, David S. *Walt Whitman's America: A Cultural Biography*. New York: Knopf, 1995.

See also LEAVES OF GRASS, 1860 EDITION; THAYER AND ELDRIDGE

"Wound-Dresser, The" (1865)

First published in *Drum-Taps* as "The Dresser" and given its present title in 1876, "The Wound-Dresser" distills Whitman's wartime hospital experiences and his urge to be the war's memorialist, "to be witness again" (section 1), in an America reconciled in the future, to the deaths and sufferings of the soldiers and his own health-destroying sacrifices. As his *Memoranda During the War* and *Specimen Days* volumes attest, he felt that deaths and agonies were the ultimate truths of the war. The poem's persona is a stoical remembrancer committed to performing his nation's grief work; in his consciousness (as in the poet's) a tragic past is projected as a dream-like continuous present.

In the Washington military hospitals, Whitman comforted thousands of ailing and dying "boys" as a bedside attendant and—rarely—as a wound-dresser: "I have some cases where the patient is unwilling anybody should do this but me" (*Whitman's Civil War* 123). He chiefly benefited the bedridden by his presence and "soothing hand" (section 4). Despite the physical and psychological breakdowns that these ministrations caused him, he felt drawn to this voluntary service: "You can have no idea how these sick & dying youngsters cling to a fellow," he wrote to his mother, "& how fascinating it is, with its hospital surroundings of sadness & scenes of repulsion and death" (*Correspondence* 1:118).

The poem's first two verse paragraphs (which together with the final paragraph form a poetic "envelope" for the central action) portray the persona as a seasoned veteran summoning up ("resuming") memories of "the mightiest armies of earth" (section 1) and his own "perils" and "joys" (section 2). But three semiautobiographical lines (originally an independent introductory poem incorporated here in 1881) confess that his strength failed him "and I resign'd myself / To sit by the wounded and soothe them, or silently watch the dead" (section 1). In an incantatory stanza (lines 20–24) he conveys the reader into the hospital milieu.

For thirty-four lines thereafter the persona becomes the ambulatory wound-dresser, moving among "my wounded" (section 2) on the ground or in the (often makeshift) hospital. "Bearing the bandages, water, and sponge" (section 2), he attends each soldier "with impassive hand, (yet deep in my breast a fire, a burning flame)" (section 3). Looking into the eyes of one dying soldier, he reflects, "I could not refuse this moment to die for you, if that would save you" (section 2). He appeals to "beautiful death" to "come quickly" (section 3). He observes a "yellow-blue countenance" and (using the unsterile sponges and homemade bandages of the time) cleans and dresses amputations and wounds with "putrid gangrene" (section 3) and blood infections that were fatal to more than half the soldiers wounded in the chest or abdomen. Although most hospital fatalities, as Whitman observed in *Memoranda During the War,* resulted from diarrhea, fevers, and pulmonary infections, the poem's wounded more poignantly represent the agonies of the armies and the wounded American nation.

Rehearsing "the experience sweet and sad" of serving the suffering soldiers and pacifying them "with soothing hand" (section 4), the poem's final stanza merges the close-ups of the empathetic healer-persona and the silently grieving Walt Whitman, perennially recalling the bittersweet embraces of these grateful soldiers.

Among the finest "hospital" or "war" poems in English, "The Wound-Dresser" demonstrates Whitman's mastery of poetic and dramatic structure, of direct and simple diction, and of conveying actions and tightly controlled depths of feeling in an intimate conversation with the reader.

Harold Aspiz

Bibliography

Aspiz, Harold. *Walt Whitman and the Body Beautiful.* Urbana: U of Illinois P, 1980.

Thomas, M. Wynn. *The Lunar Light of Whitman's Poetry.* Cambridge, Mass.: Harvard UP, 1987.

Whitman, Walt. *The Correspondence.* Ed. Edwin Haviland Miller. 6 vols. New York: New York UP, 1961–1977.

———. *Leaves of Grass: A Textual Variorum of the Printed Poems.* Ed. Sculley Bradley, Harold W. Blodgett, Arthur Golden, and William White. Vol. 2. New York: New York UP, 1980.

———. *Memoranda During the War & Death of Abraham Lincoln.* Ed. Roy P. Basler. Bloomington: Indiana UP, 1962.

———. *Specimen Days.* Vol. 1 of *Prose Works 1892.* Ed. Floyd Stovall. New York: New York UP, 1964.

———. *Walt Whitman's Civil War.* 1960. Ed. Walter Lowenfels. New York: Knopf, 1971.

See also BROWN, LEWIS KIRK; CIVIL WAR, THE; CIVIL WAR NURSING; "DRUM-TAPS"; *MEMORANDA DURING THE WAR;* SAWYER, THOMAS P.; *SPECIMEN DAYS;* WASHINGTON, D.C.

Wright, Frances (Fanny) (1795–1852)
Whitman was aware of this radical reformer, writer, and lecturer from his childhood; his father subscribed to the *Free Inquirer* (1829–1832), which was edited by Wright and Robert Dale Owen, and agreed with some of the ideas of the working class activist.

Born of a well-to-do Scottish family, Frances (Fanny) Wright was orphaned at the age of two and reared by relatives in England. She was attracted by the liberal ideas of the French Revolution and saw the United States as a place where her notions of social justice and equality might be carried out. Wright's writings and lectures in America on labor reform, women's education, class, free thinking, and free love—along with the fact that, in 1828, she was the first woman to make a lengthy political speech in America—caused the press to label her an atheist, fanatic, lewd woman, the "whore of Babylon," and the "great Red Harlot of Infidelity." Wright's antislavery experiment, the founding of Nashoba, a colony in Tennessee that offered slaves the chance to work to buy their freedom, was an economic and ideological failure.

Gay Wilson Allen argues that Whitman read his father's copies of the *Free Inquirer* and Wright's book on Epicurean philosophy, *A Few Days in Athens* (1822), and that he may have accompanied his father to hear some of Wright's New York lectures in the 1820s. In any case, Whitman was fascinated by the attractive, outspoken intellectual who brought such censure on herself by her radical ideas of democracy. Whitman once told Horace Traubel: "I never felt so glowingly toward any other woman. . . . [S]he possessed herself of my body and soul" (Traubel 500).

Whitman was drawn by Wright's stance for the workingman, by her active work for rational thought and education among all classes, and by her deism. The *Free Inquirer,* which beginning in April 1829 was published in the basement of her New York Hall of Science, argued theology and the gradual end of capital punishment, political equality for women, civil rights for all, universal and nonsectarian education, and gradual abolition, and aimed to be a forum for the exchange of ideas. The journal also supported a variety of programs aimed at helping the workingman, or mechanic, intending to bring about a more equitable distribution of wealth and a state-supported health-care system.

Reynolds claims that reading *A Few Days in Athens* taught Whitman how progressive ideas could be circulated by way of imaginative literature. Largely a dialogue between the ancient Greek philosopher Epicurus and some of his followers, this never popular novel provided Whitman with a model of deistic materialism.

The novel's notions of the interchangeability of all matter prefigure Whitman's organic view of death and belief in literal cycles of life; thus Wright's conception that all things in the natural world represent only "the different disposition of these eternal and unchangeable atoms" (qtd. in Allen 139) is echoed by Whitman's "every atom belonging to me as good belongs to you" in "Song of Myself" (section 1).

Jennifer A. Hynes

Bibliography

Allen, Gay Wilson. *The Solitary Singer: A Critical Biography of Walt Whitman.* 1955. Rev. ed. 1967. Chicago: U of Chicago P, 1985.

Eckhardt, Celia Morris. *Fanny Wright: Rebel in America.* Cambridge, Mass.: Harvard UP, 1984.

Lane, Margaret. *Frances Wright and the "Great Experiment."* Manchester, N.J.: Manchester UP, 1972.

Reynolds, David S. *Walt Whitman's America: A Cultural Biography.* New York: Knopf, 1995.

Traubel, Horace. *With Walt Whitman in Camden.* Vol. 2. 1908. New York: Rowman and Littlefield, 1961.

Wright, Frances. *A Few Days in Athens— Being the Translation of a Greek Manuscript Discovered in Herculaneum.* 1822. New York: Bliss and White, 1825.

———. *Life, Letters, and Lectures, 1834– 1844.* New York: Arno, 1972.

See also EPICURUS; *FREE INQUIRER;* INFLUENCES ON WHITMAN, PRINCIPAL; READING, WHITMAN'S

Wright, James (1927–1980)

James Wright was one of the most accomplished poets of the "Deep Image" movement, a school of poetry initiated by Robert Bly that called for poets to turn to their own psychic depths for their imagery, to seek out places of interior solitude where images resided that were resonant of a collective unconsciousness. Wright's poetry works on deep associational levels, but its imagery often is derived from his rural midwestern experience; he explores the beauty and the emptiness of often dreary lives in small Ohio and Minnesota towns, revealing at once a compassion and a cold eye. While few readers would immediately associate Wright's poetry with Whitman's, his concern with the condition of the American soul drew him to Whitman, who occasionally appears as a lost and tragic figure in Wright's poetry: "The old man Walt Whitman our countryman / Is now in America our country / Dead" (*Collected Poems* 141).

Writing at a time when Whitman had been claimed by the Beat poets, Wright in 1962 published a remarkable essay called "The Delicacy of Walt Whitman," in which he tried to wrest Whitman from the Beats by relocating his poetic power in his "delicacy of music, of diction, and of form." He saw in Whitman's work not ruggedness and bombast and formlessness and unbridled freedom, but rather "restraint, clarity, and wholeness," all suggesting a "deep spiritual inwardness" and a "deep humility" (*Collected Prose* 4). The Whitman that Wright constructed emerged in fact as a kind of forebear of the Deep Image movement, but Wright's sensitive readings of poems like "Reconciliation" and "A March in the Ranks Hard-Prest, and the Road Unknown" nonetheless demonstrated an attention to detail in sound, meter, and diction that most commentators on Whitman had ignored.

In a posthumously published poem, Wright evoked the gentle and delicate Walt Whitman that he insisted we recognize: "Walt Whitman, the chaste wanderer / Among the live-oaks, the rain, railyards and battlefields / Lifts up his lovely face / To the moon and allows it to become / A friendly ruin" (*This Journey* 86).

Ed Folsom

Bibliography

Wright, James. *Collected Poems.* Middletown, Conn.: Wesleyan UP, 1971.

———. *Collected Prose.* Ed. Annie Wright. Ann Arbor: U of Michigan P, 1983.

———. *This Journey.* New York: Vintage, 1982.

Yatchisin, George. "A Listening to Walt Whitman and James Wright." *Walt Whitman Quarterly Review* 9 (1992): 175–195.

See also LEGACY, WHITMAN'S

Y

"Year of Meteors (1859–60)" (1865)

This poem first appeared in the separate volume *Drum-Taps* in 1865, which Whitman appended to the 1867 edition of *Leaves of Grass*. "Year of Meteors" moved into a "Leaves of Grass" cluster in later editions until 1881, when Whitman finalized its placement in "Birds of Passage."

The poem memorializes a remarkable year for the nation and for Whitman himself, apparently December 1859 to November 1860, the last year before the war. It catalogues events which portend good or ill: the election of Abraham Lincoln and the execution of abolitionist zealot John Brown; the census of 1860, with its revelation of American commercial might and its tabulation of immigrants; and public sensations of that year in New York—the first-ever visit of British royalty, the Prince of Wales (later King Edward VII), in October and the June arrival of the steamship *Great Eastern*, largest in the world. First and last the poem alludes to the "comets and meteors" of 1860, celestial omens "all mottled with evil and good." In the last lines, Whitman personalizes the significance of this year, asking "what is this book, / What am I myself but one of your meteors?" (1865 *Drum-Taps*).

Thus, biographical and artistic events for Whitman may provide underlying motive for this poem. Whitman was working on "Year of Meteors" in 1860, soon after the third edition was published by Thayer and Eldridge. His new publishers launched *Leaves of Grass* with highly promising intentions and publicity, while with Whitman they planned a new volume; yet by the end of the year they were out of business, the new project abandoned, and Whitman's book in the hands of an unfriendly house. Nevertheless the third edition itself was, to Whitman, the most satisfactory yet. It included the personal and poetic breakthrough of the "Calamus" poems, which are probably the resolution of what Whitman called his "slough" of depression in 1858–1859.

Whitman's 1860 mood can be seen in lines later removed from "Year," which display a more personal and eroticized response to the Prince of Wales: "I know not why, but I loved you" (1865 *Drum-Taps*). But the poem as a whole alternates uneasily between a declamatory public voice and this more confessional one.

The mixed portents of this year 1859–1860, in perspective from five years later, signaled Whitman's breakthroughs, disappointments, Civil War silence, and resumption of publishing with the once-abandoned project that became *Drum-Taps*.

David Oates

Bibliography

Allen, Gay Wilson. *The Solitary Singer: A Critical Biography of Walt Whitman.* 1955. Rev. ed. 1967. Chicago: U of Chicago P, 1985.

Greenspan, Ezra. *Walt Whitman and the American Reader.* Cambridge: Cambridge UP, 1990.

Kaplan, Justin. *Walt Whitman: A Life.* New York: Simon and Schuster, 1980.

See also "BIRDS OF PASSAGE"; *DRUM-TAPS*

"Year that Trembled and Reel'd Beneath Me" (1865)

"Year that Trembled and Reel'd Beneath Me" first appeared in 1865 in *Drum-Taps* and was later incorporated into the 1867 edition of *Leaves of Grass*. It was probably written earlier, however, and Betsy Erkkila hypothesizes that Whitman may be referring to 1863, a year of reverses for the Union Army that included the debacles at Charleston and Chancellorsville.

Whitman's fear in "Year" of having to relinquish his "triumphant songs" in favor of "cold dirges of the baffled" contrasts greatly with his earlier war poems, particularly the optimistic, quasi-recruiting poem "Beat! Beat! Drums!" (1861). All through the summer of 1863, as Gay Wilson Allen relates, Whitman and others residing in Washington feared invasion of the capital by Robert E. Lee and his Army of Northern Virginia. In addition to the military setbacks and fear of invasion that may have influenced the poem, it is also likely that Whitman's increased contact with the wounded during his regular visits to army hospitals in Washington contributed to the "thick gloom" pervading "Year." A dismayed Whitman faced the possibility of singing "dirges," both for the Union cause and for the soldiers suffering and dying every day in area hospitals.

"Year" holds a prominent position among the shorter of Whitman's Civil War poems. Its mixture of social, political, and personal concern mark it as a uniquely Whitmanesque production that, if it does not approach the heights of "When Lilacs Last in the Dooryard Bloom'd" (1865), vividly renders the effect of the American Civil War on its most eloquent poet.

Joe Boyd Fulton

Bibliography

Allen, Gay Wilson. *The Solitary Singer: A Critical Biography of Walt Whitman.* 1955. Rev. ed. 1967. Chicago: U of Chicago P, 1985.

Erkkila, Betsy. *Whitman the Political Poet.* New York: Oxford UP, 1989.

See also CIVIL WAR, THE; "DRUM-TAPS"

"Yonnondio" (1887)

"Yonnondio" is a brief late poem, originally published in the *Critic* in 1887 and then included in "Sands at Seventy," a cluster of poems first published in *November Boughs* (1888) and added as an annex to the 1891–1892 edition of *Leaves of Grass.* The poem demonstrates Whitman's life-long love of Native American words, evident earlier in his insistence on calling Long Island "Paumanok" and New York City "Mannahatta." He liked the native edge that such names gave to the American version of the English language, and, just as he was anxious to absorb Native American words into American English, so was he determined to absorb a Native American presence into American poetry. These desires are evident in "Yonnondio," where he seeks to embed Native Americans in the evolving poem of America even while he laments what he sees as their inevitable disappearance from the American future.

The word "lament" sets the tone for this poem, for, as Whitman explains in a headnote, the word "Yonnondio" is an Iroquois term suggesting "lament for the aborigines." In mourning the loss of the natives, then, Whitman employs a native term for that mourning—a linguistic act that demonstrates his respect for Native American self-determination and self-definition even while it reenacts the American usurpation of Native American cultures. Whitman indicated to Horace Traubel that experts in native languages had contested his definition of "Yonnondio," but he stood firm: "I am sure of my correctness. There never yet was an Indian name that did not mean so much, then more, and more, and more" (Traubel 470).

Whatever the meaning of the word, its dirgelike sounding in the poem occasions a kind of magical, momentary reversal of American frontier history, as "cities, farms, factories fade," and a "misty, strange tableaux" appears, populated with "swarms of stalwart chieftains, medicine-men, and warriors." This retro-vision quickly fades, and Whitman fears that the "Race of the woods" is now "utterly lost"—that is, not only erased from the land, but also lost to utterance, erased from American memory. Whitman believed that one job of the poet, then, was to give Native Americans lines in the evolving American poem. That way, they could at least be kept alive via their names, words, and deeds, for otherwise "unlimn'd they disappear."

This twelve-line poem has often been cited by twentieth-century writers. Tillie Olsen's novel *Yonnondio* (1974) echoes the poem, and Allen Ginsberg has read it as "an odd little political poem . . . warning us of Black Mesa, of the Four Corners, of the civilization's destruction of the land and the original natives there" (251).

Ed Folsom

Bibliography

Ginsberg, Allen. "Allen Ginsberg on Walt Whitman: Composed on the Tongue." *Walt Whitman: The Measure of His Song.* Ed. Jim Perlman, Ed Folsom, and Dan Campion. Minneapolis: Holy Cow!, 1981. 231–254.

Traubel, Horace. *With Walt Whitman in Camden.* Ed. Gertrude Traubel. Vol. 5. Carbondale: Southern Illinois UP, 1964.

See also NATIVE AMERICANS (INDIANS); PLACE NAMES; "SANDS AT SEVENTY" (FIRST ANNEX)

"You Lingering Sparse Leaves of Me" (1887)

First published in *Lippincott's* Magazine (November 1887), this effective six-line lyric is enriched when linked to its companion five-line piece, "Not Meagre, Latent Boughs Alone," published at the same time in the same place. Both are found in the "Sands at Seventy" annex to *Leaves of Grass,* with "You Lingering" placed first. Both depend on the figure of a tree that Whitman equates with himself, its leaves or fruit clearly corresponding to his own late poetry.

"You Lingering" describes the stark condition of fall and winter, "Not Meagre" of spring and summer. The first, picturing his leaves as "sparse" and "lingering," adds further negative modifiers: "tokens diminute and lorn," "pallid banner-staves," and "pennants valueless . . . overstay'd of time." The second lyric looks to a warmer season when, as with his poems, "verdant leaves," "nourishing fruit," and finally "love and faith" will bloom.

Because he directly addresses the leaves in "You Lingering," using "you" five times in only six lines, there is assurance that he feels great closeness to these leaves, these poems. In the penultimate line, he defends them strongly: "Yet my soul-dearest leaves confirming all the rest." In the final line, he strengthens them still further: "The faithfulest—hardiest—last." "Last" appears to be a pun, intentional or not, yielding an appropriate double meaning.

This poem and its companion show how much Whitman learned to say in small compass without compromising his style.

David B. Baldwin

Bibliography

Whitman, Walt. *Leaves of Grass: Comprehensive Reader's Edition.* Ed. Harold W. Blodgett and Sculley Bradley. New York: New York UP, 1965.

See also AGE AND AGING; "SANDS AT SEVENTY" (FIRST ANNEX)

Young America Movement

Intellectuals with literary and political concerns were at the center of the Young America movement of the late 1830s to about 1850. Growing out of the Tetractys Club, which was founded by a small group including Evert A. Duyckinck and Cornelius Mathews, the Young Americans supported the common man, democracy, and reform. They generally promoted an inclusive nationalism rather than jingoistic chauvinism, but their political positions are complex, some, for example, opposing the Mexican War and others promoting Manifest Destiny. Their typical Jacksonian concerns had sources in Jeffersonian democracy. Whitman shared many of their positions and recalled in 1858 that John L. O'Sullivan's *United States Magazine and Democratic Review* was a "monthly magazine of profounder quality of talent than any since" (Whitman 15) and that it impressed young men at the time he contributed to it. The movement was contemporary with Old World radical initiatives such as Young Italy and Young Ireland during this period of social and political upheaval.

When seeking the intellectual and ideological sources of Whitman's nationalism, as articulated in the 1855 Preface, for example, one must take into account Young America's vigorous nationalism as expressed in the *Democratic Review,* as well as in other Locofoco periodicals to which Whitman never contributed. Duyckinck and Mathews provided magazine outlets for radical thought in periodicals such as *Arcturus* (1840–1842), *Yankee Doodle* (1846–1847), and the *Literary World* (1847–1853), but the *Democratic Review* had the largest circulation and longest life. Whitman generally agreed with the *Review's* politics and wrote for it. These publishers, editors, and writers were attempting to appeal to the new mass audiences created by the surge of Jacksonian democratic principles coupled with increasingly efficient printing technology. But they had social, political, and also literary agendas, and while interested in

English authors such as the renegade Shelley and the "divine" Shakespeare, as Herman Melville described him, they were most concerned with encouraging and promoting American writers. One readily available statement incorporating their critical values, including nationalism, is Melville's belated 1850 *Literary World* review of Nathaniel Hawthorne's *Mosses from an Old Manse* (1846), a volume Duyckinck himself proposed. Melville's notice is typical of the sort of critical writing in these new magazines which were trying to reach an expanded, possibly middle-class market. These author-journalists were middlemen purveying socially and politically important ideas and values. They were neither as partisan as the intellectually incestuous puffers Edgar Allan Poe attacked nor as objective as Edmund Clarence Stedman would be in his assessments of Whitman.

The Young America movement provided Whitman with a compatible intellectual and philosophical foundation, one that was important for his development as a journalist, thinker, and poet.

Donald Yannella

Bibliography

Chielens, Edward E., ed. *American Literary Magazines: The Eighteenth and Nineteenth Centuries.* New York: Greenwood, 1986.

Miller, Perry. *The Raven and the Whale: The War of Words and Wits in the Era of Poe and Melville.* New York: Harcourt, Brace, 1956.

Moss, Sidney. *Poe's Literary Battles: The Critic in the Context of His Literary Milieu.* Durham, N.C.: Duke UP, 1963.

Pritchard, John Paul. *Criticism in America.* Norman: U of Oklahoma P, 1956.

Stafford, John. *The Literary Criticism of "Young America": A Study in the Relationship of Politics and Literature, 1837–1850.* Berkeley: U of California P, 1952.

Whitman, Walt. *The Uncollected Poetry and Prose of Walt Whitman.* Ed. Emory Holloway. Vol. 2. Garden City, N.Y.: Doubleday, Page, 1921.

Yannella, Donald. "Cornelius Mathews." *American Literary Critics and Scholars, 1850–1880.* Vol. 64 of *Dictionary of Literary Biography.* Ed. John W. Rathbun and Monica M. Grecu. Detroit: Gale, 1988. 178–182.

———. "Evert Augustus Duyckinck." *Antebellum Writers in New York and the South.* Vol. 3 of *Dictionary of Literary Biography.* Ed Joel Myerson. Detroit: Gale, 1978. 101–109.

———. "Writing the '*Other* Way': Melville, the Duyckinck Crowd, and Literature for the Masses." *A Companion to Melville Studies.* Ed. John Bryant. New York: Greenwood, 1986. 63–81.

Yannella, Donald, and Kathleen Malone Yannella. "Evert A. Duyckinck's 'Diary: May 29–November 8, 1847.'" *Studies in the American Renaissance: 1978.* Ed. Joel Myerson. Boston: Twayne, 1978. 207–258.

See also DEMOCRATIC REVIEW; DUYCKINCK, EVERT AUGUSTUS; MATHEWS, CORNELIUS

Appendix
Genealogy

Whitman Ancestors of Walt Whitman

Before immigrating to North America, the Whitmans or Whitemans were Puritan farmers in England.

VIII   **Abijah Whit(e)man**
              b. about 1560

VII   **Zechariah Whit(e)man**
              b. 1595

Zechariah's brother, John Whit(e)man, came to North America aboard the *True Love* in 1640 and settled in Weymouth, Massachusetts. On a later voyage, or possibly the same one, Zechariah emigrated and settled in Milford, Connecticut.

VI   **Joseph Whitman**   married   Sarah Ketcham
              b. about 1640

Lived in Stratford, Connecticut, as early as 1655 but relocated to Huntington, Long Island, eventually establishing a large estate called Whitman's Great Hollow, later Whitmanvale. In Huntington, Joseph served as a constable, grand juryman, commissioner, and leather inspector. His six sons, Joseph, Nathan, Nathaniel, John, Samuel, and Zebulon, accumulated additional lands in the area.

V   **Son of Joseph Whitman**

IV   **Nehemiah Whitman**   married   Phoebe "Sarah" White
              b. about 1718?   b. about 1713
                                                  d. 1803

Nehemiah owned five hundred acres in the West Hills area of Huntington and had many slaves. "Sarah" was a strong woman who smoked tobacco, was a good rider of horses, and was a stern master to her slaves. One of their sons died in the American Revolution.

III	Jesse W. Whitman	married	Hannah Brush
	b. 29 January 1749		b. 6 October 1753
	d. 12 February 1803		d. 6 January 1834

Jesse inherited the farm and the family homestead, but the estate was divided among Jesse and Hannah's children: Jesse, Treadwell, Sarah, and Walter.

II	**Walter Whitman**	married	Louisa Van Velsor
	b. 14 July 1789		b. 22 September 1795
	d. 11 July 1855		d. 23 May 1873
	m. 8 June 1816		

Walter was raised on a remnant of the old family estate. At fifteen, he was apprenticed to a carpenter in Brooklyn and soon became a house builder, wood chopper, and farmer in the West Hills. The mature Walter was a freethinker and an admirer of Thomas Paine, but he was often moody and possibly an alcoholic. Financial success always eluded him. Louisa was attractive, jocular, an imaginative storyteller, and a good housekeeper, but she could also be miserly, argumentative, and hypochondriacal.

I	**Walter "Walt" Whitman**
	b. 31 May 1819
	d. 26 March 1892

Van Velsor Ancestors of Walt Whitman

The Van Velsors may have been descended from a Dutch noble family that fled Holland after the overthrow of William of Orange. By the late eighteenth century they owned a large farm between the towns of Cold Spring Harbor and Woodbury.

V			"Dutch Kossabone— Old Salt"

IV	**Garret Van Velsor**	married	Mary Kossabone
	b. 1742		b. about 1745
	d. 1812		d. about 1792

III	**Cornelius Van Velsor**	married	Naomi "Amy" Williams
	b. 1768		b. 1763
	d. August 1837		d. 15 February 1826

Cornelius, known as the "Major," was a garrulous, hearty horse-breeder.

II	**Louisa Van Velsor**	married	Walter Whitman

I	**Walter "Walt" Whitman**

Brush Ancestors of Walt Whitman

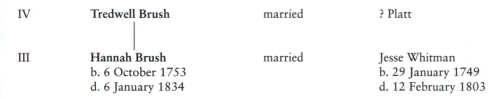

IV   **Tredwell Brush**   married   ? Platt

III   **Hannah Brush**   married   Jesse Whitman
            b. 6 October 1753   b. 29 January 1749
            d. 6 January 1834   d. 12 February 1803

Hannah was an orphan raised by her aunt, Vashiti Platt, who owned a large farm and slaves in eastern Long Island. A schoolteacher, Hannah taught Walt much about the history of Long Island and her family.

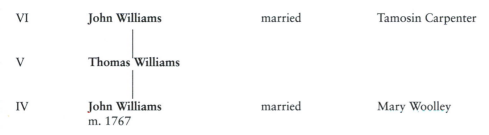

II   **Walter Whitman**   married   Louisa Van Velsor

I   **Walter "Walt" Whitman**

Williams Ancestors of Walt Whitman

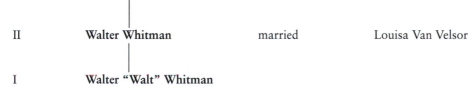

VI   **John Williams**   married   Tamosin Carpenter

V   **Thomas Williams**

IV   **John Williams**   married   Mary Woolley
            m. 1767

John was a Quaker shipmaster in the West Indies trade. He served under John Paul Jones when the *Bon Homme Richard* met the *Serapis* on 23 September 1779. He had seven daughters, and he and his only son died at sea.

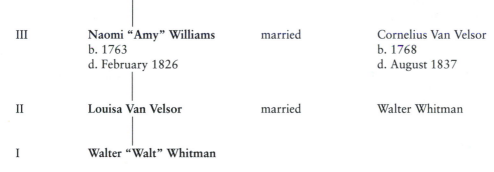

III   **Naomi "Amy" Williams**   married   Cornelius Van Velsor
            b. 1763   b. 1768
            d. February 1826   d. August 1837

II   **Louisa Van Velsor**   married   Walter Whitman

I   **Walter "Walt" Whitman**

Walter Whitman	married	Louisa Van Velsor
b. 14 July 1789		b. 22 September 1795
d. 11 July 1855		d. 23 May 1873
m. 8 June 1816		

ISSUE

1. **Jesse Whitman**
   b. 2 March 1818
   d. 21 March 1870

Jesse was a sailor and worked in the shipyards of Brooklyn. In December 1864, Walt committed Jesse to the King's County Lunatic Asylum, where he died.

2. **Walter "Walt" Whitman**
   b. 31 May 1819
   d. 26 March 1892

3. **Mary Elizabeth Whitman**   married   Ansel Van Nostrand
   b. 3 February 1821
   d. 6 August 1899
   m. 2 January 1840

Mary and Ansel moved to Greenport, Long Island, where Ansel was a shipbuilder.

   Issue: George Van Nostrand
           Fanny Van Nostrand
           Louisa Van Nostrand
           Ansel Van Nostrand
           Minnie Van Nostrand

4. **Hannah Louisa Whitman**   married   Charles Louis Heyde
   b. 28 November 1823
   d. 18 July 1908
   m. 16 March 1852

Hannah was the sister most loved by Walt; Charles was a landscape painter who shared Walt's literary interests. In 1858 Hannah and Charles settled in Burlington, Vermont. Their marriage was stormy, but they remained together for forty years. Both suffered from mental illness. Charles was eventually committed to the Vermont State Hospital in 1892.

5. **Infant**
   b. 2 March 1825
   d. 14 September 1825

6. **Andrew Jackson Whitman**   married   Nancy McClure
   b. 7 April 1827
   d. 3 December 1863

Andrew Jackson worked at the Brooklyn Navy Yard. He died from tuberculosis aggravated by alcoholism. Nancy may have become a prostitute.

Issue: James Whitman
     George Whitman
     Andrew Whitman

7. **George Washington Whitman**   married   Louisa Orr Haslam
   b. 28 November 1829   b. 2 March 1842
   d. 20 December 1901   d. 9 August 1892
   m. 14 April 1871

A soldier in the Union Army, George rose from private to brevet lieutenant colonel during the Civil War. After 1865, he worked as a water pipe inspector in Brooklyn and Camden. After a paralytic stroke in 1873, Walt lived with George and Louisa in Camden until the couple moved to Burlington County, New Jersey, in 1884. George died with an estate of almost sixty thousand dollars.

Issue: Walter Orr Whitman
       b. 4 November 1875
       d. 12 July 1876
    George Whitman
       b. July 1877 (Stillborn)

8. **Thomas Jefferson Whitman**   married   Martha Emma Mitchell
   b. 18 July 1833   b. 12 September 1836
   d. 25 November 1890   d. 19 February 1873
   m. 23 February 1859

Thomas Jefferson was a surveyor and engineer at the Brooklyn Water Works until 1867, when he was appointed superintendent in charge of constructing a new water system for Saint Louis, Missouri. Garrulous and aesthetically inclined, "Jeff" was the brother closest to Walt in temperament. Martha or "Mattie" may have been an orphan or foundling with no family. She worked hard to supplement her husband's income, enjoyed concerts and the opera, and frequently wrote to her brother-in-law Walt.

Issue: Mannahatta "Hattie" Whitman
       b. 9 June 1860
       d. 3 September 1886
    Jessie Louisa Whitman
       b. 17 June 1863

9. **Edward Whitman**
   b. 9 August 1835
   d. 30 November 1892

"Eddy" was mentally disabled and partly crippled. He lived with his mother until 1873, when he was taken in by George and Louisa. In 1883 Walt arranged for Edward to live on a farm in Moorestown, New Jersey; he was removed to an asylum in 1888, where he died four years later.

William A. Pannapacker

Bibliography

Allen, Gay Wilson. *The Solitary Singer: A Critical Biography of Walt Whitman.* 1955. Rev. ed. 1967. Chicago: U of Chicago P, 1985.

Dyson, Verne. "Walt Whitman's Ancestors." *Walt Whitman Birthplace Bulletin* 4.3 (1961): 19–24.

Hall, Martha K. "Joseph Whitman of Long Island." *Walt Whitman Birthplace Bulletin* 1.1 (1957): 3–4.

___. "Old Salt Kossabone." *Walt Whitman Birthplace Bulletin* 1.4 (1958): 13–14.

Molinoff, Katherine. *Some Notes on Whitman's Family.* Brooklyn: Comet, 1941.

Waldron, Randall H. Introduction. *Mattie: The Letters of Martha Mitchell Whitman.* Ed. Waldron. New York: New York UP, 1977. 1–26.

Index

American Indians. *See* Native Americans

American literature, 223–24, 243, 246, 317, 360, 398–99, 524, 528–29, 607, 638, 680, 683, 792, 806

American Phrenological Journal, **16**, 230, 520, 521, 625

American Renaissance, 574, 593–94

American Revolution, **18–20**, 69–70, 84, 110, 269, 313, 346, 350, 351, 393, 487, 501, 533, 679, 733, 753, 762, 779, 790–91

American Whig Review, **20**

anaphora, 52, 108, 495, 526, 585, 604, 694, 717, 751, 769

ancestors, Whitman's, 270, 781, 807–9

Anderson, Gillian, 420

Anderson, Sherwood, **21**, 36

Andrade, Joaquim de Sousa, 537

Andrade, Mário de, 537

Andrews, Stephen Pearl, 129

Andrić, Ivo, 602

androgyny, 21, 280, 600

anger, 201, 585, 722, 732

animal magnetism, 312–13, 535, 558–59

animals, 123, 210, 285, 452, 655, 669, 749

anonymous self-reviews. *See* self-reviews, Whitman's anonymous

Antoninus, Brother. *See* Everson, William

Apollinaire, Guillaume, **22–23**, 54, 233, 601

appearance and reality, 24–25, 49, 201, 279, 289, 302, 478, 565, 579, 670, 700, 718, 738

archaisms, 695

architects and architecture, **23–24**, 159, 749

Arcos, René, 232

Arendt, Erich, 248, 318

Argentina, 674, 676

Arishima, Takeo, 330

Aristidean, The, 635

aristocracy, 223, 572, 620, 703, 711

Aristotle, 321, 588

Armiño, Mauro, 675

Army Paymaster's Office, 125, 308, 576, 671, 713, 761

Arneberg, Per, 612

Arnold, George B., **25–26**, 515

Arnold, John. *See* Arnold, George B.

Arnold, Matthew, **26**, 72, 272, 478, 606
"Dover Beach," 478

art and artists, ix, 27, 102, 510, 678. *See also* painters and painting; sculptors and sculpture

art and daguerreotype galleries, **26–27**, 442, 502, 519

art criticism, 27

Arthur, Gavin, 106
Circle of Sex, The, 106

arts and crafts movement, **28–29**

Arvin, Newton, **29–30**, 60, 737
Whitman, 614

Ashton, J. Hubley, **36**, 41, 188, 265, 476

Asia, 569. *See also* China, Whitman in (reception

and influence in); Japan, Whitman in (reception and influence in)

Aspiz, Harold, 10, 163, 178, 221, 264, 271, 451, 511–12, 558, 614, 617, 648, 667, 706, 763, 797
Walt Whitman and the Body Beautiful, 614

Asselineau, Roger, 11, 22, **36–37**, 52, 57, 61–62, 147, 214, 226, 233, 426, 512, 604, 615, 675, 706, 733, 752, 770
L'Evolution de Walt Whitman, 36, 61–62, 615

associations, clubs, fellowships, foundations, and societies, **37–40**, 64–65, 68, 69, 179, 189, 269, 318, 430, 510–12, 740, 746

astronomy, 434, 617, 769

Asylum for the Insane. *See* London, Ontario, Canada

Atlantic Monthly, The, **41**, 512

Attorney General's Office, United States, 36, **41–42**, 265, 308, 576, 585, 671, 681, 745, 759, 761

Auber, Daniel François, 437, 485

Audubon, John James, 98

Australia and New Zealand, Whitman in (reception and influence in), **42–44**

autoeroticism, 109, 561, 562

autobiography, Whitman's writings as, 5, 47, 126, 132, 400–1, 442, 444, 496, 561–62, 632, 635, 650, 651, 678–80

B

Bacon, Delia, 633

Bacon, Francis, 633

Badiali, Cesare, 484, 485, 713

Baez, Joan, 422

Bailey, Gamaliel, 475

Bailey, John, 184, 258

Bailey, Margaret Lucy Shands, 475

Bailie, Helen Tufts, 69

Baker, Frank, 761

Baker, Nathan M., 197

Ballabene, Roswitha, 40

Ballou, Adin, 549, 550

Balmont, Konstantin, 600–1

Balzac, Honoré de, 606

Bancroft, George, 273

Barahona, Melvin René, 676

bard, Whitman as. *See* poet, Whitman's concept of the

Barlow, Joel, 540, 755

Barnburners and Locofocos, **48–49**, 237, 291, 344, 418, 530, 531, 570, 805

Barnshaw, Harold W., 39

Barnum, P.T., 159, 486

Barrett Collection, Clifton Waller (University of Virginia), 137, 171, 220, 400, 493, 494, 552, 686

Barrus, Clara, **49**, 90, 244, 776
Whitman and Burroughs, Comrades, 49

Barton, Clara, 127

Burroughs, Julian, 590
Burroughs, Ursula North, **89–91**, 590, 760, 761
Burton, William E., 713
Bury, Tom, 43
Bush, Professor George, 559
business records, 164–65
Butenschön, Andrea, 611
butterflies, 100, 319, 362, 468, 749
Bychowski, Gustav, 496
Byron, George Gordon, Lord, 76, 416, 593, 620, 646

C

C.C.P., 609, 797
Cable, George Washington, 510
Cady, Joseph, 191
Cairo, Illinois, 742
Calder, Ellen ("Nelly") M. Tarr O'Connor. *See* O'Connor (Calder), Ellen ("Nelly") M. Tarr
California, 792
Callow, Philip, 62, 115, 442, 483, 632, 735, 790
From Noon to Starry Night: A Life of Walt Whitman, 62
Cambon, Glauco, 324
Camden *New Republic,* 685
Camden, New Jersey, 39, **98–100**, 189, 429–30, 510, 511, 514, 515–16, 576, 621, 680, 685, 720, 740, 757, 761, 764, 778, 781, 790, 792
Campana, Dino, 324
Campion, Dan, 706
Campos, Geir, 537
Canada, response to Whitman in, 39, 67–68, **100–3**, 151, 179, 511
Canada, Whitman's travels in, 88, **103–4**, 151, 165, 402, 742, 744
canary, Whitman's, 757
Canby, Henry Seidel, 61, **104**, 164, 236, 288, 293, 614, 615, 667, 700
Walt Whitman: An American, 614
capital punishment, 22, 80, 169, 176, 264, 483
capitalism, 181, 508, 533, 707–8, 737
Cardenal, Ernesto, 676
Carducci, Giosue, 323
Carey, Henry C., 708
Caritat, Hocquet, 391
Carlisle, E. Fred, 52, 445
Carlyle, Thomas, 73, 75, **104–6**, 122, 148, 173, 176, 180, 210, 211, 215, 245, 252, 290, 301, 323, 347, 553–54, 571, 572, 573, 582, 593, 606, 669, 679, 680, 700
Sartor Resartus, 700
Shooting Niagara: And After?, 176, 245
Carman, Bliss, 102
Carnegie, Andrew, **106**, 170, 392
Carpenter, Edward, 23, 28, 37, 38, 60, 67, 73, 74, **106–7**, 280, 306, 341, 444, 561, 761
Days with Walt Whitman, 561

Carpenter, George Rice, **107**, 759
Walt Whitman, 107
carpentry business, 23, 778, 787
Carradine, John, 422
Carrillo, Enrique Gomez del, 675
Carvalho, Ronald de, 537
Cass, Lewis, 79, 82, 531, 547
Castellón, Enrique Lopez, 675
catalogues, 27, **107–8**, 206, 304–5, 337, 417, 494, 505, 518, 527, 542, 574, 604, 694–95, 698, 748
Catel, Jean, 61, 62, **108–9**, 233, 358, 561, 616
Walt Whitman: la naissance du poète, 61, 108, 616
Cather, Willa, **109–10**
Catholicism, 580
Catlin, George, 27, 450
Cattell, Ed, 686
Cattell, Henry W., 409
Cavitch, David, 354, 496, 562, 770
Celaya, Gabriel, 677
cemeteries, 678, 679, 776. *See also* Harleigh Cemetery
Cendrars, Blaise, 233, 601
Ceniza, Sherry, 25, 387, 797
Centennial edition. *See Leaves of Grass,* 1876, Author's Edition
Centennial Exposition (Philadelphia), **111–12**, 516, 557, 661
Century Illustrated Monthly Magazine, 254, 480
Cestre, Charles, 233
Chai, Leon, 594
Chainey, George, 649
Chambers, Robert, 286, 616
Vestiges of the Natural History of Creation, 616–17
Channing, Edward T., 489
Channing, William Ellery, 175, 704, 717
Chapin, William E., 365
Chapman, Frederick A., 84
Chardin, Teilhard de, 343
character, 202, 423, 581, 663
Chari, V.K., 52, 307, 426, 444, 445, 474, 504, 615, 706, 718, 770
Charvat, William, 165
Chase, Richard Volney, **113–14**, 178, 214, 289, 293, 487, 495, 644, 656, 666
Walt Whitman Reconsidered, 615
Chase, Salmon P., **114**, 747
Chase, William Merritt, 252
Chaucer, Geoffrey, 348
Cheneys, the, 78, 438
Chennevière, Georges, 232
Chesterton, G.K., 506
Chicago, Illinois, 345, 743
child (as image), 71–72, 297, 399, 495–97, 714–15
Child, Peter, 421
childhood, Whitman's, 269, 346, 404–5
children, Whitman's supposed, 59, 456, 614, 630, 671, 702

gifts to Whitman, 37, 50, 67, 72, 86, 100, 106, 131, 185, 332, 339, 434, 466, 516, 596, 647, 690, 711, 721, 729, 788, 791

Gilchrist, Alexander, 251, 252

Gilchrist, Anne Burrows, 73, 74, 116, 136, **251–52**, 405, 429, 436, 477, 503, 516, 576, 596, 629, 761, 782, 797

    "Englishwoman's Estimate of Walt Whitman, An," 73, 251, 477, 596, 629, 782, 797

    "Woman's Estimate of Walt Whitman, A." *See above* "Englishwoman's Estimate of Walt Whitman, An"

Gilchrist, Beatrice, 252

Gilchrist, Grace, 252

Gilchrist, Herbert Harlakenden, 251, **252–53**, 332, 405, 503, 621

Gilded Age, 423–24, 508, 533, 539, 736

Gilder, Jeannette L., **254**

Gilder, Joseph, 254

Gilder, Richard Watson, **254–55**, 332

Gilman, Charlotte Perkins, 511, 557

Gilman, Daniel Coit, 170

Gimbel, Richard, 430

Ginsberg, Allen, 29, 40, 249, **255**, 340, 421, 422, 571, 792, 804

Gissing, George, 53

Gita. See Bhagavad-Gita

Glass, Philip, 440

God, Whitman's concept of, 112, 214, 279, 303, 445, 453, 504, 535, 540, 563–64, 580, 581, 583, 655, 656, 669

Godwin, Parke, 234, 256, 462, 617

    "Last Half-Century, The," 617

    Out of the Past, 617

Goethe, Johann Wolfgang von, 48, 104, 248, **256**, 272, 273, 593, 600, 751

Gogol, Nikolai, 601

Gohdes, Clarence, 138

gold rush, 591

Golden, Arthur, 135, 138, 178, 202, 382, 512, 615, 763

Goldman, Emma, 741

Goldsmith, Alfred F., 57, 136

Goll, Claire, 249

Goll, Ivan, 249, 318

González de la Garza, Mauricio, 304, 604, 675

Good Gray Poet persona, 247, 318, 513–14, 598, 692, 747

Good Gray Poet, The. See O'Connor, William Douglas

Goodblatt, Chanita, 321

Goodrich, Samuel Griswold, 348

Gosse, Sir Edmund, 73, **258–59**, 596

Gostwick, Joseph, 180, 272

Gottschalk, Louis Moreau, 130

Gough, John Bartholomew, 710

Gould, Elizabeth Porter, 797

Gounod, Charles, 437, 485

Graham, Sylvester, 558

Grainger, Percy, 44

Grant, Ulysses S., 111, 242, 259, 274, 423, 532, 539, 548, 607, 698, 745, 760, 761, 765

grass (as image), 95, 200, 287, 289, 302, 311, 411, 452, 490, 534, 539, 583, 612, 655, 700, 730, 738

Gray, Fred, **259**

Gray, John F., 259

great plains and prairies, the, **259–60**, 538, 539, 680, 766

Greek philosophy, 209, 209–10, 22, 413

Greeley, Horace, 79, 159, 161, 162, 176, 458, 459, 463, 708

Greenberg, Uri Zvi, 321, 322

Greenough, Horatio, 23, 175

Greenport, Long Island, 786

Greenspan, Ezra, 159, 321

Gregg Smith Singers, 422

Gregory, Lady Augusta, 320

Grey, Ellen, 217, **260**, 616

grief, 184, 193, 194, 298, 478, 627, 634

Grier, Edward F., 135, 138, 229, 468

Griffin, James D., 666

Grisi, Giulia, 314, 485

Griswold, Rufus W., 213, **260**, 393, 457

Gross, Samuel D., 197

Grünzweig, Walter, 180

Guatemala, 676

Guerrabella, Genevra, 783

Guillén, Jorge, 677

Gunn, Thom, 74

Guo, Moruo, 118

Gurney, Ivor, 74

Gurney, Jeremiah, 519

Gurowski, Count Adam de, **260–61**, 761

Gutekunst, Frederick, 519

Guthrie, William Norman, 306

H

Hackett, James H., 3

Hale, Edward Everett, **263–64**, 465

Hale, John Parker, 89, 531

Haley, Roscoe, 12, 288

Haley, Thomas, 423

Halkin, Simon, 322

Hall, Donald, 421

Halleck, Fitz-Greene, 521

Hamblin, Thomas, 3, 4

Hamer, Harold, 38

Hamilton, Alexander, 462

Hamilton, Walter, 505

Hampson, Thomas, 441

Hamsun, Knut, 154, 611

Handel, Georg Friedrich, 437, 438, 486

Hanson, Howard, 440

Hapgood, Lyman, 25, 754

Hardie, Keir, 73

Hare, Adam, 429

Hare, Rebecca Jane, 429

London *Free Press,* 402

London, Ontario, Canada, 100, 103, 151, **402–3,**
744

Long Island Democrat, xiii, 333, **404,** 407, 530,
545

Long Island, New York, xiii, 64–65, 149, **404–6,**
592, 622, 678, 679, 685, 753, 757, 777,
779, 781, 786, 787

Long Island Patriot, xiii, 174, 269, 333, **406,** 530,
552

Long Island Star, xiii, 84, **406–7,** 530

Long Islander, The, xiii, 333, 405, **407–8,** 545, 637

Longaker, Dr. Daniel, **408–9**

Longfellow, Henry Wadsworth, 41, 70, 78, 165,
216, 243, 254, 257, 329, 385, **409–10,**
439, 571, 573, 596, 621, 626, 680, 718
"Excelsior," 409

Longinus, 694

Louis Phillipe, King, 587

Louisiana Purchase, 531, 603

Louisville, Kentucky, 742

Lourenco, Eduardo, 536

love, 194, 221–22, 363, 400–1, **410–12,** 478, 481,
495, 578, 612, 651, 655, 684, 686–87,
715–16, 768, 768–69, 782

Lovering, Henry B., 50

Loving, Jerome, 57, 335, 511–12, 546, 594, 637,
705, 706, 797
Emerson, Whitman, and the American Muse,
615

Lowell, James Russell, 32, 41, 70, 170, 175, 281,
334, **412–13,** 465, 466, 512, 571

Lowth, Robert, 694

Lozynsky, Artem, 57

Lucifer, 643, 645

Lucretius, 209, **413**
De Rerum Natura [On the Nature of Things],
209, 413, 426

Luening, Otto, 440

Lugones, Leopoldo, 676

Lunacharsky, Anatoly, 318

Lundkvist, Artur, 611–12

Luther, Martin, 228, 438

Lychenheim, Morris, 38

M

McAlister, Dr. Alexander, 39, 408, 409, 430

McCarthy, Joseph, 185

McClure, J.E., 455, 456, 671

McCormick, Edward Allan, 247

McCullagh, James C., 556

MacDiarmid, Hugh, 73

MacDonald, Wilson, 102

Macedonia, 602

Machado, Antonio, 677

MacInness, Tom, 102

McKay, David, 37, 146, 161, 165, 257, 373, 378,
379, 382, **415,** 469, 516

Mackay, John Henry, 318

MacMillan, Duane J., 214

Macpherson, James ("Ossian"), 47, 73, 315,
415–16

Macready, William Charles, 3, 4, 713, 714

Mad Poet of Broadway. *See* Clarke, McDonald

Madison, James, 547

madness. *See* insanity

Mancuso, Luke, 627

Mandelstam, Osip, 600

Manhattan, 84

Manifest Destiny. *See* expansionism

Mann, Horace, 199, 458

Mann, Thomas, 247, 250

Mannahatta. *See* Manhattan

Manske, Eva, 248

manuscripts, 57, 77, 136–38, 220, 400, 637

Manzano, Alberto, 675

Marcus Aurelius, 692

Marini, Ignazio, 713

Mario, Giuseppe, 485

Marques, Oswaldino, 537

Marr, David, 178

marriage, 59, 103, 473–74, 795

Marston, George, 477, 689

Marti, Don Francisco, 484

Martí, José, 15, 674, 675

Martin, E.K., 179, 591

Martin, Robert K., 50, 121, 274, 306, 478, 578,
604, 644, 657, 706, 716, 768
Continuing Presence of Walt Whitman, The,
631
Homosexual Tradition in American Poetry,
The, 614, 631

Martineau, Harriet, 105, 704

Martinson, Harry, 611

Marx, Karl, 180–81, 239, 305, 453, 606, 699

Marx, Leo
Machine in the Garden, The, 708

masculinity, 539, 660

Masters, Edgar Lee, 61, 288, 361, 386, **418**

masturbation, 117, 158, 745

materialism, 181, 508, 533, 637, 766

Mathews, Cornelius, **418–19,** 805

Matthiessen, F.O., 180, 288, **419,** 487, 593–94,
700, 701, 706
American Renaissance: Art and Expression in the
Age of Emerson and Whitman, 593–94

Maupassant, Guy de, 328

May, Abigail, 10, 11

May, Rollo, 238

maya. *See* illusion

Mayakovsky, Vladimir, 290, 321, 600, 601

Maynard, Laurens, 189

Mazzini, Giuseppe, 323, 698

media interpretations, 88, 151, **420–23,** 706

medicine, 271

medievalism. *See* feudalism

Melville, Herman, 70, 195, 214, 312, 331, 381,
419, 452, 593–94, 792, 806
Battle-Pieces and Aspects of the War, 190

omnibuses, **222**
onanism. *See* masturbation
opera and opera singers, 314, 323, 349, 393, 438,
   484–86, 556, 726
opera houses, 484, **713–14**
optimism, 14, 15, **486–88**, 498, 522, 533, 557,
   559, 579, 587, 604
orations, Whitman's. *See* lectures, Whitman's
oratory, 81, 109, 312, 349, 419, **489–90**, 662, 667,
   704–5, 796
Oredezh, Ivan, 601
O'Reilly, Miles, 127
organicism, **490–92**, 525–26, 543, 574, 682, 688,
   738, 746
Ormrod, James, 38
Ortiz, Simon, 450
Orvell, Miles, 27
Osceola, 450, 492
Osgood, James R., 44, 70, 71, 132, 136, 146, 161,
   373, 376, 415, 477, **492–93**, 516, 649,
   650, 689, 724
Osiris, 200, 612, 746
Osler, Dr. William, 197, **493**
Ossian. *See* Macpherson, James
Ossoli, Giovanni Angelo, 243
Ossoli, Marchesa. *See* Fuller, Margaret
O'Sullivan, John L., 175, 176, 195, 214, 418, 805
outcasts, 22, 655–56
Owen, Robert Dale, 236, 344, 801
Owen, Wilfred, 28
Oxford English Dictionary, 184, 348

P

Pacey, Desmond, 102
Pachano, Jacinto Fombona, 676
Padgett, Ron, 706
Paine, Thomas, 29, 148, 268, 312, 313, 344, 393,
   501–2, 530, 581, 587, 787, 797
   Age of Reason, The, 312, 501
painters and painting, 157, 159, 197, 252–53, 314,
   419, 432–33, 450, **502–4**, 510, 621, 735
Palgrave, Francis Turner, 72
Pall Mall Gazette, xvi
Palmer, Nettie, 43
Palmo, Ferdinand, 713
Panic of 1837, 773
pantheism, **504–5**, 669
Papini, Giovanni, 324
paradox, 13, 15, 34, 35, 113, 123, 132, 157, 220,
   279, 317, 666, 670, 708
parallelism, 12, 52, 108, 294, 337, 526, 604, 694,
   729
paralysis. *See* health, Whitman's
Parini, Jay, 387
Parke, Walter, 505
Parker, Alan, 420
Parker, Theodore, 26, 582
parodies of Whitman, 107, 129, 154, **505–6**, 514,
   661, 704

Parrington, Vernon L.
   Main Currents in American Thought, 614
Parton, James, **506**, 506–7, 796
Parton, Sara Payson Willis (Fanny Fern), 288, 393,
   506, **506–7**, 626, 792, 796, 797
Pascal, Blaise, 465
pastoralism. *See* rural life
patriotism. *See* nationalism
Paulin, Tom, 73
Pavese, Cesare, 323, 324
Paz, Mario, 324
Paz, Octavio, 675, 676
Pearce, Roy Harvey, 207, 354, 495, 554, 607, 706
Pearson, Leon, 12, 288
Pease, Donald E., 594
Peavy, Linda, 660
Pedro, Dom, II, 111
Pelham, Camden
   *Chronicles of Crime; or, the New Newgate
      Calendar,* 590
Pelli, Cesar, 24
Pennell, Elizabeth Robins, **510**, 516
Pennell, Joseph, **510**, 516
pension, Whitman's, 50, 277, 596
Perelman, Chaim, 588
periodicals devoted to Whitman, 38, 39, 40, 51,
   68, 179, **510–12**, 740, 775
Perlman, Jim, 706
Perry, Bliss, 60–61, 107, **512–13**
   Walt Whitman: His Life and Work, 60–61,
      513, 614
Perry, Nora, 797
Perse, Saint-John, 233
Persichetti, Vincent, 440
personae, 4, 13, 68, 125, 177, 203, 219, 271, 275,
   314, 334, 335, 361, **513–14**, 520, 597–
   98, 606, 624, 625, 634, 663–64, 687,
   708, 724, 754, 800–1
personalism, 173, 177, 178, 553
Peru, 675, 676
Pessoa, Fernando, **514**, 536
Peter Eckler (publishing house), 25, 193
Pfaff's Restaurant, 77, 89, 129, 130, 259, 261, 268,
   425, **514–15**, 688, 691, 698, 710, 754
Philadelphia, Pennsylvania, 111–12, **515–17**, 647,
   703–4, 741, 749, 791
Phillips, George Searle ("January Searle"), **517**
Phillips, Wendell, 568
philosophy. *See* Greek philosophy; metaphysics
photographs and photographers, Whitman's, 197,
   240, 332, 355, 359, 494, 513, **517–20**,
   597, 706
photography and photographic technique, 28, 65,
   93, 103, 110, 159, 190, 314, 442, 513,
   518–19, 574, 677, 748
phrenology, 115, 198, 219, 226, 230, 286, 347,
   442, **520–23**, 535, 557–58, 658, 669,
   714–15, 751
physicians, Whitman's, 87–88, 189, 408–9, 434, 493
Piatt, John and Sarah, 761

Rampersad, Arnold, 284

Randolph, Edmund, 148

Ransom Humanities Research Center (University of Texas), 137

Raymond, Henry J., 463, 699

reader, Whitman's relationship with, 95–96, 110, 150, 158, 172, 275, 310, 337, 349, 443, 489, 494, 561, 585, 589, 594, 622, 648–49, 653, 654, 656, 663–64, 669, 687, 708, 721, 722, 728, 734–35, 789

reading, Whitman's, 105, 149, 182, 214, 215, 243–44, 271, 280, **572–74**, 606, 614, 620, 632–33, 634, 748, 801–2

realism, 526, **574–75**

reality. *See* appearance and reality

rebellion, idea of, 19, 27, 33, 66, 93, 112–13, 155, 255, 286, 536, 791

rebirth, 579–80, 612, 623, 774

Rechnitzer, Peter A., 402

Reconstruction, 371, 372, 477, 532–33, 539, 541, **576–77**, 584, 627, 681, 736, 761

recording of Whitman's voice. *See* voice, Whitman's

Red Jacket, chief, 607

Redfield, J.S., 369

Redford, Robert, 420

Redpath, James, 423, **578–79**, 712

Rees Welsh & Co., 44, 132, 146, 372, 415, 493, 516, 678

Reeves, Harrison, 22

reform and reformers, 127, 129, 477, 530, 535, 549, 557–58, 635, 657, 709–10, 736, 740–41, 795–96, 801–2

regeneration, 15, 392, 395, 560, 534, 586, 716–17, 721, 725

reincarnation, 474, **579–80**, 612

Reinhart, Charles S., 510

Reisiger, Hans, 247

Reiss, Edmund, 30

Reitzel, William W., 179, 591

religion, 112–13, 142–45, 201, 426, 445, 504, 535, 541, 556, 563–65, 579, **580–84**, 621–22, 647, 656, 670, 686–87, 697, 755

Remini, Robert V., 506

Republican party, 175, 202, 532–33, **584–85**, 792

resurrection, 35, 392, 656, 716–17

reviews, Whitman's, 437, 486, 520, 767. *See also* self-reviews, Whitman's anonymous

reviews of Whitman's work. *See* critical reception, Whitman's contemporary

revisions, Whitman's, xi, 91, 153, 216, 295, 353, 360, 366, 373, 381–82, 409–10, 464–65, 468–69, 481, 643, 653, 687–88

Revolutionary War. *See* American Revolution

revolutions of 1848, 212, 243, 273, 463, **587–88**, 724, 805

Rexroth, Kenneth, 29

Reynolds, David S., 39, 54, 57, 62, 106, 164, 169, 202, 264, 269, 280, 327, 337, 351, 392, 409, 416, 417, 442, 464, 483, 487, 489,

508, 553, 559, 587, 590, 597, 598, 604, 609, 634, 636, 650, 654, 657, 706, 710, 735, 759, 761, 790, 801

Walt Whitman's America: A Cultural Biography, ix, 62, 155–56, 615

rhetorical theory and practice, 397, 489, **588–89**

Rhymers' Club, 589

Rhys, Ernest Percival, 73, **589–90**

Rice, Allan Thorndike, 466

Rice, T.D., 3

Rich, Adrienne, 40, 798

Richards, I.A., 589

Riggenbach, Jeff, 422

Rilke, Rainer, Maria, 248

Ripley, George, 463

Ritter, Frederick Louis, 439

Riverby, 90, **590–91**

road (as image), 93, 155, 228, 251, 301, 336, 371, 375, 663, 687, 700

Roberts Brothers, the, 371, 661

Robins, Elizabeth. *See* Pennell, Elizabeth Robins)

Rockwood, George G., 519

Rocky Mountains, **591**, 680, 743, 766

Rodgers, Cleveland, 39, 40

Roe, Charles A., **592**

Rogers, Cameron, 60

Rokha, Pablo de, 676

Rolland, Romain, 307, 318

Rolleston, Thomas William Hazen, 136, 247, 320, 341, **592**, 692

Rollins College Library (Winter Park, Florida), 137

Romains, Jules, 232, 318

romanticism, 5–6, 75–76, 213, 278, 415–16, 428, 543, **593–95**, 669, 707–8, 732

Rome brothers, 84, 332, 354, 362, 381, 467, 552, **595–96**, 757

Roosa, Dr. D.B. St. John, 77

Roosevelt, Franklin Delano, 440

Roosevelt, Theodore, 676

Ropes, John F., 213

Rorem, Ned, 440, 441

Rose, Ernestine L., 221, 795–96, 797

Rosenberg, Isaac, 74

Rossbach, Jeffrey, 605

Rossetti, Christina, 596

Rossetti, Dante Gabriel, 86, 251, 252, 596

Rossetti, William Michael, 38, 72, 73, 86, 136, 148, 239, 247, 251, 252, 282, 474, 542, 576, **596–97**, 629, 690, 761, 764

Poems [of Whitman] (1868), 72, 239, 282, 542, 576, 596, 629, 761

Poems [of Whitman] (1886), 596

Rossini, Gioacchino, 228, 437, 438, 484–85

Stabat Mater, 485, 486

roughs, 222, 513, 536, **597–99**, 763

Rourke, Constance, 289

Rousseau, Jean Jacques, 199, 428, 573, 593, 755

"Social Contract," 487

Rubin, Joseph Jay, 62, 344, 614

Rubiner, Ludwig, 249

Rudisill, Richard, 27
Ruggles, Carl, 439
Rukeyser, Muriel, 116, **599–600**
Rusev, Rusi, 602
Ruskin, John, 28, 596
Russell, George (AE), 73
Russia and other Slavic countries, Whitman in (reception and influence in), 318, **600–2**

S

Sacco, Nicola, 185
Sachithanandan, V., 307
sadomasochism, 745–46
St. Francis of Assisi, 107
St. Louis, Missouri, 433, **603**, 743, 744, 765, 783, 785
St. Paul, 151, 647, 716
Saint-Gaudens, Augustus, 170
Saintsbury, George, 73, 281, 596
Saint-Simon, Comte de, 601
Salt, Henry, 72
Sanborn, Franklin Benjamin (Frank), 37, 71, 194, 306, **605–6**
Sanchez, Luis, 675
Sand, George, 76, 428, 473, 593, **606**
    Consuelo, 486, 573, 606
    Countess of Rudolstadt, The, 473, 573, 606, 634
    Journeyman Joiner, 634
Sandburg, Carl, 28, 386, **607**
Sanders, Robert L., 441
Sanger, W.W., 335
Sankaracarya, Sri, 25
Santa Anna, Antonio Lopez de, 427
Santa Spirita, 112
Santayana, George, 328, 385, **608–9**
Santi, Enrico Mario, 675, 676
Sarony, Napoleon, 519
Sarracino, Carmine, 651
Sarrazin, Gabriel, 232, **609**
Sartre, Jean-Paul, 185
Sassoon, Siegfried, 28
Satan, 112, 214
satire, 69–70, 142, 201–3, 214, 525, 546, 672, 732
Saturday Press, 51, 129, 130, 231, 390, 495, 515, 517, **609–10**, 797
Saunders, Henry S., 22, 39, 42
Savoy, Eric, 575
Sawyer, Thomas P., 85, 150, **610**, 760
Scandinavia, Whitman in (reception and influence in), **610–12**, 616
Schabelitz, Jakob, 247, 341
Schaper, Monika, 247
Scheick, William J., 264
Schele de Vere, Maximilian, 348
Schelling, Friedrich, 97, 278, 593, 617
Schickele, René, 318
Schiller, Friedrich von, 76, 104, 323, 751
Schlaf, Johannes, 54, 247, 248, 249–50, 318
Schlegel, Friedrich, 593

Schlumberger, Jean, 250
Schmidt, Rudolf, 86, 610–11, 665
Schneidau, Herbert, 56
Schoeck, Othmar, 249
Schoff, Stephen Alonzo, 362
scholarship, trends in Whitman, 142–43, 155, 247–48, 286, 319, 321–22, 323–24, 330, 358, 419, 431–32, 510–12, 513, 553–54, 561–62, 568, 583–84, 589, 593–94, **613–16**, 644, 706
schools. See education, views on; teacher, Whitman as
Schreker, Franz, 249
Schuman, William, 439, 440
Schwiebert, John E., 110
Schwob, Marcel, 250
Schyberg, Frederik, 11, 60, 561, 598, 611, **616**
    Walt Whitman, 11, 611, 616
science, 215–16, 392, 434, 507, 508, 534, 543, 557, **616–19**, 667, 697, 769
Scotland, 646, 698
Scott, Cyril, 439
Scott, Dred, 727
Scott, Sir Walter, 47, 75, 76, 127, 227, 314, 315, 416, 444, 528, 572, 598, **619–20**, 633, 646
    Border Minstrelsy, 315
Scott, William Bell, 596
Scott, Winfield, 547
Scourby, Alexander, 422
Scribner's Monthly Magazine, 503, 688
sculptors and sculpture, **620–21**
sea, the, 92, 149, 303, 364, 405, 452, 495, 497–98, 509, 608, **621–23**, 623–24, 637, 644, 793–94, 799
Seaman, Congressman, 300
Searle, January. See Phillips, George Searle ("January Searle")
sectional strife, 81, 141–42, 365, 493, 494, 531–33, 541, **640–42**, 712, 727
Sedgwick, Theodore, 159
seer. See prophecy
self, the, 12–13, 52–53, 113, 172, 172–73, 278, 310–11, 352–53, 355–56, 366, 445, 446, 498, 505, 513, 518, 538, 561, 594, 645, 652–53, 679, 708, 733, 770, 789
self-reviews, Whitman's anonymous, 16, 176, 230, 231, 301, 381, 383, 521, 534–35, 550, **624–25**, 699, 711, 764–65, 766
Selim, Ali Mohamed, 420
Selwyn, George (Whitman pseudonym), 254
Senghor, Léopold Sédar, 5–6
sensationalism, 314, 483, 534, 587, 590, 635, 650, 710
sentimentality, 72, 191, 314, 546, 587, **625–27**, 635, 650
Seppová, Magda, 602
Serbia, 602
Sercombe, Parker, 28
Service, Robert, 102
Sessions, Roger, 421, 439, 440

Seward, William Henry, 261
sex and sexuality, 5, 10, 60–62, 115–17, 119, 161,
        217, 242–43, 249–50, 250–51, 255,
        279, 280, 297–98, 436, 446, 451, 453,
        473–74, 482, 521, 535, 558–59, 561–
        62, 564, 571, 599–600, 606, 612, 614,
        628–32, 644–45, 648–49, 655, 661, 684,
        688, 730, 739, 745–46, 763, 767, 794,
        797. *See also* autoeroticism; homoeroti-
        cism; homosexuality
Shakespeare, William, 47, 75, 125, 127, 172, 187,
        188, 223, 254, 267, 280, 282, 314, 323,
        375, 393, 400, 416, 459, 471, 487, 490,
        526, 528, 529, 572, 598, 606, 620, 625,
        632–33, 692, 702, 711, 791, 806
Shallenberg, Frank, 421
shaman, poet as, 125, 445–46
Shapiro, Karl, 431, 504
Shaw, George Bernard, 268, 347
Shaw, Quincy, 432
Shaw, Robert, 440
Shay, Frank, 57
Shelley, Percy Bysshe, 72, 76, 87, 151, 187, 323,
        543, 593, 646, 691, 702, 806
Shelton, Ron, 420
Shepard, George, 408
Shephard, Esther, 615, **634**
Shepherd, Alexander "Boss," 761
Sheridan, Philip, 257
Sherman, William Tecumseh, 212, 370
Shew, Joel, 558
ships (as image), 9, 65, 370, 473, 509, 622, 624,
        668, 775
Shively, Charley, 400
    *Calamus Lovers: Whitman's Working Class
        Camerados,* 614
Shklovsky, I.V., 600
Sholes, Hiram, 85
short fiction, Whitman's, x, 21–22, 54–55, 114–
        15, 169, 170, 175–76, 194, 224, 264,
        350–51, 351, 388–89, 396, 399, 399–
        400, 412, 416, 442, 482–83, 590,
        626, 632, 634, **635–36**, 650, 735–36,
        789–90
short poems, Whitman's, 34, 509, 527, 677, 696,
        805
Sigourney, Lydia H., 534, 626
Sill, Geoffrey M., 511
Silveira, Tasso da, 537
Silver, Rollo, 138
Simms, William Gilmore, 175
Simpson, Louis, **637**
Sinclair, Upton, 741
singers and singing, 438
Slabsides, 90
slang, 17, 337, 347, 357, 471, 526, 527, **638–39**,
        639–40, 693–94
slavery and abolitionism, 15, 80, 174, 186, 186–
        87, 193, 202, 212, 237, 314, 475–76,
        531–32, 547–48, 567, 570–71, 578,

        584, 627–28, **640–43**, 681, 749, 801
slavery, expansion of, 15, 48–49, 81, 82, 141–42,
        186, 202, 237, 344, 393, 427, 531–32,
        570–71, 584, 605, 640–42, 727, 792–93
Slenker, Elmina D., 797
Sloan, John, 37
Slote, Bernice, 109, 431
Slovenia, 602
Small, Maynard & Company, 378
Smith, Alexander, **646**
Smith, Hannah Whitall, 152, 646, 647
Smith, Henry Nash
    Virgin Land, 708
Smith, Joseph, 301
Smith, Logan Pearsall, **646–47**
Smith, Mary Whitall. *See* Costelloe,
        Mary Whitall Smith
Smith, Rachel Pearsall, 647
Smith, Robert Pearsall, 152, 516, 646, **647**
Smith, William Henry, 633
Smithie, Jack, 421
Smithtown, Long Island, 435
Smuts, Jan Christian, 6, **647–48**
Snyder, Gary, 29, 386
Snyder, John, 132
social Darwinism, 453, 569
social reform. *See* reform and reformers
socialism, 67, 249, 740
societies, Whitman. *See* associations, clubs, fellow-
        ships, foundations, and societies
Society for the Suppression of Vice, 115, 146, 492,
        630, **649–50**
Society of Friends. *See* Quakers and Quakerism
Socrates, 97, 151
Södergran, Edith, 611
sodomy, charges of, 435
soldiers, 35, 78, 85, 89, 125, 127, 142, 150, 191,
        192, 216, 222, 265, 270, 319, 345, 395,
        409, 575, 586, 636, 754
Sommer, Doris, 675
son, 789–90
sonnet, 240, 282, 400, 636, 768
Sophocles, 47, 487
soul, the, 143, 162, 167–68, 201, 257, 278, 279,
        301–3, 356, 465, 504, 507–9, 542, 543,
        565, 579, 582, 583, 607, 621–23, 624,
        629, 654, 654–55, 657–58, **669–71**, 673,
        683, 687, 722–23, 724, 738, 770
Souster, Raymond, 102
South, the American, 25, 31, 41, 113, 124, 334–
        35, 344, 365, 370, 475, 567, 584, **671–
        72**, 758
South Africa. *See* Africa, Whitman in (reception
        and influence in)
Southey, Robert, 75, 187
Southold, Long Island, 435
Soviet Union. *See* Russia and other Slavic
        countries, Whitman in (reception
        and influence in)
space, **672–74**

Spain and Spanish America, Whitman in (reception and influence in), 68, 454–55, **674–77**
Spasmodic School of Poetry, 646
Speed, Attorney General James, 476, **681**
Speed, Joshua, 144
Spencer, Herbert, 28, 215, 347, 453
Spiller, Robert E., 511
spiritualism, 26, 534–35, 559
spirituality, 123, 142–45, 163, 277, 508, 583, 606, 607
spontaneity, 525, **683–84**, 687
Spooner, Alden, 406, 552
Spooner, Edwin B., 407
Sprague, Harriet Chapman, 136
Spurzheim, Johann Gaspar, 520
Stadler, Ernst, 249
Stafford, George, 50, 99, 252, **685**, 686, 720, 742
Stafford, Harry L., 150, 189, 410, 520, 685, **685–86**, 691, 720–21, 742, 806
Stafford, Susan M., 50, 99, 252, **685**, 686, 720–21, 742
Stanbery, Henry, 42, 761
Stanford, Charles Villiers, 439, 440
Stanton, Elizabeth Cady, 436
stanzas, 695, 774
Stark, Mary Virginia, 375
stars, 156, 241, 302, 337, 395, 452, 480, 583, 692, 674, 769, 771
states' rights, 731
statues of Whitman, 100
Stedman, Edmund Clarence, 37, 61, 136, 254, 513, 515, **688–89**, 691, 806
Steffanone, Balbina, 713
Stekel, Wilhelm, 561
Stella, Joseph, 503
Stephens, A.G., 43
Sterling, Kansas, 743
Stern, J. David, 39, 430
Stern, Juliet Lit, 39, 430
Stevens, Oliver, 71, 477, 492, 649, **689**
Stevens, Wallace, 385, **689–90**
Stevenson, Robert Louis, 73, **690**
Stieglitz, Alfred, 37, 386
Stoddard, Charles Warren, **690–91**
Stoddard, Richard Henry, **691**
Stoicism, 209, 214, 419–20, 658, **691–93**
Stoker, Bram, 185, 320, 761
storms, 509, 732
Stovall, Floyd, 133, 134, 280, 335, 504
    Foreground of "Leaves of Grass," The, 614
Stowe, Harriet Beecher, 41, 166, 581
Strachey, Barbara, 152, 646
Strassburg, Robert, 439, 512
Strauch, Carl F., 656
Street and Smith, 415
stroke. *See* health, Whitman's
structure, poetic, 353, 356, 656, 801
style and technique(s), 34, 52, 54, 92, 107–8, 109, 110, 111, 121, 121–22, 130, 154, 161, 162, 166, 177, 184–85, 193–94, 195,

212–13, 219, 225, 226, 238–39, 247, 248–49, 251, 255, 257, 294, 316–17, 324, 337, 352–54, 356–57, 421, 473, 480, 490–91, 495, 505, 514, 526–27, 538, 542, 543, 571, 607, 636, 678, 679, 681–82, **693–96**, 748, 771, 774, 782, 793–94, 802
suffrage, 82, 179, 211, 221, 237, 389, 423, 530, 539, 549, 557, 761, 795
Sullivan, Louis, 23–24, 28, 386, 397
Sumner, Charles, 477
sun, 311, 452, 719
Sunset of Bon Echo, 179
Sweden, 610, 611–12
Swedenborg, Emanuel, 26, 214, 268, 312, 535, 559, **697–98**
Sweezey, Frank, 217
Swinburne, Algernon Charles, 65, 66, 72, 75, 86, 154, 214, 281, 425, 505, 506, 596, 602, 629, **698**, 703, 748
    Songs Before Sunrise, 629
    "Whitmania," 629
Swinton, John, 463, 600, **698–99**, 699
Swinton, William, 16, 21, 229, 349, 381, 593, 625, 698, **699**
    Rambles Among Words, 21, 229, 349, 593, 699
symbolism, 215, 302–3, 395, 452, 490–91, 583, 621–23, 660, 663, 672–73, 674, **699–701**, 738, 771–72
symbolist movement, the, 109, 232, 537, 689, 699–700, 701
Symonds, John Addington, 38, 60, 67, 74, 143, 144, 145, 147, 456, 561, 601, 629, 630, 671, **701–2**, 761
Symons, Arthur, 589

T

Tagore, Kshitindranath, 307
Tagore, Rabindranath, 307
Taine, Hippolyte, 48, 688
Talbot, Jesse, 84, 502
Tammanend, 703
Tammany Hall, 174, 458, 461, **703**
Tapscott, Stephen J., 200, 792
Tate, Allen, 153
Taylor, Bayard, 66, 112, 463, 505, 661, **703–4**
Taylor, Father (Edward Thompson), 70, 287, 312, 419, 471, **704–5**
Taylor, Mary, 713
Taylor, Zachary, 141, 428, 456, 531, 547, 548
teacher, Whitman as, xiii, 149, 199, 333, 384, 404, 404–5, 435, 592, 632, 709
teaching of Whitman's works, 319, **705–7**
technique. *See* style and technique(s)
technology, 5, 106, 507, 508, 518, 533, 662, **707–9**, 726, 785
temperance movement, 114, 234–36, 416, 458, 483, 535, 586–87, **709–11**. *See also* alcohol

Whitman, Walt (continued)